THIS EDITION WRITTEN AND RESEARCHED BY

Mark Beales, Tim Bewer, Joe Bindloss, Austin Bush,
David Eimer, Bruce Evans, Damian Harper, Isabella Noble

PLAN YOUR TRIP

ON THE ROAD

TRAVEL INK / GETTY IMAGES ©

WAT PHO P64, BANGKOK

ANUJAK JAIMOOK / GETTY IMAGES ©

RICE FIELDS P321, CHIANG MAI

KAMPEE PATISENA / GETTY IMAGES ©

Contents

WAT PHRA THAT DOI KONG MU P294, MAE HONG SON

Contents

ON THE ROAD

ROYAL PARK RAJAPRUEK P321, CHIANG MAI

LEELAKAJONKIJ / GETTY IMAGES ©

SAIREE BEACH, KO TAO P555

ANNAPURNA MELLOR / GETTY IMAGES ©

STEVE OGLE / GETTY IMAGES ©

10/26/2019

Item(s) Checked Out

TITLE	Gandhi / Demi.
BARCODE	33029046135620
DUE DATE	**11-16-19**
TITLE	Thailand / this edition
BARCODE	33029067122432
DUE DATE	**11-16-19**
TITLE	CBEST test
BARCODE	33029105132120
DUE DATE	**11-16-19**

Total Items This Session: 3

Thank you for visiting the library!
Sacramento Public Library
www.saclibrary.org

Love your library?
Join the Friends!
www.saclibfriends.org/join
Visit our Book Den, too.

Terminal # 85

Contents

RAILAY P655

UNDERSTAND

SURVIVAL GUIDE

SPECIAL FEATURES

Welcome to Thailand

Friendly and fun loving, exotic and tropical, cultured and historic, Thailand radiates a golden hue from its glittering temples and tropical beaches through to the ever-comforting Thai smile.

Sand Between Your Toes

With a long coastline (actually, two coastlines) and jungle-topped islands anchored in azure waters, Thailand is a tropical getaway for the hedonist and the hermit, the prince and the pauper. This paradise offers a varied menu: playing in the gentle surf of Ko Lipe, diving with whale sharks off Ko Tao, scaling the sea cliffs of Krabi, kiteboarding in Hua Hin, partying on Ko Phi Phi, recuperating at a health resort on Ko Samui and feasting on the beach wherever sand meets sea.

Sacred Spaces

The celestial world is a close confidant in this Buddhist nation, and religious devotion is colourful and ubiquitous. Gleaming temples and golden Buddhas frame both the rural and modern landscapes. Ancient banyan trees are ceremoniously wrapped in sacred cloth to honour the resident spirits, fortune-bringing shrines decorate humble homes as well as monumental malls, while garland-festooned dashboards ward off traffic accidents. Visitors can join the conversation through meditation retreats in Chiang Mai, religious festivals in northeastern Thailand, underground cave shrines in Kanchanaburi and Phetchaburi and hilltop temples in northern Thailand.

Fields & Forests

In between the cluttered cities and towns is the rural heartland, which is a mix of rice paddies, tropical forests and squat villages tied to the agricultural clock. In the north, the forests and fields bump up against toothy blue mountains decorated with silvery waterfalls. In the south, scraggy limestone cliffs poke out of the cultivated landscape like prehistoric skyscrapers. The usually arid northeast emits an emerald hue during the rainy season when tender green rice shoots carpet the landscape.

A Bountiful Table

Adored around the world, Thai cuisine expresses fundamental aspects of Thai culture: it is generous, warm, refreshing and relaxed. Each Thai dish relies on fresh, local ingredients – pungent lemongrass, searing chillies and plump seafood. A varied national menu is built around the four fundamental flavours: spicy, sweet, salty and sour. Roving appetites go on eating tours of Bangkok noodle shacks, seafood pavilions in Phuket and Burmese market stalls in Mae Sot. Cooking classes reveal the simplicity behind the seemingly complicated dishes and mastering the market is an important survival skill.

Why I Love Thailand

By Austin Bush, Writer

It's easy to say that the thing I love most about Thailand is Thai food. But then I'm reminded of that feeling of freedom during a motorcycle trip upcountry. And of the sensory overload of a busy morning market – or a night out in Bangkok. And of encounters with history and culture, the new and the old, at just about every turn. Did I mention the white-sand beaches, jungles, ancient ruins and Buddhist temples? Indeed, the food satisfies – but on second thought, Thailand offers so much more.

For more about our writers, see page 808

Above: Wat Phra That Doi Suthep (p322), Chiang Mai

Thailand

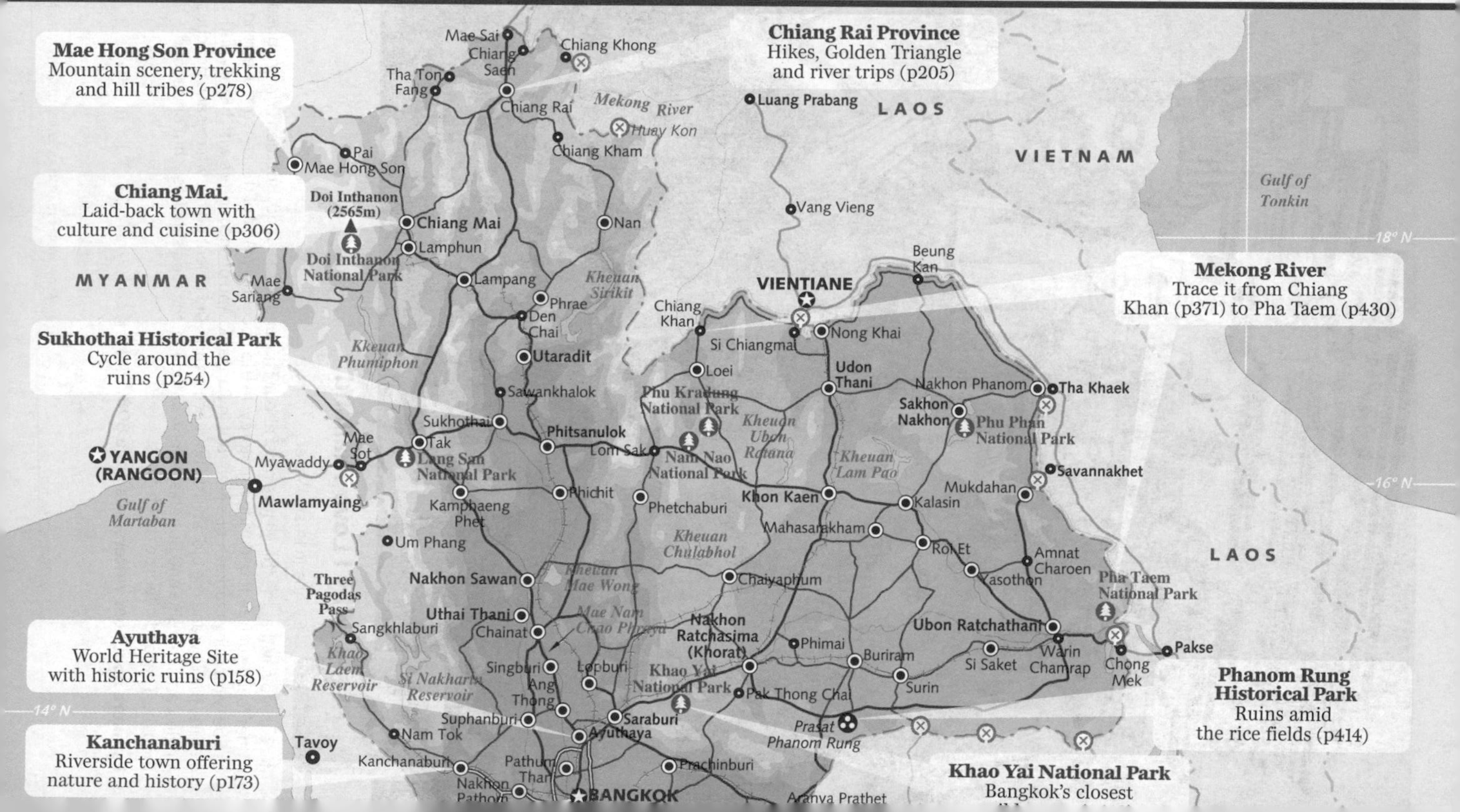
0 150 km
0 90 miles
Mae Hong Son Province
Mountain scenery, trekking and hill tribes (p278)
Chiang Mai
Laid-back town with culture and cuisine (p306)
Sukhothai Historical Park
Cycle around the ruins (p254)
Ayuthaya
World Heritage Site with historic ruins (p158)
Kanchanaburi
Riverside town offering nature and history (p173)
Chiang Rai Province
Hikes, Golden Triangle and river trips (p205)
Mekong River
Trace it from Chiang Khan (p371) to Pha Taem (p430)
Phanom Rung Historical Park
Ruins amid the rice fields (p414)
Khao Yai National Park
Bangkok's closest
MYANMAR
LAOS
VIETNAM
Gulf of Tonkin
Gulf of Martaban
18° N
16° N
14° N
YANGON (RANGOON)
VIENTIANE
BANGKOK
Mae Sai
Chiang Saen
Chiang Khong
Tha Ton
Fang
Chiang Rai
Mekong River
Huay Kon
Chiang Kham
Luang Prabang
Vang Vieng
Pai
Mae Hong Son
Doi Inthanon (2565m)
Doi Inthanon National Park
Chiang Mai
Lamphun
Nan
Mae Sariang
Lampang
Phrae
Den Chai
Kheuan Sirikit
Utaradit
Kkeuan Phumiphon
Sawankhalok
Sukhothai
Phitsanulok
Tak
Mae Sot
Myawaddy
Lang Sang National Park
Mawlamyaing
Kamphaeng Phet
Phichit
Um Phang
Lom Sak
Nam Nao National Park
Phetchaburi
Kheuan Chulabhol
Chiang Khan
Si Chiangmai
Nong Khai
Loei
Phu Kradung National Park
Kheuan Ubon Ratana
Udon Thani
Beung Kan
Nakhon Phanom
Tha Khaek
Sakhon Nakhon
Phu Phan National Park
Kheuan Lam Pao
Khon Kaen
Kalasin
Mukdahan
Savannakhet
Mahasarakham
Roi Et
Amnat Charoen
Yasothon
Pha Taem National Park
Three Pagodas Pass
Nakhon Sawan
Kheuan Mae Wong
Chaiyaphum
Uthai Thani
Chainat
Mae Nam Chao Phraya
Nakhon Ratchasima (Khorat)
Phimai
Ubon Ratchathani
Pakse
Sangkhlaburi
Khao Laem Reservoir
Si Nakharin Reservoir
Singburi
Ang Thong
Lopburi
Khao Yai National Park
Pak Thong Chai
Buriram
Si Saket
Warin Chamrap
Chong Mek
Surin
Suphanburi
Saraburi
Ayuthaya
Prasat Phanom Rung
Nam Tok
Tavoy
Kanchanaburi
Pathum Thani
Prachinburi
Nakhon Pathom
Aranya Prathet

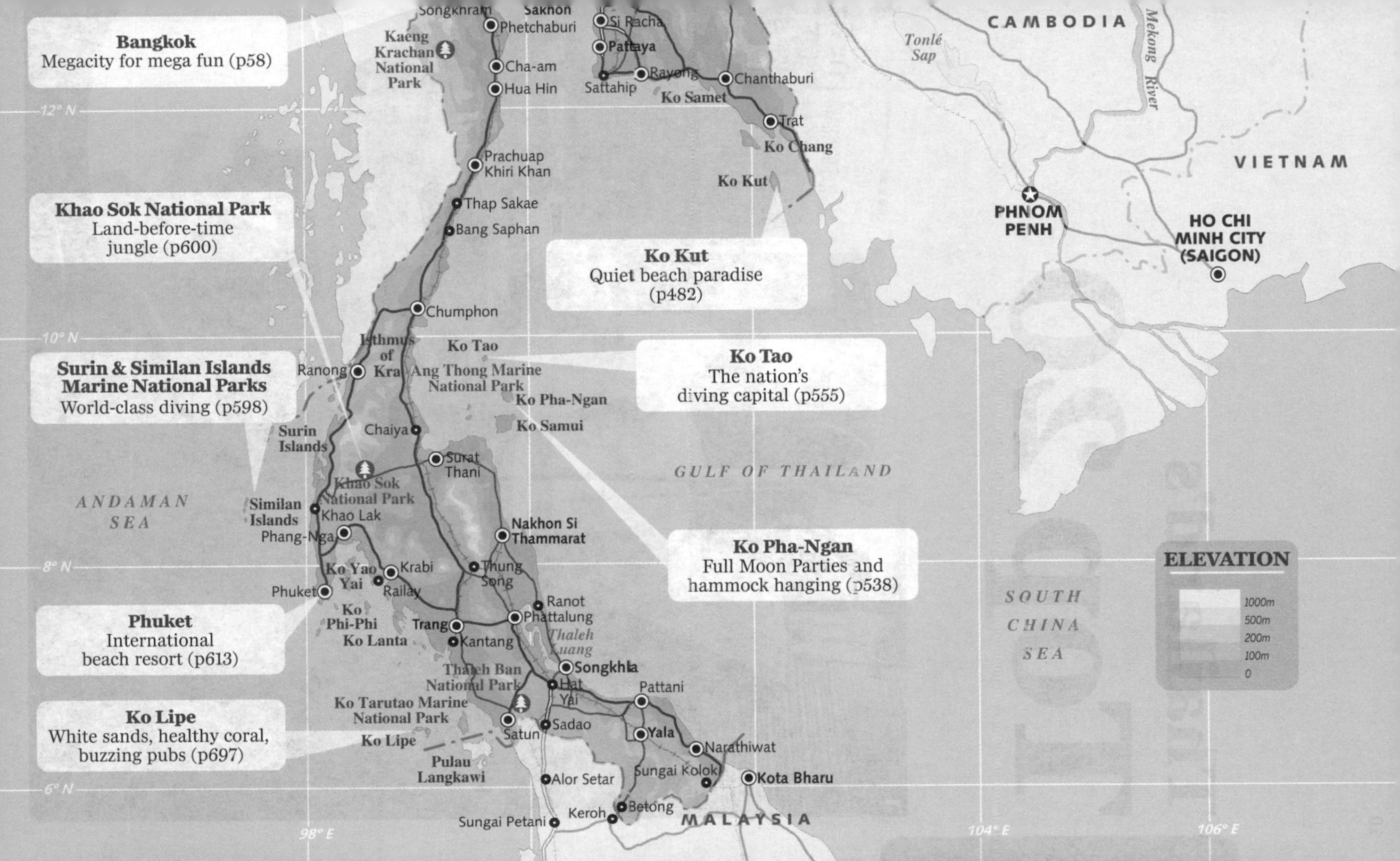

Bangkok
Megacity for mega fun (p58)
Khao Sok National Park
Land-before-time jungle (p600)
Surin & Similan Islands Marine National Parks
World-class diving (p598)
Phuket
International beach resort (p613)
Ko Lipe
White sands, healthy coral, buzzing pubs (p697)
Ko Kut
Quiet beach paradise (p482)
Ko Tao
The nation's diving capital (p555)
Ko Pha-Ngan
Full Moon Parties and hammock hanging (p538)
CAMBODIA
VIETNAM
MALAYSIA
Mekong River
Tonlé Sap
PHNOM PENH
HO CHI MINH CITY (SAIGON)
ANDAMAN SEA
GULF OF THAILAND
SOUTH CHINA SEA
ELEVATION
1000m
500m
200m
100m
0
12° N
10° N
8° N
6° N
98° E
104° E
106° E
Songkhram
Sakhon
Phetchaburi
Kaeng Krachan National Park
Cha-am
Hua Hin
Si Racha
Pattaya
Sattahip
Rayong
Chanthaburi
Ko Samet
Trat
Ko Chang
Ko Kut
Prachuap Khiri Khan
Thap Sakae
Bang Saphan
Chumphon
Isthmus of Kra
Ranong
Ko Tao
Ang Thong Marine National Park
Ko Pha-Ngan
Ko Samui
Chaiya
Surin Islands
Surat Thani
Khao Sok National Park
Similan Islands
Khao Lak
Phang-Nga
Nakhon Si Thammarat
Ko Yao Yai
Krabi
Railay
Phuket
Thung Song
Ko Phi-Phi
Ko Lanta
Trang
Kantang
Ranot
Phattalung
Thaleh Luang
Songkhla
Thaleh Ban National Park
Hat Yai
Pattani
Ko Tarutao Marine National Park
Satun
Sadao
Yala
Ko Lipe
Narathiwat
Pulau Langkawi
Alor Setar
Sungai Kolok
Kota Bharu
Keroh
Betong
Sungai Petani

Thailand's Top 20

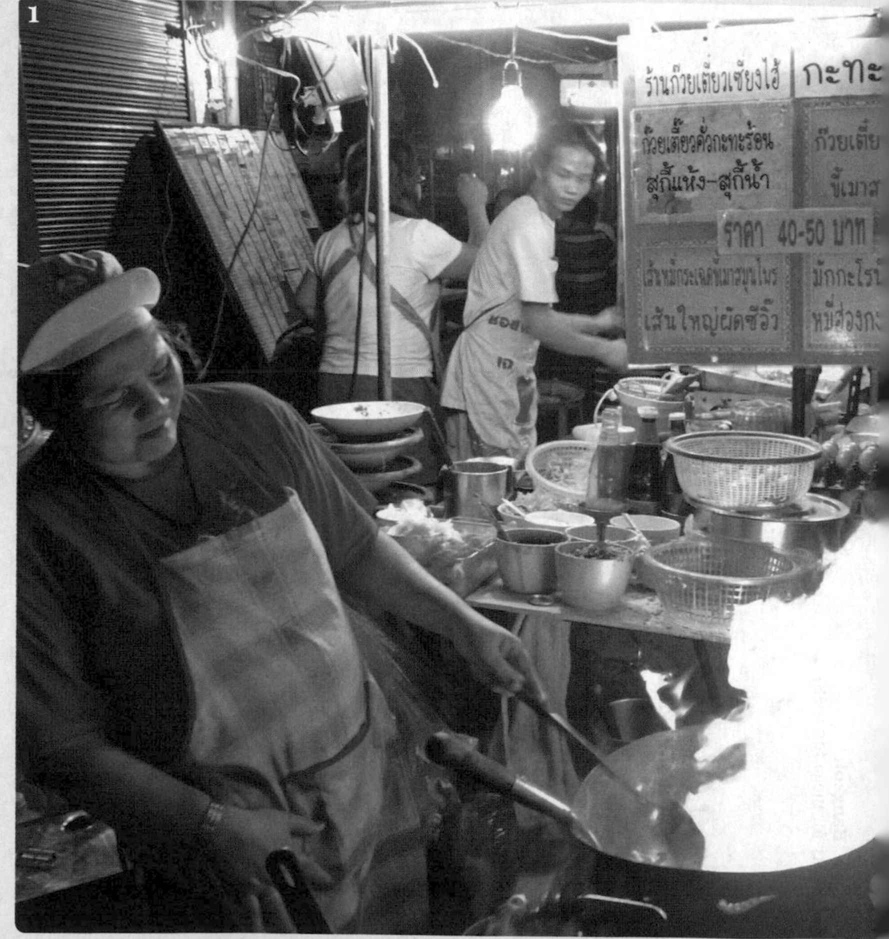

Bangkok

1 Glittering temples, towering skyscrapers, a cracking nightlife and, oh – the food! What's not to love about Bangkok (p59)? Traffic jams, humidity and political instability aside, the Thai capital is now tidier and easier to navigate than ever. Zip between golden shrines, colourful markets, glitzy mega-malls and fascinating museums, stopping to refuel at sizzling streetside food stands and some of Asia's best restaurants. Head up to one of the city's famous skybars on your first night to get your bearings in this heaving, twinkling metropolis, and prepare to dive straight in.

Chiang Mai

2 The cultural capital of the north, Chiang Mai (p306) is beloved by culture geeks, temple-spotters and families. The old city is jam-packed with temples born during the time of the once independent Lanna kingdom. The temples and winding side roads are best explored on bicycle. Cooking schools teach visitors the art of Thai food while the scenic countryside boasts jungle treks, elephant encounters and minority villages. The city enjoys fantastic dining thanks to imports such as Japanese sushi and Burmese curries, plus homegrown northern specialities and vegetarian fare. The surrounding areas are rich with traditional handicraft outlets.

KEVIN FOY / ALAMY STOCK PHOTO ©

2

WYETTE CARDOZO / GETTY IMAGES ©

Railay

3 At the tip of the Krabi peninsula are some of Thailand's most famous natural features: the soaring limestone karsts of Railay (p655), anchored in the ocean. The beaches are sugar white and the forested interior is traversed by foot traffic, not cars. No traffic jams, no transport hassles. Visitors come and go by long-tail boats. Come to lounge, swim, dive or rock climb. Beginners can learn basic skills, and some stay so long they become good enough to do a free solo on a pinnacle then tumble harmlessly into a cobalt sea.

Chiang Rai Province

4 The days of the Golden Triangle opium trade are over, but Chiang Rai (p205) still packs intrigue in the form of fresh-air fun, such as hiking and self-guided exploration. It is also a great destination for unique cultural experiences, ranging from a visit to an Akha village to a stay at the Yunnanese hamlet of Mae Salong. From the Mekong River to the mountains, Chiang Rai is arguably Thailand's most beautiful province, and if you've set your sights further, it's a convenient gateway to Myanmar and Laos.
Akha village women

Ayuthaya

5 A once vibrant, glittering capital packed with hundreds of temples, Ayuthaya (p158) today only hints at its erstwhile glory. Cycle around the brick-and-stucco ruins, which form part of a Unesco World Heritage Site, and try to imagine how the city must have looked in its prime, when it greeted merchants from around the globe. On the outskirts of the city sit several more attractions, including an enormous handicraft centre and the most eclectic royal palace you will ever see.

Phetchaburi

6 A delightful mix of culture and nature combine in this provincial capital (p486), a close and quiet alternative to the hectic streets of Bangkok. Explore an antique hilltop palace, sacred cave shrines and bustling temples. Wander the old shophouse neighbourhood filled with do-it-yourself businesses run by Thai aunties and grannies. Then head off to the wilds of Kaeng Krachan National Park to spot wild gibbons and exotic birds. Phetchaburi is also a smart layover for travellers returning from the south. Phra Nakhon Khiri Historical Park (p486)

Pai

7 Combine a beautiful mountain valley, a party scene reminiscent of a Thai island, an old-school hippie vibe and laid-back northern Thai roots and you have Pai (p278), still northern Thailand's coolest destination. Its popularity means it can get crowded, especially at the peak of Thailand's 'winter' in December and January. But a huge spread of accommodation that caters to every budget and a host of outdoor and laid-back activities means your visit won't be quite like anybody else's. Spicypai Backpackers (p284)

6

MARTIN RICHARDSON / GETTY IMAGES ©

7

Surin & Similan Islands Marine National Parks

8 The world-renowned dive sites off the Surin (p598) and Similan Islands (p606) have anchored Thailand as a global diving destination. Live-aboard trips set out from Khao Lak, allowing for more time hanging out with aquatic residents including manta rays and whale sharks. The islands are an attraction in their own right, with jungle-filled interiors and smooth white beaches surrounded by coral reefs. Manta ray, Similan Islands

Kanchanaburi

9 Once you've explored this western province's wartime past – the infamous Bridge Over the River Kwai is here – get ready to walk on the wild side in Kanchanaburi (p173), where limestone mountains gaze down upon jungle. Activities from ziplining to kayaking and elephant encounters are all on offer at this popular adventure-traveller hub. Trek past silvery waterfalls and rushing rivers in search of gibbons and some of Thailand's last tigers, then spend the night at a homestay organised through an ethnic group. Death Railway Bridge (p173)

Sukhothai Historical Park

10 Step back some 800 years in time at one of Thailand's most impressive historical parks (p254). Exploring the ruins of this former capital by bicycle is a leisurely way to wind through the crumbling temples, Buddha statues and fish-filled ponds. Worthwhile museums and some of the country's best-value accommodation round out the package. Sukhothai rarely feels crowded, but for something off the beaten track head to nearby Si Satchanalai-Chaliang Historical Park, where you might be the only one scaling an ancient stairway.

Mekong River

11 From the historic timber shophouses of Chiang Khan (p371) to the waterfalls of Pha Taem National Park (p430), northeast Thailand's glorious arc of the Mekong River offers a smorgasbord of culture and beauty. Chase the river aboard a bus, long-tail boat or even a bicycle. View the cross-pollination of Thai-Lao culture in fishing villages, Nong Khai's bizarre sculpture park and prehistoric rock paintings in Ubon Ratchathani. Those who follow this little-visited trail are rewarded with true travellers' tales to tell. Chiang Khan

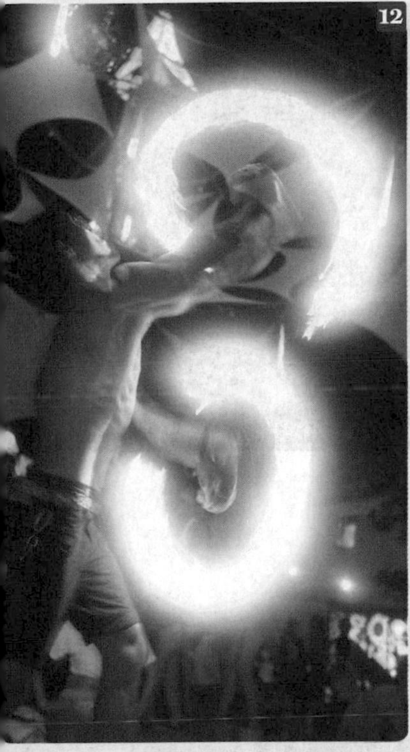

JOHN BROWN / ALAMY STOCK PHOTO ©

ALVARO LEIVA / ALAMY STOCK PHOTO ©

Ko Pha-Ngan

12 Famous for its techno-fuelled Full Moon Parties, Ko Pha-Ngan (p538) has long since graduated from being a sleepy bohemian island to an Asian Ibiza. Comfort seekers have an alternative to Ko Samui thanks to a bevy of boutique bungalows. On the northern and eastern coasts, ascetic hammock hangers can still find castaway bliss. Just offshore is Sail Rock, one of the gulf's best dive sites, while much of the island's interior is spectacular, unspoiled forest. Fire twirler at Full Moon Party, Hat Rin (p543)

Phuket

13 An international beach resort, Phuket (p613) is an easy destination for all ages. You can fly in from Bangkok (or even Dubai), and then retreat into a five-star resort or arty boutique hotel for a trouble-free tropical vacation. There are slinky stretches of sand, hedonistic party pits and world-class spas. Culture capital Phuket Town is now an attraction in its own right, plus there are day trips to mangrove forests, gibbon rescue centres and a tonne of water sports to get stuck into, from diving to surfing. Surfing, Hat Patong (p635)

Mae Hong Son Province

14 Tucked away in the country's northwest corner, this province (p278) has a lot more in common with Myanmar than anywhere else in Thailand. With its remote location, soaring mountains and unique culture and cuisine, Mae Hong Son can seem like an entirely different country. Exploration is the reason to make the journey here, and can involve tramping through one of the province's many caves, taking a hairpin turn on your motorcycle or doing a self-guided trek from Mae La-Na to Soppong. Tham Lot (p289), near Soppong

16

17

Ko Lipe

15 Where creature comforts meet laid-back island escape, Ko Lipe (p697) takes work to reach but the ever-growing devotees agree that it's worth it. The days of desertion are over, especially in the high season when the island is overrun, but it is still a wonderful blend of white-sand beaches, authentic Thai kitchens, groovy guesthouses, boutique resorts and nature adventures in the national park. The diving and living are best here during the early wet season (mid-April to June). But keep that hush-hush.

Khao Sok National Park

16 A deep, dark jungle hugs the midsection of southern Thailand. This ancient rainforest (p600) is filled with long, sweaty hiking routes up dramatic limestone formations that reward with postcard-perfect views. Birds and bats call this forest home, as does the rare *Rafflesia kerrii*, one of the stinkiest flowers on the planet. After trying out some tubing, kayaking and rafting, you can reward your outdoor work with riverside camping or sleep on the floating lake-top huts at Chiaw Lan.

Khao Yai National Park

17 This park is home to elephants, monkeys, gibbons, hornbills, pythons, bears, a million bats and even a few wily tigers. Wildlife sightings are almost at the mercy of chance, but your odds are excellent at this vast Unesco-listed reserve (p410), just a few hours out of Bangkok. And even if you don't meet many big animals, the orchids, birds, waterfalls and sense of adventure that inevitably arises when hiking in the jungle guarantee a good day. Khao Yai's mix of scenery and accessibility is hard to beat. Banded kingfishers

Ko Kut

18 Still looking for that paradise island where the crowds are thin, the water aquamarine and clear, and the beaches wide and long? Try Ko Kut (p482). There is Hat Khlong Chao, one of the most beautiful stretches of sand anywhere in Thailand, fine snorkelling and hidden waterfalls to hike to. Best of all, Ko Kut retains a supremely unhurried pace of life that visitors soon find themselves imitating. There is nothing in the way of nightlife, apart from listening to the ocean. But that's why you're here. Nam Tok Khlong Chao (p482)

Phanom Rung Historical Park

19 Perched atop an extinct volcano, the biggest and best Khmer ruin (p414) in Thailand is truly special. As you amble along the promenade, up the stairs and over the bridges, the sense of anticipation builds. And when you enter the temple, completely restored and rich with Hindu sculpture, you experience a moment of timelessness. While Phanom Rung is not as awe-inspiring as Cambodia's Angkor Wat, the experience here is impressive and different enough that you should consider visiting both.

18

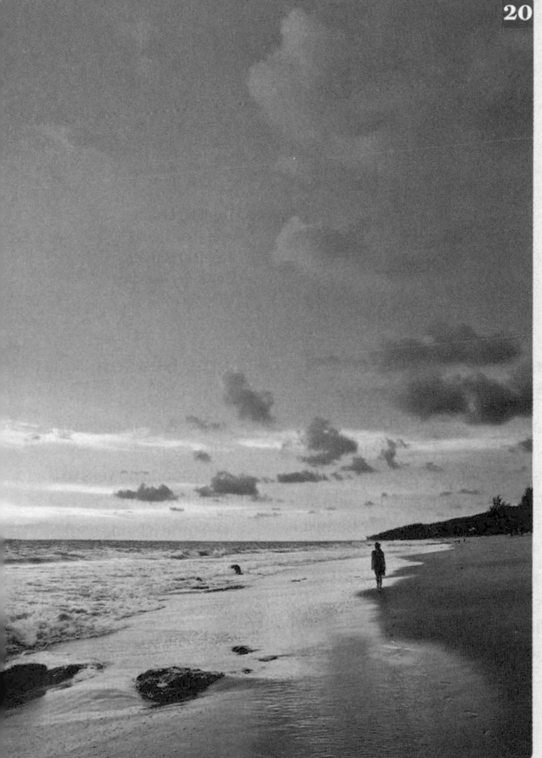

Ko Lanta

20 A beach bum's best friend, Ko Lanta (p670) sports a mellow island vibe and a parade of peachy sand. Social butterflies alight on the northern beaches for the party scene. Solitude seekers migrate southwards to low-key beach huts and a sleepy village ambience. Activities abound, from hiking through limestone caves to diving off Hin Muang and Hin Daeng, with the chance to glimpse rays and even whale sharks. Sprinkle in some culture by visiting the east coast's charismatic Old Town, home to a Muslim community and charming seafront coffee shops.

Need to Know

For more information, see Survival Guide (p757)

Currency
Thai baht (B)

Language
Thai

Visas
Usually a 30-day visa on arrival at international airports; 15-day visa at land borders; 60-day tourist visa through application at a Thai consulate.

Money
ATMs are widespread and charge a foreign-account fee (150B to 180B). Visa and MasterCard accepted at upmarket places.

Mobile Phones
Get inexpensive prepaid SIM cards for GSM phones. Bangkok and major cities have 4G.

Time
GMT plus seven hours

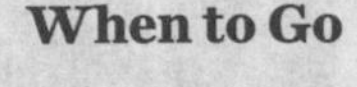

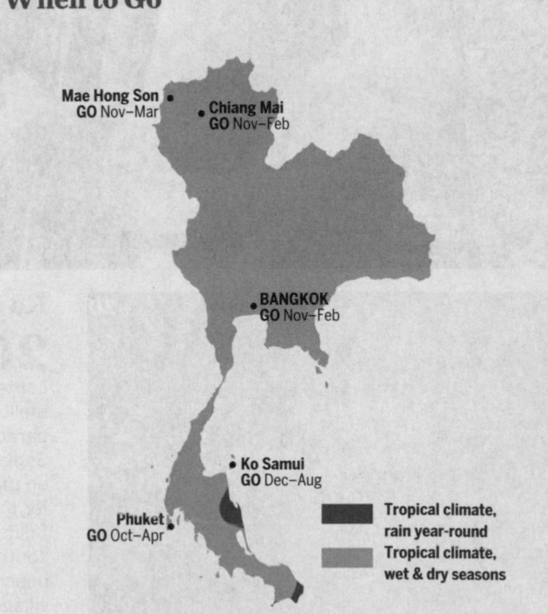

High Season
(Nov–Mar)

- A cool and dry season follows the monsoons, meaning the landscape is lush and temperatures are comfortable.
- Western Christmas and New Year's holidays bring crowds and inflated rates.

Shoulder Season
(Apr–Jun, Sep & Oct)

- April to June is generally very hot and dry, with an average Bangkok temperature of 30°C. Sea breezes in coastal areas provide natural air-con.
- September and October are ideal for the north and the gulf coast.

Low Season
(Jul–Oct)

- Monsoon season ranges from afternoon showers to major flooding.
- Some islands shut down; boat service is limited during stormy weather.
- Be flexible with travel plans.
- Rain is usually in short, intense bursts.

Useful Websites

Tourism Authority of Thailand (TAT; www.tourismthailand.org) National tourism department covering info and special events.

Thaivisa (www.thaivisa.com) Expat site for news and discussions.

Lonely Planet (www.lonelyplanet.com/thailand) Country profile and what to do and see.

Bangkok Post (www.bangkokpost.com) English-language daily.

The Nation (www.nationmultimedia.com) English-language daily.

Thai Language (www.thai-language.com) Online dictionary, Thai tutorials.

Important Numbers

Thailand country code	66
Emergency	191
International access codes	001, 007, 008, 009 (& other promotional codes)
Operator-assisted international calls	100
Tourist police	1155

Exchange Rates

Australia	A$1	26B
Canada	C$1	26B
China	Y10	55B
Euro zone	€1	39B
Japan	¥100	29B
New Zealand	NZ$1	24B
South Korea	1000W	30B
UK	£1	53B
US	US$1	36B

For current exchange rates see www.xe.com.

Daily Costs

Budget: Less than 1000B

- Basic guesthouse room: 400–1000B
- Market/street stall meal: 40–100B
- One beer: 100B
- Public transport around town: 20–50B

Midrange: 1000–3000B

- Flashpacker guesthouse or midrange hotel room: 1000–3000B
- Western lunches and seafood dinner: 150–350B
- Organised tour or activity: 1000–1500B
- Motorbike hire: 150–250B

Top End: More than 3000B

- Boutique hotel room: 3000B
- Fine dining: 350–500B
- Private tours: 2000B
- Car hire: from 800B

Opening Hours

Banks and government offices close for national holidays. Some bars and clubs close during elections and certain holidays when alcohol sales are banned. Shopping centres have banks that open late.

Banks 9.30am–3.30pm; 24hr ATMs

Bars 6pm–1am

Clubs 8pm–2am; some open later

Government Offices 8.30am–4.30pm Monday to Friday; some close for lunch

Restaurants 8am–10pm; some restaurants are open only to 3pm or 4pm

Shops 10am or 11am to 9pm

Arriving in Thailand

Suvarnabhumi International Airport (Bangkok; p774) The Airport Rail Link has a local service (45B, 30 minutes) to Phaya Thai and an express service (90B, 15 minutes) to Makkasan (Bangkok City Air Terminal) and Phaya Thai. Taxis cost 220B to 380B plus 50B airport surcharge and tolls; it's about an hour to the city. Public buses run to central Bangkok (24B to 35B, 6am to midnight).

Don Mueang International Airport (Bangkok; p774) Bus A1 runs to BTS Mo Chit; bus A2 runs to BTS Mo Chit and BTS Victory Monument. Both cost 30B and run every 30 minutes. Trains run to Hualamphong (5B to 10B, 45 minutes). Taxis cost 300B to 400B, plus 50B charges/fees. Free shuttle buses run to Suvarnabhumi 5am to midnight.

Chiang Mai International Airport (p774) Taxis from the airport are a flat 120B.

Phuket International Airport (p774) Buses run to Phuket Town (100B, every 90 minutes). Minivans run to Phuket Town (150B) and the beaches (180B). Taxis (550B) run to the beaches and Phuket Town.

Getting Around

Buses Extensive and affordable for travel between towns.

Air Cheap domestic flights.

Trains Slow but scenic from Bangkok to Chiang Mai or Surat Thani.

Car & Motorcycle Easy to rent.

Local transport Taxis and motorcycles are widely available; bargaining required.

For much more on **getting around**, see p776

First Time Thailand

For more information, see Survival Guide (p757)

Checklist

- Ensure your passport is valid for at least six months.
- Apply for a tourist visa for visits longer than 30 days from a Thai consulate.
- Organise travel insurance, diver's insurance and international driving permit.
- Visit doctor for check-up and medical clearance if intending to scuba dive.
- Inform your bank and credit-card company of your travel plans.

What to Pack

- Driving licence and international driving permit
- Thai phrasebook
- Power converter
- GSM mobile phone and charger
- A week's worth of lightweight clothes
- Hat and sunglasses
- Sandals
- Earplugs
- Raingear and dry bag if travelling in the rainy season

Top Tips for Your Trip

- Eat at the market or the street stalls for true Thai snacks.
- Hop aboard local transport. It is cheap and a great way to hang out with the locals.
- Rent a bicycle to tour towns and neighbourhoods.
- Learn a few Thai phrases and always smile.
- Avoid the first-timer scams: one-day gem sales in Bangkok, insane transport prices, dodgy tailors.
- Learn how to bargain without being a jerk.

What to Wear

In general, light, loose-fitting clothes will prove the most comfortable in the tropical heat. It's worth bringing one jacket that can double as a raincoat and keep you warm in higher elevations and on air-conditioned buses. When you visit temples, wear clothes that cover to your elbows and knees. Bring a smart outfit if you plan on clubbing in Bangkok or fine-dining in Phuket.

Sleeping

Finding a place to stay in Thailand is easy. For peace of mind, book a room for your arrival night; after that, you can wing it. However, vacancies become scarce during certain holidays and peak travel periods, so it can be beneficial to book ahead.

- **Guesthouses** Our favourites are those family-run options, usually in a converted house or apartment building. Rooms run from basic (bed and fan) to plush (private bathroom and air-con).
- **Hotels** From boutique to stodgy, hotels offer comfortable, mainly modern rooms, with extra services like breakfast included in the rate and sometimes a swimming pool.
- **Hostels** As prices and standards within Thailand's guesthouses have gone up, dorms have become better value. Good for solo travellers.

Money

Most places deal only with cash. Some foreign credit cards are accepted in high-end establishments.

ATMs are widespread but there is a foreign-transaction fee (150B to 180B) in addition to whatever fees your home bank charges. To keep ATM withdrawals to a minimum, take out as much cash as you feel comfortable carrying. Most ATMs allow 20,000B withdrawals.

Bargaining

If there is no posted price, then bargaining is acceptable. Ask the price, follow up by asking for a discount, offer a counter price and accept what is offered in return. Always smile and don't start bargaining if you're not interested in buying.

Tipping

Tipping is not standard but it is appreciated. If there are a few coins left over from a restaurant bill or metered taxi fare, it is common to offer it as a tip.

Tips for Sticking to a Budget

- Track your expenses.
- Use local transport.
- Travel with a companion to share lodging costs.
- Eat at markets.
- Save souvenir shopping until the end of your trip.
- Take buses or trains instead of planes for long-distance travel.

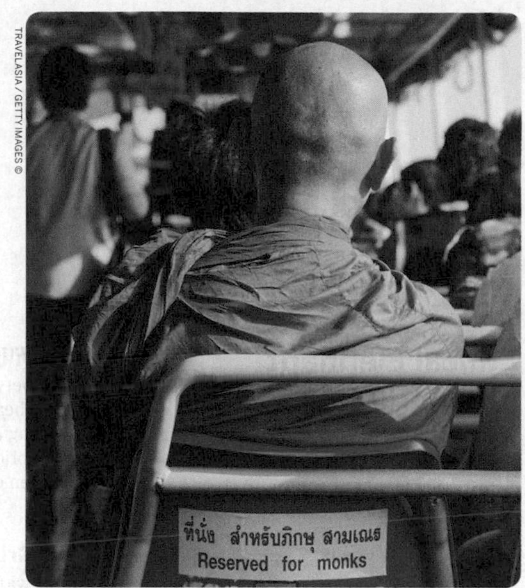

Special seats are eserved for monks on transport

Etiquette

Thais are generally very understanding and hospitable, but there are some important taboos and social conventions.

- **Monarchy** Never disrespect the royal family with disparaging remarks. Treat objects depicting the king (like money) with respect. Stand when the national and king's anthems are played.
- **Temples** Wear clothing that covers to your knees and elbows. Remove your shoes when you enter a temple building. Sit with your feet tucked behind you to avoid pointing the bottom of your feet at Buddha images. Women should never touch a monk or a monk's belongings; step out of the way on footpaths and don't sit next to them on public transport.
- **Modesty** At the beach, avoid public nudity or topless sunbathing. Wear a cover-up to and from the beach.
- **Save Face** Never get into an argument with a Thai. It is better to smile through any conflict.

Language

Tourist towns are well stocked with English speakers, though bus drivers, market vendors and taxi drivers are less fluent so it helps to know how to order food and count in Thai.

Thailand has its own script. Street signs are transliterated into English, but there is no standard system so spellings vary widely. Not all letters are pronounced as they appear ('Ph' is an aspirated 'p' not an 'f'). See Language (p787) for more information.

What's New

Ethical Elephant Interactions

With overwhelming evidence now available to support claims by animal welfare experts that elephant rides and shows are not only unsustainable, but ultimately harmful for Asia's gentle giants, more ethical elephant interactions are gaining popularity. Sanctuaries in areas such as Chiang Mai, Kanchanaburi and Surin focus on more elephant-friendly activities, such as bathing, walking with and preparing food for the pachyderms, rather than making the residents turn tricks for tourists. (p327)

Smoother Samet

The former quagmire-like roads on Ko Samet have been dramatically improved, so much so that the island's ATVs have completely vanished. All the main beaches can now be accessed in relative ease. (p457)

Airport Expansion

U-Tapao Airport, near Pattaya, is set for major expansion. At present, Bangkok Air runs flights to Ko Samui and Phuket while Air Asia flies to Kuala Lumpur in Malaysia. There are plans to launch routes to Thai provinces and Chinese cities. By 2020 the aim is to raise passenger capacity to five million people a year. (p451)

Visa Ease

Six-month, multiple-entry visas are now available for virtually all foreign visitors to Thailand. The 5000B visa will mean an end to the tiresome border-hops that long-stay travellers had to make.

Budget Flights

Hopping between cities has never been easier as cheap domestic flights have taken off. Booking ahead means flying is now a realistic option for budget travellers, as the cost is often only slightly more than going by bus.

On the Grid

An underwater cable to Ko Chang's smaller neighbours, Ko Mak and Ko Kut, began operating in late 2015, meaning they are hooked up to the national grid. Both islands now have round-the-clock electricity for the first time – great for visitors and locals alike. (p480) (p482)

Phuket Beach 'Clean Up'

Authorities have attempted to tidy up Phuket beaches by bulldozing restaurants and banning sun loungers and umbrellas. Some traders are inevitably paying little attention to such edicts and continue to offer a handful of beach mats and drinking areas. (p613)

Route into Myanmar

Travellers wanting an overland route into Myanmar can now get from from Kanchanaburi to the coastal town of Dawei. (p183)

Lao Links

A new Friendship Bridge spans the mighty Mekong River, linking up Chiang Khong in Chiang Rai and Huay Xai in Laos. (p232)

For more recommendations and reviews, see lonelyplanet.com/thailand

If You Like...

Wildlife Encounters

Khao Yai National Park Spot elephants, monkeys, snakes and creepy-crawlies in Thailand's oldest national park. (p410)

Kaeng Krachan National Park Wake up to dense morning mists, then go trekking to spot elephants and gibbons in this little-visited park, south of Bangkok. (p490)

Ao Khanom A lovely and untouristed bay south of Surat Thani that hosts pink dolphins, a rare albino breed. (p574)

Um Phang An isolated and untamed corner of Thailand where forest creatures still roam. (p274)

Chiang Mai Meet retired and rescued working elephants in sanctuaries. (p306)

Nam Nao National Park One of the best spots for ornithologists, this park is also home to elephants, leopards and tigers. (p440)

Khao Laem National Park With a mighty reservoir, this park is where visitors can jump in boats to glimpse some of the 260 species of wildlife that live here. (p187)

World-Class Pampering

Ko Samui Get lean, aligned and beautified on this wellness retreat island. (p520)

Bangkok Massages in the City of Angels are an everyday treat, like picking up dry cleaning or going to the post office. (p97)

Phuket Five-star spas make pampering an all-day affair on this resort island. (p622)

Chiang Mai This low-key city does massages for the masses without the painful 'spa' price tag. (p330)

Ko Chang As if lounging on the beach isn't enough, Ko Chang boasts top-class spas for that extra level of de-stressing. (p471)

Escaping the Crowds

Ko Tarutao Virtually deserted, Ko Tarutao's vast, empty beaches are the perfect places to enjoy seclusion. (p693)

Mae Hong Son This remote and charming border town has an addictive Thai-Burmese flavour. (p278)

Pranburi Look for dolphins and enjoy the seafood at this coastal spot. (p504)

Ko Ngai One of the quieter southern islands, Ko Ngai has superb snorkelling and top beaches. (p684)

Thai Food

Thai food is superdelicious, remarkably convenient and ridiculously cheap.

Curries Thai curry is pungent, fiery and colourful. Bangkok, southern Thailand and northern Thailand all whip up their own variations.

Isan cuisine The northeast's triumvirate dishes – *gài yâhng* (grilled chicken), *sôm·đam* (spicy green papaya salad) and *kôw nĕe·o* (sticky rice) – have converts across the country.

Seafood Grilled prawns, spicy squid stir-fries, crab curries, fried mussels – get thee to the coast and dine on the fruits of the sea.

Fruits Luscious, dessert-like tropical fruits are piled into pyramid displays at day markets or arranged like precious jewels in vendors' glass cases.

Cooking Courses Learn how to replicate the tricks of the trade at cooking schools in Bangkok (p99) or Chiang Mai (p328).

Temples & Ruins

From glittering Buddhist temples to ancient Khmer sanctuaries.

Bangkok The city's most exalted Buddha figure resides comfortably in Wat Phra Kaew, the seat of Thai Buddhism. (p58)

Ayuthaya The ruins of this fabled city stand testament to Thailand's formative years. (p158)

Sukhothai This ancient city is the capital of one of Thailand's first home-grown kingdoms. (p254)

Chiang Mai Chiang Mai's old walled city is filled with antique teak temples. (p306)

Phanom Rung This Khmer outpost built in the Angkor style has surveyed the rural landscape for centuries. (p414)

Lopburi Leaders from the Khmer and Dvaravati empires used to rule here; today hundreds of monkeys scamper around the ruins. (p167)

Shopping & Markets

Bangkok Pick from the capital's mega-malls packed with designer gear, sprawling markets like Chatuchak or chic independent shops. (p135)

Chiang Mai The bustling Night Bazaar is filled with souvenirs and antiques. Outside the city, handicraft centres make silk garments and colourful umbrellas. (p346)

Phuket Jungceylon is the island's swankiest shopping centre, while the Weekend Market has a great selection of snacks, clothes and music. (p623)

Khon Kaen Foodies swarm around the city's Walking Street market and chow down on the red sausages and sweets. (p432)

Top: Reclining Buddha at Wat Lokayasutharam (p159), Ayuthaya

Bottom: Songkran water fights, Chiang Mai

Floating lanterns at Loi Krathong festival

Hill-Tribe Culture

Chiang Mai The Karen, Lahu, Hmong and several other hill tribes live around Chiang Mai. (p306)

Chiang Rai The Akha, who live in the mountains surrounding Chiang Rai, have distinct traditions, including a giant swing festival. (p205)

Sangkhlaburi Volunteer at one of several charities in this border town that look after displaced hill tribes from Myanmar. Wang Kha is a Mon village, accessible via Thailand's longest wooden bridge. (p187)

Mae Sot A fascinatingly diverse city, where Hmong, Karen and Burmese folk stroll the streets. (p269)

Nightlife

Bangkok International DJs regularly hold court in the capital's clubs while a more chilled clientele sip mojitos from the city's sky bars. Th Khao San remains the backpackers' favourite haunt. (p126)

Phuket Clubs, live music bars and cabaret shows ensure there's plenty of post-beach action to be had. (p622)

Pattaya Mega clubs have arrived in Pattaya, aimed largely at foreign visitors. An increasing number of five-star venues have their own fancy bars, with live music on tap. (p455)

Ko Pha-Ngan Home of the Full Moon Party, buckets of whisky and almighty hangovers. (p552)

Festivals

Songkran Thailand's biggest festival is about using water to show respect. Once that's done, water fights erupt in every town.

Music festivals With a jazz festival in Hua Hin (p498), an Asian pop fest in Pattaya (p453) and international DJs in Bangkok and Ko Samui, music fans are well catered for.

Loi Krathong Every November, Thais pray for their sins to be forgiven by creating lanterns and setting them afloat in waterways.

Fruit festivals Rural towns honour their agricultural produce with a range of festivals. In Chiang Rai the lychee is revered, while Chanthaburi (p463) takes time to honour everybody's stinkiest fruit, the durian.

Month by Month

TOP EVENTS

Songkran, April

Loi Krathong, November

Ubon Ratchathani's Khao Phansaa, July

Vegetarian Festival, October

January

The weather is cool and dry, ushering in the peak tourist season.

Chinese New Year

Thais with Chinese ancestry celebrate the Chinese lunar new year *(đrùd jeen)* with a week of house-cleaning and fireworks.

February

Still in the high season, Thailand is sun and fun for anyone snowed out.

Makha Bucha

One of three holy days marking significant moments of Buddha's life, Makha Bucha *(mah·ká boo·chah)* commemorates the day when 1250 *arahants* (Buddhists who had achieved enlightenment) assembled to visit Buddha and received the principles of Buddhism; the festival falls on the full moon of the third lunar month. It is a public holiday.

Flower Festival

Chiang Mai displays its floral beauty during a three-day period. The festival highlight is the flower-decorated floats that parade through town.

March

The hot and dry season approaches and the beaches start to empty out, coinciding with Thailand's semester break ('mid term'), and students head out on sightseeing trips.

Pattaya International Music Festival

Pattaya showcases pop and rock bands from across Asia at this free music event, attracting bus loads of Bangkok university students.

Kite-Flying Festivals

During the windy season, colourful kites battle it out over the skies of Sanam Luang in Bangkok and elsewhere in the country.

Golden Mango Season

Luscious ripe mangoes come into season from March to June and are sliced before your eyes, packed in a container with sticky rice and accompanied with a sweet sauce.

April

Hot, dry weather sweeps across the land. Though the main tourist season is winding down, make reservations well in advance – the whole country is on the move for Songkran.

Songkran

Thailand's traditional new year (13–15 April) starts out as a respectful affair then degenerates into a water war. Morning visits to the temple involve colourful processions and water-sprinkling ceremonies of sacred Buddha images. Afterwards, Thais load up their water guns and head out to the streets for combat. Chiang Mai and Bangkok are the epicentres.

Poi Sang Long

This colourful Buddhist novice ordination festival held in late March/early April in Mae Hong Son and Chiang Mai sees young

Top: Colourful floats for the Flower Festival (p30) in Chiang Mai
Bottom: Spirit masks worn at the Phi Ta Khon (p32) parade in Dan Sai

Shan (Tai Yai) boys between the ages of seven and 14 parading in festive costumes, headdresses and make-up.

May

Leading up to the rainy season, festivals encourage plentiful rains and bountiful harvests. Prices are low and tourists are few but it is still remorselessly hot.

Royal Ploughing Ceremony

This royal ceremony employs astrology and ancient Brahman rituals to kick off the rice-planting season. Sacred oxen are hitched to a wooden plough and part the ground of Sanam Luang in Bangkok.

Rocket Festival

In the northeast, where rain can be scarce, villagers craft painted bamboo rockets *(bâng fai)* that are fired into the sky to encourage precipitation. This festival is celebrated in Yasothon, Ubon Ratchathani and Nong Khai.

Visakha Bucha

The holy day of Visakha Bucha *(wí·săh·kà boo·chah)* falls on the 15th day of the waxing moon in the sixth lunar month and commemorates the date of the Buddha's birth, enlightenment and *parinibbana* (passing away).

June

In some parts of the country, the rainy season is merely an afternoon shower, leaving the rest of the day for music and merriment. This month is a shoulder season.

Chanthaburi Fruit Festival

Held at the end of May or the start of June, this festival in Chanthaburi is an opportunity to enjoy an abundance of fruit: mangosteen, rambutan, longkong, longan, salak and the ever-pungent durian.

Hua Hin Jazz Festival

Jazz groups descend on this royal retreat for a musical homage to the king, an accomplished jazz saxophonist and composer.

Phi Ta Khon

The Buddhist holy day of Bun Phra Wet is given a Carnival makeover in Dan Sai village in northeast Thailand. Revellers disguise themselves in garish 'spirit' costumes and parade through the streets wielding wooden phalluses and downing rice whisky. Dates vary between June and July.

July

The start of the rainy season ushers in Buddhist Lent, a period of reflection and meditation. Summer holidays bring an upsurge in tourists.

Asahna Bucha

The full moon of the eighth lunar month commemorates Buddha's first sermon, in which he described the religion's four noble truths. It is considered one of Buddhism's holiest days.

Khao Phansaa

The day after Asahna Bucha marks the beginning of Buddhist Lent (the first day of the waning moon in the eighth lunar month), the traditional time for men to enter the monastery. In Ubon Ratchathani, traditional candle offerings have grown into a festival of elaborately carved wax sculptures.

August

Overcast skies and daily showers mark the middle of the rainy season.

HM the Queen's Birthday

The Thai Queen's Birthday (12 August) is a public holiday and national mother's day.

October

Religious preparations for the end of the rainy season and the end of Buddhist Lent begin. The monsoons are reaching the finish line (in most of the country).

Vegetarian Festival

A holiday from meat is taken for nine days in adherence with Chinese beliefs of mind and body purification. In Phuket the festival gets extreme, with entranced marchers turning themselves into human shish kebabs.

Ork Phansaa

The end of the Buddhist Lent (three lunar months after Khao Phansaa) is marked by the *gà·tĭn* ceremony, in which new robes are given to the monks by merit-makers.

King Chulalongkorn Day

Rama V is honoured on the anniversary of his death at the Royal Plaza in Dusit. Held on 23 October.

November

The cool, dry season has arrived and if you get here early enough, you'll beat the tourist crowds. The beaches are inviting and the landscape is lush.

Surin Elephant Round-up

Held on the third weekend of November, Surin celebrates its most famous residents. Note that the festival carries some animal welfare concerns.

Loi Krathong

One of Thailand's most beloved festivals, Loi Krathong is celebrated on the first full moon of the 12th lunar month. Small origami-like boats (called *kràthong* or *grà·tong*) festooned with flowers and candles are sent adrift in the waterways.

Lopburi Monkey Festival

During the last week of November, the town's troublesome macaques get pampered with their very own banquet, while merit-makers watch merrily.

December

The peak of the tourist season has returned with fair skies, busy beach resorts and a holiday mood.

HM the King's Birthday

Honouring the king's birthday on 5 December, this public holiday hosts parades and merit-making events. Everyone wears pink shirts, pink being the colour associated with the monarchy.

Itineraries

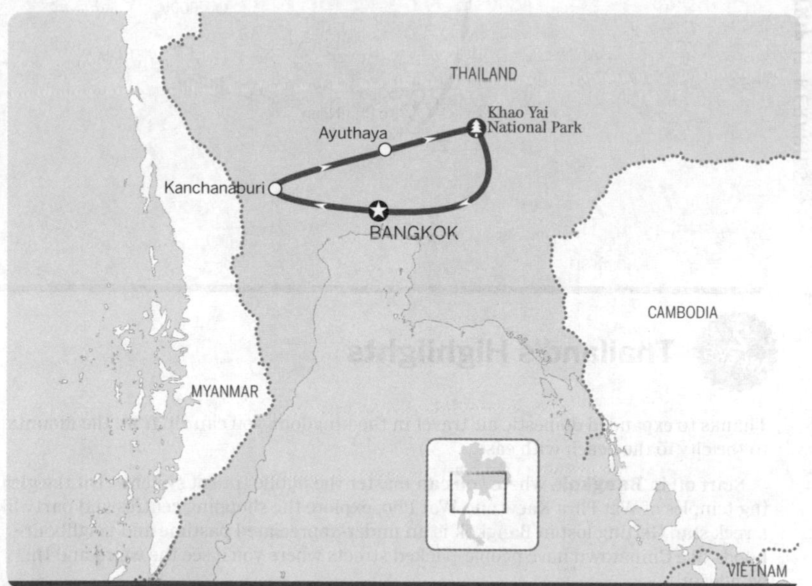

Bangkok & Around

If time is not on your side, you can still explore jungles, temples and Thai culture – they are all within easy reach of **Bangkok**.

After a quick look around the capital's major temples and markets and hitting its top restaurants, embark on the wonderfully scenic train ride to **Kanchanaburi**. Here, enjoy a dip in the seven-tiered Erawan waterfall before visiting the Hellfire Pass Memorial, a poignant tribute to the thousands of prisoners of war who died making the Death Railway during WWII. Nearby forests are ideal for short hikes or adventure activities, such as ziplining over the forest canopies or giving elephants a bath in the River Kwai.

Next, jump in a minivan bound for **Ayuthaya** and cycle around the impressive ruins of this erstwhile capital. Finally, head over to **Khao Yai National Park** (transiting through Pak Chong). Spend a day hiking through the jungle in search of elephants and tigers and a night camping under the stars before winding your way back to Bangkok.

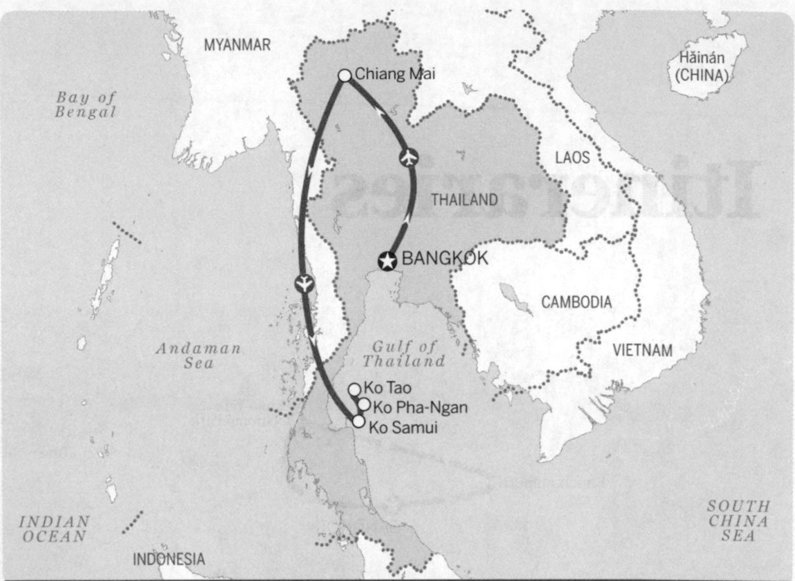

Thailand's Highlights

Thanks to expanded domestic air travel in the kingdom, you can zip from the mountains to the city to the beach with ease.

Start off in **Bangkok**, where you can master the public transit system, visit the gleaming temples of Wat Phra Kaew and Wat Pho, explore the shopping centres and party like a rock star. Getting lost in Bangkok is an under-appreciated pastime and neighbourhoods like Chinatown have people-packed streets where you'll see the weird and the wonderful.

Fly (or take the scenic train) to **Chiang Mai**, which can keep you busy for several days with its Thai cooking classes, temples, monk chats, markets and fabulous food. Take a road trip to the surrounding countryside, where you can hike to hill-tribe villages, meet rescued elephants and zipline through the forest. Don't forget to visit the cool highlands of Doi Suthep or Doi Inthanon, two famous northern mountains.

Ready for some beach time? Take a direct flight from Chiang Mai south to the tropical island of **Ko Samui**, where you can choose to live it up in a five-star resort or villa, or relax in a low-key beach bungalow in one of the island's quieter corners (yes, fortunately some still exist).

Make a day trip to uninhabited Ang Thong Marine National Marine Park before a stop at **Ko Pha-Ngan**; an easy boat trip from Ko Samui. Head to one of its famous Full Moon Parties, or time your visit to miss the crowds and enjoy some laid-back hammock hanging instead. Next door is tiny **Ko Tao**, Thailand's diving-certification headquarters; there are plenty of shallow reefs near the shore for snorkellers, too.

Head back to Samui to fly on to your next destination, or make your way back to Bangkok for some last-minute shopping.

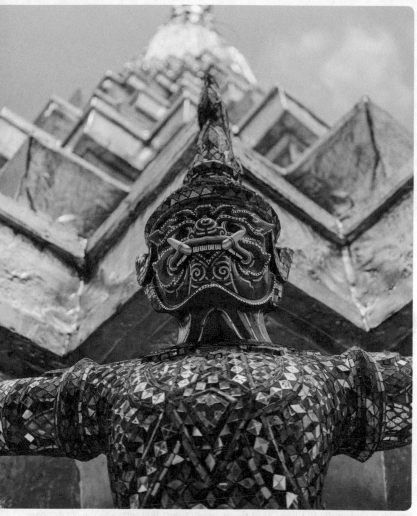

Top: Wat Phra Kaew (p61), Bangkok
Bottom: Monk Chat session (p328) at Wat Chedi Luang (p311), Chiang Mai

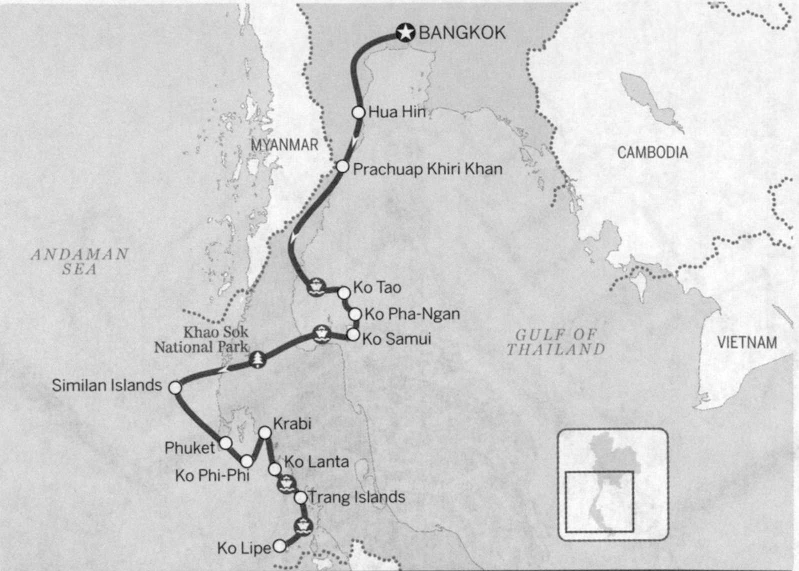

Best of Southern Thailand

Hitting all of Thailand's top beaches in one trip isn't easy, but with some serious island-hopping you can do it and still have bags of hammock time. This trip takes you there by land and sea, but if you need to hurry up, hop on a flight along the way.

From **Bangkok**, dip south into **Hua Hin**, an upmarket resort town where all the top hotel chains have a spot on the beach, then on to **Prachuap Khiri Khan**, where you can hire a bike and check out the curvy coast, bays and laid-back beach scene.

Now for some island time, first stop **Ko Tao** (via Chumphon). Sign up for a dive course or enjoy a few days of snorkelling before island-hopping to **Ko Pha-Ngan** for Full Moon Party fun or an other-side-of-the-island escape. Retire to the resort island of **Ko Samui** for some pampering (or, if you've the energy, more partying), from where it's a short ferry ride to transport hub Surat Thani. Buses leave hourly for **Khao Sok National Park**, where you can enjoy some jungle time in one of the world's oldest rainforests before making the short transfer to Khao Lak, a sleepy beach resort that serves as the perfect base for dive trips to the world-famous **Similan Islands** and, to the north, the Surin Islands. Consider spending a few days on a live-aboard to linger in the underwater world full of rays, sharks and seahorses. Once you surface, go south to **Phuket** – Thailand's largest island – and gulp down the numerous attractions and activities on offer here (don't miss a day trip to Ao Phang-Nga).

From Phuket, jump in a boat bound for **Ko Phi-Phi**, a party island that stays up all night and still looks fantastic in the morning. From here you can return to the mainland and explore the gorgeous coastline of **Krabi** (be sure to take a long-tail boat to Railay beach, regarded as one of the finest in Thailand) or ferry straight to **Ko Lanta** to collapse in a hammock and drink in the bucolic island life. Continue south by ferry past the beautiful **Trang Islands** to increasingly popular but still relatively undeveloped **Ko Lipe**, and catch a speedboat back to the mainland when you're ready to begin your journey home.

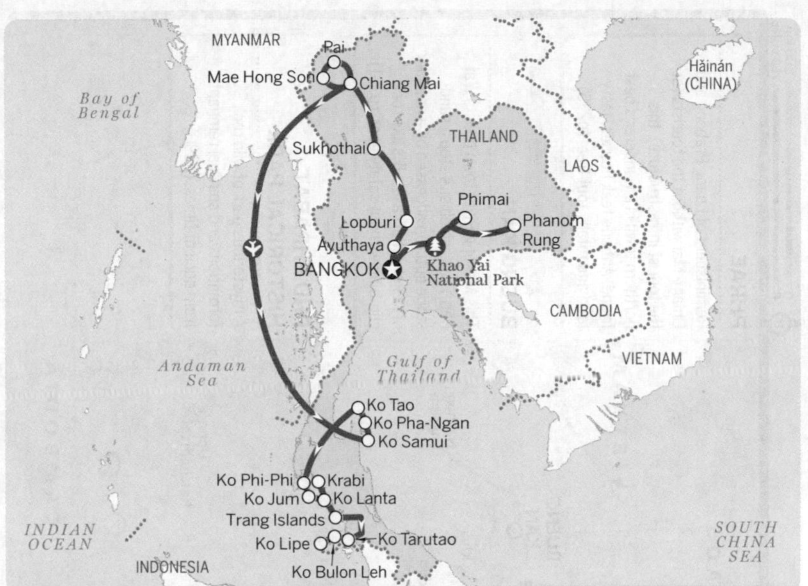

The Grand Tour

A fully rounded trip to Thailand meanders through almost every corner of the kingdom. If you need to save time, hop on a flight – planes go everywhere.

Start off in **Bangkok**, and then take a train north to the ancient capital of **Ayuthaya**. Make a brief detour to the monkey town of **Lopburi**. From here, follow the culture trail north to **Sukhothai**, where you can cycle through the crumbling ruins of another ancient capital. Hightail it to **Chiang Mai**, the 'rose of the north', and cycle around the old temples. Then switchback into the mountains to the party scene of **Pai**. Climb deeper into the hills to the Myanmar-influenced town of **Mae Hong Son**. Loop back to Chiang Mai.

By now the beach is calling, so fly to the Gulf of Thailand and thread through **Ko Samui** for its resort-island trappings, **Ko Pha-Ngan** for beach bumming and partying, and **Ko Tao** for diving and snorkelling.

Get over to the Andaman Coast and its limestone mountains jutting out of the sea. **Ko Phi-Phi** is the prettiest, priciest and partiest of them all. Little **Ko Jum** holds tight to a fast-disappearing beach-shack, hippie vibe. **Ko Lanta** has gentrified into a package-tour destination, but the dive scene is the real attraction. Rock climbers opt for mainland **Krabi**, particularly Railay.

If you've got the itch for more sand then continue down the peninsula to the **Trang Islands**, another collection of limestone sea mountains lapped by gin-clear water. Or opt for the idyllic islands offshore from Satun. There's also emerging and midrange **Ko Bulon Leh**, rustic **Ko Tarutao** and laid-back **Ko Lipe**.

Or, you could skip the beaches south of Krabi and instead take a cultural antidote to the northeast, Thailand's agricultural heartland. Transit through Bangkok and then crawl through the jungles of **Khao Yai National Park**. From here, head to Nakhon Ratchasima (Khorat), a transit point for trips to the Angkor ruins at **Phimai**. Follow the Khmer trail east to **Phanom Rung**, the most important and visually impressive of the Angkor temples in Thailand. Surrounding Phanom Rung are a handful of smaller, more remote and forgotten temples with regal ambience.

Off the Beaten Track: Thailand

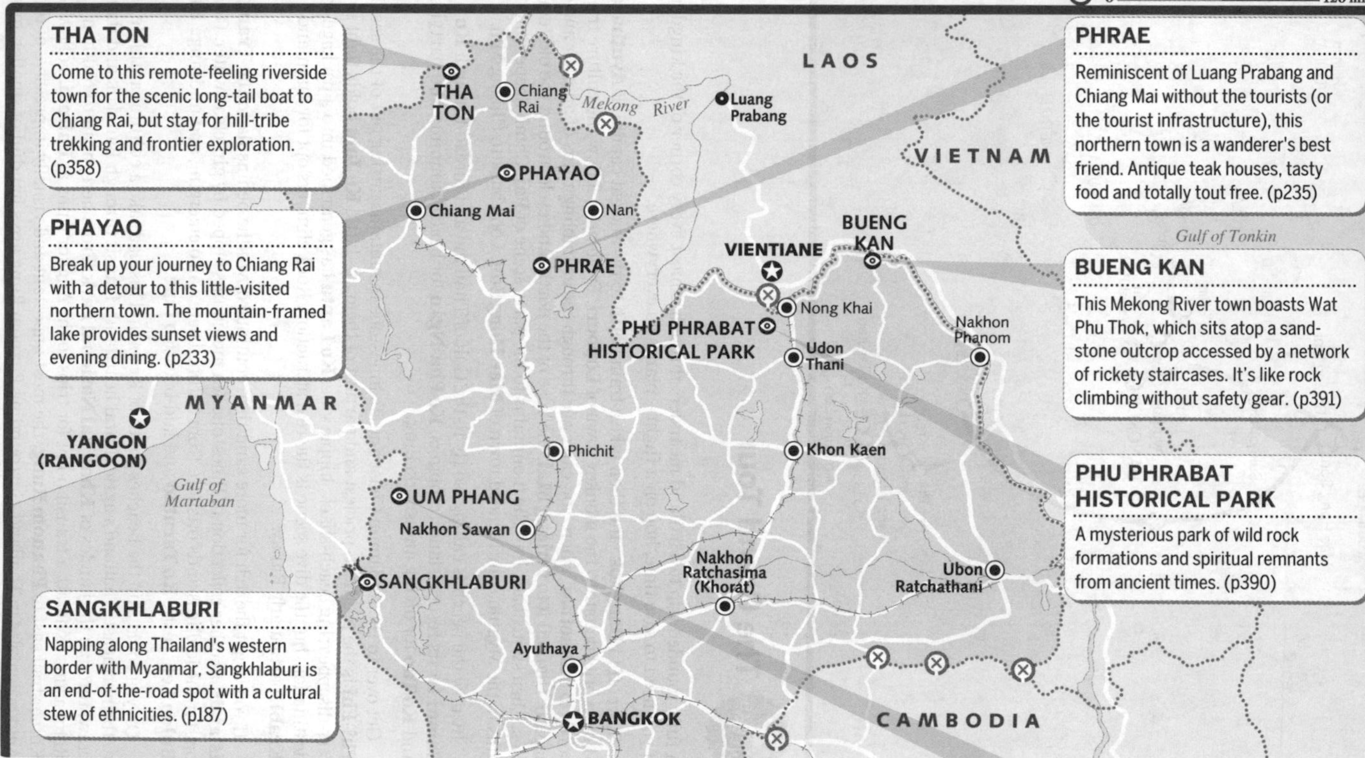
0 200 km
0 120 miles
N
THA TON
Come to this remote-feeling riverside town for the scenic long-tail boat to Chiang Rai, but stay for hill-tribe trekking and frontier exploration. (p358)
PHAYAO
Break up your journey to Chiang Rai with a detour to this little-visited northern town. The mountain-framed lake provides sunset views and evening dining. (p233)
SANGKHLABURI
Napping along Thailand's western border with Myanmar, Sangkhlaburi is an end-of-the-road spot with a cultural stew of ethnicities. (p187)
PHRAE
Reminiscent of Luang Prabang and Chiang Mai without the tourists (or the tourist infrastructure), this northern town is a wanderer's best friend. Antique teak houses, tasty food and totally tout free. (p235)
BUENG KAN
This Mekong River town boasts Wat Phu Thok, which sits atop a sandstone outcrop accessed by a network of rickety staircases. It's like rock climbing without safety gear. (p391)
PHU PHRABAT HISTORICAL PARK
A mysterious park of wild rock formations and spiritual remnants from ancient times. (p390)
LAOS
VIETNAM
MYANMAR
CAMBODIA
Gulf of Tonkin
Gulf of Martaban
Mekong River
THA TON
Chiang Rai
Luang Prabang
PHAYAO
Chiang Mai
Nan
PHRAE
VIENTIANE
BUENG KAN
Nong Khai
PHU PHRABAT HISTORICAL PARK
Udon Thani
Nakhon Phanom
YANGON (RANGOON)
Phichit
Khon Kaen
UM PHANG
Nakhon Sawan
SANGKHLABURI
Nakhon Ratchasima (Khorat)
Ubon Ratchathani
Ayuthaya
BANGKOK

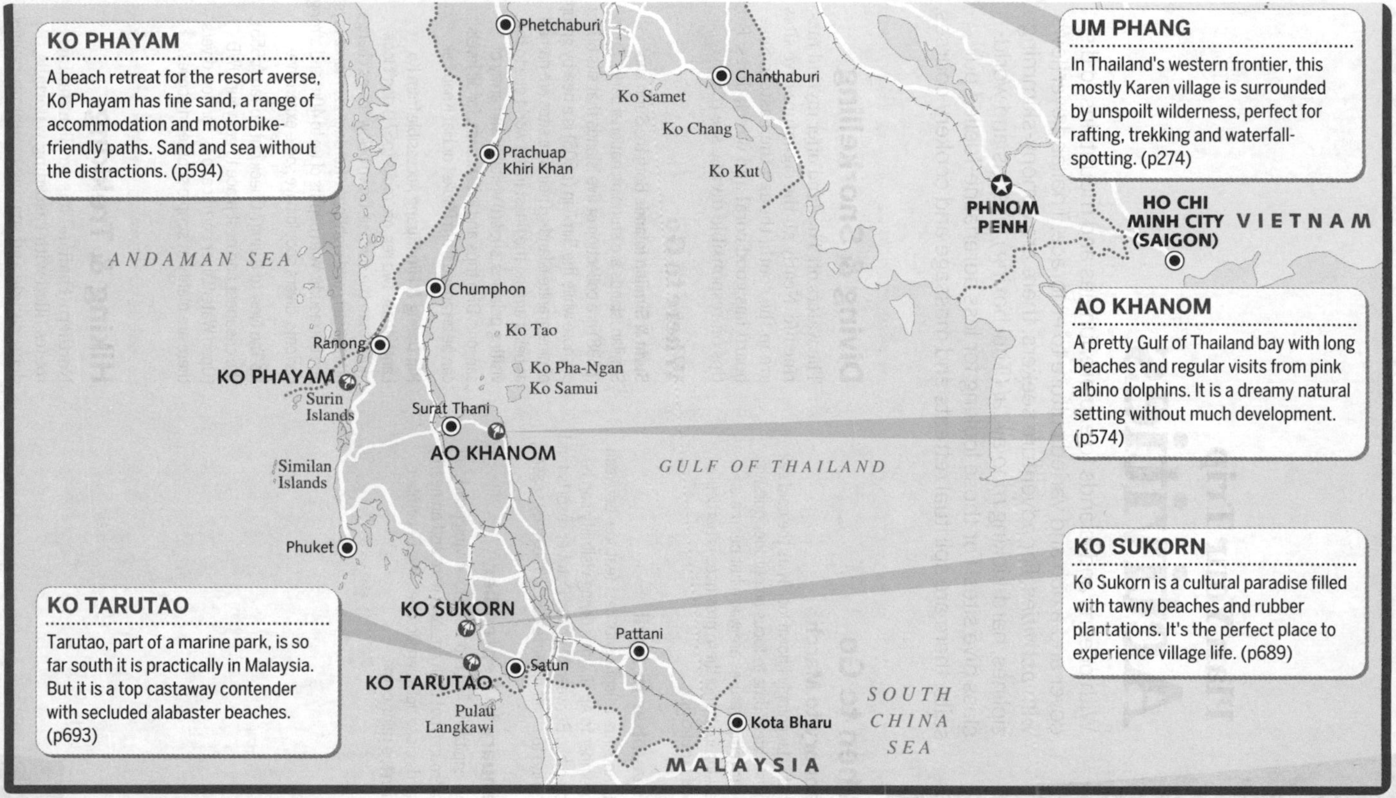

KO PHAYAM

A beach retreat for the resort averse, Ko Phayam has fine sand, a range of accommodation and motorbike-friendly paths. Sand and sea without the distractions. (p594)

UM PHANG

In Thailand's western frontier, this mostly Karen village is surrounded by unspoilt wilderness, perfect for rafting, trekking and waterfall-spotting. (p274)

AO KHANOM

A pretty Gulf of Thailand bay with long beaches and regular visits from pink albino dolphins. It is a dreamy natural setting without much development. (p574)

KO SUKORN

Ko Sukorn is a cultural paradise filled with tawny beaches and rubber plantations. It's the perfect place to experience village life. (p689)

KO TARUTAO

Tarutao, part of a marine park, is so far south it is practically in Malaysia. But it is a top castaway contender with secluded alabaster beaches. (p693)

Phetchaburi
Chanthaburi
Ko Samet
Ko Chang
Ko Kut
Prachuap Khiri Khan
PHNOM PENH
HO CHI MINH CITY (SAIGON)
VIETNAM
ANDAMAN SEA
Chumphon
Ko Tao
Ranong
KO PHAYAM
Ko Pha-Ngan
Ko Samui
Surin Islands
Surat Thani
AO KHANOM
Similan Islands
GULF OF THAILAND
Phuket
KO SUKORN
Pattani
KO TARUTAO
Satun
Pulau Langkawi
Kota Bharu
SOUTH CHINA SEA
MALAYSIA

Plan Your Trip
Activities

With oceans and islands to explore, jungles and mountains to discover and a rich and varied culture to embrace, Thailand overflows with activities. For adventure seekers, there are canopy-skimming ziplines, hard-kicking *moo·ay tai* (Thai boxing) lessons and world-class dive sites. For those looking for less adrenaline-fuelled pursuits, there are spiritual retreats and massage and cookery courses.

When to Go

January to March

What is laughingly known locally as the cold season is a great time to focus on outdoor pursuits, as the temperatures are warm but bearable. Trekking in the northern provinces is particularly good around now.

November to April

The Andaman displays its best features between November to April, when diving visibility can be incredible. Between May and October resorts tend to grind to a halt or close due to the rainy season.

January to September

Dive capital Ko Tao is primed for diving nearly all year round, but many resorts here and on nearby islands close between October and December when the rains come.

Diving & Snorkelling

The waters off Thailand offer myriad marine life. Nearly all the signature dive sites are in the south, though the Eastern Seaboard has good coral and wreck dives. For tips on responsible diving, see p759.

Where to Go

Surin & Similan Islands Both the Surin and Similan islands are stunning national parks. Surin (p598) is a collection of five islands that sits 60km offshore while the Similan (p606) is a nearby group of nine granite islands. Their dive sites are named as being among the finest in the world due to the visiting pelagics, superb visibility and array of canyons. Dive trips and liveaboards, for all levels, can be arranged from Phuket or Hat Khao Lak.

Hin Daeng & Hin Muang Accessible from Ko Lanta, these two remote rocks (p671) don't look much from the surface. Down below things change dramatically and sightings often include manta rays and barracuda. With depths of up to 40m and strong currents, divers should have some experience.

Ko Tao New to diving? Check out Ko Tao (p555), the cheapest and best place to get your OWD (Open Water Diver certification). For non-divers, there are plenty of simple snorkelling coves.

Hiking & Trekking

Northern Thailand has excellent hiking routes filled with cascading waterfalls, dense jungle and soaring mountain ranges.

Stay overnight with hill tribes or pitch a tent with nature as your only neighbour. Along with treks, guides can arrange cycling, kayaking and rafting excursions.

Where to Go

Chiang Mai Chiang Mai (p324) is the main jumping-off point for treks, such as day trips to Doi Inthanon (p361), Thailand's highest mountain. Hardcore trekkers head to more remote spots such as Um Phang Wildlife Sanctuary (p274), home to the kingdom's largest waterfall, or learn survival skills from guides who grew up near the jungles.

Loei Loei (p365) has some spectacular trekking options. Among them is Phu Kradueng National Park (p376), where you can take the 5.5km trail to the plateau, or experience the relatively cooler climes of the pine forests and savannah.

Thai Cooking

Learning how to cook authentic Thai food is high on many visitors' to-do list. Many Thai chefs are happy to share their secrets and take tourists on trips to markets to teach them about specific ingredients. See p44 for more details about cooking courses.

Where to Go

Chiang Mai To master Thailand's northern cuisine, pick one of the numerous cookery schools in Chiang Mai (p328). Some focus on vegetarian or organic options.

Kanchanaburi Earn bragging rights back home by learning how to create the perfect *pàt tai* and green curries after taking an Apple & Noi's Thai Cooking Course (p179). Most of the ingredients are organic and home-grown.

Moo·ay Tai (Thai Boxing)

Thai boxing training camps put you through your paces with packages that involve general fitness and ring work.

Where to Go

Pattaya Fairtex Sports Club (p453) has excellent facilities aimed at training foreign visitors with any level of fitness or fighting experience. National champions and MMA (mixed martial arts) fighters also drop in to spar.

Chiang Mai The northern capital has several top *moo·ay tai* gyms, including Lanna Muay Thai Boxing Camp (p330) and Chai Yai Muay Thai (p330), where everyone from national champions to total beginners comes to train.

Meditation & Spiritual Retreats

Thais often go on spiritual retreats to rejuvenate themselves. You can join them at temples or meditation centres.

Where to Go

Phuket The island (p613) has several top spots offering retreats aimed at foreigners. It also has several good-quality yoga schools.

Ubon Ratchathani The northeast is the heartland of Thailand's forest meditation temples (p428). For a monastic lifestyle, try Wat Pa Nanachat (p429).

Climbing

Thailand has a range of climbing options, from total beginner to those who rival Spiderman. Most climbs are in the south, but the north has several challenging peaks.

Where to Go

Railay Scaling these limestone crags while surrounded by azure seas and a fabulous beach makes Railay (p655) the number-one climbing site in Thailand. More than 700 bolted routes can be assaulted with the help of guides or on your own.

Lopburi Khao Chin Lae (p169) This 240m-high limestone peak is surrounded by sunflower fields. Guides in Lopburi can arrange transport and explain the routes.

Surfing & Kiteboarding

The monsoon's midyear swell creates surfable barrels off Phuket, while almost year-round gusty winds lure kiteboarders to the east coast.

Where to Go

Phuket The best waves arrive between June and September, when annual surfing competitions are held on Hat Kata Yai, (p615) Phuket's most popular surf spot, and Hat Kalim, just north of Patong.

Hua Hin Thailand's kiteboarding, or kitesurfing, capital Hua Hin (p497) is blessed with strong, gusty winds, shallow water and a long beach off which to practise your moves.

Kôw soy (curry noodle sou

Plan Your Trip

Eat & Drink Like a Local

Incendiary curries, oodles of noodles, fresh seafood and the tropical fruit you've been dreaming about – Thailand has it all. But what many visitors aren't aware of is that by eating in guesthouse restaurants and tourist-frequented stalls, they're often experiencing a Westernised version of Thai food. To experience the true flavours of Thailand, you need to familiarise yourself with the dishes of Thailand's various regions and ethnic groups.

SIMON REDDY / ALAMY STOCK PHOTO ©

The Year in Food

Summer (March to June)

Thailand's hot season is the best time of year for fruit. Durian, mangoes, mangosteen and lychees are all at their juicy peak during these months.

Rainy Season (July to October)

One event to look out for during the rainy season is Thailand's annual Vegetarian Festival (typically held in late September or early October). The festival is celebrated particularly in places with large Chinese populations, such as Bangkok, Phuket Town and Trang.

Winter (November to January)

During Thailand's brief cool season, open-air beer halls, many serving spicy Thai drinking snacks, spring up in the larger cities.

Food Experiences

Top Local Restaurants

Bann Kun Pra (p165) Offers many versions of Ayuthaya's famous river prawn, including grilled with herbs and fried with tamarind sauce.

Krua Apsorn (p116) This award-winning Bangkok restaurant has a thick menu of decadent Bangkok- and central Thailand–style fare.

Jay Fai (p118) Lauded Bangkok shophouse that specialises in seafood-heavy stir-fries that blur the line between Thai and Chinese cuisines.

Khao Soi Lam Duan Fah Ham (p342) Chiang Mai's top bowl of *kôw soy* – northern Thailand's famous curry noodles – served to enthusiastic lunchtime crowds.

Huen Phen (p342) Delicious, northern-style curries, soups and *nám prík* (chilli sauces with vegetables to dip) are whisked up in a dining room crammed with wood carvings in Chiang Mai's old city.

Larp Khom Huay Poo (p286) Simple but profoundly delicious northern-style *lâhp* (a type of minced meat 'salad') at this Pai restaurant.

Hua Hin Koti (p501) You know a restaurant in Thailand is good when the queue for a table stretches around the corner.

Gai Yang Rabeab (p436) Some of the best *gài yâhng* (grilled chicken) you'll get in Isan in breezy, busy Khon Kaen surrounds.

Chowlay (p478) True to its 'if it swims, we have it' motto, this Ko Chang pier restaurant has an epic seafood menu and great bay views.

Fisherman's Restaurant (p551) This romantic Ko Pha-Ngan place, right by the sea, hits all the right notes, especially with its delectable Thai seafood and serene ambience. Book super early during the full moon.

Krua Thara (p654) One of Thailand's very best seafood kitchens attracts domestic tourists from around the country to Krabi.

Krua Talay (p577) A feast of flavour and texture, the seafood dishes at this excellent restaurant are one of the highlights of a visit to Nakhon Si Thammarat.

Suay (p621) An outstanding Thai fusion menu at this Phuket restaurant blends seasonal, local ingredients into elegantly creative concoctions such as mangosteen *sôm đam*.

In Town (p510) Fantastic seafood and views of Prachuap Khiri Khan's awesome bay at this local's favourite.

Suanmagmai Resort (p190) Perfectly prepared food, including many uncommon dishes such as fried duck bills and fern salad, a Sangkhlaburi regional speciality.

Mum Aroy (p449) – Discover why seafood on the eastern seaboard is so highly rated by cracking open some crabs and munching on prawns at this hugely popular Si Racha spot.

Cooking Courses

A standard one-day course usually features a shopping trip to a local market to choose ingredients, followed by preparation of curry pastes, soups, curries, salads and desserts.

Amita Thai Cooking Class (p99), Bangkok

Chiang Mai Thai Cookery School (p328), Chiang Mai

Suwannee (p209), Chiang Rai

Buchabun Art & Crafts Collection (p498), Hua Hin

Apple & Noi's Thai Cooking Course (p179), Kanchanaburi

Koon Travel & Butler (p434), Khon Kaen

Koh Chang Thai Cookery School (p472), Ko Chang

Samui Institute of Thai Culinary Arts (p523), Ko Samui

Borderline Shop cookery course (p270), Mae Sot

Pai Cookery School (p282), Pai

Suay Cooking School (p619), Phuket

Regional Specialities

Unlike the way it is often touted abroad, Thai food is anything but a single entity. It is made up of a vast repertoire of ingredients, cooking techniques and dishes that can often pinpoint a particular province, or even a town.

Bangkok & Central Thai Cuisine

When foreigners think of Thai food, they're often thinking of the dishes of Bangkok and the central plains. A wealth of agriculture, access to the sea and the influence of foreign cuisines have come together in a cuisine that is both sophisticated and diverse.

Northern Thai Cuisine

You may have heard of *kôw soy* (curry noodle soup), but most people, including many Thais, would be hard-pressed to name more than a few northern Thai dishes. In addition to being the country's least-known regional cuisine, northern Thai food is probably also the most seasonal, largely due to the north's elevation and climate.

Northeastern Thai Cuisine

Northeastern Thai food is undoubtedly the country's most rustic regional cooking style, and is most likely indicative of what the ethnic Tai people have been eating for hundreds, if not thousands, of years. Spicy, tart flavours and simple cooking methods, such as grilling and soups, dominate the northeastern kitchen, in which the predominant carb is sticky rice.

Southern Thai Cuisine

Although you might not notice it in the guesthouse food you're served, the dishes of Thailand's southern provinces are arguably the country's spiciest. Eat outside the tourist track and you'll find an entire inventory of incendiary soups, piquant curries and full-flavoured stir-fries.

Ethnic Specialities

In addition to geography, the country's predominant minorities – Muslims and the Chinese – have had different but profound influences on the local cuisine.

Islamic World–Influenced Thai Cuisine

Muslims are thought to have first visited Thailand during the late 14th century. Along with the Quran, they brought with them a halal (religiously permissible) cuisine based on meat and dried spice from their homelands in India and the Middle East. Nearly 700 years later, the impact of this culinary commerce can still be felt.

While some typical dishes such as roti, a fried bread similar to the Indian paratha, have changed little, if at all, others such as *gaang mát·sà·màn* are a unique blend of Thai, Indian and Middle Eastern cooking styles and ingredients. In more recent years, additional dishes have arrived through contact with Thailand's neighbour to the south, Malaysia.

Common Islamic world–influenced Thai dishes to look out for include the following:

➡ *Gaang mát·sà·màn* – 'Muslim curry' is a rich coconut-milk-based dish, which, unlike most Thai curries, gets much of its flavour from dried spices. As with many Thai-Muslim favourites, there is an emphasis on the sweet.

Amita Thai Cooking Class (p99), Bangkok

➡ *Kôw mòk* – *biryani*, a dish found across the Islamic world, also has a foothold in Thailand. Here the dish is typically made with chicken and is served with a sweet-and-sour dipping sauce and a bowl of chicken broth.

➡ *Má·đà·bà* – Known as *murtabak* in Malaysia and Indonesia, these are roti that have been stuffed with a savoury or sometimes sweet filling and fried until crispy.

➡ *Sà·đé* (satay) – The savoury, peanut-based dipping sauce served with these grilled skewers of meat is often mistakenly associated with Thai cooking.

➡ *Sà·làt kàak* – Literally 'Muslim salad' (*kàak* is a somewhat derogatory word used to describe people or things of South Asian and/or Muslim origin), this dish combines iceberg lettuce, chunks of firm tofu, cucumber, hard-boiled egg and tomato, all topped with a sweet peanut sauce.

➡ *Súp hăhng woo·a* – Oxtail soup, possibly a Malay contribution, is even richer and often more sour than the 'Buddhist' Thai *đôm yam*.

Thai-Chinese Cuisine

Immigrants from southern China have been influencing Thai cuisine for centuries, and it was Chinese labourers and vendors who most likely introduced the wok and several varieties of noodle dishes to Thailand.

Thai-Chinese dishes you're likely to run across include the following:

➡ *Bà·mèe* – Chinese-style wheat and egg noodles are typically served with slices of barbecued pork, a handful of greens and/or wontons.

➡ *Gŏo·ay đěe·o kôo·a gài* – Wide rice noodles fried with little more than egg, chicken, squid and garlic oil. A popular dish in Bangkok's Chinatown.

➡ *Kôw kăh mŏo* – Braised pork leg served over rice, often with sides of greens and a hard-boiled egg, is the epitome of the Chinese-style one-dish meal.

➡ *Kôw man gài* – Chicken rice, originally from the Chinese island of Hainan, is now found in just about every corner of Thailand.

➡ *Sah·lah·Ƀow* – Chinese-style steamed buns are a favourite at old-school Chinese-style coffeeshops across Thailand.

Ko Yao Noi (p611), Ao Phang-Ng

Choose Your Beach

It's a terrible dilemma: Thailand has too many beaches to choose from. Choices can be daunting even for those visiting a second time and development is so rapid that where you went five years ago may now be completely different. Here, we break it down so that you can find your dream beach.

Best Beaches for...

Relaxation and Activities

Ko Mak Beach bar scene, explorably flat and vast expanses of sand.

Ko Phayam Bike back roads to empty beaches or parties.

Hat Mae Nam Quiet Ko Samui beach close to lots of action.

Ko Bulon Leh Chilled-out vibe but lots to do.

Local Culture

Ko Yao Noi Thai-Muslim fishing island with beautiful karst scenery.

Ko Sukorn Agricultural and fishing gem filled with mangroves and water buffalo.

Ko Phra Thong Look for rare orchids with *chow lair* (Moken; 'sea gypsies').

Hua Hin Mingle with middle-class Thais in this urban beach getaway.

Quick & Easy Access from Bangkok

Nowadays the closest beaches to Bangkok aren't necessarily the quickest and easiest to get to. There are international flights direct to Phuket and Ko Samui that allow you to skip the big city altogether, and flights from Bangkok (and some Southeast Asian countries) can shuttle you to several southern towns with ease.

If you don't want or can't afford to fly, but are still short on time, the closest beach island to Bangkok is Ko Samet (count on around four hours' total travel time) while the closest beach resorts are Bang Saen (one hour by bus) and Pattaya (1½ hours). The next-closest stops by land are the beach towns of Cha-am (2½ hours) and Hua Hin (three hours). It takes around six hours to get to Ko Chang, which beats the minimum of 10 hours to reach the lower gulf islands. If you're in a hurry and want to take the bus, anywhere on the Andaman Coast is not your best choice.

To Party or Not to Party

Where

A big percentage of travellers to southern Thailand aim to party, and the local tourism industry happily accommodates them with an array of thumping beach bars lining many of the main beaches.

Luckily, it's as easy to escape the revelry as it is to join in. The main party zones are well known to be just that. Anywhere you go that's not a major tourist enclave will have peace and quiet on offer.

The Girly-Bar Issue

Bangkok, Pattaya and Phuket are the capitals of push-up bras and 'hello meesta', while Hat Lamai on Ko Samui is the centre of this small universe in the lower gulf islands. Islands like Ko Chang and mid-sized towns such as Hat Yai and Ao Nang have small enclaves of questionable massage parlours and bars with the telltale pole dancer silhouette on the sign, but they won't be in your face. Smaller islands and towns will be clear of this sort of thing, at least on the surface.

Your Party Level

Level One: Dead Calm Surin and Similan Islands, Laem Son National Park, Hat Pak Meng and Hat Chang Lang

Level Two: A Flicker of Light Ko Tarutao, Ko Libong, Prachuap Khiri Khan

Level Three: There's a Bar Ko Yao Islands, Ao Khanom, Ko Kut

Level Four: Maybe a Few Bars Hat Khao Lak, Ko Muk, Ao Thong Nai Pan (Pha-Ngan)

Level Five: Easy to Find a Drink Hua Hin, Bo Phut (Samui), Ao Nang

Level Six: There's a Beach-Bar Scene Ko Mak, Ko Phayam, Railay

OVERVIEW OF THAILAND'S ISLANDS & BEACHES

BEACHES	PACKAGE TOURISTS	BACK-PACKERS	FAMILIES	PARTIES	DIVE/ SNORKEL	PERSONALITY
Ko Chang & Eastern Seaboard						
Ko Samet	✓	✓	✓	✓		pretty beach, easy getaway from Bangkok
Ko Chang	✓	✓		✓	✓	international resort, jungle interior
Ko Wai		✓	✓		✓	primitive day tripper, deserted in the evening
Ko Mak	✓	✓	✓			mediocre beach, great vibe
Ko Kut	✓	✓	✓			lovely semi-developed island, great for solitude
Hua Hin & the Upper Gulf						
Hua Hin	✓	✓	✓			international resort, easy access to Bangkok
Pranburi & Around	✓					quiet & close to Bangkok
Ban Krut			✓			low-key, popular with Thais
Bang Saphan Yai		✓	✓			cheap mainland beach
Ko Samui & the Lower Gulf						
Ko Samui	✓	✓	✓	✓		international resort for social beach-goers
Ko Pha-Ngan	✓	✓	✓	✓	✓	popular beaches, with boozy Hat Rin
Ko Tao	✓	✓	✓	✓	✓	dive schools galore
Ang Thong		✓	✓			gorgeous karst scenery
Ao Khanom		✓	✓			quiet, little known
Phuket & the Andaman Coast						
Ko Chang (Ranong)		✓	✓		✓	rustic
Ko Phayam		✓	✓			quict, little known
Surin & Similan Islands		✓	✓		✓	dive sites accessed by live-aboards
Ko Yao	✓	✓	✓			poor beaches but nice vibe, great scenery
Phuket	✓	✓	✓	✓	✓	international resort for social beach-goers
Ao Nang	✓	✓	✓		✓	touristy, close to Railay
Railay	✓	✓	✓			rock-climbing centre
Ko Phi-Phi	✓	✓		✓	✓	pretty party island
Ko Jum	✓	✓	✓			mediocre beach, nice vibe
Ko Lanta	✓	✓	✓		✓	emerging package scene
Trang Islands	✓	✓	✓		✓	Ko Ngai is good for kids
Ko Bulon Leh		✓	✓		✓	quiet, pretty beaches
Ko Tarutao		✓	✓			developing national park
Ko Lipe	✓	✓	✓	✓	✓	hot spot, good for visa runs
Ko Adang		✓			✓	popular with day trippers

Level Seven: Magic Milkshake Anyone? Ko Lanta, Ko Chang, Ban Tai (Pha-Ngan)

Level Eight: I Forget What Eight Was For Hat Lamai (Samui), Ko Lipe, Ko Samet

Level Nine: What Happened Last Night? Hat Chaweng (Samui), Pattaya, Ko Tao

Level Ten: Don't Tell Me What Happened Last Night Patong (Phuket), Ko Phi-Phi, Hat Rin (Ko Pha-Ngan)

Resort-Town Personalities

The personality of a Thai resort town depends a lot on the prices. In places where midrange options dominate, you'll usually find package tourists, rows of beach loungers and umbrellas along the beach, and plenty of big boats full of snorkelling tours.

At upscale places things settle down. The ritzier beaches of Phuket like Surin and Ao Ban Tao are among the quieter on the island yet still have plenty of dining and cocktail options. Ko Kut off the eastern seaboard has lovely resorts on some of the country's most unspoiled beaches, while the more secluded beaches of northeastern Ko Samui have some of the most luxurious resorts in Thailand. Once you go very high end, privacy and seclusion become a bigger part of the picture.

There are a few remaining beach huts that are often found on some of the country's most secluded beaches.

Activities

What there is to do besides lounging on the beach is the deciding factor for many visitors when choosing a beach.

Diving & Snorkelling

Thailand is a diving and snorkelling paradise. The Andaman Coast and Ko Tao in the lower gulf have the best undersea views in the country. Islands like Ko Samui and Ko Lanta that don't have great snorkelling from the beach will have snorkelling tours to nearby sites where you'll see some corals and fish, and a turtle or shark if you're lucky.

Climbing

Railay is the best-known place to climb in southern Thailand; it has the best set-up for beginners and a fun scene. Ko Phi-Phi has some great climbing options alongside its lively party scene and abundance of water and land activities, and there are less busy and more off-the-beaten-path climbing options around the appealing mainland town of Krabi. The Ko Yao islands are slowly getting bolted and offer horizons to more seasoned climbers. Ko Tao also attracts rock climbers.

Hiking

The mainland national parks like Khao Sok have the most jungle-walking opportunities, but more forested islands such as Ko Chang, Ko Pha-Ngan and even Phuket have

WHEN TO GO

REGION	JAN-MAR	APR-JUN	JUL-SEP	OCT-DEC
Bangkok	hotter towards Mar	hot & humid	rainy season	cooler towards Dec
Eastern Seaboard	peak season; thins towards Mar	rainy season begins in May	smaller islands close for the monsoon	cooler weather; low hotel rates
Southern Gulf	hot & dry	hot & dry	occasional rains & strong winds	occasional rains & strong winds
Lower Gulf	clear & sunny	hot & dry	clear & sunny, increasing wind & rain on Ko Tao	monsoon & rough waters
Northern Andaman	high season; high prices	fringe season with iffy weather	rainy season & surf season	high season picks up again
Southern Andaman	high season	monsoons usually begin in May	some resorts close for rainy season	crowds return with the sun

SHARON LAPKIN / GETTY IMAGES ©

New Year's Eve fireworks, Ao Nang (p651)

great hiking, often to waterfalls or vistas looking across the blue sea.

Culture

For a taste of authentic Thai culture, head out of the main tourist zones to coastal towns like Trang, Surat Thani or Nakhon Si Thammarat, to lesser known islands like Ko Si Chang or Ko Sukorn, or to the less visited parts of islands like the south coast of Ko Samui or the east coast of Ko Lanta. But even tourist central Patong or Ko Phi-Phi can give you a taste of what's beyond resort land, just by eating at food stalls and talking to the owners, smiling a lot and being open to interactions with locals.

Dangers

If renting a scooter or motorbike, you may not be insured. Insurance is not included in most rentals and your own insurance may not cover the cost of any accident. It is likely that you will be liable for medical expenses and repair or replacement costs for any damaged vehicle. If you don't have a Thai driving licence or an international driving licence, you will also be driving illegally (many rental outfits don't check). If you do rent, watch out for sand or grit on the road (especially if braking), drive slowly (under 40km/h), particularly after rain, and avoid alcohol.

Drownings are common. Pay attention to red- and yellow-flag warnings and be aware that many beaches do not have life guards. Also beware of rip tides, which can carry you out to sea. If caught in a rip tide in deep water, do not fight against it as you may rapidly, and dangerously, tire. It is more advisable to try to call for help, but go with the flow and conserve energy; the rip tide will take you further out to sea, but you should be able to swim back. Rip tide channels are quite narrow, so another technique is to gradually swim parallel to the shore when caught in a rip tide and you should escape it.

Signs on some beaches warn of box jellyfish, so check before swimming. Stings from box jellyfish can be fatal, and although there are few deaths, there were two fatalities in Ko Pha-Ngan waters in a 12-month period between 2014 and 2015.

Plan Your Trip

Travel with Children

Looking for an exotic destination that the kids can handle? Thailand has it: beaches, mountains, elephants, sparkling temples and bustling markets; there's something for each age range. Plus Thais are serious 'cute' connoisseurs and exotic-looking foreign children trump stuffed animals and fluffy dogs.

Thailand for Children

Small foreign children are instant celebrities in Thailand and attract paparazzi-like attention. Babies do surprisingly well with their new-found stardom, soaking up adoration from gruff taxi drivers who transform into loving uncles wanting to play a game of peekaboo (called *'já ǎir'*). If you've got a babe in arms, food vendors will often hold the child while you eat, or take the child for a brief stroll to visit the neighbours.

At a certain age, kids can develop stranger anxiety, which doesn't mix well with the Thai passion for children. For the preschool set, who are becoming self-conscious but still have major cute quotient, stick to tourist centres instead of trotting off to far-flung places where foreigners, especially children, will attract too much attention. A polite way to deflect spectators is to say the child is 'shy' *('ki aye')*.

Older children should be safe from Thai attention, though they might get nervous about the cities' natural chaos and the confusion that arises from being in a new place and having to negotiate transport. Consider giving your children a role in travel planning: reading the map, setting up an itinerary or carrying the water bottles. You're moulding future travellers.

Best Regions for Kids

Eastern Seaboard & Ko Chang

Shallow seas are kind to young swimmers and the low evening tides makc for good beach-combing. Older children will like the interior jungle, elephant interactions and mangrove kayaking.

Upper Gulf

Hua Hin has a long sandy coastline for pint-sized marathons and hillside temples for monkey spotting. Phetchaburi's cave temples contain bats.

Ko Samui & Lower Gulf

Older children can snorkel at Ko Tao without worry. Ko Samui, especially its northern beaches, is a hit with pram-pushers and toddlers, while Hat Chaweng is social and commercial; ideal for teens.

Phuket & Andaman Coast

Phuket has amusements galore (we recommend the surf schools), though steer clear of the Patong party scene. There are at least a dozen islands along this coast where families can frolic in the sea.

Chiang Mai

Families come in droves during European summer holidays to expose their kids to culture, walk among elephants and cycle about town.

Thai cities can be claustrophobic and the heat can make it tiring to wear out energetic children. Staying at a hotel or resort with a pool will give the kids enough exercise not to bounce off the proverbial walls.

To smooth out the usual road bumps of dragging children from place to place, check out Lonely Planet's *Travel with Children,* which contains useful advice on how to cope with kids on the road, with a focus on travel in developing countries.

Children's Highlights

Children will love the beaches, as most are shallow, gentle bays good for beginner swimmers. The further south you go, the clearer the water. The bays are often fringed with near-shore reefs and curious fish swim by for a visit.

Animal amusements abound in Thailand, though standards are often below those in the West. Chiang Mai is the centre of elephant tourism, where tourists can interact with pachyderms and learn about their plight. Wherever you take the kids, however, remember that elephant tourism is an activity commonly associated with animal welfare issues. Many beach resorts, such as Phuket and Ko Chang, also have wildlife encounters. Lopburi is overrun with monkeys that cause all sorts of mayhem.

Outdoor activities – trekking, ziplining, bamboo rafting – will appeal to older children. Chiang Mai, Kanchanaburi, southern beach resorts and tourist centres in Northern Thailand all have a variety of nature sports that are family friendly.

Bangkok has the above-ground BTS (Skytrain), shopping malls complete with escalators (a preschool favourite) and the city's immense shopping options will appeal to tweens and teens.

Getting around has its rewards. Loads of kids like overnight train journeys, where they can be assigned lower sleeping berths with views of the stations. Speedboats are another hit.

Temples can also be engaging places for children. The climb to hilltop temples, marvelling at resident monkeys and cave shrines, is a great energy-absorber. Merit-making at a Buddhist temple is surprisingly child-friendly – there are the burning joss sticks, the bowing in front of the Buddha and the rubbing of gold leaf on the central image. It is a very active process that can involve the kids. Most temples have a fortune-telling area, where you shake a bamboo container until a numbered stick falls out. The number corresponds to a printed fortune. A variation on this is to make a donation into a pot (or in some cases an automated machine) cor-

STORIES FOR THE SCRAPBOOK

After two children and four trips to Thailand with them as my research assistants, these are some of the tales that we share at the dinner table when they feel like going on a memory walkabout.

'My son's last visit to Thailand was when he was four and we researched the eastern seaboard together. At the time his highlights were the hotels that had two complimentary soaps (four-year-olds are easily impressed); 7-Elevens, where his babysitter would buy him cookies; and pineapple ('Dad, have you ever heard of pineapple before?' he asked during a phone call home). The mosquito net we slept under in Ko Kut became our very own bat cave. And his great triumph was when he outran the Thai ladies on the beach who wanted to shower him with love pinches.

On my most recent trip, I brought my one-year-old daughter along to break in her passport. We were based in Chiang Mai and she loved all of Thailand's cats and dogs, waved at passersby and was well photographed by Thais and Chinese tourists. She screeched wildly for noodles and protested violently when I didn't get off at every stop on Bangkok's BTS. She was surprised when we returned home that strangers didn't want to hold her.'

By Lonely Planet Thailand guidebook writer, China Williams

responding to the day of the week you were born and retrieve the attached fortune.

Planning & Practicalities

Amenities specially geared towards young children – such as child-safety seats for cars, high chairs in restaurants or nappy-changing facilities in public restrooms – are virtually nonexistent in Thailand. Therefore parents will have to be resourceful in seeking out substitutes or just do without.

Baby formula and nappies (diapers) are available at minimarkets and 7-Elevens in the larger towns and cities, but sizes are usually small, smaller and smallish. If your kid wears size 3 or larger, head to Tesco Lotus, Big C or Tops Market stores. Nappy rash cream is sold at pharmacies.

Hauling around little ones can be a challenge. Thailand's footpaths are often too crowded to push a pram, especially full-size SUV versions. Instead opt for a compact umbrella stroller that can squeeze past the fire hydrants and mango carts and can be folded up and thrown in a túk-túk (pronounced *đúk đúk;* three-wheeled motorised vehicle). A baby pack is also useful, but make sure the child's head doesn't sit higher than yours: there are lots of hanging obstacles poised at forehead level.

Eating with Kids

Worrying about food occupies considerable parental bandwidth and the vagaries of children's food preferences are further complicated by a cuisine known for its spiciness. Luckily, even Thai children are shielded from chillies and there are a handful of child-friendly dishes that every server can recommend. Because of the heat, remember to keep your little ones well hydrated, either with water or a variety of fruit juices, including fresh young coconuts or lime juice (a surprising hit with kids).

- *kài jee·o* (omelette) – more oily than the French style but a safe, non-spicy restaurant or street-stall option.
- *gài yâhng/tôrt* (grilled/fried chicken) – common market and street stall meal.
- *kôw něe·o* (sticky rice) – straight-up carbs but picky eaters won't resist; sold in markets alongside grilled or fried chicken.
- *gài pàt mét má·môo·ang* (chicken stir-fried with cashew nuts) – mild stir-fry, popular at restaurants.
- *kôw man gài* (Hainanese chicken rice) – a popular morning and afternoon meal sold at speciality shops.

Health & Safety

For the most part, parents needn't worry too much about health concerns. Regular hand washing should be enforced. Thai children are bathed at least twice a day and powdered afterwards to reduce skin irritation from the humid climate; foreigners should aim for at least daily showers. Children should be warned not to play with animals as rabies is relatively common and some pets (not to mention wild monkeys) may be aggressive.

Dengue is an increasing concern in Thailand and reached a 20-year-high rate of infection during the rainy season of 2013. Parents should take care to prevent mosquito bites (a difficult task) in children. Repellent creams containing 12% DEET are widely available from 7-Elevens and other convenience stores, but pack some from home before you travel. If your child is bitten, there are a variety of locally produced balms that can reduce swelling and itching. All the usual health precautions apply.

Children familiar with urban environments will do well in Thailand's cities, where traffic is chaotic and pedestrian paths are congested. Thai cities are very loud and can be a sensory overload for young children. Be sure that your child understands street safety guidelines as it will be difficult to focus on your instructions amid all the street noise outside.

Regions at a Glance

Bangkok & Around

Culture
Food
Nightlife

Classic Siam

The great temples along Mae Nam Chao Phraya (Chao Phraya River) are national pilgrimage sites cradling revered religious symbols and the country's greatest displays of classical art and architecture.

More is Better

The residents of this multi-wát city love to eat. Food can be found in every nook and cranny, from noodle pushcarts and grease-stained wok shops to fine dining and fashion-minded cafes. All of Bangkok's expat communities have their culinary outposts, providing exotic flavours to all.

Toast the Stars

The quintessential night out in Bangkok is still a plastic table filled with sweating Chang beers, but rooftop bars, with cool breezes and fizzy cocktails, make better Instagram pictures. Hip university students are always out on the town, filling indie clubs or pop discos.

p58

Central Thailand

Culture/History
Mountains
Getaways

Rest & Ruins

The ruins of Ayuthaya, Thailand's greatest empire, are a Unesco World Heritage Site. Amiable Lopburi and its ancient ruins are ruled by troops of monkeys. Kanchanaburi has poignant memorials to the POWs who worked on the Death Railway during WWII.

Mountain Journeys

Kanchanaburi is the gateway to the misty mountains of western Thailand. Rivers and waterfalls carve the contours and a collection of national parks make this one of Thailand's wildest corners.

Remote Relaxation

Sangkhlaburi and Thong Pha Phum are intoxicating end-of-the-road getaways that are easy to reach, but hard to leave.

p155

Northern Thailand

Culture/History
Mountains
Food

Ancient Kingdoms

The remains of ancient city-states, with their fortressed walls and Buddhist monuments, are dotted throughout northern Thailand. Sukhothai is the most atmospheric.

Misty Mornings

The mountains here form some of the country's most dramatic scenery. Winding roads and scenic vistas, home to the high-altitude villages of ethnic minorities, are the highlights of provinces such as Chiang Rai and Mae Hong Son.

Comfort Food, Northern Style

The north's cooler climate has shaped a menu of dishes characterised by sour and bitter notes, many influenced by Thai, Shan and Yunnanese cuisine. The region's most famous dish is *kôw soy,* a curry served over noodles.

p191

Chiang Mai Province

Culture/History
Food
Outdoor Adventures

Lanna Latitudes

A refreshing counterpoint to Bangkok's mayhem, Chiang Mai showcases northern Thailand's history and culture in its fortified city. Culture geeks come for sightseeing or courses in cooking, language and massage.

Curries & Noodles

Northern Thailand has its own versions of standard Thai dishes, reflecting its cooler climate and proximity to Yunnan and Myanmar. Chiang Mai converts carnivores with its vegetarian health food.

Commute into the Hills

Just beyond the city limits is a mountainous landscape that can be explored on hikes, river paddles or via zipline. Outdoor adventures for families, athletes and nature lovers.

p304

Northeastern Thailand

Culture/History
Outdoors
Festivals

Ancient Angkor

The Lower Isan region is the site of the Ancient Khmer Hwy, and remnants of the mighty Khmer empire are still to be seen in Phanom Rung and Phimai, as well as many other imposing temples.

Mountains & Rivers

The region's national parks include the evergreen forests of Khao Yai and the eerie rock formations of Phu Phrabat. The Mekong River draws visitors for its wild scenery and riverside resorts.

Community Spirit

In the hot season northeasterners busy themselves with having fun. The Rocket Festivals and Phi Ta Khon festival are wild and spectacular affairs.

p364

Ko Chang & Eastern Seaboard

Beaches
Diving/Snorkelling
Small Towns

Island Vibes

Jungle-covered Ko Chang is loved for its tropical ambience and thriving party scene. Quiet Ko Kut excels in seaside seclusion, Ko Mak boasts a laid-back island vibe and little Ko Wai has the prettiest views you have ever seen.

Scuba Fun

Surrounding Ko Chang is a national marine park filled with beginner-friendly dives. Seamounts and rock pinnacles serve as shelter for schooling fish and turtles.

Provincial Prominence

Often-overlooked Chanthaburi is famous for its weekend gem market and restored waterfront community, while Trat, a transit link to Ko Chang, has a simple charm.

p444

Hua Hin & the Upper Gulf

Culture/History
Beaches
Food

Royal Coast

Successive Bangkok kings escaped to this coastal getaway, which includes Phetchaburi and its historic hilltop palace and cave shrines, and Hua Hin, which still serves as the king's seaside retreat.

Surf & Turf

Beach lovers looking for a sense of place will find it in Prachuap Khiri Khan, a mellow town with karst-studded bays, and Hua Hin, a mod-con seaside resort ideal for families and honeymooners.

Beach Grub

With its proximity to Bangkok and popularity with domestic tourists, this region excels in local-style seafood, served in the raucous Hua Hin night market, by roaming vendors in Cha-am or at oceanfront restaurants.

p484

Ko Samui & the Lower Gulf

Beaches
Diving/ Snorkelling
Nightlife

Bronzing Bodies

The three sister islands of the lower gulf have been pursued by island-hoppers for decades. Professional Samui caters to resort-style vacations with stunning sugar-white beaches, while Ko Pha-Ngan is more bohemian with cosy coves.

Diver Down

The warm gentle seas and wallet-friendly prices keep Ko Tao beloved for dive training, but Ko Pha-Ngan is close behind.

Rave at the Moon

Ko Pha-Ngan becomes a huge uni campus during its Full Moon Parties when people storm the beach to rave at the moon. Booze buckets, Day-Glo paint and drunken foolishness abound.

p517

Phuket & the Andaman Coast

Scenery
Beaches
Diving/ Snorkelling

Karst Cathedrals

Limestone mountains jut out of jewel-coloured waters with monumental stature. A variety of sports, based in Krabi, Trang and Ko Yao, turn the pinnacles into a breathtaking outdoor playground.

Goldilocks Beaches

Andaman beaches come in every shape and flavour. Phuket excels in comfort for the masses and top-end luxury. Laid-back Ko Lanta and the increasingly popular Ko Phayam are well worth a look.

Cousteau Territory

Big fish, coral gardens, sunken wrecks – diving and snorkelling sites here include the world-renowned Similan Islands and Surin Islands Marine National Parks.

p587

On the Road

Bangkok & Around

Includes ➡

Why Go?

The rumours are true: Bangkok is everything you've heard it is. It's also much, much more.

Yes, the city's traffic can be brutal, but the BTS (Skytrain) or Chao Phraya Express Boat can whisk you across town in no time. There are indeed pockets of sleaze, but much more prominent than the go-go bars are Bangkok's surprisingly sophisticated bars and nightlife. The street food is justifiably legendary, but did you know that the city is also home to internationally acclaimed chefs? And you're much more likely to come across a hip hostel or a homey guesthouse than the type of budget nightmare described in *The Beach*.

What this means is that somewhere in Bangkok's eclectic jumble – glittering Buddhist temples edging glassy skyscrapers, monks sharing the sidewalk with teen fashionistas, outdoor markets next door to air-conditioned malls – is something for just about everyone.

Best Places to Eat

- nahm (p121)
- Eat Me (p120)
- Krua Apsorn (p116)
- Jay Fai (p118)
- MBK Food Island (p124)

Best Places to Stay

- AriyasomVilla (p112)
- Phra-Nakorn Norn-Len (p114)
- Siam Heritage (p108)
- Bangkok Tree House (p115)
- Lamphu Treehouse (p104)

When to Go

- Bangkok is rated by the World Meteorological Organization as one of the world's hottest cities. There's little fluctuation in the temperature, and the average high sways between a torrid 32°C and a sweltering 34°C.
- The rainy season runs approximately May to October, when the city receives as much as 300mm of rain monthly.
- Virtually the only break from this relentless heat and humidity comes during winter, a couple of weeks of relative coolness in December/January.

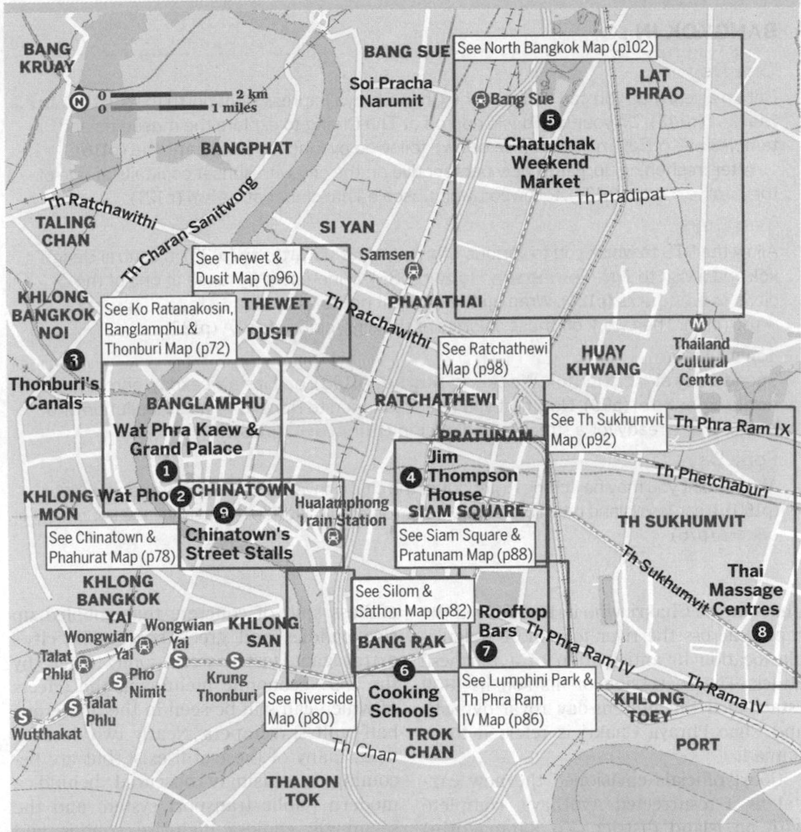

Bangkok & Around Highlights

1. Basking in the glow of all that gold at **Wat Phra Kaew & Grand Palace** (p61).
2. Taking in the immense Buddha statue at **Wat Pho** (p61).
3. Skipping between sightseeing spots on a **cruise of Thonburi's canals** (p76).
4. Encountering the best of Thai architecture and artwork at **Jim Thompson House** (p83).
5. Burning baht at **Chatuchak Weekend Market** (p138).
6. Learning to make authentic Thai dishes at one of Bangkok's **cooking schools** (p99).
7. Toasting the stars and the twinkling skyscraper lights atop one of the city's **rooftop bars** (p127).
8. Being blissfully pounded into submission at one of Bangkok's terrific-value **Thai massage centres** (p99).
9. Eating yourself into a stupor at **Chinatown's street stalls** (p119).
10. Getting out of Bangkok and visiting the canalside town of **Amphawa** (p152).

History

Now the centre of government and culture in Thailand, Bangkok was a historical miracle during a time of turmoil. Following the fall of Ayuthaya in 1767, the kingdom fractured into competing forces, from which General Taksin emerged as a decisive unifier. He established his base in Thonburi, on the western bank of Mae Nam Chao Phraya (Chao Phraya River), a convenient location for sea trade from the Gulf of Thailand. Taksin proved more of a military strategist than a popular ruler. He was later deposed by another important military general,

BANGKOK IN...

One Day

Get up as early as you can and take the Chao Phraya Express Boat north to **Nonthaburi Market** (p142). On your way back, hop off at Tha Chang to explore the museums and temples of **Ko Ratanakosin** (see below), followed by lunch in **Banglamphu** (p116).

After freshening up, gain a new perspective on the city with sunset cocktails at one of the **rooftop bars** (p127), followed by an upscale Thai dinner at **nahm** (p121).

Two Days

Allow the BTS to whisk you to various **shopping destinations** (p135) in central Bangkok and a visit to **Jim Thompson House** (p83), punctuated by lunch at one of the city's **food courts** (p124). Wrap up the daylight hours with a **traditional Thai massage** (p99). Then work off those calories at the nightclubs of **RCA** (p132).

Three Days

Spend a day at **Chatuchak Weekend Market** (p138), or if it's a weekday, enrol in a **cooking school** (p99). Now that you're accustomed to Bangkok's noise, pollution and traffic, you're ready for a street-food dinner in **Chinatown** (p119).

Four Days

At this point you may be itching to get out of the city. Convenient escapes include **Ko Kret** (p150), a car-less island north of Bangkok, or a long-tail boat ride through **Thonburi's canals** (p76).

Chao Phraya Chakri, who in 1782 moved the capital across the river to a more defensible location in anticipation of a Burmese attack. The succession of his son in 1809 established the present-day royal dynasty, and Chao Phraya Chakri is referred to as Rama I.

Court officials envisioned the new capital as a resurrected Ayuthaya, complete with an island district (Ko Ratanakosin) carved out of the swampland and cradling the royal court (the Grand Palace) and a temple to the Emerald Buddha (Wat Phra Kaew). The emerging city, which was encircled by a thick wall, was filled with stilt and floating houses ideally adapted to seasonal flooding.

Modernity came to the capital in the late 19th century as European aesthetics and technologies filtered east. During the reigns of Rama IV (King Mongkut; r 1851–68) and Rama V (King Chulalongkorn; r 1868–1910), Bangkok received its first paved road (Th Charoen Krung, formerly known as New Road) and a new royal district (Dusit) styled after European palaces.

Bangkok was still a gangly town when soldiers from the American war in Vietnam came to rest and relax in the city's go-go bars and brothels. It wasn't until the boom years of the 1980s and 1990s that Bangkok exploded into a fully fledged metropolis crowded with hulking skyscrapers and an endless spill of concrete that gobbled up rice paddies and green space. The city's extravagant tastes were soon tamed by the 1997 economic meltdown, the effects of which can still be seen in the numerous half-built skyscrapers. Nearly two decades later, many of these still exist, but are becoming increasingly obscured behind a modern public transport system and the seemingly endless high rise condos and vast glass-fronted mega-malls that have come to define the Bangkok of today.

Sights

Ko Ratanakosin เกาะรัตนโกสินทร์

Welcome to Bangkok's birthplace. The vast city we know today emerged from Ko Ratanakosin, a tiny virtual island ('Ko') made by dredging a canal around Mae Nam Chao Phraya during the late 18th century. Within this area you'll find the glittering temples and palaces that most visitors associate with the city. Ko Ratanakosin's riverfront setting is also home to several museums, markets and universities. All these sights are within walking distance of each other and are best visited early in the morning before the day comes to a boil.

The Chao Phraya Express Boat piers at Phra Chan, Maharaj, Chang and Tien are the easiest way to reach the area. Alternatively, take the BTS to National Stadium or Ratchathewi, or the MRT to Hua Lamphong, followed by a short taxi ride.

★ Wat Phra Kaew & Grand Palace

BUDDHIST TEMPLE

(วัดพระแก้ว, พระบรมมหาราชวัง; Map p72; Th Na Phra Lan; admission 500B; 8.30am-3.30pm; Chang Pier, Maharaj Pier, Phra Chan Tai Pier) **FREE** Also known as the Temple of the Emerald Buddha, **Wat Phra Kaew** is the colloquial name of the vast, fairy-tale compound that also includes the former residence of the Thai monarch, the Grand Palace.

This ground was consecrated in 1782, the first year of Bangkok rule, and is today Bangkok's biggest tourist attraction and a pilgrimage destination for devout Buddhists and nationalists. The 94.5-hectare grounds encompass more than 100 buildings that represent 200 years of royal history and architectural experimentation.

Housed in a fantastically decorated *bòht* (ordination hall), the **Emerald Buddha** is the temple's primary attraction.

Except for an anteroom here and there, the buildings of the **Grand Palace** are now put to use by the king only for certain ceremonial occasions, such as Coronation Day, and are largely off-limits to visitors. Formerly, Thai kings housed their huge harems in the inner palace area, which was guarded by combat-trained female sentries. Outer palace buildings that visitors can view include **Borombhiman Hall**, a French-inspired structure that served as a residence for Rama VI (King Vajiravudh; r 1910–25). The building to the west is **Amarindra Hall** (open from Monday to Friday), originally a hall of justice and more recently, used for coronation ceremonies, and is the only palace building that tourists are generally allowed to enter. The largest of the palace buildings is the **Chakri Mahaprasat**, the Grand Palace Hall. Last is the Ratanakosin-style **Dusit Hall**, which initially served as a venue for royal audiences and later as a royal funerary hall.

Guides can be hired at the ticket kiosk; ignore offers from anyone outside. An audio guide can be rented for 200B for two hours.

Admission for the complex includes entrance to Dusit Palace Park, which includes Vimanmaek Teak Mansion and Abhisek Dusit Throne Hall.

★ Wat Pho

BUDDHIST TEMPLE

(วัดโพธิ์/วัดพระเชตุพน, Wat Phra Chetuphon; Map p72; Th Sanam Chai; admission 100B; 8.30am-6.30pm; Tien Pier) You'll find (slightly) fewer tourists here than at Wat Phra Kaew, but Wat Pho is our fave among Bangkok's biggest sights. In fact, the compound incorporates a host of superlatives: the city's largest reclining Buddha, the largest collection of Buddha images in Thailand and the country's earliest centre for public education.

Almost too big for its shelter is Wat Pho's highlight, the genuinely impressive **Reclining Buddha**.

The grounds of Wat Pho cover 8 hectares, with the major tourist sites on the northern side of Th Chetuphon and the monastic facilities found on the southern side. The temple compound is also the national headquarters for the teaching and preservation of traditional Thai medicine, including Thai massage, a mandate legislated by Rama III when the tradition was in danger of extinction. The massage school has two **massage pavilions** (Wat Pho, Th Sanam Chai; Thai massage per hr 420B; 9am-6pm; Tien Pier) within the temple area and additional rooms within the training facility (p99) outside the temple.

DRESS FOR THE OCCASION

Many of Bangkok's biggest tourist attractions are sacred places, and visitors should dress and behave appropriately. In particular at Wat Phra Kaew & Grand Palace, Wat Arun and in Dusit Palace Park, dress rules are strictly enforced. If you're wearing shorts or a sleeveless shirt you will not be allowed into the temple grounds – this applies to both men and women. If you're showing a bit too much calf or ankle, expect to be shown into a dressing room and issued with a sarong (rental is free, but you must provide a 200B deposit). Officially, sandals and flip-flops are not permitted, though the guards are less zealous in enforcing this rule. Regardless, footwear should always be removed before entering any main *bòht* (chapel) or *wí·hǎhn* (sanctuary). When sitting in front of a Buddha image, tuck your feet behind you to avoid the highly offensive pose of pointing your feet towards a revered figure.

Wat Phra Kaew & Grand Palace

EXPLORE BANGKOK'S PREMIER MONUMENTS TO RELIGION AND REGENCY

The first area tourists enter is the Buddhist temple compound generally referred to as Wat Phra Kaew. A covered walkway surrounds the area, the inner walls of which are decorated with the **murals of the *Ramakian*** ❶ and ❷. Originally painted during the reign of Rama I (r 1782–1809), the murals, which depict the Hindu epic the *Ramayana*, span 178 panels that describe the struggles of Rama to rescue his kidnapped wife, Sita.

After taking in the story, pass through one of the gateways guarded by ***yaksha*** ❸ to the inner compound. The most important structure here is the ***bòht*, or ordination hall** ❹, which houses the **Emerald Buddha** ❺.

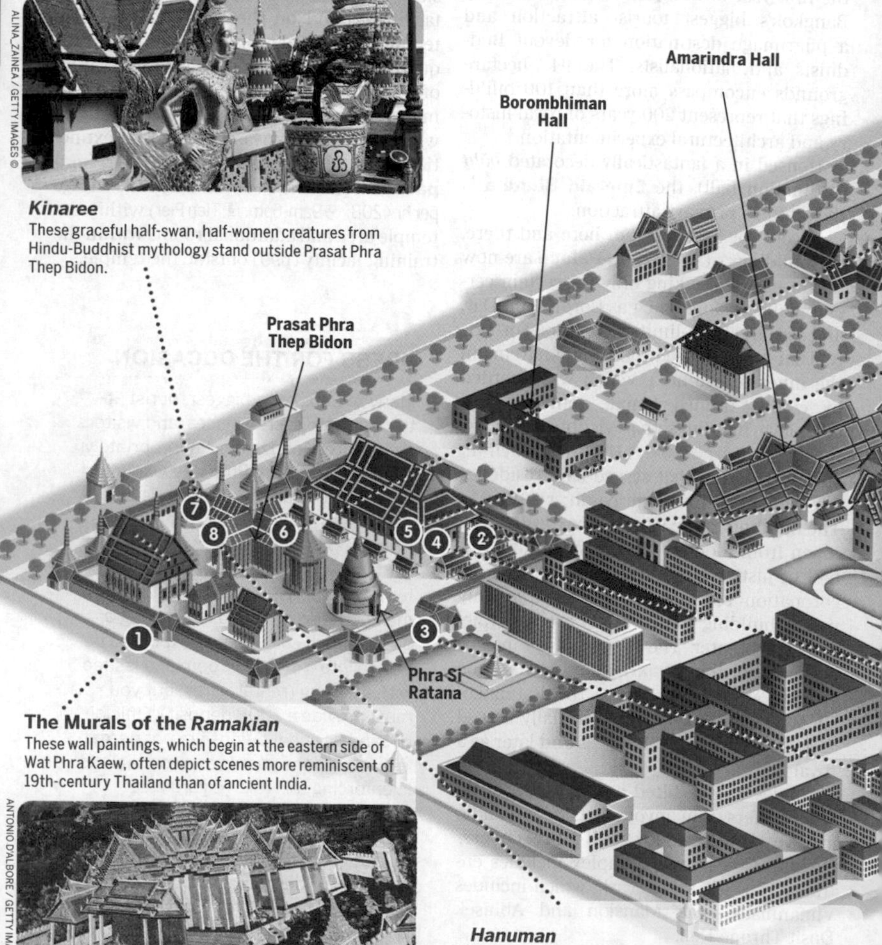

Kinaree
These graceful half-swan, half-women creatures from Hindu-Buddhist mythology stand outside Prasat Phra Thep Bidon.

The Murals of the *Ramakian*
These wall paintings, which begin at the eastern side of Wat Phra Kaew, often depict scenes more reminiscent of 19th-century Thailand than of ancient India.

Hanuman
Rows of these mischievous monkey deities from Hindu mythology appear to support the lower levels of two small *chedi* near Prasat Phra Thep Bidon.

Head east to the so-called Upper Terrace, an elevated area home to the **spires of the three primary *chedi*** 6. The middle structure, Phra Mondop, is used to house Buddhist manuscripts. This area is also home to several of Wat Phra Kaew's noteworthy mythical beings, including beckoning ***kinaree*** 7 and several grimacing **Hanuman** 8.

Proceed through the western gate to the compound known as the Grand Palace. Few of the buildings here are open to the public. The most noteworthy structure is **Chakri Mahaprasat** 9. Built in 1882, the exterior of the hall is a unique blend of Western and traditional Thai architecture.

The Three Spires
The elaborate seven-tiered roof of Phra Mondop, the Khmer-style peak of Prasat Phra Thep Bidon, and the gilded Phra Si Ratana *chedi* are the tallest structures in the compound.

Emerald Buddha
Despite the name, this diminutive statue (it's only 66cm tall) is actually carved from nephrite, a type of jade.

The Death of Thotsakan
The panels progress clockwise, culminating at the western edge of the compound with the death of Thotsakan, Sita's kidnapper, and his elaborate funeral procession.

9

Chakri Mahaprasat
This structure is sometimes referred to as *fa·ràng sài chá·dah* (Westerner in a Thai crown) because each wing is topped by a *mon·dòp*: a spire representing a Thai adaptation of a Hindu shrine.

Dusit Hall

***Bòht* (Ordination Hall)**
This structure is an early example of the Ratanakosin school of architecture, which combines traditional stylistic holdovers from Ayuthaya along with more modern touches from China and the West.

Yaksha
Each entrance to the Wat Phra Kaew compound is watched over by a pair of vigilant and enormous *yaksha*, ogres or giants from Hindu mythology.

Wat Pho

A WALK THROUGH THE BIG BUDDHAS OF WAT PHO

The logical starting place is the main *wi·hăhn* (sanctuary), home to Wat Pho's centrepiece, the immense **Reclining Buddha** ❶. Apart from its huge size, note the **mother-of-pearl inlays** ❷ on the soles of the statue's feet. The interior walls of the *wí·hăhn* are covered with murals depicting previous lives of the Buddha, and along the south side of the structure are 108 bronze monk bowls; for 20B you can buy 108 coins, each of which is dropped in a bowl for good luck.

Exit the *wí·hăhn* and head east via the two **stone giants** ❸ who guard the gateway to the rest of the compound. Directly south of these are the four towering **royal *chedi*** ❹.

Continue east, passing through two consecutive **galleries of Buddha**

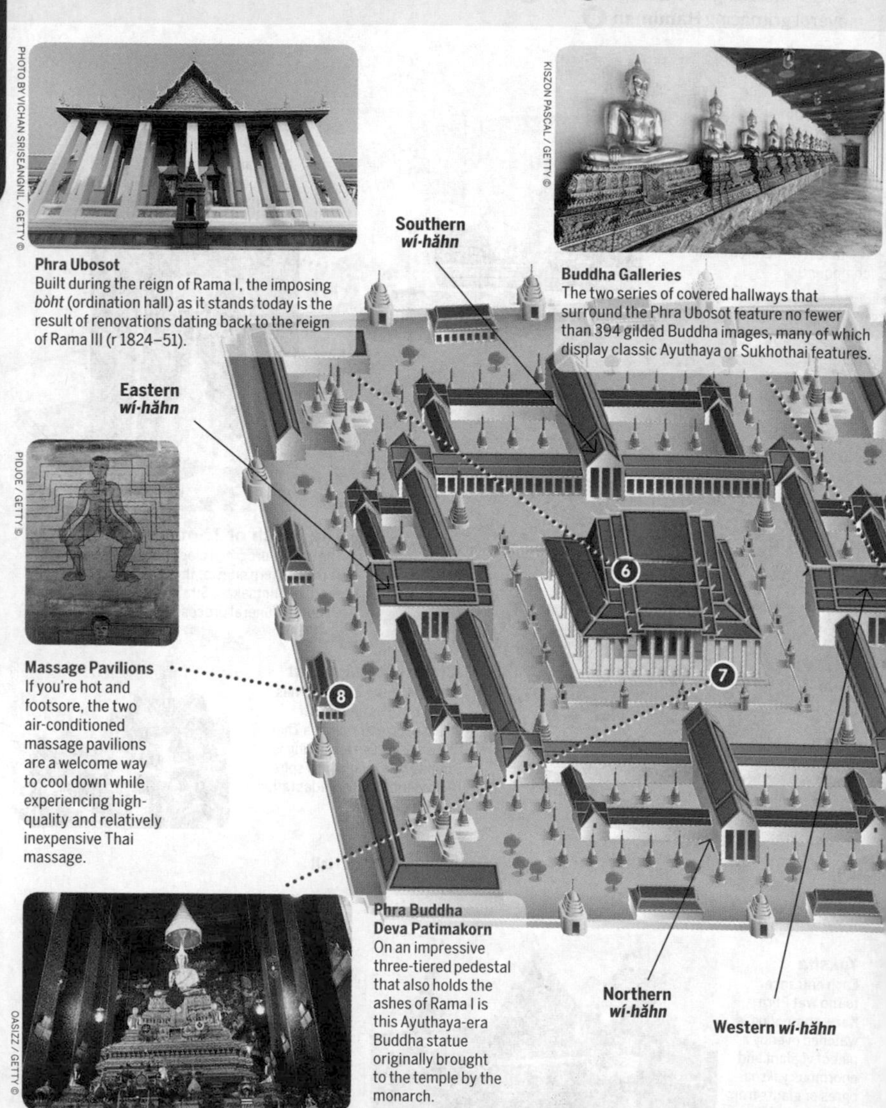

Phra Ubosot
Built during the reign of Rama I, the imposing *bòht* (ordination hall) as it stands today is the result of renovations dating back to the reign of Rama III (r 1824–51).

Buddha Galleries
The two series of covered hallways that surround the Phra Ubosot feature no fewer than 394 gilded Buddha images, many of which display classic Ayuthaya or Sukhothai features.

Massage Pavilions
If you're hot and footsore, the two air-conditioned massage pavilions are a welcome way to cool down while experiencing high-quality and relatively inexpensive Thai massage.

Phra Buddha Deva Patimakorn
On an impressive three-tiered pedestal that also holds the ashes of Rama I is this Ayuthaya-era Buddha statue originally brought to the temple by the monarch.

statues ❺ linking four *wí·hăhn*, two of which contain notable Sukhothai-era Buddha statues; these comprise the exterior of **Phra Ubosot** ❻, the immense ordination hall that is Wat Pho's second-most noteworthy structure. The base of the building is surrounded by bas-relief inscriptions, and inside is the notable Buddha statue, **Phra Buddha Deva Patimakorn** ❼.

Wat Pho is often referred to as Thailand's first university, a tradition that continues today in an associated traditional Thai medicine school and, at the compound's eastern extent, two **massage pavilions** ❽.

Interspersed throughout the eastern half of the compound are several additional minor *chedi* and rock gardens.

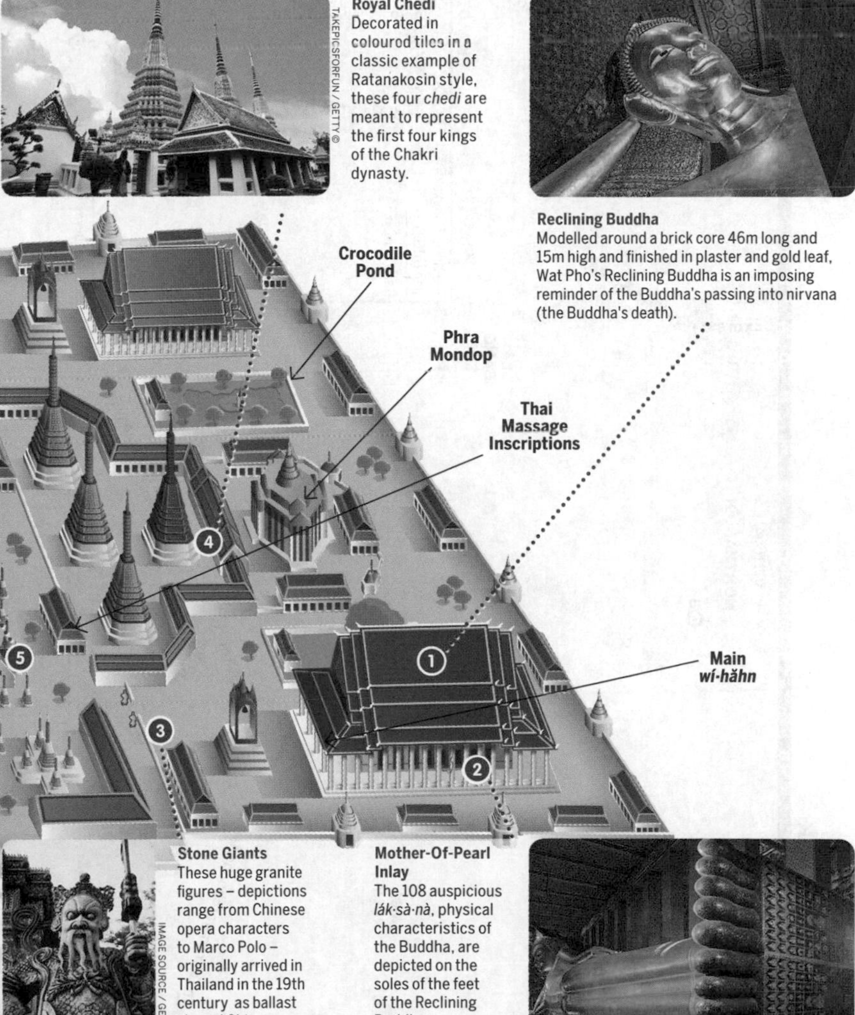

Royal Chedi
Decorated in coloured tiles in a classic example of Ratanakosin style, these four *chedi* are meant to represent the first four kings of the Chakri dynasty.

Reclining Buddha
Modelled around a brick core 46m long and 15m high and finished in plaster and gold leaf, Wat Pho's Reclining Buddha is an imposing reminder of the Buddha's passing into nirvana (the Buddha's death).

Stone Giants
These huge granite figures – depictions range from Chinese opera characters to Marco Polo – originally arrived in Thailand in the 19th century as ballast aboard Chinese junks.

Mother-Of-Pearl Inlay
The 108 auspicious *lák·sà·nà*, physical characteristics of the Buddha, are depicted on the soles of the feet of the Reclining Buddha.

Greater Bangkok

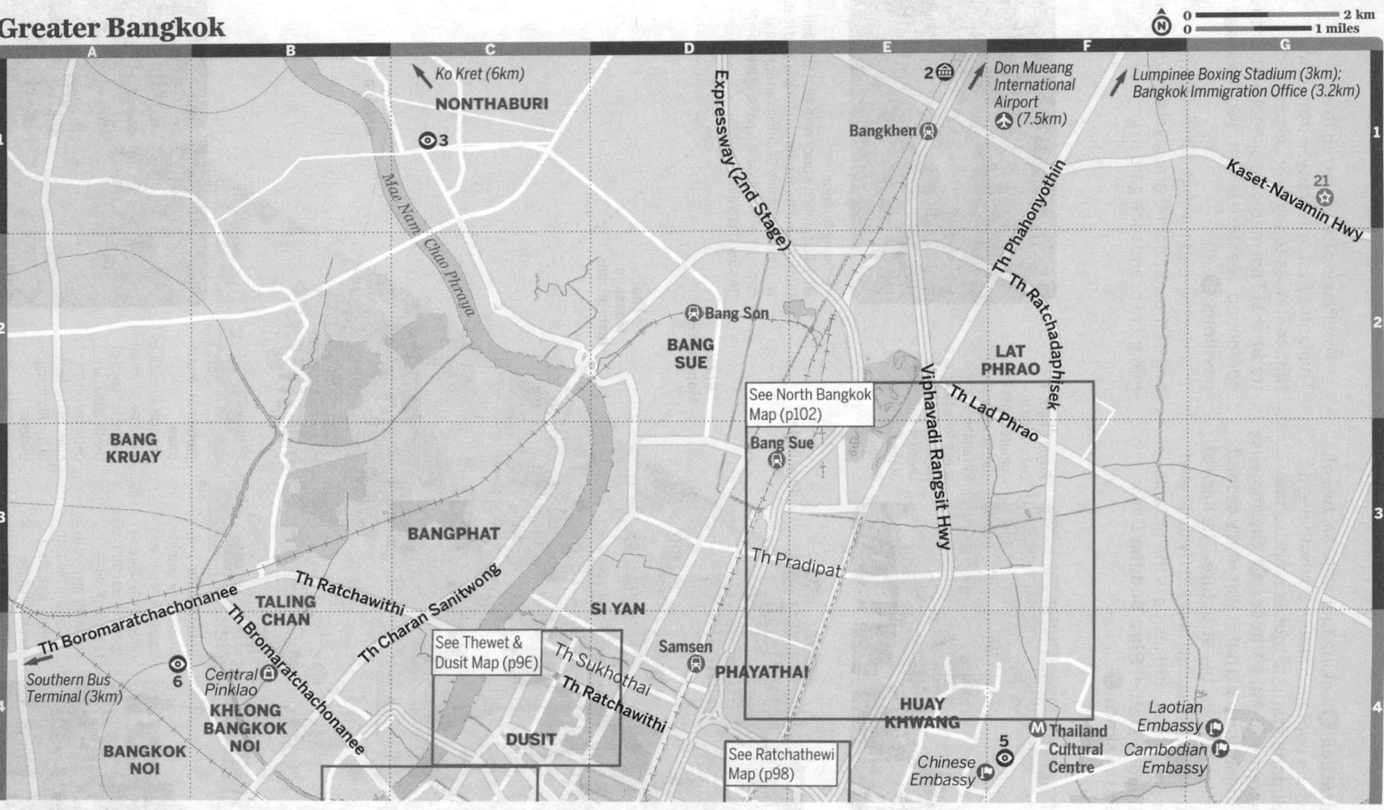
0 2 km
0 1 miles
A
B
C
D
E
F
G
1
2
3
4
Ko Kret (6km)
NONTHABURI
3
Mae Nam Chao Phraya
Expressway (2nd Stage)
2
Don Mueang International Airport (7.5km)
Lumpinee Boxing Stadium (3km); Bangkok Immigration Office (3.2km)
Bangkhen
Th Phahonyothin
Kaset-Navamin Hwy
21
Th Ratchadaphisek
Bang Son
BANG SUE
LAT PHRAO
See North Bangkok Map (p102)
Viphavadi Rangsit Hwy
Th Lad Phrao
Bang Sue
BANG KRUAY
BANGPHAT
Th Pradipat
Th Ratchawithi
TALING CHAN
Th Charan Sanitwong
SI YAN
Th Boromaratchachonanee
Th Bromaratchachonanee
See Thewet & Dusit Map (p96)
Th Sukhothai
Samsen
PHAYATHAI
Th Ratchawithi
Southern Bus Terminal (3km)
6
Central Pinklao
KHLONG BANGKOK NOI
BANGKOK NOI
DUSIT
See Ratchathewi Map (p98)
HUAY KHWANG
5
Thailand Cultural Centre
Chinese Embassy
Laotian Embassy
Cambodian Embassy

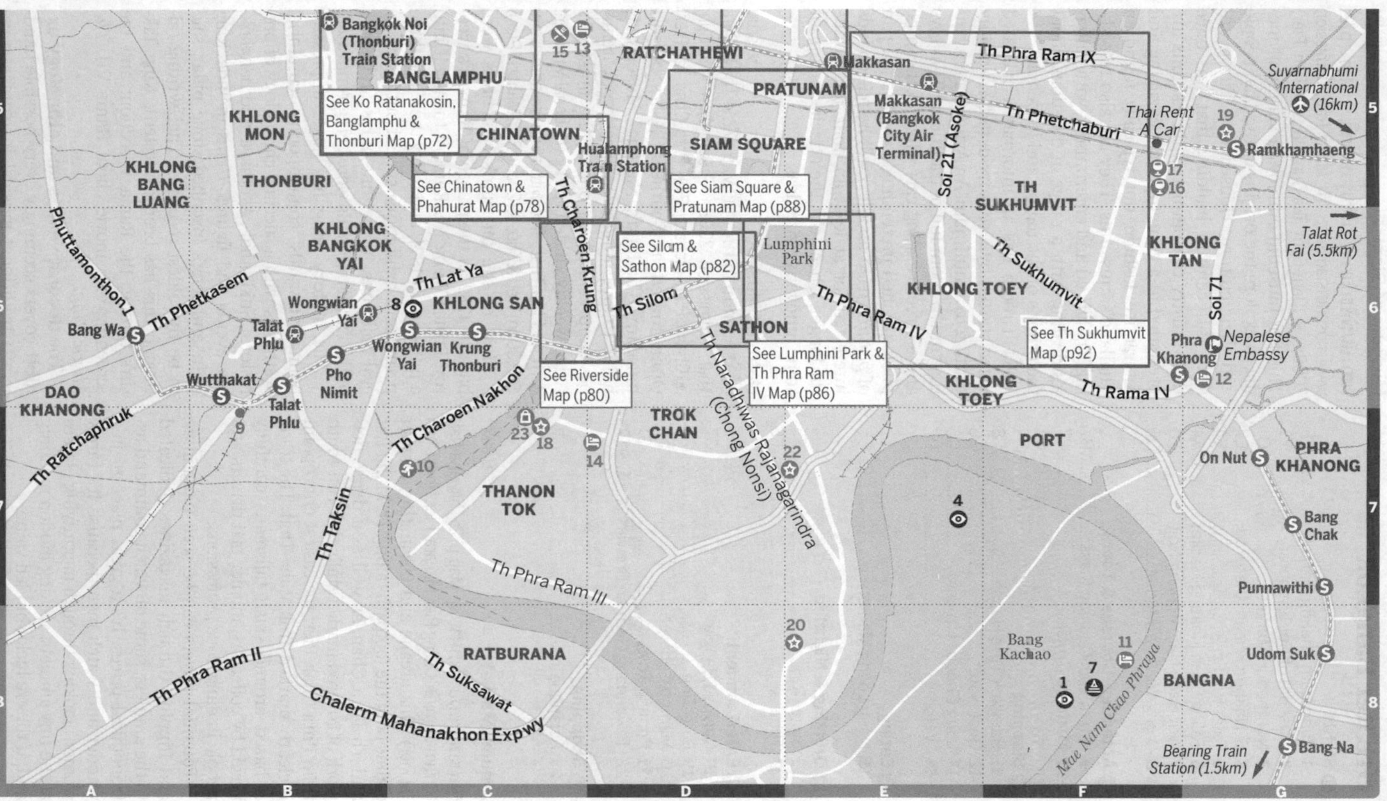
Bangkok Noi (Thonburi) Train Station
BANGLAMPHU
See Ko Ratanakosin, Banglamphu & Thonburi Map (p72)
15
13
RATCHATHEWI
Makkasan
Th Phra Ram IX
PRATUNAM
Makkasan (Bangkok City Air Terminal)
Soi 21 (Asoke)
Th Phetchaburi
Thai Rent A Car
19
Ramkhamhaeng
Suvarnabhumi International (16km)
KHLONG MON
CHINATOWN
Hualamphong Train Station
SIAM SQUARE
17
16
TH SUKHUMVIT
KHLONG BANG LUANG
THONBURI
See Chinatown & Phahurat Map (p78)
Th Charoen Krung
See Siam Square & Pratunam Map (p88)
Talat Rot Fai (5.5km)
Phuttamonthon 1
KHLONG BANGKOK YAI
See Silom & Sathon Map (p82)
Lumphini Park
Th Sukhumvit
KHLONG TAN
Th Lat Ya
KHLONG TOEY
Soi 71
Th Phetkasem
Wongwian Yai
8
KHLONG SAN
Th Silom
Th Phra Ram IV
Bang Wa
Talat Phlu
Wongwian Yai
Krung Thonburi
SATHON
See Th Sukhumvit Map (p92)
Phra Khanong
Nepalese Embassy
Pho Nimit
See Riverside Map (p80)
See Lumphini Park & Th Phra Ram IV Map (p86)
12
Wutthakat
Talat Phlu
Th Naradhiwas Rajanagarindra (Chong Nonsi)
KHLONG TOEY
Th Rama IV
DAO KHANONG
Th Charoen Nakhon
TROK CHAN
9
23
18
14
PORT
PHRA KHANONG
Th Ratchaphruk
On Nut
22
10
THANON TOK
4
Th Taksin
Bang Chak
Th Phra Ram III
Punnawithi
20
RATBURANA
Bang Kachao
11
Udom Suk
Th Phra Ram II
Th Suksawat
7
BANGNA
1
Chalerm Mahanakhon Expwy
Mae Nam Chao Phraya
Bearing Train Station (1.5km)
Bang Na
A
B
C
D
E
F
G
5
6
7
8

Greater Bangkok

Sights
1 Bang Nam Pheung Market F8
2 Museum of Contemporary Art E1
3 Nonthaburi Market C1
4 Si Nakhon Kheun Khan Park E7
5 Talat Rot Fai 2 F4
6 Taling Chan Floating Market A4
7 Wat Bang Nam Pheung Nok F8
8 Wong Wian Yai Market C6

Activities, Courses & Tours
9 Amita Thai Cooking Class B7
10 Manohra Cruises C7

Sleeping
11 Bangkok Tree House F8
12 Beat Hotel G6
13 Loog Choob Homestay C5
14 W Home D7

Eating
15 Nang Loeng Market C5

Drinking & Nightlife
16 Sugar Ray F5
17 Tuba F5

Entertainment
18 Calypso Bangkok C7
19 Lam Sing G5
20 Mambo Cabaret E8
21 Parking Toys G1
22 Tawandang German Brewery E7

Shopping
23 Asiatique C7

Amulet Market MARKET

(ตลาดพระเครื่องวัดมหาธาตุ; Map p72; Th Maha Rat; 7am-5pm; Chang Pier, Maharaj Pier, Phra Chan Tai Pier) This arcane and fascinating market claims both the footpaths along Th Maha Rat and Th Phra Chan, as well as a dense network of covered market stalls that run south from Phra Chan Pier; the easiest entry point is clearly marked Trok Maha That. The trade is based around small talismans carefully prized by collectors, monks, taxi drivers and people in dangerous professions.

Potential buyers can be seen bargaining and flipping through magazines dedicated to the amulets, some of which command astronomical prices. It's a great place to just wander and watch men (because it's rarely women) looking through magnifying glasses at the tiny amulets, seeking hidden meaning and, if they're lucky, hidden value.

Museum of Siam MUSEUM

(สถาบันพิพิธภัณฑ์การเรียนรู้แห่งชาติ; Map p72; www.museumsiam.org; Th Maha Rat; admission 300B; 10am-6pm Tue-Sun; ; Tien Pier) This fun museum employs a variety of media to explore the origins of the Thai people and their culture. Housed in a European-style 19th-century building that was once the Ministry of Commerce, the exhibits are presented in a contemporary, engaging and interactive fashion not typically found in Thailand's museums. They are also refreshingly balanced and entertaining, with galleries dealing with a range of questions about the origins of the nation and its people.

Each room has an informative narrated video started by a sensory detector, keeping waiting to a minimum. An Ayuthaya-era battle game, a room full of traditional Thai toys and a street vending cart where you can be photographed pretending to whip up a pan of *pàt tai* (fried noodles) will help keep kids interested for at least an hour, and adults for longer. Check out the attached shop for some innovative gift ideas.

National Museum MUSEUM

(พิพิธภัณฑสถานแห่งชาติ; Map p72; 4 Th Na Phra That; admission 200B; 9am-4pm Wed-Sun; Chang Pier, Maharaj Pier, Phra Chan Tai Pier) Often touted as Southeast Asia's biggest museum, Thailand's National Museum is home to an impressive collection of items, best appreciated on one of the museum's twice-weekly guided **tours** (National Museum, 4 Th Na Phra That; free with museum admission; 9.30am Wed & Thu; Chang Pier, Maharaj Pier).

Most of the museum's structures were built in 1782 as the palace of Rama I's viceroy, Prince Wang Na. Rama V turned it into a museum in 1874, and today there are three permanent exhibitions spread out over several buildings. At the time of research some of the exhibition halls were being renovated.

The **history wing** has made impressive bounds towards contemporary curatorial aesthetics with a succinct chronology of prehistoric, Sukhothai-, Ayuthaya- and Bangkok-era events and figures. Gems include King Ramkamhaeng's inscribed stone pillar, said to be the oldest record of Thai writing (although this has been contested); King Taksin's throne; the Rama V section; and the screening of a movie about Rama VII, *The Magic Ring*.

The **decorative arts and ethnology exhibit** covers seemingly every possible handicraft: traditional musical instruments, ceramics, clothing and textiles, woodcarving, regalia and weaponry. The **archaeology and art history wing** has exhibits ranging from prehistoric to the Bangkok period.

In addition to the main exhibition halls, the **Bhuddhaisawan (Phutthaisawan) Chapel** includes some well-preserved murals and one of the country's most revered Buddha images, Phra Phuttha Sihing. Legend claims the image came from Sri Lanka, but art historians attribute it to the 13th-century Sukhothai period.

National Gallery ART GALLERY
(พิพิธภัณฑสถานแห่งชาติ/หอศิลป์เจ้าฟ้า; Map p72; www.facebook.com/TheNationalGalleryBangkok; 4 Th Chao Fa; admission 200B; ⊙9am-4pm Wed-Sun; Chang Pier, Maharaj Pier, Phra Chan Tai Pier) Housed in a building that was the Royal Mint during the reign of Rama V, the National Gallery's permanent exhibition is admittedly a rather dusty and dated affair. Secular art is a relatively new concept in Thailand and most of the country's best examples of fine art reside in the temples for which they were created – much as historic Western art is often found in European cathedrals. As such, most of the permanent collection here documents Thailand's homage to modern styles.

More interesting are the rotating exhibits held in the spacious rear galleries; take a look at the Facebook page or the posters out front to see what's on.

Lak Meuang MONUMENT
(ศาลหลักเมือง; Map p72; cnr Th Sanam Chai & Th Lak Meuang; ⊙6.30am-6.30pm; Chang Pier, Maharaj Pier, Phra Chan Tai Pier) Serving as the spiritual keystone of Bangkok, Lak Meuang is a phallus-shaped wooden pillar erected by Rama I during the foundation of the city in 1782. Part of an animistic tradition, the city pillar embodies the city's guardian spirit (Phra Sayam Thewathirat) and also lends a practical purpose as a marker of a town's crossroads and measuring point for distances between towns.

If you're lucky, *lá·kon gâa bon* (a commissioned dance) may be in progress. Brilliantly costumed dancers measure out subtle movements as gratitude to the guardian spirit for granting a worshipper's wish.

Banglamphu บางลำพู

Next to Ko Ratanakosin, Banglamphu encompasses both the most characteristically old-school-Bangkok part of town as well as Th Khao San, a brash, neon-lit decompression zone for backpackers. Depending on which

LOCAL KNOWLEDGE

BI: AN AMULET VENDOR

Bi, a long-standing vendor at Bangkok's Amulet Market, gives us the lowdown on the precious talismans for sale here.

How long have you been selling amulets? My father opened this stall. I've been here around 10 years.

Who are your customers? All types of people are interested in amulets: men, women, people who believe in the power of amulets, investors, collectors.

What kind of powers do the amulets have? Some amulets do things like protect people from danger. Others are more specific and can prevent weapons from working properly.

Where do the powers come from? Amulets are blessed by monks. But this doesn't mean that they work for anybody; you have believe in them as well!

How much can amulets sell for? In Thai, we say that we rent an amulet, because it sounds disrespectful to buy a sacred object. Also, we believe that we just hold onto these amulets temporarily before passing them along. We have amulets that range from a couple hundred baht to millions of baht.

Are all the amulets at this market ancient and valuable? Some shops sell copies; they'll usually tell you. But some vendors will try to trick people. Just because an amulet is old doesn't mean it's valuable; it depends on what is popular at the time.

How can you tell if an amulet's real or fake? I have a magnifying glass, and I know what marks to look for. But the technology is very advanced nowadays, so it's getting easy to fool people.

one you fancy, it's not difficult to escape the other – another of Banglamphu's charms. Many classic Bangkok-style buildings are found in this area, as well as lots of authentic Bangkok-style cuisine and culture.

Ways to reach this 'hood include the Chao Phraya Express Boat piers at Phra Athit/Banglamphu, or the canal boat stop at Phanfa Leelard Pier. Alternatively, take the BTS to National Stadium or Ratchathewi, or the MRT to Hua Lamphong, followed by a short taxi ride.

Golden Mount BUDDHIST TEMPLE

(ภูเขาทอง, Phu Khao Thong; Map p72; off Th Boriphat; admission to summit of Golden Mount 10B; ⊙7.30am-5.30pm; klorng boat to Phanfa Leelard Pier) Even if you're wát-ed out, you should tackle the brisk ascent to the Golden Mount. Serpentine steps wind through an artificial hill shaded by gnarled trees, some of which are signed in English, and past graves and pictures of wealthy benefactors. At the peak, you'll find a breezy 360-degree view of Bangkok's most photogenic side.

The hill was created when a large stupa, under construction by Rama III (King Phranangklao; r 1824–51), collapsed because the soft soil beneath would not support it. The resulting mud-and-brick hill was left to sprout weeds until Rama IV (King Monkut; r 1851–68) built a small stupa on its crest. Rama V later added to the structure and housed a Buddha relic from India (given to him by the British government) in the stupa. The concrete walls were added during WWII to prevent the hill from eroding.

In November there's a festival in the grounds that includes an enchanting candlelight procession up the Golden Mount.

Wat Suthat BUDDHIST TEMPLE

(วัดสุทัศน์; Map p72; Th Bamrung Meuang; admission 20B; ⊙8.30am-9pm; klorng boat to Phanfa Leelard Pier) Other than being just plain huge and impressive, Wat Suthat also holds the highest royal temple grade. Inside the *wí·hăhn* (sanctuary for a Buddha sculpture) are intricate *Jataka* (stories of the Buddha) murals and the 8m-high **Phra Si Sakayamuni**, Thailand's largest surviving Sukhothai-period bronze, cast in the former capital of Sukhothai in the 14th century. Today, the ashes of Rama VIII (King Ananda Mahidol; r 1935–46) are contained in the base of the image.

Behind the *wí·hăhn,* the *bòht* is the largest of its kind in the country. To add to its list of 'largests', Wat Suthat holds the rank of Rachavoramahavihan, the highest royal temple grade. It also maintains a special place in the national religion because of its association with the Brahman priests who perform important ceremonies, such as the Royal Ploughing Ceremony in May. These priests also perform religious rites at two Hindu shrines near the wát – **Dhevasathan** (เทวสถาน (โบสถ์พราหมณ์); Map p72; ⊙dawn-dusk; klorng boat to Phanfa Leelard Pier) FREE on Th Din So, and the smaller **Vishnu Shrine** (Map p72; ⊙dawn-dusk; klorng boat to Phanfa Leelard Pier) FREE on Th Unakan.

Ban Baat NEIGHBOURHOOD

(บ้านบาตร; Map p72; Monk's Bowl Village; off Soi Ban Bat; ⊙9am-5pm; klorng boat to Phanfa Leelard Pier) FREE The residents of Ban Baat inhabit the only remaining village of three established in Bangkok by Rama I (King Phraphutthayotfa; r 1782–1809) to produce *bàht,* the distinctive bowls used by monks to receive morning food donations. Tourists – not temples – are among the customers these days, and a bowl purchase is usually rewarded with a demonstration of how the bowls are made.

To find the village – today reduced to a single alleyway – from Th Bamrung Meuang, turn down Soi Ban Bat, then take the first right.

As cheaper factory-made bowls are now the norm, the artisanal tradition has shrunk to one extended family. You can observe the process of hammering the bowls together from eight separate pieces of steel, said to represent Buddhism's eightfold path. The joints are then fused with melted copper wire, and the bowl is beaten, polished and coated with several layers of black lacquer.

Wat Ratchanatdaram BUDDHIST TEMPLE

(วัดราชนัดดาราม; Map p72; Th Mahachai; ⊙8am-5pm; klorng boat to Phanfa Leelard Pier) FREE This temple was built for Rama III (King Phranangklao; r 1824-51) in the 1840s, and its design is said to derive from metal temples built in India and Sri Lanka more than 2000 years ago.

THA OR PIER?

Tâh, often transliterated as *tha*, is the Thai word for 'pier', which explains why some of the signs for the Chao Phraya Express Boat stops say Tha XXX instead of XXX Pier.

THANON KHAO SAN

Th Khao San, better known as Khao San Rd, is genuinely unlike anywhere else on earth. It's an international clearing house of people either entering the liberated state of travelling in Southeast Asia or returning to the coddling bonds of First World life, all coming together in a neon-lit melting pot in Banglamphu. Its uniqueness is probably best illustrated by a question: apart from airports, where else could you share space with the citizens of dozens of countries at the same time, people ranging from first-time backpackers scoffing banana pancakes to 75-year-old grandparents ordering G&Ts, and everyone in between, including hippies, hipsters, nerds, glamazons, package tourists, global nomads, people on a week's holiday and those taking a gap year, people of every colour and creed looking at you looking at them looking at everyone else?

Th Khao San (*kâw săhn*, meaning 'uncooked rice') is perhaps the most high-profile bastard child of the age of independent travel. Of course, it hasn't always been this way. For its first two centuries or so it was just another unremarkable road in old Bangkok – to see what it was like back in the day, stop into the new **Khaosan Museum** (1st fl, 201 Th Khao San; 9am-9pm; Phra Athit/Banglamphu Pier) FREE. The first guesthouses appeared in 1982, and as more backpackers arrived throughout the '80s the old wooden homes were converted one by one into low-rent dosshouses. By the time Alex Garland's novel *The Beach* was published in 1997, with its opening scenes set in the seedier side of Khao San, staying here had become a rite of passage for backpackers coming to Southeast Asia.

The publicity from Garland's book and the movie that followed pushed Khao San into the mainstream, romanticising the seedy and stereotyping the backpackers it attracted as unwashed and counterculturalist. It also brought the long-simmering debate about the relative merits of Th Khao San to the top of backpacker conversations across the region. Was it cool to stay on KSR? Was it uncool? Was this 'real travel' or just an international anywhere surviving on the few baht Western backpackers spent before they headed home to start their high-earning careers? Was it really Thailand at all?

Perhaps one of Garland's characters summed it up most memorably when he said: 'You know, Richard, one of these days I'm going to find one of those Lonely Planet writers and I'm going to ask him, what's so fucking lonely about the Khao San Road?'

Today more than ever the answer would have to be: not that much. With the help of all that publicity, Khao San continued to evolve, with bedbug-infested guesthouses replaced by boutique hotels, and downmarket TV bars showing pirated movies transformed into hip design bars peopled by flashpackers in designer threads. But the most interesting change has been in the way Thais see Khao San.

Once written off as home to cheap, dirty *fa·ràng kêe ngók* (stingy foreigners), Banglamphu has become just about the coolest district in Bangkok. Attracted in part by the long-derided independent traveller and their modern ideas, the city's own counterculture kids have moved in and brought with them a tasty selection of small bars, organic cafes and shops. Indeed, Bangkok's indie crowd has proved to be the Thai spice this melting pot always lacked.

Not that Khao San has moved completely away from its backpacker roots. The strip still anticipates every traveller need: meals to soothe homesickness, cafes and bars for swapping travel tales about getting to the Cambodian border, tailors, travel agents, teeth whitening, secondhand books, hair braiding and, of course, the perennial Akha women trying to harass everyone they see into buying wooden frogs. No, it's not very lonely at all...

At the back of the compound, behind the formal gardens, is a well-known market selling *prá krêu·ang* (Buddhist amulets) in all sizes, shapes and styles.

Sao Ching-Cha MONUMENT

(เสาชิงช้า, Giant Swing; Map p72; Th Bamrung Meuang; 24hr; klorng boat to Phanfa Leelard Pier) FREE

This spindly red arch – a symbol of Bangkok – formerly hosted a Brahman festival in honour of Shiva, in which participants would swing in ever higher arcs in an effort to reach a bag of gold suspended from a 15m-high bamboo pole. Whoever grabbed the gold could keep it, but that was no mean feat, and deaths were as common as successes. A photo

Ko Ratanakosin, Banglamphu & Thonburi

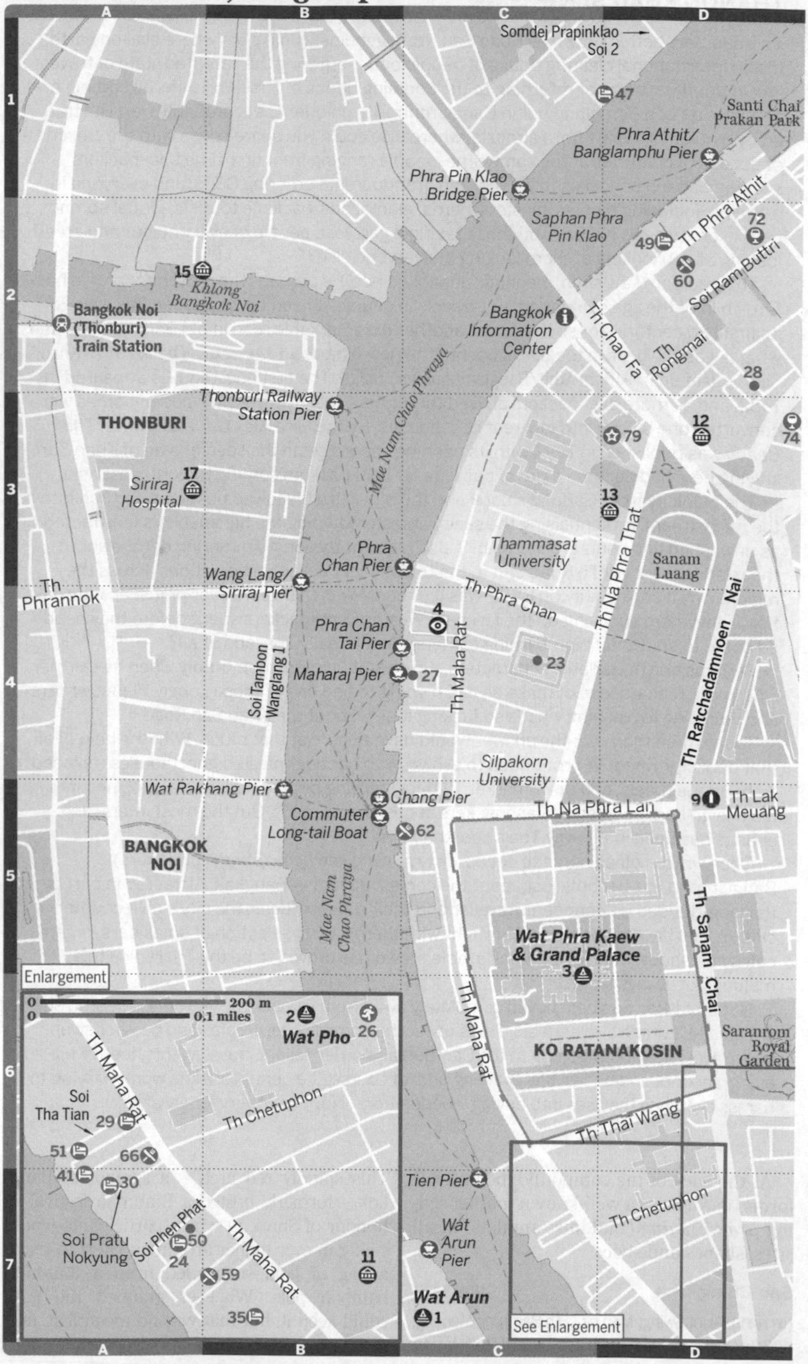

Somdej Prapinklao Soi 2
47
Santi Chai Prakan Park
Phra Athit/ Banglamphu Pier
Phra Pin Klao Bridge Pier
Saphan Phra Pin Klao
49
Th Phra Athit
72
60
Soi Ram Buttri
15
Khlong Bangkok Noi
Bangkok Noi (Thonburi) Train Station
Bangkok Information Center
Th Chao Fa
Th Rongmai
28
Thonburi Railway Station Pier
Mae Nam Chao Phraya
THONBURI
79
12
74
17
Siriraj Hospital
13
Thammasat University
Sanam Luang
Phra Chan Pier
Wang Lang/ Siriraj Pier
Th Phrannok
Th Phra Chan
Th Na Phra That
4
Th Ratchadamnoen Nai
Phra Chan Tai Pier
Th Maha Rat
23
Maharaj Pier
27
Soi Tambon Wanglang 1
Silpakorn University
Wat Rakhang Pier
Chang Pier
Th Na Phra Lan
9
Th Lak Meuang
Commuter Long-tail Boat
62
BANGKOK NOI
Mae Nam Chao Phraya
Th Sanam Chai
Wat Phra Kaew & Grand Palace
3
Th Maha Rat
Enlargement
0 200 m
0 0.1 miles
2
Wat Pho
26
KO RATANAKOSIN
Saranrom Royal Garden
Th Maha Rat
Soi Tha Tian
29
Th Chetuphon
Th Thai Wang
51
66
41
30
Tien Pier
Th Chetuphon
Soi Phen Phat
Soi Pratu Nokyung
50
24
Th Maha Rat
Wat Arun Pier
11
59
Wat Arun
1
35
See Enlargement

A B C D
1 2 3 4 5 6 7

0 500 m
0 0.25 miles
BANGLAMPHU
PHAHURAT
Th Samsen
Soi 1
Soi 2
Soi 3
Soi 4
Soi 6
Th Chakraphatdi Phong
Th Kraisi
Th Tani
Th Rambuttri
Th Khao San
Soi Damnoen Klang Neua
Th Ratchadamnoen Klang
Soi Damnoen Klang Tai
Th Tanao
Th Din So
Th Mahanop
Soi Nava
Th Phraeng Nara
Th Bamrung Meuang
Th Prachathipatai
Th Wisut Kasat
Th Phra Sumen
Th Ratchadamnoen Nok
Th Nakhon Sawan
Th Lan Luang
Phanfa Leelard Pier
Th Damrong Rak
Khlong Saen Saeb
Khlong Phadung Kasem
Tourism Authority of Thailand
Th Mahachai
Th Boriphat
Soi Ban Bat
Th Wora Chak
Rommaninat Park
Khlong Lod
Soi Phraya Si
See Chinatown & Phahurat Map (p78)
Th Atsadang
Th Triphet
Th Burapha
Th Charoen Krung
Th Chakrawat
Th Phahurat
Th Yaowarat
Th Suapa

Ko Ratanakosin, Banglamphu & Thonburi

Top Sights
1 Wat Arun ... C7
2 Wat Pho ... B6
3 Wat Phra Kaew & Grand Palace ... C5

Sights
4 Amulet Market ... C4
5 Ban Baat ... H5
6 Corrections Museum ... G6
7 Dhevasathan ... F5
8 Golden Mount ... H4
Khaosan Museum ... (see 82)
9 Lak Meuang ... D5
10 Mahakan Fort ... G4
11 Museum of Siam ... B7
12 National Gallery ... D3
13 National Museum ... D3
14 Phra Sumen Fort & Santi Chai Prakan Park ... E1
15 Royal Barges National Museum ... A2
16 Sao Ching-Cha ... F5
17 Siriraj Medical Museum ... A3
18 Vishnu Shrine ... F5
19 Wat Bowonniwet ... F2
20 Wat Ratchanatdaram ... G4
21 Wat Suthat ... F5

Activities, Courses & Tours
22 Bangkok Bold Cooking Studio ... G3
23 Center Meditation Wat Mahadhatu ... C4
24 Chetawan Traditional Massage School ... A7
25 Grasshopper Adventures ... F3
26 Massage Pavilions ... B6
27 Muay Thai Lab ... C4
National Museum Tours ... (see 13)
28 Sor Vorapin Gym ... D2

Sleeping
29 Arom D Hostel ... A6
30 Arun Residence ... A7
31 Asadang ... E6
32 Baan Dinso ... F4
33 Baan Noppawong ... F3
34 Bhuthorn ... E5
35 Chakrabongse Villas ... B7
36 Chern ... G5
37 Diamond House ... E1
38 Feung Nakorn Balcony ... E6
39 Fortville Guesthouse ... E1
40 Hotel Dé Moc ... G2
41 Inn A Day ... A7
42 Khaosan Immjai ... E1
43 Lamphu Treehouse ... G2
44 NapPark Hostel ... E2
45 Old Capital Bike Inn ... G3
46 Pannee Residence ... F3
47 Praya Palazzo ... D1
48 Rambuttri Village Inn ... E2
49 Riva Surya ... D2
50 Royal Tha Tien Village ... A7
51 Sala Ratanakosin ... A6
52 Sourire ... G3
53 Suneta Hostel Khaosan ... F2
54 The Warehouse ... E4
55 Villa Cha-Cha ... E2
56 Villa Phra Sumen ... G3

Eating
57 Arawy Vegetarian Food ... F4
58 Chote Chitr ... E5
59 Err ... B7
60 Hemlock ... D2
61 Jay Fai ... G5
62 Khunkung ... C5
63 Krua Apsorn ... F4
64 Likhit Kai Yang ... H2
65 May Kaidee's ... E1
66 Pa Aew ... A6
67 Shoshana ... E2
68 Thamna ... F1
69 Thip Samai ... G4

Drinking & Nightlife
70 Center Khao Sarn ... E3
71 Hippie de Bar ... E3
72 Madame Musur ... D2
73 Phra Nakorn Bar & Gallery ... E3
Rolling Bar ... (see 43)
Roof ... (see 51)
74 The Bank ... D3
75 The Club ... E3

Entertainment
76 Ad Here the 13th ... E1
77 Brick Bar ... E3
78 Brown Sugar ... G3
79 National Theatre ... D3
80 Ratchadamnoen Stadium ... H2

Shopping
81 Heritage Craft ... E5
82 Thanon Khao San Market ... E3

Information
Office of the National Museum ... (see 13)

illustrating the risky rite can be seen at the ticket counter at adjacent Wat Suthat.

The Brahmans once enjoyed a mystical position within the royal court, primarily in the coronation rituals. But after the 1932 revolution the Brahmans' waning power was effectively terminated and the festival, including the swinging, was discontinued during the reign of Rama VII (King Prajadhipok; r 1925–35).

In 2007, the Giant Swing was replaced with the current model, which was made from six giant teak logs from Phrae, in northern Thailand. The previous version is kept at the National Museum.

Phra Sumen Fort & Santi Chai Prakan Park NOTABLE BUILDING, PARK

(ป้อมพระสุเมรุ, สวนสันติชัยปราการ; Map p72; Th Phra Athit; 5am-9pm; Phra Athit/Banglamphu Pier) FREE Formerly the site of a sugar factory, today **Santi Chai Prakan Park** is a tiny patch of greenery with a great river view and lots of evening action, including comical communal aerobics classes. The riverside pathway heading southwards makes for a serene promenade.

The park's most prominent landmark is the blindingly white **Phra Sumen Fort**, which was built in 1783 to defend the city against a river invasion.

Named for the mythical Phra Sumen (Mt Meru) of Hindu-Buddhist cosmology, the octagonal brick-and-stucco bunker was one of 14 city watchtowers that formerly punctuated the old city wall alongside Khlong Rop Krung (now Khlong Banglamphu but still called Khlong Rop Krung on most signs). Apart from **Mahakan Fort** (ป้อมมหากาฬ; Map p72; Th Ratchadamnoen Klang; 24hr; klorng boat to Phanfa Leelard Pier) FREE, this is the only one still standing.

Wat Bowonniwet BUDDHIST TEMPLE

(วัดบวรนิเวศวิหาร; Map p72; www.watbowon.org; Th Phra Sumen; 8.30am-5pm; Phra Athit/Banglamphu Pier) FREE Founded in 1826, Wat Bowonniwet (known colloquially as Wat Bowon) is the national headquarters for the Thammayut monastic sect, a reformed version of Thai Buddhism. The rest of us should visit the temple for the noteworthy murals in its *bòht*, which include Thai depictions of Western life (possibly copied from magazine illustrations) during the early 19th century.

Because of its royal status, visitors should be particularly careful to dress properly for admittance to this wát – shorts and sleeveless clothing are not allowed.

Rama IV (King Mongkut; r 1851–68), who set out to be a scholar, not a king, founded the Thammayut sect and began the royal tradition of ordination at this temple. In fact, Mongkut was the abbot of Wat Bowon for several years. Rama IX (King Bhumibol Adulyadej; r 1946–present) and Crown Prince Vajiralongkorn, as well as several other males in the royal family, have been ordained as monks here.

Thonburi ธนบุรี

Directly across the river from Banglamphu is Thonburi, which served a brief tenure as the Thai capital after the fall of Ayuthaya. It's calm enough on the right bank of the Mae Nam Chao Phraya to seem like another province. The attractions here are relatively few, but *fàng ton* (the colloquial name for the district) is a great area for aimless wandering among leafy streets.

The Chao Phraya Express Boat piers at Saphan Somdet Phra Pin Klao, Thonburi Railway Station, Wang Lang/Siriraj, Wat Rakhang and Wat Arun are the easiest way to reach the sights.

★ Wat Arun BUDDHIST TEMPLE

(วัดอรุณฯ; Map p72; www.watarun.net; off Th Arun Amarin; admission 50B; 8am-6pm; cross-river ferry from Tien Pier) After the fall of Ayuthaya, King Taksin ceremoniously clinched control here on the site of a local shrine and established a royal palace and a temple to house the Emerald Buddha. The temple was renamed after the Indian god of dawn (Aruna) and in honour of the literal and symbolic founding of a new Ayuthaya.

At time of research, the spire of Wat Arun was closed until 2016 due to renovation. Visitors can enter the compound, but cannot climb the tower.

It wasn't until the capital and the Emerald Buddha were moved to Bangkok that Wat Arun received its most prominent characteristic: the 82m-high Ƅrahng (Khmer-style tower). The tower's construction was started during the first half of the 19th century by Rama II and later completed by Rama III. Not apparent from a distance are the floral **mosaics** made from broken, multihued Chinese porcelain, a common temple ornamentation in the early Ratanakosin period, when Chinese ships calling at the port of Bangkok discarded tonnes of old porcelain as ballast.

Also worth an inspection is the interior of the *bòht*. The main Buddha image is said to have been designed by Rama II (King Phraphutthaloetla Naphalai; r 1809–24) himself. The **murals** date from the reign of Rama V (King Chulalongkorn; r 1868–1910); particularly impressive is one that depicts Prince Siddhartha encountering examples of birth, old age, sickness and death outside his

DON'T MISS

EXPLORING THONBURI'S CANALS

Bangkok was formerly known as the Venice of the East, as the city used to be criss-crossed by an advanced network of *klorng* (also spelt *khlong*), man-made canals that inhabitants used both for transport and to ship goods. Today, cars and motorcycles have superseded boats, and the majority of Bangkok's canals have been filled in and covered by roads, or are fetid and drying up. Yet a peek into the watery Bangkok of yesteryear can still be had west of Mae Nam Chao Phraya, in Thonburi.

Thonburi's network of canals and river tributaries still carries a motley fleet of water-craft, from paddle canoes to rice barges. Homes, trading houses and temples are built on stilts with front doors opening out to the water. According to residents, these waterways protect them from the seasonal flooding that plagues the capital. **Khlong Bangkok Noi** is lined with greenery and historic temples; smaller **Khlong Mon** is largely residential. **Khlong Bangkok Yai** was in fact the original course of the river until a canal was built to expedite transits. Today, long-tail boats that ply these and other Thonburi canals are available for charter at Chang Pier and Tien Pier, both on Ko Ratanakosin. Prices at these piers are slightly higher than elsewhere and allow little room for negotiation, but you stand the least chance of being taken for a ride or being hit up for tips and other unexpected fees.

Trips generally traverse Khlong Bangkok Noi and Khlong Mon, taking in the Royal Barges National Museum, Wat Arun and a riverside temple with fish feeding. Longer trips diverge into Khlong Bangkok Yai, which can include a visit to an orchid farm. On weekends, you have the option of visiting the **Taling Chan Floating Market** (p140). However, it's worth pointing out that to actually disembark and explore any of these sights, the most common tour of one hour (1000B, up to six people) is simply not enough time; you'll most likely need 1½ hours (1300B) or two hours (1500B). Most operators have set tour routes, but if you have a specific destination in mind, you can request it. Tours are generally conducted from 8am to 5pm.

If you'd prefer something longer or more personalised, **Pandan Tour** (☎02 689 1232, 087 109 8873; www.thaicanaltour.com; tours from 2295B) conducts a variety of mostly full-day tours. A budget alternative is to take the one-way only **commuter long-tail boat** (Chang Pier, off Th Maha Rat; 25B; ⏰4.30am-7.30pm; ⛴Chang Pier) from Chang Pier to Bang Yai, at the distant northern end of Khlong Bangkok Noi, although foreigners are sometimes discouraged from doing so.

palace walls, an experience that led him to abandon the worldly life. The ashes of Rama II are interred in the base of the presiding Buddha image.

Frequent cross-river ferries run over to Wat Arun from Tien Pier (3B).

Royal Barges National Museum MUSEUM

(พิพิธภัณฑสถานแห่งชาติเรือพระราชพิธี/เรือพระที่นั่ง; Map p72; Khlong Bangkok Noi or 80/1 Th Arun Amarin; admission 100B, camera 100B; ⏰9am-5pm; ⛴Phra Pin Klao Bridge Pier) The royal barges are slender, fantastically ornamented vessels used in ceremonial processions. The tradition dates back to the Ayuthaya era, when travel (for commoners and royals) was by boat. When not in use, the barges are on display at this Thonburi museum.

The most convenient way to get here is by motorcycle taxi from Phra Pin Klao Pier (ask the driver to go to *reu·a prá têe nâng*). The museum is also an optional stop on long-tail boat trips through Thonburi's canals.

Suphannahong, the king's personal barge, is the most important of the six boats on display here. Made from a single piece of timber, it's said to be the largest dugout in the world. The name means Golden Swan, and a huge swan head has been carved into the bow. Lesser barges feature bows that are carved into other Hindu-Buddhist mythological shapes such as the *naga* (mythical sea serpent) and *garuda* (Vishnu's bird mount).

Historic photos help envision the grand processions in which the largest of the barges would require a rowing crew of 50 men, plus seven umbrella bearers, two helmsmen and two navigators, as well as a flagsman, rhythm keeper and chanter. Today, the royal barge procession is an infrequent occurrence, most recently performed in 2012 in honour of the king's 85th birthday.

Chinatown & Phahurat เยาวราช/พาหุรัด

Bangkok's Chinatown (called Yaowarat after its main thoroughfare, Th Yaowarat) is the urban explorer's equivalent of the Amazon Basin. The highlights here aren't necessarily tidy temples or museums, but rather a complicated web of tiny alleyways, crowded markets and delicious street stalls. Unlike other Chinatowns around the world, Bangkok's is defiantly ungentrified, and getting lost in it is probably the best thing that you could do.

The neighbourhood dates back to 1782 when Bangkok's Chinese population, many of whom were labourers hired to build the new capital, were moved here from today's Ko Ratanakosin area by the royal rulers. Little has changed since then, and you can still catch conversations in various Chinese dialects, buy Chinese herbal cures and taste Chinese dishes not available elsewhere in Thailand.

At the western edge of Chinatown is a small but thriving Indian district, called Phahurat. It's a seemingly endless bazaar uniting Bollywood fabric, photogenic vendors selling *paan* (betel nut for chewing), several shops stocked with delicious northern Indian–style sweets and dozens of Indian-owned stores selling all kinds of fabric and clothes. The easiest way to reach most of the sights listed below is via the MRT stop at Hua Lamphong. Alternatively, the Chao Phraya Express Boat piers at Saphan Phut/Memorial Bridge, Ratchawong and Marine Department will also get you close.

★ Wat Traimit (Golden Buddha) BUDDHIST TEMPLE

(วัดไตรมิตร, Temple of the Golden Buddha; Map p78; Th Mittaphap Thai-China; admission 40B; ⌚8am-5pm; ⛴Ratchawong Pier, Ⓜ Hua Lamphong exit 1) The attraction at Wat Traimit is undoubtedly the impressive 3m-tall, 5.5-tonne, **solid-gold Buddha image**, which gleams like, well, gold. Sculpted in the graceful Sukhothai style, the image was 'discovered' some 40 years ago beneath a stucco/plaster exterior, when it fell from a crane while being moved to a new building within the temple compound.

It has been theorised that the covering was added to protect it from marauding hordes, either during the late Sukhothai period or later in the Ayuthaya period when the city was under siege by the Burmese. The temple itself is said to date from the early 13th century.

Donations and a constant flow of tourists have proven profitable, and the statue is now housed in a new four-storey marble structure. The 2nd floor of the building is home to the **Phra Buddha Maha Suwanna Patimakorn Exhibition** (Map p78; Wat Traimit (Golden Buddha), Th Mittaphap Thai-China; admission 100B; ⌚8am-4pm Tue-Sun; ⛴Ratchawong Pier, Ⓜ Hua Lamphong exit 1), which has exhibits on how the statue was made, discovered and came to arrive at its current home, while the 3rd floor is home to the **Yaowarat Chinatown Heritage Center** (Map p78; Wat Traimit (Golden Buddha), Th Mittaphap Thai-China; admission 100B; ⌚8am-4pm Tue-Sun; ⛴Ratchawong Pier, Ⓜ Hua Lamphong exit 1), a small but engaging museum with multimedia exhibits on the history of Bangkok's Chinatown and its residents.

Talat Mai MARKET

(ตลาดใหม่; Map p78; Soi Yaowarat 6/Charoen Krung 16; ⌚6am-6pm; ⛴Ratchawong Pier, Ⓜ Hua Lamphong exit 1 & taxi) With nearly two centuries of commerce under its belt, New Market is no longer an entirely accurate name for this strip of commerce. Regardless, this is Bangkok's, if not Thailand's, most Chinese market, and the dried goods, seasonings, spices and sauces will be familiar to anyone who's ever spent time in China. Even if you're not interested in food, the hectic atmosphere (be on guard for motorcycles squeezing between shoppers) and exotic sights and smells culminate in something of a surreal sensory experience.

While much of the market centres on cooking ingredients, the section north of Th Charoen Krung (equivalent to Soi 21, Th Charoen Krung) is known for selling incense, paper effigies and ceremonial sweets – the essential elements of a traditional Chinese funeral.

Phahurat NEIGHBOURHOOD

(พาหุรัด; Map p78; Th Chakkaraphet; ⌚9am-5pm; ⛴Saphan Phut/Memorial Bridge Pier, Pak Klong Taladd Pier) Heaps of South Asian traders set up shop in Bangkok's small but bustling Little India, where everything from Bollywood movies to bindis is sold by enthusiastic, small-time traders. It's a great area to just wander through, stopping for masala chai and a Punjabi sweet as you go.

The bulk of the action unfolds along unmarked Soi ATM, which runs alongside the large India Emporium shopping centre.

The emphasis is on cloth, and Phahurat proffers boisterously coloured textiles,

Chinatown & Phahurat

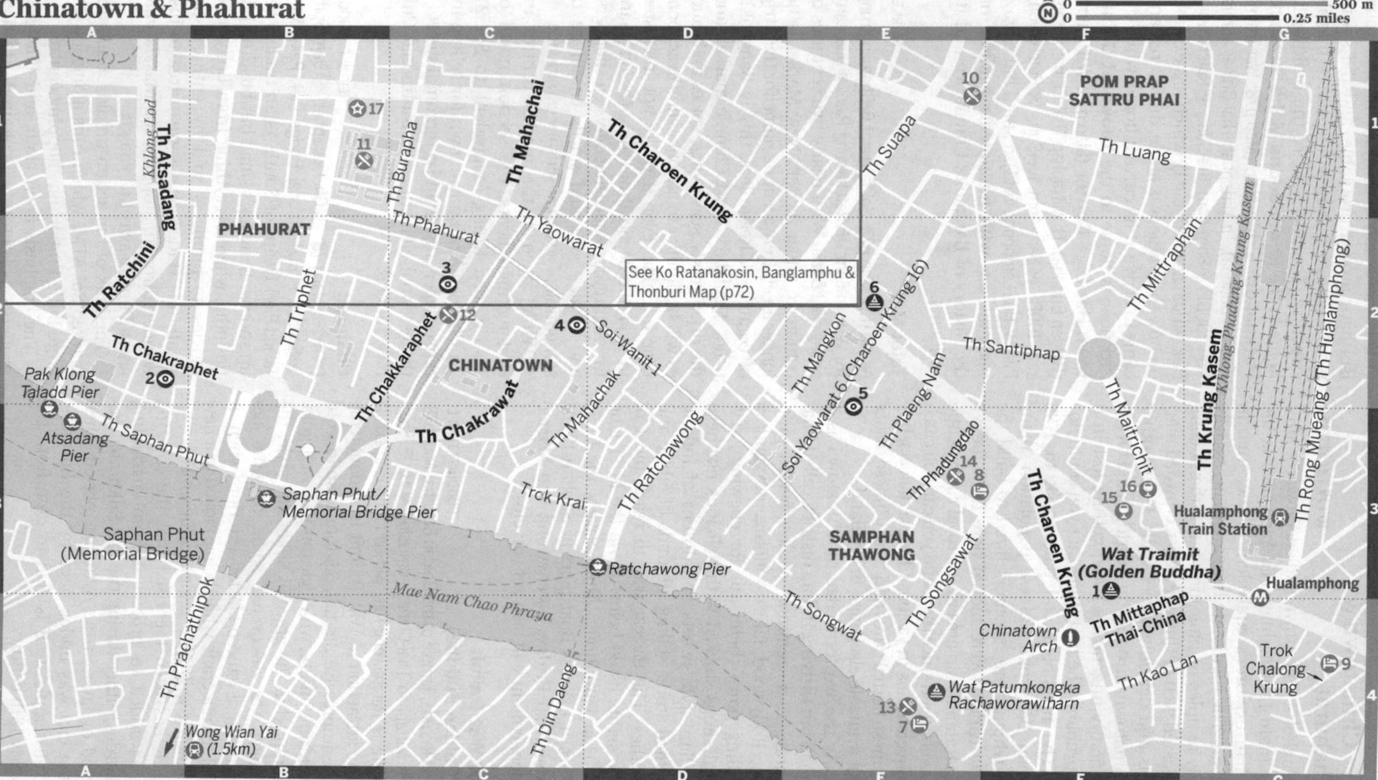

Chinatown & Phahurat

Top Sights

1 Wat Traimit (Golden Buddha) ... F3

Sights

2 Pak Khlong Talat ... A2
3 Phahurat ... C2
Phra Buddha Maha Suwanna Patimakorn Exhibition ... (see 1)
4 Sampeng Lane ... C2
5 Talat Mai ... E2
6 Wat Mangkon Kamalawat ... E2
Yaowarat Chinatown Heritage Center ... (see 1)

Sleeping

7 Loy La Long ... E4
8 Shanghai Mansion ... E3
9 Siam Classic ... G4

Eating

10 Nay Hong ... E1
11 Old Siam Plaza ... B1
12 Royal India ... C2
13 Samsara ... E4
14 Thanon Phadungdao Seafood Stalls ... E3

Drinking & Nightlife

15 El Chiringuito ... F3
16 Tep Bar ... F3

Entertainment

17 Sala Chalermkrung ... B1

traditional Thai dance costumes, tiaras, sequins, wigs and other accessories to make you look like a cross-dresser, a *mŏr lam* (Thai country music) performer, or both. Amid the spectacle of colour there are also good deals on machine-made Thai textiles and children's clothes.

Wat Mangkon Kamalawat BUDDHIST TEMPLE

(วัดมังกรกมลาวาส; Map p78; cnr Th Charoen Krung & Th Mangkon; 6am-6pm; Ratchawong Pier, Hua Lamphong exit 1 & taxi) FREE Clouds of incense and the sounds of chanting form the backdrop at this Chinese-style Mahayana Buddhist temple. Surrounding the temple are vendors selling food for the gods – steamed lotus-shaped dumplings and oranges – which are donated to the temple in exchange for merit. Dating back to 1871, it's the largest and most important religious structure in the area, and during the annual Vegetarian Festival, religious and culinary activities are particularly active here.

Riverside ข้างแม่น้ำ

This stretch of Mae Nam Chao Phraya was formerly Bangkok's international zone, and today retains a particularly Chinese and Muslim feel.

The BTS stop at Saphan Taksin, and the Chao Phraya Express Boat piers at Central/Sathon and Oriental are the easiest ways to reach this area.

Bangkokian Museum MUSEUM

(พิพิธภัณฑ์ชาวบางกอก; Map p80; 273 Soi 43, Th Charoen Krung; admission by donation; 10am-4pm Wed-Sun; Si Phraya/River City Pier) A collection of three antique structures built during the early 20th century, the Bangkokian Museum illustrates an often-overlooked period of Bangkok's history.

The main building was built in 1937 as a home for the Surawadee family and was finished by Chinese carpenters on time and for less than the budgeted 2400B (which would barely buy a door handle today). This building and the large wooden one to the right, which was added as a boarding house to help cover costs, are filled with the detritus of postwar family life and offer a fascinating window into the period. The third building, at the back of the block, was built in 1929 as a surgery for a British doctor, though he died soon after arriving in Thailand.

Talat Noi NEIGHBOURHOOD

(ตลาดน้อย; Map p80; off Th Charoen Krung; 7am-7pm; Marine Department Pier) This microcosm of soi life is named after a small *(nóy)* market *(đà·làht)* that sets up between Soi 22 and Soi 20, off Th Charoen Krung. Wandering here you'll find streamlike soi turning in on themselves, weaving through noodle shops, grease-stained machine shops and people's living rooms.

Old Customs House HISTORIC BUILDING

(กรมศุลกากร; Map p80; Soi 36, Th Charoen Krung; Oriental Pier) The country's former Customs House was once the gateway to Thailand, levying taxes on traders moving in and out of the kingdom. It was designed by an Italian architect and built in the 1890s; the front door opened onto its source of income (the river) and the grand facade was ceremoniously decorated in columns and transom windows.

Today, with its sagging shutters, peeling yellow paint and laundry flapping on the balconies, the crumbling yet hauntingly

Riverside

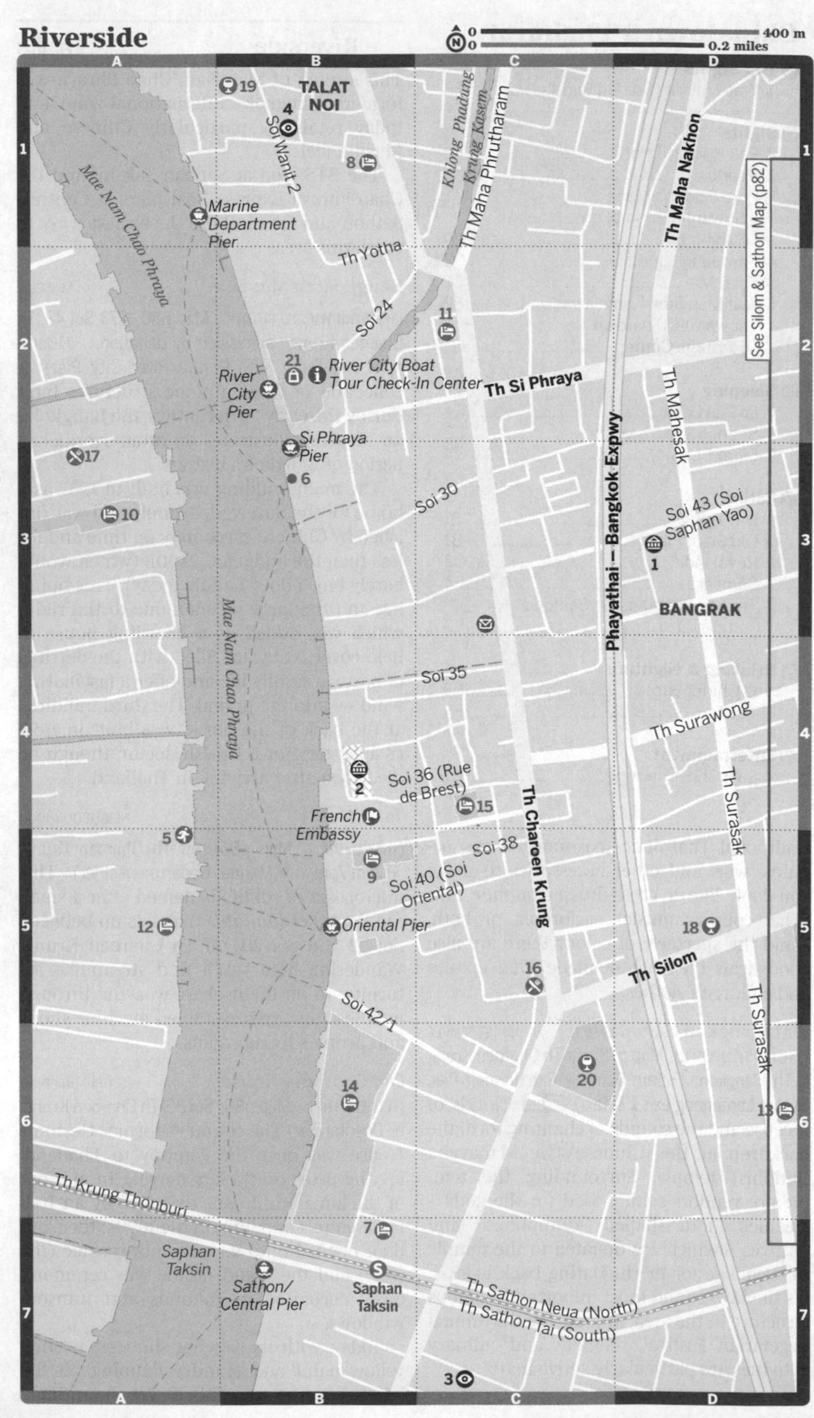

0 400 m
0 0.2 miles
TALAT NOI
Soi Wanit 2
Khlong Phadung Krung Kasem
Th Maha Phrutharam
Th Maha Nakhon
Mae Nam Chao Phraya
Marine Department Pier
Th Yotha
Soi 24
River City Boat Tour Check-In Center
River City Pier
Th Si Phraya
Si Phraya Pier
Th Mahesak
Phayathai – Bangkok Expwy
Soi 30
Soi 43 (Soi Saphan Yao)
BANGRAK
Soi 35
Th Surawong
Soi 36 (Rue de Brest)
Th Charoen Krung
Th Surasak
French Embassy
Soi 38
Soi 40 (Soi Oriental)
Oriental Pier
Th Silom
Soi 42/1
Th Krung Thonburi
Saphan Taksin
Sathon/ Central Pier
Saphan Taksin
Th Sathon Neua (North)
Th Sathon Tai (South)
See Silom & Sathon Map (p82)

Riverside

Sights
1 Bangkokian Museum ... D3
2 Old Customs House ... B4
3 Sathorn Unique Tower ... C7
4 Talat Noi ... B1

Activities, Courses & Tours
Chao Phraya Princess ... (see 21)
Chaophraya Cruise ... (see 21)
Co van Kessel Bangkok Tours ... (see 21)
Grand Pearl ... (see 21)
5 Oriental Spa ... A5
6 Wan Fah ... B3
White Orchid ... (see 21)

Sleeping
7 Glur Bangkok ... B7
8 Loftel 22 ... B1
9 Mandarin Oriental ... B5
10 Millennium Hilton ... A3
11 Oldtown ... C2
12 Peninsula Hotel ... A5
13 Saphaipae ... D6
14 Shangri-La Hotel ... B6
15 Swan Hotel ... C4

Eating
Lord Jim's ... (see 9)
16 Muslim Restaurant ... C5
17 Never Ending Summer ... A3

Drinking & Nightlife
18 Maggie Choo's ... D5
19 River Vibe ... B1
20 Sky Bar ... C6
Viva & Aviv ... (see 21)

Entertainment
Bamboo Bar ... (see 9)
Sala Rim Naam ... (see 5)

Shopping
21 River City ... B2

beautiful building serves as a residence for members of Bangkok's fire brigade, not to mention a popular destination for wedding shoots. And hard-core movie buffs with a keen eye will recognise the Old Customs House from its cameo appearance in Wong Kar Wai's film *In the Mood for Love* (2000).

Silom & Sathon สีลม/สาธร

The business district of Th Silom has only a handful of tourist attractions scattered among the corporate hotels, office towers and wining-and-dining restaurants.

The BTS stops at Sala Daeng, Chong Nonsi and Surasak, and the MRT stops at Si Lom are the easiest ways to reach these areas.

MR Kukrit Pramoj House HISTORIC BUILDING
(บ้านหม่อมราชวงศ์คึกฤทธิ์ปราโมช; Map p82; 02 286 8185; Soi 7, Th Naradhiwas Rajanagarindra/Chong Nonsi; admission adult/child 50/20B; 10am-4pm; S Chong Nonsi exit 2) Author and statesman Mom Ratchawong Kukrit Pramoj (1911–95) once resided in this charming complex now open to the public. Surrounded by a manicured garden famed for its Thai bonsai trees, the five teak buildings introduce visitors to traditional Thai architecture, arts and to the former resident, who served as prime minister of Thailand in 1974 and 1975, wrote more than 150 books (including the highly respected *Four Reigns*) and spent 20 years decorating the house.

Queen Saovabha Memorial Institute ZOO
(สถานเสาวภา; Map p82; Snake Farm; cnr Th Phra Ram IV & Th Henri Dunant; admission adult/child 200/50B; 9.30am-3.30pm Mon-Fri, to 1pm Sat & Sun; ; M Si Lom exit 1, S Sala Daeng exit 3) Thailand's snake farms tend to gravitate towards carnivalesque rather than humanitarian, except at the Queen Saovabha Memorial Institute. Founded in 1923, the snake farm gathers antivenin by milking the snakes' venom, injecting it into horses, and harvesting and purifying the antivenin they produce. The antivenins are then used to treat human victims of snake bites. Regular milkings (11am Monday to Friday) and snake-handling performances (2.30pm Monday to Friday and 11am Saturday and Sunday) are held at the outdoor amphitheatre.

The leafy grounds are home to a few caged snakes (and a constant soundtrack of Western rock music), but the bulk of the attractions are found in the Simaseng Building, at the rear of the compound. The ground floor houses several varieties of snakes in glass cages.

Sri Mariamman Temple HINDU TEMPLE
(วัดพระศรีมหาอุมาเทวี/วัดแขก; Map p82; Wat Phra Si Maha Umathewi; cnr Th Silom & Th Pan; 6am-8pm; S Surasak exit 3) FREE Arrestingly flamboyant, the Sri Mariamman Hindu temple is a wild collision of colours, shapes and deities. It was built in the 1860s by Tamil immigrants and features a 6m facade of

Silom & Sathon

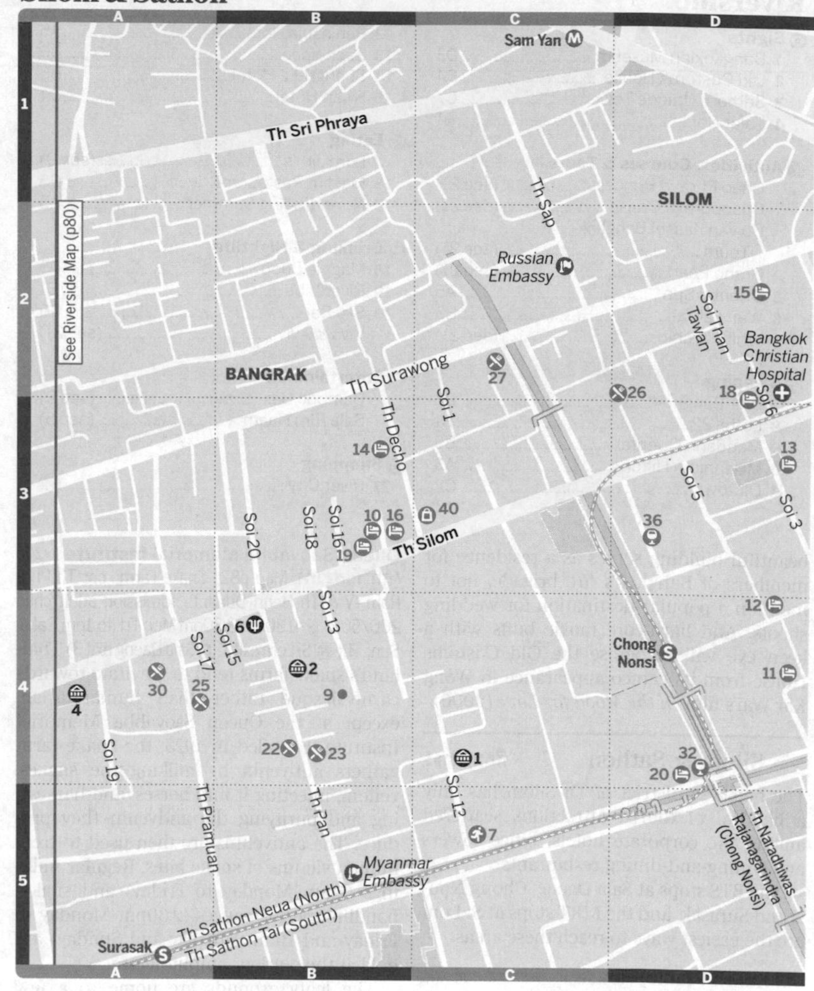

intertwined, full-colour Hindu deities. While most of the people working in the temple hail from the Indian subcontinent, you will likely see plenty of Thai and Chinese devotees praying here as well. This is because the Hindu gods figure just as prominently in their individualistic approach to religion.

The official Thai name of the temple is Wat Phra Si Maha Umathewi, but it's often referred to as Wat Khaek – *kàak* being a common expression for people of Indian descent. The literal translation is 'guest', an obvious euphemism for any group of people not particularly wanted as permanent residents; hence most Indian Thais aren't fond of the term.

Lumphini Park & Th Phra Ram IV สวนลุมพินี/ถนนพระราม ๔

The main attraction in this hyper-urban part of town is, rather paradoxically, the city's single largest green zone.

The easiest ways to reach the area are via the BTS stop at Sala Daeng or the MRT stops at Si Lom and Lumphini.

★Lumphini Park PARK

(สวนลุมพินี; Map p86; bounded by Th Sarasin, Th Phra Ram IV, Th Witthayu/Wireless Rd & Th Ratchadamri; 4.30am-9pm; ; Lumphini exit 3, Si Lom exit 1, Sala Daeng exit 3, Ratchadamri exit 2) Named after the Buddha's place of birth in Nepal, Lumphini Park is the best way to escape Bangkok without actually leaving town. Shady paths, a large artificial lake and swept lawns temporarily blot out the roaring traffic and hulking concrete towers.

There are paddleboats for lovers, playgrounds for the kids and enormous monitor lizards for the whole family. One of the best times to visit the park is before 7am, when the air is fresh (well, relatively so for Bangkok) and legions of Thai-Chinese are practising t'ai chi. The park reawakens with the evening's cooler temperatures – aerobics classes collectively sweat to a techno soundtrack. Late at night the borders of the park are frequented by streetwalking prostitutes, both male and female.

Siam Square & Pratunam สยามสแควร์/ประตูน้ำ

Commerce, mainly in the form of multistorey mega-malls, forms the main attraction in this part of town, but there are a couple of sights that don't involve credit cards.

The BTS stop at Siam or Chit Lom, or the canal boat stop at Hua Chang Pier will put you close to most of these sights.

★Jim Thompson House HISTORIC BUILDING

(Map p88; www.jimthompsonhouse.com; 6 Soi Kasem San 2; adult/student 150/100B; 9am-6pm, compulsory tours every 20 min; klorng boat to Sapan Hua Chang Pier, National Stadium exit 1) This jungly compound is the former home of the eponymous American silk entrepreneur and art collector. Born in Delaware in 1906, Thompson briefly served in the Office of Strategic Services (the forerunner of the CIA) in Thailand during WWII. He settled in Bangkok after the war, when his neighbours' handmade silk caught his eye and piqued his business sense; he sent samples to fashion houses in Milan, London and Paris, gradually building a steady worldwide clientele.

In addition to textiles, Thompson also collected parts of various derelict Thai homes and had them reassembled in their current location in 1959. Some of the homes were brought from the old royal capital of Ayuthaya; others were pulled down and floated across the *klorng* (canal; also spelt *khlong*) from Baan Khrua, including the first building you enter on the tour. One striking departure from tradition is the way each wall has its exterior side facing the house's interior, thus exposing the wall's bracing system. His small but splendid Asian art collection and his personal belongings are also on display in the main house.

Thompson's story doesn't end with his informal reign as Bangkok's best-adapted foreigner, however. While out for an afternoon walk in the Cameron Highlands of western Malaysia in 1967, Thompson mysteriously

Silom & Sathon

Sights
1 H Gallery ... C4
2 Kathmandu Photo Gallery ... B4
3 MR Kukrit Pramoj House ... E5
4 Number 1 Gallery ... A4
5 Queen Saovabha Memorial Institute ... E1
Silom Galleria ... (see 4)
6 Sri Mariamman Temple ... B4
Tang Gallery ... (see 4)
Thavibu Gallery ... (see 4)

Activities, Courses & Tours
7 Health Land ... C5
8 Ruen-Nuad Massage Studio ... E4
9 Silom Thai Cooking School ... B4

Sleeping
10 Amber ... B3
11 Café Ice Residence ... D4
12 Glow Trinity Silom ... D4
13 HQ Hostel ... D3
14 Lub*d ... B3
15 Siam Heritage ... D2
16 Silom Art Hostel ... B3
17 Silom One ... E2
18 Smile Society ... D2
19 Triple Two Silom ... B3
20 W Bangkok ... D4

Eating
21 Benjarong ... F2
22 Bonita Cafe & Social Club ... B4
23 Chennai Kitchen ... B4
24 Eat Me ... E3
25 Kalapapruek ... A4
26 Soi 10 Food Centres ... D2
27 Somboon Seafood ... C2
28 Somtam Convent ... E3
29 Sushi Tsukiji ... E2
30 Taling Pling ... A4

Drinking & Nightlife
31 Balcony ... E2
32 Cé La Vi ... D4
33 Cloud 47 ... E3
34 DJ Station ... F2
35 G.O.D ... F2
36 Namsaah Bottling Trust ... D3
37 Tapas Room ... E2
38 Telephone Pub ... E2

Entertainment
39 Patpong ... E2

Shopping
40 House of Chao ... C3
41 Jim Thompson ... E2
42 July ... F2
43 Patpong Night Market ... E2

disappeared. That same year his sister was murdered in the USA, fuelling various conspiracy theories. Was it communist spies? Business rivals? Or a man-eating tiger? Although the mystery has never been solved, evidence revealed by American journalist Joshua Kurlantzick in his profile of Thompson, *The Ideal Man,* suggests that the vocal anti-American stance Thompson took later in his life may have made him a potential target of suppression by the CIA.

Beware well-dressed touts in soi near the Thompson house who will tell you it is closed and try to take you on a dodgy buying spree.

Erawan Shrine MONUMENT
(ศาลพระพรหม; Map p88; cnr Th Ratchadamri & Th Phloen Chit; 6am-11pm; Chit Lom exit 8) FREE The Erawan Shrine was originally built in 1956 as something of a last-ditch effort to end a string of misfortunes that occurred during the construction of a hotel, at that time known as the Erawan Hotel.

After several incidents ranging from injured construction workers to the sinking of a ship carrying marble for the hotel, a Brahmin priest was consulted. Since the hotel was to be named after the elephant escort of Indra in Hindu mythology, the priest determined that Erawan required a passenger, and suggested it be that of Lord Brahma. A statue was built and, lo and behold, the misfortunes miraculously ended.

Although the original Erawan Hotel was demolished in 1987, the shrine still exists, and today remains an important place of pilgrimage for Thais, particularly those in need of some material assistance. Those wanting to make a wish at the statue should ideally come between 7am and 8am, or 7pm and 8pm, and should offer a specific list of items that includes candles, incense, sugar cane or bananas, all of which are almost exclusively given in multiples of seven. Particularly popular are teak elephants, with money from the sale of these items donated to a charity run by the current hotel, the Grand Hyatt Erawan. And as the tourist brochures depict, it is also possible to charter a classical Thai dance, often done as a way of giving thanks if a wish is granted.

A bomb exploded near the shrine in August 2015, killing 20 and slightly damaging the shrine. It was repaired and reopened just two days later.

Lingam Shrine MONUMENT

(ศาลเจ้าแม่ทับทิม; Map p88; Swissôtel Nai Lert Park, Th Witthayu/Wireless Rd; 24hr; klorng boat to Wireless Pier, S Phloen Chit exit 1) FREE Every village-neighbourhood has a local shrine, either a sacred banyan tree tied up with coloured scarves or a spirit house. But it isn't every day you see a phallus garden like this lingam shrine, tucked back behind the staff quarters of the Swissôtel Nai Lert Park.

When facing the entrance of the hotel, follow the small concrete pathway to the right, which winds down into the building beside the car park. The shrine is at the end of the building next to the *klorng*.

Clusters of carved stone and wooden shafts surround a spirit house and shrine built by millionaire businessman Nai Loet to honour Jao Mae Thap Thim, a female deity thought to reside in the old banyan tree on the site. Someone who made an offering

TOUGH TIMES AT THE ERAWAN SHRINE

One of the more clichéd tourist images of Bangkok is that of elaborately dressed classical Thai dancers performing at the Hindu shrine in front of the Grand Hyatt Erawan Hotel. Although not a fabrication, as with many things in Thailand, there is a great deal hidden behind the serene facade.

After 50 years of largely benign existence, the Erawan Shrine became a point of focus when, just after midnight on 21 March 2006, 27-year-old Thanakorn Pakdeepol, a man with a history of mental illness and depression, destroyed the highly revered, gilded plaster image of Brahma with a hammer. Thanakorn was almost immediately attacked and beaten to death by two Thai rubbish collectors in the vicinity. Although the government ordered a swift restoration of the statue, the incident became a galvanising omen for the protest movement opposing then prime minister Thaksin Shinawatra, which was in full swing at the time. At a rally the following day, protest leader Sondhi Limthongkul suggested that the prime minister had masterminded the image's destruction in order to replace the deity with a 'dark force'. Rumours spreading through the capital claimed that Thaksin had hired Cambodian shamans to put spells on Thanakorn so that he would perform the unspeakable deed. In response, Thanakorn's father was quoted as saying that Sondhi was 'the biggest liar I have ever seen'. Thaksin, when asked to comment on Sondhi's accusations, simply replied, 'That's insane.' A new statue, which incorporated pieces of the previous one, was installed a month later, and Thaksin has remained in exile since 2008.

In 2010, the Ratchaprasong Intersection, where the shrine is located, became the main gathering point for anti-government Red Shirt protesters, who occupied the area for several months. Images of the predominately lower-class, rural protesters camped out in front of Ratchaprasong's luxury storefronts became a media staple. When the Red Shirts were forcibly cleared out by the military on 19 May, five people were killed and fleeing protesters set fire to the nearby CentralWorld mall.

CentralWorld was renovated in 2012, but a year later Ratchaprasong Intersection yet again became a major protest site, this time occupied by opponents of Thaksin's sister, Yingluck Shinawatra, then prime minister. The protests were known colloquially as Shutdown Bangkok (complete with protest merchandise featuring the computer shutdown icon), and this time media images of the largely middle- and upper-class urban protesters in front of chic malls drew comparisons rather than contrasts. On 20 May 2014, the Thai Army declared martial law and took over the government in a coup d'etat, leading the protesters to disperse.

Yet the most significant event in the shrine's history came on the evening of 17 August 2015, when a bomb planted in the Erawan Shrine compound exploded, killing 20 and injuring more than 120 people, an apparent act of terrorism that Prime Minister Prayut Chan-o-cha described as the 'worst incident that has ever happened' in Thailand. At the time of research, two suspects had been arrested, although their motives remain unclear.

Why so much turmoil associated with a shrine that most believe to have positive powers? Some feel that the Erawan Shrine sits on land that carries long-standing, and potentially conflicting supernatural powers. Others feel that the area is currently spiritually overcrowded, as other nearby structures also have their own potentially competing Hindu shrines. What's certain is that in Thailand, politics, faith, fortune and tragedy are often linked.

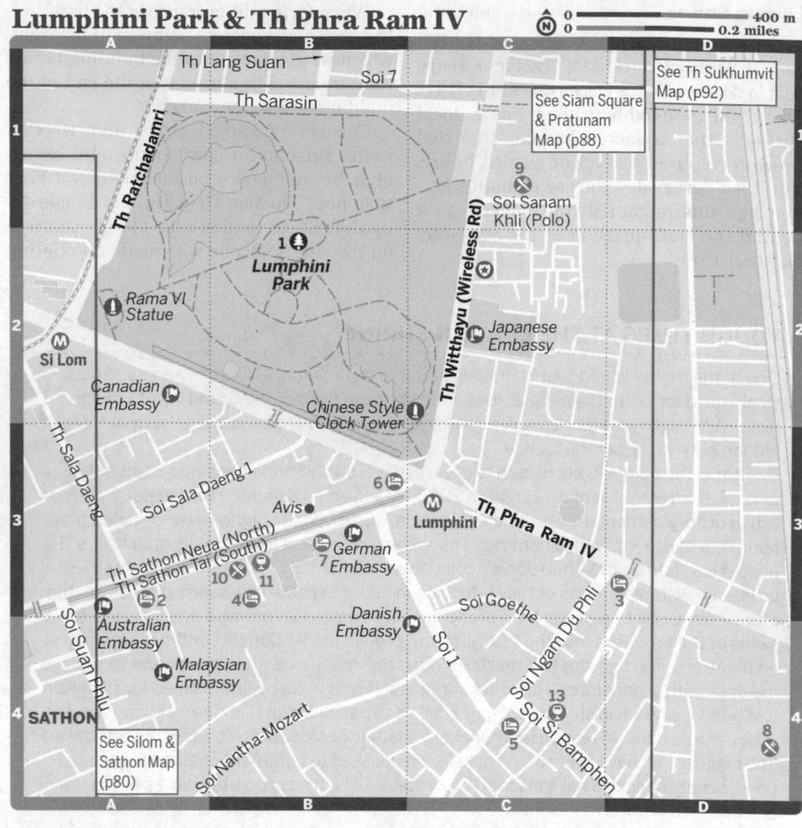

Lumphini Park & Th Phra Ram IV

Top Sights

1 Lumphini Park ... B2

Sleeping

2 Chaydon Sathorn ... A3
3 ETZzz Hostel ... D3
4 Metropolitan by COMO ... B3
5 S1 Hostel ... C4
6 Sofitel So ... B3
7 Sukhothai Hotel ... B3

Eating

8 Issaya Siamese Club ... D4
9 Kai Thort Jay Kee ... C1
10 nahm ... B3

Drinking & Nightlife

11 Moon Bar ... B3
Park Society ... (see 6)
12 Smalls ... A4
13 Wong's Place ... C4

shortly after the shrine was built had a baby, and the shrine has received a steady stream of worshippers – mostly young women seeking fertility – ever since.

Sukhumvit สุขุมวิท

More time will be spent here eating, drinking and perhaps sleeping (there is a high concentration of hotels in the area) rather than sightseeing.

The BTS, with mutiple stops along the road, is the easiest way to reach the area.

★ Siam Society & Ban Kamthieng MUSEUM

(สยามสมาคม & บ้านคำเที่ยง; Map p92; www.siam-society.org; 131 Soi 21/Asoke, Th Sukhumvit; admission adult/child 100B/free; ⌚9am-5pm Tue-Sat; M Sukhumvit exit 1, S Asok exit 3 or 6) Ban Kamthieng transports visitors to a northern Thai village complete with informative displays of daily rituals, folk beliefs and everyday household chores, all within the setting of a traditional wooden house. This museum is operated by and shares space with the Siam Society, the publisher of the renowned *Journal of the Siam Society* and a valiant preserver of traditional Thai culture.

Thewet & Dusit เทเวศน์/ดุสิต

Bangkok's royal district is one of wide streets, monuments and greenery.

The Chao Phraya Express Boat pier at Thewet is the easiest way to reach the area. Alternatively, take the BTS to Phaya Thai, followed by a short taxi ride.

Dusit Palace Park MUSEUM, HISTORIC SITE

(วังสวนดุสิต; Map p96; bounded by Th Ratchawithi, Th U Thong Nai & Th Nakhon Ratchasima; admission adult/child 100/20B, or free with Grand Palace ticket; 9.30am-4pm Tue-Sun; Thewet Pier, S Phaya Thai exit 2 & taxi) Following his first European tour in 1897, Rama V (King Chulalongkorn; r 1868–1910) returned with visions of European castles and set about transforming these styles into a uniquely Thai expression, today's Dusit Palace Park. Today, the current king has yet another home (in Hua Hin) and this complex now holds a house museum and other cultural collections.

BANGKOK'S ART GALLERIES

Although it seems to cater to the inner philistine in all of us, Bangkok has a low-key but burgeoning art scene. In recent years, galleries seem to have been opening on a weekly basis, and Bangkok also acts as something of a regional art hub with works by emerging artists from places such as Myanmar and Cambodia. To find out what's happening while you're in town, pick up a free copy of the excellent *BAM!* (www.facebook.com/bangkokartmap).

Our picks of the city's better galleries:

Kathmandu Photo Gallery (www.kathmanduphotobkk.com; Map p82; 87 Th Pan; 11am-7pm Tue-Sun; S Surasak exit 3) FREE Bangkok's only gallery wholly dedicated to photography is located in a restored Sino-Portuguese shophouse. The small upstairs gallery plays host to changing exhibitions by local and international artists and photographers.

Silom Galleria (Map p82; 919/1 Th Silom; 11am-10pm; S Surasak exit 3) FREE Not a gallery per se, but the top floors of this abandoned-feeling mall are home to some of Bangkok's best commercial galleries: **Number 1 Gallery** (www.number1gallery.com; 4th fl) features edgy contemporary Thai art, **Tang Gallery** (5th fl) showcases the work of contemporary Chinese artists and **Thavibu** (www.thavibu.com; 4th fl) focuses on the work of Vietnamese and Burmese artists.

Bangkok Art & Culture Centre (BACC; Map p88; www.bacc.or.th; cnr Th Phayathai & Th Phra Ram I; 10am-9pm Tue-Sat; S National Stadium exit 3) FREE This large, modern building in the centre of Bangkok has become one of the more significant players in the city's contemporary arts scene. As well as its three floors and 3000 sq metres of gallery space, the centre also contains shops, private galleries, cafes and an art library.

100 Tonson Gallery (Map p88; www.100tonsongallery.com; 100 Th Ton Son; 11am-7pm Thu-Sun; S Chit Lom exit 4) FREE Generally regarded as one of the city's top commercial galleries, 100 Tonson hosts a variety of contemporary exhibitions of all genres by local and international artists.

H Gallery (Map p82; www.hgallerybkk.com; 201 Soi 12, Th Sathon Neua/North; 10am-6pm Wed-Sat, by appointment Tue; S Chong Nonsi exit 1) FREE Leading commercial gallery for emerging Thai abstract painters.

Museum of Contemporary Art (MOCA; Map p66; www.mocabangkok.com; 3 Th Viphawadee Rangsit; admission 180B; 10am-6pm Tue-Sun; S Mo Chit exit 1 & taxi) A huge new complex north of town, MOCA spans five floors of pieces by the cream of the crop of Thailand's contemporary artists. It's *the* place to go to take in the spectrum of modern Thai art from breathtaking to not-so-good.

Siam Square & Pratunam

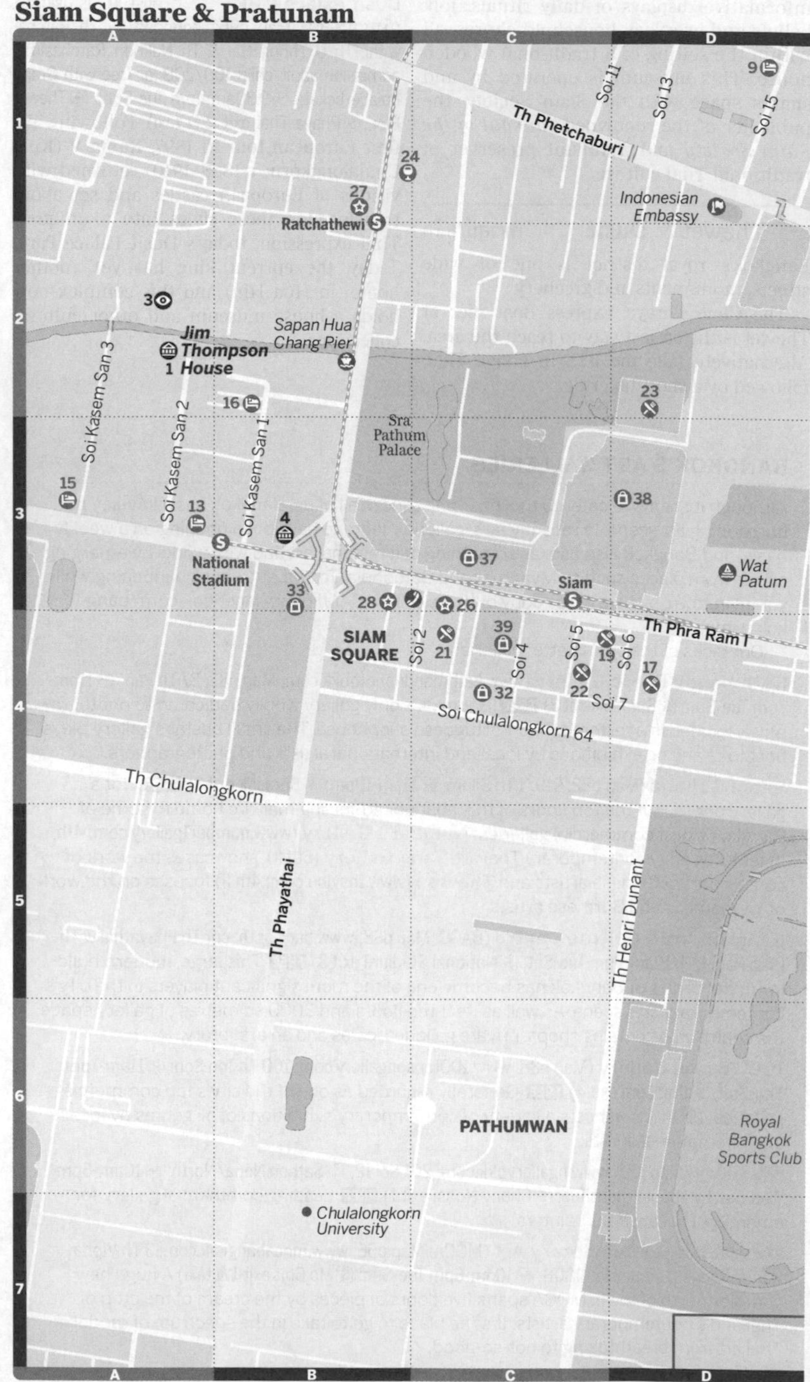

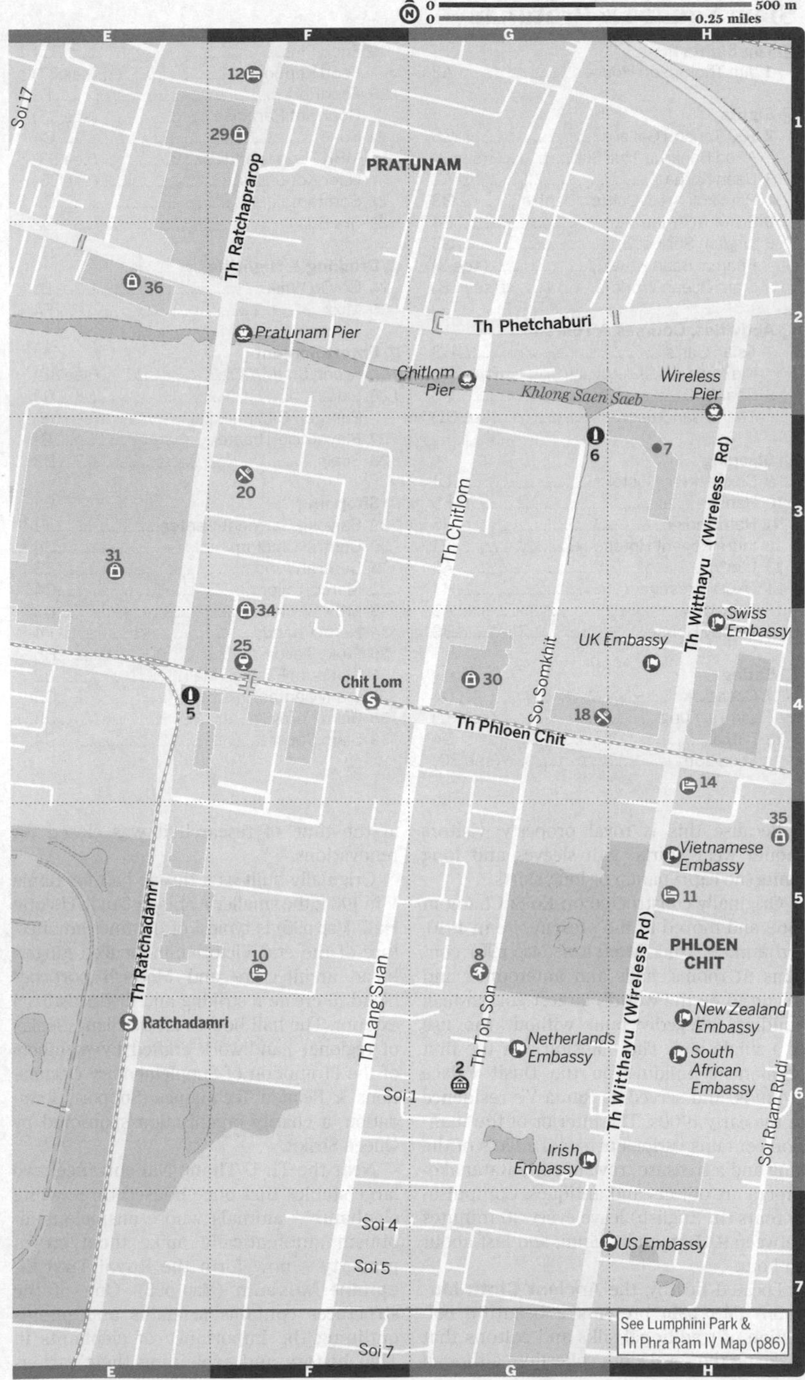

See Lumphini Park & Th Phra Ram IV Map (p86)

Siam Square & Pratunam

Top Sights
1 Jim Thompson House A2

Sights
2 100 Tonson Gallery G6
Aood Bankrua Thai Silk .... (see 3)
3 Baan Khrua A2
4 Bangkok Art & Culture Centre B3
5 Erawan Shrine E4
6 Lingam Shrine G3
Phamai Baan Krua .... (see 3)
Siam Ocean World .... (see 38)

Activities, Courses & Tours
7 Asian Oasis H3
KidZania .... (see 38)
8 Spa 1930 .... G5
Thann Sanctuary .... (see 31)

Sleeping
9 Boxpackers Hostel D1
10 Hansar F5
11 Hotel Indigo H5
12 Indra Regent Hotel F1
13 Lub*d A3
14 Okura Prestige H4
15 Siam@Siam A3
16 Wendy House B2

Eating
17 Coca Suki D4
Din Tai Fung .... (see 31)
18 Eathai G4
Food Loft .... (see 30)
19 Food Plus C4
Food Republic .... (see 37)
20 FoodPark F3
Gourmet Paradise .... (see 38)
21 Koko C4
MBK Food Island .... (see 33)
Nuer Koo .... (see 38)
22 Somtam C4
23 Sra Bua D2

Drinking & Nightlife
24 Co-Co Walk B1
25 Mixx F4

Entertainment
Krung Sri IMAX .... (see 38)
26 Lido C3
Paragon Cineplex .... (see 38)
27 Playhouse Theater Cabaret B1
28 Scala B3

Shopping
29 Baiyoke Garment Center F1
30 Central Chidlom G4
31 CentralWorld E3
32 Marco Tailor C4
33 MBK Center B3
34 Narai Phand F4
35 Pinky Tailors H5
36 Platinum Fashion Mall E2
37 Siam Center C3
38 Siam Paragon D3
39 Siam Square C4

Because this is royal property, visitors should wear shirts with sleeves and long pants (no capri pants) or long skirts.

Originally constructed on Ko Si Chang in 1868 and moved to the present site in 1910, **Vimanmek Teak Mansion** (Map p96) contains 81 rooms, halls and anterooms, and is said to be the world's largest golden-teak building, allegedly built without the use of a single nail. The mansion was the first permanent building on the Dusit Palace grounds, and served as Rama V's residence in the early 1900s. The interior of the mansion contains various personal effects of the king and a treasure trove of early Ratanakosin-era art objects and antiques. Compulsory tours (in English) leave every 30 minutes between 9.45am and 3.15pm, and last about an hour.

Located nearby, the **Ancient Cloth Museum** (Map p96) presents a beautiful collection of traditional silks and cottons that make up the royal cloth collection, although at the time of research it was closed for renovations.

Originally built as a throne hall for Rama V in 1904, the smaller **Abhisek Dusit Throne Hall** (Map p96) is typical of the finer architecture of the era. Victorian-influenced gingerbread architecture and Moorish porticoes blend to create a striking and distinctly Thai exterior. The hall houses an excellent display of regional handiwork crafted by members of the Promotion of Supplementary Occupations & Related Techniques (Support) foundation, a charity organisation sponsored by Queen Sirikit.

Near the Th U Thong Nai entrance, two large stables that once housed three white elephants – animals whose auspicious albinism automatically make them crown property – now form the **Royal Thai Elephant Museum** (Map p96). One of the structures contains artefacts and photos outlining the importance of elephants in Thai history and explaining their various rankings according to physical characteristics. The second stable holds a life-sized model of the king's first royal white elephant. Draped in royal vestments, the statue is more or less treated as a shrine by the visiting Thai public.

Wat Benchamabophit BUDDHIST TEMPLE
(วัดเบญจมบพิตร (วัดเบญฯ); Map p96; cnr Th Si Ayuthaya & Th Phra Ram V; admission 20B; ⏲8am-6pm; Thewet Pier, S Phaya Thai exit 3 & taxi) You might recognise this temple from the back of the 5B coin. Made of white marble imported from Italy, the distinctive *bòht* (ordination hall) of Wat Ben, as it's colloquially known, was built in the late 19th century under Rama V. The base of the central Buddha image, a copy of Phitsanulok's revered Phra Phuttha Chinnarat, contains his ashes.

The structure is a unique example of modern Thai temple architecture, as is the interior design, which melds Thai features with European influences: the red carpets, the gold-on-white motifs painted repetitively on the walls, the walls painted like stained-glass windows and the royal blue wall behind the central Buddha image are strongly reminiscent of a European palace. It is not all that surprising when you consider how enamoured Rama V was with Europe – just walk across the street to visit Dusit Palace Park for further evidence.

The courtyard that is situated behind the *bòht* has 53 Buddha images (33 originals and 20 copies) representing every *mudra* (gesture) and style from Thai history, making this the ideal place to compare Buddhist iconography. If religious imagery isn't your thing, this temple still offers a pleasant stroll beside landscaped canals filled with blooming lotus and Chinese-style footbridges.

Ratchathewi ราชเทวี

Aside from a couple of sights, Ratchathewi represents a more suburban side of Bangkok. The area is most easily reached via the BTS.

OFF THE BEATEN TRACK

BIZARRE BANGKOK MUSEUMS

If looking at stuffed tigers and Buddha statues just isn't doing it for you, then consider a visit to one of these quirky institutions.

Siriraj Medical Museum (พิพิธภัณฑ์นิติเวชศาสตร์สงกรานต์นิยมเสน; Map p72; 2nd fl, Adulyadejvikrom Bldg, Siriraj Hospital; admission 200B; ⏲10am-4pm Wed-Mon; Wang Lang/Siriraj Pier, Thonburi Railway Station Pier) Various appendages, murder weapons and crime-scene evidence, including a bloodied T-shirt from a victim stabbed to death with a dildo, are on display at these three linked museums – collectively dubbed the Museum of Death – dedicated to anatomy, pathology and forensic science. The easiest way to reach the museum is by taking the river-crossing ferry from Chang Pier to Wang Lang/Siriraj Pier in Thonburi. At the exit to the pier, turn right (north) to enter Siriraj Hospital and follow the green museum signs.

Ancient City (เมืองโบราณ, Muang Boran; www.ancientcitygroup.net/ancientsiam/en; 296/1 Th Sukhumvit, Samut Prakan; admission adult/child 9am-4pm 700/350B, 4-7pm 350/175B; ⏲9am-7pm; S Bearing exit 1) Don't have the time to see Thailand's most famous historic monuments? Then consider visiting scaled-down versions of them in what claims to be the largest open-air museum in the world. It's an excellent place to explore by bicycle (daily hire 50B) as it's usually quiet and rarely crowded. Ancient City lies east of Bangkok outside Samut Prakan, which is most conveniently accessed via the park's shuttle bus from BTS Bearing station (see website for departure times).

Corrections Museum (พิพิธภัณฑ์ราชทัณฑ์; Map p72; Rommaneenart Park, 436 Th Mahachai; ⏲9am-4pm Mon-Fri; klorng boat to Phanfa Leelard Pier) FREE Learn about the painful world of Thai-style punishment at what's left of this former jail. Life-sized models re-enact a variety of horrendous executions and punishments, encouraging most visitors to remain law-abiding citizens for the remainder of their visits.

Th Sukhumvit

Phra Ram 9
Th Phra Ram IX
Th Phra Ram IX
Th Watthana Tham
20
Makkasan (Bangkok City Air Terminal)
Soi 21 (Asoke)
43
44
33
Th Phetchaburi
Tourism Authority of Thailand
Nana Nua Pier
Nana Chard Pier
Phetchaburi
Asoke-Phetchaburi Pier
Indian Visa Centre
RCA (Royal City Ave)
Budget
47
50
Th Phetchaburi
Th Kamphaeng Phet 7
Khlong Saen Saeb
9
Bumrungrad International Hospital
SUKHUMVIT
Soi 1
Soi 3 (Nana)
Soi 5
40
Soi 21 (Asoke)
Italthai Pier
Wat Mai Chonglom Pier
Baan Don Mosque Pier
Soi Thong Lor Pier
Phloen Chit
Soi 11
Soi 13
Soi 15
Israeli Embassy
Indian Embassy
Soi 39
28
39
19
34
51
55
Nana
60
Soi 11/1
56
Soi 4
Soi 6
Soi 19
13
Soi 23
Soi 31
23
Siam Society & Ban Kamthieng
37
1
Sukhumvit
41
35
Soi 2
Soi Phrom Si 2
Soi Thong Lor 20 (Soi Ekamai 21)
0 1 km
0 0.5 miles

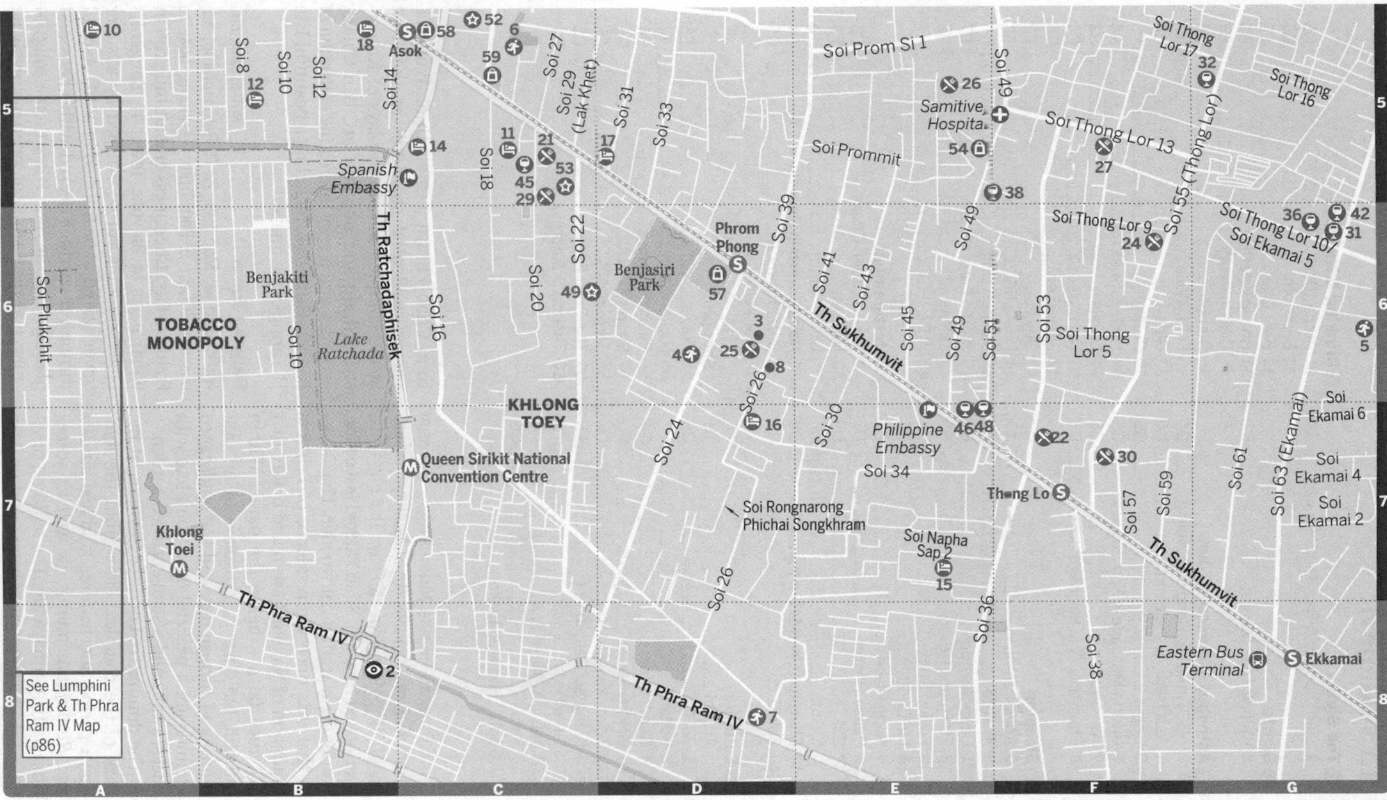
Th Sukhumvit
Th Ratchadaphisek
Th Phra Ram IV
Soi Prom Si 1
Soi Prommit
Soi Thong Lor 17
Soi Thong Lor 16
Soi Thong Lor 13
Soi 55 (Thong Lor)
Soi Thong Lor 9
Soi Thong Lor 10/
Soi Ekamai 5
Soi Thong Lor 5
Soi Ekamai 6
Soi Ekamai 4
Soi Ekamai 2
Soi 63 (Ekamai)
Soi 61
Soi 59
Soi 57
Soi 53
Soi 51
Soi 49
Soi 45
Soi 43
Soi 41
Soi 39
Soi 38
Soi 36
Soi 34
Soi 33
Soi 31
Soi 30
Soi 29 (Lak Khet)
Soi 27
Soi 26
Soi 24
Soi 22
Soi 20
Soi 18
Soi 16
Soi 14
Soi 12
Soi 10
Soi 8
Soi Napha Sap 2
Soi Rongnarong Phichai Songkhram
Soi Plukchit
Asok
Phrom Phong
Thong Lo
Ekkamai
Eastern Bus Terminal
Samitive Hospital
Spanish Embassy
Philippine Embassy
Benjasiri Park
Benjakiti Park
Lake Ratchada
TOBACCO MONOPOLY
KHLONG TOEY
Queen Sirikit National Convention Centre
Khlong Toei
See Lumphini Park & Th Phra Ram IV Map (p86)

Th Sukhumvit

Top Sights
1 Siam Society & Ban Kamthieng C4

Sights
2 Khlong Toey Market B8

Activities, Courses & Tours
3 ABC Amazing Bangkok Cyclists D6
4 Asia Herb Association D6
5 Coran G6
6 Divana Massage & Spa C5
7 Fun-arium D8
8 Phussapa Thai Massage School D6

Sleeping
9 AriyasomVilla A3
10 Atlanta A5
11 Baan Sukhumvit C5
12 FU House Hostel B5
13 Fusion Suites C4
14 Ma Du Zi C5
15 Napa Place E7
16 Pause Hostel D7
17 S31 .... D5
S-Box .... (see 17)
18 Sheraton Grande Sukhumvit B5
19 Suk 11 .... B4

Eating
20 Anotai D1
21 Bei Otto C5
22 Bo.lan F7
23 Game Over G4
24 Gokfayuen F6
25 Jidori-Ya Kenzou D6
26 Klang Soi Restaurant E5
27 Little Beast F5
28 Nasir Al-Masri A4
29 Saras C5
30 Soul Food Mahanakorn F7

Drinking & Nightlife
31 Arena 10 .... G6
32 Badmotel G5
33 Beer Cap E2
34 Cheap Charlie's B4
35 Club Insanity B4
36 Demo G6
Funky Villa .... (see 36)
37 Glow C4
38 Grease F5
39 Hyde & Seek A4
40 Levels B3
41 Narz C4
42 Nung-Len G6
43 Onyx E2
44 Route 66 .... E2
45 Scratch Dog C5
46 Studio Lam E7
47 Taksura F2
48 WTF E7

Entertainment
49 Friese-Green Club C6
50 House F3
Living Room .... (see 18)
51 Nana Entertainment Plaza A4
52 Soi Cowboy C5
53 Titanium C5

Shopping
54 Duly E5
55 Nickermann's A4
56 Raja's Fashions B4
57 Shop @ TCDC D6
58 Terminal 21 .... C5
59 ThaiCraft Fair C5
60 Thanon Sukhumvit Market B4

Suan Pakkad Palace Museum MUSEUM

(วังสวนผักกาด; Map p98; Th Si Ayuthaya; admission 100B; ⌚9am-4pm; Ⓢ Phaya Thai exit 4) An overlooked treasure, Suan Pakkad is a collection of eight traditional wooden Thai houses that was once the residence of Princess Chumbon of Nakhon Sawan and before that a lettuce farm – hence the name. Within the stilt buildings are displays of art, antiques and furnishings, and the landscaped grounds are a peaceful oasis complete with ducks, swans and a semi-enclosed garden.

The diminutive **Lacquer Pavilion**, at the back of the complex, dates from the Ayuthaya period and features gold-leaf *Jataka* and *Ramayana* murals, as well as scenes from daily Ayuthaya life. The building originally sat in a monastery compound on Mae Nam Chao Phraya, just south of Ayuthaya. Larger residential structures at the front of the complex contain displays of Khmer-style Hindu and Buddhist art, Ban Chiang ceramics and a very interesting collection of historic **Buddhas**, including a beautiful late U Thong–style image.

Baiyoke Tower II NOTABLE BUILDING

(ตึกใบหยก ๒; Map p98; 22 Th Ratchaprarop; admission 300B; ⌚9am-11pm; klorng boat to Pratunam Pier) Cheesiness and altitude run in equal parts at Baiyoke Tower II, Bangkok's tallest building (to be usurped by a 'super tower' slated to be finished in 2016). Ascend through a corridor decked with aliens and planets (and the *Star Wars* theme song) to emerge at the 84th-floor, open-air revolving

OFF THE BEATEN TRACK

BAAN KHRUA

The canal-side neighbourhood of **Baan Khrua** (บ้านครัว; Map p88; klorng boat to Sapan Hua Chang Pier, S Ratchathewi exit 1, National Stadium exit 1) dates back to the turbulent years at the end of the 18th century, when Cham Muslims from Cambodia and Vietnam fought on the side of the new Thai king and were rewarded with this plot of land east of the new capital. The immigrants brought their silk-weaving traditions with them, and the community grew when the residents built Khlong Saen Saeb to better connect them to the river.

The 1950s and '60s were boom years for Baan Khrua after Jim Thompson hired the weavers and began exporting their silks across the globe. The last 50 years, however, haven't been so great. Silk production was moved elsewhere following Thompson's disappearance, and the community spent 15 years successfully fighting to stop a freeway being built right through it. Through all this, many Muslims moved out of the area; today it is estimated that only about 30% of the population is Muslim, the rest primarily immigrants from northeast Thailand.

Today's Baan Khrua consists of old, tightly packed homes threaded by tiny paths barely wide enough for two people to pass. There's a mosque and two family-run outfits, **Phamai Baan Krua** (www.phamaibaankrua.com; Soi 9, Soi Phaya Nak; 8.30am-5pm; klorng boat to Sapan Hua Chang Pier, S Ratchathewi exit 1, National Stadium exit 1) and **Aood Bankrua Thai Silk** (02 215 9864; Soi 9, Soi Phaya Nak; 9am-8pm; klorng boat to Sapan Hua Chang Pier, S Ratchathewi exit 1, National Stadium exit 1), which continue to be involved in every step of silk cloth production, from the dyeing of threads to weaving the cloth by hand on old wood looms. Of the two, Phamai Baan Krua claims to be the original. Run by English- and German-speaking Niphon Manuthas, the company continues to produce the type of high-quality handwoven silk that originally attracted Jim Thompson, although at much cheaper prices than that sold across the *klorng*.

Baan Khrua is an easy stop after visiting the Jim Thompson House; simply cross the bridge over the canal at the end of Soi Kasem San 3. Alternatively, from the BTS stop at Ratchathewi, enter Soi Phaya Nak, take the third left (the soi that leads to Da-Rul-Fa-La Mosque), following it to the canal; turn right and look for the signs.

platform that looks over a city whose concrete sprawl can appear never-ending.

Activities

Meditation

Although at times Bangkok may seem like the most un-Buddhist place on earth, there are several places where instruction in Theravada Buddhist meditation is offered in English.

Center Meditation Wat Mahadhatu MEDITATION
(Map p72; 02 223 3813, 02 222 6011; Section 5, Wat Mahathat, Th Maha Rat; donations accepted; lessons 7am, 1pm & 6pm; Chang Pier, Maharaj Pier, Phra Chan Tai Pier) Located within Wat Mahathat, this small centre offers informal daily meditation classes. Taught by English-speaking Prasuputh Chainikom (Kosalo), classes last three hours. Longer periods of study, which include accommodation and food, can be arranged, but students are expected to follow a strict regimen of conduct.

House of Dhamma MEDITATION
(Map p102; 02 511 0439; www.houseofdhamma.com; 26/9 Soi 15, Th Lat Phrao; fee by donation; lessons 10am-5pm Wed-Sun; M Lat Phrao exit 3) Helen Jandamit has opened her suburban Bangkok home to meditation retreats and two-day classes in *vipassana* (insight meditation). Check the website to see what workshops are on offer and be sure to reserve a spot at least a week in advance.

Thai Boxing

Training in *moo·ay tai* (also spelt *muay thai*) for foreigners has increased in popularity in the last decade or so and many camps all over the country are tailoring their programs for foreign fighters. The following camps provide instruction in English and accept men and women. The website Muay Thai Camps (www.muaythaicampsthailand.com) contains additional information on Thailand's various training centres.

MuayThai Institute MARTIAL ARTS
(02 992 0096; www.muaythai-institute.net; Rangsit Stadium, 336/932 Th Prachatipat, Pathum Thani;

Thewet & Dusit

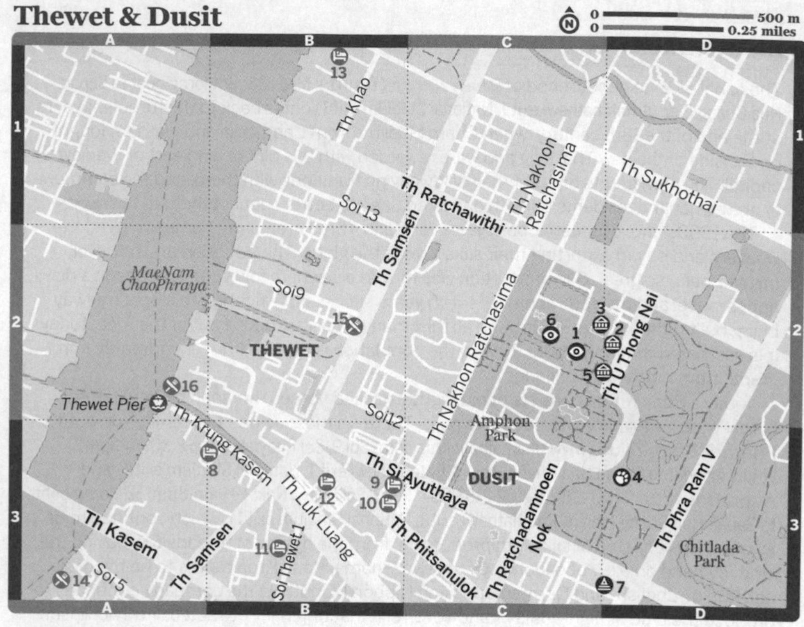

Thewet & Dusit

Sights

- 1 Abhisek Dusit Throne Hall C2
- 2 Ancient Cloth Museum D2
- 3 Dusit Palace Park C2
- 4 Dusit Zoo D3
- 5 Royal Thai Elephant Museum C2
- 6 Vimanmek Teak Mansion C2
- 7 Wat Benchamabophit D3

Sleeping

- 8 Baan Manusarn B3
- 9 Baan Tepa Boutique House B3
- 10 Hi Baan Thewet B3
- 11 Phra-Nakorn Norn-Len B3
- 12 SSIP Boutique B3
- 13 The Siam B1

Eating

- 14 Khinlom Chom Sa-Phan A3
- 15 Krua Apsorn B2
- 16 Steve Café & Cuisine A2

10-day course from 8000B; M Chatuchak Park exit 2 & taxi, S Mo Chit exit 3 & taxi) Associated with the respccted World Muay Thai Council, the institute offers a fundamental course in Thai boxing (consisting of three levels of expertise), as well as courses for instructors, referees and judges.

Fairtex Muay Thai MARTIAL ARTS

(☎086 776 0488; www.fairtexbangplee.com; 99/5 Mu 3, Soi Buthamanuson, Th Thaeparak, Samut Prakan; tuition & accommodation per day 1450-1850B; S Chong Nonsi exit 2 & taxi) A popular, long-running Thai-boxing camp south of Bangkok.

Muay Thai Lab MARTIAL ARTS

(Map p72; ☎02 024 1326; www.muaythailab.net; 2nd fl, Maharaj Pier, Th Maha Rat; lessons from 990B; 11am-8pm; Maharaj Pier, Chang Pier, Phra Chan Tai Pier) Muay Thai Lab is a new, impressive one-stop centre for everything related to Thai boxing. Start in the lobby, which has free displays on the history and culture of Thai boxing and a small shop stocked with both souvenirs and gear, before heading to the open-air rooftop gym, which looks over Mae Nam Chao Phraya.

Drop-ins are encouraged to join the introductory lessons, which take place from 11am to 3pm daily; the fee includes clothing and equipment, access to a locker and showers, and a towel.

Sor Vorapin Gym MARTIAL ARTS

(Map p72; ☎02 282 3551; www.thaiboxings.com; 13 Th Kasab; per session/month 500/9000B; lessons 7.30-9.30am & 3-5pm; Phra Athit/Banglamphu Pier) Conveniently located steps from Th

Khao San, this gym offers training in Thai boxing for foreign students of both genders.

Thai Massage

A good massage is the birthright of every Bangkokian, and the joy of every visitor. Correspondingly, places offering massage are everywhere in Bangkok, and they range dramatically in quality, depending on if they offer massage or 'massage'. To avoid the latter, stay clear of the places that advertise via hard-selling, scantily dressed women.

If it is your first time in the hands of a Thai masseur/masseuse, it is probably a good idea to discard any previous massage experience, as many visitors find the experience equal parts painful and relaxing. Traditional Thai massage is based on yogic techniques for general health that involve pulling, stretching, bending and manipulating pressure points. If done well, a traditional massage will leave you sore but revitalised. A full-body Thai massage can also involve herbal heat compresses (oil treatments are generally associated with 'sexy' massage).

Depending on the neighbourhood, prices for massages in small parlours are 200B to 350B for a foot massage and 300B to 600B for a full-body massage.

Health Land MASSAGE

(Map p82; 02 637 8883; www.healthlandspa.com; 120 Th Sathon Neua/North; 2hr massage 500B; 9am-11pm; S Surasak exit 3) This, the main branch of a long-standing Thai massage mini-empire, offers good-value, no-nonsense massage and spa treatments in a tidy environment. See website for additional branches.

Ruen-Nuad Massage Studio MASSAGE

(Map p82; 02 632 2662; 42 Th Convent; massage per hr 350B; 10am-9pm; M Si Lom exit 2, S Sala Daeng exit 2) Set in a refurbished wooden house, this charming place successfully avoids both the tackiness and New Agedness that characterise most Bangkok Thai-massage joints. Prices are relatable, too.

Asia Herb Association MASSAGE

(Map p92; 02 261 7401; www.asiaherbassociation.com; 33/1 Soi 24, Th Sukhumvit; Thai massage per hr 500B, Thai massage with herbal compress 1½hr 1100B; 9am-2am; S Phrom Phong exit 4) With multiple branches along Th Sukhumvit, this Japanese-owned chain specialises in massage using *Ъrà·kóp* (traditional Thai herbal compresses) filled with 18 different herbs.

Coran MASSAGE

(Map p92; 02 726 9978; www.coranbangkok.com; 94-96/1 Soi Ekamai 10, Soi 63/Ekamai, Th Sukhumvit; Thai massage per hr 600B; 11am-10pm; S Ekkamai exit 4 & taxi) A classy, low-key spa housed in a Thai villa. Aroma and Thai-style massage are also available.

Spas

Unless you've spent your entire visit in an air-conditioned bubble (which is entirely possible in today's Bangkok), at some point you may want to rid yourself of the negative effects of the city's urban environment. This can take the form of a simple scrub or multistage treatments with a customised choice of aromas and oils and a team of staff. There are countless spas in Bangkok, many of them situated in the city's high-end hotels with high-end price tags to match.

Oriental Spa SPA

(Map p80; 02 659 9000; www.mandarinoriental.com/bangkok/luxury-spa; Mandarin Oriental, 48 Soi 40/Oriental, Th Charoen Krung; massage/spa packages from 2900B; 9am-10pm; Oriental Pier or hotel shuttle boat from Sathon/Central Pier) Regarded as among the premier spas in the world, the Oriental Spa sets the standard for Asian-style spa treatment. Depending on where you flew in from, the jet-lag massage might be a good option, but all treatments require advance booking.

Spa 1930 SPA

(Map p88; 02 254 8606; www.spa1930.com; 42 Th Ton Son; Thai massage from 1000B, spa packages from 3500B; 9.30am-9.30pm; S Chit Lom exit 4) Discreet and sophisticated, Spa 1930 rescues relaxers from the contrived spa ambience of New Age music and ingredients you'd rather see at a dinner party. The menu is simple (face, body care and body massage) and the scrubs and massage oils are logical players.

Thann Sanctuary SPA

(Map p88; 02 658 6557; www.thann.info/thann_sanctuary.php; 2nd fl, CentralWorld, Th Ratchadamri; Thai massage from 2000B, spa treatments from 2800B; 10am-9pm; S Chit Lom exit 9 to Sky Walk, Siam exit 6 to Sky Walk) This local brand of herbal-based cosmetics has launched a series of mall-based spas – perfect for post-shopping therapy.

Divana Massage & Spa SPA

(Map p92; 02 261 6784; www.divanaspa.com; 7 Soi 25, Th Sukhumvit; massage from 1100B, spa

Ratchathewi

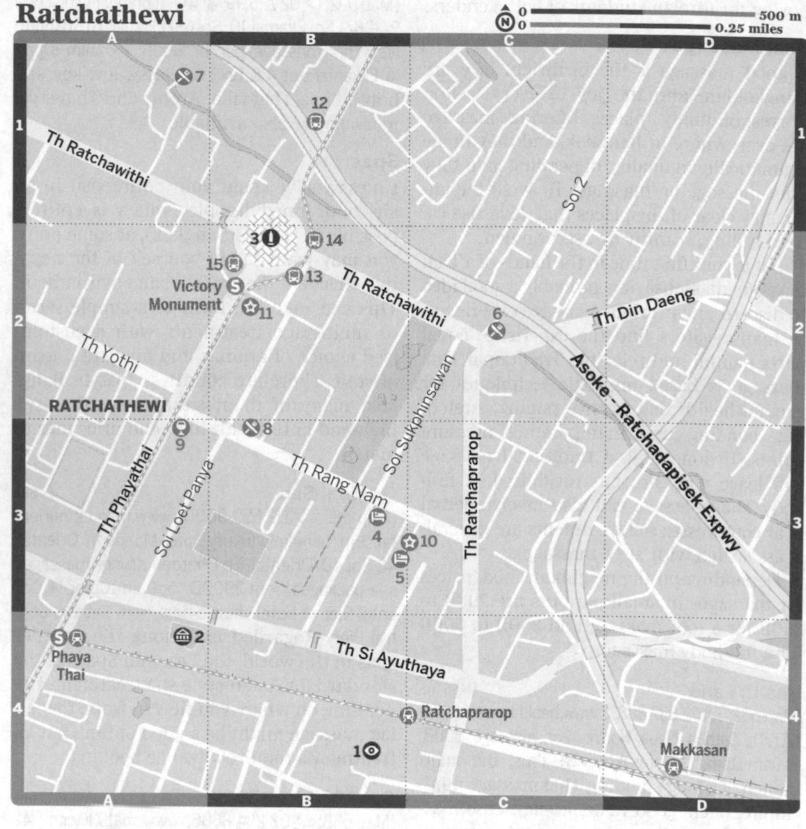

Ratchathewi

Sights
1 Baiyoke Tower II B4
2 Suan Pakkad Palace Museum A4
3 Victory Monument B2

Sleeping
4 Bizotel B3
5 K Maison B3

Eating
6 Pathé C2
7 Sam-Ang Kulap A1
8 Tida Esarn B3

Drinking & Nightlife
9 Sky Train Jazz Club A3

Entertainment
10 Raintree C3
11 Saxophone Pub & Restaurant B2

Transport
12 Minivans to Aranya Prathet (for Cambodian border), Mae Klong (for Amphawa) & Nakhon Pathom B1
13 Minivans to Ayuthaya & Ban Phe (for Ko Samet) B2
14 Minivans to Chanthaburi, Kanchanaburi, Phetchaburi & Suvarnabhumi International Airport B2
15 Minivans to Pak Chong (for Khao Yai National Park) & Southern Bus Terminal B2

packages from 2650B; ⏲11am-11pm Mon-Fri, 10am-11pm Sat & Sun; M Sukhumvit exit 2, S Asok exit 6) Divana retains a unique Thai touch with a private setting in a garden house.

 Courses

Cooking

Imagine the points you'll rack up if you can make authentic Thai dishes for your friends back at home. A visit to a Thai cooking school has become a must-do for many Bangkok itineraries, and for some visitors it's a highlight of their trip.

Courses range in price and value, but a typical half-day course should include at least a basic introduction to Thai ingredients and flavours, and a hands-on chance to both prepare and cook at least four dishes. Most schools offer a revolving cast of dishes that changes on a daily basis, making it possible to study for a week without repeating a dish. Many courses include a visit to a market, and nearly all lessons include a set of printed recipes and end with a communal lunch consisting of your handiwork.

★Amita Thai Cooking Class COOKING COURSE
(Map p66; ☎02 466 8966; www.amitathaicooking.com; 162/17 Soi 14, Th Wutthakat, Thonburi; 3000B; ⏲lessons 9.30am-1pm Thu-Tue; ⛴klorng boat from Maharaj Pier) One of Bangkok's most charming cooking schools is held in this canalside house in Thonburi. Taught by the delightfully enthusiastic Piyawadi 'Tam' Jantrupon, a course here includes a romp through the garden and instruction in four dishes. The fee covers transport, which in this case takes the form of a boat ride from Maharaj Pier.

Helping Hands COOKING COURSE
(☎080 434 8686; www.cookingwithpoo.com; courses 1500B; ⏲lessons 8.30am-1pm) This popular cooking course was started by a native of Khlong Toey's slums and is held in her neighbourhood. Courses, which must be booked in advance, span three dishes and include a visit to Khlong Toey Market and transport to and from Emporium Shopping Centre.

Bangkok Bold Cooking Studio COOKING COURSE
(Map p72; ☎098 829 4310; www.bangkokbold.com; 503 Th Phra Sumen; courses 2000B; ⏲lessons 9am-1pm & 2-5pm; ⛴klorng boat to Phanfa Leelard Pier) The newest venture by a team that previously ran a popular cooking school on Th Khao San, Bold offers two daily courses of instruction in three Thai dishes, with lessons taught in a chic shophouse setting.

Silom Thai Cooking School COOKING COURSE
(Map p82; ☎084 726 5669; www.bangkokthaicooking.com; 68 Soi 13, Th Silom; courses 1000B; ⏲lessons 9am-1pm, 1.40-5.30pm & 6-9pm; S Chong Nonsi exit 3) Spread over two simple but charming facilities; lessons at Silom Thai Cooking School include a visit to a local market and instruction for six dishes in four hours, making it the best bang for your baht. Hotel pick-up in central Bangkok is available.

Thai Massage

Chetawan Traditional Massage School MASSAGE
(Map p72; ☎02 622 3551; www.watpomassage.com; 392/32-33 Soi Phen Phat; lessons from 2500B, Thai massage per hr 420B; ⏲lessons 9am-4pm, massage 9am-6pm; ⛴Tien Pier) Associated with the nearby temple of the same name, this institute offers basic and advanced courses in traditional massage; basic courses offer 30 hours spread over five days and cover either general massage or foot massage. Thai massage is also available for nonstudents.

The school is outside the temple compound in a restored Bangkok shophouse in unmarked Soi Phen Phat.

The school's advanced-level course spans 60 hours, requires the basic course as a prerequisite, and covers therapeutic and healing massage. Other advanced courses include oil massage and aromatherapy, and infant and child massage.

Phussapa Thai Massage School MASSAGE
(Map p92; ☎02 204 2922; www.thaimassage-bangkok.com/nuat1_egl.htm; 25/8 Soi 26, Th Sukhumvit; tuition from 6000B; ⏲massage 11am-11pm, lessons 9am-4pm; S Phrom Phong exit 4) Run by a longtime Japanese resident of Bangkok, the basic course in Thai massage here spans 30 hours over five days; there are shorter courses in foot massage and self massage. Thai massage is also available for 300B per hour.

☞ Tours

If you would like someone to guide you through Bangkok, recommended outfits include **Tour with Tong** (☎081 835 0240; www.tourwithtong.com; tours from 1000B), whose team conducts tours in and around Bangkok, and **Thai Private Tour Guide** (☎082 799 1099; www.thaitourguide.com; tours from 2000B), whose guides have garnered heaps of positive feedback.

Walking & Speciality Tours

Although the pollution and heat are significant obstacles, Bangkok is a fascinating city to explore on foot.

Bangkok Private Tours WALKING TOUR
(www.bangkokprivatetours.com; tours from US$150) Themed walking tours of Bangkok.

Bangkok Food Tours WALKING TOUR
(☎095 943 9222; www.bangkokfoodtours.com; tours from 1150B) Half-day culinary tours of Bangkok's older neighbourhoods.

Chili Paste Tours FOOD TOUR
(☎085 143 6779, 094 552 2361; www.foodtoursbangkok.com; tours from 1800B) Half-day food tours of Bangkok's older neighbourhoods.

Bicycle Tours

Although some cycling tours tackle Bangkok's urban neighbourhoods, most take advantage of the nearby lush, undeveloped district to the south known as the Phrapradaeng Peninsula (also known as Bang Kachao), where narrow walkways criss-cross irrigation canals that feed small-scale fruit plantations and simple villages.

Grasshopper Adventures BICYCLE TOUR
(Map p72; ☎02 280 0832; www.grasshopperadventures.com; 57 Th Ratchadamnoen Klang; half-/full-day tours from 1100/1600B; ⏲8.30am-6.30pm; ⛴klorng boat to Phanfa Leelard Pier) This lauded outfit runs a variety of unique bicycle tours in and around Bangkok, including a night tour and a tour of the city's green zones.

ABC Amazing Bangkok Cyclists BICYCLE TOUR
(Map p92; ☎081 812 9641; www.realasia.net; 10/5-7 Soi Aree, Soi 26, Th Sukhumvit; tours from 1300B; ⏲daily tours at 8am, 10am, 1pm & 6pm; Ⓢ Phrom Phong exit 4) A long-running operation offering morning, afternoon and all-day bike tours of Bangkok and its suburbs.

Co van Kessel Bangkok Tours BICYCLE TOUR
(Map p80; ☎02 639 7351; www.covankessel.com; ground fl, River City, 23 Th Yotha; tours from 950B; ⏲6am-7pm; ⛴River City Pier) This originally Dutch-run outfit offers a variety of tours in Chinatown, Thonburi and Bangkok's green zones, many of which also involve boat rides. Tours depart from the company's office in the River City shopping centre.

Bangkok Bike Rides BICYCLE TOURS
(☎02 381 7490; www.bangkokbikerides.com; tours from 1000B) A division of tour company Spice Roads, this outfit offers a variety of cycling tours, both urban and rural, including a night tour of Bangkok. Pick-up is available.

River & Canal Trips

Glimpses of Bangkok's past as the 'Venice of the East' are still possible today, even though the motor vehicle has long since become the city's conveyance of choice. Along the river and the canals is a motley fleet of watercraft, from paddled canoes to rice barges. In these areas many homes, trading houses and temples remain oriented towards life on the water, providing a fascinating glimpse into the past when Thais still considered themselves *jôw nám* (water lords).

The most obvious way to commute between riverside attractions is on the public ferries run by Chao Phraya Express Boat (p149). The terminus for most northbound boats is Nonthaburi Pier and for most southbound boats it's Sathon/Central Pier, the latter linked with Saphan Taksin BTS station, although some boats run as far south as Wat Ratchasingkhon.

For a more customised view, you might consider chartering a long-tail boat along the city's canals; see p76 for details on this.

A little faster than the days of sailing ships, river cruises from Bangkok north to the ruins of the former royal capital of Ayuthaya take in all the romance of the river. Most trips include a guided tour of Ayuthaya's ruins with a stop at the summer palace of Bang Pa-In.

Asian Oasis BOAT TOUR
(Map p88; ☎088 809 7047, 081 496 4516; www.asian-oasis.com; 7th fl, Nai Lert Tower, 2/4 Th Witthayu/Wireless Rd; 2-day trip 6450-10,450B; ⏲9am-5pm Mon-Fri; Ⓢ Phloen Chit exit 1) Cruise the Chao Phraya River aboard a fleet of rice barges with old-world charm and modern conveniences. Trips include either an upstream or downstream journey to/from Ayuthaya with bus transfer in the opposite direction. Costs vary according to season and direction.

Thanatharee BOAT TOUR
(☎02 440 1979; www.thanatharee.com; 2-day trip 10,800-17,300B) Overnight boat tours to Ayuthaya on a restored wooden barge with six cabins.

BANGKOK FOR CHILDREN

There aren't a whole lot of attractions in Bangkok designed to appeal to little ones, but there's no lack of locals willing to provide attention. The website www.bangkok.com/kids has an excellent spread of things to do for kids, and www.bambiweb.org is a useful resource for parents of young children in Bangkok.

If visiting with young kids, keep in mind that car seats are almost nonexistent, and even if you bring your own, most taxis have no seatbelt in the back. For moving by foot, slings are often more useful than prams as Bangkok's sidewalks are famously uneven.

Kid-Friendly Museums

The recently renovated **Children's Discovery Museum** (Map p102; Th Kamphaengphet 4, Queen Sirikit Park; ⏲9am-5pm Tue-Fri, 10am-6pm Sat & Sun; 🚻; Ⓜ Chatuchak Park exit 1, Ⓢ Mo Chit exit 1) FREE features interactive displays ranging in topic from construction to culture.

Although not specifically child-targeted, the **Museum of Siam** (p68) has lots of interactive exhibits that will appeal to children.

Outside of town, **Ancient City** (p91) recreates Thailand's most famous monuments. They're linked by bicycle paths and were practically built for being climbed on.

Play Centres & Parks

For kid-specific play centres, consider **Fun-arium** (Map p92; ☎02 665 6555; www.funarium.co.th; 111/1 Soi 26, Th Sukhumvit; admission 110-320B; ⏲9am-6pm Mon-Thu, to 7pm Fri-Sun; Ⓢ Phrom Phong exit 1 & taxi), central Bangkok's largest, or the impressive **KidZania** (☎02 683 1888; www.bangkok.kidzania.com/en; 5th fl, Siam Paragon, 991/1 Th Phra Ram I; adult 425-500B, child 425-1000B; ⏲10am-5pm Mon-Fri, 10.30am-8pm Sat & Sun; Ⓢ Siam exits 3 & 5).

Lumphini Park (p83) is a trusty ally in the cool hours of the morning and evening for kite-flying (during February and March), swan boats and stretching the legs and lungs.

Rainy-day Fun

MBK Center (p136) and **Siam Paragon** (p136) both have bowling alleys to keep the older ones occupied. **Krung Sri IMAX** (Map p88; ☎02 129 4635; www.majorcineplex.com/en/cinema/paragon-cineplex/; 5th fl, Siam Paragon, 991/1 Th Phra Ram I; tickets 250-1200B; Ⓢ Siam exits 3 & 5) screens special-effects versions of Hollywood action flicks and nature features.

Zoos & Animals

Dusit Zoo (สวนสัตว์ดุสิต (เขาดิน); Map p96; www.dusitzoo.org; Th Ratchawithi; adult/child 150/70B; ⏲8am-6pm; ⛴Thewet Pier, Ⓢ Phaya Thai exit 3 & taxi) covers 19 hectares with caged exhibits of more than 300 mammals, 200 reptiles and 800 birds, including relatively rare indigenous species such as banteng, gaur, serow and some rhinoceros. There are shady grounds plus a lake in the centre with paddleboats for hire and a small children's playground.

A massive underwater world has been recreated at the **Siam Ocean World** (สยามโอเชี่ยนเวิร์ล; Map p88; www.siamoceanworld.com; basement, Siam Paragon, 991/1 Th Phra Ram I; adult/child from 990/790B; ⏲10am-9pm; Ⓢ Siam exits 3 & 5) shopping-centre aquarium. Gaze into the glass-enclosed deep-reef zone or view the daily feeding of penguins and sharks.

Kids can view lethal snakes become reluctant altruists at the adjacent antivenin-producing **Queen Saovabha Memorial Institute** (p81).

Festivals & Events

In addition to the national holidays, there's always something going on in Bangkok. Many Thai holidays are based on the lunar calendar, which varies from year to year, so check the website of the Tourism Authority of Thailand (p145) or the Bangkok Information Center (p145) for exact dates.

February & March

Chinese New Year CULTURAL

(⏲Jan or Feb) Thai-Chinese celebrate the lunar New Year with a week of house-cleaning, lion dances and fireworks. Most festivities are siyuated around Chinatown. Dates vary every year.

North Bangkok

North Bangkok

Top Sights

1 Chatuchak Weekend Market B2

Sights

2 Children's Discovery Museum B2
3 Or Tor Kor Market B2

Activities, Courses & Tours

4 House of Dhamma C1

Sleeping

5 Mystic Place A3
6 Siamaze D3
7 The Yard A4
8 Yim Huai Khwang Hostel D4

Eating

9 AJH Vegetarians A4
10 Fatbird A3
11 Khua Kling Pak Sod A4

Kite-Flying Season CULTURAL

(Mar) During the windy season, colourful kites battle it out over the skies of Sanam Luang and Lumphini Park.

April & May

Songkran CULTURAL

(mid-Apr) The celebration of the Thai New Year has morphed into a water war with high-powered water guns and water balloons being launched at suspecting and unsuspecting participants. The most intense water battles take place on Th Khao San.

Royal Ploughing Ceremony CULTURAL

(May) His Majesty the King (or lately the Crown Prince) commences rice-planting season with a ceremony at Sanam Luang.

August

Queen's Birthday CULTURAL

(12 Aug) The queen's birthday is recognised as Mother's Day throughout the country. In

Bangkok, festivities centre on Th Ratchadamnoen and the Grand Palace.

September & October

Vegetarian Festival FOOD
(Sep or Oct) A 10-day Chinese-Buddhist festival wheels out yellow-bannered streetside vendors serving meatless meals. The greatest concentration of vendors is found in Chinatown. Dates vary.

King Chulalongkorn Day CULTURAL
(23 Oct) Rama V is honoured on the anniversary of his death at the Royal Plaza in Dusit. Crowds of devotees come to make merit with incense and flower garlands.

November

Loi Krathong CULTURAL
(early Nov) A beautiful festival where, on the night of the full moon, small lotus-shaped boats made of banana leaf and containing a lit candle are set adrift on Mae Nam Chao Phraya.

Wat Saket Fair FAIR
(Nov) The grandest of Bangkok's temple fairs (*ngahn wát*) is held at Wat Saket and the Golden Mount around Loi Krathong. The temple grounds turn into a colourful, noisy fair selling flowers, incense, bells, saffron cloth and tonnes of Thai food.

December

King's Birthday/Father's Day CULTURAL
(5 Dec) Locals celebrate their monarch's birthday with lots of parades and fireworks.

Sleeping

If your idea of the typical Bangkok hotel was influenced by *The Hangover Part II*, you'll be pleased to learn that the city is home to a diverse spread of modern hostels, guesthouses and hotels. To make matters better, much of Bangkok's accommodation offers excellent value, and competition is so intense that fat discounts are almost always available.

Ko Ratanakosin

Arom D Hostel HOSTEL $
(Map p72; 02 622 1055; www.aromdhostel.com; 336 Th Maha Rat; incl breakfast dm 800B, r 2250-2500B; ; Tien Pier) The dorm beds and rooms here are united by a cutesy design theme and a host of inviting communal areas including a rooftop deck, computers, a ground-floor cafe and TV room. Private rooms don't have much space, but they do have style. The posted rates are typically subject to hefty discounts.

Royal Tha Tien Village HOTEL $$
(Map p72; 095 151 5545; www.facebook.com/theroyalthatienvillage; 392/29 Soi Phen Phat; r 1200B; ; Tien Pier) These 12 rooms spread over two converted shophouses are relatively unassuming, but TV, fridge, air-con, lots of space and shiny wood floors, not to mention a cosy homestay atmosphere, edge this place into the recommendable category. It's popular, so be sure to book ahead.

Inn A Day HOTEL $$$
(Map p72; 02 221 0577; www.innaday.com; 57-61 Th Maha Rat; incl breakfast r 3500-4200B, ste 7500-9000B; ; Tien Pier) Inn A Day wows with its hyper-cool retro/industrial theme (the hotel is located in a former sugar factory) and its location (it towers over the river and Wat Arun). The 11 rooms aren't huge, but they include unique touches such as clear neon shower stalls, while the top-floor suites have two levels and huge clawfoot tubs.

Chakrabongse Villas HOTEL $$$
(Map p72; 02 622 1900; www.chakrabongse-villas.com; 396/1 Th Maha Rat; incl breakfast r 5000B, ste 10,000-25,000B; ; Tien Pier) This almost fairy-tale-like compound incorporates three sumptuous but cramped rooms and four larger suites and villas, some with great river views, all surrounding a functioning royal palace dating back to 1908. There's a pool, jungle-like gardens and an elevated deck for romantic riverside dining. No walk-ins.

Sala Ratanakosin HOTEL $$$
(Map p72; 02 622 1388; www.salaresorts.com/rattanakosin; Soi Tha Tian; incl breakfast r 4000-6300B, ste 12,100B; ; Tien Pier) Sala boasts a sleek, modernist feel – a somewhat jarring contrast with the former warehouse it's located in. The 15 rooms are decked out in black and white, and boast open-plan bathrooms and big windows looking out on the river and Wat Arun – they can't be described as vast, but will satisfy the fashion-conscious.

Banglamphu & Around

★ **Chern** HOSTEL $
(Map p72; 02 621 1133; www.chernbangkok.com; 17 Soi Ratchasak; dm 400B, r 1400-1900B; ; klorng boat to Phanfa Leelard Pier) The

vast, open spaces and white, overexposed tones of this hostel converge in an almost afterlife-like feel. The eight-bed dorms are above average, but we particularly like the private rooms, which, equipped with attractively minimalist touches, a vast desk, TV, safe, fridge and heaps of space, are a steal at this price.

Fortville Guesthouse HOTEL $
(Map p72; 02 282 3932; www.fortvilleguesthouse.com; 9 Th Phra Sumen; r 870-1120B; Phra Athit/Banglamphu Pier) With an exterior that combines elements of a modern church and/or castle, and an interior that relies on mirrors and industrial themes, the design concept of this hotel – undergoing a renovation at the time of research – is tough to pin down. The rooms themselves are stylishly minimal, and the more expensive ones include perks such as a fridge and balcony.

Khaosan Immjai HOSTEL $
(Map p72; 02 629 3088; www.khaosanimmjai.com; 240 Soi 1, Th Samsen; dm incl breakfast 350-420B; Phra Athit/Banglamphu Pier) There's nothing flashy or particularly exceptional about this hostel. But a homely feel and positive feedback edge it into the recommendable column. Dorms, which range from four to 14 beds, are clean, done out in pastel tones and have ample natural light. There is access to lots of convenient amenities (washing machines, computers, etc), although none of these are free.

SHOULD I STAY ON THANON KHAO SAN?

Th Khao San is synonymous with budget accommodation in Bangkok, but this doesn't necessarily mean it's the only or even the best place in Bangkok for a cheap room. The main drag can be exceedingly loud and hectic, with lots of touts. If you want to be close to the action but not in the thick of it, there are increasingly attractive options spanning all price levels on outlying streets such as riverside Th Phra Athit, leafy Soi Ram Buttri and the residential side streets off Th Samsen. During the high season (December to February), however, it's probably a wise idea to take the first vacant bed you come across. The best time of day to find a vacancy is around check-out time, at 10am or 11am.

★Lamphu Treehouse HOTEL $$
(Map p72; 02 282 0991; www.lamphutreehotel.com; 155 Wanchat Bridge, off Th Prachathipatai; incl breakfast r 1650-2500B, ste 3500-4500B; klorng boat to Phanfa Leelard Pier) Despite the name, this attractive midranger has its feet firmly on land, and as such represents brilliant value. The wood-panelled rooms are attractive and inviting, and the rooftop bar, pool, internet cafe, restaurant and quiet canalside location ensure that you may never feel the need to leave. An annexe a couple blocks away increases your odds of snagging an elusive reservation.

★Feung Nakorn Balcony HOTEL $$
(Map p72; 02 622 1100; www.feungnakorn.com; 125 Th Fuang Nakhon; incl breakfast dm 700B, r 1650B, ste 2100-4700B; Saphan Phut/Memorial Bridge Pier, Pak Klong Taladd Pier) Located in a former school, the 42 rooms here surround an inviting garden courtyard and are generally large, bright and cheery. Amenities such as a free minibar, safe and flat-screen TV are standard, and the hotel has a quiet and secluded location away from the strip, with capable staff. A charming and inviting (if not particularly great-value) place to stay.

The Warehouse HOTEL $$
(Map p72; 02 622 2935; www.thewarehousebangkok.com; 120 Th Bunsiri; r incl breakfast 2380-2680B; klorng boat to Phanfa Leelard Pier) Wooden pallets as furniture, yellow and black wall art, and exposed fittings and other industrial elements contribute to the factory theme here. Against all odds, the Warehouse pulls it off, and what you get are 36 rooms that are fun, functional and relatively spacious, if not stupendous value.

Sourire HOTEL $$
(Map p72; 02 280 2180; www.sourirebangkok.com; Soi Chao Phraya Si Phiphat; r incl breakfast 1500-3500B; klorng boat to Phanfa Leelard Pier) More home than hotel, the 38 rooms here exude a calming, matronly vibe. Soft lighting, comfortable and sturdy wood furniture, and the friendly, aged owners complete the package.

To reach the hotel, follow Soi Chao Phraya Si Phiphat to the end and knock on the tall brown wooden door situated immediately on your left.

Villa Cha-Cha HOTEL $$
(Map p72; 02 280 1025; www.villachacha.com; 36 Th Tani; r 1400-2200B; Phra Athit/Banglamphu Pier) Wind your way between

Balinese statues, lounging residents, a rambling restaurant and a tiny pool to emerge at this seemingly hidden but popular hotel. Rooms are capable – bar the frequently clumsy stabs made at interior design (think art-school nude portraits) – but the real draw is the hyper-social, resort-like atmosphere.

Diamond House HOTEL **$$**

(Map p72; ☎02 629 4008; www.thaidiamondhouse.com; 4 Th Samsen; r 1100-1700B; ❄@📶; ⛴Phra Athit/Banglamphu Pier) Despite sharing real estate with a Chinese temple, there's no conflict of design at this eccentric hotel. Most rooms have raised-platform beds, and are outfitted with stained glass, dark, lush colours and eclectic furnishings. There's a lack of windows, and some of the rooms can seem pretty tight, but a rooftop deck and an outdoor jacuzzi (!) are attempts to make up for this.

Hotel Dé Moc HOTEL **$$**

(Map p72; ☎02 282 2831; www.hoteldemoc.com; 78 Th Prachathipatai; r incl breakfast 1650-1850B; ❄@📶🏊; ⛴klorng boat to Phanfa Leelard Pier) With high ceilings and generous windows, the rooms at this 1960s-era hotel seem spacious, although the furnishings, like the exterior, are still stuck in the previous century. The grounds include an inviting and retro-feeling pool and cafe, and complimentary transport to Th Khao San and free use of bikes are thoughtful perks.

Rambuttri Village Inn HOSTEL **$$**

(Map p72; ☎02 282 9162; www.rambuttrivillage.com; 95 Soi Ram Buttri; r incl breakfast 850-2350B; ❄📶🏊; ⛴Phra Athit/Banglamphu Pier) Located just off the main drag, this midsized hotel has an abundance of relatively characterless, yet clean, comfortable good-value rooms. A ground-floor courtyard with restaurants and shops also makes it a convenient place to stay.

Pannee Residence HOTEL **$$**

(Map p72; ☎02 629 4560; 117 Th Din So; r incl breakfast 1100-1700B; ❄@📶; ⛴klorng boat to Phanfa Leelard Pier) Pannee is a multistorey hotel offering tidy, if somewhat character-anaemic, rooms. The cheapest rooms are small, but like all the others include a safe, TV and fridge. An upper-floor patio with outdoor rain showers and daybeds for sunbathing provides a bit more room to stretch, and proximity to Bangkok's big sights makes the decision easy.

Old Capital Bike Inn HOTEL **$$$**

(Map p72; ☎02 629 1787; www.oldcapitalbkk.com; 609 Th Phra Sumen; r incl breakfast 3190-6590B; ❄@📶; ⛴klorng boat to Phanfa Leelard Pier) The dictionary definition of a honeymoon hotel, this antique shophouse has 10 rooms that are decadent and sumptuous, blending rich colours and heavy wood furnishings. A recent management change and refurbishment has seen the introduction of a bicycle theme, and bikes can be borrowed for free.

Praya Palazzo HOTEL **$$$**

(Map p72; ☎02 883 2998; www.prayapalazzo.com; 757/1 Somdej Prapinklao Soi 2; incl breakfast r 4145-5334B, ste 7118-11,282B; ❄📶🏊; ⛴hotel shuttle boat from Phra Athit/Banglamphu Pier) After lying dormant for nearly 30 years, this elegant 19th-century mansion in Thonburi has been reborn as an attractive riverside boutique hotel. The 17 rooms can seem rather tight, and river views can be elusive, but the meticulous renovation, handsome antique furnishings and bucolic atmosphere convene in a boutique with authentic old-world charm.

Riva Surya HOTEL **$$$**

(Map p72; ☎02 633 5000; www.rivasuryabangkok.com; 23 Th Phra Athit; r incl breakfast 6950-10,350B; ❄@🏊; ⛴Phra Athit/Banglamphu Pier) A former condo has been transformed into one of the more design-conscious hotels in this part of town. The 68 rooms are decked out in greys and blacks, with contemporary furnishings, and in the case of the Riva Rooms, great river views, although not always tonnes of space.

Villa Phra Sumen HOTEL **$$$**

(Map p72; ☎080 085 0085; www.villaphrasumen.com; 457 Th Phra Sumen; incl breakfast r 3000-3300B, ste 4500-6000B; ❄@📶; ⛴klorng boat to Phanfa Leelard Pier) Surrounding a garden and edging the canal, the new Villa Phra Sumen boasts a secluded, secret feel. Gain access to the compound and inside you'll find 34 rooms that range from somewhat tight (and likewise overpriced) standard rooms to dual-level suites, all of which come equipped with balconies and contemporary amenities, and are looked after by service-minded staff.

Chinatown & Phahurat

Siam Classic GUESTHOUSE **$**

(Map p78; ☎02 639 6363; 336/10 Trok Chalong Krung; r incl breakfast 450-1200B; ❄@📶; ⛴Ratchawong Pier, Ⓜ Hua Lamphong exit 1) The

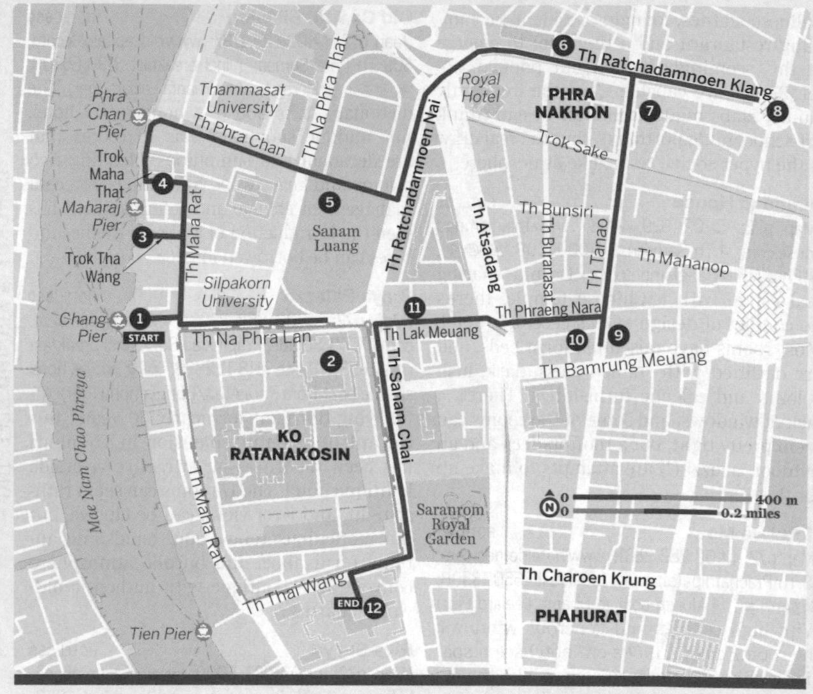

City Walk Old Bangkok

START CHANG PIER
END WAT PHO
LENGTH ABOUT 4KM; FOUR TO SIX HOURS

The bulk of Bangkok's 'must-see' destinations are in and around the former royal district, Ko Ratanakosin. It's best to start early to beat both the heat and the hordes. Remember to dress modestly to gain entry to the temples. Also ignore any strangers offering advice on sightseeing or shopping.

Start at 1 **Chang Pier**. Proceed east to the main gate of 2 **Wat Phra Kaew & Grand Palace** (p61), two of Bangkok's most famous attractions. Backtrack, then head north along Th Maha Rat, and immediately after passing the cat-laden newsstand (you'll know it when you smell it), turn left into 3 **Trok Tha Wang**, a narrow alleyway holding a hidden classic Bangkok neighbourhood.

Turn left into crowded Trok Maha That to discover the cramped 4 **amulet market** (p68). Exiting the market at Tha Phra Chan, cross Th Maha Rat and continue east until you reach 5 **Sanam Luang**, the 'Royal Field'.

Cross Th Ratchadamnoen Nai and go north, turning right at the Royal Hotel onto 6 **Th Ratchadamnoen Klang**, Bangkok's own Champs-Élysées. Continuing east, at the intersection with Th Tanao, you'll see the 7 **October 14 Memorial**, commemorating the civilian demonstrators who were killed on 14 October 1973 by the military during a pro-democracy rally. In the distance you'll see the 8 **Democracy Monument**, erected in 1932.

After a lunch stop at 9 **Poj Spa Kar** or 10 **Chote Chitr** (p117), enter Th Phraeng Nara, crossing Khlong Lod, and continue west along Th Lak Meuang to the home of Bangkok's city spirit, 11 **Lak Meuang** (p69).

Head south along Th Sanam Chai and turn right onto Th Thai Wang, which will escort you to the entrance of 12 **Wat Pho** (p61), home of the giant Reclining Buddha.

rooms here don't include much furniture, and the cheapest don't include air-con or en suite bathrooms, but an effort has been made at making them feel comfortable, tidy and even a bit stylish. An inviting ground-floor communal area encourages meeting and chatting, and the whole place exudes a welcoming homestay vibe.

Oldtown HOSTEL $

(Map p80; 02 639 4879; www.oldtownhostelbkk.com; 1048-1054 Soi 28, Th Charoen Krung; dm 230-270B, r 800B; ; Marine Department Pier, M Hua Lamphong exit 1) The dorms and rooms at this new, shophouse-bound hostel all share bathrooms and are relatively plain, but this is made up for by lots of communal space, including a vast lobby with a pool table, kitchen, computers and comfy chairs, and an adjoining cafe.

Shanghai Mansion HOTEL $$$

(Map p78; 02 221 2121; www.shanghaimansion.com; 479-481 Th Yaowarat; incl breakfast r 3000-4000B, ste 4500B; ; Ratchawong Pier, M Hua Lamphong exit 1 & taxi) Easily the most consciously stylish place to stay in Chinatown, if not in all of Bangkok. This award-winning boutique hotel screams Shanghai circa 1935 with stained glass, an abundance of lamps, bold colours and cheeky Chinatown kitsch. If you're willing to splurge, ask for one of the bigger street-side rooms with tall windows that allow more natural light.

Riverside

Swan Hotel HOTEL $$

(Map p80; 02 235 9271; www.swanhotelbkk.com; 31 Soi 36/Rue de Brest, Th Charoen Krung; r incl breakfast 1200-2000B; ; Oriental Pier) The 1960s-era furnishings date this classic Bangkok hotel despite relatively recent renovations. But the rooms are airy and virtually spotless, and the antiquated vibe provides the Swan, in particular its pool area, with a fun, groovy vibe.

Mandarin Oriental HOTEL $$$

(Map p80; 02 659 9000; www.mandarinoriental.com; 48 Soi 40/Oriental, Th Charoen Krung; incl breakfast r 14,150-30,000B, ste 26,700-160,000B; ; Oriental Pier, or hotel shuttle boat from Sathon/Central Pier) For the true Bangkok experience, a stay at this grand old riverside hotel is a must. The majority of rooms are in the modern and recently refurbished New Wing, but we prefer the old-world ambience of the Garden and Authors' Wings, the latter of which was undergoing a significant renovation at the time of research.

Peninsula Hotel HOTEL $$$

(Map p80; 02 861 2888; www.peninsula.com; 333 Th Charoen Nakhon; incl breakfast r 17,000-25,000B, ste 30,000-140,000B; ; hotel shuttle boat from Sathon/Central Pier) After nearly 20 years in Bangkok, the Pen still seems to have it all: the location (towering over the river), the rep (it's consistently one of the top-ranking luxury hotels in the world) and one of the highest levels of service in town. If money is no obstacle, stay on one of the upper floors where you literally have all of Bangkok at your feet.

Shangri-La Hotel HOTEL $$$

(Map p80; 02 236 7777; www.shangri-la.com; 89 Soi 42/1; incl breakfast r 10,000-14,100B, ste 14,800-124,800B; ; S Saphan Taksin exit 1) A convenient location near the BTS, generous rates, a resort-like riverside atmosphere, a huge selection of rooms (with more than 800, it's one of the city's largest hotels), and ample activities and amenities make the Shangri-La a clever choice for families.

Millennium Hilton HOTEL $$$

(Map p80; 02 442 2000; www.bangkok.hilton.com; 123 Th Charoen Nakhon; incl breakfast r 4300-6200B, ste 6800-34,300B; ; hotel shuttle boat from Sathon/Central Pier) As soon as you enter the dramatic lobby, it's obvious that this is Bangkok's youngest, most modern riverside hotel. Rooms, all of which boast river views, carry on the theme and are decked out with funky furniture and Thai-themed photos. A glass elevator and an artificial beach are just some of the fun touches.

Silom & Sathon

HQ Hostel HOSTEL $

(Map p82; 02 233 1598; www.hqhostel.com; 5/3-4 Soi 3, Th Silom; incl breakfast dm 330-520B, r 890-990B; ; M Si Lom exit 2, S Sala Daeng exit 2) HQ is a flashpacker hostel in the polished-concrete-and-industrial-style mould. It includes four- to 10-bed dorms, a few private rooms (some with en suite bathroom) and inviting communal areas in a narrow multistorey building in the middle of Bangkok's financial district.

★ **Smile Society** HOTEL $$

(Map p82; 081 442 5800, 081 444 1596; www.smilesocietyhostel.com; 30/3-4 Soi 6, Th Silom; incl breakfast dm 420B, r 900-1880B; ; M Si

Lom exit 2, S Sala Daeng exit 1) Part boutique, part hostel, this four-storey shophouse combines small but comfortable and well-equipped rooms and dorms with spotless shared bathrooms. A central location, overwhelmingly positive guest feedback, and helpful, English-speaking staff are other perks. And a new and virtually identical annexe next door helps with spillover as Smile Society gains more fans.

Amber HOTEL **$$**
(Map p82; 02 635 7272; www.amberboutiquesilom.com; 200 Soi 14, Th Silom; r incl breakfast 1650-2150B; ; S Chong Nonsi exit 3) Spanning design themes such as Moroccan, Sino-Portuguese and Modern, it's easy to assume that Amber might emphasise style over comfort. But nothing here is flashy or overwrought, and what you'll get are 19 excellent-value, spacious rooms with lots of amenities and natural light, in a quiet location.

Silom One HOTEL **$$**
(Map p82; 02 635 5130; www.silomone.com; 281/15 Soi 1, Th Silom; r 2500-3500B; ; M Si Lom exit 2, S Sala Daeng exit 2) Barely squeezing into the midrange bracket is this hotel with 10 rooms that boast an almost Japanese minimalism. You can't beat its convenient location in a dead-end alley, steps away from public transport and heaps of street food.

★**Siam Heritage** HOTEL **$$$**
(Map p82; 02 353 6101; www.thesiamheritage.com; 115/1 Th Surawong; incl breakfast r 4900-5700B, ste 7000-13,500B; ; M Si Lom exit 2, S Sala Daeng exit 1) Tucked off busy Th Surawong, this hotel overflows with homey Thai charm – probably because the owners also live in the same building. The 73 rooms are decked out in silk and dark woods with classy design touches and thoughtful amenities. There's an inviting rooftop garden/pool/spa, and it's all cared for by a team of professional, accommodating staff. Highly recommended.

Glow Trinity Silom HOTEL **$$$**
(Map p82; 02 231 5050; www.glowbyzinc.com/trinity-silom; 150 Soi Phiphat 2; r incl breakfast 3500-4200B; ; S Chong Nonsi exit 2) A sophisticated hotel with rates that weigh in at just above midrange, Glow has spacious-feeling, modern, tech-equipped rooms, professional service, and pool and fitness facilities just next door.

Triple Two Silom HOTEL **$$$**
(Map p82; 02 627 2222; www.tripletwosilom.com; 222 Th Silom; incl breakfast r 3200-3500B, ste 7900B; ; S Chong Nonsi exit 3) A renovation has left the rooms here resembling sleek modern offices – in a good way. With all the space, huge bathrooms and inviting-looking beds, you'll be inspired to relax, not work. Guests can use the rooftop garden, but have to go next door to the sister Narai Hotel for the swimming pool and fitness centre.

W Bangkok HOTEL **$$$**
(Map p82; 02 344 4000; www.whotels.com/bangkok; 106 Th Sathon Neua/North; incl breakfast r 9000-10,350B, ste 11,250-154,350B; ; S Chong Nonsi exit 1) A bold, brash, big-chain newbie, the W has correspondingly youngish rooms with cheeky touches (think Thai-boxing-themed furnishings) and high-tech amenities. Glitter and glass, a lobby bar and a pool that glows are some of the other touches that make this a frontrunner for Bangkok's clubbiest hotel.

Lumphini Park & Th Phra Ram IV

ETZzz Hostel HOSTEL **$**
(Map p86; 02 286 9424; www.etzhostel.com; 5/3 Soi Ngam Du Phli; dm 250-350B, r 900B; ; M Lumphini exit 1) This narrow shophouse includes dorms ranging in size from four to 12 beds, and two private rooms (the latter equipped with en suite bathroom), all of which are united by a neat, primary colour theme and a convenient location near the MRT.

Chaydon Sathorn HOTEL **$$**
(Map p86; 02 343 6333; www.chaydonsathorn.com; 31 Th Sathon Tai/South; r incl breakfast 1500-2500B; ; M Lumphini exit 2) The former King's Hotel has been reborn as a no-frills midranger, located right in the middle of the embassy district. The primary colours and bold lines of the design scheme make up for the lack of natural light in some rooms. Online discounts available through the website.

★**Metropolitan by COMO** HOTEL **$$$**
(Map p86; 02 625 3333; www.comohotels.com/metropolitanbangkok; 27 Th Sathon Tai/South; incl breakfast r 4500-6500B, ste 7500-40,000B; ; M Lumphini exit 2) The exterior of Bangkok's former YMCA has changed relatively little, but a peek inside reveals one of the city's sleekest, sexiest hotels. A 2014 renovation has all 171 rooms looking better than ever in striking tones of black, white and yellow.

A CHEAT SHEET TO BANGKOK ACCOMMODATION

At first glance, deciding where to lay your head in Bangkok appears to be an insurmountable task: there are countless hotels in virtually every corner of this sprawling city. Making the job slightly easier is the fact that where you stay is largely determined by your budget, as well as your need for access to eating, drinking or shopping.

Ko Ratanakosin, Banglamphu & Thonburi Banglamphu still holds the bulk of Bangkok's budget accommodation, as well as lots of eating, drinking and shopping options, in a location somewhat isolated from the rest of Bangkok. A few midrange and top-end places have sprung up in Ko Ratanakosin, although the immediate area has a lack of eating and drinking options.

Chinatown & Phahurat The bulk of Chinatown's accommodation is budget, and lots of street food and access to Hualamphong Train Station are perks, although you'll most likely want to go elsewhere for nightlife.

Riverside The city's most legendary luxury hotels are largely found along this stretch of Mae Nam Chao Phraya. Wining and dining are also largely upscale.

Silom & Sathon The city's financial district along Th Silom is not the most charming area of town, but accommodation spans from budget to top end, and the area allows convenient access to restaurants, nightspots and to the BTS and MRT. Th Sathon is home to several top-end hotels, but the area as a whole lacks atmosphere.

Lumphini Park & Th Phra Ram IV Lots of budget digs on Soi Ngam Duphli, near Th Sathon, although not much in the way of eating or drinking.

Siam Square & Pratunam With options that span from budget to midrange, a location at the intersection of the two BTS lines or a brief-ish taxi ride to older parts of town, and super-easy access to food and shopping, the area around Siam Sq is about as convenient as it gets in ever-expanding Bangkok.

Sukhumvit There's a bit of everything along this road, from the odd backpacker hostel to sex tourist hovels and five-star luxury. The former two are largely located between Soi 1 and Soi 4, while the latter doesn't begin to appear until you reach Soi 12 or so. Perks include access to food from virtually every corner of the globe, heaps of nightlife options and easy access to both the BTS and MRT.

Thewet & Dusit The area stretching from riverside Thewet inland to Dusit is home to a handful of low-key-feeling budget and midrange places. Not much in terms of eating or drinking, but it's not far to Banglamphu.

Ratchathewi For all the perks of 'downtown' Bangkok (mass transit, food, nightlife, shopping) but none of the touts, consider a stay in this area.

North Bangkok A bit of everything, from modern hostels to artsy midrangers, most boasting a surburban vibe. Relatively easy links to other parts of the city, and access to good eating, drinking and shopping options.

Greater Bangkok Accommodation in Bangkok's outer burbs means a less hectic setting, good value and, depending on location, convenient airport access. Transport can be inconvenient, and there is sometimes a lack of drinking and entertainment options.

It's worth noting that the City rooms tend to feel a bit tight, while in contrast the two-storey penthouse suites are like small homes.

Sukhothai Hotel HOTEL **$$$**
(Map p86; ☎02 344 8888; www.sukhothai.com; 13/3 Th Sathon Tai/South; incl breakfast r 12,800-16,800B, ste 17,800-80,000B; ❄@📶🏊; Ⓜ Lumphini exit 2) This is one of Bangkok's classiest luxury options, and, as the name suggests, the Sukhothai employs brick stupas, courtyards and antique sculptures to create a peaceful, almost temple-like atmosphere. The rooms contrast this with high-tech TVs, phones and, in some cases, toilets.

Sofitel So HOTEL **$$$**
(Map p86; ☎02 624 0000; www.sofitel.com; 2 Th Sathon Neua/North; incl breakfast r 7750-10,700B, ste 13,200-50,000B; ❄@📶🏊; Ⓜ Lumphini exit 2)

BANGKOK'S BEST HOSTELS

If you're on a shoestring budget, Bangkok has heaps of options for you, ranging from hi-tech, pod-like dorm beds in a brand-new hostel to modern bunk beds in a Chinatown shophouse. (And if you decide that you need a bit more privacy, nearly all of Bangkok's hostels also offer private rooms.) At the places listed here, we found the bathrooms to be clean and convenient, so sharing will hardly feel like a compromise. Some of our picks:

Lub*d (Map p88; 02 634 7999; www.siamsquare.lubd.com; Th Phra Ram I; dm 590B, r 1550-2000B; ; National Stadium exit 1) The title is a play on the Thai *làp dee,* meaning 'sleep well', but the fun atmosphere at this modern-feeling hostel might make you want to stay up all night. Diversions include an inviting communal area stocked with games and a bar, and thoughtful facilities range from washing machines to a theatre room. If this one's full, there's another branch just off **Th Silom** (02 634 7999; www.silom.lubd.com; 4 Th Decho; dm 550-600B, r 1250-1900B; ; Chong Nonsi exit 2).

Silom Art Hostel (Map p82; 02 635 8070; www.silomarthostel.com; 198/19-22 Soi 14, Th Silom; dm 380-450B, r 1200B; ; Chong Nonsi exit 3) Quirky, bright and fun, Silom Art Hostel combines recycled materials, unconventional furnishings and colourful wall paintings to culminate in a hostel that's quite unlike anywhere else in town. It's not all about style though: beds and rooms are functional and comfortable, with lots of appealing communal areas.

Loftel 22 (Map p80; www.loftel22bangkok.com; 952 Soi 22, Th Charoen Krung; dm 350B, r 900-1350B; ; Marine Department Pier, Hua Lamphong exit 1) Stylish, inviting dorms and private rooms (all with shared bathrooms) have been coaxed out of these two adjoining shophouses. Friendly service and a location in one of Chinatown's most atmospheric corners round out the package.

NapPark Hostel (Map p72; 02 282 2324; www.nappark.com; 5 Th Tani; dm 440-650B; ; Phra Athit/Banglamphu Pier) This popular hostel features dorm rooms of various sizes, the smallest and most expensive of which boasts six pod-like beds outfitted with power points, mini-TV, reading lamp and wi-fi. Cultural-based activities and inviting communal areas ensure that you may not actually get the chance to plug in.

Saphaipae (Map p80; 02 238 2322; www.saphaipae.com; 35 Th Surasak; incl breakfast dm 450B, r 1000-1600B; ; Surasak exit 1) The bright colours, chunky furnishings and bold murals in the lobby of this hostel give Saphaipae the feel of a day-care centre for travellers – a vibe that continues through to the playful communal areas and rooms. Dorms and rooms are thoughtful and well-equipped, and there are heaps of helpful travel resources and facilities.

Suneta Hostel Khaosan (Map p72; 02 629 0150; www.sunetahostel.com; 209-211 Th Kraisi; dm incl breakfast 490-590B, r incl breakfast 1180B; ; Phra Athit/Banglamphu Pier) A pleasant, low-key atmosphere, a unique, retro-themed design (some of the dorm rooms resemble sleeping car carriages), a location just off the main dra, and friendly service are what make Suneta stand out.

Yim Huai Khwang Hostel (Map p102; 02 118 6038; www.yimhuaikhwang.com; 70 Th Pracha Rat Bamphen; incl breakfast dm 450-550B, r 1556-3000B; ; Huay Khwang exit 1) A new suburban hostel decked out in an eclectic, colourful fashion, with dorm rooms ranging in size from four to six comfortable, high-tech bunk beds. Yes, it's far from any sights, but it's very close to the MRT.

S1 Hostel (Map p86; 02 679 7777; www.facebook.com/S1hostelBangkok; 35/1-4 Soi Ngam Du Phli; dm 330-380B, r 700-1300B; ; Lumphini exit 1) A huge new hostel with dorm beds decked out in a simple yet attractive primary-colour scheme. A host of facilities (laundry, kitchen, rooftop garden) and a convenient location within walking distance of the MRT.

Glur Bangkok (Map p80; 02 630 5595; www.glurbangkok.com; 45 Soi 50, Th Charoen Krung; incl breakfast dm 400-650B, r 800-1200B; ; Sathon/Central Pier, Saphan Taksin exit 1) A narrow shophouse with three attractive-and-comfy eight-bed dorms. Space is limited, but Glur makes the most of it with fun and functional communal areas, including a ground-floor cafe.

Taking inspiration from (and featuring amazing views of) adjacent Lumphini Park, this is one of a handful of large-yet-hip name-brand hotels to open in Bangkok over the last few years. The four elements-inspired design theme has no two rooms looking quite the same, but all are spacious and stylish, contemporary and young.

Siam Square & Pratunam

Wendy House HOSTEL $

(Map p88; ☎02 214 1149; www.wendyguesthouse.com; 36/2 Soi Kasem San 1; r incl breakfast 750-2000B; ❄@📶; S National Stadium exit 1) The rooms at this long-standing budget option are small and basic, but are exceedingly clean and relatively well equipped (TV, fridge) for this price range.

Boxpackers Hostel HOSTEL $

(Map p88; ☎02 656 2828; www.boxpackershostel.com; 39/3 Soi 15, Th Phetchaburi; incl breakfast dm 500-800B, r 1260-1530B; ❄📶; S Ratchathewi exit 1 & taxi) A contemporary, sparse hostel with dorms ranging in size from four to 12 double-decker pods – some of which are double beds. Communal areas are inviting, and include a ground-floor cafe and a lounge with pool table. A linked hotel also offers 14 small but similarly attractive private rooms.

Indra Regent Hotel HOTEL $$

(Map p88; ☎02 208 0022; www.indrahotel.com; 120/126 Th Ratchaprarop; incl breakfast r 2500-4200B, ste 5000-12,500B; ❄📶🏊; S Ratchathewi exit 4) A classic Bangkok hotel dating back to 1971, nearly half of its 500 rooms have been renovated, but the Indra Regent still retains charming touches of its past. Rooms are comfortable, spacious and well equipped – if somewhat conservative – and with the cheapest just squeezing into the midrange, represent decent value.

Siam@Siam HOTEL $$$

(Map p88; ☎02 217 3000; www.siamatsiam.com; 865 Th Phra Ram I; r incl breakfast 5467-9200B; ❄@📶🏊; S National Stadium exit 1) A seemingly random mishmash of colours and industrial/recycled materials in the lobby here result in a style one could only describe as 'junkyard chic' – but in a good way, of course. The rooms, which largely continue the theme, are found between the 14th and 24th floors, and offer terrific city views. There's a spa, a rooftop restaurant and an 11th-floor pool.

Hansar HOTEL $$$

(Map p88; ☎02 209 1234; www.hansarbangkok.com; 3 Soi Mahadlekluang 2; ste incl breakfast 5000-24,000B; ❄@📶🏊; S Ratchadamri exit 4) The Hansar can claim that elusive intersection of style and value. All 94 rooms here are handsome and feature huge bathrooms and giant desks, but the smallest (and cheapest) studios are probably the best deal, as they have a kitchenette, washing machine, stand-alone tub, free wi-fi and, in most, a balcony.

Okura Prestige HOTEL $$$

(Map p88; ☎02 687 9000; www.okurabangkok.com; 57 Th Witthayu/Wireless Rd; incl breakfast r 14,000-25,000B, ste 29,000-150,000B; P❄@📶🏊; S Phloen Chit exit 5) The Bangkok venture of this Japanese chain – the first branch outside of its homeland – is, unlike other recent, big-name openings in Bangkok, distinctly unflashy. But we like the minimalist, almost contemplative feel of the lobby and the 240 rooms, and the subtle but thoughtful, often distinctly Japanese touches. Significant online discounts are available.

Hotel Indigo HOTEL $$$

(Map p88; ☎02 207 4999; www.ihg.com; 81 Th Witthayu/Wireless Rd; incl breakfast r 3599-8599B, ste 15,599-20,599B; ❄@📶🏊; S Phloen Chit exit 5) An international chain with local flavour, the Indigo has borrowed from the history and culture of this corner of Bangkok to arrive at a hotel that is retro, modern, Thai and artsy all at the same time. Many of the 192 rooms overlook some of the greener areas of Bangkok's embassy district, and all are decked out with colourful furnishings and functional amenities.

Sukhumvit

Suk 11 HOSTEL $

(Map p92; ☎02 253 5927; www.suk11.com; 1/33 Soi 11, Th Sukhumvit; r incl breakfast 535-1712B; ❄@📶; S Nana exit 3) Extremely well run and equally popular, this rustic guesthouse is an oasis of woods and greenery in the urban jungle that is Th Sukhumvit. The rooms are basic, clean and comfy, if a bit dark, while the cheapest of them share bathrooms. Although the building holds nearly 70 rooms, you'll still need to book at least two weeks ahead.

Pause Hostel HOSTEL $

(Map p92; ☎02 108 8855; www.onedaybkk.com; Oneday, 51 Soi 26, Th Sukhumvit; incl breakfast dm 450-550B, r 1300-2000B; ❄@📶; S Phrom Phong exit 4) Attached to a cafe/co-working space is this modern, open-feeling hostel. Dorms span four to eight beds, and like the private rooms (only some of which have en suite bathrooms) are united by a handsome industrial-design theme and inviting, sun-soaked communal areas.

Atlanta HOTEL **$**

(Map p92; ☎02 252 1650; www.theatlantahotelbangkok.com; 78 Soi 2, Th Sukhumvit; incl breakfast r 750-1050B, ste 950-1950B; ; S Nana exit 2) Defiantly antiquated and equal parts frumpy and grumpy, this crumbling gem has changed very little since its 1952 construction. The opulent lobby stands in stark contrast to the simple rooms, and the anti-sex-tourist warnings are frantic in tone, but the inviting pool (allegedly the country's first hotel pool) and delightful restaurant (for guests only) are just enough incentive to get past these.

Napa Place HOTEL **$$**

(Map p92; ☎02 661 5525; www.napaplace.com; 11/3 Soi Napha Sap 2; incl breakfast r 2200-3100B, ste 3400-4100B; ; S Thong Lo exit 2) Hidden in the confines of a typical Bangkok urban compound is what must be the city's homeliest accommodation. The 12 expansive rooms have been decorated with dark woods from the family's former lumber business and light-brown cloths from the hands of Thai weavers, while the cosy communal areas might not be much different from the suburban living room you grew up in.

S-Box HOTEL **$$**

(Map p92; ☎02 262 0991; www.sboxhotel.com; 4 Soi 31, Th Sukhumvit; r incl breakfast 1000-2524B; ; S Phrom Phong exit 5) The name says it all: the rooms here are little more than boxes – albeit attractive, modern boxes with stylish furniture and practical amenities. The cheapest are pod-like and lack natural light, while the more expensive have floor-to-ceiling windows.

Fusion Suites HOTEL **$$**

(Map p92; ☎02 665 2644; www.fusionbangkok.com; 143/61-62 Soi 21/Asoke, Th Sukhumvit; r incl breakfast 1700-2400B; ; M Sukhumvit exit 1, S Asok exit 1) A disproportionately funky hotel for this price range, with unconventional furnishings providing the rooms here with heaps of style, although the cheapest can be a bit dark.

Baan Sukhumvit HOTEL **$$**

(Map p92; ☎02 258 5630; www.baansukhumvit.com; 392/38-39 Soi 20, Th Sukhumvit; r incl breakfast 1320-1650B; ; M Sukhumvit exit 1, S Asok exit 1) With only 12 rooms, this hotel exudes an approachable, cosy feel. Rooms lack bells and whistles, but are subtly attractive; the more expensive include a bit more space, a bathtub and a safe. There's another branch nearby on Soi 18.

★ **AriyasomVilla** HOTEL **$$$**

(Map p92; ☎02 254 8880; www.ariyasom.com; 65 Soi 1, Th Sukhumvit; r incl breakfast 6650-14,750B; ; S Phloen Chit exit 3) Located at the end of Soi 1 behind a wall of tropical greenery, this beautifully renovated 1940s-era villa is one of the worst-kept accommodation secrets in Bangkok. The 24 rooms are spacious and meticulously outfitted with thoughtful Thai design touches and sumptuous, beautiful antique furniture. There's also a spa and an inviting tropical pool. Book well in advance.

Sheraton Grande Sukhumvit HOTEL **$$$**

(Map p92; ☎02 649 8888; www.sheratongrandesukhumvit.com; 250 Th Sukhumvit; incl breakfast r 11,000-13,800B, ste 19,000-56,000B; ; M Sukhumvit exit 3, S Asok exit 2) This conveniently located, business-oriented hotel offers some of the biggest rooms in town and fills them with a generous spread of amenities. Guest feedback is overwhelmingly positive, and by the time you read this, ongoing renovations will be making what was already a very good hotel an excellent one.

Ma Du Zi HOTEL **$$$**

(Map p92; ☎02 615 6400; www.maduzihotel.com; cnr Th Ratchadaphisek & Soi 16, Th Sukhumvit; incl breakfast r 7062-7651B, ste 10,593-15,301B; ; M Sukhumvit exit 3, S Asok exit 6) The name is Thai for 'come take a look', somewhat of a misnomer for this reservations-only, no-walk-ins hotel. If you've gained access, behind the gate you'll find a modern, sophisticated midsized hotel steeped in dark, chic tones and designs. We particularly like the immense bathrooms, equipped with a walk-in tub and minimalist shower.

S31 HOTEL **$$$**

(Map p92; ☎02 260 1111; www.s31hotel.com; 545 Soi 31, Th Sukhumvit; incl breakfast r 6000-7000B, ste 9000-10,000B; ; S Phrom Phong exit 5) The bold patterns and graphics of its interior and exterior make the S31 a fun, youthful choice. Thoughtful touches like kitchenettes with large fridge, super-huge beds and courses (Thai boxing and yoga) prove that the style also has substance.

BANGKOK'S BEST SMALL HOTELS

Although the big chains dominate the skyline, Bangkok is also home to several attractive hotels and guesthouses that have fewer than 10 rooms. Some of our faves:

Arun Residence (Map p72; ☎02 221 9158; www.arunresidence.com; 36-38 Soi Pratu Nokyung; r incl breakfast 3500-4200B, ste incl breakfast 5800B; ; Tien Pier) Although strategically located on the river directly across from Wat Arun, this multilevel wooden house boasts much more than just great views. The six rooms here manage to feel both homey and stylish, some being tall and loft-like, while others join two rooms. The best are the top-floor, balcony-equipped suites.

Loy La Long (Map p78; ☎02 639 1390; www.loylalong.com; 1620/2 Th Songwat; dm incl breakfast 1300B, r incl breakfast 2100-4000B; ; Ratchawong Pier, M Hua Lamphong exit 1 & taxi) Rustic, retro, charming – the six rooms in this 100-year-old wooden house can lay claim to more than their fair share of personality. And united by a unique location elevated over Mae Nam Chao Phraya complete with breezy, inviting nooks and crannies, the whole place is also privy to a hidden, almost secret, feel. The only hitch is in finding it; to get there, proceed to Th Songwat and cut directly through Wat Patumkongka Rachaworawiharn to the river.

W Home (Map p66; ☎02 291 5622; www.whomebangkok.com; Yaek 8, Soi 79, Th Charoen Krung; r incl breakfast 1500-1600B; ; S Saphan Taksin exit 2 & taxi) It's admittedly off the grid, but that's part of the charm at this 60-year-old renovated house. Welcoming hosts, four small but attractive and thoughtfully furnished rooms (although only one with en suite bathroom), inviting communal areas and an authentic homestay atmosphere round out the package. Soi 79 branches off Th Charoen Krung about 1km south of Saphan Taksin; W Home is about 250m east of the main road.

Bhuthorn (Map p72; ☎02 622 2270; www.thebhuthorn.com; 96-98 Th Phraeng Phuthon; r incl breakfast 4500-6300B; ; Saphan Phut/Memorial Bridge Pier, Pak Klong Taladd Pier) Travel a century back in time by booking one of the three rooms in this beautiful antique shophouse located in a classic Bangkok neighbourhood. They're not particularly huge, but are big on atmosphere and come equipped with both antique furnishings and modern amenities. The sister hotel, **Asadang** (☎085 180 7100; www.theasadang.com; 94-94/1 Th Atsadang; r incl breakfast 3900-6000B; ; Saphan Phut/Memorial Bridge Pier, Pak Klong Taladd Pier), a couple of blocks away, offers a similar package.

Café Ice Residence (Map p82; ☎02 636 7831; cafeiceresidences@gmail.com; 44/4 Soi Phiphat 2; r incl breakfast 2100-3000B; ; S Chong Nonsi exit 2) More home than hotel, the nine rooms in this spotless, classy villa are inviting, spacious and comfortable. Outfitted with subtle yet attractive furnishings, they also share a location with a Thai restaurant and a quiet street.

Loog Choob Homestay (Map p66; ☎085 328 2475; www.loogchoob.com; 463/5-8 Th Luk Luang; incl breakfast r 2100B, ste 3600-4400B; ; Thewet Pier, S Phaya Thai exit 3 & taxi) Five rooms in a former gem factory outside the tourist zone might sound iffy, but the rooms here are stylish and inviting, and come supplemented with a huge array of thoughtful amenities and friendly, heartfelt service.

Baan Noppawong (Map p72; ☎02 224 1047; www.facebook.com/baannoppawong; 112-114 Soi Damnoen Klang Tai; incl breakfast r 2500-3200B, ste 4200-4990B; ; klorng boat to Phanfa Leelard Pier) If your grandma ran a hotel in Bangkok, it might resemble the seven rooms in this fastidiously tidy antique house. Rooms don't have much space, but are light-filled, comfortable and homely, and attractively decorated with antique furnishings. A secluded location augments the homestay vibe.

Baan Dinso (Map p72; ☎02 621 2808; www.baandinso.com; 113 Trok Sin; r incl breakfast dm 650B, r 1000-2600B; ; klorng boat to Phanfa Leelard Pier) This antique wooden villa may not represent the best value in Bangkok, but for accommodation with a nostalgic feel and palpable sense of place, it's almost impossible to beat. Of the nine small-yet-spotless rooms, only five have en suite bathrooms, while all have access to functional and inviting communal areas.

AIRPORT ACCOMMODATION

The vast majority of visitors to Bangkok generally need not consider the airport hotel rigmarole as taxis are cheap and plentiful, and light early-morning traffic means the trip shouldn't take too long. That said, those worried about a super-early departure or late arrival may consider a stay at one of the following:

Novotel Suvarnabhumi Airport Hotel (02 131 1111; www.novotelairportbkk.com; Suvarnabhumi International Airport; incl breakfast r 5613-6200B, ste 8043B; ; Phra Khanong exit 3 & taxi, Suvarnabhumi Airport & hotel shuttle bus) Has 600-plus luxurious rooms; located within the Suvarnabhumi International Airport compound.

The Cottage (02 727 5858; www.thecottagesuvarnabhumi.com; 888/8 Th Lad Krabang; r incl breakfast 900-2700B; ; Phra Khanong exit 3 & taxi, Suvarnabhumi Airport & hotel shuttle bus) Near the Suvarnabhumi International Airport compound and within walking distance of food and shopping is this solid midranger with airport shuttle.

Amari Airport Hotel (02 566 1020; www.amari.com/donmuang; 333 Th Choet Wutthakat; r 2190-2590B, ste 2590-3590B; ; Chatuchak Park exit 2 & taxi, Mo Chit exit 3 & taxi) Located directly opposite Don Mueang International Airport.

Significant discounts can be found online, and more branches are on Soi 15 and Soi 33.

Thewet & Dusit

Hi Baan Thewet HOTEL $

(Map p96; 02 281 0361; www.hi-baanthewet.com; 25/2 Th Phitsanulok; r incl breakfast 500-750B; ; Thewet Pier) The rather institutional lobby here stands in contrast to the 14 pleasant, vaguely old-school-themed rooms. Some are on the small side and could use windows, but inviting communal areas and the leafy, quiet, off-the-beaten-track location make up for this.

Baan Manusarn GUESTHOUSE $$

(Map p96; 02 281 2976; www.facebook.com/baanmanusarn; Th Krung Kasem; r incl breakfast 1400B; ; Thewet Pier) Steps from Thewet Pier is this inviting vintage shophouse with four rooms. All feature beautiful wood floors and lots of space – with the two Family rooms being the most generous – and half boasting balconies.

SSIP Boutique HOTEL $$

(Map p96; 02 282 6489; www.ssiphotelthailand.com; 42 Th Phitsanulok; r incl breakfast 2200-3500B; ; Thewet Pier) Handsome tiles, heavy wood furniture, antique furnishings: the 20 rooms here have been meticulously styled to emulate an old-school Bangkok feel. But modern amenities (TV, fridge, safe) and thoughtful staff ensure a thoroughly contemporary stay.

★ **Phra-Nakorn Norn-Len** HOTEL $$$

(Map p96; 02 628 8188; www.phranakorn-nornlen.com; 46 Soi Thewet 1; r incl breakfast 2200-4200B; ; Thewet Pier) Set in an enclosed garden compound decorated like the Bangkok of yesteryear, this bright and cheery hotel is a fun and atmospheric, if not necessarily stupendous-value place to stay. Although the 31 rooms are attractively furnished with antiques and paintings, it's worth noting that they don't include TV or in-room wi-fi, a fact made up for by daily activities, massage and endless opportunities for peaceful relaxing.

The Siam HOTEL $$$

(Map p96; 02 206 6999; www.thesiamhotel.com; 3/2 Th Khao; incl breakfast r 14,950-22,327B, villa 26,271-36,912B; ; Thewet Pier, or hotel shuttle boat from Sathon/Central Pier) Zoom back to the 1930s in this contemporary riverside hotel, where art deco influences, copious marble and beautiful antiques define the look. Rooms are spacious and well appointed, while villas up the ante with rooftop balcony and plunge pool. Yet it's not just about navel-gazing, with activities ranging from Thai boxing lessons to a private theatre to keep you busy.

Ratchathewi

Bizotel HOTEL $$

(Map p98; 02 245 2424; www.bizotelbkk.com; 104/40 Th Rang Nam; r incl breakfast 1800B; ; Victory Monument exit 4) Attractive, bright and stuffed with useful amenities: you could be fooled into believing that the rooms at this new hotel cost twice this much. A location in a relatively quiet part of town is another bonus, and helpful, friendly staff seal the deal.

K Maison HOTEL $$$

(Map p98; ☎02 245 1953; www.kmaisonboutique.com; Soi Ruam Chit; incl breakfast r 2675-3975B, ste 8375B; ; S Victory Monument exit 4) The lobby, with its virginal white, swirling marble and streaks of blue, sets the tone of this new boutique hotel. The 21 rooms follow suit, and are handsome in a delicate and attractively sparse way. Lest you think it's all about image, K Maison appears to be functional and comfortable.

North Bangkok

The Yard HOSTEL $

(Map p102; ☎089 677 4050; www.theyardhostel.com; 51 Soi 5, Th Phahonyothin; incl breakfast dm 550-650B, r 1500B; ; S Ari exit 1) This fun hostel is comprised of 10 converted shipping containers. Predictably, neither the dorm nor private rooms are huge (nor great value), but are attractive and cosy, and have access to inviting communal areas ranging from the eponymous lawn (which also functions as a bar) to a kitchen.

Mystic Place HOTEL $$

(Map p102; ☎02 270 3344; www.mysticplacebkk.com; 224/5-9 Th Pradiphat; r incl breakfast 1530-1870B; @; S Saphan Khwai exit 2 & taxi) This hotel unites 36 rooms, each of which is individually and playfully designed. One we checked out combined a chair upholstered with stuffed animals and walls covered with graffiti, while another was swathed in eye-contorting op art. Heaps of fun and perpetually popular, so be sure to book ahead.

Greater Bangkok

Siamaze HOSTEL $

(Map p102; ☎02 693 6336; www.siamaze.com; Soi 17, Th Ratchadaphisek; incl breakfast dm 390-490B, r 1200-1960B; @; M Sutthisan exit 4) Siamaze is an unflashy, casual budget hotel with spacious private rooms and tech-outfitted bunk-bed dorms. The latter share big, clean bathrooms and access to thoughtful, convenient facilities. If you're OK staying away from the main tourist drag, it's an excellent deal.

Beat Hotel HOTEL $$

(Map p66; ☎02 178 0077; www.beathotelbangkok.com; 69/1 Th Sukhumvit; r incl breakfast 2000-2500B; @; S Phra Khanong exit 3) This new, art-themed hotel has a vibrant, youthful vibe that kicks off in the lobby. The 54 rooms continue this feeling, ranging in design from those with colourful floor-to-ceiling wall art to others painted in a monochromatic bold hue. It's worth shelling out for the super-huge Deluxe rooms.

★**Bangkok Tree House** HOTEL $$$

(Map p66; ☎082 995 1150; www.bangkoktreehouse.com; near Wat Bang Na Nork, Phrapradaeng; bungalow incl breakfast 6000-10,000B; @; S Bang Na exit 2 & taxi) Located in the lush green zone known as the Phrapradaeng Peninsula. To get to Bangkok Tree House, take the BTS to Bang Na and then a taxi for the short ride to the pier at Wat Bang Na Nork. From there, take the river-crossing ferry (4B, 5am to 9.30pm), and continue by motorcycle taxi (10B) or on foot (call ahead for directions).

The 12 multilevel bungalows here are stylishly sculpted from sustainable and recycled materials, resulting in a vibe that calls to mind a sophisticated, eco-friendly summer camp. Thoughtful amenities include private computers equipped with movies, free mobile-phone and bicycle use, and free ice cream. Significant online discounts are available.

Eating

Probably the safest of the city's infamous carnal pleasures, food is serious business in Bangkok. Attracting hungry visitors from across the globe, the city's eateries also draw natives from disparate ends of the city, happy to brave traffic or floods for a bowl of noodles or a plate of rice.

The selection is enormous and diverse, with eating places in Bangkok ranging from wheeled carts that set up shop on a daily basis to chic dining rooms in five-star hotels. In our experience the tastiest eats are generally found somewhere in between, at decades old, family-run shophouse restaurants serving a limited repertoire of dishes.

The influences are also vast, and you'll find everything from Thai-Chinese to Thai-Muslim, not to mention most regional domestic cuisines. And if at some point you do tire of *gŏo·ay đěe·o* (rice noodles) and curries, Bangkok has an ever-expanding selection of high-quality international restaurants, encompassing everything from French cuisine to hole-in-the-wall Japanese ramen houses.

Ko Ratanakosin

Bangkok's royal district has an abundance of sights but a relative dearth of restaurants – a pity considering the potential riverfront views.

Pa Aew CENTRAL THAI $

(Map p72; Th Maha Rat, no roman-script sign; mains 20-60B; ⏲10am-5pm Tue-Sat; Tien Pier) Pull up a plastic stool for some rich, seafood-heavy, Bangkok-style fare. It's a bare-bones, open-air curry stall, but for taste, Pa Aew is one of our favourite places to eat in this part of town.

There's no English-language sign; look for the exposed trays of food directly in front of the Krung Thai Bank near the corner with Soi Pratu Nokyung.

Err THAI $$

(Map p72; www.errbkk.com; off Th Maha Rat; dishes 65-360B; ⏲11am-late Tue-Sun; ❄; Tien Pier) Think of all those different smoky, spicy, crispy, meaty bites you've encountered on the street. Now imagine them assembled in one funky, retro-themed locale, and coupled with tasty Thai-themed cocktails and domestic microbrews. If Err (a Thai colloquialism for agreement) seems to good too be true, we empathise, but insist that it's true.

Khunkung CENTRAL THAI $$

(Navy Club; Map p72; 77 Th Maha Rat; mains 70-450B; ⏲11am-2pm & 6-10pm Mon-Fri, 11am-10pm Sat & Sun; ❄; Chang Pier, Maharaj Pier, Phra Chan Tai Pier) The restaurant of the Royal Navy Association has one of the few coveted riverfront locations along this stretch of Mae Nam Chao Phraya. Locals come for the combination of views and cheap and tasty seafood-based eats – ostensibly not for the cafeteria-like atmosphere.

Khunkung is just off the main road; look for the sign on Th Maha Rat that says 'Navy Club'.

MONDAYS OFF

Fans of street food be forewarned that all of Bangkok's stalls close on Monday for compulsory street cleaning (the results of which are never entirely evident come Tuesday morning). If you happen to be in the city on this day, take advantage of the lull to visit one of the city's upscale hotel restaurants, which virtually never close.

Banglamphu

Despite the faux *pàt tai* and tame *đôm yam* of Th Khao San, Banglamphu is one of the city's most famous eating areas. Decades-old restaurants and legendary hawkers line the streets in this leafy corner of Old Bangkok, and you could easily spend an entire day grazing the southern end of Th Tanao alone.

Although you'd be wisest to get your domestic nosh away from the main drag, the foreign influence on Th Khao San has led to a few import standouts.

Nang Loeng Market THAI $

(Map p66; btwn Soi 8-10, Th Nakhon Sawan; mains 30-80B; ⏲10am-2pm Mon-Fri; Thewet Pier, S Phaya Thai exit 3 & taxi) Dating back to 1899, this atmospheric fresh market offers a charming glimpse of old Bangkok – not to mention a great place to grab a bite. Nang Loeng is renowned for its Thai sweets, and at lunchtime it's also an excellent place to fill up on central-Thai-style curries or Chinese-influenced noodles.

★ **Likhit Kai Yang** NORTHEASTERN THAI $$

(Map p72; off Th Ratchadamnoen Nok, no roman-script sign; mains 50-280B; ⏲9am-9pm; ❄; Thewet Pier, S Phaya Thai exit 3 & taxi) Located just behind Ratchadamnoen Stadium (avoid the grotty branch directly adjacent to the stadium), this decades-old restaurant is where locals come for a northeastern-Thai-style meal before a Thai boxing match. The friendly English-speaking owner will steer you through the ordering process, but don't miss the deliciously herbal, eponymous 'charcoal roasted chicken'.

The restaurant has no English-language sign; look for the huge yellow banner.

★ **Krua Apsorn** THAI $$

(Map p72; www.kruaapsorn.com; Th Din So; mains 80-400B; ⏲10.30am-8pm Mon-Sat; ❄; klorng boat to Phanfa Leelard Pier) This homely dining room is a favourite of members of the Thai royal family and restaurant critics alike. Just about all of the central and southern Thai dishes are tasty, but regulars never miss the chance to order the decadent 'stir-fried crab with yellow chilli' or the *tortilla Española*–like 'omelette with crab'.

There's another branch on Th Samsen in **Thewet & Dusit** (Map p96; www.kruaapsorn.com; 503-505 Th Samsen; mains 80-400B; ⏲10.30am-7.30pm Mon-Fri, to 6pm Sat; ❄; Thewet Pier).

THE FLAVOURS OF BANGKOK

In Bangkok, the geography of the central plains, influences of the country's predominate minorities and the wealth of the royal palace have all served to shape the local cuisine.

The people of central Thailand are particularly fond of sweet/savoury flavours, and many dishes include freshwater fish, pork, coconut milk and palm sugar – common ingredients in the central Thai plains. Because of their proximity to the Gulf of Thailand, Bangkok eateries also serve a wide variety of seafood. Muslim immigrants introduced a variety of dried spices, and Chinese labourers and vendors introduced a huge variety of noodle and wok-fried dishes to central Thailand as many as 200 years ago. And culinary spillover from the royal court meant that Bangkok's food was particularly refined and sophisticated, often employing unusual and exotic ingredients. It is this version of Thai food, often known as royal Thai cuisine, that has come to define Thai food outside of the country's borders.

You can't say you've tried Bangkok-style Thai food unless you've tasted at least a couple of the following:

Đôm yam Lemon grass, galangal, kaffir lime leaf and lime juice give this soup its characteristic tang; fresh chillies or an oily chilli paste provide it with its legendary sting. Available just about everywhere, but it's hard to beat the version served at **Krua Apsorn** (p116).

Gŏo·ay đěe·o reu·a Known as boat noodles because they were previously served from small boats along the canals of central Thailand, these intense pork- or beef-based bowls are among the most full-flavoured of Thai noodle dishes. Several restaurants near Bangkok's Victory Monument, including **Sam-Ang Kulap** (Soi 18, Th Ratchawithi, no roman-script sign; dishes from 30B; ⏲8am-5pm; S Victory Monument exit 3), serve the dish.

Gŏo·ay đěe·o kôo·a gài Wide rice noodles fried with little more than egg, chicken, preserved squid and garlic oil is a humble but delicious Thai-Chinese dish available at **Nay Hong** (off Th Yukol 2, no roman-script sign; mains 35-50B; ⏲4-10pm; ⛴Ratchawong Pier, M Hua Lamphong exit 1 & taxi) and other stalls in Bangkok's Chinatown.

Kôw mòk Biryani, a dish found across the Muslim world, also has a foothold in Bangkok. Here the dish is typically made with chicken and is served with a sweet-and-sour dipping sauce and a bowl of chicken broth. We love the old-school version served at long-standing staple, **Muslim Restaurant** (1354-6 Th Charoen Krung; mains 40-140B; ⏲6.30am-5.30pm; ⛴Oriental Pier, S Saphan Taksin exit 1).

Máh hór With origins in the palace, this is a Thai appetiser that pairs chunks of mandarin orange or pineapple and a sweet/savoury/peppery topping made from pork, chicken, peanuts, sugar, peppercorns and coriander root. Available as part of the set dinner at **nahm** (p121).

Mèe gròrp Crispy noodles made the traditional way, with a sweet/sour flavour (a former palace recipe), are a dying breed. Long-standing Banglamphu restaurant **Chote Chitr** (146 Th Phraeng Phuthon; mains 60-200B; ⏲11am-10pm; ⛴klorng boat to Phanfa Leelard Pier) serves an excellent version of the dish.

Pàt tai Thin rice noodles stir-fried with dried and/or fresh shrimp, bean sprouts, tofu, egg and seasonings, traditionally served with lime halves and a few stalks of Chinese chives and a sliced banana flower. **Thip Samai** (313 Th Mahachai; mains 50-250B; ⏲5pm-2am; ⛴klorng boat to Phanfa Leelard Pier) is probably Bangkok's most lauded destination for what is arguably Thailand's most famous dish.

Yen đah foh Combining a slightly sweet crimson-coloured broth with a variety of fish balls, cubes of blood and crispy greens, *yen đah foh* is probably both the most intimidating and popular noodle dish in Bangkok. Available at **Soi 10 Food Centres** (Soi 10, Th Silom; mains 20-60B; ⏲8am-3pm Mon-Fri; M Si Lom exit 2, S Sala Daeng exit 1).

CHINATOWN'S VEGETARIAN FESTIVAL

During the annual Vegetarian Festival in September or October, Bangkok's Chinatown becomes a virtual orgy of nonmeat cuisine. The festivities centre on Chinatown's main street, Th Yaowarat, and the **Talat Noi** (p79) area, but food shops and stalls all over the city post yellow flags to announce their meat-free status.

Celebrating alongside the ethnic Chinese are Thais who look forward to the special dishes that appear during the festival period. Most restaurants put their normal menus on hold and instead prepare soy-based substitutes for standard Thai dishes like *dôm yam* (Thai-style spicy/sour soup) and *gaang kĕe·o wăhn* (green curry). Even Thai regional cuisines are sold (without the meat, of course). Yellow Hokkien-style noodles often make an appearance in the special festival dishes, usually in stir-fried dishes along with meaty mushrooms and big hunks of vegetables.

Along with abstinence from meat, the 10-day festival is celebrated with special visits to the temple, often requiring worshippers to dress in white.

Shoshana ISRAELI **$$**

(Map p72; 88 Th Chakraphatdi Phong; mains 70-240B; 10am-midnight; ; Phra Athit/Banglamphu Pier) One of Khao San's longest-running Israeli restaurants, Shoshana resembles your grandparents' living room right down to the tacky wall art and plastic placemats. Feel safe in ordering anything deep-fried – they do an excellent job of it – and don't miss the deliciously garlicky eggplant dip.

Hemlock THAI **$$**

(Map p72; 56 Th Phra Athit; mains 75-280B; 4pm-midnight Mon-Sat; ; Phra Athit/Banglamphu Pier) Taking full advantage of its cosy shophouse location, this perennial favourite has enough style to feel like a special night out, but doesn't skimp on flavour or preparation. And unlike at other similar places, the eclectic menu here reads like an ancient literary work, reviving old dishes from aristocratic kitchens across the country, not to mention several meat-free items.

★ **Jay Fai** CENTRAL THAI **$$$**

(Map p72; 327 Th Mahachai; mains 180-1000B; 3pm-2am Mon-Sat; klorng boat to Phanfa Leelard Pier) You wouldn't think so by looking at her bare-bones dining room, but Jay Fai is known far and wide for serving Bangkok's most expensive *pàt kêe mow* ('drunkard's noodles'; wide rice noodles fried with seafood and Thai herbs).

Jay Fai is located in a virtually unmarked shophouse on Th Mahachai, directly across from a 7-Eleven.

Chinatown & Phahurat

When you mention Chinatown, most Bangkokians immediately dream of street food.

On the western side of the neighbourhood is Phahurat, Bangkok's Little India, filled with small Indian and Nepali restaurants tucked into the tiny soi off Th Chakkaraphet.

Old Siam Plaza SWEETS **$**

(Map p78; cnr Th Phahurat & Th Triphet; mains 30-90B; 10am-7pm; ; Saphan Phut/Memorial Bridge Pier, Pak Klong Taladd Pier) Sugar junkies, be sure to include this stop on your Bangkok eating itinerary. The ground floor of this shopping centre is a candyland of traditional Thai sweets and snacks, most made right before your eyes.

Samsara JAPANESE, THAI **$$**

(Map p78; Soi Khang Wat Pathum Khongkha; mains 110-320B; 4pm-midnight Tue-Thu, to 1am Fri-Sun; ; Ratchawong Pier, Hua Lamphong exit 1 & taxi) Combining Japanese and Thai dishes, Belgian beers and an artfully ramshackle atmosphere, Samsara is easily Chinatown's most eclectic place to eat. It's also very tasty, and the generous riverside breezes and views simply add to the package.

The restaurant is at the end of tiny Soi Khang Wat Pathum Khongkha, just west of the temple of the same name.

Thanon Phadungdao Seafood Stalls THAI **$$**

(Map p78; cnr Th Phadungdao & Th Yaowarat; mains 100-600B; 4pm-midnight Tue-Sun; Ratchawong Pier, Hua Lamphong exit 1 & taxi) After sunset, these two opposing open-air restaurants – each of which claims to be the original – become a culinary train wreck of outdoor barbecues, screaming staff, iced seafood trays and sidewalk seating. True, the vast majority of diners are foreign tourists, but this has little impact on the cheerful setting, the fun experience and the cheap bill.

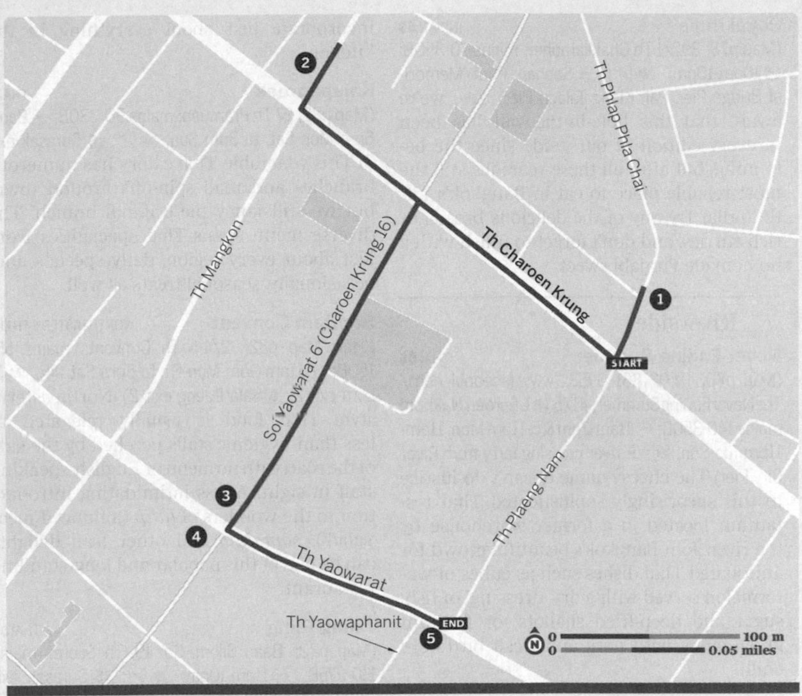

City Walk
Chinatown Eats Tour

START CNR TH PLAENG NAM & TH CHAROEN KRUNG
END CNR TH YAOWAPHANIT & TH YAOWARAT
LENGTH ABOUT 1KM; TWO TO THREE HOURS

Street food rules in Chinatown, making the area ideal for a culinary adventure. Although many vendors stay open late, the more popular stalls tend to sell out quickly, so the best time to feast in this area is from 7pm to 9pm. Don't try this walk on a Monday, when most of the city's street vendors stay at home. Bringing a friend (or three) and sharing is a good way to ensure that you can try as many dishes as possible.

Start your walk at the intersection of Th Plaeng Nam and Th Charoen Krung. Head north along Th Phlap Phla Chai, staying on the right-hand side for about 50m, until you reach 1 **Nai Mong Hoi Thod**, a shophouse restaurant renowned for its delicious *or sòo·an* (oysters fried with egg and a sticky batter).

Backtrack to Th Charoen Krung and turn right. Upon reaching Th Mangkon make a right; on your left-hand side you'll see 2 **Jek Pui**, a table-less stall famous for its Chinese-style Thai curries.

Cross Th Charoen Krung again, turn left, and continue east until you reach Soi Yaowarat 6/Charoen Krung 16, also known as Talat Mai, the area's most famous strip of commerce. At the end of the alley you'll see a gentleman making 3 **gŏo·ay đěe·o kôo·a gài**, rice noodles fried with chicken, egg and garlic oil.

Upon emerging at Th Yaowarat, cross over to the busy market area directly across the street. The first vendor on the right, 4 **Nay Lek Uan**, sells *gŏo·ay jáp nám săi*, an intensely peppery broth containing noodles and pork offal.

Returning to Th Yaowarat, turn right and continue until the next intersection. On the corner of Th Yaowaphanit and Th Yaowarat you'll see 5 **Mangkorn Khao**, a stall selling *bà·mèe* (Chinese-style wheat noodles) and barbecued pork.

Royal India INDIAN $$

(Map p78; 392/1 Th Chakkaraphet; mains 70-350B; ⌚10am-10pm; ❄✍; ⛴Saphan Phut/Memorial Bridge Pier, Pak Klong Taladd Pier) Yes, we're aware that this hole-in-the-wall has been in every edition of our guide since the beginning, but after all these years it's still the most reliable place to eat in Bangkok's Little India. Try any of the delicious breads or rich curries, and don't forget to finish with a homemade Punjabi sweet.

Riverside

Never Ending Summer THAI $$

(Map p80; ☎02 861 0953; www.facebook.com/TheNeverEndingSummer; 41/5 Th Charoen Nakhon; mains 140-350B; ⌚11am-2pm & 5-11pm Mon, 11am-11pm Tue-Sun; ❄; ⛴river-crossing ferry from River City Pier) The cheesy name doesn't do justice to this surprisingly sophisticated Thai restaurant located in a former warehouse by the river. Join Bangkok's beautiful crowd for antiquated Thai dishes such as cubes of watermelon served with a dry 'dressing' of fish, sugar and deep-fried shallots, or fragrant green curry with pork and fresh bird's-eye chilli.

Lord Jim's INTERNATIONAL $$$

(Map p80; ☎02 659 9000; www.mandarinoriental.com/bangkok/fine-dining/lord-jims; Mandarin Oriental Hotel, 48 Soi 40/Oriental, Th Charoen Krung; buffet 2050-2943B; ⌚noon-2.30pm Mon-Fri, 11.30am-3pm Sat, 11am-3pm Sun; ❄✍; ⛴Oriental Pier or hotel shuttle boat from Sathon/Central Pier) Even if you can't afford to stay at the Oriental, you should save up for the hotel's decadent riverside buffet. Dishes such as foie gras are standard, and weekends, when reservations are recommended, see additional seafood stations.

Silom & Sathon

Th Silom has a bit of everything, from old-school Thai to some of the city's best upscale international dining.

Chennai Kitchen INDIAN $

(Map p82; 107/4 Th Pan; mains 70-150B; ⌚10am-3pm & 6-9.30pm; ❄✍; **S** Surasak exit 3) This thimble-sized mom-and-pop restaurant puts out some of the best southern Indian vegetarian food in town. Yard-long *dosai* (a crispy southern Indian bread) is always a good choice, but if you're feeling indecisive (or exceptionally famished) go for the banana-leaf *thali* (set meal) that seems to incorporate just about everything in the kitchen.

Kalapapruek THAI $

(Map p82; 27 Th Pramuan; mains 90-330B; ⌚8am-6pm Mon-Sat, to 3pm Sun; ❄✍; **S** Surasak exit 3) This venerable Thai eatery has numerous branches and mall spin-offs around town, but we still fancy the original branch. The diverse menu spans Thai specialities from just about every region, daily specials and, occasionally, seasonal treats as well.

Somtam Convent NORTHEASTERN THAI $

('Hai'; Map p82; 2/4-5 Th Convent; mains 55-150B; ⌚11am-9pm Mon-Fri, to 5pm Sat; ❄; **M** Si Lom exit 2, **S** Sala Daeng exit 2) Northeastern-style Thai food is usually relegated to less-than-hygienic stalls perched by the side of the road with no menu or English-speaking staff in sight. A less intimidating introduction to the wonders of *lâhp* (a minced meat 'salad'), *sôm·đam* and other Isan delights can be had at this popular and long-standing restaurant.

Taling Pling THAI $$

(Map p82; Baan Silom, Soi 19, Th Silom; mains 110-275B; ⌚11am-10pm; ❄✍; **S** Surasak exit 3) Don't be fooled by the flashy interior; long-standing Taling Pling continues to serve a thick menu of homely, full-flavoured Thai dishes. It's a good starting point for rich, southern and central Thai fare such as *gaang kôo·a* (crabmeat curry with wild betel leaves), with tasty pies and cakes and refreshing drinks rounding out the choices.

Sushi Tsukiji JAPANESE $$

(Map p82; 62/19-20 Th Thaniya; sushi per item 60-700B; ⌚11.30am-2.30pm & 5.30-10.30pm; ❄; **M** Si Lom exit 2, **S** Sala Daeng exit 1) Our pick of the numerous Japanese joints along Th Thaniya is Tsukiji, named after Tokyo's famous seafood market. Dinner at this sleek sushi joint will leave a significant dent in the wallet, so instead come for lunch on a weekday, when Tsukiji does generous sushi sets for a paltry 297B.

★ **Eat Me** INTERNATIONAL $$$

(Map p82; ☎02 238 0931; www.eatmerestaurant.com; Soi Phiphat 2; mains 275-1400B; ⌚3pm-1am; ❄✍; **M** Si Lom exit 2, **S** Sala Daeng exit 2) The dishes here, with descriptions like 'charred whitlof and mozzarella salad with preserved lemon and dry aged Cecina beef' may sound all over the map or perhaps somewhat pretentious, but they're actually just plain tasty.

A casual-yet-sophisticated atmosphere, excellent cocktails, a handsome wine list, and some of the city's best desserts also make this one of our favourite places in Bangkok to dine.

Benjarong THAI $$$
(Map p82; ☎02 200 9000; www.dusit.com; ground fl, Dusit Thani Hotel, 946 Th Phra Ram IV; set lunch 650-750B, set dinner from 1700B, mains 390-1200B; ⏰11am-2.30pm & 6-10pm Mon-Fri, 6-10pm Sat; ❄; M Si Lom exit 3, S Sala Daeng exit 4) The Dusit Thani's signature Thai restaurant has emerged from a revamp with a sumptuous, decadent dining room and a new captain, the Danish chef Morten Nielsen. Not surprisingly, the dishes blend Western cooking techniques and Thai ingredients, with the occasional foray into other regions of Asia; think tasty twists such as 'crispy sweet pork ribs and salted Sriracha cabbage'.

Somboon Seafood CHINESE-THAI $$$
(Map p82; ☎02 233 3104; www.somboonseafood.com; cnr Th Surawong & Th Naradhiwas Rajanagarindra/Chong Nonsi; mains 120-900B; ⏰4-11.30pm; ❄; S Chong Nonsi exit 3) Somboon, a hectic seafood hall with a reputation far and wide, is known for doing the best curry-powder crab in town. Soy-steamed sea bass *(Ƀlah grà·pong nêung see·éw)* is also a speciality and, like all good Thai seafood, should be enjoyed with an immense platter of *kôw pàt Ƀoo* (fried rice with crab) and as many friends as you can gather together.

Lumphini Park & Th Phra Ram IV

Kai Thort Jay Kee NORTHEASTERN THAI $$
(Polo Fried Chicken; Map p86; 137/1-3 Soi Sanam Khli/Polo; mains 50-350B; ⏰11am-9pm; ❄; M Lumphini exit 3) Although the *sôm·đam*, sticky rice and *lâhp* of this former street stall give the impression of a northeastern-Thai-style eatery, the restaurant's namesake deep-fried bird is more southern in origin. Regardless, smothered in a thick layer of crispy deep-fried garlic, it is none other than a truly Bangkok experience.

★ **nahm** THAI $$$
(Map p86; ☎02 625 3388; www.comohotels.com/metropolitanbangkok/dining/nahm; ground fl, Metropolitan Hotel, 27 Th Sathon Tai/South; set lunch 550-1500B, set dinner 2300B, dishes 280-750B; ⏰noon-2pm Mon-Fri, 7-10.30pm daily; ❄; M Lumphini exit 2) Australian chef-author David Thompson is the man behind one of Bangkok's – and if you believe the critics, the world's – best Thai restaurants. Using ancient cookbooks as his inspiration, Thompson has given new life to previously extinct dishes with exotic descriptions such

BANGKOK'S VEGETARIAN RESTAURANTS

Vegetarianism is a growing trend among urban Thais, but meat-free restaurants are still generally few and far between.

Banglamphu has the greatest concentration of vegetarian-friendly restaurants, thanks to the preponderance of nonmeat-eating *fa·ràng* (foreigners). In this part of town, there's long-standing **Arawy Vegetarian Food** (Map p72; 152 Th Din So; mains from 30B; ⏰7am-8pm; 🖉; ⛴klorng boat to Phanfa Leelard Pier) and **May Kaidee's** (Map p72; www.maykaidee.com; 33 Th Samsen; mains 80-120B; ⏰9am-10pm; ❄🖉; ⛴Phra Athit/Banglamphu Pier), the latter with a vegetarian cookery school. Restaurants such as **Shoshana** (p118) and **Hemlock** (p118) have lots of meat-free options.

Elsewhere in Bangkok, **AJH Vegetarians** (Map p102; Banana Family Park, Th Phahonyothin; mains 15-30B; ⏰7am-2pm Tue-Sun; 🖉; S Ari exit 1), **Anotai** (Map p92; www.facebook.com/pages/Anotai/40116588503; 976/17 Soi Rama 9 Hospital, Th Phra Ram IX; mains 150-300B; ⏰10am-9.30pm Thu-Tue; ❄🖉; M Phra Ram 9 exit 3 & taxi), **Bonita Cafe & Social Club** (Map p82; 56/3 Th Pan; mains 160-250B; ⏰11am-10pm Wed-Mon; ❄📶🖉; S Surasak exit 3), **Chennai Kitchen** (p120), **Saras** (p124) and **Thamna** (Map p72; 175 Th Samsen; mains 90-190B; ⏰11am-3pm & 5-9pm Mon-Sat; ❄🖉; ⛴Thewet Pier) are all vegetarian-specific restaurants. As well, **Issaya Siamese Club** (p122), **Koko** (Map p88; 262/2 Soi 3, Siam Sq; mains 75-250B; ⏰11am-9pm; ❄🖉; S Siam exit 2) and stall C8 at the **MBK Food Island** (p124) offer a generous selection of meat-free menu items.

During the Vegetarian Festival in October, the whole city goes mad for tofu. Stalls and restaurants indicate their nonmeat menu with yellow banners; Chinatown has the highest concentration of stalls.

as 'smoked fish curry with prawns, chicken livers, cockles, chillies and black pepper'.

Dinner is best approached via the multi-course set meal, while lunch means *kà·nŏm jeen*, thin rice noodles served with curries.

If you're expecting bland, gentrified Thai food meant for foreigners, prepare to be disappointed. Reservations recommended.

Issaya Siamese Club THAI **$$$**
(Map p86; ☎02 672 9040; www.issaya.com; 4 Soi Sri Aksorn; mains 150-580B; ⏰11.30am-2.30pm & 6-10.30pm; ❄✍; Ⓜ Khlong Toei exit 1 & taxi) Housed in a charming 1920s-era villa, Issaya is Thai celebrity chef Ian Kittichai's first effort at a domestic outpost serving the food of his homeland. Dishes alternate between somewhat saucy, meaty items and lighter dishes using produce from the restaurant's organic garden.

The restaurant can be a bit tricky to find, and is best approached in a taxi via Soi Ngam Du Phli.

Siam Square & Pratunam

If you find yourself hungry in this part of central Bangkok, you're largely at the mercy of shopping-mall food courts and chain restaurants. However, this is still Thailand, and if you can ignore the prefabricated atmosphere, the food can often be quite good.

Nuer Koo CHINESE-THAI **$**
(Map p88; 4th fl, Siam Paragon, 991/1 Th Phra Ram I; mains 85-970B; ⏰11.30am-9.15pm; ❄; Ⓢ Siam exits 3 & 5) Is this the future of the noodle stall? Mall-bound Nuer Koo does a luxe version of the formerly humble bowl of beef noodles. Choose your cut of beef (including Kobe beef from Japan), enjoy the rich broth and cool air-con, and quickly forget about the good old days.

Somtam NORTHEASTERN THAI **$**
(Map p88; 392/14 Soi 5, Siam Sq; mains 75-120B; ⏰10.45am-9.30pm; ❄; Ⓢ Siam exit 4) It can't

LOCAL KNOWLEDGE

PONGTAWAT 'IAN' CHALERMKITTICHAI: BANGKOK CHEF

Pongtawat 'Ian' Chalermkittichai is a native of Bangkok, a former host of *Iron Chef: Thailand* and other television cookery programs, an author, the chef/owner of **Issaya Siamese Club** (p122) and perhaps most significantly, the inspiration for two flavours of Lay's potato chips.

What are the flavours of Bangkok food? Central Thai food is complex, it doesn't just have one level of flavour. It doesn't rely on ingredients that have very intense flavours. It's rich; curries in the central Thai region have coconut milk. And you can get any ingredients here: we're close to the sea so you can get seafood, and there's also freshwater fish and food from where the sea and rivers meet.

What are some classic Bangkok-style dishes? Curries served over rice; wok-fried dishes and Thai-Chinese dishes; lots of noodles, such as *pàt tai* or boat noodles. Some people still make royal Thai dishes, but these are really rare. One example is pomelo salad; it's very refreshing because of all the herbs and fresh ingredients, and has a nice texture from the pomelo and crispy fried shallots, and lots of flavour from chilli paste and kaffir lime leaf.

What are some good stalls and restaurants for Bangkok-style food? I like the boat noodles near Pratunam Pier; **Jay Fai** (p118) does a great crab omelette; **Krua Apsorn** (p116) does a good green curry with chicken, and a good fried *pàk kràchèt* (water mimosa; a type of vegetable).

What part of Bangkok is a good introduction to local food? Th Thong Lor has some good choices. There's a sticky rice vendor who's been there for 30 years, a good oyster omelette vendor, good braised duck noodles, and good restaurants such as **Soul Food Mahanakorn** (p125).

A good Bangkok market? I like to take people to **Wong Wian Yai Market** (Th Charoen Rat; ⏰5-10pm; Ⓢ Wongwian Yai exit 1). People call it the Lao Market because there's lots of stuff from the countryside, lots of herbs, and things like frogs, and some good seafood. There's also a lot of cooked food, as well as Thai-style snacks and sweets.

DON'T MISS

MAE NAM CHAO PHRAYA DINNER CRUISES

A dinner cruise along Mae Nam Chao Phraya is touted as an iconic Bangkok experience, and several companies cater to this. Yet it's worth mentioning that, in general, the vibe can be somewhat cheesy, with loud live entertainment and mammoth boats so brightly lit inside you'd never know you were on the water. The food, typically served as a buffet, usually ranges from mediocre to forgettable. But the atmosphere of the river at night, bordered by illuminated temples and skyscrapers, and the cool breeze chasing the heat away, is usually enough to trump all of this.

A good one-stop centre for all your dinner cruise needs is the **River City Boat Tour Check-In Center** (Map p80; www.rivercity.co.th; ground fl, River City, 23 Th Yotha; ⌚10am-10pm; Si Phraya/River City Pier, or shuttle boat from Sathon/Central Pier), where tickets can be purchased for **Grand Pearl** (02 861 0255; www.grandpearlcruise.com; 2000B; ⌚cruise 7.30-9.30pm; Si Phraya/River City Pier), **Chaophraya Cruise** (02 541 5599; www.chaophrayacruise.com; 1700B; ⌚cruise 7-9pm; Si Phraya/River City Pier), **Wan Fah** (02 622 7657; www.wanfah.in.th/eng/dinner; 1300B; ⌚cruise 7-9pm; Si Phraya/River City Pier), **Chao Phraya Princess** (02 860 3700; www.thaicruise.com; 1400B; ⌚cruise 7.50-9.50pm; Si Phraya/River City Pier) and **White Orchid** (02 438 8228; www.thairivercruise.com; 1400B; ⌚cruise 7.20-9.45pm; Si Phraya/River City Pier). All cruises depart from River City Pier; take a look at the websites to see exactly what's on offer.

For something slightly more upscale, consider **Manohra Cruises** (02 476 0022; www.manohracruises.com; adult 875-1250B, child 1750-2500B; hotel shuttle boat from Sathon/Central Pier). Taking place on a restored teak rice barge, this outfit is markedly classier, and serves what is probably the best food of Bangkok's various dinner cruises. It departs from Anantara Bangkok Riverside Resort & Spa, accessible via hotel shuttle boat from Sathon/Central Pier.

compete with the street stalls for flavour and authenticity, but if you need to be seen, particularly while in air-conditioned and trendy surroundings, this is a good place to sample northeastern Thai specialities. Expect a line at dinner.

Food Plus THAI $

(Map p88; btwn Soi 5 & Soi 6, Siam Sq; mains 30-70B; ⌚9am-3pm Tue-Sun; S Siam exit 2) This claustrophobic alleyway is bursting with the wares of several *ráhn kôw gaang* (rice and curry stalls). Everything is made ahead of time, so simply point to what looks tasty. You'll be hard-pressed to spend more than 100B, and the flavours are unanimously authentic and delicious.

Din Tai Fung CHINESE $$

(Map p88; 7th fl, CentralWorld, Th Ratchadamri; dishes 65-315B; ⌚11am-10pm; S Chit Lom exit 9 to Sky Walk, Siam exit 6 to Sky Walk) Most come to this lauded Taiwanese chain for the *xiao long bao*, broth-filled 'soup' dumplings. And so should you. But the other northern-Chinese-style dishes are just as good, and justify exploring the more remote regions of the menu.

Coca Suki CHINESE, THAI $$

(Map p88; 416/3-8 Th Henri Dunant; mains 98-788B; ⌚11am-11pm; S Siam exit 6) Immensely popular with Thai families, *sù·gêe* takes the form of a bubbling hotpot of broth and the raw ingredients to dip therein. Coca is one of the oldest purveyors of the dish, and this branch reflects the brand's efforts to appear more modern. Insider tip for fans of spice: be sure to request the tangy *tom yam* broth.

Sra Bua THAI $$$

(Map p88; 02 162 9000; www.kempinski.com/en/bangkok/siam-hotel/dining; ground fl, Siam Kempinski Hotel, 991/9 off Th Phra Ram I; mains 650-890B, set meals 1350-2700B; ⌚noon-3pm & 6-10.30pm; S Siam exits 3 & 5) Helmed by a Thai and a Dane whose Copenhagen restaurant, Kiin Kiin, snagged a Michelin star, Sra Bua takes a correspondingly international approach to Thai food. Putting local ingredients through the wringer of molecular gastronomy, the couple have created unconventional Thai dishes such as 'warm lobster with frozen curry pearls'. Reservations recommended.

DON'T MISS

BANGKOK'S BEST FOOD COURTS

The Siam Square area is home to some of Bangkok's biggest malls, which means that it's also home to more than its share of mall-based food courts. They're a great way to dip your toe in the sea of Thai food as they're generally cheap, clean, air-conditioned and have English-language menus. At most, paying is done by exchanging cash for vouchers or a temporary credit card at one of several counters; your change is refunded at the same desk.

MBK Food Island (Map p88; 6th fl, MBK Center, cnr Th Phra Ram I & Th Phayathai; mains 35-150B; 10am-10pm; ; National Stadium exit 4) Undergoing a renovation when we stopped by in 2015, the granddaddy of the genre is set to continue its offer of dozens of vendors selling Thai-Chinese, regional Thai and international dishes.

Gourmet Paradise (Map p88; ground fl, Siam Paragon, 991/1 Th Phra Ram I; mains 35-500B; 10am-10pm; ; Siam exits 3 & 5) The perpetually busy Gourmet Paradise unites international fast-food chains, domestic restaurants and food court–style stalls, with a particular emphasis on the sweet stuff.

Food Republic (Map p88; 4th fl, Siam Center, cnr Th Phra Ram I & Th Phayathai; mains 30-200B; 10am-10pm; ; Siam exit 1) The city's handsomest food court has a good mix of Thai and international (mostly Asian) outlets in an open, modern-feeling locale. We particularly fancied the Thai-Muslim dishes at the stall called 'Curry Rice'.

Food Loft (Map p88; www.centralfoodloft.com; 6th fl, Central Chidlom, 1027 Th Phloen Chit; mains 65-950B; 10am-10pm; ; Chit Lom exit 5) This department store pioneered the concept of the upscale food court, and mock-ups of the Indian, Italian, Japanese and other international cuisines aid in the decision-making process.

Eathai (Map p88; www.facebook.com/EathaibyCentral; basement, Central Embassy, 1031 Th Phloen Chit; mains 60-360B; 10am-10pm; ; Phloen Chit exit 5) This expansive new food court spans Thai – and only Thai – dishes from just about every corner of the country, including those from several famous Bangkok restaurants and stalls.

FoodPark (Map p88; 4th fl, Big C, 97/11 Th Ratchadamri; mains 30-90B; 9am-9pm; ; Chit Lom exit 9 to Sky Walk) The selections here may not inspire you to move East, but they are abundant and cheap, and are representative of the kind of 'fast food' Thais enjoy eating.

Sukhumvit

This seemingly endless ribbon of a road is where to go if, for the duration of a meal, you wish to forget that you're in Thailand.

Gokfayuen CHINESE $

(Map p92; www.facebook.com/wuntunmeen; 161/7 Soi Thong Lor 9; mains 69-139B; 11am-11.30pm; ; Thong Lo exit 3 & taxi) This new place has gone to great lengths to recreate classic Hong Kong dishes in Bangkok. Couple your (house-made) wheat-and-egg noodles with roasted pork, steamed vegetables with oyster sauce, or the Hong Kong–style milk tea.

Klang Soi Restaurant THAI $

(Map p92; Soi 49/9 Th Sukhumvit; mains 80-250B; 11am-2.30pm & 5-10pm Tue-Sun; ; Phrom Phong exit 3 & taxi) If you had a Thai grandma who lived in the Sukhumvit area, this is where she'd eat. The mimeographed menu spans old-school specialities from central and southern Thailand, as well as a few Western dishes.

Located at the end of Soi 49/9, in the Racquet Club complex.

Saras INDIAN $

(Map p92; www.saras.co.th; Soi 20, Th Sukhumvit; mains 90-200B; 9am-10.30pm; ; Sukhumvit exit 2, Asok exit 4) Describing your restaurant as a 'fast-food feast' may not be the cleverest PR move we've encountered, but it's a pretty spot-on description of this Indian restaurant. Order at the counter to be rewarded with crispy *dosai* (crispy southern Indian bread), meat-free regional set meals or rich curries (dishes are brought to your table). We wish all fast food could be this satisfying.

Game Over AMERICAN $$

(Map p92; www.gameover.co.th; Liberty Plaza, 1000/39 Soi 55/Thong Lor, Th Sukhumvit; mains 160-340B; 11.30am-2.30pm & 5.30-11.30pm Tue-

Sun, 5.30-11.30pm Mon; ❄; S Thong Lo exit 3 & taxi) Indulge your inner teen by playing *Call of Duty* while downing some of Bangkok's best burgers at this new video-game centre/restaurant. For the old at heart there's Scrabble and an impressive selection of imported microbrews.

★ Jidori-Ya Kenzou JAPANESE $$$
(Map p92; off Soi 26, Th Sukhumvit; dishes 60-350B; ⏲ 5pm-midnight Mon-Sat; ❄; S Phrom Phong exit 4) This cosy Japanese restaurant does excellent tofu dishes, delicious salads, and even delicious desserts; basically everything here is above average, but the highlight is the smoky, perfectly seasoned chicken skewers.

Little Beast INTERNATIONAL $$$
(Map p92; ☎ 02 185 2670; www.facebook.com/littlebeastbar; 44/9-10 Soi Thong Lor 13; mains 300-750B; ⏲ 5.30pm-1am Tue-Sat, 11am-4pm Sun; ❄ 📶; S Phrom Phong exit 3 & taxi) With influences stemming from modern American cuisine, Little Beast isn't very Bangkok, but it is very good. Expect meaty mains, satisfying salads and some of the best desserts in town (the ice-cream sandwiches alone are worth the visit).

Nasir Al-Masri MIDDLE EASTERN $$$
(Map p92; 4/6 Soi 3/1, Th Sukhumvit; mains 160-370B; ⏲ 24hr; ❄ 🖉; S Nana exit 1) One of several Middle Eastern restaurants on Soi 3/1, Nasir Al-Masri is easily recognisable by its floor-to-ceiling stainless steel 'theme'. Middle Eastern food often means meat, meat and more meat, but the menu here also includes several delicious vegie-based *mezze* (small dishes).

Bo.lan THAI $$$
(Map p92; ☎ 02 260 2962; www.bolan.co.th; 24 Soi 53, Th Sukhumvit; set meals 980-2680B; ⏲ noon-2.30pm & 7-10.30pm Thu-Sun, 11.30am-10.30pm Tue & Wed; ❄ 🖉; S Thong Lo exit 1) Upscale Thai is often more garnish than flavour, but Bo.lan has proven to be the exception. Bo and Dylan (Bo.lan is a play on words that also means 'ancient') take a scholarly approach to Thai cuisine, and generous set meals featuring full-flavoured Thai dishes are the results of this tuition (à la carte is not available; meat-free meals are). Reservations recommended.

Bei Otto GERMAN $$$
(Map p92; ☎ 02 260 0869; www.beiotto.com; 1 Soi 20, Th Sukhumvit; mains 185-995B; ⏲ 11am-midnight; ❄ 🖉; M Sukhumvit exit 2, S Asok exit 4) Claiming a Bangkok residence for more than 30 years, Bei Otto's major culinary bragging point is its pork knuckles, reputedly the best in town. A good selection of German beers and an attached delicatessen with brilliant breads and super sausages make it even more attractive to go Deutsch.

Soul Food Mahanakorn THAI $$$
(Map p92; ☎ 02 714 7708; www.soulfoodmahanakorn.com; 56/10 Soi 55/Thong Lor, Th Sukhumvit; mains 140-300B; ⏲ 5.30pm-midnight; ❄ 🖉; S Thong Lo exit 3) Soul Food gets its interminable buzz from its dual nature as both an inviting restaurant – the menu spans tasty interpretations of rustic Thai dishes – and a bar serving deliciously boozy, Thai-influenced cocktails. Reservations recommended.

Thewet & Dusit

While Thewet may lack in culinary diversity, it excels in riverfront views.

Khinlom Chom Sa-Phan THAI $$
(Map p96; ☎ 02 628 8382; www.khinlomchomsaphan.com; 11/6 Soi 3, Th Samsen; mains 95-2500B; ⏲ 11.30am-midnight; ⛴ Thewet Pier) Locals come to this open-air restaurant for the combination of riverfront views and tasty, seafood-based eats. It's popular, so be sure to call ahead to book a riverfront table.

Steve Café & Cuisine THAI $$
(Map p96; www.stevecafeandcuisine.com; 68 Soi 21, Th Si Ayuthaya; mains 160-390B; ⏲ 11.30am-2.30pm Mon-Fri, 11.30am-11pm Sat & Sun; ⛴ Tha Thewet) The cheesy name is seemingly a cover for this sophisticated, house-bound, riverside Thai restaurant. The menu spans a good selection of Thai dishes, and service is friendly and efficient, even when the place is mobbed.

To get here, enter Th Si Ayuthaya and walk through Wat Thevaratkunchong until you reach the river; locals will help point the way.

Ratchathewi

Tida Esarn NORTHEASTERN THAI $
(Map p98; 1/2-5 Th Rang Nam; mains 40-300B; ⏲ 10.30am-10.30pm; S Victory Monument exit 2) Tida Esarn sells country-style Thai food in a decidedly urban setting. Appropriately, foreigners provide the bulk of the restaurant's customers, but the kitchen still insists on serving full-flavoured Isan-style dishes such as *súp nòr mái,* a tart salad of shredded bamboo.

Pathé THAI, INTERNATIONAL **$$**
(Map p98; www.patherestaurant.com; 507 Th Ratchawithi; mains 94-275B; ⏲7am-midnight; ❄; S Victory Monument exit 4) The modern Thai equivalent of a 1950s-era American diner, this popular place combines solid Thai food, a fun atmosphere and a jukebox playing scratched records. The menu is equally eclectic, and combines Thai and Western dishes and ingredients; be sure to save room for the deep-fried ice cream.

North Bangkok

Khua Kling Pak Sod SOUTHERN THAI **$$**
(Map p102; ☎02 617 2553; www.khuaklingpaksod.com; 24 Soi 5, Th Phahonyothin; mains 150-380B; ⏲11am-2.30pm & 5.30-9.30pm; ❄; S Ari exit 1) Southern Thai is probably the country's spiciest regional cuisine, so if you're going to sweat over dinner, why not do so in white-tablecloth comfort. Recommended dishes include the eponymous *khua kling*, minced meat fried in an incendiary curry paste, or *moo hong*, fragrant, almost candy-like braised pork belly, a Chinese-Thai speciality of Phuket.

Fatbird INTERNATIONAL **$$**
(Map p102; ☎02 619 6609; www.facebook.com/fatbird; Soi 7/Ari, Th Phahonyothin; mains 160-300B; ⏲5.30pm-midnight Tue-Sun; ❄; S Ari exit 3) The dishes here, which range from tater tots to 'tom-yum-kung fried rice', don't quite cut it for dinner. But approach them as bar snacks, especially when combined with Fatbird's great drinks, eclectic shophouse atmosphere and fun soundtrack, and you have yourself a winner.

Drinking & Nightlife

Once infamous as an anything-goes nightlife destination, in recent years Bangkok has been edging towards teetotalism with strict regulations limiting the sale of alcohol and increasingly conservative closing times. Regardless, the city still boasts a fun bar and club scene, and there are diverse options if you find 2am too early to go to bed.

Bangkok's bars cover the spectrum from English-style pubs where you can comfortably sit with a pint and the paper to chic dens where the fair and beautiful go to be seen, not to imbibe. But many visitors associate Bangkok with the kind of watering holes that don't have an address – found just about everywhere in the city. Think streetside seating, plastic chairs, auto exhaust and tasty dishes that are absent-mindedly nibbled between toasts. Bangkok is also one of the few big cities in the world where nobody seems to mind if you slap a bar on the roof of a skyscraper. Most bars close at midnight, and smoking has been outlawed at all indoor (and some quasi-outdoor) entertainment places.

Bangkok's nightclub scene is as fickle as a ripe mango, and that really fun disco you found on your last trip a few years ago is most likely history today. To find out what is going on when you're in town, check listings rag **BK**, the *Bangkok Post* Friday supplement, **Guru**, or **Siam2nite** (www.siam2nite.com). Alternatively, check in with organisers of hugely popular DJ events such as **Dudesweet** (www.dudesweet.org) or **Paradise Bangkok** (www.facebook.com/paradisebangkok). Cover charges for nightclubs range from 100B to 800B and usually include a drink or two. Since 2004, authorities have ordered most of Bangkok's clubs to close by 1am. A complicated zoning system sees venues in designated 'entertainment areas', including Royal City Ave/RCA, Th Silom, and parts of Th Sukhumvit, open until 2am (sometimes as late as 3am), but even these 'later' licences are subject to police whimsy.

Ko Ratanakosin, Banglamphu & Thonburi

Romantic riverside drinking dominates the bar scene in Ko Ratanakosin, while rowdy Th Khao San is one of the city's best areas for a night out.

Hippie de Bar BAR
(Map p72; www.facebook.com/hippie.debar; 46 Th Khao San; ⏲3pm-2am; Phra Athit/Banglamphu Pier) Our vote for Banglamphu's best bar, Hippie boasts a funky retro vibe and indoor and outdoor seating, all set to the type of indie/pop soundtrack that you're unlikely to hear elsewhere in town. Despite being located on Th Khao San, there are surprisingly few foreign faces, and it's a great place to make some new Thai friends.

Madame Musur BAR
(Map p72; 41 Soi Ram Buttri; ⏲8am-1am; Phra Athit/Banglamphu Pier) Saving you the trip north to Pai, Madame Musur pulls off that elusive combination of 'northern Thailand meets *The Beach* meets Th Khao San'. It's a fun place to chat, drink and people-

DON'T MISS

BANGKOK'S BEST ROOFTOP BARS

In previous years, Bangkok's rooftop bars were largely the realm of well-heeled tourists, but nowadays they comprise a diverse spread, with options ranging from basic to formal. Yet it's worth noting that nearly all of Bangkok's hotel-based rooftop bars have strictly enforced dress codes barring access to those wearing shorts and/or sandals (even sparkly sandles, ladies – pack a pair of heels).

Moon Bar (Map p86; www.banyantree.com/en/web/banyantree/ap-thailand-bangkok/vertigo-and-moon-bar; 61st fl, Banyan Tree Hotel, 21/100 Th Sathon Tai/South; ⊙5pm-1am; M Lumphini exit 2) An alarmingly short barrier at this rooftop bar is all that separates one from the street, 61 floors down. Located on top of the Banyan Tree Hotel, Moon Bar claims to be among the highest alfresco bars in the world.

River Vibe (Map p80; 8th fl, River View Guesthouse, off Soi Charoen Phanit; ⊙7.30-11pm; Marine Department Pier, M Hua Lamphong exit 1 & taxi) Can't afford the overpriced cocktails at Bangkok's upscale rooftop bars? The excellent river views from the top of this guesthouse will hardly feel like a compromise.

Cloud 47 (Map p82; https://www.facebook.com/thecloud47; 47th fl, United Center, 323 Th Silom; ⊙5pm-1am; M Si Lom exit 2, S Sala Daeng exit 2) If you like a bit of elbow room – say, enough to hold a cricket match – consider this rooftopper. Spread out and enjoy live music and a location in the middle of the city's financial district, where there are impressively tall buildings in just about every direction.

Sky Bar (Map p80; www.lebua.com/sky-bar; 63rd fl, State Tower, 1055 Th Silom; ⊙6pm-1am; Sathon/Central Pier, S Saphan Taksin exit 3) Descend the Hollywood-like staircase to emerge at this bar that juts out over the Bangkok skyline and Chao Phraya River. Scenes from *The Hangover Part II* were filmed here, and while it doesn't come cheap, the bar's 'hangovertini' cocktail is actually quite drinkable.

Roof (Map p72; www.salaresorts.com/rattanakosin; 5th fl, Sala Rattanakosin, 39 Th Maha Rat; ⊙5pm-midnight Mon-Thu, to 1am Fri-Sun; Tien Pier) Although not as lofty as the others, the riverside Roof compensates with what is arguably Bangkok's best view of Wat Arun.

Park Society (Map p86; 29th fl, Sofitel So, 2 Th Sathon Neua/North; ⊙5pm-2am; M Lumphini exit 2) Gazing down at the green expanse of Lumphini Park, abruptly bordered by tall buildings on most sides, you can be excused for thinking that Bangkok almost, kinda, sorta feels like Manhattan. The drink prices at Park Society will also remind you of New York City, although there are monthly promotions.

Phra Nakorn Bar & Gallery (Map p72; www.facebook.com/Phranakornbarandgallery; 58/2 Soi Damnoen Klang Tai; ⊙6pm-1am; klorng boat to Phanfa Leelard Pier) In addition to charming views of old Bangkok, the breezy rooftop of this artsy bar also offers cheap and tasty Thai food.

Sky Train Jazz Club (Map p98; cnr Th Rang Nam & Th Phayathai; ⊙5pm-2am; S Victory Monument exit 2) An evening at this comically misnamed bar is more like chilling on the rooftop of your stoner buddy's flat than any jazz club we've ever been to. But there are indeed views of the BTS, jazz on occasion and a scrappy speakeasy atmosphere. To find it, look for the sign and proceed up the graffiti-strewn stairway until you reach the roof.

watch, and, serving a short menu of northern Thai dishes (from 100B to 200B), it's also not a bad place to eat.

The Club CLUB
(Map p72; www.facebook.com/theclubkhaosanbkk; 123 Th Khao San; admission 120B Fri & Sat; ⊙9pm-2am; Phra Athit/Banglamphu Pier) Located right in the middle of Th Khao San, this cavernlike dance hall hosts a good mix of locals and backpackers; check the Facebook page for upcoming events and guest DJs.

Center Khao Sarn BAR
(Map p72; Th Khao San; ⊙24hr; Phra Athit/Banglamphu Pier) The open-air terrace here offers ringside seats for the human parade along Th Khao San. The upstairs bar hosts late-night bands.

Rolling Bar BAR

(Map p72; Th Prachathipatai; ⏲5pm-midnight; ⛴klorng boat to Phanfa Leelard Pier) An escape from hectic Th Khao San is a good enough excuse to schlep to this quiet canalside boozer. Live music and salty bar snacks are reasons to stay.

Chinatown & Phahurat

Other than a few new bars on Soi Nana, there's little in the realm of non-dodgy nightlife in Bangkok's Chinatown. Instead, fuel up on street eats here first, then head to nearby Banglamphu or Silom for drinks.

★ Tep Bar BAR

(Map p78; www.facebook.com/TEPBAR; 69-71 Soi Nana; ⏲5pm-midnight Tue-Sun; Ⓜ Hua Lamphong exit 1) We never expected to find a bar this sophisticated – yet this fun – in Chinatown. Tep does it with a Thai-tinged, contemporary interior, tasty signature cocktails, Thai drinking snacks, and come Friday to Sunday, raucous live Thai music performances.

El Chiringuito BAR

(Map p78; ☎086 340 4791; www.facebook.com/elchiringuitobangkok; 221 Soi Nana; ⏲6pm-midnight Thu-Sun; Ⓜ Hua Lamphong exit 1) Come to this retro-feeling bar for sangria, Spanish gin and bar snacks, or the revolving art exhibitions. Opening hours can be sporadic, so call or check the Facebook page before heading out.

Silom & Sathon

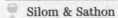

Lower Silom is Bangkok's gaybourhood, but the area as a whole has several fun bars and dance clubs for all comers.

Smalls BAR

(Map p86; 186/3 Soi Suan Phlu; ⏲8.30pm-late; Ⓜ Lumphini exit 2 & taxi) The kind of new bar that feels like it's been here forever, Smalls combines a cheekily decadent interior, an inviting rooftop and live music on Thursdays and Fridays. The eclectic house cocktails are strong, if sweet, and bar snacks range from rillettes to quesadillas.

Namsaah Bottling Trust BAR

(Map p82; www.namsaah.com; 401 Soi 7, Th Silom; ⏲5pm-2am; Ⓜ Si Lom exit 2, Ⓢ Sala Daeng exit 2) Namsaah is all about twists. From its home (a former mansion incongruously painted hot pink and decked out in a dark, clubby vibe), to the cocktails (classics with a tweak or two) and the bar snacks and dishes (think *pàt tai* with foie gras), everything's a little bit off in just the right way.

Tapas Room CLUB

(Map p82; 114/17-18 Soi 4, Th Silom; admission 100B; ⏲7pm-2am; Ⓜ Si Lom exit 2, Ⓢ Sala Daeng exit 1) Although it sits staunchly at the front of Bangkok's pinkest street, this long-standing two-level disco manages to bring in just about everybody. Come from Thursday to Saturday, when the combination of DJs and live percussion brings the body count to critical level.

LOCAL KNOWLEDGE

BANGKOK'S AFTER-HOURS SCENE

With most pubs and dance clubs closing around 2am, One Night in Bangkok is not quite what it used to be. Thankfully, there are a few places around town that have gained sufficient 'permission' to stay open until the morning hours.

Off Soi Ngam Duphli, **Wong's Place** (Map p86; 27/3 Soi Si Bamphen; ⏲9pm-late Tue-Sun; Ⓜ Lumphini exit 1), a long-standing backpacker bar, is so late-night it's best not to show up before midnight. Near Th Khao San, the elevated setting of **The Bank** (Map p72; 3rd fl, 44 Th Chakraphatdi Phong; ⏲6pm-late; ⛴Phra Athit/Banglamphu Pier) appears to lend it some leniency with the city's otherwise strict closing times. And in 'new' Bangkok, admittedly cheesy clubs such as **Club Insanity** (Map p92; www.clubinsanitybangkok.com; Soi 12, Th Sukhumvit; admission 200B; ⏲8pm-late; Ⓜ Sukhumvit exit 3, Ⓢ Asok exit 2), **Levels** (Map p92; www.levelsclub.com; 6th fl, Aloft, 35 Soi 11, Th Sukhumvit; admission 500B; ⏲9pm-late; Ⓢ Nana exit 3), **Mixx** (Map p88; www.mixx-discotheque.com/bangkok; basement, InterContinental Hotel, 973 Th Phloen Chit; admission 300B; ⏲10pm-2am; Ⓢ Chit Lom exit 7), **Narz** (Map p92; www.narzclubbangkok.net; 112 Soi 23; admission from 400B; ⏲9pm-2am; Ⓜ Sukhumvit exit 2, Ⓢ Asok exit 3) and **Scratch Dog** (Map p92; basement, Windsor Suites Hotel, 8-10 Soi 20, Th Sukhumvit; admission 400B; ⏲midnight-late; Ⓜ Sukhumvit exit 2, Ⓢ Asok exit 4) employ a Top 40 hip-hop and R&B soundtrack to propel partiers into the morning hours.

Cé La Vi CLUB

(Map p82; www.kudeta.com/bangkok; 38th & 39th fl, Sathorn Square Complex, 98 Th Sathon Neua/North; 11am-1am Mon-Thu, to 3am Fri & Sat; S Chong Nonsi exit 1) Spanning multiple bars, three restaurants and two clubs, the formerly named Ku Dé Ta remains the biggest thing on Bangkok's club scene – literally and figuratively. Expect an entry fee of 500B after 10pm on Fridays and Saturdays.

Riverside

Viva & Aviv BAR

(Map p80; www.vivaaviv.com; ground fl, River City, 23 Th Yotha; 11am-midnight; Si Phraya/River City Pier) An enviable riverside location, casual open-air seating and a funky atmosphere make this restaurant-ish bar a contender for one of Bangkok's best sunset cocktail destinations.

Maggie Choo's BAR

(Map p80; www.facebook.com/maggiechoos; basement, Novotel Bangkok Fenix Silom, 320 Th Silom; 7.30pm-2am Sun-Thu, to 3am Fri & Sat; S Surasak exit 1) A former bank vault with a Chinatown opium-den vibe, secret passageways and lounging women in silk dresses. With all this going on, it's easy to forget that Maggie Choo's is actually a bar, although you'll be reminded by the creative and somewhat sweet cocktails, and a crowd that blends selfie-snapping locals and curious tourists.

Siam Square & Pratunam

Bangkok's most central zone is home to just a handful of bars.

Co-Co Walk BAR

(Map p88; 87/70 Th Phayathai; 5pm-midnight; S Ratchathewi exit 2) This covered compound is a loud, messy smorgasbord of pubs, bars and live music popular with Thai university students on a night out. We'd list a few specific bars here, but they'd most likely all have changed names by the time you read this – it's just that kinda place.

Hyde & Seek BAR

(Map p92; www.hydeandseek.com; ground fl, Athenee Residence, 65/1 Soi Ruam Rudi; 11am-1am; S Phloen Chit exit 4) The English-inspired bar snacks and meals here have earned Hyde & Seek the right to call itself a gastropub. But we reckon the real reasons to come are one of Bangkok's best liquor cabinets and some of the city's most sophisticated cocktails.

Sukhumvit

This long street is home to Bangkok's most sophisticated bars and clubs.

★WTF BAR

(Map p92; www.wtfbangkok.com; 7 Soi 51, Th Sukhumvit; 6pm-1am Tue-Sun; ; S Thong Lo exit 3) Wonderful Thai Friendship (what did you think it stood for?) is a funky and friendly neighbourhood bar that also packs in a gallery space. Arty locals and resident foreigners come for the old-school cocktails, live music and DJ events, poetry readings, art exhibitions and tasty bar snacks. And we, like them, give WTF our vote for Bangkok's best bar.

Tuba BAR

(Map p66; www.facebook.com/tubabkk; 34 Room 11-12 A, Soi Thong Lor 20/Soi Ekamai 21; 11am-2am; S Ekkamai exit 1 & taxi) Part storage room for over-the-top vintage furniture, part restaurant, part friendly local boozer; this quirky bar certainly doesn't lack in diversity – nor fun. Indulge in a whole bottle (they'll hold onto it if you don't finish it) and don't miss the moreish chicken wings or the delicious deep-fried *lâhp* (a tart/spicy salad of minced meat).

Sugar Ray BAR

(Map p66; www.facebook.com/pages/Sugar-Ray-Youve-Just-Been-Poisoned/234918586711793; off Soi Ekamai 21; 8pm-2am Wed, Fri & Sat; S Ekkamai exit 1 & taxi) Run by a team of fun and funky Thai dudes who make flavoured syrups, Sugar Ray is a fun, funky hidden bar serving fun, funky cocktails; think an Old Fashioned made with aged rum, orange and cardamom syrup, and garnished with a piece of caramelised bacon.

Badmotel BAR

(Map p92; www.facebook.com/badmotel; 331/4-5 Soi 55/Thong Lor, Th Sukhumvit; 5pm-1am; S Thong Lo exit 3 & taxi) Badmotel blends the modern and the kitschy, the cosmopolitan and the Thai, in a way that has struck a nerve among Bangkok hipsters. This is manifested in drinks that combine Hale's Blue Boy, a Thai childhood drink staple, with rum, and bar snacks such as *naam prik ong* (a northern Thai-style dip), here served with pappadams.

Studio Lam BAR

(Map p92; www.facebook.com/studiolambangkok; Soi 51, Th Sukhumvit; 6pm-1am Tue-Sun; S Thong Lo exit 3) This new venue is an extension of uberhip record label ZudRangMa, with a Jamaican-style sound system custom-built for world and retro-Thai DJ sets and the occasional live show. Its Thai-influenced signature drinks bring Studio Lam to the present day.

Grease CLUB
(Map p92; www.greasebangkok.com; 46/12 Soi 49, Th Sukhumvit; ⏲6pm-2am Mon-Sat; S Phrom Phong exit 3 & taxi) Bangkok's youngest-feeling, hottest nightclub is also one of its biggest – you could get lost here in the four floors of dining venues, lounges and dance floors.

Cheap Charlie's BAR
(Map p92; Soi 11, Th Sukhumvit; ⏲4.30-11.45pm Mon-Sat; S Nana exit 3) There's never enough seating, and the design concept is best described as 'junkyard', but on most nights this chummy, open-air beer corner is a great place to meet everybody from package tourists to resident English teachers.

Arena 10 CLUB
(Map p92; Soi Thong Lor 10/Soi Ekamai 5; S Ekkamai exit 2 & taxi) This open-air entertainment zone is the destination of choice for Bangkok's young and beautiful – for the moment at least. **Demo** (www.facebook.com/demobangkok; Arena 10, Soi Thong Lor 10/Soi Ekamai 5; ⏲9pm-2am; S Ekkamai exit 2 & taxi) combines blasting beats and a NYC warehouse vibe, while **Funky Villa** (www.facebook.com/funkyvillabkk; Arena 10, Soi Thong Lor 10/Soi Ekamai 5; ⏲7pm-2am; S Ekkamai exit 2 & taxi), with its outdoor seating and Top 40 soundtrack, is more chilled.

There's a 400B entrance fee for foreigners on Friday and Saturday.

Glow CLUB
(Map p92; 96/415 Soi Prasanmit; admission from 350B; ⏲10pm-1am Mon-Wed, 10pm-3am Thu, 10pm-4am Fri & Sat; M Sukhumvit exit 2, S Asok exit 3) This self-proclaimed 'boutique' club starts things early in the evening as a lounge boasting an impressive spectrum of vodkas. As the evening progresses, enjoy tunes ranging from hip hop (Fridays) to electronica (Saturdays) and everything in between.

Nung-Len CLUB
(Map p92; www.nunglen.net; 217 Soi 63/Ekamai, Th Sukhumvit; ⏲6pm-1am Mon-Sat; S Ekkamai exit 1 & taxi) Young, loud and Thai, Nung-Len (literally 'sit and chill') is a popular den of live music and uni students on buzzy Th Ekamai. Get there before 10pm or you won't get in at all.

☆ Entertainment

Shame on you if you find yourself bored in Bangkok. The city's nightlife is as diverse as that of virtually any modern city, with a whole realm of options that don't contain the term 'go-go'. And even if you're usually in bed by 10pm, Bangkok still offers interesting post-dinner diversions, from flash cinemas to traditional cultural performances.

Gà·teu·i Cabaret

Over the last few years, *gà·teu·i* (trans women, also spelt *kathoey*) cabaret has emerged to become a staple of the Bangkok tourist

LGBT BANGKOK

Bangkok is so gay it makes San Francisco look like rural Texas. With out-and-open nightspots and annual pride events, the city's LGBT community enjoys an unprecedented amount of tolerance considering attitudes in the rest of the region. It should be mentioned, however, that recent years have seen a sharp rise in HIV and other STDs among gay men in Bangkok; when in town, be sure to play it safe.

Local listings mags such as BK (www.bk.asia-city.com) can point you in the direction of the bars and clubs that are hot when you're in town. The Lesbian Guide to Bangkok (www.bangkoklesbian.com) is the only English-language tracker of the lesbian scene.

Lower Th Silom is Bangkok's unofficial gaybourhood, and highlights include tiny Soi 2, which is lined with dance clubs such as **DJ Station** (Map p82; www.dj-station.com; 8/6-8 Soi 2, Th Silom; admission from 150B; ⏲10pm-2am; M Si Lom exit 2, S Sala Daeng exit 1), the busiest and arguably most famous gay nightclub in Thailand, if not Asia. Virtually next door is Soi 2/1 where bars like **G.O.D** (Guys on Display; Map p82; Soi 2/1; admission 280B; ⏲8pm-late; M Si Lom exit 2, S Sala Daeng exit 1) are not averse to a little shirtless dancing. A more casual scene is found on Soi 4, home to long-standing streetside bars **Balcony** (Map p82; www.balconypub.com; 86-88 Soi 4, Th Silom; ⏲5.30pm-2am; 📶; M Si Lom exit 2, S Sala Daeng exit 1) and **Telephone** (Map p82; www.telephonepub.com; 114/11-13 Soi 4, Th Silom; ⏲6pm-1am; 📶; M Si Lom exit 2, S Sala Daeng exit 1).

BANGKOK'S SILVER SCREENS

Movies are a fantastic deal in Bangkok. At 120B, the ticket price is a fraction of what you'd pay for a seat at home, the theatres are almost all new, and best of all, you can drink beer.

But the Thais didn't stop there. With its 16 screens and 3000-plus seats, few can rival **Paragon Cineplex** (Map p88; 02 129 4635; www.paragoncineplex.com; 5th fl, Siam Paragon, 991/1 Th Phra Ram I; S Siam exits 3 & 5). In addition to Thailand's largest IMAX screen, the options here include the Blue Ribbon Screen, a cinema with a maximum of 72 seats, where you're plied with pillows, blankets, complimentary snacks and drinks, and of course, a 15-minute massage; and Enigma, where in addition to a sofa-like love seat designed for couples, you'll be served cocktails and food (as well as blankets and a massage).

The retro-inclined can opt for the old-school standalone theatres across the street at Siam Sq, including **Scala** (Map p88; 02 251 2861; Soi 1, Siam Sq; S Siam exit 2) and **Lido** (02 252 6498; www.apexsiam-square.com; btwn Soi 2 & Soi 3, Siam Sq; S Siam exit 2). For something artsy, there's RCA's **House** (Map p92; www.houserama.com; 3rd fl, RCA Plaza, RCA/Royal City Ave; M Phetchaburi exit 1 & taxi), or for something really cosy, the eight-seat **Friese-Green Club** (FGC; Map p92; 087 000 0795; www.facebook.com/pages/The-Friese-Greene-Club/371737282944797; 259/6 Soi 22, Th Sukhumvit; S Phrom Phong exit 6).

Nearly all movies in Thailand offer screenings with English subtitles. All films are preceded by the Thai royal anthem and everyone is expected to stand respectfully for its duration. And despite the heat and humidity on the streets, keep in mind that all of Bangkok's movie theatres pump the air-con with such vigour that a jumper is an absolute necessity – unless you're going Blue Ribbon class, that is.

circuit. **Calypso Bangkok** (Map p66; 02 688 1415; www.calypsocabaret.com; Asiatique, Soi 72-76, Th Charoen Krung; admission adult/child 900/600B; show times 8.15pm & 9.45pm; shuttle ferry from Sathon/Central Pier), **Mambo Cabaret** (Map p66; 02 294 7381; 59/28 Yannawa Tat Mai; tickets 800-1000B; show times 7.15pm & 8.30pm; S Chong Nonsi exit 2 & taxi) and **Playhouse Theater Cabaret** (Map p88; 02 215 0571; www.playhousethailand.com; 5 Ratchadapisek Rd, Chompol Sub-District, Chatuchak; admission adult/child 1200/600B; show times 7pm & 8.20pm; S Ratchathewi exit 1) host choreographed stage shows featuring Broadway high kicks and lip-synched pop tunes.

Go-Go Bars

Although technically illegal, prostitution is fully 'out' in Bangkok, and the influence of organised crime and healthy kickbacks mean that it will be a long while before the existing laws are ever enforced. Yet, despite the image presented by much of the Western media, the underlying atmosphere of Bangkok's red-light districts is not necessarily one of illicitness and exploitation (although these factors do inevitably exist); rather, it has an aura of tackiness and boredom.

Patpong (Map p82; Th Phat Phong & Soi Phat Phong 2; 4pm-2am; M Si Lom exit 2, S Sala Daeng exit 1), arguably one of the world's most famous red-light districts, earned its notoriety during the 1980s for its wild sex shows involving everything from ping-pong balls to razors to midgets on motorbikes. Today it is more of a circus for curious spectators than real sex tourists. These days, **Soi Cowboy** (Map p92; Soi Cowboy; 4pm-2am; M Sukhumvit exit 2, S Asok exit 3) and **Nana Entertainment Plaza** (Map p92; Soi 4, Th Sukhumvit; 4pm-2am; S Nana exit 2) are the real scenes of sex for hire.

Live Music

Music is an essential element of a Thai night out, and just about every pub worth its salted peanuts has a house band. For the most part this means perky Thai pop covers or tired international standards (if you've left town without having heard a live version of *Hotel California,* you haven't really been to Bangkok), but an increasing number of places are starting to deviate from the norm with quirky and/or inspired bands and performances.

★ **Brick Bar** LIVE MUSIC

(Map p72; www.brickbarkhaosan.com; basement, Buddy Lodge, 265 Th Khao San; admission 150B Sat & Sun; 8pm-1.30am; Phra Athit/Banglamphu Pier) This basement pub, one of our fave destinations in Bangkok for live music,

WORTH A TRIP

RCA/ROYAL CITY AVENUE

By day a bland-looking strip of offices, come Friday and Saturday nights, Royal City Avenue – known to everybody as RCA – transforms into one of Bangkok's most popular nightlife zones. Although some of the bigger clubs can draw thousands, keep in mind that they often require an ID check and also maintain a dress code (no shorts, sandals).

The easiest way to approach RCA is via taxi from the MRT stop at Phra Ram 9; taxis generally can't enter RCA itself, so you'll have to U-turn or cross busy Th Phet Uthai on foot. Some standout venues:

Onyx (Map p92; www.facebook.com/onyxbkk; RCA/Royal City Ave; admission from 400B; 8pm-3.30am; M Phra Ram 9 exit 3 & taxi) Probably the most sophisticated club along RCA – evidenced by the hefty entry fee and the coiffed and coddled clientele. Check the Facebook page for upcoming DJ events.

The Beer Cap (Map p92; www.facebook.com/beercapbkk; 21/66 RCA/Royal City Ave; 6pm-2am; M Phra Ram 9 exit 3 & taxi) The beats and bright lights of EDM not your thing? Prefer craft beer to vodka shots? Then head to this casual beer bar with heaps of imported brews.

Route 66 (Map p92; www.route66club.com; 29/33-48 RCA/Royal City Ave; admission 300B; 8pm-2am; M Phra Ram 9 exit 3 & taxi) This vast club has been around just about as long as RCA has, but frequent facelifts and expansions have kept it relevant. Top 40 hip-hop rules the main space here, although there are several different themed 'levels', featuring anything from Thai pop to live music.

Taksura (Map p92; RCA/Royal City Ave; 6pm-2am; M Phra Ram 9 exit 3 & taxi) If you're fuelling up for the clubs, the spicy *gàp glâem* (Thai drinking snacks) here won't disappoint.

hosts a nightly revolving cast of bands for an almost exclusively Thai crowd – many of whom will end the night dancing on the tables. Brick Bar can get infamously packed, so be sure to get there early.

★ Parking Toys — LIVE MUSIC

(Map p66; 02 907 2228; www.parkingtoys.in.th; 17/22 Soi Mayalap, off Kaset-Navamin Hwy; 4pm-2am; M Chatuchak Park exit 2 & taxi, S Mo Chit exit 3 & taxi) One of Bangkok's best venues for live music, Parking Toys hosts an eclectic revolving cast of fun bands ranging in genre from rockabilly to electro-funk jam acts.

Living Room — LIVE MUSIC

(Map p92; 02 649 8888; www.thelivingroomat bangkok.com/en; Level 1, Sheraton Grande Sukhumvit, 250 Th Sukhumvit; 6pm-midnight; M Sukhumvit exit 3, S Asok exit 2) Don't let looks deceive you: every night this bland hotel lounge transforms into the city's best venue for live jazz. True to the name, there's comfy, sofa-based seating, all of it within earshot of the music. Enquire ahead of time to see which sax master or hide-hitter is in town.

Lam Sing — LIVE MUSIC

(Map p66; www.facebook.com/iSanLamSing; 57/5 Th Phet Phra Ram; 9.30pm-4am; S Ekkamai exit 1 & taxi) Even Ziggy Stardust–era David Bowie has nothing on this dark, decadent, rhinestone-encrusted den, one of Bangkok's best venues for *mŏr lam* and *lôok tûng*, music with roots in Thailand's rural northeast. Come for raucous live-music performances accompanied by tightly choreographed, flagrantly costumed backup dancers.

There's no English-language sign here, but most taxi drivers are familiar with the place.

Tawandang German Brewery — LIVE MUSIC

(Map p66; www.tawandang.co.th; cnr Th Phra Ram III & Th Naradhiwas Rajanagarindra/Chong Nonsi; 5pm-1am; S Chong Nonsi exit 2 & taxi) It's Oktoberfest all year round at this hangar-sized music hall. The Thai-German food is tasty, the house-made brews are entirely potable, and the nightly stage shows make singing along a necessity. Music starts at 8.30pm.

Titanium — LIVE MUSIC

(Map p92; www.titaniumbangkok.com; 2/30 Soi 22, Th Sukhumvit; 8pm-1am; S Phrom Phong exit 6) Many come to this cheesy 'ice bar' for the chill, the skimpily dressed working girls and the flavoured vodka, but we come for Unicorn, the all-female house band, who rock the house every night from 9.30pm to 12.30am.

Saxophone Pub & Restaurant LIVE MUSIC
(Map p98; www.saxophonepub.com; 3/8 Th Phayathai; 7.30pm-1.30am; S Victory Monument exit 2) After nearly 30 years, Saxophone remains Bangkok's premier live-music venue – a dark, intimate space where you can pull up a chair just a few metres away from the band and see their every bead of sweat. If you prefer some mystique in your musicians, watch the blues, jazz, reggae or rock from the balcony.

Ad Here the 13th LIVE MUSIC
(Map p72; www.facebook.com/adhere13thbluesbar; 13 Th Samsen; 6pm-midnight; Phra Athit/Banglamphu Pier) Located beside Khlong Banglamphu/Khlong Rob Krung, this closet-sized blues bar is everything a neighbourhood joint should be: lots of regulars, cold beer and heart-warming tunes delivered by a masterful house band (starting at 10pm). Everyone knows each other, so don't be shy about mingling.

Brown Sugar LIVE MUSIC
(Map p72; www.brownsugarbangkok.com; 469 Th Phra Sumen; 5pm-1am Tue-Thu, to 2am Sat & Sun; klorng boat to Phanfa Leelard Pier, Phra Athit/Banglamphu Pier) This long-standing, live music staple has found a cosy new home in old Bangkok. The live music starts at 8pm most nights.

Bamboo Bar LIVE MUSIC
(Map p80; 02 236 0400; www.mandarinoriental.com/bangkok/fine-dining/the-bamboo-bar; ground fl, Mandarin Oriental, 48 Soi 40/Oriental, Th Charoen Krung; 5pm-1am Sun-Thu, to 2am Fri & Sat; Oriental Pier or hotel shuttle boat from Sathon/Central Pier) Recently renovated and looking better than ever, the Oriental's Bamboo Bar remains one of the city's premier locales for live jazz. The music starts at 9pm nightly.

Raintree LIVE MUSIC
(Map p98; Soi Ruam Chit; 6pm-1am Mon-Sat; S Victory Monument exit 2) This rustic pub is one of the few remaining places in town to hear 'songs for life', Thai folk music with roots in the political movements of the 1960s and '70s. Tasty bar snacks also make it a clever place to have a bite to eat.

Traditional Arts

National Theatre THEATRE
(Map p72; 02 224 1342; 2 Th Ratchini; tickets 60-100B; Chang Pier, Maharaj Pier, Phra Chan Tai Pier) The National Theatre holds performances of *kŏhn* (masked dance-drama based on stories from the *Ramakian*) at 2pm on the first and second Sundays of the month from January to September, and *lá·kon* (Thai dance-dramas) at 2pm on the first and second Sundays of the month from October to December. Tickets go on sale an hour before performances begin.

Sala Chalermkrung THEATRE
(Map p78; 02 222 0434; www.salachalermkrung.com; 66 Th Charoen Krung; tickets 800-1200B; shows 7.30pm Thu & Fri; Saphan Phut/Memorial Bridge Pier, M Hua Lamphong exit 1 & taxi) This art deco Bangkok landmark, a former cinema dating to 1933, is one of the few remaining places *kŏhn* can be witnessed. The traditional Thai dance-drama is enhanced here by laser graphics, high-tech audio and English subtitles. Concerts and other events are also held; check the website for details.

Sala Rim Naam THEATRE
(Map p80; 02 437 3080; www.mandarinoriental.com/bangkok/fine-dining/sala-rim-naam; Mandarin Oriental Hotel, Soi 40/Oriental, Th Charoen Krung; tickets adult/child 1999/1700B; dinner & show 8.15-9.30pm; Oriental Pier or hotel shuttle boat from Sathon/Central Pier) The historic Mandarin Oriental hosts dinner theatre in a sumptuous Thai pavilion located across the river in Thonburi. The price is well above the average, reflecting the means of the hotel's client base, but the performance gets positive reviews.

Thai Boxing (Moo·ay tai)

Thai boxing's best of the best fight it out at Bangkok's two boxing stadiums: **Lumpinee Boxing Stadium** (02 282 3141; www.muaythailumpinee.net/en; 6 Th Ramintra; tickets 3rd-class/2nd-class/ringside 1000/1500/2000B; M Chatuchak Park exit 2 & taxi, S Mo Chit exit 3 & taxi) and **Ratchadamnoen Stadium** (off Th Ratchadamnoen Nok; tickets 3rd-class/2nd-class/ringside 1000/1500/2000B; Thewet Pier, S Phaya Thai exit 3 & taxi). You'll note that tickets are not cheap, and these prices are exponentially more than what Thais pay. To add insult to injury, the inflated price offers no special service or seating, and at Ratchadamnoen Stadium foreigners are sometimes corralled into an area with an obstructed view. As long as you are mentally prepared for the financial jabs from the promoters, you'll be better prepared to enjoy the real fight.

PATPONG

Super Pussy! Pussy Collection! The neon signs leave little doubt about the dominant industry in Patpong, arguably the world's most infamous strip of go-go bars and clubs running 'exotic' shows. There is enough skin on show in Patpong to make Hugh Hefner blush, and a trip to the upstairs clubs could mean you'll never look at a ping-pong ball or a dart the same way again.

For years opinion on Patpong has been polarised: some see it as an exploitative, immoral place that is the very definition of sleaze, for others a trip to Bangkok is about little more than immersing themselves in planet Patpong. But Patpong has become such a caricature of itself that in recent times a third group has emerged: the curious tourist. Whatever your opinion, what you see in Patpong or in any of Bangkok's other high-profile 'adult entertainment' areas depends as much on your personal outlook on life as on the quality of your vision.

Prostitution is technically illegal in Thailand but there are as many as 2 million sex workers, the vast majority of whom – women and men – cater to Thai men. Many come from poorer regional areas, such as Isan in the northeast, while others might be students helping themselves through university. Sociologists suggest Thais often view sex through a less moralistic or romantic filter than Westerners. That doesn't mean Thai wives like their husbands using prostitutes, but it's only recently that the gradual empowerment of women through education and employment has led to a more vigorous questioning of this very widespread practice.

Patpong actually occupies two soi that run between Th Silom and Th Surawong in Bangkok's financial district. The two streets are privately owned by – and named for – the Thai-Chinese Patpongpanich family, who bought the land in the 1940s and initially built Th Phat Phong and its shophouses; Soi Phat Phong 2 was laid later. During the Vietnam War the first bars and clubs opened to cater to American soldiers on 'R&R'. The scene and its international reputation grew through the '70s and peaked in the '80s, when official Thai tourism campaigns made the sort of 'sights' available in Patpong a pillar of their marketing.

These days Patpong has mellowed considerably, if not matured. Thanks in part to the popular night market that fills the street after 5pm, it draws so many tourists that it has become a sort of sex theme park. There are still plenty of stereotypical middle-aged men ogling pole dancers, sitting in dark corners of the so-called 'blow-job bars' and paying 'bar fines' to take girls to hotels that charge by the hour. But you'll also be among other tourists and families who come to see what all the fuss is about.

Most tourists go no further than stolen glances into the ground-floor go-go bars, where women in bikinis drape themselves around stainless-steel poles. Others will be lured to the dimly lit upstairs clubs by men promising sex shows. But it should be said that the so-called erotic shows usually feature bored-looking women performing acts that feel not so much erotic as demeaning to everyone involved. Several of these clubs are also infamous for their scams, usually involving the nonperforming (ie clothed, if just barely) staff descending on wide-eyed tourists like vultures on fresh meat. Before you know it you've bought a dozen drinks, racked up a bill for thousands of baht, and followed up with a loud, aggressive argument flanked by menacing-looking bouncers and threats of 'no money, no pussy!'

Fights are held throughout the week, alternating between the two stadiums. Ratchadamnoen, Bangkok's oldest and most venerable venue, hosts matches on Monday, Wednesday and Thursday from 6.30pm to around 11pm, and Sunday at 3pm and 6.30pm. Lumpinee, in a new building far north of the city centre, hosts matches on Tuesdays and Fridays from 6.30pm to 11pm, and on Saturdays from 4pm to 8.30pm and 9pm to 12.30am. Aficionados say the best-matched bouts are reserved for Tuesday nights at Lumphini and Thursday nights at Ratchadamnoen. There is a total of eight to 10 fights of five rounds apiece. The stadiums don't usually fill up until the main events, which normally start around 8pm or 9pm.

There are English-speaking 'staff' standing outside the stadiums who will practically tackle you upon arrival. Although there have been a few reports of scamming, most of these assistants help steer visitors to the foreigner ticket windows and hand out a fight roster; they can also be helpful in telling you which fights are the best match-ups between contestants. (Some say that welterweights, between 135lb and 147lb, ie 61.2kg and 66.7kg, are the best.) To keep everyone honest, though, remember to purchase tickets from the ticket window, not from a person outside the stadium.

As a prematch warm-up, grab a plate of *gài yâhng* (grilled chicken) and other northeastern dishes from the restaurants surrounding the Ratchadamnoen Stadium.

Shopping

Welcome to a true buyer's market. Home to one of the world's largest outdoor markets, numerous giant upscale malls and sidewalk-clogging bazaars on nearly every street, it's impossible not to be awed by the amount of commerce in Bangkok. However, despite the apparent scope and variety, Bangkok really excels in one area when it comes to shopping: cheap stuff. Although luxury items and brand names are indeed available in Bangkok, prices are high, and you'll find much better deals at online warehouses in the US or bargain-basement sales in Hong Kong. Ceramics, dirt-cheap T-shirts, fabric, Asian knick-knackery and yes, if you can deal with the guilt, pirated items, are Bangkok's bargains.

The difficulty is finding your way around, since the city's intense urban tangle sometimes makes orientation difficult. A good shopping companion is *Nancy Chandler's Map of Bangkok,* with annotations on all sorts of small and out-of-the-way shopping venues and *đà·làht* (markets).

Antiques

Real Thai antiques are rare and costly. Most Bangkok antique shops keep a few authentic pieces for collectors, along with lots of pseudo-antiques or traditionally crafted items that look like antiques.

River City ANTIQUES

(Map p80; www.rivercity.co.th; 23 Th Yotha; ⏲10am-10pm; ⛴Si Phraya/River City Pier, or shuttle boat from Sathon/Central Pier) Several upscale art and antique shops occupy the 3rd and 4th floors of this riverside mall, but, as with many antique stores in Bangkok, the vast majority of pieces appear to come from Myanmar and, to a lesser extent, Cambodia.

A free shuttle boat to River City departs from Sathon/Central Pier every 30 minutes, from 10am to 8pm.

House of Chao ANTIQUES

(Map p82; 9/1 Th Decho; ⏲9.30am-7pm; S Chong Nonsi exit 3) This three-storey antique shop, appropriately located in an antique shophouse, has everything necessary to deck out your fantasy colonial-era mansion. Particularly interesting are the various weather-worn doors, doorways, gateways and trellises that can be found in the covered area behind the showroom.

Department Stores & Shopping Centres

Bangkok may be crowded and polluted, but its department stores are modern oases of order. They're also downright frigid, and Sunday afternoons see a significant part of Bangkok's population crowding into the city's indoor malls to take advantage of the air-con. By no accident, the BTS stations also

THE WAR ON THE GEM SCAM

We're begging you, if you aren't a gem trader, don't buy unset stones in Thailand – full stop. Countless tourists are sucked into the prolific and well-rehearsed gem scam in which they are taken to a store by a helpful stranger and tricked into buying bulk gems that can supposedly be resold in their home country for 100% profit. The expert con artists (part of a well-organised cartel) seem trustworthy and convince tourists they need a citizen of the country to circumvent tricky customs regulations. Guess what, the gem world doesn't work like that, and what most tourists end up with are worthless pieces of glass. By the time you sort all this out, the store has closed, changed names and the police can do little to help.

Want to know more or want to report a scam? Visit 2bangkok.com and navigate down to the 'Gem Scam' page for years' worth of tracking the phenomenon. The tourist police can also help to resolve some purchase disputes, but don't expect miracles.

have shaded walkways delivering passengers directly into nearby stores without ever having to set foot on ground level.

The selection is surprisingly good at Bangkok's shopping centres, but don't expect any bargains – most imported items cost more than they would elsewhere. Another quirk is that shop assistants follow you around the store from rack to rack. This is the definition of Thai 'service' rather than an indication that they've sniffed you out as a shoplifter. And be sure you're satisfied with an item, as returns are largely unheard of. Most shopping centres are open from 10am to 10pm.

★MBK Center SHOPPING CENTRE
(Map p88; www.mbk-center.com; cnr Th Phra Ram I & Th Phayathai; ⏲10am-10pm; S National Stadium exit 4) This colossal shopping mall underwent an extensive renovation in 2015 and is set to retain its role as one of Bangkok's top attractions. On any given weekend, half of Bangkok's residents (and most of its tourists) can be found here combing through a seemingly inexhaustible range of small stalls and shops that span a whopping eight floors.

MBK is Bangkok's cheapest place to buy mobile phones and accessories (4th floor). It's also one of the better places to stock up on camera gear (ground floor and 5th floor), and the expansive food court (6th floor) is one of the best in town.

Siam Paragon SHOPPING CENTRE
(Map p88; www.siamparagon.co.th; 991/1 Th Phra Ram I; ⏲10am-10pm; S Siam exits 3 & 5) As much air-conditioned urban park as it is a shopping centre, in addition to shops Siam Paragon is home to Siam Ocean World (p101), Paragon Cineplex (p131) and Gourmet Paradise (p124), a huge basement-level food court. On the 3rd floor is Kinokuniya, Thailand's largest English-language bookstore.

CentralWorld SHOPPING CENTRE
(Map p88; www.centralworld.co.th; Th Ratchadamri; ⏲10am-10pm; S Chit Lom exit 9 to Sky Walk, Siam exit 6 to Sky Walk) Spanning eight storeys of more than 500 shops and 100 restaurants, CentralWorld is one of Southeast Asia's largest shopping centres. In addition to an ice rink, you'll find an extra-huge branch of bookstore B2S, and you could spend an hour sniffing around the fragrances at Karmakamet on the 3rd floor.

Terminal 21 SHOPPING CENTRE
(Map p92; www.terminal21.co.th; cnr Th Sukhumvit & Soi 21/Asoke; ⏲10am-10pm; M Sukhumvit exit 3, S Asok exit 3) Seemingly catering to a Thai need for wacky objects to be photographed in front of, this new mall is worth a visit for the spectacle as much as the shopping. Start at the basement-level 'airport' and proceed upwards through 'Paris', 'Tokyo' and other city-themed floors. Who knows, you might even buy something.

Central Chidlom SHOPPING CENTRE
(Map p88; www.central.co.th; 1027 Th Phloen Chit; ⏲10am-10pm; S Chit Lom exit 5) Generally regarded as the country's best department store for quality and selection, Central has 13 branches across Bangkok in addition to this, the chain's chichi flagship.

Fashion & Textiles

In recent years Bangkok has become something of a fashion-conscious and, increasingly, fashion-generating city. Local designers such as Senada Theory, Flynow and Tango have shown the city harbours a style scene that can compete on the international catwalk. More affordable looks are exhibited by the city's trendy teens who strut their distinctive 'Bangkok' style in the various shopping areas.

★Siam Square SHOPPING CENTRE
(Map p88; Th Phra Ram I; ⏲11am-9pm; S Siam exits 2, 4 & 6) This open-air shopping zone is ground zero for teenage culture in Bangkok. Pop music blares out of tinny speakers, and gangs of hipsters in various costumes ricochet between fast-food restaurants and closet-sized boutiques. It's a great place to pick up labels and designs you're guaranteed not to find anywhere else, though most outfits require a barely there waistline.

Siam Center SHOPPING CENTRE
(Map p88; www.siamcenter.co.th; Th Phra Ram I; ⏲10am-9pm; S Siam exit 1) Siam Center, Thailand's first shopping centre, was built in 1976 but, since a recent nip and tuck, hardly shows its age. Its 3rd floor is one of the best locations to check out established local labels such as Flynow III, Senada Theory and Tango.

Baiyoke Garment Center CLOTHING
(Map p88; cnr Th Phetchaburi & Th Ratchaprarop; ⏲10am-10pm; klorng boat to Pratunam Pier, S Ratchathewi exit 4) This rabbit warren of stalls is the undisputed epicentre of Bangkok's garment district. The vendors spill

ONE NIGHT IN BANGKOK... IS NOT ENOUGH TO HAVE A SUIT MADE

Many tourists arrive in Bangkok with the notion of getting clothes custom-tailored at a bargain price, which is entirely possible. Prices are almost always lower than what you'd pay at home, but common scams ranging from commission-hungry túk-túk *(pronounced đúk đúk)* drivers to shoddy workmanship and inferior fabrics make bespoke tailoring in Bangkok a potentially disappointing investment. To maximise your chances of walking away feeling (and looking) good, read on.

You get what you pay for If you sign up for a suit, two pants, two shirts and a tie, with a couple of silk ties thrown in for US$169 (a very popular offer in Bangkok), the chances are it will look and fit like a sub-US$200 wardrobe. And although an offer may seem great on the surface, the price may fluctuate significantly depending on the fabric you choose.

Have a good idea of what you want If it's a suit you're after, should it be single- or double-breasted? How many buttons? What style trousers? Of course, if you have no idea then the tailor will be more than happy to advise. Alternatively, bring a favourite garment from home and have it copied.

Set aside a week to get clothes tailored Shirts and trousers can often be turned around in 48 hours or less with only one fitting, but no matter what a tailor may tell you, it takes more than one and often more than two fittings to create a good suit. Most reliable tailors will ask for two to five sittings. Any tailor who can sew your order in less than 24 hours should be treated with caution.

Reputable tailors include:

Pinky Tailors (Map p88; www.pinkytailor.com; 888/40 Mahatun Plaza, Th Phloen Chit; ⌚10am-7pm Mon-Sat; S Phloen Chit exits 2 & 4) Custom-made shirts and suit jackets have been Mr Pinky's speciality for more than 35 years. Located behind the Mahatun Building.

July (Map p82; ☎02 233 0171; www.julytailor.com; 30/6 Th Sala Daeng; ⌚9am-6pm Mon-Sat; M Si Lom exit 2, S Sala Daeng exit 4) Tailor to Thailand's royalty and elite alike, the suits here don't come cheap and the cuts can be somewhat conservative, but the quality is unsurpassed.

Marco Tailors (Map p88; 430/33 Soi 7, Siam Sq; ⌚9am-7pm Mon-Fri; S Siam exit 2) Dealing solely in men's suits, this long-standing and reliable tailor has a wide selection of banker-sensibility wools and cottons.

Duly (Map p92; ☎02 662 6647; www.laladuly.co.th; Soi 49, Th Sukhumvit; ⌚10am-7pm; S Phrom Phong exit 1) High-quality Italian fabics and experienced tailors make Duly one of the best places in Bangkok to commission a sharp shirt.

Raja's Fashions (Map p92; ☎02 253 8379; www.rajasfashions.com; 160/1 Th Sukhumvit; ⌚10.30am-8pm Mon-Sat; S Nana exit 4) One of Bangkok's more famous tailors, Raja's gets a mixed bag of reviews, but the majority swear by the service and quality.

Nickermann's (Map p92; ☎02 252 6682; www.nickermanns.net; basement, Landmark Hotel, 138 Th Sukhumvit; ⌚10am-8.30pm Mon-Sat, noon-6pm Sun; S Nana exit 2) Corporate ladies rave about Nickermann's tailor-made power suits: pants and jackets that suit curves and busts. Formal ball gowns are another area of expertise.

from the covered market area to dozens of nearby shops selling similarly cheap T-shirts, bags and other no-brand clothing items.

Jim Thompson HANDICRAFTS
(Map p82; www.jimthompson.com; 9 Th Surawong; ⌚9am-9pm; M Si Lom exit 2, S Sala Daeng exit 3) The surviving business of the international promoter of Thai silk, the largest Jim Thompson shop sells colourful silk handkerchiefs, place mats, wraps and cushions. The styles and motifs appeal to older, somewhat more conservative tastes.

Platinum Fashion Mall CLOTHING
(Map p88; www.platinumfashionmall.com; Th Phetchaburi; ⌚9am-8pm; klorng boat to Pratunam Pier, S Ratchathewi exit 4) Linked with Bangkok's garment district, which lies just north across Th Phetchaburi, this five-storey mall is stocked with an enormous selection of cheap, no-name couture.

Handicrafts, Souvenirs & Decor

The tourist markets have tonnes of factory-made pieces that pop up all along the tourist route. The shopping centres sell products with a little better quality at proportionally higher prices, but the independent shops sell the best items all round.

A bimonthly **Thai Craft Fair** (Map p92; www.thaicraft.org; 3rd fl, Jasmine City Bldg, cnr Soi 23 & Th Sukhumvit; ⏲10am-3pm; M Sukhumvit exit 2, S Asok exit 3) is held in Bangkok, featuring the wares of more than 60 Thai artisans.

Heritage Craft HANDICRAFTS
(Map p72; 35 Th Bamrung Meuang; ⏲11am-6pm Mon-Fri; klorng boat to Phanfa Leelard Pier) Handicrafts with a conscience: this new boutique is an atmospheric showcase for the quality domestic wares of ThaiCraft (p138), some of which are produced via fair trade practices. Items include silks from Thailand's northeast, baskets from the south and jewellery from the north, and there's also an inviting on-site cafe.

Shop @ TCDC HANDICRAFTS
(Map p92; www.tcdc.or.th/shop; 5th fl, Emporium, cnr Soi 24 & Th Sukhumvit; ⏲10.30am-9pm Tue-Sun; S Phrom Phong exit 2) This shop, attached to the TCDC design library/museum, is a great place to pick up one-of-a-kind souvenirs, such as fragrant soaps and candles, kitchen aprons resembling Thai boxing shorts, unique postcards and cheeky housewares – all dreamt up by Thai designers.

Narai Phand SOUVENIRS
(Map p88; www.naraiphand.com; ground fl, President Tower, 973 Th Phloen Chit; ⏲10am-8pm; S Chit Lom exit 7) Souvenir-quality handicrafts are given fixed prices and comfortable air-conditioning at this government-run facility. You won't find anything here that you haven't already seen at all of the tourist street markets, but it is a good stop if you're pressed for time or are spooked by haggling.

Markets

Although air-conditioned malls have better PR departments, open-air markets are the true face of commercial Bangkok, and are where you'll find the best bargains.

Markets are best approached as sights rather than shopping destinations.

★**Chatuchak Weekend Market** MARKET
(ตลาดนัดจตุจักร, Talat Nat Jatujak; Map p102; www.chatuchak.org; Th Phahonyothin; ⏲9am-6pm Sat & Sun; M Chatuchak Park exit 1, Kamphaeng Phet exits 1 & 2, S Mo Chit exit 1) Among the largest markets in the world, Chatuchak seems to unite everything buyable, from used vintage sneakers to baby squirrels. Plan to spend a full day here, as there's plenty to see, do and buy. But come early, ideally around 10am, to beat the crowds and the heat.

There is an information centre and a bank with ATMs and foreign-exchange booths at the **Chatuchak Park Office** near the northern end of the market's Soi 1, Soi 2 and Soi 3. Schematic maps and toilets are located throughout the market.

On Friday nights from around 8pm to midnight, several vendors, largely those selling clothing, accessories and food, open up shop in Chatuchak. There are a few vendors on weekday mornings, and a daily vegetable, plant and flower market opposite the market's southern side. One section of the latter, known as the **Or Tor Kor Market** (องค์กรตลาดเพื่อเกษตรกร; Map p102; Th Kamphaengphet 1; ⏲8am-6pm; M Kamphaeng Phet exit 3), sells fantastically gargantuan fruit and seafood, and has a decent food court as well.

Once you're deep in the bowels of Chatuchak, it will seem like there is no order and no escape, but the market is arranged into relatively coherent sections. Use the clock tower as a handy landmark.

➡ ***Antiques, Handicrafts & Souvenirs***
Section 1 is the place to go for Buddha statues, old LPs and other random antiques. More secular arts and crafts, such as musical instruments and hill-tribe items, can be found in Sections 25 and 26. **Baan Sin Thai** (Section 24, Stall 130, Soi 1, Chatuchak Weekend Market, Th Phahonyothin; ⏲9am-6pm Sat-Sun; M Kamphaeng Phet exits 1 & 2, Chatuchak Park exit 1, S Mo Chit exit 1) sells a mixture of *kŏhn* masks and old-school Thai toys, all of which make fun souvenirs, and **Kitcharoen Dountri** (Section 8, Stall 464, Chatuchak Weekend Market, Th Phahonyothin; ⏲9am-6pm Sat-Sun; M Chatuchak Park exit 1, Kamphaeng Phet exits 1 & 2, S Mo Chit exit 1) specialises in Thai musical instruments, including flutes, whistles, drums and CDs of classical Thai music. Other quirky gifts include the lifelike plastic Thai fruit and vegetables at **Marché** (Section 17, Stall 254, Soi 1), or their scaled-down miniature counterparts nearby at **Papachu** (Section 17, Stall 23, Chatuchak Weekend Market, Th Phahonyothin;

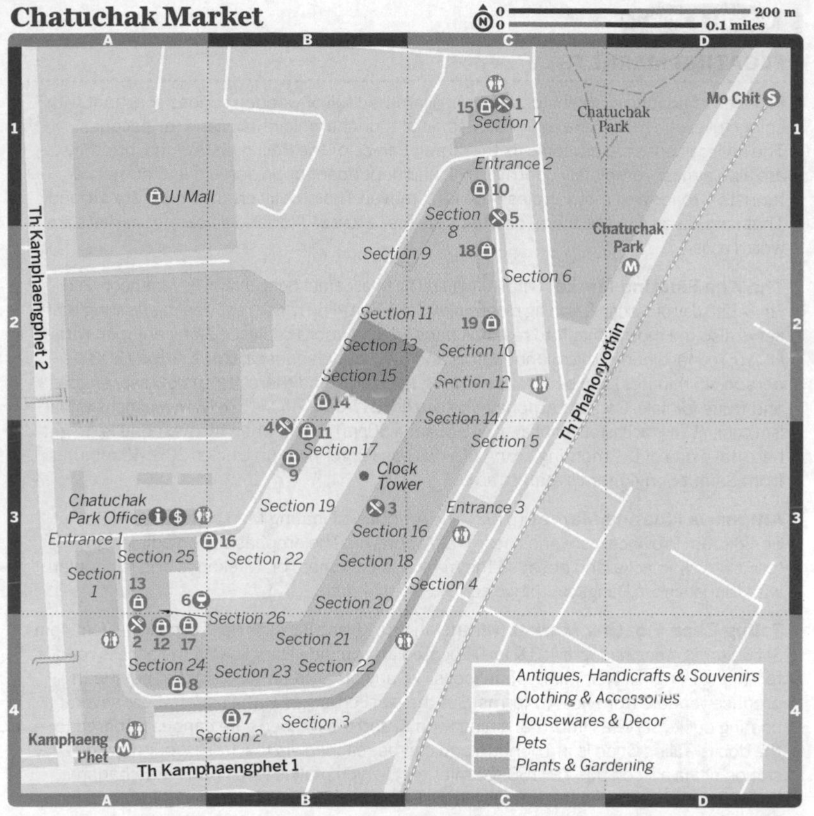

Chatuchak Market

Eating

1 Café Ice C1
2 Foontalop A4
3 Saman Islam B3
4 Toh-Plue B3
5 Viva 8 ....C1

Drinking & Nightlife

6 Viva's A3

Shopping

7 AnyaDharu Scent Library B4
8 Baan Sin Thai A4
9 D-narn B3
10 Kitcharoen Dountri C1
11 Marché B3
12 Meng A4
13 Orange Karen Silver A3
14 Papachu B2
15 Pariwat A-nantachina C1
16 PL Bronze B3
17 Spice Boom A4
18 Ton-Tan C2
19 Tuptim Shop C2

9am-6pm Sat-Sun; M Chatuchak Park exit 1, Kamphaeng Phet exits 1 & 2, S Mo Chit exit 1).

Clothing & Accessories

Clothing dominates most of Chatuchak, starting in Section 8 and continuing through the even-numbered sections to 24. Sections 5 and 6 deal in used clothing for every Thai youth subculture, from punks to cowboys, while Soi 7, where it transects Sections 12 and 14, is heavy on the more underground hip-hop and skate fashions. Somewhat more sophisticated independent labels can be found in Sections 2 and 3, while tourist-sized clothes and textiles are in Sections 8 and 10.

WORTH A TRIP

FLOATING MARKETS

Pictures of floating markets (*đà·làht nám*) jammed full of wooden canoes pregnant with colourful exotic fruits have defined the official tourist profile of Thailand for decades. The idyllic scenes are as iconic as the Grand Palace or the Reclining Buddha, but they are also almost completely contrived for, and dependent upon, foreign and domestic tourists – roads and motorcycles have long moved Thais' daily errands onto dry ground. That said, if you can see them for what they are, a few of Thailand's floating markets are worth a visit.

Tha Kha Floating Market (ตลาดน้ำท่าคา; Tha Kha, Samut Songkhram; ⏲7am-noon, 2nd, 7th & 12th day of waxing & waning moons plus Sat & Sun) The most 'real'-feeling floating market is also the most difficult to reach. A handful of vendors coalesce along an open rural *klorng* (canal) lined with coconut palms and old wooden houses. **Boat rides** (20B per person, 45 minutes) can be arranged along the canal, and there are lots of tasty snacks and fruits for sale. Contact Amphawa's **tourist office** (☎034 752847; www.amphawatourism.com; 71 Th Prachasret, Amphawa; ⏲8.30am-4.30pm) to see when the next one is. To get here, take one of the morning *sŏrng·tăa·ou* (passenger pick-up trucks, 20B, 45 minutes) from Samut Songkhram's market area.

Amphawa Floating Market (p152) The Amphawa Floating Market, located in Samut Songkhram Province, convenes near Wat Amphawa. The emphasis is on edibles and tourist knick-knacks, and because the market is only there on weekends and is popular with tourists from Bangkok, things can get pretty hectic.

Taling Chan Floating Market (ตลาดน้ำตลิ่งชัน; Khlong Bangkok Noi, Thonburi; ⏲7am-4pm Sat & Sun; S Wongwian Yai exit 3 & taxi) Located just outside Bangkok on the access road to Khlong Bangkok Noi, Taling Chan looks like any other fresh-food market busy with produce vendors from nearby farms. But the twist emerges at the canal where several floating docks serve as informal dining rooms, and the kitchens are canoes tethered to the docks. Taling Chan is in Thonburi and can be reached via taxi from Wongwian Yai BTS station or via air-con bus 79 (16B, 25 minutes), which makes stops on Th Ratchadamnoen Klang. Long-tail boats from any large Bangkok pier can also be hired for a trip to Taling Chan and the nearby Khlong Chak Phra.

Damnoen Saduak Floating Market (ตลาดน้ำดำเนินสะดวก; Damnoen Saduak, Ratchaburi; ⏲7am-noon) This 100-year-old floating market – the country's most famous – is now essentially a floating souvenir stand filled with package tourists. This in itself can be a fascinating insight into Thai culture, as the vast majority of tourists here are Thais, and watching the approach to this cultural 'theme park' is instructive. But beyond the market, the residential canals are quite peaceful and can be explored by hiring a boat (per person 100B) for a longer duration. Trips stop at small family businesses, including a Thai candy maker, a pomelo farm and a knife crafter. Air-con bus 79, with stops on Th Ratchadamnoen Klang, and **minivans** (off Th Phayathai; S Victory Monument exit 3) from the Victory Monument both connect to the Southern Bus Terminal in Thonburi, from where you can find buses to Damnoen Saduak (80B, two hours, frequent from 6am to 9pm).

Don Wai Market (ตลาดดอนหวาย; Don Wai, Nakhon Pathom; ⏲6am-6pm) Not technically a swimmer, this market claims a riverbank location in Nakhon Pathom Province, having originally started out in the early 20th century as a floating market for pomelo and jackfruit growers and traders. As with many tourist attractions geared towards Thais, the main attraction is food, including fruit, traditional sweets and *bèt pah·lóh* (five-spice stewed duck), which can be consumed aboard large boats that cruise Mae Nam Nakhorn Chaisi (60B, one hour). The easiest way to reach Don Wai Market is to take a minibus (45B, 35 minutes) from beside Central Pinklao in Thonburi.

For accessories, several shops that are situated in Sections 24 and 26, such as **Orange Karen Silver** (Section 26, Stall 229, Soi 34/8,), specialise in chunky silver jewellery and semiprecious uncut stones.

➡ *Eating & Drinking*

Lots of Thai-style eating will stave off Chatuchak rage (cranky behaviour brought on by dehydration or hunger), and numerous food stalls set up shop between Sections 6 and 8. Long-standing standouts include **Foontalop** (Section 26, Stall 319, no roman-script sign; mains 20-70B; ⏲10am-6pm Sat-Sun), a popular Isan restaurant; **Café Ice** (Section 7, Stall 267; mains 250-490B; ⏲10am-6pm Sat-Sun), a Western-Thai fusion joint that does good, if overpriced, *pàt tai* (fried noodles) and tasty fruit shakes; **Toh-Plue** (opposite Section 17; mains 150-400B; ⏲noon-8pm Sat & Sun), which does all the Thai standards; and **Saman Islam** (Section 16, Stall 34, Soi 24; mains 40-100B; ⏲10am-6pm Sat-Sun), a Thai-Muslim restaurant that serves a tasty chicken biryani. **Viva 8** (www.facebook.com/Viva8JJ; Section 8, Stall 371; mains 150-300B; ⏲9am-10pm Sat & Sun) features a DJ and, when we stopped by, a chef making huge platters of paella. And as evening draws near, down a beer at **Viva's** (Section 26, Stall 161; ⏲10am-10pm Sat & Sun), a cafe-bar with live music.

➡ *Housewares & Decor*

The western edge of the market, particularly Sections 8 to 26, specialises in all manner of housewares, from cheap plastic buckets to expensive brass woks. This area is a particularly good place to stock up on inexpensive Thai ceramics, ranging from celadon to the traditional rooster-themed bowls from Lampang.

PL Bronze (Section 25, Stall 185, Soi 4; ⏲9am-6pm Sat & Sun) has a huge variety of stainless-steel flatware, and **Ton-Tan** (Section 8, Stall 460, Soi 15/1; ⏲9am-6pm Sat & Sun) deals in coconut- and sugar-palm-derived plates, bowls and other utensils.

Those looking to spice up the house should stop by **Spice Boom** (Section 26, Stall 246, Soi 8; ⏲9am-6pm Sat & Sun), where you can find dried herbs and spices for both consumption and decoration. Other notable olfactory indulgences include the handmade soaps, lotions, salts and scrubs at **D-narn** (Section 19, Stall 203, Soi 1; ⏲9am-6pm Sat & Sun), and the fragrant perfumes and essential oils at **AnyaDharu Scent Library** (Section 3, Stall 3, Soi 43/2; ⏲9am-6pm Sat-Sun).

For less utilitarian goods, Section 7 is a virtual open-air gallery – we particularly liked **Pariwat A-nantachina** (Section 7, Stall 117, Soi 63/3; ⏲9am-6pm Sat-Sun) for Bangkok-themed murals. Several shops in Section 10, including **Tuptim Shop** (Section 10, Stall 261, Soi 19; ⏲9am-6pm Sat-Sun), sell new and antique Burmese lacquerware. **Meng** (Section 26, Stall 195, Soi 8; ⏲9am-6pm Sat-Sun) features a dusty mish-mash of quirky antiques from both Thailand and Myanmar.

➡ *Pets*

Puppies and kittens are sold in Sections 13 and 15. Soi 9 of the former features several shops that deal solely in clothing for pets. It's also worth noting that this section has, in the past, been associated with the sale of illegal wildlife, although much of this trade has been driven underground.

➡ *Plants & Gardening*

The interior perimeter of Sections 2 to 4 feature a huge variety of potted plants, flowers, herbs, fruits, and the accessories needed to maintain them. Many of these shops are also open on weekday afternoons.

★ Talat Rot Fai — MARKET

(ตลาดรถไฟ; www.facebook.com/taradrodfi; Soi 51, Th Srinakharin; ⏲6pm-1am Thu-Sun; S Udom Suk exit 2 & taxi) The emphasis at this night market is on the retro, from vintage clothes to kitschy antiques. And with stalls and food trucks, VW-van-based bars and land-bound pubs, and even a few hipster barber shops, it's also much more than just a shopping destination.

If this isn't enough vintage for you, consider the recently opened and slightly smaller (yet more convenient to reach) **Talat Rot Fai 2** (Map p102; Esplanade Complex, 99 Th Ratchadaphisek; ⏲6pm-1am Thu-Sun; S Thailand Cultural Centre exit 4), on Th Ratchadaphisek. To get here, take the MRT to Thailand Cultural Centre and walk through the Esplanade mall.

★ Thanon Khao San Market — SOUVENIRS

(Map p72; Th Khao San; ⏲10am-midnight; ⛴ Phra Athit/Banglamphu Pier) The main guesthouse strip in Banglamphu is a day-and-night shopping bazaar peddling all the backpacker 'essentials': foul-mouthed T-shirts, bootleg MP3s, hemp clothing, fake student ID cards, knock-off designer wear, selfie sticks, orange juice and, of course, those croaking wooden frogs.

OFF THE BEATEN TRACK

MARKETS AS SIGHTS

Even if you don't have a shopping list, several of Bangkok's produce and wholesale markets are well worth a visit. Here are some of our favourites:

Pak Khlong Talat (ปากคลองตลาด, Flower Market; Map p78; Th Chakkaraphet; 24hr; Pak Klong Taladd Pier, Saphan Phut/Memorial Bridge Pier) This sprawling wholesale flower market has become a tourist attraction in its own right. The endless piles of delicate orchids, rows of roses and stacks of button carnations are a sight to be seen, and the shirtless porters wheeling blazing piles of colour set the place in motion. The best time to come is late at night, when the goods arrive from upcountry.

Nonthaburi Market (ตลาดนนทบุรี; Map p66; Tha Nam Nonthaburi, Nonthaburi; 5-9am; Nonthaburi Pier) Exotic fruits, towers of dried chillies, smoky grills and the city's few remaining rickshaws form a very un-Bangkok backdrop at this, one of the most expansive and atmospheric produce markets in the area. Come early though, as most vendors are gone by 9am. To get to the market, take the Chao Phraya Express Boat to Nonthaburi Pier, the northernmost stop for most lines. The market is a two-minute walk east along the main road from the pier.

Sampeng Lane (สำเพ็ง; Map p78; Soi Wanit 1; 8am-6pm; Ratchawong Pier, M Hua Lamphong exit 1 & taxi) This crowded wholesale market runs roughly parallel to Th Yaowarat, bisecting the two districts of Chinatown and Phahurat. Pick up the narrow artery from Th Ratchawong and follow it through its many manifestations – from handbags, homewares, hair decorations, stickers, Japanese-animation gear and plastic beeping key chains.

Khlong Toey Market (ตลาดคลองเตย; Map p92; cnr Th Ratchadaphisek & Th Phra Ram IV; 5-10am; M Khlong Toei exit 1) This wholesale market, one of the city's largest, is inevitably the origin of many of the meals you'll eat during your stay in Bangkok. Although some corners of the market can't exactly be described as photogenic, you'll still want to bring a camera to capture the cheery fishmongers and stacks of durians. Get there early, ideally before 10am, when most vendors have already packed up and left.

Asiatique MARKET
(Map p66; www.thaiasiatique.com; Soi 72-76, Th Charoen Krung; 4-11pm; shuttle boat from Sathon/Central Pier) One of Bangkok's more popular night markets, Asiatique takes the form of warehouses of commerce next to Mae Nam Chao Phraya. Expect clothing, souvenirs and quite a few dining and drinking venues.

To get here, take one of the frequent, free shuttle boats from Sathon/Central Pier that run from 4pm to 11.30pm.

Bang Nam Pheung Market MARKET
(ตลาดบางน้ำผึ้ง; Map p66; Bang Kachao, Phrapradaeng; 8am-3pm Sat & Sun; S Bang Na exit 2 & taxi) An easy escape from the city, this buzzy, weekends-only market is located on the Phrapradaeng Peninsula, a vast rural-feeling district. Because it's a Thai market, the emphasis is on food, and it's a great place for unrestrained outdoor snacking.

To get there, take the BTS to Bang Na and jump in a taxi for the short ride to the pier at Wat Bang Na Nork. From there, take the river-crossing ferry (4B) followed by a short motorcycle taxi (10B) ride.

Thanon Sukhumvit Market SOUVENIRS
(Map p92; btwn Soi 3 & Soi 15, Th Sukhumvit; 11am-11pm Tue-Sun; S Nana exits 1 & 3) Knock-off clothes and watches, adult DVDs, Chinese throwing stars and other questionable items dominate this market catering mainly to package tourists.

Patpong Night Market SOUVENIRS
(Map p82; Th Phat Phong & Soi Phat Phong 2; 6pm-midnight; M Si Lom exit 2, S Sala Daeng exit 1) You'll be faced with the competing distractions of strip-clubbing and shopping in this infamous area. And true to the area's illicit leanings, pirated goods make a prominent appearance even amid a wholesome crowd of families and straight-laced couples. Bargain with determination, as first-quoted prices tend to be astronomically high.

Information

DANGERS & ANNOYANCES

You are more likely to be charmed rather than coerced out of your money in Bangkok. Practised con artists capitalise on Thailand's famous friendliness and a revolving door of clueless tourists. Bangkok's most heavily touristed areas – Wat Phra Kaew, Wat Pho, Jim Thompson House, Th Khao San, Erawan Shrine – are favourite hunting grounds for these scallywags. The best prevention is knowledge, so before hitting the ground, become familiar with the more common local scams.

If you've been scammed, the tourist police can be effective in dealing with some of the 'unethical' business practices and crime. But in general you should enter into every monetary transaction with the understanding that you have no consumer protection or recourse.

EMERGENCY

If you have a medical emergency and need an ambulance, contact the English-speaking hospitals listed here. In case of a police or safety issue, contact the following emergency services:

Police (191) The police contact number functions as the de facto universal emergency number in Thailand, and can also be used to call an ambulance or report a fire.

Tourist Police (24hr hotline 1155) The best way to deal with most problems requiring police (usually a rip-off or theft) is to contact the tourist police, who are used to dealing with foreigners and can be very helpful in cases of arrest.

INTERNET & TELEPHONE ACCESS

The ubiquity of smartphones has meant that internet cafes are an almost extinct species in Bangkok, although you can still find a couple in touristy areas such as Th Khao San.

Wi-fi, provided mostly free of charge, is ubiquitous around Bangkok especially in mall-based cafes and restaurants.

A convenient place to take care of your communication needs in the centre of Bangkok is **TrueMove** (Map p88; www.truemove.com; Soi 2, Siam Sq; 7am-10pm; S Siam exit 4). It has high-speed internet computers equipped with Skype, sells phones and mobile subscriptions, and can also provide information on city-wide wi-fi access for computers and phones.

MEDIA

Daily newspapers are available at streetside newsagents. Monthly magazines are available in most bookstores.

Bangkok 101 (www.bangkok101.com) A tourist-friendly listings magazine.

Bangkok Post (www.bangkokpost.com) The city's English-language newspaper.

BK (www.bk.asia-city.com) Online version of Bangkok's best listings magazine.

Coconuts Bangkok (bangkok.coconuts.co) Bangkok-centric news site with an emphasis on the weird and wacky.

Nation (www.nationmultimedia.com) An English-language daily with a heavy focus on business.

COMMON BANGKOK SCAMS

Commit these classic rip-offs to memory and join us in our ongoing crusade to outsmart Bangkok's crafty scam artists.

Closed today Ignore any 'friendly' local who tells you an attraction is closed for a Buddhist holiday or for cleaning. These are set-ups for trips to a bogus gem sale.

Túk-túk rides for 20B Say goodbye to your day's itinerary if you climb aboard this ubiquitous scam. These alleged 'tours' bypass all the sights and instead cruise to all the fly-by-night gem and tailor shops that pay commissions.

Flat-fare taxi ride Flatly refuse any driver who quotes a flat fare (usually between 100B and 150B for in-town destinations), which will usually be three times more expensive than the reasonable meter rate. Walking beyond the tourist area will usually help in finding an honest driver. If the driver has 'forgotten' to put the meter on, just say, 'Meter, *kâ/kráp*' (for female/male).

Tourist buses to the south On the long journey south, well-organised and connected thieves have hours to comb through your bags, breaking into (and later resealing) locked bags, searching through hiding places and stealing credit cards, electronics and even toiletries. This scam has been running for years but is easy to avoid simply by carrying valuables with you on the bus.

Friendly strangers Be wary of smartly dressed men who approach you asking where you're from and where you're going. Their opening gambit is usually followed with: 'Ah, my son/daughter is studying at university in (your city)' – they seem to have an encyclopaedic knowledge of major universities. As the tourist authorities here pointed out, this sort of behaviour is out of character for Thais and should be treated with suspicion.

Not the Nation (www.notthenation.com) Thailand's answer to the *Onion*.

MEDICAL SERVICES

Thanks to its high standard of hospital care, Bangkok is fast becoming a destination for medical tourists shopping for more affordable dental check-ups, elective surgery and cosmetic procedures. Pharmacists (chemists) throughout the city can diagnose and treat most minor ailments (Bangkok belly, sinus and skin infections etc).

The following hospitals offer 24-hour emergency services, and the numbers here should be contacted if you need an ambulance or immediate medical attention. Most of these hospitals also have daily clinics with English-speaking staff.

Bangkok Christian Hospital (Map p144; ☎ 02 625 9000; www.bch.in.th/en; 124 Th Silom; M Si Lom exit 2, S Sala Daeng exit 1) Modern hospital in central Bangkok.

BNH (Map p82; ☎ 02 686 2700; www.bnhhospital.com; 9 Th Convent; M Si Lom exit 2, S Sala Daeng exit 2) Modern, centrally located hospital.

Bumrungrad International Hospital (Map p92; ☎ 02 667 1000; www.bumrungrad.com/thailandhospital; 33 Soi 3, Th Sukhumvit; S Phloen Chit exit 3) An internationally accredited hospital.

Samitivej Hospital (Map p92; ☎ 02 022 2222; www.samitivejhospitals.com; 133 Soi 49, Th Sukhumvit; S Phrom Phong exit 3 & taxi) Modern hospital in Bangkok.

MONEY

Regular bank hours in Bangkok are generally 8.30am to 3.30pm, although branches in busy areas and shopping malls are open later. ATMs are common in all areas of the city. Many Thai banks also have currency-exchange bureaus; there are also exchange desks within eyeshot of most tourist areas. Go to 7-Eleven shops or other reputable places to break 1000B bills; don't expect a vendor or taxi to be able to change a bill 500B or larger.

POST

Main Post Office (Map p80; ☎ 02 233 1050; Th Charoen Krung; ⏰ 8am-8pm Mon-Fri, to 1pm Sat & Sun; ⛴ Oriental Pier) Bangkok's main post office.

TOILETS

Public toilets in Bangkok are few and far between and your best bet is to head for a shopping centre, fast-food restaurant or our favourite, a luxury hotel (just waltz in as if you're staying there). Shopping centres might charge 2B to 5B for a visit; some newer shopping centres have toilets for the disabled. Despite what you'll hear, squat toilets are a dying breed in Bangkok.

TOURIST INFORMATION

Official tourist offices distribute maps, brochures and advice on sights and activities. Don't confuse these free services with the licensed travel agents that book tours and transport on a commission basis. Often, travel agencies incorporate elements of the official national tourism organisation name (Tourism Authority of Thailand; TAT) into their own name to mislead tourists.

Bangkok Information Center (Map p72; ☎ 02 225 7612-4; www.bangkoktourist.com; 17/1 Th Phra Athit; ⏰ 9am-7pm Mon-Fri, to 5pm Sat & Sun; ⛴ Phra Athit/Banglamphu Pier) City-specific tourism office providing maps, brochures and directions. Kiosks and booths are found around town; look for the green-on-white symbol of a mahout on an elephant.

Tourism Authority of Thailand (TAT; ☎ call centre 1672; www.tourismthailand.org) Head office (TAT; Map p92; ☎ 02 250 5500, call centre 1672; www.tourismthailand.org; 1600 Th Phetchaburi Tat Mai; ⏰ 8.30am-4.30pm; M Phetchaburi exit

THE INSIDE SCOOP

Several Bangkok residents, local and foreign, have taken their experiences to the 'small screen' and maintain blogs and websites about living in Bangkok. Some of the more informative and/or entertaining include:

2Bangkok (www.2bangkok.com) News sleuth and history buff follows the city's headlines from today and yesterday.

Global Post (www.globalpost.com/bio/patrick-winn) Patrick Winn, this online news agency's senior Southeast Asia correspondent, is based in Bangkok and has a knack for uncovering the city's wacky occurences.

Greg To Differ (gregtodiffer.com) 'Stories, rants and observations on expat life in Asia's craziest city.'

Kathy MacLeod (www.kathymacleod.blogspot.com) A Bangkok life, in comic format.

Richard Barrow in Thailand (www.richardbarrow.com) Full time Bangkok-based blogger covering everything from travel to news.

Still Life in Moving Vehicles (www.lifeinmovingvehicle.blogspot.com) Photo blog depicting 'Bangkok from the passenger seat'.

2); Banglamphu (TAT; Map p72; ☎ 02 283 1500, call centre 1672; cnr Th Ratchadamnoen Nok & Th Chakraphatdi Phong; ⊙8.30am-4.30pm; klorng boat to Phanfa Leelard Pier); Suvarnabhumi International Airport (TAT; ☎ 02 134 0040, call centre 1672; www.tourismthailand.org; 2nd fl, btwn Gates 2 & 5, Suvarnabhumi International Airport; ⊙24hr).

ℹ Getting There & Away

AIR

Bangkok has two airports. **Suvarnabhumi International Airport** (☎ 02 132 1888; www.suvarnabhumiairport.com), 30km east of central Bangkok, began commercial international and domestic service in 2006 after several years of delay. The airport's name is pronounced *sù·wan·ná·poom,* and it inherited the airport code (BKK) previously used by the old airport at Don Mueang. The airport website has real-time details of arrivals and departures.

Bangkok's former international and domestic **Don Mueang International Airport** (☎ 02 535 1253; www.donmueangairportthai.com), 25km north of central Bangkok, was retired from commercial service in September 2006, only to reopen later as Bangkok's de-facto budget hub.

The following carriers service domestic destinations to/from Bangkok's two airports:

Air Asia ☎ 02 515 9999; www.airasia.com

Bangkok Airways ☎ 1771; www.bangkokairways.com

Happy Air ☎ 02 216 5151; www.happyair.co.th

Nok Air ☎ 1318; www.nokair.com

Orient Thai ☎ 02 229 4100, call centre 1126; www.flyorientthai.com/en/home

Solar Air ☎ 02 535 2456; www.solarair.co.th

Thai Lion Air ☎ 02 529 9999; www.lionairthai.com

Thai Smile ☎ 02 118 8888; www.thaismileair.com

BUS

Bangkok is the centre for bus services that fan out all over the kingdom. For long-distance journeys to popular tourist destinations it is advisable to buy tickets directly from the bus companies at the bus stations, rather than through travel agents in tourist centres such as Th Khao San. There are three main bus terminals – two of which are an inconvenient distance from the centre of the city – and a terminal at the public transport centre at Suvarnabhumi International Airport with inter-provincial departures. Allow an hour to reach all terminals from most parts of Bangkok.

Eastern Bus Terminal (Map p92; ☎ 02 391 2504; Soi 40, Th Sukhumvit; Ⓢ Ekkamai exit 2) The departure point for buses to Pattaya, Rayong, Chanthaburi and other points east, except for Aranya Prathet. Most people call it *sà·tăh·nee èk·gà·mai* (Ekamai station). It's near the Ekkamai BTS station.

Northern & Northeastern Bus Terminal (Mo Chit; Map p102; ☎ northeastern routes 02 936 2852, ext 602/605, northern routes 02 936 2841, ext 325/614; Th Kamphaeng Phet; Ⓜ Kamphaeng Phet exit 1 & taxi, Ⓢ Mo Chit exit 3 & taxi) Located just north of Chatuchak Park, this hectic bus station is also commonly called *kŏn sòng mŏr chít* (Mo Chit station) – not to be confused with Mo Chit BTS station. Buses depart from here for all northern and northeastern destinations, as well as international destinations including Pakse (Laos), Phnom Penh (Cambodia), Siem Reap (Cambodia) and Vientiane (Laos).

Southern Bus Terminal (Sai Tai Mai; ☎ 02 422 4444, call centre 1490; Th Boromaratchachonanee) The city's southern bus terminal lies a long way west of the centre of Bangkok. Commonly called *săi đâi mài,* it's among the more pleasant and orderly in the country. Besides serving as the departure point for all buses south of Bangkok, transport to Kanchanaburi and western Thailand also departs from here.

Suvarnabhumi Public Transport Centre (☎ 02 132 1888; Suvarnabhumi Airport) Located 3km from Suvarnabhumi International Airport, this terminal has relatively frequent departures to points east and northeast including Aranya Prathet (for the Cambodian border), Chanthaburi, Ko Chang, Nong Khai (for the Lao border), Pattaya, Rayong, Trat and Udon Thani. It can be reached from the airport by a free shuttle bus.

TRAIN

Hualamphong Train Station (☎ 02 220 4334, call centre 1690; www.railway.co.th; off Th Phra Ram IV; Ⓜ Hua Lamphong exit 2) Hualamphong is the terminus for the main rail services to the south, north, northeast and east.

Hualamphong has the following services: shower room, mailing centre, luggage storage, cafes and food courts. To get to the station from Sukhumvit take the MRT to the Hua Lamphong stop. From western points (Banglamphu, Thewet), take bus 53.

Bangkok Noi Train Station (☎ 02 418 4310, call centre 1690; www.railway.co.th; off Th Itsaraphap; ⛴ Thonburi Railway Station, Wang Lang/Siriraj Pier, Ⓢ Wongwian Yai exit 4 & taxi) Also known as Thonburi train station, this station handles infrequent (and overpriced for foreigners) services to Nakhon Pathom, Kanchanaburi and Nam Tok.

Wong Wian Yai (☎ 02 465 2017, call centre 1690; www.railway.co.th; off Th Phra Jao Taksin; Ⓢ Wongwian Yai exit 4 & taxi) This tiny hidden station is the jumping-off point for the commuter line to Samut Sakhon (also known as Mahachai).

Getting Around

Bangkok may seem chaotic and impenetrable at first, but its transport system is gradually improving, and although you'll almost certainly find yourself stuck in traffic at some point, the jams aren't as legendary as they used to be. For most of the day and night, Bangkok's 70,000 clean and dirt-cheap taxis are the most expedient choice – although it's important to note that Bangkok traffic is anything if not unpredictable. During rush hour, the BTS, MRT, river ferries, *klorng* (canal, also spelt *khlong*) ferries are much wiser options. Locals and many local expats swear by the ubiquitous motorcycle taxis, but the accidents we've seen suggest that they're not really worth the risk.

A good, up-to-date resource for public transportation in Bangkok is www.transitbangkok.com.

TO/FROM THE AIRPORT

Bangkok is served by two airports: the vast majority of flights are out of Suvarnabhumi International Airport, while the budget airlines operate out of Don Mueang International Airport. If you need to transfer between the two, pencil in *at least* an hour, as the two airports are at opposite

TRANSPORT TO/FROM BANGKOK

DESTINATION	AIR	BUS	MINIVAN	TRAIN
Ayuthaya		53-68B; 1½hr; hourly 5am-7pm (from Northern & Northeastern Bus Terminal)	60B; 1hr; every 25min 6am-9pm (from Victory Monument)	15-185B; 1½hr; 40 departures 4.20am-11.53pm
Chiang Mai	from 790B; 1-1½hr; frequent daily (from Don Mueang International Airport); from 1265B; frequent daily (from Suvarnabhumi International Airport)	500-778B; 9½-11hr; hourly 5.40am-10.05pm (from Northern & Northeastern Bus Terminal)		231-1454B; 12-15hr; 5 departures 12.45-10pm
Chiang Rai	from 790B; 1¼hr; 12 daily (from Don Mueang International Airport); from 1090B; 1¼hr; 7 departures daily (from Suvarnabhumi International Airport)	601-868B; 11-12hr; hourly 6.30am-12.30pm & 7-9.30pm (from Northern & Northeastern Bus Terminal)		
Hat Yai	from 1440B; 1½hr; frequent departures daily (from Don Mueang International Airport); 1900B; 1½hr; 5 departures daily (from Suvarnabhumi International Airport)	514-1028B; 13hr; frequent 2-9.15pm (from Southern Bus Terminal)		259-1590B; 12-15hr; 6 departures 1-10.40pm
Khon Kaen	from 700B; 55 minutes; 7 departures daily (from Don Mueang International Airport); from 1300B; 55 minutes; 3 departures daily (from Suvarnabhumi International Airport)	260-498B; 10-11hr; hourly 4am-11pm (from Northern & Northeastern Bus Terminal)		77-1168B; 9-11hr; 4 departures 8.20am-8.45pm
Mae Sot	from 1114B; 65 minutes; 4 departures daily (from Don Mueang International Airport)	297-638B; 7-8hr; hourly 8.15-9am & 9.15-10.40pm (from Northern & Northeastern Bus Terminal)		

ends of town. Minivans run between the two airports from 5.30am to 5pm (50B).

Suvarnabhumi International Airport

The following ground transport options leave directly from the Suvarnabhumi terminal to in-town destinations: metered taxis, hotel limousines, airport rail link, private vehicles and some minivans. If there are no metered taxis available kerbside or if the line is too long, you can take the airport shuttle to the taxi stand at the public-transport centre.

Airport Rail Link (☎ call centre 1690; www.srtet.co.th) Connects Suvarnabhumi International Airport and the BTS (Skytrain) stop at Phaya Thai (45B, 30 minutes, from 6am to midnight) and the MRT (Metro) stop at Phetchaburi (45B, 25 minutes, from 6am to midnight).

Bus & Minivan A public transport centre is 3km from the airport and includes a bus terminal with buses to a handful of provinces and inner-city-bound buses and minivans. A free airport shuttle connects the transport centre with the passenger terminals. Bus lines city-bound tourists are likely to use include line 551 to BTS Victory Monument station (40B, frequent from 5am to 10pm) and 552 to BTS On Nut (20B, frequent from 5am to 10pm). From these points,

TRANSPORT TO/FROM BANGKOK

DESTINATION	AIR	BUS	MINIVAN	TRAIN
Nong Khai		337-675B; 10hr; hourly 8.30-9.45pm (from Northern & Northeastern Bus Terminal)		213-1317B; 12hr; 3 departures 6.30-8.45pm
Pak Chong (for Khao Yai National Park)		130-140B; 3hr; hourly 4am-1pm (from Northern & Northeastern Bus Terminal)	160B; 2½hr; hourly 7am-8pm (from Victory Monument)	
Phuket	from 1400B; 75 minutes; frequent departures daily (from Don Mueang International Airport); from 1790B; 75 minutes; frequent departures daily (from Suvarnabhumi International Airport)	482-938B; 12-15hr; every 30 minutes 7.30am-8.20pm (from Southern Bus Terminal)		
Sukhothai	from 1695B; 1hr; 2 departures daily (from Suvarnabhumi International Airport)	265-342B; 6-7hr; hourly 9am-noon & 9.45-10pm (from Northern & Northeastern Bus Terminal)		
Trat	from 2550B; 1hr; 3 departures daily (from Suvarnabhumi International Airport)	248-275B; 5½hr; frequent 4-9.45am (from Eastern Bus Terminal); 243B; 6hr; 5 departures 7.30am-10pm (from Northern & Northeastern Bus Terminal)	300B; 5hr; hourly 5am-5pm (from Victory Monument); 300B; 5hr; hourly 9am-5pm (from Northern & Northeastern Bus Terminal)	
Ubon Ratchathani	from 1400B; 70min; 9 departures daily (from Don Mueang International Airport); from 1400B; 70min; 3 departures daily (from Suvarnabhumi International Airport)	356-790B; 10-11hr; hourly 6.40am-9.45pm (from Northern & Northeastern Bus Terminal)		205-1280B; 8½-12hr; 6 departures 5.45am-10.25pm

you can continue by public transport or taxi to your hotel. There are also buses and minivans to destinations east including Chanthaburi, Hua Hin, Ko Chang, Pattaya and Trat.

Relatively frequent minivans to Don Mueang International Airport wait on floor 1, outside door 8 (50B, 40 minutes, from 5.30am to 5pm).

From town, you can take the BTS to On Nut, then from near the market entrance opposite Tesco Lotus, take minivan 552 (20B, frequent from 5am to 10pm); BTS to Udom Suk and bus A3 (30B, frequent from 6am to 8.30pm); or BTS to Victory Monument, then one of the infrequent minivans to Suvarnabhumi International Airport (40B, from 5am to 8pm).

Taxi As you exit the terminal, ignore the touts and all the signs pointing you to overpriced 'official airport taxis'; instead, descend to floor 1 to join the generally fast-moving queue for a public taxi. Cabs booked through these desks should always use their meter, but they often try their luck so insist by saying, 'Meter, please'. Typical metered fares from the airport are as follows: 200B to 250B to Th Sukhumvit; 250B to 300B to Th Khao San; 400B to Mo Chit. Toll charges (paid by the passengers) vary between 25B and 70B. Note that there's an additional 50B surcharge added to all fares departing from the airport, payable directly to the driver.

Don Mueang International Airport

Bus & Minivan From outside the arrivals hall, there are two airport bus lines from Don Mueang: A1 makes a stop at BTS Mo Chit (30B, frequent from 7.30am to 11.30pm); while the less frequent A2 makes stops at BTS Mo Chit and BTS Victory Monument (30B, every 30 minutes from 7.30am to 11.30pm).

Relatively frequent minivans also departing from outside the arrivals hall link Don Mueang International Airport and Suvarnabhumi International Airport (50B, 1hr, from 5.30am to 5pm).

Public buses stop on the highway in front of the airport. Useful lines include 29, with a stop at Victory Monument BTS station before terminating at Hualamphong Train Station (24 hours); line 59, with a stop near Th Khao San (24 hours); and line 538, stopping at Victory Monument BTS station (4am to 10pm); fares are approximately 23B.

Taxi As at Suvarnabhumi, public taxis leave from outside the arrivals hall and there is a 50B airport charge added to the meter fare.

Train The walkway that crosses from the airport to the Amari Airport Hotel also provides access to Don Mueang Train Station, which has trains to Hualamphong Train Station every one to 1½ hours from 4am to 11.30am and then roughly every hour from 2pm to 9.30pm (from 5B to 10B).

BICYCLE

Keen-eyed bicycle enthusiasts may have noticed a new green protected bike lane that runs along parts of Banglamphu and Ko Ratanakosin. The track is part of Pun Pun (www.punpunbikeshare.com), an initiative that includes 50 bicycle hire stations across town and a clearly marked (although not always protected) bike path.

To borrow a bike, you'll first need to register online (http://pcc.punpunbikeshare.com/member/). You then pick up a smartcard at one of eight staffed stations. The card costs 320B and includes 100B of credit; the bikes are free for the first 15 minutes, then cost approximately 10B per subsequent hour.

BOAT

Once the city's dominant form of transport, public boats still survive along the mighty Mae Nam Chao Phraya and on a few interior *klorng*.

Canal Routes

Canal taxi boats run along Khlong Saen Saep (Banglamphu to Ramkhamhaeng) and are an easy way to get between Banglamphu and Jim Thompson House, the Siam Sq shopping centres (get off at Sapan Hua Chang Pier for both) and other points further east along Th Sukhumvit – after a mandatory change of boat at Pratunam Pier. These boats are mostly used by daily commuters and pull into the piers for just a few seconds – jump straight on or you'll be left behind. Fares range from 9B to 19B and boats run from 5.30am to 7.15pm from Mondays to

INTERNATIONAL BUSES FROM BANGKOK

Bangkok's Northern & Northeastern Bus Terminal (Mor Chit) is a jumping-off point for a small but growing number of government-run, international bus routes.

DESTINATION	COST	DURATION	FREQUENCY
Pakse (Laos)	900B	12hr	8pm & 9pm
Phnom Penh (Cambodia)	750B	14hr	1.30am
Siem Reap (Cambodia; for Angkor Wat)	750B	8hr	8am & 9am
Vientiane (Laos)	900B	12hr	8pm

MINIVANS TO/FROM BANGKOK

Privately run minivans, called *rót đôo*, are a fast and relatively comfortable way to get between Bangkok and its neighbouring provinces. Minivans bound for a number of destinations wait at various points around the **Victory Monument** (อนุสาวรีย์ชัย; cnr Th Ratchawithi & Th Phayathai; ⌚24hr; S Victory Monument exit 2).

DESTINATION	COST	DURATION	FREQUENCY
Aranya Prathet (for Cambodian border)	230B	3½hr	hourly 4.20am-6.30pm
Ayuthaya	60B	1hr	every 30min 6am-9pm
Ban Phe (for Ko Samet)	200B	3hr	hourly 6am-8pm
Chanthaburi	200B	3hr	hourly 5.30am-6pm
Kanchanaburi	120B	2hr	hourly 6am-6pm
Nakhon Pathom	60B	1hr	frequent 6am-9pm
Pak Chong (for Khao Yai)	160B	2hr	hourly 7am-8pm
Pattaya	150B	2hr	hourly 6am-8pm
Phetchaburi	100B	2hr	every 45min 5.15am-8pm
Samut Songkhram (Mae Klong; for Amphawa)	70B	1½hr	frequent 6am-9pm
Southern Bus Terminal	35B	20min	frequent 8am-9pm

Fridays, from 6am to 6.30pm on Saturdays, and from 6am to 6pm on Sundays.

River Routes

Chao Phraya Express Boat (☎02 623 6001; www.chaophrayaexpressboat.com) operates the main ferry service along Mae Nam Chao Phraya. The main pier is known as Tha Sathon, Saphan Taksin or sometimes Central Pier, and connects to the BTS at Saphan Taksin station.

Boats run from 6am to 8pm. You can buy tickets (10B to 40B) at the pier or on board; hold on to your ticket as proof of purchase (an occasional formality).

The most common boats are the orange-flagged express boats. These run between Wat Rajsingkorn, south of Bangkok, to Nonthaburi, north, stopping at most major piers (15B, frequent from 6am to 7pm). A blue-flagged tourist boat (40B, every 30 minutes from 9.30am to 5pm) runs from Sathon/Central Pier to Phra Athit/Banglamphu Pier with stops at eight major sightseeing piers and barely comprehensible English-language commentary. Vendors at Sathon/Central Pier tout a 150B all-day pass, but unless you plan on doing a lot of boat travel, it's not great value.

River Crossing Boats

There are also flat-bottomed cross-river ferries that connect Thonburi and Bangkok. These piers are usually next door to Chao Phraya Express Boat piers, boats cost 3B per crossing and run from approximately 7am to 7pm.

BTS & MRT

The elevated **BTS** (☎02 617 6000, tourist information 02 617 7341; www.bts.co.th), also known as the Skytrain (*rót fai fáh*), whisks you through 'new' Bangkok (Silom, Sukhumvit and Siam Sq). The interchange between the two lines is at Siam station, and trains run frequently from 6am to 11.45pm. Fares range from 15B to 52B, or 140B for a one-day pass. Most ticket machines only accept coins, but change is available at the information booths.

Bangkok's **MRT** (☎02 354 2000; www.bangkokmetro.co.th) or Metro is helpful for people staying in the Sukhumvit or Silom area to reach the train station at Hualamphong. Fares cost from 16B to 42B, or 120B for a one-day pass. The trains run frequently from 6am to midnight.

BUS

Bangkok's public buses are run by the **Bangkok Mass Transit Authority** (☎02 246 0973, call centre 1348; www.bmta.co.th). As the routes are not always clear, and with Bangkok taxis being such a good deal, you'd really have to be pinching pennies to rely on buses as a way to get around Bangkok. However, if you're determined, air-con bus fares range from 10B to 23B, and fares for fan-cooled buses start at 6.50B. Most of the bus lines run between 5am and 10pm or 11pm, except for the 'all-night' buses, which run from 3am or 4am to midmorning. You'll most likely require the help of thinknet's *Bangkok Bus Guide*.

CAR

For short-term visitors, you will find parking and driving a car in Bangkok more trouble than it is worth. If you need private transport, consider hiring a car and driver through your hotel or hire a taxi driver that you find trustworthy. One reputable operator is **Julie Taxi** (☎091 098 4553, 081 846 2014; www.facebook.com/

BANGKOK TAXI TIPS

- Never agree to take a taxi that won't use the meter; these drivers park outside hotels and in tourist areas. Simply walk a block or two and get one that's passing by instead.
- Bangkok taxi drivers will generally not try to 'take you for a ride' as happens in some other countries; they make more money from passenger turnover.
- It's worth keeping in mind that many Bangkok taxi drivers are in fact seasonal labourers fresh from the countryside and may not know their way around.
- If a driver refuses to take you somewhere, it may be because he needs to return his rental cab before a certain time, not because he doesn't like you.
- Very few Bangkok taxi drivers speak much English; an address written in Thai can help immensely.
- Older cabs may be less comfortable but often have more experienced drivers because they are driver-owned, as opposed to the new cabs, which are usually hired.

TourWithJulieTaxi), which offers a variety of vehicles and excellent service.

But if you still want to give it a go, all the big car-hire companies have offices in Bangkok. Rates start at around 1000B per day for a small car. A passport plus a valid licence from your home country (with English translation if necessary) or an International Driving Permit are required for all rentals.

Reliable car-hire companies include **Avis** (Map p86; ☎02 251 1131; www.avisthailand.com; 40 Th Sathon Neua/North; ⏲8am-6pm; Ⓜ Lumphini exit 2), **Budget** (Map p92; ☎02 203 9294; www.budget.co.th; 19/23 Bldg A, RCA/Royal City Ave; ⏲8am-7pm; Ⓜ Phra Ram 9 exit 3 & taxi) and **Thai Rent A Car** (Map p66; ☎02 737 8888; www.thairentacar.com; 2371 Th Phetchaburi Tat Mai; ⏲8.30am-5.30pm Mon-Sat; Ⓢ Thong Lo exit 3 & taxi), all of which also have counters at Suvarnabhumi and Don Mueang International Airports.

MOTORCYCLE TAXI

Forming the backdrop of modern Bangkok, teams of cheeky, numbered and vested motorcycle-taxi drivers can be found at the end of just about every long street. A ride to the end *(sùt soy)* or mouth *(bàhk soy)* of an average soi usually costs 10B to 15B. Longer journeys should be negotiated in advance, and can range from 20B to 100B.

Helmets are occasionally available upon request, although considering the way some of these guys drive, any body part is at risk. In particular, keep your legs tucked in – the drivers are used to carrying passengers with shorter legs than those of the average Westerner. Women wearing skirts should sit side-saddle and gather any extra cloth to avoid it catching in the wheel or drive chain.

TAXI

Although many first-time visitors are hesitant to use them, in general Bangkok's taxis are new and spacious and the drivers are courteous and helpful, making taxis a good way to get around.

All taxis are required to use their meters, which start at 35B, and fares to most places within central Bangkok cost 60B to 90B. Freeway tolls – 25B to 70B depending on where you start – must be paid by the passenger.

Taxi Radio (☎1681; www.taxiradio.co.th) and other 24-hour 'phone-a-cab' services are available for 20B above the metered fare.

App-based alternatives to the traditional taxi that operate in Bangkok include **All Thai Taxi** (www.allthaitaxi.com), **Easy Taxi** (www.easytaxi.com/th), **Grab Taxi** (www.grabtaxi.com/bangkok-thailand) and **Uber** (www.uber.com/cities/bangkok).

TÚK-TÚK

A ride on Thailand's most emblematic three-wheeled vehicle is an experience particularly sought after by new arrivals, but it only takes a few seconds to realise that most foreigners are too tall to see anything beyond the low-slung roof.

Túk-túk (pronounced *đúk đúk*) drivers also have a knack for smelling crisp bills and can potentially take you and your wallet far away from your desired destination. In particular, beware of drivers who offer to take you on a sightseeing tour for 20B – it's a touting scheme designed to pressure you into purchasing overpriced goods. A short trip on a túk-túk will cost at least 60B.

AROUND BANGKOK

If you're itching to get out of the capital, but don't have a lot of time, consider a day trip to one of the neighbouring towns and provinces. On Bangkok's doorstep are all of Thailand's provincial charms – you don't have to go far to find ancient religious monuments, floating markets, architectural treasures and laid-back fishing villages.

Ko Kret เกาะเกร็ด

POP 6174

An easy rural getaway from Bangkok, Ko Kret is an artificial 'island', the result of a canal having been dug nearly 300 years ago to shorten an oxbow bend in Mae Nam Chao Phraya. The area is one of Thailand's oldest settlements of Mon people, who were a dominant people of central Thailand between the 6th and 10th centuries AD. Today, Ko Kret is a popular weekend getaway, known for its hand-thrown terracotta pots and its busy weekend market.

Sights & Activities

There are a couple of temples worth peeking into, such as the leaning stupa at **Wat Poramai Yikawat** (วัดปรมัยยิกาวาส; Ko Kret, Nonthaburi; 9am-5pm; 166 & river-crossing ferry from Wat Sanam Neua) FREE, but the real highlight is taking in the bucolic riverside atmosphere. A 6km paved path circles the island, and can be easily completed on foot or by bicycle, the latter available for rent from the pier (per day 40B). Alternatively, it's possible to charter a boat for up to 10 people for 500B; the typical **island tour** stops at a batik workshop, a sweets factory and, on weekends, a floating market.

Ko Kret is known for its **hand-thrown terracotta pots**, sold at markets throughout Bangkok; order an iced coffee from just about any vendor on the island and you'll get a small pot as a souvenir. From Wat Poramai Yikawat, go in either direction to find both abandoned kilns and working pottery centres on the east and north coasts.

If you come to Ko Kret on a weekday you'll likely to be the only visitor. On weekends, things change drastically as Ko Kret is an extremely popular destination for urban Thais. There's heaps more food, drink and things for sale, but with this come the crowds.

Eating

On weekends, droves of Thais flock to Ko Kret to eat deep-fried snacks and Thai-style sweets. One snack to look for is *khâw châa,* an unusual but delicious Mon dish of savoury titbits served with chilled fragrant rice.

Pa Ka Lung THAI $
(Restaurant River Side; Ko Kret, Nonthaburi; mains 30-60B; 8am-4pm Mon-Fri, to 6pm Sat & Sun; cross-river ferry from Wat Sanam Neua)
An open-air food court with an English-language menu and sign, Pa Ka Lung serves *khâw châa* and other dishes.

Getting There & Away

Ko Kret is in Nonthaburi, about 15km north of central Bangkok. To get there, take bus 166 from the Victory Monument or a taxi to Pak Kret, before boarding the cross-river ferry (2B, from 5am to 9pm) that leaves from Wat Sanam Neua.

Around Bangkok

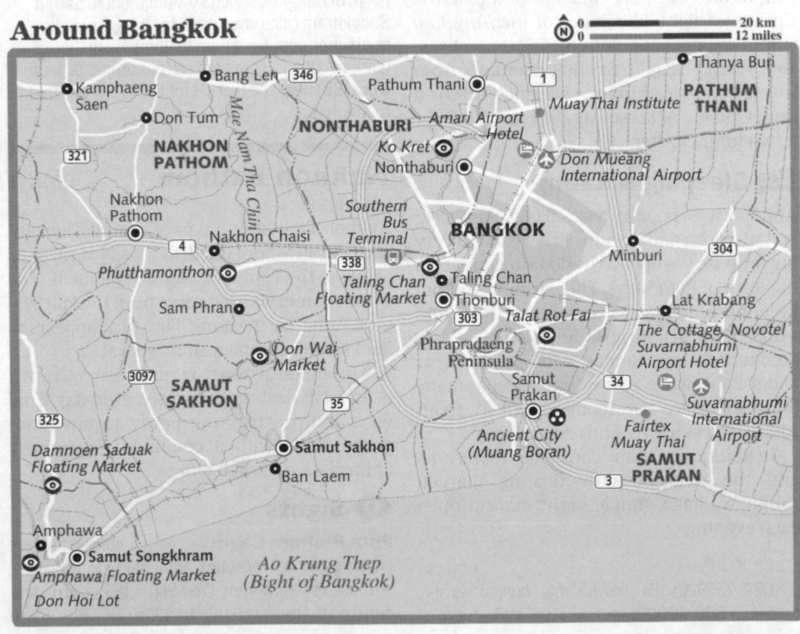

Amphawa อัมพวา

POP 5000

This canalside village has become a popular destination for city folk who seek out its quintessentially 'Thai' setting. This urban influx has sparked a few signs of gentrification, but the canals, old wooden buildings, atmospheric cafes and quaint waterborne traffic still retain heaps of charm. From Friday to Sunday, Amphawa puts on a floating market. Alternatively, visit on a weekday and you'll probably be the only tourist.

Sights & Activities

Steps from Amphawa's central footbridge is **Wat Amphawan Chetiyaram** (วัดอัมพวันเจติยาราม; off Rte 6006, Amphawa; dawn-dusk) FREE, a graceful temple believed to be located at the place of the family home of Rama II, and which features accomplished murals. A short walk from the temple is **King Buddhalertla (Phuttha Loet La) Naphalai Memorial Park** (อุทยานพระบรมราชานุสรณ์ พระบาทสมเด็จพระพุทธเลิศหล้านภาลัย (อุทยาน ร. ๒); off Rte 6006, Amphawa; 20B; 8.30am-5pm), a museum housed in a collection of traditional central Thai houses set on 1.5 landscaped hectares. Dedicated to Rama II, the museum contains a library of antiques from early-19th-century Siam.

At night **long-tail boats** zip through Amphawa's sleeping waters to watch the Christmas light–like dance of the *hìng hôy* (fireflies), most populous during the wet season. From Friday to Sunday, operators from several piers lead tours, charging 60B for a seat. Outside of these days, it costs 500B for a two-hour charter.

Sleeping & Eating

Amphawa is popular with Bangkok's weekend warriors, and it seems like virtually every other house has opened its doors to tourists in the form of homestays. These can range from little more than a mattress on the floor and a mosquito net to upscale guesthouse-style accommodation. Rooms with fan start at about 250B while rooms with air-con, many of which share bathrooms, begin at about 1000B. Prices are half this on weekdays.

In addition to many canalside restaurants and the weekends-only floating market, Amphawa has a simple **night market** open each evening.

Baan Ku Pu HOTEL $$

(034 725920; Th Rim Khlong; bungalows incl breakfast 800-4000B;) A Thai-style 'resort' featuring wooden bungalows in a relatively peaceful enclave.

ChababaanCham Resort HOTEL $$$

(081 984 1000; www.chababaancham.com; Th Rim Khlong; r incl breakfast 1500-2400B;) Located just off the canal, this place has attractive, modern and spacious duplex-style rooms, the more expensive of which come equipped with a rooftop lounge area.

Ploen Amphawa Resort HOTEL $$$

(081 458 9411; www.ploenamphawa.com; Th Rim Khlong; r incl breakfast 1400-3000B;) Not a resort at all, but rather a handful of rooms in a refurbished wooden home in the thick of the canal area.

Amphawa Floating Market MARKET $

(ตลาดน้ำอัมพวา; Amphawa; dishes 20-40B; 4-9pm Fri-Sun) If you're in Amphawa on a weekend, plan your meals around this fun market where grilled seafood and other dishes are served directly from boats.

Getting There & Away

From Bangkok's **Southern Bus Terminal** (p145), board any bus bound for Damnoen Saduak and ask to get off at Amphawa (80B, two hours, frequent from 6am to 9pm).

Alternatively, frequent minivans run from a **stop** (Map p98; Th Phahonyothin; S Victory Monument) north of Bangkok's Victory Monument to Samut Songkhram (also known as Mae Klong; 70B, 1½ hours, frequent from 6am to 9pm). From there, you can hop in a *sŏrng·tăa·ou* (passenger pick-up truck; 8B) near the market for the 10-minute ride to Amphawa.

Nakhon Pathom นครปฐม

POP 120,000

Nakhon Pathom is a typical central Thai city, with Phra Pathom Chedi as a visible link to its claim as the country's oldest settlement. The town's name, which derives from the Pali 'Nagara Pathama' meaning 'First City', appears to lend some legitimacy to this boast.

The modern town is quite sleepy, but it is an easy destination to see everyday Thai ways and practise your newly acquired language skills with a community genuinely appreciative of such efforts.

Sights

Phra Pathom Chedi BUDDHIST TEMPLE

(พระปฐมเจดีย์; museum admission by donation; museum 9am-4pm Wed-Sun) FREE In the centre of town, rising to 127m is one of the

OFF THE BEATEN TRACK

THE LONG WAY TO AMPHAWA

Amphawa is only 80km from Bangkok, but if you play your cards right, you can reach the town via a long journey involving trains, boats, a motorcycle ride and a short jaunt in the back of a truck. Why? Because sometimes the journey is just as interesting as the destination.

The adventure begins at Thonburi's **Wong Wian Yai** (p145) train station. Just past the Wong Wian Yai traffic circle is a food market that camouflages the terminus of this commuter line. Get one of the hourly trains (10B, one hour, from 5.30am to 8.10pm) to Samut Sakhon.

After 15 minutes on the rattling train the city density yields to squat villages. From the window you can peek into homes, temples and shops built a carefully considered arm's length from the passing trains. Further on, palm trees, patchwork rice fields and marshes filled with giant elephant ears and canna lilies line the route, punctuated by whistle-stop stations.

The backwater farms evaporate quickly as you enter **Samut Sakhon**, popularly known as Mahachai because it straddles the confluence of Mae Nam Tha Chin and Khlong Mahachai. This is a bustling port town, several kilometres upriver from the Gulf of Thailand, and the end of the first rail segment. Before the 17th century it was called Tha Jiin (Chinese Pier) because of the large number of Chinese junks that called here.

After working your way through one of the most hectic fresh markets in the country, you'll come to a vast harbour clogged with water hyacinths and wooden fishing boats. A few rusty cannons pointing towards the river testify to the existence of the town's crumbling fort, built to protect the kingdom from sea invaders.

Take the ferry across to Baan Laem (3B to 5B), jockeying for space with motorcycles that are driven by school teachers and people running errands. If the infrequent 5B ferry hasn't already deposited you there, take a motorcycle taxi (10B) for the 2km ride to **Wat Chawng Lom** (วัดช่องลม; Ban Laem, Samut Sakhon; ⏲ dawn-dusk), home to the Jao Mae Kuan Im Shrine, a 9m-high fountain in the shape of the Mahayana Buddhist Goddess of Mercy that is popular with regional tour groups. Beside the shrine is Tha Chalong, a train stop with three daily departures for Samut Songkhram at 8.10am, 12.05pm and 4.40pm (10B, one hour). The train rambles out of the city on tracks that the surrounding forest threatens to engulf, and this little stretch of line genuinely feels a world away from the big smoke of Bangkok.

The jungle doesn't last long, and any illusion that you've entered a parallel universe free of concrete is shattered as you enter **Samut Songkhram**. And to complete the seismic shift you'll emerge directly into a hubbub of hectic market stalls. Between train arrivals and departures these stalls are set up directly on the tracks, and must be hurriedly cleared away when the train arrives – it's quite an amazing scene.

Commonly known as Mae Klong, Samut Songkhram is a tidier version of Samut Sakhon and offers a great deal more as a destination. Owing to flat topography and abundant water sources, the area surrounding the provincial capital is well suited to the steady irrigation needed to grow guava, lychee and grapes. From Mae Klong Market pier (*tâh đà·làht mâa glorng*), you can charter a boat (1000B) or hop in a *sŏrng·tăa·ou* (8B) near the market for the 10-minute ride to Amphawa.

tallest Buddhist monuments in the world. The original stupa was erected in the early 6th century by the Theravada Buddhists of Dvaravati. But, in the early 11th century the Khmer king, Suriyavarman I of Angkor, conquered the city and built a Brahman *prang* (Hindi/Khmer-style stupa) over the sanctuary. The Burmese of Bagan, under King Anawrahta, sacked the city in 1057 and the *prang* lay in ruins until Rama IV (King Mongkut) had it restored in 1860.

On the eastern side of the monument, in the *bòht*, is a **Dvaravati-style Buddha** seated in a European pose similar to the one in Wat Phra Meru in Ayuthaya. It may, in fact, have come from there.

Also of interest are the many examples of Chinese sculpture carved from a greenish stone that came to Thailand as ballast in the bottom of 19th-century Chinese junks. Opposite the *bòht* is a **museum**, with some interesting Dvaravati sculpture and lots of old junk. Within the *chedi* complex is **Lablae Cave**, an artificial tunnel containing the shrine of several Buddha figures.

The **wát** surrounding the stupa enjoys the kingdom's highest temple rank, Rachavoramahavihan; it's one of only six temples so

WORTH A TRIP

PHRAPRADAENG PENINSULA: BANGKOK'S GREEN LUNG

If you've been to any of Bangkok's rooftop bars, you may have noticed the rural-looking zone just southeast of the city centre. Known in English as the Phrapradaeng Peninsula, the conspicuously green finger of land is surrounded on three sides by Mae Nam Chao Phraya, a feature that seems to have shielded it from development.

Most people visit the peninsula for the **Bang Nam Pheung Market** (ตลาดบางน้ำผึ้ง; Bang Kachao, Phrapradaeng; ⏲8am-3pm Sat & Sun; Ⓢ Bang Na exit 2 & taxi), a fun, weekends-only market with an emphasis on food. While you're there, also check out the wonderfully dilapidated **Wat Bang Nam Pheung Nok** (วัดบางน้ำผึ้งนอก; Bang Kachao, Phrapradaeng, Samut Prakan; ⏲dawn-dusk; Ⓢ Bang Na exit 2 & taxi) FREE, a 250-year old Buddhist temple.

For something more active, the area is on the itinerary of many Bangkok bike tours, which take advantage of the peninsula's elevated walkways. Alternatively, there's **Si Nakhon Kheun Khan Park** (สวนศรีนครเขื่อนขันธ์; Bang Kachao, Phrapradaeng, Samut Prakan; ⏲6am-7pm; Ⓢ Bang Na exit 2 & taxi) FREE, a vast botanical park with a large lake and birdwatching tower.

If you're really enjoying the Phrapradaeng Peninsula, you can extend your stay by overnighting at **Bangkok Tree House** (p115).

To get to Phrapradaeng, take the BTS to Bang Na and jump in a taxi for the short ride to the pier at Wat Bang Na Nork via Th Sanphawut. From there, take the river-crossing ferry (4B) followed by a short motorcycle taxi (10B) ride, if you're going to Bang Nam Pheung Market.

honoured in Thailand. King Rama VI's ashes are interred in the base of the Sukhothai-era Phra Ruang Rochanarit, a large standing Buddha image in the wát's northern *wí·hăhn*.

Phutthamonthon BUDDHIST MONUMENT
(พุทธมณฑล; ⏲dawn-dusk) FREE Southeast of the city stands this Sukhothai-style standing Buddha designed by Corrado Feroci. At 15.8m, it is reportedly the world's tallest, and it's surrounded by a 400-hectare landscaped park that contains sculptures representing the major stages in the Buddha's life.

All Bangkok–Nakhon Pathom buses pass by the access road to the park at Phra Phutthamonthon Sai 4; from there you can walk, hitch or flag down a *sŏrng·tăa·ou* into the park itself. From Nakhon Pathom you can also take a white-and-purple Salaya bus; the stop is on Th Tesa across from the post office.

Eating

Nakhon Pathom has an excellent **market** along the road between the train station and Phra Pathom Chedi; its *kôw lăhm* (sticky rice and coconut steamed in a length of bamboo) is reputed to be the best in Thailand.

Getting There & Away

Nakhon Pathom is 64km west of Bangkok. The city doesn't have a central bus station, but most transport arrives and departs from near the market and train station.

The most convenient and fastest way to get to Nakhon Pathom is via minivan, which depart from a **stop** (p152) north of Bangkok's Victory Monument (60B, one hour, frequent 6am to 6pm).

There are also more frequent trains from Bangkok's Hualamphong station throughout the day (14B to 60B, one hour).

Central Thailand

Includes ➡

Best Places to Eat

- ➡ Blue Rice (p181)
- ➡ Bann Kun Pra (p165)
- ➡ Suanmagmai Resort (p190)
- ➡ Naan Stop Curry (p171)

Best Places to Stay

- ➡ Tamarind Guesthouse (p164)
- ➡ FloatHouse River Kwai (p184)
- ➡ Oriental Kwai Resort (p180)
- ➡ Ayothaya Riverside House (p163)
- ➡ P Guesthouse (p189)
- ➡ Good Times Resort (p179)

Why Go?

The past is never far behind in central Thailand. Cycle around the temple ruins in Ayuthaya and you can imagine how grand this former capital must have once been. Visit the memorials and Death Railway in Kanchanaburi and you'll find new empathy for the WWII prisoners of war who suffered there.

Central Thailand doesn't just do history, though. Nature is a major player here, with the jagged mountain ranges that dominate Kanchanaburi's horizons hosting spectacular waterfalls, deep caves and some of Thailand's few remaining wild tigers. In the region's multi-ethnic northwest, lethargic Sangkhlaburi encourages lakeside lazing near the gateway to Myanmar, or you can sleep among the trees in lush Thong Pha Phum National Park.

Lopburi combines both nature and history in its own unique way, as hundreds of monkeys scamper among the Khmer-era temples in what was once Thailand's second capital.

When to Go

➡ Central Thailand experiences the country's three seasons in equal measure: hot from February to June, rainy from June to October and cool (relatively speaking) from October to January. The one constant is the humidity.

➡ Because of altitude, it is cooler (sometimes genuinely cold) and wetter in Sangkhlaburi and surrounding national parks than in other areas. Ayuthaya and Lopburi sit in a wide-open plain that receives similar amounts of rain and heat as Bangkok.

Central Thailand Highlights

1. Getting up early and walking over the **Saphan Mon** (p188) wooden bridge in laid-back Sangkhlaburi.
2. Watching the monkey mayhem in **Lopburi** (p170).
3. Cycling around the temple ruins in **Ayuthaya** (p158).
4. Spending a night up high in a tree house at **Thong Pha Phum National Park** (p186).
5. Visiting the Death Railway and WWII museums in **Kanchanaburi** (p173).
6. Clambering up the seven levels at **Erawan waterfall** (p183), one of Thailand's most impressive falls.

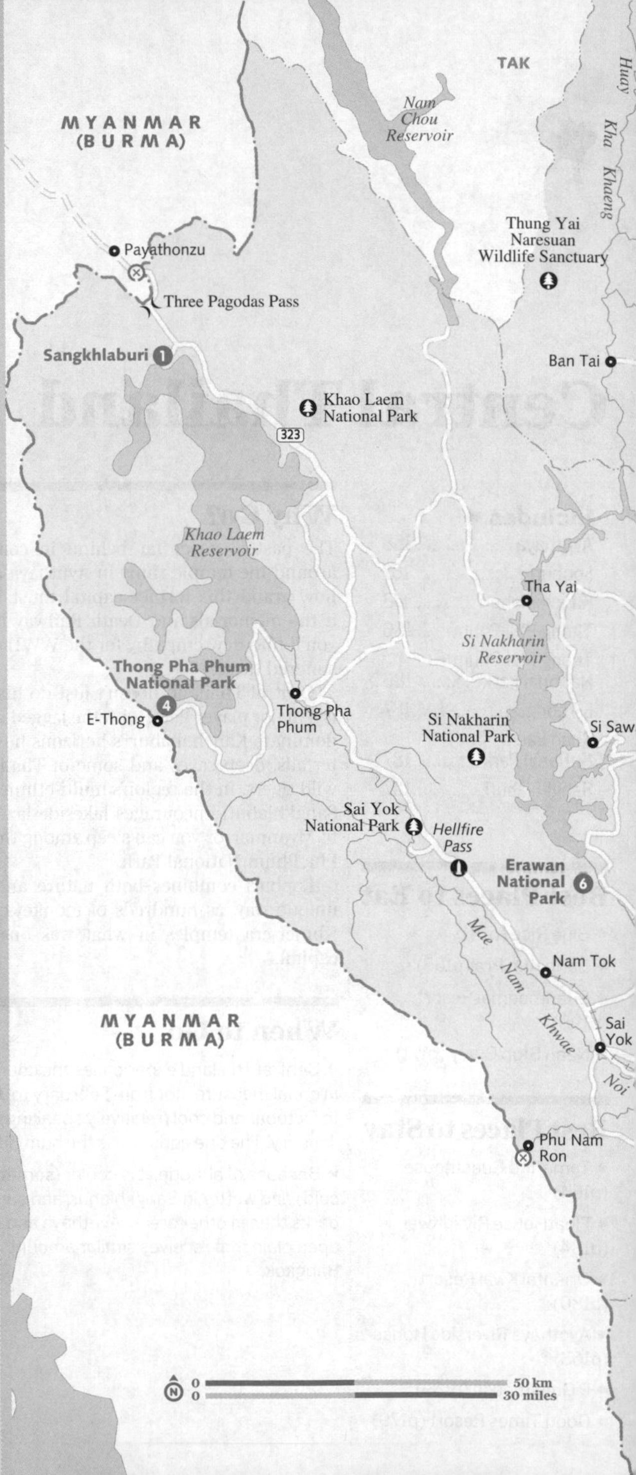

Sawang Yai
Thap Huay Salao
Huay Kha Khaeng Wildlife Sanctuary
Hua Thanon
Phaisali
NAKHON SAWAN
1
1
Uthai Thani
Hang Nam
Tak Fa
Wong Sawang
UTHAI THANI
Thung Men
Wat Sing
32
Ta Khli
Chainat
Nong Muang
333
Hua Chang
Chang Thong
CHAINAT
311
11
Ban Rai
Nong Pun
Ban Mee
Hankha
LOPBURI
Huay Taphoen
Singburi
Krasiaw Reservoir
Dan Chang
Huay Krasiaw
SINGBURI
1
2 Lopburi
Sam Chuk
Chaloem Ratanakosin National Park
Nong Khon
333
ANG THONG
Sa Krachom
SUPHANBURI
Ang Thong
32
Nong Ri
Suphanburi
309
ANCHANABURI
U-Thong
AYUTHAYA 3
Bophloi
AYUTHAYA
Thung Khok
Bang Pa In
Mae Nam Khwae Yai
3358
Bang Sai
Lat Ya
23
340
Kamphaeng Saen
Mae Nam Tha Chin
5 Kanchanaburi
Pathum Thani
Don Mueang Airport
Dan Makham Tia
Nakhon Pathom
Nonthaburi
338
4
Nong Tak Ya
Thonburi
BANGKOK
Chom Beung
35
Ratchaburi
Samut Sakhon
Samut Prakan
RATCHABURI

AYUTHAYA PROVINCE

Ayuthaya พระนครศรีอยุธยา

POP 83,217

Once one of the world's wealthiest and most cosmopolitan cities, Ayuthaya's gilded temples and treasure-laden palaces glittered from kilometres away. Today the dozens of ruins offer a tantalising glimpse into its glorious past. Many sites have been partially restored, so it's easy to imagine how they must have looked in their prime.

Between 1350 and 1767 Ayuthaya was the capital of Siam, which at its peak ruled over an area larger than England and France combined. Home to over a million people, the island city was one of Asia's major trading ports and international merchants visiting from around the globe were left in awe.

The empire fell in 1767 when an invading Burmese army thoroughly sacked the city, looting most of its treasures and enslaving thousands of its citizens. Independence was restored within a year, but the capital was moved to what is now Bangkok and Ayuthaya was left largely abandoned for decades. Major restoration work began in 1969 and it's now a Unesco World Heritage site.

Most people visit as a day trip, hitting just the major attractions, but this requires leaving a lot off your plate. Two days offers a far more rewarding visit, and lets you admire the ruins lit up at night.

Sights

At its zenith, Ayuthaya was home to over 400 temples. Today dozens of them have been partially restored, leaving the naked stupas, roofless chapels and headless Buddha images to evocatively tell the kingdom's tale.

It's easy to get between the sites by bicycle, though hiring a guide for some historical detail is useful. A special pass for the six main ruins costs 220B, lasts 30 days and can be bought at each site.

There's also a lot beyond the heart of the historical park to interest cultural explorers, such as cycling past minor but attractive ruins in the green expanse of Sri Nakharin Park, seeing local life on car-free Ko Lai island and admiring Ratanakosin-era temple mural paintings.

The ruins are symbols of both royalty and religion, two fundamental elements of Thai society, so remember to show respect.

On the Island

The sites listed are in central Ayuthaya.

★Wat Phra Si Sanphet RUIN

(วัดพระศรีสรรเพชญ์; admission 50B; ⌚8am-6pm) This ruined temple's three magnificent stupas are one of the iconic images of Ayuthaya. Built in the late 15th century, Wat Phra Si Sanphet was a royal temple inside palace grounds, and these were the models for Bangkok's Wat Phra Kaew and Royal Palace. It was Ayuthaya's largest temple and once contained a 16m-high standing Buddha (Phra Si Sanphet) covered with 143kg (or more, depending on the source) of gold, which was melted down by Burmese conquerors.

★Wihan Phra Mongkhon Bophit BUDDHIST TEMPLE

(วิหารพระมงคลบพิตร; ⌚8am-5pm) FREE Next to Wat Phra Si Sanphet, this sanctuary hall houses one of Thailand's largest bronze Buddha images. The 12.5m-high figure (17m with the base) was badly damaged by a lightning-induced fire around 1700, and again when the Burmese sacked the city. The Buddha and the building were repaired in the 20th century. In 1956 the Burmese Prime Minister donated 200,000B to restore the building, an act of belated atonement for his country's sacking of the city 200 years before.

★Wat Ratchaburana RUIN

(วัดราชบูรณะ; admission 50B; ⌚8am-6pm) The *prang* (Hindu/Khmer-style stupa) in this temple is one of the best extant versions in the city, with detailed carvings of lotus and mythical creatures. You can climb inside the *prang* to visit the brightly painted crypt, if you aren't afraid of heights, small spaces or bats. The temple was founded in 1424 by King Borom Rachathirat II on the cremation site for his two brothers who died while fighting each other for the throne.

Wat Phra Ram RUIN

(วัดพระราม; admission 50B; ⌚8am-6pm) Wat Phra Ram may mark the cremation site of King U Thong, though its history is unclear. It has one of the tallest *prang* in Ayuthaya, though the surrounding grounds are less extensive than the better-known sites. One good reason to visit is that few other people do.

Wat Mahathat RUIN

(วัดมหาธาตุ; Th Chee Kun; admission 50B; ⏲8am-6pm) The most photographed image in Ayuthaya is here: a sandstone Buddha head that lies tangled within a bodhi tree's entwined roots. The central *prang* once stood 43m high and it collapsed on its own long before the Burmese sacked the city. It was rebuilt in more recent times, but collapsed again in 1911. Founded in 1374, during the reign of King Borom Rachathirat I, it was the seat of the supreme patriarch and the kingdom's most important temple.

Ayutthaya Tourist Center MUSEUM

(ศูนย์ท่องเที่ยวอยุธยา; ☎035 246076; ⏲8.30am-4.30pm) FREE A good first stop in Ayuthaya, the excellent upstairs museum puts everything in context with displays about the temples and daily life. Also upstairs is the tiny but interesting **Ayutthaya National Art Museum**. Downstairs is the tourist information centre.

Wat Lokayasutharam RUIN

(วัดโลกยสุธาราม; off Th Khlong Thaw; ⏲dawn-dusk) FREE This temple ruin features an impressive 42m-long reclining Buddha, ostensibly dating back to the early Ayuthaya period. A visit is worth the short bike trip it takes to reach it.

Wat Suwandararam BUDDHIST TEMPLE

(วัดสุวรรณดาราราม; ⏲dawn-dusk) FREE Although there was a temple here in the Ayuthaya era, the present buildings are from the current reign, with the *bòht* (ordination hall) built by King Rama I and the adjacent *wí·hăhn* (sanctuary) by King Rama IV. Both have fascinating murals inside that show, among other things, daily life from that day and age and stories from the life of King Naresuan. Notice the *bòht*'s boat-like concave design, a typical feature of late Ayuthaya style that remained popular in the early Ratanakosin era.

Chao Sam Phraya National Museum MUSEUM

(พิพิธภัณฑสถานแห่งชาติเจ้าสามพระยา; cnr Th Rotchana & Th Si Sanphet; adult/child 150B/free; ⏲9am-4pm; P) The largest museum in the city displays many of the treasures unearthed during excavations of the ruins, including the golden treasures found in the crypts of Wat Mahathat and Wat Ratchaburana.

Ayuthaya Historical Study Centre MUSEUM

(ศูนย์ศึกษาประวัติศาสตร์อยุธยา; Th Rotchana; adult/child 100/50B; ⏲9am-4pm; P) This modern museum funded by Japan features exhibitions on the lives of traditional villagers and the foreign communities during the Ayuthaya kingdom, plus a few dioramas of the city's former glories. You'll have to ask someone to open the downstairs gallery.

Chantharakasem National Museum MUSEUM

(พิพิธภัณฑสถานแห่งชาติจันทรเกษม; Th U Thong; admission 100B; ⏲9am-4pm Wed-Sun) The museum is within the grounds of Wang Chan Kasem (Chan Kasem Palace), built for King Rama IV at the site of a palace used by King Naresuan and seven subsequent Ayuthayan kings. The museum is large, but the collection (Buddhist art, pottery, ancient weapons, lacquered cabinets and original furnishings) isn't – the highly decorated buildings themselves are the main attraction.

Thai Boat Museum MUSEUM

(พิพิธภัณฑ์เรือไทย; ☎035 241195; www.thaiboatmuseum.com; Th Ho Rattanachai; admission by donation; ⏲9am-noon & 1-5pm) This interesting little private museum is full of wooden boats, both real and artistic miniatures, many of which still ply Ayuthaya's rivers today.

Million Toy Museum MUSEUM

(พิพิธภัณฑ์ล้านของเล่นเกริกยุ้นพันธ์; ☎081 890 5782; www.milliontoymuseum.com; Th U Thong; adult/child 50/20B; ⏲9am-4pm Tue-Sun; P) Chances are your favourite childhood toy is enjoying retirement here among the tin soldiers, dolls and Godzillas, all lovingly displayed in this two-storey museum. It isn't just toys; the collection of pottery and old coconut scrapers is also of interest.

Off the Island

On the opposite side of the water that envelops central Ayuthaya are several famous temples. You can reach some sites by bicycle, but others require a motorbike. Evening boat tours around the island are another way to see the highlights.

★**Wat Chai Wattanaram** RUIN

(วัดไชยวัฒนาราม; admission 50B; ⏲8am-6pm) This is the most impressive off-island site thanks to its 35m-high Khmer-style central *prang* and overall good condition. It was built by King Prasat Thong beginning in

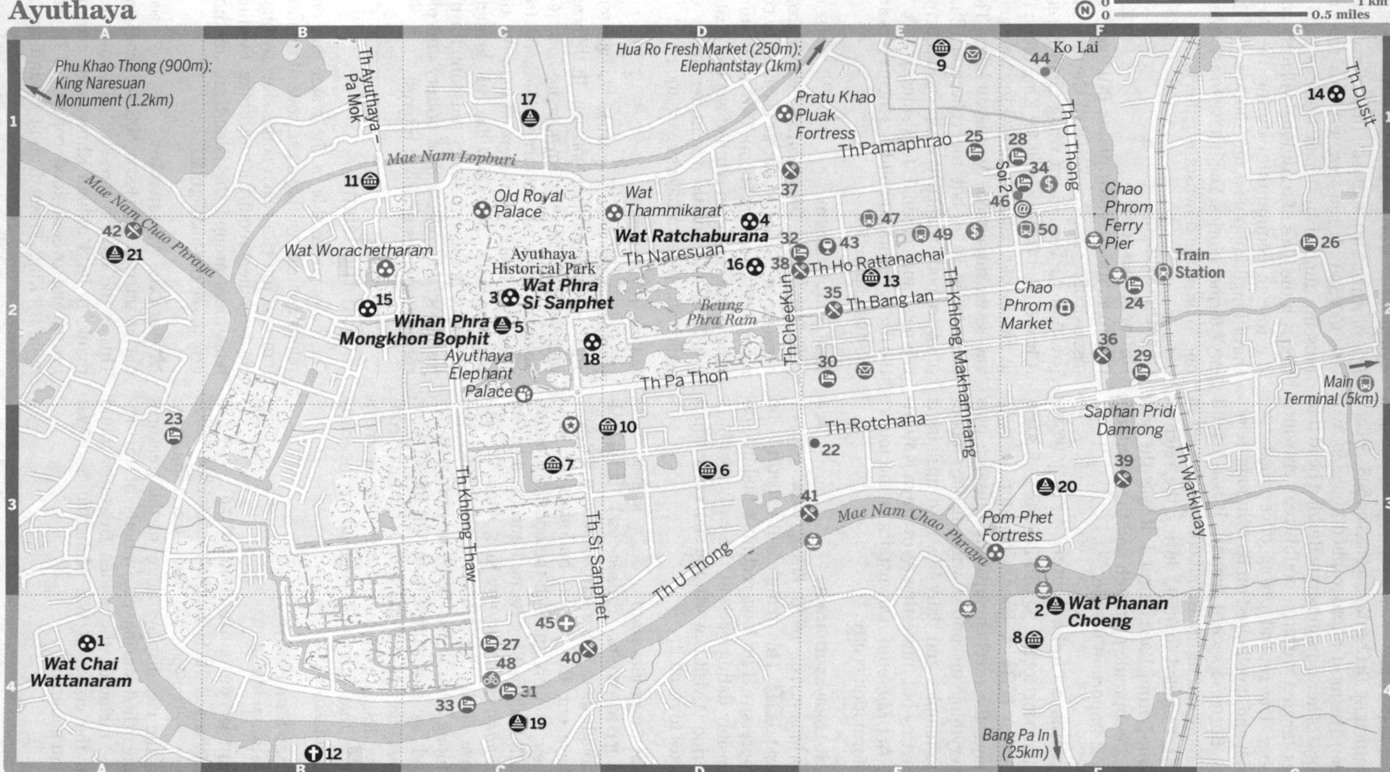
Ayuthaya
0 1 km
0 0.5 miles
Phu Khao Thong (900m); King Naresuan Monument (1.2km)
Th Ayuthaya – Pa Mok
Hua Ro Fresh Market (250m); Elephantstay (1km)
Ko Lai
Th Dusit
Pratu Khao Pluak Fortress
Th Pamaphrao
Mae Nam Lopburi
Th U Thong
Soi 2
Old Royal Palace
Wat Thammikarat
Wat Ratchaburana
Chao Phrom Ferry Pier
Mae Nam Chao Phraya
Wat Worachetharam
Ayuthaya Historical Park
Wat Phra Si Sanphet
Th Naresuan
Th Ho Rattanachai
Train Station
Wihan Phra Mongkhon Bophit
Beung Phra Ram
Th Cheekun
Th Bang Ian
Th Khlong Makhamriang
Chao Phrom Market
Ayuthaya Elephant Palace
Th Pa Thon
Main Terminal (5km)
Saphan Pridi Damrong
Th Rotchana
Th Watkluay
Th Khlong Thaw
Th Si Sanphet
Mae Nam Chao Phraya
Pom Phet Fortress
Th U Thong
Wat Phanan Choeng
Wat Chai Wattanaram
Bang Pa In (25km)

Ayuthaya

Top Sights
- 1 Wat Chai Wattanaram ... A4
- 2 Wat Phanan Choeng ... F4
- 3 Wat Phra Si Sanphet ... C2
- 4 Wat Ratchaburana ... D2
- 5 Wihan Phra Mongkhon Bophit ... C2

Sights
- 6 Ayuthaya Historical Study Centre ... D3
- 7 Ayutthaya Tourist Center ... C3
- 8 Raan Hollanda ... F4
- 9 Chantharakasem National Museum ... E1
- 10 Chao Sam Phraya National Museum ... D3
- 11 Million Toy Museum ... B1
- 12 St Joseph Church ... B4
- 13 Thai Boat Museum ... E2
- 14 Wat Kudi Dao ... G1
- 15 Wat Lokayasutharam ... B2
- 16 Wat Mahathat ... D2
- 17 Wat Na Phra Men ... C1
- 18 Wat Phra Ram ... C2
- 19 Wat Phutthai Sawan ... C4
- 20 Wat Suwandararam ... F3
- 21 Wat Tha Ka Rong ... A2

Activities, Courses & Tours
- 22 Ayutthaya Boat & Travel ... E3

Sleeping
- 23 Ayothaya Riverside House ... A3
- 24 Baan Are Gong ... F2
- 25 Baan Lotus Guest House ... E1
- 26 Baan Thai House ... G2
- 27 Baifern ... C4
- 28 Chantana Guesthouse ... F1
- 29 Krungsri River Hotel ... F2
- 30 Promtong Mansion ... E2
- 31 Sala Ayutthaya ... C4
- 32 Tamarind Guesthouse ... D2
- 33 Thong Come Homestay ... C4
- 34 Tony's Place ... F1

Eating
- 35 Bang Ian Night Market ... E2
- 36 Bann Kun Pra ... F2
- 37 Lung Lek ... D1
- 38 Malakor ... D2
- 39 Pae Krung Gao ... F3
- 40 Roti Sai Mai Stalls ... C4
- 41 Sai-Thong ... E3
- 42 Talat Nam Wat Tha Ka Rong ... A2
- Tony's Place ... (see 34)

Drinking & Nightlife
- 43 Coffee House ... E2

Information
- 44 Immigration ... F1
- 45 Phra Nakorn Si Ayuthaya Hospital ... C4
- 46 Tour With Thai ... F1
- Tourism Authority of Thailand ... (see 7)

Transport
- 47 Bus ticket office ... E2
- 48 Lung Nuat ... C4
- 49 Minivans to Bangkok ... E2
- 50 Talat Ta Rot Chao Phrom Bus Stop ... F2

1630 (and taking around 20 years) to honour his mother, and the design's resemblance to Cambodia's Angkor Wat is intentional.

★ **Wat Phanan Choeng** BUDDHIST TEMPLE

(วัดพนัญเชิง; admission 20B; ⏲dawn-dusk) A bevy of popular merit-making ceremonies makes this a hectic temple on weekends. The signature attraction is the 19m-high Phra Phanan Choeng Buddha, which was created in 1324 and sits inside a soaring *wí·hăhn* (open 8am to 5pm) surrounded by 84,000 small Buddha images lining the walls. It's even more imposing than the big Buddha at Wihan Phra Mongkhon Bophit. People come here daily to cover their heads with the end of the big Buddha's robe, a ceremony that other temples normally only do on major holidays.

The buildings in front of the big Buddha have historic murals, and the **Jao Mae Soi Dok Mak Chinese shrine** facing the river is especially colourful.

★ **Wat Yai Chai Mongkhon** RUIN

(วัดใหญ่ชัยมงคล; admission 20B; ⏲6am-6pm) King U Thong founded this temple in 1357 to house monks returning from ordination in Sri Lanka and in 1592 King Naresuan built its fantastic bell-shaped *chedi* after a victory over the Burmese. The landscaped gardens make this one of Ayuthaya's most photogenic ruins. There's a 7m-long reclining Buddha near the entrance and the local belief is that if you can get a coin to stick to the Buddha's feet, good luck will come your way.

Wat Kudi Dao RUIN

(วัดกุฎีดาว; ⏲8am-4.30pm) **FREE** Though it's not yet near Indiana Jones levels, forest is slowly reclaiming this attractive ruin. The massive main stupa has collapsed, but several buildings still stand. It's northeast of the train station, well beyond the realm of most of Ayuthaya's visitors, so you'll likely have it to yourself. **Wat Maheyong** (admission 50B; ⏲8am-4.30pm), a bit to the east, is larger, but less interesting, although the walled corridor leading to the *ubosot* (chapel) is an unusual feature.

Wat Tha Ka Rong BUDDHIST TEMPLE
(วัดทาการอง; dawn-dusk; P) FREE Just northwest of the island sits this bizarre temple, full of interesting statues: Buddhist, Hindu, animist and just-for-fun. Behind the *waiing* skeletons, the collection of Buddha images from neighbouring countries, the fish tanks and the larger-than-life-size monks are a historic *ubosot,* wrecked wooden boat and weekend floating market (p165).

Wat Phutthai Sawan BUDDHIST TEMPLE
(วัดพุทไธศวรรย์; dawn-dusk) FREE This still-active temple, the first built off the island, is one of the few places the Burmese didn't destroy, although time took a toll eventually. You can climb up inside the massive Khmer-style *prang.* It's a stunning scene when lit up at night.

Phu Khao Thong STUPA
(เจดีย์ภูเขาทอง; dawn-dusk; P) Originally built by the Burmese during a 15-year occupation, the top section of this huge white stupa was added later by Thais and you can climb the 79 stairs up to the midpoint for views of the surrounding rice paddies. The larger-than-life statue at the front is a memorial to the all-conquering King Naresuan. Surrounding him are reliefs of some of his heroic exploits, including wrestling a crocodile, and dozens of statues of fighting cockerels.

Wat Na Phra Men BUDDHIST TEMPLE
(วัดหน้าพระเมรุ; admission 20B; dawn-dusk; P) This temple was one of the few to escape the wrath of Burma's invading army in 1767 since it served as their main base. The *bôht* is massive, larger than most modern ones, and the very holy main Buddha image wears 'royal attire', which was very common in the late Ayuthaya era. Despite what the English sign inside says, it's made of bronze, not gold.

Elephant Kraal HISTORIC SITE
(เพนียดคล้องช้าง) FREE Wild elephants were once rounded up and kept in this restored *kraal* (stockade), built from hundreds of teak logs. The king would come out to look on as the animals were chosen for work or war. It's not currently in use. Instead elephants who aren't out working at the historical park are kept chained up in the back. **Elephantstay** (080 668 7727; www.elephantstay.com; from 12,000B per person incl accommodation) offers people the chance to spend time working with the elephants here. Three-day minimum.

Ayuthaya Floating Market MARKET
(ตลาดน้ำอโยธยา; 9am-5pm Mon-Fri, to 6pm Sat & Sun; P) FREE Not an actual floating market, rather a highly kitsch tourist trap full of souvenir shops and selfie-snapping spots set on wooden platforms above the water. It is, however, a good place for snacking and there are afternoon cultural shows. Avoid the neighbouring Ayodia Inter Market with its dubious animal attractions.

Tours

A variety of tours around the city and beyond are available. They can be booked through your guesthouse, though you may get more options and flexibility by talking to a travel agent such as **Tour With Thai** (035 231084; www.tourwiththai.com; Soi 2, Th Naresuan; 8.30am-6.30pm). The most promoted trip is a two-hour afternoon boat ride (200B per person) making quick stops at Wat Phanan Choeng, Wat Phutthai Sawan and Wat Chai Wattanaram. It's a convenient, though rushed, way to see these three worthy, but distant, sites.

For something different, **Ayutthaya Boat and Travel** (081 733 5687; www.ayutthaya-boat.com; Th Chee Kun; 9am-5pm Mon-Sat) does cycling and paddling tours with homestay accommodation and can organise dinner on a teak rice barge.

There are also overnight **boat tours** (p166) from Bangkok to Ayuthaya.

Festivals & Events

Wai Kru Muay Thai Ceremony CULTURAL
Thai boxing fighters and fans flock to Ayuthaya in mid-March to show respect to the masters. Activities during the week-long festival include *moo·ay tai (muay Thai)* matches and lessons, sword-making demonstrations and *yant* tattooing.

Ayutthaya World Heritage Fair LIGHT SHOW
The sound-and-light shows (500B) at Wat Mahathat are the highlight of this mid-December event.

Sleeping

Most backpackers head for Soi 2, Th Naresuan, but the area around the ferry landings (on both sides of the river) in front of the train station is also backpackery, with lots of low-priced rooms. Both spots are tiny, so you can quickly roam the areas looking for a guesthouse that fits your vibe.

Staying along the river on the west side of the island is less convenient, but very pleasant – although be warned that most of the dinner cruises, and there are many on weekends, have karaoke machines.

★ **Ayothaya Riverside House** GUESTHOUSE $
(081 644 5328; r without bath 400B, r on boat 1500B; ❄📶) Across the Chao Phraya on the west side of town, this wonderful guesthouse provides a very different experience from most due to its untouristed neighbourhood setting. Regular rooms are simple shared-bath and fan affairs in an old wooden house, but this is also the only place in town where you can sleep on a boat.

Befitting its casual character, the owners are as friendly as can be.

★ **Baan Lotus Guest House** GUESTHOUSE $
(☎035 251988; Th Pamaphrao; dm 200B, s 250B, d & tw 350-600B; P❄📶) Near, but completely separate from, the backpacker strip, this converted teak schoolhouse with a large deck out back is a real treat, and the owner is just as charming as the building. It's

FOREIGN QUARTER

One reason Ayuthaya's rulers thrived was their adroit diplomacy and tolerance towards other cultures and religions. At its peak, over 40 ethnic groups resided here. People from nearby places, such as the Mon, Lao and Khmer, as well as the Chinese, lived more or less freely among the locals. Those from further away, such as Indians, Persians, Javanese and Malay, were given land, mostly to the south of the island, by the king to create their own settlements.

The Portuguese, who arrived in 1511, were the first Europeans to reach Siam and they were granted land to settle here in the 1540s. They were followed in the next century by the Dutch, English, Spanish and French. The Europeans' brought arms and other luxuries and returned mostly with tin, deerskins, sappan wood and rice.

In 1767 these settlements met the same fate as the rest of the city, though three nations have memorialised their ancient Thai ties with information centres.

The area southwest of the river junction is semi-rural and ideal for cycling. A Persian community was here, east of **Wat Phutthai Sawan** (p162), in the historical heyday and the area is now one of many Muslim districts around the modern city.

Baan Hollanda (บ้านฮอลันดา; www.baanhollanda.org; admission 50B; ⏲9am-5pm Wed-Sun; P) This informative exhibition, built next to excavated foundations of some original trading-post buildings, chronicles Thai-Dutch relations from the time the Dutch East India Company (VOC) arrived in Ayuthaya in 1604 up to the present. Downstairs is a little cafe with Dutch coffee and cocoa. Be sure to admire the adjacent boatyard on your way in. The English village was just to the south and there was a Chinese village nearby, but nothing remains of either.

Japanese Village (หมู่บ้านญี่ปุ่น; adult/child 50/20B; ⏲8am-5pm; P) This interesting exhibition, located 1km south of Baan Hollanda, details the lives of the estimated 1500 Japanese who came to settle in Ayuthaya in the early 17th century. Some came to trade, but most were Christians fleeing persecution in their homeland. There are two exhibition halls, each with a video presentation, and a small Japanese garden.

St Joseph Church (วัดนักบุญยอแซฟ; ⏲8.30am-noon & 1-4.30pm Mon-Sat, 10.30-11.30am Sun) In 1673 King Narai gave the French land next to the Christian Vietnamese settlement and also donated money towards building the first St Joseph Church. The original wooden church was replaced by a brick building in 1695 and it's been modified since then. Many locals living around the church today are Catholic.

Portuguese Village (หมู่บ้านโปรตุเกส; ⏲9am-4pm) The focus of the Portuguese village is a burial-site excavation with several skeletal remains of Portuguese settlers on display in an open pit. In front is the foundation of the 1540 St Dominic Church, the first church built in Thailand and one of three at what was the largest of the European communities. Note the Thai-style spirit house with figures of St Joseph and St Paul inside.

LOCAL KNOWLEDGE

TAILOR-MADE TÚK-TÚKS

Túk-túks in Ayuthaya are different from the classic Thai design thanks to their strange dome-shaped fronts. Resembling Darth Vader's iconic mask, they zip around in a variety of colours and designs. One veteran driver remembers these distinctive taxis looking the same for more than 50 years. It's thought they may have first been made in Japan, which could explain the samurai-like curved front.

so chill that almost nothing happens after 6pm, including check-in.

Chantana Guesthouse GUESTHOUSE $
(035323200; chantanahouse@yahoo.com; 12/22 Soi 2, Th Naresuan; r incl breakfast 300-450B;) This spic-and-span spot is rather plain, but offers probably the best value on the backpacker strip. Staff are friendly, though English is limited. Splash out an extra 50B for a room with a balcony.

Baan Are Gong GUESTHOUSE $
(035 235592; siriporntan@yahoo.com.sg; Soi Satani Rot Fai; r 380-1300B;) Two minutes from the train station, Baan Are Gong fills a century-old teak building right on the river and is run by a welcoming family. It's not the cheapest lodging in this spot, but it's got the most character. The least-expensive rooms have shared bathrooms.

★**Tamarind Guesthouse** GUESTHOUSE $$
(089 010 0196; tamarindthai2012@gmail; off Th Chee Kun; r incl breakfast 600-1200B;) There's a creative mix of old and new in this modified wooden house and the service couldn't be more friendly. Hidden away in a little back street directly across from Wat Mahathat, Tamarind manages to be both a peaceful getaway and right in the thick of things.

★**Baifern** GUESTHOUSE $$
(035 242051; www.baifernhomestay.com; Th Khlong Thaw; r 800-1700B;) One of the classiest guesthouses around; all but the cheapest rooms have creative decorations and the lounge under the wooden house is very inviting. Very quiet and friendly.

Tony's Place GUESTHOUSE $$
(035 252578; www.tonyplace-ayutthaya.com; Soi 2, Th Naresuan; r 200-1200B;) Tony's remains the flashpackers' top choice thanks to rooms that are actually attractive, a mini-pool and the chance to swap travel tips with fellow visitors. Cheaper rooms have fans and shared bathrooms.

Thong Come Homestay GUESTHOUSE $$
(083 990 0601; http://thongcomehomestay.webiz.co.th; Th U Thong; r 700B;) Not the best value in town, but Thong Come's two simple rooms are perched right up against the river, making them ideal for lazy lounging. If it's full, Ban Bua and Seven Seas are similar and in the same small spot.

Promtong Mansion GUESTHOUSE $$
(089 165 6297; www.promtong.com; off Th Pa Thon; r 850-1550B;) Though it lacks the character of Ayuthaya's top guesthouses, the helpful owner and friendly staff run a tight ship. Rooms are big and well furnished and it's a convenient but quiet location. Guests can use the pool at the family's other hotel, 1km away.

Sala Ayutthaya BOUTIQUE HOTEL $$$
(035 242588; www.salaayutthaya.com; Th U Thong; r incl breakfast 4700-9400B;) Artistically combining Ayuthaya's ancient aesthetic with modern flair, Sala Ayutthaya is a beautiful place. The night-time view of an illuminated Wat Phutthai Sawan, directly across the river, is stunning.

Baan Thai House BOUTIQUE HOTEL $$$
(080 437 4555; www.baanthaihouse.com; r incl breakfast 2400-3800B;) These Thai-style villas, especially the three in historic teak houses, and well-kept grounds ensure a Zen-like stay. There's an on-site spa for post-ruin relaxation.

Krungsri River Hotel HOTEL $$$
(035 244333; www.krungsririver.com; 27/2 Th Rotchana; r/ste incl breakfast 1900/4500B;) All the comfort you expect from an international-style four-star hotel, plus big views from the rooms in front and a good Italian restaurant.

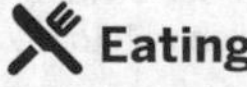

Eating

Centuries of mingling with foreign traders has resulted in a rich tapestry of food options. River prawns, Thai-Muslim snacks and especially boat noodles (legend says they were created here) are the defining dishes. The many riverside restaurants tend to be expensive, but worth it.

Roti Sai Mai Stalls SWEETS $
(Th U Thong; ⌚8am-8pm) The dessert *roh đee săi măi* (silk thread roti) was invented in Ayuthaya and is sold all over town, though the shops fronting the hospital are the most famous. Buy a bag then make your own by rolling together thin strands of melted palm sugar and wrapping them inside the roti.

Talat Nam Wat Tha Ka Rong MARKET $
(⌚8am-5pm Sat & Sun) Buying your food at this floating market, where vendors serve from boats tied up to large rafts, is a great experience, though finding space at a table is less fun. It's on the Chao Phraya river behind its namesake temple (p162).

Malakor THAI $
(Th Chee Kun; dishes 40-200B; ⌚restaurant noon-10pm, coffee shop 8am-4pm; 📶🖉) Malakor has a big menu, low prices, a great cook and a relaxing little wooden hut to enjoy it all in. You will, however, need to be patient with the service side of things. The bakery, fruit juices and coffee at the ground-floor coffee shop are great, too.

Lung Lek NOODLES $
(Th Chee Kun; mains 30-50B; ⌚8.30am-4pm) Everybody's favourite noodle emporium, Uncle Lek has long served some of the most notable *gŏo ay đĕe o reu a* in town.

Tony's Place INTERNATIONAL, THAI $
(Soi 2, Th Naresuan; dishes 70-300B; 📶🖉) Set at the front of the eponymous guesthouse, Tony's offers simple but tasty Thai/Western dishes, a few vegie nibbles and plenty of fellow travellers to chat with.

Bang Ian Night Market MARKET $
(Th Bang Ian; ⌚4-8.30pm) This big, busy night market at the end of its namesake street is a great noshing destination. It's also ideally situated for a visit either before or after seeing the ruins illuminated at night.

★ **Bann Kun Pra** THAI $$
(☎035 241978; www.bannkunpra.com; Th U Thong; dishes 70-420B; ⌚11am-9.30pm) Far more intimate than most of Ayuthaya's riverside restaurants, this century-old teak house is a great place to sit and watch river life pass by. The inventive menu is loaded with seafood and has several versions of the local river prawn, including grilled with herbs and fried with tamarind sauce. There are some lovely but pricey guest rooms here, too.

★ **Pae Krung Gao** THAI $$
(Th U Thong; dishes 60-1000B; ⌚10am-9.30pm; 📶) A wonderfully cluttered riverside restaurant serving top-notch Thai food – seemingly half the crowd is here for the grilled river prawns. The English-language menu is limited, so if you know what you like, just ask.

Sai-Thong THAI, NORTHEASTERN THAI $$
(Th U Thong; dishes 60-350B; ⌚10.30am-9.30pm; P🖉👪) One of many big restaurants with riverside decks along this stretch of the Chao Phraya, Sai-Thong doesn't bother much with decoration since the food is good enough to keep the locals coming back.

Drinking & Nightlife

Most travellers limit their nightlife to the pack of street-side bars on Soi 2, Th Naresuan. For a wholly Thai night out, there's the oddly named **Coffee House** (Th Naresuan) bar, where live music starts at 8pm nightly.

Information

DANGERS & ANNOYANCES

When cycling, put bags around your body, not in baskets where they could be snatched. At night many packs of dogs roam the streets – avoid eye contact and be sure to keep your distance.

EMERGENCY

Tourist Police (☎035 241446; Th Si Sanphet)

IMMIGRATION

Immigration (☎035 328411; Th U Thong; ⌚8.30am-noon & 1-4.30pm)

MEDICAL SERVICES

Phra Nakorn Si Ayuthaya Hospital (☎035 211888; Th U Thong) Has an emergency centre and English-speaking doctors.

MONEY

All the major banks have offices (and ATMs) on Th Naresuan, though the only weekend service is the **Krungthai exchange booth** (Amporn Department Store; ⌚10am-5.30pm). There's also an exchange booth open daily at Bang Pa In Palace.

POST

Main Post Office (Th U Thong; ⌚8.30am-4.30pm Mon-Fri, 9am-noon Sat)

TRANSPORT TO/FROM AYUTHAYA

Bus

DESTINATION	FARE (B)	DURATION (HR)	FREQUENCY
Bangkok (Rangsit)	40	¾	frequent (minivan)
Bangkok (Victory Monument)	60	1½	frequent (minivan)
Bangkok's Northern (Mo Chit) station	50	1	frequent (minivan)
Chiang Mai	419-837	8-10	frequent
Lopburi	80	1½-1¾	every 30min (minivan)
Saraburi	45	1½	frequent
Sukhothai	266-342	7	frequent
Suphanburi	45	1½	frequent (minivan)

Train

DESTINATION	FARE (B)	DURATION (HR)	FREQUENCY
Bang Pa In	3-12	1¼	18 daily
Bangkok (Hualamphong station)	15-66	1½-2½	frequent
Chiang Mai	211-1398	11-14	5 daily
Nong Khai	202-1262	9-11	4 daily
Pak Chong	53-465	2-3	10 daily

TOURIST INFORMATION

Tourism Authority of Thailand (TAT; ☎035 246076; tatyutya@tat.or.th; Th Si Sanphet; ⏰8.30am-4.30pm) Has an information counter with maps and good advice at the Ayutthaya Tourist Center (p159).

ℹ Getting There & Away

BOAT

There are no public boats between Bangkok and Ayuthaya and the 'cruises' available through travel agencies in Bangkok are really bus tours with a short boat ride through Bangkok at the start or end.

There are, however, two companies that make overnight trips from Bangkok in restored wooden rice barges. **Anantara Cruises** (www.bangkok-cruises.anantara.com) has a three-day trip that goes all the way to the city, while **Mekhala** (www.mekhala.com) only sails as far as Bang Pa In and you visit the historic park either by bus or bike.

BUS

Ayuthaya's minivan bus stop (*đà·làht tâh rót jôw prom*) is just south of the backpacker strip. Minivans to Suphanburi (transfer here for Kanchanaburi), Saraburi (transfer here for Pak Chong and Khorat) and various places in Bangkok (most people will want Victory Monument) leave from here. There's a second Bangkok departure point one block west.

For places further away, you'll need to go out to the main bus terminal 3km east of the island, off Th Rotchana, though you can buy tickets for Chiang Mai and Sukhothai from a **bus ticket office** (⏰6am-5pm) on Th Naresuan. For a túk-túk from the terminal to the old city, try for 100B, but expect to pay 150B. Or you can ride the purple *sŏrng·tăa·ou* (7B).

Many people just pay premium prices to book tickets at their hotel. The mark-up includes transport to the station and usually a shower before departure. They also sell seats in private minivans to Kanchanaburi (400B, 3½ hours) and Th Khao San (200B, 1½ hours) that pick up at the hotels.

TRAIN

The train is usually slower than buses and minibuses, except for those to Khao Yai National Park (Pak Chong station). For Bangkok, most trains stop at Bang Sue station before arriving at Hualamphong.

If you are visiting Ayuthaya as a day trip before boarding an overnight train, note that there is luggage storage at the train station and most guesthouses offer showers for about 30B.

Getting Around

Cycling is the ideal way to see the city. Most guesthouses hire bicycles (40B to 50B per day) and motorcycles (250B to 300B) and there are also several shops in front of Wat Mahathat and Wat Ratburana. If you're staying in the southwest of the island, **Lung Nuat** (088 233 2537; Th U Thong; 7am-8pm) has you covered.

Túk-túk are readily available. The driver's initial offer is certain to be high, but for most trips on the island the rate should be around 50B. The going rate per hour is 200B, but multi-hour trips get discounts.

The river ferries cost 5B per person plus 5B for a bike. The ferry nearest the train station operates 5am to 7.30pm, and the western-most can carry motorcycles.

Short elephant rides past the temples are available, but it's worth considering the animal welfare issues (see p759) involved with elephant rides before choosing this option.

Around Ayuthaya

★ Bang Pa In Palace PALACE

(พระราชวังบางปะอิน; admission 100B; 8am-4pm, last entrance 3.15pm) An eclectic assortment of architectural styles makes this a palace like no other. First used in the 17th century, it was revived in the 19th century by Kings Rama IV and V, the latter of whom added most of its European styling. Highlights include the stunning Chinese-style Wehart Chamrun, the colourful observatory Ho Withun Thasana and a Thai pavilion that appears to float in the middle of a pond.

In 1880 Queen Sunanda and her daughter drowned during a journey to the palace. Thai law forbade courtiers from touching the queen, so nobody dared jump in and save her. As a result of the tragedy King Rama V changed the law. A marble obelisk memorial is in the palace grounds. Self-drive carts (400B for one hour, 100B per hour thereafter) are available. Note the relatively early closing time.

Wat Niwet Thamaprawat, on an island next to the palace, has the most unlikely *bòht*. Designed to resemble a cathedral, its Gothic-style stained-glass windows and knights in armour stand in contrast to the Buddha images. Take a free, monk-operated cable car there from the palace parking lot.

To reach the palace, take the train from Ayuthaya (3B, 15 minutes) and then jump on a motorcycle taxi (20B) to the palace, which is 1.7km away.

Bang Sai Arts & Crafts Centre CULTURAL CENTRE

(ศูนย์ศิลปาชีพบางไทร; adult/child 100/50B, bird park additional 20B; 9am-5pm) This centre preserves traditional Thai art by offering 30 training courses, ranging from ceramics to silks to khon masks, and visitors can walk around and see them all. Other attractions on the 180-hectare site include **Sala Phra Ming Kwan** pavilion, which has galleries and sells a wide range of goods; a park with traditional houses from around the kingdom; a bird park and an aquarium. Avoid coming on non-holiday Mondays, when most things are closed.

There's no public transport from Ayuthaya.

LOPBURI PROVINCE

Lopburi ลพบุรี

POP 161,040

Temple ruins and mischievous monkeys are the headline attractions in laid-back Lopburi. They're easy to see in a day-long visit before catching overnight transport up to Chiang Mai, but stay longer and you can venture out of the city for rock climbing, sunflower fields and bat caves.

One of Thailand's oldest cities, Lopburi developed during the Dvaravati period (6th to 10th centuries), when it was known as Lavo. What remains today is the architecture and artwork of the subsequent Khmer and Ayuthaya empires. King Narai (r 1657–88) made it a second capital and hosted many foreign dignitaries here.

But it's the furry modern-day residents that really define the city. Hundreds of monkeys live in and around two of the major ruins and most visitors, both Thai and foreign, come here specifically to experience the monkey mayhem.

Sights

All of Lopburi's main sites reside in a conveniently compact area and can be visited in a leisurely day. If you're staying overnight, take a stroll through the city after dark to see the ruins and shrine lit up, each to very different effect.

There is a one-day, four-temple pass for 150B, but it's kind of pointless since the fourth place, **Kraison Siharat**, is far from the other three and not nearly as interesting.

Lopburi

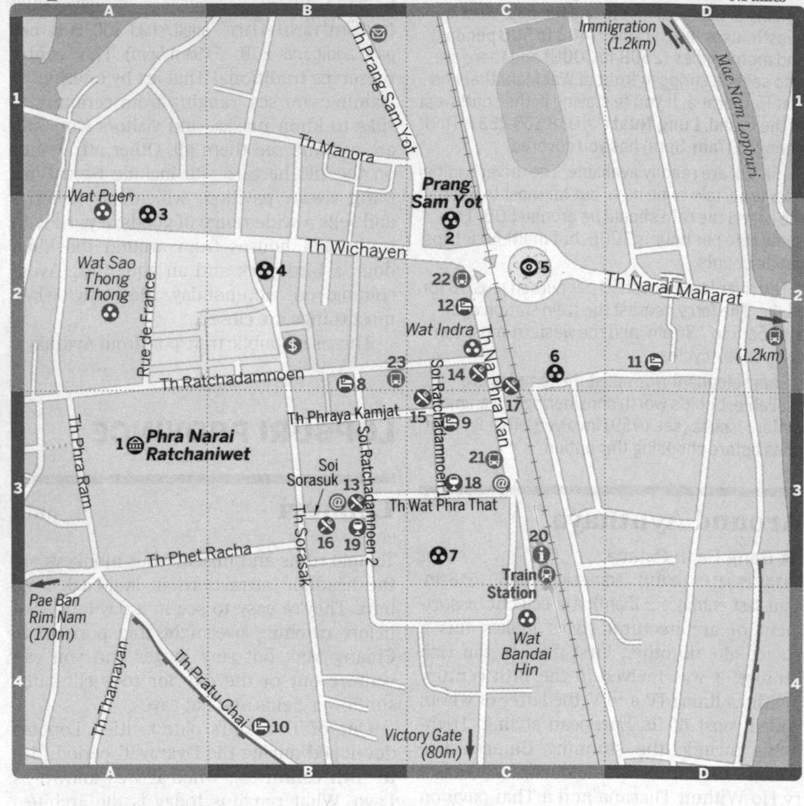

Lopburi

Top Sights

1	Phra Narai Ratchaniwet	A3
2	Prang Sam Yot	C2

Sights

3	Ban Wichayen	A2
4	Prang Khaek	B2
5	San Phra Kan	C2
6	Wat Nakhon Kosa	C2
7	Wat Phra Si Ratana Mahathat	C3

Sleeping

8	Nett Hotel	B2
9	Noom Guesthouse	C3
10	Pafun Resort	B4
11	Pee Homestay	D2
12	Sri Indra Hotel	C2

Eating

13	Baan Sahai	B3
14	Khao Tom Hor	C2
15	Matini	C3
16	Naan Stop Curry	B3
17	Night Market	C2
	Noom Guesthouse	(see 9)

Drinking & Nightlife

18	Come Inn Bar	C3
19	Sahai Phanta	B3

Information

20	Tourism Authority of Thailand	C3

Transport

21	Minivans to Bangkok	C3
22	Minivans to Bangkok	C2
23	Sŏrng·tăa·ou to bus station	B2

★Prang Sam Yot RUIN

(ปรางค์สามยอด; Th Wichayen; admission 50B; ⌚6am-6pm) The impressive Prang Sam Yot and its huge resident troop of monkeys are Lopburi's most famous attraction. The three linked towers were built by the Khmer in the 13th century as a Buddhist temple, though it was later converted to Shiva worship. There are two ruined headless Buddha images inside, while a third, more complete Buddha sits photogenically in front of the main *prang*. A heavy metal door keeps the monkeys out, but visitors can go inside.

San Phra Kan SHRINE

(ศาลพระกาฬ; Th Wichayen; ⌚5.30am-6pm) FREE Lopburi's holiest place sits in the old town's roundabout. It has a modern (built 1951) shrine in front of a Khmer-era laterite base from a toppled *prang* that was previously known as *săhn sŏong* ('tall shrine'). The principal statue inside is a four-armed Vishnu body in Lopburi-Khmer style with an Ayuthaya-era Buddha head attached.

On the shrine's north side is a monkey feeding station where milk, biscuits, fruit and more are laid out, and to the south a *lam* dance troupe performs daily. Both activities are done as thanks to the gods after wishes are granted.

★Phra Narai Ratchaniwet MUSEUM

(พระนารายณ์ราชนิเวศน์; entrance Th Sorasak; admission 150B; ⌚8.30am-4pm Wed-Sun) Plan to spend a few hours at this former royal palace, now home to the Somdet Phra Narai National Museum, which houses excellent displays of local history. Built starting in 1665 with help from French and Italian engineers, the palace was used to welcome foreign dignitaries. It was abandoned after King Narai's death, but reclaimed by King Rama IV and the main displays, covering the 3500 years of the province's known history, are in his residence.

Many of King Rama IV's belongings are on display on the 3rd floor. Next door are displays in memory of King Narai and out back are the Phra Pratiap Buildings (used primarily by queens, consorts and other women who travelled with the king), some of which have displays of handicrafts and home and farm tools still used in modern times.

After seeing the museum displays, take some time to roam the manicured palace grounds full of trees and ruins, including King Narai's elephant stables and a banquet room for receiving foreign visitors.

Enter through Pratu Phayakkha gate on Th Sorasak.

Wat Phra Si Ratana Mahathat RUIN

(วัดพระศรีรัตนมหาธาตุ; Th Na Phra Kan; admission 50B; ⌚8.30am-4.30pm) This Khmer wát, built beginning in the 12th century, has been heavily modified over the centuries and makes for a great photo opportunity. The central *prang* is the tallest in Lopburi and it retains a good amount of original stucco, as do many of the surrounding stupas. The northwestern one has U Thong–style angels; their oblong faces and unusual halos are rare.

Ban Wichayen RUIN

(บ้านวิชาเยนทร์; Chao Phraya Wichayen; Th Wichayen; admission 50B; ⌚9am-4pm) This compound, built in European style by King Narai, served as the residence of foreign ambassadors and also contained the palace of Greek trader Constantine Phaulkon, who became a key adviser to the king. The middle of the three buildings was a Catholic church. Though in a serious state of ruin, they still manage to look majestic.

Wat Nakhon Kosa RUIN

(วัดนครโกษา) FREE This is the base of what was clearly once a very big *chedi* built during the Dvaravati period, probably in the 12th century. More buildings were added in the Khmer and Ayuthaya eras, though few traces remain. To the rear is a collection of damaged Buddha images.

Prang Khaek RUIN

(ปรางค์แขก) FREE The oldest monument in Lopburi, this 11th-century trio of towers has Khmer-style brickwork and was possibly once a temple to the Hindu god Shiva. King Narai had it rebuilt after it collapsed.

Activities

It's hardly the next Krabi, but there is a **rock-climbing** scene at Khao Chin Lae (p171), with dozens of routes up the pinnacle behind Wat Pa Suwannahong. Noom Guesthouse (p170) hires gear and leads full- and half-day trips suitable for beginners. If you head there on your own, the monks want you to register and follow their posted rules, which include dressing respectfully while at the temple.

MONKEY MAGIC

Grown men arm their catapults, old women grab 2m-long poles and toy crocodiles peer out from shop windows. Welcome to Lopburi, a town that fights a losing battle to keep its iconic monkeys at bay. Hundreds of rhesus and crab-eating macaques (and cross-breeds of the two species) roam a wide swath of the old city via its rooftops and power cables. They climb on cars, slide down sunshades and squabble over scraps, putting on a nonstop show that has put 'Monkey City' on the travel map.

Many locals loathe their simian neighbours, but the monkeys are never harmed due to the belief that they are disciples of the Hindu god Hanuman (in the Thai version of the *Ramayana*, Rama gave this land to Hanuman, who founded the city), and so to injure one would be seriously bad karma. It will only take a few minutes in town, however, for you to understand why many residents support plans to round some up and ship them to a forest outside of town.

Care should be taken around the monkeys. They may be cute, but they are wild animals. Don't carry open food (or anything that could be mistaken for food) within the monkey zone, or expect a dash-and-grab robbery. If you do suffer a mugging, don't resist, as the monkeys sometimes bite, which can lead to infection. It's also prudent to avoid walking below them unless you're carrying an umbrella.

At **Prang Sam Yot** (p169) and **San Phra Kan** (p169), where most of the monkeys live, the interactions are usually more playful. Stand still long enough and some will sneak up to untie your shoelaces, steal your hat or jump on your back.

Festivals & Events

King Narai Fair CULTURAL
(mid-Feb) Held annually at the Phra Narai Ratchaniwet, there are re-enactments of period ceremonies and other cultural activities, including a 'retro market'. There is also the obligatory sound-and-light show.

Monkey Festival CULTURAL
(late Nov) Beautiful buffet tables full of fruits and sweets are set out four times during the day for the monkeys to devour. There's also a street fair and dance shows. It's usually the last Sunday in November.

Sleeping

Budget rooms are the only choice in the old town, and the new town surprises with its lack of genuinely good choices.

★**Noom Guesthouse** GUESTHOUSE $
(036 427693; www.noomguesthouse.com; Th Phraya Kamjat; dm 150B, r 200-500B;) Easily the most *fa·ràng*-friendly spot in town, Noom's options are either classic shared-bath rooms in the wooden house or cosy little garden bungalows out back.

Pee Homestay HOMESTAY $
(086 164 2184; www.lopburimassage.com; Soi Phromachan; r 200-450B;) On the wrong side of the tracks...in a good way. Staying with super-friendly Ganaree, a beautician and massage therapist, gives you a very local experience. Her three upstairs rooms are on the shortlist of contenders for cleanest guest rooms in Thailand.

Pafun Resort HOTEL $
(086 706 4931; Th Pratu Chai; r 500B;) The newest hotel (it's not a resort) in the old town, Pafun is tucked a bit out of the way along the old city wall, but giving up some convenience gets you the best rooms available near the ruins.

Nett Hotel HOTEL $
(036 411738; netthotel@hotmail.com; off Th Ratchadamnoen; r 250-550B;) The Nett remains the best of the old-school hotels near the ruins since rooms are reasonably clean and have seen some renovation in recent years. Better than the rooms, though, is the caged rooftop, which offers good monkey watching. The cheapest rooms are fan-only and have cold-water showers.

Sri Indra Hotel HOTEL $
(036 411261; 3-4 Th Na Phra Kan; r 200-350B;) Rooms are basic – bad mattresses and no hot water – but the view out your window offers a front-row seat for monkey watching. Most rooms are fan-only.

Benjatara Boutique Place Resort HOTEL $$
(036 422608; www.benjataralopburi.com; r 550-700B;) Though not truly boutique, the

modern, clean and well-run Benjatara provides the best rooms in Lopburi. It's only just barely *in* Lopburi, though, as it is along the Saraburi highway, 5.5km from the old town.

Eating & Drinking

Your best bet for an inexpensive dinner in the old town is the modest **night market** (Th Na Phra Kan; ⌚3-11pm).

There isn't much nightlife in Lopburi, especially the old town, and so most travellers end up tipping back beers at Noom Guesthouse or Matini, but it only takes a little effort to go local. Just a block south of those two is the roadside **Come Inn Bar** (Th Wat Phra That) and a block west of it is **Sahai Phanta** (Soi Sorasak) with its Carabao-style house band taking the stage nightly.

★Naan Stop Curry INDIAN $
(Soi Sorasak; dishes 70-180B; ⌚11am-10pm; 📶✎) Not your stereotypical stuffy white-linen Indian restaurant. Here you get a small menu of family recipes prepared fresh when you order, along with a sociable owner and a rock-and-roll soundtrack. It doesn't always open for lunch.

Pae Ban Rim Nam THAI $
(dishes 95-350B; ⌚10am-10pm; P) This floating restaurant, specialising in seafood, is the most pleasant eating place in the old town. You can feed the fish while waiting for your food to arrive.

Khao Tom Hor CHINESE, THAI $
(Th Na Phra Kan; dishes 50-150B; ⌚5pm-3am) Constantly busy Khao Tom Hor offers Thai-Chinese dishes, including *salid tôrd* (deep-fried salted fish). Service is speedy and the food is delicious.

Matini INTERNATIONAL, THAI $
(Th Phraya Kamjat; dishes 50-350B; ⌚9am-late; 📶✎) Free pool, a Blues Brothers' motif on the wall and good food (both Thai and Western) make this Lopburi's chillest backpacker spot. And though the name may look like a typo, 'Matini' means 'come here' in Thai.

Baan Sahai THAI $
(Soi Sorasak; dishes 40-249B; ⌚11am-10pm; 📶) Unmistakably Thai, but with a touch of European flair, this little spot chooses to call itself a bistro. The English menu is very limited, so if you don't see what you're after, just ask; it probably has it. We recommend the brownies for dessert.

Noom Guesthouse THAI, INTERNATIONAL $
(Th Phraya Kamjat; dishes 50-150B; ⌚8am-9.30pm; 📶✎) Noom sets itself apart with its big breakfast menu spanning muesli to *jóhk* (boiled rice).

Information

There are several banks in the northern half of old Lopburi, though none open evenings or weekends.

OFF THE BEATEN TRACK

KHAO CHIN LAE

This jagged mountain visible in the distance from Lopburi city is a lovely sight, especially at its east end. At **Wat Khao Chin Lae**, which has a muster of peacocks and its own troop of monkeys, you can climb the 436 steps up to the big white Buddha for superb views of the mountain and also the **sunflower fields** (blooming November to January) to the south, which are Lopburi's second claim to fame, after its monkeys. The 240m sheer peak at **Wat Pa Suwannahong**, on the far east end, looks remarkably like a Khmer *prang* (stupa) as you approach. This is the main point for **rock climbing** (p169).

The tall peak set off from the rest is **Kao Ta Kla**, home to a large **bat cave**. Just before sunset thousands of bats emerge for their nocturnal hunt. The best viewing is from the parking lot at **Wat Suwankiri**, right next to it.

Just 3km east of the mountain is **Ang Sap Lek**, a reservoir lined by restaurants with bamboo piers for eating lunch and dinner out over the water.

It's possible to visit all these places with a hired motorcycle from **Noom Guesthouse** (p170), though there's little English signage. Noom also does afternoon tours (1200B for four people) that include all these sties plus **Wat Phra Puttachai**, the famous Buddha footprint temple in nearby Saraburi Province. If you just want to see the sunflowers, a bus heading to Wang Muang (15B, 30 minutes) can drop you off near some.

TRANSPORT TO/FROM LOPBURI

Bus & Minivan

DESTINATION	FARE (B)	DURATION (HR)	FREQUENCY
Ayuthaya	80	1½	every 30min (minivan)
Bangkok (Victory Monument)	110-120	2	frequent (minivan)
Chiang Mai	502-582	9-12	12.30pm, 10.30pm, 11pm, midnight
Nakhon Ratchasima (Khorat)	127-164	3½	7 daily
Nakhon Ratchasima (Khorat)	130	3½	every 30min (minivan)
Pak Chong	70	2	every 30min (minivan)

Train

DESTINATION	FARE (B)	DURATION (HR)	FREQUENCY
Ayuthaya	13-58	¼-1½	18 daily
Bangkok (Hualamphong station)	28-123	2-3½	17 daily
Chiang Mai	212-1353	9-12	5 daily
Phitsanulok	99-1046	3-5	11 daily

Immigration (☎036 424686; Th Phra Piya; ⊙8.30am-4.30pm Mon-Fri) Out in the new town, just south of Phra Narai Circle.
Muang Narai Hospital (☎036 616300; Th Pahonyohtin)
Post Office (Th Prang Sam Yot)
Tourism Authority of Thailand (TAT; ☎036 770096; tatlobri@tat.or.th; Th Na Phra Kan; ⊙8.30am-4.30pm) Inside the train station.

ℹ Getting There & Away

BUS & MINIVAN

Because Lopburi lies well off the main north–south highway, bus service to faraway points is quite limited. Kanchanaburi requires two connections: Ang Thong or Ayuthaya and then Suphanburi. Because there is no ticket counter at the **bus station** (Sa Kaew Circle), which is 2km from the old town, you should buy Chiang Mai tickets through Noom Guesthouse (p170).

Minivans to Bangkok depart from two spots on Th Na Phra Kan. Minivans to Ayuthaya depart from the bus station, but will pick up passengers on Th Sorasak, south of Th Ratchadamnoen, if they have seats available. As with minivans everywhere in Thailand, big bags require their own tickets.

TRAIN

The **train station** (Th Na Phra Kan) is in the old town. Luggage storage costs 15B per bag per day and is open 24 hours.

ℹ Getting Around

Blue *sŏrng·tăa·ou* (8B) run from Th Ratchadamnoen to the bus station. Săhm·lór and motorcycle taxis will go anywhere in the old town for 20B.

KANCHANABURI PROVINCE

Given the jaw-dropping natural beauty of Kanchanaburi, it seems paradoxical that the area is primarily renowned for the horrors that occurred on the Death Railway in WWII. The provincial capital's war memorials are a mandatory stop before heading deeper into the province to explore thick jungle and visit beautiful waterfalls and caves in the many parks and preserves that comprise the Western Forest Complex, one of Asia's largest protected areas. The hiking here is among Thailand's best.

Remote and relaxed Sangkhlaburi, in the far north, is one of Thailand's most ethnically diverse towns. And since many of the residents arrived to escape persecution and violence in Myanmar, a large number of foreign volunteers come here to help.

And if Sangkhlaburi isn't far-flung enough for you, the dilapidated border outpost of E-Thong should be on your itinerary.

Kanchanaburi กาญจนบุรี

POP 94,602

Today the provincial town of Kanchanaburi is busy and modern, but the WWII memorials and museums are a reminder of darker times. Japanese forces used Allied prisoners of war (POWs) and conscripted Asian labourers to build a rail route to Myanmar. The harrowing story became famous after a fictional tale, based loosely on the real events, was told in Pierre Boulle's book *The Bridge Over the River Kwai* and the 1957 movie based on the book. Roads east of the bridge are named after countries involved in the conflict.

Because so many of the parks and historic sites in the surrounding countryside are easily accessible, Kanchanaburi is an ideal base for exploring some of Thailand's wild west.

Sights

In Town

★Death Railway Bridge HISTORIC SITE

(สะพานข้ามแม่น้ำแคว, Bridge Over the River Kwai) The famous 300m railway bridge still retains its power and symbolism, especially if you visit early or late enough in the day to bypass the tourist scrum. Its centre was destroyed by Allied bombs in 1945, so only the outer curved spans are original. Nothing remains of a second (wooden) bridge the Japanese built 100m downstream. You're free to roam over the bridge. Stand in one of the safety points along the bridge if a train appears.

The three old trains in the park near the station were used during WWII. Across the river, pop in to the **Chinese temple** on the right and view the bridge from its tranquil garden.

During the last weekend of November and first weekend of December a tasteful and informative **sound-and-light show** tells the history.

★Thailand–Burma Railway Centre MUSEUM

(ศูนย์รถไฟไทย-พม่า; www.tbrconline.com; 73 Th Jaokannun; adult/child 140/60B; ⌚9am-5pm) This modern, informative museum explains Kanchanaburi's role in WWII and ensures that the deaths remain a tragedy, not a statistic. The galleries tell the history of the railway, how prisoners were treated and what happened after the line was completed. Upstairs is a display of wartime artefacts, including one POW's darts fashioned from old razors, and a diorama showing how Hellfire Pass got its name. Be sure to take time to watch the poignant video from POW survivors.

KANCHANABURI IN...

Two Days

The main attractions are centrally located, so you can see everything in town in a day. The **Kanchanaburi War Cemetery**, **Thailand–Burma Railway Centre** and **Death Railway Bridge** are must-sees, and a coffee and a stroll along the charming **Heritage Walking Street** on the other side of town really rounds out the day. For your second day, head outside to **Erawan Falls** and **Hellfire Pass Memorial**.

Four Days

With two more days, either make a rush visit to **Sangkhlaburi**, where misty morning boat rides and Burmese food await, or add two more days of travelling around the capital, being sure to hit **Muang Sing Historical Park** and **Wat Tham Seua**. Spend at least one night in a national park – **Sai Yok** is a logical choice.

One Week

After visiting magical **Sangkhlaburi**, take a gorgeous detour up to **E-Thong** on the Burmese border and spend a night in a treetop hut at **Thong Pha Phum National Park**.

Kanchanaburi Province

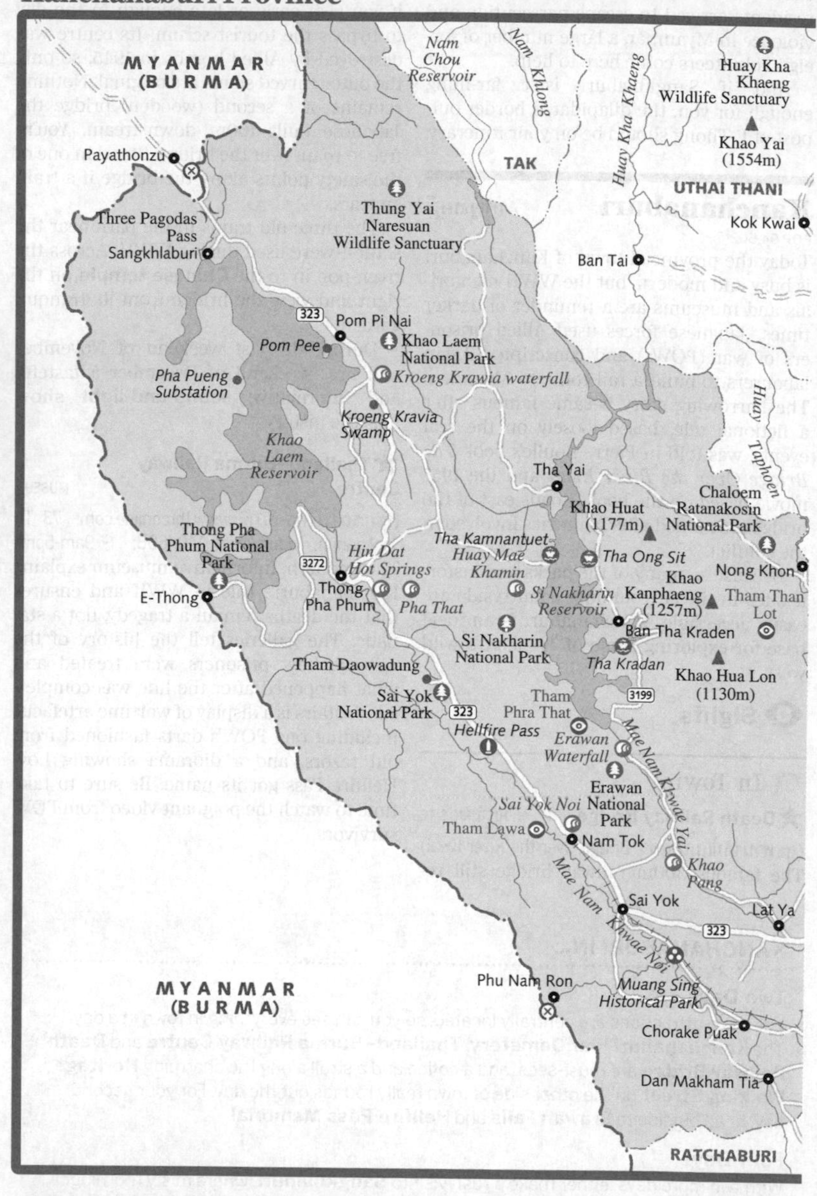

★ **Kanchanaburi War Cemetery** CEMETERY (สุสานทหารพันธมิตรดอนรัก; Th Saengchuto; ⏲24hr) The largest of Kanchanaburi's two war cemeteries, immaculately maintained by the Commonwealth War Graves Commission, is right in town. Of the 6981 soldiers buried here, nearly half were British; the rest came mainly from Australia and the Netherlands. As you stand at the cemetery entrance, the entire right-hand side contains British victims, the front-left area contains Australian graves, the rear left honours Dutch soldiers

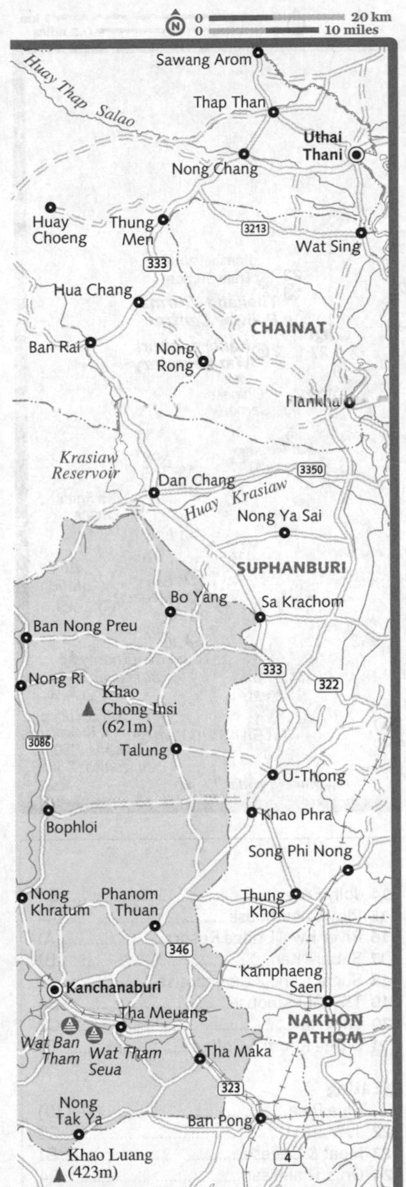

and unknown soldiers, and those who were cremated lie at the furthest spot to the left.

All remains of American POWs were returned to the USA. If you're looking for the resting place of a loved one, a register is kept at the entrance.

Heritage Walking Street AREA

(ถนนปากแพรก) This wonderful old street offers a glimpse of a bygone Kanchanaburi. Many shops date from the turn of the 20th century and the variety of buildings include Sino-Portuguese, Thai, Vietnamese and Chinese styles. Yellow signs reveal the history and architecture of nearly 20 of them. During WWII the Japanese rented several buildings here as offices, residences, a prison and a brothel.

The walk begins at the restored **City Gate**. Built in 1831, it's the last remaining of the original eight gates. Just behind it is a statue of King Rama III, who ordered the city relocated to this site, and off to the side is the 1931 **Governor's Residence**.

Jeath War Museum MUSEUM

(พิพิธภัณฑ์สงคราม; Th Wisuttharangsi; admission 50B; ⌚8am-5pm) This small museum contains correspondence and artwork from former POWs that detail their harsh living conditions, plus various personal effects and war relics, including an Allied bomb dropped to destroy the bridge that didn't explode. The main reason to come, however, is that one of the three galleries is built from bamboo in the style of the shelters (called *attap*) the POWs lived in.

Jeath is an acronym of the warring countries involved in the railway: Japan, England, Australia/USA, Thailand and Holland. This acronym is also used on many signs outside the WWII Museum.

The Jeath museum is run by the monks of the adjacent Wat Chaichumphon (Wat Tai), which is worth a wander because it has many interesting statues and shrines, including one fashioned from a WWII-era boat dredged out of the river.

WWII Museum MUSEUM

(พิพิธภัณฑ์สงครามโลกครั้งที่สอง; Th Mae Nam Khwae; admission 40B; ⌚8am-6pm) Perhaps the best thing to say about this place is that the view of the Death Railway Bridge is great. The top of the tower in the northwest corner is the best viewpoint. The museum itself is an eclectic, ramshackle but well-intentioned collection of artefacts. Most relate to the war, including trains, Japanese motorcycles and old helmets. Other rooms contain items of interest to the owners, including cigarettes, jade carvings, gems and paintings of former Miss Thailands.

Though its educational value is limited, just about everyone will find something of

Kanchanaburi

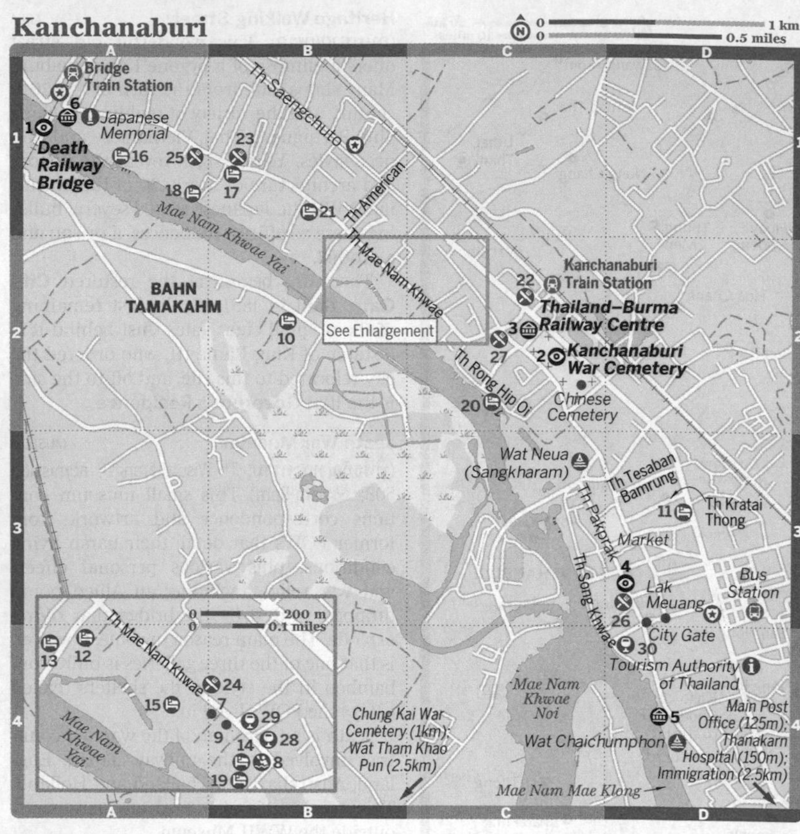

Kanchanaburi

Top Sights
1 Death Railway Bridge ... A1
2 Kanchanaburi War Cemetery ... C2
3 Thailand–Burma Railway Centre ... C2

Sights
4 Heritage Walking Street ... D3
5 Jeath War Museum ... D4
6 WWII Museum ... A1

Activities, Courses & Tours
Apple & Noi's Thai Cooking Course ... (see 10)
AS Mixed Travel ... (see 10)
7 Good Times Travel ... B4
8 River Kwai Canoe Travel Services ... B4
9 Toi's Tours ... B4

Sleeping
10 Apple's Retreat ... B2
11 Baan Ma Feung ... D3
12 Blue Star Guest House ... A4
13 Good Times Resort ... A4
14 Jolly Frog ... B4
15 Ploy Guesthouse ... A4
16 River Kwai Bridge Resort ... A1
17 Sabai@Kan ... B1
18 Sugar Cane 2 Guesthouse ... A1
19 T&T Guesthouse ... B4
20 Tara Raft ... C2
21 U Dee Room & Coffee ... B1

Eating
Blue Rice ... (see 10)
22 JJ Market ... C2
23 Meat & Cheese ... B1
24 On's Thai-Issan ... B4
25 Pai-Kan ... A1
26 Sitthisang ... D3
27 Zap Zap ... C2

Drinking & Nightlife
28 Buddha Bar ... B4
Pal Bar ... (see 28)
29 Sugar Member ... B4
30 Tam Nan ... D4

interest here. Between the two buildings is a stupa with coloured bowls decorating the exterior and a large bell hanging inside.

Outside Town

★Wat Tham Seua BUDDHIST TEMPLE
(วัดถ้ำเสือ; dawn-dusk; P) FREE The centrepiece of this hilltop temple is a striking 18m-tall Buddha covered in a golden mosaic. It's an important merit-making stop for Thais and one of the methods is to drop coins in small trays on a conveyor belt that carries the donations up to a central bowl. Surrounding it are several styles of stupa. The biggest, 69m and nine storeys tall, is full of murals of Kanchanaburi's history, mostly war related, and Buddha images, including many seldom-seen postures.

The namesake 'Tiger Cave' is at the base of the hill, to the right of the cable car (20B). The Chinese-style temple next door is **Wat Tham Khao Noi**, which is more interesting outside than in.

The temples are 12km southeast of town. After crossing the city's southernmost bridge, make the first left and follow the river. There's no public transport.

Wat Ban Tham BUDDHIST TEMPLE
(วัดบ้านถ้ำ; stairway 8am-5pm; P) FREE In the countryside around Kanchanaburi city, cave temples are almost as common as 7-Elevens inside the city, and this is one of the most interesting. Walk up the steps and into the dragon's mouth to reach the large, main cave. A section of one big rock is said to resemble Bua Kli, an innocent woman killed by her husband in Thai folklore, and is consequently 'dressed' throughout the year.

Above her is a Phra Siwali (an important disciple of the Buddha) statue illuminated by a single shaft of sunlight each cloudless morning. Continuing up the mountain (on the metal spiral staircase at the cave entrance) takes you to some minor shrines and major views. **Tham Man Wichit** cave, near the top, has steps and lights and some lovely rock formations.

You'll pass the temple 4km before Wat Tham Seua.

Chung Kai War Cemetery CEMETERY
(สุสานทหารพันธมิตรช่องไก่; 7am-6pm) FREE Chung Kai was the site of one of the biggest Allied prisoner-of-war camp during WWII and prisoners built their own hospital and church close to here. Smaller and less visited, but just as well maintained, as the cemetery in town, 1400 Commonwealth and 300 Dutch soldiers are honoured here. The cemetery is near the river, 2.5km southwest of the Wat Neua bridge and can easily be reached by bicycle.

Wat Tham Khao Pun BUDDHIST TEMPLE
(วัดถ้ำเขาปูน; admission 30B; 6am-6pm) The nearest cave to the city has a marked path through its many chambers. It's easy overall, but you'll need to duck through several passages. The chamber painted white near the exit was a Japanese wartime hospital. Outside, in a replica bamboo barracks, is a little museum containing POW photos. Follow the road to the back and you'll have a lovely view over the Mae Nam Khwae Noi. The temple is 4km out of town, past Chung Kai War Cemetery.

Activities

Tours & Trekking

Tours are a convenient way to see the main sights outside the city, though if you have a small group it may be cheaper to hire a driver and do things on your own. Day trips generally cost 800B to 1100B per person, including admission fees and lunch. Kanchanaburi is rich with natural wonders, and many of the standard tours also include bamboo rafting and short jungle treks.

Pretty much all companies offer the same itineraries for the same prices – Erawan waterfall, Hellfire Pass and the Death Railway's 'wooden bridge' is popular. But more adventurous options such as cycling tours and overnight jungle trekking, usually staying in a Karen village, are available if enough people are interested, so ask around. As a rule of thumb, the further north you go, the wilder things get.

Remember that the posted prices are usually negotiable. Also, trips will be cancelled if not enough people sign up, so check where things stand before booking.

AS Mixed Travel (034 512017; www.applesguesthouse.com; Apple's Retreat), **Good Times Travel** (034 624441; www.good-times-travel.com; Th Mae Nam Khwae) and **Toi's Tours** (034 514209; www.toistours.com; Th Mae Nam Khwae) are reputable agencies, though there are many others. If you really want to learn about the area's WWII history, then do a half- or full-day tour with the expert guides from the Thailand-Burma Railway Centre (p173).

Elephant Interactions

There are two ethical elephant projects (no riding or circus tricks) available in Kanchanaburi. Both pick up visitors in town and bring them out to the countryside. Children get reduced prices.

Besides being good for the elephants, many people consider spending their time walking with, washing and feeding rescued and retired elephants to be a more rewarding experience than just sitting in a chair on a working elephant's back. Generally the programs are a mix of visiting and volunteering and you'll also be expected to help with chores.

For elephant-based tours booked with other companies in town, you can ask to substitute elephant trekking with more pachyderm-friendly elephant bathing.

Elephant Haven ELEPHANT INTERACTION
(☎053 272855; www.elephantnaturepark.org) This new project from Chiang Mai's renowned Elephant Nature Park (p761) has both a day trip (2500B per person) and an overnight (5800B) option. The day version is just spending time with the elephant, not helping with chores, and the two-day option includes a visit to the Death Railway's nearby Tham Krasae bridge.

Elephants World ELEPHANT INTERACTION
(☎086 335 5332; www.elephantsworld.org) Elephants World has regular one- (2500B per person) and two-day (4500B) work-for-the-elephants programs, and also accepts volunteers for month-long stays.

Kayaking

River Kwai Canoe Travel Services KAYAKING
(☎034 512346; riverkwaicanoe@yahoo.com; Th Mae Nam Khwae) Takes you out of town and lets you paddle back. The three-hour, 15km trip is most popular, but longer and shorter trips are available.

Courses

On's Thai-Issan (p181) vegetarian restaurant offers a short, informal cooking class.

WHY BRIDGE THE RIVER KHWAE?

Japan's construction of the 'Death Railway' was an astonishing feat of engineering. Built by hard labour rather than modern machines, the Allied prisoners of war and conscripted workers who toiled to build it paid a terrible price. Well over 12,000 POWs and as many as 90,000 labourers died due to disease, poor hygiene, lack of medical equipment and brutal treatment by camp guards. Many Thais risked their lives to aid the POWs, but there was only so much they could do.

The 415km railway was built during the WWII-era Japanese occupation of Thailand (1941–45) and its objective was to secure an overland supply route to Burma (Myanmar) for the Japanese conquest of other west Asian countries.

Construction began in October 1942 at existing stations at Thanbyuzayat in Myanmar and Nong Pladuk (Ban Pong) in Thailand, and on 16 October, 1943 the rails were joined 37km south of Three Pagodas Pass.

Working conditions were relatively good at the start, but even then, food supplies were meagre. Cholera, malaria and dysentery were rife, and Japanese and Korean guards employed barbaric punishments for anyone who stepped out of line. As the Japanese demand for faster construction grew, conditions worsened.

Because of the mountainous terrain, there were 688 bridges built along the route. Most were wooden trestle bridges, such as those at the oft-visited Tham Krasae. The bridge that spans the 'River Kwai' near Kanchanaburi city (dubbed the **Death Railway Bridge**, see p173) was the only steel bridge built in Thailand; Burma had seven. It was bombed several times by the Allies, but the POWs were sent to rebuild it.

When the war's tide turned, the railway became an escape path for Japanese troops. After the war the British took control of the railway on the Burmese side and ripped up 4km of the tracks leading to Three Pagodas Pass for fear of the route being used by Karen separatists.

On the Thai side, the State Railway of Thailand (SRT) assumed control and continues to operate trains on 130km of the original route between Nong Pladuk, south of Kanchanaburi, and Nam Tok.

Apple & Noi's Thai Cooking Course COOKING COURSE
(www.applesguesthouse.com; Apple's Retreat) If you don't know your *sôm·đam* from your *đôm yam* then Khun Noi can assist. Her very popular one-day course (1550B) starts at the local market and ends, four dishes later, at the dining table. Longer, more-in-depth courses are available.

Sleeping

Travellers congregate around Th Mae Nam Khwae, which is centrally located and walking distance from both the bridge and the train station. Much of the accommodation here, both budget and midrange, sits alongside or literally on the river. Most are set back far enough from the road that noise from the street's many bars isn't an issue, but overall the further north you go the more peaceful and pleasant the area is. The days of party boats tormenting this stretch of the river are thankfully gone, though the rumble of long-tail boats and jet skis will always be a part of the river scene during the day.

Being just 130km from Bangkok, many city folk come here for the weekend, so reservations at this time are advisable.

In Town

Blue Star Guest House GUESTHOUSE $
(034 624733; www.bluestar-guesthouse.com; 241 Th Mae Nam Khwae; r 200-750B; P ❄ ☎) Nature wraps itself around Blue Star's super-basic but fairly priced waterside huts, creating a jungly vibe. Better, more modern rooms sit up on solid land. Overall, one of the best budget choices in town.

T&T Guesthouse GUESTHOUSE $
(034 514846; Th Mae Nam Khwae; s 150B, d 250-550B) The family that owns this little riverside spot lives here, making it as much a homestay as a guesthouse, with all the good (friendliness) and bad (noise) this can sometimes bring. The main rooms are good value, though you'll have to manually flush the toilet, while the raft rooms are just a mattress on the floor.

Sugar Cane 2 Guesthouse GUESTHOUSE $
(034 514988; Th Cambodia; r 200-550B; P ❄ ☎) Though it feels like it's way out in the countryside, Sugar Cane 2 is just a 10-minute walk to the main tourist cluster. Overall it has little character, but the landside rooms are good and the raft rooms are above average.

Jolly Frog GUESTHOUSE $
(034 514579; 28 Soi China; s 100B, d 180-320B, f 400B; P ❄ ☎) The Jolly Frog's heyday has long passed, but since the grungy rooms are among the cheapest in town, it remains popular with backpackers. The communal atmosphere and hammocks in the garden are other selling points.

★Good Times Resort HOTEL $$
(087 162 4949; www.good-times-resort.com; r incl breakfast 1150-2700B; P ❄ ☎ ≈) Although the road to the resort doesn't inspire confidence, get past the car park and you'll find a little riverside oasis with large, attractive rooms plus good service and dining.

★Sabai@Kan HOTEL $$
(034 625544; www.sabaiatkan.com; 317/4 Th Mae Nam Khwae; r 1400-1700B, f 2100B, incl breakfast; P ❄ ☎ ≈) With the kind of king-size beds you just want to jump on, this pretty boutique hotel does everything well. Rooms overlook a swimming pool and garden and have heaps of natural light. Service is excellent.

LOCAL KNOWLEDGE

DON'T BE A BUFFALO

The movie *The Bridge on the River Kwai* made the waterway famous, but also left a generation pronouncing it incorrectly. You should talk about the River Khwae (sounds like 'square' without the 's' and 'r') and not Kwai (sounds like 'why'). Pronounce it like the film and you'll be referring to the River Buffalo, which Thais find amusing.

During the war, the bridge didn't cross the River Khwae either. Though the railway ran next to the River Khwae for much of its length, the bridge, in fact, crossed the River Mae Klong – Pierre Boulle had it wrong when he wrote his book.

After the movie (filmed in Sri Lanka, so its bridge bears no resemblance to the real thing), tourists began visiting Kanchanaburi to see the bridge. To avoid confusion and disappointment, the Mae Klong officially became the Khwae Yai ('yai' means 'big') in 1960.

Ploy Guesthouse GUESTHOUSE $$
(☎090 964 2653; www.ploygh.com; 79/2 Th Mae Nam Khwae; r 660-1750B; P ❄ @ ☎ ≋) Ploy has stylish rooms with dark-wood furnishings, and ground-floor rooms have little window gardens. Its back-porch area is one of the nicest places in town to relax along the river.

Apple's Retreat GUESTHOUSE $$
(☎034 512017; www.applesguesthouse.com; 153/4 Mu 4, Ban Tamakham; r incl breakfast 990B; P ❄ ☎) Almost like a chic homestay, Apple and Noi offer simple but stylish rooms, a friendly welcome and bags of local knowledge in a quiet part of town. While the restaurant is on the river, the rooms are across the road. Unlike most places at this price, rooms lack a TV and fridge.

Tara Raft GUESTHOUSE $$
(☎086 396 7349; www.tararoom.com; Th Rong Hip Oi; r 700-900B; ❄ ☎) Though it's just 300m from the bustle of Th Mae Nam Khwae, there's an entirely different atmosphere along Rong Hip Oi road: peaceful and very local. The overall character of Tara could be better, but the rooms are by far the best raft rooms in town – bright, nicely decorated, and they even have mini-fridges and in-room safes.

While Tara is the best of the bunch, there are three cheaper options in this little spot. The ageing **VN Guesthouse** remains the first choice of most backpackers, **Rainbow Guesthouse** is the homiest and the old wooden walkways give the run-down **River Guesthouse** the most character.

U Dee Room & Coffee GUESTHOUSE $$
(☎085 360 3666; Th Mae Nam Khwae; r 750B) The rooms here, above a small coffee shop near but not quite part of the tourist scene, are bright, sparkling clean and fairly quiet. It all adds up to a guaranteed good night's sleep. There's no lobby, so service is only available when the coffee shop is open, generally 9am to 6pm, unless you make other arrangements.

River Kwai Bridge Resort RESORT $$
(☎034 514522; www.riverkwaibridgeresort.com; 8 Th Vietnam; r incl breakfast 1300-1950B; P ❄ ☎ ≋) This secluded garden resort within walking distance of the Death Railway Bridge (you can see half of it from the restaurant) has ageing but still good bungalows. Staff are friendly and keen to help.

Baan Ma Feung GUESTHOUSE $$
(☎034 511090; Th Saengchuto; r 650B; ❄ ☎) This place is a pleasant little surprise, as long as you're OK with the location, well away from the river and the main concentration of restaurants. Rooms are cosy and clean and if it was in the main tourist area it would often be full.

Though the entrance is along the main road, the rooms are set back, keeping the traffic noise at bay.

Outside Town

★**Ban Sabai Sabai** GUESTHOUSE $$
(☎089 040 5268; www.bansabaisabai.com; 102/3 Mu 4, Nong Bua; r 300-650B, f 1400-1600B; ❄ ☎) Out in the countryside, just a few kilometres from town along Hwy 323, this friendly place lives up to its name: 'Relaxation House'. The various rooms around the garden are all cosy and guests are made to feel right at home. It's easy to reach by bus, or they can pick you up in town. Motorcycle hire is available.

★**Oriental Kwai Resort** RESORT $$$
(☎034 588168; www.orientalkwai.com; 194/5 Mu 1, Tambon Lat Ya; r incl breakfast 2300-4900B; ❄ ☎ ≋) This wonderful Thai-Dutch-run spot, 13km northwest of town, almost 2km off the road to Erawan National Park, has lovely, well-appointed cottages in a semi-wild garden full of birds. Two of the cottages are designed for families and can sleep up to six people. It should be no surprise that it's often full, so book in advance if possible.

X2 River Kwai RESORT $$$
(☎034 552124; www.X2resorts.com; r 18,750-22,500B, ste 33,750-37,500B, incl breakfast; P ❄ ☎ ≋) This new place, 10km southwest of the city, combines a trendy design with a peaceful and scenic stretch of the Mae Nam Khwae Noi. Room choices include walk-in pool access or a huge balcony. The rack rates are ridiculous, but you can book online for up to 75% off. You'll need your own transport.

Eating

Riverside restaurants take top spot when it comes to eating options. Th Mae Nam Khwae has lots of good Thai food if you get out of your guesthouse. Local restaurants are more prevalent on the northern half of the road, but can be found in all parts. Another good option for authenticity is **JJ Market** (Th Saengchuto; ⏲5.30-10pm) near the train station, though it's mostly takeaway rather than sit-down.

★Blue Rice THAI $
(www.applesguesthouse.com; 153/4 Mu 4 Ban Tamakahm; dishes 135B; ⏲11am-2pm & 6-10pm; P 📶 ✐) A perfect riverside setting, brilliant menu and fantastic flavours make this a winner. Chef Apple puts a fresh, gourmet spin on Thai classics such as the eponymous rice, *yam sôm oh* (pomelo salad) and chicken-coconut soup with banana plant.

Pai-Kan THAI $
(Th Mae Nam Khwae; dishes 35-159B; ⏲11am-10pm; 📶) Scribble down your order in the little notebook then watch as the cooks go to work in the open kitchen. Thai dishes are simple but flavoursome and wholly authentic. There are many less-common dishes such as seaweed soup and *sôm·đam* made from cucumber instead of papaya.

On's Thai-Issan VEGETARIAN $
(☎087 364 2264; www.onsthaiissan.com; Th Mae Nam Khwae; dishes 50B; ⏲10am-10pm; ❄ ✐) The Thai (and a little Isan) vegetarian and vegan food on offer here is so good that there are many carnivorous diners. Friendly On will even be happy to teach you how to make it. A two-hour, three-dish cookery course costs 600B.

Sitthisang CAFE $
(Th Pakprak; bakery items 35-65B; ⏲8am-6pm; ❄ 📶) Hunker down with a bit of history – plus some cake and coffee – in this cosy little spot. The proud owners have kept it as one of the most beautiful and best-preserved buildings along the Heritage Walking Street.

Zap Zap THAI, NORTHEASTERN THAI $
(Th Mae Nam Khwae; dishes 35-220B; ⏲11am-10pm; 📶) Though it has a broad Thai menu, including green curry and *pàt tai,* it's the spicy Isan-style salads that keep the tables packed from open to close. For a blend of both cuisines, try the 'fried papaya salad'.

Meat & Cheese INTERNATIONAL, THAI $$
(Th Mae Nam Khwae; dishes 70-3300B; ⏲11am-11pm; ❄ 📶) This popular place prides itself on its steaks, but the wood-fired pizzas are the real stars. There's a live band after 9pm.

🍷 Drinking & Nightlife

Both tourists and expats spend their evenings along Th Mae Nam Khwae, which is packed with bars, especially the far southern end. Many have pools tables and show soccer matches on TV. Some also have prostitutes. **Sugar Member** (Th Mae Nam Khwae), **Buddha Bar** (Th Mae Nam Khwae) and **Pal Bar** (Th Mae Nam Khwae) all attract young Thai crowds. For true budget drinking, street-side bars offer shots of local spirits for 10B.

Th Song Khwae, along the river in the centre of town, offers a wider variety of bars, most not getting started until late. The live band playing Thai country music makes **Tam Nan** (Th Song Khwae) the standout choice down here.

ℹ Information

EMERGENCY

Tourist Police (☎034 512795; Th Saengchuto)

IMMIGRATION

Immigration (☎034 564279; Hwy 3209; ⏲8.30am-noon & 1-4.30pm Mon-Fri)

INTERNET ACCESS

Internet cafes, starting at 10B an hour, can be found along Th Mae Nam Khwae.

MEDICAL SERVICES

Thanakarn Hospital (☎034 622370; Th Saengchuto) This is the best-equipped hospital to deal with foreign visitors.

MONEY

Most major Thai banks can be found on Th Saengchuto near the bus terminal. Three exchange booths in front of the World War II Museum open daily during normal business hours.

POST

Main Post Office (Th Saengchuto; ⏲8.30am-4.30pm Mon-Fri, 9am-noon Sat & Sun)

TOURIST INFORMATION

The **Tourism Authority of Thailand** (TAT; ☎034 511200; tatkan@tat.or.th; Th Saengchuto; ⏲8.30am-4.30pm) office has maps and helpful staff, but it's located out past the bus station. You can also get limited information at the little **tourist police booth** (⏲9am-4pm) at the Death Railway Bridge.

ℹ Getting There & Away

BUS

Kanchanaburi's **bus station** (☎034 515907) is in the centre of town just off Th Saengchuto, and these days minivans outnumber buses. (Remember, with a minivan, if you have a big bag, you need to buy it a seat.) For Ayuthaya, you'll need to go to Suphanburi first. If heading south, it's quickest to transfer at Ratchaburi rather than Bangkok, but only old, 2nd-class

BUSES TO/FROM KANCHANABURI

DESTINATION	FARE (B)	DURATION (HR)	FREQUENCY
Bangkok's Khao San Rd	120	2½	frequent (minivan)
Bangkok's Northern (Mo Chit) bus terminal	120	2½	frequent (minivan)
Bangkok's Southern (Sai Tai Mai) bus terminal	110	2½	every 30min
Bangkok's Southern (Sai Tai Mai) bus terminal	100	2	frequent (minivan)
Bangkok's Victory Monument	120	2½	frequent (minivan)
Chiang Mai	594	10-11	9am, 7pm
Nong Khai (via Khorat)	533-829	11	9am, 6.30pm
Ratchaburi	50	2	frequent
Sangkhlaburi	130	5	6 daily between 6am & 1.30pm
Sangkhlaburi	175	3½	frequent (minivan)
Suphanburi	50-65	2	every 40min

buses go there. Minivans to Bangkok depart until around 8pm.

There are also minivans to Bangkok catering to tourists and these pick up passengers along Th Mae Nam Khwae. Tickets, sold from dozens of shops, cost anywhere from 20B to 60B more per person. The only routes that are worth using are Suvarnabhumi Airport (500B, three hours), Hua Hin (430B, 4½ hours) and Ayuthaya (380B, 3½ hours), since there is no direct service to these places from the bus station.

TRAIN

Kanchanaburi is on the Bangkok Noi–Nam Tok rail line (trains don't use Hualamphong station), which includes a portion of the Death Railway. The SRT promotes this as a historic route, and so charges foreigners 100B for any one-way journey along the line, regardless of the distance. The trains are 3rd class, meaning wooden benches and no air-con, and you should not expect them to run on time. So, if you are planning a day trip to Kanchanaburi, take a bus.

The most interesting part of the journey begins after Kanchanaburi as the train crosses the Death Railway Bridge and terminates at Nam Tok station (two hours, 6.07am, 10.35am and 4.26pm), which is near Hellfire Pass. Most people headed from Kanchanaburi to Nam Tok board the train at the little **station** next to the Death Railway Bridge, so to be sure you get a seat (the left side of the train has the best views), board in town instead. Another option is a 'special car'. A tour company with a table next to the tourist police booth sells 300B tickets that include a cushion, a snack and a guaranteed seat.

Trains to Bangkok Noi (three hours) depart at 7.19am and 2.48pm.

ℹ Getting Around

BICYCLE & MOTORCYCLE

Motorcycles can be rented at guesthouses and shops along Th Mae Nam Khwae for 200B per day. Bicycle rentals cost 50B.

BOAT

Long-tail boats can be hired near the Death Railway Bridge and the Jeath War Museum. The standard program is a 1½-hour trip to Chung Kai War Cemetery, Wat Tham Khao Pun and either the bridge or the museum, depending on where you begin. The set price for up to six people is 800B, but this is sometimes negotiable.

PUBLIC TRANSPORT

Motorcycle taxis, many with sidecars that can carry several people and large luggage, are much more common than túk-túks. A trip from the bus station to the guesthouse area will probably cost you 50B.

Yellow and blue *sŏrng·tăa·ou* run up and down Th Saengchuto (get off at the cemetery if you want the guesthouse area) for 10B per passenger. You can board them on the west edge of the bus station. Orange *sŏrng·tăa·ou* do more work as taxis than they do running regular routes.

Around Kanchanaburi

The major attractions around Kanchanaburi could all be squeezed into a rushed day trip if you have your own transport, but it takes at least two days to do them properly. If you plan to spend a night at a national park on a weekend, it's best to book rooms in advance.

All but Muang Sing are easily reached by public transport. If you leave in the morning, you can ride the train up to Nam Tok and then use the regular buses along Hwy 323 to visit Hellfire Pass and Sai Yok National Park.

Erawan National Park อุทยานแห่งชาติเอราวัณ

Famed for its seven-tiered waterfall, **Erawan National Park** (☎034 574222; adult/child 300/200B) is an extremely popular (ie crowded) place for locals and visitors alike. **Erawan waterfall** (trail open 8am to 5pm) gets its name as some people think the top level resembles Erawan, the three-headed elephant of Hindu mythology. Walking to the first three tiers is easy, but after that walking shoes and some endurance are needed to complete the 2km hike. Bring a bathing costume as you can swim with the nibbling fish in the ethereal blue waters at each level, but be wary of monkeys who may snatch belongings while you're taking a dip. Level four has a natural rock slide and level six usually has the fewest swimmers.

Elsewhere in this 550-sq-km park, **Tham Phra That** is a cave with a variety of shimmering limestone formations. Geologists find the caves of interest due to a clearly visible fault line. Contact the visitor centre before driving the 12km out there and a guide will meet you with paraffin lamps. There are several other fantastic caves in the park, but all are currently closed to the general public and may or may not reopen.

Mixed deciduous forest covers over 80% of the park, but there are also some dry evergreen and dry dipterocarp forests with big swaths of bamboo. Tigers, elephants, sambar deer, gibbons, red giant flying squirrels, king cobras and hornbills call the park home, but they don't frequent the waterfall area.

Park **bungalows** (☎02 562 0760; www.dnp.go.th; bungalows 800-2400B) sleep between two to eight people. Tent hire is 50B to 300B and if you bring your own tent, there's a 30B fee.

Buses from Kanchanaburi (50B, 1½ hours, eight daily from 8am to 5.40pm) go right to the visitor centre. The last bus back to town is at 4pm, and on weekends it will be packed. Touts at the bus station will try to talk you into hiring a private driver instead of taking the bus, but this isn't necessary.

Nam Tok บ้านน้ำตก

Nam Tok is the final railway station. This fact, more than the attractions here, is what brings most travellers. But there is plenty to see and do if you'd rather not just turn around and head straight back.

Though the trains stop at the station, the track continues for another 1.5km and you can follow it to **Nam Tok Sai Yok Noi** waterfall. It's quite beautiful, though also crowded with Thai families playing and picnicking,

GETTING TO MYANMAR: PHU NAM RON TO HTEE KHEE

This crossing is new and still something of an adventure, though overall things are easy enough. Myanmar visas are not available at the border.

Getting to the border There are buses (70B, two hours) and minivans (100B, 1½ hours) from Kanchanaburi's bus station right to the border starting at 9am. If you leave early you can make it to Dawei in a day, though there are guesthouses in Phu Nam Ron if you need them.

At the border After getting stamped out of Thailand wait for the new shuttle (50B) or take a motorcycle taxi to Myanmar immigration. Formalities are hassle-free, though a bit slow, on both sides.

Moving on Not far from immigration, you'll be introduced to minivan drivers who will take you to Dawei for 800B per person, though this is sometimes negotiable. You can also do it for less if you find a truck driver willing to take you. It's five hours (more with a truck) through the beautiful mountains to Dawei on what is still a mostly dirt and sometimes rough road, though improvements are under way.

TIGER TRAVESTY

The Tiger Temple near Kanchanaburi is perhaps the most controversial tourist attraction in Thailand. It started in 1999 as a rescue shelter for orphaned tiger cubs, but later it became a very profitable tourist attraction and a breeding program has increased the tiger population to near 150.

Despite being caught breaking the law and providing substandard care for its tigers, not following even the most basic conservation protocol and long facing accusations (including by the temple's former veterinarian) that it sells tigers to overseas buyers for pets and body parts, the Tiger Temple continues to draw throngs of tourists.

The alleged misdeeds have been widely reported in both Thai and foreign media and the Department of National Parks, Wildlife and Plant Conservation has threatened to remove the tigers (it *has* taken Asiatic black bears and other illegally held animals away from the temple), but no actual charges have ever been filed and the temple denies everything.

It should also be pointed out that many insurance companies do not cover visits to here or other places like it. While attacks are rare, they do happen. In May 2015 one tiger mauled the Tiger Temple's abbot.

from around July to November. Also here, at the literal end of the line, is an old **WWII steam train**.

Up above the falls, 100m straight back from the wooden bridge, is little **Sai Yok Cave**. Two Buddha images are lit up by natural light while at the back is a holy snake-shaped rock you can only see if you bring a torch. Although this is part of Sai Yok National Park, no admission fees are collected.

Beautiful **Wang Badan Cave**, part of (and thus subject to fees for) Erawan National Park, is closed and there's no decision on when, or even if, it will reopen.

Much more appealing than the waterfall, beautiful **Tham Lawa** is one of our favourite caves in Thailand. The 280m walking trail passes through several large caverns with not only imposing stalactites and stalagmites, but many other weirdly shaped rocks. The path is lit, but dimly. Bring a torch (or hope to borrow one from the rangers) for the full experience. You do need to pay Sai Yok National Park admission here. It's signed 20km from Sai Yok Noi.

Many people come to Nam Tok just to stay at either **River Kwai Resotel** (☎02 642 5497; www.riverkwairesotel.net; r incl breakfast 2400-3450B; P❄@🛜🏊) or **FloatHouse River Kwai** (☎02 642 5497; www.thefloathouseriverkwai.com; r incl breakfast 5250B; P❄🛜), sister lodges with completely different styles. Resotel is a riverside resort with bungalows around a lush garden, while FloatHouse has truly gorgeous and luxurious raft rooms. Both are very near Tham Lawa.

Just outside town, 3km south of the falls, is the more modest **Boutique Raft Resort** (☎034 634191; www.boutiqueraft-riverkwai.com; r incl breakfast 2500-3000B; P❄🛜) while **Chokchai Hotel** (☎089 550 4361; r 250-450B, f 1000B; P❄🛜) has basic but OK rooms on the highway between the falls and the village.

Trains to Kanchanaburi (100B, two hours) depart the station at 5.20am, 12.55pm and 3.30pm, while buses between Kanchanaburi (45B to 55B, 1¼ hours) and Thong Pha Phum (70B, one hour) pass through at least every half-hour. Six buses go all the way to Sangkhlaburi (80B to 90B, four hours), the last leaving about 2.30pm.

Chokchai Hotel rents motorcycles for 300B a day and can arrange cars with drivers.

Lawa cave is just a short way from the river, so you can reach it by boat from Pak Saeng Pier, next to Boutique Raft Resort. It takes one hour and 1200B to go there and back.

Hellfire Pass Memorial ช่องเขาขาด

The poignant **Hellfire Pass Memorial** (☎034 919605; Rte 323; ⏲museum 9am-4pm, grounds 7.30am-6pm) FREE is a beautiful tribute to those who died while building the Burma-Thailand Railway in WWII.

Start your visit at the museum and get the free audio guide, which has detailed descriptions of the area and fascinating anecdotes from survivors. Then walk down (via a long staircase) to the trail that follows the original rail bed.

Near the start of the route is the infamous cutting known as Hellfire Pass (locally referred to as Konyu Cutting), which is the largest along the railway's entire length. The area earned its name following the final 'Speedo' construction period where shifts of 500 prisoners worked 16 to 18 hours a day. The glow from burning torches cast eerie shadows of the Japanese guards and of the gaunt prisoners' faces, so that the scene was said to resemble Dante's Inferno.

Thc full route is 4km and ends at Compressor Cutting, though Thai officials have closed the last 1.5km, so for the foreseeable future the walk ends near Hin Tok Cutting. Pick-up service at the end of the route is available if arranged in advance.

The museum is 80km northwest of Kanchanaburi on Hwy 323 and can be reached by Sangkhlaburi and Thong Pha Phum buses (55B to 65B, 1½ hours, every 30 minutes). The last bus back to Kanchanaburi passes here around 5pm.

Sai Yok National Park อุทยานแห่งชาติไทรโยค

The 958-sq-km **Sai Yok National Park** (☎034 686024; www.dnp.go.th; adult/child 300/200B) is home to limestone mountains, waterfalls, caves and some extremely rare animals. Because there are numerous sights right around the visitor centre, along well-marked and maintained trails (most open to bikes), it's easy to explore independently. And it never gets nearly as crowded as Erawan.

The best-known attraction is **Nam Tok Sai Yok Yai** (Sai Yok Yai Waterfall), where a stream makes a short drop into the Mae Nam Khwae Noi river. The bigger Nam Tok Sai Yok Lek is on the other side of the suspension bridge. Both waterfalls are small, but beautiful because of how they flow out of the forest.

Other destinations right near the falls are a **natural spring**, riverside **viewpoints**, old Japanese soldiers' **stoves**, and **long-tail boat hire** (400B per half-hour).

The world's smallest mammal (3cm long), the very rare Kitti's hog-nosed bat, was first spotted here in 1973. They hang out, literally, at **Tham Kang Kao** ('Bat Cave'), 2km from the visitor centre, along with many regular-sized bats. Take a torch. Along the walk to Bat Cave you can take a short detour to the foundation of a **Death Railway bridge**. Just past the bridge, keep your eyes peeled for an unmarked original stretch of the track.

Another animal species discovered at Sai Yok (in 1983) is the red, white and blue Rachinee crab, but you're unlikely to see it. Nor will you likely encounter any elephants, gaurs, tapirs or sambar deer, since big animals prefer the remote western side of the park. You might, however, see barking deer and water monitors near the bridge.

Beautiful **Tham Doawadueng** cave is rich with both rock formations and animals: bats, crickets and snakes. There are lights, but not stairs, so the entrance can be treacherous when wet. A ranger will accompany you in, and though it's not required, a tip is deserved. Bats stream out just before sunset, except during the hot season. It's 6km northwest of the park entrance by road, or you can hire a boat for 1000B return, but you'll have a 1.5km uphill walk to the cave.

There are park **bungalows** (☎02 562 0760; www.dnp.go.th; bungalows 800-2100B) and a campground (tent hire 270B), but the raft resorts around the bridge, including the clean and comfortable **Krit Raft House** (☎081 942 8107; r 1000B) and **@Raft** (☎081 805 6467; r incl breakfast 1000-2000B), are a better choice. There are also floating restaurants plus many food stalls at the parking area.

The visitor centre is 95km northwest of Kanchanaburi. Sangkhlaburi–Kanchanaburi buses (60B, 1½ hours) pass the turn-off to the park. The visitor centre is 3km off the highway. Motorcycle taxis (20B) wait near, but not right at the junction. When leaving the park, the visitor centre can call them. The last bus back to Kanchanaburi passes around 5pm.

Muang Sing Historical Park อุทยานประวัติศาสตร์เมืองสิงห์

Muang Sing (admission 100B; ⏲8am-4.30pm), or Lion City, preserves the remains of a 13th-century Khmer outpost that may have been a relay point for trade along Mae Nam Khwae Noi. The restored ruins show a Bayon style of architecture and were built for Mahayana Buddhism.

The park's remaining shrines are constructed mostly of laterite blocks and are spread around a 102-hectare forested compound surrounded by a huge city wall. Around the wall are additional layers of ramparts and moats, which are visible outside the main entrance. The ponds inside the wall were probably used for religious purposes.

There are two large main monuments and the remants of two others. The principal shrine, **Prasat Muang Sing**, is in the centre and faces east (the cardinal direction of most Angkor temples). Inside are replica statues of the eight-armed Bodhisattva Avalokitesavara and the goddess Prajnaparamita; the latter was probably installed in the other large shrine.

Outside the wall, right next to the river, is a **burial site** that shows two skeletons, pottery and jewellery thought to date back 2000 years.

Muang Sing is 40km west of Kanchanaburi. Tha Kilen train station (100B) is a 1.5km walk away, but it's best to come with your own transport since the trains are infrequent and the grounds are large.

Thong Pha Phum ทองผาภูมิ

Overlooked by mountains – and most tourists – Thong Pha Phum is a small but busy junction town that people exploring the national parks of northern Kanchanaburi will probably pass through.

About the only things to do in town are stroll through the **municipal market**, where many of the vendors are ethnically Burmese, and walk out on the **suspension bridge** over the river. On the other bank is **Wat Tha Kanun**. If you walk past it you'll reach a long stairway going up to the **stupa** that seems to float over the town at night.

Outside of town, it's worth a drive to the top of **Vajiralongkorn Dam** (⏲6am-6pm), 7km northwest, which creates the massive Kheuan Khao Laem lake. The views are beautiful and a troop of monkeys lives there. Twenty kilometres south, just off the Sangkhlaburi–Kanchanaburi highway is the popular (ie crowded) **Hin Dat Hot Spring** (adult/child 60/40B; ⏲6am-10pm). The *bòr nám rórn* (hot springs) were originally developed by Japanese soldiers during the war and now have three soothing geothermal pools (plus a fourth exclusively for monks) and a massage pavilion.

Despite a bevy of oddities, such as the toilet-roll holders being outside the bathrooms, the newly built **Thong Phaphum Place** (☎034 599544; Th Thetsaban 14; r 600-1200B; P❄📶) is the best hotel in town. It's behind the market: look for the 'Free WiFi' sign. A less expensive choice is **S. Boonyong Hotel** (☎081 889 7246; Th Thetsaban; r 280-500B, f 1500B; P❄📶), 200m northwest of the market, with old but clean rooms and bungalows.

Getting There & Away

You can catch the mostly old fan buses to Kanchanaburi (80B to 110B, three hours, every 30 minutes) and Sangkhlaburi (70B to 80B, two hours, three daily) at the market or along the road on their way out of town. The minivan terminal, also for Kanchanaburi (115B, two hours, every 30 minutes) and Sangkhlaburi (80B, 1½ hours, every 30 minutes), is 200m northwest of the main market.

Comfortable air-conditioned buses to Bangkok's Northern (Mo Chit) terminal (185B to 238B, five hours, 9.30am and 11am) via Kanchanaburi leave from **Krua Ngaw Bah** (☎034 599377) restaurant, opposite the orange Thanachart Bank near the southern entrance to town.

Local *sŏrng·tăa·ou* to places such as Kaeng Krawia waterfall (35B, one hour, frequent) and Hin Dat Hot Spring (40B, 45 minutes, every 30 minutes) depart from the market.

Thong Pha Phum National Park อุทยานแห่งชาติทองผาภูมิ

Thong Pha Phum National Park (☎034 510979; adult/child 100/50B), near the end of ear-popping Hwy 3272, crosses a serrated mountain range along the Myanmar border and is one of the most beautiful but least-known places in Thailand. It bills itself as the 'Land of Fog and Freezing Rainforest', which in travellers terms means waking up early to see the cold-season fog filling the valleys and bringing warm clothes.

It's best known among foreign travellers for its **tree-top accommodation** (☎034 510979; r 800-2000B). These 6m-to-10m-tall 'Tarzan' rooms are quite rustic, with electricity only in the early evening and roofs that tend to leak when it rains, but the views are superb. The rooms down on solid ground are in better shape. There's also a campground; tent hire costs 270B.

The park is wildlife rich, and while you won't likely spot elephants, tigers or bears, marbled cats, palm civets, serow (Asian mountain goats) and Fea's muntjac often wander through the visitor centre/lodging area. You'll surely meet Wan Waew, the wild-but-tame great hornbill.

Thais know the park for the ranger-led overnight treks (16km round trip) to **Chang Pheuk mountain**, through grassland much of the way, offering 360-degree views over Myanmar. It's possible from October to January and costs 1200B for up to 10 trekkers. Porters are available. People rarely trek elsewhere, but rangers can lead you through the forest to various waterfalls and viewpoints.

You can drive to within 300m of **Jokkadin Waterfall**, which falls 30m with force. It's 2km southwest of the visitor centre then 3km down a steep side road.

The latter half of the 62km ride from Thong Pha Phum is along one of Thailand's most remote and winding roads. It's paved, but rough in many spots. Yellow *sŏrng·tăa·ou* to E-Thong pass the visitor centre.

E-Thong อีต่อง

The frontier village of E-Thong, 8km past Thong Pha Phum National Park visitor centre, was once a bustling, fairly cosmopolitan place with fresh seafood in the markets and an international population. But the tin and tungsten mines, which gained the name *mĕuang pĕe·lôrk* (Ghost Mine) because so many people died here, began to close in the 1980s and the ponds and large buildings in and around the town, plus about 300 mostly elderly residents, are all that's left.

The Myanmar border is closed, even to locals, but you can walk up to the giant Thai flag on the ridge. If the air is clear (which doesn't happen often), you can see the Andaman Sea.

E-Thong is almost like a ghost town most of the year, but on cold-season weekends it fills with young Bangkokians and thus there are several modern homestays, including **Hill House** (☎080 781 5702; r low/high season 600/1000B).

Another choice is the improbable **Somsak Mining Forest Glade** (☎081 325 9471; per person incl all meals 1600B), run by 'Auntie Glen', an Australian woman who has lived here for decades. The 5km road there requires 4WD, but they can pick you up. The home-cooked meals include her popular cakes, which can also be bought in town.

Hong Noi Restaurant (☎080 788 5919; dishes from 30B; ⊙7am-7.30pm) has excellent Thai food and the daughter speaks a little English, so it's a good place to get advice.

Yellow *sŏrng·tăa·ou* (70B, two hours, 10.30am and 11.30pm) run departing from Thong Pha Phum. The return trips leave at 6.30am and 7am.

Khao Laem National Park

อุทยานแห่งชาติเขาแหลม

With the mighty Khao Laem Reservoir at its heart and limestone mountains all around, the 1497-sq-km **Khao Laem National Park** (☎034 510431; adult/child 200/100B) is a particularly beautiful place. But despite the park's size and potential, **Kroeng Krawia waterfall**, a wide, gentle cascade flowing through a small patch of forest, is pretty much all anybody ever visits. It's 34km north of Thong Pha Phum along the main road and entrance is free. A park visitor centre lies across the road.

Another spot you can visit without your own transport is **Kroeng Krawia Swamp**, which can be productive for birdwatchers in the cool season. The trailhead is 5km south of the waterfall and you can walk around it in about two hours; rangers must accompany you.

There's **lodging** (☎02 562 0760; www.dnp.go.th; bungalows 1200-1800B) and camping at Kroeng Krawia Swamp, but things are more inviting and attractive at **Pom Pee** (☎02 562 0760; www.dnp.go.th; bungalows 900B), 9km north of Kaeng Krawia waterfall, which has sunset views over the lake.

From Thong Pha Phum, *sŏrng·tăa·ou* go to Kroeng Krawia waterfall (35B, one hour, every 30 minutes).

Sangkhlaburi สังขละบุรี

POP 6877

For many travellers Sangkhlaburi is the end of the line, but for many residents it represents the start of a new journey. Few places in Thailand have such a melange of ethnic identities, with Karen and Mon plus a few Lao and Burmese outnumbering Thai. Most were born here, but many came across the Myanmar border looking for a safer, more stable life.

Though it's a fairly remote, sleepy place, Sangkhlaburi's popularity with Thai tourists means it's full of resorts and restaurants. A host of NGOs, from heavy hitters such as the American Refugee Committee to small personal projects, also attract a steady stream of foreign volunteers providing a small

LOCAL KNOWLEDGE

LIVING ON THE EDGE

On the way up the steps of **Chedi Luang Phaw Uttama**, visitors face a challenge. A Buddha footprint is in the middle of the stairs and resting on it are dozens of coins. If you can make your coin balance on its edge, good luck will follow you.

international spark. See p761 if you'd like to join them.

It's a great place to hang out. The serpentine ride here, past jungle, floating villages and gorgeous views over Kheuan Khao Laem (Khao Laem Reservoir) is itself reason enough to come.

Sights & Activities

★Saphan Mon BRIDGE

(สะพานมอญ) Sangkhlaburi's iconic, 440m wooden bridge, one of the largest in the world, connects the main town, home mostly to Thai and Karen, with the Mon settlement. Although the buildings and shops on the Mon side aren't any different from other Thai villages, the many cheroot-smoking women, sarong-wearing men and faces covered in yellow cream make it stand out.

At the Mon end of the bridge is a typical Thai **souvenir market** where Karen shirts and dresses are popular. Follow the street uphill from the bridge and turn left on the main road to visit the **Mon market**.

A 70m section of the bridge collapsed during torrential rain in 2013 and the floating bamboo bridge built right afterwards is still there, but not for long. Once it breaks up it won't be rebuilt.

★Khao Laem Reservoir LAKE

(เขื่อนเขาแหลม) A boat ride on this gigantic lake is a must. The lake was formed in the 1980s when the Vajiralongkorn Dam (p186; known locally as Khao Laem Dam) was constructed across Mae Nam Khwae Noi near Thong Pha Phum. Two of the many villages submerged under the new lake were moved up to their present location and the bridge was built to connect them. About all that remains now are ruined buildings from three temples.

The nearest temple, just visible from the bridge, is **Wat Wang Wiwekaram Gao** (*gao* means old) and this was the site of the Mon village. When the lake rises to its highest point only the very top of the *ubosot* and bell tower stay dry. Nearby, **Wat Si Suwannaram Gao** was the temple in the Thai-Karen village. It emerges when the lake is very low, while **Wat Somdet Gao** sits in the forest high on a hill and stays dry year-round. (The new Wat Somdet is the temple with the many big Buddha images along the road into town.)

Trips from the wooden bridge costs 500B (up to six people) and take one hour for all three temples, or 300B for just Wat Wang Wiwekaram Gao.

The calm of early morning, when grey mist envelops the surrounding mountains, is the best time to go.

Wat Wang Wiwekaram BUDDHIST TEMPLE

(วัดวังก์วิเวการาม; ⊙dawn-dusk) FREE Poking out of the forest above town, this temple is the spiritual centre of Thailand's Mon people. The *wí·hăhn* with three green and yellow towers is a shrine to the highly respected monk Luang Phaw Uttama who died in 2006 and whose body lies inside. Born in Myanmar, he fled to Thailand in 1949 to escape the civil war and became a cornerstone of the Mon community in both countries, as well as a noted Buddhist leader across Thailand.

Chedi Luang Phaw Uttama BUDDHIST TEMPLE

(เจดีย์พุทธคยา) FREE Six hundred metres southeast of Wat Wang Wiwekaram, this striking stupa is constructed in the style of the Mahabodhi *chedi* in Bodhgaya, India. Its gold-painted art deco–like surface is full of niches holding little Buddha images. Around it are an unusual bell tower and another souvenir market.

Mon National Cultural Center CULTURAL CENTRE

(ศูนย์วัฒนธรรมมอญ ประเทศไทย; ⊙9am-5pm) FREE Though this small cultural centre wasn't designed for visitors, they're most welcome, and the staff are happy to answer questions. The display room doesn't have much, but the orchestra instruments are works of art, and on weekends and school holidays you stand a good chance of running into children practising. To reach the centre, head uphill from the Saphan Mon bridge and turn right on Soi 2, cross another wooden bridge and then climb up the hill for about 250m.

Sangkhlaburi Cultural Center CULTURAL CENTRE

(ศูนย์วัฒนธรรม อำเภอสังขละบุรี; ☎086 178 4096; Th Sangkhlaburi; ⊙8am-4pm Mon-Fri, to noon Sat

& Sun) FREE This little cultural centre mostly works to promote appreciation of Karen, Mon and Thai culture to local children. The main hall has a small collection of mostly baskets, but it's worth making the trip just to see the old-style farmers' hats. To find it, walk to the east side of town and head south past the school to near Soi 7.

Wat Si Suwannaram BUDDHIST TEMPLE
(วัดศรีสุวรรณาราม) FREE Karen women come to this prominent temple, near the main lodging zone, most days to weave cotton. The building they work in also has a small, dusty display of old baskets and bowls.

Sangkhlaburi Jungle Trekking TREKKING
(085 425 4434; jarunsaksri1@gmail.com) The forest around Sangkhlaburi is much more wild and far less visited than most trekking destinations in northern Thailand, and 'Jack' has years of experience as a guide around here. The prime option is six or seven days along the Myanmar border from Sangkhlaburi to Um Phang (p274), staying in Karen villages along the way.

Shorter treks through the Unesco World Heritage–listed Thung Yai Wildlife Sanctuary are also possible.

Courses

Scenns COOKING, LANGUAGE
(080 602 3184; www.scenns.com) Classically trained, thoroughly charming dancer Sai runs serious Thai cookery, dance and language classes. Rooms are available.

Sleeping

The best lodging zone begins 1km south of the bus station along Th Sri Sukwankiri. Most spots down here sit above the reservoir and have bridge views. They also get a lot of boat noise. It is very prudent to make reservations for Saturday nights, or any time around a public holiday. Or better still, just come on a weekday when the town is far more peaceful and appealing.

★ **P Guesthouse** GUESTHOUSE $
(034 595061; www.p-guesthouse.com; Th Sri Sukwankiri; r 300-950B; P) You don't normally get views like this for 300B. Stone and log-built rooms gaze upon the scenic waters at this family-run spot. There are two choices: fan rooms share cold-water, squat-toilet bathrooms, while air-con rooms have the best views (especially room 7). Both are good value for Sangkhlaburi. The restaurant is expensive, but it's a fantastic place to lounge. It runs good day trips in the surrounding forest.

J Family Homestay HOMESTAY $
(034 595511; per person 150B;) This is a great little spot if you want a very local experience. Rooms are just mattresses on the floor with shared bathroom. The family is a great source of local info. It's signed one road east of Th Sri Sukwankiri.

Phuthan Resort GUESTHOUSE $$
(084 750 1648; r 800-1600B;) Though it's away from the river – hence no view – these cute wooden bungalows are good value for Sangkhlaburi.

Ban Thor Phan HOTEL $$$
(081 824 3369; www.banthorphan.com; r incl breakfast 2500-36,000B;) This colourful, labyrinthine place feels more like a fantasy village than a hotel. Rooms are comfortable and well appointed and usually discounts up to 50% are available on weekdays. A clothing shop here helps support an orphanage and the owners also offer yoga, 'crystal singing bowl therapy' and more.

Eating & Drinking

Sangkhlaburi's **market** is a fascinating place to stroll and eat since there is as much Myanmar food as Thai. The **night market** (4.30-9.30pm) takes place next door and the **Walking Street Market** (5-10pm Sat) is a block over in front of the hospital. The latter is closed during the rainy season.

A small restaurant at the village end of the bridge serves Mon foods, but every local we talked to advised us to head up the hill to Nai Bon's nameless **ráhn kăi kôw morn** (Mon food shop; dishes 30B) instead. No English is spoken, but you can just look in the pots to choose. *Kà·nŏm jeen* (rice noodles with fish sauce) the best-known Mon food, is available in the **fresh market** across the street until about 10am.

FLOAT YOUR STAY AWAY

Lake House Adventure (02 630 9371; www.lakehouseadventure.com; dm/d 13,500/35,800B, meals incl) runs four-night houseboat excursions from Sangkhlaburi, with various activities and trips each day. There are low-season discounts.

THREE PAGODAS PASS ด่านเจดีย์สามองค์

Though the name evokes vivid images, the reality is nothing like what you might imagine. The pagodas, originally just piles of rock put up in the Ayuthaya era, are petite and surrounded by a market selling mostly gems, jade and cigarettes. They mark the pass used by both Thailand and Myanmar when they've invaded each others' territory. Next to it is a short piece of track to commemorate the tragedy of the Death Railway.

Thais and Burmese can cross the border to visit the town of Payathonzu, but this route has long been closed to others. There's no indication of when it might fully reopen.

Just 2.5km before the pass is a signed turn-off to **Kaeo Sawan Bandan Cave**. Several large, lit (the switch is down next to the big Buddha) chambers can be visited, though there aren't many formations.

Much further off the main road and, in our opinion, not really worth the effort needed to get there (in the rainy season it's a muddy mess) or the cost (rangers may or may not make you pay the 200B park entry fee) is **Takhian Thong waterfall**. You'll probably have the place to yourself, though, which is nice.

Green *sŏrng·tăa·ou* go from Sangkhlaburi's bus station (30B, 40 minutes, every 40 minutes) right to the pagodas.

Two bars along Th Sri Sukwankiri, **Garden Home** and **Blue Rock**, can fill a Western-food fix if you need one, and are good places to meet volunteers and get advice on the region.

Baan Unrak Bakery BAKERY $
(Th Sri Sukwankiri; snacks 25-90B; ⏲8am-7.30pm Mon-Sat; ✎) Vegetarians will love this meatless (mostly vegan) cafe, which is part of the Baan Unrak organisation.

★ **Suanmagmai Resort** THAI $$
(dishes 40-450B; ⏲10am-9.30pm; ☏) The English part of the menu will leave you scratching your head (the deep-fried 'platypus' is really duck bills) – the pictures can help out some – but you can be sure whatever you get will be perfectly prepared. It's a great place to try something new since there are several local specialities like the fern salad and 'spicy soup with (cat)fish'. It's 300m directly north of the Mon Bridge.

Shopping

Visitors interested in Karen weaving can pick up authentic products at the Baan Unrak Bakery; the products are made by the Baan Unrak women's cooperative.

Weaving for Women CLOTHING, HANDICRAFTS
(www.weavingforwomen.org; Th Sri Sukwankiri) A fairly informal place, genuine Karen clothes are woven and sewn here. Modern scarves, bags and more are also available.

Information

The town centre has most services visitors might need, including banks (SCB is recommended), internet (on Soi 3), hospital, post office and a 7-Eleven. **Immigration** (☎034 595335; ⏲8.30am-noon & 1-4.30pm Mon-Fri) is on the way to Three Pagodas Pass, 1.5km north of the junction.

Getting There & Away

A parking lot on the west edge of the town serves as Sangkhlaburi's bus station, but only four old Kanchanaburi (130B, four hours, 6.30am, 8am, 9.30am and 1pm) buses and local transport use it. Tickets for air-con buses to Bangkok's Mo Chit terminal (238B to 306B, seven hours, 7.45am and 9.30am) are sold about 20m in front of the station. Minivans to Kanchanaburi (175B, 3½ hours, frequent) go from the other side of town, just two blocks from the bus station.

The minivans' only regular stop between Sangkhlaburi and Kanchanaburi is Thong Pha Phum, so if you want to stop anywhere else, such as Sai Yok National Park, you need to pay the full Kanchanaburi fare.

Getting Around

J Family Homestay (p189) and P Guesthouse (p189) hire bikes (100B a day) and motorcycles (200B). The latter also has canoes. Contact **Baan Job** (☎093 994 0790; Th Sri Sukwankiri), next to P Guesthouse, if you'd like to hire a car and driver to explore anywhere in northern Kanchanaburi.

A motorbike taxi between guesthouses and the town centre or the bridge costs 20B.

Northern Thailand

Includes ➡

Best Places to Eat

- Larp Khom Huay Poo (p286)
- Muu Thup (p302)
- Khao Soi Pa Orn (p231)
- Lung Eed (p211)
- Bamee Chakangrao (p268)

Best Places to Stay

- Fern Resort (p295)
- Boklua View (p246)
- Phu Chaisai Resort & Spa (p218)
- Riverside Guest House (p201)
- Pukha Nanfa Hotel (p243)

Why Go?

What can't you do in northern Thailand?

The region's premier draw is its nature, and northern Thailand's rugged geography is a playground for outdoor pursuits ranging from a rafting excursion in Um Phang to a hike among wild orchids in Mae Hong Son.

For those drawn to the human side of things, there's also northern Thailand's buffet of cultural attractions and experiences. The region is regarded as the birthplace of much of what is often associated with Thai culture, and is a great place to take part in activities ranging from exploring a Buddhist temple in Phrae to taking part in a homestay in rural Sukhothai or sampling a local dish at Lampang's evening market.

In the north, even niche players are catered for: intrepid explorers can head off on a hill-tribe trek in Mae Sariang or on a road trip to Phayao, history buffs can travel back in time at Sukhothai Historical Park, and we'd argue that even the most devout beach bum could be converted by the inland party scene in Pai.

When to Go

- Winter (November to January) is the time to head to northern Thailand, when daytime temperatures at the higher elevations are a relatively comfortable 20°C to 23°C. Night-time temperatures can, in some places, dip perilously close to freezing.
- From March to May, the hottest time of year, daytime temperatures climb close to 40°C and smoke from slash-and-burn agriculture can fill the skies.
- The rainy season (June to October) should generally be avoided if you plan to do any hiking.

Northern Thailand Highlights

1 Exploring nature reserves such as Phitsanulok's **Phu Hin Rong Kla National Park** (p253) or Mae Hong Son's **Salawin National Park** (p303)

2 Hiking and rafting in remote Um Phang, where the end of the road leads to **Nam Tok Thilawsu** (p275), Thailand's most beautiful waterfall

3 Investigating the unique culture of remote Chinese outposts such as **Mae Salong** (Santikhiri; p216)

4 Discovering little-visited cities such as **Phayao** (p233) or **Phrae** (p235)

5 Time-travelling back to Thailand's golden age at **Sukhothai** (p254) and **Si Satchanalai-**

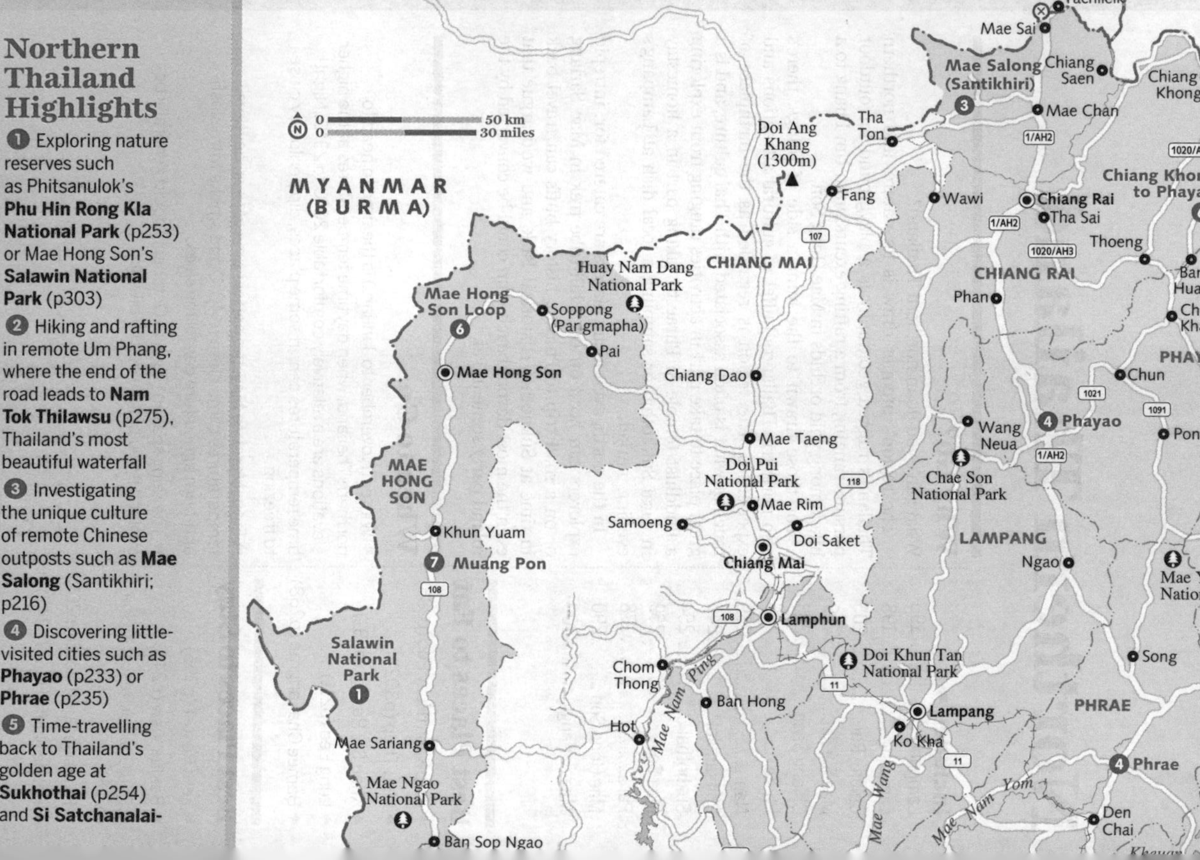

Chaliang Historical Parks (p262)

6 Hiring a vehicle and driving the **Mae Hong Son Loop** (p285) or the route from **Chiang Khong to Phayao** (p233)

7 Diving head first into northern Thai life at community-based homestays such as those in **Muang Pon** (p300) or **Ban Na Ton Chan** (p257)

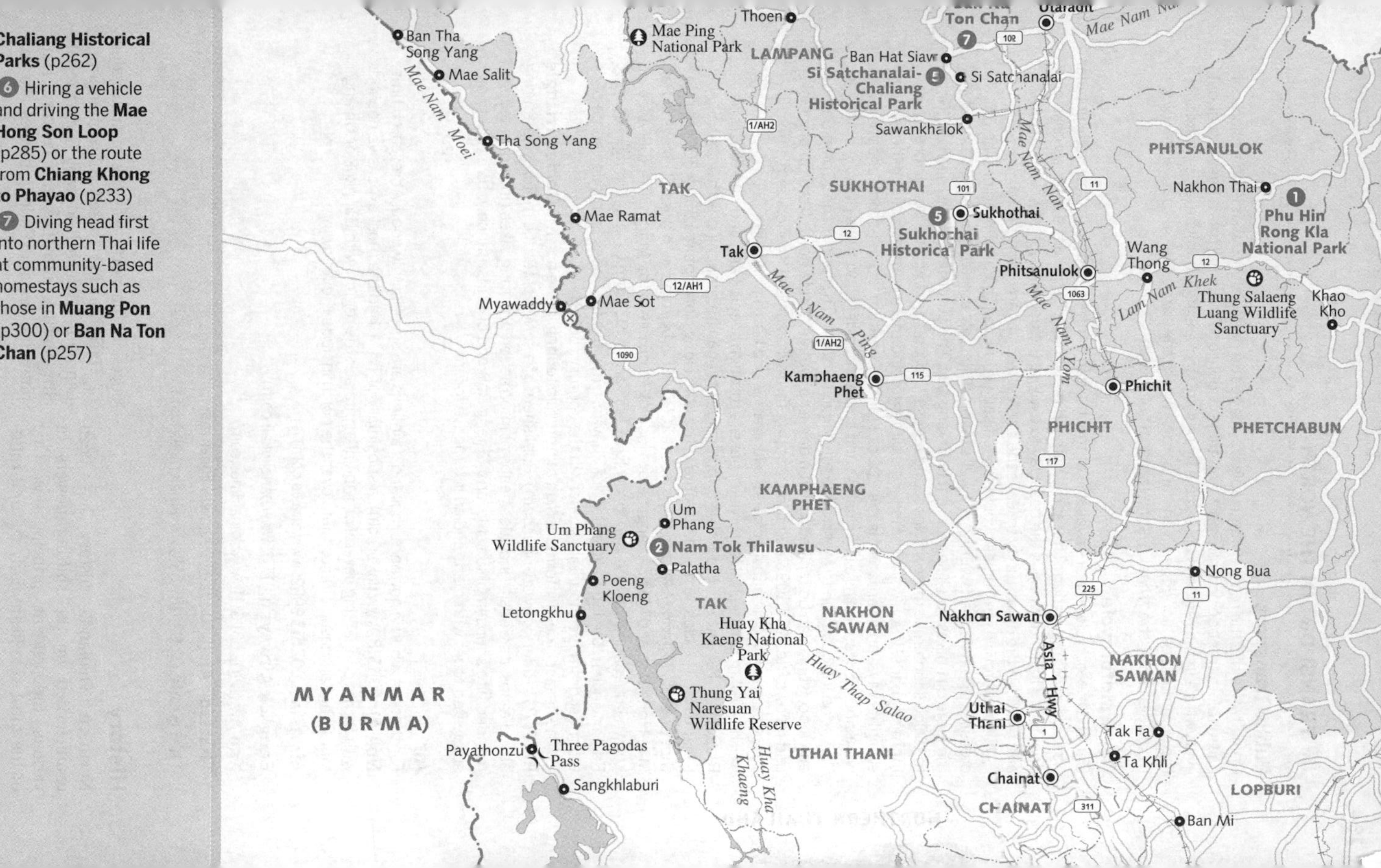

TRANSPORT IN THE NORTH

Public Transport

Going by train is the most comfortable way to get up north, although it is quite slow compared to other modes of transport, and there is only one main northern line. Just about everywhere in the region is accessible by bus and increasingly minivan, except among the communities along the Myanmar border, where the *sŏrng·tăa·ou* (passenger pick-up truck, also spelt *songthaew*) is the transport of choice.

Car & Motorcycle

Car and motorcycle hire are available at most urban centres, and an increasingly popular way of exploring northern Thailand is with a hired vehicle. Despite the obvious risks of driving in Thailand, hiring is the best way to explore the countryside at your own pace, and provides the opportunity to leave the beaten track at any moment.

For motorcycle hire, unless you're specifically intending to go off-road or plan on crossing unpaved roads during the wet season, it's highly unlikely you'll need one of the large dirt bikes you'll see for rent in Chiang Mai. The automatic transmission 110cc to 150cc scooterlike motorcycles found across Thailand are fast and powerful enough for most roads. If you want something a bit larger and more comfortable on those long straight-ways, an alternative is the 200cc Honda Phantom, a Thai-made chopper wannabe. For general hire information and safety considerations, see p000.

A good introduction to motorcycle touring in northern Thailand is the 100km Samoeng loop, which can be tackled in half a day. The route extends north from Chiang Mai and follows Rtes 107, 1096 and 1269, passing through excellent scenery and ample curves, and providing a taste of what a longer ride up north will be like.

The 470km Chiang Rai loop, which passes through scenic Fang and Tha Ton along Rtes 107, 1089 and 118, is another popular ride that can be broken up with a stay in Chiang Rai. The classic northern route is the Mae Hong Son loop (p285), a 600km ride that begins in Chiang Mai and takes in Rte 1095's 1864 curves with possible stays in Pai, Mae Hong Son and Mae Sariang, before looping back to Chiang Mai via Rte 108. A lesser known but equally fun ride is to follow Rtes 1155 and 1093 from Chiang Khong in Chiang Rai Province to the little-visited city of Phayao, a day trip that passes through some of the most dramatic mountain scenery in the country (p233).

The best source of information on motorcycle touring in the north is **Golden Triangle Rider** (GT Rider; www.gt-rider.com). Publishers of a series of terrific motorcycle-touring-based maps, its website includes heaps of information on hiring bikes (including recommended hire shops in Chiang Mai and Chiang Rai) and bike insurance, plus a variety of suggested tours with maps and an interactive forum.

Air

For those in a hurry, northern Thailand's air links are surprisingly good. At research time, **Nok Air** (☎1318; www.nokair.com), a subsidiary of THAI, had the most expansive network, with flights connecting several provincial capitals in the region with Bangkok or Chiang Mai. Other domestic airlines that cover the north include the following:

Air Asia (☎02 515 9999; www.airasia.com)

Bangkok Airways (☎1771; www.bangkokair.com)

Kan Air (☎02 551 6111; www.kanairlines.com)

Thai Lion Air (☎02 529 9999; www.lionairthai.com)

Thai Smile (☎02 118 8888; www.thaismileair.com)

History

Northern Thailand's history has been characterised by the shifting powers of various independent principalities. One of the most significant early cultural influences in the north was the Mon kingdom of Hariphunchai (based in contemporary Lamphun), which held sway from the late 8th century until the 13th century. Hariphunchai art and Buddha images are particularly distinctive, and many good examples can be found at the Hariphunchai National Museum in Lamphun.

The Thais, who are thought to have migrated south from China around the 7th century, united various principalities in the 13th century – this resulted in the creation of Sukhothai and the taking of Hariphunchai from the Mon. In 1238 Sukhothai declared itself an independent kingdom under King Si Intharathit and quickly expanded its sphere of influence. Because of this, and the significant influence the kingdom had on Thai art and culture, Sukhothai is considered by Thais to be the first true Thai kingdom.

In 1296 King Mengrai established Chiang Mai after conquering Hariphunchai. Later, in the 14th and 15th centuries, Chiang Mai, in an alliance with Sukhothai, became a part of the larger kingdom of Lan Na Thai (Million Thai Rice Fields), popularly referred to as Lanna. This empire extended as far south as Kamphaeng Phet and as far north as Luang Prabang in Laos. The golden age of Lanna was in the 15th century, and for a short time during this period, the Sukhothai capital was moved to Phitsanulok, and Chiang Mai increased in influence as a religious and cultural centre. However, during the 16th century, many of Lan Na Thai's important alliances weakened or fell apart, ultimately leading to the Burmese capturing Chiang Mai in 1556. Burmese control of Lanna lasted for the next two centuries. The northern Thais regrouped after the Burmese took Ayuthaya in 1767, and under King Kawila, Chiang Mai was recaptured in 1774 and the Burmese were pushed north.

In the late 19th century, Rama V of Bangkok made efforts to integrate the northern region with the centre to ward off the colonial threat. The completion of the northern railway to Chiang Mai in 1921 strengthened those links until the northern provinces finally became part of the kingdom of Siam in the early part of the 20th century.

Language

Thailand's regional dialects vary greatly and can even be unintelligible to native speakers of Thai not familiar with the vernacular being spoken. *Găm méuang*, the northern Thai dialect, is no exception and, in addition to an entirely different set of tones to master, possesses a wealth of vocabulary specific to the north. The northern dialect also has a slower rhythm than Thailand's three other main dialects, an attribute reflected in the relaxed, easygoing manner of the people who speak it.

Northern Thai also has its own writing system, based on an old Mon script that was originally used only for Buddhist scripture. The script became so popular during the Lanna period that it was exported for use by the Thai Lü in China, the Khün in the eastern Shan State, and other Thai–Kadai-speaking groups living between Lanna and China. Few northerners nowadays can read the northern Thai script – often referred to as Lanna script – and it is mostly used in signage to add a northern Thai cultural flavour.

LAMPHUN PROVINCE

This tiny province southeast of Chiang Mai consists of little more than a small city surrounded by farms, villages and an easily accessible national park.

Lamphun ลำพูน

POP 14,000

Essentially a culture stop for Chiang Mai sightseers, this provincial capital sits quietly along the banks of Mae Kuang, a tributary of Mae Ping.

There's not much fanfare regarding its superlative as one of Thailand's oldest cities. The old fortress wall and ancient temples are surviving examples of Lamphun's former life as the northernmost outpost of the ancient Mon Dvaravati kingdom, then known as Hariphunchai (AD 750–1281). During part of this period, the city was ruled by Chama Thewi, a Mon queen who has earned legendary status among Thailand's constellation of historic rulers.

The 26km voyage along a former highway between Chiang Mai and Lamphun is one of the city's primary attractions. It's a beautiful country road, stretches of which are canopied by tall dipterocarp trees.

Sights

Wat Phra That Hariphunchai BUDDHIST TEMPLE

(วัดพระธาตุหริภุญชัย; Th Inthayongyot; admission 20B; ⌚6am-9pm) This temple, Lamphun's most famous, spans back to the Mon period, having originally been built on the site of

NORTHERN THAILAND CHEAT SHEET

Northern Thailand covers a relatively big area, spanning lots of places, people and culture. It can all be a bit overwhelming, so to help you plan your trip, we've offered a few thematic leads:

Best for handicrafts Nan

Most exotic fresh market Mae Sot

Best for local food Chiang Rai

Best for noodles Sukhothai

Best for friendly locals Phrae

Best for cultural hiking Chiang Rai Province

Best for nature hiking Mae Hong Son Province

Best for ancient architecture Lampang

Best for ancient ruins nobody knows about Kamphaeng Phet

Best backpacker party scene Pai

Best off-the-beaten-track town Phayao

Queen Chama Thewi's palace in 1044 (or 1108 or 1157 according to some datings). The temple boasts some interesting architecture, a couple of fine Buddha images and two old *chedi* (stupas) in the original Hariphunchai style. The compound lay derelict until Khruba Siwichai, a famous northern Thai monk, ordered renovations in the 1930s.

The tallest of the ancient *chedi*, Chedi Suwan, is a narrow brick spire dating from 1418 that sits 21m high. The newer *chedi*, 46m-high Phra Maha That Chedi, is regarded as a textbook example of 15th-century Lanna architecture with its square pedestal rising to a rounded bell shape.

Hariphunchai National Museum MUSEUM
(พิพิธภัณฑสถานแหงชาติหริภุญไชย; Th Inthayongyot; admission 100B; ⌚9am-4pm Wed-Sun) Across the street from Wat Phra That Hariphunchai is the informative Hariphunchai National Museum. Inside is a collection of Mon and Lanna artefacts and Buddhas from the Dvaravati kingdom, as well as a stone inscription gallery with Mon and Thai Lanna scripts. There is a small bookshop with some English titles.

Wat Chama Thewi BUDDHIST TEMPLE
(วัดจามเทวี; Th Chamadevi; ⌚dawn-dusk) FREE An unusual Hariphunchai *chedi* can be seen at Wat Chama Thewi. The structure dates to around the 13th century, but has been restored many times since then and is now a mixture of several schools of architecture. Each side of the *chedi* has five rows of three Buddha figures, diminishing in size on each higher level. The standing Buddhas, although recently sculpted, are in Dvaravati style.

It's located about 1.5km from Wat Phra That Hariphunchai; you can take a motorcycle taxi (20B) from in front of the national museum.

Festivals & Events

Songkran WATER FESTIVAL
Should Chiang Mai's water fight be too wet and wild for your taste, Lamphun hosts a milder, more traditional affair in mid-April.

Lam Yai Festival CULINARY
During the second week of August, Lamphun hosts the annual festival spotlighting its primary agricultural product. It features floats made of fruit and, of course, a Miss Lam Yai contest.

Sleeping & Eating

You're unlikely to stay overnight as Lamphun is so close to Chiang Mai. There is a string of decent **noodle shops** (Th Inthayongyot; mains 30-90B) located on Lamphun's main street, just south of Wat Phra That Hariphunchai.

Dao Kanong NORTHERN THAI $
(340 Th Charoen Rat/Th Chiang Mai-Lamphun; mains 30-90B; ⌚9.30am-8pm) For something more substantial, long-standing Dao Kanong has a huge selection of northern Thai dishes. It's 1.5km north of Wat Phra That Hariphunchai.

Shopping

Kad Khua Moong Tha Sing MARKET
(⌚9am-6pm) Located behind Wat Phra That Hariphunchai, Kad Khua Moong Tha Sing is a souvenir market selling local items such as dried *lam yai* (longan fruit) and silk.

Getting There & Away

Frequent blue *sŏrng·tăa·ou* (passenger pick-up trucks) and purple buses bound for Lamphun leave from Chiang Mai's Chang Pheuak terminal, a stop on Th Praisani in front of Talat Warorot, and from another stop on the eastern side of the river on Th Chiang Mai-Lamphun, just south of the Tourist Authority of Thailand (TAT) office, during daylight hours (25B, 30 minutes). Both can drop you off on Th Inthayongyot at the stop in front of the national museum and Wat Phra That Hariphunchai.

Minibuses and *sŏrng·tăa·ou* (25B, 30 minutes, from 6am to 5.30pm) return to Chiang Mai from the stop in front of the national museum or from the city's bus terminal on Th Sanam.

Doi Khun Tan National Park อุทยานแห่งชาติดอยขุนตาล

Doi Khun Tan National Park NATURE RESERVE
(☎053 546 335, accommodation 02 562 0760; www.dnp.go.th; admission 200B; ⏲8am-5pm) This 225-sq-km national park straddles the mountains between Lamphun and Lampang Provinces. It ranges in elevation from 350m at the bamboo forest lowlands to 1363m at the pine-studded summit of Doi Khun Tan. Wildflowers, including orchids, ginger and lilies, are abundant. At the park headquarters there are maps of well-marked trails that range from short walks around the headquarters' vicinity to trails covering the mountain's four peaks; there's also a trail to **Nam Tok Tat Moei** (7km round trip). The park is very popular on cool-season weekends.

Intersecting the mountain slopes is Thailand's longest train tunnel (1352m), which opened in 1921 after six years of manual labour by thousands of Lao workers (several of whom are said to have been killed by tigers).

Bungalows (500B to 2700B) sleeping between two and nine people are available near the park headquarters, where there's also a restaurant.

The main access to the park is from the Khun Tan train station. To check timetables and prices from various destinations, call the **State Railway of Thailand** (☎1690; www.railway.co.th) or check its website. Once at the Khun Tan station, cross the tracks and follow a steep, marked path 1.3km to the park headquarters. By car, take the Chiang Mai–Lampang highway to the Mae Tha turn-off then follow the signs along a steep unpaved road for 18km.

LAMPANG PROVINCE

Formerly associated with the logging trade, today Lampang is more closely linked to industries such as mining and ceramics. It's a vast, mountainous province known for its natural beauty, a pleasant provincial capital, and for some of northern Thailand's most emblematic Buddhist temples.

SPEAKING NORTHERN THAI

Northerners used to take offence when outsiders tried speaking *găm méuang* (the colloquial name for the northern dialect) to them, an attitude that dates back to a time when central Thais considered northerners to be very backward and made fun of their dialect. Nowadays, most northerners are proud of their native language, and speaking a few words of the local lingo will go a long way in getting them to open up. The following are words and phrases that will help you talk to, flirt with, or perhaps just win some smiles from the locals.

Ôo găm méuang bòr jâhng I can't speak northern Thai.

A yăng gór? What did you say?

An née tôw dai? How much is this?

Mee kôw nêung bòr? Do you have sticky rice?

Lám đáa đáa Delicious

Mâan lâ Yes/That's right.

Yin dee nôe Thank you

Bòr mâan No

Gàht Market

Jôw (A polite word used by women; equivalent to the central Thai *ka*.)

Lampang ลำปาง

POP 59,000

Boasting lumbering elephants, the elegant mansions of former lumber barons and impressive (and in many cases, timber-based) Lanna-era temples, Lampang seems to unite every northern Thai cliché – but in a good way. Despite all this, the city sees relatively few visitors, giving it more of an undiscovered feel than some of the more touristed destinations in the north.

History

Although Lampang Province was inhabited as far back as the 7th century in the Dvaravati period, legend has it that Lampang city was founded by the son of Hariphunchai's (modern-day Lamphun's) Queen Chama Thewi, and the city played an important part in the history of the Hariphunchai kingdom.

Like Chiang Mai, Phrae and other older northern cities, modern Lampang was built as a walled rectangle alongside a river (in this case, Mae Wang). At the end of the 19th and beginning of the 20th century, Lampang, along with nearby Phrae, became an important centre for the domestic and international teak trade. A large British-owned timber company brought in Burmese supervisors familiar with the teak industry in Burma to train Burmese and Thai loggers in the area. These well-paid supervisors, along with independent Burmese teak merchants who plied their trade in Lampang, sponsored the construction of more than a dozen temples in the city, a legacy that lives on in several of Lampang's most impressive wát and the beautiful antique homes along Th Talad Gao.

USE YOUR MELON

Diminutive Wat Suchadaram, at Wat Phra Kaew Don Tao, is said to be located on the former melon patch *(dorn đôw)* of Mae (Mother) Suchada, a pious local woman. It is said that during a time of famine, a monk appeared and was given an unusually shaped melon by Mae Suchada. Upon opening the melon, the monk found a large green gem inside, and with the help of Mae Suchada, as well as the divine intervention of Indra, the gem was shaped into a Buddha image.

Villagers suspected the collaboration between the monk and Mae Suchada of being a bit too friendly, and in a fit of rage, beheaded Suchada. Upon later realising their mistake (the beheading led to yet another famine), a temple was built in the woman's honour. Today the Emerald Buddha image is held at Wat Phra That Lampang Luang (p203).

Sights & Activities

Wat Phra Kaew Don Tao BUDDHIST TEMPLE

(วัดพระแก้วดอนเต้า; off Th Phra Kaew; admission 20B; ⊙dawn-dusk) The main *chedi* shows Hariphunchai influence, while the adjacent *mon·dòp* (the small square-sided building with a spire) was built in 1909. The *mon·dòp* is decorated with glass mosaic in typical Burmese style and contains a Mandalay-style Buddha image. From 1436 to 1468, Wat Phra Kaew Don Tao was among four wát in northern Thailand to have housed the Emerald Buddha (now in Bangkok's Wat Phra Kaew).

A display of Lanna artefacts can be viewed in the wát's **Lanna Museum** (admission by donation; ⊙7am-6pm).

Adjacent to the temple complex, **Wat Suchadaram** dates back to 1809 and is named after Mae Suchada, the central figure in a local legend.

Th Talad Gao NEIGHBOURHOOD

(ถนนตลาดเกา) Lampang's multicultural history can be seen along this riverside street, which is lined with old homes, temples and shophouses showcasing Thai, English, Chinese and Burmese architectural styles. It's also where the town's weekly Walking Street (p202) market is held.

Wat Pongsanuk Tai BUDDHIST TEMPLE

(วัดปงสนุกใต้; Th Pongsnook; ⊙dawn-dusk) FREE Despite having lost much of its character in a renovation, the *mon·dòp* at Wat Pongsanuk Tai is still one of the few remaining local examples of original Lanna-style temple architecture, which emphasised open-sided wooden buildings. To get an idea of what it was like previously, look at the carved wooden gateway at the entrance to the north stairway.

A couple of informal museums on the temple grounds display local artefacts, but they include little English explanation.

Baan Sao Nak MUSEUM
(บ้านเสานัก; 85 Th Radwattana; admission 50B; 10am-5pm) A huge Lanna-style house built in 1895 and supported by 116 square teak pillars, Baan Sao Nak was once owned by a local *kun·yǐng* (a title equivalent to 'Lady' in England); it now serves as a local museum. The entire house is furnished with mildly interesting Burmese and Thai antiques, but the structure itself and its manicured garden are the highlights.

Dhanabadee Ceramic Museum MUSEUM
(พิพิธภัณฑ์เซรามิคธนบดี; www.dhanabadeeceramic museum.com; off Soi 1, Th Phrabat; admission 100B; 9am-5pm) Dhanabadee claims to be the first producer of the emblematic 'chicken bowls' used across Thailand. In 2013, the company opened its doors to visitors and began running guided tours that span a history of the chicken bowl in Thailand and the various steps involved in making them. The museum is located about 500m south of Th Phahonyothin/AH2.

Wat Chedi Sao BUDDHIST TEMPLE
(วัดเจดีย์ซาว; Th Pratuma; dawn-dusk) FREE This temple is named for the 20 (*sow* in northern Thai) whitewashed Lanna-style *chedi* on its grounds. But the wát's real treasure is a solid-gold, 15th-century seated Buddha on display in a glassed-in pavilion, built over a square pond.

The Buddha image is said to contain a piece of the Buddha's skull in its head and an ancient Pali-inscribed golden palm leaf in its chest; precious stones decorate the image's hairline and robe. A farmer reportedly found the figure next to the ruins of nearby Wat Khu Kao in 1983.

Monks stationed at Wat Chedi Sao make and sell herbal medicines; the popular *yah·mòrng* is similar to Tiger Balm.

The wát is located about 6km north of town, via Th Phra Kaew; a round-trip motorcycle taxi here should cost about 60B.

Phum Lakhon Museum MUSEUM
(พิพิธภัณฑ์เมืองของชาวลำปาง; cnr Th Chatchai & Th Thakhrao Noi; 8.30am-4.30pm Mon-Fri) FREE A brief but engaging museum that employs multimedia displays to tell the story of the history, people and culture of Lampang.

Wat Si Rong Meuang BUDDHIST TEMPLE
(วัดศรีรองเมือง; Th Thakhrao Noi; dawn-dusk) FREE Wat Si Rong Meuang was built in the late 19th century by Burmese artisans. The temple building was constructed in the Burmese 'layered' style, with tin roofs gabled by intricate woodcarvings.

Wat Si Chum BUDDHIST TEMPLE
(วัดศรีชุม; Th Thipawan; dawn-dusk) FREE Yet another of Lampang's ornate, Burmese-style temples, Wat Si Chum dates back to 1912.

Horse Carts
Lampang is the only town in Thailand where horse carts are still found. Now fully relegated to tourists, you can't miss the brightly coloured carts that drip with plastic flowers and are handled by Stetson-wearing drivers. A 30-minute tour (300B) goes along Mae Wang while a one-hour tour (300B) stops at Wat Phra Kaew Don Tao and Wat Si Rong Meuang.

Horse carts can be found waiting on Th Suandawg, across from Pin Hotel, and at another stall on Th Boonyawat, just east of the market, from around 5am to 9pm.

Sleeping

Akhamsiri Home HOTEL $
(054 228 791; www.akhamsirihome.com; 54/1 Th Pamaikhet; r 590B;) The tagline here ought to be 'Midrange amenities at a budget price'. The large cool rooms are located in a tidy residential compound and all have TV, fridge and a garden/balcony. Communicating in English may be problematic.

Chita Coffee & Guesthouse GUESTHOUSE $
(054 323 370; www.facebook.com/chitacoffeeguesthouse; 143 Th Talad Gao; r 350-650B;) Smack dab in the middle of historic Th Talad Gao, Chita offers relatively stylish budget rooms above a cafe. The cheapest are closet-sized, fan-cooled and share a bathroom.

Baan Chiangrai HOTEL $
(054 221 961; 336/9 Th Bahnchiengrai; r 590B;) Seven stylish and contemporary-feeling rooms above a coffee shop. All have flatscreen TV and vast desks. Good value.

TT&T Guest House GUESTHOUSE $
(054 221 303; 82 Th Pa Mai; r 350-550B;) This long-standing place has an appropriately old-school backpacker vibe. Rooms are bare and most bathrooms are shared, but the pleasant riverfront location and expansive chill-out areas downstairs make up for this.

Lampang

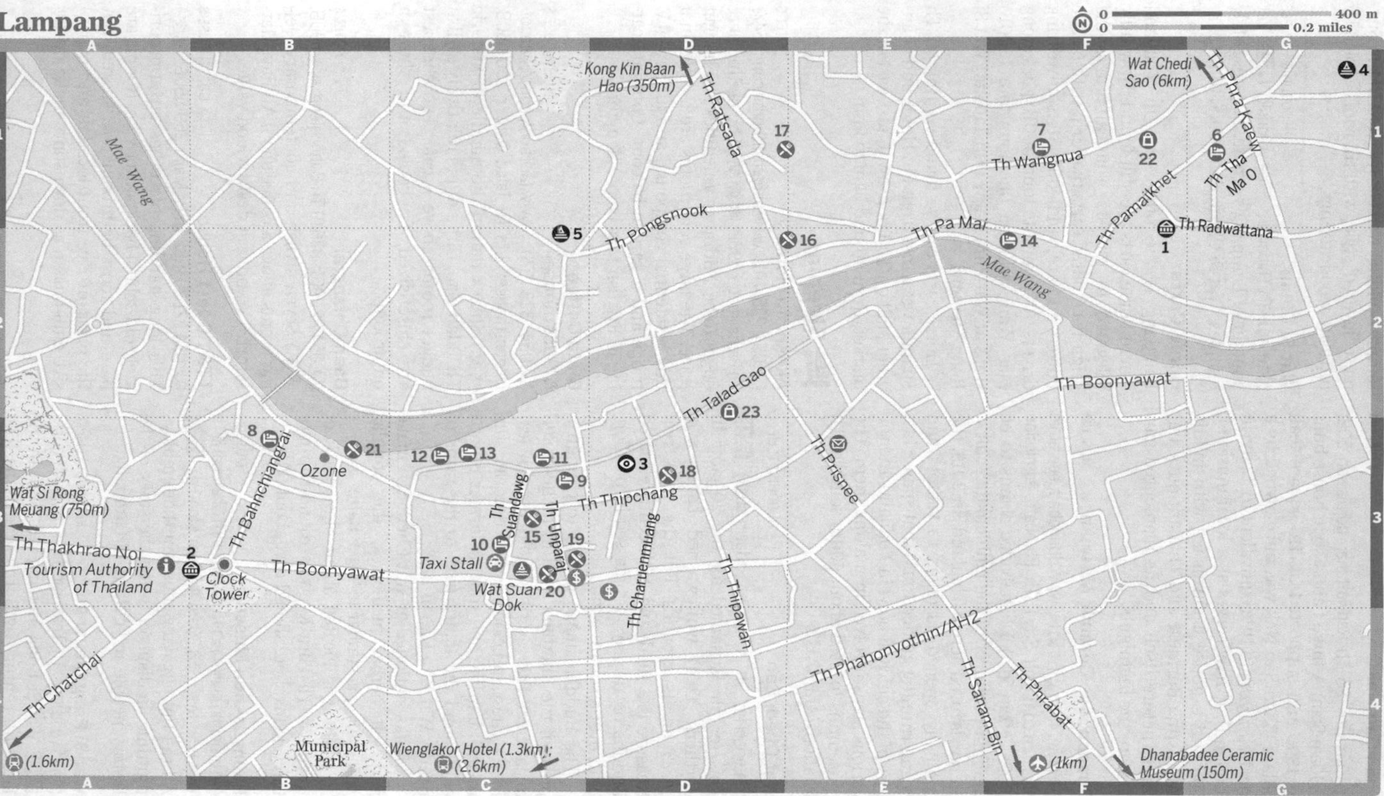
0 400 m
0 0.2 miles
A B C D E F G
1 2 3 4
Mae Wang
Kong Kin Baan Hao (350m)
Th Ratsada
Wat Chedi Sao (6km)
Th Phra Kaew
Th Wangnua
Th Tha Ma O
Th Pamaikhet
Th Radwattana
Th Pongsnook
Th Pa Mai
Th Boonyawat
Th Talad Gao
Th Prisnee
Ozone
Th Bahnchiangrai
Wat Si Rong Meuang (750m)
Th Thipchang
Th Suandawg
Th Upparaj
Th Charuenmuang
Th Thipawan
Th Thakhrao Noi
Tourism Authority of Thailand
Clock Tower
Th Boonyawat
Taxi Stall
Wat Suan Dok
Th Phahonyothin/AH2
Th Sanam Bin
Th Phrabat
Th Chatchai
(1.6km)
Municipal Park
Wienglakor Hotel (1.3km); (2.6km)
(1km)
Dhanabadee Ceramic Museum (150m)
1 2 3 4 5 6 7 8 9 10 11 12 13 14 15 16 17 18 19 20 21 22 23

Lampang

★ Riverside Guest House GUESTHOUSE $$
(054 227 005; www.theriverside-lampang.com; 286 Th Talad Gao; r 350-900B, ste 1800-2000B;) Although still mostly within budget range, this leafy compound of refurbished wooden houses is one of the more pleasant places to stay in Lampang, if not all of northern Thailand. It couldn't be any nearer the river, shaded tables for chatting or eating abound, and motorcycle rental and other tourist amenities are available.

Try to score one of the two upstairs rooms in the main structure that feature vast balconies overlooking Mae Wang, or the huge two-room suite.

Auangkham Resort GUESTHOUSE $$
(054 221 305; www.auangkhamlampang.com; 49-51 Th Wangnua; r 900-1100B;) Not a resort at all, but rather an exceptionally well run, boutique-style guesthouse. The 14 rooms feel bright and airy, and all have balconies overlooking an attractive garden. The homey service complements the peaceful vibe, and there are bonus perks such as the free use of bicycles and a location steps from Friday's Cultural Street (p202) market.

R-Lampang GUESTHOUSE $$
(054 225 278; www.r-lampang.com; 278 Th Talad Gao; r 250-1000B;) Cute is the underlying aesthetic at this compound next to Mae Wang. Wind through brightly coloured halls decked with teddy bears to emerge at spacious air-con rooms and two rather tight fan-cooled, shared-bathroom budget rooms. An attached shop sells drinks and souvenirs.

Pin Hotel HOTEL $$
(054 221 509; pin.hotel@yahoo.com; 8 Th Suandawg; r incl breakfast 625-1500B;) Spotless, spacious and secluded, the vast rooms here come decked out with cable TV, minibar and large bathrooms, but not a lot of character. Making up for this is the fact that the Pin is within walking distance of most sights in 'downtown' Lampang.

Prink HOTEL $$
(08 3589 6921; 262-264 Th Talad Gao, no roman-script sign; r 650-800B;) One of Th Talad Gao's noblest historic buildings has been turned into a stylish boutique hotel. The eight rooms, located above a cafe and ice-cream shop, share a fun retro design theme – and bathrooms – although some lack windows and feel somewhat claustrophobic. Avoid this by requesting one of the more expensive balcony rooms.

Wienglakor Hotel HOTEL $$$
(054 316 430-5; www.lampangwienglakor.com; 138/35 Th Phahonyothin; r 1200-1600B, ste 3500B, all incl breakfast;) If you're going upscale, this is Lampang's best choice. The lobby is tastefully decorated in a teak and northern Thai temple theme, a design that continues into the rooms. Deluxe rooms feature an added sitting area and walk-in closet, and the hotel's attractive outdoor dining area with carp pond is a classy, natural touch. It's about 1.5km west of the centre of Lampang, at the junction of Th Phahonyothin/AH2 and Th Duangrat.

Eating

For a relatively small town, Lampang boasts a pretty decent repertoire of restaurants,

DON'T MISS

KHUN MANEE

Khun Manee (35 Th Ratsada, no roman-script sign; ⌚7am-7pm) Lampang is known for its addictive *kôw đaan* (deep-fried rice cakes seasoned with watermelon juice and drizzled with palm sugar). You can pick up a few bags and watch the sweets being made at this homey factory just off Th Ratsada – look for the white, illuminated sign with green letters.

ranging from good northern Thai to acceptable Western fare, and a few things in between.

Aroy One Baht THAI $
(cnr Th Suandawg & Th Thipchang; mains 30-100B; ⌚4-11pm) Some nights it can seem like everybody in Lampang is here, and understandably so: the food is tasty and embarrassingly cheap, and the setting in a wooden house is a lot of fun.

Mae Hae NORTHERN THAI $
(1017 Th Upparaj, no roman-script sign; mains 20-50B; ⌚11am-7pm) Boost your Lampang foodie street cred by eating at this unassuming and long-standing northern Thai–style restaurant. There's no menu, so simply point to the soup, curry, dip or salad that looks tastiest. Look for the light blue building.

Phat Thai Yay Fong THAI $
(Th Boonyawat, no roman-script sign; mains 35-60B; ⌚5-10pm) How do northern Thais take their *pàt tai*? With minced pork and pork rinds, of course. This popular stall is located just east of Wat Suan Dok.

Evening Market MARKET $
(Th Ratsada; ⌚4-8pm) Self-caterers or those interested in local eats will want to check out Lampang's evening market, where steaming baskets of sticky rice and dozens of sides to dip it in are on daily display.

Kong Kin Baan Hao NORTHERN THAI $$
(72 Th Jama Thewi, no roman-script sign; mains 50-250B; ⌚10am-midnight) This local favourite is most popular after dark when a bottle of whisky is regarded as a typical side dish. Flip through the English-language menu's Local Cuisine pages for northern Thai staples such as *gaang kaa gòp* (a herb-laden soup with frog) or *lâhp kôo·a* (*lâhp* that has been stir-fried with local spices).

It's located about 1km outside of town. To get there, head north on Th Ratsada, crossing the river, and turn left at the stoplight. Do a U-turn at the next stoplight; the restaurant is on the left – look for the trees.

Long Jim AMERICAN $$
(Th Charuenmuang; pizzas 115-130B; ⌚5-9pm Tue-Fri, to 10pm Sat & Sun; 📶✎) New York–style pizza – available by the slice on Saturday and Sunday – as well as pasta dishes, soups and salads, all overseen by an authentic American.

Riverside INTERNATIONAL, THAI $$
(328 Th Thipchang; mains 80-210B; ⌚10am-10pm) This wooden shack that appears to be on the verge of tumbling into Mae Wang is a hit with both visiting and resident foreigners. Live music, a full bar and a thick menu of local and Western dishes bring in the crowds.

Shopping

Walking Street MARKET
(⌚4-10pm Sat & Sun) Lampang has its own Walking Street market along charming Th Talad Gao. On Saturday and Sunday evenings, the usual traffic is replaced by souvenir, handicraft and food stalls.

Cultural Street MARKET
(Th Wangnua; ⌚5-8pm Fri) A Cultural Street market, similar to the Walking Street, is held across the river on Th Wang Nuea every Friday evening.

Information

Several banks with ATMs can be found along Th Boonyawat.

Post Office (Th Prisnee; ⌚8.30am-4.30pm Mon-Fri, 9am-noon Sat)

Tourism Authority of Thailand (TAT; ☎054 237 229, nationwide 1672; Th Thakhrao Noi; ⌚9am-4pm Mon-Fri) The helpful folks here can provide decent maps of the area and details about local sights and activities.

Getting There & Away

Lampang's airport – being rebuilt when we were in town – is about 1.5km south of the centre of town, at the eastern end of Th Phahonyothin/AH2. At research time, **Bangkok Airways** (☎Lampang 054 821 522, nationwide 1771; www.bangkokair.com; Lampang Airport; ⌚8.30-11.30am & 12.30-6.30pm), with three daily flights to/from Bangkok's Suvarnabhumi International Airport (1420B, 1½ hours), and **Nok Air** (☎Lampang 09 4494 3440, nationwide 1318; www.nokair.com; Lampang Airport;

TRANSPORT TO/FROM LAMPANG

Bus

DESTINATION	FARE (B)	DURATION (HR)	FREQUENCY
Bangkok	361-722	9	frequent 7.30-11.30am & 6.30-9pm
Chiang Mai	51-143	2	half-hourly 2am-11pm
Chiang Rai	108-194	4	frequent 6.30am-3pm
Mae Sai	238	6	12.40pm
Mae Sot	245	4	3 departures 10am-4.30pm
Nan	158-316	4	7 departures 9am-midnight
Phitsanulok	164-203	4½	hourly 6.30am-8.45pm
Phrae	83-165	2	11 departures 9am-midnight
Sukhothai	220-319	3½	hourly 6.30am-8.45pm

Train

DESTINATION	FARE (B)	DURATION (HR)	FREQUENCY
Bangkok	256-1872	12	6 daily
Chiang Mai	23-413	3	6 daily
Phitsanulok	48-1542	5	6 daily

⌚8am-8pm), with three daily flights to/from Bangkok's Don Muang International Airport (1300B, 1½ hours), were the only airlines operating out of Lampang. Taxis from the airport to downtown cost 50B per person, or 100B to book the whole car.

Lampang's **bus and minivan terminal** (☎054 218 219; cnr Th Phahonyothin/AH2 & Th Chantarasurin) is nearly 2km south of the centre of town; frequent *sŏrng·tăa·ou* (20B, 15 minutes, 3am to 9pm) run between the station and town. Minibuses head to Chiang Mai (71B, 1½ hours, hourly from 6.30am to 4pm) and Phrae (85B, two hours, half-hourly from 7.10am to 4.30pm).

Lampang's historic **train station** (☎054 217024, nationwide 1690; www.railway.co.th; Th Phahonyothin), dating back to 1916, is about 2.5km from the centre of town, a fair hike from most accommodation. A túk-túk (pronounced *đúk đúk*) between here and the centre of town should run around 80B.

ℹ Getting Around

Getting around central Lampang is possible on foot. The Tourism Authority of Thailand office has free bicycle rental from 10am to 4pm; bring your passport. For destinations outside of town, there is a **taxi stall** (☎054 217233; Th Suandawg; ⌚6.30am-5pm) near the Pin Hotel.

Both bicycles and motorcycles are available for rent at **Ozone** (395 Th Thipchang; bicycle/motorcycle per day 60/200B; ⌚9am-8pm).

Around Lampang

Wat Phra That Lampang Luang วัดพระธาตุลำปางหลวง

Wat Phra That Lampang Luang BUDDHIST TEMPLE

(off Rte 1034; ⌚dawn-dusk) FREE This ancient Buddhist temple compound houses several interesting religious structures, including what is arguably the most beautiful wooden Lanna temple in northern Thailand, the open-sided **Wihan Luang**. Dating back to 1476 and thought to be the oldest-standing wooden structure in the country, the impressive *wí·hăhn* (sanctuary) features a triple-tiered wooden roof supported by immense teak pillars and early 19th-century *Jataka* murals (stories of the Buddha's previous lives) painted on wooden panels around the inside upper perimeter. A huge, gilded *mon·dòp* in the back of the *wí·hăhn* contains a Buddha image cast in 1563.

OFF THE BEATEN TRACK

WAT LAI HIN

Wat Lai Hin (วัดไหล่หิน; off Rte 1034; dawn-dusk) If you're visiting Wat Phra That Lampang Luang and you've got your own transport, you might also consider a visit to beautiful Wat Lai Hin, also near Ko Kha. Built by artists from Kyaingtong (also known as Kengtung or sometimes Chiang Tung), Myanmar, the tiny temple is one of the most characteristically Lanna temples around. It was a significant influence on the design of the Dhara Dhevi hotel in Chiang Mai, not to mention a set for the 2001 Thai historical blockbuster, *Suriyothai*. There's an interesting folk museum on the grounds that the monks can unlock for you.

If coming from Ko Kha, the temple is located about 6km down a road that turns off 1km before reaching Wat Phra That Lampang Luang.

The small and simple **Wihan Ton Kaew**, to the north of the main *wí·hăhn*, was built in 1476, while the tall Lanna-style *chedi* behind the main *wí·hăhn*, raised in 1449 and restored in 1496, is 45m high.

Wihan Nam Taem, to the north of the *chedi*, was built in the early 16th century and, amazingly, still contains traces of the original murals, making them among the oldest in the country.

South of the main *chedi*, **Wihan Phra Phut** dates back to the 13th century and is the oldest structure in the compound.

Unfortunately, only men are allowed to see a camera obscura image of the *wí·hăhn* and *chedi* in the **Haw Phra Phutthabaht**, a small white building behind the *chedi*. The image is projected (upside down) onto a white cloth, and clearly depicts the colours of the structures outside.

The lintel over the entrance to the compound features an impressive dragon relief, once common in northern Thai temples but rarely seen today. This gate allegedly dates to the 15th century.

In the arboretum outside the southern gate of the wát, there are three museums. One displays mostly festival paraphernalia and some Buddha figures. Another, called House of the Emerald Buddha, contains a miscellany of coins, banknotes, Buddha figures, silver betel-nut cases, lacquerware and other ethnographic artefacts, along with three small heavily gold-leafed Buddhas placed on an altar behind an enormous repoussé silver bowl. The third, a small museum, features shelves of Buddha figures, lacquered boxes, manuscripts and ceramics, all well labelled in Thai and English.

Getting There & Away

Wat Phra That Lampang Luang is 18km southwest of Lampang in Ko Kha. To get there by public transport from Lampang, flag a blue eastbound *sŏrng·tăa·ou* (20B) on Th Boonyawat. From the Ko Kha *sŏrng·tăa·ou* stop, it's a 3km chartered motorcycle taxi ride to the temple (60B). Alternatively, you can charter a *sŏrng·tăa·ou* from Lampang's bus station for 400B, or taxis will take you there and back for around the same price.

If you're driving or cycling from Lampang, head south on Th Phahonyothin/AH2 and take the Ko Kha exit, then follow the road over a bridge and bear right. Follow the signs and continue for 3km over another bridge until you see the temple on the left.

Thai Elephant Conservation Center & Around ศูนย์อนุรักษ์ช้างไทย

Hang Chat, 33km southeast of Lampang via Rte 11, is home to a few attractions, the centrepiece of which are two separate centres dedicated to elephants.

Thai Elephant Conservation Center ELEPHANT INTERACTION

(TECC; 054 829 333; www.thailandelephant.org; Rte 11; adult/child 200/100B; elephant bathing 9.40am & 1.10pm) This popular centre promotes the role of the Asian elephant in ecotourism. Yet it's worth mentioning that it also offers elephant shows and rides, which animal welfare experts claim can be harmful for the animals.

In addition to the shows, there is an exhibit on the history and culture of elephants, an elephant art gallery, an elephant graveyard, and elephant rides through the surrounding forest. For those keen on delving deeper into pachyderm culture, the TECC's Mahout Training School offers an array of programs ranging in duration from one day to one month.

All proceeds from the entrance fee and souvenir shops go to the on-site elephant hospital, which cares for old, abandoned and sick elephants from all over Thailand, as well as supporting research and breeding programs.

FAE's Elephant Hospital ELEPHANT INTERACTION
(Friends of the Asian Elephant; ☎08 1881 2269; www.elephant-soraida.com; off Rte 11; admission by donation; ⊙8am-5pm) Located next door to the Thai Elephant Conservation Center (but not affiliated) is this hospital, which claims to be the first of its kind in the world. Although visitors are appreciated and provided for, keep in mind that this is a functioning medical facility: there are no guided tours and no elephant art. Donations are greatly appreciated.

Sleeping & Eating

The Thai Elephant Conservation Center grounds have accommodation and three restaurants.

Homestay Program HOTEL $
(☎054 829 333; www.thailandelephant.org; Thai Elephant Conservation Center; per person 500B; @) Those enrolled in the TECC's multiday homestay programs live and eat with a mahout at these basic fan-cooled bungalows; accommodation and food are included in the price of tuition. Rooms – exclusive of meals – are also available for non-students.

Chang Thai Resort RESORT $$
(☎08 9634 6341; www.thailandelephant.org; Thai Elephant Conservation Center; bungalows 1000-1500B; ❄📶) The TECC's one- and two-room bungalows are modern and comfortable.

Shopping

Thung Kwiang Market MARKET
(ตลาดทุ่งเกวียน; Rte 11; ⊙7am-6pm) Located about 5km southeast of the Thai Elephant Conservation Center, this covered market is a crash course in northern Thai food and handicrafts, with everything from *rót dòo·an* (deep-fried worms, a northern speciality) to the distinctive rooster bowls made in Lampang.

Getting There & Away

The Thai Elephant Conservation Center and surrounds can be reached by Chiang Mai–bound minivan bus or *sŏrng·tăa·ou* (30B to 70B, 40 minutes) from Lampang's bus station. Let the driver know where you are headed and get off at the Km 37 marker for the two elephant centres. The TECC is 1.5km from the highway, and shuttle buses will take you inside. Alternatively, you can charter a blue *sŏrng·tăa·ou* for 600B at Lampang's bus station, or a taxi for about 1000B.

CHIANG RAI PROVINCE

Chiang Rai, Thailand's northernmost province, has a bit of everything: the mountains in the far east are among the most dramatic in the country, the lowland Mekong River floodplains to the northeast are not unlike those one would find much further south in Isan, and the province shares borders with Myanmar and Laos. In terms of people, it's also among Thailand's most ethnically diverse provinces and is home to a significant minority of hill tribes, Shan and other Tai groups, and more recent Chinese immigrants.

Chiang Rai เชียงราย

POP 70,000

Chiang Rai Province has such a diversity of attractions that its capital is often overlooked. This small delightful city is worth getting to know, however, with its relaxed atmosphere, good-value accommodation and great local food. It's also the logical base from which to plan excursions to the more remote corners of the province.

Founded by Phaya Mengrai in 1262 as part of the Lao-Thai Lanna kingdom, Chiang Rai didn't become a Siamese territory until 1786 and a province until 1910.

Sights

Mae Fah Luang Art & Culture Park MUSEUM
(ไร่แม่ฟ้าหลวง; www.maefahluang.org/rmfl; 313 Mu 7, Ban Pa Ngiw; adult/child 200B/free; ⊙8am-5pm Tue-Sun) In addition to a museum that houses one of Thailand's biggest collections of Lanna artefacts, this vast, meticulously landscaped compound includes antique and contemporary art, Buddhist temples and other structures. It's located about 4km west of the centre of Chiang Rai; a túk-túk or taxi here will run around 100B.

Haw Kaew, the park's museum, has a permanent collection of mostly teak-based artefacts and art from across the former Lanna region, as well as a temporary exhibition room.

Haw Kham, a temple-like tower built in 1984 from the remains of 32 wooden houses, is arguably the park's centrepiece. The immense size of the structure – allegedly influenced by Lanna-era Wat Pongsanuk in Lampang – with its Buddha image seemingly hovering over white sand (the latter imported from Ko Samet), and sacred, candle-lit aura culminate in a vibe not unlike the place of worship of an indigenous cult.

You'll probably have to ask staff to open up **Haw Kham Noi**, a structure housing folksy but beautiful Buddhist murals taken from a dismantled teak temple in Phrae.

Hilltribe Museum & Education Center MUSEUM

(พิพิธภัณฑ์และศูนย์การศึกษาชาวเขา; www.pdacr.org; 3rd fl, 620/25 Th Thanalai; admission 50B; ⏲8.30am-6pm Mon-Fri, 10am-6pm Sat & Sun) This museum and cultural centre is a good place to visit before undertaking any hill-tribe trek. Run by the nonprofit Population & Community Development Association (PDA), the displays are underwhelming in their visual presentation, but contain a wealth of information on Thailand's various tribes and the issues that surround them.

A visit begins with a 20-minute slide show on Thailand's hill tribes, followed by self-guided exploration among exhibits that include the typical clothing of six major tribes, examples of bamboo usage, folk implements and other anthropological objects. The curator is passionate about his museum and, if present, will talk about the different hill tribes, their histories, recent trends and the community projects that the museum helps fund.

The PDA also runs highly recommended treks.

Oub Kham Museum MUSEUM

(พิพิธภัณฑ์อูบคำ; www.oubkhammuseum.com; Th Nakhai; adult/child 300/100B; ⏲8am-5pm) This slightly zany museum houses an impressive collection of paraphernalia from virtually every corner of the former Lanna kingdom. The items, some of which truly are one of a kind, range from a monkey-bone food taster used by Lanna royalty to an impressive carved throne from Chiang Tung (Kyaingtong), Myanmar. It's located about 2km west of the town centre and can be a bit tricky to find; túk-túk will go here for about 60B.

Guided tours (available in English) are obligatory and include a walk through a gilded artificial cave holding several Buddha statues, complete with disco lights and fake torches! The grounds of the museum are equally kitschy and include a huge golden *naga* statue (a mythical serpent-like being with magical powers), waterfalls and fountains. An equal parts bizarre and enlightening experience.

Wat Phra Kaew BUDDHIST TEMPLE

(วัดพระแก้ว; Th Trairat; ⏲temple 7am-7pm, museum 9am-5pm) FREE Originally called Wat Pa Yia (Bamboo Forest Monastery) in the local dialect, this is the city's most revered Buddhist temple. The main prayer hall is a medium-sized, well-preserved wooden structure. The octagonal *chedi* behind it dates from the late 14th century and is in typical Lanna style. The adjacent two-storey wooden building is a museum housing various Lanna artefacts.

Legend has it that in 1434 lightning struck the temple's *chedi*, which fell apart to reveal the Phra Kaew Morakot, or Emerald Buddha (actually made of jade). After a lengthy journey that included a long stopover in Vientiane, Laos, this national talisman is now ensconced in the temple of the same name in Bangkok.

In 1990, Chiang Rai commissioned a Chinese artist to sculpt a new image from Canadian jade. Named the Phra Yok Chiang Rai (Chiang Rai Jade Buddha), it was intentionally a very close but not exact replica of the Phra Kaew Morakot in Bangkok, with dimensions of 48.3cm across the base and 65.9cm in height, just 0.1cm shorter than the original. The image is housed in the impressive Haw Phra Yoke, the walls of which are decorated with beautiful modern murals, some depicting the journey of the original Phra Kaew Morakot, as well as the elaborate ceremony that saw the current image arrive at its new home in Chiang Rai.

Tham Tu Pu & Buddha Cave BUDDHIST TEMPLE

(ถ้ำตูปู/ถ้ำพระ; ⏲dawn-dusk) FREE Cross the Mae Fah Luang Bridge (located just northwest of the city centre) to the northern side of Mae Nam Kok and you'll come to a turnoff for both Tham Tu Pu and the Buddha Cave. Neither attraction is particularly amazing on its own, but the surrounding country is beautiful and would make an ideal destination for a lazy bike or motorcycle ride.

Follow the road 1km, then turn off onto a dirt path 200m to the base of a limestone cliff where there is a steep set of stairs leading to a main chamber holding a dusty Buddha statue; this is **Tham Tu Pu**.

Continue along the same road for 3km more (the sign says 'Buddha Images Cave') and you'll reach **Buddha Cave**, a cavern by Mae Nam Kok containing a tiny but active Buddhist temple, a lone monk and numerous cats. The temple was one of several destinations on a visit to the region by King Rama V in the early 20th century.

Chiang Rai

Chiang Rai

Sights
- 1 Hilltribe Museum & Education Center C2
- 2 Wat Jet Yot B4
- 3 Wat Klang Wiang B2
- 4 Wat Phra Kaew A1
- 5 Wat Phra Singh A1

Activities, Courses & Tours
- 6 Chaow Nang Studio C2
- PDA Tours & Travel .... (see 1)

Sleeping
- 7 Baan Bua Guest House B4
- 8 Baan Warabordee C4
- 9 Chook Dee Friend House B3
- 10 Diamond Park Inn C4
- 11 FUN-D Hostel D3
- 12 Golden Triangle Inn B3
- 13 Moon & Sun Hotel C2
- 14 Na-Rak-O Resort C4
- 15 Orchids Guest House B3
- 16 The North B3
- 17 Wiang Inn B4

Eating
- 18 Khao Soi Phor Jai B3
- 19 Muang Thong B4
- 20 Namnigew Pa Nuan B4
- 21 Phu Lae C2
- 22 Rosprasert Muslim Food A3

Drinking & Nightlife
- 23 BaanChivitMai Bakery B4
- 24 Cat Bar B4
- 25 Doi Chaang B3
- 26 Easy House B3
- 27 Pangkhon Coffee B3

Shopping
- 28 Night Bazaar B3
- 29 Walking Street B2

Transport
- 30 Budget Rent-A-Car B3
- 31 Chiang Rai Big Bike Rental B3
- 32 Fat Free B3
- 33 Interprovincial Bus Station C4
- 34 ST Motorcycle B3

WORTH A TRIP

HEAVEN & HELL

Lying just outside Chiang Rai are Wat Rong Khun and Baan Dum, two of the province's most touted, bizarre – and worthwhile – destinations.

Wat Rong Khun (วัดร่องขุ่น; White Temple; off Rte 1/AH2; ⏲8am-5pm Mon-Fri, to 5.30pm Sat & Sun) FREE Whereas most of Thailand's Buddhist temples have centuries of history, Wat Rong Khun's construction began in 1997 by noted Thai painter-turned-architect Chalermchai Kositpipat. Seen from a distance, the temple appears to be made of glittering porcelain; a closer look reveals that the appearance is due to a combination of whitewash and clear-mirrored chips. It's located about 13km south of Chiang Rai. To get here, hop on one of the regular buses that run from Chiang Rai to Chiang Mai or Phayao (20B).

To enter the temple, you must walk over a bridge and pool of reaching arms (symbolising desire), where inside, instead of the traditional Buddha life scenarios, the artist has painted contemporary scenes representing *samsara* (the realm of rebirth and delusion). Images such as a plane smashing into the Twin Towers and, oddly enough, Keanu Reeves as Neo from *The Matrix* (not to mention Elvis, Hello Kitty and Superman, among others), dominate the one finished wall of this work in progress. The temple suffered minor damage in an earthquake in 2014.

Baan Dum (บ้านดำ; Black House; off Rte 1/AH2; ⏲9am-noon & 1-5pm) FREE The bizarre brainchild of Thai National Artist Thawan Duchanee, and a rather sinister counterpoint to Wat Rong Khun, Baan Dum unites several structures, most of which are stained black and ominously decked out with animal pelts and bones. It's located 13km north of Chiang Rai in Nang Lae; any Mae Sai–bound bus will drop you off here for around 20B.

The centrepiece is a black, cavernous temple-like building holding a long wooden dining table and chairs made from deer antlers – a virtual Satan's dining room. Other buildings include white, breast-shaped bedrooms, dark phallus-decked bathrooms, and a bone- and fur-lined 'chapel'. The structures have undeniably discernible northern Thai influences, but the dark tones, flagrant flourishes and all those dead animals coalesce in a way that is more fantasy than reality.

Wat Phra Singh BUDDHIST TEMPLE
(วัดพระสิงห์; Th Singhaclai; ⏲dawn-dusk) FREE This temple dates back to the late 14th century, and its oldest surviving original buildings are typical northern Thai–style wood structures with low, sweeping roofs. The main *wí·hăhn* houses impressive wooden doors thought to have been carved by local artists, as well as a copy of Chiang Mai's sacred Phra Singh Buddha.

Wat Jet Yot BUDDHIST TEMPLE
(วัดเจ็ดยอด; Th Jetyod; ⏲dawn-dusk) FREE The seven-spired *chedi* at Wat Jet Yot is similar to that of its Chiang Mai namesake but without stucco ornamentation. Of more aesthetic interest is the wooden ceiling of the front verandah of the main *wí·hăhn*, which features a unique Thai astrological fresco.

Wat Klang Wiang BUDDHIST TEMPLE
(วัดกลางเวียง; cnr Th Ratanaket & Th Uttarakit; ⏲dawn-dusk) FREE This temple appears contemporary but probably dates back at least 500 years. Extensive remodelling in the early 1990s has left several structures in the temple with a unique 'modern Lanna' style, but the elegant *hŏr đrai* (manuscript depository – the temple library) appears to have retained its original form.

Wat Phra That Doi Chom Thong BUDDHIST TEMPLE
(วัดพระธาตุดอยจอมทอง; off Th Kraisorasit; ⏲dawn-dusk) FREE King Mengrai, Chiang Rai's founder, first surveyed the site for the city from this peak, just west of contemporary Chiang Mai's centre. The Lanna-style *chedi* found at the top most likely dates from the 14th to 16th centuries and may cover an earlier Mon *chedi* inside. The hilltop compound is also home to Chiang Rai's 'city navel'.

Activities

Nearly every guesthouse and hotel in Chiang Rai offers hiking excursions in hill-tribe country, some of which have grassroots, sustainable or nonprofit emphasis.

In general, trek pricing depends on the type of activities and the number of days and participants. Rates, per person, for two people, for a two-night trek range from 2900B to 5800B. Generally everything from accommodation to transport and food is included in this price.

Mirror Foundation TREKKING

(☎053 737 616; www.thailandecotour.org) Although its rates are higher, trekking with this NGO helps support the training of its local guides. Treks range from one to three days and traverse the Akha, Karen and Lahu villages of Mae Yao District, north of Chiang Rai.

PDA Tours & Travel TREKKING

(☎053 740 088; www.pda.or.th/chiangrai/package_tour.htm; Hilltribe Museum & Education Center, 3rd fl, 620/25 Th Thanalai; ⏲8.30am-6pm Mon-Fri, 10am-6pm Sat & Sun) One- to three-day treks are available through this NGO. Profits go back into community projects that include HIV/AIDS education, mobile health clinics, education scholarships and the establishment of village-owned banks.

Rai Pian Karuna TREKKING

(☎082 195 5645; www.facebook.com/raipiankaruna) This new, community-based social enterprise conducts one- and multi-day treks and homestays at Akha, Lahu and Lua villages in Mae Chan, north of Chiang Rai. Other activities, from weeklong volunteering stints to cooking courses, are also on offer.

Thailand Hilltribe Holidays TREKKING

(☎085 548 0884; www.thailandhilltribeholidays.com) Sustainably minded guided tours and homestays in and around Chiang Rai.

Suwannee COOKING COURSE

(☎084 740 7119; www.suwanneethaicookingclass-chiangrai.blogspot.com; lessons 1250B; ⏲courses 9.30am-2pm) Suwannee's cooking courses involve a visit to a local market and instruction in cooking four dishes. Her house is about 3km outside the city centre, but she can pick you up at most centrally located hotels and guesthouses.

Cook Thai Yourself COOKING COURSE

(☎081 844 9913; www.cookthaiyourself.wix.com/home; lessons from 950B; ⏲lessons 9.30am-3pm) Thai cookery lessons in a semi-rural location, 20 minutes from Chiang Rai. Transportation is included in the fee.

Chiang Rai Bicycle Tours BICYCLE TOUR

(☎053 774 506, 085 662 4347; www.chiangraibicycletour.com; tours from 1400B) Offers a variety of two-wheel-based excursions in the areas surrounding Chiang Rai.

Chaow Nang Studio CULTURAL

(645/7 Th Uttarakit; ⏲10am-7pm) Dress up like a member of Lanna royalty and have your portrait (from 1000B) taken for posterity – a must-do activity for Thai visitors to Chiang Mai and Chiang Rai. It has a huge array of costumes and backdrops.

Sleeping

Chiang Rai has a great selection of places to stay, and price increases have been incremental over recent years, making accommodation in the town good value. Most budget places are in the centre of town, clustered around Th Jetyod; the majority of midrange places are a brief walk from 'downtown'; and Chiang Rai's upscale accommodation is generally located outside the centre of town.

In Town

Moon & Sun Hotel HOTEL $

(☎053 719 279; 632 Th Singhaclai; r 500-600B, ste 800B; ❄📶) Bright and sparkling clean, this little hotel offers large, modern, terrific-value rooms. Some feature four-poster beds, while all come with desk, cable TV and refrigerator. Suites have a separate, spacious sitting area.

Baan Warabordee HOTEL $

(☎053 754 488; baanwarabordee@hotmail.com; 59/1 Th Sanpanard; r 500-600B; ❄📶) A handsome, good-value hotel has been made from this three-storey Thai villa. Rooms are decked out in dark woods and light cloths, and are equipped with air-con, fridge and hot water.

FUN-D Hostel HOSTEL $

(☎053 712 123; www.facebook.com/FunDHostel-ChiangRai; 753 Th Phahonyothin; dm 260-290B, r 800B, all incl breakfast; ❄@📶) This is a lively-feeling hostel located, appropriately, above a restaurant-bar-cafe. Dorms are spacious and bright, and range from six to eight beds, the more expensive of which have semi-private, en suite bathroom facilities.

Baan Bua Guest House GUESTHOUSE $

(☎053 718 880; www.baanbua-guesthouse.com; 879/2 Th Jetyod; r 250-550B; ❄@📶) This quiet guesthouse consists of a strip of 11 bright green rooms surrounding an inviting garden. Rooms are simple, but unanimously clean and cosy.

The North HOTEL $
(☎053 719 873; www.thenorth.co.th; 612/100-101 Sirikon Market; dm 200B, r 390-490B;) This hotel has provided the drab market/bus station area with a bit of colour. The 15 rooms here combine both Thai and modern design, some attached to inviting chill-out areas.

Orchids Guest House GUESTHOUSE $
(☎053 718 361; www.orchidsguesthouse.com; 1012/3 Th Jetyod; r 450-500B;) This collection of spotless rooms in a residential compound is a good budget catch. In addition to accommodation, various services are available, including internet, laundry, taxi transfer and trekking.

Chook Dee Friend House GUESTHOUSE $
(☎09 4672 7921; cnr Th Jetyod & Th Thaiviwat; dm 120B, r 150-350B;) The rooms are basic, and the hyperchilled reggae vibe doesn't exactly spell sky-high standards of service, but for those who fancy a social backpacker scene, this is your place.

Baan Rub Aroon GUESTHOUSE $$
(☎053 711 827; www.baanrubaroon.net; 893 Th Ngummuang; r incl breakfast 650-2000B;) The rooms in this handsome villa, located just west of the city centre, aren't quite as charming as the exterior suggests, and most share bathrooms, but it's a good choice if you're looking for a quiet homey stay.

Diamond Park Inn HOTEL $$
(☎053 754 960; www.diamondparkinnchiangrai-resort.com; 74/6 Th Sanpanard; r 1300B, ste 1500-1600B, all incl breakfast;) Aggressive marketing copy aside ('Whenever you are at Chiang Rai. Stay at The Diamond Park Inn'), this vast hotel is a safe midrange choice. Rooms are attractive, with modern furniture and beds on an elevated platform. The more expensive rooms have tubs, wide balconies and are big enough to feel slightly empty.

Golden Triangle Inn HOTEL $$
(☎053 711 339; 590 Th Phahonyothin; r incl breakfast 1000B;) Undergoing a much-needed renovation at the time of research, the 32 rooms here call to mind an expansive Thai home (including the occasional lived-in untidiness this can entail), with tile or wood floors, wooden furniture and twin beds.

Na-Rak-O Resort HOTEL $$
(☎08 1951 7801; www.facebook.com/narakoresort; off Th Sanpanard; r incl breakfast 750B;) *Nâh·rák* is Thai for 'cute', a spot-on description of this small hotel. Rooms are bright and airy, with big bathrooms and a colourful design theme that calls to mind a daycare centre.

Wiang Inn HOTEL $$$
(☎053 711 533; www.wianginn.com; 893 Th Phahonyothin; r 2400-3200B, ste 6100-10,000B, all incl breakfast;) The funky, 1970s-era exterior is an accurate indicator of this centrally located, business-class hotel's age, but a recent renovation means the rooms are well maintained and include a few Thai decorative touches.

Outside of Town

Ben Guesthouse GUESTHOUSE $
(☎053 716 775; www.benguesthousechiangrai.com; 351/10 Soi 4, Th Sankhongnoi; r 200-800B, ste 1000-1200B;) Ben is one of the best budget-to-midrange places we've encountered in the north. The absolutely spotless compound has a bit of everything, from fan-cooled cheapies to immense suites, not to mention a pool. It's 1.2km from the centre of town, at the end of Soi 4 on Th Sankhongnoi (the street is called Th Sathanpayabarn where it intersects with Th Phahonyothin). A túk-túk costs 60B.

Chezmoi GUESTHOUSE $$
(☎08 9148 5257, 08 9747 5683; www.chezmoimyhome.com; 34/2 Th Sankhongnoi; r incl breakfast 550-1500B;) The seven rooms in this home-studio are fashionably sparse with clean shared bathrooms, and are looked after by a friendly, welcoming family. Chezmoi is about 1.5km from the centre of town at the western end of Th Sankhongnoi (the street is called Th Sathanpayabarn where it intersects with Th Phahonyothin) – a 60B túk-túk ride.

De Hug HOTEL $$
(☎053 711 789; www.dehughotel.com; Rte 1211; r incl breakfast 1100-1800B;) A new, four-storey hotel complex with vast rooms, all outfitted with modern amenities and furniture. Despite its relatively large scale, De Hug manages to feel homey. The hotel is 2km west of the town centre, across from the Oub Kham Museum; túk-túk will go here for about 60B.

Legend of Chiang Rai HOTEL $$$
(☎053 910 400; www.thelegend-chiangrai.com; 124/15 Th Kohloy; r 6500-9800B, bungalows 13,500B, all incl breakfast;) One of

the few hotels in town to boast a riverside location, this upscale resort feels like a traditional Lanna village. Rooms are romantic and luxuriously understated with furniture in calming creams and rattan. The riverside infinity pool and spa are the icing on the comfort-filled cake. The resort is about 500m north of Th Singhaclai.

Le Meridien Chiang Rai Resort HOTEL $$$
(☎053 603 333; www.lemeridien.com; 221/2 Th Kwaewai; r 5000-7500B, ste 18,000-20,000B, all incl breakfast; ❄@🛜🏊) Chiang Rai's grandest upscale resort is about 2km outside of the city centre on a beautiful stretch of Mae Nam Kok. Rooms are immense and decked out in greys, whites and blacks, and the compound includes two restaurants and an infinity pool, in addition to the usual amenities of a hotel in this price range.

Eating

Come mealtime, you'll inevitably be pointed in the direction of Chiang Rai's night bazaar, but the food there is generally pretty dire – you've been warned. Instead, if you're in town on a weekend, hit the vendors at Chiang Rai's open-air markets – Thanon Khon Muan and the Walking Street – which feature a good selection of local dishes.

★ **Lung Eed** NORTHERN THAI $
(Th Watpranorn; mains 40-100B; ⌚11.30am-9pm Mon-Sat) One of Chiang Rai's most delicious dishes is available at this simple shophouse restaurant. There's an English-language menu on the wall, but don't miss the sublime *lap kai* (minced chicken fried with local spices and topped with crispy deep-fried chicken skin, shallots and garlic). The restaurant is on Th Watpranorn about 150m east of Rte 1/AH2.

Khao Soi Phor Jai THAI $
(Th Jetyod, no roman-script sign; mains 35-60B; ⌚7.30am-5pm) Phor Jai serves mild but tasty bowls of the eponymous curry noodle dish, as well as a few other northern Thai staples. Look for the open-air shophouse with the blue interior.

Paa Suk NORTHERN THAI $
(Th Sankhongnoi, no roman-script sign; mains 10-25B; ⌚8.30am-3pm) Paa Suk does big, rich bowls of *kà·nŏm jeen nám ngée·o* (a broth of pork or beef and tomatoes served over fresh rice noodles). The restaurant is between Soi 4 and Soi 5 of Th Sankhongnoi (the street is called Th Sathanpayabarn where it intersects with the southern end of Th Phahonyothin); look for the yellow sign.

Namnigew Pa Nuan VIETNAMESE, THAI $
(Th Sanpanard, no roman-script sign; mains 10-120B; ⌚9am-5pm) This semi-concealed place serves a unique mix of Vietnamese and northern Thai dishes. Tasty food, friendly service and a fun barnlike atmosphere make us wish it was open for dinner as well.

DON'T MISS

CAFE CULTURE, CHIANG RAI STYLE

The relatively small town of Chiang Rai has an enviable spread of high-quality, Western-style cafes. This is largely due to the fact that many of Thailand's best coffee beans are grown in the more remote corners of the province. Some of the town's better cups can be found at the following:

BaanChivitMai Bakery (www.baanchivitmai.com; Th Prasopsook; ⌚8am-7pm Mon-Fri, to 6pm Sat & Sun; 🛜) In addition to a proper cup of joe made from local beans, you can snack on surprisingly authentic Swedish-style sweets and Western-style meals and sandwiches at this popular bakery. Profits go to BaanChivitMai, an organisation that runs homes and education projects for vulnerable, orphaned or AIDS-affected children.

Doi Chaang (542/2 Th Ratanaket; ⌚7am-10pm; 🛜) Doi Chaang is the leading brand among Chiang Rai coffees, and its beans are now sold as far abroad as Canada and Europe.

Pangkhon Coffee (Th Sookathit; ⌚7am-10pm; 🛜) Combine coffee brewed from local beans with views of Chiang Rai's gilded clock tower.

Roast (Th Sankhongluang; ⌚7.30am-5pm) This 'drip bar' treats local beans with the utmost respect. Th Sankhongluang is a block south of Chiang Rai Technical College, about 1.2km from the centre of town.

NORTHERN CUISINE

Much like the language, Thailand's food seems to take a slightly different form every time you cross a provincial border. The cuisine of Thailand's northern provinces is no exception and is indicative of the region's seasonal and relatively cool climate, not to mention a love for pork, vegies and all things deep fried.

Traditionally, the residents of Thailand's north ate almost exclusively *kôw nĕe·o* (sticky rice), known in the local dialect as *kôw nêung*. Coconut milk rarely makes its way into the northern kitchen, and northern Thai cuisine is probably the most seasonal and least spicy of Thailand's regional schools of cooking, often relying on bitter or other dried spice flavours.

Paradoxically (and unfortunately), it can be difficult to find authentic local food in northern Thailand. Outside of Chiang Mai and the other large cities in northern Thailand, there are relatively few restaurants serving northern-style dishes, and the vast majority of authentic local food is sold from stalls in 'to go' bags. However, if you manage to come across a restaurant serving northern-style food, some must-try dishes include:

Gaang hang·lair Burmese in origin (*hang* is a corruption of the Burmese *hin,* meaning curry), this rich pork curry is often seen at festivals and ceremonies. Try a bowl at Phu Lae (p213), in Chiang Rai.

Kâap mŏo Deep-fried pork crackling is a common, delicious side dish in northern Thailand.

Kôw gân jîn Banana leaf packets of rice mixed with blood, steamed and served with garlic oil. Available at Paa Suk (p211), in Chiang Rai.

Kôw soy This popular curry-based noodle dish is possibly Burmese in origin and was probably introduced to northern Thailand by travelling Chinese merchants. A mild but tasty version is available at Khao Soi Phor Jai (p211), in Chiang Rai.

Kà·nŏm jeen nám ngée·o Fresh rice noodles served with a meaty and tart pork- and tomato-based broth. An excellent bowl can be got at Paa Suk (p211), in Chiang Rai.

Lâhp kôo·a Literally 'fried *lâhp*', this dish takes the famous Thai minced-meat 'salad' and fries it with a mixture of unique dried spices. Try the version at Pu Som Restaurant (p243), in Nan.

Lôo Raw blood mixed with curry paste and served over deep-fried intestines and crispy noodles – the most hardcore northern dish of all, and one often associated with Phrae Province.

Năam Fermented raw pork, a sour delicacy that tastes much better than it sounds.

Nám prík nùm Green chillies, shallots and garlic that are grilled then mashed into a stringy and spicy paste served with sticky rice, parboiled vegies and deep-fried pork crackling. Available at just about every evening market in northern Thailand.

Nám prík òrng A chilli dip of Shan origin made from tomatoes and minced pork – a northern Thai bolognese of sorts. Available at Banpleng Restaurant (p296), in Mae Hong Son.

Sâi òo·a A grilled pork sausage seasoned with copious fresh herbs. Available at Muu Thup (p302), in Mae Sariang.

Đam sôm oh The northern Thai version of *sôm·đam* (spicy green papaya salad) substitutes pomelo for green papaya.

Đôm yam The northern Thai version of this Thai soup staple is flavoured with some of the same dried spices that feature in *lâhp kôo·a*.

Muang Thong CHINESE, THAI $

(cnr Th Sanpanard & Th Phahonyothin; mains 30-100B; ⌚24hr) Comfort food for Thais and travellers alike: this long-standing open-air place serves the usual repertoire of satisfyingly salty and spicy Chinese-Thai dishes.

Rosprasert Muslim Food THAI $

(Th Isaraparb; mains 35-80B; ⌚7am-8pm) This open-air restaurant next to the mosque on Th Isaraparb dishes up tasty Thai-Muslim favourites, including *kôw mòk gài* (the Thai version of chicken biryani).

Phu Lae THAI $

(673/1 Th Thanalai; mains 80-320B; ⌚11.30am-3pm & 5.30-11pm; ❄) This air-conditioned restaurant is popular with Thai tourists for its tasty but somewhat gentrified northern Thai fare. Recommended local dishes include the *gaang hang·lair* (pork belly in a rich Burmese-style curry) served with cloves of pickled garlic and *sâi òo·a* (herb-packed pork sausages).

Drinking & Nightlife

Th Jetyod is Chiang Rai's rather tacky drinking strip, on which there are a couple of standouts.

Cat Bar BAR

(1013/1 Th Jetyod; ⌚5pm-1am) Cat Bar has a pool table and live music from 10.30pm.

Easy House BAR

(cnr Th Jetyod & Th Pemavipat; ⌚5pm-midnight) Easy House has a friendly, open-air vibe and a dinner menu.

Shopping

Walking Street MARKET

(Th Thanalai; ⌚4-10pm Sat) If you're in town on a Saturday evening be sure not to miss the open-air Walking Street, an expansive street market focusing on all things Chiang Rai, from handicrafts to local dishes. The market spans Th Thanalai from the Hilltribe Museum to the morning market.

Thanon Khon Muan MARKET

(Th Sankhongnoi; ⌚6-9pm Sun) Come Sunday evening, the stretch of Th Sankhongnoi from Soi 2 heading west is closed to traffic, and in its place are vendors selling clothes, handicrafts and local food. Th Sankhongnoi is called Th Sathanpayabarn where it intersects with the southern end of Th Phahonyothin.

Night Bazaar MARKET

(off Th Phahonyothin; ⌚6-11pm) Adjacent to the bus station off Th Phahonyothin is Chiang Rai's night market. On a much smaller scale than the one in Chiang Mai, it is nevertheless an OK place to find an assortment of handicrafts and touristy souvenirs.

Information

There are several banks with foreign exchange and ATMs on both Th Phahonyothin and Th Thanalai.

Internet (Th Jetyod; per hour 20B; ⌚7am-midnight Mon-Fri, 9am-midnight Sat & Sun)

Overbrook Hospital (☎053 711 366; www.overbrook-hospital.com; Th Singhaclai) English is spoken at this modern hospital.

Tourism Authority of Thailand (TAT; ☎053 744 674, nationwide 1672; tatchrai@tat.or.th; Th Singhaclai; ⌚8.30am-4.30pm) English is limited, but staff here do their best to give advice and can provide a small selection of maps and brochures.

Tourist Police (☎053 740 249, nationwide 1155; Th Uttarakit; ⌚24hr) English is spoken and police are on standby around the clock.

Getting There & Away

AIR

Chiang Rai International Airport (Mae Fah Luang International Airport; ☎053 798000; www.chiangraiairportonline.com) is approximately 8km north of the city. The terminal has airline offices, restaurants, a money exchange, a post office and several car-rental booths. Taxis run into town from the airport for 200B. From town, a metered trip with **Chiang Rai Taxi** (☎053 773477) will cost around 120B.

There are 12 daily flights to Bangkok's Don Muang International Airport (390B to 1090B, 1 hour 20 minutes) and seven to Bangkok's Suvarnabhumi International Airport (1090B to 1800B, one hour 20 minutes).

Air Asia (☎053 793 543, nationwide 02 515 9999; www.airasia.com; Chiang Rai International Airport; ⌚8am-9pm) Flies to/from Bangkok's Don Muang International Airport.

Bangkok Airways (☎053 793 006, nationwide 1771; www.bangkokair.com; Chiang Rai International Airport; ⌚7am-8.30pm) Connects with Bangkok's Suvarnabhumi International Airport.

China Eastern (☎nationwide 02 636 6980; www.flychinaeastern.com; ⌚8.30am-5pm) At research time, Chiang Rai International Airport's only international destination was a daily flight to Kunming (9000B, 1½ hours), in China.

Kan Air (☎053 793 339, nationwide 02 551 6111; www.kanairlines.com; Chiang Rai International Airport; ⌚8.30am-8pm) Daily flight to/from Chiang Mai (1490B, 35 minutes).

Nok Air (☎053 793000, nationwide 1318; www.nokair.co.th; Chiang Rai International Airport; ⌚8am-7pm) Flies to/from Bangkok's Don Muang International Airport.

Thai Lion Air (☎nationwide 02 529 9999; www.lionairthai.com; Chiang Rai International Airport; ⌚8am-8pm) Flies to/from Bangkok's Don Muang International Airport.

Thai Smile (☎053 798200, nationwide 02 118 8888; www.thaismileair.com; Chiang Rai International Airport; ⌚8am-8pm) Flies to/from Bangkok's Suvarnabhumi International Airport.

BUSES TO/FROM CHIANG RAI

DESTINATION	FARE (B)	DURATION (HR)	FREQUENCY
Bangkok	493-935	11-12	frequent 7am-7pm (new bus station)
Chiang Khong	65	2	frequent 6am-5pm (interprovincial bus station)
Chiang Mai	140-280	3-7	hourly 6.30am-7.30pm (new bus station)
Chiang Mai	144-288	7	frequent 6.15am-6.45pm (interprovincial bus station)
Chiang Saen	38	1½	frequent 6.20am-7pm (interprovincial bus station)
Fang	120	2½	8am (new bus station)
Khon Kaen	445-668	11-12	6 departures 9am-7.30pm
Lampang	108-151	4-5	5 departures 12.45-4.30pm (new bus station)
Lampang	102-156	5	6 departures 6.30-11am (interprovincial bus station)
Luang Prabang (Laos)	950	16	1pm (new bus station)
Mae Chan (for Mae Salong/Santikhiri)	25	45min	frequent 5am-7.30pm (interprovincial bus station)
Mae Sai	39	1½	frequent 6am-6.30pm (interprovincial bus station)
Mae Sot	412	12	8.15am & 8.45am (new bus station)
Nakhon Ratchasima (Khorat)	630-745	12-13	6 departures 6.30am-7.20pm (new bus station)
Nan	164	6	9.30am (interprovincial bus station)
Phayao	47	1½-2	hourly 10am-3.30pm (new bus station)
Phayao	44	2	frequent 9.30am-3.10pm (interprovincial bus station)
Phitsanulok	260-335	6-7	hourly 6.15am-7.20pm (new bus station)
Phrae	157	4	half-hourly 6am-6pm (new bus station)
Sukhothai	255	8	hourly 7.30am-noon (new bus station)

MINIVANS TO/FROM CHIANG RAI

DESTINATION	FARE (B)	DURATION (HR)	FREQUENCY
Chiang Saen	45	1½	hourly 6.20am-5.40pm (interprovincial bus station)
Mae Sai	46	1½	frequent 6.30am-6pm (interprovincial bus station)
Phayao	63	1	half-hourly 6am-6pm
Phrae	165	3½	half-hourly 6am-6pm (new bus station)
Sop Ruak (Golden Triangle)	50	2	hourly 6.20am-7pm (interprovincial bus station)

BUS

Buses bound for destinations within Chiang Rai Province, as well as a couple of minivans and mostly slow fan-cooled buses bound for a handful of destinations in northern Thailand, depart from the **interprovincial bus station** (053 715952; Th Prasopsook) in the centre of town. If you're heading beyond Chiang Rai (or are in a hurry), you'll have to go to the **new bus station** (053 773989), 5km south of town on Rte 1/AH2; frequent *sŏrng·tăa·ou* linking it and the interprovincial station run from 6am to 5.30pm (15B, 15 minutes).

BOAT

Passenger boats ply Mae Nam Kok between Chiang Rai and Tha Ton, in Chiang Mai, stopping at Ban Ruam Mit along the way. Boats depart from the **CR Pier** (053 750009; 7am-4pm), 2km northwest of town; a túk-túk to the pier should cost about 80B.

Getting Around

TAXI & TÚK-TÚK

Chiang Rai Taxi (053 773477) operates inexpensive metered taxis in and around town. A túk-túk ride anywhere within central Chiang Rai should cost around 60B.

MOTORCYCLE & BICYCLE

In addition to most guesthouses, several places along Th Jetyod hire motorcycles, with rates starting at 200B for 24 hours.

Chiang Rai Big Bike Rental (09 1627 9367; www.crbigbikerentals.com; Th Thaiviwat; per day 400-1800B)

ST Motorcycle (053 713652; 1025/34-35 Th Jetyod; per day 150-1000B; 8am-7pm)

Fat Free (053 752532; 542/2 Th Baanpa Pragarn; per day 80-450B; 9am-6pm) Bicycle hire can be arranged here.

CAR

A number of car rental companies have offices in town or at the airport.

Avis Rent-A-Car (053 793827, nationwide 02 251 1131; www.avisthailand.com; Chiang Rai International Airport; 7.30am-9pm)

Budget Rent-A-Car (053 740443, 053 740442; www.budget.co.th; Golden Triangle Inn, 590 Th Phahonyothin; 8am-6pm)

Hertz (053 798252, nationwide 02 266 4666; www.hertzthailand.com; Chiang Rai International Airport; 8am-8pm)

Sixt (053 793999, nationwide 1798; www.sixtthailand.com; Chiang Rai International Airport; 8am-9pm)

Thai Rent A Car (053 793393; www.thairentacar.com; Chiang Rai International Airport; 8am-8pm)

Ban Ruam Mit & Around บ้านรวมมิตร

Ruam Mit means 'mixed', an accurate descriptor of this riverside village, a convenient jumping-off point for the surrounding hilly area that's home to ethnic groups including Thai, Karen, Lisu and Akha. And only 20km from Chiang Rai via a recently paved road, Ban Ruam Mit's ethnic diversity and natural beauty are more accessible than ever.

Sights & Activities

Most visitors come to Ban Ruam Mit for the elephant camp. But a better, not to mention more sustainable, reason is hiking among the surrounding area's numerous villages and to visit the hot springs and national park.

Pha Soet Hot Spring HOT SPRINGS

(บ่อน้ำพุร้อนผาเสริฐ; Ban Pha Soet; adult/child 30/10B; ⏲8am-6pm) The hot water from this natural spring has been redirected into a communal pool; for a more private experience, rooms are also available (from 50B to 100B). Ban Pha Soet is located about 3km west of Ban Ruam Mit.

Lamnamkok National Park NATURE RESERVE

(อุทยานแห่งชาติลำน้ำกก; ⏲8am-4.30pm) Dating back to 2002, this is one of Thailand's youngest national parks. The area is home to waterfalls and, most notably, a hot spring. The latter is a short walk from the headquarters, while longer excursions require a guide. The park headquarters are about 3km west of Ban Ruam Mit.

Sleeping & Eating

There are a few basic eateries in Ban Ruam Mit, and each of the hotels has its own restaurant.

Akha Hill House HOTEL $

(☎08 9997 5505; www.akhahill.com; r 150-300B, bungalows 400-1100B; ❄📶) On a steep hillside approaching an Akha village is this beautifully situated yet generally underwhelming hotel. Accommodation ranges from fan-cooled, shared-bathroom rooms to spacious, air-con bungalows. Most stay as part of trekking packages, which get mixed reviews. It's located about 5km south of Ban Pha Soet.

★Bamboo Nest de Chiang Rai GUESTHOUSE $$

(☎09 5686 4755, 08 9953 2330; www.bamboo nest-chiangrai.com; bungalows incl breakfast 800-1800B) The Lahu village that's home to this unique accommodation is only 23km from Chiang Rai but feels a world away. Bamboo Nest takes the form of simple but spacious bamboo huts perched on a hill overlooking tiered rice fields. The only electricity is provided by solar panels, so leave your laptops in town and instead take part in activities that range from birdwatching to hiking.

Bamboo Nest is located about 2km from the headquarters of Lamnamkok National Park; free transport to/from Chiang Rai is available for those staying two nights or more.

Mae Kok Siri Cottage HOTEL $$

(☎08 8914 4142; Ban Ruam Mit; bungalows incl breakfast 950-2300B; ❄) Located at the western end of Ban Ruam Mit is this new, tidy compound uniting five riverfront, fan-cooled bamboo cottages and, behind them, four larger air-con villas. There are a couple of similar places in town.

Getting There & Away

From Chiang Rai, the easiest way to get to Ban Ruam Mit is via boat. A daily passenger boat departs from the CR Pier, 2km northwest of Chiang Rai, at 10.30am (100B, about one hour); a charter will run about 800B. In the opposite direction, boats stop in Ban Ruam Mit around 2pm.

Mae Salong (Santikhiri) แม่สลอง (สันติคีรี)

POP 20,000

For a taste of China without crossing any international borders, head to this atmospheric village perched on the back hills of Chiang Rai.

Mae Salong was originally settled by the 93rd Regiment of the Kuomintang (KMT), who had fled to Myanmar from China after the establishment of communist rule in 1949. The renegades were forced to leave Myanmar in 1961 when the then Rangoon-based government decided it wouldn't allow the KMT to legally remain in northern Myanmar. Crossing into northern Thailand with their pony caravans, the ex-soldiers and their families settled into mountain villages and re-created a society like the one they had left behind in Yunnan.

Generations later, this unique community persists, and the Yunnanese dialect of Chinese still remains the lingua franca, residents tend to watch Chinese, rather than Thai, TV, and you'll find more Chinese than Thai food. And although Mae Salong is now thoroughly on the beaten track, the distinctly Chinese vibe, hilltop setting, and abundance of hill tribes and tea plantations converge in a destination quite unlike anywhere else in Thailand. It's a great place to kick back for a couple of days, and the surrounding area is ripe for self-guided exploration.

Sights

Morning Market MARKET

(⏲6-8am) A tiny but quite interesting morning market convenes at the T-intersection near Shin Sane Guest House. The market attracts town residents and tribespeople from the surrounding districts.

All-Day Market MARKET

An all-day market forms at the southern end of town and unites vendors selling hill-tribe handicrafts, shops selling tea and a few basic restaurants.

Wat Santikhiri VIEWPOINT

(วัดสันติคีรี) To soak up the great views from Wat Santikhiri go past the market and ascend 718 steps (or drive if you have a car). The wát is of the Mahayana tradition and Chinese in style.

Viewpoint VIEWPOINT

Past Khumnaiphol Resort and further up the hill is a viewpoint with some teashops, and a famous KMT general's tomb. It is sometimes guarded by a former soldier who will describe (in Thai or Yunnanese) the history of the KMT in the area.

Chinese Martyr's Memorial Museum MUSEUM

(admission 20B; ⌚8am-6pm) South of the turn-off to the KMT general's tomb is the Chinese Martyr's Memorial Museum, an elaborate Chinese-style building that houses displays on the KMT experience – battles, migration, culture – in Thailand.

Activities

Shin Sane Guest House and Little Home Guesthouse have free maps showing approximate trekking routes to Akha, Lisu, Mien, Lahu and Shan villages in the area. Nearby Akha and Lisu villages are less than half a day's walk away.

Shin Sane Guest House leads horseback treks to four nearby villages for 500B for about three or four hours.

Sleeping

The last couple of years have seen an accommodation boom in Mae Salong. Don't fret if your first pick is full: there are many, many budget and midrange places to choose from. The competition means that prices are often negotiable, except during the high season (November to January). And the cool weather means that few places have air-con.

OFF THE BEATEN TRACK

BAN THOET THAI

Located in a narrow river valley about 20km north of Mae Salong, Ban Thoet Thai (บ้านเทอดไทย) is a multiethnic village with a remote, border-town vibe and an interesting back story.

The village is probably most famous for having formerly served as the base of Khun Sa, the Shan narco-warlord known as the Opium King. Until the early 1980s, proximity to the Golden Triangle, rough, mountainous terrain and lack of sealed roads meant that the outside world was essentially cut off from Ban Thoet Thai (then known as Ban Hin Taek – Broken Stone Village), allowing Khun Sa to establish a virtual monopoly on the world opium trade. Displays on the man and on Shan culture and history can be seen at the **Khunsa Museum** (⌚8am-5pm) FREE, located in his former headquarters, about 500m north of the market area. Don't miss the VIP Living Room that boasts a creepy life-sized model of Khun Sa.

Ban Thoet Thai was also allegedly the first settlement of Akha in Thailand, and today is also home to many Shan and Chinese, not to mention other groups including Thai Lü, Lahu, Hmong, Lua and Lisu. Approximately 6km northwest of town along a very steep road is **Ban Ah Hai**, a picturesque Akha village that's also home to a unique adobe Buddhist temple. The owner of Rim Taan Guest House can provide directions or even lead an informal tour.

The best place to stay is **Rim Taan Guest House** (☎053 730209; 15 Mu 1; r & bungalows 350-2000B; ❄📶), located roughly in the middle of town, with basic fan bungalows and air-con rooms in an attractive stream-side garden. Next door, **Restaurant Ting Ting** (mains 40-150B; ⌚7am-9pm) has a thick English-language menu of tasty Chinese dishes. There are ATMs at the town's 7-Eleven and an **internet cafe** (per hour 20B; ⌚9am-11pm) nearby.

To Ban Thoet Thai, blue *sŏrng·tăa·ou* make stops in front of Mae Salong's 7-Eleven between 7am and 5pm (60B, 40 minutes); in the opposite direction, trucks depart from Ban Thoet Thai's market area from 6am to 5pm (60B).

In Town

All accommodation is located on, or just off, the main road.

Saeng A Roon Hotel GUESTHOUSE **$**
(053 765029; r 300-400B;) Conveniently located near the market area, this hotel offers rooms that are basic but clean; those on the upper floor boast great views of the hills.

Shin Sane Guest House GUESTHOUSE **$**
(053 765026; www.maesalong-shinsane.blogspot.com; r 100B, bungalows 300B; @) The rooms at Mae Salong's oldest hotel are bare but spacious with shared bathrooms, while the bungalows are much more comfortable with en suite bathrooms and TV. Located near the morning market intersection.

Little Home Guesthouse GUESTHOUSE **$$**
(053 765389; www.maesalonglittlehome.com; bungalows 800B; @) Located near the market intersection is this handful of attractive, great-value bungalows. Rooms are tidy and sunny, and the owners are extremely friendly. A new main structure was being built when we stopped by.

Baan Hom Muen Li HOTEL **$$**
(053 765271; osmanhouse@hotmail.com; no roman-script sign; r incl breakfast 1200-1500B;) Across from Sweet Maesalong cafe, in the middle of town, this stylish place consists of 22 rooms artfully decked out in modern and classic Chinese themes. Go for the upstairs rooms in the new structure that have huge balconies with views over the surrounding tea plantations.

Khumnaiphol Resort HOTEL **$$**
(08 1493 5242; https://th-th.facebook.com/khumnaiphol.chiangrai; no roman-script sign; r 800B, bungalows 1200-1500B, all incl breakfast;) This resort has comfortable but rather tackily decorated bungalows perched on a hillside. The covered porches give great views of the tea plantations below. Cheaper rooms in the main structure are also available. It's located 1km south of town near the afternoon market intersection.

Outside of Town

Maesalong Flower Hills Resort RESORT **$$**
(053 765496; www.maesalongflowerhills.com; r 1000-7000B, bungalows 1500-5900B, all incl breakfast;) Located 2km east of Mae Salong's town centre, you can't miss this monument to flower-based landscaping. There's a variety of rooms and bungalows, and the huge pool and larger bungalows make this the logical choice for families.

Maesalong Mountain Home HOTEL **$$$**
(08 4611 9508; www.maesalongmountainhome.com; r & bungalows 1600-2500B;) Down a dirt road 1km east of Mae Salong's town centre (look for the orange sign), this boutique-feeling place is a great choice if you've got your own wheels or don't mind walking. The 14 bungalows are in the middle of a working farm and are generally bright and airy, with wide balconies and huge bathrooms.

★ **Phu Chaisai Resort & Spa** RESORT **$$$**
(053 910500; www.phu-chaisai.com; bungalows incl breakfast 3900-20,000B;) Approximately 7km from Ban Pasang (the turn-off for Mae Salong) on a remote bamboo-covered hilltop, this exceptional resort is the most unique place to stay in the area. The decidedly rustic adobe/bamboo bungalows are fittingly without TV, but have amazing views of the surrounding mountains and include access to a host of activities (spa treatment, massage, yoga, day hikes, rafting, swimming) to keep you occupied. Transport from Chiang Rai is available for 824B.

Eating

The very Chinese breakfast of *Ƅah·tôrng·gŏh* (deep-fried dough sticks) and hot soybean milk at the morning market is a great way to start the day.

In fact, many Thai tourists come to Mae Salong simply to eat Yunnanese dishes such as *màn·tŏh* (steamed Chinese buns) served with braised pork belly and pickled vegetables, or black chicken braised with Chinese-style herbs. Homemade wheat and egg noodles are another speciality of Mae Salong, and are served with a local broth that combines pork and a spicy chilli paste. They're available at several places in town.

Countless teahouses sell locally grown teas (mostly oolong and jasmine) and offer complimentary tastings.

Salema Restaurant CHINESE **$**
(mains 30-250B; 7am-8pm) One of the friendliest restaurants in town also happens to be the most delicious. Salema does tasty Muslim-Chinese dishes including a rich Yunnan-style beef curry and a deliciously tart tuna and tea leaves spicy salad. The noodle dishes are equally worthwhile and

include a beef *kôw soy*. Salema is located at the eastern end of town.

Sweet Maesalong CAFE $

(mains 45-155B; ⏲8.30am-5pm; 📶) If you require more caffeine than the local tea leaves can provide, stop by this modern cafe with an extensive menu of coffee drinks using local beans. Surprisingly sophisticated baked goods and one-plate dishes are also available. Located more or less in the middle of town.

Sue Hai CHINESE $$

(mains 40-300B; ⏲7am-9pm) Just east of the town centre, this simple family-run teashop-cum-Chinese place has an English-language menu of local specialities including local mushrooms fried with soy sauce and delicious air-dried pork fried with fresh chilli.

Information

There is an ATM at the Thai Military Bank opposite Khumnaiphol Resort, at the southern end of town. An **internet cafe** (per hour 20B; ⏲9am-11pm) can be found nearby.

Getting There & Away

Probably the easiest way to get to Mae Salong is to take a bus to Mae Chan, from where there are frequent green *sŏrng·tăa·ou* to Mae Salong (60B, half-hourly from 7.30am to 4.30pm). You can charter one for around 700B. Alternatively, it's also possible to take a Mae Sai–bound bus to Ban Pasang, from where blue *sŏrng·tăa·ou* head up the mountain to Mae Salong only when full (60B, one hour, 6am to 5pm) or when chartered for around 500B. In the reverse direction, you can flag down *sŏrng·tăa·ou* near Mae Salong's 7-Eleven.

You can also reach Mae Salong by road from Tha Ton, in Chiang Mai. Yellow *sŏrng·tăa·ou* bound for Tha Ton stop near Little Home Guesthouse at 8.20am, 10.20am, 12.20pm and 2.30pm (60B, one hour).

Getting Around

Much of Mae Salong is approachable on foot. If you want to go further (or are struggling with the hills), motorcycles can be hired at Mini, at the east of town, as well as at most guesthouses, for around 200B for 24 hours.

Mae Sai แม่สาย

POP 22,000

At first glance, Thailand's northernmost town can appear to be little more than a large open-air market. But Mae Sai serves as a convenient base for exploring the Golden Triangle and Mae Salong, and its position across from Myanmar also makes it a jumping-off point for those wishing to explore some of the more remote parts of Shan State.

Because occasional fighting within Myanmar or disputes between the Thai and Myanmar governments can lead to the border being closed temporarily, it's always a good idea to check the current situation before travelling to Mae Sai.

Sights

Wat Phra That Doi Wao BUDDHIST TEMPLE

(วัดพระธาตุดอยเวา; Soi 1, Th Phahonyothin; ⏲dawn-dusk) FREE Take the steps up the hill near the border to Wat Phra That Doi Wao for superb views over Mae Sai and Myanmar. This *wát* was reportedly constructed in memory of a couple of thousand Burmese soldiers who died fighting the KMT here in 1965 (you'll hear differing stories around town, including a version wherein the KMT are the heroes).

Sleeping

Mom Home GUESTHOUSE $

(☎053 731537; haritchayahana@gmail.com; off Th Sailomjoy; r 300-500B; ❄📶) A shiny new three-storey building holding nine rooms equipped with TV, refrigerator and hot-water showers; the price depends on whether you go with fan or air-con. Call in at the signed office at the three-way junction on Th Sailomjoy.

Maesai Guest House HOTEL $

(☎053 732021; 688 Th Wiengpangkam; bungalows 200-600B; 📶) This collection of A-frame bungalows ranges from simple rooms with shared cold-water showers to bungalows on the river with terraces and private bathrooms.

Afterglow HOTEL $

(☎053 734188; www.afterglowhostel.com; 139/5 Th Phahonyothin; r 500-800B, bungalows 500B, all incl breakfast; ❄📶) Boasting a ground-floor cafe and rooms with a minimalist feel, Afterglow is probably the hippest place to stay in Mae Sai. A new addition sees a few equally stylish bungalows out back. Inconveniently located about 4km from the border.

Khanthongkham Hotel HOTEL $$

(☎053 734222; 7 Th Phahonyothin; r 850-1500B, ste 1200-1650B, all incl breakfast; ❄📶) This hotel features huge rooms that have been tastefully decorated in light woods and brown

Mae Sai

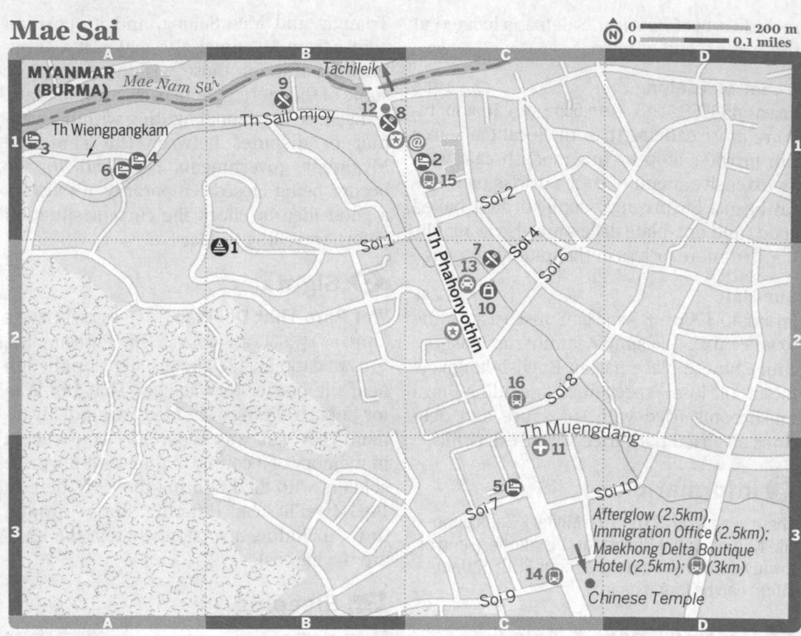

Mae Sai

Sights

1 Wat Phra That Doi Wao........B2

Sleeping

2 Khanthongkham Hotel........C1
3 Maesai Guest House........A1
4 Mom Home........A1
5 Piyaporn Place Hotel........C3
6 Sai Lom Joy........A1

Eating

7 Bismillah Halal Food........C2
8 Night Market........B1
9 Sukhothai Cuisine........B1

Shopping

10 Gem Market........C2

Information

11 Overbrook Clinic........C3
12 Thai Immigration Office........B1

Transport

13 Motorcycle Taxis to Bus Station........C2
Pornchai........(see 14)
14 Siam First........C3
15 Sŏrng·tăa·ou to Bus Station........C1
16 Sŏrng·tăa·ou to Sop Ruak & Chiang Saen........C2

cloths. Suites are exceptionally vast and like all rooms have flat-screen TVs and spacious and inviting bathrooms. A downside is that many rooms don't have windows.

Sai Lom Joy HOTEL $$
(☎09 4615 1177; www.sailomjoy.com; off Th Sailomjoy; r 1300-1500B) This charming three-storey villa surrounds a peaceful courtyard. Rooms are modern and inviting, with Thai design touches and the usual amenities.

Piyaporn Place Hotel HOTEL $$
(☎053 734511; www.piyaporn-place.com; 77/1 Th Phahonyothin; r/ste incl breakfast 800/1800B; ❄@🛜) On the main road by Soi 7, this seven-storey business hotel is good value. The large, contemporary-styled rooms have wooden floors, a small sofa and the usual business-class amenities like bathroom, cable TV and minibar.

Maekhong Delta Boutique Hotel HOTEL $$
(☎053 642517; www.maekhonghotel.com; 230/5-6 Th Phahonyothin; r incl breakfast 1000-4500B; ❄@🛜) It's an odd name, considering that the Mekong Delta is way down in Vietnam. Odder still that the rooms here are somehow reminiscent of a ski lodge. Regardless,

rooms are both modern and attractive, albeit nearly 4km from the centre of town.

Eating

An expansive **night market** (Th Phahonyothin; mains 30-60B; ⊙5-11pm) unfolds every evening along Th Phahonyothin. During the day, several **snack and drink vendors** can be found in front of the police station on Th Phahonyothin.

Bismillah Halal Food THAI $
(Soi 4, Th Phahonyothin; mains 30-100B; ⊙5am-5pm) This tiny restaurant does an excellent biryani, not to mention virtually everything else Muslim, from roti to samosa.

Sukhothai Cuisine THAI $
(399/9 Th Sailomjoy, no roman-script sign; mains 35-40B; ⊙7am-5pm) This open-air restaurant serves the namesake noodles from Sukhothai, as well as satay and a few other basic dishes. There's no English-language sign here, but it's the busy place right on the corner.

Shopping

Commerce is ubiquitous in Mae Sai, although most of the offerings are of little interest to Western travellers. One particularly common commodity is gems, and a walk down Soi 4 will reveal several open-air **gem dealers** (Soi 4, Th Phahonyothin) diligently counting hundreds of tiny semiprecious stones on the side of the street.

Information

There are several banks with ATM near the border.

Immigration Main Office (☎053 731008; Rte 110; ⊙8.30am-4.30pm Mon-Fri) Located about 3km from the border, near Soi 17.

TRANSPORT TO/FROM MAE SAI

Bus

DESTINATION	FARE (B)	DURATION (HR)	FREQUENCY
Bangkok	519-980	12	7am & frequent 4.20-5.40pm
Chiang Mai	144-288	5	9 departures 6.15am-4.30pm
Chiang Rai	39	1½	frequent 5.45am-6pm
Fang	92	3	8am & 2pm
Mae Sot	493	12	6.45am
Nakhon Ratchasima (Khorat)	514-771	15	6 departures 5am-6pm
Phayao	69-103	3	6 departures 5.15am-6pm
Phitsanulok	273-410	8	6 departures 5.15am-6pm
Phrae	164-246	5	6 departures 5.15am-6pm
Tha Ton	92	2	8am & 2pm

Minivan & Sŏrng·tăa·ou

DESTINATION	FARE (B)	DURATION (HR)	FREQUENCY
Chiang Rai	46	1	frequent minivans 6am-6pm
Chiang Saen	50	1	frequent *sŏrng·tăa·ou* 8am-noon
Fang	92	3	minivans 8am & 2pm
Sop Ruak (Golden Triangle)	50	45min	frequent *sŏrng·tăa·ou* 8am-1pm
Tha Ton	92	2	8am & 2pm

Internet Cafe (Th Phahonyothin; per hour 10B; ⌚8am-11pm) Behind the Wang Thong Hotel, by the car park.

Overbrook Clinic (☎053 734422; 20/7 Th Phahonyothin; ⌚8am-5pm) Connected to the modern hospital in Chiang Rai.

GETTING TO MYANMAR: MAE SAI TO TACHILEIK

The Mae Sai–Tachileik border is a popular visa-run destination, but there are a few caveats in crossing here for those who want to go further abroad. Border-crossing information is liable to change, so be sure to check the situation locally before you travel.

Getting to the Border

The border and Thai immigration office are a short walk from most accommodation in Mae Sai.

At the Border

After taking care of the usual formalities at the **Thai immigration office** (☎053 733261; Th Phahonyothin; ⌚6.30am-9pm), cross the bridge and head to the Myanmar immigration office. If you've already procured a Myanmar visa, you'll be allowed to proceed by land to Kyaingtong (also known as Kengtung, or sometimes Chiang Tung) or Mong La, or via air to other points in Myanmar.

If you haven't already obtained a Myanmar visa, it's relatively straightforward to cross to Tachileik for the day and slightly more complicated to get a two-week border pass to visit Kyaingtong and/or Mong La.

Day-trippers must pay a fee of 500B for a temporary ID card; your passport will be kept at the border. There is little to do in Tachileik apart from sample Burmese food and shop – the prices are about the same as on the Thai side and everyone accepts baht. There's an interesting morning market and it can be fun to hang about in the teashops.

Onwards Travel

If you'd like to visit Kyaingtong and/or Mong La but haven't already received a Myanmar visa, proceed directly to the Myanmar Travels & Tours (MTT) office. There you'll need to inform the authorities exactly where you're headed, and you'll need three photos and US$10 or 500B to process a border pass valid for 14 days; your passport will be kept at the border ensuring that you return the way you came. It's also obligatory to hire a guide for the duration of your stay. Guides cost 1000B per day (plus a 400B 'guiding tax'), and if you haven't already arranged for a Kyaingtong-based guide to meet you at the border, you'll be assigned one by MTT and will also have to pay for your guide's food and accommodation during your stay. Recommended Kyaingtong-based guides include **Leng** (☎+95 9490 31470; sairoctor.htunleng@gmail.com) and **Freddie** (Sai Yot; ☎+95 9490 31934; yotkham@gmail.com).

Kyaingtong is a sleepy but historic capital for the Shan State's Khün culture – the Khün speak a northern Thai language related to Shan and Thai Lü, and use a writing script similar to the ancient Lanna script. Places to stay include the **Princess Hotel** (☎+95 842 1319; kengtung@mail4u.com.mm; 21 Zaydankalay Rd; r incl breakfast $50-85; ❄) and the budget-oriented **Harry's Trekking House** (☎+95 842 1418; harry.guesthouse@gmail.com; 132 Mai Yang Rd; r incl breakfast US$10-20; ❄).

Mong La, on the Chinese border and under the control of the United Wa State Army, was formerly associated with the drug trade, casinos and prostitution. At the time of research, foreigners were not allowed to cross to China from Mong La.

Buses bound for Kyaingtong (K10,000, five hours, 8am to 8.30am and 11.30am to 12.30pm) depart from Tachileik's bus station, 2km and a 20B *sŏrng·tăa·ou* ride or a 50B motorcycle taxi ride from the border. Alternatively, you can charter a taxi from the same station from K65,000, or if you're willing to wait until it's full, a seat in a share taxi for K15,000 or K20,000.

There are no direct buses from Tachileik to Mong La.

For more details on Kyaingtong and Mong La, refer to Lonely Planet's *Myanmar (Burma)* guidebook.

Tourist Police (☎115; Th Phahonyothin; ⊙8.30am-6pm) With a booth in front of the border crossing before immigration.

Getting There & Away

Mae Sai's **bus station** (☎053 646403; Rte 110) is 4km from the border; shared *sŏrng·tăa·ou* ply the route between the bus station and a stop on Soi 2, Th Phahonyothin (15B, five minutes, from 6am to 6pm). Alternatively, it's a 40B motorcycle taxi ride to/from the stand at the corner of Th Phahonyothin and Soi 4.

If you're headed to Bangkok, you can avoid going all the way to the bus station by buying your tickets at **Siam First** (☎053 731504; near cnr Soi 9 & Th Phahonyothin, no roman-script sign; ⊙8am-5.30pm) – it's on the corner of Soi 9, Th Phahonyothin, next door to the motorcycle dealership.

On Th Phahonyothin, by Soi 8, is a sign saying 'bus stop'; this is where you'll find the **stop** (Th Phahonyothin) for *sŏrng·tăa·ou* bound for Sop Ruak and Chiang Saen.

Getting Around

Sŏrng·tăa·ou around town cost 15B. Motorcycle taxis cost 20B to 40B.

Motorcycles can be hired at **Pornchai** (☎053 731136; 4/7 Th Phahonyothin, no roman-script sign; per day 250B; ⊙8am-5pm). It's located near Soi 9.

Chiang Saen เชียงแสน

POP 11,000

The dictionary definition of a sleepy river town, Chiang Saen is the site of a former Thai kingdom thought to date back to as early as the 7th century. Scattered throughout the modern town are the ruins of this empire – surviving architecture includes several *chedi,* Buddha images, *wí·hăhn* pillars and earthen city ramparts. Chiang Saen later became loosely affiliated with various northern Thai kingdoms, as well as 18th-century Myanmar, but didn't become a Siamese possession until the 1880s.

Today huge river barges from China moor at Chiang Saen, carrying fruit, engine parts and all manner of other imports, keeping the old China–Siam trade route open. Despite this trade, the town hasn't changed too much over the last decade, and because of this is a pleasanter base than the comparatively hectic, touristy Sop Ruak, the so-called 'Golden Triangle', 9km east.

Chiang Saen lies across the Mekong River from the Lao town of Ton Pheung, but only locals are allowed to cross here.

Sights & Activities

Wat Phra That Pha Ngao BUDDHIST TEMPLE
(วัดพระธาตุผาเงา; off Rte 1129; ⊙dawn-dusk) FREE Located 3km south of town in the village of Sop Kham, this Buddhist temple complex contains a large prayer hall built to cover a partially excavated Chiang Saen–era Buddha statue. There is a beautiful golden teak *hŏr đrai* (manuscript depository) and a steep road leads to a hilltop pagoda and temple with views over the area and the Mekong River.

Wat Chedi Luang BUDDHIST TEMPLE
(วัดเจดีย์หลวง; Th Phahonyothin; ⊙dusk-dawn) FREE The ruins of the Buddhist Wat Chedi Luang feature an 18m octagonal *chedi* in the classic Chiang Saen or Lanna style. Archaeologists argue about its exact construction date but agree it was built some time between the 12th and 14th centuries.

Wat Pa Sak HISTORIC SITE
(วัดป่าสัก; off Rte 1290; historical park admission 50B; ⊙8.30am-4.30pm Wed-Sun) FREE About 200m from the Pratu Chiang Saen are the remains of Wat Pa Sak, where the ruins of seven monuments are visible in a historical park. The main mid-14th-century *chedi* combines elements of the Hariphunchai and Sukhothai styles with a possible Bagan influence, and still holds a great deal of attractive stucco relief work.

Wat Phra That Chom Kitti & Wat Chom Chaeng BUDDHIST TEMPLE
(วัดพระธาตุจอมกิตติ/วัดจอมแจ้ง; off Rte 1290; ⊙dawn-dusk) FREE The remains of Wat Phra That Chom Kitti and Wat Chom Chaeng can be found about 2.5km northwest of town on a hilltop. The round *chedi* of Wat Phra That Chom Kitti is thought to have been constructed before the founding of the kingdom.

Wat Pha Khao Pan BUDDHIST TEMPLE
(วัดผ้าขาวป้าน; Th Rimkhong; ⊙dawn-dusk) FREE Inside the grounds of this living wát near the river stands a magnificent Lanna-period *chedi*. The large square base contains Lanna-style walking Buddhas in niches on all four sides. The Buddha facing east is sculpted in the *mudra* ('calling for rain') pose, with both hands held pointing down at the image's sides – a pose common in Laos but not so common in Thailand.

Chiang Saen

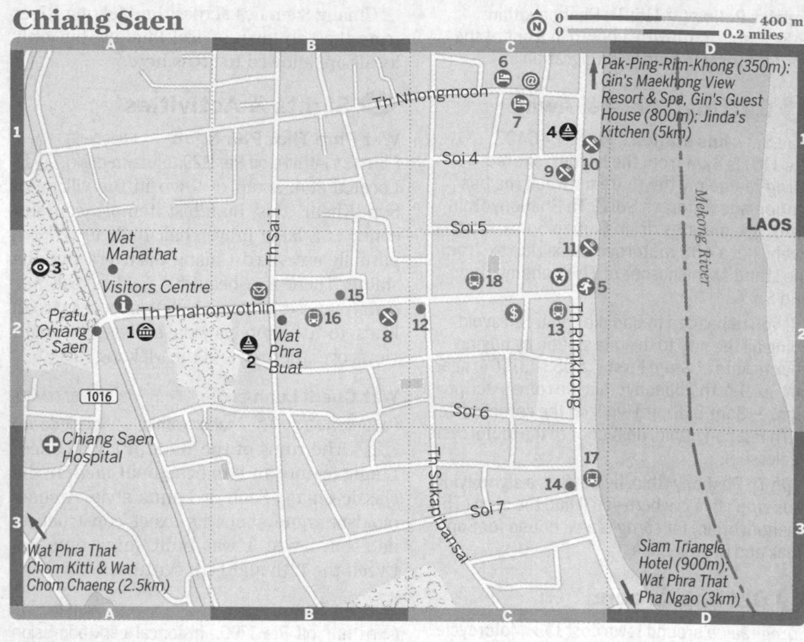

Chiang Saen

Sights
1 Chiang Saen National Museum A2
2 Wat Chedi Luang B2
3 Wat Pa Sak A2
4 Wat Pha Khao Pan C1

Activities, Courses & Tours
5 Mekong River Trips C2

Sleeping
6 Jay Nay C1
7 Sa Nae Charn Guest House C1

Eating
8 Evening Food Vendors B2
9 Kiaw Siang Hai C1
10 Riverside Food Vendors C1
11 Walking Street C2

Drinking & Nightlife
2 be 1 .... (see 9)

Information
12 Immigration Office C2

Transport
13 Buses to Chiang Rai & Chiang Mai C2
14 Chiang Saen Tour & Travel C3
15 Motorcycle Hire B2
16 Sombat Tour B2
17 Sŏrng·tăa·ou to Hat Bai C3
18 Sŏrng·tăa·ou to Sop Ruak & Mae Sai C2

Chiang Saen National Museum MUSEUM
(พิพิธภัณฑสถานแห่งชาติเชียงแสน; 702 Th Phahonyothin; admission 100B; ⌚8.30am-4.30pm Wed-Sun) This museum is a great source of local information considering its relatively small size.

Mekong River Trips RIVER CRUISE
(☎08 5392 4701; Th Rimkhong; ⌚8am-5pm) Five-passenger speedboats leave from the waterfront jetty to Sop Ruak (per boat one way/return 600/700B, one hour), or all the way to Chiang Khong (per boat one way/return 2500/3000B, 1½ hours).

Sleeping

Jay Nay GUESTHOUSE $
(☎08 1960 7551; Th Nhongmoon, no roman-script sign; r 350-400B; ❄📶) Jay Nay consists of 13 identical rooms in a two-storey complex. They're plain but new and comfy. Look for the 'Rooms For Rent' text.

Sa Nae Charn Guest House GUESTHOUSE $
(053 651138; 641 Th Nhongmoon; r 250-450B;) Run by an elderly Singaporean gentleman, the rooms here are basic yet gain more amenities (TV, air-con) the more you pay.

Gin's Maekhong View Resort & Spa HOTEL $$
(08 4485 1376; www.facebook.com/GinsMaekhongView; Th Rimkhong; r 1000-1500B, bungalows 1500B, all incl breakfast;) Here you can choose between rather tight riverside bungalows or spacious rooms in a two-storey structure. There's a pool, vast sunflower field, spa and cafe. The same folks run the budget-oriented **Gin's Guest House** (053 650847; 71 Th Rimkhong; r 300-600B, bungalows 600B;), just across the road.

Gin's is located about 1km north of the centre of Chiang Saen, near the reconstructed city walls.

Pak-Ping-Rim-Khong GUESTHOUSE $$
(053 650151; www.facebook.com/PakPingRimKhong; 484 Th Rimkhong; r incl breakfast 1200-2100B;) A new and tidy villa compound just north of town. Rooms are spacious and come equipped with air-con, TV and fridge.

Siam Triangle Hotel HOTEL $$
(053 651115; www.siamtriangle.com; 267 Th Rimkhong; r 1250-3000B, ste 6000B, all incl breakfast;) Chiang Saen's biggest hotel lacks charm, but the gigantic suites with river-view Jacuzzi tubs are pretty impressive. There's a new wing with slightly cheaper rooms across the street. The hotel is just outside Chiang Saen, about 400m south of the former city wall.

Viang Yonok GUESTHOUSE $$$
(053 650444; www.viangyonok.com; off Rte 1016; bungalows incl breakfast 2400-2950B;) The emphasis at this well-manicured compound of seven comfortable, modern bungalows is activities, and if a swimming pool, sauna, weights room, bicycles, kayaks and birdwatching aren't enough, well, you're a pretty tough customer. It's located approximately 5km west of Chiang Saen in Ban Khu Tao, off the road that leads to Mae Chan; follow the yellow signs that appear after the Esso station.

Eating & Drinking

Cheap noodle and rice dishes are available at **food stalls** (mains 30-60B) near the covered bus shelter on Th Phahonyothin. Come nightfall, **evening food vendors** (Th Phahonyothin; mains 30-60B; 4-10pm) set up just west of here. Every Saturday evening, a section of Th Rimkhong is closed to vehicle traffic for the busy **Walking Street** (mains 20-60B; 4-9pm Sat), which has lots of food.

Riverside Food Vendors THAI $
(Th Rimkhong; mains 30-60B; 4-11pm) During the dry months, riverside vendors set up mats and sell rustic food such as fish or chicken barbecued inside thick joints of bamboo, along with sticky rice and *sôm·đam* (spicy green papaya salad).

Kiaw Siang Hai CHINESE $
(44 Th Rimkhong, no roman-script sign; mains 50-200B; 8am-8pm) Serving the workers of Chinese boats that dock at Chiang Saen, this authentic Chinese restaurant prepares a huge menu of dishes in addition to the

DAY BOAT TO JINGHONG

It was previously possible to take a passenger boat along the Mekong River from Chiang Saen to Jinghong in China's Xishuangbanna, a trip of 15 hours when conditions are right. However this service was halted in 2011, when a drug-trafficking-related shooting incident led to the death of 13 Chinese sailors.

If reinstated, boats usually depart from Chiang Saen on Monday, Wednesday and Friday at 5am, but this is not set in stone and it's important to call ahead before you make plans. During the drier months (typically March to May) boats don't run, as rocks and shallows can hamper the way.

To do this trip you must already have your visa for China – several guesthouses in town can arrange this for you, but it's quicker to arrange from Chiang Mai or Bangkok. If you already have a visa, tickets can be got through **Chiang Saen Tour & Travel** (08 1993 2425; 64 Th Rimkhong; 9am-7pm) or **Maekhong Delta Travel** (053 642517; www.maekhongtravel.com; Maekhong Delta Boutique Hotel, 230/5-6 Th Phahonyothin; one way 3500B or Y820; 9am-5pm), the latter in Mae Sai.

namesake dumplings. Try the spicy Sichuan-style fried tofu or one of the Chinese herbal soups. The restaurant can be identified by the giant ceramic jars out front.

Jinda's Kitchen NORTHERN THAI $

(Rte 1290; mains 25-100B; ⌚8am-9pm; 📶) This home-bound roadside restaurant has been serving up local dishes for more than 50 years, and does a mean *kà·nŏm jeen nám ngée·o* (fresh rice noodles served with a meaty and tart pork- and tomato-based broth). It's roughly halfway between Chiang Saen and Sop Ruak.

2 be 1 BAR

(Th Rimkhong; ⌚5.30pm-midnight) By the river is this tiny bar with indoor and outdoor seating and a pool table.

Information

Chiang Saen Hospital (☎053 777017; Rte 1016) Government hospital just south of Wat Pa Sak.

Immigration Office (☎053 777118; cnr Th Phahonyothin & Th Sukapibansai; ⌚8.30am-4.30pm Mon-Fri)

Internet Cafe (Th Nhongmoon; per hour 10B; ⌚9am-9pm)

Visitors Centre (☎053 777084; Th Phahonyothin; ⌚8.30am-4.30pm Mon-Sat) Has a good relief display showing the major ruin sites as well as photos of various *chedi* before, during and after restoration.

Getting There & Away

Blue sŏrng·tăa·ou (Th Phahonyothin) bound for Sop Ruak (20B) and Mae Sai (50B) wait at a stall at the eastern end of Th Phahonyothin from 7.20am to 3pm. If you're bound for Chiang Khong, you'll need to board one of the **green sŏrng·tăa·ou** (Th Rimkhong) bound for Hat Bai at a stall on Th Rimkhong, south of the riverside immigration office, from 9am to 2pm (50B, one hour), upon reaching which you'll need to transfer to yet another *sŏrng·tăa·ou*.

Chiang Saen has no proper bus terminal, rather there is a covered **bus shelter** (Th Phahonyothin) at the eastern end of Th Phahonyothin where buses pick up and drop off passengers. From this stop there are frequent buses to Chiang Rai (37B, 1½ hours, from 5.30am to 5.30pm) and a daily bus to Chiang Mai (222B, five hours, 9am).

Sombat Tour (☎053 650788; Th Phahonyothin; ⌚8.20am-5.20pm) operates two daily VIP buses to Bangkok (1058B, 12 hours, 5pm and 5.30pm), departing from a small office on Th Phahonyothin.

Getting Around

Motorbike taxis will do short trips in town for 20B. They gather near and across from the bus stop.

A good way to see the Chiang Saen area is on two wheels. Mountain bikes and motorcycles can be rented at the **motorcycle hire shop** (☎08 9429 5798; 247/1 Th Phahonyothin, no roman-script sign; per 24hr bike/motorcycle 80/200B; ⌚8am-7pm) linked with a barber shop.

Sop Ruak สบรวก

The borders of Myanmar, Thailand and Laos meet at Sop Ruak, the so-called centre of the Golden Triangle, at the confluence of Nam Ruak and the Mekong River. The town's two opium-related museums, the House of Opium and Hall of Opium, are both worth a visit, and a boat trip is an enjoyable way to pass an hour. But the only reason to overnight here is if you've already booked a room in one of the area's outstanding luxury hotels.

Sights & Activities

Hall of Opium MUSEUM

(หอฝิ่น; Rte 1290; adult/child 200B/free; ⌚8.30am-4pm Tue-Sun) One kilometre north of Sop Ruak on a 40-hectare plot opposite the Anantara Golden Triangle Resort & Spa, the Mae Fah Luang Foundation has established the 5600-sq-metre Hall of Opium. The multimedia exhibitions include a fascinating history of opium, as well as engaging and informative displays on the effects of abuse on individuals and society. Well balanced and worth investigating.

House of Opium MUSEUM

(บ้านฝิ่น; Rte 1290; admission 50B; ⌚7am-7pm) This small museum with historical displays pertaining to opium culture is worth a peek. Exhibits include all the various implements used in the planting, harvest, use and trade of the *Papaver somniferum* resin, including pipes, weights, scales and so on, plus photos and maps with labels in English. The museum is at the southeastern end of Sop Ruak, virtually across from the huge Buddha statue at Phra Chiang Saen Si Phaendin.

Phra Chiang Saen Si Phaendin BUDDHIST TEMPLE

(พระเชียงแสนสี่แผนดิน; Rte 1290; ⌚7am-9pm) FREE The first sight you'll inevitably see in Sop Ruak is Phra Chiang Saen Si Phaendin, a giant Buddha statue financed by a

Golden Triangle & Around

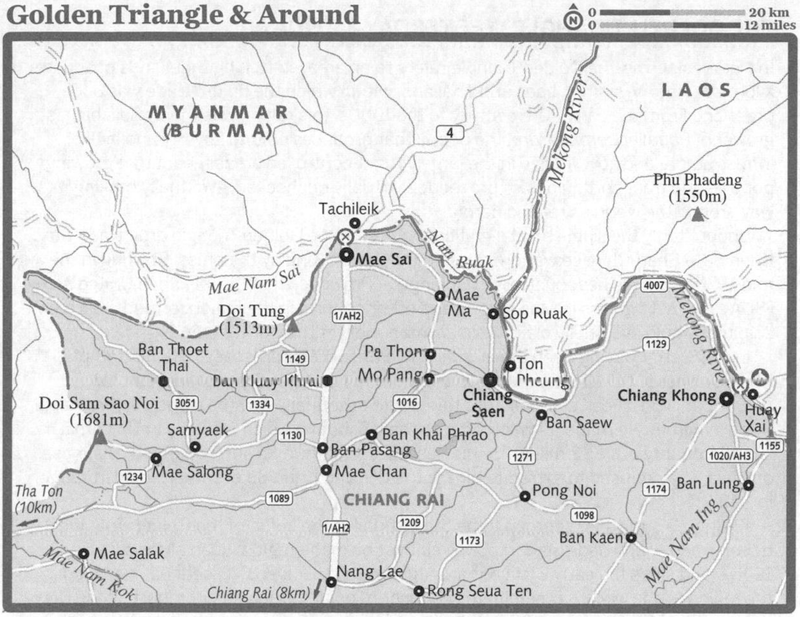

Thai-Chinese foundation. The statue straddles a boat-like platform, and visitors here are encouraged to donate by rolling coins from an elevated platform behind the statue.

Wat Prathat Pukhao BUDDHIST TEMPLE

(วัดพระธาตุภูเขา; Rte 1290; dawn-dusk) FREE Next to the House of Opium are some steps up to the Buddhist Wat Prathat Pukhao, from where you get the best viewpoint of the Mekong junction of Laos, Myanmar and Thailand.

Boat Trips

Long-tail boat trips (one-hour cruise maximum five people per boat 500B) on the Mekong River can be arranged at one of various piers throughout the day. The typical trip involves a circuit upriver for a view of the Burmese casino hotel and a stop at the Lao island of Don Sao, roughly halfway between Sop Ruak and Chiang Saen. Upon arrival in Laos, a 30B tax is collected from each visitor.

Sleeping & Eating

The only reason to stay in or around Sop Ruak is to take advantage of some of northern Thailand's best upscale lodgings; those on a budget are better off in Chiang Saen. Several tourist-oriented restaurants overlook the Mekong River.

Four Seasons Tented Camp HOTEL $$$

(053 910200; www.fourseasons.com; 2 nights all-inclusive 104,000-116,000B;) If you can fit it into your schedule (and budget), this safari-inspired resort is among the most unique accommodation experiences in Thailand. The 'tents' are appropriately luxurious and decked out in colonial-era safari paraphernalia. A minimum stay of at least two nights is required, and guests take part in daily activities ranging from longboat river excursions to spa treatments. Elephant rides and other pachyderm-related 'experiences' are also on offer, but it's worth reading up on the animal welfare issues involved with these kind of activities if considering.

Anantara Golden Triangle Resort & Spa HOTEL $$$

(053 784084; www.anantara.com; Rte 1290; r & ste per night, all-inclusive 36,500-44,000B;) This award-winning resort takes up a large patch of beautifully landscaped ground directly opposite the Hall of Opium. The rooms combine Thai and international themes, and all have balconies looking over the Mekong River. Jacuzzi, squash and tennis courts, gym, sauna and spa round out the luxury amenities, and activities such as cooking courses are included in most packages. Like the Four Seasons, elephant

THE GOLDEN TRIANGLE, YESTERDAY & TODAY

In historical terms, the Golden Triangle refers to an area, stretching thousands of square kilometres into Myanmar, Laos and Thailand, within which the opium trade was once prevalent. From the early 20th century to the 1980s, this region was the world's biggest grower of *Papaver somniferum*, the poppy that produces opium. Poverty and lack of infrastructure and governance in the largely rebel-controlled areas meant that growing poppies and transporting opium proceeded virtually unchecked, eventually making its way around the world as refined heroin.

Undoubtedly the single most significant player in the Golden Triangle drug trade was Khun Sa, a Shan-Chinese warlord dubbed the Opium King by the press. Starting in the mid-1970s from his headquarters in Chiang Rai Province, Khun Sa, his Shan United Army (SUA), ex-KMT fighters in Mae Salong and other cohorts in the region formed a partnership that would eventually claim a virtual monopoly of the world's opium trade.

In 1988, after having been the victim of two unsuccessful assassination attempts, Khun Sa offered to sell his entire crop of opium to the Australian government for AUS$50 million a year, claiming that this would essentially end the world's entire illegal trade in heroin. He made a similar offer to the US, but was dismissed by both. With a US DEA bounty of US$2 million on his head, in 1996 Khun Sa surrendered to Burmese officials. They refused to extradite him to the US, and Khun Sa eventually died in Yangon in 2007.

Khun Sa's surrender seemed to be the last nail in the coffin of the Golden Triangle opium trade – land dedicated to poppy cultivation in the region hit an all time low in 1998 – and since the early 21st century, Afghanistan's Golden Crescent has replaced the region as the world's preeminent producer of opium. But a recent report by the UN Office of Drugs & Crime claims that the trade has yet again spiked – most likely due to increased demand from China – and in 2012 Myanmar alone was thought to have produced 25% of the world's opium.

However, most agree that the contemporary Golden Triangle drug trade has shifted from opium to methamphetamines. Manufactured in Myanmar in factories with alleged links to the United Wa State Army, the drug, known in Thai as *yah bâh* (crazy drug), has become the scourge of the region, and footage of tweaked-out users holding hostages was a Thai news staple in the early 2000s. Although recent efforts to eradicate methamphetamines by Thai authorities have led to higher prices, trafficking and use are thought to have increased.

Thailand's opium growing days are long gone, but hoteliers and tour operators in Chiang Rai have been quick to cash in on the name by rebranding the tiny village of Sop Ruak as the 'Golden Triangle'. The name is undoubtedly meant to conjure up images of illicit adventure, exotic border areas and contraband caravans, but these days the only caravan you're likely to see is the endless parade of buses carrying package tourists. Sop Ruak's opium has been fully relegated to museums, and even the once beautiful natural setting has largely been obscured by ATMs, stalls selling tourist tat and the seemingly never-ending loud announcements from the various temples. Yet perhaps most tellingly, Khun Sa's formerly impenetrable headquarters in Ban Thoet Thai are today a low-key tourist attraction.

interactions are offered here, with the same issues involved.

ℹ Getting There & Away

There are frequent *sŏrng·tăa·ou* to Chiang Saen (20B, 15 minutes, from 7am to noon) and Mae Sai (45B, 30 minutes, every 40 minutes from 8am to 1pm), both of which can be flagged down along the main strip. Minivans to Chiang Rai (50B, one hour, hourly from 5.50am to 4pm) wait in the parking lot west of Phra Chiang Saen Si Phaendin. It's an easy 9km bicycle ride from Chiang Saen to Sop Ruak.

Chiang Khong เชียงของ

POP 12,000

More remote yet livelier than its neighbour Chiang Saen, Chiang Khong is historically an important market town for local hill tribes and for trade with northern Laos. At one time the city was part of a small *meu·ang* (city-state) called Juon, founded in AD 701 by King Mahathai. Over the centuries Juon paid tribute to Chiang Rai, then Chiang Saen and finally Nan before being occupied by the Siamese in the 1880s. The territory of Chiang Khong extended all the way to Yunnan Province in China until the French turned much of the Mekong's northern bank into French Indochina in 1893.

Today the riverside town is a popular travellers' gateway into Laos. In 2013, a bridge over Mae Nam Khong opened, which has facilitated transport links with China as well. From Huay Xai, on the opposite side of the Mekong, it's a two-day slow boat trip to Luang Prabang. And for those who have set their sights even further, Huay Xai is only an eight-hour bus ride from Boten, a border crossing to and from China.

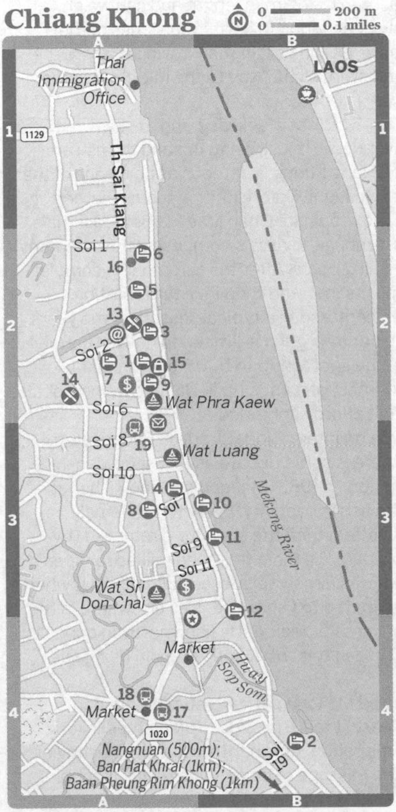

Sleeping

The vast majority of accommodation in Chiang Khong is geared towards the budget market.

In Town

Namkhong Resort HOTEL $

(☎053 791055; 94/2 Th Sai Klang; r 200-1000B; ❄📶🏊) Just off the main drag is this semi-secluded compound of tropical plants and handsome wood structures. Even the fan-cooled, shared-bathroom cheapies are charming, and the swimming pool is an added bonus.

PP Home GUESTHOUSE $

(Baan Pak Pon; ☎053 655092; baanpakpon@hotmail.co.th; off Th Sai Klang; r 350-600B; ❄📶) This rambling wooden house features large rooms with wood panelling and a couple of new rooms in an adjacent cement add-on.

Chiang Khong

0 — 200 m
0 — 0.1 miles

Chiang Khong

Sleeping
1 Baan-Fai Guest House A2
2 Baanrimtaling B4
3 Ban Tammila....A2
4 Chiang Khong Green Inn A3
5 Chiang Khong Teak Garden Hotel A2
6 Day Waterfront Hotel A2
7 Funky Box....A2
8 Namkhong Resort A3
9 Namkhong Riverside Hotel A2
10 PP Home B3
11 Rim Nam House....B3
12 River House....B3

Eating
13 Bamboo Mexican House A2
14 Khao Soi Pa Orn....A2

Drinking & Nightlife
Hub ....(see 7)

Shopping
15 Walking Street A2

Information
16 Easy Trip....A2

Transport
17 Buses to Chiang Mai & Phayao A4
Buses to Chiang Rai ....(see 18)
18 Sombat Tour A4
19 Sŏrng·tăa·ou to Hat Bai....A3

Ban Tammila HOTEL $
(☎053 791234; www.baantammila.com; 113 Th Sai Klang; r & bungalows 450-750B; ❄📶) Although the exterior looks a bit ragged, the rooms and bungalows here are neat and decorated in warm colours. Some rooms boast wide balconies and hammocks; room 12 in particular has breezy views over to Laos.

Baan-Fai Guest House GUESTHOUSE $
(☎053 791394; 108 Th Sai Klang; r 200-800B; ❄📶) A renovation has this inviting wooden house looking better than ever. The eight rooms in the main structure have air-con and en suite bathrooms, while the newer rooms are fan-cooled and share bathroom facilities; all are linked to an attached cafe.

Funky Box HOSTEL $
(☎08 2765 1839; Soi 2, Th Sai Klang; dm 100B; ❄📶) Pretty much what the name suggests: a box-like structure holding 16 dorm beds. And rest assured that it's funky in the good sense of the word.

Rim Nam House HOTEL $
(☎053 655680; abu_bumpbump@sanook.com; off Th Sai Klang; r 350-500B; ❄📶) This riverside place unites 20 mostly identical, spacious and clean budget rooms, the more expensive of which have air-con, and all boasting fridge and TV.

Chiang Khong Green Inn HOTEL $
(☎053 791009; www.chiangkhong-greeninn.com; 89/4 Th Sai Klang; r 200-500B; ❄@📶) The

THE MEKONG'S GIANT CATFISH

The Mekong River stretch that passes Chiang Khong is a traditional habitat for the *Ƀlah bèuk* (giant Mekong catfish, *Pangasianodon gigas* to ichthyologists), among the largest freshwater fish in the world. A *Ƀlah bèuk* takes at least six and possibly 12 years (no one's really sure) to reach full size, when it will measure 2m to 3m in length and can weigh up to 300kg. Although the adult fish have only been found in certain stretches of the Mekong River, it's thought that the fish originate in China's Qinghai Province (where the Mekong originates) on the Tibetan Plateau and swim all the way to the middle Mekong, where they spend much of their adult lives.

In Thailand and Laos the mild-tasting flesh is revered as a delicacy, and the fish are taken between late April and June when the river depth is just 3m to 4m and the fish are swimming upriver. Ban Hat Khrai, 1.5km from Chiang Khong, is famous as being one of the few places where *Ƀlah bèuk* are still occasionally caught. Before netting them, Thai and Lao fishermen hold a special annual ceremony to propitiate Chao Mae Pla Beuk, a female deity thought to preside over the giant catfish. Among the rituals comprising the ceremony are chicken sacrifices performed aboard the fishing boats. After the ceremony is completed, fishing teams draw lots to see who casts the first net, and then take turns casting.

In recent years only a few catfish have been captured in a typical season (some years have resulted in no catches at all). The catfish hunters' guild is limited to natives of Ban Hat Khrai, and the fishermen sell the meat on the spot for up to 500B or more per kilo (a single fish can bring 100,000B in Bangkok); most of it ends up in Bangkok, since local restaurants in Huay Xai and Chiang Khong can't afford such prices.

Although the *Ƀlah bèuk* is on the Convention on International Trade in Endangered Species (CITES) list of endangered species, there is some debate as to just how endangered it is. Because of the danger of extinction, in 1983 Thailand's Inland Fisheries Department developed a program to breed the fish in captivity. Every time a female was caught, it was kept alive until a male was netted, then the eggs were removed (by massaging the female's ovaries) and put into a pan; the male was then milked for sperm and the eggs fertilised in the pan. The program was largely unsuccessful until 2001 when 70,000 hatchlings survived. The fish were distributed to fishery centres elsewhere in the country, some of which have had moderate success breeding the fish, mostly in ponds in the central Thai province of Suphanburi. Because of this, *Ƀlah bèuk* is again being seen on menus around the country.

At the moment the greatest threats to the wild Mekong catfish's survival are dams: there are currently seven in existence and at least 11 more proposed along the Mekong River, posing potential obstacles to the fish's migration. Another threat is the blasting of Mekong River rapids in China, done to allow the passage of large ships, which is robbing the fish of important breeding grounds.

cheaper rooms in this modern-feeling backpacker joint are tight, fan-cooled and share bathrooms, but the rooms with air-con have a bit more legroom, not to mention TVs and en suite bathrooms.

River House HOTEL **$$**
(☎053 792022; theriverhouse_chiangkhong@hotmail.com; 419 Th Sai Klang; dm 150B, r 300-800B;) This homey feeling white house overlooking the Mekong River represents a great budget/midrange choice. The cheaper rooms are small, fan-cooled and share bathrooms, while the more expensive rooms are spacious and come equipped with air-con, fridge, TV and balcony.

Namkhong Riverside Hotel HOTEL **$$**
(☎053 791796; www.namkhongriverside.com; 174-176 Th Sai Klang; r incl breakfast 1300-1500B;) Having recently undergone a renovation, this modern and popular three-storey hotel holds heaps of clean, neat rooms, most with private balconies overlooking the river. It's a great midrange catch, the only downside being the noise from nightly karaoke parties.

Day Waterfront Hotel HOTEL **$$**
(☎053 791789; www.hoteldaywaterfront.com; 789 Th Sai Klang; r incl breakfast 650-900B) The rooms here are spacious and well equipped but relatively plain; the real highlight is the friendly service and the great views over to Laos.

Chiang Khong Teak Garden Hotel HOTEL **$$$**
(☎053 792008; www.chiangkhongteakgarden.com; 666 Th Sai Klang; r incl breakfast 1800-2100B;) The modern duplex bungalows at Chiang Khong's most expensive digs are well outfitted and cosy, if somewhat sterile. The price depends on garden or river view.

Outside of Town

Baanrimtaling GUESTHOUSE **$**
(☎053 791613, 08 4615 5490; maleewan_th@yahoo.com; 99/2 Soi 19, Th Sai Klang; dm 100-130B, r 150-450B;) The 13 rooms in this rambling house are pretty run-of-the-mill for this price range, and the location isn't ideal, but the homelike atmosphere and gentle service may have you staying a bit longer than you planned.

Rai Saeng Arun RESORT **$$$**
(☎08 1802 7062; www.raisaengarun.com; Rte 4007; bungalows incl breakfast 3300-3900B;) Located 22km from Chiang Khong on Rte 4007, which leads to Chiang Saen, this resort brings together 14 bungalows in a breathtaking plot of land adjacent to the Mekong River. All are stylish and comfortable, feature balconies and open-air showers, and are connected by bridged walkways over rice fields. Considerable discounts are available during the low season.

Eating & Drinking

On Wednesday and Saturday during the tourist season (from around November to May), Chiang Khong's main drag hosts a **Walking Street** (Th Sai Klang; mains 30-60B; ⊙6-10pm Wed & Sat Nov-May), which has a decent selection of local eats.

★ **Khao Sol Pa Orn** THAI **$**
(Soi 6, Th Sai Klang, no roman-script sign; mains 30-40B; ⊙8am-4pm) You may think you know *kôw soy,* the famous northern curry noodle soup, but the version served in Chiang Khong forgoes the curry broth and replaces it with clear soup topped with a rich, spicy minced pork mixture. Several non-noodle dishes are also available.

Nangnuan THAI **$**
(Ban Hat Khrai; mains 30-150B; ⊙8am-9pm) Freshwater fish from the Mekong is the emphasis here, and it's prepared in a variety of ways, as the extensive English-language menu describes. Located at the end of the road that leads to Ban Hat Khrai, about 1km south of town.

Baan Pheung Rim Khong THAI **$**
(Ban Hat Khrai, no roman-script sign; mains 40-150B; ⊙10am-10pm) A scruffy but tasty riverside shack where locals go to eat fish-based dishes. Located at the end of the road that leads to Ban Hat Khrai, about 1km south of town.

Bamboo Mexican House INTERNATIONAL **$$**
(Th Sai Klang; mains 70-250B; ⊙7.30am-8.30pm;) Run by the manager of a now-defunct guesthouse who learned to make Mexican dishes from her American and Mexican guests. To be honest, though, we never got past the coffee and tasty homemade breads and cakes. Opens early, and boxed lunches can be assembled for the boat ride to Luang Prabang.

Hub BAR
(Soi 2, Th Sai Klang; ⊙noon-midnight) After having cycled around the world in record time, Brit Alan Bate decided to plant roots in Chiang Khong and opened this tiny, fun cycling-themed pub.

GETTING TO LAOS: CHIANG KHONG TO HUAY XAI

Late 2013 saw the completion of the Fourth Thai-Lao Friendship Bridge over the Mekong River. Since then, foreigners are no longer allowed to cross to Huay Xai by boat, which has made getting to Laos both less convenient and more expensive for most tourists.

Getting to the Border

The jumping-off point is the Friendship Bridge, around 10km south of Chiang Khong, a 150B săhm·lór ride from downtown or the bus stop market area.

At the Border

After completing border formalities at the **Thai immigration office** (☎053 792824; ⏰7am-8.30pm), you'll board a shuttle bus (from 20B) across the 630m span. On the Lao side, foreigners can purchase a 30-day visa for Laos upon arrival in Huay Xai for US$30 to US$42, depending on nationality. On your return to Thailand, unless you've already received a Thai visa, immigration will grant you permission to stay in the country for 15 days.

Onwards Travel

From the Lao side of the bridge, it's an exorbitant 100B/25,000K per person for a săhm·lór ride to the boat pier or Huay Xai's new bus terminal. Bus destinations from Huay Xai include Luang Nam Tha (60,000K to 85,000K, 4½ hours, 8.30am and 10am), Luang Prabang (145,000K to 170,000K, 12 hours, 8.30am, 10am and 6pm), Udomxai (90,000K to 100,000K, nine hours, 9.30am), Vang Vieng (215,000K, 24 hours, 10am) and Vientiane (250,000K, 24 hours, 10am).

If time is on your side, the daily slow boat (1000B/250,000K, around 10.30am) to Luang Prabang takes two days, including a night in the village of Pak Beng. Avoid the noisy fast boats (350,000K, six to seven hours, frequent from 9am to 11am) as there have been reports of bad accidents. Booking tickets through a Chiang Khong–based agent such as Easy Trip costs slightly more, but they arrange tickets for you and provide transport and a boxed lunch for the boat ride.

If you already hold a Chinese visa, it's also possible to go directly to China from Chiang Khong. After obtaining a 30-day Lao visa on arrival in Huay Xai, simply board one of the buses bound for Mengla (120,000K, eight hours, 8.30am) or Kunming (430,000K, 18 hours, 10.30am), which are both in China's Yunnan Province.

ℹ Information

A handful of banks along Th Sai Klang have ATMs and foreign-exchange services.

Easy Trip (☎053 655174, 08 9635 5999; www.discoverylaos.com; 183 Th Sai Klang; ⏰9am-7pm) This professional travel agency can help you arrange boat or bus transport in Laos.

Internet (Th Sai Klang; per hour 30B; ⏰10am-10pm) On the main street across from Bamboo Mexican House.

ℹ Getting There & Away

Chiang Khong has no central bus terminal; buses pick up and drop off passengers at various points near the market, south of the centre of town. If you're going to Bangkok, buy tickets in advance at **Sombat Tour** (☎053 791644; Rte 1020). If you're bound for Chiang Saen, you'll first need to take a *sŏrng·tăa·ou* to Hat Bai from a stall on Th Sai Klang (50B, one hour, around 8am), where you'll need to transfer to another Chiang Saen–bound *sŏrng·tăa·ou*.

Alternatively, Nok Air (p213) now offer minivan transfer to/from Chiang Khong via the airport in Chiang Rai, about two hours away.

DESTINATION	FARE (B)	DURATION (HR)	FREQUENCY
Bangkok	650-1019	13	7am, 7.25am & frequent departures 3pm-4pm
Chiang Mai	279-434	6-7	7.15am, 9.45am & 10.30am
Chiang Rai	65-126	2½	hourly 5am-3pm
Phayao	151	3	10.30am

ℹ Getting Around

A săhm·lór between the bus station and Friendship Bridge, the border crossing to Laos, costs 150B.

PHAYAO PROVINCE

Phayao พะเยา

POP 20,000

Few people, including many Thais, are aware of this quiet but attractive northern city. In an overzealous effort to remedy this, a tourist brochure we came across described Phayao as the Vienna of Southeast Asia. Although this is just *slightly* stretching the truth, Phayao is certainly one of the pleasanter towns in northern Thailand. Its setting on Kwan Phayao, a vast wetland, gives the town a back-to-nature feel that's utterly lacking in most Thai cities, and the tree-lined streets, temples and old wooden houses of 'downtown' Phayao provide a pleasing old-school Thai touch.

The little-visited town is the perfect place to break up your journey to or from Chiang Rai, and can also serve as a bookend to a drive from Chiang Khong.

Sights & Activities

★Kwan Phayao LANDMARK

(กว๊านพะเยา; Th Chaykawan) This vast body of water is the largest swamp in northern Thailand and a symbol of Phayao. Although naturally occurring, the water level is artificially controlled, otherwise the wetlands would go dry outside of the wet season. Framed by mountains, the swamp is in fact more scenic than the name suggests, and is the setting for what must be among the most beautiful sunsets in Thailand.

Rowing crews can be seen practising in the evenings, and there's a pier at the southern end of Th Chai Kwan where there are **boat rides** (per person 20B; ⏲8am-6pm) to what remains of **Wat Tiloke Aram**, a submerged 500-year-old temple. There are ambitious plans to rebuild the temple, one of many submerged religious structures in Kwan Phayao.

In addition to lost Buddhist artefacts, there are at least 50 types of fish native to these waters, and there's a **small fish breeding area** where for 5B you can feed the fish.

Wat Sri Khom Kham BUDDHIST TEMPLE

(วัดศรีโคมคำ; Th Chaykawan; ⏲dawn-dusk) FREE Phayao's most important temple is thought to date back to 1491, but its present structure was finished in 1923. The immense prayer hall holds the Phra Jao Ton Luang, the largest Chiang Saen–era Buddha statue in the country. Legend has it that the construction

OFF THE BEATEN TRACK

THE LONG WAY TO PHAYAO

If you're in Chiang Khong and happen to have your own wheels, we have an excellent suggestion for a drive. Routes 1155 and 1093 are among Thailand's most dramatic roads, hugging steep mountainsides along the Thailand–Laos border and passing waterfalls, incredible vistas and national parks. If you need a destination you can continue all the way to Phayao, a little-visited town with ample accommodation and good food.

From Chiang Khong, the trip is as straightforward as heading south on Rte 1020 and following the signs to **Phu Chi Fa**, a national park near the Lao border. For Thailand, the signs are unusually clear, but a good companion is the *Golden Triangle* map, published by Golden Triangle Rider (p194).

At the mountaintop village of Doi Pha Tang, consider a quick detour to **Pratu Siam** (1653m), one of Thailand's most impressive viewpoints. There is basic lodging and food here.

Route 1093 narrows and the roadside becomes markedly less populated as you approach **Phu Chi Fa**, a mountaintop that offers high-altitude views into Laos. There are a few different ways to approach the peak, the most popular being via Ban Rom Fah Thai. There is a variety of accommodation and some basic restaurants on either side of Phu Chi Fa.

Upon passing Phu Chi Fa, stay on Rte 1093 and follow the signs to **Ban Huak**. This is a picturesque village in Phayao Province, 2km from the Lao border. There's a border market on the 10th and 30th of every month, and homestay-style accommodation in the town, and nearby **Nam Tok Phu Sang** is a unique waterfall of thermally heated water.

From Ban Huak, follow signs to Chiang Kham, then take Rte 1021 to Chun, from where it's a straight shot to Phayao (via Dok Kham Tai).

If you do the drive in one go, allow at least six hours, including stops for taking photos, coffee and a meal.

of the statue, which stands 18m high, took more than 30 years. It's not the most beautiful or well-proportioned Buddha image in Thailand, but it certainly is impressive. The temple is about 2km from the northern end of Th Chaykawan.

The ordination hall that is elevated over Kwan Phayao features graceful modern wall paintings. Also on the grounds of the wát is a Buddhist sculpture garden that includes gory, larger-than-life depictions of Buddhist hell.

Phayao Cultural Exhibition Hall MUSEUM
(หอวัฒนธรรมนิทัศน์; Th Chaykawan; admission 40B; ⊙8.30am-4.30pm) This two-storey museum is packed with artefacts and a good amount of information on local history and culture in English. Standout items include a unique 'black' Buddha statue and a fossil of two embracing crabs labelled 'Wonder Lover'. It's next door to Wat Sri Khom Kham, about 2km from the northern end of Th Chaykawan.

Wat Li BUDDHIST TEMPLE
(วัดลี; off Hwy 1 Asia; ⊙temple dawn-dusk, museum 9am-3pm) FREE Just off Rte 1 opposite the turn-off to Phayao, this Buddhist temple features a small museum with a decent variety of items from the Chiang Saen era.

Wat Phra That Jom Thong BUDDHIST TEMPLE
(วัดพระธาตุจอมทอง; off Th Chaykawan; ⊙dawn-dusk) FREE This is an attractive *chedi* on a wooded hilltop 3km from the centre of town.

Sleeping

Huanpak Jumjai GUESTHOUSE $
(☎054 482659; 37/5-6 Th Prasat; r 600B; ❄📶) Rooms here are spacious, clean and decked out in handsome wood. It's located just off Th Chaykawan, a short walk from the waterfront. There are many similar places along the waterfront.

Gateway Hotel HOTEL $$
(☎054 411333; 7/36 Soi 2, Th Pratu Khlong; r 900-1100B, ste 2000-2500B, all incl breakfast; ❄📶🏊) Ostensibly Phayao's grandest hotel, the rooms here have seen a much-needed renovation. It's next door to the bus station.

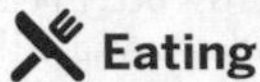

Eating

For such a small town, Phayao has an abundance of food. There are literally dozens of lakefront restaurants at the edge of Kwan Phayao, beginning at Th Thakawan and extending all the way to the public park.

Khao Soi Saeng Phian NORTHERN THAI $
(Th Thakawan, no roman-script sign; mains 25-40B; ⊙9am-3pm) One of the better bowls of *kôw soy* in this neck of the north is available at this family-run restaurant, a block from the waterfront.

Kaat Boran MARKET $
(Th Chaykawan; mains 30-60B; ⊙6-10pm) This largely food-based night market sets up every evening near the King Ngam Muang monument.

Night Market THAI $
(Th Rob Wiang; mains 30-60B; ⊙6-10pm) An extensive night market convenes along the north side of Th Rob Wiang every evening.

Chue Chan THAI $$
(Th Chaykawan; mains 80-240B; ⊙10am-10.30pm; ❄) Of all the waterfront restaurants, this place has received the most acclaim from the various Thai food authorities. The lengthy menu, which has both pictures and English, spans tasty dishes you won't find elsewhere, such as stuffed pig leg or sour fish fried with egg.

BUSES TO/FROM PHAYAO

In addition to buses, there are also minivans to Chiang Rai (63B, one hour, half-hourly from 7.15am to 7pm) and Phrae (102B, two hours, half-hourly from 7.15am to 7pm).

DESTINATION	FARE (B)	DURATION (HR)	FREQUENCY
Bangkok	416-832	11	frequent 8.30am-9.45am & 6-9pm
Chiang Khong	115	3½	12.10pm & 4.40pm
Chiang Mai	162-241	5	6 departures 7.15am-6pm
Chiang Rai	50-92	3	frequent 4am-3pm
Lampang	65-100	3	hourly 6.30am-5.30pm
Mae Sai	104-162	3	7 departures 4am-6.15pm
Nan	95-122	4	8am & noon

Information

There are several banks along Th Donsanam, near the town's morning market, many with ATM and exchange services. Internet access is available at **Internet@Cafe** (Th Pratu Khlong; per hour 20B; ⏰10am-10pm) and other shops dotting Th Donsanam.

Getting There & Away

Phayao's **bus station** (☎054 431488; Th Pratu Khlong), at the northern end of Th Chaykawan, is quite busy, primarily because the city lies on the main north–south highway. Because of this, if you're bound for Bangkok, it's possible to hop on one of the 40 or so buses that pass through the station from points further north.

PHRAE PROVINCE

Phrae is a rural, mountainous province most often associated with teak. Despite a nationwide ban on logging, there's not a whole lot of the hardwood left, and the little that does exist is under threat.

Phrae แพร่

POP 18,000

Walking around the older parts of Phrae one is struck by similarities with the historic Lao city of Luang Prabang: ample greenery, traditional wood buildings and scenic temples dominate the scenery, and monks form a significant part of the traffic. The city's residents must be among the friendliest folks in Thailand, and Phrae's location on the banks of Mae Nam Yom and its ancient wall also invite comparisons with Chiang Mai. Yet despite all this, Phrae is a little-visited city and a great destination for those who require little more than a few low-key attractions, good local food and cheery company.

Sights

In Town

Wat Luang BUDDHIST TEMPLE

(วัดหลวง; Soi 1, Th Kham Leu; ⏰dawn-dusk) FREE This is the oldest wát in Phrae, probably dating from the founding of the city in the 12th or 13th century.

The verandah of the main *wí·hăhn* is in the classic Luang Prabang–Lan Xang style but has unfortunately been bricked in with laterite. Opposite the front of the *wí·hăhn* is Pratu Khong, part of the city's original entrance gate. No longer used as a gate, it now contains a statue of Chao Pu, an early Lanna ruler.

Phra That Luang Chang Kham, the large octagonal Lanna-style *chedi*, sits on a square base with elephants supporting it on all four sides. As is sometimes seen in Phrae and Nan, the *chedi* is occasionally swathed in Thai Lü fabric.

Also on the temple grounds is a **museum** displaying temple antiques, ceramics and religious art dating from the Lanna, Nan, Bago and Mon periods. The 16th-century, Phrae-made sitting Buddha on the 2nd floor is particularly exquisite. There are also some 19th-century photos with English labels on display, including some gruesome shots of a beheading. The museum is usually open weekends only, but the monks will sometimes open it on weekdays on request.

Wat Phra Non BUDDHIST TEMPLE

(วัดพระนอน; Th Phra Non Neua; ⏰dawn-dusk) FREE Located west of Wat Luang is a 300-year-old wát named after its highly revered reclining Buddha image. The *bòht* (chapel) was built around 200 years ago and has an impressive roof with a separate, two-tiered portico and gilded, carved, wooden facade with *Ramayana* scenes. The adjacent *wí·hăhn* contains the Buddha image, swathed in Thai Lü cloth with bead and foil decoration.

Wat Jom Sawan BUDDHIST TEMPLE

(วัดจอมสวรรค์; Th Ban Mai; ⏰dawn-dusk) FREE Outside the old city, this temple was built by local Shan in the late 19th and early 20th centuries, and shows Shan and Burmese influences throughout. An adjacent copper-crowned *chedi* has lost most of its stucco to reveal the artful brickwork beneath. Since a recent renovation, Wat Jom Sawan is more of a museum piece than a functioning temple.

Wat Phra Baht Ming Meuang BUDDHIST TEMPLE

(วัดพระบาทมิ่งเมือง; Th Charoen Meuang; ⏰dawn-dusk) FREE Across from the post office within the old city, Wat Phra Baht Ming Meuang combines two formerly separate temple compounds (one of which contains a museum that is sporadically open), a Buddhist school, an old *chedi*, an unusual octagonal drum tower made entirely of teak and the highly revered Phra Kosai, which closely resembles the Phra Phuttha Chinnarat in Phitsanulok.

Phrae

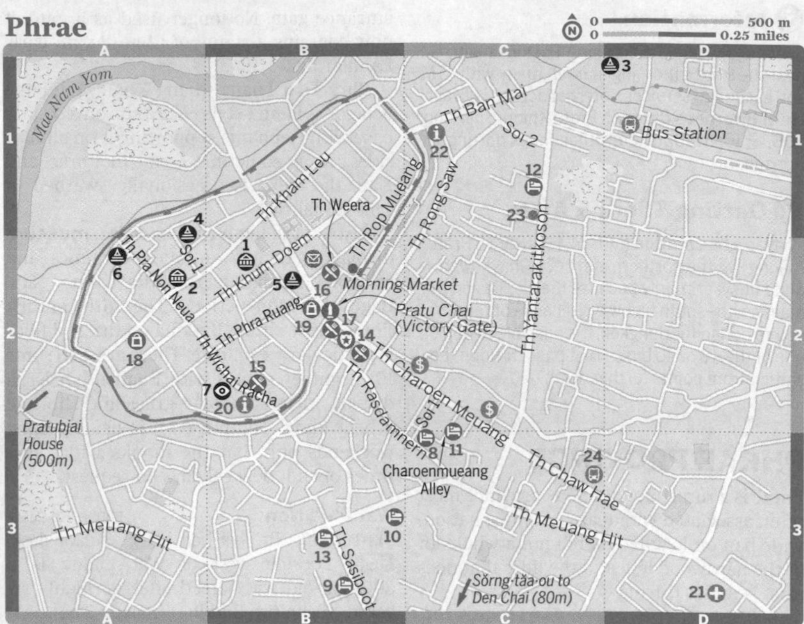

Phrae

Sights
1 Khum Jao Luang B2
2 Vongburi House A2
3 Wat Jom Sawan D1
4 Wat Luang A1
5 Wat Phra Baht Ming Meuang B2
6 Wat Phra Non A2
7 Wichairacha House B2

Sleeping
8 Bua Khao C3
9 Huern na na B3
10 Nakhon Phrae Tower B3
11 Nana C3
12 Paradorn Hotel C1
13 Phoomthai Garden B3

Eating
14 Gingerbread House Café & Gallery B2
15 Khao Soi Klang Wiang B2
Night Market .... (see 19)
16 Pan Jai B2
17 Saeng Fah Laep B2

Shopping
18 Kat Korng Kow A2
19 Maw Hawm Anian B2

Information
20 Nok Bin B2
21 Phrae Hospital D3
22 Tourism Authority of Thailand C1

Transport
23 Sang Famotor C1
24 Sŏrng·tăa·ou to Wat Phra That Cho Hae C3

Outside of Town

Phae Meuang Phi NATURE RESERVE

(แพะเมืองผี; off Rte 101; 6am-6pm) FREE The name Phae Meuang Phi means Ghost-Land, a reference to these bizarre pillars of soil and rock that look like giant fungi, most likely the result of erosion, not the paranormal. The park is located approximately 18km northeast of Phrae off Rte 101; getting there by public transport is not an option. You can charter a *sŏrng·tăa·ou* for about 600B or talk to Khun Kung at Nok Bin (p238) for alternatives.

The area has been made a provincial park; a few walking trails and viewpoints are recent additions. There are picnic pavilions in the park and food vendors selling *gài yâhng* (grilled chicken), *sôm·đam* (papaya salad) and sticky rice near the entrance.

Wat Phra That Cho Hae BUDDHIST TEMPLE
(วัดพระธาตุชอแฮ; off Rte 1022; ⌚dawn-dusk) FREE Named for the cloth that worshippers wrap around it, this hilltop wát is famous for its 33m-high gilded *chedi*. Like Chiang Mai's Wat Phra That Doi Suthep, it is an important pilgrimage site for Thais living in the north.

The temple is 9km southeast of town off Rte 1022. *Sŏrng·tăa·ou* between Phrae and Phra That Cho Hae (20B) depart from a stop near Talat Phrae Preeda, on Th Chaw Hae, from 6am to 4.30pm; outside of these hours *sŏrng·tăa·ou* can be chartered for 400B.

Tiered *naga* stairs lead to the temple compound. The interior of the *bòht* is rather tackily decorated with a gilded wooden ceiling, rococo pillars and walls with lotus-bud mosaics. The Phra Jao Than Jai Buddha image here, which resembles the Phra Phuttha Chinnarat in Phitsanulok, is reputed to impart fertility to women who make offerings to it.

Sleeping

Bua Khao HOTEL $
(☎054 511372; 8 Soi 1, Th Charoen Meuang, no roman-script sign; r 350-600B; ❄📶) Tucked just off the main road, this flagrant teak compound has mostly small rooms and rather hard beds, but the service is friendly and it has heaps of character.

Paradorn Hotel HOTEL $
(☎054 511177; kanthatham@hotmail.com; 177 Th Yantarakitkoson; r 330-800B, ste 900B, all incl breakfast; ❄📶) A decent budget choice a short walk from the bus terminal. The fan-cooled rooms have private balconies.

Nana HOTEL $
(☎054 521985; 346/2 Th Charoen Meuang, no roman-script sign; r 400-500B; ❄📶) The vast rooms here are outfitted with likewise huge TVs and fridges; the more expensive rooms pack in even more furniture. Nana is on the tiny side street labelled Charoenmeuang Alley; look for the yellow sign.

Phoomthai Garden HOTEL $$
(☎054 627359; www.phoomthaitravel.com; 31 Th Sasiboot; r incl breakfast 1200-2000B; ❄@📶) Although it's a bit of a hike from the old town, this boutique hotel is the best all-round choice in Phrae. The rooms are attractive, modern and comfortable, and all have balconies overlooking the hotel's garden. It's about 300m south of the former town wall on Th Sasiboot.

Nakhon Phrae Tower HOTEL $$
(☎054 521321; www.nakornphraetower.com; 3 Th Meuang Hit; r 650-800B, ste 1800-2500B, all incl breakfast; ❄📶) A tall, business-class hotel, Nakhon Phrae Tower lies just outside the old city. Expect the usual bland-but-functional amenities of a provincial Thai hotel of this price range, and great views of town.

Huern na na HOTEL $$$
(☎054 524800; 7/9 Th Sasiboot; r 2600, ste 5000-5500B, all incl breakfast; ❄📶≋) Rooms at Phrae's most sophisticated hotel are spacious and come decked out in both contemporary and northern Thai–style themes, as well as thoughtful amenities – suites throw in a Jacuzzi or kitchenette. You'll find it off Th Sasiboot, about 250m south of Th Meuang Hit.

Eating & Drinking

Phrae's entertainment zone is the road leading to the bus station; there you'll fine several loud bars and karaoke joints.

Pan Jai NORTHERN THAI $
(2 Th Weera, no roman-script sign; mains 20-40B; ⌚7am-10pm) During the day, the emphasis here is on *kà·nŏm jeen* (fresh rice noodles served with various curries and herbs). At night, locals come for *mŏo gà·tá* (DIY barbecue). Look for the yellow sign.

Gingerbread House Café & Gallery THAI $
(Th Charoen Meuang; mains 50-120B; ⌚8.30am-6pm Mon-Fri, to 7pm Sat & Sun; ❄📶) This modern cafe offers air-con and an English-language menu of quick, light, fried-rice-type dishes. There's a small handicrafts shop here.

Khao Soi Klang Wiang NORTHERN THAI $
(Th Wichai Racha, no roman-script sign; mains 35-50B; ⌚10am-2pm) This place does just one dish: fat bowls of *kôw soy*. Order a regular or jumbo bowl supplemented with beef, pork or chicken. It's the bright yellow place just opposite Nok Bin.

Saeng Fah Laep THAI $
(Th Charoen Meuang, no roman-script sign; mains 10-40B; ⌚9am-7pm) This friendly family sells Thai sweets, including a tasty *kôw nĕe·o má·môo·ang* (mango sticky rice). There's no English sign, but it's the old shophouse just west of the police station.

Night Market THAI $
(Th Rop Mueang; mains 30-60B; ⊙6-10pm) A small but fun night market convenes around the Pratu Chai (Victory Gate) intersection every evening.

 Shopping

Phrae is known for the distinctive *sêua môr hôrm,* the indigo-dyed cotton farmer's shirt seen all over northern Thailand. The cloth is made in Ban Thung Hong, just outside of the city.

Maw Hawm Anian CLOTHING
(36 Th Charoen Meuang, no roman-script sign; ⊙7am-8.30pm) A good place to buy *môr hôrm* in town, about 60m from the south-eastern gate (Pratu Chai) into the old city.

Kat Korng Kow MARKET
(Th Kham Leu; ⊙2-8pm Sat) Every Saturday afternoon Phrae hosts Kat Korng Kow, an open-air market held at the western end of Th Kham Leu.

Information

Nok Bin (☎08 1423 5599; 24 Th Wichai Racha; ⊙10am-5pm) Khun Kung, a local journalist, and her husband have created a cheery cafe that also functions as an informal information centre for visitors. The couple prints a tourist map of Phrae that is updated regularly, and can also arrange bicycle or motorcycle hire.

Phrae Hospital (☎054 522444; Th Chaw Hae) Southeast of town.

Tourism Authority of Thailand (TAT; ☎054 521127, nationwide 1627; tatphrae@tat.or.th; Th Ban Mai; ⊙8.30am-4.30pm) Brand new office just east of the centre of town.

 Getting There & Away

At research time, the only airline operating out of Phrae's airport was **Nok Air** (☎054 522189, nationwide 1318; www.nokair.com; Phrae Airport; ⊙8am-5pm), with a daily flight (1600B, one hour) to/from Bangkok's Don Muang International Airport. From the airport, 2.5km east of the city centre, **Ko Ngian** (☎08 7179 5056; ⊙8am-5pm Mon-Sat) can provide transport to your hotel (100B).

DON'T MISS

PHRAE'S ANTIQUE HOUSES

The lucrative teak trade led to Phrae being home to more than its fair share of beautiful antique mansions, some of which are open for visitors to peek inside.

Vongburi House (บ้านวงศ์บุรี; 50 Th Kham Leu; admission 30B; ⊙9am-5pm) The two-storey teak house of the last prince of Phrae has been converted into a private museum. It was constructed between 1897 and 1907 for Luang Phongphibun and his wife Chao Sunantha, who once held a profitable teak concession in the city. Inside, many of the house's 20 rooms display late 19th-century teak antiques, documents (including early 20th-century slave concessions), photos and other artefacts from the bygone teak-dynasty era.

Pratubjai House (บ้านประทับใจ; admission 40B; ⊙8am-5pm) Known in Thai as Baan Pratubjai (Impressive House), this is a large northern Thai–style teak house that was built using more than 130 teak logs, each over 300 years old. It's rather tackily decorated, so don't take the moniker 'impressive' too seriously. It's somewhat difficult to find; your best bet is to exit at the west gate of the former city wall and follow the signs, turning right after the school. A săhm·lór here should cost about 60B.

Wichairacha House (บ้านวิชัยราชา; 8 Th Wichai Racha; ⊙dawn-dusk) FREE This beautiful teak mansion is thought to have been built in 1898 by Cantonese artisans. Efforts are being made to turn the house into a museum, though at the time of research the work was far from complete.

Khum Jao Luang (คุ้มเจ้าหลวง; Th Khum Doem; ⊙8.30am-5pm) FREE Built in 1892, this imposing building, sporting a mixture of Thai and European architectural styles, was the home of the final Lord, or Chao Luang, of Phrae. The structure subsequently served as a governor's residence, and is today a museum on local history (no English signage). Ask to see the basement, which was used to punish and house slaves and prisoners.

TRANSPORT TO/FROM PHRAE

Bus

DESTINATION	FARE (B)	DURATION (HR)	FREQUENCY
Bangkok	692	8	frequent 9.30am-12.30pm & 6.30-9pm
Chiang Mai	151-302	4	frequent 6am-6.40pm
Chiang Rai	164-320	4	hourly 6am-6.40pm
Lampang	87-174	2	hourly 6am-6.40pm
Mae Sai	200-412	5	6 departures 5am-11.40pm
Nan	90-179	2	frequent 3am-6.50pm
Phayao	106-213	2	hourly 6am-6.40pm
Phitsanulok	191	3	frequent 6am-10.30pm
Sukhothai	127-164	3	5 departures 10am-2.20pm

Minivan

DESTINATION	FARE (B)	DURATION (HR)	FREQUENCY
Ban Huay Kon (border with Laos)	180	5	4 departures 3am-7.10pm
Chiang Rai	150	4½	hourly 6am-6.40pm
Lampang	78	2	hourly 6am-5.50pm
Nan	78	2	frequent 3am-6.50pm
Phayao	100	2	hourly 6am-6.40pm

Train

DESTINATION	FARE (B)	DURATION (HR)	FREQUENCY
Bangkok	155-1291	9-11	8 daily
Chiang Mai	72-549	4-6	7 daily
Lampang	50-968	2	4 daily
Phitsanulok	30-348	3½	8 daily

Unlike most cities in Thailand, Phrae's **bus and minivan terminal** (☎054 511800; off Th Yantarakitkoson) is located within walking distance of a few accommodation options.

Phrae's closest rail link, **Den Chai station** (☎054 613260, nationwide 1690; www.railway.co.th), is 23km south of town. There are frequent **blue sŏrng·tăa·ou** (Th Yantakarakitkoson) to Den Chai (40B, 40 minutes, from 6.30am to 5.30pm), departing from a stop in front of Phrae Vocational College, or you can charter one for 400B.

Getting Around

A săhm·lór within the old town costs around 40B. Motorcycle taxis are available at the bus terminal; a trip from here to Pratu Chai (Victory Gate) should cost around 40B. **Sang Famotor** (☎054 521598; 163/8 Th Yantarakitkoson; per 24hr 200B; ⊙8.30am-4.30pm Mon-Sat) is a motorcycle dealership that also hires out bikes.

NAN PROVINCE

Tucked into Thailand's northeastern corner, Nan is a remote province to be explored for its natural beauty. Nan's ethnic groups are another highlight and differ significantly from those in other northern provinces. Outside Mae Nam Nan Valley, the predominant hill tribes are Mien, with smaller numbers of Hmong, while dispersed throughout Nan are four lesser-known groups seldom seen outside this province: the Thai Lü, Mabri, Htin and Khamu.

Nan น่าน

POP 20,000

Due to its remote location, Nan is not the kind of destination most travellers are going to stumble upon. But if you've taken the time to get here, you'll be rewarded by a city rich in both culture and history.

Many of Nan's residents are Thai Lü, the ancestors of immigrants from Xishuangbanna, in southwestern China. This cultural legacy is seen in the city's art and architecture, particularly in its exquisite temples. A Lanna influence on the town can also be seen in the remains of the old city wall and several early wát.

History

For centuries Nan was an isolated, independent kingdom with few ties to the outside world. Ample evidence of prehistoric habitation exists, but it wasn't until several

Nan

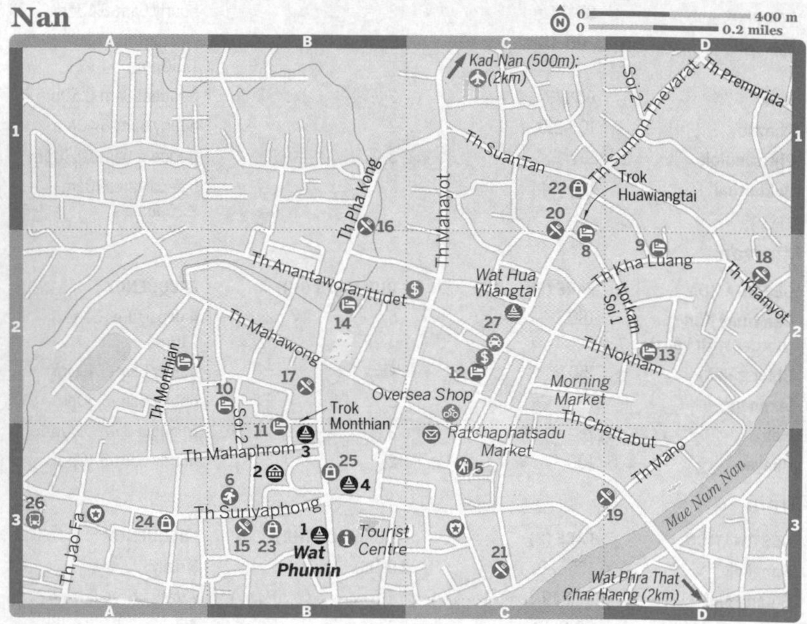

Nan

Top Sights
1 Wat Phumin B3

Sights
2 Nan National Museum B3
3 Wat Hua Khuang B3
4 Wat Phra That Chang Kham B3

Activities, Courses & Tours
5 Fhu Travel C3
Nan Seeing Tour .... (see 12)
6 Nan Touring B3

Sleeping
7 Banban Nannan Library A2
8 Fah Place C2
9 Nan Boutique Hotel D2
10 Nan Guest House B2
11 Nan Lanna Hotel B3
12 Pukha Nanfa Hotel C2
13 Srinual Lodge D2
14 Sukkasem Hotel B2

Eating
15 Hot Bread B3
16 Night Market B1
17 Nor Nan B2
18 Pu Som Restaurant D2
19 Rak Khun D3
20 Som Tam Thawt C1
21 Wan Da C3

Shopping
22 Amnouy Porn & Jangtrakul C1
Nan Silver .... (see 12)
23 OTOP B3
24 Peera A3
25 Walking Street B3

Transport
26 Bus Station A3
27 Thana Sin Motors C2

small *meu·ang* (city-states) consolidated to form Nanthaburi in the mid-14th century that the city became a power to contend with. Towards the end of the 14th century Nan became one of the nine northern Thai-Lao principalities that comprised Lan Na Thai (Lanna). The city-state flourished throughout the 15th century under the name of Chiang Klang (Middle City), which was a reference to its position situated approximately midway between Chiang Mai (New City) and Chiang Thong (Golden City, today's Luang Prabang). The Burmese took control of the kingdom in 1558 and transferred many of the inhabitants to Burma as slaves; the city was all but abandoned until western Thailand was wrested from the Burmese in 1786. The local dynasty then regained local sovereignty and it remained semi-autonomous until 1931, when Nan finally (and reluctantly) accepted full Bangkok sponsorship.

Sights

★Wat Phumin BUDDHIST TEMPLE

(วัดภูมินทร; cnr Th Suriyaphong & Th Pha Kong; dawn-dusk) FREE Nan's most famous Buddhist temple is celebrated for its exquisite murals that were executed during the late 19th century by a Thai Lü artist named Thit Buaphan. The exterior of the temple takes the form of a cruciform *bòht* (chapel) that was constructed in 1596 and restored during the reign of Chao Anantavorapitthidet (1867–74). The ornate altar in the centre of the *bòht* has four sides, with four Sukhothai-style sitting Buddhas facing in each direction.

Nan National Museum MUSEUM

(พิพิธภัณฑสถานแหงชาติน่าน; Th Pha Kong; admission 100B; 9am-4pm Wed-Sun) Housed in the 1903 vintage palace of Nan's last two feudal lords, this museum first opened its doors in 1973. In terms of collection and content, it's one of the country's better provincial museums, and has English labels for most

DON'T MISS

THE MURALS OF WAT PHUMIN

Wat Phumin is northern Thailand's Sistine Chapel, and the images on its walls are now found on everything from knick-knacks at Chiang Mai's night bazaar to postcards sold in Bangkok. Yet despite the seemingly happy scenes depicted, the murals were executed during a period that saw the end of Nan as a semi-independent kingdom. This resulted in several examples of political and social commentary manifesting themselves in the murals, rarities in Thai religious art.

The murals commissioned by Jao Suliyaphong, the last king of Nan, include the *Khaddhana Jataka,* a relatively obscure story of one of the Buddha's lives that, according to Thai historian David K Wyatt in his excellent book, *Reading Thai Murals,* has never been illustrated elsewhere in the Buddhist world. The story, which is on the left side of the temple's northern wall, depicts an orphan in search of his parents. Wyatt argues that this particular tale was chosen as a metaphor for the kingdom of Nan, which also had been abandoned by a succession of 'parents', the Thai kingdoms of Sukhothai, Chiang Mai and Ayuthaya. At roughly the same time as the murals were painted, Nan was fully incorporated into Siam by King Rama V, and much of its territory was allotted to France. Apparent discontent with this decision can be seen in a scene on the western wall that shows two male monkeys attempting to copulate against a background that, not coincidentally, according to Wyatt, resembles the French flag.

The murals are also valuable purely for their artistic beauty, something that is even more remarkable if you step back and consider the limited palette of colours that the artist, Thit Buaphan, had to work with. The paintings are also fascinating for their fly-on-the-wall depictions of local life in Nan during the end of the 19th century. A depiction of three members of a hill tribe on the western wall includes such details as a man's immense goitre and a barking dog, suggesting this group's place as outsiders. Multiple depictions of a man wearing a feminine shawl, often seen performing traditionally female-only duties, are among the earliest depictions of *gà·teu·i* (ladyboys; also spelt *kàthoey*). And in what must be one of the art world's most superfluous cameos, the artist painted himself on the western wall, flirting with a woman. Considering that the murals took Thit Buaphan more than 20 years to complete, we'll allow him this excess.

items. It was closed for renovations when we were in town, but is expected to reopen with much the same focus.

The ground floor has ethnological exhibits covering the various ethnic groups found in the province. Among the items on display are silverwork, textiles, folk utensils and tribal costumes.

On the 2nd floor are exhibits on Nan history, archaeology, local architecture, royal regalia, weapons, ceramics and religious art. Of the latter, the museum's collection of Buddha images includes some rare Lanna styles as well as the floppy-eared local styles. Also on display on the 2nd floor is a rare 'black' elephant tusk said to have been presented to a Nan lord over 300 years ago by the Khün ruler of Chiang Tung (Kyaingtong).

Wat Phra That Chae Haeng BUDDHIST TEMPLE
(วัดพระธาตุแช่แห้ง; off Rte 1168; ⏲dawn-dusk) FREE Located two kilometres past the bridge that spans Mae Nam Nan, heading southeast out of town, this Buddhist temple dating from 1355 is the most sacred wát in Nan Province. It's set in a square walled enclosure on top of a hill with a view of Nan and the valley. A round-trip motorcycle taxi here from the centre of Nan will run about 100B.

The Thai Lü–influenced *bòht* features a triple-tiered roof with carved wooden eaves and dragon reliefs over the doors. A gilded Lanna-style *chedi* sits on a large square base next to the *bòht;* visit late in the day and the structure practically glows in the afternoon light.

Wat Phra That Chang Kham BUDDHIST TEMPLE
(วัดพระธาตุช้างค้ำ; cnr Th Suriyaphong & Th Pha Kong; ⏲dawn-dusk) FREE This is the second-most important temple in the city after Wat Phra That Chae Haeng. The founding date is unknown, but the main *wí·hăhn*, reconstructed in 1458, has a huge seated Buddha image and faint murals that have been partially recovered. The *chedi* behind the *wí·hăhn* is thought to date to around the same time as the temple was founded, and features elephant supports similar to those seen in Sukhothai and Si Satchanalai.

Next to the *chedi* is a small, undistinguished *bòht* from the same era. Wat Phra That Chang Kham's current abbot tells an interesting story involving the *bòht* and a Buddha image that was once kept inside. According to the abbot, in 1955 art historian AB Griswold offered to purchase the 145cm-tall Buddha inside the small *bòht*. The image appeared to be a crude Sukhothai-style walking Buddha moulded of plaster. After agreeing to pay the abbot 25,000B for the image, Griswold began removing the image – but as he did it fell and the plaster around the statue broke away to reveal an original Sukhothai Buddha of pure gold underneath. Needless to say, the abbot made Griswold give it back, much to the latter's chagrin. Did Griswold suspect what lay beneath the plaster? The abbot refuses to say.

The image is now kept behind a glass partition in the *hŏr đrai* (manuscript library) adjacent to the *wí·hăhn,* the largest of its type in Thailand.

Wat Hua Khuang BUDDHIST TEMPLE
(วัดหัวขวง; cnr Th Mahaphrom & Th Pha Kong; ⏲dawn-dusk) FREE This temple features a distinctive Lanna/Lan Xang–style *chedi* with four Buddha niches, an attractive wooden *hŏr đrai* and a noteworthy *bòht* with a Luang Prabang–style carved wooden verandah. Inside is a carved wooden ceiling and a huge *naga* altar. The temple's founding date is unknown, but stylistic cues suggest that this may be one of the city's oldest wát.

 Activities

Nan has nothing like the organised trekking industry found in Chiang Rai and Chiang Mai, and many visitors, particularly Thais, opt to float rather than walk. White-water rafting along Mae Nam Wa, in northern Nan, is only possible when the water level is high (September to December), and is said to be best during the early part of the rainy season. The rapids span from classes I to IV, and pass through intact jungle and remote villages.

Nan Touring RAFTING
(☎08 1961 7711; www.nantouring.com; 11/12 Th Suriyaphong; 3 days & 2 nights per person 5900B; ⏲9am-5pm) This outfit offers a variety of rafting trips for groups of at least five people.

Nan Seeing Tour CYCLING TOUR
(☎08 1472 4131; Th Sumon Thevarat; tours per day from 4500B; ⏲8am-7pm) Offers van-based tours in and around town. Nan Coffee functions as the office.

Fhu Travel TREKKING
(☎054 710636, 08 1287 7209; www.fhutravel.com; 453/4 Th Sumon Thevarat; trekking per person 1700B; ⏲9am-6pm) This established outfit currently offers one-day treks around Nan.

Sleeping

Fah Place HOTEL $
(☎054 710222; 237/8 Th Sumon Thevarat; r 400-500B; ❄📶) The rooms here are vast and have been outfitted with attractive teak furniture, including the kind of puffy inviting beds you'd expect at places that charge several times this much; a terrific bargain. The same people also run the similar **Sukkasem Hotel** (☎054 772555; sukksasemnan@gmail.com; 119-121 Th Anantaworarittidet; r 400-1000B; ❄📶).

Nan Guest House HOTEL $
(☎054 771849, 08 1288 8484; www.nanguest-house.net; 57/15 Soi 2, Th Mahaphrom; r 250-430B; ❄@📶) In a quiet residential area a short walk from Nan's most famous temples, this long-standing and well-maintained place has spotless, spacious rooms, half of which have private hot-water bathrooms, air-con, TV and fridge.

Banban Nannan Library GUESTHOUSE $
(☎08 9859 5898; www.facebook.com/BanbanNannan; 14/1 Th Monthian; r 350-700B; 📶) Although the four rooms in this wooden house are simple, the setting, which spans an inviting garden, the eponymous library and a homely atmosphere, more than make up for this.

Srinual Lodge HOTEL $$
(☎054 710174; www.facebook.com/srinuallodge-fanpage; 40/5 Th Nokham; r 800-1400B, ste 1800B; ❄📶) This two-storey brick structure holds a couple dozen rooms decked out in a *faux rustique* style with logs, bamboo and local textiles. Despite the earthy design theme, the rooms look comfortable and it's about as close as you'll get to sleeping near Mae Nam Nan.

Nan Lanna Hotel HOTEL $$
(☎054 772720; Trok Monthian; r 600-800B; ❄📶) Cool rooms with not much natural light, but with lots of space, big bathrooms and attractive retro-themed design touches.

★ **Pukha Nanfa Hotel** HOTEL $$$
(☎054 771111; www.pukhananfahotel.co.th; 369 Th Sumon Thevarat; r incl breakfast 2500-4600B; ❄@📶) The former and forgettable Nan Fah Hotel has been meticulously transformed into this charming boutique lodging. The 14 rooms are cosy and classy, with aged wood accentuated by touches such as local cloth, handicrafts and art. Antique adverts and pictures add to the old-world feel, and to top it off, the place is conveniently located and has more-than-capable staff.

Nan Boutique Hotel HOTEL $$$
(☎054 775532; www.nanboutiquehotel.com; 1/11 Th Kha Luang; r incl breakfast 1800-3200B; ❄📶) This super-tidy suburban-feeling compound lacks the old-school character of some of Nan's other choices, but makes up for this with some of the city's most modern and well-equipped rooms, free pickup and drop-off, free bicycles, and an on-site spa.

Eating & Drinking

Despite its other charms, Nan has one of the least inspiring restaurant scenes in northern Thailand.

The town's **night market** (Th Pha Kong; mains 30-60B; ⏰5-11pm) provides a few decent food stall offerings. Better yet is Nan's Saturday Walking Street (p244), where dishes and tables are provided for the take-away northern Thai–style food.

Pu Som Restaurant NORTHERN THAI $
(203/1 Th Khamyot, no roman-script sign; mains 35-90B; ⏰10am-10pm) The emphasis here is on meat, served in the local style as *lâhp* (a type of minced meat 'salad') or *néu·a·nêung* (beef steamed over herbs and served with a delicious galangal-based dip). There's no English-language sign; look for the illuminated 'est cola' ad.

Hot Bread INTERNATIONAL, THAI $
(38/1-2 Th Suriyaphong; mains 25-140B; ⏰7am-4pm; 🖉) This charming, retro-themed cafe and restaurant has a generous menu of Western-style breakfast dishes – including the eponymous and delicious homemade bread – and other Western and Thai items. Come for *kôw soy* (noodle soup) in the mornings.

Rak Khun THAI $
(Th Mano, no roman-script sign; mains 70-200B; ⏰5-10pm) This open-air convocation of foldable tables and fluorescent lights – barely a restaurant by Western standards – is a hit among locals. Don't miss *gài tôrt má·kwàan* (chicken fried with local spices) or *yam pàk gòot* (a salad of ferns).

Wan Da THAI $
(Th Kha Luang; mains 30-50B; ⏰8am-5pm) This local legend serves just about everything from curries ladled over rice to satay, but those in the know come for *kà·nŏm jeen* (fresh rice noodles served with various toppings).

Som Tam Thawt THAI $
(Th Sumon Thevarat, no roman-script sign; mains 35-60B; ⏰10am-9pm Tue-Sun) This tiny restaurant

is known for its *sôm·đam tôrt:* deep-fried *sôm·đam* (papaya salad), an equal parts crunchy and refreshing snack. It also does fruit smoothies and other basic dishes. Located roughly across from Fah Place hotel.

Nor Nan THAI $

(Lanna & Art Shop, Th Pha Kong; mains 70-180B; 8am-10pm;) A contemporary-feeling cafe-restaurant, with a short (Thai language only) menu of Thai dishes and brief selection of imported beers.

Shopping

Nan is one of the best places in northern Thailand to pick up some souvenirs, and good buys include local textiles, especially the Thai Lü weaving styles, which typically feature red and black designs on white cotton in floral, geometric and animal designs. A favourite is the *lai nám lăi* (flowing-water design) that shows stepped patterns representing streams, rivers and waterfalls. Local Hmong appliqué and Mien embroidery are of excellent quality. Htin grass-and-bamboo baskets and mats are worth a look, too.

Walking Street MARKET

(Th Pha Kong; 5-10pm Sat) Every Saturday afternoon the stretch of Th Pha Kong in front of Nan National Museum is closed and vendors selling food, textiles, clothing and local handicrafts set up shop.

Kad-Nan MARKET

(43 Th Mahayot; 10am-10pm) This open-air mall is Nan's answer to Bangkok's Chatuchak Weekend Market. Here you'll find shops selling local knick-knacks, art and clothing, plus restaurants, coffee shops and bars. The market is technically open from 10am, but evening, when most shops and restaurants are open and live music gives the place a fair-like atmosphere, is the best time to visit.

Amnouy Porn & Jangtrakul HANDICRAFTS

(Th Sumon Thevarat; 8am-7pm) These adjacent shops sell a variety of local goods with an emphasis on textiles and clothing.

OTOP HANDICRAFTS

(Th Suriyaphong; 8.30am-6pm) The showroom of this government-funded development initiative has everything from local snacks to silverware.

Peera HANDICRAFTS

(26 Th Suriyaphong; 8am-7pm) A short walk from Wat Phumin, this place offers high-quality local textiles, mostly comprised of women's skirts and blouses.

Nan Silver HANDICRAFTS

(430/1 Th Sumon Thevarat; 7.30am-6.30pm) This small but classy shop sells a huge variety of locally designed and produced silver items.

BUSES TO/FROM NAN

In addition to buses, there are also minivans to Ban Huay Kon (border with Laos; 100B, three hours, five departures from 5am to 9.30am) and Phrae (78B, two hours, half-hourly 5.30am to 6pm).

DESTINATION	FARE (B)	DURATION (HR)	FREQUENCY
Bangkok	400-801	10-11	frequent 8-10am & 7-7.30pm
Chiang Mai	242-451	6	frequent 7.30am-10.30pm
Chiang Rai	171	6	9am
Lampang	158-316	4	frequent 7.30am-10.30pm
Phayao	200	4	1.30pm
Phitsanulok	196	4	5 departures 7.45am-5.15pm
Phrae	98	2½	frequent 7.30am-10.30pm
Pua (for Doi Phu Kha National Park)	50	2	hourly 6am-6pm

GETTING TO LAOS: BAN HUAY KON TO MUANG NGEUN

Located 140km north of Nan, Ban Huay Kon is a sleepy village in the mountains near the Lao border. There's a border market on Saturday mornings, but most will come here because of the town's status as an international border crossing to Laos.

Getting to the Border

To Ban Huay Kon, there are five daily minivans originating in Phrae and stopping in Nan between 5am and 9.30am (100B, three hours). In the opposite direction, minivans bound for Nan (100B, three hours), Phrae (180B, five hours) and Den Chai (for the train; 200B) leave Ban Huay Kon at 9am, 10am, 11.45am, 12.45pm and 3pm.

At the Border

After passing the Thai immigration booth, foreigners can purchase a 30-day visa for Laos for US$30 to US$42, depending on nationality. There is an extra US$1 or 50B charge after 4pm and on weekends.

Onwards Travel

You can then proceed 2.5km to the Lao village of Muang Ngeun, where you could stay at the Phouxay Guesthouse; if you're heading onward, continue to the tiny Passenger Car Station beside the market, from where *sŏrng·tăa·ou* leave for Hongsa (40,000K, 1½ hours) between 2pm and 4pm.

Information

Tourist Centre (054 751169; Th Pha Kong; 8.30am-noon & 1-4.30pm) Opposite Wat Phumin, this helpful information centre is hidden behind vendors and coffee shops.

Getting There & Away

Nan's recently renovated Nan Nakhon Airport is located about 3km north of town. **Air Asia** (Nan 054 772635, nationwide 025 159999; www.airasia.com; Nan Nakhon Airport; 9am-5.30pm) and **Nok Air** (Nan 09 1119 9834, nationwide 1318; www.nokair.com; Nan Nakhon Airport; 8am-6pm) has flights to Bangkok's Don Muang International Airport (890B to 1200B, 1½ hours, six daily), while **Kan Air** (Nan 09 0907 1811, nationwide 02 551 6111; www.kanairlines.com; Nan Nakhon Airport; 8am-8.30pm) flies to/from Chiang Mai (1890B, 45 minutes, daily). **Klay Airport Taxi** (08 6188 0079; Nan Nakhon Airport) has airport transfers for about 100B per person.

From Nan, all buses, minivans and *sŏrng·tăa·ou* leave from the **bus station** (054 711662; Th Jao Fa) at the southwestern edge of town. A motorcycle taxi between the station and the centre of town costs 30B.

If you're connecting to the train station at Den Chai in Phrae, you can hop on any bus bound for Chiang Mai or Bangkok.

Getting Around

Săhm·lór around town cost 30B to 40B. Metered taxis can be hailed at **Nan Taxi** (08 4610 7777, 054 773555).

Motorcycles can be hired (from 200B) at **Oversea Shop** (054 710258; 488 Th Sumon Thewarat; 8.30am-5.30pm) and **Thana Sin Motors** (TS; 08 9953 0896; 1-7 Th Sumon Tevarat; 8am-5pm Mon-Sat), and at several guesthouses.

Around Nan

Wat Nong Bua วัดหนองบัว

Wat Nong Bua BUDDHIST TEMPLE

(dawn-dusk) FREE The neat and tidy Thai Lü village of Nong Bua, near the town of Tha Wang Pha, approximately 30km north of Nan, is famous for the Lü-style Wat Nong Bua. Featuring a typical two-tiered roof and carved wooden portico, the *wí·hăhn* design is simple yet striking – note the carved *naga* heads at the roof corners. Inside the *wí·hăhn* are rustic but beautiful *Jataka* murals thought to have been painted by Thit Buaphan, the same mural artist whose work can be seen at Wat Phumin. Donations left at the altar are for the temple's upkeep and restoration.

There is a model Thai Lü house directly behind the wát where weaving is done and you can buy attractive local textiles.

Nong Bua is about 30km north of Nan. To get there, take a northbound bus or *sŏrng·tăa·ou* (35B) to Tha Wang Pha. Get off at Samyaek Longbom, walk west to a bridge over Mae Nam Nan and turn left. Continue until you reach another small bridge, after which Wat Nong Bua will be on your right. It's a long 3km from the highway to the wát.

Doi Phu Kha National Park อุทยานแห่งชาติดอยภูคา

Doi Phu Kha National Park NATIONAL PARK
(☎08 2194 1349, accommodation 02 562 0760; www.dnp.go.th; admission 200B) This national park is centred on 2000m-high Doi Phu Kha, the province's highest peak, in Amphoe Pua and Amphoe Bo Kleua, about 75km northeast of Nan. There are several Htin, Mien, Hmong and Thai Lü villages in the park and vicinity, as well as a couple of caves and waterfalls, and endless opportunities for forest walks. The park headquarters has a basic map and staff can arrange a local guide for walks or more extended excursions around the area, plus rafting on Nam Wa. The park is often cold in the cool season and especially wet in the wet season.

The park offers a variety of **bungalows** (two to seven people 300B to 2000B), and there is a nearby restaurant and basic shop.

To reach the national park by public transport you must first take a bus or *sŏrng·tăa·ou* to Pua (50B, two hours, hourly from 7am to 5pm). Get off at the 7-Eleven then cross the highway to board one of the three daily *sŏrng·tăa·ou* (50B, 30 minutes) that depart at 7.30am, 9.30am and 11.30am.

Ban Bo Luang บ้านบ่อหลวง

Ban Bo Luang (also known as Ban Bo Kleua, or Salt Well Village) is a picturesque Htin village southeast of Doi Phu Kha National Park where the long-standing occupation has been the extraction of salt from local salt wells. It's easy to find the main community salt wells, which are more or less in the centre of the village.

If you have your own transport, the village is a good base for exploring the nearby national parks, Doi Phu Kha and **Khun Nan National Park** (อุทยานแหงชาติขุนนาน; ☎054 778140; adult/child 100/50B; ⏲8am-4.30pm). The latter is located a few kilometres north of Ban Bo Luang and has a 2km walk from the visitor centre that ends in a viewpoint looking over local villages and nearby Laos. Accommodation (bungalows 800B to 1600B) and a basic restaurant are available.

There is a handful of places to stay in Ban Bo Luang. By far the best of these is **Boklua View** (☎08 1809 6392; www.bokluaview.com; r & bungalows incl breakfast 1850B; ❄📶), an attractive and well-run hillside resort overlooking the village and the Nam Mang that runs through it. The resort has its own garden and serves good food (be sure to try Chef Toun's chicken deep-fried with northern Thai spices). If Boklua View is booked, a few simple 'resorts' and homestay-style accommodation are available around town.

A few small restaurants serve basic dishes in Ban Bo Luang; the best is probably **Hua Saphan** (no roman-script sign; mains 70-120B; ⏲9am-9pm), located at the foot of the bridge.

At the time of research, Bo Luang's only ATM did not accept foreign cards, so bring cash.

To reach Ban Bo Luang from Nan, take a bus to Pua (50B, two hours, hourly from 6am to 6pm). Get off at the 7-Eleven and cross the highway to take the *sŏrng·tăa·ou* that terminates in the village (80B, one hour, departing 7.30am, 9.30am and 11.30am). To Pua, *sŏrng·tăa·ou* leave from near Bo Luang's T-intersection at 9am, 10.30am and 12.30pm.

PHITSANULOK PROVINCE

Phitsanulok พิษณุโลก

POP 84,000

Phitsanulok sees relatively few independent travellers but a fair amount of package tourists, probably because the city is a convenient base from which to explore the attractions of historical Sukhothai, Si Satchanalai and Kamphaeng Phet. The frenetic and extremely friendly city also boasts some interesting sites and museums, chief of which is Wat Phra Si Ratana Mahathat, which contains one of the country's most revered Buddha images.

Those willing to forge their own path can also use the city as a base to visit the nearby national parks and wildlife sanctuaries of Thung Salaeng Luang (p252) and Phu Hin Rong Kla (p252), the former strategic headquarters of the Communist Party of Thailand.

Sights

★Wat Phra Si Ratana Mahathat BUDDHIST TEMPLE
(วัดพระศรีรัตนมหาธาตุ; Th Phutta Bucha; ⏲temple 6am-9pm, museum 9am-5.30pm Wed-Sun) FREE The main *wí·hăhn* at this temple, known by locals as Wat Yai, appears small from the outside, but houses the Phra Phuttha Chinnarat, one of Thailand's most revered and copied Buddha images. This famous bronze statue is probably second in importance

Phitsanulok

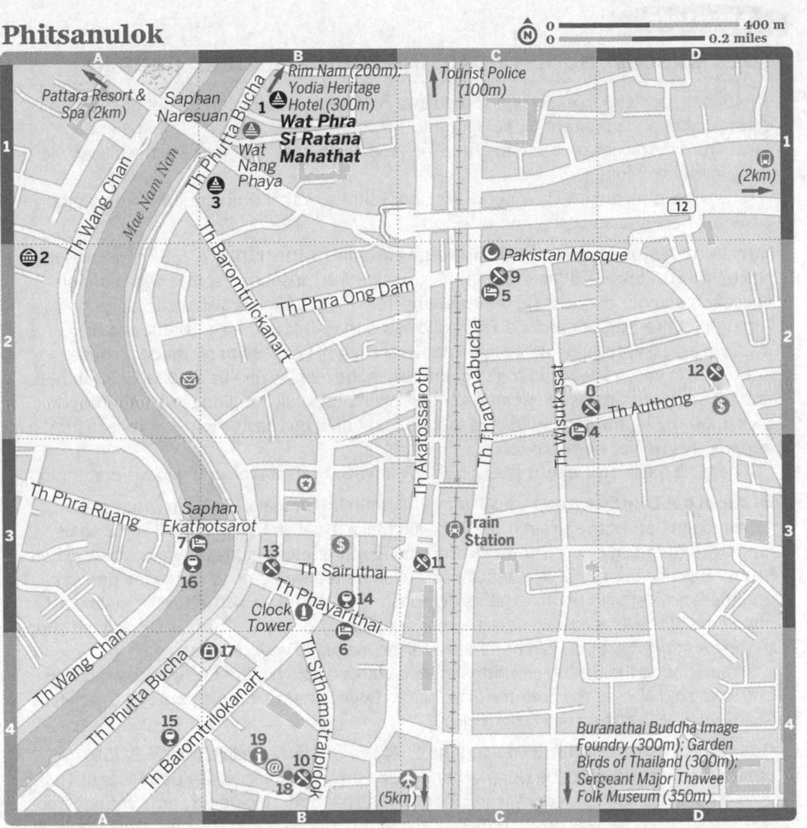

Phitsanulok

Top Sights

1 Wat Phra Si Ratana Mahathat B1

Sights

2 Museum of Phitsanulok A2
3 Wat Ratburana B1

Sleeping

4 Ayara Grand Palace C2
5 Golden Grand Hotel C2
6 Lithai Guest House B4
7 River Homestay A3

Eating

8 Ban Mai C2
9 Fah-Ke-Rah C2
10 Jaroen Rat B4
11 Night Market C3
12 Night Market D2
13 Paknang B3

Drinking & Nightlife

14 Amarin in Town B3
15 Camper A4
16 Shew Shew A3

Shopping

17 Night Bazaar B4

Information

18 Golden House Tour B4
19 Tourism Authority of Thailand B4

only to the Emerald Buddha in Bangkok's Wat Phra Kaew.

The story goes that construction of this wát was commissioned under the reign of King Li Thai in 1357. When it was completed, King Li Thai wanted it to contain three high-quality bronze images, so he sent for well-known sculptors from Si Satchanalai, Chiang Saen and Hariphunchai (Lamphun), as well as five Brahman priests. The first two

DON'T MISS

FOLK MUSEUM, BUDDHA-CASTING FOUNDRY & BIRD GARDEN

A nationally acclaimed expert on Thai folkways, former military cartographer, Buddha statue caster and apparent bird aficionado, Sergeant Major Thawee Buranakhet has taken from his diverse experiences and interests to create three very worthwhile attractions in Phitsanulok.

The museums are on Th Wisutkasat, about 1km south of Phitsanulok's train station; a túk-túk here should cost about 60B.

Sergeant Major Thawee Folk Museum (พิพิธภัณฑ์พื้นบ้านจ่าทวี; 26/38 Th Wisutkasat; adult/child 50/25B; ⏲8.30am-4.30pm) This fascinating museum displays a remarkable collection of tools, textiles and photographs from Phitsanulok Province. It's spread throughout five traditional-style Thai buildings with well-groomed gardens, and the displays are all accompanied by informative and legible English descriptions. Those interested in cooking will find much of interest in the display of a traditional Thai kitchen and the various traps used to catch game. Male visitors will feel twinges of empathetic pain upon seeing the display that describes traditional bull castration – a process that apparently involves no sharp tools.

There's a basic **aquarium** featuring fish native to Phitsanulok in the same compound.

Buranathai Buddha Image Foundry (โรงหล่อพระบูรณะไทย; 26/43 Th Wisutkasat; ⏲8am-5pm) Across the street from Sergeant Major Thawee Folk Museum and also belonging to Sergeant Major Thawee is the small Buranathai Buddha Image Foundry, where bronze Buddha images of all sizes are cast. Visitors are welcome to watch the process, and there are detailed photo exhibits demonstrating the lost-wax method of metal casting. Some of the larger images take a year or more to complete. There is a small gift shop at the foundry where you can purchase bronze images of various sizes.

In addition to the Buddha foundry, there is also a display of fighting cocks, which are bred and sold all over the country. (The official English name for this part of the facility is The Centre of Conservative Folk Cock.)

Garden Birds of Thailand (สวนนกไทย; 26/43 Th Wisutkasat; adult/child 50B/25B; ⏲8am-5pm) Attached to the Buranathai Buddha Image Foundry is Garden Birds of Thailand, a collection of cages containing indigenous Thai birds, including some endangered species such as the very pretty pink-chested jamu fruit-dove and the prehistoric-looking helmeted hornbill. Unfortunately, the cages are generally rather small and don't reflect the birds' natural environments.

castings worked well, but the third required three attempts before it was decreed the best of all. Legend has it that a white-robed sage appeared from nowhere to assist in the final casting, then disappeared. This last image was named the Chinnarat (Victorious King) Buddha and it became the centrepiece in the *wí·hăhn*. The other two images, Phra Chinnasi and Phra Si Satsada, were later moved to the royal temple of Wat Bowonniwet in Bangkok.

The image was cast in the late Sukhothai style, but what makes it strikingly unique is the flame-like halo around the head and torso that turns up at the bottom to become dragon-serpent heads on either side of the image. The head of this Buddha is a little wider than standard Sukhothai, giving the statue a very solid feel.

Another sanctuary to one side has been converted into a free **museum**, displaying antique Buddha images, ceramics and other historic artefacts.

Despite the holiness of the temple, endless loud broadcasts asking for donations, Thai musicians, a strip of vendors hawking everything from herbs to lottery tickets, several ATM machines and hundreds of visitors all contribute to a relentlessly hectic atmosphere. Come early (ideally before 7am) if you're looking for quiet contemplation or simply wish to take photos, and regardless of the time be sure to dress appropriately – no shorts or sleeveless tops.

Wat Ratburana BUDDHIST TEMPLE
(วัดราชบูรณะ; Th Phutta Bucha; ⏲dawn-dusk) FREE Across the street from Wat Phra Si Ratana Mahathat, Wat Ratburana draws

fewer visitors but in some ways is more interesting than its famous neighbour. In addition to a *wí·hăhn* with a 700-year-old gold Buddha, there's a *bòht* with beautiful murals thought to date back to the mid-19th century, and two wooden *hŏr đrai*.

The temple is also home to a few quirky attractions that offer a fascinating insight into the practices of Thai Buddhism. The most apparent of these is a large wooden boat decked with garlands that originally served to transport King Rama V on an official visit to Phitsanulok. Today the boat is thought to grant wishes to those who make an offering and crawl under its entire length three or nine times. Next to the *wí·hăhn* is a sacred tree with ladders on either side that visitors climb up, leave an offering, then ring a bell and descend, again repeating the action a total of three or nine times. And directly adjacent to the tree is an immense gong that, when rubbed the right way, creates a unique ringing sound.

Near each of these attractions you'll find somebody stationed who, in addition to selling the coins, incense and flowers used in offerings, will also instruct visitors in exactly how to conduct each particular ritual, including how many times to pass, what to offer and what prayer to say.

Museum of Phitsanulok MUSEUM
(พิพิธภัณฑ์เมืองพิษณุโลก; Pibulsongkram Rajabhat University, Th Wang Chan; ⌚8.30am-4.30pm) **FREE** A new but bare-bones museum with mostly text-based displays on local history and culture. Upstairs are additional displays on the five southernmost provinces of northern Thailand – Phetchabun, Phichit, Tak, Phitsanulok and Uttaradit – but virtually none of the information is in English.

Sleeping

Lithai Guest House HOTEL $
(☎055 219626; 73/1-5 Th Phayarithai; r incl breakfast 300-580B; ❄📶) The light-filled 60 or so rooms here don't have much character but they are clean. Air-con rooms include perks such as large private bathrooms with hot water, cable TV, fridge and breakfast.

River Homestay HOTEL $
(☎055 249226; off Th Wang Chan; r 550-650B; ❄📶) Reviving a type of accommodation once common in Phitsanulok, the six rooms here are located on a moored houseboat. Rooms are tight but attractive, with semi-open bathrooms and sharing an open TV area.

Ayara Grand Palace HOTEL $$
(☎055 909993; www.ayaragrandpalacehotel.com; Th Authong; r 1100-1200B, ste 1600-2800B, all incl breakfast; ❄@📶🏊) The '90s-era pastels, fake fireplaces and relentless flower theme of this hotel give it an undeniably cheesy feel. But it's all in good fun, and the vast suites – the most expensive of which is decked out with an electric massage chair – are pretty good value.

Golden Grand Hotel HOTEL $$
(☎055 210234; www.goldengrandhotel.com; 66 Th Thammabucha; r 690-850B, ste 2500B, all incl breakfast; ❄@📶) The mint green furniture, carpet and curtains date this 1970s-era business-class hotel. But rooms are spacious and clean, if slightly faded and musty, and an ongoing renovation will hopefully impart the suites with the colour schemes and furniture of the current era.

Pattara Resort & Spa HOTEL $$$
(☎055 282966; www.pattararesort.com; 349/40 Th Chaiyanupap; r 3800-4000B, villa 7500-9000B, all incl breakfast; ❄@📶🏊) This natural-feeling resort about 2km east of the centre of Phitsanulok has a lot going for it. Rooms feel vast and all have equally huge bathrooms with tubs, as well as wide balconies that look out over lotus ponds and a pool. Better yet, go for one of the two pool villas with private pool, or the two floating villas built over the lotus pond.

Yodia Heritage Hotel BOUTIQUE HOTEL $$$
(☎055 214677; www.yodiaheritage.com; 89/1 Th Phutta Bucha; r 3300-4500B, ste 8900B, all incl breakfast; ❄@📶🏊) Located along a quiet stretch of Mae Nam Nan is this boutique hotel, which boasts huge suites with large tubs, and a semi-private swimming pool.

Eating

Phitsanulok takes its cuisine seriously. The city is particularly obsessive about night markets, and there are no fewer than three dotted in various locations around town. The most touted, Phitsanulok's night bazaar (p250), focuses mainly on clothing, but the southernmost restaurant along the strip specialises in *pàk bûng loy fáh* (literally 'floating-in-the-sky morning glory vine'), in which the cook fires up a batch of the eponymous vegetable in a wok and then flings it through the air to a waiting server who catches it on a plate. If you're lucky, you'll be here when a tour group is trying to catch the flying vegetables, but is actually dropping *pàk bûng* all over the place.

A **night market** (Th Phra Ong Dam; mains 30-60B; ⏲5pm-midnight) lines either side of Th Phra Ong Dam north of Th Authong, and there's a very busy **night market** (off Th Akatossaroth; mains 30-60B; ⏲4-8pm) just south of the train station that features mostly takeaway items including *kôw nĕe·o hòr* (tiny banana-leaf parcels of sticky rice with various toppings). There are two vendors opposite each other near the Th Akatossaroth entrance to the market.

Another dish associated with Phitsanulok is *gŏoay·đĕe·o hôy kăh* (literally 'legs-hanging' noodles). The name comes from the way customers sit on the floor facing the river, with their legs dangling below.

Paknang CHINESE, THAI **$**
(Th Sairuthai; mains 40-280B; ⏲10am-10pm) This corner of old Phitsanulok has a distinctly old-world Chinese feel, an excellent pairing with the tasty Chinese-style dishes at this long-standing restaurant.

Fah-Ke-Rah THAI **$**
(786 Th Phra Ong Dam; mains 20-60B; ⏲7am-9pm) There are several Thai-Muslim cafes near the Pakistan Mosque on Th Phra Ong Dam, and this is probably the best of them. Thick *roh·đee* (crispy dough 'pancakes') is served up with rich curries, and fresh yoghurt is made daily.

Jaroen Rat VEGETARIAN, THAI **$**
(Th Sithamatraipidok, no roman-script sign; mains 15-40B; ⏲8am-3pm; 🖉) This simple place serves a choice of vegetarian dishes paired with husky brown rice. There are at least three other meat-free places along the same strip – look for the yellow banners.

Rim Nan THAI **$**
(5/4 Th Phutta Bucha, no roman-script sign; mains 20-35B; ⏲9am-4pm) Just north of Wat Phra Si Ratana Mahathat, Rim Nan is one of a few similar restaurants along Th Phutta Bucha that offer *gŏoay·đĕe·o hôy kăh* ('legs-hanging' noodles) and 'alternative' seating.

★**Ban Mai** THAI **$$**
(93/30 Th Authong, no roman-script sign; mains 100-290B; ⏲11am-10pm; ❄) Dinner at this local favourite is like a meal at your grandparents' place: opinionated conversation resounds, frumpy furniture abounds and an overfed cat appears to rule the dining room. The likewise homey dishes include *gaang pèt bèt yâhng* (grilled duck curry) and *yam đà krái* (herbal lemongrass salad). Look for the yellow compound across from the Ayara Grand Palace hotel.

Drinking & Nightlife

Amarin in Town BAR
(Th Phayarithai; ⏲6pm-midnight) With eight beers on tap and about 50 different bottles in the refrigerator, this is the place to come if you want to forget about Chang or Singha for a night.

Camper BAR
(Th Baromtrilokanart; ⏲7pm-midnight) An open-air, ramshackle convocation of falling-apart retro furniture, local hipsters, draught beer and live music, Camper is as loose and fun as it sounds.

Shew Shew BAR
(off Th Wang Chan; ⏲6pm-midnight) As the only remaining floating pub in Mae Nam Nan, Shew Shew is a dying breed. Snacks and more substantial Thai dishes are available.

Shopping

Night Bazaar MARKET
(Th Phutta Bucha; ⏲7pm-midnight) Distinctly more workday and less crafty than northern Thailand's other night markets, Phitsanulok's night bazaar is worth a visit if you need some cheap clothes or a foot massage.

Information

Several banks in town offer foreign-exchange services and ATMs. There are also several ATMs inside the Wat Phra Si Ratana Mahathat compound.

@net (off Th Baromtrilokanart; per hour 8B; ⏲24hr) Internet access.

Golden House Tour (☎055 259973; 55/37-38 Th Baromtrilokanart; ⏲7am-7pm Mon-Sat) This experienced travel agency can book airline tickets and arrange ground transport in and around Phitsanulok.

Tourism Authority of Thailand (TAT; ☎055 252742, nationwide 1672; tatphlok@tat.or.th; 209/7-8 Th Baromtrilokanart; ⏲8.30am-4.30pm) Off Th Baromtrilokanart, with helpful staff who hand out free maps of the town and a walking-tour sheet. This office also oversees the provinces of Sukhothai, Phichit and Phetchabun.

Tourist Police (☎1155; Th Akatossaroth)

Getting There & Away

Phitsanulok's **airport** (☎055 301002) is about 5km south of town; a taxi counter can arrange trips to/from town for 150B. **Air Asia**

TRANSPORT TO/FROM PHITSANULOK

Bus

DESTINATION	FARE (B)	DURATION (HR)	FREQUENCY
Bangkok	304-472	5-6	hourly 6.20am-11.30pm
Chiang Mai	232-237	6	frequent 5.40am-12.40pm
Chiang Rai	300	7-8	4 departures 8am-10.30am
Kamphaeng Phet	59-83	3	hourly 5am-6pm
Lampang	203	4	frequent 5.40am-12.40pm
Lom Sak (for Green Route)	68	1-2	5 departures 7am-5pm
Mae Sai	309-336	7	3 departures 5am-1pm
Mae Sot	242	4	1am & 2.30am
Nakhon Thai (for Phu Hin Rong Kla National Park)	52-73	2	hourly 5am-6pm
Nan	204	6	3 departures 7.30am-11.30am
Phayao	218-303	4	4 departures 8am-10.30am
Phrae	127	4	3 departures 6am-3.30pm
Sukhothai	57-94	1	frequent 7.20am-4.45pm
Sukhothai Historical Park	58	1½	4 departures 7.15am-12.40pm

Minivan

DESTINATION	FARE (B)	DURATION (HR)	FREQUENCY
Mae Sot	157	4	4 departures 8am-3pm
Phrae	147	4	7 departures 5am-6.30pm
Sukhothai	50	1	half-hourly 5am-6pm
Sukhothai Historical Park	70	1½	half-hourly 5am-6pm

Train

DESTINATION	FARE (B)	DURATION (HR)	FREQUENCY
Bangkok	69-1664	5-7	10 daily
Chiang Mai	65-1645	7-9	6 daily
Lampang	158-1042	5	5 daily

(☎Phitsanulok 09 4719 3645, nationwide 02 515 9999; www.airasia.com; Phitsanulok Airport; ⊙6am-6.30pm) and **Nok Air** (☎Phitsanulok 055 301051, nationwide 1318; www.nokair.co.th; Phitsanulok Airport; ⊙6am-9pm) have flights to/from Bangkok's Don Muang International Airport (690B to 1100B, 55 minutes, five daily), and **Kan Air** (☎Phitsanulok 08 6395 0718, nationwide 02 551 6111; www.kanairlines.com; Phitsanulok Airport; ⊙8am-5pm) to/from Chiang Mai (1990B, one hour, four weekly).

The city's **bus station** (☎055 212090; Rte 12) is 2km east of town on Hwy 12; túk-túk and motorcycle taxis to/from town cost 60B. Transport options out of Phitsanulok are good as it's a junction for several bus and minivan routes.

Phitsanulok's **train station** (☎Phitsanulok 055 258005, nationwide 1690; www.railway.co.th; Th Akatossaroth) is within walking distance of accommodation and offers a left-luggage service. The station is a significant train terminal and virtually every northbound and southbound train stops here.

Getting Around

Rides on the town's Darth Vader–like săhm·lór start at about 60B. Outside the train station there's a sign indicating prices for different destinations around town. Phitsanulok now also has a small fleet of **taxis** (☎055 338888).

Hire cars out of Phitsanulok's airport cost from around 1200B per day:

Avis (☎Phitsanulok 08 9969 8672, nationwide 02 251 1130; www.avisthailand.com; ⌚7am-9pm)

Budget (☎Phitsanulok 018 208644, nationwide 02 203 9222; www.budget.co.th; ⌚7am-6pm)

Sixt (☎Phitsanulok 055 301044, nationwide 1789; www.sixtthailand.com; ⌚7am-10pm)

Thai Rent A Car (☎Phitsanulok 055 301058, nationwide 02 737 8888; www.thairentacar.com; ⌚7am-8.30pm)

Phu Hin Rong Kla ภูหินร่องกล้า

Between 1967 and 1982, the mountain that is known as Phu Hin Rong Kla served as the strategic headquarters for the Communist Party of Thailand (CPT) and its tactical arm, the People's Liberation Army of Thailand (PLAT). The remote, easily defended summit was perfect for an insurgent army. China's Yunnan Province is only 300km away and

OFF THE BEATEN TRACK

THE GREEN ROUTE

Route 12, which runs along the scenic, rapid-studded Lam Nam Khek between Phitsanulok and Lom Sak, is known as the Green Route. Off this road are waterfalls, resorts and the Phu Hin Rong Kla and Thung Salaeng Luang National Parks.

The Phitsanulok TAT office distributes a good map of the attractions along this 130km stretch of road. You may want to bypass the first two waterfalls, **Nam Tok Sakhunothayan** (at the Km 33 marker) and **Kaeng Song** (at the Km 45 marker), which on weekends can be overwhelmed with visitors. The third, **Kaeng Sopha** (at the Km 72 marker), is a larger area of small falls and rapids where you can walk from rock formation to rock formation – there are more or fewer rocks depending on rainfall. When there's enough water (typically from September to November) any of the resorts along this section can organise **white-water rafting** trips on Lam Nam Khek.

Further east along the road is the 1262-sq-km **Thung Salaeng Luang National Park** (☎055 268019, accommodation 02 562 0760; www.dnp.go.th; admission 300-500B; ⌚8am-5pm), one of Thailand's largest and most important wildlife sanctuaries. The entrance is at the Km 80 marker, where the park headquarters has information on walks and accommodation.

If you have your own wheels, you can turn south at the Km 100 marker onto Rte 2196 and head for **Khao Kho** (Khow Khor), another mountain lair used by the Communist Party of Thailand (CPT) during the 1970s.

If you've made the side trip to Khao Kho you can choose either to return to the Phitsanulok–Lom Sak highway, or take Rte 2258, off Rte 2196, until it terminates at Rte 203. On Rte 203 you can continue north to Lom Sak or south to Phetchabun.

Resort-style accommodation can be found along most of the Green Route, with budget accommodation clumping near Kaeng Song, around Km 45, and at the various **national parks** (☎02 562 0760; www.dnp.go.th; tent sites 30B, 2-8 person tents 150-600B, bungalows 300-5000B). Several restaurants are located on the banks of Nam Khek, most taking full advantage of the views and breezes.

Buses between Phitsanulok and Lom Sak cost 68B, and run from 7am to 5pm. For more freedom it's best to do this route with your own wheels; cars can be hired via several companies at Phitsanulok's airport.

it was here that CPT cadres received their training in revolutionary tactics. (This was until the 1979 split between the Chinese and Vietnamese communists, when the CPT sided with Vietnam.)

For nearly 20 years the area around Phu Hin Rong Kla served as a battlefield for Thai troops and the communists. In 1972 the Thai government launched an unsuccessful major offensive against the PLAT. The CPT camp at Phu Hin Rong Kla became especially active after the Thai military killed hundreds of students in Bangkok during the October 1976 student-worker uprising. Many students subsequently fled here to join the CPT, setting up a hospital and a school of political and military tactics.

By 1978 the PLAT ranks here had swelled to 4000. In 1980 and 1981 the Thai armed forces tried again and were able to recapture some parts of CPT territory. But the decisive blow to the CPT came in 1982, when the government declared an amnesty for all the students who had joined the communists after 1976. The departure of most of the students broke the spine of the movement, which had become dependent on their membership. A final military push in late 1982 resulted in the surrender of the PLAT, and Phu Hin Rong Kla was declared a national park in 1984.

Sights & Activities

Phu Hin Rong Kla National Park NATURE RESERVE
(อุทยานแหงชาติภูหินรองกลา; ☎055 233527; www.dnp.go.th; admission 500B; ⏲8.30am-5pm) The park covers about 307 sq km of rugged mountains and forest, much of it covered by rocks and wildflowers. The elevation at park headquarters is about 1000m, so the area is refreshingly cool even in the hot season. The main attractions don't tend to stray too far from the main road through the park and include the remains of the CPT stronghold – a rustic meeting hall, the school of political and military tactics – and the CPT administration building. Across the road from the school is a waterwheel designed by exiled engineering students.

Phu Hin Rong Kla can become quite crowded on weekends and holidays; for a more peaceful visit schedule for midweek.

If you're not interested in the modern history of Phu Hin Rong Kla, there are waterfalls, hiking trails and scenic views, as well as some interesting rock formations – jutting boulders called Lan Hin Pum and an area of deep rocky crevices where PLAT troops would hide during air raids, called Lan Hin Taek. Ask at the visitor centre for maps.

Pha Chu Thong HISTORIC SITE
(Flag Raising Cliff) A 1km trail leads to Pha Chu Thong (sometimes called Red Flag Cliff), where the communists would raise the red flag to announce a military victory. Also in this area is an air-raid shelter, a lookout and the remains of the main CPT headquarters – the most inaccessible point in the territory before a road was constructed by the Thai government.

The buildings in the park are made out of wood and bamboo and have no plumbing or electricity – a testament to how primitive the living conditions were.

There is a small **museum** at the park headquarters that displays relics from CPT days, although there's not a whole lot of English explanation. At the end of the road into the park is a small White Hmong village.

Sleeping & Eating

The Golden House Tour (p250) travel agency, near the TAT office in Phitsanulok, can help book accommodation.

Thailand's Royal Forest Department CAMPGROUND $
(☎02 562 0760; www.dnp.go.th; 2-8 person tents 150-600B, bungalows 800-2400B) Bungalows for three to 15 people, in three different zones of the park, must be booked in advance via this organisation. You can also pitch a tent or rent one, and rent sleeping bags (60B). There are restaurants and food vendors located near the camping ground and bungalows.

Getting There & Away

The park headquarters is about 125km from Phitsanulok. To get here, first take an early bus to Nakhon Thai (57B to 73B, two hours, hourly from 5am to 6pm). From there, near the market, you can charter a *sŏrng·tăa·ou* to the park (700B). As a day trip from Phitsanulok, Golden House Tour (p250) charges 2500B for car and driver; petrol is extra. This is a delightful trip if you're on a motorcycle since there's not much traffic along the way, but a strong engine is necessary to conquer the hills to Phu Hin Rong Kla.

SUKHOTHAI PROVINCE

Sukhothai สุโขทัย

POP 37,000

The Sukhothai (Rising of Happiness) kingdom flourished from the mid-13th century to the late 14th century. This period is often viewed as the golden age of Thai civilisation, and the religious art and architecture of the era are considered to be the most classic of Thai styles. The remains of the kingdom, today known as *meu·ang gòw* (old city), feature around 45 sq km of partially rebuilt ruins, which are one of the most visited ancient sites in Thailand.

Located 12km east of the historical park on Mae Nam Yom, the market town of New Sukhothai is not particularly interesting. Yet its friendly and relaxed atmosphere, good transport links and excellent-value accommodation make it a pleasant base from which to explore the old city ruins.

History

Sukhothai is typically regarded as the first capital of Siam, although this is not entirely accurate. The area was previously the site of a Khmer empire until 1238, when two Thai rulers, Pho Khun Pha Muang and Pho Khun Bang Klang Hao, decided to unite and form a new Thai kingdom.

Sukhothai's dynasty lasted 200 years and spanned nine kings. The most famous was King Ramkhamhaeng, who reigned from 1275 to 1317 and is credited with developing the first Thai script – his inscriptions are also considered the first Thai literature. Ramkhamhaeng eventually expanded his kingdom to include an area even larger than that of present-day Thailand. But a few kings later in 1438, Sukhothai was absorbed by Ayuthaya.

> **THE FIRST KINGDOM?**
>
> The establishment of Sukhothai in 1238 is often described as the formation of the first Thai kingdom. But the kingdom of Chiang Saen had already been established 500 years earlier, and at the time of Sukhothai's founding, other Thai kingdoms such as Lanna and Phayao also existed. Sukhothai's profound influence on the art, language, literature and religion of modern Thai society, not to mention the immense size of the kingdom at its peak in the early 13th century, are doubtlessly reasons for the proliferation of this convenient, but technically incorrect, historical fact.

Sights

Sukhothai Historical Park HISTORIC SITE

(อุทยานประวัติศาสตร์สุโขทัย; Map p255; ☎055 697527) The Sukhothai Historical Park ruins are one of Thailand's most impressive World Heritage sites. The park includes the remains of 21 historical sites and four large ponds within the old walls, with an additional 70 sites within a 5km radius. The ruins are divided into five zones, the central, northern and eastern of which each has a separate 100B admission fee.

The architecture of Sukhothai temples is most typified by the classic lotus-bud *chedi,* featuring a conical spire topping a square-sided structure on a three-tiered base. Some sites exhibit other rich architectural forms introduced and modified during the period, such as bell-shaped Sinhalese and double-tiered Srivijaya *chedi*.

Despite the popularity of the park, it's quite expansive and solitary exploration is usually possible. Some of the most impressive ruins are outside the city walls, so a bicycle or motorcycle is essential to fully appreciate everything.

Central Zone

This is the historical park's **main zone** (admission 100B, plus per bicycle/motorcycle/car 10/20/50B; ⏰6.30am-7pm Sun-Fri, to 9pm Sat) and home to arguably some of the park's most impressive ruins. An audio guide (150B), available in English, Japanese or Thai, can be rented at the ticket booth. On Saturday night much of the central zone is illuminated and remains open until 9pm.

Wat Mahathat BUDDHIST TEMPLE

(วัดมหาธาตุ; Map p255) Completed in the 13th century, the largest wát in Sukhothai is surrounded by brick walls (206m long and 200m wide) and a moat that is believed to represent the outer wall of the universe and the cosmic ocean.

The *chedi* spires feature the famous lotus-bud motif, and some of the original stately Buddha figures still sit among the ruined columns of the old *wí·hăhn*. There are 198 *chedi* within the monastery walls – a lot to

Sukhothai Historical Park

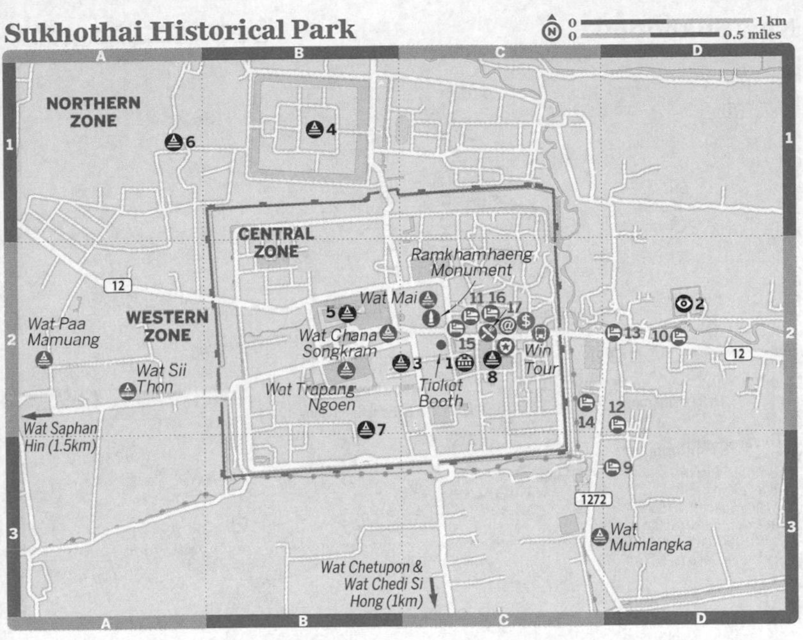

Sukhothai Historical Park

Sights

1 Ramkhamhaeng National Museum.......... C2
2 Wat Chang Lom.......... D2
3 Wat Mahathat.......... C2
4 Wat Phra Phai Luang.......... B1
5 Wat Sa Si.......... B2
6 Wat Si Chum.......... A1
7 Wat Si Sawai.......... B2
8 Wat Trapang Thong.......... C2

Sleeping

9 Le Charme Sukhothai.......... D3
10 Legendha.......... D2
11 Old City Guest House.......... C2
12 Orchid Hibiscus Guest House.......... D2
13 PinPao Guest House.......... D2
14 Tharaburi Resort.......... C2
15 Vitoon Guesthouse.......... C2
16 Wake Up @ Muang Kao.......... C2

Eating

17 Coffee Cup.......... C2

explore in what is believed to be the former spiritual and administrative centre of the old capital.

Ramkhamhaeng National Museum MUSEUM
(พิพิธภัณฑสถานแหงชาติรามคําแหง; Map p255; admission 150B; 9am-4pm) A good starting point for exploring the historical park ruins is this museum. A replica of the famous Ramkhamhaeng inscription, said to be the earliest example of Thai writing, is kept here among an impressive collection of Sukhothai artefacts. Admission to the museum is not included in the ticket to the central zone.

Wat Si Sawai BUDDHIST TEMPLE
(วัดศรีสวาย; Map p255) Just south of Wat Mahathat, this Buddhist shrine (dating from the 12th and 13th centuries) features three Khmer-style towers and a picturesque moat. It was originally built by the Khmers as a Hindu temple.

Wat Sa Si BUDDHIST TEMPLE
(วัดสระศรี, Sacred Pond Monastery; Map p255) Wat Sa Si sits on an island west of the bronze monument of King Ramkhamhaeng (the third Sukhothai king). It's a simple, classic Sukhothai-style wát containing a large Buddha, one *chedi* and the columns of the ruined *wí·hăhn*.

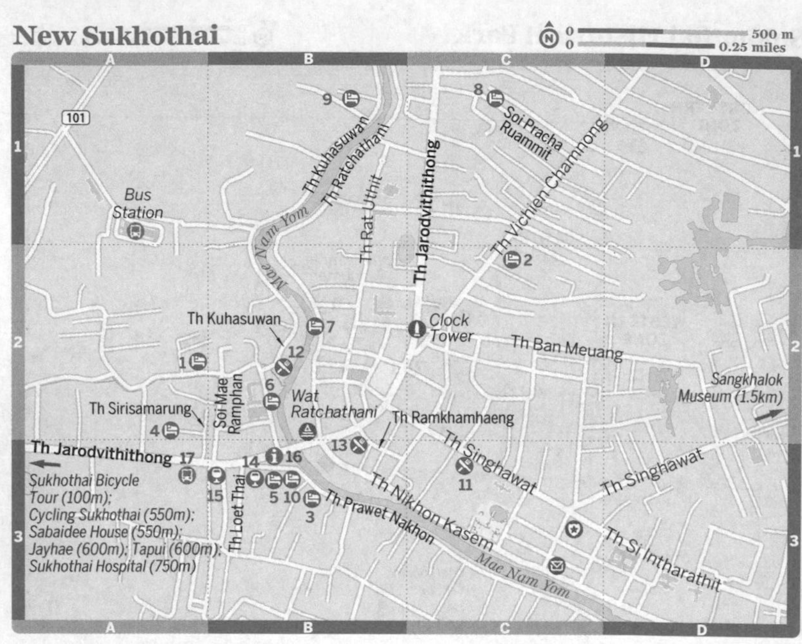

New Sukhothai

Sleeping

1 4T Guesthouse A2
2 At Home Sukhothai C2
3 Ban Thai B3
4 Blue House A2
5 Foresto B3
6 J&J Guest House B2
7 Lotus Village B2
8 Ruean Thai Hotel C1
9 Sila Resort B1
10 TR Room & Bungalow B3

Eating

11 Dream Café C3
12 Fueang Fah B2
13 Night Market B3

Drinking & Nightlife

14 Chopper Bar B3
15 Poo Restaurant B3

Information

Kasikorn Bank .... (see 16)
16 Tourism Authority of Thailand B3

Transport

17 Sŏrng·tăa·ou to Sukhothai Historical Park A3

Wat Trapang Thong BUDDHIST TEMPLE

(วัดตระพังทอง; Map p255) Next to the Ramkhamhaeng National Museum, this small, still-inhabited wát with fine stucco reliefs is reached by a footbridge across the large lotus-filled pond that surrounds it. This reservoir, the original site of Thailand's Loi Krathong festival, supplies the Sukhothai community with most of its water.

Northern Zone

The **northern zone** (admission 100B, plus per bicycle/motorcycle/car 10/20/50B; ⌚6.30am-5.30pm), 500m north of the old city walls, is easily reached by bicycle.

Wat Si Chum BUDDHIST TEMPLE

(วัดศรีชุม; Map p255) This wát is northwest of the old city and contains an impressive *mon·dòp* with a 15m, brick-and-stucco seated Buddha. This Buddha's elegant, tapered fingers are much photographed. Archaeologists theorise that this image is the 'Phra Atchana' mentioned in the famous Ramkhamhaeng inscription. A passage in the *mon·dòp* wall that leads to the top has been blocked so that it's no longer possible to view the *Jataka* inscriptions that line the tunnel ceiling.

Wat Phra Phai Luang BUDDHIST TEMPLE
(วัดพระพายหลวง; Map p255) This somewhat isolated wát features three 12th-century Khmer-style towers, bigger than those at Wat Si Sawai in the Central Zone. This may have been the centre of Sukhothai when it was ruled by the Khmers of Angkor prior to the 13th century.

Western Zone

The **western zone** (admission 100B, plus per bicycle/motorcycle/car 10/20/50B; ⏲8am-4.30pm), at its furthest extent 2km west of the old city walls, is the most expansive. In addition to Wat Saphan Hin, several mostly featureless ruins can be found. A bicycle or motorcycle is necessary to explore this zone.

Wat Saphan Hin BUDDHIST TEMPLE
(วัดสะพานหิน) Located on the crest of a hill that rises about 200m above the plain, the name of the wát, which means 'stone bridge', is a reference to the slate path and staircase that leads up to the temple, which are still in place.

All that remains of the original temple are a few *chedi* and the ruined *wí·hăhn*, consisting of two rows of laterite columns flanking a 12.5m-high standing Buddha image on a brick terrace. The site is 3km west of the former city wall and gives a good view of the Sukhothai ruins to the southeast and the mountains to the north and south.

Other Sites

A few worthwhile destinations lie outside the more popular paid zones.

Sangkhalok Museum MUSEUM
(พิพิธภัณฑสังคโลก; Rte 1293; adult/child 100/50B; ⏲8am-5pm) This small but comprehensive museum is an excellent introduction to ancient Sukhothai's most famous product and export, its ceramics.

The ground floor displays an impressive collection of original Thai pottery found in the area, plus some pieces traded from Vietnam, Myanmar and China. The 2nd floor features examples of non-utilitarian pottery made as art, including some beautiful and rare ceramic Buddha statues.

The museum is about 2.5km east of the centre of New Sukhothai; a túk-túk here will run about 100B.

Wat Chang Lom HISTORIC SITE
(วัดช้างล้อม; Map p255; off Rte 12) FREE Off Rte 12 in the eastern zone, Wat Chang Lom (Elephant Circled Monastery) is about 1km east of the main park entrance. A large bell-shaped *chedi* is supported by 36 elephants sculpted into its base.

Wat Chetupon HISTORIC SITE
(วัดเชตุพน) FREE Located 1.4km south of the old city walls, this temple once held a four-sided *mon·dòp* featuring the four classic poses of the Buddha (sitting, reclining, standing and walking). The graceful lines of the walking Buddha can still be made out today.

Wat Chedi Si Hong HISTORIC SITE
(วัดเจดีย์สี่ห้อง) FREE Directly across from Wat Chetupon, the main *chedi* here has retained much of its original stucco relief work, which shows still vivid depictions of elephants, lions and humans.

Activities

Cycling Sukhothai BICYCLE TOUR
(☎055 612519, 08 5083 1864; www.cycling-sukhothai.com; off Th Jarodvithithong; half-day 750B, full day 950-990B, sunset tour 400B) A resident of Sukhothai for nearly 20 years, Belgian cycling enthusiast Ronny Hanquart's rides follow themed itineraries such as the Historical

OFF THE BEATEN TRACK

BAN NA TON CHAN HOMESTAY

Homestay Program (☎08 9885 1639; www.homestaynatonchan.blogspot.com; per person incl breakfast & lunch 500B) The residents of Ban Na Ton Chan, a picturesque village in rural Sukhothai, have formed a worthwhile and award-winning homestay program. Approximately 20 households are involved, and the fee includes breakfast and dinner (for lunch you can try *kôw Ђóep*, a local noodle dish), and involvement in daily activities such as cooking, furniture-making and weaving.

The locals are keen to open their homes and share their knowledge, but it must be noted that the level of English ability among the villagers is low.

The village is 15km east of Rte 101, down a signed turn-off north of Ban Hat Siaw. A motorcycle taxi from Ban Hat Siaw will take people here for 150B.

Park Tour, which also includes stops at lesser-seen wát and villages. Its office is based about 1.2km west of Mae Nam Yom, in New Sukhothai; free transport can be arranged.

Sukhothai Bicycle Tour BICYCLE TOUR
(☎08 6931 6242; www.sukhothaibicycletour.com; 34/1 Th Jarodvithithong; half-day 750B, full day 1050-1150B) A bicycle-based tour outfit that gets overwhelmingly positive feedback.

Festivals & Events

Loi Krathong CULTURAL
Sukhothai Historical Park is one of the most popular destinations to celebrate this holiday. In addition to the magical floating lights, there are fireworks, folk-dance performances and a light-and-sound production. Held over five days in November.

Sleeping

Most accommodation is in New Sukhothai, which is home to some of the best-value budget accommodation in northern Thailand. Clean, cheerful hotels and guesthouses abound, with many places offering attractive bungalows, free pick-up from the bus station and free use of bicycles. There are an increasing number of options near the park, many of them in the upscale bracket. Prices tend to go up during the Loi Krathong festival.

New Sukhothai

TR Room & Bungalow GUESTHOUSE $
(Map p256; ☎055 611663; www.sukhothaibudget-guesthouse.com; 27/5 Th Prawet Nakhon; r 300-450B, bungalows 600B; ❄@📶) The rooms here are basic and lack character, but figure among the tidiest we've encountered in northern Thailand. For those needing a bit more legroom, there are five wooden bungalows out back.

Ban Thai HOTEL $
(Map p256; ☎055 610163; banthai_guesthouse@yahoo.com; 38 Th Prawet Nakhon; r 200-500B, bungalows 350-550B; ❄📶) None of the rooms here are particularly remarkable, but the convergence of a friendly atmosphere, an attractive garden setting and low prices culminate in a winner.

Sabaidee House HOTEL $
(☎055 616303; www.sabaideehouse.com; 81/7 Th Jarodvithithong; r 200-600B; ❄📶) This cheery guesthouse in a semi-rural setting has seven attractive bungalows and four rooms in the main structure. It's off Th Jarot Withithong about 200m before the intersection with Rte 101; look for the sign.

4T Guesthouse HOTEL $
(Map p256; ☎055 614679; fourthouse@yahoo.com; 122 Soi Mae Ramphan; r 300-400B, bungalows 600-800B; ❄📶🏊) Hardly a leaf is out of place at this expansive budget resort. There's a smorgasbord of bungalows and spacious rooms to consider, and the swimming pool makes the decision even easier.

Lotus Village HOTEL $$
(Map p256; ☎055 621484; www.lotus-village.com; 170 Th Ratchathani; r 900-1500B, bungalows 1300-2900B, all incl breakfast; ❄@📶) Village is an apt label for this peaceful compound of wooden bungalows elevated over lotus ponds. Smaller, mostly fan-cooled rooms in a wooden building are also available, and an attractive Burmese-Indian design theme runs through the entire place. Both the breakfast and staff here get great reports, and an on-site spa offers a variety of services.

At Home Sukhothai GUESTHOUSE $$
(Map p256; ☎055 610172; www.athomesukhothai.com; 184/1 Th Vichien Chamnong; r 450-900B, bungalows 900B, all incl breakfast; ❄@📶) Located in the 50-year-old childhood home of the proprietor, the simple but comfortable rooms here – both those fan-cooled in the original structure and the newer air-con ones – really do feel like home. A new addition sees four bungalows overlooking a pond. The only downside is the relative distance from 'downtown' Sukhothai.

Sila Resort HOTEL $$
(Map p256; ☎055 620344; 3/49 Th Kuhasuwan; r 230-500B, bungalows 750-1200B; ❄@📶) We couldn't help but think of Disneyland when we first encountered this compound of flowering trees, a gingerbread Thai villa, wood bungalows, statues, resort-like A-frames and a restaurant. And like Disneyland, it comes together in a cheerful, colourful package looked after by smiling people. The only downside is that it's a fair hike from the centre of New Sukhothai.

J&J Guest House GUESTHOUSE $$
(Map p256; ☎055 620095; 12 Th Kuhasuwan; bungalows 600-700B; ❄📶) Located in a manicured garden by the river, the eight bungalows here are attractive, cool and relatively spacious. They're identical, and price depends on whether you go with fan or air-con.

WORTH A TRIP

FARMER FOR A DAY

Organic Agriculture Project (☎055 647290; half-day incl lunch 900B; ⏰8am-5pm Thu-Tue) Sukhothai's Organic Agriculture Project allows visitors to take part in traditional Thai farm activities.

Taking place at Sukhothai Airport's organic farm, the half-day begins by donning the outfit of a Thai rice farmer and riding an *ee đăan* (a traditional utility vehicle) to gather duck eggs. This is followed by riding a buffalo, checking into an orchid farm, witnessing the stages of rice production and, ultimately, planting or gathering rice. The session ends with an informal cooking lesson and meal using organic produce from the farm.

Up to this point, the project has primarily hosted Thai visitors, and non-Thai speakers will most likely need to bring or hire a translator. This can be arranged via the concierge at the nearby Sukhothai Heritage Resort (p264).

The compound is also home to a **restaurant** (mains 50-120B; ⏰8am-5pm Thu-Tue) serving dishes made from the farm's organic produce.

The project is located on the same road as Sukhothai's airport, 27km from New Sukhothai off Rte 1195, and is not accessible by public transport. If you don't have your own wheels, you can arrange a ride with the Sukhothai Airport's minivan service (p262).

Foresto HOTEL $$
(Map p256; ☎08 3213 4112; www.forestosukhothai.com; 16/1-3 Th Prawet Nakhon; r 800-1500B; ❄@📶) In a semi-secluded, green area off the main guesthouse drag is this union of 12 spacious, stylish rooms. More rooms were being planned at the time of research.

Blue House HOTEL $$
(Map p256; ☎055 64863; www.sukhothaibluehouse.wordpress.com; off Th Sirisamarung; r 600-800B; ❄@📶) A big villa with 18 rooms, all equipped with en suite bathrooms, air-con, TV, refrigerator and hot-water showers. If you don't need such creature comforts, consider the linked Green House, where fan-cooled rooms with shared bathroom run from 100B to 300B.

★**Ruean Thai Hotel** HOTEL $$$
(Map p256; ☎055 612444; www.rueanthaihotel.com; 181/20 Soi Pracha Ruammit; r incl breakfast 1480-4200B; ❄@📶🏊) At first glance, you may mistake this eye-catching complex for a Buddhist temple or a traditional Thai house. The rooms on the upper level follow a distinct Thai theme, while the poolside rooms are slightly more modern, and there's a concrete building with simple air-con rooms out the back. Service is both friendly and flawless, and the whole place boasts a resort-like feel. Call for free pick-up from the bus station.

Sukhothai Historical Park

Vitoon Guesthouse GUESTHOUSE $
(Map p255; ☎055 697045; 49 Rte 12; r 300-900B; ❄📶) The better of the two budget options within walking distance of the old city, the fan rooms here are starkly bare, but the air-con rooms, in a newer building, are spotless and represent a good deal.

Old City Guest House GUESTHOUSE $
(Map p255; ☎055 697515; 28/7 Rte 12; r 200-900B; ❄📶) This vast budget complex features heaps of rooms in a variety of styles and states, most with air-con and TV; ask to see a few before you make a decision.

Orchid Hibiscus Guest House HOTEL $$
(Map p255; ☎055 633284; www.orchidhibiscus-guesthouse.com; 407/2 Rte 1272; r/bungalows 900/1300B; ❄📶🏊) This collection of rooms and bungalows is set in relaxing, manicured grounds with a swimming pool as a centrepiece and the self-professed 'amazing breakfast' (100B) as a highlight. Rooms are spotless and fun, featuring colourful design details and accents. It's on Rte 1272 about 500m off Rte 12 – the turn-off is between the Km 48 and Km 49 markers.

Wake Up @ Muang Kao GUESTHOUSE $$
(Map p255; ☎055 697153; www.facebook.com/WakeUpAtMuangKaoBoutiqueHotel; 1/1 Rte 12; r incl breakfast 1100-1500B; ❄@📶) If there's a homestay equivalent to flashpacker, Wake Up has nailed it. The five rooms here are spacious and tasteful, come decked out with local touches and are looked after by a friendly local couple. A breath of fresh air in Old Sukhothai.

PinPao Guest House HOTEL $$
(Map p255; ☎055 633284; www.pinpaoguesthouse.com; Rte 12; r 900B; ❄@📶🏊) PinPao is home to 10 of the most gaily coloured

WORTH A TRIP

BOON LOTT'S ELEPHANT SANCTUARY

Boon Lott's Elephant Sanctuary (www.blesele.org; per person per night incl meals & transfers 5000B) Located 8km from the village of Baan Tuek in Sukhothai Province, this brilliant elephant sanctuary allows guests to observe rescued and retired working pachyderms interact in their natural environment. It welcomes overnight and multi-day visitors, with guests involved in all aspects of sanctuary life, from walking elephants to grazing grounds, to planting vegetation. Three teak guesthouses each sleep two people; book ahead.

rooms we've seen anywhere, although many lack windows and can be rather dark. The inviting pool and sunbathing area go quite a distance in making up for this. It's on Rte 12, directly opposite the turn-off to Rte 1272.

Tharaburi Resort HOTEL $$$
(Map p255; ☎055 697132; www.tharaburiresort.com; 321/3 Rte 1272; dm 600B, r incl breakfast 1500-4200B, ste incl breakfast 5000-6000B; ❄@📶🏊) This sumptuous-feeling place features three traditional-feeling structures divided into 13 rooms, suites and even a few dorms. Rooms are themed (Moroccan, Japanese, Chinese), using faux antiques and silks, while the suites feel like a small home. A stylish, if somewhat overpriced, choice.

Le Charme Sukhothai HOTEL $$$
(Map p255; ☎055 633333; www.lecharmesukhothai.com; 9/9 Rte 1272; r & bungalows 2500-4500B; ❄📶🏊) It may not look like much from a distance, but a closer look reveals an inviting cluster of bright bungalows linked by an elevated wooden walkway, lush gardens and lotus ponds. Rooms are large and simply but tastefully decorated, with inviting balconies looking out over all that water.

Legendha HOTEL $$$
(Map p255; ☎055 697215; www.legendhasukhothai.com; Rte 12; r 1600-4400B, villa 7500B, all incl breakfast; ❄@📶🏊) Water, greenery and traditional structures come together at this lauded resort, culminating in the feel of a northern Thai village. Service-minded staff, a pool and a location relatively close to the historical park are other perks.

Eating & Drinking

New Sukhothai

Sukhothai's signature dish is *gŏo·ay đĕe·o sù·kŏh·tai* (Sukhothai-style noodles), which features a slightly sweet broth with different preparations of pork, ground peanuts and thinly sliced green beans.

Jayhae THAI $
(Th Jarodvithithong; mains 30-50B; ⏲8am-4pm) You haven't been to Sukhothai if you haven't tried the noodles at Jayhae, an extremely popular restaurant that also serves *pàt tai* and tasty coffee drinks.

Tapui THAI $
(Th Jarodvithithong, no roman-script sign; mains 30-50B; ⏲7am-3pm) Consisting of a brick floor with a tin roof over it, Tapui claims to be the first shop in Sukhothai to have sold the city's namesake dish, *gŏo·ay đĕe·o sù·kŏh·tai*. Located about 1.3km west of Mae Nam Yom.

Fueang Fah THAI $
(Map p256; 107/2 Th Khuhasuwan, no roman-script sign; mains 50-350B; ⏲10am-10pm) Pretend you're a local in the know and take a meal at this long-standing riverside restaurant. The speciality is freshwater fish dishes, such as the tasty fried fish, the first item on the barely comprehensible English-language menu. It's just after the bridge on Th Khuhasuwan.

Night Market MARKET $
(Map p256; Th Ramkhamhaeng; mains 30-60B; ⏲6-11pm) A wise choice for cheap eats is New Sukhothai's tiny night market. Most vendors here are accustomed to accommodating foreigners and even provide bilingual menus.

Dream Café THAI $$
(Map p256; 86/1 Th Singhawat; mains 80-350B; ⏲5-11pm; ❄🍷) A meal at Dream Café is like dining in an antique shop. Eclectic but tasteful furnishings and knick-knackery abound, staff are equal parts competent and friendly, and, most importantly of all, the food is good. Try one of the well-executed *yam* (Thai-style 'salads'), or one of the dishes that feature freshwater fish, a local speciality.

Chopper Bar BAR
(Map p256; Th Prawet Nakhon; ⏲10am-12.30am; 📶) Both travellers and locals congregate at this restaurant-bar from morning till hangover for food (mains 30B to 150B), drinks and live music. Take advantage of Sukhothai's cool evenings on the rooftop terrace.

Poo Restaurant BAR
(Map p256; 24/3 Th Jarodvithithong; 11am-midnight;) Unfortunately named and deceptively simple, Poo has a small selection of Belgian beers.

Sukhothai Historical Park

Along the road that leads to the historical park is a string of food stalls and simple tourist-oriented restaurants.

Coffee Cup INTERNATIONAL, THAI $
(Map p255; Rte 12; mains 30-150B; 8am-10pm;) The better of the strip of backpacker restaurants near the historical park

Information

There are banks with ATMs scattered all around the central part of New Sukhothai, particularly in the area west of Mae Nam Yom, and several in Old Sukhothai as well.

Smile Internet Cafe (Rte 12; per hour 10B; 9am-10pm) Internet access in Old Sukhothai; located across from Wat Trapang Thong.

Sukhothai Hospital (055 610280; Th Jarodvithithong) Located just west of New Sukhothai.

Tourism Authority of Thailand (TAT; Map p256; 055 616228, nationwide 1672; Th Jarodvithithong; 8.30am-4.30pm) Near the bridge in New Sukhothai, this new office has a pretty good selection of maps and brochures.

Tourist Police (1155; Rte 12)

Getting There & Away

Sukhothai's airport is located a whopping 27km north of town off Rte 1195. **Bangkok Airways** (Sukhothai Airport 055 647224,

TRANSPORT TO/FROM SUKHOTHAI

Bus

DESTINATION	FARE (B)	DURATION (HR)	FREQUENCY
Bangkok	266-342	6-7	half-hourly 7.50am-10.40pm
Chiang Mai	214-293	5-6	5 departures 6.20am-2am
Chiang Rai	255	9	4 departures 6.40-11.30am
Kamphaeng Phet	57-72	1½	frequent 7.50am-10.40pm
Khon Kaen	244-357	7	frequent 8.30am-midnight
Lampang	170-220	3	5 departures 6.20am-2am
Mae Sot	191	3	1.30am & 3.30am
Nan	193	4	3pm
Phitsanulok	43-54	1	hourly 6am-midnight
Sawankhalok	28	1	hourly 6.40am-6pm
Si Satchanalai	49	1½	hourly 6.40am-6pm

Minivan & Sŏrng·tăa·ou

DESTINATION	FARE (B)	DURATION (HR)	FREQUENCY
Kamphaeng Phet	60	2	frequent *sŏrng·tăa·ou* 7am-4.30pm
Mae Sot	130	3	4 minivan departures 9.15am-4.15pm
Phitsanulok	40	1	3 minivan departures 8.50am-2pm
Sukhothai Historical Park	30	30min	frequent *sŏrng·tăa·ou* 6am-6pm

nationwide 1771; www.bangkokair.com; Sukhothai Airport; ⏰7.30-11.30am & 12.30-5.30pm) is the only airline operating here, with two daily flights to/from Bangkok's Suvarnabhumi International Airport (1695B, 1¼ hours). There is a **minivan service** (☎055 647220; Sukhothai Airport; one way 180B) between the airport and New Sukhothai. Alternatively, Air Asia (p250) and Nok Air (p251) now offer minivan transfer to/from both Old and New Sukhothai via the airport in Phitsanulok, less than an hour away.

Sukhothai's minivan and **bus station** (☎055 614529; Rte 101) is almost 1km northwest of the centre of New Sukhothai; a motorcycle taxi between here and central New Sukhothai should cost around 50B, or you can hop on any *sŏrng·tăa·ou* bound for Sukhothai Historical Park, which make a stop at the bus station on their way out of town (20B, 10 minutes, frequent from 6am to 6pm).

Alternatively, if you're staying near the historical park, **Win Tour** (Rte 12; ⏰6am-9.40pm) have an office where you can board buses to Bangkok (342B, six hours, 8.20am, 12.30pm and 9.50pm) and Chiang Mai (228B, five hours, six departures from 6.50am to 2pm).

Getting Around

A săhm·lór ride within New Sukhothai should cost no more than 40B.

Relatively frequent *sŏrng·tăa·ou* run between New Sukhothai and Sukhothai Historical Park (30B, 30 minutes, from 6am to 6pm), leaving from a stop on Th Jarot Withithong. Motorcycle taxis go between the town or bus station and the historical park for 120B.

The best way to get around the historical park is by bicycle, which can be rented at shops outside the park entrance for 30B per day (6am to 6pm).

The park operates a tram service (40B, one hour, from 8am to 5pm) that stops at three temples in the central zone, though it only departs when there are 10 passengers and explanation is in Thai only.

Motorbikes can be rented starting at about 250B for 24 hours and are available at Poo Restaurant (p261) and nearly every guesthouse in New Sukhothai.

COMBINED ADMISSION

An admission fee of 220B allows entry to Si Satchanalai, Wat Chao Chan (at Chaliang) and the Si Satchanalai Centre for Study & Preservation of Sangkalok Kilns.

Si Satchanalai-Chaliang Historical Park

อุทยานประวัติศาสตร์ศรีสัชนาลัย

Set among hills, the 13th- to 15th-century ruins of the old cities of Si Satchanalai and Chaliang, 50km north of Sukhothai, are in the same basic style as those in the Sukhothai Historical Park, but the setting is more rural and arguably more peaceful. The park covers roughly 720 hectares and is surrounded by a 12m-wide moat. Chaliang, 1km southeast, is an older city site (dating to the 11th century), though its two temples date to the 14th century.

The nearby towns of Ban Hat Siaw and Sawankhalok are the main centres for the area.

Sights & Activities

Si Satchanalai

This **zone** (admission 100B, plus car 50B; ⏰8am-6pm) contains the majority of ruins. An **information centre** (⏰8am-4.30pm) at the park distributes free maps and has a small exhibit outlining the history and attractions. **Bike hire** (per day 30B; ⏰9am-4pm) is available near the entrance gate.

Wat Chang Lom HISTORIC SITE

(วัดช้างล้อม) This fine temple, marking the centre of the old city of Si Satchanalai, has elephants surrounding a bell-shaped *chedi* that is somewhat better preserved than its counterpart in Sukhothai. An inscription states that the temple was built by King Ramkhamhaeng between 1285 and 1291.

Wat Khao Phanom Phloeng HISTORIC SITE

(วัดเขาพนมเพลิง) On the hill overlooking Wat Chang Lom are the remains of Wat Khao Phanom Phloeng, including a *chedi*, a large seated Buddha and stone columns that once supported the roof of the *wí·hăhn*. From here you can make out the general design of the once-great city. The slightly higher hill west of Phanom Phloeng is capped by a large Sukhothai-style *chedi* – all that remains of **Wat Khao Suwan Khiri**.

Wat Chedi Jet Thaew HISTORIC SITE

(วัดเจดีย์เจ็ดแถว) Located next to Wat Chang Lom, these ruins contain seven rows of *chedi*, the largest of which is a copy of one at Wat Mahathat in Sukhothai. An interesting

Si Satchanalai-Chaliang Historical Park

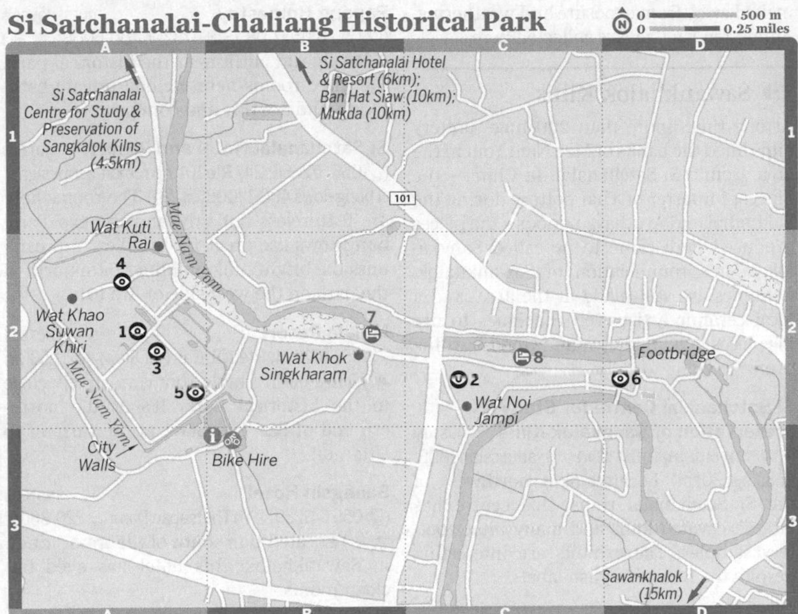

Si Satchanalai-Chaliang Historical Park

Sights

1 Wat Chang Lom A2
2 Wat Chao Chan C2
3 Wat Chedi Jet Thaew A2
4 Wat Khao Phanom Phloeng A2
5 Wat Nang Phaya A2
6 Wat Phra Si Ratana Mahathat D2

Sleeping

7 Homestay B2
8 Papong Homestay C2

brick-and-plaster *wí·hăhn* features barred windows designed to look like lathed wood (an ancient Indian technique used all over Southeast Asia).

Wat Nang Phaya HISTORIC SITE
(วัดนางพญา) South of Wat Chedi Jet Thaew, this *chedi* is Sinhalese in style and was built in the 15th or 16th century, a bit later than the other monuments at Si Satchanalai. Stucco reliefs on the large laterite *wí·hăhn* in front of the *chedi* – now sheltered by a tin roof – date from the Ayuthaya period when Si Satchanalai was known as Sawankhalok. Goldsmiths in the district still craft a design known as *nahng pá·yah,* modelled after these reliefs.

Chaliang

The older site of Chaliang, a short bike ride from Si Satchanalai, has two temples of note.

Wat Phra Si Ratana Mahathat HISTORIC SITE
(วัดพระศรีรัตนมหาธาตุ; admission 20B; 8am-4.30pm) These ruins consist of a large laterite *chedi* (dating back to 1448–88) between two *wí·hăhn*. One of the *wí·hăhn* holds a large seated Sukhothai Buddha image, a smaller standing image and a bas-relief of the walking Buddha, exemplary of the flowing, boneless Sukhothai style. The other *wí·hăhn* contains some less distinguished images.

Wat Chao Chan HISTORIC SITE
(วัดเจ้าจันทร์; admission 100B; 8am-5pm) The central attraction here is a large Khmer-style tower similar to later towers built in Lopburi and probably constructed during the reign of Khmer King Jayavarman VII (1181–1217). The tower has been restored and is in fairly good shape. The roofless *wí·hăhn* on the right contains the laterite outlines of a large standing Buddha that has all but

melted away from exposure and weathering. Admission isn't always collected here.

Sawankhalok Kilns

At one time, more than 200 huge pottery kilns lined the banks of Mae Nam Yom in the area around Si Satchanalai. In China – the biggest importer of Thai pottery during the Sukhothai and Ayuthaya periods – the pieces produced here came to be called Sangkalok, a mispronunciation of Sawankhalok. Ceramics are still made in the area, and a local ceramic artist even continues to fire his pieces in an underground wood-burning oven.

Si Satchanalai Centre for Study & Preservation of Sangkalok Kilns MUSEUM
(ศูนย์ศึกษาและอนุรักษ์เตาสังคโลก; admission 100B; 8am-4.30pm) Located 5km northwest of the Si Satchanalai ruins, this centre has large excavated kilns and many intact pottery samples. The exhibits are interesting despite the lack of English labels.

Sawankhalok

Sawanworanayok National Museum MUSEUM
(พิพิธภัณฑสถานแห่งชาติสวรรควรนายก; 69 Th Phracharat; admission 50B; 9am-4pm Wed-Sun) In Sawankhalok town, near Wat Sawankhalam on the western river bank, this state-sponsored museum houses an impressive collection of 12th- to 15th-century artefacts. The ground floor focuses on the area's ceramic legacy, while the 2nd floor features several beautiful bronze and stone Sukhothai-era Buddha statues.

Sleeping & Eating

There's little in the way of accommodation or food near any of the historical sites. Alternatives include Sawankhalok, 15km to the south, or Ban Hat Siaw, about 9km north of the park.

Homestay GUESTHOUSE $
(055 631063, 08 4048 8595; r 600B;) A local artist has opened her family's home-studio to guests. A single room, separate from the house, is equipped with private bathroom and air-con. Look for the 'Homestay' sign directly across from Wat Khok Singkharam, near the entrance to Si Satchanalai.

Papong Homestay GUESTHOUSE $
(055 631557, 08 7313 4782; r 400-600B;) A locally run outfit near the historical park, the three rooms here include private bathrooms and are tidy and comfortable.

Si Satchanalai Hotel and Resort HOTEL $
(055 672666; 247 Rte 101, no roman-script sign; r & bungalows 400-1200B;) The rooms here are featureless but tidy, and the expansive bungalows are great for families. You can't miss the bright pink buildings 6km north of the park on the west side of Rte 101.

Mukda Resort HOTEL $
(055 671024; Rte 101, Ban Hat Siaw; r 220-500B;) Tidy, comfortable rooms relatively close to the historical park. It's at the northern end of Ban Hat Siaw, at the turn-off to Uttaradit.

Saengsin Hotel HOTEL $
(055 641259; 2 Th Thetsaban Damri; r 220-360B;) Located 1km south of the train station in Sawankhalok, this hotel has aged but clean rooms.

Sukhothai Heritage Resort RESORT $$$
(055 647564; www.sukhothaiheritage.com; 999 Mu 2; r 3400-4600B, ste 6600-8900B, all incl breakfast;) Approximately 32km from Si Satchanalai Historical Park near Sukhothai Airport is this upscale yet rural-feeling, isolated resort. Seemingly a continuation of the historical park, the low-lying brick and peak-roofed structures are interspersed by green fields and calming lotus-filled ponds, culminating in a temple-like environment. The rooms take you back to the contemporary world with large flat-screen TVs and modern furniture.

Getting There & Away

BUS

Si Satchanalai-Chaliang Historical Park is off Rte 101 between Sawankhalok and Ban Hat Siaw. From New Sukhothai, take a Si Satchanalai bus (49B, 1½ hours, hourly from 6.40am to 6pm) or one of four buses to Chiang Rai between 6.40am and 11.30am (46B), and ask to get off at *meu·ang gòw* (old city).

To get to the park from Sawankhalok, you can hop on just about any northbound line from the town's government **bus station** (055 642037), south of the train station on Rte 1180 (around 20B, 30 minutes, frequent from 7am to 5pm).

TRAIN

Sawankhalok's original train station is one of the local sights. King Rama VI built a 60km railway spur from Ban Dara (a small town on the main northern trunk) to Sawankhalok just so that he could visit the ruins. Amazingly, there's a daily special express from Bangkok to Sawankhalok (482B, seven hours, 10.50am). The train heads back to Bangkok at 7.40pm, arriving in the city at 3.30am. You can also take this train to Phitsanulok (328B, 3½ hours, 5.55pm). It's a 'Sprinter' – 2nd class air-con and no sleepers. The fare includes dinner and breakfast.

Getting Around

You can hire bicycles (p262) from near the food stalls at the entrance to the historical park.

KAMPHAENG PHET PROVINCE

Kamphaeng Phet กำแพงเพชร

POP 30,000

Located halfway between Bangkok and Chiang Mai, Kamphaeng Phet translates as 'Diamond Wall', a reference to the apparent strength of this formerly walled city's protective barrier. This level of security was necessary, as the city helped to protect the Sukhothai and later Ayuthaya kingdoms against attacks from Burma or Lanna. Parts of the wall can still be seen today, as well as impressive ruins of several religious structures. The modern city stretches along a shallow section of Mae Nam Ping and is one of Thailand's pleasanter provincial capitals.

Sights & Activities

Kamphaeng Phet Historical Park HISTORICAL PARK

(อุทยานประวัติศาสตร์กำแพงเพชร; 8am-6pm) A Unesco World Heritage site, the Kamphaeng Phet Historical Park features the ruins of structures dating back to the 14th century, roughly the same time as the better-known kingdom of Sukhothai. Kamphaeng Phet's Buddhist monuments continued to be built up until the Ayuthaya period, nearly 200 years later, and thus possess elements of both Sukhothai and Ayuthaya styles, resulting in a school of Buddhist art quite unlike anywhere else in Thailand.

The park consists of two distinct sections: a formerly walled city just north of modern Kamphaeng Phet, and a larger compound about 1.5km further north.

In general, the ruins are not nearly as well restored as those of Sukhothai, but they are smaller, more intimate and less visited.

Walled City

Just north of modern Kamphaeng Phet, this **walled zone** (admission 100B; 8am-6pm) is the origin of the city's name, and was formerly inhabited by *gamavasi* ('living in the community') monks. It's a long walk or an approximately 40B motorcycle taxi ride from the centre of town.

Wat Phra Kaew HISTORIC SITE

(วัดพระแกว) This former temple, adjacent to what is believed to have been the royal palace (now in ruins), dominates the walled city. There's an immense reclining Buddha and several smaller, weather-corroded Buddha statues that have assumed slender, porous forms, reminding some visitors of the sculptures of Alberto Giacometti.

Wat Phra That HISTORIC SITE

(วัดพระธาตุ) The ruins of this temple are distinguished by a large round-based brick and laterite Kamphaeng Phet–style *chedi* surrounded by columns.

Outside of Town

The majority of Kamphaeng Phet's ruins are found in this expansive zone (admission 100B), located about 1.5km north of the city walls. The area was previously home to *aranyavasi* ('living in forests') monks, and in addition to Wat Phra Si Iriyabot and Wat Chang Rob, contains more than 40 other former compounds, including an additional six currently being excavated, although most are not much more than flat-brick foundations with the occasional weather-worn Buddha image.

There is an excellent **visitor centre** (8am-4.30pm) at the entrance where **bicycle hire** (per day 30B) can be arranged.

A motorcycle taxi from central Kamphaeng Phet to the entrance will run about 80B.

COMBINED ADMISSION

An admission fee of 150B allows entry to both the former walled city of Kamphaeng Phet and the larger compound outside of town.

Kamphaeng Phet

Kamphaeng Phet

Sights

1 Kamphaeng Phet National Museum C2
2 Kamphaeng Phet Regional Museum C2
3 Shiva Shrine C2
4 Wat Khu Yang D3
5 Wat Phra Borommathat A3
6 Wat Phra Kaew B2
7 Wat Phra That B2

Sleeping

8 Chakungrao Riverview C4
9 Grand View Resort B3
10 Ko Chokchai Hotel D4
11 Navarat Heritage Hotel C4
12 Scenic Riverside Resort A1
13 Three J Guest House D3

Eating

14 Bamee Chakangrao D4
15 Kitti D4
16 Mae Ping Riverside B3
17 Night Market C4

Drinking & Nightlife

18 Rong Tiam C3

Wat Phra Si Iriyabot HISTORIC SITE

(วัดพระสี่อิริยาบถ) The highlight here is a towering *mon·dòp* (the small square building with a spire in a wát) that contains the shattered remains of standing, sitting, walking and reclining Buddha images, all sculpted in the classic Sukhothai style.

Wat Chang Rob HISTORIC SITE

(วัดช้างรอบ) Translated as the Elephant-Encircled Temple, this ruin is just that – a temple buttress that has 68 elephants which are covered in stucco.

Other Sights

Kamphaeng Phet National Museum MUSEUM
(พิพิธภัณฑสถานแหงชาติกำแพงเพชร; Th Pindamri; admission 100B; ⌚9am-4pm Wed-Sun) Kamphaeng Phet's visit-worthy museum has undergone an extensive renovation. It's home to an expansive collection of artefacts from the Kamphaeng Phet area, including an immense Shiva statue that is the largest bronze Hindu sculpture in the country. The image was formerly located at the nearby **Shiva Shrine** until a German missionary stole the idol's hands and head in 1886 (they were later returned). Today a replica stands in its place.

Kamphaeng Phet Regional Museum MUSEUM
(พิพิธภัณฑเฉลิมพระเกียรติกำแพงเพชร; Th Pindamri; admission 10B; ⌚9am-4.30pm) Being renovated when we stopped by, the regional museum is a series of Thai-style wooden structures on stilts set among nicely landscaped grounds. There are three main buildings in the museum featuring displays ranging from history and prehistory to the various ethnic groups that inhabit the province.

Wat Phra Borommathat BUDDHIST TEMPLE
(วัดพระบรมธาตุ; off Rte 1078; ⌚dawn-dusk) FREE Across Mae Nam Ping are the ruins of Wat Phra Borommathat, located in an area that was settled long before Kamphaeng Phet's heyday although visible remains are post-classical Sukhothai. The compound has a few small *chedi* and one larger *chedi* of the late Sukhothai period which is now crowned with a Burmese-style umbrella added early in the 20th century.

Wat Khu Yang BUDDHIST TEMPLE
(วัดคูยาง; Soi 1, Soi Ratchavithee; ⌚dawn-dusk) FREE Located just north of central Kamphaeng Phet, this Buddhist temple contains a handsome wooden *hŏr đrai* (manuscript library) dating back to the 19th century.

Phra Ruang Hot Springs HOT SPRINGS
(บ่อน้ำร้อนพระร่วง; admission 30B; ⌚8.30am-6pm) Along the road to Sukhothai, 20km from Kamphaeng Phet, this complex of hot springs is the Thai version of a rural health retreat. The reputedly therapeutic hot waters have been diverged into seven private bathing rooms (50B), and there's also several places offering traditional Thai massage. There is no public transport to the hot springs, but transport can be arranged at Three J Guest House.

Sleeping

Three J Guest House GUESTHOUSE $
(☎055 713129, 08 1887 4189; www.threejguesthouse.com; 79 Soi 1, Soi Ratchavitee; r 250-800B; ❄@🛜) The cheapest bungalows at this welcoming guesthouse are fan-cooled and share a clean bathroom while the more expensive have air-con. There's heaps of local information, and bicycles and motorcycles are available for hire.

Ko Chokchai Hotel HOTEL $
(☎055 711531; 19-43 Soi 8, Th Ratchadumnoen 1, no roman-script sign; r 280-340B; ❄🛜) This imposing building with smallish but tidy rooms is a decent budget choice, especially if you want to be in 'downtown' Kamphaeng Phet.

Navarat Heritage Hotel HOTEL $$
(☎055 711211; www.navaratheritage.com; 2 Soi 21, Th Tesa 1; r incl breakfast 800-2500B; ❄🛜) The '70s-era Navarat has undergone a renovation, erasing most signs of the hotel's true age. The rooms are slightly overpriced, but are modern, spacious and cosy, some boasting nice views of the river.

Chakungrao Riverview HOTEL $$
(☎055 714900; www.chanukungraoriverview.com; 149 Th Thesa 1; r 1000-1300B, ste 3500B, all incl breakfast; ❄@🛜) At Kamphaeng Phet's poshest digs rooms are tastefully decked out in dark woods and forest green and feature balconies with river or city views. Suites are huge and are generally available at a considerable discount.

Grand View Resort HOTEL $$
(☎055 721104; 34/4 Mu 2, Nakhon Chum; r & bungalows incl breakfast 290-890B; ❄🛜) One of a handful of semi-rural 'resorts' on the western bank of Mae Nam Ping, there's a variety of accommodation here, but the highlight is the six floating raft bungalows.

Scenic Riverside Resort HOTEL $$$
(☎055 722009; www.scenicriversideresort.com; 325/16 Th Thesa 2; bungalows incl breakfast 1000-3500B; ❄🛜🏊) Picture a Greek fishing village in which the interior design has been overseen by a teenaged Thai girl, and you start to get an idea of this wacky but fun resort. The eight dome-shaped, whitewashed villas here are decked out with stuffed dolls and other kitsch, but are spacious and share a pool and a pleasant riverside location.

BUSES TO/FROM KAMPHAENG PHET

In addition to the buses listed here, there are minivans to Mae Sot (120B, three hours, frequent from 8am to 6pm) and Sukhothai (60B, one hour, 2.30pm), and *sŏrng·tăa·ou* to Sukhothai (60B, two hours, three departures from 8am to noon).

DESTINATION	FARE (B)	DURATION (HR)	FREQUENCY
Bangkok	220-330	5	frequent 8am-1.30am
Chiang Mai	218-328	5	8 departures 11.30am-1am
Chiang Rai	291-374	7	5 departures noon-10.30pm
Lampang	161	4	8 departures 11.30am-1am
Mae Hong Son	509	11	8.30pm
Nan	239	6	1.30pm
Phitsanulok	61-85	2½	hourly 5am-6pm
Phrae	169	4	1.30pm
Sukhothai	57-74	1	hourly noon-4am

Eating & Drinking

Kamphaeng Phet doesn't have a reputation as a culinary destination, but there are a few mildly interesting offerings.

★Bamee Chakangrao THAI $
(cnr Soi 9 & Th Rachadumnoen 1, no roman-script sign; mains 30-35B; ⌚8.30am-3pm) Thin wheat and egg noodles *(bà·mèe)* are a speciality of Kamphaeng Phet, and this famous restaurant is one of the best places to try them. The noodles are made fresh every day behind the restaurant, and pork satay is also available. Look for the green banners on the corner.

Night Market THAI $
(Th Thesa 1; mains 30-60B; ⌚4-10pm) For cheap Thai eats, a busy night market sets up every evening near the river just north of the Navarat Heritage Hotel.

Mae Ping Riverside THAI $
(50/1 Mu 2, Nakhon Chum, no roman-script sign; mains 40-120B; ⌚11am-11pm) Decent eats, draught beer and live music can be found here, on the west bank of Mae Nam Ping. There are a few other similar riverside places along this strip.

Kitti CHINESE, THAI $$
(cnr Th Vijit 2 & Th Bamrungrat, no roman-script sign; mains 50-1200B; ⌚10am-2pm & 4-10pm; ❄) Long-standing Kitti excels at seafood-forward, Chinese-style dining. Try the unusual but delicious fried chicken with cashew nuts, which also includes pickled garlic and slices of sweet pork.

Rong Tiam BAR
(Soi 9, Th Thesa 1, no roman-script sign; ⌚6pm-1am) Live music (from 8.30pm), snacks and beer are available at this friendly pub located in a converted antique shophouse.

Information

Most major banks have branches with ATMs along the main streets near the river and on Th Charoensuk. There's an **internet cafe** (Soi 8, Th Rachadumnoen 1; per hour 15B; ⌚9am-9pm) in town.

Getting There & Away

Kamphaeng Phet's **bus station** (☎055 799103; Rte 101) is about 1km west of Mae Nam Ping. Motorcycles (50B) and *sŏrng·tăa·ou* (20B, frequent from 7.30am to 3pm) run between the station and town. If coming from Sukhothai or Phitsanulok, get off in the old city or at the roundabout on Th Thesa 1 to save yourself the trouble of having to get a *sŏrng·tăa·ou* back into town.

Alternatively, if you're bound for Bangkok (295B, five hours, frequent from 9am to 11pm) you can circumvent the bus station altogether by buying tickets and boarding a bus at **Win Tour** (☎055 713971; Th Kamphaeng Phet), near the roundabout.

Getting Around

There are very few motorcycle taxis or túk-túk in Kamphaeng Phet. As such it's wise to consider hiring a bicycle or motorbike – Three J Guest House has both (per day bicycle/motorcycle 50/200B).

TAK PROVINCE

Tak is a vast, mountainous province whose proximity to Myanmar has resulted in a complex history and unique cultural mix. There are Hmong, Musoe (Lahu), Lisu and White and Red Karen settlements throughout the west and north, while western Tak in particular has always been in distinct contrast with other parts of Thailand because of strong Karen and Burmese cultural influences. Today the Thailand-Myanmar border districts of Mae Ramat, Tha Song Yang and Mae Sot are dotted with refugee camps, an outcome of years of fighting between the Karen National Union (KNU) and the Myanmar government.

Perhaps due its relative isolation, much of Tak still remains quite wild. The linked Um Phang Wildlife Sanctuary, Thung Yai Naresuan National Park, Huay Kha Kaeng Wildlife Sanctuary and Khlong Lan and Mae Wong National Parks together form one of Thailand's largest wildlife corridors and one of the largest intact natural forests in Southeast Asia.

Yet with the opening of Myanmar's first land border at Mae Sot–Myawaddy in 2013, Tak finds itself less isolated, and it remains to be seen how its new role as an increasingly important international crossroads will change the province.

Mae Sot แม่สอด

POP 52,000

Despite its remote location and relatively small size, Mae Sot is among the most culturally diverse cities in Thailand. Walking down the streets of the town, you'll see a fascinating ethnic mixture of Burmese men in their *longyi* (sarongs), Hmong and Karen women in traditional hill-tribe dress, bearded Muslims, Thai army rangers and foreign NGO workers. Burmese and Karen are spoken as much as Thai, shop signs along the streets are in Thai, Burmese and Chinese, and most of the temple architecture is Burmese. Mae Sot has also become the most important jade and gem centre along the border, with much of the trade controlled by Chinese and Muslim immigrants from Myanmar.

Around Tak & Mae Sot

Although there aren't many formal sights in Mae Sot, and many visitors come simply for a visa run, many end up staying longer than expected. The multicultural vibe, not to mention a vibrant market, fun activities and good food have become attractions in their own right.

Sights & Activities

Border Market MARKET
(ตลาดริมน้ำเมย; Rte 105; ⏲7am-7pm) Alongside Mae Nam Moei on the Thai side is a market that sells a mixture of workaday goods from Myanmar, black-market clothes, cheap Chinese electronics and food, among other things. It's 5km west of Mae Sot; *sŏrng·tăa·ou* depart from a spot on Th Chid Lom between approximately 6am and 6pm (20B).

Herbal Sauna SAUNA
(Wat Mani, Th Intharakhiri; admission 20B; ⏲3-7pm) Wat Mani has separate herbal sauna facilities for men and women. The sauna is towards the back of the monastery grounds, past the monks' *gù·đì* (living quarters).

Cookery Course COOKING COURSE
(☎055 546584; borderlineshop@yahoo.com; Borderline Shop, 674/14 Th Intharakhiri; lessons 1000B; ⏲lessons 9am-noon & 3-6pm Tue-Sun) The courses here include instruction in four Shan, Burmese and Karen dishes, a trip to the market, a cookbook, and the chance to share the results in the adjoining cafe. The course cost decreases with bigger groups. Held at Borderline Shop (p272).

Yoga For Life YOGA
(☎08 3092 2772; Irawadee Resort, 758/1 Th Intharakhiri; ⏲classes 9.30-10.30am, 4.50-5.30pm & 6-7pm Mon-Sat, 7.15-8.15pm Tue & Thu) Daily yoga instruction, held at Irawadee Resort.

Festivals & Events

Thai Boxing Competition SPORTS
Around April, Thai and Burmese boxers meet for a competition in the traditional style, held somewhere outside town. Five-round matches are fought in a circular ring; the first four rounds last three minutes, the fifth has no time limit. With their hands bound in hemp, boxers fight till first blood or knockout. You'll have to ask around to find the changing venue for this annual slugfest.

Sleeping

Many places in Mae Sot are in the budget range and cater to NGO workers who tend to stay for the long-term.

Phan Nu House GUESTHOUSE $
(☎08 1972 4467; 563/3 Th Intharakhiri; r 250-500B; ❄📶) This place consists of 29 large rooms in a residential strip just off the street. Most rooms are equipped with air-con, TV, fridge and hot water, making them a good deal.

Bai Fern Guesthouse HOTEL $
(☎055 531349; www.bai-fern.com; 660 Th Intharakhiri; r 150-350B; ❄📶) Set just off the road in a large house, the shared-bathroom budget rooms here are tidy but plain. Service is friendly, and a stay includes use of a kitchen, fridge and wi-fi in the communal area.

Krissana Guest House GUESTHOUSE $
(☎08 8158 7877; 63/4 Soi Ban Tung; r 350-450B; ❄@📶) Located on a quiet street, this place features vast rooms in polished concrete, beds on an elevated platform, and tight, round-shaped bathrooms. The price depends on whether you opt for fan or air-con.

Ban Thai Guest House HOTEL $$
(☎055 531590; banthai_mth@hotmail.com; 740 Th Intharakhiri; r 350-1200B; ❄@📶) This tiny neighbourhood of converted Thai houses includes spacious, stylish air-con rooms with Thai-style furniture, axe lounging pillows and Thai textiles, and a couple of fan-cooled, shared bathroom rooms in the main structure. The whole package is neat, homey and comfortable, not to mention popular with long-stay NGO workers, so booking ahead is a good idea.

Picturebook Guesthouse HOTEL $$
(☎09 0459 6990; www.picturebookthailand.org; 125/4-6 Soi 19, Th Intharakihiri; r incl breakfast 600-800B; ❄📶) Located in an attractive garden, the 10 rooms here, with their smooth concrete, artsy details and custom wood furniture, call to mind trendy dorms. Staff are friendly and keen to help, and are part of a not-for-profit training program. You'll find the hotel in unmarked Soi 19, directly behind the J2 hotel, about 1km east of Mae Sot.

Baan Rabiangmai HOTEL $$
(☎055 532144; www.baanrabiangmai.in.th; 3/3 Th Don Kaew; r incl breakfast 950-2000B; ❄📶) Baan Rabiangmai is the type of clean, homey, no-fuss hotel every town should have. The 19 rooms come thoughtfully equipped with kitchenette, big fridge, sitting area, flat-screen TV and a small balcony.

J2 HOTEL $$
(☎055 546999; www.facebook.com/j2hotel; 149/8 Th Intharakhiri; r incl breakfast 850-1900B;

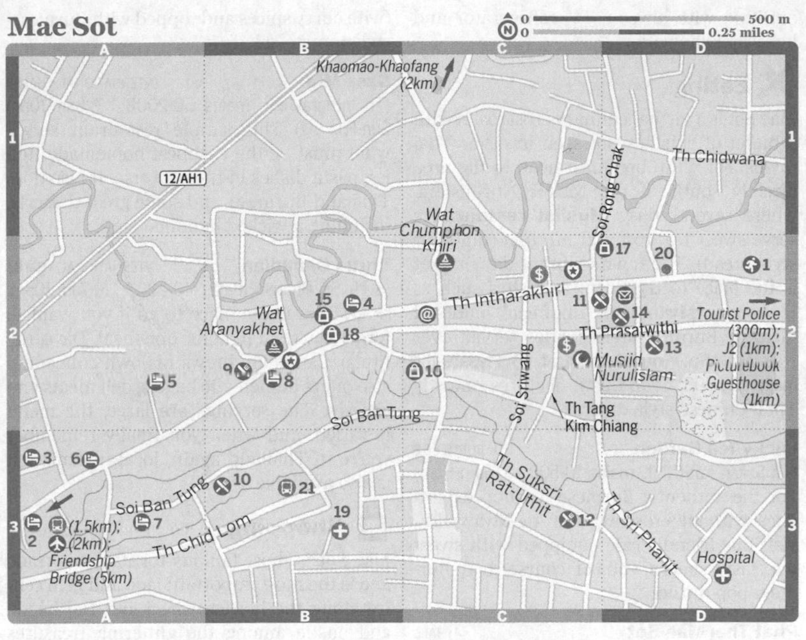

Mae Sot

Activities, Courses & Tours
- Cookery Course .... (see 15)
- 1 Herbal Sauna D2
- Yoga For Life .... (see 6)

Sleeping
- 2 Arisa House A3
- 3 Baan Rabiangmai A3
- 4 Bai Fern Guesthouse B2
- 5 Ban Thai Guest House A2
- 6 Irawadee Resort A3
- 7 Krissana Guest House A3
- 8 Phan Nu House B2

Eating
- Borderline Teashop .... (see 15)
- 9 Casa Mia B2
- 10 Famous Ray's B3
- 11 Khrua Canadian C2
- 12 Lucky Tea Garden C3
- 13 Night Market D2
- 14 Phat Thai Mae Sot D2

Shopping
- 15 Borderline Shop B2
- 16 Municipal Market C2
- 17 Walking Street D2
- 18 WEAVE B2

Information
- 19 Phra Wo Hospital B3

Transport
- 20 Mr Park D2
- 21 Sŏrng·tăa·ou to Border Market/Friendship Bridge B3

❄@📶) The bright new J2 has large rooms decked out in an intriguing minimalist-retro theme – think repro '60s- and '70s-era furniture. Rooms aren't a steal, but you're paying for style, and the J2 is probably the most image-conscious hotel in town. Located about 1km east of the centre of Mae Sot.

Irawadee Resort HOTEL **$$**
(☎055 535430; www.irawadee.com; 758/1 Th Intharakhiri; r/ste incl breakfast 1200/2100B; ❄📶) The Irawadee has modern-feeling rooms decked out in a Burmese – or is it an imperial Chinese – theme. Bathrooms are spacious with open-air showers. Unabashedly gaudy, but fun and comfortable.

Arisa House HOTEL **$$**
(☎055 535111; www.barnarisa.com; Th Intharakhiri; r incl breakfast 690-1000B; ❄📶) There's little flair here, but the 35 rooms in this four-storey building are large, modern and come

outfitted with air-con, TV, refrigerator and hot-water showers.

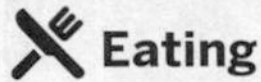

Eating

Mae Sot is a virtual culinary crossroads with a buffet of cuisines not seen in other Thai towns. For a fun breakfast head to the area directly south of the Musjit Nurulislam, where several busy **Muslim restaurants** serve sweet tea, roti and *nanbya* (tandoor-style bread). The town's vibrant day market is the place to try Burmese dishes such as *mohinga* (Myanmar's unofficial national dish) or Burmese-style curries served over rice. Mae Sot's **night market** (Th Prasatwithi; mains 30-60B; 6-11pm) features mostly Thai–Chinese-style dishes.

Lucky Tea Garden BURMESE $
(Th Suksri Rat-Uthit; mains 10-50B; 6am-6pm) For the authentic Burmese teashop experience without crossing over to Myawaddy, visit this friendly cafe equipped with sweet tea, tasty snacks and, of course, bad Burmese pop music.

Phat Thai Mae Sot THAI $
(Th Prasatwithi, no roman-script sign; mains 25-45B; noon-9pm) This cosy place serves *pàt tai* with a local twist: toppings of pork rind and barbecued pork. Look for the rustic, semi-open-air wood building.

Borderline Teashop BURMESE $
(Borderline Shop, 674/14 Th Intharakhiri; mains 35-55B; 7.30am-9pm Tue-Sun;) A cosy cafe with tasty Burmese-style salads, noodle dishes and sweets. If you like what you ate, consider enrolling in the linked cookery course (p270).

★**Khaomao-Khaofang** THAI $$
(www.khaomaokhaofang.com; 382 Rte 105; mains 120-280B; 11am-10pm) Like dining in a gentrified jungle, Khaomao-Khaofang replaces chandeliers with hanging vines, and interior design with orchids and waterfalls. Try one of the several delicious-sounding *yam* (Thai-style spicy salads) featuring ingredients ranging from white turmeric to local mushrooms. The restaurant is north of town between the Km 1 and Km 2 markers on Rte 105, which leads to Mae Ramat.

Famous Ray's AMERICAN $$
(Soi Ban Tung; mains 110-330B; 11.30am-9pm;) Just burgers here, including creative variations such as Thai (with *pàt tai* seasoning and sautéed morning glory) or Burmese (with curry spices and topped with Burmese-style tomato salad).

Casa Mia INTERNATIONAL, THAI $$
(Th Intharakhiri; mains 50-200B; 8am-10pm Sun-Fri;) This simple restaurant serves what must be the cheapest homemade Italian pasta dishes in the universe. It also does Thai and Burmese, and some great desserts, including a wicked banoffee pie.

Khrua Canadian INTERNATIONAL, THAI $$
(3 Th Sri Phanit; mains 40-280B; 7am-10pm;) This is the place to go if you want to forget you're in Asia for one meal. Dave, the titular Canadian, brews his own coffee and also offers homemade bagels, deli meats and cheeses. The servings are large, the menu is varied, and when you finally remember you're in Thailand again, local information is also available.

Shopping

Mae Sot is most famous for its gems trade and is the most important jade and gem centre along the border. Check out the hustle and bustle among the glittering treasures in the gem shops along Th Prasatwithi, just east of the morning market.

Municipal Market MARKET
(off Th Prasatwithi; 6am-6pm) Mae Sot's municipal market is among the largest and most vibrant we've encountered anywhere in Thailand. There's heaps of exotic stuff from Myanmar, including Burmese book shops, sticks of *thanaka* (the source of the yellow powder you see on many faces), bags of pickled tea leaves and velvet thong slippers from Mandalay.

Borderline Shop HANDICRAFTS
(www.borderlinecollective.org; 674/14 Th Intharakhiri; 9am-7pm Tue-Sun) Selling arts and crafts made by refugee women, the profits from this shop go back into a women's collective and a child-assistance foundation. The upstairs gallery sells paintings and the house is also home to a tea garden and cookery course.

WEAVE HANDICRAFTS
(www.weave-women.org; 656 Th Intharakhiri; 9am-5pm Mon-Sat) One of two branches in northern Thailand, this shop specialises in bright handcrafted cloth goods created by displaced women from Myanmar.

Walking Street MARKET
(Soi Rong Chak; ⏲5-9pm Sat) Every Saturday evening the small street by the police station is closed to traffic, and in its place are vendors selling handicrafts, clothes and food.

Information

Several centrally located banks have ATMs. There is no official tourist office in Mae Sot, but the Khrua Canadian restaurant is a good source of local information.

Immigration (☎055 563000; Th Intharakhiri; ⏲8.30am-4.30pm) Located next to the Friendship Bridge, this office can do visa extensions.

net @ all (Th Intharakhiri; per hour 15B; ⏲9am-10pm) Internet access.

Tourist Police (☎1155; 738/1 Th Intharakhiri) Located east of the centre of town.

Getting There & Away

Mae Sot's tiny **airport** (☎055 563620; Th Asia) is about 2km west of town. At research time, **Kan Air** (☎Mae Sot 09 0907 1817, nationwide 02 551 6111; www.kanairlines.com; Mae Sot Airport), with flights to/from Bangkok's Don Muang International Airport and Chiang Mai, and **Nok Air** (☎Mae Sot 055 563883, nationwide 1318; www.nokair.co.th; Mae Sot Airport; ⏲8am-5pm), with flights to/from Bangkok's Don Muang International Airport, were the only airlines operating out of Mae Sot.

All long-distance *sŏrng·tăa·ou*, minivans and buses leave from Mae Sot's **bus station** (☎055 563435; Th Asia), located 1.5km west of town; a motorcycle taxi to/from here should cost about 50B.

Getting Around

Most of central Mae Sot can be navigated on foot. Motorcycle taxis and săhm·lór charge 40B for trips within the centre of town. Mae Sot also has a **taxi service** (☎09 8101 9345; www.facebook.com/taximaesot); service between the airport and town costs 60B.

Sŏrng·tăa·ou to the Friendship Bridge leave from a stop on Th Chid Lom (20B, 15 minutes, frequent from 6am to 6pm).

There are car-hire outlets at Mae Sot's airport and many guesthouses hire motorbikes for around 250B for 24 hours:

Hertz (☎Mae Sot 09 5695 2469, nationwide 02 266 4666; www.hertzthailand.com; Mae Sot Airport; ⏲9.30am-6.30pm)

TRANSPORT TO/FROM MAE SOT

Air

DESTINATION	FARE (B)	DURATION	FREQUENCY
Bangkok (Don Muang International Airport)	1600	65min	4 daily
Chiang Mai	1290	40min	1 daily

Bus

DESTINATION	FARE (B)	DURATION (HR)	FREQUENCY
Bangkok	333-666	7-8	frequent 8am-9.50pm
Chiang Mai	259-333	5-6	6am & 10am
Chiang Rai	488	9	6am & 10am
Kamphaeng Phet	120	3	4 departures 10am-8.30pm
Lampang	248	4	8am
Mae Sai	535	12	3 departures 6am-10am
Phitsanulok	158	4	4 departures 7am-1pm
Sukhothai	120	3	4 departures 7am-1pm

Minivan & Sŏrng·tăa·ou

DESTINATION	FARE (B)	DURATION (HR)	FREQUENCY
Kamphaeng Phet	140	3	hourly minivans 8am-4pm
Mae Sariang	200	6	hourly *sŏrng·tăa·ou* 6am-noon
Um Phang	120	4	hourly *sŏrng·tăa·ou* 7am-3pm

GETTING TO MYANMAR: MAE SOT TO MYAWADDY

The 420m Friendship Bridge links Mae Sot and Myawaddy, in Myanmar's Kayin State.

Getting to the Border

Sŏrng·tăa·ou make trips from Mae Sot to the Friendship Bridge from 6am to 6pm (20B).

At the Border

Immigration procedures are taken care of at the **Thai immigration booth** (☎055 563004; ⊙5.30am-8.30pm) at the Friendship Bridge. Cross to the **Myanmar immigration booth** (☎+95 0585 0100; ⊙5am-8pm, Myanmar time), where, if you've already procured a Myanmar visa in Bangkok or elsewhere, you'll be allowed to stay overnight or proceed to other destinations. Otherwise you must pay a fee of 500B for a temporary ID card at the Myanmar immigration booth, which allows you to stay in Myawaddy until 8pm the same day; your passport will be kept at the border.

Myawaddy is a fairly typical Burmese town, with a number of monasteries, schools, shops and so on. The most important temple is Shwe Muay Wan (Dar Tu Kalair St), a traditional bell-shaped *chedi* (stupa) gilded with many kilos of gold and topped by more than 1600 precious and semiprecious gems. Another noted Buddhist temple is Myikyaungon (Nat Shin Naung St), called Wat Don Jarakhe in Thai and named for its gaudy, crocodile-shaped sanctuary. Myawaddy's 1000-year-old earthen city walls, probably erected by the area's original Mon inhabitants, can be seen along the southern side of town.

Onwards Travel

About 200m from the border, on the corner with Pattamyar St, is a glut of white share taxis (called 'vans' by the Burmese). Cars depart when full between 6am and 5pm – on even-numbered days only; destinations include Mawlamyine (10,000K to 15,000K, six hours), Hpa-an (7500K to 10,000K, six hours) and Yangon (25,000K, 14 hours). There's also a bus to Yangon (12,000K, 16 hour), departing from a small office on Pattamyar St at 5am daily.

Mr Park (☎055 533900; 304-304/1 Th Intharakhiri; per 24hr 150-200B; ⊙8am-5.30pm Mon-Sat) This retail shop hires motorbikes.

Thai Rent A Car (☎Mae Sot 09 9060 0500, nationwide 02 737 8888; www.thairentacar.com; Mae Sot Airport; ⊙9.30am-6.30pm)

Mae Sot to Um Phang

Route 1090 goes south from Mae Sot to Um Phang, 150km away. This stretch of road used to be called the Death Highway because of the guerrilla activity in the area that hindered highway development. Those days ended in the 1980s, but lives are still lost because of brake failure or treacherous turns on this steep, winding road through incredible mountain scenery.

Along the way there are two waterfalls, **Nam Tok Thararak** (น้ำตกธารารักษ์; Rte 1090; ⊙6am-6pm) FREE, 26km from Mae Sot, and **Nam Tok Pha Charoen** (น้ำตกพาเจริญ; Rte 1090; ⊙6am-6pm) FREE, 41km from Mae Sot. Nam Tok Thararak streams beside a picturesque *chedi* and over limestone cliffs and calcified rocks with a rough texture that makes climbing the falls easy. It's been made into a park of sorts, with benches right in the stream at the base of the falls for cooling off and a couple of outhouse toilets nearby; on weekends food vendors set up here. The turn-off isn't clear; look for the sign indicating Chedi Kho.

Just beyond Ban Rom Klao 4 – roughly midway between Mae Sot and Um Phang – is **Um Piam**, a very large Karen and Burmese refugee village with around 20,000 refugees that were moved here from camps around Rim Moei. There are also several Hmong villages in the area.

Sŏrng·tăa·ou to Um Phang depart from Mae Sot's bus station hourly from 7am to 3pm (120B, four hours).

Um Phang & Around อุ้มผาง

Sitting at the junction of Mae Nam Klong and Huay Um Phang, Um Phang is a remote village populated mostly by Karen. Many of the Karen villages in this area are quite traditional, and elephants are a common sight, especially in **Palatha**, a traditional Karen village 25km south of Um Phang. *Yaeng* (elephant saddles) and other tack used for elephant wrangling are a common sight on the verandahs of the houses in this village.

Yet the majority of visitors come to Um Phang for nature, not culture. The area borders the Um Phang Wildlife Sanctuary, a popular destination for rafting and hiking that is also home to Nam Tok Thilawsu, the largest waterfall in Thailand.

Sights

Nam Tok Thilawsu WATERFALL
(น้ำตกทีลอซู) Located in the **Um Phang Wildlife Sanctuary** (เขตรักษาพันธุ์สัตว์ป่าอุ้มผาง; 055 577318, 08 8427 5272; admission 200B, plus car 30B; 8am-4.30pm), this waterfall is Thailand's largest, measuring an estimated 200m high and up to 400m wide during the rainy season.

You can camp (30B) at the sanctuary headquarters, although you'll have to bring your own tent, and it's best to book ahead from November to January. This is also the only time of year the sanctuary's basic restaurant is guaranteed to be open.

Thais, particularly fanatical about such things, consider **Nam Tok Thilawsu** to be the most beautiful waterfall in the country. There's a shallow cave behind the falls and several levels of pools suitable for swimming. The best time to visit is after the rainy season (November and December) when the 200m to 400m limestone cliffs alongside Mae Nam Klong are streaming with water and Nam Tok Thilawsu is at its best.

The easy 1.5km path between the sanctuary headquarters and falls has been transformed into a **self-guided nature tour**. Surrounding the falls on both sides of the river are some of Thailand's thickest stands of natural forest, and the hiking in the vicinity of Nam Tok Thilawsu can be superb. The forest here is said to contain more than 1300 varieties of palm; giant bamboo and strangler figs are also commonplace.

The vast majority of people visit the falls as part of an organised tour, but it's also possible to go more or less independently. If you've got your own wheels, take the turn-off to Rte 1167 just north of Um Phang. After 12km, turn left at the police checkpoint onto Rte 1288. Continue 6km until you reach the sanctuary checkpoint, where you're expected to pay the entry fee. It's another 25km along a mostly paved road to the sanctuary headquarters.

It's easy to book a truck just about anywhere in Um Phang (round trip around 2000B). Alternatively, you can take a Poeng Kloeng–bound *sŏrng·tăa·ou* to the sanctuary checkpoint (30B, hourly from 6.30am to 3.30pm), and organise transport from there (round trip around 1800B).

Tham Ta Khu Bi CAVE
(ถ้ำตะโคะบิ) FREE From Ban Mae Klong Mai, just a few kilometres north of Um Phang via the highway to Mae Sot, Rte 1167 heads southwest along the Thailand–Myanmar border. Along the way is the cave system of Tham Ta Khu Bi, which in Karen allegedly means 'Flat Mango'. There are no guides here, so be sure to bring your own torch.

Villages

Route 1288, which leads to the checkpoint for Um Phang Wildlife Sanctuary, continues more than 70km, terminating in **Poeng Kloeng** (บ้านเปิงเคลิ่ง), a Karen, Burmese, Talaku and Thai trading village on the Myanmar border.

Poeng Kloeng is a pretty nondescript border town where the main occupations appear to be selling black-market cigarettes from Myanmar and the production of betel nut. The real reason to make the schlep here is to visit the neighbouring village of **Letongkhu** (เลตองคุ).

Located 12km south of Poeng Kloeng along a rough uphill track, according to what little anthropological information is available, the villagers belong to the Lagu or Talaku sect, said to represent a form of Buddhism mixed with shamanism and animism. Each village has a spiritual and temporal leader called a *pu chaik* (whom the Thais call *reu·sĕe* – *'rishi'*, or 'sage') who wears his hair long – usually tied in a topknot – and dresses in white, yellow or brown robes, depending on the subsect.

Evangelistic Christian missionaries have infiltrated the area and have tried to convert the Talaku, thus making them sensitive to outside visits. If you do visit Letongkhu, take care not to enter any village structures without permission or invitation. Likewise, do not take photographs without permission. Overnight stays are not generally permitted.

From the *sŏrng·tăa·ou* station in Um Phang there are *sŏrng·tăa·ou* to Poeng Kloeng approximately hourly from 6.30am to 3.30pm (100B, 2½ hours). There's no regular transport to Letongkhu, and if you're not willing to walk or hitch from Poeng Kloeng or organise a guided visit to the village, a 4WD will do the trip from Um Phang for about 5000B.

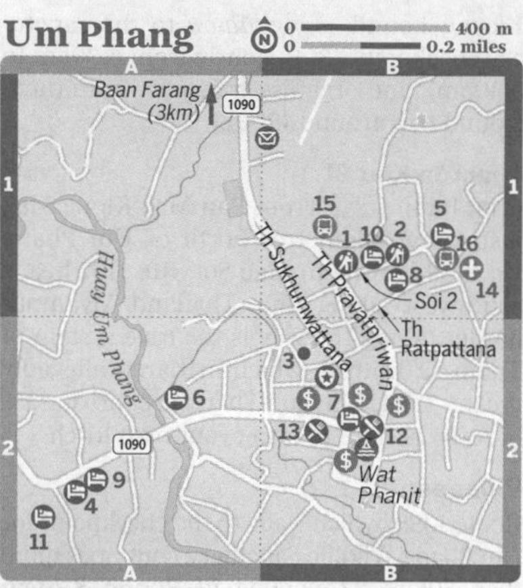

Um Phang

Activities, Courses & Tours
1 Boonchuay Tour ... B1
2 Napha Tour ... B1
Trekker Hill ... (see 10)
3 Umphang House ... B2

Sleeping
4 Ban Phurkchaya ... A2
5 Comesing Homestay ... B1
6 Garden Huts ... A2
7 K & K Guest House ... B2
8 Phudoi Camp Site & Resort ... B1
9 Se Heng Chai Resort ... A2
10 Trekker Hill ... B1
11 Tu Ka Su Cottage ... A2

Eating
12 Evening Market ... B2
13 Wae Kam Der ... B2

Drinking & Nightlife
Ban Kru Sun ... (see 7)

Information
14 Hospital ... B1

Transport
15 Sŏrng·tăa·ou to Mae Sot ... B1
16 Sŏrng·tăa·ou to Poeng Kloeng ... B1

Activities

Virtually every guesthouse in Um Phang can arrange combination trekking and rafting trips in the area. Yet because Um Phang is dominated by Thai tourists, only a handful of guides speak English or have experience in dealing with foreign visitors.

A typical three-day, two-night trip involves both rafting and hiking, with a popular optional activity being elephant rides, though animal welfare experts claim that this can be harmful for the animals. The majority involve trips to Nam Tok Thilawsu and beyond, and longer or shorter trips may also be arranged.

Rafting trips range from one-day excursions along Mae Klong, from Um Phang to Nam Tok Thilawsu, to three-day trips from Palatha to Nam Tok Thi Lo Re, another impressive waterfall. Most rafting is only possible between November and January.

Another area for rafting is Um Phang Khi, northeast of Um Phang. Officially there are 47 (some rafting companies claim 67) sets of rapids rated at class III (moderate) and class IV (difficult) during the height of the rainy season. The rafting season for Um Phang Khi is short – August to October only – as at other times of the year the water level isn't high enough.

Costs are all-inclusive and start at about 4000B per person (for two people) for a three-day rafting and trekking excursion.

Trekker Hill TREKKING, RAFTING
(☎055 561090; Soi 2, Th Pravatpriwan) This recommended outfit has the greatest number of English-speaking guides and offers a variety of treks running from two to three days.

Boonchuay Tour TREKKING, RAFTING
(☎055 561020, 08 1379 2591; Th Pravatpriwan; ⏲1-6pm) Mr Boonchuay offers a variety of treks and rafting trips led by guides who can speak English and have experience in dealing with foreign trekkers.

Umphang House TREKKING, RAFTING
(☎055 561511, 08 9568 5273; www.umphanghouse.webs.com; Soi 4, Th Sukhumwattana; ⏲8am-5pm) This outfit offers a variety of tours led by English-speaking guides, many with an emphasis on elephant rides, an activity now more commonly associated with animal welfare issues.

Napha Tour TREKKING, RAFTING
(☎055 561287, 08 1855 8754; Soi 2, Th Pravatpriwan) Napha has an emphasis on rafting and offers a variety of programs and English-speaking guides.

Sleeping

Most places in Um Phang cater to large groups of Thai visitors, so individual foreign travellers can be met with a bit of confusion. Likewise, many of the rooms in town are designed for four or more people, but singles or couples can usually negotiate lower rates, especially in the wet season.

Se Heng Chai Resort HOTEL $
(☎055 561605; Rte 1090, no roman-script sign; r 500B; ❄📶) Just west of town, this 'resort' has 13 clean, modern-feeling rooms in a two-storey building. It's the tallest building on the hill.

K & K Guest House GUESTHOUSE $
(☎08 7846 1087; Th Sukhumwattana; r 350-500B; ❄📶) Eight rooms in a modern shophouse right in the middle of the hustle and bustle of 'downtown' Um Phang.

Comesing Homestay GUESTHOUSE $
(☎08 1813 9742; off Th Pravatpriwan; r 300B) The eponymous guide has opened his rambling wooden home to visitors. The three rooms are simple, and share communal areas with the family. Pay another 100B and two home-cooked meals are thrown in.

Trekker Hill HOTEL $
(☎055 561090; Soi 2, Th Pravatpriwan; r 300-500B; 📶) This rustic collection of huts on a steep hillside is a decent place to stay, and rooms have hot water and views of the valley and Um Phang.

Tu Ka Su Cottage HOTEL $$
(☎055 561295; www.tukasu.webs.com; off Rte 1090; r 800-1500B; ❄📶) This is the most comfortable and best-run accommodation in Um Phang. The attractive collection of brick-and-stone, multiroom cottages is surrounded by flower and exotic fruit gardens, and all rooms come equipped with air-con, hot water, TV, fridge and semi-outdoor bathrooms.

Baan Farang HOTEL $$
(☎08 0115 5678; off Rte 1090; r incl breakfast 500-1000B; 📶) Located 3km from Um Phang, off Rte 1090 near the intersection that leads to Thilawsu, this attractive plot of land has seven cosy huts, the more expensive of which are riverside.

Phudoi Camp Site & Resort HOTEL $$
(☎055 561049; www.phudoi.com; Th Ratpattana; tents 150B, r 500-1200B; ❄📶) Primarily catering to its prebooked tour clients, Phudoi has bungalows set on a well-landscaped hillside near the village centre. The log cabin–style bungalows are spacious and have verandahs. There's also a camping area and a restaurant with the same name.

Garden Huts HOTEL $$
(☎055 561093, 08 7073 7509; Rte 1090; r 300-1500B; 📶) Operated by a sweet older lady, this collection of budget bungalows of varying degrees of comfort and size and a new building front the river. It features pleasant sitting areas and a well-cared-for garden.

Ban Phurkchaya HOTEL $$
(☎055 561308, 08 9926 8 7976; www.banphurkchaya.com; Rte 1090, no roman-script sign; r incl breakfast 700-1000B; ❄📶) A compound of cutesy rooms in and around a modern villa, all of which appear clean and comfortable. There's no English sign here, but you'd have to struggle to miss the huge flower-decked letters out front.

Eating & Drinking

Um Phang has several simple restaurants.

Wae Kam Der THAI $
(Rte 1090, no roman-script sign; mains 30-120B; ⏰10am-8pm) One of the better eateries in town, with a couple of *kà·nŏm jeen* (fresh rice noodles served with curry) dishes *du jour*, as well as a menu of Thai-style salads. Look for the semi-open structure with clay pots.

Evening Market THAI $
(Soi 9, Th Pravatpriwan; mains 20-60B; ⏰3-9pm Fri & Sat) On Friday or Saturday evenings, there's a small but good evening market.

Ban Kru Sun CAFE
(Th Sukhumwattana; mains 20-35B; ⏰6.30am-8.30pm; 📶) Owned by a Thai musician, this souvenir shop also does decent coffee and other drinks.

Information

There are now two large banks and four ATMs in Um Phang.

Getting There & Away

Sŏrng·tăa·ou to Mae Sot depart from a stop at the northern end of Th Pravatpriwan (130B, four hours, hourly from 6.30am to 12.30pm). *Sŏrng·tăa·ou* to Poeng Kloeng depart from a stop on Th Ratpattana, opposite the hospital (100B, 2½ hours, hourly from 6.30am to 3.30pm).

Mae Sot to Mae Sariang

Route 105 runs north along the Myanmar border from Mae Sot all the way to Mae Sariang (226km) in Mae Hong Son Province. The winding, paved road passes through the small communities of Mae Ramat, Mae Salit, Ban Tha Song Yang and Ban Sop Ngao (Mae Ngao). The thick forest in these parts still has a few stands of teak and the Karen villages continue to use the occasional work elephant.

Nam Tok Mae Kasa, between the Km 13 and Km 14 markers, is an attractive waterfall fronting a cave. There's also a hot spring in the nearby village of **Mae Kasa**.

In **Mae Ramat**, don't miss **Wat Don Kaew**, behind the district office, which houses a large Mandalay-style marble Buddha.

At Km 58, after a series of roadblocks, you'll pass **Mae La**, where it's estimated that 60,000 Burmese refugees live. The village is at least 3km long and takes a couple of minutes to drive past, bringing home the significant refugee problem that Thailand faces.

There are extensive limestone caverns at **Tham Mae Usu**, at Km 94 near Ban Tha Song Yang (not to be confused with the village of the same name further north). From the highway it's a 2km walk to Tham Mae Usu; note that it's closed in the rainy season, when the river running through the cave seals off the mouth.

At the northern end of Tak Province, you'll reach **Ban Tha Song Yang**, a Karen village attractively set at the edge of limestone cliffs by Mae Nam Moei. This is the last significant settlement in Tak before you begin climbing uphill and into the dense jungle and mountains of Mae Ngao National Park, in Mae Hong Son Province.

Ban Sop Ngao, little more than a roadside village that is home to the park headquarters, is the first town you'll come to in Mae Hong Son. From there it's another 40km to Mae Sariang, where there's ample food and accommodation.

Sleeping & Eating

There aren't too many places to stay and eat along this route. The most convenient base is Tha Song Yang (the town near Km 90, not the village of the same name at the northern edge of Tak Province), as there are a few restaurants in town. Mae Salit, further north, also has basic accommodation and food.

Thasongyang Hill Resort HOTEL $
(055 589088; Km 85 marker, Rte 105, Ban Tha Song Yang; r 300-500B;) North of Tha Song Yang, accommodation here takes the form of either large modern rooms in a long building or attractive bungalows in a flower-lined garden. There are a couple of similar hotels in the area, but this place is the nicest.

Per-pron Resort HOTEL $
(08 1774 5624; 110 Mu 2; bungalows 300-350B) Just south of Mae Salit, this place has a few rustic bungalows looking over Mae Nam Moei.

Getting There & Away

Sŏrng·tăa·ou to Mae Sariang depart from Mae Sot's bus station (200B, six hours, hourly from 6am to noon).

MAE HONG SON PROVINCE

Accessible only by vomit-inducing windy mountain roads or a dodgy flight to the provincial capital, Mae Hong Son is arguably Thailand's remotest province. Thickly forested and mountainous, and far from the influence of sea winds, the temperature seldom rises above 40°C, while in January it can drop to 2°C. The air is often misty with ground fog in the winter and smoke from slash-and-burn agriculture during the hot season. Mae Hong Son's location along the border with Myanmar means that it is also a crossroads for ethnic minorities (mostly Karen, with some Hmong, Lisu and Lahu), Shan and Burmese immigrants.

Although the province is firmly on the tourist trail, with many resorts opening in the area around the capital, the vast majority of visitors don't seem to make it much further than Pai.

Pai ปาย

POP 2000

Spend enough time in northern Thailand and eventually you'll hear the comparisons between Pai and Bangkok's Khao San Road. Although this is definitely a stretch, in recent years the small town has started to resemble something of a Thai island getaway – without the beaches. Guesthouses appear to outnumber private residences in the 'downtown' area, a trekking agency or restaurant is never more than a few steps away and the nights buzz with the sound of live music and partying.

However, unlike Khao San or the islands, Pai (pronounced more like the English 'bye', not 'pie') is just as popular among Thais as foreigners. During the peak of the cool season (December and January), thousands of Thais from Bangkok crowd into the town, making parts of it feel more like the Chatuchak Weekend Market than a village in Mae Hong Son. Traffic jams aren't unusual during this time of year, and accommodation becomes so scarce that many are forced to rough it in tents.

Despite all this, the town's popularity has yet to negatively impact its nearly picture-perfect setting in a mountain valley.

There's heaps of quiet accommodation outside the main drag, a host of natural, lazy activities to keep visitors entertained, a vibrant art and music scene, and the town's Shan roots can still be seen in its temples, quiet back streets and fun afternoon market.

Sights

Most of Pai's sights are outside the city centre, making hiring a motorcycle a necessity.

Wat Phra That Mae Yen BUDDHIST TEMPLE
(วัดพระธาตุแม่เย็น; dawn-dusk) FREE This temple sits atop a hill and has good views overlooking the valley. To get there, walk 1km east from the main intersection in town to get to the stairs (353 steps) that lead to the top. Or, if you've got wheels, take the 400m sealed road that follows a different route.

Wat Nam Hoo BUDDHIST TEMPLE
(วัดน้ำฮู; Ban Nam Hoo; dawn-dusk) FREE Wat Nam Hoo is about 2km west of Pai and houses a sacred Buddha image said to have once emitted holy water from its head. The place is popular with visiting Thais and there's a small market on the grounds.

Ban Santichon VILLAGE
(บ้านสันติชล) It's a living, breathing Chinese village, but the cheesy photo ops, piped-in music, restaurants serving Yunnanese food, tea tasting, pony rides, a tacky re-creation of the Great Wall of China and **mountaintop viewpoint** (admission 20B; 4.30am-6pm) can make parts of Ban Santichon seem more like a Chinese-themed Disneyland. Located about 4km west of Pai.

Tha Pai Hot Springs HOT SPRINGS
(บ่อน้ำร้อนท่าปาย; adult/child 300/150B; 7am-6pm) Across Mae Nam Pai and 7km southeast of town via a paved road is this well-kept local park. A scenic stream flows through the park, which mixes with the hot springs in places to make pleasant bathing areas. The water is also diverted to a couple of nearby spas.

Pai Canyon NATURE RESERVE
(กองแลนปาย) FREE Located 8km from Pai along the road to Chiang Mai, a paved stairway here culminates in an elevated lookout over high rock cliffs and the Pai valley. The latter can be followed by a dirt trail, but lacking shade, is best done in the morning or afternoon.

Memorial Bridge LANDMARK
(สพานประวัติศาสตรท่าปาย; Rte 1095) To us it may look like an antiquated bridge, but to the thousands of Thais who stop here during the tourist season it's one of several crucial photo ops along the '762 curves' to Pai. Located 9km from Pai along the road to Chiang Mai, the bridge was originally built by Japanese soldiers during WWII.

Waterfalls

There are a few waterfalls around Pai that are worth visiting, particularly after the rainy season (October to early December). The closest and the most popular, **Nam Tok Mo Paeng**, has a couple of pools that are suitable for swimming. The waterfall is about 8km from Pai along the road that also leads to Wat Nam Hoo – a long walk indeed, but suitable for a bike ride or short motorcycle trip. Roughly the same distance in the opposite direction is **Nam Tok Pembok**, just off the road to Chiang Mai. The most remote is **Nam Tok Mae Yen**, a couple of hours' walk down the rough road east of Pai, just after the turn-off to Fluid.

Mae Hong Son Province

Activities

Massage & Spa Treatments

There are plenty of traditional Thai massage places charging from around 150B an hour. Reiki, crystal healing, acupuncture, reflexology and other non-indigenous methods of healing are also available; keep your eyes

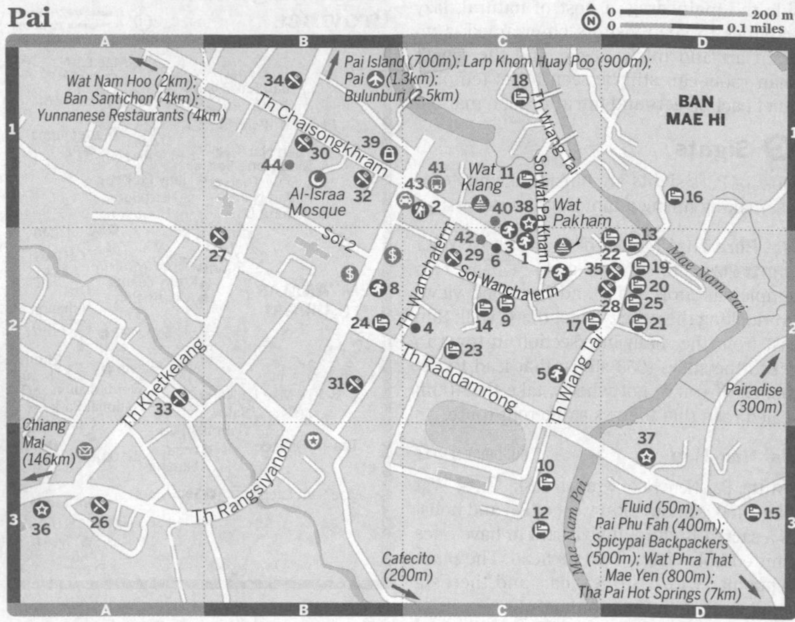

Pai

Activities, Courses & Tours

1 Back-Trax C2
2 Duang Trekking C1
3 Pai Adventure Rafting C2
4 Pai Cookery School C2
5 Pai Traditional Thai Massage C2
6 Savoei (A Taste of Pai) C2
7 Thai Adventure Rafting C2
8 Thom's Pai Elephant Camp B2

Sleeping

9 Baankanoon C2
10 Baantawan Guest House C3
11 Breeze of Pai Guesthouse C1
12 Giant Guest House C3
13 Hotel des Artists D2
14 Mr Jan's Guest House C2
15 Pai Chan D3
16 Pai Country Hut D1
17 Pai Fah C2
18 Pai River Villa C1
19 Pai RiverCorner D2
20 Pai Village Boutique Resort & Farm D2
21 Pai Vimaan Resort D2
22 Rim Pai Cottage D2
23 Tayai's Guest House C2
24 TTK B2
25 Villa De Pai D2

Eating

26 Baan Benjarong A3
27 Evening Market B2
28 Good Life D2
Khanom Jeen Nang Yong .... (see 3)
29 Mama Falafel C2
Maya Burger Queen .... (see 17)
30 Nong Beer B1
31 Om Garden Cafe B2
32 Pai Siam Bistro B1
33 Saengthongaram Market A2
34 Thai Style BBQ Buffet B1
TTK .... (see 24)
35 Witching Well D2

Entertainment

36 Bebop A3
37 Don't Cry D3
38 Edible Jazz C1

Shopping

39 Walking Street B1

Transport

40 Aya Service C1
41 Bus Station C1
42 Duan-Den C2
43 Motorcycle Taxi Stand C1
44 North Wheels B1

open for signs or refer to the monthly *Pai Events Planner*. In addition to these, a few local businesses, all of which are located approximately 1.5km northweast of Tha Pai Hot Springs (p279), have taken advantage of the area's healing thermal waters.

Pai Traditional Thai Massage MASSAGE
(PTTM; ☎08 3577 0498; www.pttm_2001@hotmail.com; 68/3 Soi 1, Th Wiang Tai; massage per 1/1½/2hr 180/270/350B, sauna per visit 100B, 3-day massage course 2500B; ⏲9am-9pm) This long-standing and locally owned outfit offers very good northern Thai massage, as well as a sauna (cool season only) where you can steam yourself in medicinal herbs. Three-day massage courses begin every Monday and Friday and last three hours per day. The friendly couple that do the massages and teach the course are accredited and are graduates of Chiang Mai's Old Medicine Hospital.

Spa Exotic SPA
(☎053 065 722; www.spaexotic.com; 86 Mu 2, Ban Mae Hi; thermal water soak 120B; ⏲8am-11pm) This resort channels the hot water from Tha Pai Hot Springs into its bungalow bathrooms and an open-air pool; the latter is open to the public.

Pai Hotsprings Spa Resort SPA
(☎053 065748; www.paihotspringsparesort.com; 84-84/1 Mu 2, Ban Mae Hi; thermal water soak 100B, 1hr massage 350B) A resort-style hotel that also offers massage (from 8am to 5pm) and thermal water soaks (from 6am to 7pm).

Aroma Pai Spa SPA
(☎053 065745; www.aromapaispa.com; 110 Mu 2, Ban Mae Hi; thermal water soak 80B, spa treatments 850-1500B; ⏲8am-10pm) Offers soaks in private rooms and in a communal pool, as well as a variety of spa treatments.

Rafting & Kayaking

Rafting along Mae Nam Pai during the wet season (approximately June to February) is a popular activity here. The trip runs from Pai to Mae Hong Son, which, depending on the amount of water, can traverse rapids from class I to class V. Rates are all-inclusive (rafting equipment, camping gear, dry bags, insurance and food) and run from 1500B to 1800B per person for a one-day trip and from 1800B to 2500B per person for two days.

Pai Adventure Rafting RAFTING
(☎053 699385; www.thailandpai.net; 28 Th Chaisongkhram; ⏲8am-10pm) The one- to two-day white-water rafting trips offered by this recommended outfit can be combined with hiking and other activities. Also offers a jungle survival course upon request.

Thai Adventure Rafting RAFTING
(☎053 699111; www.thairafting.com; Th Chaisongkhram; ⏲8am-5pm) This French-run outfit leads one- and two-day rafting excursions. On the way, rafters visit a waterfall, a fossil reef and hot springs; one night is spent at the company's permanent riverside camp.

Back-Trax RAFTING
(☎053 699739; backtraxtour@gmail.com; 85 Th Chaisongkhram; ⏲8am-10pm) With more than a decade of experience, this company offers multiday rafting excursions, inner tubing trips, hiking and, of course, reiki lessons.

Trekking

Guided treks range in cost from about 800B to 1000B per person per day, in groups of two or more, and are all-inclusive. Most treks focus on the Lisu, Lahu and Karen villages in and around neighbouring Soppong (Pangmapha). Treks can be booked through guesthouse-based agencies or through specific outfitters, including all of the rafting outfits listed above.

Duang Trekking TREKKING
(☎053 699101; Duang Guesthouse, Th Chaisongkhram; ⏲8am-9pm) This is one of the established local agencies for trekking.

Other Activities

Fluid GYM
(Ban Mae Yen; admission 60B; ⏲9am-6.30pm) This pool and gym complex is located just outside of town, about 600m east of the bridge.

Thom's Pai Elephant Camp ELEPHANT INTERACTION
(☎053 699286; www.thomelephant.com; Th Rangsiyanon; elephant rides per person 800-1200B; ⏲8am-9pm) Pai's most established elephant outfitter has an office in town. You can choose between riding bareback or in a seat, and some rides include swimming with the elephants. Rides include a soak in the hot-spring-fed tubs afterwards. It's worth noting that animal welfare experts claim elephant rides can be harmful for these gentle giants, with arguments in favour of admiring elephants instead of clambering all over them.

Courses

The curriculum of courses available in Pai range from drumming to circus arts; check

LOCAL KNOWLEDGE

PAI BEFORE THE BUZZ

Today Pai is an established stop on the backpacker trail and one of northern Thailand's most talked about destinations. Yet according to Joe Cummings, author of the original edition of the *Thailand* guidebook, Pai in the early '80s was little more than 'a string of wooden houses, shophouses and two wát'. Since those days, Joe has continued to live in Thailand, having contributed to more than 30 books on the region, and maintains a home in Pai.

When did you first go to Pai? In early 1981 I rented a 250cc dirt bike in Chiang Mai and set out for Mae Hong Son. I was researching the 1st edition of Lonely Planet *Thailand* and was warned not to be on the road after 5pm because 'communists and bandits' came out after dark.

What do you remember of that visit? I stayed at the only place that rented rooms, Wiang Pai Hotel, a two-storey teak building with six rooms, a shared toilet and shower, and a one-room opium den out back. I liked Pai but throughout the 1980s I assumed it would always be just a one-night stopover for people on the way to Mae Hong Son.

What do you think of the Pai of today? Have you ever regretted including it in the guidebook? Pai got popular for a good reason. It's the most beautiful valley in Thailand, for my tastes at least (and by now I've seen most of them), it's still pretty chill and there's lots to do in the area. [I have] no regrets writing about Pai. Word of mouth travels much faster than guidebook prose anyway, so there was no way to keep it a secret.

What are some worthwhile things to do, see or eat in Pai? I still like hiking around Nam Tok Pembok. And the Yunnanese cuisine (p286) in Ban Santichon makes a nice change from the Thai and *fa·ràng* food in town.

listings rags such as the *Pai Events Planner* (PEP) or the **Pai Explorer** (www.paiexplorer.com) to see what's on when you're in town.

Pai Cookery School COOKING COURSE
(☎08 1706 3799; Th Wanchalerm; lessons 600-750B; ⏱lessons 11am-1.30pm & 2-6.30pm) With a decade of experience, this outfit offers a variety of daily courses covering three to five dishes. The afternoon course involves a trip to the market for ingredients. Contact a day in advance.

Savoei (A Taste of Pai) COOKING COURSE
(☎08 5620 9918; Th Chaisongkhram; lessons 600-800B; ⏱lessons 9.30am-1.30pm & 4-8pm) Full-day classes here involve a visit to the fresh market and instruction in six dishes, while half-day courses cover four dishes.

Sor Wisarut THAI BOXING
(☎08 3321 2230; www.facebook.com/SorWisarutMuayThaiGym; Ban Mae Hi; lessons 300-400B; ⏱lessons 8-10am & 3-5pm) Wanachai and Emanuel lead instruction in Thai boxing at this rustic gym about 1km outside of town, on the turn-off just after Fluid.

Xhale Yoga Pai YOGA
(www.xhaleyogapai.com; 5 days 14,000B) Need some time out? Sign up for a five-night yoga retreat (Monday to Saturday) in the foothills outside Pai. Courses suit beginners to intermediates and include accommodation, stand-out meals, yoga and meditation classes, plus an excursion to a nearby hot spring. Instructor Bhud is all smiles, laughter and sunshine, and the vibe is welcoming and non-competitive. Pick-up from Aya bus stop in Pai is provided.

Sleeping

Despite several years of growth, Pai's accommodation has slowed only slightly, and the rumour on the ground during our visit was that there were more than 500 hotels, guesthouses and resorts. Although 'downtown' Pai has seen relatively little change in this respect over the last few years, on our last visit there were several new resorts in an approximate 3km circle around the town. Yet despite the glut of accommodation, during the height of the Thai tourist season (December and January), accommodation in Pai can be nearly impossible to come by, although tents are available for about 100B. Keep in mind that prices fluctuate significantly in Pai, and nearly all the midrange and top-end accommodation cut their prices, sometimes by as much as 60%, during the off season.

In Town

Pai's popularity, particularly among domestic tourists, has resulted in a glut of midrange and upscale places. But there are still some cheap rooms just outside of the centre of town, which is where you should base yourself if you're coming to Pai with preconceived notions of an idyllic, rural stay.

Pai Country Hut HOTEL $

(☎08 7779 6541; www.paicountryhut.com; Ban Mae Hi; bungalows incl breakfast 300-800B; wi-fi) The bamboo bungalows here are utterly simple, but are tidy and most have bathrooms and inviting hammocks. Although it's not exactly riverside, it's the most appealing of several similar budget places close to the water.

TTK GUESTHOUSE $

(☎053 098093, 8/10 Th Raddamrong; r 350-450B; wi-fi) Set behind the Israeli restaurant of the same name, the rooms here lack both natural light and interior design, but are spotless and conveniently located.

Mr Jan's Guest House GUESTHOUSE $

(☎053 699554; 18 Soi Wanchalerm; r 300-1000B; air-con wi-fi) One of Pai's longest-standing guesthouses, the rooms here are set around a medicinal herb garden, although they can be plain and somewhat dark.

Giant Guest House GUESTHOUSE $

(☎053 698059; www.giantguesthouse.com; Th Wiang Tai; bungalows 200-400B; wi-fi) It isn't the most comfortable or service-minded accommodation Pai has to offer, but nobody else comes close to Giant for that old-school hippie, authentic Pai vibe.

Pai River Villa HOTEL $$

(☎053 699796; pairivervillaresort@gmail.com; 7 Th Wiang Tai; bungalows incl breakfast 900-1500B; air-con wi-fi) This place boasts some of the more attractive midrange accommodation in town. The air-con bungalows are spacious and stylish, and have wide balconies that encourage lazy riverside relaxing and mountain viewing, while the fan-cooled bungalows are a significantly tighter fit.

Baankanoon GUESTHOUSE $$

(☎053 699453; www.baankanoonpai.com; 33 Soi Wanchalerm; bungalows 500-1200B; wi-fi) Consisting of 14 bright duplex and free-standing bungalows around a 100-year-old *kà·nŭn* (jackfruit) tree, this locally owned place is quiet, clean and cosy.

Pai Fah HOTEL $$

(☎08 8409 1151; 77 Th Wiang Tai; r 900-1200B; air-con @ wi-fi) This self-professed 'boutique house' takes the form of 14 simple but bright and clean rooms in a two-storey villa steps from all the action. Rooms with air-con are more expensive.

Breeze of Pai Guesthouse HOTEL $$

(☎08 1998 4597; www.facebook.com/BreezeOfPai; Soi Wat Pa Kham; r 500B, bungalows 800B; air-con wi-fi) This well-groomed compound near the river consists of nine plain but clean and spacious rooms and six A-frame bungalows. It's close to the action without the noise pollution. A loyal customer base means you'll probably have to book ahead.

Tayai's Guest House GUESTHOUSE $$

(☎053 699579; off Th Raddamrong; r & bungalows 800-1200B; air-con wi-fi) Simple but clean fan and air-con rooms and bungalows in a quiet, leafy compound just off the main drag.

Villa De Pai HOTEL $$

(☎053 699109; www.villadepai.net; 87/1 Th Wiang Tai; bungalows 1000-2000B; wi-fi) A mix of new and old, clean and conveniently located riverside bungalows. Rates include breakfast during the high season.

★ Pai Village Boutique Resort & Farm HOTEL $$$

(☎053 698152; www.paivillage.com; 88 Th Wiang Tai; bungalows incl breakfast 1900-3200B; air-con @ wi-fi) This well-maintained place has a collection of 26 wooden bungalows set among winding garden pathways. The rooms don't leave heaps of room to stretch, but they do have floor-to-ceiling sliding windows, large and quite plush bathrooms, as well as spacious terraces with rattan mats and axe cushions to best enjoy the greenery. Huge off-season discounts available.

Baantawan Guest House HOTEL $$$

(☎053 698116; www.baantawanpai.com; 117 Th Wiang Tai; r 1200-3000B, bungalows 2000-3000B, all incl breakfast; air-con @ wi-fi) The older and more charming riverside two-storey bungalows made with salvaged teak are the reason to stay here, but there are also spacious (and less expensive) rooms in a large two-storey building. Service is first-rate and it's located on a relatively isolated (read: quiet) stretch of the river.

Rim Pai Cottage HOTEL $$$

(☎053 699133; www.rimpaicottage.com; 99/1 Th Chaisongkhram; bungalows 1500-3500B; air-con wi-fi) The homelike bungalows (which include breakfast from October to February) are spread out along a secluded and beautifully wooded section of Nam Pai. There are countless cosy riverside corners to relax in and a palpable village-like feel about the whole place. Tip: opt for one of the original wooden bungalows, as the newer concrete ones have markedly less charm.

Hotel des Artists HOTEL $$$
(☎053 699539; www.hotelartists.com; 99 Th Chaisongkhram; r incl breakfast 4000-4800B; ❄📶) This former Shan mansion has been turned into an attractive boutique hotel. The 14 slightly crowded rooms mingle pan-Asian and Western design elements in a tasteful, attractive package. Twin beds are on an elevated platform and all rooms have balconies, those with riverside views being slightly larger and more expensive.

Pai RiverCorner HOTEL $$$
(☎053 699049; www.pairivercorner.com; 94 Th Chaisongkhram; r incl breakfast 3900-6400B; ❄📶🏊) A no-brainer for the design-conscious traveller, the nine rooms here include beautiful Thai furniture, gorgeous colours and lots of deluxe details. All rooms have river-facing balconies and some have lounges and interior spa pools.

Pai Vimaan Resort HOTEL $$$
(☎053 699403; www.paivimaan.com; 73 Th Wiang Tai; r 2500-300B, bungalows 5000-6000B, all incl breakfast; ❄📶) The highlight here is the five riverside tented bungalows. Huge and equipped with air-con, Jacuzzi, TV and other modern amenities, they redefine camping. The resort's two-storey bungalows are bright and airy, with the top-floor rooms allowing great views of the river, and there are also rooms in the main wooden structure.

Outside of Town

If you've got your own wheels, you'll find many options outside of the centre of Pai. Most are targeted towards domestic rather than foreign tourists, which means they fall in the mid- and upper range of the price spectrum, and typically take the form of air-con-equipped bungalow compounds.

Amy's Earth House GUESTHOUSE $
(☎08 6190 2394; www.amyshouse.net; Ban Mae Khong; dm 200B, bungalows 400-600B; 📶) Amy's claims to have been the first adobe accommodation in Pai. Mud bungalows are simple but spacious, have open-air showers, and are on a landscaped hillside looking over the valley. The hotel is about 3.5km from the centre of town, off the road to Mae Hong Song – look for the well-posted turn-off just after the airport runway, about 1.3km from Pai.

Spicypai Backpackers HOTEL $
(☎08 5263 5147; www.spicyhostels.com; Mae Yen; dm 150B; 📶) The bamboo dorms here look like they could have featured in an episode of *Survivor*. Communal areas ranging from a communal kitchen to fire pit continue the rustic feel. It's about 750m east of Mae Nam Pai, just off the road that leads to Thai Pai Hot Springs.

★Bueng Pai Farm GUESTHOUSE $$
(☎08 9265 4768; www.paifarm.com; Ban Mae Hi; bungalows 1000-2000B; 📶🏊) Located in a rural setting, the 12 spacious, fan-cooled bungalows here are strategically and attractively positioned around a vast pond stocked with freshwater fish. There's a campfire during the winter months, and a pool, communal kitchen and fishing equipment are available year-round. Bueng Pai is about 2.5km east of Pai, off the road that leads to Tha Pai Hot Springs; look for the sign.

★Pairadise HOTEL $$
(☎053 698065; www.pairadise.com; Ban Mae Hi; bungalows 900-1500B; ❄📶🏊) This neat resort looks over the Pai Valley from atop a ridge just outside of town. The bungalows are stylish, spacious and include gold-leaf lotus murals, beautiful rustic bathrooms and terraces with hammocks. All surround a spring-fed pond that is suitable for swimming. You'll find it about 750m east of Mae Nam Pai; look for the sign just after the bridge.

Pai Chan HOTEL $$
(☎08 1180 3064; www.paichan.com; Ban Mae Hi; bungalows incl breakfast 500-1400B; 📶🏊) Pai Chan doesn't look like much from the parking lot, but a closer look reveals attractive and comfortable heavy wooden bungalows that lack modern amenities (including air-con), but make up for this with balconies overlooking rice fields or an inviting pool. It's about 200m east of Mae Nam Pai.

PuraVida HOTEL $$
(☎08 9635 7556; www.puravidapai.com; Wiang Nua; bungalows incl breakfast 1430B; ❄📶) A friendly Dutch-Thai couple look after these eight cute bungalows on a well-manicured hillside in the quiet Wiang Nua area. The honeymoon bungalow offers a bit more privacy, and all rooms are equipped with air-con, TV, fridge and hot water. PuraVida is about 4km from the centre of town off the road to Mae Hong Song; look for the well-posted turn-off about 1km from Pai.

OFF THE BEATEN TRACK

MAE HONG SON LOOP

One of the most popular motorcycle riding tours in northern Thailand is the circuitous route that begins in Chiang Mai and passes through the length of Mae Hong Son Province before looping back to the city – a round trip of nearly 600km.

The Mae Hong Son loop really begins 34km north of Chiang Mai when you turn onto Rte 1095 and lean into the first of its 1864 bends. It's slow going, and you start climbing almost immediately; however, the good thing about this route is that potential for overnight stops is ample – many of the towns with good accommodation and food are less than 70km apart – giving riders the chance to reclaim the blood flow to their bottoms. Convenient overnight stops include Pai, 130km from Chiang Mai, Soppong, another 40km up the road, and Mae Hong Son, 65km from Soppong.

Upon reaching Khun Yuam, 70km south of Mae Hong Son, you can opt to take Rte 1263 to Mae Chaem, before continuing back to Chiang Mai via Doi Inthanon, the country's highest peak, or you can continue south to Mae Sariang and follow Rte 108 all the way back to Chiang Mai via Hot, although the distances between towns here are greater and best done on a more powerful and more comfortable motorcycle.

An excellent driving companion is Golden Triangle Rider's *Mae Hong Son Loop Guide Map*, available at most bookshops in Chiang Mai. The map shows accurate distances between locations along the loop, as well as potential side trips and other helpful information.

Sipsongpanna HOTEL **$$**

(053 698259; www.facebook.com/paisipsongpanna; Wiang Nua; bungalows incl breakfast 1000-1200B;) The five adobe-style riverside bungalows here are rustic and quirky with a mix of bright colours, beds on elevated platforms and sliding-glass doors opening to wide balconies. There are also still a few original wooden bungalows, though these are being phased out. The hotel is about 2.5km from the centre of town off the road to Mae Hong Son; look for the well-posted turn-off, about 1km from Pai.

Pai Phu Fah HOTEL **$$**

(08 1906 2718; www.paiphufah.com; Ban Mae Hi; r & bungalows 300-1500B;) There's a decent, if tight, range of accommodation here, from bungalows to rooms, all in a quiet, rural setting at the edge of a photogenic rice field. It's about 650m east of Mae Nam Pai, along the road to Thai Pai Hot Springs.

Phu Pai HOTEL **$$$**

(053 065111; www.phupai.com; Mae Na Theung; bungalows incl breakfast 2100-3800B;) This self-professed 'art resort' is an attractive, remote-feeling gathering of 40 locally styled luxury bungalows. Views are the focus here, with most bungalows edging rice fields and an infinity pool framing the Pai Valley.

The hotel is about 4km from the centre of town off the road to Mae Hong Son; look for the well-posted turn-off just after the airport runway, about 1.3km from Pai.

Bulunburi HOTEL **$$$**

(053 698302; www.bulunburi.com; Ban Pong; bungalows incl breakfast 1300-4500B;) Set in a tiny secluded valley of rice fields and streams, the seductively bucolic location is as much a reason to stay here as the attractive accommodation. The 11 bungalows, which range from tight fan-cooled rooms to huge two-bedroom houses, are well equipped and stylish.

Bulunburi is about 2.5km from the centre of town along the road to Mae Hong Son; look for the well-posted turn-off, about 1km from Pai.

Pripta HOTEL **$$$**

(053 065750; www.pripta.com; 90 Mu 3, Mae Hi; bungalows incl breakfast 3500-5000B;) This hillside compound features 12 chic bungalows perched at the edge of the Pai Valley. Rooms are huge, with tall ceilings, and feature vast balconies with outdoor tubs with water supplied by the nearby hot springs. It's about 7km from Pai, between Tha Pai Hot Springs and Rte 1095.

Pai Island RESORT **$$$**

(053 699999; www.paiislandresort.com; bungalows incl breakfast 5000-6500B;) Intertwining Pacific Island and African themes is this quirky and popular resort. Accommodation takes the form of 10 free-standing, private-feeling luxury villas located on islands connected by bridges, each equipped with Jaccuzzi and expansive semi-outdoor bathrooms. It's located about 700m north of town, along the road that leads to Mae Hong Son.

Pai Treehouse HOTEL **$$$**
(☎08 1911 3640; www.paitreehouse.com; Mae Hi; bungalows incl breakfast 1000-6500B; ❄📶) Even if you can't score one of the three treehouse rooms here (they're popular), there are several other attractive bungalows, many near the river. On the vast grounds you'll also find elephants and floating decks on Mae Nam Pai, all culminating in a family-friendly atmosphere. The resort is 6km east of Pai, just before Tha Pai Hot Springs.

Eating

At first glance, Pai has a seemingly impressive range of restaurants, but a few meals will reveal that the quality of food is generally pretty mediocre.

During the morning, there's takeaway food at **Saengthongaram market** (Th Khetkelang; mains 30-60B; ⊙6-11am). For tasty take-home local-style eats, try the **evening market** (Th Raddamrong; mains 30-60B; ⊙3-7pm) that unfolds every afternoon from about 3pm to sunset. And every evening during the tourist season several vendors set up along Th Chaisongkhram and Th Rangsiyanon, selling all manner of food and drink from stalls and refurbished VW vans.

★**Larp Khom Huay Poo** NORTHERN THAI **$**
(Ban Huay Pu; mains 50-80B; ⊙9am-8pm) Escape the wheatgrass and tofu crowd and get your meat on at this unabashedly carnivorous local eatery. The house special (and the dish you must order) is *larp moo kua*, northern-style *lâhp* (minced pork fried with local herbs and spices). Accompanied by a basket of sticky rice, a plate of bitter herbs and an ice-cold Singha, it's the best meal in Pai. The restaurant is about 1km north of town, on the road to Mae Hong Son.

★**Yunnanese Restaurants** CHINESE **$**
(no Roman-script sign; mains 30-250B; ⊙7am-8pm) Several open-air restaurants in Ban Santichon, 4km west of Pai, serve the traditional dishes of the town's Yunnanese residents. Choices include *màntŏ* (steamed buns), here served with pork leg stewed with Chinese herbs, hand-pulled noodles and several dishes using unique local crops and exotic ingredients such as black chicken.

Om Garden Cafe INTERNATIONAL **$**
(off Th Raddamrong; mains 60-120B; ⊙8.30am-5pm Tue-Sun; 🖉) Fresh-pressed juices, meat-free takes on international dishes, barefoot and/or flute-playing patrons: basically everything you'd expect at a place called Om Garden, except that the food is actually good. Dishes range from Middle Eastern meze to breakfast burritos, as well as a good selection of salads and pastries.

Witching Well INTERNATIONAL **$**
(www.witchingwellrestaurant.com; 97 Th Wiang Tai; mains 70-150B; ⊙8am-10pm; 📶🖉) This buzzy foreigner-run place is where to come if you're looking for authentic sandwiches, pasta, cakes and pastries. It also does good coffee and the kind of sophisticated breakfasts you're not likely to find elsewhere in Pai.

Maya Burger Queen AMERICAN **$**
(www.facebook.com/MayaBurgerQueen; Th Wiang Tai; mains 90-1450B; ⊙2-10pm; 🖉) Burgers are a big deal in Pai, and arduous research led us to believe that Maya does the best job. Everything is homemade, from the soft, slightly sweet buns to the rich garlic mayo that accompanies the thick-cut fries.

Good Life INTERNATIONAL **$**
(Th Wiang Tai; mains 35-190B; ⊙8am-11pm; 📶🖉) Kefir, kombucha, beet juice and wheatgrass are indicators of the vibe of this eclectic and popular cafe. But don't fear: soft drinks are available, as is a thick menu of Thai and international dishes, many of which are meat-free.

TTK ISRAELI **$**
(The Thai Kebab; Th Raddamrong; mains 100-180B; ⊙8.30am-9.30pm; 📶🖉) The expansive menu here spans Israeli dishes from standards to surprises, with a few breakfast options thrown in for good measure.

Cafecito TEX-MEX **$**
(www.facebook.com/cafecitopai; mains 70-160B; ⊙9am-6pm Fri-Wed; 🖉) Tacos, burritos, quesadillas and tacos: Cafecito serves the Tex-Mex staples, all overseen by an American. Lots of meat-free options, and it also doubles as a cafe. It's located about 600m south of Th Rangsiyanon, on the unmarked street adjacent to Pai's police station.

Khanom Jeen Nang Yong THAI **$**
(Th Chaisongkhram, no roman-script sign; mains 25-30B; ⊙7am-10pm) This place specialises in *kà·nŏm jeen* (thin rice noodles served with your choice of a curry-like broth). It's located in the same building as Pai Adventure Rafting.

Nong Beer THAI **$**
(cnr Th Khetkalang & Th Chaisongkhram; mains 40-200B; ⊙8am-8pm) A long-standing go-to for cheap and authentic Thai eats ranging from *kôw soy* to curries ladled over rice.

Mama Falafel ISRAELI $
(Soi Wanchalerm; set meals 100-110B; 2.30-10pm Mon-Sat;) This friendly native of Pai has been cooking up tasty felafel, hummus, schnitzel and other Israeli faves since 2002; the set meals win in both quality and quantity.

Pai Siam Bistro INTERNATIONAL $
(Th Chaisongkhram; mains 70-140B; 9am-10pm;) Cosy place with a menu spanning your standard Thai-International dishes, as well as Mediterranean-influenced specials and some decent cakes and pastries.

Baan Benjarong CENTRAL THAI $$
(179 Th Rangsiyanon; mains 90-170B; 11am-9pm) Emulate local families and come to this classy home-based restaurant at the edge of a rice field. Menu items such as stewed, salted crabs in coconut milk and a salad of banana flower, shrimp and chicken culminate in some of the better Thai food in town.

Thai Style BBQ Buffet THAI $$
(Th Khetkelang; per person 150B; 4-10pm) As the name suggests, this is *mŏo gà·tá*, the DIY barbecue so beloved by northern Thais. Yet unlike most places, the meat and veg are of good quality and there's live music.

Drinking & Entertainment

There are dozens of bars in Pai, most of which seem to have the approximate lifespan of a fruit fly. You will, however, find some interesting, long-standing live-music places in and around town.

Edible Jazz LIVE MUSIC
(www.ediblejazz.com; Soi Wat Pa Kham; 4-11pm) Stroke a cat and nurse a beer while listening to acoustic guitar performances, every night around 8.30pm. Depending on who's in town, the open-mike night on Sunday can be surprisingly good.

Bebop LIVE MUSIC
(Th Rangsiyanon; 8pm-1am) This legendary box is popular with both locals and travellers and has live music nightly (from about 10pm), emphasising blues, R&B and rock.

Don't Cry BAR
(Th Raddamrong; 6pm-late) Located just across the river, this is the kind of reggae bar you thought you left behind on Ko Phangan. Soporifically chilled out, featuring both live music and a club, and open until the last guy goes home.

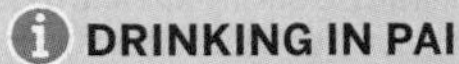

DRINKING IN PAI 101

As a general guide to downtown Pai's drinking scene, most of the open-air and VW van–based cocktail bars are found along Th Chaisongkhram; Th Wiang Tai is where you'll find Pai's highest concentration of bars, many with a reggae vibe; Th Rangsiyanon is where most of the guesthouse-style restaurant-bars with a diverse soundtrack and a dinner menu are located; and a knot of open-air reggae-style bars can be found at the eastern end of Th Raddamrong, just across the bridge.

Shopping

Walking Street MARKET
(Th Chaisongkhram & Th Rangsiyanon; 6-10pm) Every evening during the tourist season, from November to February, a walking street forms in the centre of town.

Information

Internet cafés are a dying breed, although we saw a couple at the western end of Th Chaisongkhram (20B to 30B per hour).

Several exchange booths and ATMs can be found along Th Rangsiyanon and Th Chaisongkhram.

Pai Explorer (www.paiexplorer.com) is the free local English-language map. The *Pai Events Planner* (PEP) is a free monthly newsletter that covers cultural events, travel destinations and some restaurant and bar openings; you can find it around town.

Getting There & Away

AIR

Pai's airport is around 1.5km north of town along Rte 1095. At research time, **Kan Air** (053 699955, nationwide 025 516111; www.kanairlines.com; Pai Airport; 8.30am-5.30pm) was the only airline operating out of the town, with connections to/from Chiang Mai. Alternatively, Air Asia offers bus transfer to Pai from Chiang Mai International Airport (1990B, 20 minutes, 11am) daily from December to March and on Friday, Saturday and Sunday from April to November.

BUS & MINIVAN

Pai's tiny **bus station** (Th Chaisongkhram) is the place to catch slow, fan-cooled buses:

Chiang Mai 80B, three to four hours, noon
Mae Hong Son 80B, three to four hours, 11am
Soppong (Pangmapha) 45B, 1½ hours, 11am

More efficient minivans to Chiang Mai and destinations in Mae Hong Son also depart from here:

Chiang Mai 150B, three hours, hourly from 7am to 5pm

Mae Hong Son 150B, 2½ hours, 8.30am

Soppong (Pangmapha) 100B, one hour, 8.30am

Aya Service and Duan-Den also run air-con minivan buses to Chiang Mai (from 150B to 200B, three hours, hourly from 7am to 5.30pm).

Getting Around

Most of Pai is accessible on foot. Motorcycle taxis wait at the taxi stand across from the bus station. Sample fares are 50B to Ban Santichon and 100B to Nam Tok Mo Paeng. For local excursions you can hire bicycles or motorcycles in town.

Aya Service (053 699888; www.ayaservice.com; 22/1 Th Chaisongkhram; motorcycles per 24hr 100-1800B; 7am-10pm) This busy outfit has more than 100 bikes.

Duan-Den (053 699966; 20/1 Th Chaisongkhram; per 24hr 100-250B; 7am-9pm) Lots of smaller motoryclces available here.

North Wheels (094 7196119; www.northwheels.com; Th Khetkelang; motorcycle/car per 24hr 140/1200B; 8am-8pm) Motorcycle and car hire.

Soppong สบป่อง

Soppong (also sometimes known as Pangmapha, actually the name of the entire district) is a small market village a couple of hours northwest of Pai and about 70km from Mae Hong Son. There's not much to see in town, but the surrounding area is defined by dense forests, rushing rivers and dramatic limestone outcrops and is *the* place in northern Thailand for caving.

There are several Shan, Lisu, Karen and Lahu villages that can easily be visited on foot.

Sights & Activities

If you're in Soppong on Tuesday morning, check out the town's rustic **market**.

The best source of information on caving and trekking in the area is the owner of Cave Lodge (p290). Experienced local guides and recommended kayaking, hiking and caving trips in the area can be arranged here. It's located near Tham Lot, the most accessible cave in the area, 9km from Soppong.

Sleeping & Eating

All accommodation, much of which is found along Soppong's main road, is clearly marked by signs. There's little in the way of food in Soppong, but virtually every guesthouse has a restaurant attached.

★Soppong River Inn HOTEL $$
(053 617107; www.soppong.com; Rte 1095; r & bungalows 200-2450B;) Combining rooms in a couple of rambling riverside structures and a handful of free-standing basic bungalows, this is the most attractive place in Soppong. Set among lush gardens with winding paths, the rooms have heaps of character and are all slightly different; the River Rim Cottage, with a private balcony situated right over the river, is our fave. It's at the western edge of town, within walking distance of the bus station.

Little Eden Guesthouse HOTEL $$
(053 617054; www.littleeden-guesthouse.com; Rte 1095; r & bungalows 400-1800B;) The five A-frame bungalows around a pleasant pool are well maintained and include hot-water showers. And the four rooms in the new building are spacious and attractive. But it's the beautiful two-storey 'houses' that make this place special. Perfect for families or a group of friends, they are stylishly decorated with living rooms, interesting nooks and crannies, and terraces with hammocks.

Baan Cafe Nature Resort HOTEL $$
(053 617081; khunjui@yahoo.com; Rte 1095; r 600B, bungalows 1200B;) Located near the bridge, about 750m west of Soppong's bus stop, this place combines spotless rooms and house-like bungalows in a park setting by Nam Lang. The bungalows include fireplaces, have balconies looking over the river and are terrific value. Baan Cafe is also one of the better restaurants in town (open 7.30am to 7.30pm) and serves locally grown coffee.

Lemonhill Garden GUESTHOUSE $$
(053 617039; Rte 1095; r & bungalows 500-1500B;) Due to its location across from the town bus stop, this guesthouse is probably the most popular place in town, though it must be said that there are nicer places to stay. There's a mishmash of accommodation ranging from rooms to bungalows – check out a few before coming to a decision – and a restaurant (open 7am to 6pm).

Rock RESORT $$$
(☎053 617134; www.therockresort.com; Rte 1095; r & bungalows incl breakfast 800-2500B; ❄📶) You can't miss this place, located about 1.5km west of town. The bungalows are scattered across a manicured riverbank pockmarked with rock formations, and there are also a few rooms equipped with TV, fridge and air-con. A suspension bridge links the grounds with adjacent flower gardens. Rock is geared towards Thai tourists and communicating in English might be a problem.

Information

Soppong's police station is 1.5km west of the town. There are a couple of ATMs in the centre of town near the petrol station.

Getting There & Around

Motorcycle taxis stationed at the bus stop in Soppong will take passengers to Tham Lot or the Cave Lodge for 70B per person; private pick-up trucks will take you and up to five other people for 300B.

Motorcycles can be hired at **Castrol Bike Point** (☎053 617185; Rte 1095; ⏱7am-6pm), at the western edge of town, for 250B per day.

Buses and minivans stop near the town's market, roughly opposite the petrol station.

Bus services:

Chiang Mai 105B, six hours, 10.30am

Mae Hong Son 45B, three hours, 12.30pm

Pai 45B, 1½ hours, 10.30am

Minivan services:

Chiang Mai 250B, four hours, hourly 8.30am to 6pm

Mae Hong Son 100B, two hours, hourly 9.30am to 6.30pm

Pai 100B, one hour, hourly 8.30am to 6.30pm

Around Soppong

Tham Lot ถ้ำลอด

Tham Lot CAVE
(admission from 150B; ⏱8am-5.30pm) Located about 9km north of Soppong is Tham Lot (pronounced *tâm lôrt* and also known as *tâm nám lôrt*), a large limestone cave with impressive stalagmites, 'coffin caves' and a wide stream running through it. Along with Tham Nam Lang further west, it's one of the largest known caves in Thailand. The total length of the cave is 1600m, and the stream runs through it for 600m.

OFF THE BEATEN TRACK

THE CAVES OF PANGMAPHA

The 900-sq-km area of Pangmapha district is famous for its high concentration of cave systems, where over 200 have been found. Apart from Tham Lot, one of its most famous is **Tham Nam Lang**, which is 20km northwest of Soppong near Ban Nam Khong. It's 8.5km long and thought to be one of the largest caves in the world in terms of volume.

Many of the caves are essentially underground river systems, some of which boast waterfalls, lakes and sandy 'beaches'. *Cryptotora thamicola*, an eyeless, waterfall-climbing troglobitic fish that forms its own genus, is found in only two caves in the world, both of which are in Pangmapha. Other caves contain little or no life, due to an abundance of noxious gases or very little oxygen.

More than 85 of the district's 200 limestone caverns are known to contain ancient teak coffins carved from solid teak logs. Up to 9m long, the coffins are typically suspended on wooden scaffolds inside the caves. The coffins have been carbon-dated and shown to be between 1200 and 2200 years old. The ends are usually carved and Thai archaeologists have identified at least 50 different design schemes.The local Shans know these burial caves as *tâm pěe* (spirit caves) or *tâm pěe maan* (coffin caves). It is not known who made them or why they were placed in the caves, but as most caves have fewer than 10 coffins it indicates that not everyone was accorded such an elaborate burial. Similar coffins have been found in karst areas west of Bangkok and also in Borneo, China and the Philippines, but the highest concentration of coffin caves from this period is in Pangmapha.

The easiest coffins to visit are in the **coffin cave** (Rte 1095; admission 20B; ⏱8.30am-5pm) just past Pangmapha Hospital, 2km west of Soppong, and the coffin caves in Tham Lot, 9km northeast of Soppong. Several caves that scientists are investigating at the moment are off limits to the public, but John Spies at Cave Lodge (p290) may know which caves are possible to explore. His book, *Wild Times*, is also a great informal guide to the area's caves.

Apart from the main chamber there are also three side chambers – Column Cavern, Doll Cave and Coffin Cave – that can be reached by ladders. It takes around two hours to explore the whole thing. Access to parts of the cave may be limited between August and October because of water levels.

At the entrance, you must hire a gas lantern and guide for 150B (one guide leads one to three people) to take you through the caverns; visitors are not permitted to tour the caves alone. Rafts (up to three people, one way 300B, return 400B) from the entrance to the exit take in the Column Cavern, Doll Cave and Coffin Cave. If going one way you can walk back from outside the cave (20 minutes), but only during the dry season (from approximately November to May). In the dry season it may be possible to wade to the Doll Cave and then take a raft through to the exit (200B). Try to be at the exit at sunset when hundreds of thousands of swifts pour into Tham Lot and cling to their bedtime stalagmites.

A **Nature Education Centre** (⌚8am-5.30pm) on the grounds has basic displays on the area as well as displays of pottery remains found in the cave.

Sleeping & Eating

A row of **outdoor restaurants** (mains 20-60B; ⌚9am-6pm) outside the Tham Lot park entrance offer simple Thai fare.

★**Cave Lodge** GUESTHOUSE $$
(☎053 617203; www.cavelodge.com; dm 120B, r 250-300B, bungalows 400-2000B;) Open since 1986 and run by John Spies, the unofficial expert on the area, this is one of the more legendary places to stay in northern Thailand (and probably the first guesthouse in Mae Hong Son). The 20 rooms here are basic but unique and varied. The setting on a wooded hillside above Nam Lang is beautiful and options for adventure abound.

Choose from caving and kayaking trips (the latter possible from approximately February to May), guided or unguided hikes (good maps are available), or just hang out in the beautiful communal area. The traditional Shan herbal sauna is an experience and the custom ovens bake bread and other treats. Tham Lot is a short walk away.

Mae La-Na แม่ละนา

Set in a picturesque mountain valley located 6km off Rte 1095, this tiny, remote Shan village feels like a lost corner of the world. The most famous local attraction is **Tham Mae La-Na**, a 12km-long cavern with a stream running through it. Although local guides are willing to take people inside, in reality the cave lacks the appropriate infrastructure to support visitors, who run a serious risk of permanently damaging delicate cave formations and disturbing the habitat of sensitive cave fish. A better bet is to check out the nearby **Tham Pakarang** (Coral Cave) and **Tham Phet** (Diamond Cave), both of which feature good wall formations. Guides (200B) can be arranged at the main village shop and petrol station. Some of the caves may not be accessible during the rainy season.

Mae La-Na is also a good base for some inspiring **walks**. Some of Mae Hong Son's most beautiful scenery is within a day's ramble, and there are several Red and Black Lahu villages nearby. It's also possible to walk a 15km half-loop all the way from Mae La-Na to Tham Lot. Khun Ampha at Maelana Garden Home can provide a basic map.

The Mae La-Na junction is 13km west of Soppong. A motorcycle taxi here from Soppong costs 200B. Along the way you'll pass the Black Lahu village of **Jabo**, which also has a coffin cave.

Sleeping & Eating

Homestay Program GUESTHOUSE $
(per person per night 100B) Two dozen homes in Mae La-Na have collaborated to form a homestay program; fees go back into a community fund. Meals can be prepared for 100B per person. Enquire at the sporadically staffed wooden office at the entrance to town or at any home with a 'homestay' sign.

Maelana Garden Home GUESTHOUSE $
(☎08 1706 6021; r & bungalows 200-500B;) At the edge of town towards Tham Mae La-Na, this beautiful farmlike compound combines rooms in two wooden houses and a few A-frame bamboo bungalows. Authentic Shan meals can be prepared for 100B per person. Call ahead – transport can be arranged for 150B from Rte 1095 or from Soppong for 400B – or ask for Khun Ampha at the village shop/petrol station.

Mae Hong Son แม่ฮ่องสอน

POP 7000

With its remote setting and surrounding mountains, Mae Hong Son fits many travellers' preconceived notion of how a northern

Thai city should be. A palpable Burmese influence and a border-town feel don't clash with this image, and best of all, there's hardly a túk-túk or tout to be seen. This doesn't mean Mae Hong Son is uncharted territory – tour groups have been coming here for years – but the city's potential as a base for activities, from boat trips to trekking, ensures that your visit can be quite unlike anyone else's.

Mae Hong Son is best visited between November and February when the town is at its coolest and most beautiful. During the rainy season (June to October), travel to the more remote corners of the province can be difficult because there are few paved roads. During the hot season (approximately February to May), Mae Nam Pai valley fills with smoke from swidden agriculture. The only problem with going in the cool season is that the nights are downright cold – you'll need at least one sweater and a thick pair of socks for mornings and evenings.

History

Mae Hong Son has been isolated from Thailand geographically, culturally and politically for most of its relatively short existence. The city was founded as an elephant training outpost in the early 19th century, and remained little more than this until 1856, when fighting in Burma caused thousands of Shan to pour into the area. In the years that followed, Mae Hong Son prospered as a centre for logging and remained an independent kingdom until 1900, when King Rama V incorporated the area into the Thai kingdom.

Sights

With their bright colours, whitewashed stupas and glittering zinc fretwork, Mae Hong Son's Burmese- and Shan-style temples will have you scratching your head wondering which country you're in.

Wat Jong Klang BUDDHIST TEMPLE
(วัดจองกลาง; Th Chamnansatit; ⏲dawn-dusk) FREE Wat Jong Klang houses 100-year-old glass *Jataka* paintings and a **museum** (admission by donation; ⏲8am-6pm) with 150-year-old wooden dolls from Myanmar that depict some of the more gruesome aspects of the wheel of life. The temple is lit at night and is reflected in Nong Jong Kham – a popular photo op for visitors.

Wat Jong Kham BUDDHIST TEMPLE
(วัดจองคำ; Th Chamnansatit; ⏲dawn-dusk) FREE Next door to Wat Jong Klang, this temple was built nearly 200 years ago by Thai Yai (Shan) people, who make up about half of the population of Mae Hong Son Province.

Wat Hua Wiang BUDDHIST TEMPLE
(วัดหัวเวียง; Th Phanich Wattana; ⏲dawn-dusk) FREE This wát, just west of Mae Hong Son's market, is recognised for its *bòht* (chapel) boasting an elaborate tiered wooden roof and a revered bronze Buddha statue from Mandalay (Myanmar).

Wat Kam Kor BUDDHIST TEMPLE
(วัดก้ำก่อ; Th Pha Doong Muay Do; ⏲dawn-dusk) FREE This Burmese-style temple is known for its unique covered walkway.

Wat Phra Non BUDDHIST TEMPLE
(วัดพระนอน; Th Pha Doong Muay Do; ⏲dawn-dusk) FREE Wat Phra Non is home to the largest reclining Buddha in town.

Activities

Trekking

Mae Hong Son's location at the edge of mountainous forest makes it an excellent base for hikes into the countryside. Trekking here is not quite the large-scale industry it is elsewhere, and visitors willing to get their boots muddy can expect to find relatively untouched nature and isolated villages.

Multiday hikes in groups of two people range from 1000B to 3000B per person, per day. As is the case elsewhere in Thailand, the per-day rates drop significantly with a larger group and a longer trek.

Nature Walks TREKKING
(☎08 9552 6899; www.naturewalksthai-myanmar.com) Treks here might cost more than elsewhere, but John, a native of Mae Hong Son, is the best guide in town. Hikes range from day-long nature walks to multiday journeys across the province. John can also arrange custom nature-based tours, such as the orchid-viewing tours he conducts from March to May. Email or call John to get in touch with him.

Friend Tour TREKKING
(☎053 611647, 08 6180 7031; PA Motor, 21 Th Pradit Jong Kham; ⏲8am-6.30pm) With nearly 20 years' experience, this recommended outfit offers trekking and rafting excursions, as well as day tours.

Mae Hong Son

Namrin Tour HIKING

(☎053 614454; off Th Pradit Jong Kham; ⏰9am-7pm) Mr Dam advertises 'bad sleep, bad jokes', but his treks get good reports.

Boat Trips

Long-tail boat trips on the nearby Mae Nam Pai are popular, and the same guesthouses and trekking agencies that organise treks from Mae Hong Son can arrange river excursions. The most common trip sets off from Tha Pong Daeng, 4km southwest of Mae Hong Son. Boats travel 15km downstream to the 'long-neck' village of Huay Pu Keng (700B, one hour), or all the way to the border outpost of Ban Nam Phiang Din (800B, 1½ hours), 20km from the pier, before returning. Boats can accommodate a maximum of eight passengers.

Mud Spa

Phu Klon country club SPA

(☎053 282579; www.phuklon.co.th; mud treatments 80-700B, massage per hour 250-450B; ⏰8am-6.30pm) This self-professed country club is touted as Thailand's only mud treatment spa. Phu Klon is 16km north of Mae Hong Son in Mok Champae. If you haven't got your own wheels, you can take the daily Ban Ruam Thai– or Mae Aw–bound *sŏrng·tăa·ou* (25B), but this means you might have to find your own way back. Discovered by a team of geologists in 1995, the mud here is pasteurised and blended with herbs before being employed in various treatments. There's thermal mineral water for soaking, and massage is also available.

☞ Tours

Rosegarden Tours TOUR

(☎053 611681; www.rosegarden-tours.com; 86/4 Th Khunlumprapas; tours from 600B; ⏰8.30am-10pm) The English- and French-speaking guides at this long-standing agency focus on cultural and sightseeing tours.

Mae Hong Son

Sights

1 Wat Hua Wiang B1
2 Wat Jong Kham C3
3 Wat Jong Klang C3
Wat Jong Klang Museum .... (see 3)
4 Wat Kam Kor B3
5 Wat Phra Non A3

Activities, Courses & Tours

6 Friend Tour C2
7 Namrin Tour B3
8 Rosegarden Tours B2
9 Tour Merng Tai B3

Sleeping

10 Baan Mai Guest House D2
11 Baiyoke Chalet Hotel B2
12 Coffee Morning D2
13 Friend House C2
14 Jongkham Place C2
15 Mountain Inn & Resort B4
16 Palm House C3
17 Piya Guesthouse B3
18 Romtai House C3

Eating

Ban Din Coffee .... (see 13)
19 Banpleng Restaurant B4
20 Fern Restaurant B3
La Tasca .... (see 11)
21 Maesribua C2
22 Morning Market C1
23 Night Market C1
24 Night Market B3
25 Salween River Restaurant & Bar C2

Drinking & Nightlife

26 Crossroads B2
27 Sunflower B2

Shopping

28 Maneerat B2
29 Manerplaw/Ethnic Echoes B2
30 Walking Street C3

Transport

31 JD C2
PA Motor .... (see 6)
32 Sŏrng·tăa·ou to Mae Aw (Ban Rak Thai) C1
33 Sŏrng·tăa·ou to Ban Ruam Thai (Pang Ung) C1
34 Titan B2

Tour Merng Tai TOUR
(☎053 611979; www.tourmerngtai.com; 89 Th Khunlumprapas) This outfit mostly does city-based van tours and cycling tours, but can also arrange treks.

Festivals & Events

Poi Sang Long Festival RELIGIOUS
Wat Jong Klang and Wat Jong Kham are the focal point of this March festival, where young Shan boys are ordained as novice monks in the ceremony known as *boò·at lôok gâa·ou*. As part of the Shan custom, the boys are dressed in ornate costumes (rather than simple white robes) and wear flower headdresses and facial make-up.

Jong Para Festival RELIGIOUS
An important local event, this festival is held towards the end of the Buddhist Rains Retreat around October – it's three days before the full moon of the 11th lunar month, so it varies from year to year. The festival begins with local Shan bringing offerings to monks in the temples in a procession marked by the carrying of models of castles on poles. Folk theatre and dance, some of it unique to northwest Thailand, is performed on the wát grounds.

Loi Krathong CULTURAL
During this national holiday in November – usually celebrated by floating *grà·tong* (small lotus floats) on the nearest pond, lake or river – Mae Hong Son residents launch balloons called *grà·tong sà·wăn* (heaven *grà·tong*) from Doi Kong Mu.

Sleeping

Mae Hong Son generally lacks inspiring accommodation, although there are a couple of standout midrange options outside the centre of town. Because it's a tourist town, accommodation prices fluctuate with the seasons, and outside of the high season (November to January) it's worth pursuing a discount.

In Town

Friend House GUESTHOUSE $
(☎053 620119; 20 Th Pradit Jong Kham; r 200-500B; 📶) The super-clean though characterless rooms here run from the ultra basic, which share hot-water bathrooms, to larger rooms with private bathrooms.

Coffee Morning HOTEL $
(☎053 612234; 78 Th Singha-nat Barm Rung; r 500-600B; @📶) This old wooden house unites a

DON'T MISS

WAT PHRA THAT DOI KONG MU

Wat Phra That Doi Kong Mu (วัดพระธาตุดอยกองมู; ⊙dawn-dusk) FREE Climb the hill west of town, Doi Kong Mu (1500m), to visit this temple compound, also known as Wat Plai Doi. Two Shan *chedi*, erected in 1860 and 1874, enshrine the ashes of monks from Myanmar's Shan State. Around the back of the wát you can see a tall, slender, standing Buddha and catch views west of the ridge. There's also a cafe and a tourist market. The view of the sea of fog that collects in the valley each morning is impressive; at other times you get wonderful views of the town and surrounding valleys.

On Th Pha Doong Muay Do is a long stairway leading to the top of Wat Phra That Doi Kong Mu (it's easier than it might appear), otherwise a motorcycle taxi costs 120B return.

cafe-bookshop and three basic rooms. Considering that bathrooms are shared, the rates aren't exactly a steal, but easy access to coffee and an artsy atmosphere make up for it.

Baan Mai Guest House GUESTHOUSE $
(☎09 3136 0577; www.facebook.com/BaanMaiGuestHouse; 26/1 Th Chamnansatit; r incl breakfast 300B) The three simple fan-cooled rooms in a cosy wooden house near Nong Jong Kham have an authentic homestay feel.

Palm House GUESTHOUSE $
(☎053 614022; 22/1 Th Chamnansatit; r 400-1000B; ❄📶) This two-storey cement building offers several characterless but large, clean rooms with TV, fridge, hot water and fan/air-con. A new annexe was being built when we were in town. The helpful owner speaks English and can arrange transport.

Piya Guesthouse HOTEL $$
(☎053 611260; piyaguesthouse@hotmail.com; 1/1 Th Khunlumprapas; bungalows 700B; ❄📶🏊) Steps from Mae Hong Son's central lake is this compound of bungalows ringing a garden and a tiny pool. Rooms come equipped with air-con, fridge, TV and hot showers. It's all clean and inviting, and couldn't be more conveniently located.

Romtai House GUESTHOUSE $$
(☎053 612437; www.maehongson-romtai.com; Th Chamnansatit; r 400-600B, bungalows 800B; ❄📶) Hidden behind both the lakeside temples and a bland-looking reception area, this place has a huge variety of accommodation ranging from spacious, clean rooms to bungalows looking over a lush garden with fishponds.

Jongkham Place GUESTHOUSE $$
(☎053 614294; 4/2 Th Udom Chaonited; r 500-800B, bungalows 800B, ste 1200-1500B; ❄📶) This family-run place by the lake has a few rooms, four attractive wooden bungalows and two penthouse-like suites. Most accommodation includes TV, fridge and air-con.

Mountain Inn & Resort HOTEL $$
(☎053 611803; www.mhsmountaininn.com; 112/2 Th Khunlumprapas; r 1200-1500B, ste 2500B, all incl breakfast; ❄@📶🏊) Clean, cosy rooms with Thai decorative touches, air-con, TV and fridge are the standard here. There is a pretty courtyard garden with small ponds, a pool, and benches and parasols. Superior rooms are a better deal than the Deluxe as they include a terrace overlooking the pool.

Baiyoke Chalet Hotel HOTEL $$$
(☎053 613132; www.baiyokehotel.com; 90 Th Khunlumprapas; r incl breakfast 1380-1800B; ❄📶) This place intertwines convenient location and comfortable lodging. As established in the lobby, the rooms are tastefully outfitted in hardwood and subtle local themes. A downside is that the restaurant-lounge downstairs can get quite loud, so request a room away from the street or on an upper level. Low-season rates are almost 50% less.

Outside of Town

Sang Tong Huts HOTEL $$
(☎053 611680; www.sangtonghuts.org; Th Maka Santi; bungalows 700-3000B; @📶🏊) This clutch of rustic bungalows in a wooded area just outside of town is one of Mae Hong Son's more character-filled places to stay. Accommodation is spacious, comfortable and well designed, and the tasty baked goods and pool make up for the distance from the town centre. It's popular among repeat visitors to Mae Hong Son, so it pays to book ahead.

Sang Tong Huts is about 1km northeast of Th Khunlumprapas, just off Th Maka Santi – if going towards Pai, turn left at the intersection before the town's northernmost stoplight and follow the signs.

Pana Huts GUESTHOUSE $$
(☎053 614331; www.panahuts.com; 293/9 Th Maka Santi; r & bungalows 600-800B; 📶) Set in a

wooded area outside of town, the five bamboo huts here all have hot-water bathrooms and terraces. The inviting communal area is equally rustic, with its thatched teak leaf roof, wooden benches and enclosed campfire for chilly nights.

Pana Huts is about 1km northeast of Th Khunlumprapas, just off Th Maka Santi – if going towards Pai, turn left at the intersection just before the town's northernmost stoplight and follow the signs.

★Fern Resort RESORT **$$$**
(☎053 686110; www.fernresort.info; off Rte 108; bungalows incl breakfast 2500-3500B; ❄@📶🏊) This long-standing ecofriendly resort is one of the pleasanter places to stay in northern Thailand. The 35 wooden bungalows are set among tiered rice paddies and streams and feature stylishly decorated interiors. There's no TV, but dogs, a pool, pétanque court and the nearby nature trails at the adjacent Mae Surin National Park are more than enough to keep you occupied. The only downside is that the resort is 7km south of town, but free pick-up is available from the airport and bus terminal, and regular shuttles run to/from town, stopping at Fern Restaurant.

Imperial Tara Mae Hong Son Hotel HOTEL **$$$**
(☎053 684444-9; www.imperialhotels.com; Rte 108; r 3800B, ste 5000-6600B, all incl breakfast; ❄@📶🏊) Rooms in this upmarket, 104-room hotel all have wooden floors and balconies and are tastefully decorated. French windows that open onto a terrace make a pleasant change from the standard business hotel layout. Facilities include a sauna, swimming pool and fitness centre. It's about 2km south of town.

Eating & Drinking

Mae Hong Son's **morning market** (off Th Phanich Wattana; mains 10-30B; ⏰6-9am) is a fun place to have breakfast. Several vendors at the northern end of the market sell unusual dishes such as *tòo·a poo ùn,* a Burmese noodle dish supplemented with thick chickpea porridge and deep-fried chickpea flour cakes and tofu. Other vendors along the same strip sell a local version of *kà·nŏm jeen nám ngée·o* (thin rice noodles served

LONG-NECKED KAYAN VILLAGES

These villages are Mae Hong Son's most touted – and most controversial – tourist attraction. The 'long-necked' moniker originates from the habit of some Kayan women (sometimes also referred to as Padaung, a Shan term) of wearing heavy brass coils around their necks. The coils depress the collarbone and rib cage, which makes their necks look unnaturally stretched. A common myth claims if the coils are removed, a woman's neck will fall over and she will suffocate. In fact the women attach and remove the coils at will and there is no evidence that this deformation impairs their health at all.

Nobody knows for sure how the coil custom got started. One theory is that it was meant to make the women unattractive to men from other tribes; another story says it was so tigers wouldn't carry the women off by their throats. Most likely it is nothing more than a fashion accessory. Until relatively recently the custom was largely dying out, but money from tourism, and undoubtedly the influence of local authorities eager to cash in on the Kayan, have reinvigorated it.

Regardless of the origin, the villages are now on every group tour's itinerary, and have become a significant tourist draw for Mae Hong Son. The villages are often derided as human zoos, and there are certainly elements of this, but we find them more like bizarre rural markets, with the women earning much of their money by selling souvenirs and drinks. The Kayan we've talked to claim to be happy with their current situation, but the stateless position they share with all Burmese refugees is nothing to be envied, and these formerly independent farmers are now reliant on aid and tourists to survive.

Any of the three Kayan settlements outside Mae Hong Son can be visited independently, if you have transportation, or any travel agency in Mae Hong Son can arrange a tour. The most-touted Kayan village is **Huai Seua Thao**, about 7km from Mae Hong Son. More remote, but definitely not off the beaten track, is **Kayan Tayar**, near the Shan village of Ban Nai Soi, 35km northwest of Mae Hong Son. Another 'long-necked' community is based at **Huay Pu Keng** and is included on long-tail boat tours departing from Tha Pong Daeng. All collect an entry fee from non-Thais of 250B per person.

with a pork- and tomato-based broth) often topped with *kàhng pòrng*, a Shan snack of battered-and-deep-fried vegetables.

The city also has two good night markets: the **night market** (Th Phanich Wattana; mains 20-60B; ⌚4-8pm) near the airport offers mostly takeaway northern Thai-style food, while the **night market** (Th Khunlumprapas; mains 10-60B; ⌚4-9pm) at the southern end of Th Khunlumprapas has more generic Thai food. Several vendors at Mae Hong Song's Walking Street market also sell a variety of dishes, some local, during the tourist season.

Maesribua NORTHERN THAI $
(cnr Th Pradit Jong Kham & Th Singha-nat Barm Rung; mains 20-40B; ⌚8am-1pm) Like the Shan grandma you never had, Auntie Bua prepares a generous spread of local-style curries, soups and dips on a daily basis.

Chom Mai Restaurant THAI $
(off Rte 108, no roman-script sign; mains 40-290B; ⌚8.30am-3.30pm;) The English-language menu here is limited, but don't miss the deliciously rich *kôw soy* (northern-style curry noodle soup) or *kôw mòk gài* (the Thai version of biryani). Chom Mai is located about 4km south of Mae Hong Son, along the road that leads to Tha Pong Daeng – look for the Doi Chaang coffee sign.

Ban Din Coffee CHINESE $
(Th Pradit Jong Kham, no roman-script sign; mains 30B; ⌚7am-9pm) If you didn't make it up to Mae Aw (Ban Rak Thai), be sure to stop by this open-air restaurant selling delicious and unique noodle dishes, dried fruit, tea and other specialities of Mae Hong Son's Chinese/Yunnanese residents.

Banpleng Restaurant NORTHERN THAI $
(108 Th Khunlumprapas; mains 35-120B; ⌚9am-10pm Mon-Sat) This open-air restaurant does a handful of tasty local dishes – you're safe going with anything that says 'Maehongson style' on the English-language menu.

Salween River Restaurant & Bar INTERNATIONAL, THAI $
(www.salweenriver.com; 23 Th Pradit Jong Kham; mains 60-330B; ⌚8am-10pm;) Salween is your typical traveller's cafe: a few old guidebooks, free wi-fi and a menu ranging from burgers to Burmese. Yet unlike most traveller's cafes, the food here is good; don't miss the Burmese green tea salad.

Fern Restaurant INTERNATIONAL, THAI $
(Th Khunlumprapas; mains 65-180B; ⌚10.30am-10pm;) The Fern is almost certainly Mae Hong Son's most upscale restaurant, but remember, this is Mae Hong Son. Nonetheless, service is professional and the food is decent. The expansive menu covers Thai and local dishes, with quite a few meat-free options. There is live lounge music some nights.

La Tasca ITALIAN $$
(Th Khunlumprapas; mains 60-190B; ⌚10am-10pm;) This cosy place has been serving homemade pasta, pizza and calzone for as long as we can remember and is one of the few places in town to do relatively authentic Western food.

Crossroads BAR
(61 Th Khunlumprapas; ⌚8am-1am;) This friendly bar-restaurant is a crossroads in every sense, from its location at one of Mae Hong Son's main intersections to its clientele that ranges from wet-behind-the-ears backpackers to hardened locals. And there's steak (from 180B to 250B).

Sunflower BAR
(Th Pradit Jong Kham; ⌚7.30am-10pm) It's technically a restaurant (mains 50B to 320B), but Sunflower's draught beer, live lounge music, views of the lake and tacky artificial waterfall also make it a decent bar.

Shopping

A few souvenir shops can be found near the southern end of Th Khunlumprapas.

Walking Street MARKET
(Th Pradit Jong Kham; ⌚5-10pm Oct-Feb) From October to February the roads around Jong Kham Lake become a lively Walking Street market, with handicrafts and food vendors.

Manerplaw/Ethnic Echoes HANDICRAFTS
(Th Khunlumprapas; ⌚10am-10pm) These linked shops specialise in hill-tribe garb.

Maneerat HANDICRAFTS
(80 Th Khunlumprapas, no roman-script sign; ⌚8am-9pm) Maneerat has a good selection of Shan and Burmese items.

Information

Most of the banks at the southern end of Th Khunlumprapas have ATMs.

Maehongson Living Museum (27 Th Singha-nat Barm Rung; ⌚7am-5pm;) An attractive wooden building – actually Mae Hong Son's former bus depot – has been turned into a museum on local culture, food and architecture, though the bulk of information is only in Thai. There are a few maps and brochures in English, and there's also free wi-fi and bike rental for only 15B per day.

Titan (Th Khunlumprapas; per hour 15B; ⌚9am-9pm) Internet is available here.

Tourism Authority of Thailand (TAT; ☎053 612982, nationwide 1672; www.tourismthailand.org/Mae-Hong-Son; Th Ni-wet Pi-sarn; ⌚8.30am-4.30pm) Basic tourist brochures and maps can be picked up here.

Tourist Police (☎053 611812, nationwide 1155; Th Singha-nat Barm Rung; ⌚8.30am-4.30pm)

Getting There & Away

For many people the time saved flying from Chiang Mai to Mae Hong Son versus bus travel is worth the extra baht. At research time, **Kan Air** (☎053 613188, nationwide 02 551 6111; www.kanairlines.com; Mae Hong Son Airport; ⌚7.30am-5pm) was the only airline operating out of Mae Hong Son's airport, with three daily flights (1590B, 35 minutes). A túk-túk into town costs about 80B.

Mae Hong Son's bus and minivan station is 1km south of the city; a túk-túk or motorcycle ride to/from here costs 60B. **Prempracha Tour** (☎053 684100; Mae Hong Son Bus Station, Th Nawa Khotchasan) runs bus services within the province; **Sombat Tour** (☎053 684222; Mae Hong Son Bus Station, Th Nawa Khotchasan) operates connections between Mae Hong Son and Bangkok.

Getting Around

The centre of Mae Hong Son can easily be covered on foot, and it's one of the few towns in Thailand that doesn't seem to have a motorcycle taxi at every corner. A few can be found near the entrance to the morning market, and charge 20B to 40B for trips within town. There are also a few túk-túk who charge from 40B per trip within town.

Because most of Mae Hong Son's attractions are outside of town, renting a motorcycle or bicycle is a wise move.

PA Motor (☎053 611647, 08 6180 7031; 21 Th Pradit Jong Kham; per day motorbike 150-250B, car 1500-3000B; ⌚8am-6.30pm) Hires motorbikes and cars.

JD (☎08 4372 6967; Th Ni-wet Pi-sarn; per day 150-200B; ⌚8am-6.30pm) Hires motorbikes.

Titan (Th Khunlumprapas; per day 100B; ⌚9am-9pm) Hires good-quality mountain bikes.

Around Mae Hong Son

Pha Bong Hot Springs บ่อน้ำร้อนผาบ่อง

Pha Bong Hot Springs HOT SPRINGS
(private bath/bathing room 50/400B; ⌚8am-sunset) Eleven kilometres south of the capital in the Shan village of Pha Bong is this public park with hot springs. You can take a private bath or rent a room, and there's also massage (per hour 150B). The springs can be reached on any southbound bus.

Tham Pla National Park อุทยานแห่งชาติถ้ำปลา

Tham Pla National Park NATURE RESERVE
(Rte 1095; adult/child 100/50B; ⌚8am-6pm) The most touted attraction of this national park is Tham Pla (Fish Cave), a water-filled cavern where hundreds of soro brook carp thrive. A 450m path leads from the park entrance to a suspension bridge that crosses a stream and continues to the cave. The park is 16km north of Mae Hong Son and can be reached by hopping on any northbound bus.

A statue of a Hindu *rishi* (sage) called Nara, said to protect the holy fish from danger, stands nearby the cave. The fish grow up to 1m long and are found only in the provinces of Mae Hong Son, Ranong, Chiang Mai, Rayong, Chanthaburi and Kanchanaburi. They eat vegetables and insects, although the locals believe them to be vegetarian and feed them only fruit and vegetables, which can be purchased at the park entrance.

It's all a bit anticlimactic, but the park grounds are a bucolic, shady place to hang out. Food and picnic tables are available.

Mae Aw (Ban Rak Thai) & Around แม่ออ

A worthwhile day trip from the provincial capital is to Mae Aw (also known as Ban Rak Thai), an atmospheric Chinese outpost right at the Myanmar border, 43km north of Mae Hong Son.

The road to Mae Aw is a beautiful route that passes through tidy riverside Shan villages such as **Mok Champae** before suddenly climbing through impressive mountain scenery. Stops can be made at **Pha Sua Waterfall**, about 5km up the mountain, and **Pang Tong Summer Palace**, a rarely used royal compound a few kilometres past the waterfall.

TRANSPORT TO/FROM MAE HONG SON

Bus

DESTINATION	FARE (B)	DURATION (HR)	FREQUENCY
Bangkok	742-865	15	3pm & 4pm
Chiang Mai	118	8	8.30am (northern route)
Chiang Mai	185-333	9	8am, 10.30am, 8pm & 9pm (southern route)
Khun Yuam	43-88	2	8am, 10.30am, 8pm & 9pm
Mae Sariang	97-182	4	8am, 10.30am, 8pm & 9pm
Pai	66	4½	8.30am
Soppong (Pangmapha)	41	2	8.30am

Minivan & Sŏrng·tăa·ou

DESTINATION	FARE (B)	DURATION (HR)	FREQUENCY
Ban Ruam Thai (Pang Ung)	80	1	*sŏrng·tăa·ou* 9.30am & 3.30pm
Chiang Mai	250	6	hourly minivans 7am-5pm
Mae Aw (Ban Rak Thai)	80	1	*sŏrng·tăa·ou* noon & 3pm
Pai	150	2½	hourly minivans 7am-5pm
Soppong (Pangmapha)	100	1½	hourly minivans 7am-5pm

For an interesting detour, at Ban Na Pa Paek take a left and continue 6km to the Shan village of **Ban Ruam Thai**. There are several basic places to stay and eat here, and the road ends 500m further at **Pang Ung**, a peaceful mountain reservoir surrounded by pines that is immensely popular among Thai day trippers in search of a domestic Switzerland.

From Ban Na Pa Paek it's 6km further to Mae Aw. Located on the edge of a reservoir and surrounded by tea plantations, the town was established by Yunnanese KMT fighters who originally fled from communist rule in 1949; the town's population and architecture remain very Chinese. The main industries are tourism and tea, and there are numerous places to taste the local brew, as well as several restaurants serving Yunnanese cuisine.

There's a brief dirt road to a border crossing (for locals only), but it's not advisable to do any unaccompanied hiking here, as the area is an occasional conflict zone and an infamous drug smuggling route.

Sleeping & Eating

Ping Ping Guest House GUESTHOUSE **$**
(☎08 44481 9707; Mae Aw; r 300-400B) This place and other similar outfits ringing Mae Aw's reservoir offer basic accommodation in adobe-style bungalows.

Guest House & Home Stay GUESTHOUSE **$$**
(☎08 3571 6668; Ban Ruam Thai; r 400-2500B) The first guesthouse in Ban Ruam Thai (there are now numerous 'homestays' offering accommodation from 200B to 400B), this place consists of several simple brick huts positioned on a slope surrounded by coffee plants, tea plants and fruit trees.

Gee Lee Restaurant CHINESE **$$**
(Mae Aw, no roman-script sign; mains 60-180B; ⊙8am-7pm) This was one of the first places in Mae Aw to serve the town's Yunnanese-style Chinese dishes to visitors. Stewed pork leg and stir-fried local vegies are the specialities. It's at the corner of the lake, just before the intersection that leads to the centre of the village.

Getting There & Away

There are four daily *sŏrng·tăa·ou* that head towards Mae Aw: two depart from a stall east of the market and only go as far as Ban Ruam Thai (80B, one hour, 9.30am and 3.30pm), and two depart from a stall opposite the market and terminate in Mae Aw (80B, one hour, noon and 3pm). The latter depart only when full, which can sometimes be a couple of hours after the scheduled departure time. Because of this, it's probably worth getting a group of people together and chartering a vehicle; the *sŏrng·tăa·ou* drivers we talked to quoted from 1200B to 1600B for either destination, while any tour agency in Mae Hong Son will arrange a vehicle for around 1500B. Heading back to Mae Hong

Son, *sŏrng·tăa·ou* leave Ban Ruam Thai at 5.30am and 11am, and Mae Aw at 8am.

Alternatively, the route also makes a brilliant motorcycle ride – just make sure you have enough petrol, as the only station is in Ban Na Pa Paek, at the end of a very long climb.

Khun Yuam ขุนยวม

POP 7000

Between Mae Sariang and Mae Hong Son, where all northbound buses make their halfway stop, is the quiet hillside town of Khun Yuam. There are a couple of places to stay and a few notable sights, and this little-visited town is a nice break from more 'experienced' destinations nearby.

Sights

Most of Khun Yuam's sights are located outside of town and you'll need private transport to reach them.

Thai-Japan Friendship Memorial Hall MUSEUM
(Rte 108; adult/child 100/50B; 8am-4.30pm) At the northern end of town is the recently renovated Thai-Japan Friendship Memorial Hall. After watching a brief film on the history of Khun Yuam, you'll find displays and artefacts that document the period when the Japanese occupied Khun Yuam in the closing weeks of the war with Burma, as well as local history and culture. After they had recovered, some of the Japanese soldiers stayed in Khun Yuam and married; the last Japanese soldier who settled in the area died in 2000.

Wat To Phae BUDDHIST TEMPLE
(วัดตอแพ; dawn-dusk) FREE About 6km to the west of Khun Yuam, the atmospheric Wat To Phae sits alongside a rural stream and boasts a Mon-style *chedi* and an immaculate Burmese-style *wí·hăhn*. Inside the latter, take a look at the large, 150-year-old Burmese *kalaga* (embroidered and sequined tapestry) that's kept behind curtains to one side of the main altar.

Ban Mae U Khaw VILLAGE
(บ้านแม่อูคอ) On the slopes of Doi Mae U Khaw, 25km from Khun Yuam via Rte 1263, is the Hmong village of Ban Mae U Khaw. During late November the area blooms with scenic Mexican sunflowers, known locally as *dòrk boo·a dorng*. This event is popular among Thais and accommodation in the town is booked out.

Nam Tok Mae Surin WATERFALL
(น้ำตกแม่สุรินทร์; admission 200B) Approximately 50km from Khun Yam is the 100m-high Nam Tok Mae Surin, part of Mae Surin National Park and reportedly Thailand's highest waterfall.

Sleeping & Eating

In Khun Yuam you'll find a collection of modest rice and noodle shops along the east side of Rte 108, towards the southern end of town. Most of these close by 5pm or 6pm.

Mithkhoonyoum Hotel HOTEL $
(053 691057; 63 Rte 108; r 400-800B;) On the main road through the town centre, this long-standing place has simple, clean rooms with private bathrooms, the more expensive of which were recently renovated and look better than ever.

Ban Farang HOTEL $$
(053 622086; www.banfarang-guesthouse.com; 499 Th Ratburana; dm 150B, r & bungalows 800-1600B, all incl breakfast;) Off the main road towards the northern end of town (look for the signs near the bus stop), the exceedingly tidy bungalows here are set on a wooded hillside. The cheaper fan rooms are plain and dark but have a terrace, while the more expensive rooms come with air-con, fridge and TV.

Yoont HOTEL $$
(053 691531; yoontkhunyuam@hotmail.com; 92 Rte 108; r incl breakfast 700-1200B;) Yoont is comprised of 12 rooms in a tall concrete building located in the middle of Khun Yuam's main strip. Rooms are relatively

WORTH A TRIP

MAE SAKUT NATURE TRAIL

Mae Sakut Nature Trail (admission 20B; 8am-5pm) Don't have the time for a trek in Mae Hong Son? A taste of the area's natural beauty can be got by tackling this nature trail, part of Nam Tok Mae Surin National Park. In a relatively easy 5km loop, you'll pass through bamboo forests, teak woods, waterfalls, wildflower fields (in season) and viewpoints.

The trailhead is about 7km north of Mae Hong Son, along the same road that leads to Fern Resort; proceed about 200m past the resort to the roadblock where you're expected to park your vehicle and pay the entry fee.

OFF THE BEATEN TRACK

MUANG PON

Muang Pon Homestay Program
(☎08 4485 5937; per night incl breakfast & dinner 350B) For the last decade, the residents of Muang Pon, a picturesque and traditional Shan village just south of Khun Yuam, have collaborated in a homestay program. Approximately 15 households are involved, and the fee includes breakfast and dinner, and involvement in daily activities such as making traditional handicrafts, cooking local-style sweets, taking part in agriculture and sightseeing. The locals are keen to open their homes and share their knowledge, but it must be noted that the level of English ability among the villagers is low.

Muang Pon is about 12km south of Khun Yuam; any Mae Sariang– or Chiang Mai–bound bus can drop you off here.

spacious and stylish – if slightly overpriced – and there's an inviting rooftop chill-out area.

Information

There are a couple of banks with ATMs along the main strip.

Getting There & Away

Buses stop regularly at Khun Yuam on their runs between Mae Sariang and Mae Hong Son. The bus station is at the northern end of town.

Six daily buses depart for Chiang Mai (150B to 275B, seven to eight hours) between 8am and 10.30pm; there are also two minivan departures (300B, 5½ hours, 7am and 2pm). Four daily buses depart for Mae Hong Son (43B to 80B, 1½ hours) between 3pm and 4am; six depart for Mae Sariang (60B to 120B, two hours), between 8am and 10.30pm. Minivans also go to Mae Sariang (150B, 1½ hours) at 7am and 2pm.

Mae Sariang แม่สะเรียง

POP 20,000

Little-visited Mae Sariang is gaining a low-key buzz for its riverside setting and potential as a launching pad for sustainable tourism and hiking opportunities. There are several hill-tribe settlements in the greater area, particularly around Mae La Noi, 30km north of the city, and the area south of Mae Sariang is largely mountainous jungle encompassing both Salawin and Mae Ngao National Parks.

Sights

Mae Sariang Museum MUSEUM
(พิพิธภัณฑ์แมสะเรียง; Th Wiang Mai; ⏲8.30am-4.30pm) FREE Located in the imposing, temple-like structure near the highway junction is this museum dedicated to local culture. There's no explanation in English, but the life-sized dioramas that depict the customs of Mae Sariang's northern Thai, Shan, Karen and Lua inhabitants are worth a look.

Wat Jong Sung & Wat Si Bunruang BUDDHIST TEMPLE
(วัดจองสูง/วัดศรีบุญเรือง; off Th Wiang Mai; ⏲dawn-dusk) FREE These two adjacent Burmese-Shan temples, Wat Jong Sung and Wat Si Bunruang, are located just off Mae Sariang's main street. Built in 1896, Wat Jong Sung is the more interesting of the two and has slender, Shan-style *chedi* and wooden monastic buildings.

Phra That Jom Thong BUDDHIST TEMPLE
(พระธาตุจอมทอง; off Rte 105; ⏲dawn-dusk) FREE You may have spotted this giant, golden hilltop Buddha statue, from where there's great views over Mae Sariang. It's located about 3km south of town, just off the road that leads to Mae Sot.

Activities

The area surrounding Mae Sariang is probably one of the best in northern Thailand for trekking, nature tours and other outdoor pursuits. This is due not only to the area's natural beauty and cultural diversity, but also because of a new breed of responsible and community-based touring and hiking outfits that have sprung up here. Prices range from 1500B to 5000B per day, per person, for groups of at least two people.

Mae Sariang Tours TREKKING, RAFTING
(☎08 8404 8402; www.facebook.com/maesariang.man) Mae Sariang Man, as the owner of this company prefers to be known, is an experienced trekker who leads environmentally conscious and community-based treks and rafting trips in the jungles and national parks surrounding his native city and in Sop Moei, further south. He has no office in town; call or look at his Facebook page to arrange an excursion.

Dragon Sabaii Tours TREKKING
(☎08 5548 0884; www.thailandhilltribeholidays.com; Th Mongkolchai) This outfit emphasises

eco- and cultural tourism primarily in the Mae La Noi area just north of Mae Sariang. Activities range from non-intrusive tours of hill-tribe villages to homestays, 'volunteerism', and cooking and farming with hill tribes, all of which are designed to directly benefit local communities.

Piak Private Tours TREKKING
(☎09 3179 9786; piak1003@hotmail.com) An independent, experienced guide, Piak gets positive feedback for his tours and treks. Call or email to arrange an excursion

NG River Guides RAFTING
(☎053 681139, 08 9756 6443; www.ng-river-guides.com; 258/1 Th Mae Sariang; ⌚9am-5pm) Bobby, the local behind this outfit, conducts rafting and kayaking excursions along Mae Nam Yuam, at its wet peak from October to December. Half-day trips, descending from Mae La Noi to Mae Sariang, start at 1200B per day, per person, in groups of two or more. Greater distances and overnight trips can also be arranged.

Bobby also leads catch and release fly-fishing expeditions in Mae Ngao and Mae La Noi; prices start at 9000B per day, per person, in groups of two or more.

Northwest Tour TREKKING
(☎053 682860, 08 9700 9928; Northwest Guest House, 81 Th Laeng Phanit) This outfit can arrange treks to natural areas and Karen villages in Mae Sariang and Sop Moei Districts.

Mae Sariang

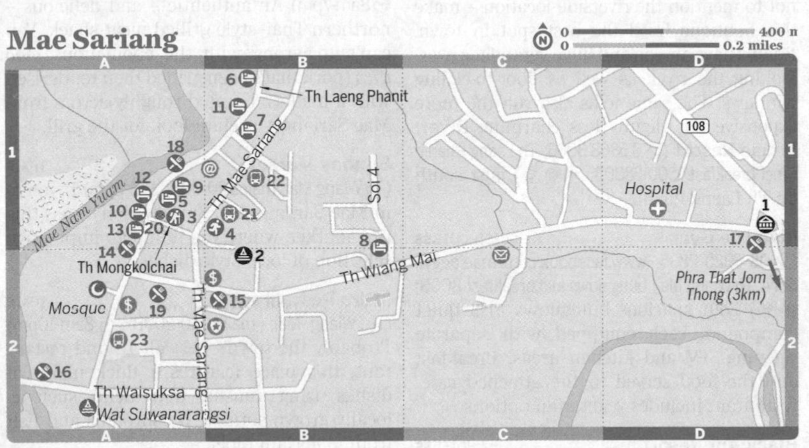

Mae Sariang

Sights
1 Mae Sariang Museum D1
2 Wat Jong Sung & Wat Si Bunruang B2

Activities, Courses & Tours
3 Dragon Sabaii Tours A1
4 NG River Guides B1
Northwest Tour .... (see 9)

Sleeping
5 Above The Sea A1
6 Black Ant Resort B1
7 Huen-Kham-Kong B1
8 Mae Loe Gyi B1
9 Northwest Guest House A1
10 Pang Sariang A1
11 River Bank Guest House B1
12 Riverhouse Hotel A1
13 Riverhouse Resort A1

Eating
14 Coriander in Redwood A2
15 Intira Restaurant B2
16 Kai Yang Rai Khwan A2
17 Muu Thup D1
18 Sawaddee Restaurant & Bar A1
19 Sunday Market A2

Transport
20 Bike Rental Shop A1
Bus Station .... (see 21)
21 Prempracha Tour B1
22 Sombat Tour B1
23 Sŏrng·tăa·ou to Mae Sam Laep A2

Sleeping

Northwest Guest House GUESTHOUSE $
(08 9700 9928; patiat_1@hotmail.com; 81 Th Laeng Phanit; r 250-350B;) The eight rooms in this cosy wooden house are mattress-on-the-floor simple, but get natural light and are relatively spacious. Trekking and other excursions can be arranged here.

Pang Sariang GUESTHOUSE $
(053 682333; 2 Th Laeng Phanit, no roman-script sign; r 250-300B;) A villa with four homey-feeling, simple rooms. Look for the sign that says Guest House & Restaurant.

Riverhouse Hotel HOTEL $$
(053 621201; www.riverhousehotels.com; 77 Th Laeng Phanit; r incl breakfast 1000-1300B;) The combination of teak and stylish decor – not to mention the riverside location – make this boutique hotel the best spot in town. Rooms have air-con and huge verandahs overlooking the river, as well as floor-to-ceiling windows. The same folks also run the more expensive but slightly less charming **Riverhouse Resort** (0 5368 3066; Th Laeng Phanit; r incl breakfast 1500-2800B;), just south on Th Laeng Phanit.

Mae Loe Gyi GUESTHOUSE $$
(08 6920 2835; www.facebook.com/maeloegyi; Soi 4, Th Wiang Mai; bungalows incl breakfast 800B;) Four spacious bungalows in a quiet compound, each equipped with separate sleeping, TV and kitchen areas. Breakfast and the food served in the attached cafe restaurant includes vegetarian options.

Black Ant Resort HOTEL $$
(053 682123; www.blackantcoffee-resort.com; 113 Th Laeng Phanit; r incl breakfast 1000-1200B;) Black Ant has rooms on each side of Th Laeng Phanit. All are large and well outfitted, with some boasting unique quirks such as a tree growing in the middle of the room.

Huen-Kham-Kong HOTEL $$
(053 682416; www.huenkhamkong.com; 102 Th Laeng Phanit; bungalows 800-900B;) The six cutesy bungalows here appear comfortable, come equipped with TV, fridge, air-con and bicycle, and are looked after by some friendly folks.

River Bank Guest House GUESTHOUSE $$
(053 682787; Th Laeng Phanit; r 300-1500B;) Rooms in this attractive riverside house are decked out in hardwood and have lots of natural light. It's worth shelling out 200B more for the rooms on the upper floor as the cheaper rooms feel cramped and have comically small TVs. A highlight here is the stylish and inviting riverside balcony.

Above The Sea HOTEL $$
(09 1859 5264; www.abovetheseamaesariang.com; Th Laeng Phanit; r incl breakfast 800B;) This new place has eight rooms, decked out in an artsy, industrial-chic style, with an attached bar-restaurant.

Eating & Drinking

Th Laeng Phanit, north of the junction with Th Mongkolchai, is home to a strip of ever-changing riverside bars.

★ **Muu Thup** NORTHERN THAI $
(Th Wiang Mai, no roman-script sign; mains 50-80B; 8am-7pm) An authentic – and delicious – northern Thai–style grilled meat shack. You can't go wrong with the eponymous *mŏo đúp* (pork that's been grilled then tenderised with a mallet). Located roughly across from Mae Sariang Museum; look for the grill.

Sunday Market THAI $
(Th Wiang Mai; mains 20-60B; 3-8pm) If you're in Mae Sariang on a Sunday, don't miss this tiny market, where you'll find an impressive selection of local-style dishes.

Intira Restaurant THAI $
(Th Wiang Mai; mains 50-200B; 8am-10pm) Probably the town's best all-around restaurant, this place features a thick menu of dishes using unusual ingredients such as locally grown shiitake mushrooms and fish from Mae Nam Moei.

Kai Yang Rai Khwan THAI $
(Th Waisuksa, no roman-script sign; mains 30-180B; 9am-2pm Tue-Sun) Head here for the Isan holy trinity of grilled chicken, papaya salad and sticky rice. This simple place is at the foot of the bridge crossing.

Sawaddee Restaurant & Bar THAI $
(Th Laeng Phanit; mains 40-150B; 5pm-midnight;) Like a beachside bar, this is a great place to recline with a beer and watch the water (in this case Mae Nam Yuam). There's a lengthy menu with lots of options for vegetarians.

Coriander in Redwood THAI $$
(Th Laeng Phanit; mains 50-420B; 10am-10pm Mon-Sat) The city's poshest restaurant, this attractive wooden structure makes a big deal of its steaks, but we'd suggest sticking with Thai dishes such as the various *nám prík*

TRANSPORT TO/FROM MAE SARIANG

Bus

DESTINATION	FARE (B)	DURATION (HR)	FREQUENCY
Bangkok	590-689	12	7pm & 7.30pm
Chiang Mai	100-180	4-5	4 departures 12.30pm-1am
Khun Yuam	60-120	2-3	7 departures 12.30pm-4am
Mae Hong Son	100-200	3-4	7 departures 12.30pm-4am

Minivan & Sŏrng·tăa·ou

DESTINATION	FARE (B)	DURATION (HR)	FREQUENCY
Chiang Mai	200	3½	6 minivan departures 7am-5pm
Khun Yuam	150	1½	minivan 10.30am & 5.30pm
Mae Sam Laep	80	1½	frequent *sŏrng·tăa·ou* 6.30am-3.30pm
Mae Sot	250	6	frequent *sŏrng·tăa·ou* 6.30am-12.30pm

(chilli-based dips). There's also ice cream and iced coffee drinks for an afternoon cooler.

ℹ Information

Mae Sariang has several banks with ATMs, mostly along the western end of Th Wiang Mai. There's an **internet cafe** (Th Laeng Phanit; per hour 10B; ⊙9am-10pm) in town. Christian and Beng at Sawaddee Restaurant & Bar are good sources of information for small-but-fun destinations and activities in the area.

ℹ Getting There & Away

Located at the **bus station** (Th Mae Sariang), **Prempracha Tour** (☎053 681347) conducts buses and minivans between Mae Sariang and Mae Hong Song. With an office just north of the bus station, **Sombat Tour** (☎053 681532; Th Mae Sariang) handles buses to Bangkok.

ℹ Getting Around

Motorcycles and bicycles are available for hire at the **bike rental shop** (☎08 1181 3695; off Th Laeng Phanit; bike/motorcycle hire per 24hr 50/200B; ⊙7am-7pm), as well as at Northwest Guest House.

Around Mae Sariang

Salawin National Park

Salawin National Park NATIONAL PARK

(อุทยานแหงชาติสาละวิน; ☎053 071429; admission 200B) This national park covers 722 sq km of protected land in Mae Sariang and Sop Moei districts. The park is heavily forested with teak and Asian redwood and is home to what is thought to be the second-largest teak tree in Thailand. There are numerous hiking trails, and it's also possible to travel by boat along Mae Nam Salawin to the park's outstation at Tha Ta Fang. The main headquarters are 6km from Mae Sariang and have bungalow-style accommodation (600B to 1200B), which can be booked via the **Royal Forest Department** (☎02 562 0760; www.dnp.go.th/parkreserve).

Mae Sam Laep

Mae Sam Laep VILLAGE

(แมสามแลบ) The riverside trading village of Mae Sam Laep is nearly at the end of a 50km winding mountain road from Mae Sariang, within the boundaries of Salawin National Park. Populated by Burmese refugees, it has a raw, border-town feel.

The village acts as a launching point for boat trips along Mae Nam Salawin. The trips pass through untouched jungle, unusual rock formations along the river and, occasionally, enter Myanmar. From the pier at Mae Sam Laep it's possible to charter boats south to Sop Moei (approximately 2000B, 1½ hours), 25km from Mae Sam Laep, and north to the Salawin National Park station at Tha Ta Fang (approximately 1500B, one hour), 18km north of Mae Sam Laep. There are passenger boats as well, but departures are infrequent and, unless you speak Thai, difficult to negotiate.

Sŏrng·tăa·ou from Mae Sariang to Mae Sam Laep (80B, 1½ hours, frequent from 6.30am to 3.30pm) depart from a stop on Th Laeng Phanit near the morning market.

Chiang Mai Province

Best Places to Eat

- ➡ SP Chicken (p340)
- ➡ Talat Pratu Chiang Mai (p341)
- ➡ Ginger & Kafe @ The House (p342)
- ➡ Tengoku (p344)
- ➡ Chiang Dao Nest (p357)

Best Places to Stay

- ➡ Anantara Resort & Spa (p338)
- ➡ Rachamankha (p336)
- ➡ Baan Orapin (p338)
- ➡ Mo Rooms (p336)
- ➡ Awanahouse (p334)

Why Go?

Thailand's northern capital is an overnight train ride and light years away from the bustle and bombast of Bangkok. Wrestled from Burmese control by the kingdom of Siam, the former capital of the Lanna people is a captivating collection of glimmering monasteries, manic markets, modern shopping centres, and quiet residential streets that would not look amiss in a country village.

Chiang Mai is more country retreat than mega-metropolis, but this historic city has evolved into a major traveller centre, luring everyone from backpacking teenagers to young families, round-the-world retirees and a huge contingent of youthful tourists from China, who are redefining the traveller experience in the city.

Historic monasteries and cooking courses are just part of the picture. The surrounding province is a jumble of forested hills, and thrill seekers flock here for rafting, hiking, mountain biking and other adrenaline-charged activities, while less energetic visitors interact with elephants, soak in hot springs and wander around experimental farms and lush botanic gardens.

When to Go

- ➡ Chiang Mai is at its best during the cool season, roughly from November to February, when temperatures are mild and rain is scarce.
- ➡ The hot season runs from March until June, and the mercury regularly climbs above 35°C; pick a hotel with a pool!
- ➡ Songkran in April is Chiang Mai's biggest festival – and biggest party – but book well ahead for transport and accommodation.

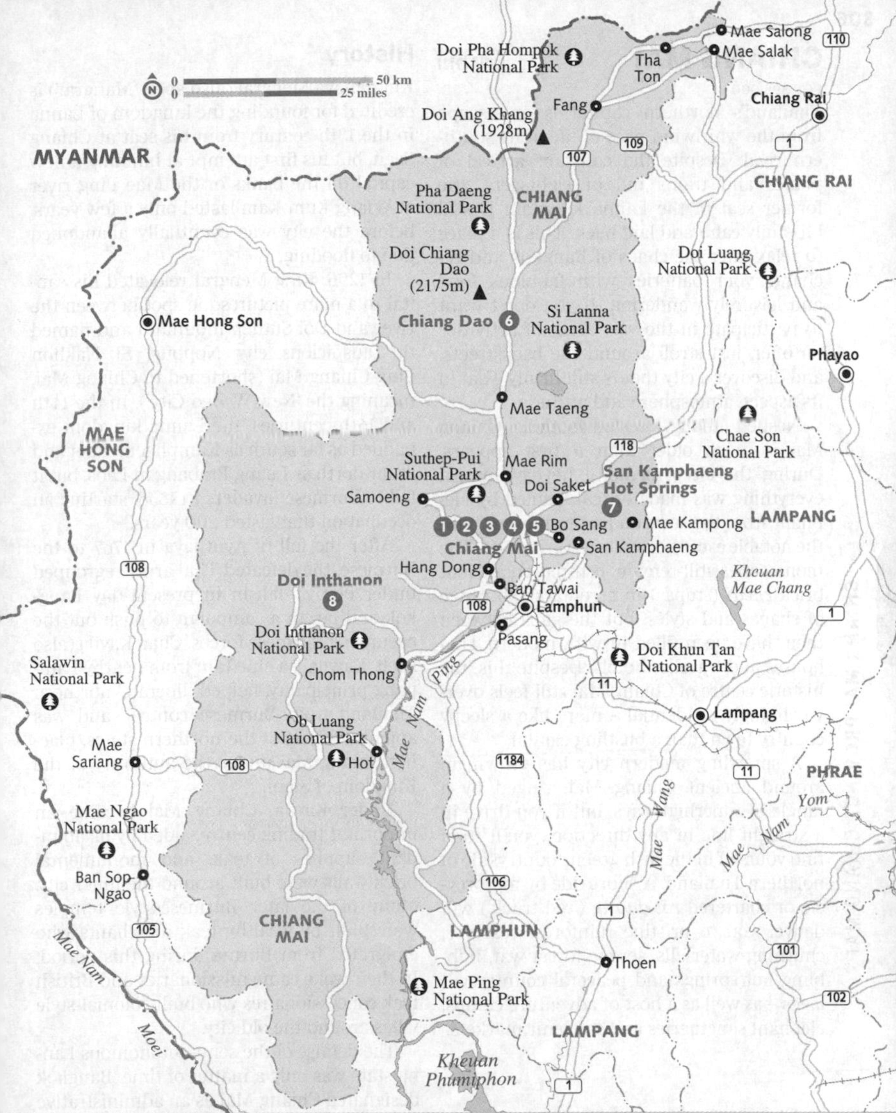

Chiang Mai Province Highlights

1. Taking in Chiang Mai's golden trinity – **Wat Phra Singh** (p307), **Wat Chedi Luang** (p311) and **Wat Phra That Doi Suthep** (p322).
2. Meeting monks at **Monk Chat** (p328) and discovering what motivates Chiang Mai's men in orange.
3. Learning how to make green curry during a Chiang Mai **cooking class** (p328).
4. Joining the human shopping parade at the **Saturday Walking Street** and **Sunday Walking Street** (p316).
5. Plunging into the commercial beehive of **Talat Warorot** (p317).
6. Exploring the mystical **Chiang Dao cave** (p356) in Chiang Dao.
7. Jungle bathing in the **hot springs** (p361) at San Kamphaeng.
8. Scaling **Doi Inthanon** (p361) to see plunging falls and modernist *chedi* (stupas).

CHIANG MAI เชียงใหม่

POP 398,000

Thailand's northern capital is an escape from the whirlwind pace of life of its southern rival. Despite the constant arrival of planes and trains full of sightseers, the former seat of the Lanna kingdom is still blissfully calm and laid-back. This is a place to relax after the chaos of Bangkok and recharge your batteries with fabulous food and leisurely wandering. If you don't want to participate in the vast array of activities on offer, just stroll around the backstreets, and discover a city that is still firmly Thai in its aspect, atmosphere and attitude.

Nestled among forested foothills, Chiang Mai is much older than it first appears. During the city's medieval heyday, almost everything was made of teak hauled by elephant from the surrounding rainforest, with the notable exception of its towering wát. The monasteries still remain, centred on ancient brick *chedi* (stupas) in a remarkable range of shapes and styles, but the gaps between them have been filled in with modern Thai houses and traveller hotels. Despite this, the historic centre of Chiang Mai still feels overwhelmingly residential – more like a sleepy country town than a bustling capital.

A sprawling modern city has grown up around ancient Chiang Mai, ringed by a tangle of superhighways, but if you drive in a straight line in any direction, you'll soon find yourself in the lush green countryside of northern Thailand. A short ride by motorcycle or chartered *rót daang* ('red truck') will deliver you to pristine rainforest reserves, churning waterfalls, serene forest wát, bubbling hot springs and peaceful country villages – as well as a host of adventure camps, elephant sanctuaries and souvenir markets.

PARK LIFE IN CHIANG MAI

The old city's only public park, **Suan Buak Hat** (Map p308; Th Bamrungburi; ⏲5am-9pm) is a delightful spot to unwind. As the sun slides towards the horizon, locals gather to jog along the running tracks, run around the playground (if they're little), feed the fish in the ponds, or buy bunches of lychees from the vendors out front and sit on rented reed mats (10B) enjoying the balmy evening temperatures.

History

King Phaya Mengrai (also spelt 'Mangrai') is credited for founding the kingdom of Lanna in the 13th century from his seat at Chiang Saen, but his first attempt at building a new capital on the banks of the Mae Ping river at Wiang Kum Kam lasted only a few years, before the city was eventually abandoned due to flooding.

In 1296, King Mengrai relocated his capital to a more picturesque spot between the river and Doi Suthep mountain and named the auspicious city Nopburi Si Nakhon Ping Chiang Mai (shortened to Chiang Mai, meaning the 'New Walled City'). In the 14th and 15th centuries, the Lanna kingdom expanded as far south as Kamphaeng Phet and as far north as Luang Prabang in Laos, but it fell to Burmese invaders in 1556, starting an occupation that lasted 200 years.

After the fall of Ayuthaya in 1767 to the Burmese, the defeated Thai army regrouped under Phraya Taksin in present-day Bangkok and began a campaign to push out the occupying Burmese forces. Chao Kavila (also spelt 'Kawila'), a chieftain from nearby Lampang principality, helped 'liberate' northern Thailand from Burmese control, and was appointed king of the northern states, placing Chiang Mai under the authority of the Kingdom of Siam.

Under Kavila, Chiang Mai became an important trading centre, aided by its abundant supplies of teak, and monumental brick walls were built around the inner city. Many of the later Burmese-style temples were built by wealthy teak merchants who emigrated from Burma during this period. In their wake came missionaries and British teak concessionaires who built colonial-style villas around the old city.

The demise of the semi-autonomous Lanna state was only a matter of time. Bangkok designated Chiang Mai as an administrative unit in 1892 in the face of expanding colonial rule in neighbouring Burma and Laos, and the Lanna princess Dara Rasmi was sent to Bangkok to become one of the official consorts of King Rama V, cementing ties between the two royal families.

The completion of the northern railway to Chiang Mai in 1922 finally linked the north with central Thailand, and in 1933 Chiang Mai officially became a province of Siam. Even so, Chiang Mai remained relatively undeveloped until 2001, when prime minister and Chiang Mai native Thaksin Shinawatra sought to modernise the city by expanding the airport and building superhighways.

Though the prime minister's grand vision was interrupted when he was ousted from power in 2006, many loyal Thaksin supporters remain in positions of power, and a high-speed rail link to Bangkok is slated for construction by 2019.

Sights

Chiang Mai overflows with temples, markets and museums, but don't overlook the sights outside of the old city, both inside and outside the fringing highways.

Old City เมืองเก่า

Within the old city, temples dominate the skyline, orange-robed monks weave in and out of the tourist crowds and the atmosphere is more like a country town than a heaving modern city. However, the residential feel of the old city is changing as government offices move out, residents sell up and developers move in.

Wát & Religious Sites

The highlight of any visit to the old city is exploring the temples that burst out on almost every street corner, attracting hordes of pilgrims, tourists and local worshippers. For a calmer experience, visit late in the afternoon, when the tourist crowds are replaced by monks attending evening prayers. Visitors are welcome but should follow the standard rules of Buddhist etiquette: stay quiet during prayers, keep your feet pointed away from Buddha images and monks, and dress modestly (covering shoulders and knees).

★Wat Phra Singh BUDDHIST TEMPLE

(วัดพระสิงห์; Map p312; Th Singharat; admission to main wí·hăhn 20B; ⏲5am-8.30pm) Chiang Mai's most revered temple, Wat Phra Singh is dominated by an enormous, mosaic-inlaid *wí·hăhn* (sanctuary). Its prosperity is plain to see from the lavish monastic buildings

WHAT, MORE WÁT?

If you still have a taste for more Thai religious architecture, there are dozens more historic wát scattered around the old city and the surrounding streets. Here are some good places to start your explorations.

Wat Inthakhin Saduemuang (วัดอินทขิลสะดือเมือง; Map p312; donations appreciated; ⏲6am-6pm) Marooned in the middle of Th Inthawarorot, this was the original location of the Làk Meuang (city pillar), and the gilded teak *wí·hăhn* (sanctuary) is one of the most perfectly proportioned buildings in the city.

Wat Phan On (วัดพันอ้น; Map p312; Th Ratchdamnoen; donations appreciated; ⏲6am-5pm) Set with gilded Buddhas in alcoves decorated with *lai·krahm* stencilling, the gold *chedi* (stupa) at this prosperous wát is visited by scores of devotees after dark. The courtyard becomes a food court during the Sunday Walking Street market.

Wat Jet Lin (วัดเจ็ดลิน / วัดหนองจลิน; Map p312; Th Phra Pokklao; donations appreciated; ⏲4am-6pm) This friendly wát was used for the coronation of Lanna kings in the 16th century; today you can see a collection of giant gongs, a big old *mon·dòp*-style *chedi* and a large gilded Buddha with particularly graceful proportions.

Wat Lokmoli (วัดโลกโมฬี; Map p312; Th Chaiyaphum; donations appreciated; ⏲6am-6pm) An elegant wooden complex dotted with terracotta sculptures. The *wí·hăhn* is topped by a three-tiered roof and the tall, barrel-shaped *chedi* still has some of its original stucco.

Wat Chomphu (วัดชมพู; Map p312; Soi 1, Th Chang Moi Kao; donations appreciated; ⏲6am-6pm) Just north of Th Tha Phae, this calm monastery has a gorgeous gilded stupa with gold elephants, restored as a tribute to the king in 1999.

Wat Ou Sai Kham (วัดอู่ทรายคำ; Map p312; Th Chang Moi Kao; donations appreciated; ⏲7am-6pm) This friendly neighbourhood wát has an impressive collection of jade Buddhas and jade and nephrite boulders in its main *wí·hăhn*.

Wat Mahawan (วัดมหาวัน; Map p312; Th Tha Phae; donations appreciated; ⏲6am-6pm) A handsome, whitewashed wát that shows the obvious influence of the Burmese teak traders who used to worship here. The *chedi* and Burmese-style gateways are decorated with a stucco menagerie of angels and mythical beasts.

Chiang Mai

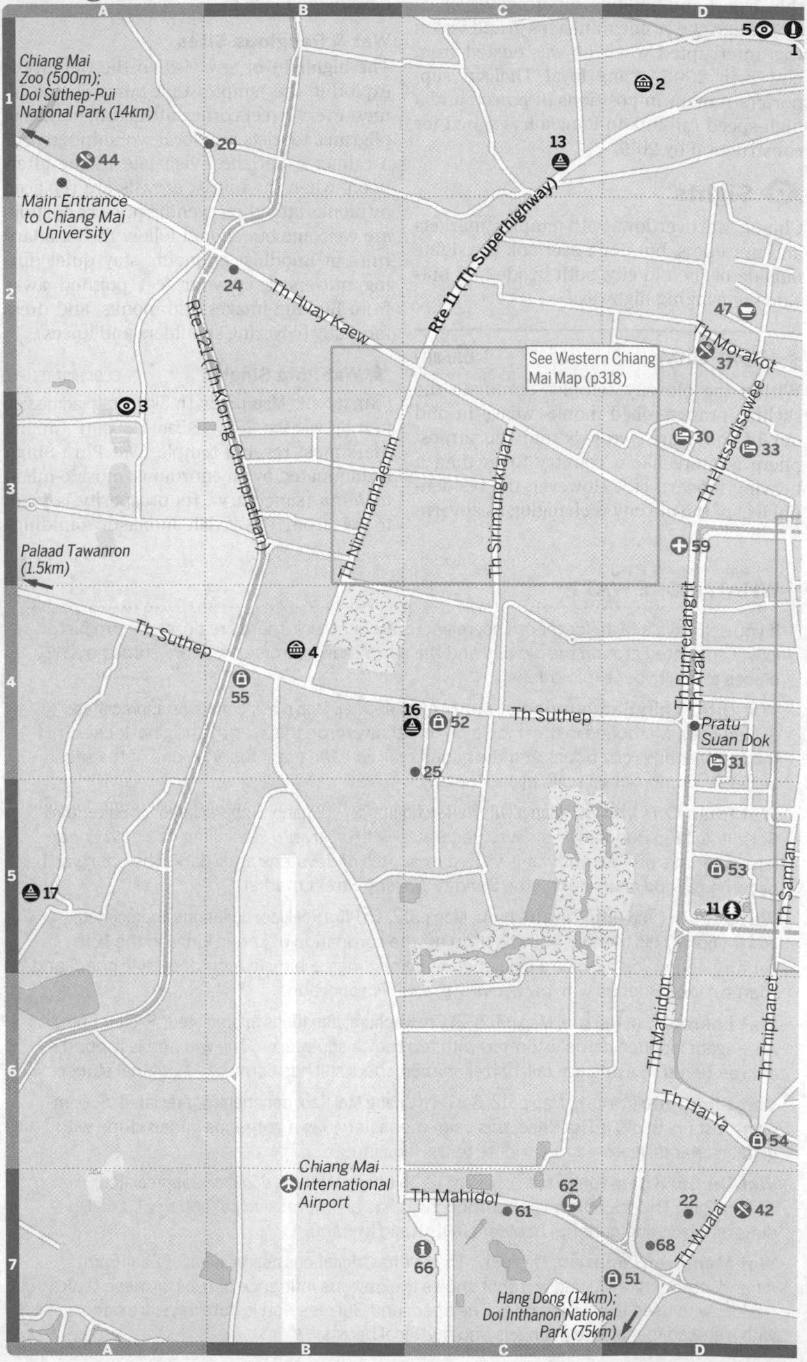

A
B
C
D
1
2
3
4
5
6
7
Chiang Mai Zoo (500m); Doi Suthep-Pui National Park (14km)
Main Entrance to Chiang Mai University
Palaad Tawanron (1.5km)
Th Huay Kaew
Rte 121 (Th Klorng Chonprathan)
Rte 11 (Th Superhighway)
Th Nimmanhaemin
Th Sirimungklajarn
See Western Chiang Mai Map (p318)
Th Morakot
Th Hutsadisawee
Th Suthep
Th Bunreuangrit
Th Arak
Pratu Suan Dok
Th Samlan
Th Mahidon
Th Thiphanet
Th Hai Ya
Th Wualai
Th Mahidol
Chiang Mai International Airport
Hang Dong (14km); Doi Inthanon National Park (75km)
1
2
3
4
5
11
13
16
17
20
22
24
25
30
31
33
37
42
44
47
51
52
53
54
55
59
61
62
66
68

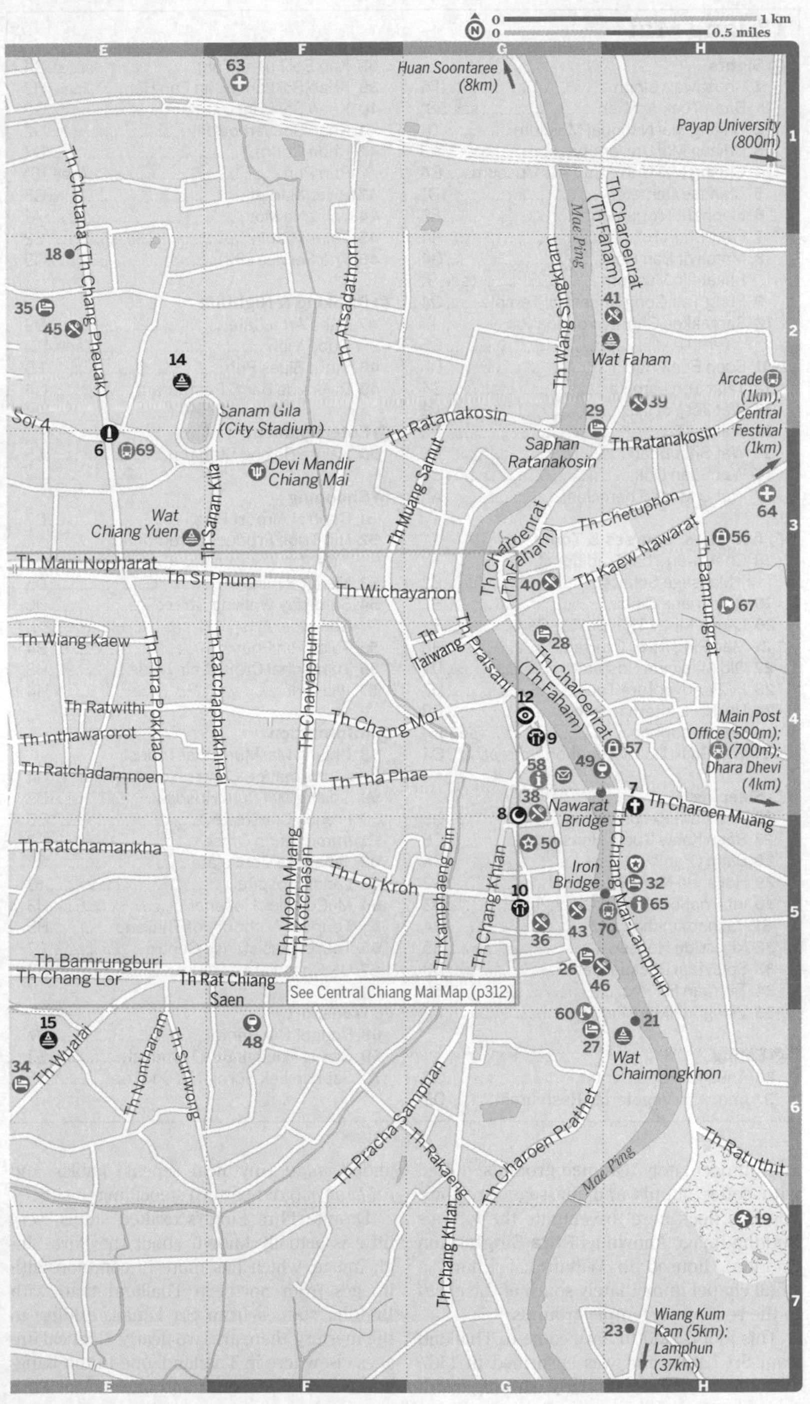

Huan Soontaree (8km)
Payap University (800m)
Th Chotana (Th Chang Pheuak)
Th Atsadathorn
Mae Ping
Th Wang Singkham
Th Charoenrat (Th Faham)
Wat Faham
Arcade (1km); Central Festival (1km)
Sanam Gila (City Stadium)
Soi 4
Th Ratanakosin
Saphan Ratanakosin
Devi Mandir Chiang Mai
Th Muang Samut
Wat Chiang Yuen
Th Sanan Kila
Th Chetuphon
Th Kaew Nawarat
Th Bamrungrat
Th Mani Nopharat
Th Si Phum
Th Wichayanon
Th Taiwang
Th Praisani
Th Wiang Kaew
Th Phra Pokklao
Th Ratchaphakhinai
Th Chaiyaphum
Th Ratwithi
Th Inthawarorot
Th Chang Moi
Th Ratchadamnoen
Th Tha Phae
Main Post Office (500m); (700m); Dhara Dhevi (4km)
Nawarat Bridge
Th Charoen Muang
Th Ratchamankha
Th Loi Kroh
Iron Bridge
Th Chiang Mai-Lamphun
Th Moon Muang
Th Kotchasan
Th Kamphaeng Din
Th Chang Khlan
Th Bamrungburi
Th Chang Lor
Th Rat Chiang Saen
See Central Chiang Mai Map (p312)
Wat Chaimongkhon
Th Wualai
Th Nontharam
Th Suriwong
Th Pracha Samphan
Th Rakaeng
Th Charoen Prathet
Th Ratuthit
Wiang Kum Kam (5km); Lamphun (37km)

Chiang Mai

Sights
1 Anusawari Singh D1
Baan Tuek Art Center .... (see 58)
2 Chiang Mai National Museum D1
3 Chiang Mai University A3
4 Chiang Mai University Art Museum B4
5 Chinese Cemetery D1
6 Elephant Monument E3
7 First Church H4
8 Matsayit Ban Haw G4
Philatelic Museum .... (see 9)
9 Pung Tao Gong Ancestral Temple G4
10 Samakkee Charity Foundation Temple G5
11 Suan Buak Hat D5
12 Talat Ton Lam Yai G4
13 Wat Jet Yot C1
14 Wat Ku Tao E2
15 Wat Srisuphan E6
16 Wat Suan Dok C4
17 Wat U Mong Thera Jan A5

Activities, Courses & Tours
18 Chetawan Thai Traditional Massage School E2
19 Gymkhana Club H7
20 Lanna Muay Thai Boxing Camp B1
21 Mae Ping River Cruise H6
22 Old Medicine Hospital D7
23 Peak Adventure Tour H7
24 UniTEFL International B2
Wat Srisuphan .... (see 15)
25 Wat Suan Dok Meditation Retreat C4

Sleeping
26 Anantara Resort & Spa G5
27 Baan Kaew Guest House G6
28 Baan Orapin G4
29 Hollanda Montri G2
30 International Hotel Chiangmai D3
31 Rachamankha D4
32 Riverside House H5
33 Spicythai Backpackers D3
34 Tri Yaan Na Ros E6
35 Viangbua Mansion E2

Eating
36 Anusarn Food Center G5
37 Imm Aim Vegetarian Restaurant D2
38 Kao Soi Fueng Fah G4
39 Khao Soi Lam Duan Fah Ham H2
40 Khao Soi Prince G3
41 Khao Soi Samoe Jai H2
42 Khun Churn D7
Pun Pun .... (see 16)
43 River Market G5
44 Talat Na Mor A1
45 Talat Thanin E2
46 The Service 1921 .... G5

Drinking & Nightlife
47 Akha Ama Cafe D2
Good View .... (see 49)
48 Pinte Blues Pub F6
49 Riverside Bar & Restaurant G4

Entertainment
50 Kalare Boxing Stadium G5

Shopping
51 Central Airport Plaza D7
52 Hill-Tribe Products Promotion Centre C4
53 Mengrai Kilns D5
54 Saturday Walking Street D6
Sop Moei Arts .... (see 28)
55 Talat Ton Phayom B4
56 Thai Tribal Crafts Fair Trade H3
57 Vila Cini H4

Information
58 Chiang Mai Municipal Tourist Information Centre G4
59 Chiang Mai Ram Hospital D3
60 French Consulate G6
61 Immigration Office C7
62 Japanese Consulate C7
63 Lanna Hospital F1
64 McCormick Hospital H3
65 Tourism Authority of Thailand H5
66 Tourist Assistance Centre C7
67 UK Consulate H3

Transport
68 Budget Car Rental D7
69 Chang Pheuak Bus Terminal E3
70 Saphan Lek Sŏrng·tăa·ou Stop H5

and immaculately trimmed grounds, dotted with coffee stands and massage pavilions. Pilgrims flock here to venerate the famous Buddha image known as **Phra Singh** (Lion Buddha), housed in Wihan Lai Kham, a small chapel immediately south of the *chedi* to the rear of the temple grounds.

This idol is said to have come to Thailand from Sri Lanka and was enshrined in 1367, and the chapel is similarly striking, with gilded *naga* (mythical sepent) gables and *lai·krahm* (gold-pattern stencilling) inside.

Despite Phra Singh's exalted status, very little is actually known about the Phra Singh image, which has more in common with images from northern Thailand than with Buddha statues from Sri Lanka. Adding to the mystery, there are two nearly identical images elsewhere in Thailand, one in the Bangkok National Museum and one in Wat Phra

Mahathat Woramahawihaan in Nakhon Si Thammarat. Regardless of its provenance, the statue has become a focal point for religious celebrations during the Songkran festival.

As you wander the monastery grounds, note the raised temple library, housed in a dainty teak and stucco pavilion known as **Ho Trai**, decorated with bas-relief angels in the style of Wat Jet Yot (see p324). The temple's main *chedi,* rising over a classic Lanna-style octagonal base, was constructed by King Pa Yo in 1345; it's often wrapped in bolts of orange cloth by devotees.

★**Wat Chedi Luang** BUDDHIST TEMPLE

(วัดเจดีย์หลวง; Map p312; Th Phra Pokklao; donations appreciated; ⏲6am-6pm) Wat Chedi Luang is not quite as grand as Wat Phra Singh, but its towering, ruined Lanna-style *chedi* (built in 1441) is much taller and the sprawling compound around the stupa is powerfully atmospheric. The famed Phra Kaew (Emerald Buddha), now held in Bangkok's Wat Phra Kaew, resided in the eastern niche until 1475; today, you can view a jade replica, given as a gift from the Thai king in 1995 to celebrate the 600th anniversary of the *chedi.*

This was possibly the largest structure in ancient Chiang Mai but the top of the *chedi* was destroyed by either a 16th-century earthquake or by cannon fire during the recapture of Chiang Mai from the Burmese in 1775 (nobody knows for sure). Like most of the ancient monuments in Chiang Mai, Chedi Luang was in ruins when the city began its modern renaissance, but a restoration project by Unesco and the Japanese government in the 1990s stabilised the monument and prevented further degradation.

As you wander around the *chedi*, you can easily spot the restoration work on the four *naga* stairways in each of the cardinal directions. The base of the stupa has five elephant sculptures on the southern face – four are reproductions, but the elephant on the far right is the original brick and stucco. The restorers stopped short of finishing the spire, as nobody could agree what it looked like.

In the main *wí·hăhn* is a revered standing Buddha statue, known as **Phra Chao Attarot**, flanked by two disciples. There are more chapels and statues in teak pavilions at the rear of the compound, including a huge reclining Buddha and a handsome

NAVIGATING CHIANG MAI

Chiang Mai is an easy city to navigate. The old city sees little traffic except on its main thoroughfares, and most explore by bike or on foot, using túk-túk (pronounced *đúk đúk*) and *rót daang* (shared taxis) to reach attractions outside this compact central area. A copy of Nancy Chandler's *Map of Chiang Mai,* available in local bookshops, will help you wander the old city with confidence.

Heading out from the old city, Rte 107 runs north, Rte 108 runs south and Rte 106 runs southeast. These radial routes intersect with a complicated outer ring road made up of two superhighways, Rte 11 (Th Superhighway) and Rte 121 (Th Klorng Chonprathan). If you are driving yourself, it's almost always easier to stick to the roads radiating out from the centre rather than trying to navigate via the superhighways. When travelling beyond the old city, directions are often given in relationship to the old city's four cardinal gates.

Pratu Tha Phae (east) Head east from here along Th Tha Phae to reach the riverside, Talat Warorot and the Night Bazaar.

Pratu Chang Pheuak (north) Head north from here along Th Chotana (Th Chang Pheuak) to reach the Chang Pheuak Bus Terminal and Rte 107 to northern Chiang Mai Province.

Pratu Suan Dok (west) Head west from here along Th Suthep to reach Chiang Mai University, Doi Suthep and the entertainment district of Th Nimmanhaemin.

Pratu Chiang Mai (south) Head southwest from here along Th Wualai for the Saturday Walking Street market and Rte 108 to southern Chiang Mai Province.

When entering or leaving the old city by road, you'll have to navigate the complicated traffic system along the city moat. Traffic on the ring road inside the moat moves in an anticlockwise direction; traffic on the ring road outside the moat moves clockwise. To get between these two thoroughfares, you must cross the moat and make a U-turn. As none of the crossings line up with the cardinal gates, you will almost always have to drive past where you want to go and then come back on the far side.

Central Chiang Mai

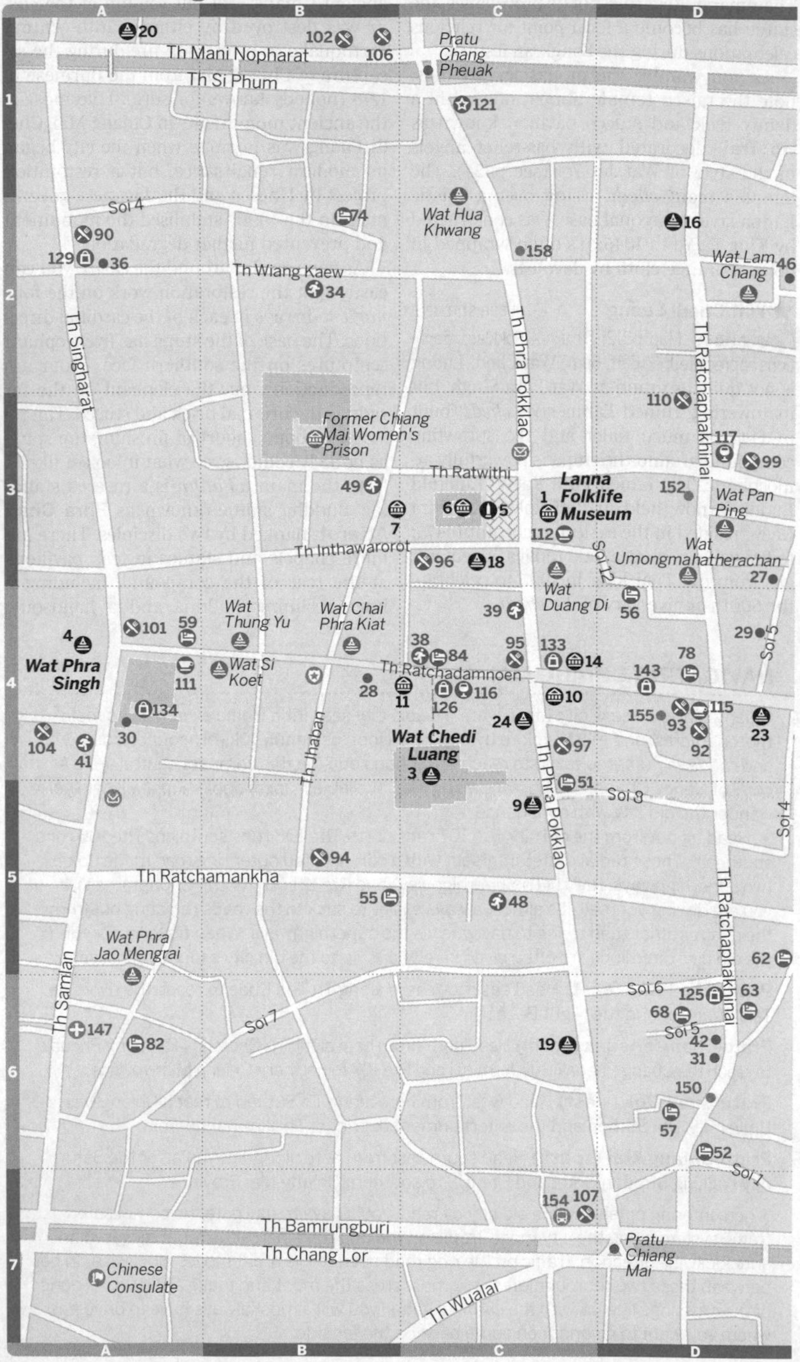

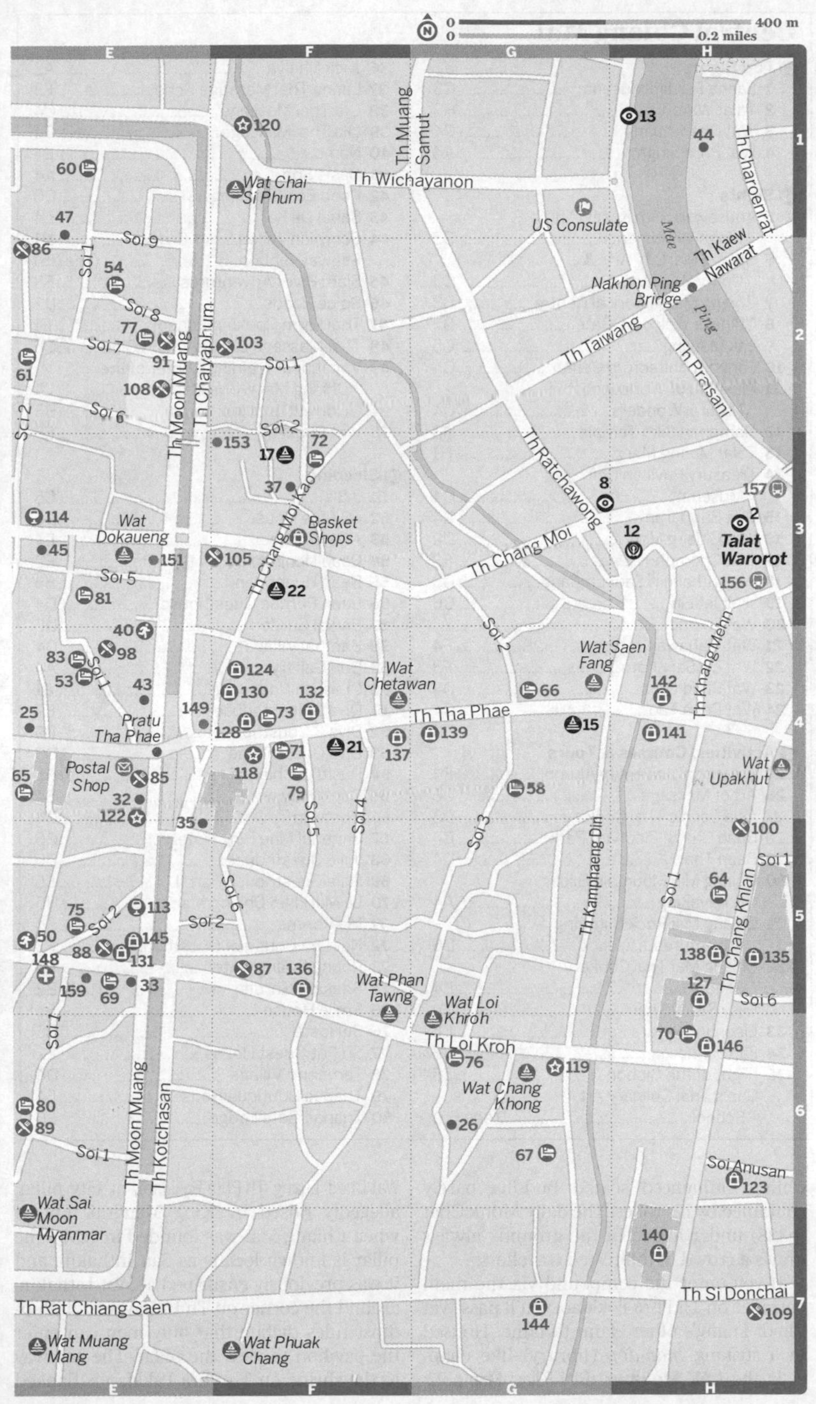

Th Wichayanon
Th Muang Samut
Wat Chai Si Phum
US Consulate
Th Kaew Nawarat
Nakhon Ping Bridge
Mae Ping
Th Charoenrat
Th Taiwang
Th Prasani
Th Chaiyaphum
Th Moon Muang
Soi 9
Soi 8
Soi 7
Soi 6
Soi 1
Soi 2
Th Ratchawong
Th Chang Moi
Th Chang Moi Kao
Basket Shops
Wat Dokaueng
Soi 5
Talat Warorot
Th Khang Mehn
Wat Saen Fang
Wat Chetawan
Th Tha Phae
Pratu Tha Phae
Postal Shop
Wat Upakhut
Soi 4
Soi 3
Th Kamphaeng Din
Th Chang Khlan
Soi 6
Wat Phan Tawng
Wat Loi Khroh
Th Loi Kroh
Wat Chang Khong
Th Kotchasan
Soi Anusan
Wat Sai Moon Myanmar
Th Rat Chiang Saen
Th Si Donchai
Wat Muang Mang
Wat Phuak Chang

Central Chiang Mai

Top Sights
1 Lanna Folklife Museum C3
2 Talat Warorot H3
3 Wat Chedi Luang C4
4 Wat Phra Singh A4

Sights
5 Anusawari Sam Kasat (Three Kings Monument) C3
6 Chiang Mai City Arts & Cultural Centre C3
7 Chiang Mai Historical Centre B3
8 Chinese Welcome Gate G3
9 Làk Meuang C5
10 Lanna Architecture Center C4
11 Museum of World Insects & Natural Wonders C4
12 Namdhari Sikh Temple H3
13 Talat Muang Mai H1
14 Treasury Pavilion Coin Museum C4
15 Wat Bupparam G4
16 Wat Chiang Man D2
17 Wat Chomphu F3
18 Wat Inthakhin Saduemuang C3
19 Wat Jet Lin C6
20 Wat Lokmoli A1
21 Wat Mahawan F4
22 Wat Ou Sai Kham F3
23 Wat Phan On D4
24 Wat Phan Tao C4

Activities, Courses & Tours
25 American University Alumni E4
26 Art of Massage G6
27 Asia Scenic Thai Cooking D3
28 Baan Chang Elephant Park B4
29 Baan Thai D4
30 Chiang Mai Mountain Biking & Kayaking A4
31 Chiang Mai Rock Climbing Adventures D6
32 Chiang Mai Thai Cookery School E4
Easy Study Thai .... (see 140)
33 Elephant Nature Park E5
34 Fah Lanna B2
35 Flight of the Gibbon E5
Gap's Thai Culinary Art School .... (see 65)
36 Jack Chaiya A2
37 Lanna Thai Massage School F3
38 Lila Thai Massage C4
39 Lila Thai Massage C4
40 Namo E4
41 Oasis Spa A4
42 Pooh Eco-Trekking D6
43 Sabai De Ka E4
44 Scorpion Tailed River Cruise H1
Segway Gibbon .... (see 35)
45 Siam River Adventures E3
46 Spice Roads D2
47 Thai Farm Cooking School E1
48 Thai Massage Conservation Club C5
49 Vocational Training Center of the Chiang Mai Women's Correctional Institution B3
50 Wat Phakkao E5

Sleeping
51 3 Sis C5
52 60 Blue House D6
53 Awanahouse E4
54 Baan Hanibah Bed & Breakfast E2
55 Baan Huenphen B5
56 Baan Pordee Guesthouse D4
57 Banjai Garden D6
58 Banthai Village G4
59 Buri Gallery A4
60 Charcoa House E1
61 Diva 2 Guesthouse E2
62 Diva 3 Guesthouse D5
63 Diva Guesthouse D6
64 DusitD2 Chiang Mai H5
65 Gap's House E4
66 Hostel In Town G4
67 Imperial Mae Ping Hotel G6
68 Julie Guesthouse D6
69 Julie Guesthouse Part II E5
70 Le Meridien Chiang Mai H6
71 Mo Rooms F4
72 Nat Len Boutique Guesthouse F3
73 Roong Ruang Hotel F4
74 Shakara Garden B2
75 Smile House 1 .... E5
76 SoHostel G6
77 Sri Pat Guest House E2
78 Tamarind Village D4
79 Thapae Boutique House F4
80 Thapae Gate Lodge E6

Chinese-influenced seated Buddha barely contained by his robes. The daily Monk Chat (p328) under a tree in the grounds always draws a crowd of interested travellers.

If you enter the compound via the main entrance on Th Phra Pokklao, you'll pass Wat Chedi Luang's other claim to fame. Housed in a striking *mon·dòp* (library)–like chapel is the **Làk Meuang** (City Pillar; Map p312; Wat Chedi Luang, Th Phra Pokklao), or city pillar, allegedly raised by King Mengrai himself when Chiang Mai was founded in 1296. The pillar is known locally as Sao Inthakin, and it was previously enshrined at Wat Inthakin, around the corner on Th Inthawarorot. Buddhist rules dictate that only men can enter the pavilion to view the pillar. The gateway to the shrine on Th Phra Pakklao is flanked

81 TJR Boutique House E3
82 Tropical Inn A6
83 Vieng Mantra E4
84 Villa Duang Champa C4

Eating
85 AUM Vegetarian Food E4
86 Blue Diamond E2
87 Chez Marco Restaurant & Bar F5
88 Dada Kafe E5
89 Dash E6
90 Fern Forest Cafe A2
91 Ginger & Kafe @ The House E2
92 Girasole D4
Good Morning Chiang Mai .... (see 82)
93 Hot Chilli D4
94 Huen Phen B5
95 Khaow Tom 1B C4
96 Kiat Ocha C3
97 La Fourchette C4
98 Lert Ros E4
99 New Delhi D3
100 Night Market H5
101 Pak Do Restaurant A4
102 Party Buffet B1
Ruen Tamarind .... (see 78)
103 Salad Concept F2
104 SP Chicken A4
105 Swan F3
106 Talat Pratu Chang Pheuak B1
107 Talat Pratu Chiang Mai C7
108 Talat Somphet E2
109 Whole Earth Restaurant H7
110 Yok Fa D3

Drinking & Nightlife
111 Akha Ama Cafe A4
112 Café de Museum C3
113 John's Place E5
Raming Tea House .... (see 142)
114 UN Irish Pub E3
115 Wawee Coffee D4
116 Writer's Club & Wine Bar C4
117 Zoe In Yellow D3

Entertainment
118 Inter F4
119 Loi Kroh Boxing Stadium G6
120 Nabé F1
121 North Gate Jazz Co-Op C1
122 Thapae Boxing Stadium E4

Shopping
123 Anusarn Night Bazaar H6
124 Backstreet Books F4
125 Chaitawat Bikeshop D6
126 Chiang Mai Cotton C4
127 Chiang Mai Night Bazaar H5
128 Elements F4
129 Ethnic Lanna A2
130 Gecko Books F4
131 Gecko Books E5
Ginger .... (see 91)
132 Herb Basics F4
133 Herb Basics C4
134 HQ Paper Maker A4
135 Kalare Night Bazaar H5
Kesorn Arts .... (see 142)
136 KukWan Gallery F5
137 Nakorn Kasem F4
138 Night Bazaar H5
139 Nova G4
140 Pantip Plaza H7
141 Praewphun Thai Silk H4
142 Siam Celadon H4
143 Sunday Walking Street D4
144 Suriwong Book Centre G7
145 Thai Tribal Crafts Fair Trade E5
146 Vila Cini H6

Information
147 Center of Thai Traditional & Complementary Medicine A6
148 Mungkala Traditional Medicine Clinic E5

Transport
149 Air Asia E4
150 Mr Mechanic D6
151 Mr Mechanic E3
152 Mr Mechanic D3
153 North Wheels F3
154 Pratu Chiang Mai Sŏrng·tăa·ou Stop C7
155 SM Travel D4
156 Sŏrng·tăa·ou to San Kamphaeng H3
157 Talat Warorot Sŏrng·tăa·ou Stop H3
158 Thai Airways International C2
159 Tony's Big Bikes E5

by *yaksha* (guardian demons) and Lanna warriors are depicted in bas relief on the gates.

Wat Phan Tao BUDDHIST TEMPLE
(วัดพันเตา; Map p312; Th Phra Pokklao; donations appreciated; 6am-6pm) Without doubt the most atmospheric wát in the old city, this teak marvel sits in the shadow of Wat Chedi Luang. Set in a compound full of fluttering orange flags, the monastery is a monument to the teak trade, with an enormous prayer hall supported by 28 gargantuan teak pillars and lined with dark teak panels, enshrining a particularly graceful gold Buddha image. The juxtaposition of the orange monks' robes against this dark backdrop during evening prayers is particularly sublime.

WEEKEND SHOPPING

As Bangkok has Chatuchak Weekend Market, so Chiang Mai has its weekend 'walking streets' – carnival-like street markets that close off main thoroughfares in the city on Saturday and Sunday for a riot of souvenir shopping, street performances and hawker food.

As the sun starts to dip on Saturday afternoon, the **Saturday Walking Street** (ถนนเดินวันเสาร์; Map p308; Th Wualai; ⏲4pm-midnight Sat) takes over Th Wualai, running southwest from Pratu Chiang Mai. There is barely space to move as locals and tourists from across the world haggle vigorously for carved soaps, novelty dog collars, woodcarvings, Buddha paintings, hill-tribe trinkets, Thai musical instruments, T-shirts, paper lanterns and umbrellas, silver jewellery, herbal remedies, you name it.

An eclectic soundtrack is provided by street performers – blind guitar players, crooners, precocious school children with headset microphones – and food vendors fill every courtyard and alleyway. There are more stellar street-food offerings at nearby **Talat Pratu Chiang Mai** (p341). To escape the crowds, duck into **Wat Srisuphan** (p319), whose silver *ubosot* (ordination hall) is illuminated in rainbow colours after dark.

On Sunday afternoon, the whole shebang moves across the city to Th Ratchadamnoen for the equally boisterous **Sunday Walking Street** (ถนนเดินวันอาทิตย์; Map p312; Th Ratchadamnoen; ⏲4pm-midnight Sun), which feels even more animated because of the energetic food markets that open up wát courtyards along the route. If you went to Th Wualai on Saturday, you'll recognise many of the same sellers and buskers that you spotted the night before. The markets are a major source of income for local families and many traders spend the whole week hand-making merchandise to sell on Saturday and Sunday.

Above the facade is a striking image of a peacock over a dog, representing the astrological year of the former royal resident's birth. The monastery is one of the focal points for celebrations during the Visakha Bucha festival in May or June, when monks light hundreds of butter lamps around the pond in the grounds.

Wat Chiang Man BUDDHIST TEMPLE

(วัดเชียงมั่น; Map p312; Th Ratchaphakhinai; donations appreciated; ⏲6am-6pm) Chiang Mai's oldest temple was established by the city's founder, Phaya Mengrai, sometime around 1296. In front of the *ubosot* (ordination hall), a stone slab, engraved in 1581, bears the earliest known reference to the city's founding. The main *wí·hăhn* also contains the oldest known Buddha image created by the Lanna kingdom, cast in 1465.

A smaller, second *wí·hăhn* enshrines the city's guardian images, the bas-relief marble Phra Sila Buddha, believed to have been carved in Sri Lanka more than 1000 years ago, and the tiny crystal Phra Sae Tang Khamani Buddha, reportedly crafted for the king of Lopburi in around 200 AD.

The sacred images are housed inside a handsome, *mon·dòp*-like altar known as a *khong phra chao*, a distinctive feature of ancient Lanna temples. The monastery has a glorious *chedi*, with an elephant-flanked stucco base and a gilded upper level.

Anusawari Sam Kasat (Three Kings Monument) MONUMENT

(อนุสาวรีย์สามกษัตริย์; Map p312; Th Phra Pokklao) Marking the centrepoint of the old administrative quarter of Chiang Mai, the bronze Three Kings Monument commemorates the alliance forged between by Phaya Ngam Meuang of Phayao, Phaya Mengrai of Chiang Mai and Phaya Khun Ramkhamhaeng of Sukhothai in the founding of the city. The monument is a shrine for local residents, who swing by after work to leave offerings.

The square is a favourite promenade spot for families after dark, with vendors selling 'helicopter' toys inspired by dipterocarp seeds.

Museums

The old city has three excellent historical museums – the Lanna Folklife Museum, Chiang Mai City Arts & Cultural Centre and the Chiang Mai Historical Centre – located in a series of Thai-colonial-style buildings that used to house the city administration. You can buy a single ticket covering all three, valid for a week, for 180/80B (adult/child).

★Lanna Folklife Museum MUSEUM

(พิพิธภัณฑ์พื้นถิ่นล้านนา; Map p312; Th Phra Pokklao; adult/child 90/40B; ⏲8.30am-5pm Tue-Sun) Set inside the Thai-colonial-style former Provincial Court, dating from 1935, this imaginative museum recreates Lanna village life in a series of life-sized dioramas that explain everything from *lai·krahm* stencilling and *fon lep* (a mystical Lanna dance with long, metal false fingernails) to the intricate symbolism of different elements of Lanna-style monasteries.

This is the best first stop before heading to the many wát dotted around the old city.

Chiang Mai City Arts & Cultural Centre MUSEUM
(หอศิลปวัฒนธรรมเชียงใหม่; Map p312; www.cmocity.com; Th Phra Pokklao; adult/child 90/40B; ⏲8.30am-5pm Tue-Sun) Set in the former Provincial Hall, a handsome Thai-colonial-style building from 1927, this museum provides an excellent primer on Chiang Mai history. Dioramas, photos, artefacts and audiovisual displays walk visitors through the key battles and victories in the Chiang Mai story, from the first settlements to the arrival of the railroad. Upstairs is a charming recreation of a wooden Lanna village. The museum gift shop is exceptionally well stocked with lacquerware, jewellery and even metal false fingernails for the *fon lep* dance.

Chiang Mai Historical Centre MUSEUM
(หอประวัติศาสตร์เมืองเชียงใหม่; Map p312; Th Ratwithi; adult/child 90/40B; ⏲8.30am-5pm Tue-Sun) Housed in an airy Lanna-style building behind the Chiang Mai City Arts & Culture Centre, this appealing museum covers the history of Chiang Mai Province, with displays on the founding of the capital, the Burmese occupation and the modern era of trade and unification with Bangkok. Downstairs is an archaeological dig of an ancient temple wall.

Museum of World Insects & Natural Wonders MUSEUM
(Map p312; www.thailandinsect.com; Th Ratchadamnoen; adult/child 100/70B; ⏲9.30am-4.30pm) Thailand's giant butterflies and creepy crawlies are showcased at this little museum operated by a malaria researcher and his entomologist wife. As well as pinned and mounted specimens, there are info panels on insect-borne diseases and surreal paintings of nudes with mosquitoes. There's a small **branch** (Map p318; www.thailandinsect.com; Soi 13, Th Nimmanhaemin; admission adult/child 200/100B; ⏲9am-5pm Mon-Sat, 9am-4pm Sun) in the Th Nimmanhaemin zone.

Treasury Pavilion Coin Museum MUSEUM
(Map p312; Th Ratchadamnoen, Treasury Pavilion; ⏲8.30am-noon & 1-4.30pm) FREE It's worth ducking into this small government museum to see the bizarre shapes that Thai money has taken over the years, from hammered coins to round silver balls and ingots.

East of the Old City

Beyond Pratu Tha Phae is Chiang Mai's traditional commercial quarter, with sprawling bazaars and old-fashioned shophouses running down to the riverbank.

★**Talat Warorot** MARKET
(ตลาดวโรรส; Map p312; cnr Th Chang Moi & Th Praisani; ⏲6am-5pm) Chiang Mai's oldest public market, Warorot (also spelt 'Waroros') is a great place to connect with the city's Thai soul. Alongside souvenir vendors you'll find stalls selling items for Thai households: woks, toys, fishermen's nets, pickled tea leaves, wigs, sticky-rice steamers, Thai-style sausages, *kâab mŏo* (pork rinds), live catfish and statues for spirit houses. It's easy to spend half a day wandering the walkways, watching locals browsing, and haggling for goods that have a practical use back home.

JEEN HOR

In ancient times, Chiang Mai straddled one of Asia's famous crossroads: the southern spur of the Silk Road. Chinese-Muslim traders from Yunnan Province (China) drove their horse-drawn caravans south through the mountains to the Indian Ocean to trade with the merchant ships of seafaring powers. To the Thais of Chiang Mai, these caravans were a strange sight and the traders were nicknamed *jeen hor* (galloping Chinese), a reference to their strange beasts of burden.

The focus for this horse-trading was the market district known as **Ban Haw**, near the present Night Bazaar, where you'll still find a thriving Yunnanese Muslim community. Traders worship at the 100-year-old **Matsayit Ban Haw** (Hedaytul Islam Mosque; Map p308; Soi 1, Th Charoen Prathet (Halal St)), founded by later arrivals from China. Along Halal St are a number of simple restaurants selling Thai-Muslim-style food, including excellent *kôw soy* (curried chicken and noodles), *kôw mòk gài* (chicken *biryani*) and *néu·a òp hŏrm* ('fragrant' dried beef).

Western Chiang Mai

Western Chiang Mai

Sights
1 Museum of World Insects & Natural Wonders B3

Activities, Courses & Tours
2 Burma Study Center B3

Sleeping
3 Artel Nimman B3
4 Baan Say-La A2
5 Bunk Boutique D2
6 Bunthomstan Guesthouse B2
7 Kantary Hills A3
8 Nimman Boutique Resort B3
9 Sakulchai Place D1
10 Yesterday Hotel A2

Eating
11 Ai Sushi D2
12 Anchan Noodle C3
13 Esan Cafe A2
14 I-Berry B3
15 Salad Concept A2
16 Salsa Kitchen D2
17 Smoothie Blues A2
18 Tengoku B2
19 Tong Tem Toh A2

Drinking & Nightlife
20 Beer Republic B2
21 Blar Blar Bar B2
22 Soho Bar D2
23 Warmup Cafe A3
24 Year Garage B3

Entertainment
25 Sangdee Gallery C3
26 Sudsanan C2

Shopping
27 Chabaa A2
28 Doi Tung A1
29 Ginger A1
30 Kad Suan Kaew Shopping Center D3
31 Maya Lifestyle Shopping Center B1
32 Shinawatra Thai Silk D2
33 Srisanpanmai A1
34 Studio Naenna B1
The Booksmith .... (see 33)

You will know that you have arrived at the market when traffic comes to a standstill and carts laden with merchandise weave in between the cars. The location by the river is no coincidence; historically, most of the farm produce sold in Chiang Mai was delivered here by boat along the Mae Ping river.

Adjacent to Talat Warorot is Talat Ton Lam Yai, the city's main flower market, and to the south are more bazaars, full of 'wet and dry' footstuffs, fabric vendors, Chinese goldsmiths and apparel stalls. The northern end of the bazaar area is thronged by fruit vendors selling bushels of lychees, longans, mangosteens and rambutans. Săhm·lór (cycle-rickshaws) – now rarely seen in the city – wait to shuttle shoppers home with their produce.

Talat Ton Lam Yai MARKET

(ตลาดต้นลำไย; Map p308; Th Praisani; 24hr) Adjacent to Talat Warorot, Talat Ton Lam Yai morphs from a covered household market into an animated flower market (*gàht dòrk mái*), flanking the river on Th Praisani. Florists here are almost architects, assembling blooms and banana leaves into fantastically elaborate sculptures for festivals and home shrines. The smell of jasmine floats like perfume along the passageways, and drivers stop outside day and night to purchase strings of miniature roses and jasmine blossoms to sweeten their cabs.

Though the market is open 24/7, the bulk of its trade takes place after dark, away from the wilting daytime heat. The market goes into overdrive for big festivals such as Loi Krathong and the Flower Festival.

Talat Muang Mai MARKET

(ตลาดเมืองใหม่; Map p312; Th Praisani; 24hr) Chiang Mai's main wholesale fruit market is a riot of activity every morning, when enormous cargoes of mangoes, durians, rambutans, longans, watermelons, Malay apples, passionfruit and just about any other tropical fruit you could mention are unloaded from trucks along the east bank and sold on to juice-stand owners and market traders.

Chinatown NEIGHBOURHOOD

(Th Chang Moi) The area dominated by the Warorot and Ton Lam Yai markets doubles as the city's small Chinatown, marked by a flamboyant **Chinese welcome gate** (Map p312) across Th Chang Moi. Dotted around the bazaar area are several small Confucian temples, a handful of Chinese apothecaries and lots of Chinese jewellery shops, decorated in brilliant red, a symbol of good fortune. However, the area has lost some of its prominence with the construction of the vast new **Samakkee Charity Foundation temple** (Map p308; Th Loi Kroh; 6am-10pm) FREE.

South of the flower market on Th Praisani, the **Pung Tao Gong Ancestral Temple** (Map p308; Th Praisani; 6am-6pm) FREE was founded in 1876, but the shrine fell into ruin as the city's Chinese population declined. The temple was reconstructed as part of the city's 700th anniversary celebrations in 1995, complete with towering pagodas and writhing dragons, and two shophouses in front were removed to improve the flow of *chi*. A small parade winds through the streets for Chinese New Year.

Wat Bupparam BUDDHIST TEMPLE

(วัดบุปผาราม; Map p312; Th Tha Phae; donations appreciated; 6am-6pm) This highly ornate temple shows the clear influence of the Burmese teak merchants who immigrated to Chiang Mai during the 19th century. The eye-catching dharma hall has a *mon·dòp* (library) downstairs and a large prayer room above, but the most striking feature is the gorgeous, wonky *wí·hăhn* on the grounds, built from teak inlaid with mirror mosaics in the classic Lanna style. The *chedi* at the rear of the compound is in the Burmese Mon style, with four stucco *singha* (lions) around the base.

South of the Old City

The main highway running southwest from the old city, Th Wualai is famous for its **silver shops** and the entire street reverberates to the sound of smiths hammering intricate religious designs and ornamental patterns into bowls, jewellery boxes and decorative plaques made from silver or, more often, aluminium. This is also the location for the energetic Saturday Walking Street market (p316).

Wat Srisuphan BUDDHIST TEMPLE

(วัดศรีสุพรรณ; Map p308; Soi 2, Th Wualai; donations appreciated; 6am-6pm) It should come as no surprise that the silversmiths along Th Wualai have decorated their patron monastery with the same fine craftsmanship shown in their shops. The 'silver' *ubosot* at Wat Srisuphan is covered inside and out with silver, nickel and aluminium panels, embossed with elaborate repoussé-work designs. The effect is like a giant jewellery box, particularly after dark when the monastery is illuminated by coloured lights.

Wat Srisuphan was founded in 1502, but little remains of the original wát except for some teak pillars and roof beams in the main *wí·hăhn*. The murals inside show an interesting mix of Taoist, Zen and Theravada Buddhist elements. Note the gold and silver Ganesha statue beneath a silver *chatra* (umbrella) by the *ubosot,* a sign of the crossover between Hinduism and Buddhism in Thailand.

Because this is an active ordination hall, only men may enter the *ubosot.*

Wiang Kum Kam HISTORIC SITE

(เวียงกุมกาม; Rte 3029; tour by horse cart/tram 300/400B; ⌚8am-5pm) The first attempt at founding a city on the banks of the Mae Ping river, Wiang Kum Kam served as the Lanna capital for 10 years from 1286, but the city was abandoned in the 16th century due to flooding. Today, the excavated ruins are scattered around the winding lanes of a sleepy village 5km south of Chiang Mai. The centuries haven't been kind to Wiang Kum Kam, but the brick plinths and ruined *chedi* give a powerful impression of its former magnificence.

The landmark monument of the ruins is **Wat Chedi Liam**, with a soaring stucco *chedi* divided into dozens of niches for Buddha statues, an architectural nod to India's famous Mahabodhi Temple. In fact, this spire was created as part of a rather fanciful restoration by a Burmese trader in 1908. Over 1300 inscribed stone slabs, bricks, bells and *chedi* have been excavated at the site and some pieces are displayed at the visitor centre. The most important archaeological discovery was a four-piece stone slab, now housed at the Chiang Mai National Museum, inscribed with one of the earliest known examples of Thai script.

Most people explore the ruins by horse cart or tram, starting from the visitor centre on Rte 3029; if you come with your own transport via Th Chiang Mai–Lamphun (Rte 106), follow the signed road past a small roundabout with a fountain and turn left at the T-junction to reach Wat Chedi Liam.

West of the Old City

Modern Chiang Mai has sprawled west from the old city towards Doi Suthep and the Chiang Mai University, but there are a few historic sites dotted around the streets.

Wat Suan Dok BUDDHIST TEMPLE

(วัดสวนดอก; Map p308; Th Suthep; donations appreciated; ⌚6am-10pm) Built on a former flower garden in 1373, this important monastery enshrines the other half of the sacred Buddha relic that was transported by white elephant to Wat Phra That Doi Suthep. The main *chedi* is a gilded, bell-shaped structure that rises dramatically above a sea of immaculate white memorial *chedi* honouring members of the Thai royal family, with the misty ridge of Doi Suthep soaring behind.

The hangar-like main *wí·hăhn* contains a huge standing Buddha statue that almost touches the ceiling. Take some time to wander the memorial garden of whitewashed *chedi* in front of the monastery, which contain the ashes of generations of Lanna royalty.

Mahachulalongkorn Buddhist University is located on the same grounds and foreigners often join the popular Monk Chat and English-language meditation retreats.

Wat U Mong Thera Jan BUDDHIST TEMPLE

(วัดอุโมงค์; Map p308; Soi Wat U Mong, Th Khlong Chonprathan; donations appreciated; ⌚6am-6pm) Not to be confused with the small Wat U Mong in the old city, this historic forest wát is famed for its sylvan setting in the forest, and its ancient *chedi,* which rises above a brick platform wormholed with passageways, built around 1380 for the 'mad' monk Thera Jan. As you wander the arched tunnels, you can see traces of the original murals and a number of old and venerated Buddha images. The scrub forest around the platform is scattered with centuries' worth of broken Buddha images.

The attendant monks raise cows, deer, chickens and, curiously, English bull terriers, and in the grounds is a pretty, artificial lake, surrounded by *gù·đì* (monastic cottages). Check out the emaciated black stone Buddha in the Burmese style behind the *chedi.*

Wat U Mong is 600m south of Th Suthep near Chiang Mai University; be sure to ask the driver to take you to 'Wat U Mong Thera Jan' so you end up at the right monastery. If coming with your own transport, look for the signs to Srithana Resort on Th Suthep.

Chiang Mai University UNIVERSITY

(มหาวิทยาลัยเชียงใหม่, CMU; Map p308; www.cmu.ac.th; Th Huay Kaew & Th Suthep; entry adult/child 60/30B; ⌚9am-5pm) The main campus of Chiang Mai's famous public university occupies a 2.9-sq-km wedge of land about 2km west of the city centre, partly covered by forest and open greenery. It's a peaceful place to wander and there are bike lanes throughout the campus and plenty of cafes for pit stops.

The entry fee for tourists – introduced after Chinese tourists started dressing up in school uniforms and sneaking into classes! – is charged at the **Information Center** near the Th Huay Kaew entrance; this includes a tram ride to the Ang Kaew reservoir in the grounds.

ONE MILLION RICE FIELDS

Once upon a time, northern Thailand was as separate and foreign to Bangkok as Cambodia or Laos is today. The northern kingdom of Lanna (meaning 'one million rice fields') had its own dialect, writing system, religious and social customs and tribal ethnicity. A concerted effort to create a unified 'Thai' identity began after WWII, and Lanna traditions declined in the face of massive influence from the south. Nevertheless, if you scratch the surface, you can still find traces of Lanna identity and even glimmers of Lanna national pride.

Carved crossed gables known as *kalae* (a legacy of animist tribal cults) still adorn buildings across Chiang Mai, and the Northern Thai dialect continues to be spoken by millions of *kun meu·ang* (people of the north). Religious festivals in Chiang Mai erupt in a riot of noise and colour, as *piphat* bands strike up traditional tunes and devotees perform Lanna dances in outrageously colourful costumes. Songkran (p331), a festival introduced to Thailand from the north, is celebrated with particular aplomb in Chiang Mai.

More tantalising glimpses of old Lanna can be seen at Anusawari Singh (p324), just beyond Hwy 11 in the north of the city, where Chao Kavila built two stucco lions on an artificial island to scare off would-be Burmese invaders. The lions are the focus of boisterous celebrations as part of the Suep Jata Muang festival in June, when older residents of Chiang Mai dance and make offerings to Chiang Mai's guardian spirits. Chao Kavila is also credited with building the stucco guardian elephants in the Elephant Monument (p324) by the bus station on Th Chotana (Th Chang Pheuak).

The animist origins of the Lanna kingdom are even more tangible at the Pu Sae Ya Sae festival, held 10 days after Suep Jata Muang at Mae Hia in the forest below Wat Phra That Doi Kham (p322). According to legend, Doi Kham mountain was once the domain of two evil giants known as Pu Sae and Ya Sae, but Buddha appeared to the giants and convinced them to pursue a life of dharma, saving the people of Mae Hia. To invoke blessings from the giants, a water buffalo is sacrificed and skinned by a village shaman, who becomes possessed by the spirit of Pu Sae.

Chiang Mai University Art Museum GALLERY
(Map p308; www.finearts.cmu.ac.th; Th Nimmanhaemin; ⌚9am-5pm Tue-Sun) **FREE** The Faculty of Fine Arts displays temporary exhibitions of contemporary Thai and international artists at its own gallery near the Th Nimmanhaemin/Th Suthep junction, but there's no permanent collection. Some shows take place at the **Baan Tuek Art Center** (Map p308; Th Tha Phae; ⌚3-8pm Tue-Sun) **FREE** on Th Tha Phae.

Chiang Mai Night Safari ZOO
(เชียงใหม่ไนท์ซาฟารี; ☎053 999000; www.chiangmainightsafari.com; Rte 121; tours adult/child 800/400B; ⌚11am-10pm; 👪) This expansive animal park is open day and night, but the real action happens after dark, when you can view all sorts of critters from the back of an open-sided tram. With animal shows and musical fountains, it's all a little bit Las Vegas. Despite having come under fire from animal welfare experts for alleged poor animal management, it remains popular with families, with lots of big predators and African herbivores on display. Predator Prowl and Savannah Safari tours leave at fixed times, day and night.

There's also the **Jaguar Trail** (adult/child 100/50B), a 1.2km walk around the lake, passing enclosures with all the usual zoo favourites. The Night Safari is about 12km from central Chiang Mai, just west of Rte 121. Most people come on package tours arranged through hotels and tour agencies, with transport included.

Come late in the afternoon before the Night Safari to enjoy the excellent children's playground.

Royal Park Rajapruek GARDENS
(อุทยานหลวงราชพฤกษ์; www.royalparkrajapruek.org; Rte 121, Mae Hia; adult/child 100/50B; ⌚8am-6pm) Close to the Night Safari, this sprawling formal garden is another venture honouring the king and queen, with 21 themed gardens donated by international governments as part of Chiang Mai's International Horticultural Exposition in 2006. It sounds a bit corporate on paper, but the complex is actually lush, green and peaceful, with a vast wát-shaped central pavilion full of slightly OTT displays honouring the Thai royal family.

Wat Phra That Doi Kham BUDDHIST TEMPLE
(วัดพระธาตุดอยคำ; Mae Hia; donations appreciated; 6am-6pm) Reached via a steep *naga* stairway through the forest, this handsome wát looms above the city from the hillside above Royal Park Rajapruek. With its gilded *chedi*, supersized Buddha statues and panoramic city views it's an attractive and quieter alternative to Wat Phra That Doi Suthep. The easiest way to get here is by rented motorcycle or chartered *rót daang;* follow the signs for Royal Park Rajapruek from Rte 121 and go right at the roundabout before the entrance.

Chiang Mai Zoo ZOO
(สวนสัตว์เชียงใหม่; www.chiangmaizoo.com; 100 Th Huay Kaew; adult/child 150/70B, combined zoo & aquarium ticket 290/200B; 8am-4.30pm;) Chiang Mai Zoo is better than many zoos in the region when it comes to animal welfare, and the setting, sprawled across the forested slopes of Doi Suthep, is gorgeous. As well as animals from across the globe, including penguins in their own refrigerated ice-house, the zoo has several special exhibits requiring separate admission, including an impressive **aquarium** (adult/child 225/175B), the **panda house** (adult/child 100/50B) and the **snow dome** (150/100B), where locals come for their first taste of the cold stuff. You also stand a good chance of seeing giant bugs crawling out of the surrounding jungle.

The zoo monorail is dormant, but a shuttle bus (adult/child 30/20B) pootles around the grounds, and provides access to the slightly neglected upper reaches of the grounds, which are a steep hike from the entrance. Many enclosures sell bananas and other healthy snacks for the animals; kids will love the ruckus of feeding emus and other exotic beasties.

Doi Suthep-Pui National Park NATIONAL PARK
(อุทยานแห่งชาติดอยสุเทพ – ปุย; 053 210244; Th Huay Kaew; adult/child 100/50B, car 30B; camping per person 60B, bungalows 400-2500B; 8am-sunset) Often bearing a crown of clouds, sultry **Doi Suthep** (1676m) and **Doi Pui** (1685m) are two of northern Thailand's most sacred peaks. A dense cloak of jungle envelops the twin summits, which soar dramatically on the fringes of Chiang Mai. A 265-sq-km area on the slopes of the mountains, encompassing both summits, is preserved as a national park, attracting hordes of nature lovers, and legions of pilgrims who come to worship at Wat Phra That Doi Suthep.

As you climb, lowland rainforest gives way to cloud forest, full of mosses and ferns, providing a haven for more than 300 bird species and 2000 species of ferns and flowering plants. The park is also a renowned destination for mountain biking, and several Chiang Mai–based agencies run technical mountain-biking tours along trails that were once used as hunting and trade routes by hill-tribe villagers.

The park accommodation makes a comfortable base from which to explore and a trail runs for 2km from the campground to the summit of Doi Suthep, though the only view is of eerie mists swirling between the trees.

As with other national parks in the area, Doi Suthep is blessed with many thundering waterfalls, including **Nam Tok Monthathon**, about 2.5km off the paved road, which surges into a series of pools that hold water year-round. Swimming is best during or just after the monsoon, but you'll have to pay the national park fee to visit. Closer to the start of the road to Doi Suthep, **Nam Tok Wang Bua Bahn** is free, and full of frolicking locals, although this is more a series of rapids than a proper cascade.

Above the Bhubing Palace are a couple of Hmong villages. **Ban Doi Pui** is off the main road and is basically a tourist market at altitude; it's more interesting to continue to **Ban Kun Chang Kian**, a coffee-producing village about 500m down a dirt track just past the Doi Pui campground (ask the park staff for directions). *Rót daang* run from the Wat Phra That Doi Suthep parking lot to both Ban Doi Pui (60B) and Ban Kun Chang Kian (200B return).

The entrance to the park is 16km northwest of central Chiang Mai. Shared *rót daang* leave from Chiang Mai University (Th Huay Kaew entrance) to various points within the national park. One-way fares start at 40B to Wat Phra That Doi Suthep and 70B to Bhubing Palace. You can also charter a *sŏrng·tăa·ou* (passenger pick-up truck) for a half-day of exploring for 500B to 600B.

★ Wat Phra That Doi Suthep BUDDHIST TEMPLE
(วัดพระธาตุดอยสุเทพ; Th Huay Kaew, Doi Suthep; admission 30B; 6am-6pm) Overlooking the city from its mountain throne, Wat Phra That Doi Suthep is one of northern Thailand's most sacred temples, and its founding legend is learned by every school kid in Chiang Mai. The wát itself is a beautiful example of northern Thai architecture, reached via a strenuous, 306-step staircase flanked by mosaic *naga*; the climb is intended to help devotees accrue Buddhist

merit, but less energetic pilgrims can take a funicular-style lift for 20B.

The monastery was established in 1383 by King Keu Naone to enshrine a piece of bone, said to be from the shoulder of the historical Buddha. The bone shard was brought to Lanna by a wandering monk from Sukhothai and it broke into two pieces at the base of the mountain, with one piece being enshrined at Wat Suan Dok. The second fragment was mounted onto a sacred white elephant who wandered the jungle until it died, in the process selecting the spot where the monastery was later founded.

The terrace at the top of the steps is dotted with breadfruit trees, small shrines, rock gardens and monuments, including a statue of the white elephant that carried the Buddha relic to its current resting place. Before entering the inner courtyard, children pay their respects to a lizard-like guardian dragon statue known as 'Mom'.

Steps lead up to the inner terrace, where a walkway circumnavigates the gleaming golden *chedi* enshrining the relic. The crowning five-tiered umbrella marks the city's independence from Burma and its union with Thailand. Pilgrims queue to leave lotus blossoms and other offerings at the shrines surrounding the *chedi*, which are studded with Buddha statues in an amazing variety of poses and materials.

Within the monastery compound, the Doi Suthep Vipassana Meditation Center (p328) conducts a variety of religious outreach programs for visitors.

Rót daang run to the bottom of the steps to the temple from several points in Chiang Mai, including from in front of the zoo (40B per passenger) and in front of Wat Phra Singh (50B per passenger), but they only leave when they have enough passengers. A charter ride from the centre will cost 300B, or 500B return. Many people cycle up on mountain-biking tours from Chiang Mai, and you can also walk (p324) from the university.

Bhubing Palace GARDENS

(พระตำหนักภูพิงค์, Phra Tamnak Bhu Bing; www.bhubingpalace.org; Th Huay Kaew, Doi Suthep; admission 50B; ⌚8.30-11.30am & 1-3.30pm) Above Wat Phra That Doi Suthep, the grounds of the royal family's winter palace are open to the public (when the royals aren't visiting). Thanks to the mountain's cool climate, the royal gardeners are able to raise 'exotic' species such as roses, attracting lots of Thai

TEAK-ERA CHIANG MAI

Chiang Mai was never colonised by European powers, but the city has many of the hallmarks of European influence, dating back to the time when teak concessionaires from Britain and the US built fortunes on the timber being hauled from the surrounding forests.

One of the most striking colonial relics is the weatherboard **First Church** (Map p308; Th Chiang Mai-Lamphun), just south of Nawarat Bridge on the east bank, founded by the Laos Mission from North Carolina in 1868. Just south of here, the Iron Bridge was built as a homage to the demolished Nawarat Bridge, whose steel beams were fabricated by engineers from Cleveland in England. Local folklore states that the famous memorial bridge in Pai is not a WWII relic but a 1970s fake, built using reclaimed beams from Chiang Mai's Nawarat Bridge.

If you head in the other direction along the west bank, you'll pass the colonial-style former **Main Post Office**, which now houses a small **philatelic museum** (Map p308; Th Praisani; ⌚9am-4pm Tue-Sun) FREE. Similar Thai-Colonial administrative buildings spread out around the junction of Th Ratwithi and Th Phra Pokklao in the old city, where the former **Provincial Hall**, now the **Chiang Mai City Arts & Cultural Centre** (p317), and **Provincial Courthouse** (now the **Lanna Folklife Museum** (p316)) show the clear influence of the British 'gentlemen foresters' who controlled 60% of Chiang Mai's teak industry in the 19th and 20th centuries.

Many of the teak concessionaires' mansions have fallen into disrepair, but the colonial style of architecture was adopted by the Lanna royal family. One of the most impressive surviving teak-era mansions is the **Lanna Architecture Center** (Map p312; www.lanna-arch.net; 117 Th Ratchadamnoen; ⌚8.30am-4.30pm Mon-Fri) FREE, formerly owned by prince Jao Maha In, built between 1889 and 1893; it displays some interesting models showing the changing face of Lanna architecture through the centuries. The former British Consulate, now **The Service 1921 restaurant** (p343) at the Anantara Resort, and the **Darapirom Palace** (p354) in Mae Rim are also fine examples of this hybrid style.

WALKING TO DOI SUTHEP

At the start of every academic year in July, the entire first-year class from Chiang Mai University embarks on a pilgrimage on foot to Wat Phra That Doi Suthep, to introduce new students to the spirit of the city, believed to reside in the mountain. More ambitious students make the ascent via a muddy footpath, which starts close to the TV tower near the back entrance to Chiang Mai Zoo and continues through the grounds of Wat Phalad. To get to the start of the path, go to the end of the university perimeter wall on Th Suthep and then follow the signposted road on the right towards Palaad Tawanron to reach the back entrance to the zoo; bear left at this fork and you'll reach the TV tower and a brown sign showing the start of the trail.

sightseers. More interesting is the **reservoir** in the grounds, brought to life by fountains that dance to the king's own musical compositions. You can rent a 'trolley car' (golf cart) to explore for 400B.

North of the Old City

From Pratu Chang Pheuak (White Elephant Gate), it's a short walk north to the **Elephant Monument** (Map p308), whose twin elephant statues in stucco pavilions are said to have been erected by King Chao Kavila in 1800.

Wat Jet Yot BUDDHIST TEMPLE

(วัดเจ็ดยอด; Map p308; Rte 11/Th Superhighway; donations appreciated; ⏲8.30am-5pm) Beyond Rte 11 in the north of the city, this historic wát still has much of its original stucco intact, and gives a strong impression of what other wát in the city would have looked like in their heyday. The monastery was built to host the eighth World Buddhist Council in 1477, and its historic *wí·hăhn* is decorated with time-worn stucco bas reliefs of *deva* (angelic Buddhist spirits).

Topped by *jèt yôrt* (seven spires), representing the seven weeks Buddha spent in Bodhgaya in India after his enlightenment, the old *wí·hăhn* is believed to be a replica of Bodhgaya's Mahabodhi Temple, but scholars believe that the plans were copied from a clay votive tablet showing the temple in distorted perspective. Dotted around the compound are more chapels and *chedi,* as well as lots of mature ficus trees propped up with wooden stakes by devotees seeking merit.

Wat Ku Tao BUDDHIST TEMPLE

(วัดกู่เต้า; Map p308; Soi 6, Th Chotana/Th Chang Pheuak; donations appreciated; ⏲6am-6pm) North of the old city, behind the Muang Chiang Mai sports stadium, photogenic Wat Ku Tao dates from 1613 and incorporates many Burmese and Confucian elements. The distinctive *chedi* is said to resemble a stack of watermelons, hence the name (*tao* means 'melon' in the Northern Thai dialect). Contained inside are the ashes of Tharawadi Min, son of the Burmese king Bayinnaung, who ruled over Lanna from 1578 to 1607.

Chiang Mai National Museum MUSEUM

(พิพิธภัณฑสถานแห่งชาติเชียงใหม่; Map p308; ☎053 221308; Rte 11/Th Superhighway; ⏲9am-4pm Wed-Sun) Operated by the Fine Arts Department, this museum is the primary caretaker of Lanna artefacts and Northern Thai history, but most of the galleries were closed at the time of research for refurbishment, and only the ground floor, with Buddhist statues, *howdahs* (elephant carriages) and dioramas of historical scenes, was open to the public. When the museum reopens, expect the old admission fee of 100B to be reinstated.

Bags and cameras must be left in the free lockers by the ticket desk. To make a visit more worthwhile, combine your trip with a visit to Wat Jet Yot and the Chinese cemetery.

Chinese Cemetery CEMETERY

(Map p308; Soi 1, Th Chotana/Th Chang Pheuak; ⏲6am-6pm) Tucked away on a quiet soi behind the National Museum, this peaceful cemetery is lined with elegant Chinese gravestones, whose level of ornamentation provides a good indication of the former wealth of their occupants. Nearby are the curious **Anusawari Singh** (Map p308; Soi 1, Th Chotana/Th Chang Pheuak), two stucco lions said to have been erected by King Chao Kavila himself.

Activities

Outdoor escapes are easy in Chiang Mai, with tropical rainforests, looming mountains, rushing rivers, hill-tribe villages, and sanctuaries and camps full of elephants all within an hour's drive of the city. Dozens of operators offer adventure tours, exploring the forested mountains and waterways on foot, or by bike, raft, all-terrain-vehicle and even zipline.

The operators listed below have a good reputation for the quality of their trips, but there are many imitators offering less impressive versions of the same activities. To guarantee that you'll get what you're expecting, book directly with the providers, rather than booking through a tour agent, to whom you'll also pay an additional commission.

Adventure Activities

Forested mountains rise up around Chiang Mai like green giants, starting right at the city limits. Just 15km from the old city, Doi Suthep National Park is watered by crashing cascades and criss-crossed by hiking and mountain-biking trails that are regarded as some of the finest in the country. For a taste of the jungle, consider taking a rented motorcycle to the top of Doi Suthep, or around the Mae Sa–Samoeng Loop (p354), which winds across the lower slopes of the mountain. Rock climbers head to Crazy Horse Buttress, an impressive set of limestone cliffs behind the Tham Meuang On cave, 35km east of Chiang Mai, off Rte 1317 between San Kamphaeng and Ban Huai Kaew.

The closest rushing river for white-water rafting and kayaking is the wild and frothy Mae Taeng, which carves a path through the mountains near Chiang Dao. The long white-water season runs from July to March, and operators follow a 10km stretch of the river with rapids from grade II to grade V. Note that the river is prone to flash flooding after heavy monsoon rain and can be dangerous at these times; when choosing a white-water operator take a careful look at their safety equipment and procedures.

Flight of the Gibbon ZIPLINING
(Map p312; ☎053 010660; www.treetopasia.com; 29/4-5 Th Kotchasan; day tour 3599B) Much copied but never equalled, this adventure outfit started the zipline craze, with nearly 5km of wire and staging platforms strung up like a spiderweb in the forest canopy near Ban Mae Kampong, an hour's drive east from Chiang Mai. As well as day trips, it offers multiday, multi-activity tours that include a night at a village homestay.

Chiang Mai Mountain Biking & Kayaking MOUNTAIN BIKING
(Map p312; ☎053 814207; www.mountainbikingchiangmai.com; 1 Th Samlan; tours 1250-2300B) This specialist operator offers recommended kayaking trips on the Mae Ping and full-day guided mountain-biking tours (using imported bikes) to Doi Suthep-Pui National Park and further afield, including the popular ascent to Wat Phra That Doi Suthep.

HIKING IN CHIANG MAI

Thousands of visitors trek into the hills of northern Thailand each year hoping to see fantastic mountain scenery, interact with traditional tribespeople and meet elephants, and a huge industry has grown up to cater to this demand, but the experience is very commercial and may not live up to everyone's notion of adventure.

The standard package involves a one-hour minibus ride to Mae Taeng or Mae Wang, a brief hike to an elephant camp, an elephant ride, bamboo rafting and, for multiday tours, an overnight stay in or near a hill-tribe village. Many budget guesthouses pressure their guests to take these trips because of the commissions paid, and may ask guests to stay elsewhere if they decline.

While these packages are undeniably popular, they visit elephant camps that have a questionable record on elephant welfare. Hill-tribe trips can also disappoint as many of the villages now house a mix of tribal people and Chinese and Burmese migrants, and have abandoned many aspects of the traditional way of life. Rafting can also be a tame drift on a creek, rather than an adrenaline-charged rush over white water.

If you crave real adventure, you'll have to be a bit more hands-on about organising things yourself. To get deep into the jungle, rent a motorcycle and explore the national parks north and south of Chiang Mai; Chiang Dao is an excellent place to base yourself for jungle exploration. To see elephants in humane, natural conditions, spend a day at **Elephant Nature Park** (p326), then raft real white water with **Siam River Adventures** (p326). To encounter traditional hill-tribe culture, you'll need to travel to more remote areas than you can reach on a day trip from Chiang Mai; your best bet is to travel to Tha Ton and book a multiday trek from there.

Siam River Adventures RAFTING
(Map p312; ☎089 515 1917; www.siamrivers.com; 17 Th Ratwithi; rafting per day from 1800B) With more than a decade of experience, this outfit running white-water-rafting and kayaking trips has a good reputation for safety and professionalism. The guides have specialist rescue training and additional staff are located at dangerous parts of the river with throw ropes. Trips can be combined with elephant encounters and overnight village stays.

Spice Roads BICYCLE TOUR
(Map p312; ☎053 215837; www.spiceroads.com; 1 Soi 7, Th Moon Muang; cycling tours from 1000B) Offers a wide range of cycling tours, using impressively maintained, imported bicycles, from half-day trips around Chiang Mai city to serious mountain-biking trails in the surrounding countryside.

Peak Adventure Tour ADVENTURE SPORTS
(Map p308; ☎053 800567; www.thepeakadventure.com; 302/4 Th Chiang Mai-Lamphun; tours 900-2500B) The Peak offers a variety of adventure trips, including quad biking, abseiling, trekking, white-water rafting and rock climbing, as well as photography tours of Chiang Mai by săhm·lór.

Pooh Eco-Trekking TREKKING
(Map p312; ☎053 208538; www.pooh-ecotrekking.com; 59 Th Ratchaphakhinai; 2-day tours per person from 3500B) The owners of this adventure tour agency take the eco part of their name seriously, offering above-average hill-tribe treks and other adventure tours.

Chiang Mai Rock Climbing Adventures ROCK CLIMBING
(CMRCA; Map p312; ☎053 207102; www.thailandclimbing.com; 55/3 Th Ratchaphakhinai; climbing course from 3195B) CMRCA maintains many of the climbs at the limestone Crazy Horse Buttress, with bolted sport routes in the French 6a to 7a+ range. As well as climbing and caving courses for climbers of all levels, it runs a shuttle bus to the crag at 8am (300B return; book one day before). You can rent all the gear you need here, either piece by piece, or as a 'full set' for two climbers (1875B).

Elephant Interactions

Chiang Mai is one of Thailand's most famous destinations for elephant encounters, with dozens of elephant camps, though many still offer packages of elephant rides, circus-like sideshows and buffalo cart rides or bamboo rafting on the nearest river. Better camps offer interaction in place of exploitation; visitors walk with, feed and wash the elephant herds, but avoid activities that are harmful to the animals' welfare.

★ **Elephant Nature Park** ELEPHANT INTERACTION
(Map p312; ☎053 818754; www.elephantnaturepark.org; 1 Th Ratchamankha; 1-/2-day tour 2500/5800B) One of the first sanctuaries for rescued elephants in Chiang Mai, Elephant Nature Park has led the movement to abandon rides and shows and put elephant welfare at the top of the agenda, under the guidance of founder Sangduen (Lek) Chailert. In place of circus routines, visits are focused on interaction – the day is spent wandering with mahouts and their charges, helping to feed and wash elephants.

The elephants here have been rescued from logging camps and tourist shows, and, instead of being subjected to hooks and chains, they are allowed to form their own family groups and follow as closely as possible the natural behaviour of a wild herd. The most rewarding experience of all is seeing the natural interaction between the elephants, with baby elephants having trunk tug-of-wars, families enjoying shared mud baths and older elephants taking care of blind and disabled members of the herd.

The park is in the Mae Taeng valley, 60km from Chiang Mai, and day trips include a vegetarian buffet lunch. Longer volunteering packages are also available.

Thai Elephant Care Center ELEPHANT INTERACTION
(☎053 206247; www.thaielephantcarecenter.com; Mae Sa; half/full day 2000/3000B) This small centre at Mae Sa, about 25km northwest of Chiang Mai, was set up to provide care for elderly elephants retired from logging camps and elephant shows. There are no rides and visitors feed the old-timers with ground grass, herb balls and bananas and help out at bath-time, as well as visiting the cemetery for elephants who have died of old age.

Elephant Retirement Park ELEPHANT INTERACTION
(☎081 961 9663; www.elephantretirementpark.com; San Pa Yang, Mae Taeng; tours from 2600B) An ethical operator at Mae Taeng offering walking, feeding and bathing encounters with elephants, but no rides; the herd are allowed to maintain their own family units.

Baan Chang Elephant Park ELEPHANT INTERACTION
(Map p312; ☎053 814174; www.baanchangelephantpark.com; 147/1 Th Ratchadamnoen; 1-/2-day tours from 2900/6900B) Located in Mae Taeng, 50 minutes north of Chiang Mai, Baan Chang makes an effort to educate visitors about elephants and conservation issues, though the herd here is chained and packages include bareback elephant rides, which, while better than *howdah* rides, are still discouraged by animal welfare groups. Packages include basic mahout training, and elephant bath-time.

Patara Elephant Farm ELEPHANT INTERACTION
(☎081 992 2551; www.pataraelephantfarm.com; Baan Pong; day tour 3800-5800B) About 30km west of Chiang Mai, off Rte 1269, Khun Pat's elephant camp focuses on the interaction between mothers and babies. Visitors become 'elephant owners' for a day and help with health inspections, feeding, bathing and exercising the animals. While riding is offered, it is bareback only.

Other Activities

Namo YOGA
(Map p312; ☎053 326648; www.namochiangmai.com; 109/1 Th Moon Muang; classes 220B;

ETHICAL ELEPHANT INTERACTIONS

Elephants have been used as beasts of burden in Thailand for thousands of years, hauling logs from the teak forests and transporting the carriages of Thai royalty. The elephant-headed deities Erawan and Ganesha are revered by Buddhists and Hindus alike, and even the outline of Thailand resembles an elephant's head, with its trunk extending down into the isthmus.

With the nationwide ban on logging in 1989, thousands of working elephants suddenly found themselves out of a job, and herders and mahouts (elephant drivers) looked for new ways to generate revenue from their animals. So were born Chiang Mai's elephant camps, where former logging herds now entertain visiting tourists with circus-style displays and rides through the forest. However, growing awareness of animal welfare issues is shining a new spotlight on this industry and its practices.

Elephant rides are particularly problematic, with just one of the many issues including the fact that *howdahs* (carriages) used to carry tourists place severe strain on elephant's spines and can cause debilitating damage over time. Circus-like performances also put elephants at risk of injury, and many camps keep their elephants chained and segregated, and use the traditional *ankus* and similar types of metal hooks to control their animals. Government regulations offer little to no oversight, as they still classify elephants as modes of transport, and many animals show clear signs of psychological damage, which has manifested itself in attacks on humans.

There are alternatives. Sangduen (Lek) Chailert, a pioneer of elephant welfare in northern Thailand, has successfully demonstrated that rescued elephants can be kept in conditions that closely resemble their natural environment and still generate tourist income. At Elephant Nature Park (p326) near Mae Taeng, elephants are left unchained and allowed to form their own social groups in a sprawling riverside compound. In place of elephant rides, visitors walk around the grounds with elephants and their mahouts, feeding elephants by hand with fruit and vegetables at special feeding stations and helping out at bath-time in the creek.

With the success of this model of elephant tourism, other operators are abandoning some of the more harmful practices, and there are now several outfits where you can contribute to elephant conservation without the uncomfortable feeling that you are contributing to the problem. When choosing an outfit, look at the activities on offer and how the animals are looked after. If rides are offered, bareback riding, where the rider sits on the elephants' shoulders, is less harmful than rides in wooden *howdahs*, though some insist that rides should be avoided altogether given claims by animal welfare experts that elephants undergo brutal abuse to 'learn' how to accept riders. Bareback riding is not suitable for younger children.

The elephant camps listed in this guidebook have a focus on animal welfare and by booking with these operators, you can apply pressure that will hopefully encourage more operators to put elephant welfare at the top of their agenda.

⏲10-11.30am & 6-7.30pm Mon-Sat) Tucked away down a quiet lane near Tha Phae Gate, Namo has drop-in yoga classes as well as workshops in chanting, qigong and massage.

Gymkhana Club HEALTH & FITNESS
(Map p308; ☎053 241035; www.chiengmaigymkhana.com; Th Ratuthit) Founded in 1898 by British teak merchants, the historic Gymkhana Club has tennis courts and a golf course and driving range that are open to nonmembers for a daily fee. It's southeast of the Nawarat Bridge just off Th Chiang Mai-Lamphun.

Courses

Buddhist Meditation

Several temples offer *vipassana* meditation courses and retreats, but most have strict rules and participants should dress in modest white clothes, which can typically be purchased from the temple. There is usually no set fee but donations are appropriate.

Doi Suthep Vipassana Meditation Center MEDITATION
(☎053 295012; www.fivethousandyears.org; Th Huay Kaew, Wat Phra That Doi Suthep) Set within the grounds of Wat Phra That Doi Suthep, this centre offers meditation training retreats for all levels, lasting from three to 21 days.

Northern Insight Meditation Centre MEDITATION
(☎053 278620; www.watrampoeng.net; Th Suthep Muang, Wat Ram Poeng) The intensive course of 26 days or longer at Wat Ram Poeng, 4km south of Chiang Mai, is best suited for serious meditation students; days start at 4am and meals are taken in silence.

Wat Srisuphan MEDITATION
(Map p308; ☎053 200332; 100 Th Wualai; ⏲5.30-9pm Tue, Thu & Sat) The silver temple south of the old city offers an introduction to meditation using the four postures: standing, walking, sitting and lying down.

Wat Suan Dok Meditation Retreat MEDITATION
(Map p308; ☎084 609 1357; www.monkchat.net; Th Suthep, Wat Suan Dok; 2-day retreat 500B; ⏲Tue & Wed) The Buddhist university affiliated with Wat Suan Dok conducts a two-day meditation retreat at an affiliated forest wát. Register in advance for more information.

Cooking

Chiang Mai is the most popular place in the country to learn Thai cooking, with more than a dozen schools competing for the honour of teaching you how to prepare your own curry pastes, Thai soups, stir-fries, curries and Thai puddings. Courses are typically based around one-day modules that you can bolt together to learn an entire Thai menu over a week, though some short half-day and evening courses are available. All the courses will teach you about the ingredients as well as the techniques, with trips to local markets to buy herbs and spices, or walks around the herb garden. The best courses take place at bespoke communal kitchens at country farmhouses around Chiang Mai. Along the way, you get to eat the Thai food you make and you'll leave with a recipe booklet so you can create the same magic back home.

Chiang Mai Thai Cookery School COOKING COURSE
(Map p312; ☎053 206388; www.thaicookeryschool.com; 47/2 Th Moon Muang; courses from

MONK CHAT

If you're curious about Buddhism, many Chiang Mai temples offer popular Monk Chat sessions, where novice monks get to practise their English, and tourists get to find out about the inner workings of monastery life. It's a fascinating opportunity to discover a little more about the rituals and customs that most Thai men sign up to for at least a small portion of their lives. Remember to dress modestly as a sign of respect: cover your shoulders and knees. Because of ritual taboos, women should take care not to touch the monks or their belongings, or to pass anything directly to them.

Wat Suan Dok (p320) has a room for Monk Chats from 5pm to 7pm Monday to Friday.

Wat Srisuphan (p319) holds 5.30pm to 7pm sessions just before its meditation course.

Wat Chedi Luang (p311) has a table under a tree where monks chat from 9am to 6pm daily.

Wat Phakkao (วัดผ้าขาว; Map p312; Th Ratchmankha; donations appreciated; ⏲6am-6pm) holds a low-key session from 4pm to 7pm on Saturday and Sunday.

CHIANG MAI FOR CHILDREN

Chiang Mai is very popular with families, both for its easygoing vibe and for the massive range of activities on offer. As a sensible first step, pick a hotel with a pool and plan out your days to avoid overload; chartering a *rót daang* or túk-túk will give you the independence to come and go as you please. **Suan Buak Hat** (p306) has the most convenient playground in the old city. At meal times you can find familiar Western food in the old city and shopping centres.

Set aside one day for an elephant interaction – **Elephant Nature Park** (p326) gets the balance of conservation and interaction just right – and another day for a paddle, swim and picnic at the **Mae Sa waterfalls** (p354). Wát trips are popular with kids and the compounds are green, calm and mostly traffic free; **Phra That Doi Suthep** (p322), **Suan Dok** (p320), **U Mong Thera Jan** (p320), **Chedi Luang** (p311) and **Phra Singh** (p307) have the most going on to keep small sightseers entertained. The three old-city museums (p316) have plenty of modern, kid-friendly displays, and zoo-style wildlife encounters are possible at the **Chiang Mai Zoo** (p322) and **Chiang Mai Night Safari** (p321).

For days when the temperature rises to unbearable levels, all the big shopping centres have icy air-con, multiscreen cinemas and kids' activities; Central Festival has the **Sub-Zero ice-rink** (053 288868; www.majorbowlhit.com; per hr adult/child 250/200B; 11am-10pm Mon-Fri, 10am-10pm Sat & Sun), complete with 'walkers' for first-time skaters. It's worth delaying bedtime on Saturday and Sunday for a trip to the **Walking Street markets** (p316), or for a trip to the **Night Bazaar** (p347) any night of the week.

1450B) One of Chiang Mai's first cooking schools, run by TV chef Sompon Nabnian and his team. Classes are held in a rural setting outside of Chiang Mai, and there's a special evening masterclass led by the founder, with Northern Thai delicacies.

Asia Scenic Thai Cooking COOKING COURSE
(Map p312; 053 418657; www.asiascenic.com; 31 Soi 5, Th Ratchadamnoen; half-/full-day courses from 800/1000B) On Khun Gayray's cooking courses you can study in town or at a peaceful out-of-town farm. Courses cover soups, curries, stir-fries, salads and desserts, so you'll be able to make a three-course meal after a single day.

Gap's Thai Culinary Art School COOKING COURSE
(Map p312; 053 278140; www.gaps-house.com; 3 Soi 4, Th Ratchadamnoen; 1-/2-day course 900/1800B; Mon-Sat) Affiliated with the guesthouse Gap's House, classes are held out of town at the owner's house.

Thai Farm Cooking School COOKING COURSE
(Map p312; 081 288 5989; www.thaifarmcooking.com; 38 Soi 9, Th Moon Muang; course 1300B) Teaches cooking classes at its organic farm, 17km outside of Chiang Mai; the course includes return transport from Chiang Mai.

Baan Thai COOKING COURSE
(Map p312; 053 357339; www.baanthaicookery.com; 11 Soi 5, Th Ratchadamnoen; day/evening course 1000/800B) With a handy in-town location, this school offers all-day and evening classes.

Language

As a university town, Chiang Mai is a popular place to learn the Thai language and there are also opportunities to train up as a TEFL (Teaching English as a Foreign Language) teacher.

American University Alumni LANGUAGE COURSE
(AUA; Map p312; 053 214120; www.learnthaiinchiangmai.com; 73 Th Ratchadamnoen; group course 4800B) Conducts 60-hour Thai courses, with two hours of classes daily, Monday to Friday. Private instruction is also available.

Easy Study Thai LANGUAGE COURSE
(Map p312; 089 429 9872; www.easystudythai.com; Th Chang Khlan, 3rd fl, Pantip Plaza; Thai courses from 2000B) Upstairs in the Pantip Plaza shopping centre; offers a wide range of courses in Thai, from month-long beginner packages to year-long courses.

Payap University LANGUAGE COURSE
(053 851478; http://ic.payap.ac.th; Th Kaew Nawarat, Kaew Nawarat Campus; Thai courses from 8000B) A private university founded by the Church of Christ of Thailand; offers intensive Thai language courses in 60-hour modules.

UniTEFL International LANGUAGE COURSE
(Map p308; 053 400001; www.unitefl.com; 213/2 Th Huay Kaew, P & S Bldg 3; TEFL courses

US$345-1790) Offers TEFL certificate courses ranging from 60 to 120 hours, with post-qualification placements, as well as one-year Thai language courses.

Thai Boxing

Chiang Mai has several established *moo·ay tai* (also spelt *muay Thai*) gyms that have trained national champions, and all accept foreign fighters.

Lanna Muay Thai Boxing Camp MARTIAL ARTS
(Map p308; ☎053 892102; www.lannamuaythai.com; 161 Soi Chang Khian, Th Huay Kaew; day/week/month 400/2200/8000B) Offers instruction to foreigners and Thais. The gym is famous for having trained the title-winning, transvestite boxer Parinya Kiatbusaba.

Chai Yai Muay Thai MARTIAL ARTS
(☎082 938 1364; Th Sunpiliang, Nong Hoi; day/week/month 450/1700/5000B) This school has been training Thai and foreign fighters of all levels for 30 years. It's southeast of the city, off Rte 11 near the Chiang Mai 700 Years Park.

Santai Muay Thai MARTIAL ARTS
(☎082 528 6059; www.muay-thai-santai.com; 79 Mu 9, San Kamphaeng; day/week/month 500/2500/9000B) Run by former prize fighters, with a focus on reaching competition standard. The gym is east of town.

Thai Massage

Chiang Mai has many massage schools, from tourist-focused courses to government-accredited vocational programs.

CHIANG MAI SPAS

Once upon a time in Chiang Mai, massage parlours offered little more than a mattress and a vigorous pummelling for a modest fee, but these days the focus has shifted to lavish spas, which strive to recreate the elegant lifestyle of Lanna royalty, with massage tables set in lush gardens full of birdsong and the sound of trickling water.

If you fancy going for a massage in Chiang Mai, we recommend going to one end of the spectrum or the other. If you don't fancy a lavish pampering at a posh spa, head instead to the informal massage pavilions inside Chiang Mai's monasteries or the massage services run as rehabilitation schemes for the blind and for former prison inmates.

Vocational Training Center of the Chiang Mai Women's Correctional Institution (Map p312; ☎053 122340; 100 Th Ratwithi; foot/traditional massage from 150/180B; ⏲8am-4.30pm Mon-Fri, 9am-4.30pm Sat & Sun) Offers fantastic massages performed by female inmates participating in the prison's job-training rehabilitation program. The cafe next door is a nice spot for a post-massage brew.

Lila Thai Massage (Map p312; ☎053 327043; www.chiangmaimassage.com; Th Phra Pokklao; standard/herbal massage from 200/300B; ⏲10am-10pm) Established by the former director of the Chiang Mai women's prison, Lila Thai offers post-release employment for graduates from the prison's massage training program. There are five branches in the old city, including a Th Ratchadamnoen branch (Map p312; ☎053 327243; www.chiangmaimassage.com; Th Ratchadamnoen; standard/herbal massage from 200/300B; ⏲10am-10pm).

Thai Massage Conservation Club (Map p312; ☎053 904452; 99 Th Ratchamankha; massage 180-300B; ⏲8am-9pm) A collective of traditional Thai massage practitioners, the Thai Massage Conservation Club employs all blind masseuses, who are considered to be expert practitioners because of their heightened sense of touch.

Oasis Spa (Map p312; ☎053 920111; www.oasisspa.net; 4 Th Samlan; herbal steam treatments from 600B, massages from 1700B) If you just want to be indulged, Oasis offers an upmarket take on the traditional Thai massage experience, with scrubs, wraps, massage and Ayurvedic treatments in a tranquil garden full of Lanna-style pavilions.

Fah Lanna (Map p312; www.fahlanna.com; 57/1 Th Wiang Kaew; massages from 250B; ⏲10am-10pm) Set in a Lanna-style water garden and offering a full range of spa treatments, this idyllic spa is a mass of fern fronds and water features.

Ban Hom Samunphrai (☎053 817362; www.homprang.com; 93/2a Mu 12, Tawangtan, Saraphi; steam bath 200B, massage 600-1300B) Teacher Maw Hom ('Herbal Doctor') comes from a long line of herbalists and massage therapists; as well as traditional Thai massage here, you can try a traditional herbal steam bath. It's 9km from Chiang Mai near the McKean Institute; check the website for directions.

Thai Massage School of Chiang Mai MASSAGE

(TMC; ☎053 854330; www.tmcschool.com; 203/6 Th Chiang Mai-Mae Jo; basic courses from 7500B) Northeast of town, this well-known school offers a government-licensed massage curriculum. There are three foundation levels and an intensive teacher-training program.

Old Medicine Hospital MASSAGE

(OMH; Map p308; ☎053 201663; www.thaimassageschool.ac.th; 78/1 Soi Siwaka Komarat, Th Wualai; courses 5000-6000B) The government-accredited curriculum is very traditional, with two 10-day massage courses a month, as well as shorter foot and oil massage courses.

Chetawan Thai Traditional Massage School MASSAGE

(Map p308; ☎053 410360; www.watpomassage.com; 7/1-2 Soi Samud Lanna, Th Pracha Uthit; general course 9500B) Bangkok's Wat Pho massage school established this Chiang Mai branch outside of town near Rajabhat University.

Lanna Thai Massage School MASSAGE

(Map p312; ☎053 232547; http://en.lannathaimassageschool.net; 37 Th Chang Moi Kao; courses 1800-12,000B) Close to Wat Chomphu, this reputable school is recognised by the Thai Ministry of Education and Public Health; training includes the preparation of herbal treatments using fresh ingredients.

Art of Massage MASSAGE

(Map p312; ☎083 866 2901; www.artofmassage.webs.com; Soi 3, Th Loi Kroh; courses 990-2900B) Khun Wanna gets rave reviews for her practical training sessions, limited to a maximum of two people, lasting two to three days.

Sabai De Ka MASSAGE

(Map p312; ☎081 881 3697; www.massage-chiangmai.com; 93/3 Th Moon Muang; courses 1200-5000B) Near Pratu Tha Phae, this popular school offers courses in a wide variety of massage techniques and therapies, lasting from half a day to two days.

Jack Chaiya MASSAGE

(Map p312; ☎083 154 6877; www.jackchaiya.com; 74/3 Th Wiang Kaew; 3- to 5-day courses from 7000B) Jack Chaiya was trained by his mother in *jàp sên* (literally 'nerve touch'), a Northern Thai massage technique akin to acupressure, and is passing on the wisdom at this small massage school near Wat Phra Singh.

Tours

The adventure activities operators Peak Adventure (p326), Chiang Mai Mountain Biking & Kayaking (p325) and Spice Roads (p326) all offer city tours by bike or săhm·lór.

Segway Gibbon TOUR

(Map p312; ☎084 614 4004; www.segwaygibbon.com; 29/4-5 Th Kotchasan; 2/3hr tours 1999/2299B) Run by the Flight of the Gibbon team; visiting the most popular sites by Segway.

Click and Travel CYCLING

(☎053 281553; www.chiangmaicycling.com; tours 950-5350B; 👪) Click and Travel offers family-friendly pedal-powered tours with a cultural focus, visiting temples and attractions in and outside of the city centre.

Chiang Mai Street Food Tours FOOD

(☎085 033 8161; www.chiangmaistreetfoodtours.com; tours 750B) These foodie trips through the city's morning and night markets are a great introduction to Northern Thai cuisine.

Festivals & Events

During the phenomenally popular Flower Festival, Songkran and Loi Krathong, make your travelling arrangements far in advance.

Chiang Mai Red Cross & Winter Fair CULTURAL

(Dec-Jan) This 10-day festival feels a bit like a country fair, with cultural performances and food hawkers doing a lively trade in Northern Thai cuisine. The main venue is the Chiang Mai City Arts & Cultural Centre.

Flower Festival CULTURAL

(early Feb) A riot of blooms, held over a three-day period in early February. There are flower displays, cultural performances and beauty pageants, plus a floral parade from Nawarat Bridge to Suan Buak Hat.

Chiang Mai Chinese New Year NEW YEAR

(Feb) The city's Chinese inhabitants herald the New Year in February with Chinese festival food, lion dances and the like.

Songkran NEW YEAR

(mid-Apr) The traditional Thai New Year (13 to 15 April) is celebrated in Chiang Mai with infectious enthusiasm. Thousands of revellers line up along all sides of the moat to throw water on any passers-by in the city (and each other), while more restrained Songkran rituals are held at Wat Phra Singh.

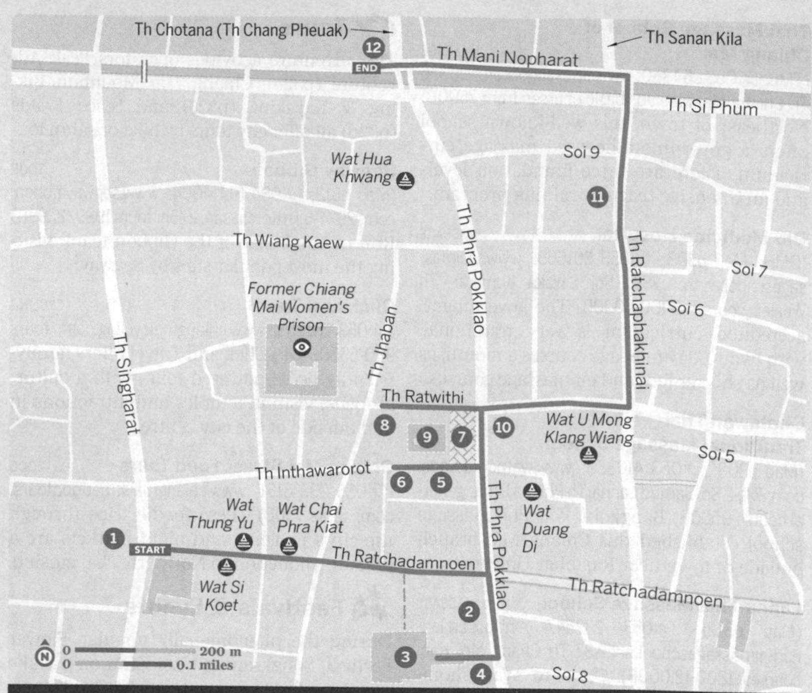

City Walk
Old City Temple Tour

START WAT PHRA SINGH
END TALAT PRATU CHANG PHEUAK
LENGTH 2.5KM; FIVE HOURS

No visit to Chiang Mai is complete without a temple tour. Start with the best, 1 **Wat Phra Singh** (p307), home to the city's most revered Buddha image, then stroll down Th Ratchadamnoen and turn right onto Th Phra Pokklao. In swift succession, you'll pass the gorgeous teak *wí·hăhn* (sanctuary) of 2 **Wat Phan Tao** (p315), and the looming mass of 3 **Wat Chedi Luang** (p311), the largest and grandest Lanna *chedi* (stupa) in the city. Perform a ceremonial circumambulation clockwise around the stupa, then duck into the 4 **Làk Meuang** (p314) to view the revered city pillar.

Turn on your heels now and follow Th Phra Pokklao north to the junction with Th Inthawarorot, where you'll see the post-card-perfect *wí·hăhn* of 5 **Wat Inthakhin Saduemuang** (p307), which enshrined the city pillar in medieval times, perched surreally in the middle of the road. This is a good time to pause for lunch at the ever-popular 6 **Ki-at Ocha** (p340). Suitably refreshed, walk another block north on Th Phra Pokklao to the 7 **Anusawari Sam Kasat** (p316; Three Kings Monument), and pay your respects to the three Lanna kings who founded Chiang Mai.

You are now in the perfect location to take in Chiang Mai's trinity of excellent city museums, the 8 **Chiang Mai Historical Centre** (p317), the 9 **Chiang Mai City Arts & Cultural Centre** (p317) and the 10 **Lanna Folklife Museum** (p316; all accessible on a combination ticket). If you can drag yourself away from the icy air-conditioning, continue north along Th Ratchaphakhinai to reach ancient 11 **Wat Chiang Man** (p316), the oldest wát in a city awash with ancient temples. To finish, walk on to the moat and enjoy the Cowboy Hat Lady's fabulous *kôw kăh mŏo* (slow-cooked pork leg with rice) at 12 **Talat Pratu Chang Pheuak** (p341).

LOCAL KNOWLEDGE

SONGKRAN IN CHIANG MAI

Introduced to Thailand from the north by Burmese invaders and wandering hill tribes, the Songkran festival (13 to 15 April) is Chiang Mai's biggest and brightest celebration. The streets become a virtual jacuzzi as thousands of litres of water are squirted and poured over all and sundry to celebrate the traditional Northern Thai New Year. The celebrations extend to all the city wát, particularly Wat Phra Singh, which is the destination for a huge procession. Traditionally, much of the water was sourced from the moat around the old city, but there are now concerns that this will have to be abandoned on health grounds because of high pollution levels. Wherever the water comes from, some of it will end up on you, so wear clothes you don't mind getting wet and leave your phone and camera in your hotel, or even better, buy a water pistol and join in the fun!

Poy Sang Long (Poy Luang) RELIGIOUS
(usually Apr) In this three-day ordination ceremony, novices at Wat Pa Pao, Wat Ku Tao and Wat Srisuphan are dressed in make-up and garish costumes representing Buddha's early life as a pampered prince.

Inthakhin Festival RELIGIOUS
(mid-May) Held at Wat Chedi Luang in mid-May, this religious festival propitiates the city's guardian deity, who resides in the city pillar, ensuring that the monsoon will arrive on time.

Loi Krathong RELIGIOUS
(Oct/Nov) Also known as Yi Peng, this lunar holiday is celebrated along the Mae Ping with the launching of small lotus-shaped boats honouring the spirit of the river, and the release of thousands of illuminated lanterns into the night sky.

Sleeping

Inspired by the hit movie *Lost in Thailand* (2011), huge numbers of Chinese travellers are flocking to Thailand on city breaks, and this is having a profound effect on the hotel scene in Chiang Mai. New hotels and guesthouses are springing up like desert flowers and traditional ideas of high and low season are going out the window. Make reservations far in advance if visiting during Chinese New Year, Songkran and other holiday periods.

Accommodation prices in the city are slowly creeping up, but you can still find a dorm bed for under 200B, a basic fan room for 400B and a respectable air-con room from 500B. Some budget guesthouses subsidise their room rates through commissions from booking treks and tours; travellers have reported being moved on for declining to book these through their guesthouse. Staff usually inform guests if they have this policy.

The top-end range is dominated mainly by business-style hotels, but there are some lovely Lanna-style hotels at the upper end of the midrange category that are arguably more appealing. At the very top of the pile are a handful of resorts that perfectly marry traditional Lanna details with futuristic tech and flawless service. Free wi-fi is standard in almost all Chiang Mai accommodation.

Old City

There are literally hundreds of places to stay in the old city, most dotted around the tiny lanes linking the main streets.

★**Gap's House** GUESTHOUSE $
(Map p312; 053 278140; www.gaps-house.com; 3 Soi 4, Th Ratchadamnoen; s/d from 370/470B;) The overgrown garden at this old backpacker favourite is a veritable jungle, providing plenty of privacy in the relaxing communal spaces. Modest budget rooms are set in old-fashioned wooden houses, and the owner runs cooking courses and dishes up a delicious nightly vegetarian buffet. No advance reservations.

★**Diva Guesthouse** GUESTHOUSE $
(Map p312; 053 273851; www.divaguesthouse.com; 84/13 Th Ratchaphakhinai; dm 120-180B, r 250-800B;) An energetic spot on busy Th Ratchaphakhinai, Diva offers the full backpacker deal – dorm beds, budget box rooms, adventure tours, net access, ambient tunes, and fried rice and *sà·dé* (grilled meat with peanut sauce) in the downstairs cafe. Accommodation ranges from dorms to family rooms and comes with either fans or air-con. The same owners run **Diva 2** (Map p312; 053 224648; Soi 2, Th Ratwithi; s/d from 180/220B;) and **Diva 3** (Map p312; 093 171 6078; Soi 3, Th Ratchamankha; dm from 170B;).

WORTH A TRIP

SUPERHIGHWAY OF YORE: MAE PING RIVER

Before the construction of the roads and railways, the Mae Ping river was the main route of transit for goods coming into Chiang Mai. The markets along the riverbank are where the Lanna kingdom came to trade with the rest of Thailand, and via the Silk Road, with the rest of Asia. The river was used to transport everything from fruit and vegetables to the giant trunks of teak trees, but trade on the river slowly died after the arrival of the railways in 1922.

The Mae Ping still traces a lazy passage through the middle of Chiang Mai, but few vessels ply its waters today, with the exception of boat tours, which provide an excellent vantage point from which to view the city. The longest-established operator is **Scorpion Tailed River Cruise** (Map p312; 081 960 9398; www.scorpiontailedrivercruise.com; Th Charoenrat; cruise 500B), which runs river tours in covered long-tail boats from a pier by Wat Srikhong (just north of the Nakhon Ping bridge). Tours pass through peaceful countryside en route to a country farm, where passengers get a snack of mango and sticky rice. **Mae Ping River Cruise** (Map p308; 081 884 4621; www.maepingrivercruise.com; 133 Th Charoen Prathet, Wat Chaimongkhon; 2hr cruise from 550B; hourly 8.30am-5.30pm) offers similar trips starting from Wat Chaimongkhon, south of the centre on Th Charoen Prathet, as well as longer cruises to **Wiang Kum Kam** (p320).

If you don't mind paddling yourself, **Chiang Mai Mountain Biking & Kayaking** (p325) offers guided kayak tours along the Mae Ping, visiting forested stretches north of the city.

Julie Guesthouse GUESTHOUSE $

(Map p312; 053 274355; www.julieguesthouse.com; 7 Soi 5, Th Phra Pokklao; dm from 90B, r without/with bathroom from 150/220B;) Julie is perennially popular, though this is as much about budget as facilities. For not much more than the price of a fruit smoothie you can get a basic dorm bed, and tiny box rooms cost only a little more. In the evenings travellers congregate on the covered roof terrace.

There's a **Th Ratchamankha branch** (Map p312; 094 628 1991; julie_chiangmai@gmx.net; 11 Th Ratchamankha; dm 120-180B) with dorms only.

Smile House 1 GUESTHOUSE $

(Map p312; 053 208661; www.smilehousechiangmai.com; 5 Soi 2, Th Ratchamankha; r with fan/air-con 350/700B;) There's a hint of the 1950s motel about this popular and friendly guesthouse, with a splash pool for kids and a bigger pool for grown-ups. It's very relaxed and the simply furnished rooms (with big windows) offer good value for money.

According to local folklore, the old house once served as the 'safe house' of Kun Sa, the infamous Shan-Chinese opium warlord.

Shakara Garden GUESTHOUSE $

(Map p312; 053 327535; shakaragarden@gmail.com; 51/1 Soi 4, Th Singharat; dm 150B, r with fan/air-con 350/450B;) The old Aoi Garden Home has been rebranded but it still offers the same old-fashioned backpacker experience at bargain rates. Basic box rooms with mossie nets are spread across a series of wooden houses, with lots of chilled-out seating areas where travellers sit and chat. Dorms are mixed; private rooms share bathrooms.

60 Blue House GUESTHOUSE $

(Map p312; 053 206120; www.60bluehouse.com; 32-33 Th Ratchaphakhinai; dm 250B, s/d from 350/400B;) This ladies-only hostel has one eight-bed dorm and clean private rooms with shared bathroom. Owner Khun Tao is a mine of local information, so guests always know where to go and what to do.

Thapae Gate Lodge GUESTHOUSE $

(Map p312; 053 207134; www.thapaegatelodge.com; 38/7 Soi 2, Th Moon Muang; r with fan/air-con from 250/500B;) An upgrade of a typical Thai house, with simple backpacker rooms and a sliding scale of amenities, from fans to air-con, extra space and balconies. It's owned by a Thai-German team, which will become obvious when you see the menu at the garden cafe!

Banjai Garden GUESTHOUSE $

(Map p312; 085 716 1635; www.banjai-garden.com; 43 Soi 3, Th Phra Pokklao; r with fan/air-con 400/500-1200B;) Set in an orderly wooden house, Banjai Garden has a calm air and a pleasant garden for hanging out. Take your pick from simple but clean fan rooms or better air-con rooms. Staying here feels a little like staying in a Thai home.

★ **Awanahouse** GUESTHOUSE $$

(Map p312; 053 419005; www.awanahouse.com; 7 Soi 1, Th Ratchadamnoen; r with fan/air-con

400/650-875B; ❄@📶🏊) The pick of the guesthouses around Pratu Tha Phae, with rooms for every budget – all kept spotless – and a mini cold-water pool under cover on the ground-floor terrace. Rooms get more comfortable and better decorated as you move up the price scale and there's a rooftop chill-out area with views across old Chiang Mai.

Staff are delightful and go the extra mile for children, so it's a big hit with families; book ahead.

★Sri Pat Guest House GUESTHOUSE **$$**
(Map p312; ☎053 218716; www.sri-patguesthouse.com; 16 Soi 7, Th Moon Muang; r 1300-1900B; ❄📶🏊) A standout flashpacker guesthouse with all the trimmings: wi-fi, pool, wood-decked communal areas, scattered Buddha carvings and smart tiled rooms with flatscreens and little Thai details. You get plenty of personality for your baht and staff are cheerful and friendly.

★Villa Duang Champa HOTEL **$$**
(Map p312; ☎053 327199; www.duangchampa.com; 82 Th Ratchadamnoen; r from 1900B; ❄📶) In a prime piece of real estate for the Sunday Walking Street market, Villa Duang Champa adds a little design-magazine chic to the backpacker experience. Set in a modernised traditional building, the spacious rooms have polished concrete floors, eclectic furniture, a hint of colonial charm and small nooks that catch the sun.

Vieng Mantra HOTEL **$$**
(Map p312; ☎053 326640; www.viengmantra.com; 9 Soi 1, Th Ratchadamnoen; s/d from 1050/1900B; ❄@📶🏊) A proper hotel tucked into winding Soi 1, Vieng Mantra creates a little oasis with its courtyard pool and landscaped gardens. Rooms range from simple standards to swanky deluxe-plus rooms with circular divans and plump silk cushions. Balconies have built-in seats with a view over the electric-blue pool.

Tropical Inn GUESTHOUSE **$$**
(Map p312; ☎086 922 3606; www.goodmorningchiangmai.com; 29/5 Soi 6, Th Ratchamankha; r 1300-1500B; ❄📶🏊) A saltwater pool, superior breakfasts and a tranquil location south of Wat Phra Singh all score points for this comfortable guesthouse in a vaguely Spanish-style villa. Rooms full of natural timber come with crisp linen and tasteful bathrooms. The Good Morning Chiang Mai cafe (p340) also serves good lunches and dinners.

Buri Gallery GUESTHOUSE **$$**
(Map p312; ☎053 416500; www.burigallery.com; 102 Th Ratchadamnoen; r 1300-2300B; ❄📶🏊) Seconds from Wat Phra Singh, Buri Gallery is a perfect base for exploring the old city. Rooms, set around a lovely pool that's ideal for families, are tucked away behind the coffeeshop and garden in a series of converted teak buildings. Although pricey, they have bits and bobs of Lanna art and the best have balconies where you can sit and enjoy the sunset.

Baan Pordee Guesthouse GUESTHOUSE **$$**
(Map p312; ☎083 764 8008; www.baanpordee.com; 6 Soi 12, Th Phra Pokklao; r from 1100B; ❄📶) A huge, open, airy balcony sets the scene at this calm, quiet guesthouse in a smart modern home, tucked away behind Wat Duang Di. Spotlessly tidy rooms face onto the garden.

Baan Hanibah Bed & Breakfast HOTEL **$$**
(Map p312; ☎053 287524; www.baanhanibah.com; 6 Soi 8, Th Moon Muang; s/d from 1000/1600B; ❄📶) Protected by a garden of fragrant frangipani trees, Baan Hanibah is a relaxed boutique escape in the heart of the old city. Behind an ornate gateway, in a converted teak house, you'll find small, quite stylish rooms with floaty drapes and Thai trim.

Charcoa House HOTEL **$$**
(Map p312; ☎053 212681; www.charcoa.com; 4 Soi 1, Th Si Phum; r 1440-1990B; ❄📶) Like a dainty *petit four*, this boutique hotel is run with precision by friendly staff, who also run the attached bakery and cafe. The decor falls somewhere between Spanish villa and Swiss B&B. It's worth staying just for the breakfast pastries.

TJR Boutique House HOTEL **$$**
(Map p312; ☎053 326525; Soi 1, Th Moon Muang; r 900-1200B; ❄@📶) Set in a new apartment-style block, TJR has huge rooms, large beds and bathrooms with tubs, plus some Thai trim to remind you where you are. Street-facing rooms enjoy views towards the mountains. Book ahead as it's popular.

★Tamarind Village HOTEL **$$$**
(Map p312; ☎053 418896-9; www.tamarindvillage.com; 50/1 Th Ratchadamnoen; r from 4500B, ste from 7800B; ❄📶🏊) Effortlessly refined, this atmospheric Lanna-style property sprawls across the grounds of an old tamarind orchard in a prime location off Th Ratchadamnoen. Walkways covered by tiled pavilions lead to secluded and beautiful spaces, and tall mature trees cast a gentle shade around the huge pool and gardens.

Design-magazine-worthy rooms are full of gorgeous tribal fabrics and artefacts.

It has a babysitting service for children aged one year or older.

The Ruen Tamarind restaurant (p342) serves beautifully presented Thai dishes and there's an opulent spa offering the full range of treatments.

★Rachamankha HOTEL **$$$**

(Map p308; ☎053 904111; www.rachamankha.com; off Soi 1, Th Samlan; r from 8040B, ste from 21,590B;) After working his magic on Tamarind Village, architect Ong-ard Satrabhandu upped the ante with his second heritage property in the lanes west of Wat Phra Singh. Entering Rachamankha is like walking into the cloisters of an ancient monastery or a medieval village. Interlinked courtyards lead to shady terracotta-tiled pavilions and opulent rooms with four-poster beds and an understated elegance that perfectly fits the mood of the hotel.

3 Sis HOTEL **$$$**

(Map p312; ☎053 273243; www.the3sis.com; 1 Soi 8, Th Phra Pokklao; d 1590-1700B;) Facing the gates to Wat Chedi Luang, 3 Sis offers large, airy rooms set around a huge open atrium, behind a streetside restaurant. The front building has fairly standard hotel rooms; the 'Vacation Lodge' at the back has much more attractive rooms with wooden floors and extra comforts. Rates are very fair for this prime location and breakfast is included.

Baan Huenphen BOUTIQUE HOTEL **$$$**

(Map p312; ☎053 281100; www.baanhuenphen.com; 117/1 Th Ratchamankha; r 1700-2850B;) Near the Northern Thai restaurant of the same name, this upgraded Thai house has large, airy rooms with immaculate bathrooms, and sit-on balconies out front. There's a lovely swimming pool and lots of Hang Dong crafts and antiques in the communal areas downstairs.

East of the Old City

While it isn't as quaint as the old city, Th Tha Phae is just as convenient for sightseeing and nightlife and is even closer to the Night Bazaar.

Hostel In Town HOSTEL **$**

(Map p312; ☎053 234292; www.hit-thapae.com; Soi 2, Th Tha Phae; dm 220B;) One of a cluster of spic-and-span backpacker hostels just east of the old city walls, 'HIT' has neat dorms with lockers, towels and a rooftop cafe. There's a women-only dorm on the 2nd floor.

SoHostel HOSTEL **$**

(Map p312; ☎053 206360; sohostel.chiangmai@gmail.com; 64/2 Th Loi Kroh; dm from 219B, r from 1500B;) Loi Kroh is better known for girlie bars than backpacker bunks, but this huge modern hostel is a good deal, just an easy stroll from the old city and the Night Bazaar. The two-tone red-and-white dorms (with six to 12 beds) are better value than the somewhat overpriced private rooms.

Roong Ruang Hotel HOTEL **$**

(Map p312; ☎053 234746; www.roongruang.com; 398 Th Tha Phae; r 500-700B;) The price is the clincher at this old-fashioned hotel on Th Tha Phae. Clean tiled rooms have little character, but higher classes have bathtubs and lots of space to spread out your stuff.

Thapae Boutique House HOTEL **$$**

(Map p312; ☎053 284295; www.thapaeboutiquehouse.com; 4 Soi 5, Th Tha Phae; r/ste from 950/1500B;) This popular flashpacker hotel has enough murals, Thai textiles and wooden trim to justify the boutique tag, and the location is handy for both the old city and the Night Bazaar. Rooms have more character than most and rates include breakfast.

Nat Len Boutique Guesthouse GUESTHOUSE **$$**

(Map p312; www.natlenboutiqueguesthouse.com; 2/4 Soi Wat Chompu, Th Chang Moi; r 650-1200B;) Quirky rooms are spread over several colourful houses at this low-key guesthouse just outside the city walls. Our favourite feature is the pale blue pool with its bubbling whirlpools, and there are lots of interesting wát in the surrounding alleyways.

Baan Kaew Guest House GUESTHOUSE **$$**

(Map p308; ☎053 271606; www.baankaew-guesthouse.com; 142 Th Charoen Prathet; r 800B;) This two-storey, apartment-style place is a good deal on the quiet east bank, but not too far from the Night Bazaar. Clean tiled rooms with white linen open onto a balcony with views across the spacious garden.

★Mo Rooms HOTEL **$$$**

(Map p312; ☎053 280789; www.morooms.com; 263/1-2 Th Tha Phae; r from 2800B;) Mo Rooms is designer in the urban mould, all exposed concrete and sculptural timbers juxtaposed with natural materials. Each of the Chinese-zodiac-themed rooms was decorated by a different Thai artist, ensuring some unique visions in interior decor – our top picks are 'Monkey' with its woven pod bed and 'Horse' with its surreal bed-tree.

There's a pebble-lined pool out back and an Asian fusion restaurant out front.

★Banthai Village HOTEL $$$
(Map p312; ☎053 252789; www.banthaivillage.com; 19 Soi 3, Th Tha Phae; r 6000-8000B, ste from 10,000B; ❄@📶🏊) Banthai does indeed resemble a country village transported to the modern city. The hotel sprawls over a series of wooden buildings with balconies, surrounding a pool and gardens with birds-of-paradise flowers. Rooms do the heritage thing, but subtly, with low wooden beds, dark wood furniture and traditional triangular Thai pillows. Hunt for discounted rates online as published rates are too high for what you get.

DusitD2 Chiang Mai HOTEL $$$
(Map p312; ☎053 999999; www.dusit.com; 100 Th Chang Khlan; r from 3768B; ❄@📶🏊) DusitD2 is a slice of modern minimalism in the chaos at the Night Bazaar. The dominant orange colour scheme spills over from the lobby into the designer rooms, and hotel facilities run to a pool and a fitness room with city views.

Le Meridien Chiang Mai HOTEL $$$
(Map p312; ☎053 253666; www.lemeridienchiangmai.com; 108 Th Chang Khlan; r from 4800B; ❄@📶🏊) This corporate hotel delivers a modern package on the doorstep of the Night Bazaar. Cool, silent corridors open onto contemporary rooms with bathrooms linked to the bedrooms by glass walls to bring in natural light. For our money, the infinity pool with mountain views is a better place to be seen! Cheaper walk-in rates are often available.

Imperial Mae Ping Hotel HOTEL $$$
(Map p312; ☎053 283900; www.imperialhotels.com; 153 Th Sridonchai; r from 2300B, ste from 4500B; ❄@📶🏊) Icy air-con welcomes you to the vast lobby of this slightly institutional tower hotel in a prime location near the Night Bazaar. The setup is old-fashioned – tinted windows, boutiques and a dulcimer player in the lobby, with standard Asian-style hotel rooms upstairs – but there's a good pool and it certainly offers respite from the heat and noise outside.

Riverside

The neighbourhoods on either bank of the riverside are less touristy, but are handy for the night market and the riverside eateries on the east bank.

Hollanda Montri GUESTHOUSE $
(Map p308; ☎053 242450; www.hollandamontri.com; 365 Th Charoenrat (Th Faham); r with fan/air-con from 400/500B; ❄📶) A good-value alternative to the old-city backpacker places, within walking distance of the riverside restaurants. Travellers rate its simple rooms and quiet riverbank location. Bike and motorcycle hire can be arranged.

★Riverside House GUESTHOUSE $$
(Map p308; ☎053 302121; www.riversidehousechiangmai.com; 101 Th Chiang Mai-Lamphun; r 700-

INVISIBLE MIGRANT WORKERS

Over the past three decades, an estimated 200,000 people have fled from Myanmar to Chiang Mai Province, escaping political violence, economic hardship and oppression in bordering Shan state. While some of these migrants have found sanctuary and opportunity in Thailand, others have found exploitation, working in almost slave-like conditions with little security or protection from abuse. Many of the 'long-necked' Padaung tribespeople put on display in tourist camps around Chiang Mai are actually indentured workers, working off fees charged by people smugglers to bring them across the border.

Facing growing international and domestic pressure, the Thai government is taking steps to reduce the influx, tightening border controls, raiding people-smuggling camps, and introducing a nationality verification process, which qualifies migrants for legal status and a minimum wage. However, allegations that the police turn a blind eye to and even participate in exploitation are widespread.

In response to this situation, a number of nongovernmental organisations are working with the Burmese migrant community in Chiang Mai, providing health care, education and legal support for displaced people. If you are interested in contributing or volunteering, contact Chiang Mai's **Burma Study Center** (Map p318; www.burmastudy.org; 302/2 Soi 13, Th Nimmanhaemin; ⏲11.30am-8pm Mon-Fri, 11.30am-6pm Sat), an umbrella for projects working with the Burmese refugee community.

1000B;) Near the Saphan Lek (Iron Bridge), this guesthouse offers great value. Rooms are spread across three blocks; you pay top dollar for the central block, by the pool and away from the traffic noise, but all the rooms are good for the money. It's a good choice for families.

★Baan Orapin GUESTHOUSE $$$
(Map p308; 053 243677; www.baanorapin.com; 150 Th Charoenrat (Th Faham); r 1700-3500B;) Set in a tranquil private garden, surrounding a stately teak house, Baan Orapin is a family affair. The owner's family have lived here since 1914, and guestrooms are in elegant villas dotted around the grounds and full of graceful furniture and fabrics. Design fans can find their own swish homewares in the posh boutiques along Th Charoenrat.

★Anantara Resort & Spa DESIGN HOTEL $$$
(Map p308; 053 253333; http://chiang-mai.anantara.com; 123 Th Charoen Prathet; r from 8230B;) Where James Bond would stay if he came to Chiang Mai, the Anantara sprawls across the grounds of the handsome former British Consulate, and it offers a perfect blend of cutting-edge modern design and period elegance. Rooms are simply gorgeous – natural timber in varied tones, floor-to-ceiling windows, flat-screens, balconies with divans – and all overlook the Zen-inspired grounds and river. The old consulate now houses The Service 1921 restaurant (p343) and there's a serene garden pool and a pond where staff place floating lanterns at night. There's a babysitting service and the hotel can provide cots, high chairs, kids' meals and car seats for families.

West of the Old City

Staying west of the old city puts you close to Chiang Mai University and Th Nimmanhaemin's bars and restaurants.

Spicythai Backpackers HOSTEL $
(Map p308; 083 477 9467; www.spicyhostels.com; 14 Th Hutsadisawee; dm 220B;) Tucked away in the student-y district north of Th Huay Kaew, this old-fashioned backpacker joint follows the classic Southeast Asian model. Beds are in simple single-sex dorms, there's a garden with hammocks and Western movies play all day long in the communal lounge. It closes most summers from June to August to accommodate Thai students.

Bunk Boutique HOSTEL $
(Map p318; 091 859 9656; bunkboutique@hotmail.com; 8/7 Th Ratchaphuek; dm 250B, r 900B;) Recently opened Bunk Boutique offers superior accommodation in four-bed dorms in a large apartment block behind Th Huay Kaew. Blond wood bunks have curtains for privacy and everyone gets a locker. You can rent a dorm as a private room if there's space.

International Hotel Chiangmai HOTEL $
(Map p308; 053 221819; www.ymcachiangmai.org; 11 Soi Sermsak, Th Hutsadisawee; r 400-1600B;) The main Chiang Mai YMCA has well-priced, if slightly worn, rooms, and the usual comfortingly institutional atmosphere. Alhough the decor is stuck in the 1980s, staff keep everything scrubbed clean and you'll get a mountain view from the upper floors.

There's a restaurant, pool and craft shop.

★Artel Nimman BOUTIQUE HOTEL $$
(Map p318; 053 213143; Soi 13, Th Nimmanhaemin; r 1350-1850B;) We're suckers for hotels with slides, so the Artel delivers in spades. The modernist building is all round windows, polished concrete, geometric forms and juxtaposed materials, and the rooms are cool, calm, creative spaces. There's a dainty cafe and, as mentioned, a slide from the balcony down to the street.

Baan Say-La GUESTHOUSE $$
(Map p318; 053 894229; www.baansaylaguesthouse.com; 4 Soi 5, Th Nimmanhaemin; r with fan/air-con 600/890B;) Set in a Nimmanhaemin shophouse, this boutique guesthouse has stylish rooms in a mixture of styles – modernist, heritage, flowery colonial – and the owners keep the place looking immaculately clean and prim. Prices are as low as you'll find this close to the action.

Bunthomstan Guesthouse GUESTHOUSE $$
(Map p318; 053 217768; www.bunthomstan.com; 7 Soi 5, Th Nimmanhaemin; r 1150-1550B;) The owner of this comfy guesthouse in a modern Thai home has a 1950s thing going on (check out the vintage petrol pump in the drive). It's a peaceful haven with some of Chiang Mai's best eating on the doorstep. Rooms are smart, spacious and deliciously air-conditioned.

Nimman Boutique Resort HOTEL $$
(Map p318; 053 222638; www.nimmanresort.com; 29 Soi 17, Th Nimmanhaemin; r from 1500B;) This efficient hotel charges rates that

actually match its facilities – pretty rare in the Nimmanhaemin neighbourhood. Runners and cushions in Thai textiles add a bit of flair to the contemporary, hotel-style rooms, and there's a garden to relax in, though you may spend more of your time sipping smoothies round the corner at I-Berry (p344). Walk-in discounts can bring rates down to the budget level.

Sakulchai Place HOTEL **$$**
(Map p318; ☎053 211982; www.sakulchaiplace.com; Soi Plubpueng, Th Huay Kaew; r 650-1100B; ❄📶) Hidden away down an anonymous lane north of Th Huay Kaew, this self-contained tower offers rooms that positively gleam. Reached via calm, cool corridors, rooms come with TVs and other modern essentials that cost twice the price in many other hotels in town. There's a decent house restaurant, but the lack of a pool may put off families.

Kantary Hills HOTEL **$$$**
(Map p318; ☎053 222111; www.kantarycollection.com; Soi 12, Th Nimmanhaemin; r 2800-7100B, apt per month from 38,000B; ❄📶🏊) Immaculately turned out Kantary Hills offers stylish hotel rooms in a vast, self-contained complex set back a bit from the Nimmanhaemin action. It's a favourite with the business and diplomatic set, and also rents out serviced apartments.

Yesterday Hotel BOUTIQUE HOTEL **$$$**
(Map p318; ☎053 213809; www.yesterday.co.th; 24 Th Nimmanhaemin; r from 1500B; ❄📶) In the heart of the action on Th Nimmanhaemin, Yesterday offers a quick trip back to the near past. Communal spaces are decorated with vintage prints, old phonographs, Bakelite phones and flashback tube TVs, and the rooms have a more subtle mid-century mood. At the time of research a new lobby area was under construction.

Elsewhere

Viangbua Mansion HOTEL **$$**
(Map p308; ☎053 411202; www.viangbua.com; 3/1 Soi Viangbua, Th Chang Pheuak; r from 750B, per week from 5600B; ❄@📶) North of Pratu Chang Pheuak, this serviced-apartment hotel is away from the action, but popular with long-stayers. Spic-and-span apartment-style rooms with fridges, lounges, balconies and TVs are rented by the day, week or month. More expensive rooms have a simple kitchen.

★**Tri Yaan Na Ros** BOUTIQUE HOTEL **$$$**
(Map p308; ☎053 273174; www.triyaannaros.com; 156 Th Wualai; r from 3675B; ❄📶🏊) South of the main tourist bustle on Th Wualai, this charming boutique hotel puts you in pole position for the Saturday Walking Street market, but the main appeal is the elegant period decor – perhaps the best recreation of a traditional Thai home in Chiang Mai. Rooms are tucked away behind the restaurant in a lovingly restored Thai house.

The rooms come with four-poster beds, flowing drapes, oodles of dark timber and antique Buddhas. There's also a peaceful courtyard pool.

★**Dhara Dhevi** RESORT **$$$**
(☎053 888888; www.dharadhevi.com; 51/4 Th Chiang Mai-San Kamphaeng, off Rte 1006; r from 17,600B; ❄@📶🏊) About 5km east of the old city, Dhara Dhevi feels like stepping back in time, taking modern standards of service and facilities with you, of course! Chiang Mai's most opulent place to stay recreates a traditional Lanna village, sprawling over grounds full of whitewashed colonades, teak pavilions, antique objets d'art and landscaped ponds and rice terraces. The rooms are positively regal, with every imaginable comfort.

You can enjoy spectacular food, indulgent massages, craft workshops, cooking courses and even rice-planting classes without ever leaving the compound.

There's a special kids club and a babysitting service so it's great for families.

Four Seasons Chiang Mai RESORT **$$$**
(☎053 298181; www.fourseasons.com; Th Mae Rim-Samoeng Kao, off Rte 1096; r from 20,000B; ❄@📶🏊) Chiang Mai's lavish Four Seasons resort is a sprawl of vaulted pavilions and self-contained residences scattered through the rainforest near Mae Rim, with landscaped gardens tended by farmers in traditional pyjamas. Rooms offer the full design-magazine experience, all flowing fabrics and antique arts, and there's a cooking school, an award-winning spa and all the expected five-star flourishes. There are special villas for families, and no extra charge for children up to 18 years old who stay in the same room with their parents.

Eating

The restaurant scene in Chiang Mai is thriving, though dominated by backpacker cafes and tourist-oriented establishments.

Without doubt, the best places to eat in Chiang Mai are the city's fabulous night markets (p341), which sprawl around the main city gates and several other locations. Everyone should have a night-market dinner at least once on their trip; many people eat at night markets every single evening.

Old City

The old city is crammed with traveller cafes but standards vary widely, and there are limited options for an upmarket dinner.

★Lert Ros NORTHEASTERN THAI $
(Map p312; Soi 1, Th Ratchadamnoen; mains 30-160B; ⌚noon-9pm) As you enter this local-style hole in the wall, you'll pass the main course: delicious whole tilapia fish, which is grilled on coals and served with a fiery Isan-style dipping sauce. Eaten with sticky rice, this simple dish is one of Chiang Mai's most delicious meals. The (tiny) menu also includes curried pork grilled in banana leaves, hot northern-style curries and *sôm·đam* (spicy green papaya salad).

★SP Chicken NORTHERN THAI $
(Map p312; 9/1 Soi 1, Th Samlan; mains 50-150B; ⌚11am-9pm) Chiang Mai's best chicken emerges daily from the broilers at this tiny cafe near Wat Phra Singh. The menu runs to salads and soups, but most people just pick a half (80B) or whole (150B) chicken, and dip the moist meat into the spicy, tangy Northern Thai dipping sauces provided.

★Kiat Ocha CHINESE, THAI $
(Map p312; Th Inthawarorot; mains 50-90B; ⌚6am-3pm) This humble Chinese-style canteen is mobbed daily by locals who can't get enough of the house *kôw man gài* (Hainanese-style boiled chicken). Each plate comes with soup, chilli sauce and blood pudding and the menu also includes wok-fried chicken and pork and *sà·đé*.

Khaow Tom 1B CENTRAL THAI $
(Map p312; 68/3 Th Ratchadamnoen; mains 60-250B; ⌚noon-midnight) This partly open-air canteen is a bit more tourist savvy than it first appears, but the Thai food is decent, the prices are right, and it's a great place to watch the hubbub on Th Ratchadamnoen. Grab your own chopsticks from the tin box on the table.

AUM Vegetarian Food VEGETARIAN $
(Map p312; 65 Th Moon Muang; mains 80-150B; ⌚10.30am-8.30pm; 🖉) One of the original health-food peddlers, AUM (pronounced 'om') attracts crowds of vegie travellers and a few vegie-curious carnivores. The menu runs from vegetable maki rolls to blue sticky rice and delicious *sôm·đam* with cashews and carrot. They make their own mushroom-based stock.

Dash CENTRAL THAI $
(Map p312; 38/2 Soi 2, Th Moon Muang; mains 85-325B; ⌚11am-11pm) A cut above the average traveller restaurant, Dash serves up flavoursome Thai curries that are full of spice, served in a smart teak house or outside on the terrace. The chocolate brownie à la mode is nothing short of spectacular.

Dada Kafe VEGETARIAN $
(Map p312; Th Ratchamankha; mains 60-140B; ⌚9am-9pm, to 6pm May & Jun; 🖉) A tiny hole in the wall that does a busy trade in vitamin-rich, tasty vegetarian health food and smoothies. Wholesome ingredients like pollen and wheatgrass are whisked into fruit shakes and the food menu includes vegie burgers, omelettes, salads, sandwiches and curries with brown rice.

Pak Do Restaurant NORTHERN THAI $
(Map p312; Th Samlan; mains 35-50B; ⌚7am-3pm) Across the street from Wat Phra Singh, Pak Do has no menu – instead, just peek inside the big metal bowls out front and pick whatever takes your fancy. Most days feature a dozen meat-based and vegetarian curries and stews, served over rice. The pork ribs in dry northern curry are superb!

Fern Forest Cafe CAFE $
(Map p312; Th Singharat; mains 90-190B; ⌚8.30am-8.30pm) A move around the corner has not diminished the appeal of this cute garden cafe, with shady tables dotted around a calm courtyard garden full of greenery. The Westernised menu has sandwiches, cakes and salads.

Blue Diamond VEGETARIAN $
(Map p312; 35/1 Soi 9, Th Moon Muang; mains 65-140B; ⌚7am-9pm Mon-Sat; 🖉) Packed with fresh produce, pre-packaged spice and herb mixes and freshly baked treats, Blue Diamond feels a little like a wholefood store. The cafe offers an adventurous menu of sandwiches, salads, curries, stir-fries and curious fusion dishes such as *đôm yam* macaroni.

Good Morning Chiang Mai INTERNATIONAL $
(Map p312; 29/5 Soi 6, Th Ratchamankha; breakfasts & mains 80-130B; ⌚8am-8pm) A favourite

FABULOUS FOOD MARKETS

Everyone knows that the best food in Chiang Mai is served on the street, and the city's night markets are fragrant, frenetic and fabulous. Every evening from around 5pm, hawker stalls set up in key locations around the old city, alongside smoothie stalls and beer and soft-drink vendors. Each stall has a speciality: you'll find everything from grilled river fish and *pàt gà prow* (chicken or meat fried with chilli and holy basil) to Western-style steaks, grilled prawns and 'Tornado potato' (a whole potato, corkscrew sliced and deep fried).

The city's day markets are also thronged by food stalls and wholesale vendors, who prepare *gàp kôw* (pre-made stews and curries served with rice) and other take-home meals for busy city workers. And of course, the **Saturday and Sunday Walking Street markets** (p316) are mobbed by food hawkers. Here's a guide to Chiang Mai's best market eats.

Talat Pratu Chiang Mai (Map p312; Th Bamrungburi; mains from 40B; ⏲4am-noon & 6pm-midnight) This heaving market sells foodstuffs and ready-made packed lunches by day and night-market treats after dark. It's mobbed nightly, particularly during Th Wualai's Saturday Walking Street.

Talat Pratu Chang Pheuak (Map p312; Th Mani Nopharat; mains from 40B; ⏲5-11pm) Sprawling west from the city's northern gate, this is one of Chiang Mai's most popular night markets, serving all the usual suspects, alongside the city's finest *kôw kăh mŏo* (slow-cooked pork leg with rice), prepared with a flourish by the 'Cowboy Hat Lady' – you can't miss her stall.

Talat Somphet (Somphet Market; Map p312; Soi 6, Th Moon Muang; mains from 30B; ⏲6am-10pm) A small local food market north of Pratu Tha Phae that transforms into a night market after hours. Many of the cooking schools do their market tours here.

Talat Ton Phayom (Map p308; Th Suthep; mains from 30B; ⏲8am-6pm) This local market off Th Suthep is a popular stop for visiting Thais who come to pick up authentic northern foodstuffs such as *kâap mŏo* (deep-fried pig skin).

Talat Warorot (p317) The grandmother of Chiang Mai markets has Northern Thai food stalls tucked in all sorts of corners (mains from 30B).

Talat Thanin (Siri Wattana; Map p308; off Th Chang Pheuak; mains 20-40B; ⏲5am-7pm) North of the old city off Th Chotana (Th Chang Pheuak), this public market specialises in takeaway meals, with vendors serving fish stews, curries, stir-fries and spicy condiments from huge pans, vats and platters.

Talat Na Mor (Map p308; Th Huay Kaew, Malin Plaza; mains from 40B; ⏲5-10pm) A cheerful night market for the college set, with low prices and lots of choice; the student restaurants nearby on Th Huay Kaew are also worth investigating.

among expats, this guesthouse cafe near Wat Phra Jao Mengrai serves big, international breakfasts, from pancake towers to continental spreads and *đôm yam*–flavoured pasta. You can eat inside, in the movie-memorabilia-covered cafe, or in the garden by the pool.

Yok Fa NORTHERN THAI **$**

(Map p312; Th Ratchaphakhinai; mains 35-45B; ⏲11am-9pm) This ma-and-pa place cooks up fresh food in the massive woks out front. There are five or six choices most days and the menu depends on what is cooking in the kitchen. *Râht nâh* (deep-fried mee noodles, softened in a slightly sweet soy gravy) is a particular speciality.

Party Buffet CHINESE **$**

(Map p312; Th Mani Nopharat; buffet 169B; ⏲4pm-6am) Don't be put off by the name – this all-night hotpot buffet is where Chiang Mai's night owls come to play. It's all-you-can-eat, so pay once and feast until the wee hours on boiled and barbecued meat, fish and veg.

Swan BURMESE **$**

(Map p312; 48 Th Chaiyaphum; mains 70-150B; ⏲11am-11pm) This worn-looking restaurant just east of the old city offers a trip across the border, with a menu of tasty Burmese dishes such as *gaang hang lay* (dry, sour pork curry with tamarind and peanuts). The backyard courtyard provides an escape from the moat traffic.

★Huen Phen NORTHERN THAI $$
(Map p312; ☎053 277103; 112 Th Ratchamankha; lunch dishes 40-60B, evening mains 80-200B; ⏲8am-3pm & 5-10pm) This antique-cluttered restaurant cooks up some true northern magic. By day, meals are served in the canteen out front, but at night, the action moves back to the atmospheric dining room, where you can sample a full range of delicious, highly spiced jungle curries, stir-fries and regional variations on *nám prík* (chilli sauces with vegetables to dip). It's phenomenally popular, so come early or face a long wait for a table.

★La Fourchette FRENCH $$
(Map p312; Th Phra Pokklao; mains 250-580B; ⏲6-10.30pm) Decked out like a 1920s living room, La Fourchette is owned by a jazz-bass-loving, French-trained Thai chef who is putting his education to excellent use in Chiang Mai. Come for excellent steaks and funky fusion dishes such as red snapper fillet with mango.

Girasole ITALIAN $$
(Map p312; ☎053 276388; Kad Klang Wiang, Th Ratchadamnoen; mains 90-260B; ⏲11am-9pm) In the tidy little Kad Klang Wiang arcade, Girasole makes a convincing claim to offer the city's best pizzas, prepared using real pepperoni and other hard-to-find ingredients. There are several spaces for eating, both inside and outside, and the menu runs to superior pasta dishes and *secondi piatti,* plus tasty gelato for dessert.

Hot Chilli CENTRAL THAI $$
(Map p312; 71A Th Ratchadamnoen; mains 150-350B; ⏲noon-midnight) The premium you pay at this trendy eatery on Th Ratchadamnoen is not for the Thai food, which is only so-so, but for the ambience. Diners sit in giant swings beneath flowing red drapes and cascades of artificial flowers.

New Delhi INDIAN $$
(Map p312; Th Ratwithi; mains 60-300B; ⏲11am-10pm) OK, you don't get much atmosphere, but this straightforward place serves up some of Chiang Mai's best Indian food.

★Ginger & Kafe @ The House CENTRAL THAI $$$
(Map p312; ☎053 419011; www.thehousethailand.com; 199 Th Moon Muang, The House; mains 90-590B; ⏲11am-11pm) Dining at the restaurant in the House boutique feels like eating in a posh Thai mansion, with antique furniture, soft sofas, fine china and lots of red velour. The Thai food is delish and lavishly presented, but watch out for hidden prices in the menu – Massaman curry costs almost twice as much with lamb as with beef!

★Ruen Tamarind NORTHERN THAI $$$
(Map p312; Tamarind Village, 50/1 Th Ratchadamnoen; mains 220-440B; ⏲11am-10.30pm; ✎) For a more sophisticated dinner, the restaurant at Tamarind Village serves superior Northern Thai food in sleek surrounds overlooking the hotel pool. Dishes such as *yum tawai gài* (spicy chicken salad with tamarind dressing) are presented as works of art, and musicians serenade diners.

East of the Old City

In the early morning, vendors sell *nám đow·hôo* (soy milk) and baton-shaped *you*

KÔW SOY SAMPLER

Chiang Mai's unofficial city dish is *kôw soy* (*khao soi*), a rich curry soup with crispy fried noodles and soft boiled noodles, coconut milk and plenty of turmeric and chilli, served with pickled vegetables. The dish has its origins with the Yunnanese traders who came to Chiang Mai along the Silk Road, and the vendors along **Halal Street** (Soi 1, Th Charoen Prathet) near the Night Bazaar still serve some of the best in town. For our baht, **Kao Soi Fueng Fah** (Map p308; Soi 1, Th Charoen Phrathet; mains 40-60B; ⏲7am-9pm) has the edge over other vendors, with full-flavoured bowls and a spotlessly clean dining room.

Another great place to try *kôw soy* is around **Wat Faham** on Th Charoenrat (Th Faham), north of the Th Ratanakosin bridge on the east bank of the Mae Ping. Our top pick is **Khao Soi Lam Duan Fah Ham** (Map p308; 352/22 Th Charoenrat (Th Faham); mains from 40B; ⏲9am-4pm), a modest-looking place that is packed to the rafters at lunchtime with hordes of locals slurping down bowls of deliciously rich *kôw soy.* Nearby **Khao Soi Samoe Jai** (Map p308; 391 Th Charoenrat (Th Faham); mains 50-70B; ⏲8am-5pm) also cooks up a spectacular bowl. Another top slurp is **Khao Soi Prince** (Map p308; 105-109 Th Kaew Nawarat; mains 30-50B; ⏲8am-3.30pm), close to the Prince Royal's College and popular with local students.

tiao (Chinese-style doughnuts) from stalls in Chiang Mai's small Chinatown (p319).

Anusarn Food Center MARKET $

(Map p308; Th Chang Khlan, Anusarn Night Bazaar; mains 60-350B; ⌚5-10pm) Behind the Anusarn market, the Anusarn Food Center has a neat gaggle of stalls selling Thai-Chinese standards, and a collection of restaurants serving live seafood cooked your way (grilled, fried, or steamed with ginger, sweet-and-sour sauce or sweet chilli). Seafood is priced by weight so make sure you know what you are spending before you commit.

River Market THAI $$

(Map p308; ☎053 234493; Th Charoen Prathet; mains 165-500B; ⌚11am-11pm) Trading on its location rather than its kitchen, River Market nevertheless scores romantic dinner points for the night-time views across the illuminated Iron Bridge. The menu covers all the usual Thai bases.

Chez Marco Restaurant & Bar FRENCH $$

(Map p312; ☎053 207032; 15/7 Th Loi Kroh; mains 150-1290B; ⌚5.30pm-midnight Mon-Sat) Despite the unpromising location in the midst of Loi Kroh's girlie-bar scene, Chez Marco cooks up wholesome French food with fresh ingredients and a bit of Gallic flair.

Whole Earth Restaurant CENTRAL THAI, INDIAN $$

(Map p312; 88 Th Si Donchai; mains 165-420B; ⌚11am-10pm) Set in a sprawling garden, this teak-house restaurant wears a coat of hanging vines and orchids. It is the sort of place Thais take visitors for Indian and Thai dishes that sound exotic but won't blow the roof off your mouth with too much chilli.

Riverside & Elsewhere

As well as eating at the restaurants, lots of people make a night of it at the riverbank situated along Th Charoenrat (Th Faham); Riverside (p345) and Good View (p345) invariably pull in a crowd.

Khun Churn VEGETARIAN $

(Map p308; Th Thiphanet, Old Chiang Mai Cultural Center; buffet 164B; ⌚8am-10pm; 📶) Moved to a slightly inconvenient location in the Old Chiang Mai Cultural Center (about 1km south of the old city walls on Rte 108), Khun Churn is best known for its all-you-can-eat meatless buffet (11am to 2.30pm), with dozens of dishes, salads, herbal drinks and Thai-style desserts.

Huan Soontaree NORTHERN THAI $$

(☎053 872707; 208 Th Patan; mains 110-200B; ⌚4-11pm Mon-Sat) Thai tourists eagerly make the pilgrimage out of town to this rustic restaurant in the hope of hearing the dulcet tones of its owner, the Thai chanteuse Soontaree Vechanont. She performs at the restaurant from around 8pm Monday to Saturday. The menu is a pleasing blend of Northern, Northeastern and Central Thai specialities.

It is 8km north of town on the west side of the river, just south of Rte 11.

★The Service 1921 SOUTHEAST ASIAN $$$

(Map p308; ☎053 253333; Anantara Resort, 123 Th Charoen Prathet; mains 250-2000B; ⌚6am-11pm) The pan-Asian restaurant at the Anantara is elegance incarnate, with wait staff in full 1920s garb and interior decor resembling the secret offices of MI6 – appropriate as the gorgeous teak villa housing the restaurant used to be the British Consulate. The food is made with top-notch ingredients, though some dishes have the spice dialled down to appeal to international palates.

The hotel also has an international restaurant in a similarly romantic location overlooking the river.

West of the Old City

Th Nimmanhaemin and the surrounding soi excel in international cuisine, but restaurants and cafes appear and vanish overnight; we've stuck to listing places below that are likely to still be in business when you finish your dessert.

★Pun Pun VEGETARIAN $

(Map p308; www.punpunthailand.org; Th Suthep, Wat Suan Dok; mains 40-75B; ⌚8am-4pm Thu-Tue; 📶) Tucked away at the back of Wat Suan Dok, this student-y cafe is a great place to sample Thai vegetarian food prepared using little-known herbs and vegetables and lots of healthy whole grains grown on its concept farm, which doubles as an education centre for sustainable living.

There's a branch called **Imm Aim Vegetarian Restaurant** (Map p308; 10 Th Santhitham; mains 40-75B; ⌚10am-9pm; 📶) near the International Hotel Chiangmai.

Esan Cafe NORTHEASTERN THAI $

(Map p318; Th Nimmanhaemin; mains 75-110B; ⌚11am-10pm) A modern, bright cafe serving delicious Isan-style salads and grills. There are half a dozen variations on *sôm·đam* and the salad dressings are fiery and superb.

Anchan Noodle CHINESE-THAI $
(Map p318; Soi 9, Th Sirimungklajarn; mains 40-60B; ⏰9am-4pm) Students love this calm cafe on a residential lane east of Th Nimmanhaemin for big bowls of Chinese-style pork, served with blue noodles or sticky rice, dyed with flower petals.

I-Berry DESSERTS $
(Map p318; Soi 17, Th Nimmanhaemin; ice creams & smoothies from 60B; ⏰10am-10pm; 📶) Mobbed day and night, this shop selling ice-cream and fruit smoothies has star power. I-Berry is owned by Thai comedian Udom Taepanich (nicknamed 'Nose' for his signature feature). When ordering, check the menu signs and order the delicious smoothies, shakes and sundaes using their rather elaborate names.

Ai Sushi JAPANESE $
(Map p318; Th Huay Kaew; mains 90-210B; ⏰5-11.30pm) Students are the ones to follow when it comes to cheap eats in Chiang Mai and Ai Sushi pulls them in in droves. The pace gets furious in the evening as diners pack it out for fresh and delicious sushi, sashimi and sides.

Salad Concept INTERNATIONAL $
(Map p318; Th Nimmanhaemin; mains 50-170B; ⏰11am-10pm; 📶🖉) Diners eat like rabbits at this salad buffet with a big choice of chemical-free greens, toppings and dressings. There's a **branch** (Map p312; Th Chaiyaphum; mains 50-170B; ⏰10am-9pm) on Th Chaiyaphum.

★**Tong Tem Toh** NORTHERN THAI $$
(Map p318; Soi 13, Th Nimmanhaemin; mains 50-170B; ⏰11am-9pm) Set in an old teak house, this trendy cafe serves deliciously authentic Northern Thai cuisine. The menu roams beyond the usual Thai standards to local specialities such as *nám prík ong* and *gaang hang lay*.

Salsa Kitchen MEXICAN $$
(Map p318; Th Huay Kaew; mains 100-240B; ⏰11am-11pm) For reasons not entirely clear, US-style Mexican food is all the rage in Chiang Mai, and this place serves some of the best. It's an expat favourite and it's often busy in the evening.

Royal Project Restaurant NORTHERN THAI $$
(Krua Silapacheep; Th Huay Kaew; mains 90-190B; ⏰9am-5.30pm) 🍃 Products from the Queen's agricultural projects are whisked into delicious salads, soups, stews, stir-fries and other healthy Thai meals at this neat government-run restaurant near the zoo. Rainbow trout and seasonal Northern Thai specialities spruce up the menu and there's an attached shop with Royal Project produce.

Smoothie Blues INTERNATIONAL $$
(Map p318; 32/8 Th Nimmanhaemin; mains 45-160B; ⏰7.30am-8pm) This expat favourite is a top spot for breakfast – croissants, pancakes, bagels, bacon and eggs, you know the drill – and they also serve good sandwiches and, not entirely surprisingly, smoothies.

★**Tengoku** JAPANESE $$$
(Map p318; ☎053 215801; Soi 5, Th Nimmanhaemin; mains 130-1650B; ⏰11am-2pm & 5.30-10pm; 📶) Chiang Mai loves Japanese food, but Tengoku leaves everywhere else in town in the shade of Mt Fuji. This sleekly modern restaurant serves superior sushi, yummy yakitori, spectacular sukiyaki and wonderful wagyu steaks, plus cheaper bento box set meals.

Palaad Tawanron CENTRAL THAI $$$
(☎053 216039; off Th Suthep; mains 160-380B; ⏰11am-midnight) Set into a rocky ravine near Doi Suthep, this restaurant inhabits a magical spot overlooking a forest reservoir, with the city lights twinkling below. The ambience and the ride here through the forest are great, the food only so-so.

To get here, go to the end of the university compound on Th Suthep and follow the signs; if you reach the back entrance to the zoo, you're on the right track.

Drinking & Nightlife

Chiang Mai has three primary areas for watering holes: the old city, the riverside and Th Nimmanhaemin. Almost everyone ends up at either Riverside (p345) or Good View (p345) on the east bank of the Mae Ping at some point in their stay.

Old City

The old city has a handful of backpacker party bars, and a larger number of more genteel, pub-style watering holes.

Zoe In Yellow BAR
(Map p312; 40/12 Th Ratwithi; ⏰11am-2am) Part of a complex of open-air bars at the corner of Th Ratchaphakhinai and Th Ratwithi, Zoe is where backpackers come to sink pitchers of cold Chang, sip cocktails from buckets, rock out to cheesy dancefloor-fillers, canoodle and swap travel stories until the wee hours.

John's Place BAR
(Map p312; Th Moon Muang; ⌚11am-midnight) This old-school traveller bar is a blur of neon lights and mismatched posters. It's far enough from the seedy Loi Kroh scene to be a convivial place to drink and the roof deck is a great spot to sip a cold beer above the commotion.

Writer's Club & Wine Bar BAR
(Map p312; 141/3 Th Ratchadamnoen; ⌚10am-midnight; 📶) Run by a former foreign correspondent, this bar and restaurant is popular with expats, and travellers looking for a more low-key drinking experience, with wine by the glass (from 140B).

UN Irish Pub PUB
(Map p312; 24/1 Th Ratwithi; ⌚11am-midnight) Chiang Mai's Irish pub offers the standard Emerald Isle package – draught Guinness, familiar pub grub, Thursday quiz nights, and international sports on the big screen.

East & South of the Old City

★ **Riverside Bar & Restaurant** BAR
(Map p308; www.theriversidechiangmai.com; 9-11 Th Charoenrat (Th Faham); mains 130-370B; ⌚10am-1am) Almost everyone ends up at Riverside at some point in their stay. Set in an old teak house, it feels like a boondocks reimagining of a Hard Rock Cafe, and bands play nightly until late. Stake out a claim on the riverside terrace or the upstairs balcony to catch the evening breezes on the Mae Ping.

They also serve good Thai and Western food, and there's a posher annexe across the road with a lounge-bar feel.

★ **Good View** BAR
(Map p308; www.goodview.co.th; 13 Th Charoenrat (Th Faham); mains 100-250B; ⌚10am-2am) Just a few metres along the riverbank from arch-rival Riverside, Good View attracts plenty of locals, with a big menu of Thai standards and sushi platters and a nightly program of rotating bands with rotating line-ups (what, so now the drummer is playing guitar and the bass player is behind the piano?).

Pinte Blues Pub BAR
(Map p308; https://bluespubchiangmai.wordpress.com; 9 Soi 1, Th Ratcha Chiangsaen; ⌚4pm-midnight) A veteran blues bar (founded in 1986) that has hopscotched around the city and currently resides on a back lane south of the moat; it offers country blues in a country-style setting.

West of the Old City

Th Nimmanhaemin is popular with CMU students and hi-so (high society) Thais, and bars open and close here faster than you can order a cold bottle of Chang. Find the latest

STIMULATING BREWS

Chiang Mai has enthusiastically adopted coffee culture, but its coffeeshops are not global chains but local independents, selling coffee sourced from the hill tribes and forest communities around the city. The high-quality arabica coffee grown here was introduced as a replacement crop for opium, and it is served hot, cold, iced and in an astonishing variety of dessert-style concoctions. All the cafes also serve Northern Thai–style iced tea, a bright orange mixture of overbrewed tea, sugar and evaporated milk, served over crushed ice. Here are some top spots for a brew.

Akha Ama Cafe (Map p308; www.akhaama.com; 9/1 Soi 3, Th Hutsadisawee, Mata Apartment; coffee from 50B; ⌚9am-9pm; 📶) A local coffeshop founded by an Akha who was the first in his village to graduate from college. There's a **branch** (Map p312; www.akhaama.com; 175/1 Th Ratchadamnoen; ⌚8am-6pm; 📶) on Th Ratchadamnoen in the old city.

Wawee Coffee (Map p312; www.waweecoffee.com; Th Ratchadamnoen, Kad Klang Wiang; drinks from 50B; ⌚8am-9pm Mon-Sat, to 11pm Sun; 📶) It's hard to go more than a few blocks in Chiang Mai without stumbling across an air-conditioned Wawee Coffee branch.

Café de Museum (Map p312; Th Ratwithi, Lanna Folklife Museum; drinks from 40B; ⌚9am-6pm Mon-Fri, to 7pm Sat & Sun; 📶) The perfect spot to refuel after touring the old-city museums, with a full range of stimulating hot, cold and iced brews.

Raming Tea House (Map p312; Th Tha Phae; drinks 50-100B; ⌚8.30am-5.30pm) This elegant Victorian-era cafe within the Siam Celadon shop serves Thai mountain teas alongside tasty Thai and Western food. Afternoon tea spreads with snacks and desserts start at 190B.

hot spots by cruising the soi and stopping wherever you find a crowd.

Beer Republic BAR

(Map p318; Soi 11, Th Nimmanhaemin; ⏲4pm-midnight Tue-Sun) There are 15 draught beers kept at this European-style beer bar in the trendiest part of Nimmanhaemin.

Year Garage BEER GARDEN

(Map p318; www.facebook.com/oneyearatnimman; Soi 17, Th Nimmanhaemin; ⏲6pm-midnight) The beer-festival ambience and good cheap eats (Thai curries, stir-fries and seafood grills) lure students in droves to this open-air beer garden on Soi 17.

Blar Blar Bar BEER GARDEN

(Map p318; Soi 5, Th Nimmanhaemin; ⏲6pm-midnight) A big and boozy bar popular with uni students and other youthful punters, with waitresses promoting branded beers and live music in the courtyard.

Warmup Cafe CLUB

(Map p318; www.facebook.com/warmupcafe1999; 40 Th Nimmanhaemin; ⏲6pm-2am) A Nimmanhaemin survivor, Warmup has been rocking since 1999, attracting a young, trendy and beautiful crowd as the evening wears on. Hip-hop spins in the main room, electronic beats reverberate in the lounge, and rock bands squeal out solos in the garden.

Soho Bar BAR

(Map p318; 20/3 Th Huay Kaew; ⏲5pm-midnight) Chiang Mai doesn't have much of an LGBT scene, but this cosy cafe-bar is gay-friendly and the affable owners make everyone feel at home.

☆ Entertainment

Live Music

As well as the dedicated music venues, the Riverside (p345) and Good View (p345) host bands nightly.

★**Sudsanan** LIVE MUSIC

(Map p318; off Th Huay Kaew; ⏲6pm-midnight) A stroll down an unlit dirt track off Th Huay Kaew will take you to a wooden house full of character and music. It's primarily a local hangout with performers playing tear-jerking *pleng pêu·a chee·wít* (songs for life). Look for the easy-to-miss signboard just west of Th Ratchaphuek.

Nabé LIVE MUSIC

(Map p312; Th Wichayanon; ⏲6pm-1am) A popular spot for Chiang Mai twenty-somethings, with cold beers, hot snacks and rocking live bands, who can actually play their instruments, singing Thai songs for a Thai audience.

Inter LIVE MUSIC

(Map p312; 271 Th Tha Phae; ⏲4pm-1am) This small wooden house packs in a lively line-up of local talent. It has that beach-shack vibe beloved by travellers everywhere and a popular pool table – though we recommend against challenging the multiple-trophy-winning lady who owns the place!

North Gate Jazz Co-Op LIVE MUSIC

(Map p312; Th Si Phum; ⏲7-11pm) This compact jazz club tends to pack in more musicians than patrons, but the music can be pretty hip (for jazz).

Sangdee Gallery LIVE MUSIC

(Map p318; www.sangdeegallery.org; 5 Soi 5, Th Sirimungklajarn; ⏲11am-midnight Tue-Sat) Part gallery, music club, bar and cafe, Sangdee is beloved by the art set, who gather here for live music, DJ sets and art shows. There's an open-mic night on Thursday.

Cinemas

All the big shopping centres have multiplex cinemas, screening the latest Thai and Hollywood films, with tickets from 100B, up to 350B for deluxe seats with waitress service. Try the Maya Lifestyle Shopping Center (p348), Central Airport Plaza (p348), Central Festival (p348), or the less flashy but cheaper Kad Suan Kaew Shopping Center (p348).

Moo·ay Tai

Chiang Mai has three *moo·ay tai* stadiums – **Thapae Boxing Stadium** (Map p312; ☎089 434 5553; Th Moon Muang; tickets 400-600B; ⏲9pm-midnight Mon-Sat), **Loi Kroh Boxing Stadium** (Map p312; ☎094 606 8029; Th Kamphaeng Din; tickets 400-600B; ⏲from 9.30pm) and **Kalare Boxing Stadium** (Map p308; ☎081 681 8029; Th Chang Khlan; tickets 400-600B; ⏲from 9pm Mon & Fri) – showcasing a mixture of Thai and international fighters, but purists may find the scene a bit contrived compared to the real deal down south.

Shopping

Chiang Mai is Thailand's handicraft centre, and an incredible volume and variety of crafts are produced and sold here, from handwoven hill-tribe textiles to woodcarving, basketry and reproduction antiques (frequently sold without that disclaimer). The Saturday and Sunday Walking Street markets (p316) are Chiang's Mai's most entertaining shopping experiences, but you can find similar handicrafts every day in the Night Bazaar (see below), and outside the city in Ban Tawai (p361), Hang Dong (p361) and Bo Sang (p360).

Old City

★Herb Basics BEAUTY

(Map p312; www.herbbasicschiangmai.com; Th Ratchadamnoen; ⏲9am-6pm Mon-Sat, 2-9pm Sun) A great stop for fragrant herbal balms, scrubs, creams, soaps and shampoos, all made in Chiang Mai with natural ingredients. There's a **branch** (Map p312; ⏲10am-8pm Mon-Sat, noon-8pm Sun) on Th Tha Phae and a small shop at the airport.

★Ginger HOMEWARES, CLOTHING

(Map p312; www.thehousethailand.com; 199 Th Moon Muang, The House; ⏲10am-10.30pm) Designer-ethnic is the prevailing aesthetic at this chichi boutique on the edge of the moat, with rooms full of cushions, clothes and toys in tribal fabrics, and dinky plates, cups and other homewares in rainbow-coloured melamine. There's a **branch** (Map p318; www.thehousethailand.com; 6/21 Th Nimmanhaemin; ⏲9.30am-7pm) on Th Nimmanhaemin.

HQ Paper Maker PAPER

(Map p312; www.hqpapermaker.com; 3/31 Th Samlan; ⏲9am-6pm) This intriguing shop sells reams of handmade mulberry paper (*săh*), in a remarkable range of colours and patterns, including gorgeous marbled sheets that resemble the end leaves of bound 19th-century books.

Mengrai Kilns CERAMICS

(Map p308; www.mengraikilns.com; 79/2 Th Arak; ⏲8am-5pm) In the southwestern corner of the old city, Mengrai Kilns keeps the tradition of Thai celadon pottery alive, with cookware, dining sets, ornaments and Western-style nativity scenes.

Chiang Mai Cotton CLOTHING

(Map p312; www.chiangmaicotton.com; Th Ratchadamnoen; ⏲10am-7pm Mon-Sat, 10am-11pm Sun) Close to Wat Chedi Luang and selling high-quality natural cotton cut for modern living.

NIGHT-TIME SHOPPING IN CHIANG MAI

At times, it can feel like the whole of Chiang Mai is an engine built to sell souvenirs, and nowhere is this feeling stronger than in the **Chiang Mai Night Bazaar** (Map p312; Th Chang Khlan; ⏲7pm-midnight), between the river and the old-city walls. As the afternoon wears on, hundreds of streetside hawkers fill the pavement on both sides of the street, selling silk boxer shorts, 'I Love Chiang Mai' T-shirts, miniature wooden spirit houses, hill-tribe silver, dried mango, carved soaps, wooden elephants, wire models of túk-túks, Buddha paintings, fabrics, teddy bear dioramas and selfie sticks. This slightly frenetic shopping experience is the modern legacy of the Yunnanese trading caravans that stopped here along the ancient Silk Road, and you'll still need to haggle hard today.

Within the Night Bazaar are two large covered markets, signposted as **Night Bazaar** (Map p312; Th Chang Khlan; ⏲7pm-midnight) and **Kalare Night Bazaar** (Map p312; Th Chang Khlan; ⏲7pm-midnight), selling more of the same, with a slight weighting towards wooden carvings, paintings and other handicrafts. The Kalare Night Bazaar is the more raucous of the two, with a blues bar on a raised podium in the centre.

South of Th Loi Kroh on Th Chang Khlan is the less claustrophobic **Anusarn Night Bazaar** (Map p312; Th Chang Khlan; ⏲5-10pm), a semi-covered market filled with tables of vendors selling hill-tribe trinkets, wooden elephants, carved soap flowers and other cottage-industry goods. It's also good for dried mango and other local preserves. Fringing the market are numerous massage and fish-nibbling-your-feet places, and there's a tacky *gà·teu·i* (ladyboy, also spelt *kàthoey*) cabaret.

For food, there are abundant fast-food joints, some excellent *kôw soy* (curry noodle soup) canteens along Halal St (Soi 1, Th Charoen Prathet) and some touristy seafood places inside the **Anusarn Food Center** (p343). There's also a noisy open-air **night market** (Map p312; Th Chang Khlan; mains from 40B; ⏲6-11pm) just north of Halal St on Th Chang Khlan, serving a good range of hawker favourites.

Túk-túks and *rót daang* (shared taxis) loiter around the junction of Th Loi Kroh and Th Chang Khlan to transport you and your purchases home for a slightly elevated fare.

Ethnic Lanna HANDICRAFTS
(Map p312; www.ethniclanna.com; Th Singharat; 9am-8pm Mon-Sat) A good selection of fair-trade tribal trinkets and textiles.

East of the Old City

Th Tha Phae is lined with small shops selling antiques of sometimes questionable lineage, and lots of bijou emporiums selling jewellery, accessories, clothes and handicrafts. For reed hats and basketware bits and bobs, try the specialist **basket shops** lined up along Th Chang Moi, just east of the city walls.

Handicrafts & Clothing

Siam Celadon CERAMICS
(Map p312; www.siamceladon.com; 158 Th Tha Phae; 8am-6pm) This long-established company sells fine cracked-glazed celadon ceramics in a lovely fretwork-covered teak building from the time of the British teak concessionaires. After browsing, stop for a cuppa at the attached Raming Tea House (p345).

Kesorn Arts HANDICRAFTS
(Map p312; 154-156 Th Tha Phae; 9am-6pm) The collector's best friend, this cluttered shop has been trading old bric-a-brac from the hills for years. It specialises mainly in textiles, lacquerware and jewellery.

Nova JEWELLERY
(Map p312; www.nova-collection.com; 201 Th Tha Phae; 10am-8pm Mon-Sat, 10am-6pm Sun) Sleekly contemporary, this high-class jewellery studio makes top-quality rings, pendants and earrings using silver, gold and precious stones.

Nakorn Kasem HANDICRAFTS
(Map p312; 231-3 Th Tha Phae; 9am-8pm Mon-Sat) One of a string of antique shops selling ceramics, statues, carvings and bronzes of hard-to-determine age and authenticity. Pick something because you like it, rather than as an investment in an heirloom.

CHIANG MAI'S SHOPPING BOOM

Chiang Mai is becoming an impressive alternative to Bangkok when it comes to global brand names and shopping centres, helped of course by the explosion of travellers on shopping city breaks from China. The airport has the usual VAT refund scheme and there are megamalls scattered around the city fringes selling everything from Gucci pumps to the latest consumer electronics.

Maya Lifestyle Shopping Center (Map p318; www.mayashoppingcenter.com; Th Huay Kaew; 11am-10pm Mon-Fri, from 10am Sat & Sun) Chiang Mai's flashiest shopping centre hides behind a geometric facade, with all the big international brands, a whole floor of electronics, a good supermarket, multiscreen cinema and excellent eating options on the 4th floor.

Central Festival (www.central.co.th; Rte 11, Faham; 11am-9pm Mon-Thu, 11am-10pm Fri, 10am-10pm Sat & Sun) Just north of the bus station on Rte 11, Chiang Mai's flashiest shopping centre is anchored around a Central department shore and Uniqlo, with tonnes of international brands, impressively catered food floors and a multiplex cinema and ice rink.

Central Airport Plaza (Map p308; www.centralplaza.co.th; Rte 1141 (Th Mahidol); 11am-9pm Mon-Fri, 10am-9pm Sat & Sun) A vast cathedral to consumerism with floor after floor of apparel, electronics and food, plus the inevitable multiscreen cinema. The 'Northern Village' on the 1st floor sells well-packaged handicrafts.

Kad Suan Kaew Shopping Center (Map p318; www.kadsuankaew.co.th; Th Huay Kaew; 10am-9pm) This low-key and slightly ageing shopping centre is where Thais come for household essentials and cheap movie nights.

Pantip Plaza (Map p312; www.pantipplaza.com; Th Chang Khlan; 10am-10pm) Near the Night Bazaar, with a good selection of legit computer gear, cameras and phones, plus all manner of accessories, software and peripherals.

Promenada Resort Mall (www.promenadachiangmai.com; Rte 3029, Tumbon Tasala; 11am-9pm Mon-Fri, 10am-9pm Sat & Sun) A little marooned in the southwest of the city, beyond Rte 11, this quieter suburban shopping centre has the inevitable cinema, food centre, kids' soft play and IT and fashion stores.

Praewphun Thai Silk CLOTHING
(Map p312; 83-85 Th Tha Phae; ⏲10am-6pm) This 50-year-old shop sells silks of all ilks, made both into clothing and loose by the metre.

Elements JEWELLERY
(Map p312; 400-402 Th Tha Phae; ⏲9.30am-9.30pm) An eclectic collection of sterling silver and stone jewellery, silk scarves and other trinkets fills this unsigned store near Pratu Tha Phae. It's good for eye-catching one-off pieces.

KukWan Gallery CLOTHING
(Map p312; 37 Th Loi Kroh; ⏲10am-7pm) Set slightly back from the road, this charming little shop sells scarves, runners, bedspreads and natural cotton and silk by the metre.

Books

Backstreet Books BOOKS
(Map p312; 2/8 Th Chang Moi Kao; ⏲8am-8pm) Backstreet, a rambling shop along 'book alley' (Th Chang Moi Kao), has a good selection of guidebooks and stacks of crime and thriller novels.

Gecko Books BOOKS
(Map p312; 2/6 Th Chang Moi Kao; ⏲9am-9pm) Gecko Books has several branches packed with used novels, guidebooks and maps, including a **Th Ratchamankha branch** (Map p312; Th Ratchamankha; ⏲11am-6pm Mon-Fri, 9am-9pm Sat & Sun).

Suriwong Book Centre BOOKS
(Map p312; 54 Th Si Donchai; ⏲8am-8pm) A Chiang Mai institution, with a well-stocked bookshop upstairs, and a magazine shop downstairs packed with international mags from *Elle* to *Wallpaper*.

Riverside

Vila Cini CLOTHING, ACCESSORIES
(Map p308; www.vilacini.com; 30-34 Th Charoenrat (Th Faham); ⏲9.30am-10.30pm) Set in an atmospheric teak house with marble floors and a narrow, rickety staircase, Vila Cini sells high-end, handmade silks and cotton textiles that are reminiscent of the Jim Thompson brand. There's a **branch** (Map p312; www.vilacini.com; Th Chang Khlan, OP Place; ⏲11am-11pm) on Th Chang Khlan.

Sop Moei Arts CLOTHING, HANDICRAFTS
(Map p308; www.sopmoeiarts.com; 150/10 Th Charoenrat (Th Faham); ⏲9am-6pm) High-end hill-tribe crafts, from off-the-loom textiles to baskets, are sold at this economic-development shop, which helps for Karen villagers in Mae Hong Son Province.

Thai Tribal Crafts Fair Trade CLOTHING, HANDICRAFTS
(Map p308; www.ttcrafts.co.th; 208 Th Bamrungrat; ⏲9am-5pm Mon-Sat) Baskets and ornate needlework from the provinces are the offerings at this missionary-backed, fair-trade shop near the McCormick Hospital. There is a **branch** (Map p312; www.ttcrafts.co.th; 25/9 Th Moon Muang; ⏲9.30am-6pm Mon-Sat) by the moat in the old city.

West of the Old City

Around affluent Th Nimmanhaemin, trendy and cosmopolitan boutiques pop up like mushrooms after rain (and vanish just as quickly).

★ **Studio Naenna** CLOTHING, HOMEWARES
(Map p318; www.studio-naenna.com; 22 Soi 1, Th Nimmanhaemin; ⏲10am-6pm) The colours of the mountains have been woven into the naturally dyed silks and cottons here, part of a project to preserve traditional weaving and embroidery. You can see the whole production process at their main **workshop** (www.studio-naenna.com; 138/8 Soi Chang Khian; ⏲9am-5pm Mon-Fri, also 9am-5pm Sat Oct-Mar), north of Th Huay Kaew.

Doi Tung ACCESSORIES, HOMEWARES
(Map p318; www.doitung.org; Th Nimmanhaemin; ⏲10am-7pm) Part of a project providing development assistance for rural communities in Chiang Rai Province, this very chic emporium is full of upscale accessories and homewares, many made from graceful handmade textiles in understated, modern colours.

Chabaa CLOTHING
(Map p318; www.atchabaa.com; 14/32 Th Nimmanhaemin, Nimman Promenade; ⏲10am-9pm) Taking ethnic fashion uptown, Chabaa is a cavern of clothes, jewellery and accessories in radiant, room-filling primary colours, sourced from Thailand, India and worldwide.

The Booksmith BOOKS
(Map p318; www.smithproject.co.th; 11 Th Nimmanhaemin; ⏲10.30am-8.30pm) This pocket-sized store is a great stop for books on the culture and customs of Thailand.

Hill-Tribe Products Promotion Centre CLOTHING, HANDICRAFTS
(Map p308; 21/17 Th Suthep; ⏲9am-5pm) Hill-tribe textiles, bags, boxes, lacquerware and

other crafts are sold at this large store near Wat Suan Dok; profits go to hill-tribe welfare programs.

Srisanpanmai CLOTHING, ACCESSORIES
(Map p318; 6 Soi 1, Th Nimmanhaemin; ⏲10am-6.30pm) The display cases here are like a library of Lanna textiles, with reams of silk and cotton shawls, scarves and hill-tribe costumes. You're guaranteed to find something to surprise the folks at home.

Shinawatra Thai Silk CLOTHING
(Map p318; www.shinawatrathaisilk.co.th; 18 Th Huay Kaew; ⏲9am-6pm) This family-owned silk shop was already a household name before the owners' nephew, Thaksin Shinawatra, became (now-exiled) prime minister. The range here is good for scarves, shirts, ties and the like.

Information

DANGERS & ANNOYANCES

Compared to Bangkok, Chiang Mai is a breeze for tourists. The hassles from *sŏrng·tăa·ou* and túk-túk drivers are minimal and there are few rip-offs to watch out for.

Probably the biggest annoyance is the traffic; during rush hour, expect long, fume-filled waits at traffic lights. Take care when crossing busy roads; motorcyclists and *rót daang* drivers rarely give way.

In March and April, smoky, dusty haze can be a problem because of farmers burning off their fields. While malaria is not a risk, dengue fever outbreaks are common in the monsoon; take steps to avoid being bitten, even in the daytime.

A popular backpacker activity is jumping off the cliffs at the so-called 'Grand Canyon', a water-filled quarry near Hang Dong; be warned that a number of travellers have drowned after losing consciousness when hitting the water.

Note that some budget guesthouses expect guests to book their tours, and have been known to evict guests who decline. Most places will be forthcoming if this is their policy.

WARNING: INSURANCE IN CHIANG MAI

When renting a motorcycle, scooter or car in Chiang Mai, check the insurance small print carefully. Some companies hire out vehicles with only basic compulsory insurance, which gives limited cover if you harm somebody else in an accident, but provides no medical cover for you and no cover for damage to the vehicle you are hiring or to any other vehicle you might collide with. If your vehicle is stolen, you could be fully liable. Play it smart and use a company that offers full insurance and breakdown cover, with the level of cover clearly spelt out in the contract.

EMERGENCY

Tourist Police (Map p308; ☎053 247318, 24hr emergency 1155; 608 Rimping Plaza, Th Charoenraj; ⏲6am-midnight) Volunteer staff speak a variety of languages.

IMMIGRATION

Immigration Office (Map p308; ☎053 201755; http://chiangmaiimm.com; off Rte 1141 (Th Mahidol); ⏲8.30am-4.30pm Mon-Fri) By the airport; handles visa extensions.

INTERNET ACCESS

Almost all hotels, guesthouses, restaurants and cafes in Chiang Mai have free wi-fi access. The city has excellent mobile-phone data coverage but roaming charges for Thailand can be crippling.

MEDIA

The weekly English-language *Chiangmai Mail* (www.chiangmai-mail.com) is a useful source of local news. Look out for the free tourist magazines *Citylife* (www.chiangmaicitylife.com), *Chang Puak* (www.changpuakmagazine.com) and *Chiang Mai Mag* (www.magazinechiangmai.com); all have interesting articles as well as maps and blanket advertising.

MEDICAL SERVICES

There are English-speaking pharmacies along Th Ratchamankha and Th Moon Muang.

Center of Thai Traditional & Complementary Medicine (Map p312; ☎053 949899; ttcmmedcmu@gmail.com; 55 Th Samlan; ⏲8am-8pm) Run by the Faculty of Medicine; offers Western medical check-ups, Thai herbal therapies and Chinese traditional medicine.

Chiang Mai Ram Hospital (Map p308; ☎053 920300; www.chiangmairam.com; 8 Th Bunreuangrit) The most modern hospital in town.

Lanna Hospital (Map p308; ☎053 999777; www.lanna-hospital.com; Rte 11 (Th Superhighway)) Modern well-equipped hospital.

McCormick Hospital (Map p308; ☎053 921777; www.mccormick.in.th; 133 Th Kaew Nawarat) Former missionary hospital; good for minor treatments.

Mungkala Traditional Medicine Clinic (Map p312; ☎053 278494; 21-27 Th Ratchamankha; ⏲9am-12.30pm & 2-7pm) Government-licensed clinic using acupuncture, massage and Chinese herbal remedies.

MONEY

All of the big Thai banks have branches and ATMs throughout Chiang Mai, including along Th Tha Phae, and most operate small exchange booths with ATMs in the old city. **Western Union** (www.westernunion.com) has booths dotted around town where you can wire money, including at the Night Bazaar.

POST

There's a small **postal shop** (Map p312; ⌚8am-8pm) on Th Ratchadamnoen, charging Thailand Post rates; staff specialise in wrapping awkwardly shaped packages to send home.

Main Post Office (☎053 241070; Th Charoen Muang; ⌚8.30am-4.30pm Mon-Fri, 9am-noon Sat & Sun) Other convenient branches on Th Samlan, Th Prasaini, Th Phra Pokklao, and at the airport and university.

TOURIST INFORMATION

Chiang Mai Municipal Tourist Information Centre (Map p308; ☎053 252557; Th Tha Phae; ⌚8.30-11.30am & 1-4.30pm Mon-Fri) City-run tourist information centre near the Night Bazaar.

Tourism Authority of Thailand (TAT; Map p308; ☎053 248604; www.tourismthailand.org; Th Chiang Mai-Lamphun; ⌚8.30am-4.30pm) English-speaking staff provide maps, and advice on travel across Thailand.

Getting There & Away

AIR

Domestic and international flights arrive and depart from **Chiang Mai International Airport** (Map p308; ☎053 270222; www.chiangmaiairportthai.com), 3km southwest of the old city.

Schedules vary with the seasons and tourist demand. **Thai Airways** (THAI; Map p312; ☎053 211044, 023 561111; www.thaiair.com; 240 Th Phra Pokklao; ⌚8.30am-4.30pm Mon-Fri) has the widest range of domestic routes, but the network of **Thai Air Asia** (Map p312; ☎053 234645; www.airasia.com; 416 Th Tha Phae; ⌚10am-8pm) is rapidly expanding, and Chiang Mai is served by many more budget airlines. Tickets to Bangkok start from 1800B with Bangkok Airways, or 2200B on Thai. Heading south, expect to pay from 2350B to Phuket, or 1650B to Surat Thani.

Direct flights linking Chiang Mai to neighbouring nations are also expanding fast, with regular flights to Yangon (from 4950B), Luang Prabang (from 5000B) and Kuala Lumpur (3340B). There are also direct flights to Singapore, Seoul and Taipei, and to Hong Kong, Shanghai, Guangzhou, Hangzhou, Chengdu and other cities in China. To reach Cambodia or Vietnam, you'll have to go via Bangkok. **SM Travel** (Map p312; ☎053 206488; http://www.yourtripthailand.com; 87-95 Th Ratchadamnoen; ⌚8.30am-5.30pm) in the old city is a good place to book flights.

The airport has luggage storage (7am to 9pm, 200B per day), a post office branch (8.30am to 8pm), banks, souvenir shops and a **tourist assistance centre** (Map p308; ☎053 281438; ⌚7am-11pm). If you have time to kill, you could just stroll back down the highway to the large Central Airport Plaza (p348).

BUS

Chiang Mai has two bus stations, and *sŏrng·tăa·ou* run from fixed stops to towns close to Chiang Mai.

Arcade Bus Terminal

About 3km northeast of the city centre, near the junction of Th Kaew Nawarat and Rte 11, Chiang Mai's main long-distance station handles all services, except for buses to Northern Chiang Mai Province. This is the place to come to travel on to Bangkok or any other major city in Thailand. A chartered *rót daang* from the centre to the bus stand will cost about 60B; a túk-túk will cost 80B to 100B.

There are two terminal buildings, with ticket booths for dozens of private and government bus companies. Nominally, **Building 2** is for towns north of Chiang Mai and **Building 3** is for towns south of Chiang Mai, but in practice, buses leave from both terminals to most destinations. There is also a third depot behind Building 2 used exclusively by the private bus company **Nakornchai Air** (☎053 262799; www.nca.co.th; Th Kaew Nawarat, Arcade Bus Terminal), which has luxury buses to Bangkok and almost everywhere else in Thailand.

Facilities for travellers are a little lacklustre; there's a parade of local-style restaurants beside the two terminal buildings, and a left-luggage office (3am to 9pm, 20B per item). If you have time to burn, head over to the **Star Avenue Lifestyle Mall** (off Rte 11, Arcade Bus Terminal; ⌚24hr) by Building 3, which has air-conditioned coffeeshops and restaurants.

There is a regular international bus service linking Chiang Mai to Luang Prabang, via Bokeo, Luang Namtha and Udom Xai. You can also travel by bus across to Nong Khai (for Vientiane).

Chang Pheuak Bus Terminal

Just north of the old city on Th Chotana (Th Chang Pheuak), the Chang Pheuak Bus Terminal is the main departure joint for journeys to the north of Chiang Mai Province. Government buses leave regularly to:

Chiang Dao (40B, 1½ hours, every 30 minutes)

Fang (80B, three hours, every 30 minutes)

Hot (50B, two hours, every 20 minutes)

Tha Ton (90B, four hours, six daily)

BUSES TO/FROM CHIANG MAI

DESTINATION	PRICE (B)	DURATION (HR)	FREQUENCY
Bangkok	420-840	9-10	frequent
Chiang Khong	280-430	6½	3 daily
Chiang Rai	140-280	3-4	hourly
Khon Kaen	440-580	12	10 daily
Khorat (Nakhon Ratchasima)	580-680	12	11 daily
Lampang	92-107	2	hourly
Lamphun	31-36	1	hourly
Luang Prabang	1200-1500	20	8am & 9am (Mon, Wed, Fri, Sun)
Mae Hong Son	140-185	6	every 1½ hours
Mae Hong Son (minivan)	250	5	hourly
Mae Sai	175-350	5	7 daily
Mae Sariang	100-200	4-5	every 1½ hours
Mae Sot	320	6	2 daily
Nan	220-280	6	7 daily
Nong Khai	from 910	12	3 daily
Pai	from 75	4	hourly
Pai (minivan)	150	3	hourly
Phayao	120-240	3	5-8 daily
Phrae	150-300	4	4-8 daily
Phuket	1826	22	1 daily
Sukhothai	from 230B	5-6	10 daily
Udon Thani	850	12	2 daily

Local blue *sŏrng·tăa·ou* run to Lamphun (25B, one hour, every 20 minutes). Air-con minibuses to Chiang Dao (150B) leave hourly from Soi Sanam Gila, behind the bus terminal.

Public Sŏrng·tăa·ou Stands

There are several stops for *sŏrng·tăa·ou* running to towns close to Chiang Mai. Fares range from 20B to 30B and services run frequently throughout the day.

Pratu Chiang Mai Sŏrng·tăa·ou Stop (Map p312; Th Bamrungburi) Serves Hang Dong, Ban Tawai and points south.

Saphan Lek Sŏrng·tăa·ou Stop (Map p308; Th Chiang Mai-Lamphun) Serves Lamphun and Lampang.

Talat Warorot Sŏrng·tăa·ou Stop (Map p312; Th Praisani) Serves Lamphun, Bo Sang, San Kamphaeng and Mae Rim.

TRAIN

Run by the State Railway of Thailand, the neglected Chiang Mai Railway Station is about 2.5km east of the old city on Th Charoen Muang. Trains run five times daily on the main line between Bangkok and Chiang Mai, but there have been derailments on this line, and with the growth of discount air travel in Thailand, the trains are mostly used by Thais. The government has promised more investment in the railways in future, including the creation of a new high-speed rail link between Chiang Mai and Bangkok. The train station has an ATM, a left-luggage room (5am to 8.45pm, 20B per item) and an advance-booking counter (you'll need your passport to book a ticket).

There are four classes of train running between Chiang Mai and Bangkok's Hualamphong station: rapid, sprinter, express and special express. Most comfortable are the overnight special express services leaving Chiang Mai at 5pm and 6pm, arriving into Bangkok at 6.15am and 6.50am. In the opposite direction, trains leave Hualamphong at 6.10pm and 7.35pm. However, schedules change regularly, so see the State Railway of Thailand website (www.railway.co.th) for the latest information.

At the time of research, fares were as follows:

3rd class (bench seat) 231B to 271B

2nd class (reclining seat) 391B to 431B

2nd-class sleeper berth (with fan) 531B to 581B

2nd-class sleeper berth (air-con) 791B to 881B

1st-class sleeper berth (air-con) 1253B to 1953B

Getting Around

TO/FROM AIRPORT

From Arrivals Exit 9 there is a licensed airport taxi service, charging a fixed fare to different locations around Chiang Mai; expect to pay 160B to reach the centre of the old town. A cheaper shuttle minibus service charges 40B to the old town, but minibuses only leave when full, and you may face pressure to charter the whole vehicle.

Another option is to walk out to the highway and flag down a *rót daang* for a charter trip to town (around 100B to the old city). Many guesthouses and hotels also provide airport transfers. From any point within the city, you can charter a túk-túk or *rót daang* to the airport for about 80B; allow 30 minutes for the journey.

BICYCLE

Cycling is a good way to get around Chiang Mai but be cautious on the ring roads circling the old city. Rickety sit-up-and-beg bikes can be rented for around 50B a day or 300B per week from guesthouses and shops around the old city. Check the bike carefully before you hire – brakes in particular can be very iffy.

If you want a superior bike, you can rent good-quality foreign-made road bikes (100B to 400B per day) and mountain bikes (250B to 800B) from **Chiang Mai Mountain Biking & Kayaking** (p325) and **Spice Roads** (p326). Spare parts for foreign bikes are available at **Chaitawat Bikeshop** (Map p312; 75/4 Ratchaphakhinai; ⏲9am-6pm Mon-Sat).

Chiang Mai also has an under-utilised shared bike scheme, **Bike@Chiangmai** (☎085 139 2410; www.bike-at.com; from per hr 20B), with five stations in the old city – at Wat Phra Singh, in front of the Lanna Folklife Museum, at Pratu Tha Phae, at Pratu Chiang Mai and at Suan Buak Hat – and more across the city. Registration fees are 220B, and there's a minimum 100B credit on the card you use to access the bikes; rental fees start at 20B for an hour.

CAR & TRUCK

Cars and pick-up trucks can be hired from rental agencies throughout the city, particularly along Th Moon Muang but stick to companies that offer full insurance (liability) coverage and breakdown cover, and check the terms so you're clear on what is and isn't included. Most companies ask for a cash deposit of 5000B to 10,000B.

Standard rental rates for small 1.5L cars, such as a Toyota Vios or Honda Jazz, start at 1500B; prices include unlimited kilometres but not petrol. Well-regarded agencies include:

Budget Car Rental (Map p308; ☎053 202871; www.budget.co.th; 201/2 Th Mahidol) Across from Central Airport Plaza.

North Wheels (Map p312; ☎053 874478; www.northwheels.com; 70/4-8 Th Chaiyaphum) Offers hotel pick-up and delivery, 24-hour emergency road service and comprehensive insurance.

Thai Rent a Car (☎053 904188; www.thairentacar.com; Chiang Mai International Airport) Located at the airport.

MOTORCYCLE

Renting a motorcycle or scooter is an extremely popular option in Chiang Mai. Agencies and guesthouses rent out everything from 100cc automatic scooters (from 150B per day) to larger Honda Dream bikes (from 250B) and full-sized road and off-road bikes up to 650cc (600B to 1300B). Smaller bikes are fine for city touring but if you plan to attempt any of the mountain roads around Chiang Mai, pick a machine with an engine size of 200cc or more.

By law, you must wear a helmet, and police frequently set up checkpoints to enforce this. You should also carry photo ID and an International Driving Permit (IDP) to present at police checkposts. In practice, police are usually happy with foreign drivers' licences, but if you can't present a licence, you'll be fined.

Saving a few baht by renting without proper insurance could cost you dearly; stick to companies offering breakdown cover and full insurance. Most policies have a 1500B excess in case of accident and a 10,000B excess if the motorbike is stolen; use the chain and padlock provided!

Most bike-hire places will ask for your passport as a security deposit. While there are rarely any problems with this, better agencies will accept a cash deposit of 5000B to 10,000B as an alternative. This cannot be paid by credit card.

For tips on touring the countryside around Chiang Mai, check out the advice at Golden Triangle Rider (www.gt-rider.com).

Mr Mechanic (Map p312; ☎053 214708; www.mr-mechanic1994.com; 135/1 Th Ratchaphakhinai; per day scooter/motorcycle/car from 150/500/1200B) Probably the best operator in town in terms of insurance and support, with a well-maintained fleet and comprehensive insurance with breakdown cover. There are other branches on Th Moon Muang (Map p312; ☎053 214708; www.mr-mechanic1994.com; 4 Soi 5, Th Moon Muang; per day scooter/motorcycle/car from 150/500/1200B) and Th Ratchaphakhinai (Map p312; ☎053 214708; www.mr-mechanic1994.com; 33 Th Ratchaphakhinai; per day scooter/motorcycle/car from 150/500/1200B).

Tony's Big Bikes (Map p312; ☎053 207124; www.chiangmai-motorcycle-rental.com; 17 Th Ratchamankha) Rents well-maintained 125cc to 400cc motorbikes. Also offers riding lessons, gives touring advice and repairs motorcycles.

PUBLIC & CHARTERED TRANSPORT

Rót daang (literally 'red trucks') operate as shared taxis, and they roam the streets picking up passengers who are heading in the direction they are travelling. There are no fixed routes so the easiest thing to do is to ask if the driver will take you where you want to go. Journeys start from 20B for a short trip of a few blocks and 40B for a longer trip (eg from the old city to Th Nimmanhaemin).

Drivers are also happy to hire out the whole vehicle for charter trips for a higher price, including day trips out into the countryside. If the vehicle is parked by the roadside instead of moving along the street, the driver is normally looking for a charter fare. Either way, there's little hassle involved; indeed, many *rót daang* are family businesses, with husbands driving and wives sitting alongside dealing with the money and route planning.

Túk-túk work only on a charter basis and are more expensive than *rót daang*, but they offer that energising wind-through-your-hair feeling and are faster in traffic. Rates start at 60B for short trips and creep up to 100B at night. Some drivers can be pushy and may try to steer you towards attractions that pay commissions.

Chiang Mai still has a few săhm·lór, which offer short transfers around Talat Warorot for 20B or so.

TAXI

It is very rare to see a metered taxi to flag down in Chiang Mai, but you can call for a pick-up from **Taxi Meter** (☎ 053 244268, 053 241955; www.taxichiangmai.com) – fares within Chiang Mai are unlikely to top 160B.

NORTHERN CHIANG MAI PROVINCE

North of Chiang Mai, the land rucks up into forested mountains on either side of the Mae Ping river as northern Thailand merges into southeastern Myanmar. With a chartered *rót daang* or rented motorcycle (with sufficient horsepower) you can roam high into the hills, visiting national parks, spectacular viewpoints, Royal Project farms and hill-tribe villages. The website www.gt-rider.com has trip reports posted by motorcylists who have made sorties through this region.

Mae Rim แม่ริม

The nearest town north of Chiang Mai, sleepy Mae Rim is an easy 30km ride from the city along Rte 107. Here you can visit the former palace of princess Dara Rasmee, and kick back at the Huay Teung Thao reservoir. Mae Rim is easily accessible by bus or *sŏrng·tăa·ou* (20B, 15 minutes) from Chiang Mai's Pratu Chang Pheuak bus terminal.

Huay Teung Thao Reservoir RESERVOIR

(อ่างเก็บน้ำห้วยตึงเฒ่า; admission 20B; ⏲7am-7pm) For Thais, a reservoir is not just a water store, it's a place for some serious R&R. At this expansive body of water just west of town, families gather to swim or splash around by the beach and picnic by the water's edge in elevated bamboo cabins. It's like a day at the beach.

To get here, follow Rte 107 and turn southwest onto Rte 121, then turn right across the bridge by the Khuang Phra Chao Lanna shrine.

Darapirom Palace MUSEUM

(admission 20B; ⏲9am-5pm Tue-Sat) Dara Rasmee, the last princess of the Lanna kingdom, lived out her days in this handsome 19th-century residence, built in classic Thai-colonial style, with tall ceilings, elegant fretwork vents and timbered verandahs. Rooms full of heirlooms, photos and personal effects recall the princess's life and times.

The palace lies in the grounds of the Mae Rim police compound on the west side of Rte 107; turn right after the police station and follow the signs past the runway for the police helicopter.

Mae Sa–Samoeng Loop แม่สา/สะเมิง

You don't have to roam far from the city limits to get into the jungle. Branching west off Rte 107 at Mae Rim, Rte 1096 winds past a string of tacky day-trip attractions – crocodile and monkey shows, elephant camps, orchid farms, shooting ranges, all-terrain-vehicle-hire companies, even a cobra farm endorsed by Sylvester Stallone – before climbing steadily into the forested **Mae Sa Valley**. The road continues in a winding loop past charging waterfalls and a series of Royal Project farms and then morphs into Rte 1269 at the turn-off to the sleepy country village of Samoeng, making for a thoroughly enjoyable 100km round-trip from Chiang Mai by rented motorcycle, or chartered *rót daang*.

Your first stop should be **Nam Tok Mae Sa** (adult/child 100/50B, car 30B; ⏲8am-4.30pm), a long chain of churning cascades set in lush tropical forest on the fringes of

Doi Suthep-Pui National Park, just 6km from the turn-off at Mae Rim. Swimming is permitted all along the stream, so you should have no problem finding a private pool to swim in, complete with waterfall-powered shower and rocky outcrop to picnic on. It's a great day trip for families, and an epic place to play pooh-sticks. If you didn't bring a packed lunch from Chiang Mai, there are some simple food vendors by the car park.

Beyond the Nam Tok Mae Sa turn-off, the road goes past the **Mae Sa Elephant Camp**, but the herd are used for old-fashioned circus shows and *howdah* rides, which are discouraged by animal welfare groups.

About 2km past the elephant camp are the **Queen Sirikit Botanic Gardens** (www.qsbg.org; Rte 1096; adult/child 100/50B, car 100B, motorcycle 30B; ⌚8.30am-4.30pm), where 227 hectares have been set aside for plantations, nature trails and vast greenhouses full of exotic and local flora. At the top of the ridge, the **Natural Science Museum** is an under-appreciated education centre, with lots of giant nature models and interactive displays for kids. The greenhouses shelter everything from jungle ferns to cacti and full-sized palms. Just downhill is a high **canopy walkway** through a copse of jungle trees; you'll be glad to have transport to get up to the top of the hill.

After the botanic gardens the road climbs into a high-altitude basin that was once a major centre for the production of opium poppies. With sponsorship from the Thai royal family, local hill-tribe farmers have been persuaded to re-seed their terraced fields with vegetables and tropical and temperate fruits and flowers. Produce from these farms is processed by Royal Project factories and sold under the Doi Kham label.

To get a taste of Royal Project produce, turn off Rte 1096 at Ban Pong Yaeng and follow the steep concrete road uphill to the Hmong village of **Nong Hoi**. Above the village, at around 1200m above sea level, you'll find the **Mon Cham Restaurant** (Nong Hoi Mai; mains 60-150B; ⌚7am-7pm), in a fantastic location at the top of the ridge. Here you can sample tasty, freshly cooked Thai food, prepared using Royal Project produce, or just sip local fruit liqueurs in a series of bamboo pavilions with spectacular views over the surrounding valleys. Accommodation is available in tents (700B) in the grounds. You'll need a reasonably powerful motorcycle to get all the way up the hill from Ban Pong Yaeng.

Further west around the valley, **Proud Phu Fah** (☎053 879389; www.proudphufah.com; Rte 1096, Km 17; r 2950-14,000B; ❄@📶🏊) is a stylish boutique hotel with elegant designer villas spread out along a trickling brook, designed to give the illusion of sleeping in the great outdoors. The open-air restaurant serves healthy Thai food (dishes 150B to 250B), with views across the lawns and mountains.

After Proud Phu Fah, the road swings around the mountain ridge, passing several spectacular viewpoints where you can pull in for photos. Before long, you'll reach the junction with Rte 1269 and the turning for the tidy village of **Samoeng**, but there's no real reason to visit except to stock up on provisions at the village 7-Eleven. There is less traffic on the return to Chiang Mai, which follows Rte 1269 all the way to Rte 121 on the outskirts of Chiang Mai.

Chiang Dao เชียงดาว

In a lush, jungle setting in the shadow of a mighty limestone mountain, Chiang Dao is where expats and Chiang Mai's growing middle classes come to escape the heat of the plains. It gets cooler still as you leave the village and climb towards the summit of Doi Chiang Dao (2175m). The forest is a popular stop for birders and trekkers, and at the base of the mountain is a highly venerated wát marking the entrance to one of Thailand's deepest limestone caverns.

Buses to Chiang Dao stop in the modern village on the east side of Rte 107, but most travellers head to the nearby village of **Ban Tham** on the west side of the highway, where all the accommodation and the famous cave temple can be found.

Sights & Activities

As well as exploring the cave temple, you can organise some impressive **treks** to bird life hot spots, scattered hill-tribe villages and the lofty summit of Doi Chiang Dao. Lodges can arrange guides and camping equipment, but only from October to May, when the trails are dry enough to trek.

Chiang Dao also has an **elephant camp**, but the package here is rather old-fashioned with *howdah* rides, performances and the inevitable mini-rafting trip, which goes against recommended practice for elephant welfare. Hill-tribe villagers congregate for the bi-weekly **market** in Chiang Dao village, held on the first and third Tuesday of each month.

Wat Tham Chiang Dao CAVE, BUDDHIST TEMPLE

(วัดถ้ำเชียงดาว, Chiang Dao Cave; admission 40B, guide fee 100B) Set in pretty grounds that teem with jungle butterflies, this forest wát was founded at the entrance to the **Chiang Dao Cave**, a chilly warren of tunnels and passageways that extends more than 10km beneath the limestone massif of Doi Chiang Dao. For local Buddhists, the cave is a popular meditation retreat, and the twisting, turning passages overflow with stalactites and stalagmites in weird and wonderful configurations.

The chambers at the start of the network of tunnels – known as Tham Sua Dao and Tham Phra Non – are illuminated by electric lights, but the most interesting section of the caves is unlit and you'll need to hire a guide with a gas lantern (100B) to explore, providing a living for a local villager in the process. The tour wriggles through narrow passageways to other large chambers – Tham Mah (735m), Tham Kaew (474m) and Tham Nam (660m) – and your guide will point out bat colonies and limestone features that have been named for their resemblance to animals; a tip (50B or so) is appropriate. At the end of the illuminated section, you'll reach a small but highly revered sleeping Buddha in a small antechamber.

Local legend says that the cave was the home of a *reu·sěe* (hermit) who convinced the spirits to create several magic wonders inside the caverns: a stream flowing from the pedestal of a solid-gold Buddha, a storehouse of divine textiles and a city of *naga*. These miraculous features are said to be much deeper inside the mountain, beyond the last of the illuminated caverns.

Doi Chiang Dao Wildlife Sanctuary NATURE RESERVE

(เขตรักษาพันธุ์สัตว์ป่าเชียงดาว, Doi Luang; Chiang Dao; admission 200B, vehicle 30B) Doi Chiang Dao rises dramatically above the surrounding plain, wrapped in a thick coat of tropical forest. This jungle wonderland is one of Thailand's top spots for birders, with more than 300 resident species. It's a steep two-day hike to the summit, which offers spectacular views over the surrounding massifs, and the mountain is one of the best spots in the world to see the giant nuthatches and Hume's pheasants. Treks can be arranged with guesthouses in Ban Tham; expect to pay around 2400/4600B for one/two days.

If you just want a taste of the marvellous scenery, take a right at the junction just before the cluster of lodges at Ban Tham and follow the gorgeously scenic, winding mountain road that climbs to the ridge through the forest. This is a challenging ride and you'll need transport with sufficient power to handle the gradients.

Wat Tham Pha Plong BUDDHIST TEMPLE

(สำนักสงฆ์ถ้ำผาปล่อง; Ban Tham; donations appreciated) FREE If you continue on the road past the Chiang Dao lodges, you'll reach the parking lot for this pretty forest wát on the edge of the Chiang Dao massif. A steep *naga* stairway climbs up through the forest to the rocky crevice where the revered meditation master Luang Pu Sim once practised.

Pha Daeng National Park NATIONAL PARK

(อุทยานแห่งชาติผาแดง; ☎053 046370; www.dnp.go.th; Ban Muang Na; admission adult/child 100/50B; camping per person 30B, bungalow 600-2500B) North of Doi Chiang Dao and reached by following Rte 1178, Pha Daeng National Park offers lush, jungle scenery and stunning bird life. Flanking the Myanmar border, the park is pockmarked by deep cave systems and has the usual full hand of scenic viewpoints, summit hikes and spurting waterfalls. Bungalow accommodation is available at the park headquarters.

Sleeping & Eating

The guesthouses are spread out along the road leading north from Wat Tham Chiang Dao on the edge of the forest. All can arrange tours, and rent bicycles and motorbikes.

The restaurant at Chiang Dao Nest is the undisputed culinary highlight of the area, but all the lodges serve meals and there's a cluster of simple **Thai restaurants** around the parking lot at Wat Tham Chiang Dao. Note that it can get cold here, particularly from October to February; bring a coat or sweater for the evenings.

Chiang Dao Hut GUESTHOUSE $

(☎053 456625; www.chiangdaohut.com; r from 400B; Wi-Fi) This cute collection of bungalows in a glade that drops down to a stream is close to Wat Tham Chiang Dao, so you'll have extra choices for dinner. The shared bathrooms have hot water and the atmosphere is appropriately laid-back and unhurried.

★ **Chiang Dao Nest** GUESTHOUSE $$
(☎053 456242; www.chiangdaonest.com; bungalow 895-1595B; @ 🛜 🏊) The guesthouse that put Chiang Dao on the map is a charming country retreat, with comfortable, bamboo-weave bungalows scattered around a gorgeous tropical garden with plenty of shady gazebos where you can kick back with a book. The award-winning restaurant here is worth the trip from Chiang Mai all by itself, with guest ales, fine wines and sophisticated modern European dishes such as seared tuna loin and saffron risotto (mains 120B to 695B).

There's a forest-flanked swimming pool with mountain views, and kids will also love the goats and toy pavilion. The owners are experts on the area and can arrange recommended trekking tours. To get here, bear left at the junction towards Tham Pha Plong.

They also run **Nest 2**, closer to Wat Tham Chiang Dao, with more well-kept bungalows and a good Thai restaurant.

Chiang Dao Roundhouses BUNGALOW $$
(☎087 496 1571; www.chiangdao-roundhouses.com; bungalow from 1200B) The lodge that everyone is talking about in Chiang Dao, this eye-catching collection of cap-shaped huts was fashioned using traditional techniques and materials such as recycled glass bottles, bamboo, rice husks, mud and straw. Bathrooms are partly open-air and the huts cluster around a breakfast room and yoga cave. It's down a small lane opposite the entrance to the Wat Tham Chiang Dao parking lot.

Malee's Nature Lovers Bungalows GUESTHOUSE $$
(☎081 961 8387; www.maleenature.com; camping per person 100B, bungalow 850-1950B; 🛜 🏊) Run by the orchid-obsessed Malee, this green-fingered spot on the road to Tham Pha Plong has simple, clean cottages with hot showers in an orchid-filled garden. The cheapest share bathrooms, while posher cabins have en suites. One is set high off the ground for birders to watch the canopy activity.

ℹ Getting There & Around

Chiang Dao is 72km north of Chiang Mai along Rte 107. It's a 150B *sŏrng·tăa·ou* ride from the bus stand in Chiang Dao village to the guesthouses near the cave temple. Buses travel to:

Chiang Mai (40B, 1½ hours, every 30 minutes)

Fang (50B, two hours, seven daily)

Tha Ton (65B, 2½ hours, seven daily)

There are also air-conditioned minivans charging 150B to either Chiang Mai or Tha Ton.

Most of the lodges rent out mountain bikes (from 100B) and motorbikes (from 300B), or you can hire a *sŏrng·tăa·ou* for about 1000B a day to drive you around the area.

Doi Ang Khang ดอยอ่างขาง

Pushed up against the border with Myanmar, the mountain valleys around **Doi Ang Khang** are known locally as 'Little Switzerland' thanks to the cool climate, which gets cold enough for frost in January, but really the resemblance ends there. Instead of chalets and yodelling you'll find peaceful green valleys full of temperate flowers and plantations of 'exotic' – to the Thais at least – fruit, such as apples, pears and strawberries, tucked into the middle of a crown-shaped circle of forested mountains.

Today, people come here to enjoy the almost-temperate climate and explore the **Royal Agricultural Station** (☎053 450107; www.angkhangstation.com; admission 50B, car 50B; ⏲6am-9pm), which sprawls out from the village of **Ban Khum** in the centre of the basin. This Royal Project was founded to provide hill-tribe villagers with an alternative source of income to growing opium, and to conduct research into which new crops could be cultivated in the cool mountain valleys of northern Thailand. Many station staff are villagers from the mixed Yunnanese, Burmese and hill-tribe villages of Pang Ma, Ban Luang, Ban Khob Dong and Ban Nor Lae, which circle the Royal Project and are also worth a visit.

Dotted around the station grounds are a string of landscaped gardens and workshops where fruit is sorted, tea is processed and herbal remedies and beauty products are mixed and tested. The main station **restaurant** – a colonial-style space with waiters in flowery pyjamas – cooks up good lowland Thai food and northern specialities, prepared using ingredients from the Royal Project. Accommodation is also available (dorms 50B, bungalows 650B to 3500B); most of the roomy bungalows have terraces or balconies where you can soak up the scenery.

There's more accommodation in Ban Khum village, the best choice being the rather lovely **Angkhang Nature Resort** (☎053 450110; www.mosaic-collection.com/angkhang; bungalows 2500-3800B; ❄ @), offering large, upscale bungalows with balconies and mountain views in cascading grounds above the Royal Project. The hotel can arrange mountain biking, trekking and mule riding in the surrounding hills. Bring a coat or sweater for the cool evenings.

Getting There & Away

To reach Doi Ang Khang, follow the looping hairpin turns of Rte 1249, which branches off Rte 107 about 13km south of Fang. There's no public transport but you can reach the station by chartered *sŏrng·tăa·ou* or with a rented motorcycle, though a bike with less than 250cc will struggle.

Leaving the mountain, consider taking the scenic back route via Rte 340 and Rte 1178, snaking through the forest and emerging in Pha Daeng National Park near Chiang Dao.

Fang ฝาง

Few foreigners stop in at Fang, which was originally founded by King Phaya Mengrai in the 13th century. This sleepy market town was once a stop for Chinese trade caravans but these days most goods come from Myanmar, including *yah bâh* (methamphetamine), which explains all the police checkpoints along the highway. Most travellers only stop here to change buses for Tha Ton or Chiang Mai, but it's worth taking an hour or two to visit the Burmese-influenced wát scattered over the hillside to the north of the traffic lights in the middle of town.

Wat Chong Paen has a distinctive green Burmese pagoda roof, and nearby is the **Queen Three Complexions monument**, with a towering gold statue of its founder. The monument honours a local queen who was said to be so beautiful that her skin changed colour depending on the time of day. Close to the market in the town centre, **Wat Chedi Ngam** is full of murals of King Bhumibol. About 5km south of Fang, **Wat Sriboonruang** (☎089 231 0581; www.templeretreatthailand.com; Sansai) hosts a popular two-week temple-stay program for foreign Buddhist devotees.

From the bus stand by the town market, local buses run to: Chiang Dao (50B, two hours, every 30 minutes), Chiang Mai (80B, 3½ hours, every 30 minutes) and Tha Ton (14B, 30 minutes, six daily).

Yellow *sŏrng·tăa·ou* run frequently from the market to Tha Ton (25B, 30 minutes) and air-con minivans run to Chiang Rai (120B, three hours) at 8.30am and 2pm; an unpredictable bus covers the same route at 2pm. Minivans also run regularly to Chiang Mai (150B) from a stand by the hospital on the highway.

Tha Ton ท่าตอน

The northernmost town in Chiang Mai Province feels a long way from the provincial capital. At one time, this jungle outpost was a key staging point for opium ferried across the border by Burmese warlord Khun Sa, but there is no legal border crossing and modern Tha Ton is a quiet backwater that sees just a trickle of tourists headed downriver towards Chiang Rai.

The trip downstream is possible from July to December – at other times, you may be the only foreigner in town. Nevertheless, there are some interesting detours in the area, including boat trips up to the Myanmar border and day trips by road to Mae Salong or the hot springs at Doi Pha Hompok National Park. The town has a sizeable population of Yunnanese migrants, who worship at the small Chinese-style mosque just south of the boat jetty.

Watch out for packs of dogs as you wander around; they can be aggressive.

Sights & Activities

Resorts in Tha Ton can arrange **treks** and **rafting trips** to a string of hill-tribe villages inhabited by Palaung, Black Lahu, Akha, Karen and Yunnanese villagers. While these are less traditional than the villages immediately across the border, they are more traditional than the tribal villages close to Chiang Mai. Expect to pay around 1000B per person for a day trek, and from 2500B for a two-day rafting tour (only possible from October to February).

Wat Tha Ton BUDDHIST TEMPLE
(วัดท่าตอน; ☎053 459309; www.wat-thaton.org; donations appreciated) **FREE** Just south of the bridge, this intriguing monastery complex sprawls west from Tha Ton over a series of forested hills. The wát buildings are spread over nine different levels and each comes with its own collection of supersized statues and stunning views north towards Myanmar or east across the Tha Ton plain.

The first level has a statue of Kuan Yin, the Chinese goddess of compassion; level three has a portly Chinese Buddha and a towering white seated Buddha in the Thai style; level four has a huge seated Buddha with a *naga* cowl; level eight crowns the hilltop, with a colourful stupa known as Chedi Kaew; and there's a huge golden standing Buddha holding a cauldron-sized begging bowl on level nine (reached via a road running across the saddle behind the *chedi*). Look out for helicopter-like dipterocarp seeds spiralling down from the canopy as you wander. Allow an hour to explore.

Chiang Rai Boat Trip BOATING
(☎053 053727; ticket 350B; ⊙departs 12.30pm) During the rainy season and for as long as water levels stay high (July to December), long-tail boats make the journey between Chiang Rai and Tha Ton daily. It's a scenic trip passing tracts of virgin forest, riverside monasteries, and villages of thatched huts with fishermen casting nets in the shallows.

The travel time is anywhere from three to five hours, depending on river conditions and on how many stops are taken along the way. Each boat takes six to 12 passengers, but operators may be reluctant to depart if there are insufficient passengers; chartering the whole boat costs 2200B. You can also make the trip (much more slowly) upriver from Chiang Rai.

Travellers often stop in the Lahu village of **Mae Salak** or the Karen village of **Ban Ruammit** and trek into the hills to find a less commercial hill-tribe experience. **Doi Wawi**, south of Mae Salak, is a large multi-ethnic community of Yunnanese, hill-tribe and Thai peoples; the Wawee chain of coffeeshops gets all its beans from this area. Nearby are dozens of hill-tribe villages, including Thailand's largest Akha community (Saen Charoen) and oldest Lisu settlement (Doi Chang), both also known for their coffee.

Sleeping & Eating

Tha Ton's guesthouses are strung out along both sides of the river by the bridge, and most can arrange treks, boat trips and motorcycle and bicycle hire. Note that some resorts close during the quiet season (January to June), when the river is too low for boat trips.

All the guesthouses have riverside restaurants and there are more coffeeshops and local restaurants on the main road south of the bridge.

Apple Resort RESORT $
(☎053 373144; applethaton@yahoo.com; r 500-1200B; ❄📶) Apple makes the most of its setting facing the boat jetty from the north bank, with budget fan-cooled bungalows in the garden and much more welcoming riverfront bungalows with fantastic front porches facing the water. There is a friendly riverside restaurant for enjoying Tha Ton's

DON'T MISS

SOAK YOUR CARES AWAY

About 10km west of Fang at Ban Meuang Chom, near the agricultural station, **Doi Pha Hompok National Park** (Doi Fang/Mae Fang National Park; ☎053 453517; www.dnp.go.th; admission adult/child 300/150B, car/motorbike/bike 30/20/10B; camping per person 30B, bungalows 1000-2000B; ⊙7am-7pm) is part national park and part public spa, with a gorgeous hot springs complex (*bor náam hórn* in Northern Thai) set in a boulder-strewn glade in the forest. Boardwalks wind across an open meadow dotted with more than 40 hot springs, with steam vents blasting up to 30m into the air and clouds of steam drifting theatrically across the footpaths. The mineral-rich spring water is cooled to a bearable temperature and piped into a series of private bathhouses (adult/child 50/20B) and a public pool (20/10B). There's also a sauna (30/10B) and masseurs are on hand to complete the package.

Fang residents come here to bathe and boil eggs in the springs at weekends, but the complex is wonderfully peaceful on weekdays. There are several cafes, and accommodation is available in simple but comfortable bungalows, or there's a campsite with tents for rent.

Beyond the hot springs complex, the rest of the park is a ruckus of forested mountains, with lots of hiking trails and forest campsites. The most popular destination is the 2285m summit of Doi Pha Hompok, Thailand's second-highest peak. Most trekkers camp below the summit and leave early to reach the top at sunrise for an epic view over the surrounding countryside. At the top of the mountain, average temperatures are a mere 2°C during winter and 14°C during summer.

To reach the park, turn off Rte 107 onto Rte 5054 and follow the signs.

best feature: the river by moonlight. Rates include breakfast.

★ **Old Tree's House** RESORT **$$**
(☎085 722 9002; www.oldtreeshouse.net; bungalows 1200-2800B; ❄📶🏊) After an uninspiring approach beside a cement works, you'll struggle to suppress the oohs and aahs as you reach the lush tropical garden at this French-Thai operation on the hillside. From the new restaurant overlooking the valley to the immaculate bamboo-weave bungalows and postcard-pretty palm-fringed pool, Old Tree's doesn't put a foot wrong. Look for the turn-off 400m past Tha Ton.

Saranya River House HOTEL **$$**
(☎053 373143; www.thatonthailand.com; r from 1000B; ❄📶🏊) A stylish modern place by the boat jetty, with a pool out back and tasteful Thai-meets-art deco interiors. A buffet breakfast is 200B extra.

Garden Home Nature Resort RESORT **$$**
(☎053 373015; gardenhome14@hotmail.com; r with fan from 300B, with air-con 800-1500B; ❄📶) Neat thatch-roofed bungalows are dotted around a calm, green compound full of lychee trees and bougainvillea at this tranquil riverside spot. There are also a few stone bungalows, and three larger, more luxurious bungalows on the river with TVs, fridges and lovely verandahs.

Thaton River View HOTEL **$$**
(☎053 053589; thatonriverview@hotmail.com; r from 1450B; ❄📶) A little worn, this hotel has a perfect riverside setting, with views from the restaurant across to the forested south bank of the river, and waterfront bungalows with polished wooden floors, connected by snaking wooden walkways. However, the price is a little steep considering the tired facilities and hit-or-miss service.

ℹ Getting There & Away

The main bus stand in Tha Ton is a long hike south along the highway, but buses also swing in at the parking lot just north of the bridge. Services include:

Bangkok (670B to1000B, 14 hours, three daily)
Chiang Dao (65B, 2½ hours, six daily)
Chiang Mai (90B, four hours, six daily)
Fang (14B, 30 minutes, six daily)

You can also get to Fang using the yellow *sŏrng·tăa·ou* (25B), which cruise the main street looking for passengers. Air-conditioned minivans charge 150B from Tha Ton to Chiang Dao; ask your guesthouse to make a booking. To reach Chiang Rai by road, take a *sŏrng·tăa·ou* to Mae Salong (60B, 1½ hours, three daily) and change, or head to Fang.

With your own car or motorcycle, you can continue to Mae Salong along Rte 107, turning off on Rte 1089, following a fully paved but sometimes treacherous mountain road, passing scattered Lisu and Akha villages. Local guesthouses rent out motorcycles for 350B per day.

SOUTHERN CHIANG MAI PROVINCE

To the immediate south of Chiang Mai is the Ping Valley, a fertile plain that runs out to densely forested hills. Southwest is Thailand's highest peak, Doi Inthanon (2565m).

San Kamphaeng & Bo Sang

สันกำแพง/บ่อสร้าง

About 14km southeast of Chiang Mai along Rte 1006, the town of **San Kamphaeng** was once famous as a production centre for cotton, silk and other handicrafts, but many of the small factories have relocated and those remaining seem a little down on their luck these days. *Sŏrng·tăa·ou* and *rót daang* drivers in Chiang Mai push trips to San Kamphaeng quite heavily, steering tourists towards factories and workshops that pay a commission, but it's easy to get here by public transport, so there's no particular need to pay into this system if you don't want to.

If you do feel inclined to visit, the most engaging option is the 'umbrella village' of **Bo Sang**, just west of San Kamphaeng, with a string of souvenir shops, showrooms and workshops, most devoted to the production of paper and bamboo umbrellas and parasols. However, prices aren't especially cheap and you'll find similar items in Chiang Mai's night market.

In late January the surprisingly untouristy **Bo Sang Umbrella Festival** *(têt·sà·gahn rôm)* features a colourful umbrella procession along Bo Sang's main street.

ℹ Getting There & Away

White *sŏrng·tăa·ou* to San Kamphaeng town (20B, 30 minutes) leave Chiang Mai frequently during the day from the lane south of Talat Warorot market; white *sŏrng·tăa·ou* to Bo Sang (20B, 25 minutes) leave from the riverside on Th Praisani.

San Kamphaeng Hot Springs

About 36km east of Chiang Mai, down a small country lane leading north from Rte 1317 at Mae On, the **San Kamphaeng Hot Springs** (053 037101; adult/child 100/50B; r from 1000B, with bathhouse from 1300B; camping per person 50B; 7am-8pm) are a delight. Set in a meandering country garden are public and private bathhouses, massage pavilions and a hot lazy river where you can soak away the tiredness from your calves. Locals flock here at weekends to picnic and boil eggs in the hot vents, which emerge from the ground at a scorching 100°C. During the week, however, things are calm and peaceful, apart from the whoosh of steam roaring out of the steam vents. If you want the full-immersion experience, a dip in the public mineral pool costs 50/30B (adult/child), while a private bathhouse costs 60B for 15 minutes. Simple but comfortable rooms are available and there's a campsite and several restaurants serving Thai meals.

For a posher stay, **Roong Aroon Hot Spring Resort** (053 939128; www.chiangmaihotspring.com; r Mon-Fri from 1600, Sat & Sun 2000B), a few kilometres past the main springs, has spic-and-span cottages and its own mineral baths, pools and vents, set in a cute garden full of rocks with a passing resemblance to animals.

Hang Dong หางดง

About 15km south of Chiang Mai on Rte 108, the village of **Hang Dong** built its fortune on the production and sale of furniture, woodcarving, antiques (both real and imitation) and handicrafts. Hang Dong's 'furniture highway' – Th Thakhilek – runs east from Rte 108 towards Ban Tawai; look for the turn-off just south of the market. Lined up along the road are dozens of antique and handicraft dealers, selling everything from elaborate antique Chinese wedding beds (with astronomical price tags) to gigantic Buddhist woodcarvings, Burmese lacquer boxes and cheaper and more portable Thai knick-knacks. Alongside are numerous shipping companies who will ship your purchases worldwide.

Stores are open from 8am to 5pm daily. Good places to browse include: **De Siam** (053 441254; www.desiam-antiques.com; Th Thakhilek) for extravagant antique beds and cabinets; **The Mandala** (081 490 9251; Th Thakhilek) for Japanese heirlooms; **Siripat Antique** (053 433246; Th Thakhilek) for repro antiques and enormous woodcarvings; **Maharaj Interiors** (087 692 1691; Th Thakhilek) for Indian doorframes and chests; **Chilli Antiques & Arts** (053 433281; 125 Th Thakhilek) for top-notch Thai and Burmese Buddhas; **World Port Services** (053 434200; www.legendscollection.com; Th Thakhilek) for portable handicrafts and Burmese lacquerware; and **Crossroads Asia** (053 434650; www.crossroadsasia.com; 214/7 Th Thakhilek, Chaiyo Plaza) for ethnic art and textiles spanning 26 countries.

Hang Dong is also the location of **Dokmai Garden** (dokmai.garden@gmail.com; 386 Mu 10, Namprae, Hang Dong; admission 300B; Jan-Jun), a private botanical garden that preserves and propagates native flora, but its future is up in the air as the owners are emigrating; email for the latest information.

It is possible to reach Hang Dong by *sŏrng·tăa·ou* from Pratu Chiang Mai (20B, 20 minutes) but it's easier to come with a chartered *rót daang* so you can also visit nearby Ban Tawai and cart your purchases home.

Ban Tawai บ้านถวาย

About 2km east of Hang Dong, **Ban Tawai Tourism Village** (www.ban-tawai.com; 9am-6pm Mon-Sat) is a vast, pedestrian-friendly tourist market, with hundreds of small shops selling handicrafts and knick-knacks to spruce up your interiors back home. This vast enterprise was kicked off by local woodcarvers, who are famous for their artistry and prodigious output. Today, carvings are produced on an industrial scale by workshops such as Sriboonmuang in Zone 5. It's all very commercial, but you'll find the same kinds of handicrafts and souvenirs that you see in Chiang Mai's walking street markets (p316), spread out across six covered 'zones'. Signs saying 'antiques made to order' should make you question the origins of anything purporting to be old.

You can reach Ban Tawai by *sŏrng·tăa·ou* from Pratu Chiang Mai (20B, 20 minutes) but if you charter a *rót daang* you can also visit nearby Hang Dong.

Doi Inthanon National Park อุทยานแห่งชาติดอยอินทนนท์

Thailand's highest peak – Doi Inthanon (often abbreviated to Doi In) – soars to 2565m above sea level, an impressive altitude for the kingdom, but a tad diminutive compared to its cousins in the Himalaya. Surrounding this granite massif is a 1000-sq-km **national park** (☎053 286730; adult/child 300/150B, car/motorcycle 30/20B; ⊙4am-6pm), dotted with hiking trails and waterfalls and enveloped in an impenetrable curtain of jungle. When the heat of Chiang Mai gets too much, locals decamp to Doi Inthanon for day trips, especially during the New Year holiday when there's the rarely seen phenomenon of frost at the summit.

Sights & Activities

The whole point of the park is to get as high as you can to experience life in a colder climate. At the summit of Doi Inthanon, the forest is dank and chilly, often partly obscured by swirls of mist due to the condensation of warm humid air from lower down the mountain. It's otherworldly, and at times a little spooky, especially if you are alone in the mist. Do as Thai visitors do and bring a jacket and an umbrella or rain poncho in case of sudden showers.

The **summit** itself is reached via a short trail near the radar station, just beyond Doi Inthanon's twin *chedi*. At the end is a 'Highest Point in Thailand' sign, and a shrine to one of the last Lanna kings (Inthawichayanon). Don't expect a rewarding view; you'll see more from the terraces of the two *chedi*. The tiny cafe by the boardwalk is frequented by exotic bird life.

The mist-shrouded upper slopes produce abundant orchids, lichen, moss and epiphytes, and 385 bird species make a home in the canopy, more than in any other habitat in Thailand. Keep an eye out for flashes of colour in the forest as electric-blue niltavas, yellow-cheeked tits and green-tailed sunbirds fly by. The best birdwatching season is from February to April, with the best chance of sightings at the *beung* (bogs) below the summit. The mountain is also home to Assamese macaques, Phayre's leaf monkeys, gibbons, Indian civets, barking deer and giant flying squirrels – around 75 mammal species in all.

Most visitors charge straight to the stupas and summit. The only easy access into the forest is the slippery **Ang Ka trail** (a 360m-long boardwalk) into the cloud forest, near the Km 48 marker. A more ambitious jungle walk is the **Kew Mae Pan Nature**

WORTH A TRIP

BAN MAE KAMPONG แม่กำปอง

About 50km northeast of Chiang Mai, hidden away in the emerald jungles above Rte 1317, the pocket-sized village of **Ban Mae Kampong** has become an offbeat retreat for travellers looking to escape the commercialism of Chiang Mai and rediscover the village way of life. Most visitors are introduced to the area on zipline tours with **Flight of the Gibbon** (p325), but it's worth coming under your own steam to explore the village and the surrounding jungle.

Perched at an altitude of about 1300m, Ban Mae Kampong is locally famous as a centre for the production of *mêeang* (pickled tea leaves), and local coffee is sold at many small coffeeshops dotted along the road through the village. The steep road continues through the forest into **Chae Son National Park** (☎054 380000; adult/child 200/100B; r from 900B), where you'll find waterfalls, hot springs and cottages in the woods.

Local residents have formed a Community Ecotourism Committee and accommodation (600B per room) is provided at a series of local homestays; you can find a room just by asking at the houses displaying a 'homestay' sign. But **Tiger Trail Thailand** (☎053 278517; www.tigertrailthailand.com) in Chiang Mai can also arrange an overnight trip by minibus, or you can join a multiday trip with Flight of the Gibbon. For more information on the village, see www.mae-kampong.com.

An alternative overnight stop is **Tharnthong Lodges** (☎081 961 538; www.tharnthonglodges.com; r 1200-4000B), a few kilometres downhill from Ban Mae Kampong, an appealing Swiss Family Robinson affair, with wooden villas strewn over a jungle garden dotted with statues – including an incongruous Easter Island head – and a restaurant overlooking a pebble stream.

There is no public transport, but the village is easy to reach with a decent-sized motorcycle or by chartered *rót daang* – just follow Rte 1317 past Mae On to Ban Huai Kaew, and follow the signed road on the right.

Trail (admission & guide fee 200B; ⏲ Oct-Jun) near the Km 42 marker, which snakes for nearly 3km, passing a string of viewpoints and a pretty waterfall; a guide is compulsory and should be arranged at the park headquarters. The views are best in the cool dry season from November to February.

Also in the park are a few hill-tribe villages, though none are particularly picturesque. Most tribal people now work at farms and flower nurseries on the lower slopes. Near the national park headquarters, the Hmong village of **Ban Khun Klang** is worth visiting for its views of the Siriphum waterfall.

Waterfalls

During the wet season, the highlands collect rain like a sponge, sending it surging down towards the plains in raging torrents over eight dramatic waterfalls. Although swimming is discouraged because of the risk of flash floods, the falls are wonderfully scenic and spectacular after rain.

The most accessible cascade is **Nam Tok Mae Klang**, near the Km 8 marker, close to the turn-off from Rte 108 (take the signposted road just before the national park entrance), but the falls can get crowded with picnickers and coach tours at weekends. Reached via a side road near the Km 21 marker and tucked into a forested basin, **Nam Tok Wachirathan** has a huge frothy mane that plummets 50m and after heavy rain it can be as loud as an AC/DC concert. There's an enticing collection of food vendors by the parking lot. Near the Km 30 marker, **Nam Tok Siriphum** (at Km 30) is a delicate ribbon of silver when viewed from nearby Ban Khun Klang village.

Chedi

About 3km before the summit, set amid lush tropical gardens, the twin stupas of **Phra Mahathat Naphamethanidon** and **Phra Mahathat Naphapholphumisiri** (Km 41-42; admission to both 40B; ⏲ 6am-6pm) were built by the Royal Thai Air Force in honour of the king and queen of Thailand, respectively. The elongated flowerbud shape of the red granite Naphamethanidon *chedi* is mirrored by the purple granite spire of the Naphapholphumisiri *chedi,* both constructed in a modernist style that marks them out from other monuments in northern Thailand. The two *chedi* enshrine Buddha images and bas reliefs of Buddhist scenes, and offer great views from their terraces.

Sleeping & Eating

Park accommodation is available in comfortable bungalows located next to the national park information centre at Ban Khun Klang village, near the Km 31 marker; the best ones overlook the water. Nearby is a roadside restaurant complex with several hawker-style eateries, and there are more food vendors at Nam Tok Wachirathan. Camping is also possible (with your own equipment) at Nam Tok Mae Pan. Alternatively, there are some OK places to stay just outside the park, near the junction of Rte 1009 and Rte 108.

Ratchaphruek Hotel HOTEL **$**
(☎ 053 341901; www.ratchaphruekhotel.com; r 350-1200B; ❄ 📶) A rather institutional hotel near the turn-off to Doi Inthanon, with somewhat old-fashioned rooms and a noisy karaoke bar; ask for a room away from the warbling.

Little Home Inthanon Resort BUNGALOW **$$**
(☎ 053 033555; www.littlehomeinthanonresort.com; huts 600-800B, r from 1000B; ❄ 📶) There's a hint of the highway motel about this bungalow operation, with an assortment of boxy bungalows roofed in red tin. The price is right though, and breakfast is included.

Touch Star Resort HOTEL **$$$**
(☎ 080 589 9168; www.touchstarresort.com; r 1000-6000B; ❄ 📶 🏊) A step up in comfort and luxury from other options around Doi Inthanon National Park, Touch Star is well signposted, down a small lane off Rte 1009, near the Km 7 marker. Rooms are in an eccentric collection of villas, from Swiss chalets to tropical bungalows.

Doiin View BUNGALOW **$$$**
(☎ 053 033567; www.doiinview.com; bungalows from 2200B; ❄ 📶) A new arrival at Chom Thong, just of Rte 1009, with cute and comfortable timber bungalows in a neat garden, and bike hire for guests.

Getting There & Away

Most visitors come with private transport or on a tour from Chiang Mai; if coming by motorcycle or moped from Chiang Mai allow 2½ hours each way.

To reach the park via public transport, you first need to take a bus from Chiang Mai to Chom Thong (60B) on Rte 108. There are occasional public *sŏrng·tăa·ou* into the park from the highway junction, but these will only take you to the summit and back. Considering the risk of getting marooned, it makes more sense to charter a whole *sŏrng·tăa·ou* for the round-trip (about 1000B).

Northeastern Thailand

Includes ➡

Best Places to Eat

- Maeya (p387)
- Khao Tom Raeng Ngan (p369)
- Rung Roj (p426)
- Jumpa-Hom (p426)
- Goodmook* (p400)

Best Places to Stay

- Mekong Riverside Resort & Camping (p373)
- Mut Mee Garden Guest House (p379)
- Loei Village (p369)
- Tohsang Khongjiam Resort (p430)
- Hotel des Artists (p413)

Why Go?

The northeast of Thailand, or Isan (pronounced *ee-săhn*) as it's usually known, stretches from the wild Mekong River (Mae Nam Khong in Thai) down to the edges of the Khorat Plateau, and is home to Thailand's best national parks and most ancient temple ruins. Rich in religious significance and influenced by nearby Cambodia and Laos, it has a culture and food all its own.

As the country's most populous region and second-largest in terms of area, this relatively dry expanse is known more for its farming, culture and hard-working people than its tourist sights. But dispel those stereotypes from your mind – while it doesn't have the beaches or wild parties, it is rich in natural attractions, historic sites and unique cultural activities. The traditional music reflects the pulse of the agrarian culture, and the people are down to earth and friendly. The place moves to its own rhythm. If you relax into it and go with the flow, you'll find a warm welcome.

When to Go

- The weather is best during the 'cool' season from November to February. It almost never rains and temperatures, while still warm, are cooler than the rest of the year.
- The hot season from March to May sees temperatures soar to the high 30s and stay there. Any rain that falls at this time is a real blessing. Travelling can be arduous, but some of the best festivals are held during this time.
- Isan is at its most beautiful during the rainy season (June to October) because the forests and rice paddies turn green and the waterfalls run wild. The rain can be a challenge, though.

History

As with all of Southeast Asia, Isan's identity and allegiance have changed over the centuries, with parts of the region being variously under the sway of Laos and Cambodia in more recent times, and in earlier times part of the ancient Chenla and Dvaravati cultures. The region's history stretches back around 5600 years, to the Ban Chiang culture, which, by at least 2100 BC, had developed bronze tools.

The Dvaravati kingdoms, about which very little is known, were in ascension from somewhere between the 7th and 10th centuries, and traces of the culture can be found at Phu Phrabat in Udon Thani and Muang Sema in Nakhon Ratchasima. The Khmers came in the 9th century and occupied the region for some 400 years. They left their iconic massive temples, examples of which can be seen over much of Isan, but notably at Phimai in Nakhon Ratchasima and Phanom Rung in Buriram.

As the Khmer empire waned, the Lan Xang (Lao) kingdom rose in power and in the 14th century campaigned south deep into what is now Isan, as far as present-day Roi Et Province. From the 17th century the region came under the sway of Siamese kings, but remained largely autonomous. In the 19th century the region was once again briefly subjected to Lao influence when the Lao prince Chao Anou, rebelling against Thai dominion, stormed into Isan and worked his forces down as far as Nakhon Ratchasima, where his plans were thwarted in part by a local hero whose exploits have taken on folkloric proportions.

In the mid-20th century a dedicated program to make Isan more 'Thai' was carried out in the interests of national solidarity. But the Thai government, with considerable help from the US, only began serious development here in the 1960s, as a way to counter communist threat. The result was an improved economy and increased opportunity, but despite rapid improvement since then, the per-capita income here remains only one-third the national average.

Language & Culture

Isan is a melting pot of Thai, Lao and Khmer influences. The Isan language, still a more common first language than Thai, is very similar to Lao. In fact, there are probably more people of Lao heritage in Isan than in Laos. On the other hand, in the southernmost provinces of Lower Isan, many villages maintain Khmer as their primary tongue.

Isan can be roughly divided into three subregions: Upper Isan, consisting of the northernmost provinces of Loei, Nong Khai, Udon Thani and Bueng Kan, as well as the provinces hugging the Mekong; Lower Isan, the southern provinces of the region stretching from Nakhon Ratchasima to Ubon Ratchathani; and Central Isan, headed by Khon Kaen and Roi Et Provinces.

UPPER ISAN

The northern regions of Isan hug the Lao border, following the curves of the Mekong as it wends its way through Thailand before going into Cambodia and Laos, and taking in some rugged and, in places, spectacular national parks.

The national and historic parks are the main attractions, but the Mekong region in particular is becoming a hot spot for riverside retreats, with some excellent resorts springing up offering luxurious relaxation in rustic surrounds.

Loei Province

Loei is Isan's westernmost province and in some ways has a lot in common with northern Thailand. It has mountains, it has ethnic minorities and it has spectacular national parks. It's a diverse, beautiful province with probably the most tourist potential of all Isan.

The people of Loei call themselves 'Thai Loei' and are proud of their culture. It is believed the Thai Loei migrated from Luang Prabang via Chiang Mai to their present location in the 1850s. Being close to the border, Loei has also seen migrations of other ethnic groups and has sizeable numbers of Tai Phuan and Tai Dam, plus a very small number of Maew (Hmong) people.

The terrain here is mountainous and temperatures fluctuate from one extreme to the other: it's one of the few provinces in Thailand where temperatures drop below 0°C.

Loei เลย

POP 22,700

Loei is a relatively small provincial capital and easy to get around. It makes a convenient base from which to explore the province's

Northeastern Thailand Highlights

❶ Broadening your horizons at **Pha Taem National Park** (p430).

❷ Spotting elephants, deer and birds in **Khao Yai National Park** (p410).

❸ Marvelling at the art and industry of the Khmer at **Phanom Rung Historical Park** (p414).

❹ Challenging your vertigo on the rickety walkways of **Wat Phu Thok** (p392).

❺ Exploring the mystical landscape of **Phu Phrabat Historical Park** (p390).

❻ Chillin' along the Mekong River at **Nong Khai** (p376).

❼ Breathing in fresh air from atop the spectacular viewpoint of **Hin Chang See** (p436).

❽ Celebrating the height of the hot season with the **rocket festival** (p442) in Yasothon.

SOUTH
CHINA SEA
VIETNAM
LAOS
CAMBODIA
0 50 km
0 25 miles
Paksan
Bueng Kan
Wat Phu Thok
Ban Kham Pia
Phu Wua
Wildlife Sanctuary
Ban Phaeng
Phon
Charoen
Ban Chaiburi/
Mae Nam Song Si
Wanon
Niwat
NAKHON
PHANOM
Tha Khaek
Nakhon
Phanom
Phang Khon
SAKON
NAKHON
Sakon
Nakhon
Renu
Nakhon
Phu Phan
National Park
That
Phanom
Mekong
River
Huay
Huat
National Park
Talat Klang
Dong Sang
Kaw
Somdet
MUKDAHAN
KALASIN
Mukdahan
Savannakhet
Nong Sung
Phra Maha
Chedi Chai
Mongkhon
Phu Pha Thoep
National Park
Loeng Nok Tha
Roi Et
Selaphum
AMNAT CHAROEN
Khemmarat
YASOTHON
Lakhon
Pheng
Yasothon
Pha Tiu
Ban Si Than
Amnat Charoen
Phana
Sam Phan Bok
Phra That
Kong Khao Noi
Ku Phra Koh Na
Pha Taem
National Park
Nam Mun
Ban Pa-Ao
Ubon
Ratchathani
Khong
Jiam
Kaeng Tana National Park
Rasi
Salai
Khuang
Nai
Warin
Chamrap
Phibun
Mangsahan
Vangtao
Chong
Mek
Si Saket
Prasat
Sikhoraphum
Kheuan
Sirinthon
Mekong
River
SI SAKET
Det Udom
SURIN
Buntharik
Sangkha
Kantharalak
UBON
RATCHATHANI
Khun
Han
Lalom
Phum
Saron
Nohn
Sung
Chuor Phnom Dangkrek
(Dangkrek Mountains)
Phu Chong Nayoi
National Park
Chong
Sa-Ngam
Khao Phra
Wihan
Phu Khok Yai
(753m)
Phnom
Bach
(581m)
Chong
Phran
Khao Phra Wihan
National Park
222
212
22
223
213
13
9
202
214
23
24

Loei Province

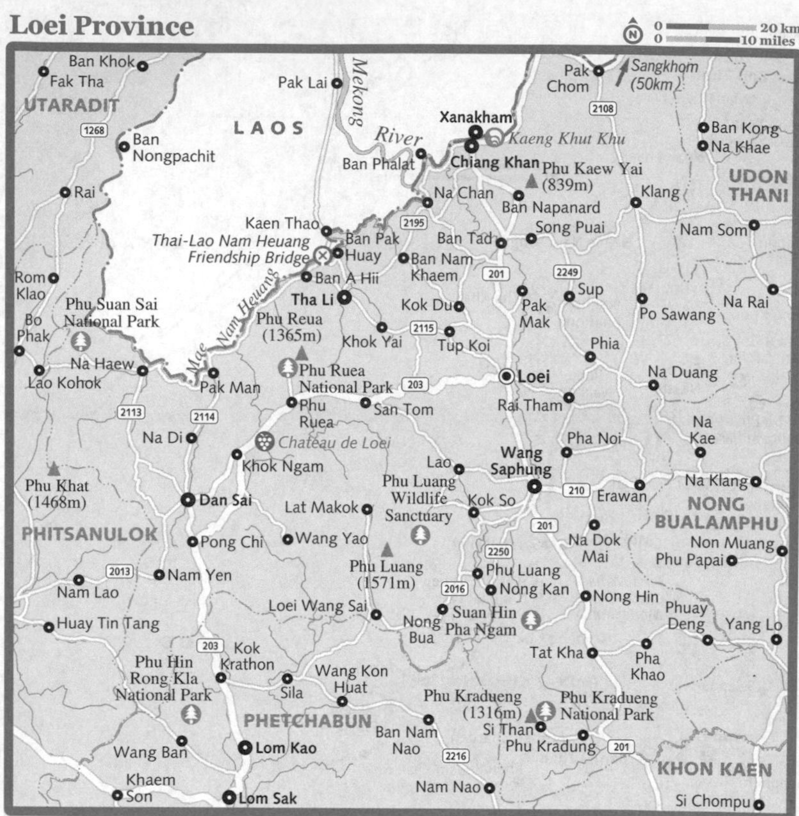

national parks and has some decent accommodation options. The forest park on the outskirts of town gives spectacular views of the town and surrounding hills.

Sights

★Phu Bo Bit Forest Park VIEWPOINT

(วนอุทยานภูบอบิด) If you want to harden up your legs for Loei's national parks, Phu Bo Bit gives you 600 steep steps to practise on, and rewards your effort with great 360-degree views of the town and the surrounding mountains. It's a decent climb, but can be done in half an hour or so each way. The park is about 6km from the town centre along Rte 2138. You can get a túk-túk there and back for about 250B, including wait time.

Many locals come up here at sunset and stay till after dark to see the lights of Loei. Needless to say, it's a popular photo spot.

Loei Museum MUSEUM

(พิพิธภัณฑ์เมืองเลย; Th Charoenrat; 8.30am-4.30pm; P) FREE This museum sits in the same stately old building as the tourist office, on the 2nd floor. It contains mostly posters and written commentary, but does have some displays on the region's Tai Phuan and Tai Dam people, along with some interesting costumes. All displays are in Thai.

Loei Cultural Centre MUSEUM

(ศูนย์วัฒนธรรมจังหวัดเลย; 042 835223; Rte 201; 8.30am-4.30pm) FREE The little Loei Cultural Centre is found 5km north of town at Rajabhat University. If you aren't visiting Dan Sai, you can see some Phi Ta Khon festival masks and photos here.

Lak Meung (City Pillar) MONUMENT

(เสาหลักเมือง; Th Sert-Si) The city pillar sits along the San Chao Pho Kut Pong Shrine, on the banks of the Mae Nam Loei, and is a great area for evening walks.

Sleeping

Sugar Guesthouse GUESTHOUSE $

(☎089 711 1975; www.sugarguesthouse.blog.com; Soi 2, Th Wisut Titep; s with fan 200-270B, d with air-con 380B; P❄@📶) This guesthouse has simple rooms, is clean and the friendly owner speaks English. It organises tours to nearby sights such as Phu Reua (2000B) and Phu Luang (1200B).

Baan Sabai HOTEL $

(☎042 811132; www.baansabailoei.com; off Th Nok Kaew; r 350-400B; P❄📶) The stylish-looking hotel has plain but decent rooms (even the cheap ones feature fridges and quality mattresses) in a quiet, convenient location. It's good value for money.

★**Loei Village** BOUTIQUE HOTEL $$

(☎042 833599; www.loeivillages.com; Soi 3, Th Nok Kaew; r incl breakfast 990B; P❄📶) From the warm welcome and cold welcome drink as you walk in the door, the focus is on service at this stylish boutique hotel. The decor is smart, and small details such as free minibar snacks and an excellent buffet breakfast make this one of the city's top choices. There are also bikes for guests' use. Staff are especially helpful.

Muanmanee Boutique Hotel BOUTIQUE HOTEL $$

(☎042 832353; www.muanmaneehotel.com; Soi 3, 35/59 Nok Kaew; r 590-690B; ❄@📶) This rather new place on a quiet cul-de-sac off Soi 3, Nok Kaew has clean, spacious rooms that are great value for the price. The lobby has an inviting lounge area and there are bikes available for guests' use.

Loei Palace Hotel HOTEL $$$

(☎042 815668; 167/4 Th Charoenrat; r 1200-2500B, ste 4000B; P❄@📶🏊) Loei's flagship hotel has helpful staff, plenty of mod cons and usually a high vacancy rate, so ask about discounts. Wi-fi reaches the first two floors only.

Eating & Drinking

There are a handful of bars situated on Th Ruamphattana.

★**Khao Tom Raeng Ngan** THAI $

(☎042 033050; 32/12 Th Sert-Si; dishes 60-200B; ⏲5pm-3am) As busy as the street it sits on, this place serves not only the rice soup *(kôw đôm)* it is named after, but hundreds of other dishes, and the place is happy to improvise if what you want isn't on the menu. The service is quick and friendly and the food won't disappoint.

Baan Yai NORTHEASTERN THAI $

(Th Maliwan; dishes 25-150B; ⏲11am-11pm) After moving from the centre of town, this genuine Isan restaurant finds itself on the main road, half hidden behind a concrete wall, making it hard to find. It looks a bit chaotic, but the food, featuring Isan country food such as ant eggs, cicadas and frogs, as well as regular Thai fare, is good. At night there is live music (which can be a good or bad thing).

Walking Street NORTHEASTERN THAI $

(Th Ruamjit; ⏲4pm-11pm) Loei's night market is a good dining destination. It's not far from the river and so makes a good place for an evening stroll.

Phuloei Coffee CAFE

(Th Ruamjai; ⏲8am-7.30pm Sun-Thu, to 8.30pm Fri & Sat; 📶) This little spot serves good locally grown coffee and delicious bakery goods.

Information

The **Tourism Authority of Thailand** (TAT; ☎042 812812; tatloei@tat.or.th; Th Charoenrat; ⏲8.30am-4.30pm) office provides a good map and has particularly helpful staff.

There are extended-hour banks and an AEON ATM located in the Big C department store on the highway.

Getting There & Away

AIR

Nok Air (☎02 900 9955; www.nokair.com) and **Air Asia** (p776) both connect Loei to Bangkok's Don Mueang Airport twice daily, with prices starting around 990B. **Loei Travel** (☎085 010 2426; www.loeitravel.com; ⏲10am-5pm Mon-Sat), inside Loei Palace Hotel, sells tickets. At time of writing, Air Asia had just added a minivan shuttle-link service from the airport to Chiang Khan.

GETTING TO LAOS: THA LI TO KAEN THAO

Foreigners can get Lao visas at the seldom-used **Thai-Lao Nam Heuang Friendship Bridge** (⏲6am-6pm) in Amphoe Tha Li, 60km northwest of Loei. The VIP service from Loei goes all the way to Luang Prabang.

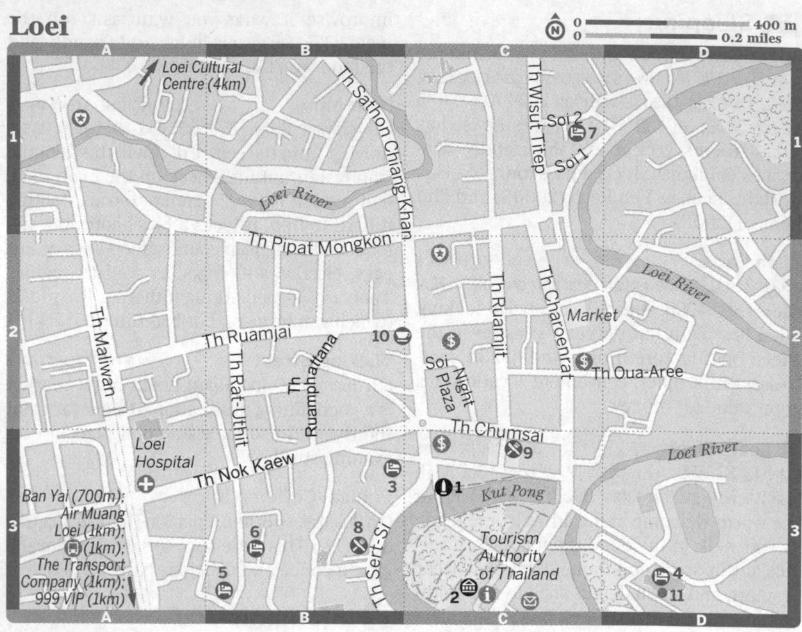

Loei

Sights
1 Lak Meung (City Pillar)......C3
2 Loei Museum......C3

Sleeping
3 Baan Sabai......B3
4 Loei Palace Hotel......D3
5 Loei Village......B3
6 Muanmanee Boutique Hotel......B3
7 Sugar Guesthouse......C1

Eating
8 Khao Tom Raeng Ngan......B3
9 Walking Street......C3

Drinking & Nightlife
10 Phuloei Coffee......B2

Transport
11 Loei Travel......D3

BUS

Loei's **bus terminal** (☎ 042 833586; Th Maliwan) has services to Udon Thani (100B, three hours, every 30 minutes), Khon Kaen (137B, 3½ hours, hourly), Khorat (275B, six hours, hourly), Phitsanulok (154B, four hours, four daily) and Chiang Mai (409B to 570B, 10 hours, four daily). The only bus to Nong Khai (130B, 6½ hours) leaves at 6am, and it's worth catching because it follows the scenic Mekong River route. It's faster, however, to go via Udon Thani.

First-class buses to Bangkok (440B, 11 hours) are frequent and there are VIP buses (666B) each evening with **Air Muang Loei** (☎ 042 832042) and **999 VIP** (☎ 042 811706).

The **Transport Company** (Borisat Khon Song; ☎ 042 811706; Loei bus terminal) has a new VIP service from Loei to Luang Prabang in Laos (700B, 10 hours), crossing the Heuang River at Tha Li, where travellers can get Lao visas. Buses leave Loei at 8am and 10am. There are also services to Saiyabuli in Laos (500B, seven hours).

Getting Around

Sŏrng·tăa·ou (shared taxi, 20B) run from the bus station through town, or you can take a túk-túk (pronounced 'đúk đúk') for about 60B.

Loei Village hotel and Muanmanee both provide bicycles free of charge to guests. Sugar Guesthouse rents bicycles (50B per day) and motorcycles (250B per day) and leads reasonably priced trips around the area. Loei Palace Hotel rents bikes (50/80B per half-/full day).

Chiang Khan เชียงคาน

POP 6100

Sitting right on the banks of the Mekong, Chiang Khan capitalises on its great location with a thriving tourist industry. With great views across to the mountains of Laos, its main attractions are a lovely esplanade along the river and the quaint wooden shophouses of its 'walking street' (which actually does have a few cars). It's a popular spot for holidaying Thais and a great place to spend a few days relaxing.

At time of writing there were plans to extend the esplanade along the Mekong all the way out to Kaeng Khut Khu, which would make it a nice 4km walk.

Sights

Kaeng Khut Khu VIEWPOINT

(แก่งคุดคู้) With the mountains making an attractive backdrop, this famous bend in the Mekong, and its small set of rapids, is a popular stop. The surrounding park has a bevy of vendors selling *má·prów gâa·ou* (coconut candy), the local speciality. It's 5km downstream from town; túk-túk drivers charge 100B per person.

Phu Thok VIEWPOINT

(ภูทอก) In the cool season, people head to nearby Phu Thok mountain for sunrise and 'sea of fog' views. If you don't have your own vehicle, ask your hotel to arrange a ride. Túk-túk charge 100B per person and then you have to ride the *sŏrng·tăa·ou* (25B per person) to the top.

Wat Si Khun Mueang BUDDHIST TEMPLE

(วัดศรีคุณเมือง; Th Chai Khong; dawn-dusk) The *bòht* (ordination hall) at Wat Si Khun Mueang, which probably dates to the Rama III era, is mostly Lao-style (in particular, note the sweeping roof), but it also freely mixes central (the lotus pillars) and northern (the guardian lions) Thai styling. It's fronted by a superb mural of the Jataka tales.

Activities

Many guesthouses arrange boat trips to Kaeng Khut Khu or further afield, and the mountain scenery makes them highly recommended. Rates swing with petrol prices, but the typical 1½-hour trip costs around 1000B for up to 10 people.

Asta Yoga House YOGA

(086 234 0011; malarinson@hotmail.com; Soi 10; 10 lessons 1400B) Khun Malarin teaches hatha yoga and can speak English. Classes are held on Monday, Wednesday, Thursday and Sunday.

Sleeping

Almost every second house along Th Chai Khong seems to have been converted into a guesthouse, and Chiang Khan's popularity means hotel owners don't need to price their rooms reasonably. But staying on the Mekong is what Chiang Khan is all about. Note that preserving the historic character of buildings often means shared bathrooms and thin walls. Most places have bicycles for hire, usually for around 50B per day.

Chiangkhan Riverview Guesthouse GUESTHOUSE $

(080 741 8055; 277 Th Chai Khong; r with fan/air-con 400/600B, with air-con & bathroom 900B;) This tasteful riverside spot has rooms with fan and air-con, shared and private bathrooms and a mix of old and new construction. The rooms, some with river views, are all dark wood and cool ambience, the terrace is very inviting and the owners are friendly.

Tiw Toy Ngoi Khong GUESTHOUSE $$

(084 797 0091; Soi 6, Th Chai Khong; r 1200B) This spotlessly clean place on the river has 10 rooms all tastefully laid out with big double beds. There's no English sign, but it's just across from the Krungthai ATM. The room prices go down considerably (to 500B) in the low season (February to October).

Suk Somboon HOTEL $$

(092 728 5288; 243/3 Th Chai Khong; s/d with breakfast 1000/1500B; P) With lovely river views and lots of dark-wood panelling, this place has a great atmosphere. The beds are big and comfortable.

Norn-Nab-Dao HOTEL $$

(086 792 0215; Th Chai Khong; r incl breakfast 800-1000B; P) Unlike many of the new places going up, this one isn't all timber, but it still has some charm nonetheless. The cutely painted rooms lie around a central courtyard.

Chiang Khan Hill Resort HOTEL $$$

(042 821285; www.chiangkhanhill.com; r 800-4000B; P) The best views of Kaeng Khut Khu are from the town's original

Chiang Khan

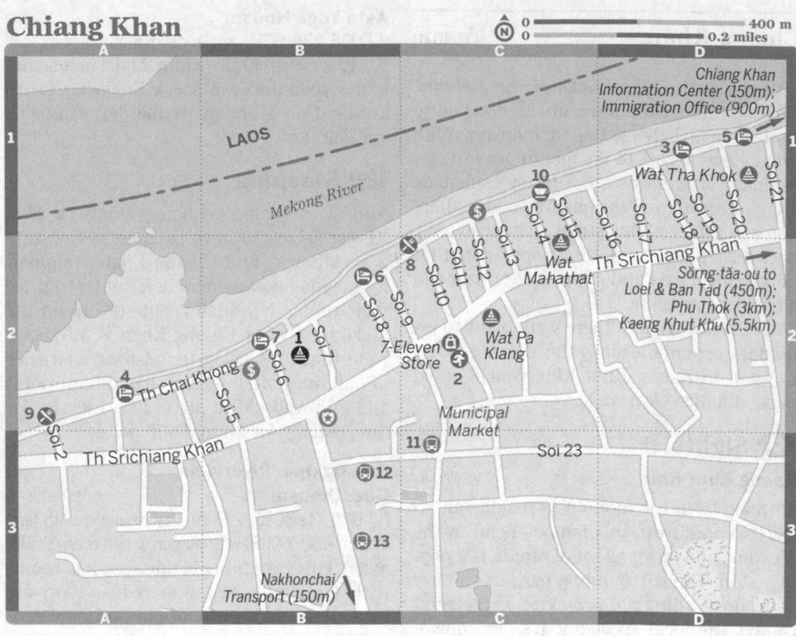

Chiang Khan

Sights

1 Wat Si Khun Mueang B2

Activities, Courses & Tours

2 Asta Yoga House C2

Sleeping

3 Chiangkhan Riverview Guesthouse D1
4 Norn-Nab-Dao A2
5 Old Chiangkhan Boutique Hotel D1
6 Suk Somboon B2
7 Tiw Toy Ngoi Khong B2

Eating

Kit Theung .... (see 6)
8 Rabiang Rim Khong C2
9 Soi Song A2

Drinking & Nightlife

10 Toffee Coffee C1

Transport

11 999 VIP C3
12 Air Muang Loei B3
13 Phu Kradung Tours B3

resort, which overlooks the rapids 5km east of town. The garden setting right on the Mekong adds to the appeal. There's a variety of rooms, ranging from 'row-house' rooms to bungalows, most of which are bright and colourful, and the restaurant is quite good.

Old Chiangkhan Boutique Hotel BOUTIQUE HOTEL $$$
(☎088 340 3999; Soi 20, Th Chai Khong; r with breakfast 1500-1700B) This stately old Thai-style home has tastefully decorated rooms all with double beds. The more expensive rooms have Mekong views.

Eating & Drinking

Soi Song THAI $
(Soi 2, Th Chai Khong; dishes 50-150B; ⏱5pm-midnight) This little place has a bit of everything: it's a restaurant with tables and chairs, a bar with lounge chairs and TV, and a pub with karaoke and snooker. The food, mainly Thai and northeastern dishes, is good and there's an English menu. Local and international beers and cocktails are available.

Rabiang Rim Khong THAI $
(Th Chai Khong; dishes 50-200B; ⏱10am-10pm) This place has been popular with locals since long before the tourism boom. The

prices have risen a bit but the quality has not dropped.

Kit Theung THAI $

(☎042 821064; 243/3 Th Chai Khong; mains 45-200B; ⏰11am-8.30pm) Attached to the Suk Somboon hotel, this restaurant shares the same dark-wood ambience and lovely views of the Mekong. The food is standard-quality Thai fare.

Toffee Coffee CAFE

(Th Chai Khong; ⏰7am-5pm) A cosy little place with nice views to the Mekong and comfortable chairs in which to relax and have a hot or iced coffee. It's attached to the Baansupichaya guesthouse.

Information

There are some full-service banks in town that exchange money, including Krungthai.

Bike hire generally costs 50B per day, while motorcycles are 250B.

Chiang Khan Information Center (Soi 21, Th Chai Khong; ⏰10am-5pm) This tourist office was in the process of moving in to its new location at time of writing, and should be open by the time you read this.

Immigration Office (☎042 821911; Soi 26, Th Chai Khong; ⏰8.30am-4.30pm Mon-Fri) For visa extensions.

Getting There & Away

Sŏrng·tăa·ou to Loei (35B, 1¼ hours) depart about every 15 minutes in the early morning, and then whenever there are enough passengers, from a stop on Th Srichiang Khan (at Soi 26). They also pick up passengers at the market and Rte 201 along the way. Nine 1st-class buses (38B, 45 minutes) leave from the **Nakhonchai Transport** (☎042 821905) terminal on Rte 201. They continue to Khorat (311B, seven hours) via Chaiyaphum (225B).

Three companies, departing from their own offices, make the run to Bangkok (10 hours) in the morning and early evening: **Air Muang Loei** (☎082 642 1629; Th Srichiang Khan Soi 23), **999 VIP** (☎089 893 2898; Soi 9) and **Phu Kradung Tours** (☎089 842 1524; petrol station, Rte 201). Tickets range from 464B to 666B.

No transport runs direct to Nong Khai. The quickest way there is via Loei and Udon Thani, but for the scenic river route take a Loei-bound *sŏrng·tăa·ou* south to Ban Tad (20B, 30 minutes), where you can catch the bus to Nong Khai that leaves Loei at 6am. Another option is to hire a car to take you to Pak Chom (about 700B), from where there are buses to Nong Khai (80B, four hours) at 10am and 3pm. There is a more roundabout way to Pak Chom involving two *sŏrng·tăa·ou*.

If you're heading west and you've got your own wheels, consider following the seldom-seen back roads along Mae Nam Heuang; they'll eventually deposit you in Dan Sai.

Pak Chom ปากชม

Around 70km east of Chiang Khan along the Mekong is the sleepy, remote town of Pak Chom. The town itself is no Chiang Khan, but its natural beauty exceeds that of its more well-known sibling, and a couple of outstanding resorts make this a place worth visiting if you're looking for rustic relaxation and natural charm. The road here from Chiang Khan has excellent views.

Sleeping

★Mekong Riverside Resort & Camping RESORT $$

(☎082 272 7472; www.mekongriverside.com; Hwy 211; villas 1200-1300B; P ❄ 📶) This delightful spot, nestled in a rubber plantation right on the Mekong, gets very positive reviews from travellers. Mike, the owner, is a fount of knowledge on the local area and can give good tips on activities and places to go. The four villas are tastefully designed and comfortable. Camping is also available. You must book in advance.

An evening boat cruise is par for the course, and the resort's restaurant, run by Mike's wife, Khun Ben, does excellent meals (dishes 80B to 400B), including international food.

★Mekong Villas RESORT $$$

(☎089 810 0498; www.mekongvillas.com; Hwy 211; s villa (sleeps 2) 3000B, r in Thai house 4000B, 3-bedroom cottage 10,000B; P ❄ 📶 🏊) If you want a taste of a bygone, genteel Thailand, this is the place for you. The stunning retreat earns kudos not only for its location on a bend in the Mekong, with sweeping views across to Laos, but also for the splendid villas, assembled from traditional Thai stately homes and retaining all the art and ambience of the originals.

There is a restaurant on the grounds that can make meals to order, a pick-up service from Loei airport and the resort's car can be hired for trips. Note that the resort does not accept walk-ins. In fact if you just show up, you probably won't get past the front gate. You need to book in advance.

Getting There & Away

At time of writing there was no direct public transport from Chiang Khan to Pak Chom. You need to get a Loei-bound bus to Ban Tad (25B, 40 minutes) then a bus from there to Pak Chom (45B, 1½ hours). A more convenient way to get there is to hire a car from Chiang Khan (700B). Onwards from Pak Chom there are old, non-air-conditioned buses to Nong Khai (80B, 3½ hours, three times daily).

Phu Ruea National Park

The 121-sq-km **Phu Ruea National Park** (อุทยานแห่งชาติภูเรือ; 088 509 5299, 042 810965; admission 200B; office 5am-8pm daily) is a popular place to escape the heat, offering vast views from the summit (1365m), reached by either a *sŏrng·tăa·ou* or a 1km footpath. For a longer hike to the top, take the easy (but usually overgrown) 2.5km trail from the lower visitor centre to 30m-tall **Nam Tok Huai Phai**, arguably the park's most scenic waterfall, and then keep going another 5.5km.

The park is 50km west of Loei on Rte 203 and buses can drop you in the town of Phu Ruea (55B, one hour), where you'll have to hitch or charter a truck (around 800B, including a few hours' wait) to the park itself. The summit is 8km from the highway.

DAN SAI & THE PHI TA KHON FESTIVAL

The Phi Ta Khon Festival in the village of Dan Sai is a unique event. Combining a Buddhist festival (called Phra Wet) with Bun Bang Fai (the rocket festival), it produces a curious cross between the drunken revelry of Carnival and the spooky imagery of Halloween.

The origins of the festival are shrouded in ambiguity, but some aspects appear to be related to tribal Tai (possibly Tai Dam) spirit cults. The dates for the festival (which occurs in the seventh lunar month, usually June) are divined by Jao Phaw Kuan, a local spirit medium who channels the information from the town's guardian deity. On the first day of the festival Jao Phaw Kuan performs a sacrifice to invite Phra Upakud (an enlightened monk with supernatural powers who chose to transform himself into a block of white marble to live eternally on the bottom of the Man River) to come to town. Locals then don wild costumes and masks for two days of dancing that's fuelled by *lôw kŏw* (rice whisky) and is full of sexual innuendo, before launching the rockets and heading to the temple to listen to sermons on the third day. The **Phi Ta Khon Museum** (พิพิธภัณฑ์ผีตาโขน; Wat Phon Chai, Th Kaew Asa; 8.30am-4.30pm) FREE is a great place to study up on how the masks are made and see some sample costumes up close.

Other attractions in Dan Sai include **Wat Neramit Wiphatsana** (วัดเนรมิตวิปัสสนา; dawn-dusk) FREE, a lovely meditation temple with striking laterite-block buildings just outside town, and nearby **Phra That Si Songrak** (พระธาตุศรีสองรัก; Rte 2113; 7am-5pm) FREE, an important *chedi* built around 1560 on what was then the Thai-Lao border to commemorate a joint resistance of the Ayuthaya and Wiang Chan (Vientiane) kingdoms against the Burmese.

If you want to stay in Dan Sai, **Dansai Resort Hotel** (089 277 1251, 042 892281; Rte 2013; r with fan 300B, with air-con 500-700B; P ❄ 📶) is a reliable and inexpensive option, while the Dan Sai **homestay** (086 862 4812, 042 892339; dm/tw or d 170/550B, with air-con 650B) program gives a great opportunity to stay with Thai families (mostly teachers who can speak a bit of English) and get familiar with local life. The crafts shop **Kawinthip Hattakham** (กวินทิพย์หัตถกรรม; 042 892339; Th Kaew Asa; 8am-7pm), which sells Phi Ta Khon masks and other festival paraphernalia and also hires bikes, has details. For something a little more upmarket, the excellent **PhuNaCome Resort** (042 892005; www.phunacomeresort.com; Rte 2013; r 4200-6000B; P ❄ @ 📶), just out of town, is a kind of luxury-organic place with a great location.

Because the date for festivities is decided each year by the local medium, it is pretty difficult to plan a trip to coincide with the festival. The tourist office is trying to persuade the village to provide advance notice of upcoming dates, but in the meantime you can email the Loei tourist office (p369) for dates.

Dan Sai is 80km east of Loei on the road to Phu Ruea. Buses between Loei (65B to 79B, 1½ hours) and Phitsanulok (73B to 102B, three hours) stop in Dan Sai, near the junction of Th Kaew Asa and Rte 2013, every couple of hours.

Sleeping

There's hot water, all-day electricity and wi-fi at the attractive **campsite** (tent hire 405B;), which also has six comfortable **bungalows** (02 562 0760; www.dnp.go.th/parkreserve; 4/6 people 2000/3000B) with TV and fridge. There are restaurants at the campsite, and many small resorts below the park with cheaper prices. Night-time temperatures can drop to near freezing in December and January, so come prepared.

Thailand Sustainable Yoga Retreat Center MEDITATION RETREAT $
(Kailash Akhara; 087 220 2384; www.dharmainc.org; shared r per person from 250B, private r 650B, cabins 800B) Although not in the national park, Kailash Akhara is in the district of Phu Ruea. This yoga/meditation retreat centre offers something completely different, making maximum use of Loei's bucolic settings with a choice of private cabin accommodation or a shared room in a beautiful guesthouse. Daily meals are provided (300B).

While meditation instruction and structured retreats are provided, established practitioners are also welcome to make use of the retreat centre and its meditation hall for their own practice. The centre offers yoga, meditation, permaculture, Thai massage and ayurveda lessons too, as well as tours.

Kailash Akhara is just off Hwy 203 (the road from Loei to Phu Reua) and about 14km from Phu Reua. A taxi from Phu Reua should cost about 300B.

THE GARDEN OF ISAN

The Phu Ruea region is famous for its flower farms and there's a riot of colours along the roadside. The cool, dry climate allows farmers to grow a variety of crops not common in Isan, such as strawberries, coffee (the Coffee Bun chain is based here and its blend includes Loei-grown beans), macadamia nuts, petunias and persimmon.

If you have realistic expectations of the wine, you might find **Chateau de Loei** (042 809521; Rte 203, Km 61; 8am-5pm) worth a visit. It released the first commercially produced Thai wine in 1995. It's a small operation compared to the attractive and well-managed wineries around Khao Yai, but visitors are welcome to taste its wines and brandies way back in the utilitarian main building.

Phu Kradueng National Park

Phu Kradueng National Park (อุทยานแหงชาติภูกระดึง; 042 870833; adult/child 400/200B; trail to summit 7am-2pm Oct-May) is one of the most popular national parks in Thailand, and spending the night atop Phu Kradueng is something of a rite of passage for many students. Capped by its eponymous peak, the park covers a high-altitude plateau cut through with trails and peppered with cliffs and waterfalls. Rising to 1316m, Thailand's second national park is always cool at its highest reaches (average year-round temperature is 20°C), where its flora is a mix of pine forest and savannah. Various forest animals, including elephants, Asian jackals, Asiatic black bears, sambar deer, serows and white-handed gibbons inhabit the 348-sq-km park.

There's a small visitor centre at the base of the mountain, but almost everything else is up top. The main trail scaling Phu Kradueng is 5.5km in length and takes about three to four hours to climb. It's strenuous, but not too challenging (unless it's wet) since there are steps at most of the steep parts. The hike is quite scenic and there are rest stops with food vendors about every 1km. Once on top, it's another 3km to the main visitor centre. You can hire porters to carry your gear balanced on bamboo poles for 30B per 1kg.

The trail that passes six waterfalls in a forested valley is the most beautiful destination, even after November, when the water has largely dried up. There are also many **clifftop viewpoints**, some ideal for sunrise and sunset, scattered around the mountain.

The park gets unbelievably crowded during school holidays (March to May and especially New Year), but it's closed June to September to allow forest regeneration.

Sleeping & Eating

Atop the mountain there's space for 5000 people to **camp** (per person with own tent 30B, 3-person-tent hire 225B), a variety of large **bungalows** (02 562 0760; www.dnp.go.th/parkreserve; bungalows 900-3600B) and many open-air restaurants. If you're arriving late, there's also camping and bungalows at the bottom.

WORTH A TRIP

THE KUNMING OF THAILAND

Locally billed as Khunming Mueang Thai ('The Thai Kunming'), due to its resemblance to the Stone Forest in Kunming, China, **Suan Hin Pha Ngam** (สวนหินผางาม; ☎042 894254; per group 100B, tractor ride per person 15B; ⏰8.30am-5.30pm) is a beautiful trip, but Kunming it isn't, and if you just ride a tractor up to the easy-to-reach viewpoint for a quick look, you might be disappointed. The real highlight is the walk there or back with your guide through the labyrinthine paths and caves. At times the hour-long route is a little rough and you need to duck through some small passageways, and if it has been raining you might get a little muddy, so be prepared. But the effort is worth it.

A second site in the same forest is a bit more adventurous. The path through **Suan Sawan** (สวนสวรรค์; ☎084 952 0591; Ban Suan Sawan; per group 100B, tractor ride per person 15B; ⏰8.30am-4pm) follows a series of metal walkways over the rocks and through some caves. The trip takes about 45 minutes, and requires a guide (with headlamp). This and the walk to Suan Hin are really the highlights of the trip. **Tham Phothisat** (ถ้ำโพธิสัตว์; per group 100B, tractor ride per person 15B; ⏰8.30am-4pm) is another cave with a similar set-up to Suan Sawan.

The sites are about 15km and 18km respectively southwest of Nong Hin. There's no public transport and hitching is highly impractical. If you want to stay the night, **Chatikorn** (☎086 249 0946; Puan Phu Subdistrict, Nong Hin; r 450-900B; P ⊖ ❄ 📶), just outside the park at the 17 Km marker on the Nong Hin–Suan Hin Pha Ngam road, has simple but comfortable bungalows and a great location, with its own iconic rock nearby.

ℹ Getting There & Away

Buses between Loei (56B, 1½ hours, every 30 minutes) and Khon Kaen (75B, two hours) stop in Phu Kradueng town where *sŏrng·tăa·ou* (20B per person, charters 300B) take people to the base of the mountain, 10km away.

Nong Khai หนองคาย

POP 47,600

Sitting on the banks of the Mekong, just across from Vientiane in Laos, Nong Khai has been popular with travellers for years. Its popularity is about more than just its proximity to Vientiane and bounty of banana pancakes. Seduced by its dreamy pink sunsets and sluggish pace of life, many visitors who mean to stay one night end up bedding down for many more.

History

Wedged between nations, Nong Khai is both a historic and physical bridgehead between Thailand and Laos. The city once fell within the boundaries of the Vientiane (Wiang Chan) kingdom, which itself vacillated between independence and tribute to Lan Xang and Siam. In 1827 Rama III gave a Thai lord, Thao Suwothamma, the rights to establish Meuang Nong Khai at the present city site, which he chose because the surrounding swamps *(nŏrng)* would aid in the city's defence.

The opening of the US$30-million, 1174m-long Saphan Mittaphap Thai-Lao (Thai-Lao Friendship Bridge) in 1992 marked a new era of development for Nong Khai as a regional trade and transport centre.

Sights

★Sala Kaew Ku SCULPTURE PARK

(ศาลาแก้วกู่; admission 20B; ⏰8am-6pm) Yes, it's cheesy, but the sheer size of the sculptures at Sala Kaew Ku can't fail to impress. Built over a period of 20 years by Luang Pu Boun Leua Sourirat, a mystic who died in 1996, the park features a weird and wonderful array of gigantic sculptures ablaze with Hindu-Buddhist imagery.

The main shrine building, almost as strange as the sculptures, is full of images of every description and provenance, photos of Luang Pu at various ages and his corpse lying under a glass dome ringed by flashing lights.

All buses headed east pass the road leading to Sala Kaew Ku (10B), which is also known as Wat Khaek. It's about a five-minute walk from the highway. Chartered túk-túk cost 150B return with a one-hour wait, or you can reach it by bike in about 30 minutes. A map handed out at the Mut Mee Guesthouse shows the scenic route. We suggest avoiding the touristy crocodile show near the entrance.

Wat Pho Chai BUDDHIST TEMPLE

(วัดโพธิ์ชัย; Th Phochai; ⏲7am-7.30pm) FREE Luang Po Phra Sai, a large Lan Xang–era Buddha image awash with gold, bronze and precious stones, sits at the hub of Nong Khai's holiest temple. The head of the image is pure gold, the body is bronze and the *ùt·sà·nít* (flame-shaped head ornament) is set with rubies. Due to the great number of miracles attributed to it, this royal temple is a mandatory stop for most visiting Thais.

Luang Po Phra Sai was one of three similar statues made for each of the daughters of Lao King Setthathirat, and they were taken as bounty after King Rama I sacked Vientiane in 1778. The awesome murals in the hall housing the Buddha image depict their travels from the interior of Laos to the banks of the Mekong, where they were put on rafts. A storm sent one of the statues to the bottom of the river, where it remains today. It was never recovered because, according to one monk at the temple, the *naga* (which lives in the river) wanted to keep it. The third statue, Phra Soem, is at Wat Pathum Wanaram, next to Siam Paragon in Bangkok. Phra Sai was supposed to accompany it, but, as the murals show, the cart carrying it broke down here and so this was taken as a sign that it wished to remain in Nong Khai.

Nong Khai Aquarium AQUARIUM

(พิพิธภัณฑ์สัตว์น้ำจังหวัดหนองคาย; admission 100B; ⏲10am-6pm Tue-Sun) First impressions may not overwhelm at this aquarium, as some of the early displays look a little shabby, but the further you go the more interesting it gets, especially the impressive giant Mekong river tank. A highlight is the 'feeding the man to the fish' performance every day at 2pm and also at 11am on Saturdays, Sundays and public holidays. It's far out of town on the Khon Kaen University campus and not served by public transport.

Tha Sadet Market MARKET

(ตลาดท่าเสด็จ; Th Rimkhong; ⏲8.30am-6pm) This covered market. is the most popular destination in town and almost everyone loves a stroll through it. It offers the usual mix of clothes, electronic equipment, food and assorted bric-a-brac, most of it imported from Laos and China, but there are also a few shops selling quirky quality stuff.

Wat Lam Duan BUDDHIST TEMPLE

(วัดลำดวน; Th Rimkhong; ⏲dawn-dusk) FREE You can easily pick out this temple on the skyline because an immense Buddha image sits atop

Around Nong Khai

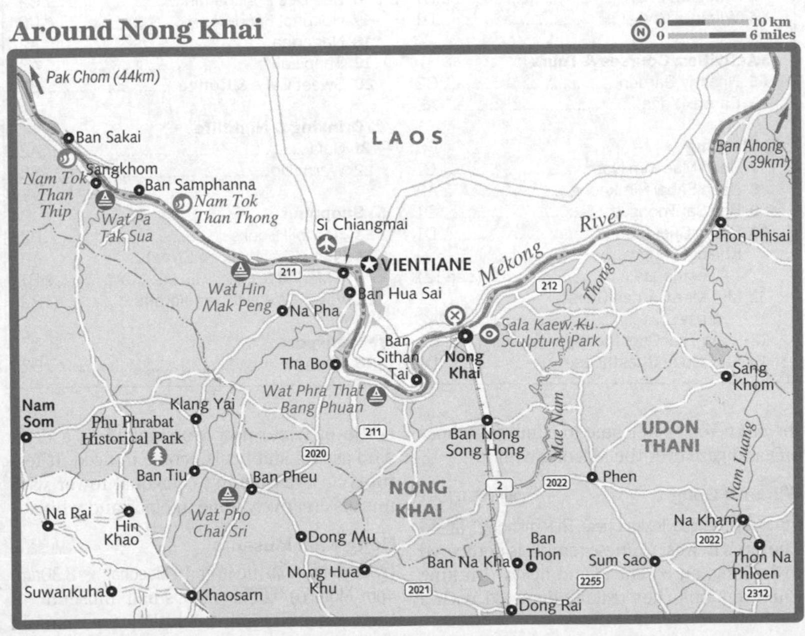

Central Nong Khai

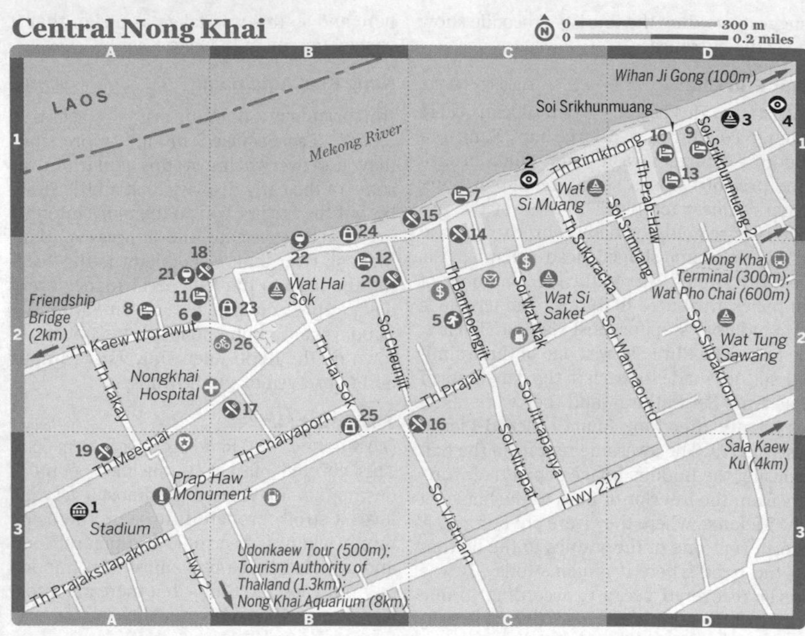

Central Nong Khai

Sights
1 Nong Khai Museum A3
2 Tha Sadet Market C1
3 Wat Lam Duan D1
4 Wihan Ji Gong D1

Activities, Courses & Tours
5 Healthy Garden C2
6 Pantrix Yoga A2

Sleeping
7 Baan Mae Rim Nam C1
8 Baan Sabai Rimkhong A2
9 Ban Sai Thong D1
10 E-San Guesthouse D1
Khiangkhong Guesthouse .... (see 12)
11 Mut Mee Garden Guest House A2
12 Ruan Thai Guesthouse B2
13 Sawasdee Guesthouse D1

Eating
14 Café Thasadej C1
15 Daeng Namnuang C1
16 Dee Dee Pohchanah C2
17 Hospital Food Court B2
18 Nagarina A2
19 Saap Lah A3
20 Sweet Cake & Coffee B2

Drinking & Nightlife
21 Gaia A2
22 Warm Up B2

Shopping
23 Hornbill Books B2
24 Nong Khai Walking Street Market B1
25 Village Weaver Handicrafts B2

Transport
26 Khun Noui B2

the *bóht*. You're welcome to climb up (shoes off) and gaze over the Mekong with it.

Wihan Ji Gong CHINESE TEMPLE

(วิหารจี้กง; Sanjao Tekka Chee; Th Rimkhong) FREE The city's newest Chinese temple is dedicated to Ji Gong, an eccentric and heavy-drinking Chinese monk (he's usually depicted with a bottle of wine) now worshipped as a deity who assists and heals people in need. It features an eye-catching octagonal tower with murals creatively done in black and white.

Nong Khai Museum MUSEUM

(พิพิธภัณฑ์จังหวัดหนองคาย; Th Meechai; ⏲8.30am-4pm Mon-Fri) FREE This small museum in the former city hall has little more than old photographs, but there's enough English labelling to make it worth a few minutes of your time, and the price is right.

Activities

Healthy Garden MASSAGE
(042 423323; Th Banthoengjit; Thai/foot massage per hr 170/200B; 8am-8pm) For the most effective massage in Nong Khai, this place has foot massage and traditional Thai massage in air-conditioned rooms.

Pantrix Yoga YOGA
(www.pantrix.net; Soi Mutmee) Pantrix offers seven-day yoga courses through Mut Mee Garden Guest House for serious students. The courses start on the 1st and 15th day of each month except May and December. The one-week courses are run by qualified yoga instructors who have been teaching for many years, and cost 7700B (they are not live-in courses).

More details can be found on the website or through Mut Mee.

Festivals & Events

During Songkran the priceless image of Luang Po Phra Sai from Wat Pho Chai is paraded around town.

Like many other cities in the northeast, Nong Khai has a **rocket festival** *(bun bâng fai),* which begins on Visakha Bucha day in late May/early June.

At the end of Buddhist Lent (Ork Phansaa) in late October/early November, there are **long-boat races** on the Mekong. These correspond with the October full moon, which is when *naga* fireballs (p380) can be seen.

One particularly fun event is Nong Khai's version of the **Chinese Dragon Festival**, held over 10 days, usually in November, with dragon dancing, acrobatics, Chinese opera and lots of firecrackers.

The **Anu Sahwaree Prap Haw Festival** (5 to 15 March) boasts the city's biggest street fair.

Sleeping

Catering to the steady flow of backpackers, Nong Khai's budget lodging selection is the best in Isan.

★**Mut Mee Garden Guest House** GUESTHOUSE $
(042 460717; www.mutmee.com; 1111/4 Th Kaew Worawut; s & d without bathroom 200-300B, d 300-420B, d with air-con 600-1400B;) Occupying a sleepy stretch of the Mekong, Nong Khai's budget classic has a garden so relaxing it's intoxicating, and most nights it's packed with travellers. Mut Mee caters to many budgets, with a huge variety of rooms (the cheapest with shared bathroom, the most expensive with an awesome balcony) clustered around a thatched-roof restaurant with expansive views of the Mekong.

The owner, Julian, freely shares his wealth of knowledge about sights and legends of the local area.

Ban Sai Thong GUESTHOUSE $
(081 975 6451; Soi 2, Th Meechai; r 600B) This newly opened traditional Thai-style home has nine rooms surrounding an open courtyard. The house has a lovely design and the rooms are spacious and have rustic verandahs with sitting areas facing onto the courtyard. There are free bikes. Price includes morning coffee and *kôw tanyápêut,* a mix of sticky rice and other grains.

It's the best of the converted Thai houses in this area.

E-San Guesthouse GUESTHOUSE $
(086 242 1860; 538 Soi Srikhunmuang; r with fan & shared bathroom 250B, with air-con 450B;) Just off the river in a small, beautifully restored wooden house ringed by a long verandah, this is an atmospheric place to stay. Bikes are free.

Ruan Thai Guesthouse GUESTHOUSE $
(042 412519; Th Rimkhong; r with fan/air-con 300/400B;) Popular for its good prices, convenient location, regular maintenance and friendly vibe. There's a mix of fan and air-con rooms, plus one wooden cottage and some flower-filled garden greenery.

Baan Sabai Rimkhong HOTEL $
(042 413545; www.baansabairimkhong.com; Th Kaew Worawut; r 490-590B, with river views 690B;) This new riverside place is a tad odd, but the prices are fair for what you get. Although it's a new building, there are a few rough spots and things may not work the way you'd expect, but the location and the view from the lobby terrace more than make up for it.

Khiangkhong Guesthouse HOTEL $
(042 422870; Th Rimkhong; r with fan/air-con 300/400B;) Catch a refreshing breeze and snag some river views from the 3rd-floor terrace (and some of the rooms) at this

GREAT BALLS OF FIRE

Methane gas? Drunken Lao soldiers? Clever monks? Or perhaps the fiery breath of the sacred *naga*, a legendary serpent-like being that populates waterways throughout Southeast Asia. Since 1983 (or for ages, depending on who you ask) the sighting of the *bâng fai pá·yah·nâhk* (loosely translated, '*naga* fireworks') has been an annual event along the Mekong River. Sometime in the early evening, at the end of the Buddhist Rains Retreat (October), which coincides with the 15th waxing moon of the 11th lunar month, small reddish balls of fire shoot from the Mekong River and float 100-or-so metres into the air before vanishing without a trace. Most claim the *naga* fireballs are soundless, but others say a hissing can be heard if you're close enough to where they emerge from the surface of the river. Most Thai and Lao see the event as a sign that resident *naga* are celebrating the end of the holiday.

There are many theories about the fireballs. One, which aired on a Thai exposé-style TV program, claimed that Lao soldiers taking part in festivities on the other side of the Mekong were firing their rifles into the air. Interestingly, the reaction to the TV program was a storm of protest from both sides of the river. Some suggest that a mixture of methane gas and phosphane, trapped below the mud on the river bottom, somehow reaches a certain temperature at exactly that time of year and is released. Many simply assume that some monks have found a way to make a 'miracle'. The latter was the premise behind a 2002 comedy film entitled *Sip Hah Kam Deuan Sip-et* (Fifteenth Waxing Moon of the Eleventh Lunar Month), released with English subtitles under the peculiar title *Mekhong Full Moon Party*.

Naga fireballs have become big business in Nong Khai Province, and curious Thais from across the country converge at various spots on the banks of the Mekong for the annual show. Little Phon Phisai, the locus of fireball-watching, hosts around 40,000 guests. Special buses (cheap or free) make the return trip to Nong Khai city, and several hotels run their own buses, where you'll get a guaranteed seat. Mut Mee Garden Guest House (p379) sails its boat there and back (2800B, including lunch and dinner).

If you don't come with the right mindset, you'll likely be disappointed. The fireball experience is more than just watching a few small lights rise from the river; it's mostly about watching Thais watching a few small lights rise from the river. And even if the *naga* doesn't send his annual greeting on the day you come (it's sometimes delayed by a day due to the vagaries of calculating the arrival of the full moon), it'll be an interesting experience.

family-run concrete tower that falls between guesthouse and hotel. The terraces are really nice. Bicycles are 30B per day.

Sawasdee Guesthouse GUESTHOUSE $
(042 420259; www.sawasdeeguesthouse.com; 402 Th Meechai; r with fan & shared bathroom 200-220B, with air-con 450-650B;) If you could judge a hotel by its cover, this charismatic guesthouse in an old Franco-Chinese shophouse would come up trumps. The tidy rooms mostly lack the old-school veneer of the exterior and lobby, but they're tidy and fairly priced. Rooms are set around an open courtyard that's great for lounging. Bicycles are 40B per day, motorbikes 250B.

Baan Mae Rim Nam HOTEL $$
(042 420256, 081 873 0636; www.baanmaerimnam.com; Soi Kheuan 3, Mekong Promenade; d 500-800B, tr 800-1100B;) Tucked down a soi right in the Tha Sadet Market and right on the riverfront, this bright-yellow building has great rooms with balconies and river views. The cheaper standard rooms out back, however, are less inviting.

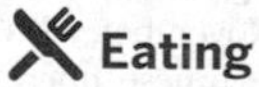

Eating

There are many restaurants in the Tha Sadet Market, and elsewhere along the promenade, that serve big river views.

★**Dee Dee Pohchanah** THAI $
(Th Prajak; dishes 45-250B; 10.30am-2am) How good is Dee Dee? Just look at the dinnertime crowds. Despite having a full house every night, this simple place is a well-oiled machine and you won't be waiting long.

Sweet Cake & Coffee THAI $
(Th Meechai; dishes 50-100B; 6am-9pm;) It's hard to categorise this place, run by a sweet old lady who makes standard Thai

dishes and also many international favourites such as baked cakes and banana pancakes. Enjoy the homely atmosphere for breakfast, lunch or dinner, or just a coffee (instant, brewed or traditional Thai).

Saap Lah THAI $

(Th Meechai; dishes 25-150B; ⌚7am-8pm) For excellent *gài yâhng, sôm·đam* and other Isan foods, follow your nose to this no-frills shop.

Daeng Namnuang VIETNAMESE $

(Th Rimkhong; dishes 60-130B; ⌚8am-8pm; P 📶) This massive river restaurant has grown into an Isan institution, and hordes of out-of-towners head home with car boots and carry-on bags (there's an outlet at Udon Thani's airport) stuffed with *năam neu·ang* (pork spring rolls).

Hospital Food Court THAI $

(Th Meechai; dishes 30-50B; ⌚7am-3pm) Don't be put off by the name – it isn't 'hospital food'. Located across from the hospital, this food court whips up Thai standards at low prices. The food is delicious, there's plenty of choice and it is conveniently located near the most popular guesthouses in town.

Nagarina THAI $$

(☎042 412211; Th Rimkhong; dishes around 100B, meals 200B; ⌚10am-9pm; 📶 ✎) Mut Mee Garden Guest House's floating restaurant, which specialises in fish, turns out the real deal. There's a sunset cruise most nights (100B; at least 10 guests needed before the cruise will go ahead) around 5pm; order food at least 30 minutes before departure.

Café Thasadej INTERNATIONAL $$

(Th Banthoengjit; dishes 60-375B; ⌚8am-late) At this little restaurant both the menu and liquor list – the latter among the best in town – span the globe.

Drinking & Nightlife

For something completely Thai, follow the Mekong-hugging Th Rimkhong east past Tha Sadet Market and you will pass a bevy of restaurants and bars, some earthy, some fashionable, churning out dinner and drinks. There are some expat-owned bars around here, too.

Gaia BAR

(Th Rimkhong; ⌚7pm-late) Much of the Mut Mee crowd, and many resident *fa·ràng*, fill this laid-back floating bar on the Mekong. There's a great drinks list, a chilled vibe and sometimes live music. It often hosts fundraisers for local charitable projects.

Warm Up BAR

(Th Rimkhong) This little place rises above, both figuratively and literally, the other bars at this end of Th Rimkhong. It looks out over the river, has a pool table and is popular with both locals and travellers.

Shopping

Village Weaver Handicrafts HANDICRAFTS

(1020 Th Prajak) This place sells high-quality, handwoven fabrics and clothing (ready-made or made to order) that help fund development projects around Nong Khai. The *mát·mèe* cotton is particularly good here.

Nong Khai Walking Street Market MARKET

(⌚4pm-10pm Sat) This street festival featuring music, handmade items and food takes over the promenade every Saturday night.

Hornbill Books BOOKS

(Soi Mut Mee; ⌚10am-7pm Mon-Sat) Buys, sells and trades books in English, French and other languages. Also sells coffee and has internet access.

Information

There are banks with extended opening hours and AEON ATMs at **Asawann** (Hwy 2; ⌚10am-9pm) shopping centre.

Immigration (☎042 990935; ⌚8.30am-noon & 1-4.30pm Mon-Fri) South of the Friendship Bridge. Offers Thai visa extensions.

Nongkhai Hospital (☎042 413461; Th Meechai) Has a 24-hour casualty department.

Tourism Authority of Thailand (TAT; ☎042 421326; tat_nongkhai@yahoo.com; Hwy 2; ⌚8.30am-4.30pm) Inconveniently located outside of town.

Getting There & Away

AIR

The nearest airport is 55km south in Udon Thani.

Udonkaew Tour (☎042 411530; Th Pranang Cholpratan; ⌚8.30am-5.30pm) travel agency runs minivans (150B per person) to/from the airport. Coming into town it'll drop you at your hotel or the bridge; going back you need to get yourself to its office. It's best to buy tickets in advance.

BUS

Nong Khai bus terminal (☎042 412679) is located just off Th Prajak, about 1.5km from the main pack of riverside guesthouses. Udon Thani (40B to 45B, one hour, every 30

GETTING TO LAOS: NONG KHAI TO VIENTIANE

This is one of the busiest Thai border crossings.

Getting to the border If you already have your Lao visa, the easiest way to Vientiane is the direct bus from Nong Khai's bus terminal (55B, one hour, six daily). There's also a bus to Vang Vieng (270B, four hours, 10am). The 5B surcharge for tickets to Laos on weekends, holidays and the 7.30am and 6pm weekday services is genuine.

If you plan to get your visa at the border (6am to 10pm), take a túk-túk there – expect to pay 100B from the bus station, but you can pay 50B from the town centre. Unless you're travelling in a large group, there's no good reason to use a visa service agency, so don't let a driver take you to one.

You can also go to Laos by train (there are immigration booths at both stations), though it doesn't go through to Vientiane, so we strongly recommend against doing it. The 15-minute ride (20B to 30B, departs 9am and 2.45pm) drops you in Thanaleng (aka Dongphasay) station just over the bridge, leaving you at the mercy of túk-túk drivers who charge extortionate prices.

At the border After getting stamped out of Thailand, you can take the minibuses (weekdays/weekends 20/30B) that carry passengers across the bridge to the hassle-free, but sometimes busy, Lao immigration checkpoint, where 30-day visas are available.

Moving on It's about 20km to Vientiane. Plenty of buses, túk-túk and taxis will be waiting for you and it's easy to find fellow travellers to share the costs.

minutes) is the most frequent destination. For those travelling west along the Mekong, there are buses to Sangkhom (60B, three hours, 7.30am, 1pm and 3pm), with the 7.30am bus continuing all the way to Loei (130B, 6½ hours). There are also buses to Khon Kaen (119B to 176B, 3½ hours, hourly), Nakhon Phanom (200B, 6½ hours, two daily), and Kanchanaburi (530B to 840B, 10 hours, 8am and 5.30pm) and minivans to Udon Thani (50B, 45 minutes, hourly) and Bueng Kan (100B to 150B, 2½ hours, eight daily).

Bangkok (380B to 490B, 11 hours) bus services are frequent in the late afternoon and early evening, but less so during the day. **Nakhonchai Air** (☎042 420285), **Chan Tour** (☎042 460205) and **999 VIP** (☎042 412679) offer VIP buses (around 720B to 760B). There's also one bus direct to Suvarnabhumi (Airport) bus station (495B, nine hours, 8pm). For Chiang Mai, you have to change at Udon's Bus Terminal 2.

TRAIN

Three express trains, one in the morning and two in the afternoon, connect Bangkok (seat 103B to 498B, 1st-class sleeper upper/lower 1117/1317B, 11½ hours) and **Nong Khai train station** (☎042 411637), which is 2km west of the city centre. There's also one cheaper evening rapid train.

Getting Around

Nong Khai is a great place for cycling due to the limited traffic and the nearby countryside. Many guesthouses let you use their bikes for free. If you need to hire one, **Khun Noui** (☎081 975 4863; Th Kaew Worawut; ⏲8am-4pm), who sets up on the roadside across from the entrance to Mut Mee, has reliable bikes (50B per day) and motorcycles (200B).

You can find metered taxis at the bus station and the bridge. Generally people agree on a price rather than use the meter. A túk-túk between the Mut Mee area and either the bus station or bridge should be 40B to 50B.

West of Nong Khai

A couple of significant temples and a lovely Mekong river town west of Nong Khai are worth a visit.

Wat Phra That Bang Phuan

Wat Phra That Bang Phuan BUDDHIST TEMPLE
(วัดพระธาตุบังพวน; ⏲dawn-dusk) Boasting a beautiful *chedi* that locals believe holds 29 Buddha relics, Wat Phra That Bang Phuan is one of the region's most sacred temples. Nobody knows when the first stupa was erected here, but after moving his capital from Luang Prabang to Vientiane in 1560, Lan Xang King Setthathirat commissioned grand temples to be built all around his kingdom, including a new stupa built here over an older one.

Rain caused it to lean precariously and in 1970 it toppled. It was rebuilt in 1977. The current one stands 34m high on a 17-sq-metre base and has many unsurfaced *chedi* around it, as well as a *naga* pond, giving the temple an ancient atmosphere, and it's this, much more than the main stupa, that makes a trip here rewarding.

The temple is 22km from Nong Khai on Rte 211. Take a Pak Chom–bound bus (20B, 45 minutes).

Wat Hin Mak Peng

Wat Hin Mak Peng BUDDHIST TEMPLE
(วัดหินหมากเป้ง; 6am-7pm) FREE Overlooking a lovely stretch of the Mekong, this vast forest temple is centred on a cliff rising out of the river. The very peaceful temple is respected by Thais because of their reverence for the founding abbot, Ajahn Thet, a disciple of Ajahn Mun Bhuridatto (p428). Several monuments in his honour, including a lifelike wax statue and a glistening *chedi,* are found around the grounds. Visitors must dress politely: no shorts above the knees or sleeveless tops.

The temple is midway between Si Chiangmai and Sangkhom. Sangkhom-bound buses from Nong Khai (50B, 2¼ hours) pass the entrance, and then it's a longish walk to the buildings.

Sangkhom สังคม

POP 3500

The little town of Sangkhom (officially named Ban Chueang), facing the Lao island of Don Klang Khong, makes a great rest stop for those following the Mekong between Nong Khai and Loei. Staring at the lovely scenery tends to dominate visitors' time here, but there are also some wonderful attractions around town.

Sights

Three-tiered **Nam Tok Than Thip** waterfall, 13km west of Sangkhom (2km off Rte 211), is the largest waterfall in the area. The lower level drops 30m and the second level, easily reached on stairs, falls 100m. The 70m top drop is barely visible through the lush forest. **Nam Tok Than Thong** waterfall, 12km east of Sangkhom, is a wider but shorter drop. Than Thong is more accessible than Than Thip, but can be rather crowded on weekends and holidays. Bear in mind that, like most Isan waterfalls, these are seasonal. Both are at full flow around July to September and dry up by February.

MEKONG BLUES

The Mekong River (in Thai, Mae Nam Khong) runs more than 4000km from the Tibetan Plateau in China to the Mekong Delta in Vietnam. It's one of the world's great rivers, and along the 800-plus kilometres of the Thai–Lao border offers some rugged and at times spectacular scenery.

The vast quantity of water makes it a priceless resource, not only for riverside villages and fisheries (it's the world's largest inland fishery) but also for hydropower companies. It is the latter that have become a potential problem for the river's future. Everyone wants a bit of that power. In an attempt to have some sort of governance over the damming of the Mekong, the Mekong River Commission was established by the governments of Cambodia, Thailand, Laos and Vietnam. The commission (in theory, at least) also works with the governments of China and Myanmar to moderate development along the river. In spite of this, hydroelectric projects are mushrooming, and at time of writing there were no less than 150 more dams being planned for the Mekong Basin, including 11 major dams proposed for the lower mainstream Mekong (the Lao, Thai and Cambodian share). This is in addition to the 82 dams that already exist.

The impact of development has already affected villages that sit alongside the river and have had to make way for the dams. In addition, water levels rise and fall dramatically dependent on dam activity, leading to flash floods. The impact on fisheries is great, with the construction of a dam creating a new ecosystem. So far the impact in Thailand has not been a major issue, but the long-term effects cannot be ignored. Hydropower is billed as 'clean' energy, but it comes at a high cost. Though it bites rural people (who benefit least from the power generated) more than the urban populations who consume most of the power, in the long term it will affect everyone.

Wat Pha Tak Sua BUDDHIST TEMPLE

(วัดผาตากเสื้อ; dawn-dusk) FREE The forest wát peering down on the town, Wat Pha Tak Sua lies just 2km away as the crow flies, but it's 19km to drive. It has amazing Mekong views; you might see the valley filled with fog on early mornings during the cold season. The footpath used by the monks every morning begins east of town just before the Km 81 pillar. Follow Soi 5 past the last house, then veer right by the mango and papaya trees.

Sleeping

★Bouy Guesthouse GUESTHOUSE $

(042 441065; toy_bgh@hotmail.com; Rte 211; r with fan 250B, with air-con 400B;) As the ever-smiling owners will tell you, Sangkhom's veteran lodge has just a few 'simple huts', but they're popular for good reason. They come with hammocks and wooden decks and the riverside location, just west of town, is wonderfully relaxing. Bike/motorbike hire is 50/200B and river trips are available. There's a restaurant, but it's not always open.

Poopae Ruenmaithai HOTEL $$

(042 441088; Rte 211; r 700-900B;) This attractive set-up, featuring wooden walkways and decorative stonework, will satisfy those who demand a certain level of comfort. Many rooms have river views and the restaurant is good. It's 1.5km east of the town centre.

Getting There & Away

There are three rickety fan-cooled buses a day from Nong Khai (60B, three hours) and the earliest of those continues all the way to Loei (70B, 3½ hours). There's no bus stop in town; wave buses down when they pass.

Udon Thani Province

Udon Thani Province is dominated by its flashy, progressive capital, but the World Heritage-listed Ban Chiang, charming Red Lotus Sea and the mysterious Phu Phrabat ensure the province is no slouch when it comes to attractions.

Udon Thani อุดรธานี

POP 143,390

Udon Thani is a big, brash city with one of the largest expat populations in Thailand. The city boomed on the back of the Vietnam War as the site of one of the largest US air bases, and it subsequently became the region's primary transport hub and commercial centre. The town itself doesn't have many must-see attractions, but there are some interesting spots in the surrounding region.

Sights

Sanjao Pu-Ya CHINESE TEMPLE

(ศาลเจ้าปู่ย่า; Th Nittayo; dawn-dusk) FREE This large, garish Chinese temple on the southern shore of Nong Bua attests to the wealth of the local Thai-Chinese merchant class. At its heart, the Pu-Ya Shrine houses small images of the Chinese gods Pu (Grandpa) and Ya (Grandma).

In front of the temple is the impressive **Udon Thani Thai-Chinese Cultural Center** (ศูนย์วัฒนธรรมไทย-จีน; Th Nittayo; 9am-7pm) FREE. It features a large garden and the **Moral Museum**, which has excellent displays about the history of the Chinese community in Udon Thani, Chinese culture and Confucius. The Pu-Ya Chinese Orchestra plays Wednesday and Friday from 5pm, and a smaller group performs Saturday and Sunday at 1pm.

Udon Sunshine Orchid Farm GARDENS

(สวนกล้วยไม้อุดรซันไฌน์; 085 747 4144; 127 Th Udorn-Nong Samrong; 8am-5pm) FREE The Udon Sunshine Orchid Farm, just northwest of town, earned fame for developing an aromatic breed of orchid and producing the first orchid-based perfume. It has since developed a hybrid of *Codariocalyx motorius ohashi leguminosae*, a succulent that 'dances' to music. If you sing or talk to the plant in a high-pitched voice, a few smaller leaves will shift back and forth. The plants are most active from November to February and from 7am to 9.30am and 4.30pm to 6.30pm.

You can buy Udon Dancing Tea (now very popular for its supposed medical benefits; each batch sells out quickly), made from the plant, along with the Miss Udon Sunshine orchids and perfumes.

To get here, go to the 'Welcome to Nongsamrong Community' sign on Rte 2024, then after 150m follow the 'Udorn Sunshine Fragrant Orchid' sign. *Sŏrng·tăa·ou* 6 and the 'yellow bus' get you close to it. A túk-túk from Udon's city centre should cost 60B to 70B.

Nong Prajak Park PARK

(สวนสาธารณะหนองประจักษ์) Udon's most popular park starts to rev up as the afternoon winds down. Much of the action takes place on the sunset-watching side of the lake, along Th Thesa. Dozens of streetside **massage** (10am-10pm) artists begin rub-downs around 10am, and paint-your-own pottery shops join in around 4pm. There's a **bike-hire** (1/2/3 seaters per hr 20/40/50B; 8am-8pm) shop on the northeast shore.

Ho Chi Minh Educational & Tourism Historical Site MUSEUM

(แหล่งศึกษาและท่องเที่ยวเชิงประวัติศาสตร์ (โฮจิมินห์); 8am-4pm) FREE During 1928 and 1929, Ho Chi Minh used the jungle around Nong Hang village as one of his bases to train soldiers and rally Isan's sizeable Vietnamese community for his resistance against the French occupation of Vietnam. This is a replica of his thatched-roof, mud-wall house, plus a big museum, which may be of interest if you are into recent Vietnamese history.

Bâhn lung hoh (Uncle Ho's House), as locals call it, is 10km from Udon. You can get nearby on *sŏrng·tăa·ou* 14 (13B, 30 minutes), which parks on Th Prajak across from Precha Night Market and runs west on Th Wattananuwong and south along Th Mukkamontri before heading out of town. It's a 750m walk from the signed junction.

Festivals & Events

For the first 15 days of December, Udon celebrates the **Thung Si Meuang Fair**, with Isan cultural performances and all the usual shopping and eating. The Pu and Ya statues from Sanjao Pu-Ya spend the first 10 days in a temporary temple in City Field. The transfers on 1 and 10 December are grand processions accompanied by a 99m-long dragon; there's also dragon dancing on 5 December.

Sleeping

The One HOTEL $

(042 244330; www.theoneud.com; Th Prajak Sinlapacom; d/tw 550/600B; P ❄ ☎) This place has modern, comfortable rooms and good security. Its location, central and near the action but away from the sleaze, is its best feature.

Intara Resort HOTEL $

(042 930490; 263/8 Soi San Chao Puya; s/d incl breakfast 500/550B; P ❄ ☎) In typical Thai style this is a resort in name only, but for the price it has a lot more atmosphere than other budget places, with surrounding gardens and nice touches such as free bicycles for guests' use. The rooms are very clean and spacious.

Top Mansion HOTEL $

(042 345015; topmansion@yahoo.com; 35/3 Th Sampanthamit; r 450-790B; P ❄ @ ☎) This popular hotel is so impressively spick and span it warrants consideration, despite being on sleazy 'Soi Falang'.

P & Mo Guesthouse GUESTHOUSE $

(081 380 1952; www.pmo-udon.com; Th Rung Sun; s/d 400/590B; ❄ @ ☎) Rooms are simple, but this friendly place is better than average value and the best of the budget hotels near the bus station. Despite its location, most rooms are in the back of the building and thus quiet.

Ban Pannarai HOTEL $

(042 304001; Th Poniyom; r with fan/air-con 300/440B; ❄ ☎) In contrast to most older hotels in Thailand, this unmissable yellow building a little way in from the street has some actual character. It could use some new mattresses, but if you want to stay near the lake on a budget, this is a good choice. Very little English is spoken. Bicycles for hire for 20B per hour.

P Mansion HOTEL $

(089 554 8636; www.pmansion-udon.com; 44/40 Th Phosri; r 400B) This newly built place not far from the bus terminal is a little less sleazy than some of the places nearby and has decent, clean rooms. They're good value and long-term rates are available.

★ **Much-che Manta** HOTEL $$

(042 245222; www.much-chemanta.com; Th Makkang; r incl breakfast 900-1600B; P ❄ @ ☎ ≋) A lovely boutique hotel that uses creative lighting, liberal use of real wood and random splashes of colour to craft a unique design. The lovely and relaxing backyard restaurant features wood-fired pizzas as part of an international menu. There is a free airport pick-up and drop-off service for guests.

Centara HOTEL $$$

(042 343555; www.centarahotelsresorts.com; Th Prajak Sinlapacom; r/ste incl breakfast 2800/5800B; P ❄ @ ☎ ≋) This large, sumptuous hotel makes a good impression in the lobby, with its attentive staff and nearby restaurant. Those impressions continue when you go up to the rooms, which are

Udon Thani

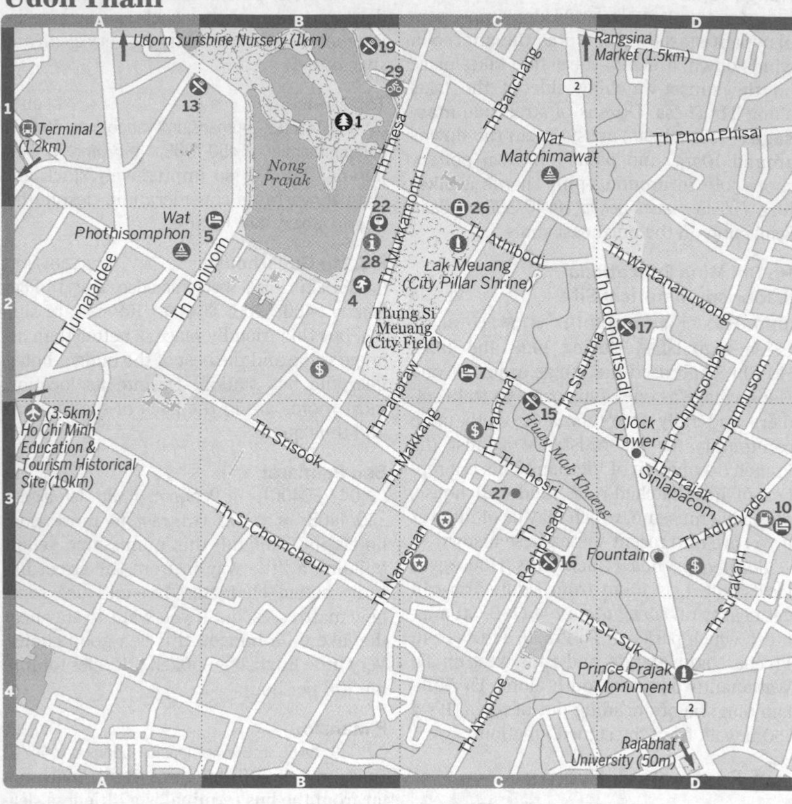

Udon Thani

Sights
1 Nong Prajak Park B1
2 Sanjao Pu-Ya F4
3 Udon Thani Thai-Chinese Cultural Center F4

Activities, Courses & Tours
4 Massage B2

Sleeping
5 Ban Pannarai B2
6 Centara E3
7 Much-che Manta C2
8 P & Mo Guesthouse E3
9 P Mansion E4
10 The One D3
11 Top Mansion E3

Eating
12 Centre Point Night Market F3
13 Good Everything A1
14 Khai Tun E4
15 Kungfu Restaurant C3
16 Maeya C3
17 Papagallo D2
18 Preecha Night Market E3
19 Rabiang Phatchanee B1
20 UD Bazaar F3

Drinking & Nightlife
21 Gib Shop E3
22 Juice Bars B2

Shopping
23 Central Plaza E3
24 Fuzzy Ken's E3
25 UD Town F4
26 Udon City Walking Street C2

Information
27 Immigration C3
28 Tourism Authority of Thailand B2

Transport
29 Bike Hire B1
30 Bus Terminal 1 .... E4
31 Chan Tour E3
32 On Time E4

stationed around a cavernous courtyard that is eerily quiet and yet strangely attractive. The rooms are a bit worn, though.

Eating & Drinking

Udonites take their night markets very seriously. The three adjoining markets in front of the train station, **Centre Point** (4pm-10pm), **Preecha** (4pm-10pm) and UD Bazaar, offer an impressive spread of food and large beer gardens.

UD Bazaar NORTHEASTERN THAI $
(Th Prajak Sinlapacom; dishes from 50B; 11am-11pm) This lively place is a great spot to get some decent cheap food. It's chock-full of vendors selling a big variety of Thai dishes and there's a stage for live music shows as well.

Khai Tun THAI $
(042 343966; 539/14 Th Nittayo; buffet 75B; 9am-10pm) The crowds are 'exhibit A' for how tasty (and cheap) this all-you-can-eat buffet is. The food, usually with some rice, noodles, curries and sweets to choose from, is great value for money.

Kungfu Restaurant BREAKFAST, CHINESE $
(042 343395; 98 Th Prajak Sinlapacom; breakfast 75B; 10am-10pm; P) This place is billed as a Chinese restaurant, but we love it for the breakfast. Here you can get good-quality Udon-style breakfasts with *kôw đôm* (boiled rice), *jòk* (rice gruel), *kài gràtá* (fried eggs served in a pan) and brewed coffee.

★ **Maeya** THAI $$
(Th Rachpusadu; dishes 55-355B; 9.10am-10.30pm; P) This delightful place defies categories. The interior decor looks like a mixture of Moroccan and art nouveau, with its whimsical tiling and frosted windows. The waiters all dress formally in black ties, and the menu stretches from grilled cheese to wild boar in red-curry sauce. It's a busy place for good reason: the food is great.

Rabiang Phatchanee THAI $$
(Th Suppakitchanya; dishes 100-350B; 9am-11pm;) This place on the lake's east shore offers all the usual Thai dishes, but also many you've probably never tried before, such as fish-stomach salad. Eat outdoors on the deck or in air-conditioned dining rooms.

Papagallo ITALIAN $$
(100/9 Th Udondutsadi; pizza 200B; 11am-10pm;) There are several Italian eateries in the Central Plaza/Soi Farang area, but we prefer this slightly less convenient place. It's very small, so easy to miss. The pizza is especially good.

Good Everything INTERNATIONAL, THAI $$$
(Th Poniyom; dishes 150-690B; 10am-10pm; P) This white cottage and garden transported from the English countryside is the polar opposite of the Soi Falang experience. It features fresh and healthy cuisine, such as lamb served with Texas-style chilli, Polish mushroom soup, Thai- and *fa·ràng*-style salads, plus quality coffees and teas. It's one of Udon's most expensive restaurants, but the many regulars consider it money well spent.

Gib Shop JUICE BAR
(Th Prajak Sinlapacom; 10.30am-9pm Mon-Fri, 10am-9pm Sat & Sun) Not all juice is created equal, and this shop on the ground floor of Central Plaza proves it. Most of the fruit and vegies are organic and you can choose to have no sugar added. There's another

WORTH A TRIP

A CAVE WITH AMAZING VIEWS

Tham Erawan (ถ้ำเอราวัณ; donations appreciated; ⌚dawn-dusk) If you're travelling from Loei to Nong Bua Lamphu, don't miss this amazing cave, 2km off the main highway in Wat Tham Erawan. The cave is in a group of rugged karst hills and is accessed by a steep but easily climbed stairway. The cave, with a big Buddha statue at its mouth, is very large and open. The climb to it goes through pockets of bamboo forest and has splendid views of the surrounding forested hills and cultivated fields.

Don't stop at the entrance: if you keep going in until the light is very dim, you'll come across another section where a hole in the roof of the cave lets down shafts of sunlight, making for a spectacular atmosphere.

The cave is tended by the monks of Wat Tham Erawan. You'll see a number of donation points in the temple, including a rather bizarre talking skeleton asking for donations for paupers' coffins. The temple is along Rte 210, just across the Nong Bualamphu Province line. Buses from Loei (25B to 35B, 1¼ hours, every 30 minutes) to Udon Thani will drop you at Ban Na Wang on the main road, 2.5km away. You can catch a túk-túk from the Sunthorn Withaya school to the cave for 200B return.

branch among the **juice bars** (Th Thesa; ⌚10am-9pm) at Nong Prajak.

☆ Entertainment

Udon has the largest and most in-your-face sex-tourism scene in Isan, and the 'Soi Falang' (Th Sampanthamit) area is rather sleazy at night – even in the day you'll have to endure 'Hallo, massaaaage'. Some travellers might find the street atmosphere uncomfortable.

The three night markets in front of the train station offer a range of diversions. Besides dining you can shop for clothes, sing karaoke, play snooker, get a tattoo and have your fortune told. On some weekends you can watch football games on the big screen or listen to live bands.

Central Plaza occasionally screens movies in their original English and also has a bowling alley.

Shopping

Central Plaza (Th Prajak Sinlapacom; ⌚10.30am-9pm Mon-Fri, 10am-9pm Sat & Sun) is Udon's biggest shopping centre and has a branch of the English-language bookstore Asia Books, though strolling the open-air **UD Town** (Th Thongyai; ⌚10am-10pm Mon-Fri, 9am-10pm Sat-Sun) is more fun.

Udon City Walking Street MARKET
(Th Athibodi; ⌚5pm-10pm Fri & Sat) With just a handful of vendors selling handmade items, Udon's Walking Street pales in comparison to the markets in Chiang Mai and Khon Kaen that inspired it.

Fuzzy Ken's BOOKS
(302/10 Th Prajak Sinlapacom; ⌚10am-11pm Mon-Fri & noon-11pm Sat) This restaurant/knick-knack shop has a bit of everything, including a good selection of secondhand books.

Information

Central Plaza and Tesco-Lotus have AEON ATMs and extended-hour banks.

Aek Udon International Hospital (☎042 342555; Th Phosri) Has a 24-hour casualty department.

Immigration (☎042 249982; Th Phosri; ⌚8.30am-noon & 1-4.30pm) Does visa extensions.

Tourism Authority of Thailand (TAT; ☎042 325406; tatudon@tat.or.th; Th Thesa; ⌚8.30am-4.30pm)

Udon Thani Map (www.udonmap.com) This map and its companion magazine, the *Udon Thani Guide*, are mostly geared towards expats, but helpful for travellers, too. They're available free at *fa·ràng*-focused businesses.

Getting There & Away

AIR

Thai Airways (THAI; ☎Udon Airport 042 246567, call centre 02 356 1111; www.thaiairways.com) connects Udon Thani to Bangkok (from 1400B) through Suvarnabhumi airport four times daily, while **Nok Air** (☎Udon Thani airport 042 348771, bookings 02 900 9955; www.nokair.com) (from 1100B) and **Air Asia** (☎02 515 9999; www.airasia.com) (from 1000B) use Don Mueang Airport four and two times daily respectively. Air Asia also has a daily direct flight to Phuket (4000B) and Nok Air goes daily direct to Chiang Mai (1800B).

Buy tickets at **On Time** (☎ 042 247792; Th Sai Uthit; ⏰ 8am-5pm Mon-Sat, 9am-3pm Sun), one of several travel agencies near Bus Terminal 1.

BUS

Buses to most destinations, including Bangkok (428B to 666B, eight to nine hours, every 30 minutes), use the downtown **Bus Terminal 1** (☎ 042 221489; Th Sai Uthit). **Chan Tour** (☎ 042 343403; ⏰ 7 daily) and **999 VIP** (☎ 042 221489) have VIP service to Bangkok. Other destinations include Bueng Kan (160B, five hours, six daily), Nakhon Phanom (160B to 209B, three hours, every 30 minutes), Khon Kaen (84B to 180B, two hours, every 30 minutes), Pattaya (511B to 636B, 11 hours, 10 daily) and Suvarnabhumi International Airport (455B, eight hours, 9pm). If you already have a Lao visa you can take the bus to Vientiane (80B, two hours, eight daily; the 6pm departure has an additional 5B fee) and Vang Vieng (320B, seven hours, 8.30am).

Bus Terminal 2 (☎ 042 214914), on the western ring road, serves many of the same destinations, plus it's the only station for western cities such as Loei (100B, three hours, every 30 minutes), Phitsanulok (238B to 306B, seven hours, 13 daily) and Chiang Mai (666B to 888B, 12 hours, 10 daily).

There are buses to Nong Khai (50B, one hour) from both terminals, but the most frequent departures are from Rangsina Market; the last departs at 9pm. There are also Nong Khai minivans (60B, 45 minutes, hourly from 6.30am to 6.30pm) from Central Plaza.

TRAIN

There are three express trains (seat 95B to 457B, 1st-class sleeper upper/lower 1077/1277B, 10½ hours) each evening and one each morning between Bangkok and **Udon Thani train station** (☎ 042 222061). There's also a cheaper evening rapid train. Four morning trains head to Nong Khai (11B to 48B, one hour).

Getting Around

Sŏrng·tăa·ou (10B) run regular routes across town. Route 6 (white) is handy since it runs up and down Th Udondutsadi (with a convenient detour to the Th Prajak-Surakarn junction), past Rangsina Market and out to Bus Terminal 2. There are also two city buses (10B). The White Bus follows Th Udondutsadi while the Yellow Bus tracks Th Phosri-Nittayo, connecting the two bus terminals in the process. The *Udon Thani Map* shows all bus and *sŏrng·tăa·ou* routes.

You can rarely flag a **taxi** (☎ 042 343239; call fee 30B) down on the street, but they park at Bus Terminal 1 and Central Plaza. Drivers don't use meters. Túk-túk (called 'skylab' here) are seemingly everywhere. The cost from Central Plaza to Nong Prajak Park is usually 50B.

Many hotels pick guests up at the airport for free, otherwise shuttle vans to the city centre cost 80B per person. **Lek Car Rental** (☎ 086 059 3028; www.lekcarrentaludonthani.com) is a reputable company and there are also many smaller car-hire outlets around Central Plaza.

Ban Chiang บ้านเชียง

What's now one of Southeast Asia's most important archaeological sites was discovered accidentally in 1966 when an anthropology student from Harvard tripped while walking through the area and found the rim of a buried pot right under his nose. Looking around he noticed many more and speculated that this might be a burial site. He was right. Serious excavations began soon after and over a million pottery pieces and dozens of human skeletons were unearthed.

The now-iconic burnt-ochre swirl-design pottery (made between 300 BC and AD 200) is just one of many styles these people created over the years. Researchers also found the earliest evidence of the manufacture of metal tools (people here began working bronze around 2000 BC) in the region.

The area was declared a Unesco World Heritage site in 1992. Archaeological digs in this village have uncovered a treasure trove of artefacts dating back to 3600 BC and overturned the prevailing theory that Southeast Asia was a cultural backwater compared to China and India at the time.

Sights

Ban Chiang National Museum MUSEUM

(พิพิธภัณฑสถานแห่งชาติบ้านเชียง; admission 150B; ⏰ 9am-4pm Tue-Sun) This excellent museum exhibits a wealth of pottery from all Ban Chiang periods, plus myriad spearheads, sickles, fish hooks, ladies' neck rings and other metal objects. The displays (with English labels) offer excellent insight into the

BAN CHIANG CRAFTS

Rice farming remains Ban Chiang's primary livelihood, but selling souvenirs now comes a close second. Some of the items, including Ban Chiang–style pottery, are made in the area. Walk down the road facing the museum to find a couple of **pottery workshops**. Just south of the Thai Phuan House is a small **women's weaving group** that mostly weaves indigo cotton.

region's distant past and, just as interestingly, how its mysteries were unravelled. Hidden out back is a room showcasing the culture of the Tai Phuan people, who migrated here about 200 years ago and founded the present town.

One kilometre east, at **Wat Pho Si Nai**, is an original burial-ground excavation pit, with a cluster of 52 individual burial sites dating to 300 BC. It shows how bodies were laid to rest with pottery. It's included in the museum ticket, though it's free on Mondays.

Wat Pa Lelai BUDDHIST TEMPLE
(วัดป่าเลไลยก์; dawn-dusk) FREE For something completely different, visit this temple 500m north of the burial site, across the little bridge. The awesome childlike murals in the two-storey building at the back are both enlightening and entertaining.

Thai Phuan House HISTORIC SITE
(บ้านไทพวน) About 300m southwest of the burial site (follow the signs for 'Phuan House which the King and Queen visited in 1972'), this traditional Isan house is promoted as an attraction, but the still-lived-in houses throughout the village are more interesting.

Sleeping & Eating

There are several restaurants on the road fronting the museum, one of which stays open for dinner.

Lakeside Sunrise Guesthouse GUESTHOUSE $
(080 193 4300; suppawat2508@gmail.com; r with/without bathroom 500/400B; P) In a countryside setting, yet within easy striking distance of the museum, this old wooden house is reason enough to spend the night in town. It's best to call ahead because the joyful owner, who speaks good English, isn't always at home.

Getting There & Around

From Udon Thani, take a bus bound for Sakon Nakhon or Nakhon Phanom and get off at Ban Nong Mek (35B, 45 minutes, every 30 minutes), where túk-túk will take one or two people the 8km to Ban Chiang and bring you back for 200B.

With a lack of hills and traffic, the countryside around Ban Chiang is a great place to explore by bike. You can rent bikes for 10B per day from the shops next to the police box east of the museum.

Red Lotus Sea

You'll see pictures of the **Red Lotus Sea** (ทะเลบัวแดง; Kumphawapi District) all over Udon as it's touted as one of the province's top attractions, but not many foreigners make it there. The trick is in the timing. The sea of lotuses really is a spectacular sight, but if you go when the lotuses are closed up you'll be disappointed. December to February is the best time, and in the morning (before 11am), but even outside of those months you might see them if you go in the morning. You need to hire a boat (300B) to go out into the middle of the lake for the best views. The tourist office can advise on the best times.

The Red Lotus Sea is not serviced directly by public transport. To get there, go along Hwy 22 to Ban Na Di. You can get a túk-túk from Na Di to the Red Lotus Sea for 300B return, including waiting time.

Ban Na Kha บ้านนาข่า

Na Kha village is one of the best fabric shopping destinations in Thailand. In the city centre is a **covered market** (085 013 1060) with dozens of shops selling a great variety of silk and cotton from Thailand and Laos. Except at the large shops on the highway, much of the fabric is handmade. **Mae Bah Pah Fai** (6.30am-6pm), across from the temple entrance, has as good a selection as any, including some century-old *kít* hanging in the back.

Before leaving, take a peek at **Wat Na Ka Taewee** (dawn-dusk), founded by a wandering monk who discovered a hole from which bellowed the sound and smoke of a *naga*. It's right behind the small *bòht*. Pottery and human skeletons unearthed during various construction projects at the temple are on display under the giant Buddha.

Udon's White Bus runs to the village, 16km north of the city.

Phu Phrabat Historical Park

No one really knows the history of this mysterious, mystical place peppered with bizarre rock formations. **Phu Phrabat** (อุทยานประวัติศาสตร์ภูพระบาท; 042 918619; admission 100B; 8am-4.30pm) is one of Isan's most compelling sights and experiences. The park consists of a collection of strange rock formations that in prehistoric times were modified to form various religious functions. Buddhist *sima* stones, presumably from the Dvaravati era about 1000 years ago, are plentiful. Cave floors have been painstakingly carved into smooth platforms. Hindu shrines also seem to have been built among the many spires, whale-sized boulders and improbably balanced rocks. If you're here at a time with few visitors, sit for a few minutes in one of the caves and soak up the ambience: it really is a special place.

One intriguing sight is **Bo Nang Usa** (บ่อนางอุษา), a man-made well carved into solid rock. It's at least 5m deep and its age is unknown. The mind boggles at the labour required to make it, and for what purpose.

In addition, prehistoric paintings on several rock overhangs, best seen at side-by-side **Tham Wua** and **Tham Khon**, show this was probably regarded as a holy site at least 1500 years earlier. A climb beyond these rock formations to **Pha Sa Dej**, at the edge of the escarpment, ends with vast views of the farms and forest beyond. A web of trails meanders past all these sites and you can see them in a leisurely two hours, but it's worth spending several more. A remoter northern loop is lovely, but not well marked, so it's easy to get lost.

The highlight of the park is **Hor Nang U-sa**, an overturned-boot-shaped outcrop with a shrine built into it. Many of these rock formations are signposted with names in Thai and English alluding to the legend of Usa and Baros, a short version of which can be read in the museum. If you're staying at the Mut Mee Garden Guest House (p379) in Nong Khai, you can read the entire tale.

South of the entrance is **Wat Phra Phutthabaht Bua Bok**, with its namesake Lao-style *chedi* covering a Buddha footprint. It also has many rocks like those in the park.

There are **campsites** (per tent with own tent 20B, 2-/8-person tent hire 50/200B) and three lovely **bungalows** (2/4/6 people 300/600/1200B) with rock-hard mattresses.

Getting There & Away

The park is 65km from Udon Thani and Nong Khai and can be visited as a day trip from either city. *Sŏrng·tăa·ou* from Nong Khai's bus station to Ban Pheu (55B, 1½ hours) travel via Tha Bo. Vehicles from Udon's Rangsina Market continue past Ban Pheu to Ban Tiu (*sŏrng·tăa·ou*/minivans 35/100B, one hour/45 minutes), the village at the base of the hill, from where a motorcycle taxi costs 100B return for the final 5km climb. Túk-túk from Ban Pheu cost around 250B return and motorcycle taxis cost half that. The last vehicle back to Nong Khai leaves at 4pm and the last to Udon at 3pm.

Wat Pho Chai Sri

Wat Pho Chai Sri BUDDHIST TEMPLE

(วัดโพธิ์ชัยศรี; dawn-dusk) With brightly painted statuary that's even more bizarre than Nong Khai's Sala Kaew Ku, this wát is a perfect add-on to Phu Phrabat and even worth a trip on its own. The life-size figures around the temple grounds are acting out scenes from Isan fables and demonstrating the punishment awaiting the wicked in the Buddhist Hell.

The temple is also home to Luang Po Naak, a very holy 1200-year-old Buddha image shaded by a seven-headed *naga* that locals believe is responsible for many miracles.

Also known as Wat Ban Waeng, the temple is about 5km out of Ban Pheu. A túk-túk costs about 100B round trip with waiting time.

Bueng Kan Province

Thailand's newest province split off from Nong Khai in 2011. It's remote and often-lovely territory and includes one of Thailand's most amazing temples and best homestay programs.

Bueng Kan บึงกาฬ

POP 4850

The only thing that qualifies as an attraction in little Bueng Kan township is the **Thai-Lao Market** (ตลาดนัดบึงกาฬ; Soi Buengkan; mornings Tue & Fri). Some of the products, such as herbs and mushrooms, sold by the Lao traders are gathered in the forest, and there's a good representation of traditional Isan fare (crates of crickets and frogs). It's also interesting to take a look at the river during the dry season since it recedes far from Bueng Kan and reaches one of its narrowest points along the Thai–Lao border.

Not surprisingly, most travellers only stop long enough to catch connecting transport to Wat Phu Thok. If you do decide to stay, the Mekong-facing **Maenam Hotel** (042 491051; Th Chansin; r 400-450B; P ⊝ ❄ @ ☜) is the best-located place in town. At the time of our visit extensive improvements were being made to the promenade along the river, which will only increase the value of the location.

The One (042 492234; www.theonehotel-bk.com; Nakhon Phanom Rd; r 790-1700B, ste 2500B; P ⊝ ❄ @ ☜ ☒), out on the highway,

GETTING TO LAOS: BUENG KAN TO PAKSAN

Although it's very rarely done, you can cross the Mekong from Bueng Kan to Paksan, but only if you already have your Lao visa.

Getting to the border Immigration (8am to 6pm) is 2.5km northwest of town. A túk-túk will cost about 60B.

At the border Boats cross the river between 8.30am and noon and between 1pm and 4.30pm when they have about 20 passengers. During lunch and after 4.30pm you'll probably need to charter the whole boat for 1000B.

Moving on Túk-túk wait on the Lao shore, though the highway and a few hotels are an easy walk from the landing.

is the top hotel in town. It offers excellent value and service for the price. The 790B rooms are a 'promotion' that has been on offer for years.

Many restaurants set up tables along the riverside promenade at dinner time, making this the best place to eat.

Buses to Nong Khai (100B to 150B, 3½ hours, eight daily), Nakhon Phanom (140B, 3½ hours, four daily) and Udon Thani (130B to 150B, 4½ hours, 12 daily) park near the old clock tower. The last departures for Nong Khai and Nakhon Phanom are at 3pm, and for Udon Thani at 4pm. You could also take one of the later Bangkok (600B) buses to Nong Khao or Udon Thani, but you may need to pay the full fare. There are also buses to Chiang Mai (800B).

Wat Phu Thok

When he first set up his monastery on remote and inaccessible Phu Thok, the forest meditation teacher Luang Pu Juan was not thinking of creating a tourist attraction. In his own words, the crevices in the sheer walls of the mountain made good places to meditate to overcome sleepiness. When you go there you'll see his point. With its network of rickety staircases and walkways built in, on and around a giant sandstone outcrop, **Wat Phu Thok** (วัดภูทอก; 6am-5pm, closed 10-16 Apr) FREE is one of the region's wonders. The precarious paths lead past shrines and *gù·đì* (monk's hut or living quarters) that are scattered around the mountain, on cliffs and in caves, and provide fabulous views over the surrounding countryside. A final scramble up roots and rocks takes you to the forest on the summit, which is considered the seventh level. If you hustle and take all the short cuts you can be up and down in about an hour, but we advise against it: this is a climb that should be savoured.

The quiet isolation entices monks and *mâa chee* (nuns) from across Thailand to come to meditate, so remember to be quiet and respectful as you explore.

Luang Pu Juan died in a plane crash in 1980 along with several other highly revered forest monks who were flying to Bangkok for Queen Sirikit's birthday celebration. A marble *chedi* containing Luang Pu Juan's belongings, some bone relics and fantastic exterior sculptures sits below the mountain amid a gorgeous garden.

Getting There & Away

Túk-túk in Bueng Kan charge 800B for the return journey to Wat Phu Thok, including a few hours of waiting time. It's cheaper to take a bus from Bueng Kan to Ban Siwilai (30B, 45 minutes), where túk-túk drivers will do the trip for 350B. If you catch an early bus to Bueng Kan, Wat Phu Thok can be visited as a day trip from Nong Khai, although there's no need to backtrack since buses from Siwilai go to Udon Thani (140B, four hours, last bus 4.45pm).

If you're driving or cycling, continue past Bueng Kan for 27km until you reach Chaiyaphon, then turn right at Rte 3024, the road signed for Chet Si and several other waterfalls. (These are in the Phu Wua Wildlife Sanctuary and make worthy detours, as much for the weird rocky landscape as the cascades. There's only water mid-May through December.) After 17.5km make a right and continue 4km more.

Phu Wua Wildlife Sanctuary

Phu Wua Wildlife Sanctuary (เขตรักษาพันธุ์สัตว์ป่าภูวัว; 084 428 5389; adult/child 100/50B) covers an area of 186 sq km and offers some superb hikes (including an overnight stop in a cave). The forest is flush with waterfalls and home to about three dozen elephants. The elephants are sometimes encountered on day walks from the village of Kham Pia, which sits near the entrance to the sanctuary, during the rainy season, but the cool season is the best time to visit (not least because of the leeches that proliferate in wet weather).

Note that Phu Wua, being a wildlife sanctuary, has accommodation but is difficult to stay in. You would have to arrange a stay in advance with the Department of National Parks. However, rangers are happy to act as guides (fee negotiable). You should contact the park in advance if you want to do this.

A better way to stay here is with Ban Kham Pia's village **homestay** (☎087 861 0601; www.bunloedhuts.jimdo.com; s 170-270B, d 200-300B, meals 50-90B) program. Khun Bunleud, who runs the program, can arrange day walks from the village and overnight stays in 'treehouses' (not for the faint-hearted) in the middle of a forest clearing about an hour's drive from the village. The standard guide fee in and around the village is 300B per day and there are motorcycles for 200B per day.

Buses between Nong Khai (150B, 3½ hours) and Nakhon Phanom (130B, three hours) will drop you at Ban Don Chik, 3km away.

Ban Ahong

If you're travelling from Nong Khai to Bueng Kan, Ban Ahong, a pretty riverside village 20km before Bueng Kan, makes a nice stop along the way. **Wat Ahong Silawat** (วัดอาฮงศิลาวาส; ⊙dawn-dusk), on its eastern edge, is built amid ruddy boulders at a river bend known as Sàdeu Námkong (the Mekong River's Navel) because of the large whirlpool that spins here June to September. It's said to be one of the deepest and narrowest sections of the Mekong. The scenery amid the massive boulders, which seem quite out of place in the context of the surrounding area, is striking and the atmosphere serene.

Buses between Nong Khai (100B, 2½ hours, six daily) and Bueng Kan can drop you at the temple.

Nakhon Phanom Province

Lao and Vietnamese influences are strong in Nakhon Phanom, a province bordered by the Mekong and full of highly revered temples. It's a region of subtleties rather than can't-miss attractions, but there are plenty of fine river views and interesting historic sites, and the colossal Wat Phra That Phanom is one of the must-sees of Isan culture.

Nakhon Phanom นครพนม

POP 22,710

Nakhon Phanom means 'City of Mountains', but the undulating sugarloaf peaks all lie across the river in Laos, so you'll be admiring rather than climbing them. The views are stunning, though, especially during a hazy sunrise. The aquarium is worth a visit and the sunset cruises are great value.

Nakhon Phanom's temples have a distinctive style. This was once an important town in the Lan Xang Empire and, after that, Thai kings sent their best artisans to create new buildings. Later a vivid French influence crossed the Mekong and jumped into the mix.

Sights & Activities

Mekong Underwater World AQUARIUM

(โลกของปลาแม่น้ำโขง; ☎042 530780; Rte 2033; admission 30B; ⊙8.30am-4pm Mon-Fri) The displays here are smaller than those at the Nong Khai aquarium, but in some ways they're more impressive, with timber finishing and better lighting. It's a good place to get up close with some rather large specimens of Mekong catfish (*Ɓlah bèuk*). It's 6km west of town along Hwy 22. *Sŏrng·tăa·ou* to Na Kae (20B, 15 minutes) pass by. You can also get a taxi from the bus station to get you there and back for 100B.

Wat Okat BUDDHIST TEMPLE

(วัดโอกาส; Th Sunthon Wijit; ⊙dawn-dusk) Predating the town, Wat Okat is home to Phra

SACRED RELICS

If you're visiting temples of deceased meditation teachers, you will inevitably see displays of bone fragments and crystalline objects given high prominence. These are 'relics' *(prá tâht)*, bone fragments collected after the monk's cremation that, over time, sometimes develop into crystals. As in many Buddhist countries, Thai Buddhists believe that the appearance of these crystalline relics is a sign of the master's enlightenment, and their colour and beauty an indication of the level of purity. Relics are highly revered and sometimes handed out to devotees. They are believed to multiply or decrease in number, or even disappear, depending on the conduct of the person looking after them.

Nakhon Phanom

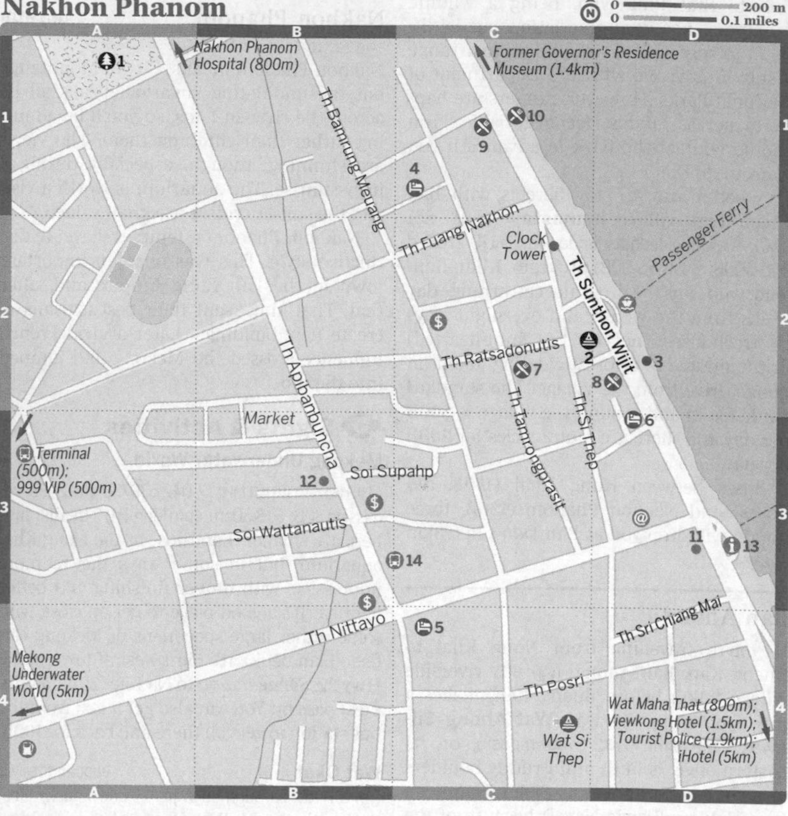

Nakhon Phanom

Sights
1 Chom Khong Park A1
2 Wat Okat C2

Activities, Courses & Tours
3 Sunset Cruise D2

Sleeping
4 777 Hometel C1
5 SP Hotel C4
6 TC Apartment D3

Eating
7 Good Morning Vietnam & Coffee C2
8 Indochina Market D2
9 Khrua Champasak C1
10 Khun Kaew Steak Corner C1

Information
11 Immigration Office D3
12 NKP Travel Centre B3
13 Tourism Authority of Thailand D3

Transport
777 Hometel .... (see 4)
14 Sŏrng·tăa·ou to That Phanom & Na Kae C3

Tiow and Phra Tiam, two sacred wooden Buddha images covered in gold that sit on the highest pedestal in the *wí·hăhn* (sanctuary). The current Tiam (on the right) is a replica because the original was stolen in 2010. The amazing mural showing the story of Phra Tiow and Phra Tiam floating across the Mekong from Laos is one of our favourites (see if you can find the backpackers).

Ho Chi Minh's House MUSEUM
(บ้านโฮจิมินห์; ☎042 522430; entry by donation; ⏲dawn-dusk) The Vietnamese community

in Ban Na Chok village, about 3.5km west of town, has built a replica of Udon Thani's Uncle Ho's House, the simple wooden house where Ho Chi Minh sometimes stayed (1928–29) while planning his resistance movement. There are more displays, some labelled in English, in the **Ho Chi Minh Museum**, which, at time of research, was being rebuilt in a bright, shiny-new structure 500m from the house. His birthday is celebrated here every 19 May.

Former Governor's Residence Museum MUSEUM
(จวนผู้ว่าราชการจังหวัดนครพนม /หลังเก่า); Th Sunthon Wijit; ⌚9am-5pm Wed-Sun) FREE This museum fills a restored 1925 mansion with photos of old Nakhon Phanom, many labelled in English, while out the back are displays about the illuminated boat procession.

Chom Khong Park PARK
(สวนชมโขง; Th Ratchathan; ⌚5am-8pm) This park used to be a prison, and models of prisoners sit in some of the old cells. You can also climb the guard towers.

Sunset Cruise BOAT TOUR
(☎086 230 5560; per person 50B) The city runs this hour-long Mekong River cruise on *Thesaban*, which docks across from the Indochina Market. Snacks and drinks are served.

Festivals & Events

Nakhon Phanom is famous for its illuminated boat procession, **Lai Reua Fai** (⌚late Oct/early Nov), during Ork Phansaa (the end of Buddhist Lent). It's a modern twist on the ancient tradition of sending rafts loaded with food, flowers and candles down the Mekong as offerings for the *naga*. Today's giant bamboo rafts hold up to 20,000 handmade lanterns, with some designers adding animation to the scenes. Boat races, music competitions and other festivities run for a week, but the boats are launched only on the night of the full moon.

Sleeping

SP Hotel HOTEL $
(☎042 513505; Th Nittayo; s/d 450/500B; P❄@📶) Plain but modern, the rooms here are less institutional than the exterior and hallways would lead you to believe, and for just a few extra baht it's better than the city's older hotels in the same price range. The furniture in the rooms is particularly impressive: made of beautifully finished timber and strong enough to jump on!

★**777 Hometel** HOTEL $$
(☎042 514777; Th Tamrongprasit; r with breakfast 590-790B; P❄@📶) Don't let the boxy exterior fool you: inside is Nakhon Phanom's most stylish hotel. It doesn't just get by on looks alone: the rooms are great, it's well managed and has some of the friendliest, most helpful staff in town. It's called *đorng jet* in Thai.

TC Apartment HOTEL $$
(☎042 512212; Th Sunthon Wijit; r 690B; P❄📶) One of many new hotels in Nakhon Phanom, TC has a great central location and big river views from the balconies of the front-facing rooms. The rooms are solid and the wi-fi strong. One big downside: the noise coming from busy Th Sunthon Wijit can be pretty terrible at night.

iHotel HOTEL $$
(☎042 543355; Th That Phanom; r incl breakfast 490-650B; P❄@📶) The stylish 'i' mixes good mattresses, 'power showers', a backyard garden and attentive staff. It looks more aligned to karaoke and snooker fans and, at 6km, may be a little far from town.

Eating & Drinking

After dinner, head to one of the laid-back, attractive bars that fill historic shophouses near the clock tower.

Indochina Market THAI $
(Th Sunthon Wijit; ⌚7am-7pm) The balcony fronting this small food court has choice seats that frame the mountain views.

Good Morning Vietnam & Coffee VIETNAMESE $
(☎087 226 3445; Th Tamrongprasit; dishes 30-50B; ⌚6am-6pm) This little corner shop still serves the same family recipes, including *năam neu·ang* (assemble-it-yourself pork spring rolls) and spicy Thai salads, that it has through four generations, not to mention decent brewed coffee.

Khrua Champasak THAI, VIETNAMESE $$
(☎042 514541; Th Sunthon Wijit; dishes 40-350B; ⌚10am-10pm) Champasak specialises in Mekong river fish. The owner, the daughter of Mekong fisherfolk, knows her fish and takes pride in her selection. The shop has both air-con and open-area sections, with clear views over the Mekong. Standard Thai and

Vietnamese fare is also served. There's no Roman-script sign, but it's opposite Khun Kaew Steak Corner.

Note that the English menu doesn't have the Mekong fish dishes. If you want to try them, ask for the Thai menu (it has pictures).

Khun Kaew Steak Corner INTERNATIONAL **$$**
(☎085 925 7979; Th Sunthon Wijit; dishes 65-475B; ⏲4-10pm Mon-Sat) Funky from the decor to the Thai-fusion pastas, this little riverside spot, owned by a Thai chef who worked for some years in Texas, makes for a nice night, especially if you can get one of the tables with a view. There are only seven tables.

Information

Bangkok Bank (Tesco-Lotus, Th Nittayo; ⏲10.30am-7pm) Keeps late hours.

Immigration Office (☎042 511235; Th Sunthon Wijit; ⏲8.30am-noon & 1-4.30pm Mon-Fri) For visa extensions.

Tourism Authority of Thailand (TAT; ☎042 513490; tatphnom@tat.or.th; Th Sunthon Wijit; ⏲8.30am-4.30pm) Covers Nakhon Phanom, Sakon Nakhon and Mukdahan Provinces.

Getting There & Away

AIR

Nok Air (☎02 900 9955; www.nokair.com) and **Air Asia** (☎02 515 9999; www.airasia.com) fly daily to/from Bangkok's Don Mueang Airport with one-way prices from 1100B. Agencies such as **NKP Travel Centre** (☎042 520999; Th Apibanbuncha; ⏲9am-6pm Mon-Sat, to 5pm Sun) sell tickets. An airport shuttle drops passengers at any in-town hotel for 100B per person.

BUS

Nakhon Phanom's **bus terminal** (☎042 513444; Th Fuang Nakhon) is west of the town centre. From here buses head to Nong Khai (200B, 6½ hours, four daily), Udon Thani (160B to 210B, 4½ hours, frequent) and Ubon Ratchathani (from 220B, 4½ hours, 7am). For Ubon most people use minivans (190B, four hours, seven daily), which go via Mukdahan (80B, 2½ hours) and That Phanom (40B, one hour). Most Bangkok (477B to 614B, 11 to 12 hours) buses depart between 7am to 8am and 5pm to 7pm. VIP service is offered by **999 VIP** (☎042 511403) for 893B and **Nakhon Chai Air** (☎042 51199) also has a service (641B).

Sŏrng·tăa·ou to That Phanom (40B, 1½ hours, frequent until 5pm) park near Kasikornbank.

GETTING TO LAOS: NAKHON PHANOM TO THA KHAEK

Getting to the border Passenger ferries cross the Mekong to Tha Khaek in Laos, but they're for Thai and Lao only. All travellers must use the Thai-Lao Friendship Bridge 3, north of the city. Buses to Tha Khaek (70/75B weekdays/weekends, eight daily) run between 8am and 5pm.

At the border All immigration formalities are handled at the bridge and Lao visas are available on arrival. Things get pretty chaotic when droves of Vietnamese workers, who don't appreciate the value of a queue, are passing through.

Moving on The bus tends to wait a long time to get more passengers, so total travel time to Tha Khaek is often more than two hours.

Getting Around

Túk-túk drivers quote 30B to 40B per person from the bus station to most places in town, and 200B for the round trip to Ban Na Chok, although you might get a taxi to do it for 100B.

Nakhon Phanom's sparse traffic makes it a good place for cycling. **777 Hometel** (☎042 514777; Th Tamrongprasit; bikes/motorbikes per day 50/200B; ⏲24hr) hires bikes.

That Phanom ธาตุพนม

POP 11,680

Towering over this small, peaceful town, the spire of the colossal *chedi* at Wat Phra That Phanom is one of the region's most emblematic symbols and one of the great pillars of Isan identity. Some historic buildings in the Mekong-hugging half of town can round out a pleasant visit. The town doesn't make much of its Mekong location as do, say, Nong Khai and Nakhon Phanom, but a new riverside promenade extension was under construction at time of research, which should liven up the river area considerably.

Sights

★**Wat Phra That Phanom** BUDDHIST TEMPLE
(วัดพระธาตุพนม; Th Chayangkun; ⏲5am-8pm) FREE This temple is a potent and beautiful place; even if you're feeling templed-out, you'll likely be impressed. At its hub is a stupa *(tâht)*, more impressive than any in present-day Laos and highly revered by Buddhists from both countries. The *tâht* is 53.6m high, and a 16kg real-gold umbrella

laden with precious gems adds 4m more to the top.

The local legend goes that the Lord Buddha travelled to Thailand and directed that one of his breast-bone relics be enshrined in a *chedi* to be built on this very site; and so it was in 535 BC, eight years after his death. Historians actually date the first construction, a short stupa (there's a **replica** of how it may have looked in a pond in front of the temple), to around the 9th century AD and modifications have been routine since then. In 1690 it was raised to 47m and you'll find replicas of this *tâht* all over Isan. The current design went up in 1941, but it toppled during heavy rains in 1975 and was rebuilt in 1978.

Behind the surrounding cloister is a shady little park and **museum** (⌚8.30am-4pm) FREE, which tells the legend (not the history) of the *tâht* and also displays a collection of pottery, gongs and some rare Buddha images.

Kong Gate MONUMENT

(ประตูโขง) Standing tall on the road in front of Wat Phra That Phanom is an arch that symbolically connects the *tâht* to the Mekong. The block of French Indochinese architecture between the arch and the river is reminiscent of old Saigon, and a few shops sell Vietnamese food.

Phra That Renu BUDDHIST TEMPLE

(พระธาตุเรณู; ⌚dawn-dusk) The Phu Thai town of Renu Nakhon, 15km northwest of That Phanom, hosts a 35m-tall *tâht* that closely resembles the previous *chedi* built in That Phanom and is considered very holy. It's located in the temple Wat That Renu, which also hosts a good **textiles market** with locally made fabrics and clothes as well as silk and cotton from Laos and elsewhere in Thailand. There's no public transport. Túk-túk drivers in That Phanom ask 300B round trip.

Festivals & Events

During the **That Phanom Festival** in late January or early February, visitors descend from all over Thailand and Laos to make merit and pay respect to the *tâht*. The streets fill with market stalls, many top *mŏr lam* (p747) troupes perform and the town hardly sleeps for nine days.

On the morning of **Ork Phansaa**, Phu Tai dancers perform their 'peacock dance' in front of the *prá tâht* (reliquary or stupa) inside the wat.

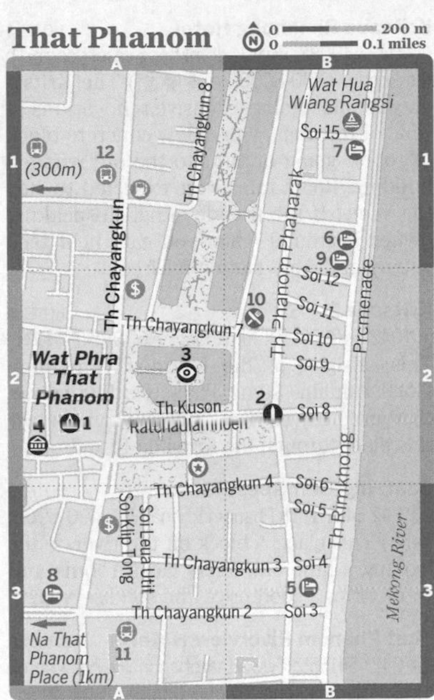

That Phanom

Top Sights
1 Wat Phra That Phanom A2

Sights
2 Kong Gate B2
3 Replica Stupa A2
4 That Phanom Museum A2

Sleeping
5 Baan-Ing-Oon Guesthouse B3
6 Kritsada 2 B1
7 Kritsada Rimkhong Hotel B1
8 Na That Phanom Place A3
9 That Phanom Riverview Hotel B1

Eating
Krua Kritsada Rimkhong (see 7)
10 Night Market B2

Transport
11 Old Bus Station A3
12 Sŏrng·tăa·ou to Nakhon Phanom A1

Sleeping

During the That Phanom Festival, rates soar and rooms are booked out well in advance.

Kritsada Rimkhong Hotel HOTEL $
(☎042 540088; www.ksdrimkhong-resort.com; Th Rimkhong; r 500-600B; P❄@📶) The Kritsada was undergoing extensive renovations at time of research, with a new concrete block of rooms going up next to the old wooden building. Room rates were expected to stay the same. If the friendly, English-speaking owner is around when you call, he'll pick you up at the bus station for free.

Kritsada 2 HOTEL $
(☎042 540088; Th Rimkhong; r 600B; P❄📶) This offshoot of the Kritsada Rimkhong Hotel contains some Thai-style bungalows right on the river-view road. You can contact this place through the Kritsada Rimkhong.

Baan-Ing-Oon Guesthouse HOTEL $
(☎042 540111; Th Phanom Phanarak; r 490-590B; ❄📶) This place, a block off the river, while looking a little old, offers clean rooms and comfort for a good price and solid service.

That Phanom Riverview Hotel HOTEL $$
(☎042 541555; www.thatphanomriverviewhotel.com; Th Rimkhong; r 850-1250B; P❄@📶) Rooms at That Phanom's biggest and best lodge are pretty plain for the price, but being large and bright helps compensate and the service and amenities are what you'd expect. Note that, despite the name, most rooms have little or no view. There are free bicycles for guests' use.

Na That Phanom Place HOTEL $$
(☎042 532148; thatphanomplace@gmail.com; Th Chayangkun; r 790B; ❄📶) Although a little far from the action, about 2km from the river, this lovely hotel has plain but stylish rooms, each featuring a unique design. It has a lovely atmosphere and the design seems to catch the breeze. There are free bikes for guests' use. Luckily it's 100m or so in from the busy highway.

Eating

Krua Kritsada Rimkhong NORTHEASTERN THAI $
(Th Rimkhong; dishes 40-200B; ⏰8am-10pm; P📶) At time of research, the old wooden restaurant on the river was in the process of being moved into new premises, under construction on the grounds of the Kritsada Rimkhong Hotel. It serves regular Thai dishes, with an emphasis on Mekong river delicacies.

Night Market NORTHEASTERN THAI $
(⏰4-10pm) That Phanom's night market is much bigger than you'd expect for a town this size. It has a good variety of food, but few places to sit.

Information

There are several regular banks in the centre of town. For weekends and evenings, there's a **Bangkok Bank** (⏰10.30am-7pm) west of town in the Tesco-Lotus shopping centre, which also has an AEON ATM.

Getting There & Around

From That Phanom's new bus station, inconveniently located west of town (a túk-túk to the river should cost 30B), there are services to Ubon Ratchathani (bus/minivan 150/185B, 4½/four hours, 14 daily) via Mukdahan (47/50B, one hour), Udon Thani (168B to 200B, four hours, six daily) via Nakhon Phanom (40B to 50B, one hour, seven daily). For Nakhon Phanom you can also take one of the *sŏrng·tăa·ou* (40B, 1½ hours, frequent until 4pm) that park north of the *tâht*. There are a few morning buses to Bangkok (435B to 871B, 10 to 11 hours), but most depart between 5pm and 7pm. One Bangkok-bound company still departs from the old bus station in town.

Mukdahan Province

Mukdahan มุกดาหาร

POP 34,294

On the banks of the Mekong, directly opposite the Lao city of Savannakhet, Mukdahan has enough of interest to fill a relaxing day or two, and the vibe is friendly.

Sights

Talat Indojin MARKET
(ตลาดอินโดจีน; Th Samran Chaikhongtai; ⏰8am-6pm) This riverside market, which stretches along and under the promenade, is a busy and colourful spectacle, with stall after stall of food, clothing and assorted trinkets from China and Vietnam, plus silk and cotton fabrics made in Isan.

Hor Kaew Mukdahan MUSEUM
(หอแก้วมุกดาหาร; Th Samut Sakdarak; admission 50B; ⏰8am-6pm) This eye-catching 65m-tall tower was built for the 50th anniversary of King Rama IX's ascension to the throne. The nine-sided base has a good museum with displays (labelled in English) on the eight ethnic

groups of the province. There are great views and a few more historical displays in 'The 360° of Pleasure in Mukdahan by the Mekong' room, up at the 50m level. The ball on the top holds a locally revered Buddha image supposedly made of solid silver.

Phu Manorom VIEWPOINT

(ภูมโนรมย์; ⊙6am-7pm) You can get an impressive view of Laos and the Mekong from this mountain south of Hor Kaew Mukdahan. The temple here has a small garden and they're constructing a massive 84m-tall Buddha image. It's a popular spot for photo ops and catches a nice breeze, too.

Wat Pa Silawiwek BUDDHIST TEMPLE

(วัดป่าศิลาวิเวก; Th Damrongmukda; ⊙dawn-dusk) FREE It's the resident monkeys rather than anything religious or artistic that makes this forest temple on the edge of town worth a visit.

Festivals & Events

Besides the ordinary activities, the **Mukdahan Thai Tribal Festival**, better known as the Red Cross Fair, held 9 to 17 January in the field fronting the provincial hall *(săh·lah glahng)*, features dancing and other cultural activities from Mukdahan's eight ethnic groups.

Sleeping

Ban Rim Suan HOTEL $

(☎042 632980; www.banrimsuan.weebly.com; Th Samut Sakdarak; s/d 350/450B; P ⊖ ❄ ☜) This place offers a good budget deal with big, airy rooms with good furnishings. It's a tad south of the centre, but that makes it convenient for dinner and drinks along the river.

Submukda Grand Hotel HOTEL $

(☎042 612666; www.submukdagrandhotel.com; Th Samut Sakdarak; r 400-500B; P ❄ ☜) This place has standard rooms, and upper-floor balconies offer good river views.

Huanum Hotel HOTEL $

(☎042 611137; 38 Th Samut Sakdarak; r with fan & shared bathroom 200-350B, with air-con 350-420B; P ❄ @ ☜) The Huanum was undergoing a renovation at time of research and the finished rooms looked bright and cheerful. The place has a breezy atmosphere and the renovations make it a good budget choice.

★**Riverview Maekhong Hotel** HOTEL $$

(☎042 633323; Th Samran Chaikhongtai; r 650B; P ❄ @ ☜) This funky place south of Talat Indojin has a great waterfront location, and the spacious layout means the river breezes are fully utilised. The rooms are a little faded but somehow it hangs together for an overall pleasant feel. Add the friendly staff, free bikes, wooden terrace overlooking the river and riverfront restaurant and it's our favourite place in Mukdahan.

Be sure to request a river view room. They have spacious balconies.

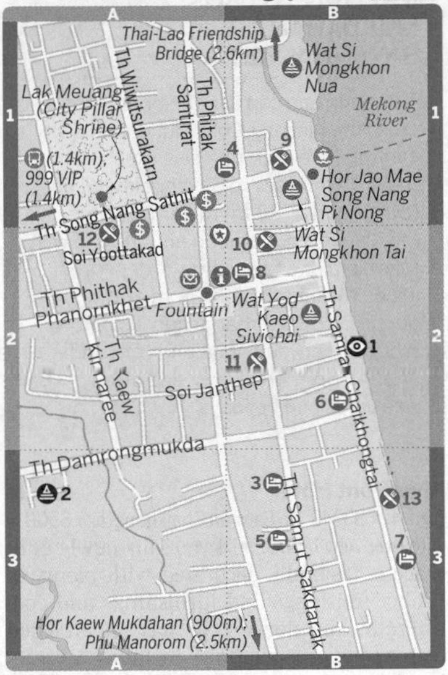

Mukdahan

Sights

1 Talat Indojin B2
2 Wat Pa Silawiwek A3

Sleeping

3 Ban Rim Suan B3
4 Huanum Hotel A1
5 River City Hotel B3
6 Riverfront Hotel B2
7 Riverview Maekhong Hotel B3
8 Submukda Grand Hotel B2

Eating

9 Goodmook* B1
10 Kufad B2
11 Kufad 2 .... B2
12 Night Market A2
13 Wine Wild Why? B3

GETTING TO LAOS: MUKDAHAN TO SAVANNAKHET

Thais and Lao can use the boats that cross the Mekong from Mukdahan's city centre, while everyone else must use the bridge. Buses to Savannakhet, Laos (50B, hourly 7.30am to 7pm) depart Mukdahan's bus station and the trip will take from one to two hours, depending on the length of the immigration queues. A 5B surcharge applies before 8.30am, between noon and 1pm and after 4.30pm weekdays, and all day weekends and holidays.

Riverfront Hotel HOTEL **$$**
(☎042 633348; Th Samran Chaikhongtai; r 850B, d with river view 1250B; P ❄ 📶) This newly built place is tastefully decorated with plenty of timber finishings and furnishings and cool (literally) tile flooring. It has an attached cafe and the room price includes a buffet breakfast. The river-view rooms have fabulous views.

River City Hotel HOTEL **$$$**
(☎042 615444; Th Samut Sakdarak; r incl breakfast 1080-1800B, ste from 3200B; P ❄ 📶 🏊) This large tower, topped by a 16th-floor revolving restaurant, is now tops in town. The suites are probably a bit much, but if you value your river outlook, the river-view standard rooms are good. There are cheaper rooms in the old wing, but they can't be recommended.

Eating

Most city-centre restaurants shut their doors early, but many out along Th Phithak Phanomkhet keep the woks sizzling late into the night.

Wine Wild Why? NORTHEASTERN THAI **$**
(Th Samran Chaikhongtai; dishes 40-150B; ⌚9am-10pm; P 📶) Housed in an atmospheric wooden building next to the river, this relaxing spot has bags of character and delicious Thai and Isan food, though it no longer serves wine.

Night Market THAI, VIETNAMESE **$**
(Th Song Nang Sathit; ⌚4-9pm) Mukdahan's night market has all the Thai and Isan classics, but it's the Vietnamese vendors that set it apart. A few sell *băhn dah* (the vendors will tell you it's 'Vietnamese pizza'), which combines soft noodles, pork, spring onions and an optional egg served on a crispy cracker.

Kufad VIETNAMESE **$**
(Th Samut Sakdarak; dishes 40-130B; ⌚8am-5pm; 📶) This family-run Vietnamese cafe is bright and clean and rightly popular. It's a good choice for breakfast if you're not in a rush. The picture menu takes the guesswork out of ordering, but leaves you clueless on the prices. There's a branch, **Kufad 2** (⌚8am-5pm), a little further down the road.

★**Goodmook*** INTERNATIONAL, THAI **$$**
(☎042 612091; Th Song Nang Sathit; dishes 70-450B; ⌚9am-10pm Tue-Sun; 📶) This delightful place is a pleasant discovery in Mukdahan – a cool, dark, inviting place with a mix of Thai and international food, art on the walls, chill music, good coffee and the best homemade cookies this side of the Mekong. It's a great place to drop in and meet other travellers, both Thai and Western.

Information

Immigration Office (☎042 674274; ⌚8.30am-4.30pm Mon-Fri) The office for visa extensions is north of town by the bridge.

Krung Thai Bank (Th Song Nang Sathit; ⌚10am-7pm) The only extended-hours bank in the city centre.

Tourism Information Centre (Th Phithak Phanomkhet; ⌚9am-4.30pm) You can pick up maps and brochures here, but don't expect staff to be able to answer your questions. There's also Thai massage and a crafts shop.

Getting There & Away

Mukdahan's **bus terminal** (☎042 630486) is on Rte 212, west of town. To get there from the centre, catch a yellow *sŏrng·tăa·ou* (10B, 6am to 5pm) running west along Th Phithak Phanomkhet. Túk-túk to the bus terminal cost 50B. There are minivans to Nakhon Phanom (80B, two hours, every 30 minutes) via That Phanom (40B, 45 minutes), and to Yasothon (84B, two hours, every 30 minutes) and Ubon Ratchathani (105B, 2½ hours, every 30 minutes). Buses go to Khon Kaen (180B to 230B, 4½ hours, every 30 minutes) and Ubon Ratchathani (75B to 135B, 3½ hours, every 30 minutes). A few Bangkok buses (420B to 790B, 10 hours) leave during the day, but most depart between 5pm and 8pm, including **999 VIP** (☎042 611478), with luxury buses (829B) at 8.30am, 8pm and 8.15pm.

If you're driving to Ubon Ratchathani, Rte 212 will zip you there in about three hours, but if you can spare a whole day, take the Mekong-hugging back roads through a gorgeous stretch of rural Thailand.

Getting Around

Rides with **Taxi Mukdahan** (☎042 613666; ⏰6am-midnight) start at 30B plus a 20B call fee, if the driver uses the meter.

Goodmook* (p400) restaurant hires bikes for 100B per day.

Phu Pha Thoep National Park

Despite only covering 48 sq km, hilly **Phu Pha Thoep National Park** (อุทยานแห่งชาติภูผาเทิบ; ☎089 619 7741; admission 200B) has a host of beautiful attractions – most famously, large mushroom-shaped rock formations. The main rock groups sits right behind the visitor centre, and wildflowers bloom around them October through December. Besides the weird rocks there are several clifftop viewpoints and **Nam Tok Phu Tham Phra**, a scenic waterfall (May to November only) with a grotto atop it holding hundreds of small Buddha images. It only takes a few hours on the well-marked trails to see all these sights. **Tham Fa Mue Daeng**, a cave with 5000-year-old hand paintings, is an 8km drive from the main park area and then a 1.5km walk.

For accommodation, there's **camping** (per person with own tent 30B, 4-/8-person tent hire 300/600B) and a three-bedroom **bungalow** (☎02 562 0760; www.dnp.go.th/parkreserve; bungalow 1800B).

The park is 15km south of Mukdahan via Rte 2034. *Sŏrng·tăa·ou* (20B, 30 minutes, every 30 minutes) to Don Tan, departing from Porn Pet Market, 300m north of Hor Kaew Mukdahan, pass the turn-off to the park. Hitching the last 1.3km to the visitor centre isn't tough, or you can ask the *sŏrng·tăa·ou* driver to detour off the route and take you; they'll probably do it for 100B. Be back at the junction by 4.30pm to guarantee finding a *sŏrng·tăa·ou* back to town.

LOWER ISAN

The provinces from Nakhon Ratchasima onwards to Ubon Ratchathani roughly conform to the Ancient Khmer Hwy, a road that during the times of the great Khmer kings led from Angkor Wat up into what is now Thailand. While the road no longer exists, traces of it remain in the form of the many temple and rest-station ruins, including the imposing Phanom Rung, that are testimony to the might the Khmer empire once achieved.

It's not only about Khmer temples. Thailand's pre-eminent national park, Khao Yai, is also in this region, along with many less-known but no less interesting parks. Some of them require a bit of leg work and an adventurous spirit, but the efforts are well rewarded.

Nakhon Ratchasima (Khorat) นครราชสีมา (โคราช)

POP 151,450

Khorat is a big, busy city with little in the way of sights, but one that for many travellers serves as the gateway to Isan. A bumper dose of urban hubbub reflects the city's affluence, and Khorat's one-time historic charm has been largely smothered under a duvet of homogenous development.

Khorat has a strong sense of regional identity (people call themselves *kon koh·râht* instead of *kon ee·săhn*) and is at its best in its quieter nooks, such as inside the east side of the historic moat, where local life goes on in a fairly traditional way.

Nakhon Ratchasima is almost universally abbreviated to the much more succinct 'Khorat'. The two terms are interchangeable.

Sights

Thao Suranari Monument MONUMENT

(อนุสาวรีย์ท้าวสุรนารี; Th Rajadamnern) FREE Thao Suranari, wife of the city's assistant governor during Rama III's reign, is something of a wonder woman in these parts. Ya Mo (Grandma Mo), as she's affectionately called, became a hero in 1826 by organising a successful prisoner revolt after Chao Anou of Vientiane had conquered Khorat during his rebellion against Siam. One version of the legend says she convinced the women to seduce the Lao soldiers and then the Thai men launched a surprise attack, saving the city.

Her monument sits photogenically in front of **Chumphon Gate**, the only original gate left standing – the other three are recent rebuilds. It was a part of the city walls erected in 1656 by French technicians on the orders of Ayuthaya King Narai. The little white building north of this gate that resembles the old fortifications is **Suranari Hall** (อาคารแสดงแสงเสียงวีรกรรมท้าวสุรนารี; Th Chumphon;

Nakhon Ratchasima (Khorat)

0 500 m
0 0.25 miles

Terminal 2 (800m); Tourist Police (900m); U-Bar (2km)
V-One (1km)
The Mall (1.3km); Bangkok Hospital (1.6km)
Hwy 2
Mae Nam Mun
Th Suranari
Th Chang Phuak
Th Mittaphap
Pratu Phonsaen
Th Thaosura Soi 1
Th Polsean
Chang Phueak Shrine
Th Burin
Vatmung Soi 2
Th Rajadamnern
Th Chumphon
Th Yommarat
Th Phonlan
Th Thaosura
Th Jant
Th Suranaree
Th Yotha
Th Chakkri
Th Manat
Th Prajak
Th Assadang
Th Kudan
Lak Meuang
Pratu Phonlan
Th Phoklang
Th Chomphon
Wat Boon
Nakhon Ratchasima (Khorat) Railway Station (1km); 100 Year Meuang Ya Market (1.5km)
Th Jomsurangyat
Th Mahat Thai
Th Wacharasrit
Th Chainarong
Th San-Prasit
Th Kamhaengsongkhram
Th Ratchanikun
Pratu Chainarong
Th Buarong
Chira

1 2 3 4 5 6 7 8 9 10 11 12 13 14 15 16 17 18 19 20 21 22 23

A B C D E F G
1 2 3 4

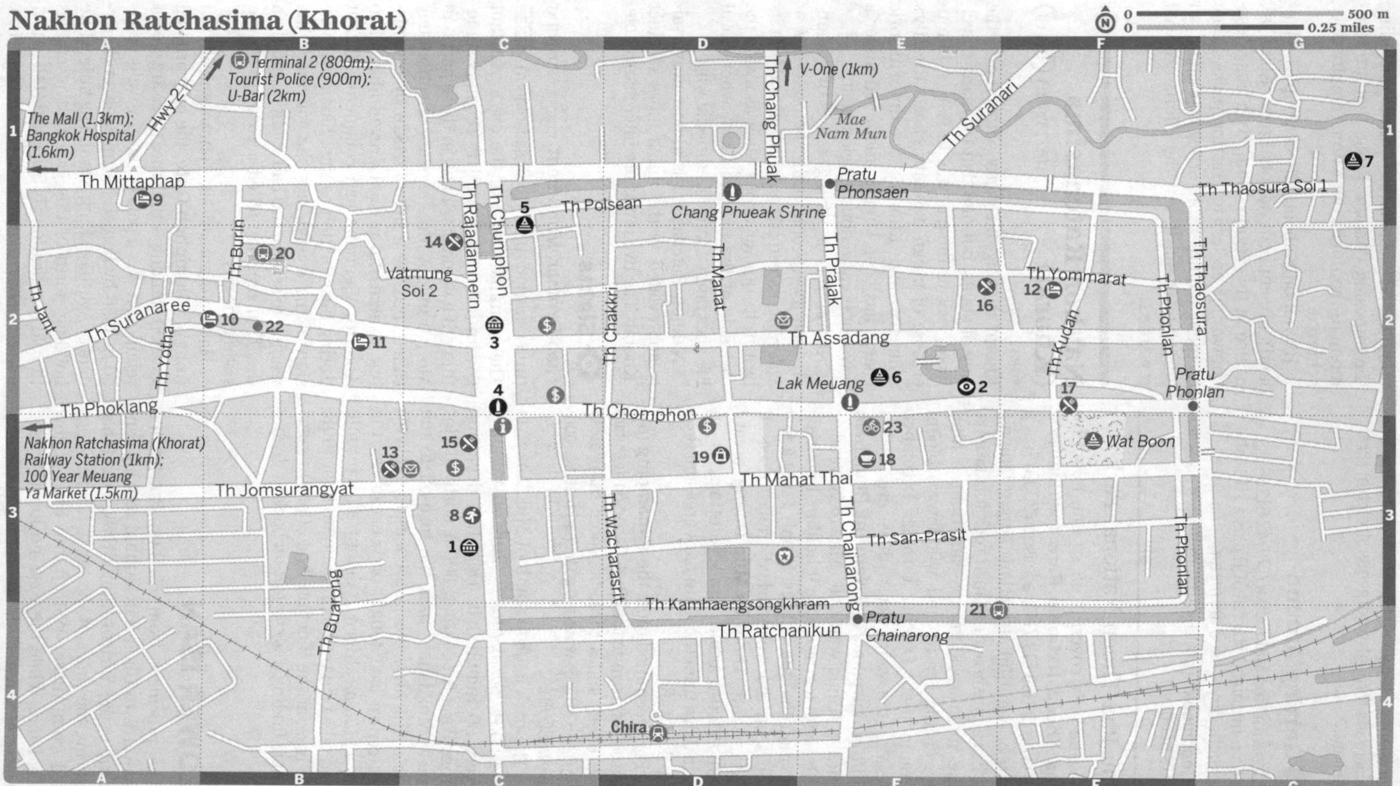

Nakhon Ratchasima (Khorat)

Sights

	Chumphon Gate	(see 4)
1	Maha Viravong National Museum	C3
2	Naranya Temple	E2
3	Suranari Hall	C2
4	Thao Suranari Monument	C2
5	Wat Phayap	C1
6	Wat Phra Narai Maharat	E2
7	Wat Salaloi	G1

Activities, Courses & Tours

8	Ratchadamnern Nuat Pheua Sukhaphap	C3

Sleeping

9	Rachaphruk Grand Hotel	A1
10	Sansabai House	B2
11	Srivichai Hotel	B2
12	Thai Inter Hotel	F2

Eating

13	Anego	B3
14	Gai Yang Saang Thai	C2
15	Ming Ter	C3
16	Rabieng Kaew	E2
17	Wat Boon Night Bazaar	F2

Drinking & Nightlife

	Bar Nana	(see 9)
18	Wawee Coffee	E3

Shopping

19	Night Bazaar Korat	D3

Transport

20	Bus Terminal 1	B2
21	Bus to Dan Kwian	E4
22	Euro Karn Chang	B2
23	Jompol Bike	E3

9am 6pm Tue-Sun) FREE, a museum of sorts with a cool diorama and even-cooler sculpted mural creatively depicting the famous battle.

Wat Salaloi BUDDHIST TEMPLE
(วัดศาลาลอย; Soi 1, Th Thaosura; dawn-dusk) FREE The city's most interesting temple was supposedly founded by Thao Suranari and her husband in 1827. Half of her ashes are interred in a small stupa (the other half are at her monument) and so there are also singing troupes on hire to perform for her spirit here. A small statue of the heroine sits praying in the pond in front of the temple's award-winning *bóht*. The temple is usually teeming with people making offerings.

Built in 1967, the *bóht* resembles a Chinese junk and holds a large gleaming-white Buddha image in 'calming the ocean' posture. It, and other buildings, are decorated with Dan Kwian pottery. Elsewhere around the grounds are a variety of spirit shrines that have nothing to do with Buddhism.

Wat Phayap BUDDHIST TEMPLE
(วัดพายัพ; Th Polsaen; dawn-dusk) FREE When the abbot of Wat Phayap learned that blasting for a quarry in Saraburi Province was destroying a beautiful cave, he rescued pieces of it and plastered the stalactites, stalagmites and other incredible rocks all over a room below his residence, creating a shrine like no other.

It looks like the products of the quarry have been put to good use, too. The temple was putting the finishing touches to a beautiful new *bóht* when we visited, made of polished granite and marble, with a marble-tiled roof.

Wat Phra Narai Maharat BUDDHIST TEMPLE
(วัดพระนารายณ์มหาราช; Th Chomphon; dawn-dusk) FREE This large temple is of interest because of three holy Khmer sandstone sculptures that were unearthed here – Phra Narai (Vishnu) is the holiest. To see them, follow the signs with red arrows back to the special **Naranya Temple** (10am-6pm) at the southeast corner (the sculptures are enclosed in the attached building).

Maha Viravong National Museum MUSEUM
(พิพิธภัณฑสถานแห่งชาติมหาวีรวงศ์; Th Rajadamnern; admission 50B; 9am-4pm Wed-Sun) Though the collection at this seldom-visited museum is very small, it's also very good. There's ancient pottery (don't miss sneaking a peek at what's stored in the back) and a variety of Buddha images spanning the Dvaravati to Rattanakosin eras.

Activities

Ratchadamnern Nuat Pheua Sukhaphap MASSAGE
(092 452 4717; 68 Th Rajadamnern; Thai massage per hr 200B, with oil 400B; 9am-9pm) This soothing place is nicely decked out and has lilting Thai music to calm the nerves. It's a genuine massage facility practicing relaxation and targeted therapeutic massage, using various traditional Thai techniques, as well as herbs and tapping.

Festivals & Events

Khorat explodes into life during the **Thao Suranari Festival** (23 March to 3 April), when the city celebrates the namesake heroine. It features parades, theatre and other events along Th Rajadamnern.

During Khao Phansaa in July, Khorat has a **candle parade**, smaller than, but similar to, that in Ubon Ratchathani.

Sleeping

★ Sansabai House HOTEL $
(☎044 255144; www.sansabai-korat.com; Th Suranaree; r 300-450B; P ❄ ☎) This place is hidden beside the Tokyo hotel, which does a much better job of advertising itself, but the obscurity fits its understated ambience. The lobby is welcoming and the rooms are constantly being refitted. There are fan rooms as well as air-con rooms.

Srivichai Hotel HOTEL $
(☎044 242194; 9-11 Th Buarong; r 400-500B) The Srivichai has decent rooms that are reliable, clean and nicely decked out with rattan furniture. One plus is that all the rooms have big bathtubs, as well as showers. There's an attached cafe and breakfast can be included for an extra 50B to 90B.

Thai Inter Hotel HOTEL $$
(☎044 247700; www.thaiinterhotel.com; Th Yommarat; r incl breakfast 650B; P ❄ @ ☎) This little hotel patches together an odd mix of styles. The lobby is homely, the rooms are comfy, if small, and the furniture a little worn. It's got a good (though not so quiet) location near decent restaurants and bars. Guests receive a discount at the nearby bar.

Rachaphruk Grand Hotel HOTEL $$
(☎044 341222; www.rachaphrukgrandhotel.com; Th Mittaphap; r incl breakfast 1200-1500B, ste 4500; P ❄ @ ☎ ≈) This grand old Chinese hotel is full of memorabilia and bric-a-brac. The rooms are spacious with designer, if dated, furnishings. There's a pool, a fitness centre with a sauna, a yoga room and many entertainment options.

V-One HOTEL $$$
(☎044 342444; www.v-onehotelkorat.com; Th Chang Phuak; r incl breakfast 1990-7900B; P ❄ @ ☎ ≈) The self-proclaimed 'Trendy & Boutique Hotel' is a brash mixture of colours and styles that sometimes feels more like a children's playroom than a three-star hotel. But in trying to be different it certainly earns an 'A' for effort. All rooms have safes and other little amenities and most are more tasteful than tacky.

Sima Thani HOTEL $$$
(☎044 213100; www.simathani.com; Th Mittaphap; r incl breakfast 1500-2000B, ste 4600-10,500B; P ❄ @ ☎ ≈) Sima Thani has the standards and amenities expected from a luxury hotel.

DON'T MISS

PÀT MÈE KOH·RÂHT

One speciality you must try once is *pàt mèe koh·râht*. It's similar to *pát tai*, but boasts more flavour and is made with a local style of rice noodle *(mèe koh·râht)*. It's widely available in Nakhon Ratchasima Province, but very rare everywhere else.

Eating

There's abundant *fa·ràng* food at the Mall.

Ming Ter VEGAN $
(Th Rajadamnern; dishes 40-80B; ⊙7.30am-6pm; ✎) There's little English at this homely vegan affair, but since it does mock-meat versions of Thai and Chinese standards, you can just order your favourites and the message will get through. Or just point to something in the buffet tray.

Gai Yang Saang Thai THAI $
(Th Rajadamnern; whole free-range chicken 140B; ⊙7.30am-8pm) Has served some of the best *gài yâhng* (grilled chicken) in Khorat for half a century.

Wat Boon Night Bazaar THAI $
(Th Chompon; ⊙5-9.30pm) This night market is less popular than Night Bazaar Korat (p405), but it's the better choice for eating. Offers Thai as well as northeastern Thai food.

★ Anego JAPANESE $$
(☎044 260530; Th Jomsurangyat; dishes 60-600B; ⊙5pm-midnight; P ❄ ☎) Step through the dark-wood doors and into a cosy little spot that is popular with both Thais and expats. It has a huge menu of Japanese dishes (with the obligatory photographs) and one page of Italian pastas.

Rabieng Kaew THAI $$
(Th Yommarat; dishes 100-300B; ⊙11am-5pm; P) This lovely spot has an antique-filled dining area and a leafy garden out back. The furni-

EATING ISAN

Isan's culinary creations are a blend of Lao and Thai cooking styles that make use of local ingredients. The holy trinity of northeastern cuisine, *gài yâhng* (grilled chicken), *sôm·đam* (spicy papaya salad) and *kôw něe·o* (sticky rice), is integral to the culture. Also crucial are chillies – a fistful of potent peppers find their way into most dishes. Outsiders, including most other Thais, are rarely fans of *Ƀlah ráh*, a fermented fish sauce (that looks like rotten mud), but Isan people consider it almost essential for good cooking. If your *sôm·đam* doesn't have this, it's not real *sôm·đam*.

Fish dominates Isan menus, with *Ƀlah dùk* (catfish), *Ƀlah chôrn* (striped snake-head) and *Ƀlah boo* (sand goby) among the most popular. These are mostly caught in the Mekong and other large rivers. Insects traditionally comprised a large part of the typical family's diet and are still very common as snacks and chilli-sauce ingredients. Purple lights shining out in the countryside are for catching giant water bugs *(maang dah)*, which make a fragrant chilli paste *(prík maang dah)*.

Following are some Isan staples.

lâhp Thailand's famous minced-meat 'salad' is actually an Isan dish and, if eaten here, it's one of the spiciest foods in Thailand. Sometimes the meat (it can be made with almost anything as a base, including mushrooms) is raw, but this is not recommended due to bacteria and parasites.

nám đòk Essentially the same as *lâhp*, but with the meat sliced and grilled rather than diced and boiled.

đôm sâap The Isan version of *đôm yam*. Usually full of innards and tendons, the soft parts of an animal left over after making *lâhp*.

súp nòr·mái Usually translated as bamboo shoot 'salad', it uses *yâh nang* leaves for flavour. It's much less spicy than *sôm·đam*.

gaang òrm This prototypical Isan curry is heavy on herbs and only mildly spicy. Like all Isan curries, there's no coconut milk.

gaang hèt Another common northeastern curry, it's the tamarind that makes it a little sour. The mix is often seasonal, depending on what mushrooms have just been picked in the forest.

sâi gròrk ee·săhn 'Isan sausage' uses fermented pork for a sour taste. Sticky rice, garlic and salt also go inside the skin.

Ƀlah pŏw Grilled fish (several freshwater species are used) coated in salt, with its stomach stuffed with pandanus leaves and lemongrass.

ture is rustic to the point of looking neglected, but it's not all about the atmosphere. The food, all big dishes meant to be shared, is good.

Drinking & Nightlife

Khorat has a glut of good Thai-style pubs. Th Mahat Thai and Th San-Prasit, around their junctions with Th Chainarong, is a good bar-hopping district.

U-Bar (Hwy 2), near the V-One Hotel, 2.5km north of the centre, and the less popular but more convenient **Bar Nana** (Th Mittaphap), at the Rachaphruk Grand Hotel, have student-filled dance floors. Both get hopping around 10pm.

Wawee Coffee COFFEE
(☎080 170 3232; Th Mahat Thai; ⏰7am-8pm; 📶) This is a great place to lounge around in, with an air-con section and also an outdoor patio overlooking a pond with brightly coloured carp. The lattes, brownies and sofas make this stylish place pretty well perfect.

Shopping

Night Bazaar Korat MARKET
(Th Manat; ⏰5-10pm) While it's got nothing on Chiang Mai's version, this night market, selling mostly clothes, attracts a lively crowd and is fun to stroll.

BUSES FROM NAKHON RATCHASIMA'S TERMINAL 2

DESTINATION	FARE (B)	DURATION (HR)	FREQUENCY
Aranya Prathet (Rong Kleua Market)	165	4	5.30am-5.30pm (5 daily)
Ayuthaya (minivan)	132	4	6am-7pm (frequent)
Buriram	99	2-3	frequent
Chiang Mai	473	12-13	3am-8.30pm (11 daily)
Khon Kaen	120-250	3-4	6am-11pm (frequent)
Khon Kaen (minivan)	129	2½	7am-5pm (hourly)
Krabi	913	15	4.50pm
Loei	275	7	5.30am-5.45pm (11 daily)
Lopburi	120	3½	6am-7pm (every 30 min)
Nang Rong	75-95	2	all day (frequent)
Nang Rong (minivan)	75	1½	5am-8pm (every 30 min)
Nong Khai	220-435	6	all day (hourly)
Surin	136-175	4	7am-7.20pm (every 30 min)
Trat	324	8	1am
Ubon Ratchathani	288-445	5-6	8am-1am (14 daily)
Udon Thani	245-300	5	frequent

100 Year Meuang Ya Market MARKET
(Th Mukhamontri; ⏲4-10pm) This market is full of kitsch, and is pretty quiet on weekdays.

The Mall SHOPPING CENTRE
(Th Mittaphap; ⏲10.30am-9pm Mon-Fri, 10am-9pm Sat & Sun) This is Isan's largest and glossiest mall. It has a small branch of Asia Books selling English-language books.

Information

The Mall has many banks with extended opening hours, and an AEON ATM.

Bangkok Bank (Th Jomsurangyat; ⏲10.30am-7pm) Bank inside Klang Plaza. There's also an AEON ATM outside by the alley entrance.

Bangkok Hospital (☎044 429999; Th Mittaphap)

Immigration (☎044 375138; ⏲8.30am-noon & 1-4pm Mon-Fri) Located in Dan Kwian village.

Post Office (Th Jomsurangyat; ⏲8.30am-10.30pm Mon-Fri, 9am-noon & 4-10.30pm Sat, 4-10.30pm Sun & holidays)

Tourism Authority of Thailand (TAT; ☎044 213666; tatsima@tat.or.th; 2102-2104 Th Mittaphap; ⏲8.30am-4.30pm) Next to Sima Thani Hotel.

Tourist Office Booth (⏲9am-5pm) Right by the Thao Suranari Monument.

Getting There & Away

BUS

Khorat has two bus terminals. **Terminal 1** (☎044 242899; Th Burin) in the city centre serves Bangkok (1st-class only) and most towns within Nakhon Ratchasima Province, including Pak Chong (60B, 1½ hours, every 20 minutes). Buses to other destinations, plus more Bangkok buses and minivans, use **Terminal 2** (bor kŏr sŏr sŏrng; ☎044 295271; Hwy 2) north of the centre. You never have to wait long for a bus to Bangkok (171B to 320B, 3½ hours) since buses from most cities in Isan pass through Khorat on their way to the capital.

There are minivans to/from Ayuthaya (132B, four hours, every 30 minutes) and Lopburi (120B, 3½ hours, hourly) from Bus Terminal 2.

TRAIN

Many trains pass through **Khorat train station** (☎044 242044), but buses are much faster. Ten daily trains go to/from Bangkok (50B to 425B, five to seven hours), via Ayuthaya. There are also nine Ubon Ratchathani (58B to 453B, five to six hours) and four Khon Kaen (38B to 170B, 3½ hours) trains.

Khorat's smaller **Chira Train Station** (☎044 242363) is closer to the old city, so it may be more convenient to get off there.

Getting Around

There are fixed *sŏrng·tăa·ou* (8B) routes through the city, but even locals find it hard to figure them out because of the dizzying array of numbers and colours representing them. Most pass the junction of Th Suranaree and Th Rajadamnern, so if you want to go somewhere, just head there and ask around. Heading west on Suranaree, yellow *sŏrng·tăa·ou* 1, with white and green stripes, will take you past the train station, the tourism office and the Mall. Heading north on Rajadamnern the white 6, with red and yellow stripes, passes the Mall more directly and the white 15, with purple stripes, goes to Bus Terminal 2.

Túk-túk cost between 40B and 70B to most places in town. Motorcycle taxis and *săhm·lór* (pedicabs), both of which are common, always cost less. Metered taxis are found only at Bus Terminal 2 and the Mall, but there's almost no chance of getting them to use the meter.

Korat Car Rental (☎ 081 877 3198; www.koratcarrental.com) is a local firm with a stellar reputation. The Sima Thani Hotel also arranges cars with drivers, some of whom speak English.

Euro Karn Chang (☎ 088 355 9393; 239-241 Th Suranaree; ⏰ 8am-5pm Mon-Sat) near Bus Terminal 1 hires motorcycles for 300/1400B per day/week, and **Jompol Bike** (☎ 081 955 2838; Th Chumphon; ⏰ 8am-5.30pm Tue-Sun) hires bicycles for 100B a day.

Around Nakhon Ratchasima

Dan Kwian ด่านเกวียน

If you have even a small interest in ceramics, you should pay Dan Kwian a visit. Just a quick trip out of Khorat, this village has been producing pottery for hundreds of years and its creations are famous for their rough texture and rust-like hue. Only kaolin sourced from this district produces such results. Most of what's made and sold these days are cheap lawn ornaments, but there's also some attractive modern pottery plus cast sandstone reproductions of ancient Khmer sculptures. If you walk through the village proper, south of the myriad shops lining the highway (turn east at the school), you'll find some families with small workshops and kilns at their houses. There's also a large workshop behind the **DinPao** shop at the north end of the highway, near the pedestrian bridge.

To get here from Khorat, hop on a bus (14B, 30 minutes) from near the southern city gate (or catch it along Th Mahat Thai) or Terminal 2 (25B, 45 minutes).

Pak Thong Chai ปักธงชัย

Pak Thong Chai became one of Thailand's most famous silk-weaving centres when Jim Thompson started buying silk here. Today there are almost a dozen large silk factories in the district and thousands of families still work hand looms at home in every village. Pak Thong Chai is known for following the latest trends, but some shops stock traditional styles such as *mát·mèe,* most of which are woven in other provinces.

Because Pak Thong Chai is a fairly large town, it's not nearly as fun to visit as other Isan silk centres such as Chonnabot (p438) or Ban Tha Sawang (p420), but **Macchada** (⏰ 8am-5pm), a shop at the city's southern end, where you can watch weavers working, is worth seeking out. There are highway signs directing you to a Silk Cultural Center, but it's been closed for years.

Pak Thong Chai is 30km south of Khorat on Rte 304. Buses (21B, one hour, frequent) leave from Terminal 1.

Ban Prasat บ้านปราสาท

About 3000 years ago a primitive agricultural culture, closely related to Ban Chiang, put down roots at Ban Prasat, near the banks of the Than Prasat River. It survived around 1500 years, planting rice, domesticating animals, fashioning coloured pottery, weaving cloth and, in later years, forging tools out of bronze. The secrets of this early civilisation were revealed during extensive archaeological digs completed in 1991.

Three **excavation pits** (admission free) with skeletons (most are replicas) and pottery left in situ are on display in the village, and a small but good **museum** (admission free; ⏰ 8am-4.30pm) houses some of the discoveries. It also explains what life was like in those days and in the village today. South of the museum, one family still does **silk weaving**, including raising their own worms and spinning their own thread. They welcome visitors to come by for a look.

Many families (some speak a little English) are part of an award-winning **homestay program** (☎ 081 725 0791; per person incl 2 meals 400B) where villagers put up visitors in their homes and show them daily activities including basketry and farming.

Reservations should be made at least a day in advance.

Ban Prasat is located 45km northeast of Khorat, off Hwy 2, and buses (35B, one hour) heading to Phimai will drop you off at the highway. A motorcycle taxi will zip you around to all the sites for 50B per person, but note that sometimes only one driver is working.

Phimai พิมาย

POP 9768

The otherwise mundane little town of Phimai has one of Thailand's finest surviving Khmer temple complexes right at its heart. Reminiscent of Cambodia's Angkor Wat, Prasat Phimai was once stood on the Ancient Khmer Hwy linking the Khmer capital of Angkor with the northern reaches of the realm. Phimai is the first of the major Khmer monuments to be reached if you're coming from Bangkok, and also one of the most picturesque. And, being located smack in the centre of this small and pleasant town, it is easily the most accessible.

Phimai is an easy day trip out of Khorat, but if you prefer the quiet life, you could always make Khorat a day trip out of Phimai instead.

Sights

★Phimai Historical Park HISTORIC SITE

(อุทยานประวัติศาสตร์พิมาย; 044 471568; Th Ananthajinda; admission 100B; 7.30am-6pm) According to the information in its **visitor centre** (8.30am-4.30pm), this temple was started by Khmer King Jayaviravarman (r AD 1002–06), although other records have it dated to as late as the 12th century. Regardless, Phimai is one of the most impressive Khmer ruins in Thailand. Though built as a Mahayana Buddhist temple, the carvings also feature many Hindu deities, and design elements at Prasat Phimai influenced Angkor-Wat.

You enter over a cruciform **naga bridge**, which symbolically represents the passage from earth to heaven, and then through the **southern gate** (which is unusual since most Khmer temples face east) of the outer wall, which stretches 565m by 1030m. A raised passageway, formerly covered by a tiled roof, leads to the inner sanctum and the 28m-tall **main shrine** built of white sandstone and covered in superb carvings. At the centre of the **Prang Brahmathat**, in front of the main shrine, is a replica stone sculpture of Angkor King Jayavarman VII sitting cross-legged and looking very much like a sitting Buddha. The original is in the Phimai National Museum.

Knowledgeable local students sometimes act as guides, but few speak English. Luckily, a free brochure provides a good overview of the complex.

Phimai National Museum MUSEUM

(พิพิธภัณฑสถานแหงชาติพิมาย; Th Tha Songkhran; admission 100B; 9am-4pm Wed-Sun) After a recent renovation this is now one of the best museums in Isan and well worth a visit. Situated on the banks of Sa Kwan, a 12th-century Khmer reservoir, the museum consists of two spacious buildings housing a fine collection of Khmer sculptures from Phimai, including many exquisite lintels, and other ruins around Lower Isan. There's also some distinctive black Phimai pottery (500 BC–AD 500) and Buddha images from various periods.

Sai Ngam PARK

(ไทรงาม; dawn-dusk) Situated a bit east of town is Thailand's largest and oldest banyan tree, a 350-plus-year-old giant spread over an island. The extensive system of interlocking branches and gnarled trunks makes the 'Beautiful Banyan' look like a small forest.

Other Historic Sites

Meru Bhramathat (Th Buchayan) FREE is a toppled brick *chedi* dating back to the late Ayuthaya period (18th century). Its name is derived from a folk tale that refers to it as the cremation site of King Bhramathat.

Three city gates remain. **Pratu Chai** (Victory Gate) FREE, the one that served the road to Angkor, is the most intact. The mounded dirt ridge alongside it shows what the ramparts formerly surrounding the entire city looked like. These city walls went up in the 13th century, as did what's now known as **Kuti Rusi** (Hermit's Quarters; dawn-dusk) FREE, a healing station built by Jayavarman VII, and **Tha Nang Sa Phom** (dawn-dusk) FREE, a laterite landing platform on the grounds of the Fine Arts Department compound; turn right immediately after entering the gate.

Phimai

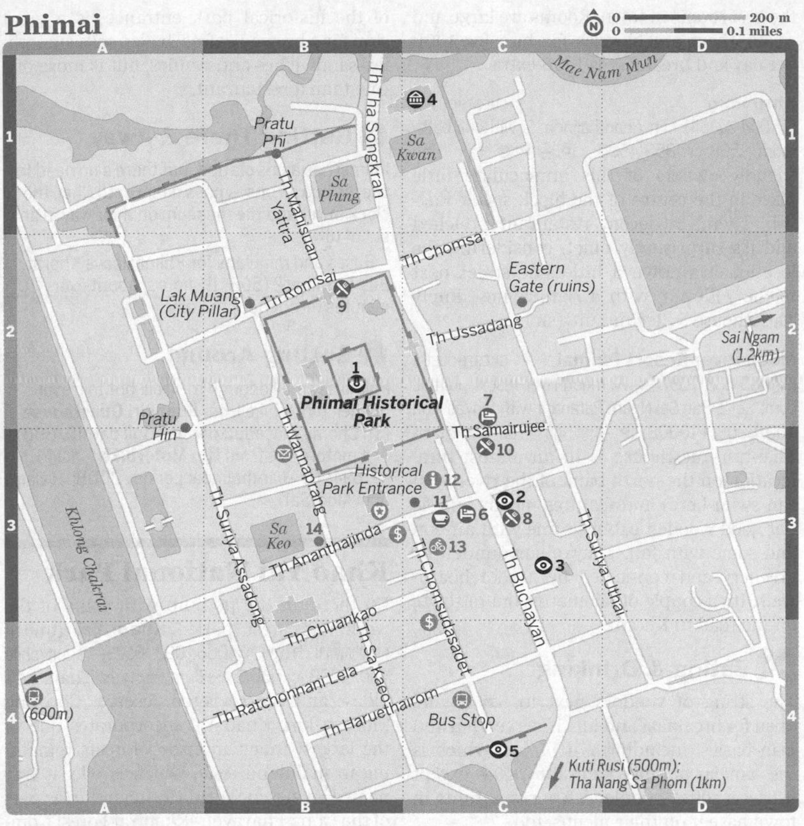

Phimai

Top Sights
1 Phimai Historical Park B2

Sights
2 Clock Tower C3
3 Meru Bhramathat C3
4 Phimai National Museum C1
5 Pratu Chai C4

Sleeping
6 Khru Pom C3
7 Phimai Paradise C2

Eating
8 Night Bazaar C3
9 Nom Neay Bakery & Coffee B2
10 Rabiang Mai C3

Drinking & Nightlife
11 Barai Coffee C3

Information
12 Phimai Historical Park Visitor Center C3

Transport
13 Boonsiri Guesthouse C3
14 Niu Motorbike B3

Festivals & Events

Staged in mid-November, the **Phimai Festival** celebrates the town's history, with cultural performances, sound-and-light shows (tickets 200B to 600B) and long-boat races.

Sleeping

Phimai Paradise HOTEL $
(044 287565; www.phimaiparadise.com; Th Samairujee; r 450-700B; P ⊖ ❄ ☜ ≋) Nothing too fancy, but this newish tower has by far

the best rooms in town. Rooms are large and clean. There are bicycles for hire for 100B per day and breakfast is 100B extra.

Khru Pom GUESTHOUSE **$**
(044 471541; Th Ananthajinda; s without bathroom 150B, r 350-450B;) The friendly owners of this immaculate little place in the centre of the block speak English. There's a decent restaurant attached and it's surprisingly quiet, considering the location. It's down a little side street next to the 7-Eleven, with a sign saying simply 'Guesthouse & Restuarant' (sic).

Moon River Resort Phimai GUESTHOUSE **$**
(085 633 7097; www.moon-river-resort-phimai.com; Soi 2, Ban Sai Ngam Patana; r with fan/air-con 400/600B, f 1000B;) This German-Thai-run guesthouse is in an almost-rural location on the north bank of the river (you can swim here) and features mostly simple but good wooden cabins, some with air-con and some with fan. They're surrounded by greenery and connected by a cool boardwalk. It's a couple of kilometres out of town, off the road to Khorat.

Eating & Drinking

The string of vendors next to Sai Ngam, open for breakfast and lunch, serve Thai and Isan basics, including *pàt pímai,* which is the same as pàt mèe koh·râht (p404) except it uses a softer noodle. A few restaurants in town have it on their menus, too.

★**Nom Neay Bakery & Coffee** BAKERY **$**
(Th Tha Songkhran; dishes 100-250B; 8.30am-5pm) It bills itself as a bakery, but this little place near the historical park entrance also does international and Thai food quite well. Brewed coffee and cakes are a speciality.

Rabiang Mai THAI **$**
(Th Samairujee; dishes 50-250B; 5pm-midnight;) This semi-fancy place is a tad on the pricey side, but the food (mostly Thai, plus some Isan and *fa·ràng* options) is quite good. It's also a bar and has live music of sorts.

Night Bazaar NORTHEASTERN THAI **$**
(Th Ananthajinda; 4-9pm) The food stalls set up along a side street to the nightly fresh market and are worth a stroll.

Barai Coffee CAFE
(085 611 5841; Th Ananthajinda; 8.30am-5pm) This delightful little place, just in front of the historical park entrance, is a great stop for a brewed coffee. It also sells smoothies, sandwiches and waffles, but is more of a cafe than a restaurant.

Getting There & Away

Phimai has a bus station, but there's no need to use it since all buses pass near Pratu Chai, the clock tower and the museum on their way in and out of town.

Buses and minivans for Phimai leave Khorat's Bus Terminal 2 (50B, 1½ hours) about every 20 minutes throughout the day.

Getting Around

Phimai is small enough to stroll, but to travel further, hire a bike from **Boonsiri Guesthouse** (Th Chomsudasadet; per half/full day 40/60B) or a motorcycle from **Niu Motorbike** (044 471694; Th Ananthajinda; per day 200B; 8am-5pm Mon-Sat).

Khao Yai National Park

Up there on the podium with some of the world's greatest parks, **Khao Yai** (อุทยานแห่งชาติเขาใหญ่; 086 092 6529; adult/child 400/200B, car 50B; 6am-6pm) is Thailand's oldest and most visited reserve. Covering 2168 sq km, Khao Yai incorporates one of the largest intact monsoon forests remaining in mainland Asia, which is why it was named a Unesco World Heritage site (as part of the Dong Phayayen–Khao Yai Forest Complex). Visiting independently is quite easy, as the mostly English-speaking staff at the **visitor centre** (086 092 6529; 8am-7pm) are very helpful.

Rising to 1351m at the summit of Khao Rom, the park's terrain covers five vegetation zones: evergreen rainforest (100m to 400m), semi-evergreen rainforest (400m to 900m), mixed deciduous forest (northern slopes at 400m to 600m), hill evergreen forest (over 1000m) and savannah and secondary-growth forest in areas where agriculture and logging occurred before it was protected.

Around 200 elephants tramp the park's boundaries. Other mammals include tigers, leopards, bears, gaur, barking deer, otters, various gibbons and macaques and some rather large pythons. Khao Yai's bird list boasts 392 species, and one of Thailand's largest populations of hornbills lives here, including the great hornbill (*nók gòk* or *nók gah·hang*).

The main entrance is south of Pak Chong, but there's a second, seldom-used southern entrance in Prachinburi Province.

Sights & Activities

Waterfalls

Khao Yai has many waterfalls. Little **Nam Tok Kong Kaew** sits right behind the visitor centre, while **Nam Tok Haew Narok** is in the far south of the park (an 800m walk from the parking area). Its three levels combine to form a 150m drop, making it the park's biggest falls. The beauty award, however, goes to 25m-high **Nam Tok Haew Suwat**, which scooped a starring role in Danny Boyle's film *The Beach*. It has water year-round and you can walk down to the bottom, but swimming isn't allowed. Though easily reached by car, Haew Suwat can also be accessed by a couple of walking trails, including the Kong Kaew–Haew Suwat Trail.

Wildlife

There are several **viewpoints** and **salt licks** (often attracting elephants in the early morning and evening) along the roads through the park. There's a good chance of seeing gibbons and hornbills on the Kong Kaew–Haew Suwat Trail, and it's probably the best footpath for spotting elephants, though encounters are unlikely; the roads are better for elephant spotting.

The **Nong Phak Chi observation tower** overlooks a little lake and a salt lick, and is one of the best wildlife-spotting sites in the park. In the early evening, deer congregate at the visitor centre and campgrounds.

Hiking

The Nong Phak Chi observation tower can be reached on a couple of walking trails. The shortest way (900m) to the tower starts 1.8km north of the visitor centre, and it's a wide, well-maintained path. Hikers can also get to the observation tower either by a 5.4km (three-hour) trail from the visitor centre, or a 3km (two-hour) path starting at Km 33. The latter is better for seeing wildlife along the way and is one of Khao Yai's best birdwatching walks. To get to Nam Tok Haew Suwat waterfall, try the mildly challenging, 8km-long (four to five hours) **Kong Kaew–Haew Suwat Trail** (Trail 1), which starts behind the visitor centre.

While the Kong Kaew–Haew Suwat Trail and walks to the tower don't require a guide, hiring one is highly recommended (except for the short route to the observation tower) because the trails aren't well trodden or well marked. We've heard from travellers who got lost and were forced to sleep in the forest overnight. Park rangers can be hired as guides (half/full day 500/1000B per group) through the visitor centre. They can also lead you on longer off-trail treks.

No matter where you hike, you should wear boots and long trousers. During the rainy season leeches are a problem. Mosquito repellent helps keep them away, but the leech socks sold in the visitor centre are much better.

Tours

Most hotels and resorts around Khao Yai arrange park tours and this is really the

BEYOND THE FOREST

The greater Pak Chong region is a popular destination and there are a couple of attractions worth a visit.

The excellent **Khao Yai Art Museum** (☎044 756060; www.khaoyaiartmuseum.com; ⏲10am-6pm) FREE has three rooms of modern art from some of Thailand's top artists, including Anupong Chantorn and Lampu Kansanoh. It's 4km east of Th Thanarat at Km 15; turn at the police box.

Thailand is the pioneer of 'New Latitude Wines' and with over a dozen wineries in the area, the Khao Yai area is now the epicentre of this increasingly respectable industry. Two of the leaders – **PB Valley** (☎036 226415; www.khaoyaiwinery.com; tours 300B; ⏲tours 10.30am, 1.30pm & 3.30pm), which corked its first bottle in 1998, and **GranMonte** (☎044 009543; www.granmonte.com; tours adult/under 20yr 300/220B; ⏲tours 10am, 11.30am, 1pm, 2.30pm & 4.30pm Sat, Sun & holidays Nov-Feb, 10.30am, 1.30pm & 3.30pm Mar-Oct), which got into the game three years later – lie along Muak Lek road (exit Km 144), the direct route from Bangkok to Khao Yai. Both are scenically set and offer tours (book in advance), tastings, luxury lodging and classy restaurants for lunch and dinner. They're 22.5km and 16km respectively from the national park gate.

ideal way to visit because a good guide will show you creatures you'll probably never see on your own. The typical day-long program (1300B to 1900B per person) includes some easy morning walks looking for wildlife and a visit to Haew Suwat waterfall. Lunch, snacks, water and, in the rainy season, 'leech socks' are always included, but sometimes the park entry fee isn't, so do some comparison shopping. Half-day trips (450B to 600B) typically stay outside the park to visit a cave, swim in a spring and watch a million or so rare wrinkle-lipped bats disgorge from a mountain-top cave. Birdwatching, camping, trekking and other speciality tours are also available. Greenleaf Guesthouse and Khaoyai Garden Lodge have long earned enthusiastic praise for their tours, as has the relative newcomer **Bobby's Apartments & Jungle Tours** (☎086 262 7006; www.bobbysjungletourkhaoyai.com), based near Tesco-Lotus in Pak Chong.

Khao Yai is one of Thailand's top **birdwatching** sites. Two noted birdwatching guides are Tony, who owns **Khao Yai Nature Life Resort** (☎081 827 8391; www.khaoyainaturelifetours.com), and **Nang** (☎089 427 1823; www.thailandyourway.com), one of Khao Yai's few female guides. Both also lead standard park tours.

The park itself offers one-hour **night safaris** (☎081 063 9241; per vehicle 500B; ⏲7pm & 8pm), using spotlights to look for animals. There are often so many vehicles during the safari that it ruins the experience. Reservations are a must (maximum eight people per vehicle).

Sleeping & Eating

There are dozens of places to stay on and near Th Thanarat (Rte 2090), the road leading to the park, and plenty more in the gateway city of Pak Chong. Budget and some midrange places offer free transport to/from town, though usually only if you book a tour with them. All but the cheapies do weekday and off-season (April to October) discounts of up to 40%.

The best setting for sleeping is, of course, in the park itself. There are **campsites** (per person with own tent 30B 3-person tent 225B) and a variety of **lodgings** (☎02 562 0760; www.dnp.go.th/parkreserve; r & bungalows 800-9000B, 30% discount Mon-Thu) available around the park, all pretty far from the visitor centre. The lodgings are rustic – no air-con, fridges or TVs – but comfortable. Note that you must book these from the national park website.

Each of the lodges reviewed serves food and there are many more restaurants along Th Thanarat, including a surprising number serving Italian food. The park itself has restaurants at all busy locations, including the visitor centre, campsites and some waterfalls, but even the campsite ones close around 6pm, so plan ahead.

★Khaoyai Garden Lodge — HOTEL $

(☎044 365178; www.khaoyaigardenlodgekm7.com; Th Thanarat, Km 7; r with fan 350B, with air-con 2000-3200B, f 2800B; P❄@📶🏊) This friendly, family-run place offers a variety of rooms (the cheapest are large, have shared hot-water bathrooms and fans and are better value than other cheapies in the area), all spread out around an attractive garden. It's great value and the restaurant-lounge in front encourages interaction with fellow guests.

Greenleaf Guesthouse — GUESTHOUSE $

(☎044 365073; www.greenleaftour.com; Th Thanarat, Km 7.5; r 200-300B; P) The common areas are chaotic and the rooms basic at best at this long-running family-owned place. But there's flexibility with families to share rooms at no extra cost, and a family bungalow that's excellent value (500B). Wi-fi only extends to the common areas. With limited number of rooms, preference is given to guests who are taking the wildlife tours.

Khao Yai Villa — HOTEL $$

(☎083 365 8588; www.khaoyaivilla.com; Th Thanarat, Km 12; r 790B; P❄📶) What these simple new rooms lack in charm, they more than make up for in value. The price is very low by Khao Yai standards.

Rimtarninn Hotel — HOTEL $$

(430 Th Mitraphap; r 850B; P❄📶🏊) If you don't want to stay along Th Thanarat, this place in Pak Chong is well worth checking out. Crammed into a small space is a lot of clever design. The six floors are tastefully set around a courtyard affair, with plenty of rough timber beams and rustic touches. Considering it's on busy Mitraphap Hwy, it's not a bad deal.

The attached **Rabiang Nam** (430 Th Mitraphap; dishes 80-150B) restaurant is right on a river bank *('rim tarn')*.

★ Hotel des Artists HOTEL $$$
(☎044 297444; hoteldesartists@gmail.com; Th Thanarat, Km 22; r 3200-4200B, villas 5000-6000B, incl breakfast; P❄@☎≋) Breaking from the Khao Yai norm, this tasteful hotel goes for French-colonial chic rather than a nature theme, though with its mountain views out the back you won't forget where you are. The rooms are gorgeous and the villas sit right by the large swimming pool.

Balios HOTEL $$$
(☎044 365971; www.balioskhaoyai.com; Th Thanarat, Km 17; r incl breakfast 3200-4000B; P❄@☎≋) Khao Yai's original luxury lodge has kept up with the times and has an attractive, vaguely Italian theme. All of the rooms have patios overlooking either the pool or the attractive gardens and are tastefully designed. There are reductions in the off-season and for advance bookings.

Jungle House HOTEL $$$
(☎044 297183; www.junglehousehotel.com; Th Thanarat, Km 19.5; r 1600-2200B; P❄☎) Rooms here are nicely arranged with stucco walls and natural timber, and most have loft areas as well. It has its own little patch of untamed forest, and with a motley collection of animals, reptiles and even its own elephants, it has the jungle vibe down pat.

Getting There & Away

Sŏrng·tăa·ou travel the 30km from Pak Chong down Th Thanarat to the park's northern gate (40B, 45 minutes) every 30 minutes from 6am to 5pm. They start their journey in front of the 7-Eleven near the artistic deer (they look like giraffes) statue. It's another 14km to the visitor centre, and park guards are used to talking drivers into hauling people up there. Some also do a side business hiring motorcycles for 500B per day. Several motorcycle shops on Pak Chong's main road do rentals for 300B per 24 hours, including **Petch Motor** (☎081 718 2400; Th Mittaphap, at Th Tesabarn 13), a bit southwest of the stoplight (look for the diamond in the window).

Only 2nd-class buses to Bangkok (128B, three hours) use the bus station, which is southwest of the traffic light at Th Thesabarn 8. Frequent 2nd-class buses and minivans to Khorat (60B, 1½ hours) stop about 500m northeast of the deer statue near *đà·l àht kàak*. Minivans to Bangkok's Victory Monument (180B, 2½ hours, hourly) park near the deer statue. You can also catch minivans (departing from Khorat) to Ayuthaya (100B, 2½ hours) and Lopburi (80B, two hours) across the street from *đà·làht kàak*, if they have empty seats when they pass through, which they usually do. Board 1st-class buses to both Bangkok (150B, 2½ hours) and Khorat (80B, one hour) across the highway from the deer statue.

You can also get to Pak Chong by train from Bangkok and Khorat, but it's much faster to go by bus or minivan. Ayuthaya, on the other hand, has no direct bus service and not many minivans, so the train (23B to 363B, two to three hours, nine daily) can be a good option.

Sung Noen สูงเนิน

A little way down the road from Pak Chong on the way to Khorat is the little town of Sung Noen, which has a couple of interesting sights.

Sights

Sema Ancient City RUIN
(เมืองเกาเสมา; Ban Hin Tang) Located in the small town of Hin Tang, just 5km from Sung Noen district, is this ancient ruin that's said to date from the Dvaravati period. An exact date for the site hasn't been established and, in fact, not much archaeological work has been done here. It's mostly crumbling foundations, though there is one pedestal that presumably once supported a Buddha image.

While it isn't spectacular, what you do get here is a sense of being off the beaten track. There's no tourist infrastructure other than a few explanatory signs and you'll most likely have the place to yourself for a wander.

Wat Dhammachak Senaram BUDDHIST TEMPLE
(วัดธรรมจักรเสนาราม; donations welcome) Also known as Wat Phra Norn (Temple of the Reclining Buddha), this temple is significant for housing a 1300-year-old reclining Buddha, carved from sandstone blocks, that dates to the Dvaravati period. It's the oldest reclining Buddha in Thailand. The face is worn considerably and the blocks that make it are askew, but it makes for an impressive sight.

Getting There & Away

Sung Noen is 63km from Pak Chong and 37km from Khorat. Minivans going to Khorat from Pak Chong will stop there. From Sung Noen it's a further 5km to Ban Hin Tang, where the temple and ruins are situated (about 500m from each other). You can hire a motorcycle from Sung Noen to take you there.

Buriram Province

The town of Buriram is a friendly place, but lacks much of interest to tourists. The province, on the other hand, has some of Thailand's must-see Khmer relics. The countryside is peppered with dozens of Khmer ruins, the crowning glory of which is Phanom Rung, a beautifully restored complex climbing to the summit of an extinct volcano. The most spectacular Angkor monument in Thailand, Phanom Rung is well worth the journey and should impress even those who've already experienced Angkor Wat in Cambodia.

Nang Rong นางรอง

POP 20,920

This workaday city is the most convenient base for visiting Phanom Rung, and a full range of services and a good selection of hotels make it a friendly and comfortable one.

Sleeping & Eating

★P California Inter Hostel GUESTHOUSE $
(☎081 808 3347; www.pcalifornianangrong.webs.com; Th Sangkakrit; r with fan 250B, with air-con 350-600B; P❄📶) This great place on the east side of town offers bright, nicely decorated rooms with value in all price ranges, including the cheapest, which have fans and cold-water showers. The more expensive have living areas with sofas. English-speaking owner Khun Wicha has a wealth of knowledge about the area and leads tours. Bikes are free, and staff speak several languages.

A motorcycle taxi from the bus station costs 50B.

Honey Inn GUESTHOUSE $
(☎044 622825; www.honeyinn.com; Soi Si Kun; r with fan/air-con 250/350B; ❄@📶) This family-run Nang Rong veteran, 1km from the bus station, is a fine choice. Motorcycle hire (250B to 300B per day) and guided tours are also available. It's north of the bus station, down a quiet soi, away from the noise; the hotel offers free pick-up from the station. The owner is a music teacher, so expect a musical time.

The Park HOTEL $$
(☎044 633778; www.theparknangrong.com; Th Praditpana; r 590-790B; P❄📶) One of several new, midrange hotels in Nang Rong, the Park is the best, with all of its fairly priced rooms around a quiet, lovely garden. It's southeast of the bus station, next to the lake.

Cabbages & Condoms HOTEL $$
(☎044 657145; Hwy 24; r with breakfast 700-1500B; P❄@📶) This Population & Community Development Association–run resort, set in beautifully shaded grounds right on the highway, is a pleasant place to stay. The rooms are large and have stone floors. There's a clothing factory on-site, opened to bring work normally found in the city to the villages.

As you might expect, condoms are a theme here, and they're even handed out for free.

The downside is that it's 6.5km west of town, though you can flag down minivans going into Nang Rong and elsewhere on the highway pretty easily.

Phob Suk THAI $$
(Hwy 24; dishes 60-360B; ⏰9am-10pm; P📶) The picture menu at this well-known restaurant near the bus station presents the typical mix of Thai, Isan and Chinese, but we recommend the city's famous *kăh mŏo* (pork-rump roast).

Getting There & Around

Nang Rong's **bus station** (☎044 631517) is on the west side of town. Most buses running to Phanom Rung Historical Park stop in Nang Rong.

Both P California and Honey Inn hire motorcycles, starting at 250B per day, and the former also has mountain bikes for 100B per day.

At time of writing the owner of P California was planning to introduce a Khao Yai–Phimai–Nang Rong shuttle service. Phone the guesthouse for details.

Phanom Rung Historical Park

The largest and best-restored Khmer monument in Thailand, **Phanom Rung** (อุทยานประวัติศาสตร์เขาพนมรุ้ง; ☎044 666251; admission 100B, combined ticket with Prasat Muang Tam 150B; ⏰6am-6pm) sits on the summit of a spent volcano 200m above the paddy fields.

The temple was erected as a Hindu monument to Shiva between the 10th and 13th centuries, the bulk of it during the reign of King Suriyavarman II (r AD 1113–50), who ruled during the apex of Angkor architecture. The complex faces east and four times a year the sun shines through all 15 sanctuary doorways. The correct solar alignment happens during sunrise from 3 to 5 April and 8 to 10 September and sunset from 5 to 7 March and 5 to 7 October (some years are one day earlier). The park extends its hours during these events and locals celebrate the **Phanom Rung Festival** around the April alignment, with ancient Brahmin ceremonies and modern sound-and-light shows.

Sights

Below the main sanctuary, above the long row of gift shops, an **information centre** (8.30am-4.30pm) houses artefacts found at the site and displays about both the construction and restoration, the latter of which took 17 years. You can pick up a free informative brochure or arrange a Thai-speaking guide (free, but tips are expected) here. Those who don't want to climb can use an upper parking lot (50B per car), but the brochure isn't available there.

One of the most remarkable aspects of Phanom Rung is the **promenade** leading to the main gate. It begins on a slope 400m east of the main tower with three earthen **terraces**. Next comes a cruciform base for what may have been a wooden pavilion. To the right of this is the **changing pavilion** (Phlab Phla), where royalty bathed and changed clothes before entering the temple complex. You then step down to a 160m-long **processional walkway** flanked by sandstone pillars with early Angkor style (AD 1100–80) lotus-bud tops. This walkway ends at the first and largest of three **naga bridges**, flanked by 16 five-headed *naga* (mythical serpents) in the classic Angkor style. As at all Khmer temples, these represent the passing from the earthly realm to the heavenly.

After crossing this bridge and climbing the stairs you come to the magnificent **east gallery** leading into the main sanctuary. The **main tower** has a gallery on each of its four sides and the entrance to each gallery is itself a smaller version of the main tower.

The craftsmanship at Phanom Rung represents the pinnacle of Khmer artistic achievement, on par with the reliefs at Angkor Wat in Cambodia. Excellent sculptures of both Shaiva and Vaishnava deities can be seen in the lintels and pediments over the doorways to the central monuments and in various other key points on the sanctuary exterior. On the east portico of the *mon·dòp* (square hall) is a Nataraja (Dancing Shiva), which is late Baphuon or early Angkor style, while on the south entrance are the remains of Shiva and Uma riding their bull mount, Nandi. The central cell of the *Ƀrah·sàht* (palace) contains a Shivalingam (phallus image) and in front of it is an evocative Nandi statue.

Getting There & Away

Sŏrng·tăa·ou (25B, 30 minutes, every 30 minutes) from in front of the old market on the east end of town in Nang Rong, and Chanthaburi-bound buses from the bus station on the west side of town, go to Ban Ta Pek, where motorcycle taxi drivers charge 200B to Phanom Rung, including waiting time.

Coming from or heading to Ubon Ratchathani (263B, 4½ hours, hourly), Surin (80B, two hours, every 30 minutes), Khorat (75B to 95B, two hours, hourly), Pak Chong (122B, 2½ hours, hourly) or Bangkok (231B to 275B, five hours, hourly), you have the option of getting off at Ban Tako, a well-marked turn-off about 14km east of Nang Rong, and waiting for one of the vehicles from Nang Rong, or just taking a motorcycle taxi (300B return) direct to Phanom Rung.

P California Inter Hostel (p414) has a half-day tour (385B per person) that takes in both Phanom Rung and Prasat Muang Tam.

Around Phanom Rung

PRASAT MUANG TAM

Prasat Muang Tam (ปราสาทเมืองต่ำ; admission 100B; 6am-6pm) is 8km to the northwest of Phanom Rung. Dating back to the late 10th century or early 11th century and sponsored by King Jayavarman V, 'Lower City' is Isan's third-most-interesting Khmer temple complex (after Phanom Rung and Phimai) in terms of size, atmosphere and quality of restoration work.

The complex, built as a shrine to Shiva, has an unusual layout. Most significantly, the five *prang* (Khmer-style stupa) are grouped three in front and two in back rather than the typical quincunx cross shape. The principal *prang*, likely representing Mt Kailasa, Shiva's home, could not be rebuilt. Four lotus-filled L-shaped ponds, representing the oceans, ring the *prang* and are themselves surrounded by whimsical five-headed *naga*. Muang Tam is the only Khmer temple with this particular arrangement, and the ponds add a lot to its appeal.

Begin your visit across the road in the small **information centre** (6am-6pm) FREE, next to **Barai Muang Tam** (a 510m-by-1090m Khmer-era reservoir), which has good displays about the site. The village has a **homestay** (089 070 8889; per person with 3 meals 500B) program, but for independent

Around Phanom Rung

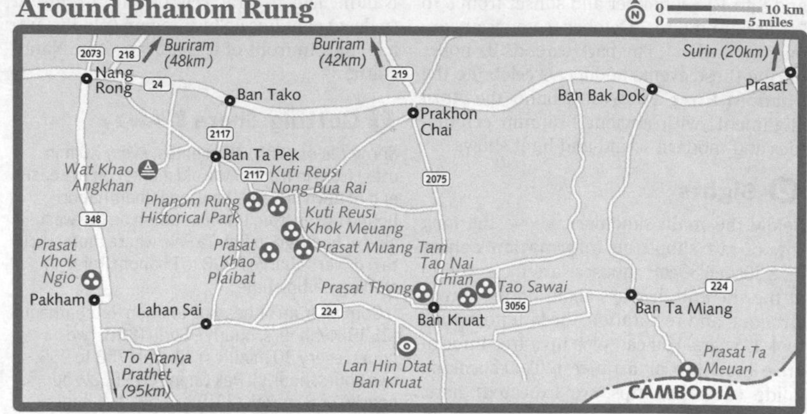

travellers the private **Tanyaporn Guesthouse** (☎087 431 3741; r 350-500B; 🅿⊖❄📶), southwest of the ruins, is an easier option.

Motorcycle-taxi drivers will add Muang Tam onto a trip to Phanom Rung for another 150B.

OTHER KHMER RUINS

For those with an insatiable appetite for Khmer ruins, the area around Phanom Rung offers a smorgasbord of lesser-known sites that, taken together, create a picture of the crucial role this region once played in the Khmer empire. Most people find these places of only minor interest, but driving through this rice-growing region offers an unvarnished look at village life and will surely make for an enlightening trip. All of the following sites, restored to some degree by the Fine Arts Department, are free of charge and open during daylight hours.

Kuti Reusi Nong Bua Rai sits right below Phanom Rung, and the similar but more atmospheric **Kuti Reusi Khok Meuang** is just northwest of Prasat Muang Tam.

Little of **Prasat Khao Plaibat** is left standing, but the adventure of finding it, along with cool views of both Phanom Rung and the Dangrek Mountains on the Cambodian border, makes it worth seeking out. The seldom-used trail starts at Wat Khao Plaibat, 3km from Prasat Muang Tam. Pass the gate next to the giant Buddha image, veer right at the *gù·đì* (monks' quarters) and slip through the barbed-wire fence. From here take the path to the right, and then a quick left up the hill and follow the strips of orange cloth tied to trees. The walk up the hill should take less than 30 minutes if you don't get lost along the way, though it's likely you will. If you ask, a monk might lead you there.

Prasat Khok Ngio, 3km before Pakham, has a small museum with old pots and Buddha images unearthed around the temple.

Prasat Thong (aka Khok Prasat), located near the market in Ban Kruat town, has recently been restored with new brick walls and is now worth a stop if you're passing through.

The sandstone used to build these ancient structures came from the widely scattered **Lan Hin Dtat Ban Kruat** (Ban Kruat Quarry), which is best seen at Wat Lan Hin Dtat, southwest of Ban Kruat town. One cutting site is near the parking lot: take the trail to the right after the Buddha statue and look to your left as you walk up the steps.

Also near Ban Kruat are **Tao Nai Chian** and the larger **Tao Sawai**, two kilns that supplied pottery to much of the Khmer empire between the 9th and 13th centuries. Today they're little more than piles of dirt and brick with roofs over them.

You can easily add Surin Province's Prasat Ta Meuan (p421) to your trip around this region. It's 55km from Phanom Rung.

WAT KHAO ANGKHAN

Although this peaceful **temple** (วัดเขาอังคาร; ⏲dawn-dusk) atop an extinct volcano has an ancient past, as evidenced by the 8th- or 9th-century Dvaravati sandstone boundary markers, it's the modern constructions that make Wat Khao Angkhan worth a visit. The flamboyant *bóht* was erected in 1982 in an unusual nouveau-Khmer style that sort of harks back to the age of empire. The wát also hosts a Chinese-style pagoda, a 29m reclining Buddha and beautiful views of the surrounding forest. If you're up for a little adventure, a trail lets you walk or mountain bike down the hill to Ban Khwao village. Though there's a map posted at the temple and signs along the way, it would be best to seek advice from P California (p414) in Nang Rong.

The temple is about 20km from either Nang Rong or Phanom Rung, with both roads horribly potholed, and there's no public transport. The route is pretty well signposted, but if you're driving you'll have to ask directions at some junctions. A motorcycle taxi should cost 200B from Ban Ta Pek and 300B from Nang Rong. P California does half-day tours (285B per person) that also include stops at silk-weaving villages.

Surin Province

Surin Province is full of Angkor-era Khmer ruins. Most are rather modest and of interest only to those with a history habit. On the other hand, the artwork at Sikhoraphum is outstanding and Prasat Ta Meuan, out in the jungle, is very evocative. The region's Khmer influence comes not only from the past, but also the present. Over one-third of the population of this province is ethnically Khmer and this remains the principal language in many villages.

Besides the temples, Surin Province is famous for the Elephant Round-up and is home to Ban Ta Klang elephant village, as well as some famous craft centres. The capital city is far less interesting than the countryside, although it does make a comfortable-enough base.

Surin สุรินทร์

POP 40,100

Surin city doesn't have much to say for itself until November, when the provincial capital explodes into life for the Surin Elephant Round-up, during which the city hosts giant scrums of pachyderms.

Sights

Surin National Museum MUSEUM

(พิพิธภัณฑสถานแห่งชาติสุรินทร์; ☎044 513358; Th Surin-Prasat; ⏰9am-4pm Wed-Sun) FREE Displays at this well-executed museum focus on the province's Khmer ruins and Surin's three ethnic groups: Lao, Khmer and Suai, the region's renowned elephant herders. It's 4km south of town on Rte 214. Catch pink *sŏrng·tăa·ou* 1 (10B) in front of the bus station or the clock tower by the fresh market *(đà·làht sòt)*.

Queen Sirikit Sericulture Center HANDICRAFT CENTRE

(ศูนย์หม่อนไหมเฉลิมพระเกียรติสมเด็จพระนางเจ้าสิริกิติ์ พระบรมราชินีนาถ (สุรินทร); ☎044 511393; Rte 226; ⏰8am-4.30pm) FREE The easiest place to see the entire silk-making process, from larva to loom, is at this research centre 4km west of town. Various displays can be seen any time and, while the silk makers only work on weekdays, a demonstration can be arranged on weekends with advance notice.

San Lak Meuang MONUMENT

(ศาลหลักเมือง; Th Luck Meuang) Surin's gorgeous city pillar shrine, just west of Th Tanasarn, is a Khmer-style *prang* with copies of Phanom Rung's famous Narai Bandhomsindhu lintel above the doors.

Festivals & Events

Surin Elephant Round-up CULTURAL

Surin celebrates its famous festival for 11 days, but the biggest crowds come on the last weekend for the main event, which features 300 elephants taking part in battle reenactments and other spectacles, such as the 'elephant buffet' on the Friday before the big show.

While the festival dates back centuries, elephant 'shows' of all kinds are contentious (p759). Elephants are forced to undergo rigorous, often torturous, 'training' to become 'tamed' enough for such shows, which is worth considering if you are planning to attend.

Tickets for the battle reenactment start at 40B, but VIP seats, which get you closest to the action, guaranteed shade and (sometimes) English commentary cost from 500B to 1000B. The festival takes place on the third weekend of November. Note that accommodation prices increase significantly during this period.

Tours

Saren Travel TOUR

(☎044 513599; 202/1-4 Th Thesaban 2; ⏰8.30am-5pm Mon-Sat) Offers tours in and around Surin Province.

Sleeping

Prices skyrocket during the Elephant Round-up and hotels fill up fast, so book as far in advance as possible if you're visiting at that time.

★ **Maneerote Hotel** HOTEL $
(044 539477; www.maneerotehotel.com; Soi Poi Tunggor, Th Krungsri Nai; s 450B, d 450-500B; P ❄ @) This quiet hotel southwest of the fresh market is hands-down the best-value place in town. Rooms are clean and modern and there's an attached restaurant and coffee shop. The optional breakfast is an extra 100B.

Baan Chang Ton HOMESTAY $
(087 459 8962; www.baanchangton.com; Th Suriyarart; r 400-500B; P ❄ @) This old wooden house has lovely dark timbers and will give you a good feel for Thai home life. The friendly owners make it a great place to stay. It's quite simple (shared bathrooms, mattresses on the floor and air-conditioning in only one room) but the atmosphere makes it special.

Guests can use the kitchen or, if arranged in advance, join the family for dinner. Bring your own towel. It's on a mostly quiet side street south of *săh·lah glahng* (provincial hall). Check-out times are flexible. You need to book in advance.

Martina Hotel HOTEL $
(044 713555; www.martinahotel.com; Th Phichilchai; r 400-550B, ste 1200B) This expansive place is a little out of town, but is still very popular due to the attractive rooms at good prices. It's modern, spacious and has great service. All rooms have the usual conveniences. There are free bicycles, but only for use in the hotel grounds (!), plus motorbikes for 250B per day.

Surin Majestic Hotel HOTEL $$
(044 713980; www.surinmajestic.com; Th Jitrbumrung; r incl breakfast 1200-1400B, ste 2200-4500B; P ❄ @) The rooms here are clean and bright, but would be much cheaper if it weren't for the location next to the bus station and plenty of extras, including a swimming pool and fitness room.

Eating & Drinking

Surin's surprisingly exuberant nightlife mostly revolves around the Thong Tarin Hotel, east of the bus station.

Steak Corner THAI $
(Hua Mum Satek; 089 888 9948; Th Suriyakan; dishes 50-270B; 3-10pm;) The owner of this place ran the popular Tang Lak around the corner, but has moved to new premises with a new name not far from the tourist office. It's popular with both Thai and *fa·ràng*. The appearance is very basic, but the food is great.

Petmanee 2 THAI $
(Th Murasart; dishes 20-80B; 9am-3pm) This simple spot south of Ruampaet Hospital by Wat Salaloi (look for the large chicken

GETTING TO CAMBODIA: SURIN & SI SAKET

Chong Chom to O Smach

Getting to the border Because of the Cambodian casinos, there are plenty of minibuses (60B, 1½ hours, frequent) from Surin's bus terminal to the Cambodian border at Chong Chom.

At the border The border is open from 7am to 8pm and Cambodian visas are available on the spot. There are many touts offering to assist you with a visa, but this will cost you extra and you can easily do it yourself at the counter.

Moving on Taxi agents wait on the Thai side of the border, but it's cheaper to deal directly with the actual drivers, who congregate near the visa office in Cambodia. You still have to bargain, though, as no prices are fixed. One seat for the two-hour ride will cost anywhere from 350B to 500B. You can also charter the whole car for 1500B to 1800B, which after around 9am, when few people travel, might be your only option.

Chong Sa-Ngam to Choam

This border crossing in Sri Saket Province sees very little traffic, despite the road to Siem Reap being in excellent shape, because it can't be done by public transport. Visas are available on arrival.

BUSES FROM SURIN

DESTINATION	FARE (B)	DURATION (HR)	FREQUENCY
Aranya Prathet	234	6	5 daily
Khon Kaen	182	4	hourly
Khorat	125-175	4	every 30min
Roi Et	104	2½	hourly
Ubon Ratchathani	105-200	3	every 2hr
Udon Thani	142	4	2.30pm

grill) is Surin's most famous purveyor of *sôm·đam* and *gài yâhng*. The *súp nòr mái* (bamboo shoot curry) is good, too. There's little English, spoken or written, but the food is so good it's worth stumbling through an order.

Night Market THAI **$**
(Th Krungsri Nai; ⌚5-10pm) A block south of the fountain, this good night market whips up a wide selection of Thai and Isan dishes.

Kit Teung Bakery & Coffee BAKERY **$**
(☎086 468 9414; Th Sanit Nikomrat; cakes 40B; ⌚7am-8pm; P 📶) This bright, modern place just southeast of the train station has some of the best coffee in town, but it really sets itself apart with a fun selection of Thai baked goods. It has an air-con inner section and a covered outdoor section with refreshing hanging plants around it.

Surin Chai Kit THAI **$**
(297 Th Tanasarn; dishes 35-55B; ⌚7am-3pm Mon-Sat) This no-frills spot whips up tasty pan-egg breakfasts and stir-fried lunches. The owners wear welcoming perma-grins and give *fa·ràng* customers a handy city map. It's just to the right of the Sang Thong Hotel.

★**Sydney Canale** INTERNATIONAL, THAI **$$**
(☎089 428 4711; 349/4 Th Tesaban 1; dishes 50-1100B; ⌚10am-3pm & 5-10pm; 📶) This place has had a makeover and a change of location, moving into impressive big premises beside a canal a few doors down from the tourist office. It has both air-con and open-air sections in a high-celinged building. This is by far our favourite choice for *fa·ràng* food in Surin.

The Australian-trained chef does a variety of dishes, including chicken lasagne and duck breast fillet with orange sauce, plus a pretty mean crème caramel and some Thai and Japanese, too.

ℹ Information

Banks in the Surin Plaza Mall are open evenings and weekends and there's an AEON ATM outside the back entrance of Petchkasem Plaza. They are both located on Th Tesabarn 1, two blocks west and one block east of the fountain respectively.

Ruampaet Hospital (☎044 513192; Th Tesabarn 1)

Tourism Authority of Thailand (TAT; ☎044 514447; tatsurin@tat.or.th; Th Tesabarn 1; ⌚8.30am-4.30pm) Across from Ruampaet Hospital.

ℹ Getting There & Away

BUS

Frequent buses from Surin's **bus terminal** (☎044 511756; Th Jitrbumrung) head to/from Bangkok (272B to 543B, seven hours). The best service is **Nakhonchai Air** (☎044 515151), which has VIP buses (389B, nine daily) from its own terminal 1km north of the train station – if coming from Bangkok, you can get off at the main bus terminal.

TRAIN

Surin train station (☎045 511295) is on the line between Bangkok (73B to 489B, seven to nine hours, nine daily) and Ubon Ratchathani (31B to 382B, two to four hours, 10 daily).

ℹ Getting Around

Surin is very convenient for travellers; virtually everything you'll want or need is within a few blocks of the bus and train stations. If you don't want to walk, túk-túk charge 40B to 50B for a trip within the centre. Surin also still has many cheaper pedicabs.

Saren Travel (p417) and Surin Chai Kit (p419) restaurant hire cars, and some of the *fa·ràng* bars on the soi behind the bus station hire motorcycles.

Around Surin

BAN TA KLANG บ้านตากลาง

The Suai village of Ban Ta Klang is a bit of a mixed bag: it's the best place to see Surin's elephants outside festival time, but if you are sensitive to animal welfare you may find some of it unpleasant. You can see elephants throughout the village, where people and pachyderms live side by side, but the main attraction is the **Elephant Study Centre** (☎044 145050; admission 100B; ⏱8.30am-4pm). The study centre runs a half-hour circus-like show, billed as a talent show, at 10am and 2pm, with painting, darts and basketball performed by the elephants. It is very tacky and you might want to give the show a miss. The elephants are clearly being goaded into doing their tricks.

Within the grounds is the excellent **Surin Project** (☎084 482 1210; www.surinproject.org), which is affiliated with the Elephant Nature Park (p761) in Chiang Mai. It works to improve the elephants' living conditions by, among other things, letting them roam inside large enclosures so they don't need to be as heavily chained. Not all the elephants living in the Study Centre are beneficiaries of the Surin Project's work, so not all elephants are equal here (the ones under the care of the Surin Project wear one chain rather than two).

If you'd like to spend some quality time with elephants, you can sign up for activities with the project to work side-by-side with the mahouts caring for the elephants, cutting food, doing construction and more. Programs include one day of volunteering (2000B, including meals) and one week of volunteering (13,000B, including lodging and meals). It's best to book ahead. The information centre is within the showgrounds. There is also a **homestay** (per person 200B, meals 50-100B) program on offer.

During Visakha Bucha day (usually in May) all Suai villages in the area host **elephant parades**, with brightly painted pachyderms carrying the men who will enter the monkhood.

Sŏrng·tăa·ou run from Surin's bus terminal (60B, 1½ hours, hourly), with the last one returning at 4pm. If you're driving, take Rte 214 north for 40km and follow the elephant signs down Rte 3027 for 22km more.

CRAFT VILLAGES

There are many craft villages in easy striking distance of Surin city and many of the products, including *pâh hohl* (a geometric pattern that bears a slight resemblence to *mát·mèe,* but isn't tie-dyed) fabric, have a Cambodian influence. Surin silks, which often use natural dyes, aren't readily available in other parts of Thailand and prices are much cheaper here.

The most famous weaving centre is Ban Tha Sawang.

WORTH A TRIP

BAN THA SAWANG

You may find the village of Tha Sawang a fascinating stop, even if you're not particularly turned on by weaving. Stationed in a number of ancient houses, fascinating in themselves, and amid some cooling gardens, are some specialist weavers working on looms that span over two storeys to create silk fabrics that are works of art.

Chansoma (จันทร์โสมา; ⏱8am-5pm) has made Tha Sawang one of the most renowned silk villages in Thailand. Its exquisite brocade fabrics *(pâh yók torng)* incorporate threads made of real gold and silver, but the weaving process is just as impressive as the finished cloth. Four women, including one sitting a floor below the others, work the loom simultaneously and collectively manage over 1000 heddles. Not surprisingly, they produce just a few centimetres per day. Many of the finished products are destined for the royal court, but you can custom order your own at an average price of 30,000B per metre. One of the pieces we saw being made on our visit was valued at 300,000B, and was expected to take another year-and-a-half to finish.

Other shops around Chansoma sell typical silks to a steady stream of Thai visitors. The village is 8km west of Surin along Rte 4026. *Sŏrng·tăa·ou* (15B, 20 minutes) run regularly from the north side of Surin's fresh market (don't wait for a return vehicle in the village, walk out to the main road) and a túk-túk should cost about 200B.

Ban Khwao Sinarin and **Ban Chok**, next-door neighbours 18km north of Surin along Rte 214 and Rte 3036, are known for silk (now mostly synthetic) and silver. One of the weaving specialities is *yók dòrk,* a simpler brocade style than what's made in Ban Tha Sawang, but it's nowadays not for sale in the village (you can see some on sale in Suwannaphum International Airport). The silver standout is *Ƅrà keuam,* a Cambodian style of bead brought to Thailand by Ban Chok's ancestors many centuries ago. You can see it, and other jewellery, being made in the **OTOP handicrafts mall** (Th Jitrbumrung; ⌚8am-5.30pm) at the east end of the villages. Big blue *sŏrng·tăa·ou* to Ban Khwao Sinarin (25B, 30 minutes, hourly) park on an unnamed soi between the fountain and Surin train station.

PRASAT TA MEUAN

Prasat Ta Meuan KHMER RUIN
(ปราสาทตาเมือน; ⌚dawn-3pm) **FREE** The most atmospheric of Surin's Khmer ruins is a series of three sites known collectively as Prasat Ta Meuan in the forest on the Cambodian border. They line the Ancient Khmer Hwy linking Angkor Wat to Phimai and this is where the road crossed the Dongrek Mountains.

The first site, **Prasat Ta Meuan** proper, was built in the Jayavarman VII period (AD 1181–1210) as a rest stop for pilgrims. It's a fairly small monument with a two-door, five-window sanctuary constructed completely of laterite blocks. One sandstone lintel, of a meditating Buddha, remains.

Just 300m south, **Prasat Ta Meuan Toht**, which was the chapel for a 'healing station', is a bit larger. Also built by Jayavarman VII, the ruins consist of a *gopura, mon·dòp* and main *prang,* all surrounded by a laterite wall.

Nearly 1km further on, next to the army base at the end of the road, is the largest site, **Prasat Ta Meuan Thom**. This Shiva shrine, built around a natural rock lingam, predates the others by as much as two centuries. Despite a somewhat haphazard reconstruction (and major damage from the years in the 1980s when it was occupied by the Khmer Rouge), this one justifies the effort it takes to get here. Three *prang* and a large hall are built of sandstone blocks on a laterite base and several smaller buildings still stand inside the boundary wall. No significant carvings remain. A stairway on the southern end (like Phimai, this temple faces south) drops to Cambodian territory, which begins at the tree line.

The sites begin 10.3km south of Ban Ta Miang (on Rte 224, 23km east of Ban Kruat) via a winding road used more by cows than cars. You need your own transport to get here and a visit is just as convenient from Phanom Rung as from Surin city. Note the closing time: because of its proximity to the border, it closes early for security reasons.

OTHER KHMER TEMPLE RUINS

The 11th-century **Prasat Ban Phluang** (admission 50B; ⌚7am-6pm), 33km south of Surin, is just a solitary sandstone *prang* without its top, but the wonderful carvings (including Indra riding his elephant Airavata – Erawan in Thai – with just a single head rather than the usual three) make it worth a stop. The *prang* was probably never completed, but some speculate it may have had a wooden top. The site sits 600m off Rte 214; the turn-off is 2.5km south of Hwy 24. Any vehicle from Prasat bound for Kap Choeng or the border can drop you nearby (30B, 30 minutes).

Prasat Sikhoraphum (admission 50B; ⌚7.30am-6pm) is a larger and more rewarding Khmer site 30km northeast of Surin. Built in the 12th century, Sikhoraphum features five brick *prang,* two of which still hold their tops, including the 32m-tall central one. Only one lintel remains, but it's a stunner. Featuring a dancing, 10-armed Shiva, it's in excellent condition and is one of the most beautiful pieces of Khmer art ever carved. Below it are the only two apsara (celestial dancers) carvings in Thailand. There's a sound-and-light show here during the Elephant Round-up. Sikhoraphum can be reached by minivan (30B, one hour, hourly) or train (7B to 50B, 30 minutes, frequent) from Surin city. The temple is very easy to get to as it's right in the town. Sikhoraphum, incidentally, is well known for its *kah-lá-maa,* a sticky, sweet black paste that is tastier than it sounds.

If you happen to be driving to Sikhoraphum, you may as well take a 400m detour off Rte 226 for a peep at **Prasat Muang Thi** (ปราสาทเมืองที; ⌚dawn-dusk) **FREE**. The three remaining brick *prang* are in sad shape (one looks like it's ready to topple), but they're so small they're kind of cute.

KHAO PHRA WIHAN NATIONAL PARK

The main attraction of the 130-sq-km **Khao Phra Wihan National Park** (อุทยานแห่งชาติเขาพระวิหาร; ☎081 264 8727; adult/child 400/200B) is one of the region's great Angkor-period monuments. Unfortunately Khao Phra Wihan ('Preah Vihear' in Khmer), which used to sit on the Thai side of the border, now comes under Cambodian rule, due largely to a campaign by the Cambodian government to make it a World Heritage site. Due to border tensions it is no longer accessible from the Thai side. The large temple complex, which the Cambodian government chooses not to restore, towers 500m above the plains, offering evocative ruins and stunning views. It is not likely to be accessible from the Thai side for the foreseeable future.

Si Saket

There's not a whole lot to do in the humdrum town of Si Saket, but if you're headed to Khao Phra Wihan, you may pass through. Si Saket is centred on its train station. The bus terminal is about 2km south, on Th Kuang Heng, and the commercial centre lies between.

Wat Lan Khuat BUDDHIST TEMPLE
(วัดล้านขวด; ⏲dawn-dusk) FREE Officially it's Wat Pa Maha Chedi Kaeo, but these days nearly everyone calls it Wat Lan Khuat, the 'Million Bottle Temple'. The temple's unique appearance is a result of creative use of thousands of bottles. It's in Khun Han, 11km south of Hwy 24 via Rte 2111. Turn west at the roundabout in the centre of Si Saket town.

Prasat Wat Sa Kamphaeng Yai KHMER RUIN
(⏲dawn-dusk) FREE Thirty kilometres west of Si Saket via Rte 226 in Amphoe Uthumphon Phisai, Prasat Wat Sa Kamphaeng Yai, built as a shrine to Shiva, features four 11th-century *prang* and two *wí·hăhn* (large hall in a Thai temple, usually open to laity). The *prang* (including the main one, which was built of sandstone but restored with brick) have lost their tops, but many lintels and other carvings remain.

The ruined sanctuary can be found on the grounds of Wat Sa Kamphaeng Yai, the *prasat's* modern successor. Buses from Si Saket (20B, 30 minutes) and Surin (55B, 1½ hours) can drop you right nearby. The train is faster and cheaper, but the station is a couple of kilometres away.

Ubon Ratchathani Province

Little-visited Ubon Ratchathani is one of Thailand's most interesting provinces. The capital city has plenty of history and charm, and nature lovers will really enjoy themselves here. The scenery along the Mekong River is often as bizarre as it is gorgeous and Pha Taem National Park has so much to see that it warrants a couple of days. Even more remote is the jungle-clad intersection of Thailand, Laos and Cambodia, now known as the 'Emerald Triangle' (inspired by northern Thailand's 'Golden Triangle') due to the magnificent jungle landscape of Phu Chong Nayoi National Park.

Ubon Ratchathani อุบลราชธานี

POP 86,800

Few cities in Thailand reward aimless wandering as richly as Ubon. Survive the usual knot of choked access roads, and the 'Royal City of the Lotus' will reveal an altogether more attractive face. Racked up against Mae Nam Mun, Thailand's second-longest river, the historic heart of the city, south of Th Kueuan Thani, has a sluggish character rarely found in the region's big conurbations. And throughout the city there are many interesting temples that even people suffering acute temple overload will enjoy.

Ubon grew prosperous as a US air base during the Vietnam War and is now a financial, educational and agricultural market centre. It's not a busy tourist destination, but it does make a great base from which to explore the province's many attractions.

Sights

Thung Si Meuang PARK
(ทุ่งศรีเมือง) The main centrepiece of this city-centre park is a huge concrete **Candle Parade statue**. The humble brick obelisk in the northeast corner is the **Monument of Merit**, erected by former allied-forces POWs (brought here for forced labour by the Japanese, who occupied Thailand during WWII)

in gratitude for the secret assistance they received from ordinary Thai citizens while in the prison camps. The **City Pillar Shrine** (San Lak Meuang) is to the south.

Wat Thung Si Meuang BUDDHIST TEMPLE
(วัดทุ่งศรีเมือง; Th Luang; ⊙dawn-dusk) FREE Built during the reign of Rama III (1824–51), with a classic *hŏr đrai* (Tripitaka hall) in excellent shape. Like many *hŏr đrai*, it rests on tall, angled stilts in the middle of a pond to protect the precious scriptures (written on palm-leaf paper) from termites. It's kept open so you can look inside. The original murals in the little *bóht* beside the *hŏr đrai* show life in that era and are in remarkably good condition.

Ubon Ratchathani National Museum MUSEUM
(พิพิธภัณฑสถานแหงชาติอุบลราชธานี; Th Kheuan Thani; admission 100B; ⊙9am-4pm Wed-Sun) Occupying the former city hall, this is a very informative museum with plenty on show, from Dvaravati-era Buddhist ordination-precinct stones and a 2500-year-old Dong Son bronze drum to Ubon textiles. The museum's most prized possession is a 9th-century Ardhanarisvara, a composite statue combining Shiva and his consort Uma into one being. It's one of just two ever found in Thailand.

Wat Si Ubon Rattanaram BUDDHIST TEMPLE
(วัดศรีอุบลรัตนาราม; Th Uparat; ⊙dawn-dusk) FREE The **bóht** (⊙8am-4pm) at this important temple resembles Bangkok's Wat Benchamabophit, but it's the 7cm-tall topaz Buddha inside that most Thais come to see. Phra Kaew Butsarakham, as it's known, was reportedly brought here from Vientiane at Ubon's founding and is one of the city's holiest possessions.

The temple has turned a beautiful old wooden *săh·lah* (hall) into a **museum** (พิพิธภัณฑวัดศรีอุบลรัตนาราม; ⊙9am-4pm Wed-Sun) FREE of religious items. The highlight is the collection of 18th-century *đôo prá đraiЂìdòk*, gorgeous boxes used for storing sacred palm-leaf texts.

Wat Phra That Nong Bua BUDDHIST TEMPLE
(วัดพระธาตุหนองบัว; Th Thammawithi; ⊙dawn-dusk) This spectacular monastery has had a makeover in recent years and the gleaming gold-and-white towers are sure to dazzle. The *chedi* at the temple loosely resembles the Mahabodhi stupa in Bodhgaya, India, and inside is another beautiful golden *chedi* (open 8am to 6pm). The latter was built in 1956 in honour of the 2500th anniversary of Buddhism. The adjacent *săh·lah* (hall) continues the golden theme, with a bright altar containing eight large sitting Buddhas and, above them, a reclining Buddha.

The temple is on the outskirts of town. To get there, take *sŏrng·tăa·ou* 10.

Ubonnithat Culture Display MUSEUM
(หอวัฒนธรรมอุบลนิทัศน์; Th Jaeng Sanit; ⊙8.30am-4pm Mon-Sat) FREE The museum in the lower level of the strikingly designed Ubon Ratchathani Art & Culture Centre at Rajabhat University contains a lot more cultural references than the National Museum. There are some relatively recent displays such as a room on Ubon's famous forest monks, including some of their teachings in English, herbal medicines, music, costumes and a lot of sculpted candles.

Activities

Ubonvej Thai Massage MASSAGE
(☎045 260345; www.ubonvejthaimassage.com; 113 Th Thepyothi; 2hr massage 350B; ⊙9.30am-midnight) The website declares boldly 'No Sex' – what this place does have is the best massage in Ubon. The premises are classy and there are many different kinds of massage to choose from.

Legacy Gym MARTIAL ARTS
(☎045 264708; www.legacygym.com; Th Srisangthong; private lessons from 600B, share-room accommodation per person per month 13,000B) This *moo·ay tai* (Thai boxing) gym is run by Ole Laursen, a former professional *moo·ay tai* fighter now living in Ubon. It's well set up for Westerners and offers accommodation and training packages. Both women and men train here (although there's no 'women-only' session) and it's suitable for both 'fighters' and those just wanting to train in fitness.

Training in Ubon provides a more settled environment than some of the more hectic *moo·ay tai* locations such as Phuket and Pattaya.

Festivals & Events

Ubon's famous **Candle Parade** (Kabuan Hae Tian) began during the reign of King Rama V, when the appointed governor decided the rocket festival was too dangerous. The original simple designs have since grown (with the help of internal frames) to gigantic, elaborately carved wax sculptures.

Ubon Ratchathani

The parade is part of **Khao Phansaa**, which usually happens in July.

Prize-winning candles go on display along Th Srinarong next to Thung Si Meuang for three days after the parade and most of them will be parked at the city's temples for several months after. Construction, also done on temple grounds, begins about a month before the parade. The festival is very popular with Thai tourists and the city's hotels are booked out long in advance.

Ubon also has **Lai Reua Fai** during Ork Phansaa, but it's a much smaller affair than that in Nakhon Phanom (p395).

Sleeping

Phadaeng Hotel HOTEL $

(045 254600; www.thephadaeng.com; Th Phadaeng; r 500-800B; P ❄ @) One of the best-value hotels in Ubon, the Phadaeng has newish, well-maintained rooms with good furnishings (including large TVs and desks) just minutes from Thung Si Meuang park. It has a large parking area that separates the rooms from the street noise. The hotel is livened up with copies of classic paintings. Bike hire costs 50B per day.

Sri Isan Hotel HOTEL $

(045 261011; www.sriisanhotel.com; 62 Th Ratchabut; s 450-600B, d 500-650B; ❄ @) The bright, cheerful lobby of this hotel is full of natural light streaming down through the atrium. The rooms have had a makeover and are bright and colourful. Sri Isan has a great location for exploration and overall it's good for the price. Bike hire is 60B per 12 hours.

★**Outside Inn** GUESTHOUSE $$

(088 581 2069; www.theoutsideinnubon.com; 11 Th Suriyat; r incl breakfast 650-790B; P ❄) A nice little garden lounge area sets the relaxed, communal vibe here. The rooms are large, comfy and fitted with tasteful-

Ubon Ratchathani

ly designed reclaimed timber furnishings. The Thai-American owners are great hosts and cook some good food, both Thai and Mexican.

It's a long walk to the town's main attractions, but there are bikes (free for guests) and motorcycles (240B to 280B per day), and *sŏrng·tăa·ou* 10 can deliver you from the bus station. Brent is a good source of local knowledge and can give advice on Ubon's attractions.

Ecoinn HOTEL $$
(☎045 254200; 152 Th Srinarong; r 800-900B; P❄📶) This snazzy new place oozes style and offers good value. The owners take pride in some green credentials, such as using locally made, natural products in the bathrooms, and a tasteful room design that allows for natural air flow to reduce the need for air-conditioning. At time of research, a wine bar was scheduled to be opened on the premises.

T3 House HOTEL $$
(☎045 263119; Soi Saphasit 1, Th Saphasit; r 600-700B; P❄📶) This hotel goes for a stylish, modern look and the rooms have plenty of nice little touches, such as rain showers. It's tucked down a small soi and has a huge parking area.

Tohsang Hotel HOTEL $$
(☎045 245531; www.tohsang.com; 251 Th Palochai; r incl breakfast 1000-1500B; P❄@📶) The tasteful decor here makes a great first impression and the service is attentive. The hotel has an interesting structure, with levels within levels of rooms. While the lobby is elegant, the rooms are a tad worn, but still adequate for the price. There's room service and free airport collection.

Next door is a priest's house and coconut plantation, which ensures a nice rural touch in the middle of town.

Sunee Grand Hotel HOTEL $$$
(☎045 352900; www.suneegrandhotel.com; Th Chayangkun; r incl breakfast 1800-2300B; P❄@📶🏊) The Sunee Grand is Ubon's best, and far less expensive than anything similar outside Isan. From the stylish light fixtures to the at-a-snap service, it will meet expectations. There's a large business centre and a piano player in the lobby, and the adjacent shopping mall has a cinema, a bowling alley and a kid-sized rooftop water park.

Eating

★ Rung Roj THAI $
(☎045 263155; Th Nakhonban; dishes 45-150B; ⏲9.30am-8.30pm Mon-Sat; ❄📶) It's surprising the prices are so low at this upmarket-looking establishment. It's an Ubon institution serving excellent food using family recipes and only fresh ingredients. From the outside it looks more like a well-to-do house than a restaurant. Look for the bold plate, fork and spoon sign.

Ros Isan NORTHEASTERN THAI $
(Th Nakhonban; ⏲4-11pm) Don't be fooled by the slightly grungy look at this place. The service is friendly and the food, focused mainly on Isan fare but also covering the Thai standards, is great. Try the *néua dàat dee·o* (dried beef strips) and *kôw něe·o* (sticky rice) for some traditional Isan energy food.

Sam Chai Cafe THAI $
(Th Phadaeng; dishes from 45B; ⏲5.30am-1.30pm) Not really a cafe, this bustling place serves *jóke* (rice gruel), *kôw đôm* (rice soup) and traditional Thai coffee. The service is lightning fast and you'll be given the bill almost as soon as you finish eating. The owner wields a microphone in front of the shop and gives a running commentary. It's not as annoying as it sounds.

Night Market THAI, VIETNAMESE $
(Th Kheuan Thani; ⏲4-11pm) Though it's smaller than you'd expect, Ubon's city-centre night market makes an excellent dining destination, especially when paired with the weekend Walking Street Market. Vendors sell Thai, Isan and Vietnamese food.

Porntip Gai Yang Wat Jaeng THAI $
(Th Saphasit; dishes 20-130B; ⏲7.30am-7pm) It looks like a tornado has whipped through this no-frills spot, but the chefs cook up a storm of their own. This is considered by many to be Ubon's premier purveyor of *gài yâhng, sôm·đam,* sausages and other classic Isan foods.

Sarin Coffee & Cake CAFE $
(Th Phrommarat; cakes from 40B; ⏲8am-5pm Mon-Thu, to 7pm Fri-Sun; ❄📶) It's a little oasis of cool on a hot day, with the regular iced coffee and some homemade cookies on hand. The sign is in Thai, but it's stylised to look like the English 'NTSU'.

Outside Inn INTERNATIONAL, THAI $
(Th Suriyat; dishes 60-200B; ⏲11am-2.30pm & 5-9pm Wed-Mon; P📶🖊) This hotel restaurant sets itself apart with good (by Thailand standards) Mexican meals, but the Thai food is delicious, too. The menu also features sandwiches and a full roster of cocktails.

Gway-tiao Gai Boran THAI $
(Th Phrommarat; dishes 35-45B; ⏲8.30am-3pm) Yes, the *gŏo·ay·đěe·o* (noodle soup) here is delicious, but we love thsi place most for its old-time feel. It's part of the revival of the old city centre.

★ Jumpa-Hom THAI $$
(☎045 260398; Th Phichitrangsan; dishes from 100B; ⏲5pm-midnight; ❄📶) One of the loveliest and most delicious restaurants in Isan, Jumpa-Hom has a large menu featuring some less-common dishes. You can dine on a water-and-plant-filled wooden deck or in the air-con dining room, which offers a choice of tables and chairs or cushions for floor seating. On the premises is the bakery **U-Bake** (cake from 50B; ⏲9am-11pm).

★ Peppers Restaurant, Bakery & Cafe INTERNATIONAL, BAKERY $$
(297/2-3 Upalisan Rd; dishes 75-450B; ⏲8am-9pm; ❄📶) Peppers, popular with both *fa·ràng* and Thai, features a broad international menu with everything from nachos to schnitzel to pub pies to *đôm yam gûng* and all-day breakfast. The bakery offerings, its real speciality, are downright delicious. There are also wines and international beers.

Drinking & Nightlife

U-Bar CLUB
(Th Thepyothi) U-Bar has long remained at the top of the heap for the college crowd, partly because the best bands from Bangkok often play here when they visit Ubon. It's moved from its old location to just around the corner, but still buzzes.

Shopping

Isan may be silk country, but Ubon is a cotton town and there are several good shops selling handwoven fabric, clothing, bags etc. **Camp Fai Ubon** (Th Thepyothi; ⏲8.30am-5pm), signed as Peaceland, has a good variety and some of its products are made with natural dyes. **Maybe** (Th Srinarong; ⏲8am-7pm) has the biggest clothing selection, though none of it's naturally dyed.

★ **Punchard** HANDICRAFTS
(☎045 265751; Th Phadaeng; ⊙9am-6.30pm) Though pricey, this is the best all-round handicrafts shop in Ubon. Specialises in silks and home-decoration products. Many of its products are a merging of old methods and designs in modern items. The shop is a great place to come and browse.

Rawang Thang HANDICRAFTS
(Th Kheuan Thani; ⊙8am-8pm Mon-Thu, to 9pm Fri-Sun) There's also Ubon cotton at this Isan-themed shop, which sells fun and funky T-shirts, pillows, postcards, picture frames and assorted bric-a-brac, most made and designed by the friendly husband-and-wife owners. They can fill you in on all things Ubon.

Walking Street Market MARKET
(Th Ratchabut; ⊙6-11pm Fri-Sun) This fun market takes over Th Ratchabut on weekends.

Information

Ying Charoen Park, near Rajabhat University, has the extended-hours banks nearest to the city centre. There are AEON ATMs at Tesco-Lotus and City Mall, both on the way to the bus station.

Tourism Authority of Thailand (TAT; ☎045 243770; tatubon@tat.or.th; 264/1 Th Kheuan Thani; ⊙8.30am-4.30pm) Has helpful staff.

Ubonrak Thonburi Hospital (☎045 260285; Th Phalorangrit) Has a 24-hour casualty department.

Getting There & Away

AIR

Air Asia (☎02 515 9999; www.airasia.com) and **Nok Air** (☎02 900 9955; www.nokair.com) fly to Bangkok's Don Mueang Airport two and seven times daily respectively for about 1400B one way. **Thai Airways** (THAI; ☎045 313340; www.thaiairways.com) flies three times a day to Bangkok's Suvarnabhumi Airport for about the same price. Kan Air has one flight a day each to Chiang Mai and Pattaya for about 1200B.

Many travel agencies, including **Sakda Travel World** (☎045 254333; www.sakdatour.com; Th Phalorangrit; ⊙8.30am-6.30pm Mon-Sat), sell tickets.

BUS

Ubon's **bus terminal** (☎045 316085) is north of town; take *sŏrng·tăa·ou* 2, 3 or 10 to the city centre. Several buses link Ubon with Bangkok: the top VIP service is offered by **999 VIP** (☎045 314299) (767B, 8.30pm) and **Nakhonchai Air** (☎045 269777) (767B, 8.20am, 1.55pm and 8.30pm).

Buses from Ubon Ratchathani:

DESTINATION	FARE (B)	DURATION (HR)	FREQUENCY
Bangkok	420-603	10	frequent
Chiang Mai	872	12	6pm
Khon Kaen	180-277	4½	every 30min
Mukdahan	75-135	3½	every 30min
Nakhon Ratchasima	286-445	5-6	14 daily
Nang Rong	263	4½	hourly
Pakse (Laos)	200	3	9.30am & 3.30pm
Rayong	605-784	13	5 daily
Surin	105-200	3	every 2hr
Udon Thani	318	6	7.30am, 8.30am & 11.30am

TRAIN

Ubon's **train station** (☎045 321004; Th Sathani) is in Warin Chamrap; take *sŏrng·tăa·ou* 2. There's an overnight express train to/from Bangkok (2nd/1st-class seat 221/460B, 2nd-class sleeper upper/lower 691/781B, 1st-class sleeper upper/lower 1080/1280B, 11½ hours) at 6.30pm. The five other departures (95B to 581B) take from 8½ to 12 hours. All trains also stop in Si Saket, Surin and Khorat.

Getting Around

Numbered *sŏrng·tăa·ou* (10B) run throughout town. TAT's free city map marks the routes, most of which pass near its office. A túk-túk trip within the centre should cost from 30B to 50B. Ubon also has a few metered **taxis** (☎045 265999) that park at the bus station and airport (flagfall 30B, call fee 20B). They're unlikely to use their meters, and charge 100B for rides into town.

Car-hire companies include **Ubon Car Rental** (☎089 629 9418; cars per day with/without driver 1500/1200B) – the driver, Thanawat, speaks good English and is a mine of local information.

Around Ubon Ratchathani

There are two famous forest temples in Warin Chamrab District, just across the river from Ubon town.

FOREST TEMPLES

When the Buddha set out on his quest for enlightenment 2500 years ago, he took to the forests, the traditional abode of ascetics and truth seekers in India at the time. The first disciples were all accepted into the monkhood and lived and practised in forests.

As the teaching spread and the order of monks increased in size, some of the monks began setting up dwellings in towns. Over time these became known as the *gamavasi* (the town dwellers), while the monks who preferred to live in the forest were called *aranyavasi* (forest dwellers). The latter were generally considered to be more intent on developing meditation and strict observance of one or more of the 13 austere practices *(dhutanga)* allowed by the Buddha, such as living at the foot of a tree, eating just one meal a day and eating only from the alms bowl.

In more modern times, town-dwelling monks have become the norm. In fact, forest-dwelling monks had all but disappeared from the landscape in Thailand when Venerable Ajahn Mun Bhuridatto (1870–1949) almost singlehandedly revived the tradition. Ajahn Mun (pronounced as in 'sun') is generally credited with the revival of the *aranyavasi* in Thailand. He is also one monk who is widely acknowledged to have attained enlightenment (unusually so, since attainments are traditionally not publicised). After his passing away, his legacy lived on in the remarkable number of students he left behind, many of whom became famous teachers in their own right.

It is said that in the early days people would run away at the sight of the sombre forest monks in their dark robes. Nowadays forest teachers are sought after by Bangkok elites, intelligentsia and faithful farmers alike, as well as truth-seeking Westerners. As a result, their temples are often flooded with donations and some have become rich. Nevertheless, the authentic forest temple will always maintain its discipline and remain first and foremost a place of spiritual endeavour. As such, it is important to enter them modestly. Since they are not tourist attractions we do not review many of them, but the following have become places of spiritual pilgrimage and so are worth adding to your itinerary (with the exception of Wat Pa Nanachat, which is exclusively for sincere practitioners). They offer a unique glimpse into a deeper side of Thai culture.

Wat Pa Sutthawat (วัดป่าสุทธาวาส; Th Suk Kasem; ⏲5am-9pm) FREE This temple in the town of Sakon Nakhon is dedicated to Ajahn Mun, who helped found the temple but didn't live here until just before his death. The final resting place of his personal effects, the **Ajahn Mun Museum** (⏲6am to 7pm), looks a bit like a modern Christian church, with arches and etched-glass windows. A bronze image of Ajahn Mun sits on a pedestal at the back and relics that remained after his cremation are in a glass box in front. Signs are in English.

Wat Nong Pa Pong The temple of renowned meditation teacher Venerable Ajahn Chah, who spent a brief but enlightening period with Ajahn Mun.

Wat Pa Nanachat (p429) Branch monastery of Wat Nong Pa Phong, built especially for non-Thais.

Wat Phu Thok (p392) Simply the most spectacular monastery in Thailand, built by Ajahn Mun disciple Venerable Ajahn Juan.

Wat Hin Mak Peng (p383) Overlooking the Mekong, this is the temple of senior Ajahn Mun disciple Luang Pu Thet.

Wat Nong Pa Phong BUDDHIST TEMPLE
(วัดหนองป่าพง; ⏲dawn-dusk) Peaceful Wat Nong Pa Phong is known for its quiet discipline and daily routine of work and meditation. The founding teacher, Luang Pu Cha, passed away in 1992, but he established nearly 100 branch monasteries and thousands of followers, including dozens of Western monks, who went on to establish branches in the UK, Europe and elsewhere. The temple is about 10km past the river. *Sŏrng·tăa·ou* 3 gets you within 2km; a motorcycle taxi (if one is available) should cost 20B.

The temple is cleverly designed so that the three-storey museum and golden *chedi,* where Luang Pu Cha's relics are interred, are sectioned off from the interior of the monastery, so that visitors do not disturb the monks' practice. The museum displays an odd assortment of items, from Luang Pu Cha's worldly possessions to world currencies, skeletons and fetuses (for reflection on birth and death).

Wat Pa Nanachat BUDDHIST TEMPLE
(วัดป่านานาชาติ; www.watpahnanachat.org; ⏲dawn-dusk) FREE Wat Pa Nanachat was opened as a branch monastery of Wat Nong Pa Phong in 1975 specifically for non-Thais, and English is the primary language. Those with previous meditation experience are welcome to apply (write to the Guest Monk, Wat Pa Nanachat, Ban Bung Wai, Amphoe Warin Chamrap, Ubon Ratchathani 34310) to stay here. Guests must follow all temple rules, including eating just one meal a day, rising at 3am and shaving heads and eyebrows.

BAN PA-AO บ้านผาอ่าว

Ban Pa-Ao village is famous for producing brass and bronze items using a unique lost-wax casting method involving long strands of wax. This is the only place in Thailand that still does it. You can watch workers creating bells, bowls and more at **Soon Thorng Leuang Ban Pa-Ao** (⏲7am-5pm) on the far side of the village. Ban Pa-Ao is also a silk-weaving village and there's a **silk centre** (⏲8am-5pm) at the entrance to the town with a shop (the quality of the *mát·mèe* here is excellent) and a couple of looms, but most weaving is done at home.

Wat Burapa Pa-Ao Nuea has a gorgeous **museum** (⏲8am-5pm) FREE holding various historical artefacts and local handicrafts; unfortunately, there are very few labels.

Ban Pa-Ao is 3.5km off Hwy 23. Buses to/from Yasothon pass the turn-off (20B, 20 minutes) and a motorcycle taxi from the highway costs 20B each way.

PHIBUN MANGSAHAN พิบูลมังสาหาร

POP 10,890

Thais often stop in the dusty town of Phibun Mangsahan to see a set of rapids called **Kaeng Sapheu**, just downstream of the Mae Nam Mun bridge. The rocky islets make 'Python Rapids' rise between February and May, but the shady park here is a pleasant stop year-round.

The tile-encrusted *bóht* at **Wat Phu Khao Kaew** (⏲dawn-dusk), on the west side of town, is covered with Khmer symbols, including apsara and dancing Shivas on the outside, while the interior walls have reliefs of important stupas from around Thailand.

Villages past the bridge as you drive toward Khong Jiam are famed for forging iron and bronze **gongs**, both for temples and classical Thai-music ensembles. You can watch the gong-makers hammering the flat metal discs and tempering them in rustic fires at many roadside workshops. People make drums, bells and cymbals here, too.

Visa extensions are available at Phibun Mangsahan's **immigration office** (☎045 441108; ⏲8.30am-noon & 1-4.30pm Mon-Fri), 1km south of the bridge on the way to Chong Mek.

Sleeping & Eating

★Kaeng Sa-Pue Riverside Hotel RESORT $$
(☎045 204318; r incl breakfast with/without river views 850/750B; P❄📶🏊) Give yourself a treat and check out this relatively unknown spot right on Kaeng Sapheu, across the river from Phibun. While the rooms may be a little tired, it punches way above its price tag, with a bright and breezy foyer looking out over the rapids, a swimming pool also with great rapids views, and carefully manicured gardens. Get a room before the prices go up.

Getting There & Away

Phibun's bus stop behind the market serves ordinary buses (35B, one hour, every 20 minutes) to Ubon's bus station (these stop to pick up passengers at Warin Market across the river) and *sŏrng·tăa·ou* to Chong Mek (35B, one hour, every 30 minutes).

Minivans between Ubon (50B) and Chong Mek (50B) stop every 30 minutes in Phibun one block behind the bus stop in front of an auto-parts store.

Sŏrng·tăa·ou (40B, 1½ hours, every 30 minutes) to Talat Ban Du (Ban Du Market), in Ubon's city centre, and Khong Jiam (40B, one hour, two each morning) park near the bridge.

KAENG TANA NATIONAL PARK

Along the road to Khong Jiam you can cross the Pak Mun Dam to **Kaeng Tana National Park** (อุทยานแห่งชาติแก่งตะนะ; ☎045 406888; admission 200B). After circling thickly forested Don Tana (Tana Island), linked to the mainland by two long suspension bridges, the Mun River roils through the park's beautiful namesake rapids and passes below some photogenic cliffs. In the rainy season the rapids lie under water, but towards the end of the dry season naturally cut holes in the rock, similar to those at Sam Phan Bok (p431), emerge. There are several good short walks from the **visitor centre** (8am-4pm): the 1.5km clifftop trail to **Lan Pha Phueng** viewpoint is especially serene. **Nam Tok Tad Ton** is a wide and lovely waterfall in the far south of the park, just 300m off the main road.

There's a **campsite** (per person with own tent 30B, 4-/8-person tent hire 150/225B) and four **bungalows** (02 562 0760; www.dnp.go.th/parkreserve; 6/10 people 1000/2000B). The simple restaurant opens during the day only.

By road, the park is 14km from Khong Jiam. There's no public transport, but boats in town will take you upriver and drop you at the park for a quick look around for 600B.

KHONG JIAM โขงเจียม

Khong Jiam sits on a picturesque peninsula at the confluence of the reddish Mekong and bluish Mun Rivers, known as Mae Nam Song Si (Two-Colour River). The multicoloured merger is usually visible from the shore, but it's best seen from a boat. When the rivers are high (June to October) the blending waters create small whirlpools, resembling boiling lava. **River tours** (089 628 6883) on a 10-person boat cost 350B (30 minutes). Other trips are available. The big boats can also take you to Kaeng Tana and Pha Taem National Parks or elsewhere along the Mekong River.

Above the town is **Wat Tham Khuha Sawan** (วัดถ้ำคูหาสวรรค์; dawn-dusk). The awesome views alone are worth the trip, but this well-known temple also has a unique nine-pointed *chedi,* an all-white *bóht,* an impressive orchid garden (blooming in the cold season), one of the biggest gongs you'll ever see and the body of the late abbot, Luang Pu Kham, on display in a glass case atop a flamboyant altar.

Naga fireballs (p380) began appearing at Khong Jiam in 2005, but they don't occur every year.

Sleeping & Eating

Khong Jiam doesn't get many *fa·ràng* visitors, but it's popular with Thais, so there's an abundance of lodging. There are several pricey restaurants near the Mae Nam Song Si, including two floating on the Mekong.

Banpak Mongkhon HOTEL $
(045 351352; www.banmongkhon.com; Th Kaewpradit; d 350-700B, tr 500B; P) This place has basic rooms housed in cute Thai-style wooden cottages, friendly, clued-in owners and lots of character, making it a great choice for any budget. There is a car for hire. Booking ahead is recommended.

★**Baansuan Rimnam Resort** HOTEL $$
(085 493 3521; Th Rimmoon; bungalows incl breakfast 800-1000B; P) This quiet spot sits in a small patch of teak forest along Mae Nam Mun. The air-con log-cabin-type bungalows match the forest location perfectly and command great views of the river. At time of research there were plans to add a restaurant. The location makes it a highly recommended option.

★**Tohsang Khongjiam Resort** HOTEL $$$
(045 351174; www.tohsang.com; r incl breakfast 2500-3890B, villas 2500-7060B, Sedhapura pool villas 12,500-14,500B; P@) This place oozes understated class and capitalises on its prime location right on the banks of Mae Nam Mun. While its upmarket nature seems a little incongruous for this stretch of rural Thailand, it's not flashy and blends in well with the rustic surrounds. The ambience is totally restful. The open-air restaurant has spectacular views.

There's a spa, and bikes and kayaks are available. It's 3.5km from town, on the south bank of the river.

Getting There & Away

All transport to town stops at the highway junction. The only direct bus to Ubon (80B, 2½ hours) leaves at 6am and departs to Khong Jiam at 2pm. You can also take the morning *sŏrng·tăa·ou* to Phibun Mangsahan (40B, one hour, 6am and 8am) and continue from there. Buses to Bangkok leave at 7.30am (2nd class 435B) and 4.30pm (1st class 560B).

Banpak Mongkhon rents bicycles (100B per day) and motorcycles (300B per day).

PHA TAEM NATIONAL PARK

Up the Mekong from Khong Jiam is a long cliff named Pha Taem, the centrepiece of awesome but unheralded **Pha Taem National Park** (อุทยานแหงชาติผาแตม; 045 252581; adult/child 400/200B). From the top you get a bird's-eye view across the river into Laos and down below a trail passes prehistoric rock paintings dating to at least 1000 BC. Mural subjects include *Ɓlah bèuk* (giant Mekong catfish), elephants, human hands, geometric designs and fish traps that look much like the huge ones still used today. The second viewing platform fronts the most im-

WORTH A TRIP

SAM PHAN BOK สามพันโบก

Visit Sam Phan Bok (3000 Holes) and you'll feel as much like you're on another planet as in another country. Eons of erosion have made Swiss cheese of this narrow, rocky Mekong bend, creating one of the most stunning moments of the river's epic journey. Water drowns it during the rainy season, but when it's fully exposed (usually between December and May) you can explore for hours. Even in the shoulder months, when it only partly protrudes, it's worth the trip. There's no shade out here, so early morning and late-afternoon visits are best. Boat rides beyond Sam Phan Bok are also very rewarding for the bucolic scenery.

Sam Phan Bok is north of Pha Taem National Park and there's no public transport. You can camp there, and a few people even hire tents in the busy season. There's accommodation, of which we prefer the simple and friendly **Song Khon Resort** (☎087 256 1696; www.songkhonresort.com; r 500-700B; P ❄) overlooking Hat Salung, a lovely stretch of river in its own right, in the nearby village of Ban Song Khon. This place has rustic rooms, but the location can't be beat. Wherever you stay, definitely book ahead on weekends and holidays during Sam Phan Bok season.

pressive batch. Unfortunately the clearing of the path for viewing the paintings has exposed the rock to the elements, resulting in some fading of the images over the years since the park was established, but they're still impressive. A **visitor centre** (⏰5am-6pm) here contains exhibits pertaining to the paintings and local ecology.

North of the cliff is **Nam Tok Soi Sawan**, a 25m-tall waterfall flowing from June to December, the same period as all the park's waterfalls. It's a 19km drive from the visitor centre and then a 500m walk, or you can hike (with a ranger) for about 15km along the top of the cliff if you arrange it in advance. What the park calls **Thailand's largest flower field** (blooming November to February) lies near the falls.

The northern half of the park holds more waterfalls, ancient art and wonderful views. **Pha Cha Na Dai** cliff serves Thailand's first sunrise view, and amazing **Nam Tok Saeng Chan** waterfall flows through a hole cut naturally into the overhanging rock. Scattered across the 340-sq-km park are many oddly eroded rocks, including four sites known as **Sao Chaliang**, which are mushroom-shaped stone formations similar to those found in Mukdahan's Phu Pha Thoep National Park.

Pha Taem has **campsites** (per person with own tent 30B, 2-/3-/4-person tent hire 150/225/300B) and five **bungalows** (☎02 562 0760; www.dnp.go.th/parkreserve; 6-person bungalows with fan 1200B, 5-person with air-con 2000B; ❄) and vendors sell snacks and fast food until about sunset. There are also a collection of 'resorts' around the entrance to the park. The pick of the bunch is **Pha Taem & Kaeng Phisamai Resort** (☎087 249 3173; www.phataemriverside.com; r with breakfast 1000B; P ❄ 📶), which has a great location right on the riverfront and spectacular views of the cliffs of Laos, and even ponies and goats.

Pha Taem is 18km from Khong Jiam along Rte 2112. There's no public transport, so the best way to get there is to hire a túk-túk in Khong Jiam (600B).

CHONG MEK ช่องเม็ก

South of Khong Jiam, at the end of Rte 217, is the small border town of Chong Mek. The new bridges over the Mekong further north have reduced traffic on this route and stolen much of the bustle from the Chong Mek Market, which used to be a big hit with Thai tourists. If you get stuck here after hours, there are cheap guesthouses north of the market.

There's no public transport that runs between Chong Mek and Khong Jiam; either go through Phibun or hire a motorcycle taxi/túk-túk/pickup truck for 250/300/500B.

PHU CHONG NAYOI NATIONAL PARK

Sitting at the heart of the 'Emerald Triangle' (a meeting of the Thai, Lao and Cambodian borders) is the little-known **Phu Chong Nayoi National Park** (อุทยานแหงชาติภูจองนายอย; ☎045 210706; adult/child 400/200B), one of Thailand's wildest corners and healthiest forests. Resident fauna includes elephants, tigers, Malayan sun bears, barking deer, gibbons, black hornbills and endangered

GETTING TO LAOS: CHONG MEK TO VANGTAO

Getting to the border Almost every traveller uses the direct Ubon Ratchathani–Pakse buses, which wait long enough to buy Lao visas at the border. Otherwise, Chong Mek's little bus terminal serves *sŏrng·tăa·ou* from Phibun Mangsahan (35B, one hour, frequent), minivans from Ubon (100B, 1¼ hours, every 30 minutes) via Phibun (50B) and buses from Bangkok (547B to 638B, 10 hours, five daily). It's nearly 1km from the bus station to the border: motorcycle taxis and túk-túk charge 20B.

At the border The border is open from 6am to 8pm and the crossing, involving walking though an underground tunnel, is largely hassle free. Lao officials sometimes try to extract additional 'stamping fees', but they're usually not too insistent.

Moving on Pakse is about an hour away in one of the frequent *sŏrng·tăa·ou* (10,000K).

white-winged ducks, though you won't likely see them.

The 686-sq-km park's primary attraction is **Namtok Huay Luang**, a waterfall that plunges 45m over a cliff in two parallel streams and has at least a little water all year. A short trail from the visitor centre leads to a viewpoint and you can walk down 274 steps to the bottom, where you can swim, though the water dries up around March. About 150m downstream is **Namtok Praon La-or**, also a pretty picture. Rangers can take visitors on short bamboo-raft trips (300B for six people) above the falls, though for various reasons this activity is intermittent. The best time for this is between October and December. Between the waterfall and the lodging/visitor centre is **Palan Pachad**, a rocky field that features many wildflowers.

Stargazing is superb here, so consider spending the night. There are six well-worn **bungalows** (☎02 562 0760; www.dnp.go.th/parkreserve; 4-/6-bed bungalows 600/1200B) plus a **campsite** (per person with own tent 30B) 2km from Huay Luang. A restaurant opens at least 9am to 4pm daily at the waterfall, and snacks and drinks are sold at the lodging area.

There's no public transport to the park and not much traffic inside it, so you'll need your own transport. Hitching requires patience.

CENTRAL ISAN

Central Isan is light on when it comes to major attractions, but it does contain the important hub and university town Khon Kaen, as well as the pleasant town of Roi Et. There are also links to some important national parks and the region contains Thailand's major deposits of dinosaur fossils.

Khon Kaen Province

Khon Kaen Province, the gateway to Isan for those arriving from northern Thailand, serves up an interesting mix of old and new. Farming and textiles still dominate life in the countryside, while things are booming in the increasingly modern capital city.

Khon Kaen ขอนแก่น

POP 122,370

As the site of the northeast's largest university and an important hub for all things commercial, Khon Kaen is youthful, educated and on the move. While it's the kind of city that's more likely to land on a best-places-to-live list than a traveller's itinerary, there are more than enough interesting attractions and good facilities to make a stop rewarding.

Sights

BUENG KAEN NAKHON บึงแก่นนคร

This 100-hectare lake is the most pleasant place in town to spend some time, and the paths hugging its shore link quite a few interesting places. There's bike hire at the market and down along the west shore across from Wat Klang Muang Kao. The latter has two- and three-seaters (30B per hour per seat).

★**Wat Nong Wang** BUDDHIST TEMPLE

(วัดหนองแวง; Th Robbung; ⏲dawn-dusk) FREE Down at the south end of the lake, **Phra Mahathat Kaen Nakhon** (⏲7am-5pm), the stunning stupa at the heart of this important temple, is Khon Kaen's one must-see. It features enlightening murals depicting Isan culture, various historical displays, including a collection of rare Buddha images on the 4th floor, and a 9th-floor observation deck.

Mahesak Shrine HINDU TEMPLE
(ศาลเจ้าพ่อมเหศักดิ์; Th Robbung) FREE This modern Khmer-style *prang* is dedicated to the Hindu god Indra. It's almost spooky at night.

Rim Bueng Market MARKET
(ตลาดริมบึง; Th Robbung; ⏲4-9pm) This fun little market, in the shadow of Wat That, features food, secondhand clothing and paint-your-own pottery stalls. During the day there are paddleboats (40B per half-hour after 5pm, 50B for any length of time that ends before 5pm) for hire.

Hong Moon Mung MUSEUM
(โฮงมูนมังเมืองขอนแกน; Th Robbung; admission 90B; ⏲9am-5pm Tue-Sat) Inside the amphitheatre, this excellent museum about Khon Kaen provides a good introduction to Isan with dioramas and displays going back to the Jurassic period.

Sanjao Bueng Tao Gong Ma CHINESE TEMPLE
(ศาลเจ้าปึงเถ่ากงม่า; Th Robbung) Sometimes called Sanjao Bueng Kaen Nakhon, this is Khon Kaen's biggest and most beautiful Chinese temple. There's a large Guan-Im (Chinese Goddess of Mercy) statue in the park across the street.

One Pillar Pagoda SHRINE
(ศาลเจ้าเสาเดียว; Th Robbung) This replica of Hanoi's iconic temple was built by Khon Kaen's sizeable Vietnamese community. It's a good sunset-watching spot.

ELSEWHERE IN KHON KAEN

Khon Kaen National Museum MUSEUM
(พิพิธภัณฑสถานแหงชาติขอนแกน; Th Lang Sunratchakan; admission 100B; ⏲9am-4pm Wed-Sun) This interesting collection of artefacts spans prehistoric times to the present. Highlights are Ban Chiang pottery and a beautiful Dvaravati *săir·mah* (temple boundary marker) depicting Princess Pimpa cleaning Lord Buddha's feet with her hair. The household and agricultural displays shed light on what you'll see out in the countryside.

Wat Pa Thama Uthayan BUDDHIST TEMPLE
(วัดธรรมอุทยาน; Th Mittaphap; ⏲dawn-dusk) This peaceful temple, 10km north of the city, has many beautiful monuments, including a 23m-tall white walking Buddha image, spread across its vast grounds. It has become a well-known meditation centre. Take *sŏrng·tăa·ou* 4 (15B) from Namuang or Prachasamoson streets; be sure to tell the driver where you are going since not all go that far.

Courses

Centrum Health Center MASSAGE
(☎089 711 8331; veenasspa@gmail.com; Soi Supatheera) Located in the same area as the Khon Kaen Centrum Hotel, Veena teaches Thai massage in English and Thai. There's also a hairdressing facility.

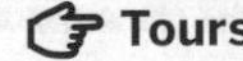

Tours

There are several great tour companies based in Khon Kaen that can show you around the province or take you all over Isan.

THE KHON KAEN ART SCENE

With its large student population, Khon Kaen has an active and growing contemporary-art scene. You can start to uncover it at the following galleries.

Art & Culture Museum (หอศิลปวัฒนธรรม มหาวิทยาลัยขอนแก่น; ⏲10am-7pm) Khon Kaen's leading arts showcase is this two-storey gallery at Khon Kaen University that features monthly installations of mostly professional artists. While open every day, it does close down regularly for a day or two to change the exhibitions.

Ton Tann Art Space & Gallery (หอศิลป์ต้นตาล; Hwy 2; ⏲4.30-10pm) In the stilted building in Ton Tann Green Market.

Lak Muang Gallery (หอศิลป์หลักเมือง; Th Srichant; ⏲10am-6pm) Hidden behind FedEx.

Khon Kaen Faculty of Fine & Applied Arts Gallery (หอศิลป์ คณะศิลปกรรมศาสตร์ มหาวิทยาลัยขอนแก่น; ⏲9am-7pm Mon-Fri) Mostly promotes student work, but sometimes artists from elsewhere exhibit here. Some months have no exhibits.

Khon Kaen

Koon Travel & Butler COOKING, MEDITATION

(☎043 332113; www.koontravel.net) Gregarious owner-guide Veena organises all kinds of tours and specialises in individually tailored meditation tours, visiting famous forest meditation temples throughout Isan, including Khon Kaen's Wat Pa Thama Uthayan. The company also arranges casual cooking classes (2000B per person), and Thai massage courses (6900B, seven days), among others.

Isan Explorer ADVENTURE TOUR

(☎085 354 9165; www.isanexplorer.com) Co-run by Lonely Planet writer Tim Bewer, Isan Explorer runs a wealth of tour options, specialising in slow-travel tours. Elephant encounters have a focus on the animals' welfare and there are many trips based on Isan's cultural attractions, plus trekking in the mountains west of Khon Kaen.

Khon Kaen Education & Travel Programs TOUR

(☎083 359 9115; www.kketp.com) Offers one-day and multiple-day tours of Isan. The outfit also runs a volunteer teaching program and Katt, the owner, offers Thai-language lessons.

Festivals & Events

The **Silk Fair** and **Phuk Siaw Festival** are held simultaneously over 12 days starting in late November. Centred on the provincial hall *(săh·lah glahng),* the festival celebrates and seeks to preserve the tradition of '*pòok sèeo*' (friend bonding), a ritual union of friends during which *fâi pòok kăan* (sacred threads) are tied around one's wrists. Other activities include a parade, Isan music and lots of shopping.

Khon Kaen

Sights
1 Hong Moon Mung D4
2 Lak Muang Gallery B2
3 Mahesak Shrine C4
4 Rim Bueng Market C4
5 Sanjao Bueng Tao Gong Ma D4
6 Ton Tann Art Space & Gallery A4

Activities, Courses & Tours
7 Centrum Health Center B2

Sleeping
8 Charoenchit House C3
9 Chonlada B2
10 Eco Place D1
Khon Kaen Centrum .... (see 7)
11 Piman Garden C1
12 Pullman Raja Orchid B4

Eating
13 Didines A4
14 Night Market C3
15 Pavilion Café B4
16 Pomodoro B4
Tawan Thong .... (see 10)

Drinking & Nightlife
17 Rads B3
18 Slove U C4
19 U-Bar B4

Entertainment
Central Plaza .... (see 20)

Shopping
20 Central Plaza A2
21 Prathammakant C3
22 Rin Thai Silk C3
23 Thammoo Art-Decor C3
Ton Tann Green Market .... (see 6)

Information
24 Très Bien Travel B4

Transport
25 Nakhonchai Air C2
26 Narujee B2
27 Old Air-conditioned Bus Terminal C2
28 Ordinary Bus Terminal C1
29 THAI B4

Sleeping

★ Eco Place HOTEL $
(27/9 Th Robmuang; r/ste 600/1500B; P ❄ 📶) This newish place has bright, light and colourful rooms with subtle stylings and offers great value. The hotel has an ecofriendly policy, using natural local products in its bathrooms and a room design that maximizes natural airflow and reduces the need for air-conditioning (which, however, is there if you want it).

Chonlada HOTEL $
(☎081 873 1387; Soi Supatheera; r 400B; ❄ 📶) A small, simple spot with decent new rooms at an excellent price. The soi is pretty quiet and the ever-smiling owners round out the experience.

Charoenchit House HOTEL $
(☎043 227300; Th Chuanchun; r 500-600B; P ❄ @ 📶) A solid budget choice, just north of the lake. The place is clean and fairly new and the rooms are attractively decorated with a fair amount of va-va-voom for the price.

★ Khon Kaen Centrum HOTEL $$
(☎081 574 0507; www.kk-centrum.com; 33/17-18 Soi Supatheera; r incl breakfast 650-850B; P ❄ 📶) What seems like an ordinary small Thai hotel sets itself apart in the details. The rooms are fairly striking in their white-themed decor and have high-quality furnishings. The owner, who lives on-site, is serious about service and cleanliness. And it's quiet because it's built at the back of the block. Bikes are available for guest use.

Piman Garden HOTEL $$
(☎043 334111; www.pimangardenhotel.com; Th Klang Muang; r 800-1500B; P ❄ 📶) Set back off the road around an attractive garden, Piman offers serenity and privacy despite its city-centre location. Rooms are well presented, though the more expensive rooms aren't the best value. Still, it's one of the best options in the price range.

Pullman Raja Orchid HOTEL $$$
(☎043 322155; www.pullmanhotels.com; off Th Prachasumran; r 2220-2720B, ste 3950-5450B, incl breakfast; P ❄ @ 📶 🏊) A stunning lobby sets the tone for Khon Kaen's top hotel. In the heart of the city it has plenty of razzle-dazzle, including a luxurious spa, pool and gym, a German microbrewery and spacious, well-equipped rooms. There are plenty of restaurants to choose from, and the service is thorough and attentive.

Insist on a room at the front, unless you want to listen to music drifting out of the nearby nightclubs.

WORTH A TRIP

A VIEW WORTH SEEING

Hin Chang See Viewpoint (จุดชมวิวหินช้างสี; admission 100B) While it's difficult to get to – there's no public transport so you have to either drive the 50km, or hire a taxi from Khon Kaen – the Hin Chang See Viewpoint is well worth the trip. More than a viewpoint, it's a wonderland of massive boulders (think 'house-sized') scattered around the scraggy forest, culminating in the lookout itself, which offers spectacular views over the Ubonrat dam. It's a lot higher and more impressive than you'd expect from the drive up.

It's part of Nam Phong National Park, but you can drive straight to the viewpoint from Khon Kaen without going through the main national park entrance, which is about 30km away on another route. To get to Hin Chang See, take Hwy 12 (Th Maliwan) until the 30km marker, then follow Rte 4064 onto Rte 5035 for another 12km. Taxis can be hired for the half-day trip from Khon Kaen for around 1500B. Khun Panya (p438) in Khon Kaen can do a day trip for 1300B (fuel not included). Koon Travel (p434) in Khon Kaen can arrange tours, including camping in the area. Isan Explorer (p434) has hiking trips that take in the spectacular views.

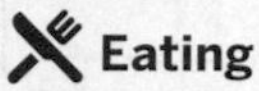

Eating

Khon Kaen has a good **night market** (Th Reunrom; 5pm-midnight) and the eastern-most block of the Saturday Walking Street Market is an awesome eating destination.

Gai Yang Rabeab NORTHEASTERN THAI $
(043 243413; Th Theparak; whole chickens 160B; 9am-3pm) Many Thais believe Khon Kaen Province makes Thailand's best *gài yâhng* (roast chicken) and this simple joint, serving an all-Isan menu, gets the most nods as best of the best in the city.

Tawan Thong VEGAN $
(043 330389; 71/1 Th Ammart; dishes 30-40B; 6am-2pm; P) Tawan Thong has moved from its previous location into large new premises with an ecofriendly design (high ceilings, open spaces). It's an all-vegie, health-food buffet. The food is so good it attracts plenty of non-vegetarian diners.

Pomodoro ITALIAN $$
(Soi Khlong Nam; dishes 150-330B; 5-11pm) In the middle of the lively area around the Pullman Raja Orchid, this place has the best Italian in town.

Didines INTERNATIONAL $$
(Th Prachasumran; dishes 60-380B; kitchen 5-10.30pm, bar until midnight) Far more successful behind the bar than in the kitchen, this stylish restaurant nonetheless has the biggest selection of *fa·ràng* food in town, including chicken cordon bleu, salmon ravioli and black-bean quesadillas. The real reason to go, however, is the selection of American microbrews and the pool table.

Pavilion Café INTERNATIONAL $$$
(Th Prachasumran; breakfast/lunch/dinner 450/550/700B; 6-10am, 11.30am-2pm & 6-10.30pm; P) The principal restaurant of the Pullman Raja Orchid hotel features an excellent international buffet, though it's not available for lunch every day.

Drinking & Nightlife

Several chill, open-air, Thai-style pubs have sprung up around the intersection of Th Reunrom and Th Prachasumran. The fast-growing Lang Mor neighbourhood, way out of town behind Khon Kaen University, has more of the same with a mostly student clientele.

★ **Slove U** CAFE
(095 651 7121; Th Sri Nual; green-tea latte 40B, fruit smoothies 90B; 8am-6pm) Khon Kaen's youthful population has spawned many good coffee shops and this friendly closet-sized one, attractively cluttered with knick-knacks, is one of our favourites.

Rads CLUB
(Th Prachasumran) The exuberant anchor of Khon Kaen's nightlife, this is a multifaceted place with live music, DJs, karaoke, 'coyote' dancers and an alfresco restaurant.

U-Bar CLUB
(Soi Khlong Nam) U-Bar packs them in with live music and some big-name bands from Bangkok.

★ Entertainment

Central Plaza CINEMA

(Th Srichant) Khon Kaen's glossiest shopping mall screens movies in English and has a bowling alley.

Shopping

Because of the variety available, Khon Kaen is arguably the best place to buy Isan handicrafts.

★ Walking Street Market MARKET

(Th Na Sunratchakan; ⌚5.30-10.30pm Sat) In the spirit of Chiang Mai's street markets, hundreds of vendors, many of them students, gather to sell handmade handbags, T-shirts, postcards, picture frames and more. Dancers, musicians and other buskers work strategic corners and the whole place is festooned with Chinese-style lanterns, adding to the festive atmosphere.

Prathammakant HANDICRAFTS

(Th Reunrom; ⌚9am-6pm) With by far the largest and best selection of handicrafts in town, including an impressively large choice of silk, this well-known store makes a perfect one-stop shop.

Thammoo Art-Decor ARTS

(☎043 320479; 79/2 Th Ruenrom; ⌚9am-6pm) This fascinating store is attached to the equally interesting Prathammakhant fabric store – you can walk from one to the other without realising you're in a different store. It has artworks, jade sculptures, souvenirs such as toy *kaan* pipes, household ornaments and Buddhas, as well as artworks made by the owner, who often paints while sitting at the desk.

Ton Tann Green Market MARKET

(Hwy 2; ⌚4-11pm) Half-market, half-mall, Ton Tann is an attractive open space where, like the Walking Street Market, many of the vendors sell modern handmade crafts. There's also a fashion zone, an art gallery and many restaurants.

Rin Thai Silk HANDICRAFTS

(☎043 220705; Th Namuang) This store creates silk dresses and skirts and also sells *mát-mèe* cloth cotton-ware. The emphasis is on quality and there are some great pieces on display. Locals, especially brides-to-be, come here for high-quality garments.

Central Plaza SHOPPING CENTRE

(Th Srichant; ⌚10.30am-9pm Mon-Thu, 10am-9pm Fri-Sun) One of the biggest shopping malls in Isan. Has a branch of the English-language Asia Books.

Information

Khon Kaen's three largest shopping malls, Central Plaza, TukCom and Fairy Plaza, have extended-hours banks. Central and Fairy have AEON ATMs.

Immigration (☎043 465242; Hwy 2; ⌚8.30am-noon & 1-4.30pm Mon-Fri) Situated north of town, near the entrance to Khon Kaen University.

Khon Kaen Ram Hospital (☎043 333800; Th Srichant) Has a 24-hour emergency room.

Tourism Authority of Thailand (TAT; ☎043 227714; tatkhkn@tat.or.th; Th Robbung; ⌚8.30am-4.30pm) Distributes maps of the city and can answer questions about surrounding provinces, too.

Très Bien Travel (☎043 322155; Pullman Raja Orchid; ⌚8.30am-5.30pm Mon-Fri, to 2pm Sat) A reliable spot for booking plane tickets.

Getting There & Away

AIR

Thai Airways (☎043 227701; www.thaiairways.com; Pullman Raja Orchid; ⌚8am-5pm Mon-Fri) operates three daily flights between Khon Kaen and Suvarnabhumi Airport in Bangkok (1300B to 3300B one way). **Air Asia** (☎02 515 9999; www.airasia.com) flies four times daily to Bangkok's Don Mueang Airport (700B to 1500B) and **Nok Air** (☎02 900 9955; www.nokair.com) flies three times daily to/from Don Mueang (700B to 2300B).

Several hotels, including the Pullman, send shuttles (70B) to meet flights at Khon Kaen Airport and you don't need to be staying at the hotels to use them. Taxis at the airport don't use their meters.

BUS

Khon Kaen is a busy transport hub and you can ride directly to nearly all cities in Isan and many beyond. A new air-conditioned **bus terminal** (Th Liang Muang Khon Kaen) has been built on the ring road south of town, and all bus services depart and arrive there. This is often referred to as Bor Kor Sor Sahm (Terminal Three). At time of writing, some of the major bus companies, such as Nakhonchai and Chan Tour, were still operating ticket offices in the old air-conditioned **terminal** (☎043 239910; Th Klang Muang) and you could get a free shuttle bus from there to the new terminal to catch your bus. Minivans still use the old air-conditioned bus terminal.

At time of writing, the **ordinary bus terminal** (☎043 237300; Th Prachasamoson), which

BUSES FROM KHON KAEN'S AIR-CON TERMINAL

Note that there are also non-air-conditioned and 2nd-class buses from the ordinary bus terminal to Loei (143B, 3½ hours, hourly), Khorat (120B, three hours, frequent), Surin (182B, four hours, hourly) and Roi Et (80B, 2½ hours, frequent), as well as to some of the destinations served by the new air-con terminal.

DESTINATION	FARE (B)	DURATION (HR)	FREQUENCY
Bangkok	280	7	6.30am-12.30am (frequent)
Chiang Mai	549-949	12	3.30am-9pm
Khorat	166	3½	8.30am-11.30pm (frequent)
Mukdahan	230	4	2.45am & 4.30am
Nakhon Phanom	243	5	7.30am-4pm (5 daily)
Nong Khai	176	3½	12.20-8pm (4 daily)
Phitsanulok	323	6	12.30-10pm (8 daily)
Roi Et	104-222	2	9am-3pm (9 daily)
Suvarnabhumi Airport	365	6½	10.50pm
Ubon Ratchathani	180-277	4½	1am-8pm (16 daily)
Udon Thani	126-180	2	5am-7pm (hourly)
Vientiane (Laos)	180	4	8am & 3pm

serves all variety of buses to almost everywhere, including all destinations within the province, was flagged to be closing in the near future, with all buses to depart from the new air-con terminal.

The best service to Bangkok is with **Nakhonchai Air** (☎ call centre 1624, 02 790 0009; www.nca.co.th), departing frequently throughout the day from the new air-con terminal. Its 'First-Class' VIP service (560B) departs at 11.15am, 11.15pm and 12.15am.

TRAIN

There's one morning and three evening express trains (seat 77B to 399B, 1st-class sleeper upper/lower 968/1168B, 8½ to nine hours) between Bangkok and **Khon Kaen train station** (☎ 043 221112). There's also a cheaper evening rapid train. Four trains go to Nakhon Ratchasima (38B to 170B, 3½ hours).

ℹ Getting Around

Sŏrng·tăa·ou (9B) ply regular routes across the city. Some of the handiest (all of which pass the old air-con terminal on Th Klangmuang) are line 4, which passes immigration; line 8, which goes to Wat Nong Wang and also northwest through the university; line 10 (going north), which passes near and sometimes in front of the Vietnamese consulate; and line 21, which goes out to the National Museum.

For individual rides, túk-túk are the most expensive way to get around (40B to 60B to most places in the centre), but they're the method most people use because it's rare to find **metered taxis** (☎ 043 465777, 043 342800; flagfall 30B, call fee 30B) on the street, and when you call for one you usually have to wait a long time. About the only places you're likely to find a taxi or motorcycle taxi (within town 20B to 30B) parked are the bus stations and Central Plaza, and the taxis here won't use their meters.

There are many car-hire outlets around Tuk-Com. **Narujee** (☎ 081 471 6524; Soi Kosa; cars per day from 1200B), which charges from 1200B for a car and 200B for a motorcycle, is a reliable choice. **Khun Panya** (☎ 092 290 9151; car per day with driver 1300B) and friends offer cars with drivers.

Chonnabot ชนบท

This small town located 55km southwest of Khon Kaen is one of Thailand's most successful silk villages and is famous for producing top-quality *mát·mèe*. The **Sala Mai Thai** (☎ 043 286218; ⏰ 9am-5pm) FREE is a silk-weaving museum 1km west of town where you can learn about the entire silk-making process, and even take a turn at a loom. Out back is an exhibition hall showing the wooden contraptions devised to spin, tie-dye and weave silk by hand, and a large machine used in factories. A pair of mock-Isan houses hold various traditional household items, and a room upstairs catalogues traditional *mát·mèe* patterns.

The museum sells silk too, but most people buy from the myriad shops on Th Sriboonruang, aka **Silk Road**, some of which also stock attractive cotton fabrics made in the nearby village of Ban Lawaan.

Khon Kaen tour companies run tours to Chonnabot and you can also go by public transport. Buses bound for Nakhon Sawan, departing from Khon Kaen's ordinary bus terminal, will drop you in Chonnabot (42B, one hour, six daily). Or take a bus (35B, one hour, every 30 minutes) or train (9B, 30 minutes, 8am and 8.30am) to Ban Phai, from where you can get a bus to Chonnabot (20B, 20 minutes, hourly).

Prasat Puay Noi

The 12th-century **Prasat Puay Noi** (ปราสาทเปือยนอย; ⏲dawn-dusk) FREE is the largest and most interesting Khmer ruin in northern Isan, though it can't compete with even some of the not-so-famous ruins further south.

From Khon Kaen catch a bus (35B, one hour, every 30 minutes) or train (9B, 30 minutes, 8am and 8.30am) to Ban Phai, then a *sŏrng·tăa·ou* to Puay Noi (35B, one hour). The last *sŏrng·tăa·ou* back to Ban Phai leaves at 2pm. If you have your own wheels, head east of Ban Phai on Hwy 23 (signposted to Borabu) for 11km to Rte 2301. Follow it and Rte 2297 for 24km.

Phu Wiang National Park

A geologist looking for uranium discovered a giant patella bone here in 1976, and the palaeontologists who were called to investigate then unearthed a fossilised 15m-long herbivore. It was later named *Phuwianggosaurus sirindhornae,* after Princess Sirindhorn. Dinosaur fever followed (explaining the myriad model dinosaurs in Khon Kaen city), more remains were uncovered, and **Phu Wiang National Park** (อุทยานแหงชาติภูเวียง; ☎043 358073; admission 200B) was born.

Enclosed **excavation sites** (⏲8.30am-4.30pm), including one with a partial skeleton of *Siamotyrannus isanensis,* an early ancestor of *Tyrannosaurus rex,* can be easily reached on trails from the visitor centre or nearby parking areas. Those who want to explore further (best done by 4WD or mountain bike) will find dinosaur footprints, waterfalls and a superb viewpoint.

Phu Wiang Museum (พิพิธภัณฑไดโนเสาร ภูเวียง; ☎043 438204; adult/child 60/30B; ⏲9am-5pm Tue-Sun), 3km before the park, has palaeontology and geology displays, including full-size models, including some animatronic models, of the dinosaur species that once lived in the area. Kids will love it. They'll also go ape over the giant photogenic dinosaur statues in nearby **Si Wiang Dinosaur Park**. Wiang Kao, the district inside the horseshoe-shaped mountains that comprise the park, is a fruit-growing area and a great place to explore by car, if you want to look at traditional village life.

The park entrance is 90km west of Khon Kaen. Buses and minivans from Khon Kaen's ordinary bus terminal go to Phu Wiang town (40B to 1000B, 1½ hours, every 30 minutes), where you can hire a túk-túk (500B return) or motorbike taxi (300B) for the remaining 19km to the park.

MÁT·MÈE WEAVING

Isan *mát·mèe* is one of Thailand's best-known weaving styles. It's a tie-dye process (*mát* is 'tie' and *mèe* is 'strands') that results in a geometric pattern repeatedly turning back on itself as it runs up the fabric. Although you wouldn't notice it without being told, most of the patterns, handed down from mother to daughter, are abstract representations of natural objects such as trees and birds.

To start, the weavers string their thread (silk or cotton) tightly across a wooden frame as wide as the finished fabric will be. Almost always working from memory, the weavers then tie plastic (traditionally the skin of banana-plant stalks was used) around bunches of strands in their desired design. The frame is then dipped in the dye (nowadays usually a chemical colour, though natural sources such as flowers and tree bark are regaining popularity), which grips the exposed thread but leaves the wrapped sections clean. The wrapping and dipping continues for multiple rounds, resulting in intricate, complex patterns that come to life on the loom. The more you see of the process, the more you understand how amazing it is that the finished product turns out so beautifully.

Nam Nao National Park

One of Thailand's most valuable nature preserves, **Nam Nao National Park** (อุทยานแห่งชาติน้ำหนาว; ☎081 962 6236; admission 200B) covers 966 sq km across the Phetchabun Mountains of Chaiyaphum and Phetchabun Provinces, just beyond Khon Kaen Province. Although it covers remote territory (this remained a People's Liberation Army of Thailand stronghold until the early 1980s), Hwy 12 makes access easy.

With an average elevation of 800m, temperatures are fairly cool year-round (*nám nŏw* means 'cold-feeling water') and frost can occur in December and January. There are both evergreen and deciduous forests, including some three-leaf pine, uncommon in Thailand, mixed with some vast bamboo groves. Nam Nao lies at the heart of the Western Isaan Forest Complex, a 6000-sq-km block of eight connected preserves (including Phu Kradueng National Park and **Phu Khiaw Wildlife Sanctuary**; permits must be acquired in advance to visit the latter), so wildlife is particularly abundant. Elephant encounters are common enough that there's an electric fence around the campground. Lucky visitors might also spot Malayan sun bears, banteng (wild cattle), Asian jackals, barking deer, gibbons, pangolins and flying squirrels. There are even a few tigers. More than 200 species of birds, including great hornbill and silver pheasant, fly through the forest and the exceptional visibility makes this one of Thailand's best birdwatching sites.

A fair system of **hiking trails** branches out from the visitor centre to several scenic overlooks. **Haewsai Waterfall** is 17km east of the visitor centre, while to the west lie the best sunrise/morning fog (5km) and sunset (11km) **viewpoints**. When the park is busy, vehicles (70B per person) deliver people to the viewpoints; reserve a seat at the visitor centre.

There are **campsites** (per person with own tent 30B, 2-6 person tent hire 250-300B), a variety of **bungalows** (☎02 562 0760; www.dnp.go.th/parkreserve; 4-12 person bungalows 1500-4000B) and some simple restaurants around the visitor centre. Accommodation must be booked via the national parks website (www.dnp.go.th).

Most buses heading west to Lom Sak or Phitsanulok from the ordinary bus terminal in Khon Kaen (120B, 2½ hours) will stop in the park. The visitor centre is 1.5km from the highway.

Ban Khok Sa-Nga Cobra Village หมู่บ้านงูจงอางบ้านโคกสง่า

The villagers of Ban Kho Sa-Nga have hit upon a unique (and dangerous) way to make a living: they run king cobra shows daily. Locals at the King Cobra Village rear hundreds of the reptiles and most families have some in boxes under their houses.

The custom began in 1951 when a travelling medicinal-herb salesman began putting on snake shows to attract customers. His plan was a success and the art of breeding and training snakes has been nurtured in this village ever since. Today the King Cobra Club of Thailand puts on **snake shows** where handlers taunt snakes and tempt fate – they often lose, as the many missing fingers show. There is even an 'honour board' showing the performers who have lost their lives as a result of the shows, and this is often played up in the commentary. If this, or the thought of children as young as five performing with snakes, upsets you, you might want to give it a miss.

The village is 50km northeast of Khon Kaen along Hwy 2 and Rte 2039. Take a Kranuan bus or minivan from Khon Kaen's ordinary bus terminal to the turn-off for Ban Khok Sa-Nga (30B, one hour, every 30 minutes) and then take a túk-túk (40B) to the showgrounds. If you're driving from Khon Kaen, consider taking the rural route that passes **Phra That Kham Kaen**, a revered *chedi* in the village of Ban Kham.

Roi Et ร้อยเอ็ด

POP 34,285

There has been a settlement at this spot for at least 2800 years, making this one of Isan's oldest cities. At one point, legend says, it had 11 city gates. In ancient writing '11' was expressed as '10-plus-1' and somehow this morphed into the city's name, which means '101'.

Except for extensive stretches of the old city moat, Roi Et's long history hasn't followed it into the 21st century. Still, the city retains a charm and sense of identity all its own. You can't call Roi Et sleepy, but it does seem to move to its own urban beat.

Roi Et

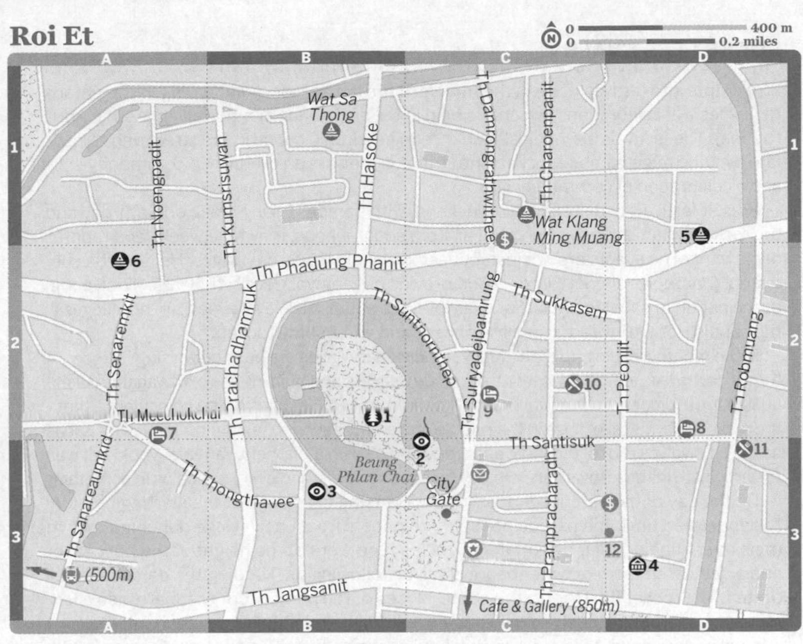

Sights

Wat Burapha BUDDHIST TEMPLE

(วัดบูรพา; Th Phadung Phanit; dawn-dusk) FREE The enormous standing Buddha towering above Roi Et's skyline is **Phra Phuttha Ratana Mongkon Mahamuni** (Luang Po Yai for short), the main attraction at this temple. Despite being of little artistic significance, it's hard to ignore. Head to toe he stands 59.2m, and from the ground to the tip of the *ùt·sà·nít* it's 67.8m. You can climb up the stairs behind him.

Roi Et National Museum MUSEUM

(พิพิธภัณฑสถานแห่งชาติร้อยเอ็ด; Th Peonjit; admission 100B; 9am-4pm Wed-Sun, closed public holidays) This interesting museum gives equal billing to ancient artefacts and Isan culture. The 3rd floor features silk weaving, including a good display showing the materials used to produce natural-dye fabrics. There are also some Lopburi-era Khmer pieces.

Bueng Phalan Chai PARK

(บึงพลาญชัย) Walking paths criss-cross the attractive, shady island and attract the usual crowd of doting couples, students, joggers and picnickers. The beloved walking Buddha statue is on the north side and the **lak meuang** (ศาลหลักเมือง; city pillar) is to the south.

Roi Et

Sights

Sleeping

Eating

Transport

Wat Neua BUDDHIST TEMPLE

(วัดเหนือ; Th Phadung Phanit; dawn-dusk) FREE This temple in the northern quarter of town has a peaceful ambience. It's known for its 1200-year-old brick *chedi* from the Dvaravati period, which has an unusual four-cornered bell-shaped form that's rare in Thailand. Also inside the cloister are some old Dvaravati *bai săir·mah* (Buddhist boundary stones) and a giant bodhi tree.

ROCKET FESTIVALS

Isan erupts into festival mode in the middle of the hot season, culminating in the riotous rocket festival celebrations, which are held in the sixth lunar month (falling around April to June). The festivals are not just a chance to get drunk, dance in the street and tempt fate by firing huge bamboo rockets into the sky: they are an exercise in community spirit and a celebration of community life.

Rocket festivals usually fall on a weekend, with parades taking place on Saturday and the rocket launches on the Sunday. Far from spontaneous, they take weeks and months of planning. The events are not just focused on single towns or villages. Held on the subdistrict *(đambon)*, district *(amper)* and provincial *(jangwàt)* levels, they also involve the participation of satellite areas. For example, at a subdistrict-level event, all the villages in the subdistrict are invited to join the parade and enter some rockets.

In the months leading up to the festival, individual villages are busy organising the costumes and music for the dancers, training the dancers and building the extravagant rocket floats for the parade – as well as the rockets themselves. (Perhaps it's no coincidence that the rocket festivals take place in the middle of the hot season, when agricultural work is least active.) It involves a lot of planning and work, and also financial help. Families who don't want to participate in the festival can help pay for the costumes, and everyone chips in something.

On the day of the parade, dancers line up outside the village at the starting point. At the appointed time, the parade begins, with people from each village dancing down the main street behind their designated sign. It's hard work at the height of the hot season and a dedicated team of water bearers will be following on, keeping the dancers hydrated. The rocket floats form the centerpieces of the parade, but there are also a few recurring characters, such as the Toad King (Phaya Khan Khak), an elephant, a squirrel and perhaps even an effigy of a 'young boy' engaging in sex. As the parade proceeds down the street, the organising committee sits and assesses with an eagle eye. The winning village for the parade gains glory rather than gold, but winning isn't the aim.

On the Sunday the rockets, which come in all sizes, are fired. Traditionally they were made of a bamboo shaft stuffed with gunpowder, but nowadays PVC pipes are becoming the vessel of choice. The largest can reach 3m in length, and accidents do happen – bear in mind that they aren't made to aeronautical standards and their trajectories are unpredictable. Add to that the large amount of alcohol being consumed and you have a saucy recipe for accidents, something the Thai government has been keen to clean up.

While many villages and towns hold rocket festivals, without a doubt the most famous of all is the **Yasothon** festival, which is officially promoted by the Tourism Authority of Thailand. This otherwise unremarkable town springs to life during festival time (second weekend in May) and if you want to stay here at that time you really need to book accommodation well in advance. The **BM Grand** (045 714262; Th Rattanakhet; s/d 400/450B; P ⊖ ❄ ≋) offers the best value in town, while the **JP Emerald Hotel** (045 724848; www.jpemeraldhotel.com; Th Prapa; r 550B, incl breakfast 700-1200B; P ❄ @ ≋) is well kept and lively.

Other towns with notable rocket festivals are Suwannaphum (first weekend of June) and Phanom Phrai (full moon of the 7th lunar month) districts in Roi Et, as well as many towns in Nong Khai and Udon Thani Provinces. Buses to Yasothon from Bangkok cost between 400B (1st class) and 624B (VIP), and there are also buses from nearby Ubon Ratchathani (90B to 105B), Mukdahan (80B to 103B) and Khon Kaen (120B to 181B).

If you're in Yasothon for the festival, you might want to check out the giant toad, a five-storey-high **toad museum** that was just being completed at time of research. It's planned to house displays about the rocket festival and associated folklore.

Roi Et Aquarium AQUARIUM

(สถานแสดงพันธุ์สัตว์น้ำเทศบาลเมืองร้อยเอ็ด; Th Sunthornthep; 8.30am-4pm Tue-Sun, closed public holidays) FREE This little aquarium with a walk-through tunnel houses fish found around Isan. Most of the tanks are somewhat plain and sad, but the walk-through tank has some rather large river fish. If you don't have a chance to see the aquariums in Nong Khai or Nakhon Phanom, it's probably worth a visit.

Sleeping

City Home Place HOTEL $

(☎043 516079; Th Thongthavee; s/d 400/440B; P ❄ 📶) The rooms here, while lacking character, are spotlessly clean and represent good value for the price. The place is fairly new and there's a small breakfast provided.

Saithip Hotel HOTEL $

(☎043 511742; Th Suriyadejbamrung; r 240-320B; P ❄ 📶) Bascially a concrete block with rows of rooms crammed in together, this is a basic cheapie. The more expensive rooms are air-con and probably a wise decision given the design of the rooms.

Roi Et City Hotel HOTEL $$

(Th Peonjit; r 950B, ste up to 7000B) This grand old place has seen better days, but from the artwork in the foyer and the style of the decor it must have been really something in its day. While a little worn, the rooms are nicely finished and the bathrooms, with bath, are spacious. The standard rooms are good value.

Eating & Drinking

White Elephant INTERNATIONAL, THAI $

(Chang Pheuak; Th Robmuang; dishes 60-350B; ⌚4-11.30pm; P 📶) This place just across the old moat has a massive Thai menu, but the specialities are German, as is the owner. It's very popular with Western visitors and has cosy timber furnishings.

Night Market NORTHEASTERN THAI $

(Th Prampracharadh; ⌚3-11pm) By day, this big roof hosts Roi Et's municipal market, but at night it shifts gears to become the city's main night market.

Cafe & Gallery COFFEE

(Th Ronnachai Chanyut; ⌚9am-6.30pm; 📶) Owned by a photographer, and full of his framed prints (for sale starting at 500B), this small coffee shop brings a welcome bit of culture to Roi Et. For a snack, try the 'spicy cake' – chocolate with chilli peppers. It's 1km south of the lake, across the street from Roi Et Hospital.

Getting There & Around

Nok Air (☎02 900 9955; www.nokair.com) has three flights daily to/from Bangkok's Don Mueang Airport, with fares from about 1000B, while **Air Asia** (☎02 515 9999; www.airasia.com) has two flights daily to/from Don Mueang. **ST Travel** (☎043 512469; Th Peonjit; ⌚8.30am-6pm Mon-Sat) sells tickets. The airport is 13km north of town.

Buses depart at least hourly from Roi Et's **bus terminal** (☎043 511939; Th Jangsanit) to Bangkok (305B to 610B, eight hours), Khon Kaen (bus and minivan 80B to 116B, 2½ hours), Ubon Ratchathani (113B to 146B, three hours) and Surin (95B, 2½ hours). The bus terminal is 1km west of the city centre. Túk-túk charge 60B to anywhere near the lake.

Ko Chang & Eastern Seaboard

Includes ➡

Best Places to Eat

- ➡ Relax (p445)
- ➡ Glass House (p454)
- ➡ Jep's Restaurant (p461)
- ➡ Chanthorn Phochana (p464)
- ➡ Pan & David Restaurant (p450)

Best Places to Stay

- ➡ Bann Makok (p483)
- ➡ Rabbit Resort (p454)
- ➡ Samed Pavilion Resort (p459)
- ➡ Baan Luang Rajamaitri (p464)
- ➡ Koh Chang Sea Hut (p475)

Why Go?

Two islands – Ko Samet and Ko Chang – are the magnets that draw travellers to the eastern seaboard. The mainland has plenty of its own attractions, though, from international resorts like Pattaya to the charismatic, old-world charm of Chanthaburi.

Ko Samet, the nearest major island to Bangkok, is a flashpacker fave where visitors sip from vodka buckets and admire the fire jugglers or head for the quieter southern coves. Further down the coast is Ko Chang, Thailand's second-largest island. Spend your days diving, chilling on the west-coast beaches or hiking through dense jungle – then recover in time to experience the island's vibrant party scene.

Fewer travellers make it to Bang Saen, though its hip seafront restaurants and long beach make it worth a stopover. Less serene is the raucous resort of Pattaya, with its hedonistic nightlife, numerous attractions and some of the best international cuisine in the kingdom.

When to Go

- ➡ The best time to visit is the end of the rainy season (usually around November) but before the start of high season (December to March) when the weather is cool, the landscape green and rates reasonable. Peak season on Ko Chang is the Christmas and New Year holiday period. Crowds thin in March, the start of the hot season.
- ➡ The rainy season runs from May to October, though there are often days or weeks with no rain at all. A few businesses on Ko Chang close, and Ko Kut, Ko Mak and Ko Wai go into hibernation with many places shut. Your best bet during monsoon is Ko Samet, which enjoys its own microclimate and stays relatively dry.

Bang Saen บางแสน

POP 42, 843

As the closest beach to Bangkok, Bang Saen is a weekend favourite for those wanting to escape city life. Recent renovations to the beachfront and a slew of new boutique hotels have boosted its popularity. During the day, the 4km-long promenade is packed with tandem bicycles and seafood stalls. By night, the string of hip restaurants and bars facing the sea draw a student crowd.

Sights & Activities

Khao Sam Muk HILL

(เขาสามมุข, Monkey Mountain) Hundreds of rhesus monkeys with greedy eyes and quick hands live on this small hill (avoid feeding them, as this just makes them more aggressive). Local folklore says the hill is named after a girl who took her life here after a doomed romance.

Wang Saen Suk BUDDHIST TEMPLE

(วังแสนสุข, Temple of Happiness; Soi 19, Sai 2; 8am-6pm) FREE Despite its name, this site contains gruesome Dante-esque statues of sinners being eternally punished. Half-human, half-animal creatures surround two huge figures by the entrance. On the flip side, there are statues depicting Thai fairy tales and more righteous behaviour. A nearby pond has giant catfish and turtles that can be fed (10B).

Mangrove Forest Conservation Centre FOREST

(038 398268; Ang Sila; 8.30am-3.30pm) FREE This forest is such a well-kept secret, many locals don't even know it's here. A 2km-long wooden walkway gives access to the mangrove forest, which is mostly shaded. Look out for the crabs, cockles and mudfish. The forest is 3km north of Ang Sila's daily fish market, also worth exploring. Ang Sila is 6km north of Bang Saen.

Wihahn Tepsatit Pra Gitichairloem CHINESE TEMPLE

(วิหารเทพสถิตพระกิตติเฉลิม; Ang Sila; 8am-5pm; P) FREE Created to mark the king's 72nd birthday, this four-storey Chinese temple is filled with intricate paintings and magnificent sculptures. Locals regularly come to make merit, and temple volunteers are happy to explain the rituals if you want to make your own offerings. The temple is on the main road in Ang Sila.

Flight of the Gibbon ZIPLINING

(089 970 5511; www.treetopasia.com; tours from 3000B) This zipline course extends 3km via 26 platforms through the forest canopy of Khao Kheow Open Zoo. It is an all-day tour with additional add-on activities, like a jungle obstacle course and a visit to the neighbouring zoo.

Sleeping

Suk Jai Guesthouse GUESTHOUSE $

(086 839 1688; Soi 1, Bang Saen Sai 1; r 500B;) The rooms may be functional rather than fancy but you will be on the beach in only a few steps. There is no English sign so look for the red-and-white-tiled wall.

Bangsaen Heritage Hotel HOTEL $$$

(038 399899; www.bs-heritagehotel.com; 50 Sai 1; r incl breakfast 2942-11,181B;) A sign of Bang Saen's recent growth comes in the form of this beautiful resort, which fuses traditional Thai design with modern twists.

Eating & Drinking

Summer's Corner CAFE $

(193/25 Th Long Had Bang Saen; dishes 100-150B; 10am-10pm;) Students from the local uni are regulars here thanks to cheery staff, creative dishes and cool decor.

Relax THAI $$

(Th Rob Khao Sum Muk; dishes 150-300B; 4pm-midnight) Aptly named, Relax lets its customers sit on the beach, sipping beer, listening to live music and snacking on grilled squid.

Getting There & Away

Minivans and buses leave from either side of Th Sukhumvit, close to the main turn off into Bang Saen. Red *sŏrng·tăa·ou* (passenger pick-up trucks) go to Si Racha (15B, 20 minutes, 5.30am to 9pm).

DESTINATION	BUS	MINIVAN
Bangkok's Eastern Bus Terminal (Ekamai)	83B; 1hr; hourly	
Bangkok's Northern Bus Terminal (Mo Chit)	95B; 1½hr; hourly	120B; 1½hr; hourly; 5am-8.30pm
Bangkok Suvarnabhumi International Airport	110B; 1hr; hourly	
Victory Monument (Bangkok)	110B; 1½ hr; hourly	
Ban Phe (for Ko Samet)		180B; 2hr; 8am-5pm

Ko Chang & Eastern Seaboard Highlights

1. Snorkelling and jungle trekking on **Ko Chang** (p468).
2. Floating the day away on the crystalline waters of **Ko Kut** (p482).
3. Swimming with the fishes in the gin-clear coves of **Ko Wai** (p479).
4. Cove-hopping on pretty **Ko Samet** (p457).
5. Strolling through the old waterfront community in **Chanthaburi** (p462).
6. Riding a tandem bike along the shady promenade in **Bang Saen** (p445).
7. Kicking back in the atmospheric wooden shophouse quarter of **Trat** (p465).
8. Escaping Bangkok's bustle with a day trip to peaceful **Ko Si Chang** (p450) and a layover in **Si Racha** (p448).
9. Admiring the modern masterpiece of Pattaya's **Sanctuary of Truth** (p451), an elaborately carved testament to the artistry of Buddhism and Hinduism.
10. Dining on seafood beside the sea everywhere – the principal reason Thais travel to the beach.

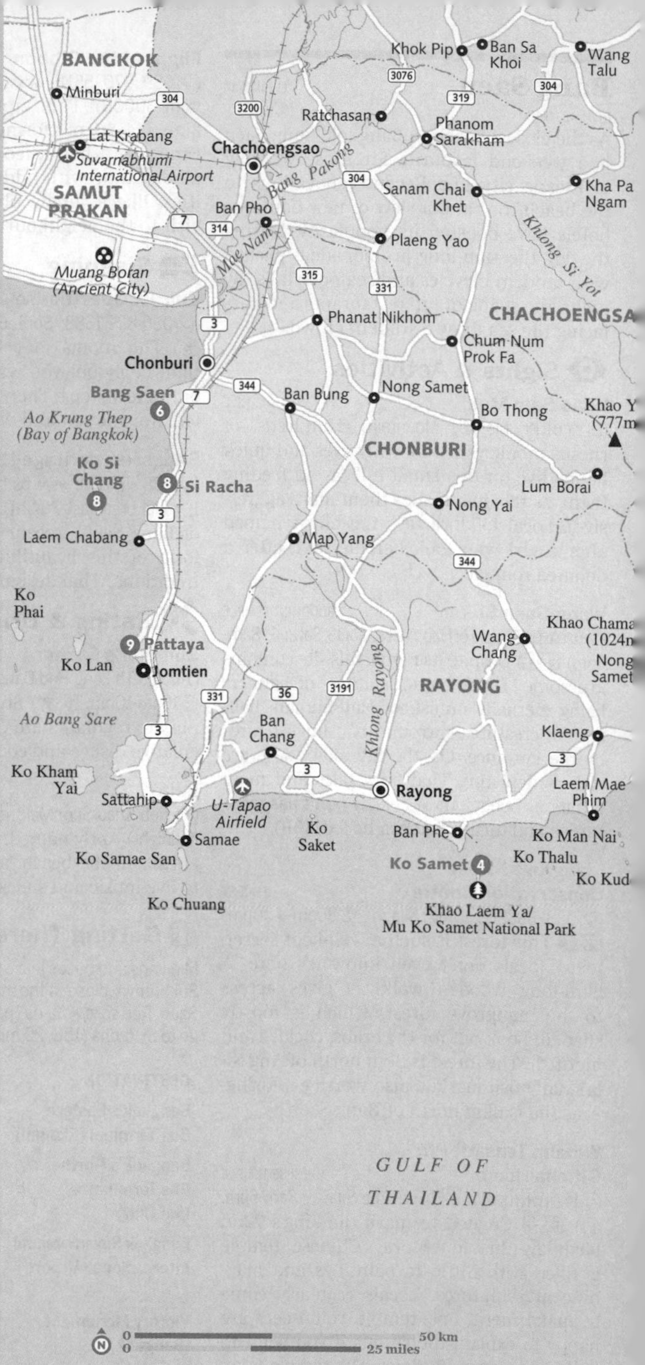

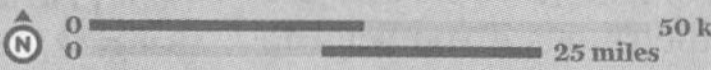

Sa Kaew
Lam Prachinburi
Watthana Nakhon
Huay Jot
Ang Sila
Non Mak Mun
Sai Yoi
Khao Chakan
Aranya Prathet
Poipet
CAMBODIA
Sai Diaw
Non Sao-Eh
Sisophon
Khlong Hat
hao Takrup (660m)
Wang Mai
Khao Daeng
Thun Khanan
CHANTHABURI
Tamun
Battambang
Khao Soi Dao Nua (1566m)
Pung Ngon
Nong Chek Soi
Takra
Ban Pakard
Psar Pruhm
Khao Chamao/ Khao Wong National Park
Pong Nam Ron
Khao Khitchakut National Park
Pailin
Si Yaek Kong Din
Nong Khla
Makham
Ban Pa-Ah
Tha Mai
Chanthaburi
Chang Thun
Nam Tok Phlio National Park
Nong Sii
aem Sadet
Chao Lao
Ta Chalap
Chak Yai
Khlung
Laem Sing
Pong
Dan Chumpon
Laem Ko Proet
Tha Chot
TRAT
CAMBODIA
Trat
Ban Noen Sung
Bang Kradan
Laem Muang
Laem Ngop
Ao Trat
Tha Sen
Ko Chang
Laem Sok
Mu Ko Chang National Marine Park
Hat Mai Rut
Ko Wai
Ko Kradat
Ko Mak
Ko Ran
Khlong Yai
Ko Mai Si
Ko Kut
Hat Lek
Krong Koh Kong
348
33
317
3395
3
3157
3159
3271
3156
318

Si Racha ศรีราชา

POP 80,088

Si Racha (pronounced 'see-ra-cha') is an unlikely blend of traditional and modern. Colourful, creaking fishing boats and squid rigs are still moored here, but these days they share the water with giant container ships from the nearby port of Laem Chabang.

Sushi restaurants and karaoke bars cater for the hundreds of Japanese employees who work at nearby industrial estates, giving the town centre a Little Tokyo vibe. The heart of Si Racha is the seafront health park.

Sights

Si Racha's attractions are limited, but the town centre makes for a pleasant stroll.

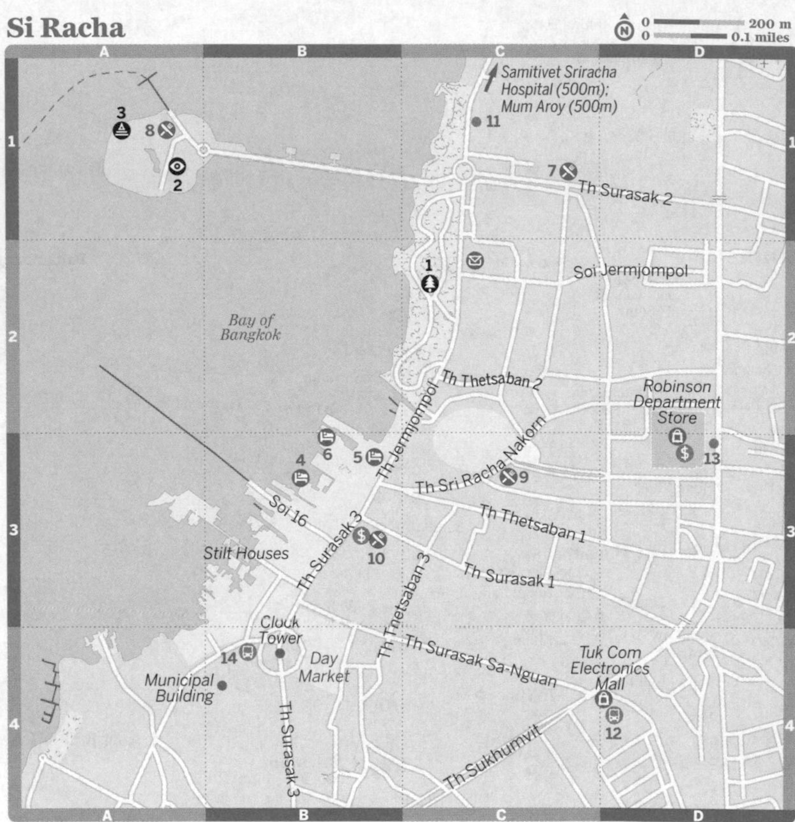

Si Racha

Sights
1 Health Park C2
2 Ko Loi A1
3 Thai-Chinese Temple A1

Sleeping
4 Samchai B3
5 Seaview Sriracha Hotel B3
6 Siriwatana Hotel B3

Eating
7 California Steak C1
8 Ko Loi Seafood Stalls A1
9 Lahp Ubon C3
10 My One B3

Information
11 Immigration Office C1

Transport
12 Buses to Bangkok D4
13 Minivans to Bangkok D3
14 Sŏrng·tăa·ou to Pattaya & Bang Saen B4

Ko Loi ISLAND

This island has a **Thai-Chinese temple** and a sunset viewing area. Below the temple is a pond, where huge turtles can be fed squid (10B). This is also where you can catch the ferry to Ko Si Chang.

Health Park PARK

Locals fill this well-maintained municipal park every evening to practise yoga, tai chi and skateboarding. The park includes a coffee shop, jogging track and play equipment.

Sleeping

The most authentic (read: basic) places to stay are the wooden hotels on the piers

Samchai HOTEL $

(☎038 311800; Soi 10, Th Jermjompol; r 350-900B; ❄📶) This pier hotel has rustic rooms and good sea views. Cheaper rooms are fan-only.

Siriwatana Hotel HOTEL $

(☎038 311037; 35 Soi Siriwatana, Th Jermjompol; r 200-380B; 📶) Locals reckon this guesthouse on stilts has been here for almost a century. Get a sea view by looking straight ahead – or down through the wooden slats.

Seaview Sriracha Hotel HOTEL $$

(☎038319000; seaview_hotel@hotmail.com; 50-54 Th Jermjompol; r incl breakfast 990-1900B; ❄@📶) Rooms are large and comfortable; try to score one at the back for sea views.

Eating

Unsurprisingly, Si Racha is famous for its seafood. You can try it Thai-, Japanese- or Korean-style.

Ko Loi Seafood Stalls SEAFOOD $

(dishes 40-160B; ⏲10am-9pm) On the Ko Loi jetty, these spots specialise in fresh seafood.

Lahp Ubon NORTHEASTERN THAI $

(Th Si Racha Nakorn; dishes 20-80B; ⏲10am-10pm) An Isan place with yummy *nám đòk mŏo* (spicy pork salad).

My One VIETNAMESE $

(14/10 Th Surasak 1; dishes 50-160B; ⏲9am-9pm) This simple Thai-Vietnamese restaurant has a variety of fresh, healthy dishes, including (non-fried) spring rolls and salads.

Mum Aroy SEAFOOD $$

(Soi 8, Th Jermjompol; dishes 60-420B; ⏲11am-10pm) Mum Aroy ('delicious corner') is *the* place to enjoy a seafood meal with views of the squid rigs. It is north of the town; turn left at Samitivet Sriracha Hospital and look for the tank with the 2m fish out front.

California Steak STEAK $$

(4/3-4 Th Surasak 2; mains 200-300B; ⏲5.30pm-midnight) This stylish steakhouse has a good range of pizzas and imported meats.

Information

Immigration Office (☎038 312571; 3/1 Th Jermjompol; ⏲8.30am-4.30pm)

Krung Thai Bank (cnr Th Surasak 1 & Th Jermjompol; ⏲8.30am-3.30pm) ATM and exchange.

Post Office (Th Jermjompol; ⏲8.30am-4.30pm Mon-Fri, 8.30am-12.30pm Sat) The post office is opposite the Health Park.

Samitivet Sriracha Hospital (☎038 324111; Soi 8, Th Jermjompol)

Getting There & Around

Minivans leave from Th Sukhumvit (Hwy 3) by Robinson Department Store and buses and minivans leave from the nearby IT mall, Tuk Com.

White *sŏrng·tăa·ou* leave from near the clock tower for Pattaya's Naklua market (40B, 45 minutes, 6am to 6pm); red *sŏrng·tăa·ou* go to Bang Saen (15B, 20 minutes, 6am to 6pm). Motorbike taxis zip around town for a cost of about 30B to 40B.

TRANSPORT TO/FROM SI RACHA

DESTINATION	BUS	MINIVAN	TRAIN
Bangkok's Eastern Bus Terminal (Ekamai)	94B; 1½hr; hourly; 5am-8pm		
Bangkok's Northern Bus Terminal (Mo Chit)	97B; 2hr; hourly; 5am-7.30pm		
Bangkok Suvarnabhumi International Airport	110B; 1hr; hourly; 5.10am-8pm		
Pattaya		40B; 30min; frequent	
Victory Monument (Bangkok)		100B; 1½hr; every 30min; 5am-8pm	
Bangkok Hualamphong			28B; 3hr; 2.52pm daily

Ko Si Chang เกาะสีชัง

POP 4,975

Once a royal beach retreat, Ko Si Chang has a fishing village atmosphere and enough attractions to make it a decent day's excursion from Si Racha, or an overnight stop for those who want to chill out. It gets busier at weekends, when Bangkok Thais come to eat seafood, pose in front of the sea and make merit at the local temples.

Sights

Phra Chudadhut Palace HISTORIC SITE

(9am-5pm Tue-Sun) FREE This former royal palace was used by Rama V (King Chulalongkorn) over the summer months, but was abandoned when the French briefly occupied the island in 1893. The main throne hall – a magnificent golden teak structure known as Vimanmek Teak Mansion – was moved to Bangkok in 1910. What's left are Victorian-style buildings set in gardenlike grounds.

Ruen Vadhana and Ruen Mai Rim Talay contain historical displays about the king's visits to the island and his public works programs, including a lecture to the local people on Western tea parties. Up the hill is Wat Atsadang Khanimit, a temple with Gothic-style windows that contains a small, consecrated chamber where Rama V used to meditate. The Buddha image inside was fashioned more than 50 years ago by a local monk. Nearby is a stone outcrop wrapped in holy cloth, called Bell Rock because it rings like a bell when struck.

San Jao Phaw Khao Yai CHINESE TEMPLE

FREE The most imposing sight on the island, this ornate Chinese temple dates back to the days when Chinese traders anchored in the sheltered waters. During Chinese New Year in February, the island is overrun with Chinese tourists. There are shrine caves, multiple platforms and a good view of the ocean. It's north of the main town.

Wat Tham Yai Phrik BUDDHIST TEMPLE

(วัดถ้ำยายปริก; www.watthamyaiprig.com; donations appreciated; 5am-6pm) FREE This Buddhist monastery is built around several meditation caves running into the island's central limestone ridge and offers fine views from its hilltop *chedi* (stupa). Monks and *mâa chee* (nuns) from across Thailand come to take advantage of the caves' peaceful environment. Someone is usually around to give informal tours and talk about Buddhism.

The body of a former nun is displayed in a small room within the grounds, a reminder of the impermanence of earthly life. Accommodation is available for those taking a meditation course.

Hat Tham Phang BEACH

On the southwest side of the island, Hat Tham Phang (Fallen Cave Beach) is the only sandy beach on the island. You can hire kayaks and there's deckchair and umbrella rental. Snorkelling is possible around the northern section.

Activities

Several locals run **snorkelling** trips to nearby Ko Khang Khao (Bat Island), which has a good beach, or you can take a speedboat (400B) there from the main pier. **Kayaks** are available (200B per hour) on Hat Tham Phang. You can paddle to Ko Khang Khao in 45 minutes.

Sichang Healing House MASSAGE

(081 572 7840; off Th Makham Thaew) The charming, English-speaking owner of this leafy haven offers a range of excellent massages (300B to 600B). She also sells homemade health products and has modest bamboo rooms for rent (300B).

Sleeping & Eating

There are a smattering of guesthouses and homestays on the island, as well as restaurants specialising in seafood.

Charlie's Bungalows GUESTHOUSE $$

(085 191 3863; www.kosichang.net; Th Makham Thaew; r 1000-1100B;) Bright, fresh, all-white bungalows set around a garden. All come with TVs and DVD players. Friendly and helpful staff. Book ahead at weekends and public holidays.

★ **Pan & David Restaurant** INTERNATIONAL, THAI $$

(038 216629; www.ko-sichang.com; 167 Mu 3, Th Makham Thaew; dishes 120-440B; 8.30am-10pm) With free-range chicken, homemade ice cream, a reasonable wine list and excellent Thai dishes, you can't go wrong here. It also has rooms available (750B to 1800B), which include converted fishing boats.

Pa Noi Rim Tahng SEAFOOD $$

(Th Makham Thaew; 100-350B; 11am-9pm) This eat-on-the-street restaurant is a favourite with locals thanks to its great seafood options. Look for the blue tables and umbrellas.

Information

The island's one small settlement faces the mainland and is the terminus for the ferry. A bumpy road network links the village with the other sights.

Pan & David's website (www.ko-sichang.com) is an excellent source of local information.

Kasikornbank (99/12 Th Atsadang; ⏲8.30am-3.30pm) Has an ATM and exchange facilities.

Post Office (Th Atsadang; ⏲8.30am-4.30pm Mon-Fri, 8.30am-12.30pm Sat) Near the pier.

Getting There & Around

Boats to Ko Si Chang leave hourly 7am to 8pm from the jetty of Ko Loi (p449) in Si Racha (one way 50B, 45 minutes). From Ko Si Chang boats shuttle back hourly from 6am to 7pm.

Motorbike taxis wait at the pier and will take you anywhere for 30B to 50B, and souped-up săhm·lór (also spelt sǎamláw) do tours of the main spots for 250B.

Motorbikes are available to rent on the pier (250B per day, 80B hourly).

Pattaya พัทยา

POP 192,372

If you long for quiet beaches and hammocks swaying in the breeze, make a sharp U-turn before arriving in Pattaya. The city's reputation as a sex capital is well deserved, with hundreds of beer bars, go-go clubs and massage parlours. But Pattaya does perennially try to lose its sex tag and many of its 10 million annual visitors instead come for the mega shopping centres and amenities. Pattaya is also home to a growing number of cultural and action-packed attractions and international restaurants.

The city is built around **Ao Pattaya**, a wide, crescent-shaped bay that was one of Thailand's first beach resorts in the 1960s when American GIs came for some R&R. North Pattaya (Pattaya Neua) is a more upmarket area while Pattaya South (Pattaya Tai) remains the nightlife hub.

To the south of Pattaya, **Jomtien** is a resort with a gay-friendly beach at Hat Dongtan, while to the north **Naklua** is also quieter, with some top-end resorts at Wong Amat.

The best beaches in the area are on **Ko Samae San**, a tiny island with good snorkelling, and the navy-run **Hat Nahng Ram**, both 35km south of Pattaya.

Sights & Activities

Sanctuary of Truth MONUMENT

(ปราสาทสัจธรรม; ☎038 367229; www.sanctuaryoftruth.com; 206/2 Mu 5, Soi Naklua 12; adult/child 500/250B; ⏲8am-6pm) Made entirely of wood (without any metal nails) and commanding a celestial view of the ocean, the Sanctuary of Truth is best described as a visionary environment: part art installation, religious shrine and cultural monument. Constructed in four wings dedicated to Thai, Khmer, Chinese and Indian religious iconography, its architecture and setting is impressive.

The ornate temple-like complex was conceived by Lek Viriyaphant, a Thai millionaire who spent his fortune on this and other heritage projects (such as Ancient City near Bangkok) that revived and preserved ancient building techniques and architecture in danger of extinction. In this case, the building continues to support hand-hewn woodworking skills as it's been under construction since 1981 and still isn't finished.

PATTAYA FOR CHILDREN

Pattaya has lots to offer younger visitors, from water parks to family-friendly farms.

Cartoon Network Amazone (☎038 237797; www.cartoonnetworkamazone.com; 888 Mu 8, Th Sukhumvit; adult/child 1290/890B; ⏲10am-6pm; 👪) The world's first Cartoon Network–themed water park includes a surfing arena, a 1km-long river and the chance to meet Ben 10.

Greta Farm (☎092 634 7979; www.gretafarm.com; 68/5 Mu 3, Th Wat Yarn; ⏲7am-11pm; 👪) Goats, horses and cows are the star attractions at this children's farm, which also includes archery, a fun park and rope bridges.

Underwater World (☎038 756879; www.underwaterworldpattaya.com; 22/22 Mu 11, Th Sukhumvit; adult/child 500/300B; ⏲9am-6pm; 👪) The area's largest aquarium is particularly child-friendly, with touch pools and koi feeding sessions.

Art in Paradise (☎038 424500; www.artinparadise.co.th; 78/34 Mu 9, Th Pattaya Sai 2; adult/child 400/200B; ⏲9am-9pm; 👪) Thais come here for the ultimate selfie as they pose amid 3D paintings of dinosaurs, waterfalls and, bizarrely, an elephant on a toilet.

Pattaya & Naklua

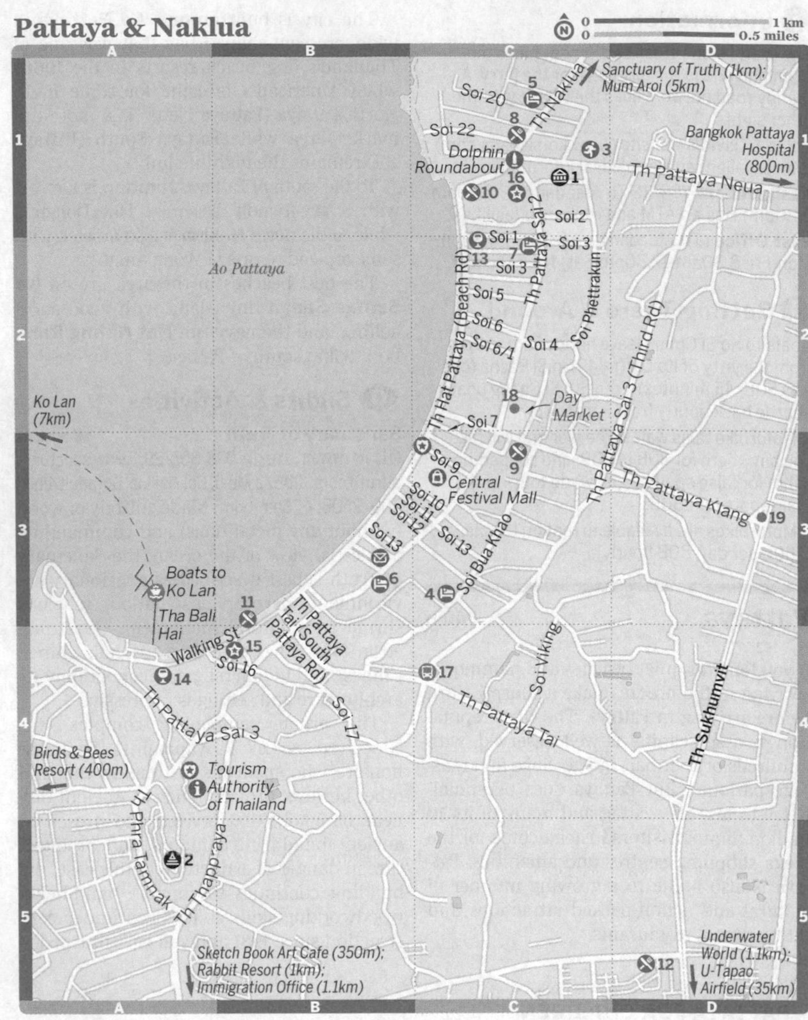

Every part of the 105m-tall building is covered with wood carvings of Hindu and Buddhist gods and goddesses.

Compulsory tours are led through the building every 30 minutes. Thai dancing is at 11.30am and 3.30pm. Motorcycle taxis can be hired from Pattaya for 50B to 70B. The sanctuary is 1km down Soi 12 off Th Naklua, about 3km from the centre of town.

Anek Kusala Sala (Viharn Sien) MUSEUM
(อเนกกุศลศาลา / วิหารเซียน); ☎038 235250; off Th Sukhumvit; admission 50B; ⊙8am-5pm) A popular stop for tour groups, this museum contains more than 300 impressive pieces of Chinese artwork, mainly bronze and brass statues depicting historical figures as well as Buddhist, Confucian and Taoist deities. Founded by Sa-nga Kulkobkiat, a Thai national who grew up in China, the museum was intended as a friendship-building project between the two countries.

The 1st floor is a crowded pavilion of Chinese immortals, from Pangu, the cosmic giant, to Guan Yin, the goddess of mercy. The 2nd-floor terrace is the museum's most dramatic, with larger-than-life-sized statues of Shaolin monks depicting different martial-arts poses.

Pattaya & Naklua

Sights
1 Art in Paradise ... C1
2 Khao Phra Tamnak ... A5

Activities, Courses & Tours
3 Fairtex Sports Club ... C1

Sleeping
4 Asia BackPackers ... C3
5 Garden Lodge Hotel ... C1
6 Nag's Head ... B3
7 Siam@Siam ... C2

Eating
8 La Baguette ... C1
9 Leng Kee ... C3
10 Mantra ... C1
11 Nang Nual ... B3
12 Thepprasit Market ... D5

Drinking & Nightlife
13 Gulliver's ... C2
14 Lima Lima ... A4

Entertainment
15 Blues Factory ... B4
16 Tiffany's ... C1

Transport
17 35 Group ... C4
18 Bangkok Airways ... C2
19 Minivans to Bangkok ... D3

Nearby is a touching collection of daily life statues that visitors place 1B coins on.

The museum is 16km south of Pattaya; take a Pattaya–Sattahip *sŏrng·tăa·ou* (25B) to the Wat Yangsangwaram turn-off. Hire a passing motorbike to go the final 5km to the museum. Ask the driver to stick around, as getting a lift back is hard to find. Private transport is 1500B.

Ko Lạn ISLAND
(เกาะลาน) Day trippers head for this small island, 7km offshore from central Pattaya. On weekends, its five beaches entertain 5000 visitors and the sea is busy with banana boats and other marine merriment. Ferries leave Pattaya's Bali Hai pier (30B, 45 minutes, five daily) at the southern end of Walking St. The last boat back from Ko Lan is at 6pm.

Khao Phra Tamnak BUDDHIST SITE
(เขาพระตำหนัก; dawn-dusk) A giant golden Buddha sits atop this forested hill between Jomtien and south Pattaya. The serene Buddha figure of Wat Phra Yai dates back to when Pattaya was a small fishing village. On a neighbouring hill is **Monument Park**, which offers great sunset views of Ao Pattaya. You can walk here from the southern end of Walking St.

Fairtex Sports Club HEALTH & FITNESS
(038 253888; www.fairtexpattaya.com; 179/185-212 Mu 5, Th Pattaya Neua; per session 800B) Burnt-out professionals, martial-arts fans and adventurous athletes head to this resort-style sports camp for training in *moo·ay tai* (Thai boxing; also spelt *muay Thai*) and a sweat-inducing vacation. Accommodation packages are available and use of the club's pool and other sports facilities are included.

Festivals & Events

Pattaya International Music Festival MUSIC
(www.pattayamusicfest.com) In mid-March, Pattaya's oceanfront esplanade is transformed into an outdoor concert venue for three days of live music. Local musicians, as well as bands from across Asia, take to the stages to perform everything from hip-hop to rock.

Sleeping

Rooms around central or south Pattaya tend to be cheaper but closer to the noisy nightlife. North Pattaya and parts of Naklua host the signature hotels, while Soi Bua Khao and Jomtien have budget options.

Jomtien Hostel HOSTEL $
(038 233416; www.jomtienhostel.com; Mu 12, Hat Jomtien; dm/r 280/550B;) Clean dorms with good bedding, 200m from the beach. Lockers are available.

Asia BackPackers HOSTEL $
(038 420528; www.asia-backpackers.com; 420/162 Mu 9, Soi Bua Khao; r 330B;) One of the few dorms in the heart of Pattaya, this no-frills place is a welcome alternative to the myriad guesthouses. Lockers are available.

Nag's Head GUESTHOUSE $
(038 425274; nagshead_pattaya@yahoo.co.th; 485/15 Th Pattaya Sai 2; r 700B;) Clean rooms and friendly staff make this a good budget option. Try and score a room away from the road.

Garden Lodge Hotel HOTEL $$
(038 429109; www.gardenlodgepattaya.net; cnr Soi 20 & Th Naklua; r 1350-3000B;) A favourite among German tourists; the rooms

PATTAYA – EXPAT CENTRAL

No other Thai city has a reputation like Pattaya's. Ever since the first US servicemen started arriving in the 1960s for some R&R, hedonism has been a permanent guest. Beer bars, go-go clubs and massage parlours are omnipresent, with thousands of prostitutes working in the city.

While Pattaya is known for sleaze, there is another side to the city. Thousands of expats from numerous countries live here, making it Thailand's only truly international city after Bangkok. Many are attracted to the resort by the quality of life, relatively low cost of living and amenities – the area has some of Thailand's finest golf courses.

Many Brits have businesses here, there is a thriving Arab community centred around Soi 16 at the south end of Walking St, and Naklua is popular with the German crowd. As a result of such diversity, there are specialist shops offering everything from South American coffee to French cheese.

It is thought that around 40,000 foreigners live in Pattaya, with many more spending part of the year here. Those numbers are likely to rise as rapid development continues; an underground tunnel to the seafront is the latest venture and new high-rise condos pop up every month to meet demand.

here are old-fashioned but surrounded by landscaped gardens and a swimming pool.

★Rabbit Resort HOTEL $$$
(☎038 251730; www.rabbitresort.com; Hat Dongtan; r incl breakfast 5000-10,990B; ❄@🛜🏊) Rabbit Resort has stylish and secluded bungalows and villas that showcase Thai design and art, all set in beachfront forest hidden between Jomtien and Pattaya Tai. With two pools (one designed for families) and superb service, the resort is an excellent option.

Birds & Bees Resort HOTEL $$$
(☎038 250556; www.cabbagesandcondoms.co.th; Soi 4, Th Phra Tamnak; r 2000-12,000B; ❄@🛜🏊) 🍃 A tropical garden resort with two pools and good-sized rooms. The resort helps fund the work of the PDA, a rural development charity run by social campaigner Mechai Viravaidya. Cheaper rooms have no views.

Siam@Siam HOTEL $$$
(☎038 930600; www.siamatpattaya.com; 390 Mu 9, Th Pattaya Sai 2; r incl breakfast 6250-15,000B; ❄@🛜🏊) Merging contemporary design with recycled materials and vibrant colours, Siam@Siam ticks every box. A rooftop restaurant, infinity pool and, ingeniously, a bar made from secondhand jeeps and túk-túks (pronounced *đúk đúks*) are some of the highlights. Rates are often flexible.

Eating

Pattaya has an eclectic range of quality international and Thai restaurants, but there are still plenty of markets and street stalls for baht-watchers.

Thepprasit Market MARKET $
(cnr Th Thepprasit & Th Sukhumvit; dishes 30-80B; ⏲4-10pm Fri-Sun) As well as intriguing knick-knacks and endless clothes stalls, this thriving weekend market has a great range of smoothies, noodles and Thai snacks.

Leng Kee CHINESE-THAI $
(Th Pattaya Klang; dishes 100-300B; ⏲24hr) Duck dishes rule the roost in this well-established Thai-Chinese restaurant, though the seafood dishes are also tasty.

★Glass House THAI $$
(☎038255922; www.glasshouse-pattaya.com; 5/22 Mu 2, Jomtien; dishes 170-380B; ⏲11am-midnight) Diners at this all-white beachfront spot plunge their toes into the warm sand as waiters deliver seafood, pizza and steak.

Mum Aroi THAI $$
(☎038 223252; 83/4 Soi 4, Th Naklua; dishes 150-420B; ⏲11am-11pm) This long-established restaurant is perched beside the sea in the fishing-village end of Naklua. Old fishing boats sit marooned offshore and crisp sea breezes envelop diners as they devour fantastic Thai food. Try *sôm·đam Ɓoo* (spicy papaya salad with crab) and *Ɓlah mèuk nêung ma·now* (squid steamed in lime juice).

Nang Nual SEAFOOD $$
(☎038 428478; Walking St; dishes 180-500B; ⏲11am-midnight) One of Pattaya's most famous seafood restaurants spreads across both sides of Walking St. The massive range

of dishes (including plenty of Western options) is good, and the fish are all on display.

Bang Sare THAI $$

(dishes 100-300B; 11am-11pm) Around 20km south of Pattaya is Bang Sare, a developing resort with a long strip of sand and some trendy, tasty international and Thai restaurants and cafes. It gets busy at weekends.

Rimpa Lapin THAI $$

(038 235515; www.rimpa-lapin.com; Hat Jomtien; dishes 150-400B; 2pm-midnight) With spectacular views looking back over the entire Pattaya bay, this clifftop restaurant conjures up excellent Thai fushion food. Reservations are needed around sunset. Private transport is required to get here.

Sketch Book Art Cafe INTERNATIONAL, THAI $$

(478/938 Mu 12, Th Tha Phraya; dishes 90-365B; 8am-10pm) This gorgeous, leafy art cafe offers pleasant respite from the normal Pattaya vibe. It's surrounded by a sprawling garden, and the restaurant's walls are covered with the owner's artwork. Smoothies are lush and the Thai food is fresh.

La Baguette BAKERY $$

(038 421707; 164/1 Mu 5, Th Naklua; dishes 160-290B; 8am-midnight) This stylish cafe has excellent salads, yummy crêpes and lots of coffee and tea options. Make a reservation if visiting at the weekend.

Mantra INTERNATIONAL $$$

(038 429591; Th Hat Pattaya; dishes 160-1240B; 6-11.30pm) One of Pattaya's top restaurants, Mantra is fun even if you can only afford a classy cocktail (from 180B). The menu combines Japanese, Thai and Western dishes. The 1690B Sunday brunch is legendary among locals.

Drinking & Nightlife

Despite the profusion of identikit beer bars, there are still some good places for a no-strings-attached drink.

Gulliver's BAR

(Th Hat Pattaya; beers from 85B; 3pm-2am) The neocolonial facade belies the sports bar inside. There are lots of screens for watching English Premier League football.

Lima Lima CLUB

(Walking St; 10pm-5am) International DJs sometimes, and a mix of Western and local party-goers. Entry is 200B.

Entertainment

Tiffany's THEATRE

(038 421700; www.tiffany-show.co.th; 464 Th Pattaya Sai 2; admission 800-1200B; 6pm, 7.30pm & 9pm) Family-friendly ladyboy show featuring lots of sequins, satin and songs, aimed largely at Chinese tour groups.

Blues Factory LIVE MUSIC

(Soi Lucky Star, Walking St; 10pm-2am) New management now runs this long-established live music venue, but the same rock and soul classics are still belted out nightly.

Information

DANGERS & ANNOYANCES

Most problems in Pattaya are alcohol-induced, especially bad driving and fights. Leave valuables in your room to be on the safe side. Avoid renting jet-skis as scams involving fictional damage are common.

EMERGENCY

Tourist Police (emergency 1155; tourist@police.go.th) The head office is beside the Tourism Authority of Thailand office on Th Phra Tamnak, with police boxes along Pattaya and Jomtien beaches.

IMMIGRATION

Immigration Office (038 252750; Soi 5, Hat Jomtien; 8.30am-4.30pm)

MEDIA

Pattaya Mail (www.pattayamail.com) is one of the city's English-language weekly newspapers. Pattaya One (www.pattayaone.net) offers an intriguing insight into the darker side of the city.

MEDICAL SERVICES

Bangkok Pattaya Hospital (038 259999; www.bangkokpattayahospital.com; 301 Mu 6, Th Sukhumvit, Naklua; 24hr) For first-class health care.

MONEY

There are banks and ATMs throughout the city.

POST

Post Office (Soi 13/2, Th Pattaya Sai 2; 8.30am-4.30pm Mon-Fri, 8.30am-12.30pm Sat)

TOURIST INFORMATION

Tourism Authority of Thailand (TAT; 038 428750; tatchon@tat.or.th; 609 Th Phra Tamnak; 8.30am-4.30pm) Located at the northwestern edge of Rama IX Park. Helpful staff have brochures and maps.

TRANSPORT TO/FROM PATTAYA

DESTINATION	BUS	MINIVAN	TRAIN	AIR
Bangkok's Eastern Bus Terminal (Ekamai)	119B; 2hr; every 30min; 4.30am-11pm	130B; 2hr; frequent		
Bangkok's Northern Bus Terminal (Mo Chit)	128B; 2½hr; every 40min; 4.30am-9pm	150B; 2½hr; frequent		
Bangkok's Southern Bus Terminal	119B; 3hr; every 2hr; 6am-6.30pm	150B; 2½hr; hourly		
Bangkok Suvarnabhumi International Airport	250B; 2hr; 7 daily; 6pm-7pm	120B; 2hr; frequent		
Bangkok Hualamphong		150B; 3½hr; 1 daily		
Aranya Prathet (for Cambodia)		260B; 5hr; hourly; 4am-6pm		
Ko Samet		160B; 1hr; hourly		
Rayong		100B; 1½hr; frequent		
Si Racha		40B; 50min; frequent	5B; 1¼hr; 1 daily	
Ko Samui				from 3890B; 1hr; daily
Phuket				from 2650B; 1½hr; daily

Getting There & Away

Pattaya's airport is **U-Tapao Airfield** (☎038 245595; www.utapao.com), 33km south of town. **Bangkok Airways** (☎038 412382; www.bangkokair.com; 179/85-212 Th Pattaya Sai 2) and **Air Asia** (www.airasia.com) fly from here.

The main bus station is on Th Pattaya Neua.

Minivans heading north to Bangkok leave from the corner of Th Sukhumvit and Th Pattaya Klang. Minivans heading for the Cambodian border leave from the junction of Th Sukhumvit and Th Pattaya Tai. The **35 Group** (☎080 070 3341; cnr Th Pattaya 3 & Th Pattaya Tai) has minivans for Ko Chang (550B), Ko Mak (750B) and Ko Kut (800B).

Pattaya Train Station (☎038 429285) is off Th Sukhumvit south of town.

Getting Around

Locally known as 'baht buses', *sŏrng·tăa·ou* do a loop along the major roads; just hop on and pay 10B when you get off. If you are going all the way to or from Naklua, you will have to change vehicles at the dolphin roundabout in Pattaya Neua. Baht buses run to the bus station from the dolphin roundabout as well. If you are going further afield, you can charter a baht bus; establish the price beforehand. Motorbikes can be hired for 200B a day.

Rayong & Ban Phe ระยอง/บ้านเพ

POP 106,737 / 17,116

You are most likely to transit through these towns en route to Ko Samet. Rayong has frequent bus connections to elsewhere and the little port of Ban Phe has ferry services to Ko Samet. Blue *sŏrng·tăa·ou* link the two towns (25B, 45 minutes, every 15 minutes).

Sleeping

Rayong President Hotel HOTEL $

(☎038 611307; www.rayongpresidenthotel.com; off Th Sukhumvit, Rayong; d/tw 400-500/550B; ❄📶) From the bus station, cross to the other side of Th Sukhumvit and walk right. Look for a Siam Commercial Bank on the corner and turn left.

Christie's Guesthouse GUESTHOUSE $

(☎038 651976; www.christiesbanphe.com; 280/92 Soi 1, Ban Phe; r 600B; ❄📶) Christie's is a comfortable place near the pier if you need a room, a meal or a book.

Eating

★**Tamnanpar** THAI $$

(www.tamnanpar-rayong.com; 167/6 Mu 7, Ban Phe; dishes 150-300B; ⏲10am-10pm) It is worth making a detour to experience this rainforest-style restaurant's incredible food and, ahem, award-winning bathrooms. There is also a waterpark on-site (adult/child 200/100B).

Getting There & Away

Minivans from Rayong's bus station go to Bangkok's eastern (Ekamai) and northern (Mo Chit) bus terminals (both 160B, 3½ hours, hourly, 4.40am to 8pm), as well as Suvarnabhumi International Airport (160B, 3½ hours, hourly, 5am to 8pm).

There are minivans to Pattaya (80B, 1½ hours, frequent), Chanthaburi (120B, two hours, frequent) and Trat (200B, three hours, frequent).

Buses opposite Ban Phe's Nuanthip pier go to/from Ekamai (166B, four hours, every two hours, 7am to 6pm).

Ban Phe also has minivan services to Laem Ngop for boats to Ko Chang (250B, three hours, three daily), Pattaya (200B, two hours, hourly) and Bangkok's Victory Monument (200B, four hours, every 40 minutes).

There are boats to/from Ko Samet (p461).

Ko Samet เกาะเสม็ด

Once the doyen of backpacker destinations, today Ko Samet shares its charms with a wider audience. The sandy shores, cosy coves and aquamarine waters attract ferry-loads of Bangkokians looking to party each weekend, while tour groups pack out many resorts. Fire-juggling shows and beach barbecues are nightly events on the northern beaches, but the southern parts of the island are far more secluded and sedate.

Despite being the closest major island to Bangkok, Ko Samet remains surprisingly underdeveloped, with a thick jungle interior crouching beside the low-rise hotels.

Sights & Activities

On some islands you beach-hop, but on Ko Samet you cove-hop. The coastal footpath traverses rocky headlands, cicada-serenaded forests and one stunning bay after another, where the mood becomes successively more mellow the further south you go.

Hat Sai Kaew BEACH

(หาดทรายแก้ว) In the island's northeastern corner, Hat Sai Kaew is the island's widest, whitest and wildest stretch of sand. Sunbathers, sarong-sellers, speedboats, jet-skis and restaurants take up almost every inch of space. At night, the scene is rambunctious, with parties and karaoke sessions.

Ao Hin Khok & Ao Phai BEACH

(อ่าวหินโคก/อ่าวไผ่) Less frenetic than their northern neighbour of Hat Sai Kaew, Ao Hin Khok and Ao Phai are two gorgeous bays separated by rocky headlands. The crowd here tends to be younger and more stylish than the tour groups who gather in Hat Sai Kaew; these two beaches are the traditional backpacker party centres of the island.

> **BYPASSING BANGKOK**
>
> An expanding network of bus and minivan services now connects the eastern seaboard with Suvarnabhumi International Airport, meaning that you don't have to transit through Bangkok for a flight arrival or departure. This is especially alluring to winter-weary visitors eager to reach a beach fast. Ko Samet is the closest prettiest beach to the airport and its southeastern beaches are serene enough for honeymooners. From the airport bus terminal, check the schedule for Rayong-bound buses and then catch a *sŏrng·tăa·ou* to reach the ferry pier to Ko Samet.

Ao Phutsa (Ao Tub Tim) BEACH

(อ่าวพุทรา / อ่าวทับทิม) South of Ao Hin Khok and Ao Phai is wide and sandy Ao Phutsa (Ao Tub Tim), a favourite for solitude seekers, families and couples who need access to 'civilisation' but not much else.

Ao Wong Deuan BEACH

(อ่าววงเดือน) Ao Wong Deuan, meaning 'crescent moon bay', is Samet's second-busiest beach, with a range of resorts and more modest guesthouses.

Ao Thian BEACH

(อ่าวเทียน) Ao Thian (Candlelight Beach), is punctuated by big boulders that shelter small sandy spots, creating a castaway ambience. It remains one of Samet's most easy-going beaches and is deliciously lonely on weekdays. On weekends, Bangkok university students serenade the stars with all-night guitar sessions.

Ao Wai BEACH

(อ่าวหวาย) Ao Wai is a lovely beach far removed from everything else (though in reality it is only 2km from Ao Thian).

Ao Prao BEACH

On the west coast, Ao Prao (Coconut Beach) is worth a visit for a sundowner cocktail, but the small beach is outsized by resorts that promise (but don't deliver) solitude.

Tours

Ko Samet, along with nine neighbouring islands, is part of the Khao Laem Ya/Mu Ko Samet National Park. While there is some development on the other islands, most visitors come for day trips. **Ko Kudee** has a

Ko Samet

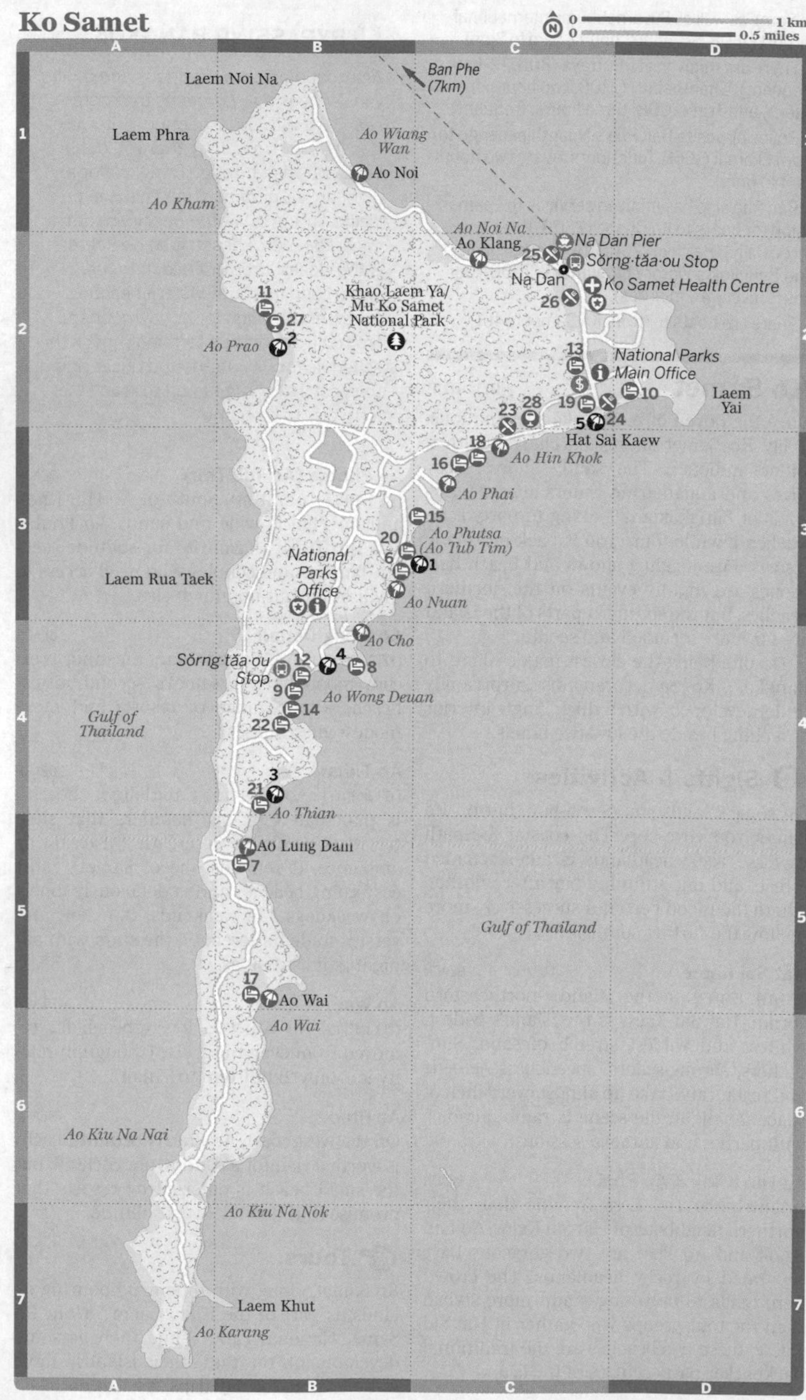

0 1 km
0 0.5 miles
Ban Phe (7km)
Laem Noi Na
Laem Phra
Ao Wiang Wan
Ao Noi
Ao Kham
Ao Noi Na
Ao Klang
Na Dan Pier
Sŏrng·tăa·ou Stop
Na Dan
Ko Samet Health Centre
Khao Laem Ya/ Mu Ko Samet National Park
Ao Prao
National Parks Main Office
Laem Yai
Hat Sai Kaew
Ao Hin Khok
Ao Phai
Ao Phutsa (Ao Tub Tim)
National Parks Office
Laem Rua Taek
Ao Nuan
Ao Cho
Sŏrng·tăa·ou Stop
Ao Wong Deuan
Gulf of Thailand
Ao Thian
Ao Lung Dam
Gulf of Thailand
Ao Wai
Ao Wai
Ao Kiu Na Nai
Ao Kiu Na Nok
Laem Khut
Ao Karang

Ko Samet

Sights

1 Ao Phutsa (Ao Tub Tim) C3
2 Ao Prao B2
3 Ao Thian B4
4 Ao Wong Deuan B4
5 Hat Sai Kaew C2

Sleeping

6 Ao Nuan Bungalows B3
7 Apache B5
Ban Thai Sang Thain .... (see 21)
8 Blue Sky B4
9 La Lune Beach Resort B4
10 Laem Yai Hut Resort D2
11 Lima Coco Resort B2
12 Malibu Garden Resort B4
13 Mossman House C2
14 Nice & Easy B4
15 Pudsa Bungalow C3
16 Samed Pavilion Resort C3
17 Samet Ville Resort B5
18 Silver Sand C3
19 Sinsamut C2
20 Tubtim Resort B3
21 Viking Holiday Resort B4
22 Vongdeuan Resort B4

Eating

23 Jep's Restaurant C2
24 Ploy C2
25 Rabeang Baan C2
26 Red Ginger C2
Sea Breeze .... (see 18)

Drinking & Nightlife

27 Ao Prao Resort B2
Baywatch Bar .... (see 9)
28 Naga Bar C2

small, pretty sandy stretch, clear water for decent snorkelling and a nice little hiking trail. Ko Man Nai is home to the **Rayong Turtle Conservation Centre**, which is a breeding place for endangered sea turtles, and has a small visitor centre.

Agents for boat tours can be found on the popular beaches and have a couple of different trips on offer (from 500B per person).

Sleeping

Though resorts are replacing bungalows, much of Ko Samet's accommodation is still simple and old-fashioned. There are a handful of sub-700B fan rooms remaining. Look for low season and weekday discounts.

A word of caution to early risers: Hat Sai Kaew, Ao Hin Khok, Ao Phai and Ao Wong Deuan are the most popular beaches and host well-amplified night-time parties.

Hat Sai Kaew

Mossman House GUESTHOUSE $
(038 644017; r 800-1300B;) On the main street, just before the national park ticket office, is this sound guesthouse, with large, comfortable rooms and leafy grounds. Choose a spot at the back for some quiet.

Sinsamut GUESTHOUSE $$
(038 644134; www.sinsamutkohsamed.com; r 1100-2500B;) This former grungy guesthouse is now a shiny boutique sleep, with bright, cheery rooms and an upstairs garden area. Check for discounts.

Laem Yai Hut Resort BUNGALOW $$
(038 644282; r 1500-2500B;) A colourful collection of 15 bungalows scattered around a shady garden on the north end of the beach. The tatty outside appearance belies the interior's modern bathrooms and soft bedding.

Ao Hin Khok & Ao Phai

★ **Samed Pavilion Resort** BOUTIQUE HOTEL $$$
(038 644420; www.samedpavilionresort.com; Ao Phai; r incl breakfast 3500-5500B;) This gorgeous boutique resort has 85 elegant, spacious rooms set around a pool.

Silver Sand HOTEL $$$
(038 644300; www.silversandsamed.com; Ao Phai; r incl breakfast 2200-4000B;) An expanding empire, Silver Sand is a mini-resort, complete with bar, restaurant and shops. It's a little impersonal but the rooms are flashpacker quality and set on a super strip of beach.

Ao Phutsa & Ao Nuan

Ao Nuan Bungalows BUNGALOW $$
(081 781 4875; bungalow fan/air-con 800-1200/1500-3000B;) Ao Nuan is Samet's one remaining bohemian bay, with no internet and access only via a dirt track. Guests hang in hammocks outside their wooden bungalows here or chill in the attached restaurant. Tents are also available (450B).

Tubtim Resort HOTEL $$
(038 644025; www.tubtimresort.com; Ao Phutsa; r incl breakfast 800-3800B;) A well-organised place with great, nightly barbecues and a range of solid, spacious bungalows of varying quality close to the beach.

Pudsa Bungalow BUNGALOW $$
(☎038 644030; Ao Phutsa; bungalow with fan/air-con 800/1700B;) Fan rooms are showing their age, but the air-con ones come with a balcony and better bedding. Check out the strange stone sculptures on the beach.

Ao Wong Deuan & Ao Thian (Candlelight Beach)

Ferry services run between Ao Wong Deuan and Ban Phe (140B return), with increased services at the weekend. To get to Ao Thian, catch a ferry to Ao Wong Deuan and walk south over the headland. It is also a quick walk from here to the west coast – look for the marked trail on Ao Thian.

Blue Sky BUNGALOW $
(☎089 936 0842; Ao Wong Deuan; r 600-1200B;) A rare budget spot on Ao Wong Deuan, Blue Sky has beaten-up bungalows set on a rocky headland.

Apache GUESTHOUSE $
(☎081 452 9472; Ao Thian; r 800-1500B;) Apache's eclectic, quirky decorations add character to this super-chilled spot. Bungalows are basic but adequate. Apache's restaurant on stilts is worth a look.

Nice & Easy HOTEL $$
(☎038 644370; www.niceandeasysamed.com; Ao Wong Deuan; r 1200-2500B;) As the name suggests, this is a very amiable place, with comfortable, modern bungalows set around a garden behind the beach.

Viking Holiday Resort HOTEL $$
(☎038 644353; thammaraksa@hotmail.com; Ao Thian; r incl breakfast 1200-2000B;) About as developed as things get around here, Viking has homely rooms. Staff are helpful and friendly. Cheaper rooms are fan-only.

BEACH ADMISSION FEE

Ko Samet is part of the Mu Ko Samet National Park and charges all visitors an entrance fee (adult/child 200/100B) upon arrival. If you can prove that you live and work in Thailand, it will only cost you 40B, the price Thais pay. The fee is collected at the national parks office; *sŏrng·tăa·ou* from the pier will stop at the gates for payment. Hold on to your ticket for later inspections. There is a 20B fee when using Na Dan pier.

Ban Thai Sang Thain HOTEL $$
(☎081 305 9408; www.banthaisangthain.com; Ao Thian; r 1700-3000B;) Thai travellers stay in many of the pavilion-style rooms in this traditional, all-wood resort. Rooms are functional rather than fab. Few staff speak English.

Malibu Garden Resort GUESTHOUSE $$
(☎038 427277; www.malibu-samet.com; Ao Wong Deuan; r incl breakfast 1950-3400B;) Set just behind the main row of beach resorts, Malibu has clean, nondescript rooms, but gets bonus points for having a pool. Staff are helpful and friendly.

La Lune Beach Resort RESORT $$$
(☎in Bangkok 02 260 3592; www.lalunebeachresort.com; Ao Wong Deuan; r incl breakfast 2500-3200B;) Meet the new face of Samet. Stylish, chic resorts like this are becoming more common – and this is the best of the bunch. The 40 rooms, all with a soft brown-and-white theme, face a central pool. Rates vary so check for discounts.

Vongdeuan Resort HOTEL $$$
(☎038 644171; www.vongdeuan.com; Ao Wong Deuan; r incl breakfast 2700-4900B;) This sprawling resort with its garden-like setting occupies much of the southern part of Ao Wong Deuan. Popular with families and efficiently run, the smart bungalows come with the best bathrooms in this part of the world.

Ao Wai

Ao Wai is a 2km walk from Ao Thian or it can be reached from Ban Phe by chartered speedboat.

Samet Ville Resort HOTEL $$$
(☎038 651682; www.sametvilleresort.com; r incl breakfast 1400-6500B;) Spread over two bays – Ao Wai and Ao Hin Kleang – this leafy, 4½-hectare resort is as secluded as it is soporific. The rooms, of which there are several types, are all a few steps from the excellent beach.

Ao Prao

Lima Coco Resort RESORT $$$
(☎in Bangkok 02 129 1140; www.limasamed.com; r incl breakfast 2590-7290B;) Ao Prao, on Samet's west coast, has three fancy resorts. Lima Coco is the least ostentatious of these, with bright, whitewashed rooms, energetic staff and beachside massages.

Eating

Most hotels and guesthouses have restaurants that moonlight as bars after sunset. The food and service won't blow you away, but there aren't many alternatives. Nightly beach barbecues, starring all manner of seafood, are an island favourite. There are cheapie Thai places in Na Dan.

Jep's Restaurant INTERNATIONAL **$**
(Ao Hin Khok; mains 60-150B; ⏲7am-11pm) Canopied by the branches of an arching tree decorated with pendant lights, this pretty place does a wide range of international, and some Thai, dishes. Leave room for dessert.

Rabeang Baan THAI **$**
(Na Dan; dishes 70-120B; ⏲8am-9pm) By the ferry terminal, this spot has good enough food to make you forget you have to leave the island. It is busier at lunch than dinner.

Red Ginger INTERNATIONAL, THAI **$$**
(Na Dan; dishes 120-320B; ⏲11am-11pm) A small but select menu of the French-Canadian chef's favourite dishes star at this atmospheric eatery between the pier and Hat Sai Kaew. Good salads, great oven-baked ribs, and some Thai food.

Sea Breeze SEAFOOD **$$**
(Ao Phai; dishes 80-500B; ⏲11am-11pm) Appropriately named: you can dine on a wide range of seafood right on Ao Phai's pretty beach. There's some Western food on the menu too.

Ploy SEAFOOD **$$**
(Hat Sai Kaew; dishes 50-400B; ⏲11am-11pm) Before heading to the island's only nightclub, right next door, crunch down on some crab and lobster at this lively restaurant. The menu is epic and the accompanying bar is constantly busy.

Drinking & Nightlife

On weekends, Ko Samet is a boisterous night-owl with tour groups crooning away on karaoke machines and the young ones slurping down beer and buckets to a techno beat. There is usually a crowd on Hat Sai Kaew, Ao Hin Khok, Ao Phai and Ao Wong Deuan.

Ao Prao Resort BAR
(Ao Prao; drinks from 90B; ⏲sunset-midnight; 📶) On the sunset-side of the island, this is a lovely sea-view restaurant perfect for a sundowner. You will need private transport to reach it.

LOCAL KNOWLEDGE

A MONSTER WELCOME

The imposing statue of a topless female giant at Na Dan pier is impossible to miss. She is an allusion to Ko Samet's most famous son, the poet Sunthorn Phu and his famous story *Phra Aphaimani*. In the tale, a prince is exiled to an undersea kingdom ruled by the lovesick female giant. A mermaid helps the prince escape to Ko Samet, where he defeats the giant by playing a magical flute.

Baywatch Bar BAR
(Ao Wong Deuan; beers from 80B; ⏲sunset-late) A good spot for after-dark beach-gazing, with a fun crowd and strong cocktails.

Naga Bar BAR
(Ao Hin Khok; beers from 70B; ⏲sunset-late) This busy beachfront bar is covered in Day-Glo art and run by a friendly bunch of locals who offer good music, lots of whisky and vodka/Red Bull buckets.

Information

There are many ATMs on Ko Samet, including those near the Na Dan pier, Ao Wong Deuan and Ao Thian.

Ko Samet Health Centre (☎038 644123; ⏲24hr) On the main road between Na Dan and Hat Sai Kaew.

National Parks Main Office (btwn Na Dan & Hat Sai Kaew; ⏲sunrise-sunset) Has another office at Ao Wong Deuan.

Police Station (☎1155) On the main road between Na Dan and Hat Sai Kaew. There's a substation at Ao Wong Deuan.

Getting There & Away

Ko Samet is accessed via the mainland piers in Ban Phe. There are many piers each used by different ferry companies, but they all charge the same fares (one way/return 70/100B, 40 minutes, hourly, 8am to 5pm) and dock at Na Dan, the main pier on Ko Samet. The last boat back to the mainland leaves at 6pm.

If you are staying at Ao Wong Deuan or further south, catch a ferry from the mainland directly to the beach (one way/return 90/140B, one hour, three daily departures).

Speedboats charge 200B to 500B one way and will drop you at the beach of your choice, but only leave when they have enough passengers.

Getting Around

Ko Samet's small size makes it a great place to explore on foot. A network of roads connects most of the island.

Green *sŏrng·tăa·ou* meet boats at the pier and provide drop-offs at the various beaches (10B to 70B, depending on the beach and number of passengers). Chartering one costs 100B to 400B.

You can rent motorcycles nearly everywhere along the northern half of the island for 300B per day. Newly improved roads mean that ATVs have bitten the dust.

Chanthaburi

จันทบุรี

POP 121,549

Chanthaburi is proof all that glitters is not gold. Here, gems do the sparkling, with precious stones ranging from sapphires to emeralds traded every weekend in a bustling street market. Nearby, wonderfully restored waterfront buildings are evidence of how the Chinese, French and Vietnamese have influenced life – and architecture – here.

Vietnamese Christians fled persecution from Cochin China (southern Vietnam) in the 19th century and came to Chanthaburi. More Vietnamese arrived in the 1920s and 1940s as they fled French rule, then a third wave in 1975 after the communist takeover of southern Vietnam. The French occupied Chanthaburi from 1893 to 1905 due to a dispute over the border between Siam and Indochina.

Head south for 25km, past the numerous salt fields, to find the quiet coastal towns of **Laem Sing** and **Chao Lao**. The latter has good beaches and accommodation.

GETTING TO CAMBODIA: BAN PAKARD TO PSAR PRUHM

Getting to the Border In Chanthaburi, **minivans** (092 037 6266) depart from a stop across the river from the River Guest House to Ban Pakard/Pong Nam Ron (150B, 1½ hours, 10am, 11am, 6.30pm).

At the Border This is a far less busy and more pleasant crossing than Poipet further north. You need a passport photo and US$20 for the visa fee.

Moving On Hop on a motorbike taxi to Pailin in Cambodia. From there, you can catch frequent shared taxis (US$5 per person, 1½ hours) to scenic Battambang. After that, you can move on to Siem Reap by boat, or Phnom Penh by bus.

Sights & Activities

★ Chantaboon Waterfront Community HISTORIC SITE

(Th Sukhaphiban) Hugging the banks of Mae Nam Chanthaburi is this charismatic part of town, filled with restored houses and elderly residents sitting around reminiscing about their Chanthaburi tales with each other. The **Learning House** (081 945 5761; 10am-4.30pm Sat & Sun) displays neighbourhood photos, paintings and architectural designs, including upstairs drawings of intricate ventilation panels that feature Chinese characters and French fleurs-de-lis.

Around 300 years ago, farmers and merchants started trading alongside the river, which provided easy transport links. Later, Chinese and Vietnamese traders and refugees came to the area. Today, the 1km-long street scene still includes many private homes, but the art galleries, coffee shops and snack stalls entice visiting Thais at weekends.

Gem Market MARKET

(ตลาดพลอย; Th Si Chan & Trok Kachang; 9am-6pm Fri-Sun) Every weekend, the normally quiet streets that are near Th Si Chan (Gem Road) burst into life as gem traders arrive to bustle and bargain. Incongruously humble considering the value of commodities on offer, people cluster around makeshift tables examining small piles of unset stones.

Buying and selling is not for the uninitiated, but it is a fascinating glimpse at a trade that has taken place here for decades. In the hills surrounding Chanthaburi, several sapphire and ruby mines once supplied the palace with fine ornaments prior to the mid-19th century when the mines were developed into commercial operations by Shan (Burmese) traders. These days, locally mined gems are of inferior international quality but the resourceful Chanthaburi traders roam the globe acquiring precious and semi-precious stones, which are in turn traded to other globetrotters.

The last remaining mine in the area is **Khao Phloi Waen**, 6km from town, which is famous locally for its 'Mekong Whiskey' yellow-coloured sapphire.

Cathedral CHURCH

(dawn-dusk) FREE Thailand's largest cathedral, situated on the east bank of Mae Nam Chanthaburi, started life as a modest chapel in 1711. Since then there have been four

Chanthaburi

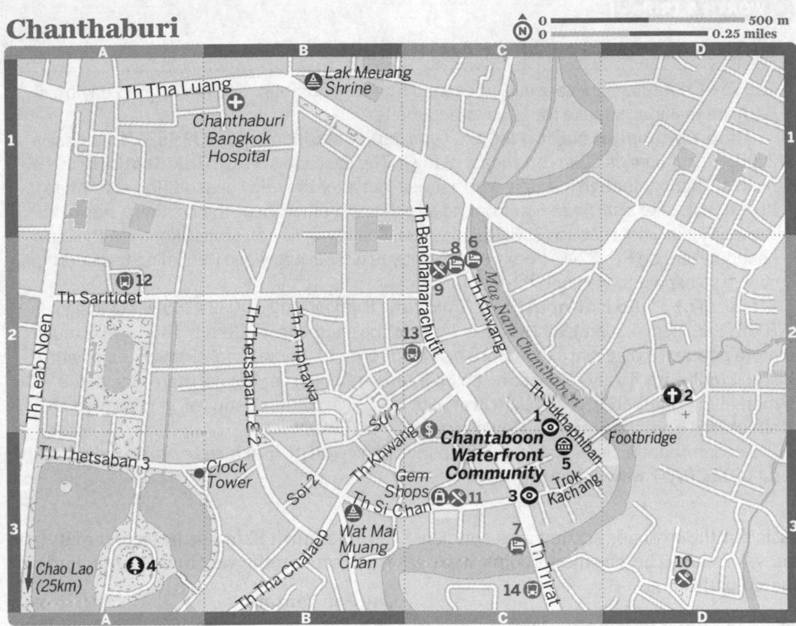

Chanthaburi

Top Sights
1 Chantaboon Waterfront Community C2

Sights
2 Cathedral D2
3 Gem Market C3
4 King Taksin Park A3
5 Learning House C3

Sleeping
6 Baan Luang Rajamaitri C2
7 River Guest House C3
8 Tamajun Hotel C2

Eating
9 Chanthorn Phochana C2
10 Jay Pen Yentafo D3
11 Muslim Restaurant C3

Transport
12 Bus Station & Minivans A2
13 Minivan Stop C2
14 Minivans to Ban Pakard/Pong Nam Ron C3

reconstructions and the current Gothic-style structure includes stained-glass windows. The statue of the Virgin Mary at the front is bedecked with more than 200,000 sapphires – a fitting link between religion and the city's famous gem trade. Cross a footbridge to access the Chantaboon Waterfront Community.

King Taksin Park PARK
(สวนสาธารณะสมเด็จพระเจ้าตากสิน; Th Tha Chalaep; ⏲dawn-dusk) The town's main oasis is filled with joggers and picnicking families. It is a pleasant spot to visit for an evening stroll.

Festivals & Events

Fruit Festival FOOD
Held at the end of May or beginning of June, Chanthaburi's annual fruit festival is a great opportunity to sample the region's superb produce, especially rambutans, mangosteens and the ever-pungent durian.

Sleeping

Several boutique and budget spots can be found near Th Sukhaphiban.

River Guest House HOTEL $
(☎039 328211; 3/5-8 Th Si Chan; r 190-490B; ❄@☜) Rooms are tiny and the beds are

WORTH A TRIP

NATIONAL PARKS NEAR CHANTHABURI

Two small national parks are easily reached from Chanthaburi, and make good day trips. Both are malarial, so take the usual precautions.

Khao Khitchakut National Park (อุทยานแห่งชาติเขาคิชฌกูฏ; ☎039 452074; admission 200B; ⏲6am-6pm) is 28km northeast of town. The cascade of **Nam Tok Krathing** is the main attraction, though it is only worth a visit just after the rainy season. To get to Khao Khitchakut, take a *sŏrng·tăa·ou* from next to the post office, near the northern side of the market in Chanthaburi (35B, 45 minutes). The *sŏrng·tăa·ou* stops 1km from the park headquarters on Rte 3249, from which point you will have to walk. Returning transport is scarce so expect to wait or hitch.

Nam Tok Phlio National Park (อุทยานแหง่ ชาติน้ำตกพลิ้ว; ☎039 434528; admission 200B; ⏲8.30am-4.30pm), off Hwy 3, is 14km to the southeast of Chanthaburi and is much more popular. A pleasant 1km nature trail loops around the waterfalls, which teem with soro brook carp. To get to the park, catch a *sŏrng·tăa·ou* from the northern side of the market in Chanthaburi to the park entrance (50B, 30 minutes). You will get dropped off about 1km from the entrance. Private transport is 1500B.

Accommodation is available at both parks; book with the **park reservation system** (☎02 562 0760; www.dnp.go.th).

basic but the riverside seating area compensates for this. The cheapest rooms have a shared bathroom.

★ **Baan Luang Rajamaitri** HISTORIC HOTEL $$
(☎039 322037; www.baanluangrajamaitri.com; 252 Th Sukhaphiban; r incl breakfast 1100-2650B; ❄📶) Named after a local philanthropist, this expertly restored hotel has elegant rooms.

Tamajun Hotel BOUTIQUE HOTEL $$
(☎039 311977; www.tamajunhotel.com; 248 Th Sukhaphiban; r incl breakfast 1500-1800B; ❄📶) From the fake grass on the stairs to the individually themed rooms, Tamajun has a fun, retro-chic feel. Riverside rooms come with a shared balcony and there's a good on-site restaurant. Weekday rates are 15% cheaper.

Eating & Drinking

Fruit Stalls FRUIT STALL $
(Th Sukhumvit; fruit 40-80B; ⏲8am-9pm; 🖉) Chanthaburi is famed for its fruit. You can taste why at the various fruit stalls that line Th Sukhumvit 8km northeast of the city (you pass them on the way into Chanthaburi).

Jay Pen Yentafo THAI $
(Wat Phai Lom; noodles 100B; ⏲9am-3.30pm) Pink-coloured noodle soup combined with crab has given this temple restaurant a great reputation with locals.

Muslim Restaurant INDIAN, THAI $
(☎081 353 5174; cnr Soi 4, Th Si Chan; dishes 50-80B; ⏲9.30am-6pm) Run by Thai Muslims, this tiny place has excellent *paratha*, *biryani*, curries and chai tea.

Chanthorn Phochana THAI $$
(102/5-8 Th Benchamarachutit; dishes 100-200B; ⏲9am-9pm) A great place to try local specialities; the *chamung* leaves with pork and Chanthaburi crab noodles are particularly good.

Information

Banks with change facilities and ATMs can be found across town.

Bank of Ayudhya (Th Khwang; ⏲8.30am-3.30pm)

TRANSPORT TO/FROM CHANTHABURI

DESTINATION	BUS	MINIVAN
Bangkok's Eastern Bus Terminal (Ekamai)	198B; 4hr; 25 daily	
Bangkok's Northern Bus Terminal (Mo Chit)	205B; 4hr; 2 daily	
Khorat	279B; 4hr; every 2 hours	
Sa Kaew	145B; 2hr; every 2 hours	
Rayong		120B; 2hr; hourly
Trat		70B; 1hr; frequent

Chanthaburi Bangkok Hospital (☎039 319888; Th Tha Luang; ⏰24hr) Part of the Bangkok group; handles emergencies.

ℹ Getting There & Around

Chanthaburi's bus station is west of the river. Minivans leave from the bus station. Motorbike taxis charge 30B to 40B for trips around town.

Trat ตราด

POP 21,590

Trat is a major transit point for Ko Chang and coastal Cambodia, with underappreciated old-world charm. The guesthouse neighbourhood occupies a wooden shophouse district, bisected by winding sois and filled with Thai street life: children riding bikes, housewives running errands and small businesses selling trinkets and necessities.

Trat's signature product is a medicinal herbal oil (known as *nám·man lĕu·ang*), touted as a remedy for everything from arthritis to bug bites and available at local pharmacies. It is produced by resident Mae Ang-Ki (Somthawin Pasananon), using a secret pharmaceutical recipe that has been handed down through her Chinese-Thai family for generations.

Sights

One booming business in Trat is **swiftlet farming**. Walk down Th Lak Meuang and you will see that the top floors of shophouses have been converted into nesting sites for birds that produce the edible nests considered a Chinese delicacy. Swiflets' nests were quite rare (and expensive) in the past because they were only harvested from precipitous sea caves by trained, daring climbers. In the 1990s, entrepreneurs figured out how to replicate the cave atmosphere in multistorey shophouses and the business has become a key operation in Trat.

Indoor Market MARKET

The indoor market sprawls east from Th Sukhumvit to Th Tat Mai and has a little bit of everything, especially all the things that you forgot to pack. Without really noticing the difference you will stumble upon the **day market** (Th Tat Mai; ⏰6-11am), selling fresh fruit, vegetables and takeaway food.

Sleeping

Trat has many budget hotels in traditional wooden houses on and around Th Thana Charoen.

★**Ban Jai Dee Guest House** GUESTHOUSE $

(☎083 589 0839; banjaideehouse@yahoo.com; 6 Th Chaimongkol; r 200B; 📶) This relaxed traditional wooden house has simple rooms with shared bathrooms (hot-water showers). Paintings and objets d'art made by the artistically inclined owners decorate the common spaces. Booking ahead is essential. Ask the owner, Serge, for travel advice.

Garden Guest House GUESTHOUSE $

(☎087 019 3111; 87/1 Th Sukhumvit; r 150-400B; 📶) A charming, elderly lady runs this guesthouse, though it feels more like a homestay as she makes such an effort. Bedding is of varying quality, so check first. All but one of the 10 rooms have shared bathrooms.

Orchid GUESTHOUSE $

(☎039 530474; orchidguesthouse@gmail.com; 92 Th Lak Meuang; r 150-500B; ❄📶) Big, slightly battered rooms in a house with a large garden. The cheapest rooms are fan-only and share bathrooms. The laid-back owner sometimes opens her attached restaurant, which serves good pizzas.

Pop Guest House GUESTHOUSE $

(☎039 512392; popgoodguesthouse@hotmail.com; 1/1 Th Thana Charoen; r 150-600B; ❄@📶)

Trat

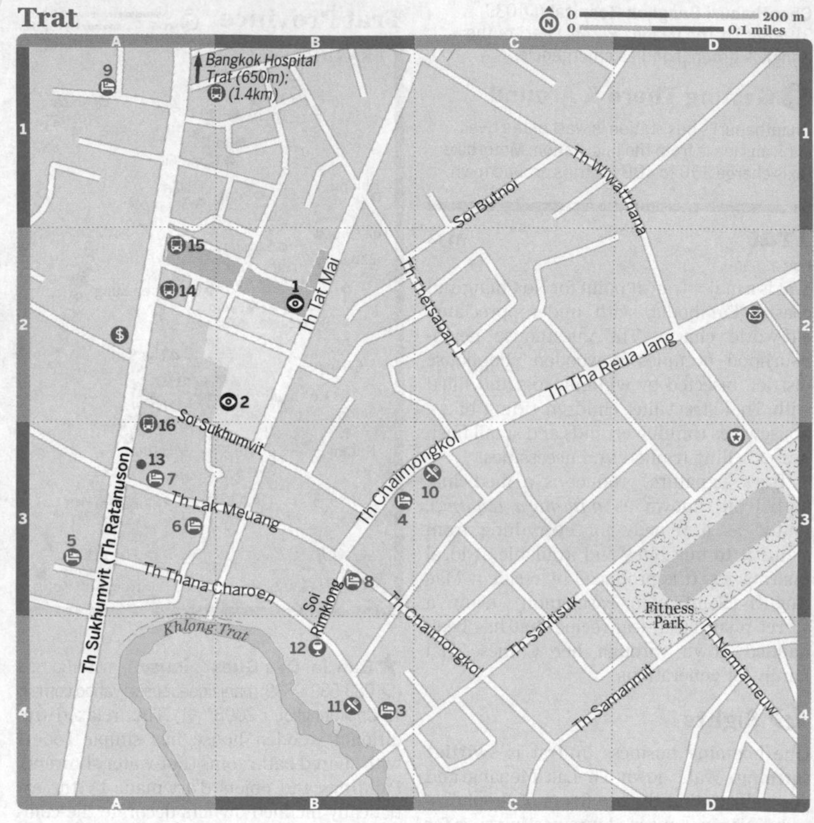

Trat

Sights
1 Day Market.......B2
2 Indoor Market.......B2

Sleeping
3 Artist's Place.......B4
4 Ban Jai Dee Guest House.......B3
5 Garden Guest House.......A3
6 Orchid.......A3
7 Pop Guest House.......A3
8 Rimklong Boutique Hotel.......B3
9 Trat Center Hotel.......A1

Eating
10 No Name Steak & Pasta.......C3
11 Pier 112.......B4

Drinking & Nightlife
12 Cafe Oscar.......B4

Transport
13 Family Tour.......A3
14 Minivans to Chanthaburi.......A2
15 Sŏrng·tăa·ou to Bus Station & Laem Ngop.......A2
16 Sŏrng·tăa·ou to Tha Centrepoint & Th Thammachat (Laem Ngop).......A3

Pop, which has two neighbouring locations, comes with somewhat uninspiring rooms in lots of guises. The staff are not particularly friendly but the restaurant is good. Cheaper rooms are fan-only.

Artist's Place GUESTHOUSE **$$**
(☎082 469 1900; pier.112@hotmail.com; 132/1 Th Thana Charoen; r incl breakfast 800-1100B; ❄📶) The individually decorated rooms, and pieces of art dotted around the adjoining garden, come courtesy of the owner, Mr Phukhao.

Trat Center Hotel HOTEL $$
(☎039 531234; www.tratcenterhotel.com; 45/65 Th Tasaban 5; r incl breakfast 900B;) Spotless, modern rooms with comfy beds at this decent midrange option. It is a five-minute walk north of the day market.

Rimklong Boutique Hotel BOUTIQUE HOTEL $$
(☎039 523388; soirimklong@hotmail.co.th; 194 Th Lak Meuang; r 1000B;) Trat's only boutique hotel has five bright, airy rooms. There's a pleasant cafe attached.

Eating & Drinking

Trat is all about market eating: head to the day market on Th Tat Mai for *gah·faa bohrahn* (ancient coffee), the night market (which is in the same location from 5pm to 9pm) or the indoor market for lunchtime noodles. Food stalls line Th Sukhumvit at night.

No Name Steak & Pasta INTERNATIONAL, THAI $
(61-65 Th Chaimongkol; dishes 50-120B; 8am-9pm Sun-Fri) Restaurant serving Thai and Western classics, plus sandwiches. It makes for a good coffee/smoothie stop, too.

Pier 112 THAI $$
(132/1 Th Thana Charoen; dishes 80-250B; 10.30am-10.30pm;) Good range of vegetarian dishes, as well as reliable curries.

Cafe Oscar BAR
(Th Thana Charoen; beers from 50B; 9am-1am) An eclectic crew of locals and expats gather at this corner bar, with wooden furniture and a retro 1970s and '80s soundtrack. In low season it opens in the evening only.

Information

Th Sukhumvit runs through town, though it is often called Th Ratanuson.

Trat Map (www.tratmap.com) is a useful online directory of businesses and attractions in Trat.

Bangkok Hospital Trat (☎039 532735; www.bangkokhospital.com; 376 Mu 2, Th Sukhumvit; 24hr) Located 400m north of the town centre.

Krung Thai Bank (Th Sukhumvit; 8.30am-3.30pm) Has an ATM and exchange facilities.

Police Station (☎1155; cnr Th Santisuk & Th Wiwatthana) A short walk from Trat's centre.

Post Office (Th Tha Reua Jang; 8.30am-4.30pm Mon-Fri, 8.30am-12.30pm Sat) East of Trat's commercial centre.

Getting There & Around

Trat's bus station is 2km out of town. Minivans leave from points along Th Sukhumvit. **Family Tour** (☎081 940 7380; cnr Th Sukhumvit & Th Lak Meuang) has minivans to Bangkok's Victory Monument and northern bus terminal (Mo Chit).

The three piers that handle boat traffic to Ko Chang, Ko Kut, Ko Mak and Ko Wai are located in Laem Ngop, about 30km southwest of Trat. For boat transport details to the islands, see those sections of each island.

Sŏrng·tăa·ou to Laem Ngop and the piers (60B per person for six passengers, 200B for the whole vehicle, 40 minutes) leave from Th Sukhumvit, just past the market.

Bangkok Airways (☎Trat airport 039 5516545, in Bangkok 02 265 5555; www.bangkokair.com) operates flights from the airport, which is 40km from town. Taxis to Trat are a rip-off at 600B; try to hail a *sŏrng·tăa·ou*.

Motorbike taxis charge 20B to 30B for local hops.

Motorbikes can be rented for 200B a day along Th Sukhumvit near the guesthouse area.

TRANSPORT TO/FROM TRAT

DESTINATION	BUS	MINIVAN	AIR
Bangkok Suvarnabhumi International Airport	261B; 5-6hr; 5 daily		from 2550B; 1hr; 2 daily
Bangkok's Eastern Bus Terminal (Ekamai)	254B; 5hr; 17 daily	270B; 4hr; every 2hr; 8.30am-4.30pm	
Bangkok's Northern Bus Terminal (Mo Chit)	261B; 5-6hr; 4 daily	270B; 4hr; every 2hr; 8.30am-4.30pm	
Chanthaburi	70B; 1hr; every 2hr; 8.15am-6pm	70B; 50min; frequent; 6am-6pm	
Hat Lek (for Cambodia)		120B; 1½hr; hourly; 5am-6pm	
Pattaya		300B; 3½hr; every 2hr; 8am-6pm	
Rayong/Ban Phe (for Ko Samet)		200B; 2½hr; every 2hr; 8am-6pm	

GETTING TO CAMBODIA: HAT LEK TO KRONG KOH KONG

Getting to the Border From Trat, the closest Thailand–Cambodia crossing is from Hat Lek to the Cambodian town of Krong Koh Kong. Minivans run to Hat Lek hourly from 5am to 6pm (120B, 1½ hours) from Trat's bus station.

At the Border This is the most expensive place to cross into Cambodia from Thailand. Visas are a steep 1500B (they are US$20 at other crossings) and payment is only accepted in baht. You will need a passport photo too. Avoid anyone who says you require a 'medical certificate' or other paperwork. The border closes at 8pm.

Moving On Take a taxi (US$10) or *moto* (US$3) to Koh Kong where you can catch onward transport to Sihanoukville (four hours, one or two departures per day) and Phnom Penh (five hours, two or three departures until 11.30am).

Thai visas can be renewed here, but visas at land borders have been shortened to 15 days.

Ko Chang เกาะช้าง

POP 12,346

With steep, jungle-covered peaks, picturesque Ko Chang (Elephant Island) retains its remote and rugged spirit – despite attempts to transform it into a package-tour destination. Sweeping bays are sprinkled along the west coast; most have super-fine sand, some have pebbles. What it lacks in sand it makes up for in an unlikely combination: accessible wilderness with a thriving party scene. Convenient forays into a verdant jungle or underwater coral gardens can be enthusiastically toasted at one of Lonely Beach's many beer and bucket parties.

Because of its relative remoteness, it is only in the past decade or so that tourists – and 24-hour electricity – have arrived. Today, it is still a slog to get here, but the resorts are now busy with Chinese package tourists, Cambodian-bound backpackers and beach-hopping couples funnelling through to more remote islands in the Mu Ko Chang National Marine Park. Along the populous west coast are virtual mini-towns with a standard of living that has outpaced the island's infrastructure. For a taste of old-school Chang, head to the southeastern villages and mangrove forests of Ban Salak Phet and Ban Salak Kok.

Sights

Although Thailand's second-largest island has accelerated into the modern world with some understandable growing pains, Ko Chang still has tropically hued seas, critter-filled jungles and a variety of water sports for athletic beach bums.

West Coast

The west coast is by far the most developed part of Ko Chang, thanks to its beaches and bays. Public *sŏrng·tăa·ou* make beach-hopping easy and affordable. Some beaches are rocky, so it's worth bringing swim boots for children. Most of the time the seas are shallow and gentle but be wary of rips during storms and the rainy season (May to October).

Hat Sai Khao BEACH

(หาดทรายขาว) The longest, most luxurious stretch of sand on the island is packed with package-tour hotels and serious sunbathers. Head to the north section of the beach to find the more secluded backpacker spot. Along the main road, the village is busy and brash – but comes with all the necessary amenities.

Hat Kai Mook BEACH

(หาดไข่มุก) The name means 'pearl beach', although the 'pearls' here are just large pebbles that pack the shore and culminate in fish-friendly headlands. Swimming and sunbathing are out but there's good snorkelling.

Ao Khlong Prao BEACH

(อ่าวคลองพร้าว) Khlong Prao's beach is a pretty sweep of sand pinned between hulking mountainous headlands and bisected by two estuaries. At low tide, beachcombers stroll the rippled sand eyeing the critters left naked by the receding water. Sprawling luxury resorts dominate here and the primary pastime is sunbathing by the pool, as high tide gobbles up much of the beach.

With hired transport, you can head in to the interior of the island to do some waterfall-spotting. The island's biggest is **Nam Tok Khlong Plu**, a three-tiered cascade with a swimmable pool. It is reached via a 600m jungle path.

Hat Kaibae BEACH

(หาดไก่แบ้) A companion beach to Khlong Prao, Hat Kaibae is a good spot for families and thirty-something couples. A slim strip of sand unfurls around an island-dotted bay far enough removed from the package-tour scene that you'll feel independent. There is kayaking to the outlying island and low tide provides hours of beachcombing.

Lonely Beach BEACH

The last thing you'll be here is lonely, as this is Ko Chang's backpacker enclave and the liveliest place to be after dark. Here, vodka buckets are passed around and the speakers turned up. The beach has pebbles at the southern tip but the rest is sandy.

Tree Top Adventure Park PARK

(www.treetopadventurepark.com; Bailan Bay; 950B; ⏲9am-5pm) Swing through the jungle like Tarzan, walk the rope bridges, or ride the ziplines, flying skateboards and bicycles at this popular attraction. Close to Bailan Bay, this is a two-hour adventure. Add on 150B for transport there and back. All tour agencies around Ko Chang can book it.

Ban Bang Bao VILLAGE

(บ้านบางเบ้า) The villagers of Bang Bao, a former fishing community built in the traditional fashion of interconnected piers, have swapped their nets for renting out portions of their homes to souvenir shops and restaurants.

At first glance, Bang Bao may look like a tourist trap, but the traders who pack the pier generally offer quality, locally made produce. Walk to the far end to see a white lighthouse and boats bound for the nearby islands. Unless you are staying in one of the pier's guesthouses, get going before dark as it can be hard to find a taxi back.

Hat Khlong Kloi BEACH

At the eastern end of Ao Bang Bao, Khlong Kloi is a sandy beach that feels a lot like a secret though there are other people here, as well as all the requisite amenities (beer, food, fruit, massage) and a few guesthouses. You'll need private transport to get out here.

Northern Interior

Ko Chang's mountainous interior is predominately protected as a national park. The forest is lush and alive with wildlife and threaded by silver-hued waterfalls.

Ban Kwan Chang ELEPHANT INTERACTION

(บ้านควาญช้าง; ☎087 811 3599; chaitientong@yahoo.com; tours 800-1300B; ⏲8am-5pm) Tours ranging from 30 minutes to one hour (800/1300B) that involve feeding, bathing and riding a pachyderm are offered in a beautiful forested setting home to 10 rescued female elephants. Owner Pittaya Homkrailas is a well-regarded conservation enthusiast who works to preserve a humane relationship between the elephant and mahout, but it's worth considering the animal welfare issues involved with elephant rides before choosing that particular option.

Transport is included in the price. Be sure to apply mozzie spray.

East Coast

The east coast is still peaceful and undeveloped, filled with undulating hills of coconut and palm trees and low-key fishing villages in the far south. You will need private transport to explore this charming coast of scenic bays and mangrove forests.

Nam Tok Than Mayom WATERFALL

(น้ำตกธารมะยม; park fee 200B; ⏲8am-5pm) A series of three falls along the stream of

WORTH A TRIP

HAT MAI RUT

If you are going through coastal withdrawal, the sliver of Trat province that extends southeast towards Cambodia is fringed by sandy beaches. One of the easiest beaches to reach is **Hat Mai Rut**, roughly halfway between Trat and the border crossing of Hat Lek. Nearby is a traditional fishing village filled with colourful wooden boats and the sights and smells of a small-scale industry carried on by generations of families. **Mairood Resort** (☎089 841 4858; 28 Mu 6; r from 1950B ; ❄@📶≋) is a lovely spot to stay overnight, with cottages by the sea and in the mangroves.

You can get to Hat Mai Rut from the Trat bus station via Hat Lek–bound *sŏrng·tăa·ou*. The resort is 3km from the Km 53 highway marker.

Ko Chang

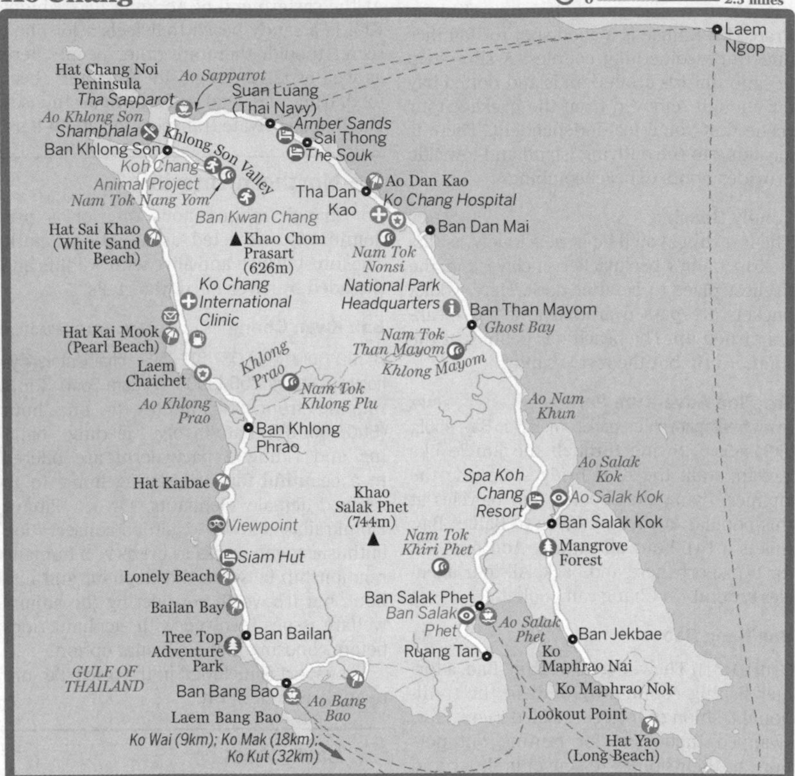

Khlong Mayom can be reached via the park office near Tha Than Mayom. The view from the top is superb and nearby there are inscribed stones bearing the initials of Rama V, Rama VI and Rama VII.

Ao Salak Kok BAY

(อ่าวสลักคอก) The dense tangle of mangroves here are protected by a group of fisherfolk who recognise their ecological importance. Mangroves are the ocean's nurseries, fostering the next generation of marine species, as well as resident birds and crustaceans, and this bay is now Ko Chang's prime ecotourism site.

Villagers, working in conjunction with Khun Pittaya, of Ban Kwan Chang elephant park, operate an award-winning program to preserve the environment and traditional way of life. They rent kayaks through the Salak Kok Kayak Station and run an affiliated restaurant.

Ban Salak Phet VILLAGE

(บ้านสลักเพชร) To discover what Ko Chang was like before the tourists came, visit Ban Salak Phet, in the far southeastern corner. This sleepy community is full of fishing boats and yawning dogs who stretch out on the roadside; it also provides access to some good treks.

Most visitors come for the seafood restaurants or to cruise the lonely byways for a secluded beach. Beyond the commercial heart of the village is **Ao Salak Phet**, a beautiful blue bay serenely guarded by humpbacked islands.

Nam Tok Khiri Phet WATERFALL

(น้ำตกคีรีเพชร) This small waterfall, 2km from Ban Salak Phet, is a 15-minute walk from the road and rewards you with a deep plunge pool. It is usually less crowded than many of the larger falls and is easily reached if you are in the neighbourhood of Ao Salak Phet.

Activities

Kayaking

Ko Chang cuts an impressive and heroic profile when viewed from the sea aboard a kayak. The water is generally calm and offshore islands provide a paddling destination that is closer than the horizon. Most hotels rent open-top kayaks (from 300B per day) that are convenient for near-shore outings and noncommittal kayakers. Some provide them for free.

KayakChang KAYAKING
(☎087 673 1753; www.kayakchang.com; Emerald Cove Resort, Khlong Prao; kayak per day from 2000B) For experienced paddlers, KayakChang rents high-end, closed-top kayaks that handle better and travel faster. They also lead multiday trips (from 4500B) to other islands in the archipelago.

Salak Kok Kayak Station KAYAKING
(☎087 748 9497; kayak rental per hr 200B) On the east side of the island, explore the mangrove swamps of Ao Salak Kok while supporting an award-winning ecotour program. Salak Kok Kayak Station rents self-guided kayaks and is a village work project designed to promote tourism without affecting the traditional way of life. They can also help arrange wooden-boat trips with a guide (200B), village homestays and hiking tours.

Hiking

Ko Chang isn't just about the beaches. The island has a well-developed trekking scene, with inland routes that lead to lush forests filled with birds, monkeys and flora. A handful of English-speaking guides grew up near the jungle and are happy to share their secrets

Mr Tan (tantrekking@hotmail.com; ☎089 645 2019) from **Evolution Tour** (☎039 557078; www.evolutiontour.com) has family-friendly hikes and more challenging eight-hour mountain treks. **Mr Raht** (kohchang_trekking@yahoo.com; ☎086 155 5693) leads one-day jungle treks around the southern and eastern parts of the island. Overnight camping can also be arranged. Treks range from 450B to 1500B.

Koh Chang Trekking HIKING
(☎081 588 3324) Birdwatchers should contact Koh Chang Trekking, which runs one- and two-day trips (950B to 1800B) into Mu Ko Chang National Marine Park and hikes to the top of Khao Chom Prasat, two nearby rocky-tipped peaks. Prices are for a group of four people.

Volunteering

Koh Chang Animal Project VOLUNTEERING
(☎089 042 2347; www.kohchanganimalproject.org; Ban Khlong Son; ⏲9am-5.30pm Mon-Sat) Abused, injured or abandoned animals receive medical care and refuge at this nonprofit centre. With local people it also works on general veterinarian services and spaying and neutering. Volunteers and donations are welcome. Travelling vets and vet nurses often drop by, while non-vets are needed to help with numerous odd jobs. Call to make an appointment.

Most *sŏrng·tăa·ou* drivers know how to get here; say you are going to 'Ban Lisa' (Lisa's House) in Khlong Son. If you have a bike, turn off the main road in Ban Khlong Son at 7-Eleven; the project is 1.5km down the road.

Massage

Sima Massage MASSAGE
(☎081 489 5171; Khlong Prao; massage per hr 250-400B; ⏲8am-10pm) On the main road and next to KaTi Culinary (p478), Sima is regarded by locals as the best massage on the island – quite an accolade in a place where a massage is easier to find than a 7-Eleven.

KO CHANG IN...

Three Days

Lie on the beach, rotate your body and repeat, with occasional forays into the ocean. Do this until you get bored, then rouse yourself out of your sun-induced stupor to explore the island. Do a **day hike** through the jungle or view the island from aboard a **kayak**. Catch a *sŏrng·tăa·ou* to **Ban Bang Bao** (p469) for lunch or an early dinner, followed by souvenir shopping. The next day rent a motorbike and explore the mangrove forest and fishing villages of the **east coast** (p469).

One Week

Migrate to the nearby islands of **Ko Wai** (p479) or **Ko Kut** (p482) for powder-soft sands, or devote a day or two giving back to the island by lending a hand at the **Koh Chang Animal Project** (p471).

DON'T MISS

DIVING & SNORKELLING KO CHANG

The dive sites near Ko Chang offer a variety of coral, fish and beginner-friendly shallow waters.

The seamounts off the southern tip of the island within the Mu Ko Chang National Marine Park are reached within a 30-minute cruise. Popular spots include **Hin Luk Bat** and **Hin Rap**, rocky, coral-encrusted seamounts with depths of around 18m to 20m. These are havens for schooling fish and some turtles. In 2013, near Hin Rap, a 30m gunship was deliberately sunk and now lies on its side.

By far the most pristine diving in the area is around **Ko Rang**, an uninhabited island protected from fishing by its marine park status. Visibility here is much better than near Ko Chang and averages between 10m and 20m. Everyone's favourite dive is **Hin Gadeng** – spectacular rock pinnacles with coral visible to around 28m. On the eastern side of Ko Rang, **Hin Kuak Maa** (also known as Three Finger Reef) is another top dive spot and is home to a coral-encrusted wall sloping from 2m to 14m and attracting swarms of marine life.

Ko Yak, **Ko Tong Lang** and **Ko Laun** are shallow dives perfect for both beginners and advanced divers. These small rocky islands can be circumnavigated and have lots of coral, schooling fish, puffer fish, morays, barracuda, rays and the occasional turtle.

About 7km offshore from Ban Bang Bao there's a popular dive to the wreck of the **HTMS Chang**, a 100m-long former Thai naval vessel purposely sunk in 2012 to form an artifical reef that now sits 30m beneath the surface.

Reef-fringed **Ko Wai** features a good variety of colourful hard and soft corals and is great for snorkelling. It is a popular day-tripping island but has simple overnight accommodation for more alone time with the reef.

The snorkelling on **Ko Mak** is not as good, but the island offers some decent dives even if the reefs don't see as many fish as elsewhere.

One-day diving trips start at 2900B. PADI Open Water certification costs 14,500B per person. Many dive shops remain open during the rainy season (May to October) but visibility and sea conditions are poor. The following are recommended dive operators:

BB Divers (☎039 558040; www.bbdivers.com) In Bang Bao with branches in Lonely Beach, Khlong Prao and Hat Sai Khao, plus outposts on Ko Kut and Ko Wai (high season only).

Lonely Beach Divers (☎080 619 0704; www.lonelybeachdivers.com) Operating out of Lonely Beach, this place offers multilingual instructors.

Courses

Koh Chang Thai Cookery School COOKING COURSE
(☎039 557243; Blue Lagoon Bungalows, Khlong Prao) Break up your lazy days with classes designed to enhance mind and body. Classes are typically five hours, include a market tour and cost 1500B per person; book ahead. Slices, dices and sautés are performed in a shady open-air kitchen beside the estuary.

Sleeping

Ko Chang's package-tour industry has distorted accommodation pricing. In general, rates have risen while quality has not, partly because hotels catering to group tours are guaranteed occupancy and don't have to maintain standards to woo repeat visitors or walk-ins. There is also a lot of copy-cat pricing, giving value-oriented visitors little choice.

During the wet season (May to October) rates drop precipitously. Consider booking ahead and shopping for online discounts during peak season (November to March), weekends and holidays.

On the west coast, Lonely Beach is the best budget option, Hat Kaibae is the best-value option and Hat Sai Khao is the most overpriced. A few accommodation options exist on the east coast at Ao Salak Kok and Ao Dan Kao.

Hat Sai Khao

The island's prettiest beach is also its most expensive. The northern and southern extremities have some budget and midrange options worth considering if you need proximity to the finest sand. The southern end of the beach is rocky and lacks sand during high tide. There's a backpacker enclave north of KC Grande Resort accessible only via the beach.

Independent Bo's GUESTHOUSE $
(r 300-800B;) The closest this beach gets to bohemian is this eclectic range of rooms that cling to the cliff. Quirky signs and a wi-fi ban in the bar add to the hippie feel. All the fan-only bungalows are different so prices vary. No reservations (and no children).

Starbeach Bungalows GUESTHOUSE $
(084 345 1079; www.starbeach-kohchang.com; bungalows 500-750B;) Ramshackle in appearance, the simple fan-only bungalows wind up the hillside and are solid enough. You are close to the prime part of the beach.

Arunee Resort GUESTHOUSE $$
(086 111 9600; aruneeresorttour@hotmail.com; r incl breakfast fan/air-con 500/1500B;) Recent renovations mean the super-cheap rooms have been replaced by bright and breezy ones. Arunee is set back from the main road and is a 50m-walk to the beach.

Rock Sand Resort GUESTHOUSE $$
(084 781 0550; www.rocksand-resort.com; r 750-3500B;) Touting itself as a flashpacker destination, this place is not really a resort. But the sea-view rooms are decent and come with shared balconies. Cheaper rooms are plain. Be prepared to wade here at high tide.

Paddy's Palms Resort HOTEL $$
(039 619083; www.paddyspalmspub.com; r incl breakfast 1100-1300B;) It may be a bit of a walk to the beach, but Paddy's compensates with a pool/jacuzzi, smart rooms and an excellent sports bar at the front.

Sai Khao Inn GUESTHOUSE $$
(081 570 1380; r 1200-1800B;) A quiet garden setting on the interior side of the road and reasonable value in the land of resorts, Sai Khao Inn has a little bit of everything – bungalows on stilts and more ordinary rooms. It's up an alley off the main road.

Keereeelé HOTEL $$
(039 551285; keeree_ele@hotmail.com; r incl breakfast 2200-2600B;) This multi-storey hotel has modern and comfortable rooms, some of which have views of the verdant mountains behind. Beds are raised off the floor Chinese-style. The hotel is on the interior side of the road, with the beach 300m away. The name means 'elephant mountain', in case you wondered.

Apple Beachfront Resort HOTEL $$
(039 551228; applebeachfrontresort@gmail.com; r incl breakfast 2800B;) Employing lots of natural materials, Apple has neat, simple rooms facing the sea or a large terraced pool area.

Ao Khlong Prao

Ao Khlong Prao is dominated by high-end resorts, with just a few budget spots peppered in between. There are a handful of cheapies on the main road that are within walking distance to the beach.

★ **Blue Lagoon Bungalows** GUESTHOUSE $$
(039 557243; www.kohchang-bungalows-bluelagoon.com; r 500-1800B;) Set beside a scenic estuary, Blue Lagoon has a variety of bungalows and rooms, or you can rent a tent (250B). A wooden walkway leads to the beach. Check out the larger family room, which was made using elephant dung. The staff, who are excellent, provide numerous activities, including yoga and cookery classes.

Lin Bungalow BUNGALOW $$
(084 120 1483; r 1500B;) A good mid-range choice, with 10 sturdy and sizeable bungalows right on the beach.

Baan Rim Nam GUESTHOUSE $$
(087 005 8575; www.iamkohchang.com; r 1300-1900B;) This converted fisherman's

DON'T FEED THE ANIMALS

On many of the around-the-island boat tours, operators amaze their guests with a stop at a rocky cliff to feed the wild monkeys. It seems innocent enough, and even entertaining, but there's an unfortunate consequence. The animals become dependent on this food source and when the boats don't come as often during the low season the young and vulnerable ones are ill-equipped to forage in the forest.

The same goes for the dive or boat trips that feed the fish leftover lunches, or bread bought on the pier specifically for this purpose. It might be a fantastic way to see a school of brilliantly coloured fish, but they then forsake the coral reefs for an easier meal, and without the daily grooming efforts of the fish the coral is soon overgrown with algae and will eventually suffocate.

NATIONAL PARK STATUS

Some areas of Ko Chang are protected and maintained as part of the Mu Ko Chang National Marine Park. Conservation efforts are a bit haphazard, but you will be required to pay a 200B park entrance fee when visiting some of the waterfalls (the waterfall reviews mention this fee where it applies). **National Park headquarters** (☎039 555080; Ban Than Mayom; ⏰8am-5pm) is on the eastern side of the island near Nam Tok Than Mayom.

Nudity and topless sunbathing are forbidden by law in Mu Ko Chang National Marine Park; this includes all beaches on Ko Chang, Ko Kut, Ko Mak and Ko Wai.

house sits over a mangrove-lined river and comes with cool, airy rooms. The English owner is well-informed about the island and keen to help. Free kayaks are provided – the beach is a three-minute paddle away.

Magic Resort BUNGALOW **$$**
(☎039 557074; www.magicresortkohchang.co.th; r incl breakfast 1300-2500B; ❄📶) Once a thriving backpacker commune, the magic here has faded a tad, but the basic beachside bungalows and neat chill-all-day garden are still popular. Wi-fi is limited to the reception area.

Sofia Garden Resort HOTEL **$$**
(☎080 095 1095; www.sofiagardenresort.net; r 1690-2200B; ❄📶🏊) Good price for the comfort factor, and there's a Finnish sauna as well as the pool, but the rooms are slightly dated and there is no direct beach access.

Keereeta Resort GUESTHOUSE **$$**
(☎039 551304; keeree_ta@hotmail.com; Hat Kai Mook; r incl breakfast 1900-2300B; ❄📶🏊) Rooms here have an extra splash of style, with warm colours and arty touches. Massage pavilions are right by the pool. The resort is just north of Ao Khlong Prao.

Aana HOTEL **$$$**
(☎039 551137; www.aanaresort.com; r 3500-6500B; ❄@📶🏊) Private villas perch prettily above the forest and Khlong Prao, kayaking distance from the beach. The cheaper rooms are a little faded for the price.

The Dewa RESORT **$$$**
(☎039 557339; www.thedewakohchang.com; r incl breakfast 7000-20,000B; ❄@📶🏊) Everything about the Dewa, the top luxury pad in these parts, is chic, from the dark-bottomed 700-sq-metre pool to the contemporary Thai-style rooms that Jim Thompson would have been proud of.

Hat Kaibae

Hat Kaibae has some of the island's best variety of accommodation, from boutique hotels to budget huts and midrange bungalows. The trade-off is that the beach is only sandy in parts.

Porn's Bungalows BUNGALOW **$**
(☎080 613 9266; www.pornsbungalows-kohchang.com; r 600-1500B) Very chilled spot at the far western end of the beach, with a popular on-site restaurant. All of the wooden bungalows are fan-only. The 1000B beachfront bungalows are a great deal.

KB Resort HOTEL **$$**
(☎039 557125; www.kbresort.com; r incl breakfast 2300-5000B; ❄@📶🏊) Yellow bungalows have cheery bathrooms and pose peacefully beside the sea.

Kai Bae Hut Resort HOTEL **$$**
(☎081 862 8426; www.kaibaehutresort.com; r incl breakfast 900-2500B; ❄📶) Sprawling across a scenic stretch of beach, Kai Bae Hut has a variety of lodging options – slightly worn fan huts, fancier concrete bungalows and modern hotel-style rooms. A large open-air restaurant fires up nightly barbecues and there's plenty of room for free-ranging kids. Cheaper rooms have fans.

Garden Resort HOTEL **$$**
(☎039 557260; www.gardenresortkohchang.com; r incl breakfast 2200-4500B; ❄@📶🏊) On the interior side of the main road, Garden Resort has large, clean bungalows dotted either side of a shady pathway that leads to a swimming pool. The bar and restaurant at the front are popular hang-outs. A sandy stretch of beach is 150m away.

The Chill RESORT **$$$**
(☎039 552555; www.thechillresort.com; r incl breakfast 5250-14,400B; ❄@📶🏊) Cleverly designed, with all ground-floor rooms opening onto one of three pools, the Chill has contemporary, bright rooms and bags of facilities. Popular with families.

Lonely Beach

A backpacker fave, Lonely Beach is one of the cheapest places to sleep on the island, though budget spots smack on the beach are harder to find. Having been ignored by the flashy resorts, the streets are filled with grungy bars and cheap guesthouses rather than spas and salons.

★BB World of Tapas HOSTEL $
(☎089 504 0543; www.bbworldoftapas.com; dm 200B, r with fan 500-600B;) Much like tapas, you get a little taste of everything here. The on-site dive school, gym, eclectic tapas menu and a chill-out zone make it a great spot to meet fellow travellers. One of the only dorms within reach of the beach.

Siam Hut GUESTHOUSE $
(☎039 619012; www.siamhutkohchang.com; r 480-680B;) Part Ibiza and part Full Moon, Siam Hut is party central on Lonely Beach. Backpackers are attracted by the cheap wooden huts that sit next to one of the few sandy strips around here. Wi-fi is available by reception.

Paradise Cottage HOTEL $
(☎081 773 9337; y_yinggg@hotmail.com; r fan/air-con 500/800-1200B;) With house music as a backdrop, hammock-clad pavilions facing the sea and comfy rooms, Paradise Cottage is tailor-made for flashpackers. At low tide a sandbank just beyond the rocks can be reached.

Little Eden GUESTHOUSE $
(☎084 867 7459; www.littleedenkohchang.com; r 700-1100B;) There are 15 bungalows here, all connected by an intricate series of wooden walkways. Rooms are quite spacious with surprisingly good bathrooms. Pleasant communal area and staff.

KLKL Hostel GUESTHOUSE $
(☎083 088 3808; r 600-1200B;) Not a true hostel as there are no dorms here. Instead, you get pleasant blue, green and pink rooms at reasonable prices. Cheaper rooms are fan-only, but all have hot water. Wi-fi is only in the bar area.

Oasis Bungalows GUESTHOUSE $$
(☎081 721 2547; www.oasis-kohchang.com; r 450-1400B;) Literally the top place in Lonely Beach – largely due to its location on the peak of a hill – Oasis has great sea views, and the scene from its 12m-tall treehouse is even more impressive. Run by a friendly Dutch couple, Oasis has roomy, midrange bungalows. Cheaper rooms are fan-only.

It's a five-minute walk to the beach.

Warapura Resort HOTEL $$
(☎039 558123; r 1900-4500B;) Warapura has a collection of adorable cottages tucked in between the village and a mangrove beach. The large, oceanfront pool is perfect for people who would rather gaze at the ocean than frolic in it.

Lonely Beach Resort BUNGALOW $$
(☎081 279 5120; www.lonelybeach.net; r 900-1300B;) The bungalows here slope downhill amid a leafy garden. They're plain but a good size and comfortable enough. The attached restaurant is a bizarre, albeit tasty, mix of Danish and Thai dishes.

Ban Bang Bao

Despite its touristy veneer, Ban Bang Bao is still a charming place to stay. Accommodation options are mainly converted pier houses overlooking the sea, with easy access to departing inter-island ferries. Daytime transport to a swimmable beach is possible thanks to the steady flow of day trippers, or Khlong Kloi beach is just to the east. Night owls should either hire a motorbike or stay elsewhere, as *sŏrng·tăa·ou* become rare and expensive after dinnertime.

Bang Bao Cliff Cottage GUESTHOUSE $
(☎085 904 6706; www.cliff-cottage.com; r 600-1200B;) Partially hidden on a verdant hillside west of the pier are a few dozen simple thatch huts overlooking a rocky cove. Most have sea views and a couple offer spectacular vistas. Scubadawgs dive school has a base here. Tents are available in the high season.

★Koh Chang Sea Hut HOTEL $$
(☎081 285 0570; www.kohchang-seahut.com; r incl breakfast 2800B;) Set at the far end of Bang Bao pier, this collection of luxurious bungalows and rooms offers near-panoramic views of the bay. Each bungalow is surrounded by a private deck where breakfast is served. Free kayaking.

Buddha View GUESTHOUSE $$
(☎039 558157; www.thebuddhaview.com; r 600-1400B;) Swish pier guesthouse popular with Bangkokians. There are only seven thoughtfully designed, all-wood rooms, four

of which come with private bathrooms. The restaurant is excellent too.

El Greco GUESTHOUSE $$
(☎086 843 8417; www.elgreco-kohchang.com; r 1200-1400B; ❄📶) There are clean rooms, slightly hard beds and great views at this simple guesthouse half-way along Bang Bao pier. The on-site Greek restaurant is worth a look.

Nirvana HOTEL $$$
(☎039 558061; www.nirvanakohchang.com; r incl breakfast 3000-4700B; ❄📶🏊) Super-deluxe, Balinese-style bungalows hidden away on a rocky, jungle-filled peninsula. Spacious rooms feature stone bathrooms and retro pop posters. This is about as removed from everything else on the island as possible, though there is a shuttle bus to Bang Bao if civilisation is required. The adjacent beach is not swimmable.

Northern Interior & East Coast

The northern and eastern parts of the island are less developed than the west coast and more isolated. You will need your own transport and maybe even a posse not to feel lonely out here, but you'll be rewarded with a quieter, calmer experience.

Jungle Way GUESTHOUSE $
(☎089 247 3161; Khlong Son Valley; r 200-500B) Set deep in the forest, accessible via a rope bridge, is this wonderful jungle hideaway. Owner and local expert Khun Ann can arrange treks from here. The fan-only bungalows are simple but adequate and the on-site restaurant is good.

Jungle Way's Facebook page is updated regularly.

The Souk GUESTHOUSE $$
(☎081 553 3194; www.thesoukkohchang.com; Ao Dan Kao; r fan/air-con 900/1500-2200B; ❄@📶) This cool spot has reasonably priced bungalows that are decked out with pop art. There are lots of chill-out spaces and a low-key, open-deck restaurant and cocktail bar, just in front of the red-sand beach. Air-con rooms include breakfast.

Amber Sands HOTEL $$$
(☎039 586177; www.ambersandsbeachresort.com; Ao Dan Kao; r 2800-4250B; ❄@📶🏊) Sandwiched between mangroves and a quiet red-sand beach, Amber Sands has smart bungalows and great sea views. The location feels a world away but it is only 15 minutes from the pier. Closes August to mid-October.

Spa Koh Chang Resort HOTEL $$$
(☎080 964 7614; www.thespakohchang.com; Ao Salak Kok; r incl breakfast 2136-3657B; ❄📶🏊) Specialising in health-care packages, including fasting, yoga and meditation, this resort has lush, peaceful surroundings that almost touch the bay's mangrove forests. Elegantly decorated bungalows scramble up a flower-filled hillside providing a peaceful getaway for some quality 'me' time. The restaurant has vegan and vegie options. No beach access.

Eating & Drinking

Virtually all of the island's accommodation choices have attached restaurants with adequate but not outstanding fare. Parties abound on the beaches and range from the more mature, restrained scene on Hat Sai Khao, to the younger and more frenetic on Lonely Beach.

West Coast

Porn's Bungalows Restaurant THAI $
(Hat Kaibae; dishes 80-180B; ⏲11am-11pm) This laid-back, dark-wood restaurant is the quintessential beachside lounge. Great barbecue. Feel free to have your drinks out-size your meal and don't worry about dressing up for dinner.

Nid's Kitchen THAI $
(nidkitchen@hotmail.com; Khlong Prao; dishes 50-150B; ⏲6-10pm) Nid's creates all the Thai standards like a wok wizard in a hut festooned with rasta imagery. Equally fine for a drink or three.

★**Barrio Bonito** MEXICAN $$
(Hat Kaibae; dishes 160-250B; ⏲5-10.30pm) Fab fajitas and cracking cocktails are served by a charming French-Mexican couple at this roadside spot in the middle of Kaibae. Authentic food and stylish surroundings.

★**Phu-Talay** SEAFOOD $$
(☎039 551300; Khlong Prao; dishes 100-320B; ⏲10am-10pm) There is a cute, homely feel at this wooden-floored, blue-and-white-decorated place perched over the lagoon. There's a sensible menu of Ko Chang classics (lots of fish) and it's far more reasonably priced than many other seafood places.

Oodie's Place

INTERNATIONAL-THAI $$

(☎039 551193; Hat Sai Khao; dishes 80-390B; ⊙11am-midnight) Local musician Oodie runs a nicely diverse operation with excellent French food, tasty Thai specialities and live music from 10pm. After all these years, it is still beloved by expats.

Baanta

THAI $$

(Khlong Prao; dishes 120-250B; ⊙noon-10pm; 📶) Baanta is run by the same folk who have the ultra-posh Panviman Resort, and the dishes here are both excellent in terms of quality and value. Expect Thai standards plus some modern twists.

Saffron on the Sea

THAI $$

(☎039 551253; Hat Kai Mook; dishes 120-350B; ⊙8am-10pm; 📶) Owned by an arty escapee from Bangkok, this friendly boutique hotel has a generous portion of oceanfront dining and a relaxed, romantic atmosphere. All the Thai dishes are prepared in the island style, more sweet than spicy.

Jea Eaw

THAI $$

(Khlong Prao; dishes 120-300B; ⊙10am-9pm) Locals fill this simple, open-air restaurant every evening due to the big flavours and prolific menu options. The prawns are recommended.

GETTING TO CAMBODIA: ARANYA PRATHET TO POIPET

Getting to the Border The easiest way to get from Bangkok to Siem Reap overland is the direct bus departing from the Northern (Mo Chit) Bus Terminal. The through-service bus trips sold on Th Khao San and elsewhere in Bangkok seem cheap and convenient, but they haven't been nicknamed 'scam buses' for nothing, and if using them you will be most likely hassled and ripped off, often quite aggressively.

If you choose to do it in stages (much cheaper than the direct Mo Chit bus), you can get from Bangkok to the border town of Aranya Prathet (aka Aran) by bus from Mo Chit, by bus or minivan from the Eastern (Ekamai) Bus Terminal, by bus from Suvarnabhumi International Airport bus station, by minivan from Victory Monument or by 3rd-class train (only the 5.55am departure will get you there early enough, at 11.35am, to reach Siem Reap the same day) from Hualamphong. Aran also has bus services about every one or two hours from other cities in the area including Khorat, Surin and Chanthaburi. All minivans, plus some buses, go all the way to the Rong Kluea Market next to the border, so there's no need to stop in Aranya Prathet city. Otherwise, you'll need to take a *sŏrng·tăa·ou* (15B), motorcycle taxi (60B) or túk-túk (pronounced *đúk đúk*; 80B) the final 7km to the border.

At the Border The border is open 7am to 8pm daily. There are many persistent scammers on the Thai side trying to get you to buy your Cambodia visa through them, but no matter what they might tell you, there's absolutely no good reason to get visas anywhere except the border. Buying them elsewhere costs more and takes longer. Don't even show your passport to anyone before you reach Thai immigration and don't change money.

After getting stamped out of Thailand – a straightforward process – follow the throng to Cambodian immigration and find the 'Visa on Arrival' sign if you don't already have a visa. Weekday mornings you might finish everything in 10 to 20 minutes, but if you arrive after noon it could take an hour or more. Weekends and holidays, when many Thais arrive to gamble and foreign workers do visa runs, are also busy. You will probably be offered the opportunity to pay a 'special VIP fee' of 200B to jump to the front of the queue. You will almost certainly be asked to pay another small 'fee', which will be called a 'stamping' or 'overtime' fee. You should refuse, though doing so might mean you have to wait a few extra minutes.

Moving On There are frequent buses and share taxis from Poipet to Siem Reap along a good sealed road from the main bus station, which is about 1km away (2000r by motorcycle taxi) around the main market, one block north of Canadia Bank off NH5. Poipet also has a second 'international' bus station 9km east of town where prices are double and which is only used by uninformed or gullible foreigners who get swept into the free shuttle that takes travellers out there. Lonely Planet's *Cambodia* guide has full details for travel on this side of the border.

Paul's Restaurant EUROPEAN $$
(☎039 551499; Hat Sai Khao; dishes 160-280B; ⏰5-10pm) Great-value German and other European dishes are served up at this clifftop restaurant, along with side orders of sarcasm from the entertaining owner.

Magic Garden THAI $$
(☎039 558027; Lonely Beach; dishes 100-220B; ⏰9am-midnight; 📶) The hippest place on Lonely Beach to have a smoothie or vodka bucket, as travellers swap tales or catch up on some reading. The menu covers Thai and Western standards.

Chowlay SEAFOOD $$
(Ban Bang Bao; dishes 100-450B; ⏰10am-midnight) 'If it swims, we have it', goes its motto, and this pier restaurant does indeed have a huge seafood menu as well as great bay views.

KaTi Culinary THAI $$
(☎081 903 0408; Khlong Prao; dishes 130-290B; ⏰11am-3pm & 6-10pm) Seafood, a few Isan dishes and the famous homemade curry sauce are the best bets here. The menu features creative smoothies, featuring lychee, lemon and peppermint, and there's a children's menu.

Northern Interior & East Coast

Blues Blues Restaurant THAI $
(Ban Khlong Son; dishes 70-150B; ⏰10am-9pm) Through the green screen of tropical plants is an arty stir-fry hut that is beloved for its expertise, efficiency and economy. The owner's delicate watercolour paintings are on display too. Take the road to Ban Kwan Chang; it's 600m ahead on the right.

Jungle Way Restaurant THAI $
(☎089 247 3161; Ban Khlong Son; dishes 70-120B; ⏰7am-9pm; 🌿) Enjoy the natural setting and home-style cooking of this guesthouse restaurant. Meal preparation takes a leisurely pace so climb up to the elevated wildlife-viewing platform to spot some jungle creatures while the wok is sizzling.

★**Shambhala** EUROPEAN $$
(Siam Royal View, Hat Chang Noi; dishes 120-390B; ⏰1-9pm Thu-Tue) Perched at the top of the island, this poolside restaurant comes with some of the cheapest cocktails around and quality Thai/international dishes, including great risotto. Perfect for a sundowner.

ℹ Information

DANGERS & ANNOYANCES

Take extreme care when driving between Ban Khlong Son south to Hat Sai Khao, as the road is steep and treacherous, with several hairpin turns. There are mud slides and poor conditions during storms. If you do rent a motorbike, ride carefully between Hat Kaibae and Lonely Beach, especially in the rainy season. Wear protective clothing when riding on a motorcycle.

The police conduct regular drug raids on the island's accommodation. If you get caught with narcotics, you could face heavy fines or imprisonment.

Be aware of the cheap minibus tickets from Siem Reap to Ko Chang; these usually involve some sort of time- and money-wasting commission scam.

Ko Chang is considered a low-risk malarial zone, meaning that liberal use of mosquito repellent is probably an adequate precaution.

EMERGENCY

Police Station (☎039 586191; Ban Dan Mai)

Tourist Police Office (☎1155) Based north of Ban Khlong Prao. Also has smaller police boxes that are located in Hat Sai Khao and Hat Kaibae.

MEDICAL SERVICES

Bang Bao Health Centre (☎039 558086; Ban Bang Bao; ⏰8.30am-4pm) For the basics.

Ko Chang Hospital (☎039 586096; Ban Dan Mai) Public hospital with a good reputation and affordably priced care; south of the ferry terminal.

Ko Chang International Clinic (☎039 551555; Hat Sai Khao; ⏰24hr) Related to the Bangkok Hospital Group; accepts most health insurances and has expensive rates.

MONEY

There are banks with ATMs and exchange facilities along all the west-coast beaches.

POST

Ko Chang Post Office (☎039 551240; ⏰9am-5pm) At the far southern end of Hat Sai Khao.

TOURIST INFORMATION

The free magazine *Koh Chang Guide* (www.koh-chang-guide.com) is widely available on the island and has handy beach maps.

The comprehensive website I Am Koh Chang (www.iamkohchang.com) is a labour of love from an irreverent Brit living on the island. It's jam-packed with opinion and information.

TRANSPORT TO/FROM KO CHANG

ORIGIN	DESTINATION	SPEEDBOAT	BUS
Bangkok's Eastern Bus Terminal (Ekamai)	Tha Thammachat		263B; 6hr; 2 daily
Tha Centrepoint (Laem Ngop)	Ko Chang	80B; 40min; hourly; 6am-7pm	
Tha Thammachat (Laem Ngop)	Ko Chang	80B; 30min; every 45min; 6.30am-7pm	
Ko Chang	Ko Kut	900B; 5hr; 2 daily	
Ko Chang	Ko Mak	600B; 2hr; 1 daily	
Ko Chang	Ko Wai	400B; 15 min; 2 daily	
Ko Chang	Bangkok Suvarnabhumi International Airport		263B; 5hr; 2pm

Getting There & Away

Whether starting from Bangkok or Cambodia, it is an all-day haul to reach Ko Chang.

Ferries from the mainland (Laem Ngop) leave from either Tha Thammachat, operated by **Koh Chang Ferry** (☎039 555188), or Tha Centrepoint with **Centrepoint Ferry** (☎039 538196). Boats from Tha Thammachat arrive at Tha Sapparot; Centrepoint ferries at a pier down the road.

Bang Bao Boat (☎039 558046; www.kohchangbangbaoboat.com) is the inter-island ferry that connects Ko Chang with Ko Mak, Ko Kut and Ko Wai during the high season. Boats leave from Bang Bao in the southwest of the island.

Speedboats travel between the islands during high season.

It is possible to go to and from Ko Chang from Bangkok's Eastern (Ekamai) bus terminal and Bangkok's Suvaranabhumi International Airport, via Chanthaburi and Trat.

Getting Around

Shared *sŏrng·tăa·ou* meet arriving boats to shuttle passengers to the various beaches (Hat Sai Khao 100B, Khlong Prao 150B and Lonely Beach 200B). Hops between neighbouring beaches range from 50B to 200B but prices rise dramatically after dark, when it can cost 500B to travel from Bang Bao to Hat Sai Khao.

Motorbikes can be hired from 200B per day. Ko Chang's hilly and winding roads are dangerous; make sure the bike is in good working order.

Ko Wai เกาะหวาย

Stunning Ko Wai is teensy and primitive, but endowed with gin-clear waters, excellent coral reefs for snorkelling and a handsome view across to Ko Chang. Expect to share the bulk of your afternoons with day trippers but have the remainder of your time in peace.

Most bungalows close from May to September when seas are rough and flooding is common.

Sleeping

Good Feeling BUNGALOW $
(☎081 850 3410; r 400-500B) There are 12 wooden bungalows here, all but one with private bathroom, spread out along a rocky headland interspersed with private, sandy coves. Good snorkelling nearby.

Ko Wai Paradise BUNGALOW $
(☎081 762 2548; r 300-800B) Simple wooden bungalows on a postcard-perfect beach. You'll share the coral out front with day trippers.

Grand Mar Hut GUESTHOUSE $
(☎081 841 3011; r 400-600B) On the rocky northeastern tip of the island is this basic and remote place; speedboat operators know it by the nearby bay of Ao Yai Ma.

Ko Wai Pakarang GUESTHOUSE $$
(☎084 113 8946; kohwaipakarang@hotmail.com; r fan/air-con 600-1200/2200-2500B; ❄@📶) Wooden and concrete bungalows, with an OK attached restaurant and helpful, English-speaking staff. Only the top-price rooms have air-con.

Koh Wai Beach Resort HOTEL $$$
(☎081 306 4053; www.kohwaibeachresort.com; r incl breakfast 2100-5900B; ❄📶) Upscale collection of spacious bungalows that are equipped with all the mod cons just a few steps from the beach and on the southern side of the island.

SPEEDBOAT TRANSPORT FROM KO WAI

DESTINATION	FARE (ONE WAY)	DURATION	FREQUENCY
Ko Chang	400B	15min	3 daily
Ko Kut	700B	1hr	3 daily
Ko Mak	300B	45min	3 daily
Laem Ngop (mainland pier)	450B	30min	4 daily

Getting There & Around

Boats will drop you off at the nearest pier to your guesthouse; otherwise you'll have to walk 15 to 30 minutes along a narrow forest trail.

Bang Bao Boat (www.kohchangbangbaoboat.com) is the archipelago's inter-island ferry, running a daily loop from Ko Chang to Ko Kut. Boats depart Ko Chang at 9.30am and noon and arrive at Ko Wai (one way 400B, 30 minutes) then continue on to Ko Mak (one way 600B, one hour) and Ko Kut (900B, two hours).

Ko Mak

เกาะหมาก

Little Ko Mak measures only 16 sq km and doesn't have any speeding traffic, wall-to-wall development, noisy beer bars or crowded beaches. The palm-fringed bays are bathed by gently lapping water and there's a relaxed vibe. But Ko Mak is not destined for island superstardom: the interior is a utilitarian landscape of coconut and rubber plantations and sand flies are a pain on some beaches.

Visiting the island is easier in the high season (December to March); during the low season (May to September) many boats stop running and bungalow operations wind down. A new underwater electricity cable means Ko Mak and Ko Kut now have 24-hour power.

Sights & Activities

The best beach on the island is **Ao Pra** in the west, but it is undeveloped and hard to reach. For now, swimming and beach strolling are best on the northwestern bay of **Ao Suan Yai**, which is a wide arc of sand and looking-glass-clear water that gets fewer sand flies than the southern beaches. It is easily accessible by bicycle or motorbike if you stay elsewhere.

Offshore is **Ko Kham**, a private island that was sold in 2008 for a reported 200 million baht. It used to be a popular day-trippers' beach; today work is slowly ongoing to create a luxury resort.

Koh Mak Divers DIVING
(☎083 297 7724; www.kohmakdivers.com; dive trips from 2400B) Koh Mak Divers runs dive trips to the Mu Ko Chang National Marine Park, about 45 minutes away.

Sleeping & Eating

Most budget guesthouses are on Ao Khao, a decent strip of sand on the southwestern side of the island, while the resorts sprawl out on the more scenic northwestern bay of Ao Suan Yai.

There are a handful of family-run restaurants on the main road between Monkey Island and Makathanee Resort. If you feel like a journey, use a meal or a sundowner as an excuse to explore different bays.

Koh Mak Cottage BUNGALOW $
(☎081 910 2723; www.kohmakcottage.com; Ao Khao; r 500B; @ 🛜) Koh Mak has 19 small and rustic bungalows. No frills, but you are right on the beach. Wi-fi is only near reception.

Monkey Island GUESTHOUSE $$
(☎085 389 0949; www.monkeyislandkohmak.com; Ao Khao; r 600-4000B; ❄ @ 🛜) The troop leader of guesthouses, Monkey Island has earthen or wooden bungalows in three creatively named models – Baboon, Chimpanzee and Gorilla – with various amenities. All have fun design touches and the hip restaurant does respectable Thai cuisine in a leisurely fashion. There's also a small children's pool. Rooms over 1500B come with air-con and breakfast.

Baan Chailay GUESTHOUSE $$
(☎080 101 4763; www.baanchailay.com; Ao Khao; r incl breakfast 1000-1600B; ❄ 🛜) A cross between a homestay and a guesthouse, you can stay in bungalows on the beach, or rooms in the family house at this friendly place at the eastern, less busy, end of Ao Khao. Foodies will appreciate the beach barbecues and bakery.

Makathanee Resort HOTEL $$
(☎087 802 7575; www.makathaneekohmak.com; Ao Khao; r incl breakfast 1200-5500B; ❄📶🏊) Floor-to-ceiling windows are open to sea views in these plush bungalows, which have deliciously soft mattresses and lots of breathing room. Some rooms are in a hotel block; the cheapest of these don't have a view but do offer great value. Professional service, and kayaks for rent (400B per day).

Baan Koh Mak BUNGALOW $$
(☎089 895 7592; www.baan-koh-mak.com; Ao Khao; r 1690-3990B; ❄📶) Each of the 18 white bungalows here comes with heaps of natural light and arty features. Wi-fi is available at the restaurant.

Ao Kao Resort GUESTHOUSE $$
(☎083 152 6564; www.aokaoresort.com; Ao Khao; r 2500-3000B; ❄📶) 🍃 In a pretty crook of the bay, Ao Kao has an assortment of Thai-style bungalows, all with balconies and easy beach access. Amenities include a range of sports options and a massage pavilion. Ao Kao Resort also gets kudos for its ecofriendly projects, which include solar panels and energy-saving schemes. Wi-fi is in the restaurant only.

Lazy Day Resort BUNGALOW $$
(☎081 882 4002; www.kohmaklazyday.com; r incl breakfast 2500-2700B; ❄📶) This professionally run operation has a dozen big bungalows stationed around an attractive garden.

Koh Mak Resort HOTEL $$$
(☎039 501013; www.kohmakresort.com; Ao Suan Yai; r incl breakfast 2800-6800B; ❄📶📺) A speedboat from Laem Ngop (450B) takes guests directly to this all-encompassing resort. Once they've arrived, they get to stay in pretty, white beachfront bungalows that offer lots of natural light. Services include kayak rentals and cookery classes.

Ko Mak & Ko Kut

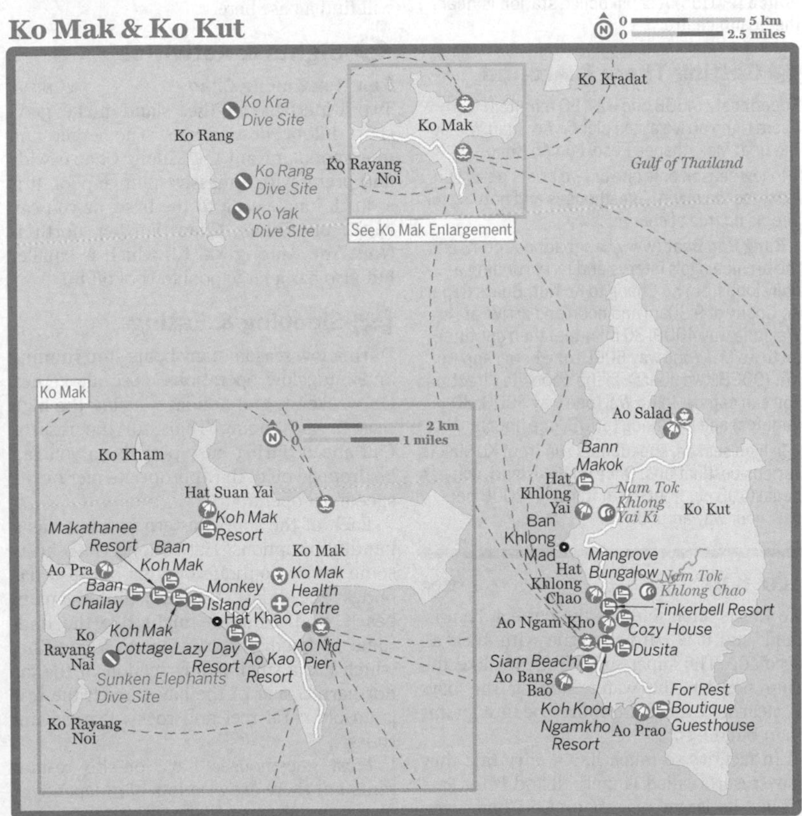

SPEEDBOAT TRANSPORT FROM KO MAK

DESTINATION	FARE (ONE WAY)	DURATION	FREQUENCY
Ko Chang	600B	45min	3 daily
Ko Kut	400B	45min	2 daily
Ko Wai	300B	30min	3 daily
Laem Ngop (mainland pier)	450B	1hr	2 daily

Information

There are no banks or ATMs on the island, so stock up on cash before visiting.

Ball's Cafe (081 925 6591; Ao Khao; 8am-9pm;) Khun Ball runs his internet cafe, coffee shop and information centre in a spot just behind Baan Koh Mak; he's an active island promoter and runs www.kohmak.com as well as environmental initiatives.

Ko Mak Health Centre (8.30am-4.30pm) Can handle basic first-aid emergencies and illnesses. It is on the cross-island road near Ao Nid Pier.

Police (1155) A small police station is near the health centre.

Getting There & Around

Speedboats (450B one way, 50 minutes) from Laem Ngop arrive at the pier on Ao Suan Yai, Ao Nid or at Makathanee Resort on Ao Khao.

In low season only one or two boats a day run from the mainland. Guesthouses and hotels pick people up free of charge.

Bang Bao Boat (www.bangbaoboat.com) is the archipelago's inter-island ferry running a daily loop from Ko Chang to Ko Kut. Boats depart Ko Chang at 9.30am and noon and arrive at Ko Wai (one way 400B, 30 minutes) then continue on to Ko Mak (one way 600B, one hour) and Ko Kut (900B, two hours). In the opposite direction, you can catch it to Ko Wai (one way 300B, 30 minutes) and Ko Chang (600B, one hour).

In high season, speedboats run from Ko Mak to various destinations. Once on the island, you can pedal (40B per hour) or motorbike (200B per day) your way around.

Ko Kut

เกาะกูด

Ko Kut is often feted as the perfect Thai island, and it is hard to argue with such an accolade. The super-soft sands are like talcum powder, the water lapping the bays is clear and there are more coconut palms than buildings.

In fact, it's so much like a fairy tale they have resorts called Tinkerbell and Peter Pan. Unlike its larger neighbour Ko Chang, you can forget about any nightlife, traffic or noise – this is where you come to do almost nothing. If you can be roused from your hammock, kayaking and snorkelling are the main activities (nearby Ko Rang is particularly good for fish gazing).

Half as big as Ko Chang and the fourth-largest island in Thailand, Ko Kut (also known as Koh Kood) has long been the domain of package-tour resorts and a seclusion-seeking elite. But the island is becoming more egalitarian, and independent travellers, especially families and couples, will find a base here.

Sights & Activities

Nam Tok Khlong Chao WATERFALL

Two waterfalls on the island make good short hiking destinations. The larger and more popular Nam Tok Khlong Chao is wide and pretty with a massive plunge pool. It is a quick jungle walk to the base, or you can kayak up Khlong Chao. Further north is **Nam Tok Khlong Yai Ki**, which is smaller but also has a large pool to cool off in.

Sleeping & Eating

During low season many boats stop running and bungalow operations close altogether. On weekends and holidays during the high season, vacationing Thais fill the resorts. Call ahead during busy periods so you can be dropped off at the appropriate pier by the speedboat operators.

Each of the southwestern beaches has a handful of options. Hat Khlong Chao hosts some pricey boutique options but also has budget guesthouses tucked behind the main beach road. Families might like the mid-range and budget options on Ao Ngam Kho, which has a small sandy section in the far northern corner of the bay, though the rest is an old coral reef and rocky. Bring swim shoes.

Most guesthouses have on-site restaurants but there are also lots of independent places, mainly specialising in seafood.

Cozy House GUESTHOUSE $

(☎089 094 3650; www.kohkoodcozy.com; Khlong Yai; r incl breakfast 600-1200B; ❄📶) The go-to place for backpackers, Cozy is a 10-minute walk from delightful Hat Khlong Yai. There are cheap and cheerful fan rooms or more comfortable wooden bungalows with air-con.

Mangrove Bungalow BUNGALOW $

(☎089 936 2093; www.kohkood-mangrove.com; Ban Khlong Chao; r incl breakfast with fan/air-con 700-1000/1500B; ❄📶) With a mangrove forest on one side and the beach a short walk away, this collection of wooden bungalows is immersed in nature. Khlong Chao waterfall is a 20-minute kayak, and short walk, away. Rooms are clean and neat. Wi-fi is by reception only.

Koh Kood Ngamkho Resort BUNGALOW $$

(☎081 825 7076; www.kohkood-ngamkho.com; Ao Ngam Kho; r incl breakfast with fan/air-con 1000/1500-2000B; ❄📶) One of the best budget-by-the-beach options. Agreeably rustic huts perch on a forested hillside over a reasonable beach. They rent kayaks (250B per day) and there's a good restaurant, where you keep your own tab.

For Rest Boutique Guesthouse HOTEL $$

(☎084 524 4321; www.kohkoodboutiquehouse.com; Ao Prao; r incl breakfast 1200-2500B; ❄📶) Almost at the southernmost point of the island is this secluded, peaceful hotel that was converted from two traditional houses on stilts. Reservations are required. Closed low season (May to September).

Dusita HOTEL $$

(☎081 707 4546; www.dusitakohkood.net; Ao Ngam Kho; r 1490-3890B; ❄) Justifiably popular with families, whose children can run wild in the huge oceanfront garden. For everyone else, well-spaced-out, slightly dated bungalows provide a perfect retreat from the real world.

Siam Beach BUNGALOW $$

(☎084 332 0788; www.siambeachkohkood.net; Ao Bang Bao; r incl breakfast 1400-2500B; ❄@📶) The bungalows on stilts may not be outstanding, but you do get to gaze at one beautiful beach from your room. The cheaper fan rooms are a good deal. Wi-fi is in the lobby area only.

★**Bann Makok** HOTEL $$$

(☎081 643 9488; www.bannmakok.com; Khlong Yai Ki; r incl breakfast 3200-3800B; ❄@📶) 🌿 This boutique hotel, tucked into the mangroves, uses recycled timbers painted in vintage colours to create a maze of eight rooms that resembles a traditional pier fishing village. Common decks and reading nooks provide peaceful spaces to listen to birdsong or get lost in a book.

Tinkerbell Resort HOTEL $$$

(☎081 826 1188; www.tinkerbellresort.com; Hat Khlong Chao; r incl breakfast 9900-12,000B; ❄@📶🏊) Natural materials, like bamboo privacy fences and thatched roof villas, sew this resort seamlessly into the landscape. The terracotta-coloured bungalows open right onto a postcard-perfect beach; the villas behind come with plunge pools. The bar is a great spot for a sundowner. Expect 40% discounts in low season.

ℹ Information

There is now one ATM on Ko Kut (though when we visited it didn't contain money). Major resorts can exchange money. A small **hospital** (☎039 525748; ⏰8.30am-4.30pm) at Ban Khlong Mad can handle minor emergencies. The **police station** (☎039 525741) is nearby. Almost all hotels and guesthouses have wi-fi.

ℹ Getting There & Around

Ko Kut is accessible from the mainland pier of Laem Sok, 22km southeast of Trat, the nearest bus transfer point.

Koh Kood Princess (☎086 126 7860; www.kohkoodprincess.com) runs an air-con boat (one way 350B, one daily, one hour 40 minutes) that docks at Ao Salad, in the northeastern corner of the island. There's free land transfer on your arrival to the island's main beaches. **Boonsiri** (☎085 921 0111; www.boonsiriferry.com) has a catamaran (one way 500B, twice daily, 1½ hours) that runs from Laem Sok to Ao Salad.

Speedboats make the crossing to/from Laem Sok (one way 500B, 1½ hours) during high season and will drop you off at your hotel's pier.

Bang Bao Boat (www.bangbaoboat.com) is the archipelago's inter-island ferry running a daily loop from Ko Chang to Ko Kut. Boats depart Ko Chang at 9.30am and noon and arrive at Ko Wai (one way 400B, 30 minutes) then continue on to Ko Mak (one way 600B, one hour) and Ko Kut (900B, two hours).

Ko Kut's roads are steep, which rules out renting a push bike unless you are a champion cyclist. Motorbikes can be rented for 300B per day.

Hua Hin & the Upper Gulf

Includes ➡

Best Places to Eat

- Rang Yen Garden (p492)
- Hua Hin Koti (p501)
- Prikhorm (p515)
- In Town (p510)
- Rabieng Rim Nam (p489)

Best Places to Stay

- Baan Bayan (p500)
- Brassiere Beach (p505)
- Away Hua Hin (p505)
- House 73 (p509)
- Pattana Guest House (p499)

Why Go?

The upper gulf has long been the favoured playground of the Thai elite. Following in the footsteps of the royal family – every Thai king from Rama IV on has spent his summers at a variety of regal holiday homes here – they in turn have inspired countless domestic tourists to flock to this stretch of coast in pursuit of fun and fine seafood.

A winning combination of outdoor activities and culture is on offer here, with historic sites, national parks and long sandy beaches ideal for swimming all an easy hop from Bangkok. Increasing numbers of foreign travellers are also drawn here, by the twin delights of an unspoiled coastline and the relaxed pace of provincial life. There's not much diving or snorkelling, but kiteboarders will be in paradise as this part of the gulf is by far the best place in Thailand to ride the wind.

When to Go

- The best time to visit is during the hot and dry season (February to June). From July to October (southwest monsoon) and October to January (northeast monsoon) there is occasional rain and strong winds, but the region tends to stay drier than the rest of the country because of a geographic anomaly.
- During stormy periods, jellyfish are often carried close to shore, making swimming hazardous. Thais get around this by swimming fully clothed.

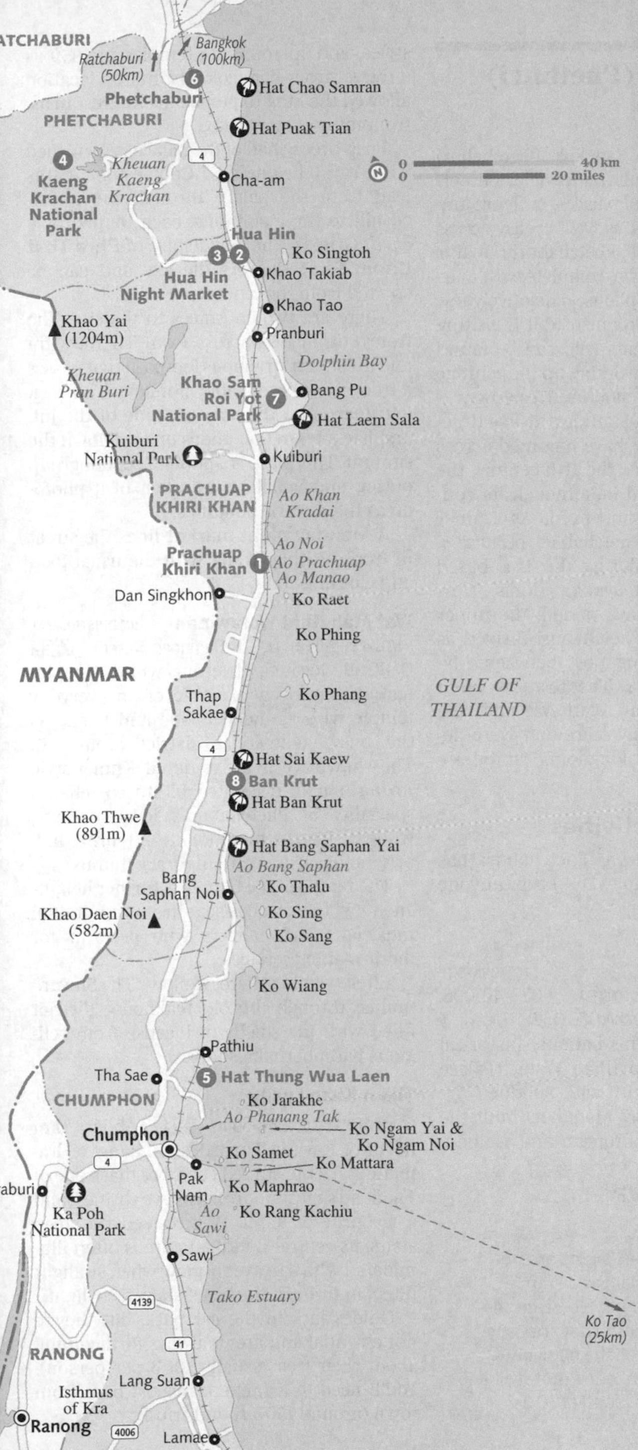

Hua Hin & the Upper Gulf Highlights

1 Motorcycling between curvaceous bays and limestone peaks in **Prachuap Khiri Khan** (p507).

2 Strolling the long blond coastline of **Hua Hin** (p493) dotted with wave-jumping kiteboarders.

3 Eating and shopping (and eating some more) at Hua Hin's **night market** (p500).

4 Escaping into the depths of **Kaeng Krachan National Park** (p490) and spotting gibbons and wild elephants.

5 Stepping off the backpacker trail on laid-back **Hat Thung Wua Laen** (p513).

6 Exploring the hilltop palace and underground caves, while dodging monkeys, in **Phetchaburi** (p486).

7 Making the pilgrimage to see the illuminated cave shrine of Tham Phraya Nakhon at **Khao Sam Roi Yot National Park** (p505).

8 Finding your own secluded strip of sand to laze on at **Ban Krut** (p511).

Phetchaburi (Phetburi)

เพชรบุรี

POP 23,235

An easy escape from Bangkok, Phetchaburi should be on every cultural traveller's itinerary. It has temples and palaces, outlying jungles and cave shrines, as well as easy access to the coast. Best of all, Phetchaburi remains a sleepy provincial town, complete with markets and old teak shophouses. Relatively few foreigners make it here; instead it is visiting groups of Thai students who can be found touring the sites and working up the courage to say 'hello' to any wandering Westerners.

Historically, Phetchaburi is a visible timeline of kingdoms that have migrated across Southeast Asia. During the 11th century the Khmer empire settled in, although its control was relatively short-lived. As Khmer power diminished, Phetchaburi became a strategic royal fort during the Thai-based Sukhothai and Ayuthaya kingdoms. During the stable Ayuthaya period, the upper gulf flourished and Phetchaburi thrived as a 17th-century trading post between Myanmar and Ayuthaya. The town is often referred to as a 'Living Ayuthaya', since the equivalent of the many relics that were destroyed in the former kingdom's capital are still intact here.

Sights & Activities

For such a small town, Phetchaburi has enough historic temples to keep anyone busy for the day.

Phra Nakhon Khiri Historical Park HISTORIC SITE

(อุทยานประวัติศาสตร์พระนครคีรี; ☎032 401006; 150B, tram return adult/child 50/15B; ⌚park & tram 8.30am-4.30pm) This national historical park sits regally atop Khao Wang (Palace Hill), surveying the city with subdued opulence. Rama IV (King Mongkut) built the palace, in a mix of European and Chinese styles, and surrounding temples in 1859 as a retreat from Bangkok. The hilltop location allowed the king to pursue his interest in astronomy and stargazing.

Each breezy hall of the palace is furnished with royal belongings. Cobblestone paths lead from the palace through the forested hill to three summits, each topped by a *chedi* (stupa). The white spire of **Phra That Chom Phet** skewers the sky and can be spotted from the city below.

There are two entrances to the site. The front entrance is across from Th Ratwithi and involves a strenuous footpath that passes a troop of unpredictable monkeys. The back entrance is on the opposite side of the hill and has a **tram** that glides up and down the summit. This place is a popular school-group outing and you'll be as much of a photo-op as the historic buildings.

A **Monday night market** lines the street in front of Khao Wang with the usual food and clothing stalls.

> **PHETCHABURI SIGHTSEEING**
>
> Some of the city's best sights are outside town, but don't let the distance deter you. Hire a *sŏrng·tăa·ou* (passenger pick-up truck) for the day (usually around 500B) to hit all the highlights. Alternatively, you can rent a motorbike (200B to 300B) or a bicycle (50B).

Wat Mahathat Worawihan BUDDHIST TEMPLE

(วัดมหาธาตุวรวิหาร; Th Damnoen Kasem) FREE Centrally located, gleaming white Wat Mahathat is a lovely example of an everyday temple with as much hustle and bustle as the busy commercial district around it. The showpiece is a five-tiered Khmer-style *prang* (stupa) decorated in stucco relief, a speciality of Phetchaburi's local artisans, while inside the main *wí·hăhn* (shrine hall or sanctuary) are contemporary murals.

The tempo of the temple is further heightened by the steady beat from traditional musicians and dancers who perform for merit-making services.

After visiting here, follow Th Suwanmunee through the old teakhouse district filled with the smells of incense from religious paraphernalia shops.

Tham Khao Luang CAVE

(ถ้ำเขาหลวง; ⌚8am-6pm) FREE About 4km north of town is Tham Khao Luang, a dramatic stalactite-stuffed chamber that's one of Thailand's most impressive cave shrines, and a favourite of Rama IV. Accessed via steep stairs, its central Buddha figure is often illuminated with a heavenly glow when sunlight filters in through the heart-shaped skylight.

Guides lurk in the car park, but they're not essential and aren't always forthcoming about their fees (usually 100B per person). You'll need to arrange transport here from town (around 150B round-trip).

At the opposite end of the chamber are a row of sitting Buddhas casting shadows on the undulating cavern wall.

The story is that Rama IV built the stone gate that separates the main chamber from a second chamber as a security measure for a couple who once lived in the cave. A figure of a prostrate body in the third chamber is said to represent the cycle of life and death but it hasn't experienced a peaceful resting place as bandits destroyed much of it in search of hidden treasures. Deeper in the cave is supposedly a rock formation that looks like Christ on the cross, but our eyes couldn't spot it. (Thais are especially imaginative at spotting familiar forms in cave stalactites.)

Around the entrance to the cave you'll meet brazen monkeys looking for handouts.

Phra Ram Ratchaniwet HISTORIC SITE

(พระรามราชนิเวศน์; ☎032 428083; Ban Peun Palace; admission 50B; ⏰8.30am-4.30pm Mon-Fri) An incredible art nouveau creation, construction of this elegant summer palace began in 1910 at the behest of Rama V (who died just after the project was started). It was designed by German architects, who used the opportunity to showcase contemporary design innovations; inside there are spacious sun-drenched rooms decorated with exquisite glazed tiles, stained glass, parquet floors and plenty of wrought-iron details.

The palace is on a military base 1km south of town; you may be required to show your passport.

While the structure is typical of Thailand in the early 20th century, a period that saw a local passion for erecting European-style buildings in an effort to keep up with the 'modern' architecture of Thailand's colonised neighbours, the scale of the palace is impressive. Check out the double-spiral staircase, which provides a classic debutante's debut, and the state-of-the-art, for the time, personal bathroom of the king.

Wat Kamphaeng Laeng BUDDHIST TEMPLE

(วัดกำแพงแลง; Th Phokarang) FREE A wonderful 12th-century remnant of the time when the Angkor (Khmer) kingdom stretched from present-day Cambodia all the way to the Malay peninsula, this ancient and once-ornate shrine was originally Hindu before Thailand's conversion to Buddhism. There is one intact sanctuary, flanked by two smaller shrines and crumbling sandstone walls, making for intriguing photo opportunities.

> **MONKEY BUSINESS**
>
> Phetchaburi is full of macaque monkeys who know no shame or fear. Having once just congregated on Khao Wang (Palace Hill), they have now spread to the surrounding streets, as well as to the road leading to Tham Khao Luang. There, they lurk by food stands, or eye up passing pedestrians as potential mugging victims. These apes love plastic bags – regarding them as a signal that you are carrying food – so be wary about displaying them. Keep a tight hold on camera bags too. Above all, don't feed or bait the monkeys. They do bite.

Tham Khao Bandai-It CAVE

(ถ้ำเขาบันไดอิฐ; donation appreciated; ⏰9am-4pm) This hillside monastery, 2km west of town, sprawls through several large caverns converted into Buddha shrines and meditation rooms. English-speaking guides (100B tip appreciated) lead tours, mainly as a precaution against the monkeys. One cavern contains a population of bats, and guides will instruct you not to look up with your mouth open (a good rule for everyday life).

Hat Puak Tian BEACH

(หาดปึกเตียน) On weekends locals come to this dark-sands beach, 20km southeast of Phetchaburi and famed for its role in Thai literature, to eat seafood and frolic in the surf. You'll need private transport to get here.

The beach is mentioned in the Thai epic poem *Phra Aphaimani,* written by Sunthorn Phu. A partially submerged statue of a giant woman standing offshore with an outstretched hand and a forlorn expression depicts a character from the poem who disguised herself as a beautiful temptress to win the love of the hero and imprison him on this beach. But he discovers her treachery (and her true ugliness) and with the help of a mermaid escapes to Ko Samet (which has nicer beaches so maybe he was onto something).

Festivals & Events

Phra Nakhon Khiri Fair CULTURAL

Centred on Khao Wang, this provincial-style celebration lasts nine days and takes place in late March and early April. Phra Nakhon Khiri is festooned with lights, there are traditional dance performances, craft and food displays, and a beauty contest.

Phetchaburi (Phetburi)

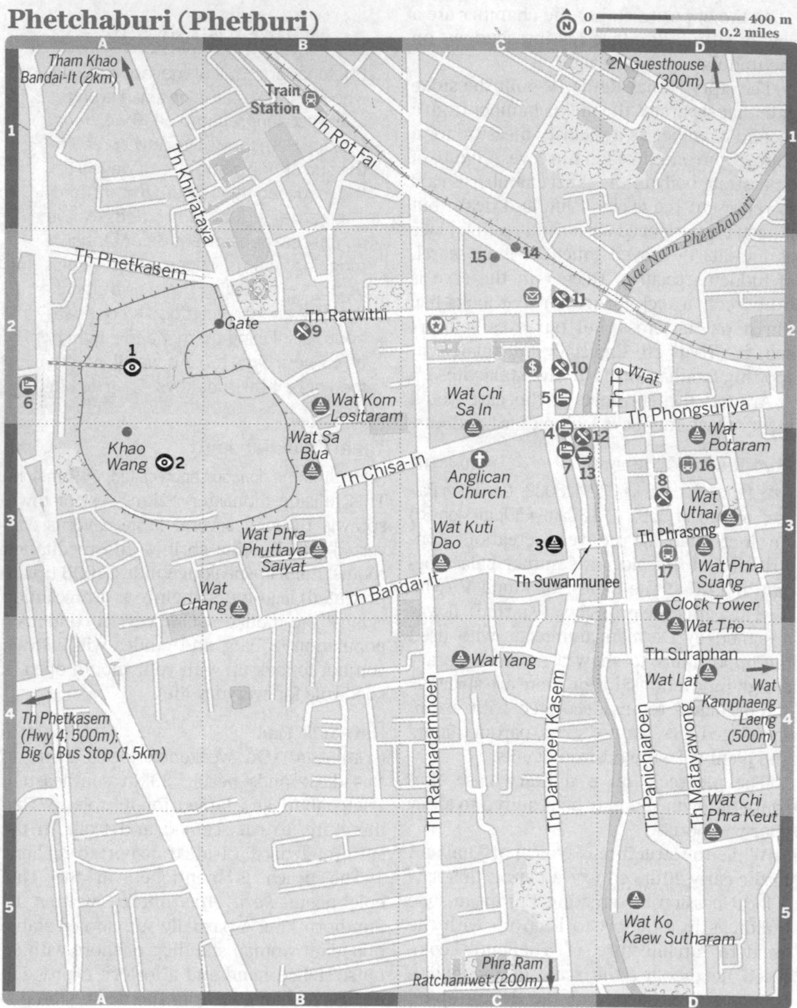

Sleeping

Once bereft of guesthouses, Phetchaburi's accommodation options have improved in recent years. But there aren't many places, so it's worth booking ahead, especially in high season (November to March).

2N Guesthouse GUESTHOUSE $

(☎081 817 1134; two_nguesthouse@hotmail.com; 98/3 Mu 2, Tambol Bankoom; d & tw 580B; ❄📶) In a secluded location away from the centre of town, the six rooms here are big and bright and come with small balconies. The friendly staff are a solid source of information and they offer free pick-ups and bicycles.

Sabaidee Resort GUESTHOUSE $

(☎086 344 4418; sabai2505@gmail.com; 65-67 Th Klongkrachang; r 250-500B; ❄📶) Basic but well-kept bungalows and rooms, some fan-only and all with shared bathrooms, are set around a small garden. There's a communal terrace overlooking the river that's a decent spot for a sundowner. The pleasant staff can arrange Thai cooking classes, and bikes (50B) and scooters (300B) can be hired.

Phetchaburi (Phetburi)

Sights
1 Phra Nakhon Khiri Historical Park A2
2 Phra That Chom Phet.......................... A3
3 Wat Mahathat Worawihan C3

Sleeping
4 J.J. Home.. C3
5 Sabaidee Resort C2
6 Sun Hotel.. A2
7 White Monkey C3

Eating
8 Day Market.. D3
9 Jek Meng B2
10 Ne & Nal... C2
11 Night Market.. C2
12 Rabieng Rim Nam C3

Drinking & Nightlife
13 Pagoda Cafe C3

Transport
14 Minivans to Bangkok............................ C2
15 Minivans to Kaeng Krachan National Park.................................... C2
16 Ordinary Buses to Cha-am & Hua Hin.. D3
17 Sŏrng·tăa·ou to Kaeng Krachan National Park.......................... D3

J.J. Home GUESTHOUSE $
(081 880 9286; a.sirapassorn@hotmail.com; 2 Th Chisa-In; r 300-500B;) On both sides of the road, the rooms here are clean and a decent deal. The more expensive options have private bathrooms, air-con and shared balconies.

White Monkey GUESTHOUSE $$
(032 898238; whitemonkey.guesthouse@gmail.com; 78/7 Th Klongkrachang; r 600-1000B;) New, if pricey, guesthouse with bright, spacious, spick-and-span rooms (the more expensive have air-con and private bathrooms), a fine communal terrace and helpful English-speaking staff who can organise trips in the area.

Sun Hotel HOTEL $$
(032 401000; www.sunhotelthailand.com; 43/33 Soi Phetkasem; r 950B;) Sitting opposite the back entrance to Phra Nakhon Khiri, the Sun Hotel has professional staff and large, modern but uninspiring rooms. There's a pleasant cafe downstairs and you can rent bikes for 20B per hour.

Eating & Drinking

Surrounded by palm sugar plantations, Phetchaburi is famous for its sweet concoctions, including *kà·nŏm môr gaang* (egg custard) and the various 'golden' desserts made from egg yolks to portend good fortune. Nearby fruit orchards produce refreshingly aromatic *chom·pôo Phet* (Phetchaburi rose apple), pineapples and golden bananas.

★**Rabieng Rim Nam** INTERNATIONAL, THAI $
(032 425707; 1 Th Chisa-In; dishes 50-100B; 8am-midnight;) This riverside restaurant serves up terrific food in an agreeable atmosphere and the English-speaking owner is a fount of tourist information. The affiliated guesthouse has a few run-down but bearable rooms (120B), all with shared bathrooms.

Jek Meng THAI $
(www.jekmeng-noodle.com; 85 Th Ratwithi; dishes 50-100B; 7am-5pm) A cut above your average hole-in-the-wall joint, you can get curries and dumplings here, as well as fried rice and noodles. It's opposite the Shell petrol station. Look for the black-and-white checked tablecloths.

Ne & Nal THAI $
(Th Damnoen Kasem; dishes 30-50B; 8am-4pm) Great slow-cooked soups in claypots are the signature dishes at this casual place. Their *gŏo·ay đĕe·o gài* (chicken noodles) comes southern style with a chicken drumstick.

Night Market MARKET $
(Th Ratwithi; 4-10pm) Big and bustling from the late afternoon, head to this market for all the standard Thai fast-food favourites and decent barbecue.

Day Market MARKET $
(6am-6pm) A good spot for watching people, the day market, north of the clock tower, has food stalls on the perimeter serving the usual noodle dishes as well as specialities such as *kà·nŏm jeen tôrt man* (thin noodles with fried spicy fishcake) and the hot-season favourite *kôw châa pét·bù·ree* (moist chilled rice served with sweetmeats).

Pagoda Cafe CAFE
(95 Th Klongkrachang; tea/coffee from 35B; 9am-6pm Tue-Sun;) A hip cafe that draws lots of students and makes a wonderful

TRANSPORT TO/FROM PHETCHABURI

DESTINATION	BUS	MINIVAN	TRAIN
Bangkok Hualamphong			34-84B; 3-4hr; 11 daily; 1.51am-4.46pm
Bangkok Southern Bus Terminal	120B; 2-3hr; frequent	100B; 2hr; hourly; 4.30am-5pm	
Bangkok Victory Monument		100B; 2hr; every 45min; 4.30am-8pm	
Cha-am (from Th Matayawong)	30B; 45min; frequent		20-30B; 1hr; 3 daily
Hua Hin (from Th Matayawong)	40B; 1½ hr; frequent		13-34B; 2hr; 11 daily; 1.51am-4.46pm
Kaeng Krachan National Park		100B; 1hr; hourly; 8.30am-5pm	

air-conditioned retreat away from the afternoon sun.

Information

There's no formal information source in town, but all the guesthouses can provide up-to-date travel tips.

Main Post Office (cnr Th Ratwithi & Th Damnoen Kasem; ⏲8.30am-4.30pm Mon-Fri, 9am-noon Sat)

Police Station (☎032 425500; Th Ratwithi) Near the intersection of Th Ratchadamnoen.

Siam Commercial Bank (2 Th Damnoen Kasem; ⏲9.30am-3.30pm Mon-Fri) You can change money here and it has an ATM (as do other nearby banks).

Getting There & Away

Air-conditioned buses to Bangkok's southern bus terminal leave from opposite the Big C department store on Th Phetkasem outside town. Southbound buses and minivans stop outside Big C. Motorcycle taxis await and charge 50B to take you into town.

Minivans to Bangkok (Victory Monument and the southern bus terminal) and Kaeng Krachan National Park leave from close to the night market.

Ordinary buses to Cha-am and Hua Hin stop in town near Th Matayawong.

Frequent rail services run to/from Bangkok's Hualamphong station. Fares vary depending on the train and class.

Getting Around

Motorcycle taxis go anywhere in the town centre for 30B to 40B. *Sŏrng·tăa·ou* (passenger pick-up trucks) cost about the same. It's a 20-minute walk (1km) from the train station to the town centre.

All the guesthouses hire out bicycles (50B per day) and motorbikes (200B to 300B per day).

Kaeng Krachan National Park อุทยานแห่งชาติแก่งกระจาน

Wake to an eerie symphony of gibbon calls as the early morning mist hangs limply above the forest canopy. Hike through lush forests in search of elephant herds and other wildlife at the communal watering holes. Or sweat through your clothes as you summit the park's highest peak. At 3000 sq km, Thailand's largest **national park** (☎032 459291; www.dnp.go.th; 300B; ⏲visitors centre 8.30am-4.30pm) is surprisingly close to civilisation but shelters an intense tangle of wilderness that sees relatively few tourists. Two rivers (Mae Nam Phetchaburi and Mae Nam Pranburi), a large lake and abundant rainfall keep the place green year-round. Animal life is prolific and includes wild elephants, deer, gibbons, boars, dusky langurs and wild cattle.

This park also occupies an interesting, overlapping biozone for birds as the southernmost spot for northern species and the northernmost for southern species. There are about 400 species of birds, including hornbills, as well as pheasants and other ground dwellers.

Activities

Hiking is the best way to explore the park. Most of the trails are signed and branch off the main road. The **Nam Tok Tho Thip** trail starts at the Km 36 marker and continues for 4km to an 18-tiered waterfall. **Phanoen Thung** (1112m) is the park's highest point and can be summited via a 6km hike that starts at the Km 27 marker. Note that most trails, including the one to Phanoen Thung, are closed during the rainy season (August to October).

The twin waterfalls of **Pa La-U Yai** and **Pa La-U Noi** in the southern section of the park are popular with day trippers on tours from Hua Hin and stay open in the rainy season, when they are in full flow. It's also possible to organise mountain biking in the park from Hua Hin.

Tourist infrastructure in Kaeng Krachan is somewhat limited and the roads can be rough. The park rangers can help arrange camping-gear rental, food and transport, which you'll need to go deep into the park where the wildlife is. There are crowds on weekends and holidays but weekdays should be mostly free of people. The best months to visit are between November and April.

Sleeping & Eating

There are various **bungalows** (02 562 0760; www.dnp.go.th/parkreserve; bungalows from 1200B) within the park, mainly near the reservoir. These sleep from four to six people and are simple affairs with fans and fridges. There are also **campsites** (per person 60-90B), including a pleasant grassy one near the reservoir at the visitors centre, and a modest restaurant. Tents can be rented at the visitors centre. Bear in mind that you can't stay overnight during the rainy season and that the campsites and bungalows are a fair distance from where the animals roam.

A&B Bungalows BUNGALOW $$
(089 891 2328; bungalow for 2 people 1000B;) On the road out to the Kaeng Krachan National Park entrance, about 3.5km before reaching the visitors centre, this family-run place is popular with birdwatching groups. There's an attached restaurant that can provide you with a packed lunch.

Getting There & Away

Kaeng Krachan is 52km southwest of Phetchaburi, with the southern edge of the park 35km from Hua Hin. If you have your own vehicle, drive 20km south from Phetchaburi on Hwy 4 to the town of Tha Yang. Turn right (west) and after 38km you'll reach the visitors centre. You use the same access road from Tha Yang if coming south from Hua Hin.

You can also reach the park by **minivan** (089 231 5810; one way 100B; hourly 8.30am-5.30pm) from Phetchaburi. Alternatively you can catch a *sŏrng·tăa·ou* (80B, 1½ hours, 6am to 2pm) from Phetchaburi (near the clock tower) to the village of Ban Kaeng Krachan, 4km before the park. From the village, you can charter transport to the park. You can also hire your own *sŏrng·tăa·ou* all the way to the park; expect to pay around 1500B for the return trip.

Minivan tours also operate from Hua Hin.

Cha-am ชะอำ

POP 35,581

Cheap and cheerful Cha-am is a popular beach getaway for working-class families and Bangkok students. On weekends and public holidays, neon-painted buses (called '*chor ching cha*'), their sound systems pumping, deliver groups of holidaymakers. It is a very Thai-style beach party, with eating and drinking marathons held around umbrella-shaded beach chairs and tables. Entertainment is provided by the banana boats that zip back and forth, eventually making a final jack-knife turn that throws the passengers into the sea. Applause and giggles usually follow from the beachside audience.

Cha-am doesn't see many foreigners; visitors are usually older Europeans who winter here instead of more expensive Hua Hin. And there are even fewer swimsuits on display as most Thais frolic in the ocean in T-shirts and shorts. But Cha-am's beach is long, wide and sandy, the grey-blue water is clean and calm, the seafood is superb, the people-watching entertaining and the prices are some of the most affordable anywhere on the coast.

Festivals & Events

Crab Festival FOOD
(Feb) In February, Cha-am celebrates one of its local marine delicacies: blue crabs. Food stalls, concerts and lots of neon turn the beachfront into a pedestrian party.

Gin Hoy, Do Nok, Tuk Meuk FOOD
(Sep) You really can do it all at this annual festival held in September. The English translation means 'Eat Shellfish, Watch Birds, Catch Squid' and is a catchy slogan for all of Cha-am's local attractions and fishing traditions. Mainly it is a food festival showcasing a variety of shellfish but there are also birdwatching events at nearby sanctuaries and squid-fishing demonstrations.

Cha'am International Kite Festival SPORTS
(Mar) Every March, kites from around Thailand and the world take to the skies over the beach for two days.

Sleeping

Cha-am has two basic types of accommodation: hotels along the beach road (Th Ruamjit) and more expensive 'condotel' developments (condominiums with a kitchen and operating under a rental program). Expect a discount on posted rates for weekday stays. For guesthouses, head to Soi 1 North off Th Ruamjit (the beach road) or raucous Soi Bus Station, a few hundred metres south of Soi 1 North.

The northern end of the beach (Long Beach) has a wider, blonder strip of sand and is the most crowded. Th Narathip divides the beach into north and south and the sois off Th Ruamjit are numbered in ascending order in both directions from this intersection.

Pa Ka Ma GUESTHOUSE **$$**
(032 433504; Soi 1 North, Th Ruamjit; r 600-1200B;) The best of the Soi 1 guesthouses: attractively designed and with better bathrooms than its competitors. Comfy beds, and the honeymoon suite has an attractive terrace. Not much English spoken.

Charlie House GUESTHOUSE **$$**
(032 433799; www.charlie-chaam.com; 241/60-61, Soi 1 North, Th Ruamjit; r 650-800B;) This quiet place boasts a lime-green lobby and modern, comfortable rooms, although the bathrooms are cramped. Don't confuse it with the institutional Charlie Place or Charlie TV on the same soi.

Cha-am Mathong Guesthouse GUESTHOUSE **$$**
(081 550 2947; www.chaammathong.com; 263/47-48 Th Ruamjit; r 600-700B;) No frills here, but the rooms are clean and you're right across from the beach. Better rooms have sea views and small balconies. The attached restaurant does brisk business during the day.

Baan Pantai Resort HOTEL **$$$**
(032 433111; www.baanpantai.com; 247/58 Th Ruamjit; r from 2000B;) Rather more upmarket than most hotels in Cha-am, this family-friendly place has a huge pool, a small fitness centre and the beach is just across the road. Rooms are big with great beds and all come with terraces.

Eating

From your deck chair you can wave down vendors selling seafood, or order from the many nearby beachfront restaurants and they'll deliver. At the far northern end of the beach, seafood restaurants with reasonable prices can be found at the fishing pier. There's also a large night market on Th Narathip close to the train station.

★ **Rang Yen Garden** THAI **$**
(032 471267; 259/40 Th Ruamjit; dishes 60-180B; 11am-10pm Nov-Apr) This lush garden restaurant is a cosy and friendly spot to feel at home after a day of feeling like a foreigner. It serves up Thai favourites and is only open in the high season.

Hello Restaurant INTERNATIONAL, THAI **$$**
(Soi Bus Station, Th Ruamjit; dishes from 155B; 10am-10pm;) The French chef here turns

ANIMAL ENCOUNTERS

Modern sensibilities have turned away from circus-like animal attractions but many well-intentioned animal lovers curious to see Thailand's iconic creatures (such as elephants, tigers and monkeys) unwittingly contribute to an industry that is poorly regulated and exploitative. Wild animals are often trapped and then disfigured to make them less dangerous (tigers sometimes have their claws and teeth removed), they are acquired as pets and then neglected or inhumanely confined, or abandoned when they are too sick or infirm to work.

Wildlife Friends Foundation Thailand runs a **wildlife rescue centre** (032 458135; www.wfft.org; Wat Khao Luk Chang), 35km northwest of Cha-am, that adopts and cares for abused and abandoned animals. Most of these animals are creatures that can't return to the wild due to injuries or lack of survival skills. The centre cares for 400 animals, including bears, tigers, gibbons, macaques, loris and birds. There is also an affiliated elephant rescue program that buys and shelters animals being used to beg on the streets.

The centre offers a **full access tour** (1800B per person) that introduces the animals and discusses their rescue histories. The tour includes a visit with the elephants (but no rides are offered) and hotel transfer from Hua Hin or Cha-am.

Those looking for a more intimate connection with the animals can volunteer to help at the centre. An average day could involve chopping vegetables to feed sun bears, cleaning enclosures and rowing out to the gibbon islands with a daily meal. Volunteers are required to stay a minimum of one week and have to make a compulsory donation (from US$455/16,152B) to the centre. Contact the centre or visit the website (www.wildlifevolunteer.org) for details.

TRANSPORT TO/FROM CHA-AM

DESTINATION	BUS	MINIVAN	TRAIN
Bangkok Hualamphong			40-90B; 4½hr; 4.55am & 2.33pm daily
Bangkok Southern Bus Terminal	155B; 3hr; frequent	160B; 2½hr; hourly; 7am-6pm	
Bangkok Victory Monument		160B; 2½hr; every 30min; 7am-6.30pm	
Hua Hin	25B; 45min; frequent	40B; 30min; frequent	30-40B; 1½hr; 2 daily
Phetchaburi	30B; 45min; frequent	50B; 30min; frequent	20-30B; 1hr; 3 daily

out high-quality international dishes, as well as Thai standards and lots of seafood.

Bella Pizza ITALIAN, THAI $$
(☎032 470980; 328/19 Th Nongjiang; pizzas from 175B; ⊙4-11pm) Located at the southern end of town (but they deliver), this popular, Italian-run pizza place has a large, quiet outdoor terrace. Thai food is on offer as well.

Information

Phetkasem Hwy runs through Cha-am's busy town centre, which is about 1km away from the beach. The town centre is where you'll find the main bus stop, banks, the main post office, an outdoor market and the train station.

There are plenty of banks along Th Ruamjit with ATMs and exchange services.

Only Chaam (www.onlychaam.com) is a useful online blog and website about visiting Cha-am.

Post Office (Th Ruamjit; ⊙8.30am-4.40pm Mon-Fri, 9am-noon Sat) On the main beach strip.

Tourism Authority of Thailand (TAT; ☎032 471005; tatphet@tat.or.th; 500/51 Th Phetkasem; ⊙8.30am-4.30pm) On Phetkasem Hwy, 500m south of town. The staff speak good English.

Getting There & Away

Buses stop on Phetkasem Hwy at the intersection with Th Narathip. Frequent buses run to/from Bangkok, Phetchaburi and Hua Hin.

Minivans to Bangkok's Victory Monument and Bangkok's southern bus terminal leave from Soi Bus Station, in between Th Ruamjit and Th Chao Lay. Other minivan destinations include Hua Hin and Phetchaburi. A private taxi to Hua Hin costs 500B.

The **train station** (Th Narathip) is west of Phetkasem Hwy. From Bangkok's Hualamphong station trains go to Cha-am and continue on to Hua Hin. Note that Cha-am is listed in the timetable only in Thai as 'Ban Cha-am'.

Getting Around

From the city centre to the beach it's a quick motorcycle ride (40B). Some drivers may try to take you to hotels that offer commissions instead of the one you requested.

You can hire motorcycles for 200B per day all along Th Ruamjit. Bicycles are a good way to get around and are available everywhere for 20B per hour or 80B per day.

Hua Hin หัวหิน

POP 59,369

Thailand's original beach resort is no palm-fringed castaway island and arguably is the better for it. Instead, it is a delightful mix of city and sea with a cosmopolitan ambience, lively markets, tasty street eats, long beaches and a fully functional infrastructure.

Hua Hin traces its aristocratic roots to the 1920s when Rama VI (King Vajiravudh) and Rama VII (King Prajadhipok) built summer residences here to escape Bangkok's stifling climate. The most famous of the two is **Phra Ratchawang Klai Kangwon** (Far from Worries Palace), 3km north of town and still a royal residence today; it's so poetically named that Thais often invoke it as a city slogan. Rama VII's endorsement of Hua Hin and the construction of the southern railway made the town *the* place to be for Thai nobility who built their own summer residences beside the sea.

In the 1980s, luxury hotels started moving in and foreign tourists began arriving in numbers. Today, all the international hotel chains have properties in Hua Hin, and a growing number of wealthy expats retire to the condominiums that dot the town. Middle-class and high-society Thais from Bangkok swoop in on weekends, making parts of the city look a lot like upper Sukhumvit.

There's a lot of money swirling around but because this is a bustling Thai town, seafood is plentiful and affordable, there's cheap public transport for beach-hopping and it takes a lot less effort (and money) to get here from Bangkok than to the southern islands.

Hua Hin

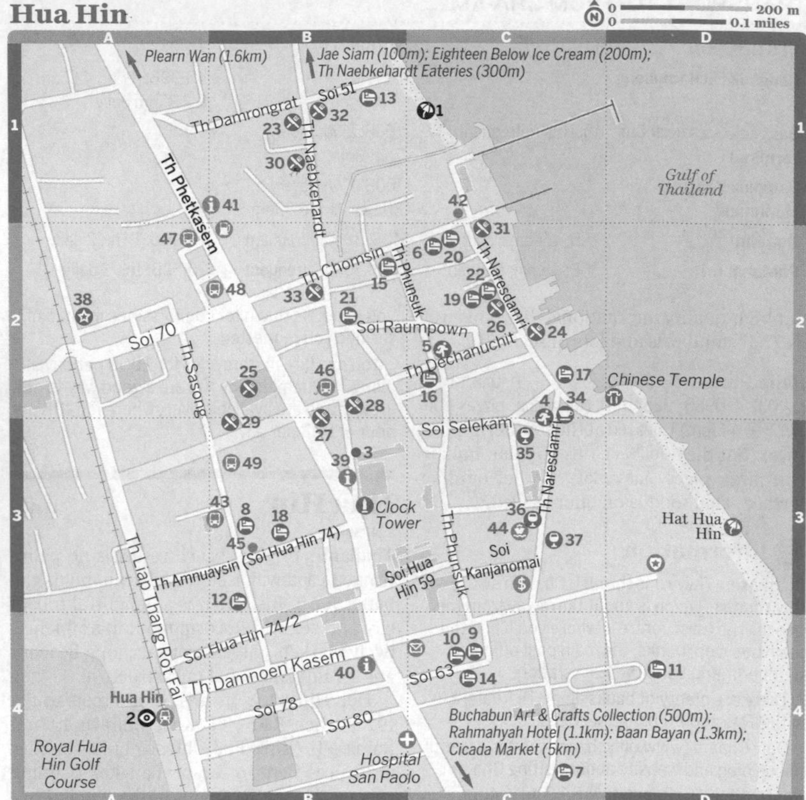

Sights

The city's beaches are numerous, wide and long; swimming is safe, and Hua Hin continues to enjoy some of the peninsula's driest weather. During the rainy season (July to September) watch out for jellyfish.

Hua Hin Town เมืองหัวหิน

A former fishing village, Hua Hin town retains links with its past with an old teak shophouse district bisected by narrow sois, pier houses that have been converted into restaurants and guesthouses, and a busy pier still in use today. South of the harbour is a rocky headland that inspired the name 'Hua Hin', which means 'Stone Head'. In the commercial heart are busy markets and shops selling all the things you forgot to pack.

Hat Hua Hin BEACH

(หาดหัวหิน; public access via eastern end of Th Damnoen Kasem) When viewed from the main public entrance, Hua Hin's beach is a pleasant but not stunning stretch of sand punctuated by round, smooth boulders. Don't be dismayed; this is the people-watching spot. If you're after swimming and sunbathing continue south where the sand is a fine white powder and the sea a calm grey-green.

The 5km beach stretches to a Buddha-adorned headland (Khao Takiab). The north end is where Thais come to photograph their friends wading ankle-deep in the sea and pony rides are offered to anyone standing still. Further south, resort towers rather than coconut trees line the interior of the beach, but that's a minor distraction if you're splashing around in the surf. Access roads lead to Th Phetkasem, where you can catch a green *sŏrng·tăa·ou* back to town.

Hua Hin Train Station HISTORIC SITE

(สถานีรถไฟหัวหิน; Th Liap Thang Rot Fai) An iconic piece of local architecture, the red-and-white pavilion that sits beside Hua

Hua Hin

Sights

1 Hat Hua Hin C1
Hat Hua Hin Neua .... (see 1)
2 Hua Hin Train Station A4

Activities, Courses & Tours

3 Hua Hin Adventure Tour B3
4 Hua Hin Golf Centre C2
5 Thai Thai Massage C2

Sleeping

6 Baan Chalelarn Hotel C2
7 Baan Laksasubha C4
8 Baan Manthana B3
9 Baan Oum-or Hotel C4
10 Ban Somboon C4
11 Centara Grand Resort & Villas D4
12 Euro-Hua Hin City Hotel YHA B3
Fulay Guesthouse .... (see 17)
13 Green Gallery B1
14 Hotel Alley C4
15 King's Home B2
16 Love Sea House C2
17 Mod C2
18 My Place Hua Hin B3
19 Pattana Guest House C2
20 Tai Tai Guest House C2
21 Tong-Mee House B2
22 Victor Guest House C2

Eating

23 Baan Tuayen Icy Beans B1
24 Chaolay C2
25 Chatchai Market B2
26 Cool Breeze C2
27 Hua Hin Koti B3
28 Jek Pia Coffeeshop B2
29 Night Market B3
30 Ratama B1
31 Sang Thai Restaurant C2
32 Sôm·đam Stand B1
33 Thanon Chomsin Food Stalls B2

Drinking & Nightlife

34 Coffee Club C2
35 El Murphy's Mexican Grill & Steakhouse C3
36 Lounge Bar C3
37 Mai Tai Cocktail & Beer Garden C3

Entertainment

38 Bang Bar A2

Information

39 Municipal Tourist Information Office B3
40 Municipal Tourist Information Office B4
41 Tourism Authority of Thailand B1
42 Tuk Tours C1

Transport

Air-con Buses to Bangkok .... (see 43)
43 Bangkok Bus Office B3
44 Lomprayah C3
45 Minivans to Bangkok B3
46 Minivans to Bangkok B2
47 Minivans to Bangkok's Victory Monument A2
48 Ordinary Buses to Phetchaburi & Cha-am B2
49 Sŏrng·tăa·ou to Khao Takiab & Buses to Pranburi B3

Hin's train station once served as the royal waiting room during Rama VI's reign. By cutting the journey time from Bangkok to a mere four hours, it was the arrival of the railway that made Hua Hin a tourist destination for the Bangkok-based monarchy and the city's elite. One hundred years later and even speeding minivan drivers fuelled by energy drinks can't do it much quicker.

North Hua Hin

The summer residences of the royal family and minor nobility dot the coast northwards from Hua Hin's fishing pier towards Cha-am.

Hat Hua Hin Neua BEACH
(หาดหัวหินเหนือ; North Hua Hin Beach; grounds 5.30-7.30am & 4-7pm) While the northern end of Hua Hin's beach is not its most spectacular section, it is lined with genteel Thai-Victorian garden estates bestowed with ocean-inspired names such as 'Listening to the Sea House'. The current king's palace lies about 3km north of town but visitors are only allowed on the **grounds** (passport ID required).

There are public access paths to the beach off Th Naebkehardt. On weekends, Th Naebkehardt is the preferred getaway for Bangkokians, some of whom still summer in the old-fashioned residences while others come to dine in the houses that have been converted into restaurants.

Plearn Wan NOTABLE BUILDING
(เพลินวาน; 032 520311; www.plearnwan.com; Th Phetkasem btwn Soi 38 & Soi 40; 9am-9pm) As much an art installation as a commercial enterprise, Plearn Wan is a recreation of the old-fashioned shophouses that once occupied the Thai-Chinese neighbourhoods of Bangkok and Hua Hin. There's a pharmacy selling

NEW ATTITUDES TOWARDS WINE

Common wisdom will tell you that tasty wine grapes don't grow alongside coconut trees. But advances in plant sciences and a global palette for wines has ushered in the geographic experiment dubbed New Latitude Wines, produced from grapes grown outside the traditional 30- to 50-degree parallels.

The New Latitudes' main challenge is to replicate the wine-producing grapes' preferred climate as best as possible. That means introducing a false dormancy or winter period through pruning, regulated irrigation and companion planting of grasses to prevent soil loss during the rainy season. If you're familiar with viticulture in the Old World, you'll be shocked to see all the cultivation rules Thai vineyards successfully break.

Wine experts have yet to crown a New Latitude that surpasses the grande dames, but they do fill a local niche. Siam Winery, the parent company of **Hua Hin Hills Vineyard**, aims to produce wines that pair with the complex flavours of Thai food. The vineyard grows colombard, chenin blanc, muscat, shiraz and sangiovese grapes, among others, and typically the citrus-leaning whites are a refreshing complement to the fireworks of most Thai dishes.

A wine drinker's palette is often altered in a hot climate. The thinner wines produced in Thailand tend to have a more satisfying effect than the bold chewy reds that pair well with a chilly spring day. Drinking red wine in Thailand has always been a challenge because the heat turns otherwise leathery notes straight into vinegar. To counteract the tropical factor, break yet another wine rule and chill reds in the refrigerator to replicate 'cellar' temperature as close as possible.

(well actually displaying) roots and powders that Thai grandmothers once used, as well as music and clothes stores.

Phra Ratchaniwet Mrigadayavan HISTORIC SITE
(พระราชนิเวศนมฤคทายวัน; ☎032 508443; admission 50B; ⊙8.30am-4pm Thu-Tue) With a breezy seaside location 12km north of Hua Hin, this summer palace was built in 1924 during the reign of Rama VI. Set in a beautiful garden with statuesque trees and stunning sea views, it's a series of interlinked teak houses with tall, shuttered windows and patterned fretwork built upon stilts forming a shaded ground-level boardwalk.

The functional but elegant style of the palace was a result of Rama VI suffering from rheumatoid arthritis; the court's Italian architect designed it to maximise air circulation and make the most of the seaside location. There's not a huge amount to see (a small selection of royal photos is on display), but it's a tranquil spot and Thais flock here to pay their respects.

The palace is within the grounds of Camp Rama VI, a military base, and you may need to show ID (passport). It is easiest to get here with private transport but you can also catch a Hua Hin–Cha-am bus and ask to be dropped off opposite the camp's front gate. Motorcycle taxis are sometimes waiting to take you the remaining 2km. As this is a royal palace, legs and arms should be covered, otherwise you'll be given a sarong-like garment to hide your limbs.

Inland from Hua Hin

Baan Silapin GALLERY
(บานศิลปิน; ☎032534830; www.huahinartistvillage.wordpress.com; Th Hua Hin-Pa Lu-U; art classes per hr adult/child 150/100B; ⊙10am-5pm Tue-Sun) Local painter Tawee Kase-ngam established this artist collective in a shady grove 4km west of Th Phetkasem. The galleries and studio spaces showcase the works of 19 artists, many of whom opted out of Bangkok's fast-paced art world in favour of Hua Hin's more relaxed atmosphere and scenic landscape of mountains and sea.

There are rotating exhibitions, while clay huts shelter the playful sculptures. **Art classes** are available for adults on Tuesday and Thursday and for children on Saturday.

Hua Hin Hills Vineyard VINEYARD
(ไร่องุ่นหัวหินฮิลล วินยารด; ☎081 701 0222; www.huahinhillsvineyard.com; Th Hua Hin-Pa Lu-U; vineyard tour 1700-2400B, wine tasting 3 glasses 290B; ⊙9am-7pm) This vineyard is nestled in a scenic mountain valley 45km west of Hua Hin. The loamy sand and slate soil feeds Rhone grape varieties that are used in their Monsoon Valley wine label. There are daily **vineyard tours** from 1700B, including wine, an excellent

three-course meal and return transport. Alternatively, you can just do the **wine tasting**.

The most expensive tour also includes the completely unnecessary option of an elephant ride. There's also a *pétanque* course, mountain biking and the picturesque Sala Wine Bar & Bistro.

A vineyard shuttle leaves the affiliated **Hua Hin Hills Wine Cellar store** (☎032 511497; 2F Villa Market, Th Phetkasem) at 10.30am and 3pm and returns at 1.30pm and 6pm; a return ticket is 300B.

Khao Takiab เขาตะเกียบ

About 7km south of Hua Hin, Monumental Chopstick Mountain guards the southern end of Hua Hin beach and is adorned with a giant standing Buddha. Atop the 272m mountain is **Wat Khao Lat**, a Thai-Chinese temple, and many resident monkeys who are not to be trusted – but the views are great. On the southern side of Khao Takiab is **Suan Son Pradipath** (Sea Pine Garden), a muddy beach maintained by the army and popular with weekending Thais. Green *sǒrng·tǎa·ou* go all the way from Hua Hin to Khao Takiab village, where you'll find loads of simple Thai eateries serving fish straight off the fishing boats that dock here.

The nearby **Cicada Market** (Th Phetkasem; dishes 45-120B; ⊙4-11pm Fri & Sat, 4-10pm Sun) hosts lots of outdoor food stalls at the weekend and is a pleasant, mellow spot with live music from 7pm. It's just before Khao Takiab on the left-hand side of the road. You can catch a green *sǒrng·tǎa·ou* (20B, 6am to 9pm) from Hua Hin's night market; a hired túk-túk (pronounced *đúk đúk;* motorised three-wheeled taxi) will cost 150B one-way.

Activities

With nine courses scattered around its environs, Hua Hin continues to be an international and domestic golfing destination.

Cycling is a scenic and affordable option for touring Hua Hin's outlying attractions, especially since hiring a taxi to cover the same ground is ridiculously expensive. Don't be spooked by the busy thoroughfares; there are plenty of quiet byways where you can enjoy the scenery.

Kiteboarders flock to Hua Hin for the strong winds that blow almost all year round.

Kiteboarding Asia KITEBOARDING
(☎081 591 4593; www.kiteboardingasia.com; 143/8 Soi 75/1, Th Phetkasem, South Hua Hin; 3-day beginner course 11,000B) This long-established company operates three beachside shops that rent kiteboarding equipment and offer lessons. The three-day introductory course teaches beginners the physical mechanics of the sport, and the instructor recommends newbies come when the winds are blowing from the southeast (January to March) and the sea is less choppy.

Hua Hin Golf Centre GOLF
(☎032 530476; www.huahingolf.com; Th Selakam; ⊙noon-9pm) The friendly staff at this pro shop can steer you to the most affordable, well-maintained courses where the monkeys won't try to run off with your balls. The company also organises golf tours and rents sets of clubs (500B to 700B per day).

KITE CRAZY

Adding to the beauty of Hua Hin's beach are the kiteboarders flying and jumping above the ocean. Hua Hin is Thailand's kiteboarding, or kitesurfing, capital, blessed with strong, gusty winds, shallow water and a long, long beach off which to practise your moves.

From here down to Pranburi the winds blow from the northeast October to December, and then from the southeast January to May: perfect for kitesurfing. Even during the May to October rainy season there are plenty of days when the wind is fine for taking to the waves. In fact, this stretch of coast is so good for kiteboarding that Hua Hin hosted the Kiteboarding World Cup in 2010.

This is also the best place in Thailand to learn how to kiteboard, with a number of schools in Hua Hin offering tuition. After three days with them you can be leaping into the air too. The schools also cater for more advanced students, and you can qualify as an instructor here as well.

But if you prefer to stay on the ground while flying a kite, then check out the **Hua Hin International Kite Festival**. Staged every two years in March 12km north of town at the Rama VI military base, it's a chance to see stunt kiters in action, as well as kites of every conceivable size and colour.

SEVEN KINGS

If anyone needed further proof of Thailand's devotion to its monarchy, then the seven giant statues of the country's most revered kings newly erected in Ratchaphakdi Park outside Hua Hin are compelling evidence. Standing 14m high and weighing in at 30 tonnes each, the bronze statues tower over the park.

Cast in different foundries in central Thailand, the statues held up traffic for weeks as they were transported south to Hua Hin in convoys of flat-bed trucks that stretched for up to 200m.

The seven kings are Ramkhamhaeng, Naresuan, Narai, Taksin, Buddha Yodfa Chulalok, Mongkut and Chulalongkorn. Their statues will be the centrepiece of the 700-million-baht park located close to Klai Kangwon Palace, where the current king spends his summers, and are funded by the fiercely patriotic military.

With the army running Thailand since a May 2014 coup, the new park is symbolic of the way the military see the monarchy as central to Thailand's national identity. The kings have been carefully chosen to represent the most glorious periods of Thai history, and to hammer home the idea that only under the monarchy can the country prosper.

Black Mountain Golf Course GOLF
(☎032 618666; www.bmghuahin.com; green fees from 1800B, caddy 300B) The best course in Hua Hin, and one that has hosted Asian PGA tournaments. About 10km west of Hua Hin, its 18 holes are carved out of jungle and an old pineapple plantation and it retains some natural creeks as water hazards.

Thai Thai Massage MASSAGE
(20/1 Th Dechanuchit; massage from 250B; ⊙10am-11pm) There are luxury spas inside all the posh hotels, however if you want something less pricey but still a cut above the average, the trained and friendly masseuses at this respectable place get excellent feedback.

Courses

Thai Cooking Course Hua Hin COOKING COURSE
(☎081 572 3805; www.thai-cookingcourse.com; 19/95 Th Phetkasem; courses 1500B) Aspiring chefs should sign up for a one-day cooking class here that includes a market visit and recipe book. The course runs only if there are a minimum of three people.

Tours

There are many travel agencies in town offering day trips to nearby national parks. Unless you're in a group, you may have to wait until enough people sign up for the trip of your choice.

Hua Hin Adventure Tour ADVENTURE TOUR
(☎095 493 6942, 032 530314; www.huahinadventuretour.com; 69/7 Th Naebkehardt) Hua Hin Adventure Tour offers active excursions, including kayaking trips in the Khao Sam Roi Yot National Park and mountain biking in Kaeng Krachan National Park.

Hua Hin Bike Tours CYCLING
(☎081 173 4469; www.huahinbiketours.com; 15/120 Th Phetkasem btwn Soi 27 & 29; tours from 2000B) A husband-and-wife team operates this cycling company that leads day-long and multiday tours to a variety of attractions in and around Hua Hin. Pedal to the Hua Hin Hills Vineyard for some well-earned refreshment, tour the coastal byways south of Hua Hin, or ride among the limestone mountains of Khao Sam Roi Yot National Park.

They also rent premium bicycles (500B per day) for independent cyclists and can recommend routes. The same couple lead long-distance charity and corporate bike tours across Thailand; visit the parent company **Tour de Asia** (www.tourdeasia.org) for more information.

Festivals & Events

King's Cup Elephant Polo Tournament CULTURAL
(⊙Aug & Sep) This annual polo tournament involving pachyderms instead of ponies takes place in late August and early September. While this event raises money for elephant-welfare issues, it must be noted that using elephants for the purpose of entertainment, as this popular event does, is an elephant welfare issue in itself. For some background on the subject, see p492.

Hua Hin Jazz Festival JAZZ
(⊙Aug) In honour of the king's personal interest in the genre, the city that hosts royal

getaways also hosts an annual jazz festival featuring Thai and international performers. All events are free.

Sleeping

Most budget and midrange options are in the old shophouse district. It is an atmospheric setting with cheap food nearby but you'll have to 'commute' to the beach, either by walking to north Hat Hua Hin (best at low tide) or catching a *sŏrng·tăa·ou* a couple of kilometres to the southern end of Hat Hua Hin.

The top-end options are beachfront resorts sprawling south from the Sofitel. All the international brands have a presence in Hua Hin but we've only listed special local options for a more intimate experience.

Hua Hin Town

Victor Guest House GUESTHOUSE $
(032 511564; victorguesthouse@gmail.com; 60 Th Naresdamri; r 390-1290B;) Popular with both Thais and foreigners, this efficient guesthouse has solid rooms, a small garden and a central location. Helpful staff and a good source of travel tips.

Fulay Guesthouse GUESTHOUSE $
(032 513145; www.fulayhuahin.net; 110/1 Th Naresdamri; r 550-1050B;) With the waves crashing underneath and the floorboards creaking, this is a fine old-school pier guesthouse. Rooms aren't huge, but the beds are good and the bathrooms are OK.

Euro-Hua Hin City Hotel YHA HOSTEL $
(032 513130; www.huahineurohotel.com; 5/15 Th Sasong; r 250-1600B;) Some dorms are fan-only, all are old-fashioned and it feels a tad institutional, but the price is right for Hua Hin and the staff are friendly. The private rooms are sizeable, if overpriced. Add 50B to these prices if you don't belong to HI. It's off the road; look for the sign.

★ **Pattana Guest House** GUESTHOUSE $$
(032 513393; 52 Th Naresdamri; r 990B;) Located in a simple teak house tucked away down a soi, this recently remodelled guesthouse features a lovely, peaceful garden. All rooms are two-storey, with bathrooms and a small living room downstairs.

King's Home GUESTHOUSE $$
(089 052 0490; huahinkingshome@gmail.com; off Th Phunsuk; r 600-1400B;) Family-run guesthouse with loads of character; it's crammed with antiques and artefacts from the owners' travels across Southeast Asia. Decent-sized rooms, and it even has a small splash pool out back. They get a lot of repeat guests, which says it all.

Baan Chalelarn Hotel HOTEL $$
(032 531288; www.chalelarnhotel.com; 11 Th Chomsin; r 1000-1800B;) Chalelarn has a lobby with wooden floors, while the 12 big rooms are equipped with king-size beds. Verandahs and breakfast are part of the perks.

Baan Oum-or Hotel HOTEL $$
(081 944 9390; baan_oum-or@hotmail.com; 77/18-19 Soi 63, Th Phetkasem; r 800-1200B;) Rooms here are big and bright. There are only six of them so book ahead.

Love Sea House GUESTHOUSE $$
(080 079 0922; siamozohlie@hotmail.com; 35 Th Dechanuchit; r 700-1200B;) Pleasant, family-run guesthouse decked out in fresh blue and white colours. Clean, good-sized rooms and a handy location.

Tai Tai Guest House GUESTHOUSE $$
(032 512891; Kallaya_Lasen@hotmail.com; 1/8 Th Chomsin; r 700-900B;) Large rooms with excellent beds, mermaid murals and OK bathrooms. The more expensive rooms have verandahs and a bit of road noise. There's a cosy communal roof terrace.

Tong-Mee House GUESTHOUSE $$
(032 530725; tongmeehuahin@hotmail.com; 1 Soi Raumpown, Th Naebkehardt; r 600-1000B;) Hidden in a quiet residential soi, this long-running guesthouse has cosy and clean rooms with balconies. Book ahead.

Mod GUESTHOUSE $$
(032 512296; www.modguesthouse.com; Th Naresdamri; r 600-800B;) Refurbished and now more comfortable (better beds) than most pier guesthouses, the more expensive rooms here come with air-con and sea views. A few cheaper rooms lack windows and are fan-only.

Ban Somboon GUESTHOUSE $$
(032 511538; www.baansomboon.com; 13/4 Soi Hua Hin 63, Th Phetkasem; r 700B;) With family photos decorating the walls and a compact garden, this place on a very quiet centrally located soi is like staying at your favourite Thai auntie's house.

Hotel Alley HOTEL $$
(032 511787; www.hotelalleyhuahin.com; 13/5 Soi Hua Hin 63, Th Phetkasem; r 1300-1600B;) Hotel Alley is tucked away down a quiet soi,

with spacious and modern rooms decorated in pastel colours. Most have balconies and breakfast is included.

Baan Manthana HOTEL $$
(☎032 514223; www.manthanahouse.com; 24/10 Th Sasong; r 900-2500B;) With three separate wings, there's always space here even during public holidays. Rooms are comfortable and proper-sized and some have balconies. There's a small pool, too.

My Place Hua Hin HOTEL $$$
(☎032 514111; www.myplacehuahin.com; 17 Th Amnuaysin, Th Phetkasem; r 1850-4500B;) A smart, amiable and efficient place in the heart of the city with stylish, good-sized rooms that qualify it for boutique status. There's a rooftop swimming pool.

Hua Hin Beaches

Rahmahyah Hotel GUESTHOUSE $$
(☎032 532106; Rahmahyah@yahoo.co.uk; 113/10 Soi Hua Hin 67, Th Phetkasem, South Hua Hin; r 800-1300B;) Across the street from Market Village, about 1km south of town, is a small guesthouse enclave tucked between the high-end resorts, with beach access. The Rahmahyah is the best of the bunch with clean, functional rooms. Guests can use the communal swimming pool opposite. Book ahead here.

★**Baan Bayan** HOTEL $$$
(☎032 533540; www.baanbayanresort.com; 119 Th Phetkasem, South Hua Hin; r 3500-21,000B;) A beautiful teak house built in the early 20th century, Baan Bayan is perfect for travellers seeking a luxury experience without the overkill of a big resort. Airy, high-ceilinged rooms, attentive staff and the location is absolute beachfront.

Baan Laksasubha HOTEL $$$
(☎032 514525; www.baanlaksasubha.com; Th 53/7 Naresdamri; r 3675-11,525B;) At this petite resort owned by a scion of the royal family there are 16 much-in-demand cottages on offer. The decor is crisp and subdued, meandering garden paths lead to the beach and there's a dedicated kids' room with toys and books. The taxi drivers will understand you better if you say 'baan lak-su-pah'.

Green Gallery HOTEL $$$
(☎032 530487; www.greenhuahin.com; 3/1 Soi Hua Hin 51, Th Naebkehardt, North Hua Hin; r 2650-12,980B;) As cute as candy, this small hotel occupies a converted colonial-style beach house that was once the vacation home of a princess and is very popular with upmarket Thais. Every room is individually decorated in a quirky, arty style. The attached restaurant is recommended.

Centara Grand Resort & Villas HOTEL $$$
(☎032 512021; www.centarahotelsresorts.com; 1 Th Damnoen Kasem; r 3720-9450B;) The historic Railway Hotel, Hua Hin's first seaside hotel, has been restored to world-class levels. Fantastic grounds, great pool, beach access, huge rooms, many restaurants and super-smooth staff.

G Resort & Mall HOTEL $$$
(☎032 515199; www.ghuahin.com; 250/201 Th Phetkasem; r 2400-5900B;) A resort and shopping centre all in one: a combo designed to appeal to Asian tourists but also attracts a fair few Westerners. It has big, modern rooms with vast beds and decent balconies. Huge pool and the beach is a 200m walk away.

Eating

Jek Pia Coffeeshop THAI $
(51/6 Th Dechanuchit; dishes from 50B; ⊙6.30am-1.20pm & 5.30-8.30pm) More than just a coffeeshop, this 50-year-old restaurant is a culinary destination specialising in an extensive array of stir-fried seafood dishes. It's wildly popular with the locals – be prepared to queue for a table – and they stick rigidly to their serving hours; get here after 7.30pm and you won't be able to order.

Night Market MARKET $
(Th Dechanuchit btwn Th Phetkasem & Th Sasong; dishes from 50B; ⊙5pm-midnight) An attraction that rivals the beach, Hua Hin's night market mixes food and clothes and draws in both locals and visitors. Lobsters and king prawns appeal to the big spenders but the fare at stir-fry stalls is just as tasty. Try *pàt pǒng gà·rèe Ɓoo* (crab curry), *gûng tôrt* (fried shrimp) and *hǒy tôrt* (fried mussel omelette).

Thanon Chomsin Food Stalls FOOD STALL $
(cnr Th Chomsin & Th Naebkehardt; dishes 35-45B; ⊙9am-9pm) If you're after 100% authentic eats, check out the food stalls congregated at this popular lunch corner. Though the setting is humble, Thais are fastidious eaters and use a fork (or their fingers with a pinch of *kôw nĕe·o*) to remove the meat from the bones of *gài tôrt* (fried chicken) rather than putting teeth directly to flesh.

WEEKENDS EATING WITH BANGKOK'S THAIS

On weekends, a different kind of tidal system occurs in Hua Hin. Bangkok professionals flow in, filling up hotels and restaurants on Th Naebkehardt, washing over the night market or crowding into nightclubs. And then come Sunday they clog the roadways heading north, obeying the pull of the upcoming work week.

Their presence is so pronounced that there is an irresistible urge to join them. And because of restaurant features on Thai TV or in food magazines, everyone goes to the same places. So don your designer sunglasses and elbow your way to a table at one of these popular spots in North Hua Hin:

Sôm·đam Stand (Th Naebkehardt; dishes from 35B; ⏲10am-2pm) Across from Iammeuang Hotel is a *sôm·đam* stand that easily wipes out the country's supply of green papayas in one weekend. Great grilled chicken too.

Baan Tuayen Icy Beans (Th Naebkehardt; dishes from 55B; ⏲7am-10pm) New hipster hang-out that draws the crowds with three different menus for breakfast, lunch and dinner. The green curry with simmered pork is famous already, as are the red bean smoothies.

Eighteen Below Ice Cream (Th Naebkehardt; ice cream from 55B; ⏲11am-5pm Wed-Mon) At the end of the road behind Baan Talay Chine Hotel, this gourmet ice-cream shop is run by a trained chef and specialises in rich and creamy flavours.

Ratama (12/10 Th Naebkehardt; dishes from 120B; ⏲10am-10pm) Visiting high-society Thais like the menu here that runs from simple noodle dishes to great, spicy seafood curries. If you're feeling very Thai, go for the hot and sour chicken-feet soup.

Jae Siam (Th Naebkehardt; dishes from 35B; ⏲9am-10pm) Cruise by this open-air noodle shop, just before the Evergreen Hotel, where Hua Hin civil servants pack in on weekdays and Bangkokians come on weekends. The shop is famous for *gŏo·ay đĕe·o mŏo đŭn* (stewed pork noodles) and *gŏo·ay đĕe·o gài đŭn* (stewed chicken noodles).

Chatchai Market MARKET $

(Th Phetkasem; dishes from 35B; ⏲daylight hours) The city's day market resides in an historic building built in 1926 with a distinctive seven-eaved roof in honour of Rama VII. There are the usual market refreshments: morning vendors selling *bah·tôrng·gŏh* (Chinese-style doughnuts) and *gah·faa boh·rahn* (ancient-style coffee spiked with sweetened condensed milk); as well as all-day noodles with freshly made wontons, and the full assortment of fresh fruit.

★**Hua Hin Koti** CHINESE, THAI $$

(☎032 511252; 16/1 Th Dechanuchit; dishes from 120B; ⏲noon-10pm) Across from the night market, this Thai-Chinese restaurant is a national culinary luminary. Thais adore the fried crab balls, while foreigners swoon over *đôm yam gûng* (shrimp soup with lemon grass). And everyone loves the spicy seafood salad *(yam tá-lair)* and deep-fried fish with ginger.

Sang Thai Restaurant SEAFOOD $$

(Th Naresdamri; dishes from 150B; ⏲10am-11pm) One of a number of long-established pier-side restaurants, Sang Thai is a Hua Hin institution and a massive operation. There's a vast choice of seafood housed in giant tanks awaiting your decision. You can eat very well for not much, or spend lots if you want to feast on prime lobster.

Chaolay SEAFOOD $$

(15 Th Naresdamri; dishes from 150B; ⏲10am-10pm) An atmospheric old-time pier restaurant and always busy. There's a big open kitchen on the ground floor enabling you to see the chefs preparing your seafood selection. Ascend the stairs to find a table.

Cool Breeze MEDITERRANEAN $$

(62 Th Naresdamri; tapas from 70B; ⏲11am-11pm; 📶) Popular tapas joint spread over two floors. The daily set lunch (260B) is a good deal. Decent wine list and an amiable spot for a drink as well.

Drinking & Entertainment

Drinking destinations in Hua Hin are stuck in a time warp of sports bars or hostess bars – and sometimes you can't tell the difference. Try the posh hotels if you want something more sophisticated.

Mai Tai Cocktail & Beer Garden BAR
(33/12 Th Naresdamri; beers from 70B, cocktails from 129B; noon-1am; wi-fi) Cheap and convivial and it always gets a crowd. Grab a table on the outdoor terrace for a pre-dinner drink.

El Murphy's Mexican Grill & Steakhouse BAR
(25 Soi Selakam, Th Phunsuk; beers from 90B, cocktails from 180B; 7am-1.30am) Every sports bar needs a gimmick and this busy spot marries Mexico and Ireland. There's a big menu, live music and a pleasant vibe, although the beers aren't cheap.

Lounge Bar COCKTAIL BAR
(156 Th Naresdamri; cocktails from 150B; 10am-midnight; wi-fi) Upmarket for a Hua Hin bar, this place has reasonably priced cocktails and outdoor seating to watch the world go by. During the day it's fine for a coffee stop.

Coffee Club CAFE
(130/2 Th Naresdamri; coffee from 90B, sandwiches from 180B; 7am-10.30pm Mon-Thu, 7am-11pm Fri-Sun; wi-fi) This Starbucks-esque cafe serves many varieties of coffee and tea, as well as solid Western breakfasts, hefty sandwiches, salads and classic Thai dishes.

Bang Bar LIVE MUSIC
(Th Liap Thang Rot Fai) North of Soi 70 along Railway Rd are a string of Thai music bars, nearly all foreigner-free. This one stays packed to the early hours, with rotating singers and bands.

Information

EMERGENCY

Tourist Police (032 515995; Th Damnoen Kasem) At the eastern end of the street.

INTERNET ACCESS

Wi-fi is available all over Hua Hin, in guesthouses and cafes.

MEDICAL SERVICES

Bangkok Hospital Hua Hin (032 616800; www.bangkokhospital.com/huahin; Th Phetkasem btwn Soi Hua Hin 94 & 106) An outpost of the well-regarded hospital chain; it's in South Hua Hin.

Hospital San Paolo (032 532576; 222 Th Phetkasem) Just south of town with emergency facilities.

MONEY

There are exchange booths and ATMs all over town.

POST

Main Post Office (Th Damnoen Kasem; 8.30am-4.30pm Mon-Fri, 9am-noon Sat)

TOURIST INFORMATION

Municipal Tourist Information Office (032 511047; cnr Th Phetkasem & Th Damnoen Kasem; 8.30am-4.30pm Mon-Fri) Provides maps and information about Hua Hin. There's another branch (032 522797; Th Naebkehardt; 9am-7.30pm Mon-Fri, 9.30am-5pm Sat & Sun) near the clock tower.

Tourism Authority of Thailand (TAT; 032 513885; 39/4 Th Phetkasem; 8.30am-4.30pm) Staff here speak English and are quite helpful; the office is north of town near Soi Hua Hin 70.

TRAVEL AGENCIES

Tuk Tours (032 514281; www.tuktours.com; 2/1 Th Chomsin; 9am-6pm) Helpful, no-pressure place that can book activities and transport all around Thailand.

USEFUL WEBSITES

Hua Hin Today (www.huahintoday.com) Expat-published newspaper.

Tourism Hua Hin (www.tourismhuahin.com) A cursory intro to the city with a good rundown on the outlying area.

Getting There & Away

The **airport** (www.huahinairport.com) is 6km north of town, but only has charter services.

Hua Hin's **long-distance bus station** (Th Phetkasem btwn Soi Hua Hin 94 & 98) is located south of town and has services that go to Chiang Mai, Prachuap Khiri Khan, Phuket, Surat Thani and Ubon Ratchathani. Buses to Bangkok leave from a bus company's in-town **office** (Th Sasong), near the night market. Buses to Bangkok Suvarnabhumi International Airport leave from the long-distance bus station.

Ordinary buses depart from north of the market on Th Phetkasem, and destinations include Cha-am and Phetchaburi.

Lomprayah offers a bus-boat combination from Hua Hin to Ko Tao (1050B, seven to eight hours, 8.30am), as well as to Ko Pha-Ngan (1300B, nine hours, 8.30am) and Ko Samui (1400B, 10 hours, 8.30am).

Minivans go to Bangkok's southern bus terminal and Victory Monument. They leave from near the night market and from an office that is situated on the corner of Th Phetkasem and Th Chomsin.

There are frequent trains running to/from Bangkok's Hualamphong station and other stations on the southern railway line.

TRANSPORT TO/FROM HUA HIN

DESTINATION	BUS	MINIVAN	TRAIN
Bangkok Hualamphong			44-622B; 4-6hr; 13 daily; 12.45am-4.01pm
Bangkok Southern Bus Terminal	180B; 4½hr; 8 daily; 3am-9pm		
Bangkok Suvarnabhumi International Airport	294B; 5hr; 7 daily; 6am-6pm		
Bangkok Victory Monument		180B; 4hr; every 30min; 6am-7pm	
Cha-am	25B; 40min; frequent		20-30B; 2 daily
Chiang Mai	813B; 12hr; 3 daily; 8am, 5.30pm & 6pm		
Phetchaburi	40B; 1½hr; frequent		30-40B; 12 daily
Phuket	1011B; 9-10hr; 2 daily; 10am & 9pm		
Surat Thani	787B; 7-8hr; 2 daily; 10am & 10pm		
Ubon Ratchathani	695B; 13hr; 1 daily; 6pm		

Getting Around

Green *sŏrng·tăa·ou* depart from the corner of Th Sasong & Th Dechanuchit, near the night market, and travel south on Th Phetkasem to Khao Takiab (20B). Pranburi-bound buses (20B) depart from the same stop.

Túk-túk fares in Hua Hin are outrageous and start at a whopping 100B and barely budge from there. Motorcycle taxis are much more reasonable (40B to 50B) for short hops.

Motorcycles (200B to 300B per day) and bicycles (50B to 100B per day) can be hired from shops on Th Damnoen Kasem and Th Chomsin. **Thai Rent A Car** (☎ 02 737 8888; www.thairentacar.com) is a professional car-rental agency with competitive prices, a well-maintained fleet and hotel drop-offs.

Hua Hin to Pranburi

South of Hua Hin are a series of beaches framed by dramatic headlands that make great day trips when Hua Hin beach feels too urban.

Hat Khao Tao หาดเขาเต่า

About 13km south of Hua Hin, a barely inhabited beach stretches several kilometres south from Khao Takiab to Khao Tao (Turtle Mountain). It's far quieter and less developed than Hua Hin's beach: there are no high-rises, no beach chairs, no sarong sellers and no horseback riders.

The mountain has a sprawling temple dedicated to almost every imaginable deity: Buddha, Guan Yin (Chinese goddess of Mercy), Vishnu and even the Thai kings. Follow the trail towards the oceanfront to hike up to the Buddha on the hill.

To get here, take a Pranburi-bound bus from Hua Hin and ask to be dropped off at the turn-off for Khao Tao (20B); a motorbike taxi can take you to the temple (20B). A motorbike from Hua Hin will cost 200B one way. Return transport is rare, though you can always walk or flag down a ride as people are usually coming and going from the temple.

Hat Sai Noi หาดทรายน้อย

About 20km south of Hua Hin, a scenic cove, Hat Sai Noi, drops off quickly into the sea, providing a rare opportunity for deep-water swimming. Mostly patronised by Thais, nearby are all the amenities: simple seafood restaurants and even small guesthouses. For ideal seclusion, come on a weekday. The beach is south of Khao Tao on a lovely road that passes a reservoir and is lined with bougainvillea and limestone cliffs. To get there take a Pranburi-bound bus from Hua Hin and ask to be dropped off at the turn-off for Khao Tao (20B); then ask a motorcycle taxi to take you to Hat Sai Noi (60B). Getting back to the highway will be difficult but enquire at one of the restaurants for assistance.

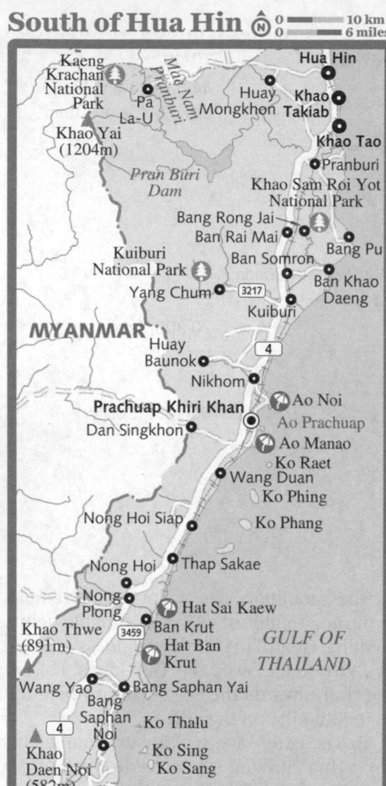

Pranburi & Around

POP 24,789

Continuing along the highway south from Hua Hin leads to the country 'suburb' of Pranburi district, which has become a popular coastal alternative for Bangkok Thais. Ever-more popular, some even go so far as to call it the 'Thai Riviera'. Locally, the fishing village and nearby beaches are known by a more humble name: **Pak Nam Pran** (mouth of the Pranburi River), which designates its geographic location only.

A coastal road separates a string of small villa-style resorts, and an increasing number of condo developments, from the beach. With each successive rainy season, the ocean claims more sand and a breakwater is being constructed along parts of the coastline. Since most of the visitors are Thai, the disappearing beach is of minor consequence. Instead, most domestic tourists come for sea views and the village's primary product: dried squid. Every morning the squid boats dock in the river, unload their catch and begin the process of sun-drying. It is a pungent but interesting affair with large drying racks spread out across town.

Bordering the river is an extensive mangrove forest, protected by the **Pranburi Forest Park** (☎032 621608). Within the park is a wooden walkway that explores the mangroves from the perspective of a mud-dweller, and a sea-pine-lined beach and accommodation facilities. The park also offers boat trips along the river and small canals.

The coastal road provides a pleasant trip to **Khao Kalok** (Skull Mountain), a mammoth headland that shelters a beautiful bay on the southern side. This southern beach is wide and sandy and far removed from the hubbub of Hua Hin and even from Pak Nam Pran for that matter, though it does get busy on weekends. Lazing along this stretch are several secluded boutique resorts that are ideal for honeymooners, or anyone looking to escape the crowds without travelling too far from civilisation.

The next southern bay is often called **Dolphin Bay**, because of the seasonal visits (February to May) from bottlenose dolphins and finless porpoise. Sculpted, jungle-covered islands sit scenically offshore and the beach is a lovely, wide strip of powdery sand. This area is a family favourite because the resorts are value-oriented, traffic is minimal and nightlife is nonexistent. You're also a few kilometres from the northern entrance to Khao Sam Roi Yot National Park.

Sleeping & Eating

It is mainly high-end here but not all of the beach resorts earn the price tag so be discerning when making online reservations for places not listed below. That said, this area has some of the best seaside boutique hotels in Thailand, making it a fine place to splash out.

Beach House GUESTHOUSE **$$**
(☎087 164 6307; karl@beachhousepranburi.com; Pak Nam Pran; r 700-1200B;) One of the cheapest options around, this affable, English-run guesthouse has comfortable, decent-sized rooms. It caters mainly to young kiteboarders; you can learn to kitesurf here and the wind is as good, if not better, than Hua Hin. The attached restaurant does a decent Sunday roast lunch.

★ Away Hua Hin HOTEL $$$
(☎089 144 6833; www.away-huahin.com; south of Khao Kalok; r 4500-6000B; ❄📶🏊) A boutique resort without pretence, and one of the more affordable in the area, its seven antique teak houses have been transported to this coastal patch of paradise and outfitted with huge, comfy beds and swish bathrooms.

The amiable owners, a Thai-Australian family, set a homey mood where breakfast is enjoyed at a common table in the 'big' house, providing instant camaraderie. Some villas offer extreme privacy while others accommodate families. The beach is just across the road.

★ Brassiere Beach HOTEL $$$
(☎032 630554; www.brassierebeach.com; Dolphin Bay; r 3000-9000B; ❄📶🏊) A delicious combination of privacy and personality; these 12 stucco villas abut the mountains of Khao Sam Roi Yot National Park and face a secluded beach, 100m from the nearest paved road. The rooms have an uncluttered Spanish colonial feel, some with roof decks and most with open-air showers. Ideal for people who want to leave the world behind for a while.

La a natu Bed & Bakery HOTEL $$$
(☎032 689941; www.laanatu.com; south of Khao Kalok; r 4488-15,888B; ❄📶🏊) Turning the Thai rice village into a luxury living experience is what La a natu does, and it does it with panache. The thatched roof villas rising on stilts have rounded modern corners and a Flintstones-esque playfulness to their design.

Each villa is private but evocative of traditional rustic lifestyles, with living quarters on the ground floor and often steep, ladderlike stairs leading to the sleeping area. Great food on offer too, and then there's the semi-private beach right on your doorstep.

Dolphin Bay Resort HOTEL $$$
(☎032 559333; www.dolphinbayresort.com; Dolphin Bay; r 1690-13,680B; ❄@📶🏊) The resort that defined Dolphin Bay as a family-friendly retreat offers a low-key holiday camp ambience with a variety of standard-issue, value-oriented bungalows and apartments, as well as a few very expensive ones. The grounds are large enough for kids to roam safely, there are two big pools and there's a great sandy beach opposite.

Palm Beach Resort & Hotel HOTEL $$$
(☎085 921 5533; www.palm-beachresort.com; Pak Nam Pran; r 2000-3000B; ❄📶🏊) Right by the beach and newly renovated, the 10 spacious rooms here are tastefully furnished and very comfortable. The staff are pleasant.

Khao Kalok Restaurant THAI $$
(Khao Kalok; dishes 90-300B; ⏰11am-10pm) At the southern base of the mountain, this open-air restaurant provides a front-row view of the moored fishing boats. Tasty dishes, like *gaang kĕe·o wăhn* (green curry), *Ƀlah mèuk gà·prow* (squid stir-fried with basil) and even the standard *pàt pàk roo·am* (stir-fried vegetables) arrive at a leisurely pace.

ℹ Getting There & Around

Pranburi is 35km south of Hua Hin and accessible by ordinary bus from Hua Hin's night market (20B). You'll be dropped off on the highway where you can catch a *sŏrng·tăa·ou* to Pak Nam Pran.

There is also a minivan service from Bangkok's Victory Monument to Pranburi (200B); if you're going to Dolphin Bay (sometimes referred to as Khao Sam Roi Yot Beach), you'll have to negotiate an additional fare with the driver (usually 100B).

If you want to explore the area, you'll need to rent a motorbike as public transport isn't an option.

Khao Sam Roi Yot National Park

อุทยานแห่งชาติเขาสามร้อยยอด

Towering limestone outcrops form a rocky jigsaw-puzzled landscape at this 98-sq-km **park** (☎032 821568; www.dnp.go.th; adult/child 200/100B), whose name means Three Hundred Mountain Peaks. There are also caves, beaches and coastal marshlands to explore for outdoor enthusiasts and birdwatchers.

With its proximity to Hua Hin, the park is well travelled by day trippers and contains a mix of public conservation land and private shrimp farms, so don't come expecting remote virgin territory.

Rama IV and a large entourage of Thai and European guests came here on 18 August 1868 to see a total solar eclipse (apparently predicted by the monarch himself) and to enjoy a feast prepared by a French chef. Two months later the king died from malaria, contracted from mosquito bites inflicted here. Today the risk of malaria in the park is low but the mosquitoes can be pesky, especially during the rainy season.

The **Khao Daeng Visitors Centre** in the southern end of the park has the largest collection of tourist information and English-speaking rangers. Maps are handed out at the entrance gates.

Travel agencies in Hua Hin run day trips to the park. Hua Hin Bike Tours (p498) offers cycling and hiking tours.

Sights & Activities

The maps provided at the park checkpoints are often in Thai. The following sites are listed in geographical order from north to south.

Tham Kaew CAVE

(ถ้ำแก้ว) Tham Kaew is a series of underground chambers and narrow passageways accessed by a steep scramble 128m up the mountain. It's not a popular stop, even though the stalactites and limestone formations here glitter with calcite crystals (hence the cave's name, 'Jewel Cave'). You can hire lamps from the booth at the footpath's entrance. The path can be slippery and dangerous.

Tham Phraya Nakhon & Hat Laem Sala CAVE

(ถ้ำพระยานคร/หาดแหลมศาลา) The park's most-visited attraction is this revered cave sheltering a royal *săh·lah* (meeting hall; often spelled *sala*) built for Rama V in 1890 that is often bathed in streams of light. It's accessed via a walking trail from the picturesque sandy beach of **Hat Laem Sala**, flanked on three sides by limestone hills and casuarinas.

The beach hosts a small visitors centre, restaurant, bungalows and campsites. The cave trail is 450m long and is steep, rocky and at times wet, so don't come in your flip-flops. Once there you'll find two large caverns with sinkholes – the meeting hall is the second of the two.

Reaching Laem Sala requires alternative travel since there is no road connection. It is reached by boat from Bang Pu (400B return), which sits beachfront from the turn-off from Tham Kaew. Alternatively, you can follow the steep footpath from Bang Pu for a 20-minute hike to the beach.

Tham Sai CAVE

(ถ้ำไทร) Sitting at the end of a 280m hillside trail, Tham Sai features a large single cavern filled with stalactites and stalagmites. Be careful of steep drop-offs inside and slippery footings. Usually, only more adventurous types undertake this cave. Villagers rent out lamps near the cave mouth. It is just north of Hat Sam Phraya.

Hat Sam Phraya BEACH

(หาดสามพระยา) This shady casuarina-lined beach is about 1km long and is a pleasant stop for a swim after a sweaty hike. There is a restaurant and toilets.

Khao Daeng HIKING

(เขาแดง) The turn-off to the trail winds through towering mountains promising a rewarding hike. The 30-minute steep trail that leads to the top of Khao Daeng delivers spectacular views of limestone cliffs against a jagged coastline.

Khlong Khao Daeng BIRDWATCHING

(คลองเขาแดง) You can hire a boat at Wat Khao Daeng for a cruise (500B, 50 minutes) along the canal in the morning or afternoon. Before heading out, chat with your prospective guide to see how well they speak English. Better guides will know the English names of common waterfowl and point them out to you.

Thung Sam Roi Yot BIRDWATCHING

(ทุ่งสามร้อยยอด) The country's largest freshwater marsh is recognised as a natural treasure and provides an important habitat for songbirds, waterbirds, amphibians and other wetland species. It sits in the western

BIRDS OF A FEATHER

At the intersection of the East Asian and Australian migration routes, Khao Sam Roi Yot National Park is home to as many as 300 migratory and resident bird species, including yellow bitterns, cinnamon bitterns, purple swamp hens, water rails, ruddy-breasted crakes, bronze-winged jacanas, grey herons, painted storks, whistling ducks, spotted eagles and black-headed ibises. The park is one of only two places in the country where the purple heron breeds.

Waterfowl are most commonly seen in the cool season from November to March. The birds come from as far as Siberia, China and northern Europe to winter here. Common places for birdwatchers are the Mangrove Centre, Khlong Khao Daeng and even some of the beaches.

Thai Birding (www.thaibirding.com) provides more in-depth information about the park's bird species and where to spot them.

WORTH A TRIP

WHERE THE ELEPHANTS ARE

Want to see herds of wild elephants enjoying an evening bath surrounded by the sounds of the jungle? Although urbanised Thailand seems hundreds of kilometres away from such a natural state, **Kuiburi National Park** (☎032 646292; Hwy 3217; adult/child 200/100B), southwest of Khao Sam Roi Yot National Park, shelters one of the country's largest herds of wild elephants (around 230 of them). The park provides an important habitat link between the rugged Myanmar border and Kaeng Krachan National Park, forming one of the largest intact forest tracts in Southeast Asia. The herds can frequently be found bathing at the watering ponds near the Pa Yang substation, which is equipped with wildlife-viewing platforms. You'll also likely spot barking deer, wild cattle and the inevitable monkeys.

Trekking and elephant-spotting tours include English-speaking guides and transport and can be arranged through the park headquarters.

Bungalow **accommodation** (☎02 562 0760; www.dnp.th.go/parkreserve; bungalows 1800B) is available for overnight stays with advance reservations.

corner of the park accessible from Hwy 4 (Th Phetkasem) at the Km 275.6 marker; hold on to your entrance-fee ticket to avoid having to pay again.

Mangrove Walk WALKING

Located behind the visitors centre in the southern end of the park is a 900m wooden boardwalk that circumnavigates a mangrove swamp popular for birdwatching and crab spotting. There are guides available for hire from the centre depending on availability and English-language skills.

Sleeping & Eating

There are private resorts within 4km of the park at Dolphin Bay.

National Parks Department CAMPGROUND $$

(☎02 562 0760; www.dnp.go.th/parkreserve; tent sites 160-225B, visitors centre bungalows 1200-1400B, Hat Laem Sala bungalows 1600-3000B) The National Parks Department hires out bungalows (sleeping up to six people) at Hat Laem Sala and at the visitors centre; advance reservations are required. You can pitch a tent at campsites near the Khao Daeng viewpoint, Hat Laem Sala or Hat Sam Phraya. There are basic restaurants at all these locations, as well as lots of monkeys.

Getting There & Away

The park is around 40km south of Hua Hin, and best visited by vehicle. There are two main entrances into the park. The turn-off for the northern entrance is at Km 256 marker on Hwy 4 (Th Phetkasem). The southern entrance is off the Km 286.5 marker.

If there's a group of you, a taxi from Hua Hin is 1500B return. You can also visit on day tours from there. Alternatively, you can catch a minivan from Bangkok's Victory Monument to Pranburi (200B) and then hire a motorcycle to tour the park independently. You can also negotiate with the minivan driver to drop you off at the entrance to the park but then you won't have transport inside.

Prachuap Khiri Khan ประจวบคีรีขันธ์

POP 33,521

A sleepy seaside town, Prachuap Khiri Khan is a delightfully relaxed place; one of the real jewels of this part of Thailand. The broad bay is a tropical blue punctuated by bobbing fishing boats and there are tremendous beaches close by, all overlooked by honeycombed limestone mountains – scenery that you usually have to travel to the southern Andaman to find.

In recent years, foreigners have discovered Prachuap's charms and begun defecting from the overdeveloped Samui archipelago. Families especially are flocking here. But their numbers are still small compared to better-known destinations, leaving plenty of room on the beaches, at the hilltop temples and the many excellent seafood restaurants.

Sights & Activities

Khao Chong Krajok VIEWPOINT

(เขาช่องกระจก) At the northern end of town, Khao Chong Krajok ('Mirror Tunnel Mountain', so named for the mountain-side hole that seemingly reflects the sky) provides a beloved Prachuap tradition: climbing to the **temple** at the top, dodging ill-behaved monkeys and enjoying a view of the coastline.

Prachuap Khiri Khan

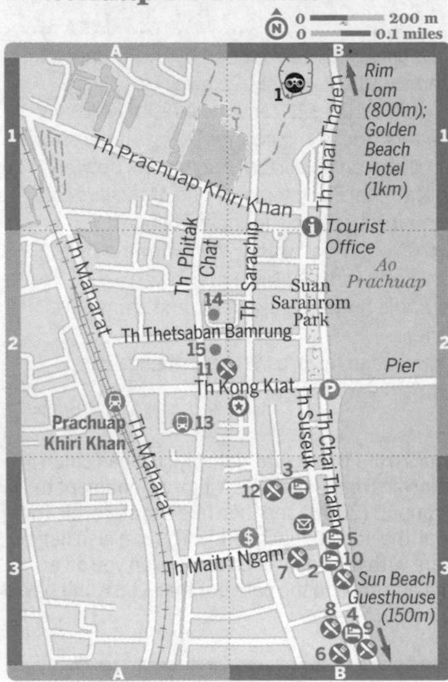

Prachuap Khiri Khan

Sights

1 Khao Chong Krajok B1

Sleeping

2 House 73 .... B3
3 Maggie's Homestay B3
4 Prachuap Beach Hotel B3
5 Thur Hostel B3

Eating

6 Ciao Pizza B3
7 Day Market B3
8 Grandma's B3
9 In Town B3
10 Longmug-Paa Lord B3
11 Night Market A2
12 Suan Krua B3

Drinking & Nightlife

Top Deck .... (see 5)

Transport

13 Air-con Buses to Hua Hin, Cha-am, Phetchaburi & Bangkok A2
14 Minivans to Ban Krut, Bang Saphan Yai & Chumphon A2
15 Minivans to Hua Hin & Bangkok A2

A long flight of stairs leads to a mountaintop temple established by Rama VI. From here there are perfect views of the town and the bay and even the border with Myanmar, just 12km away.

Don't bring food, drink or plastic bags with you as the monkeys will assume they're prizes worth having.

Ao Prachuap BAY

(อ่าวประจวบ) The town's crowning feature is Ao Prachuap (Prachuap Bay), a gracefully curving bay outlined by an oceanfront esplanade. In the cool hours of the morning and evening, locals run, shuffle or promenade along this route enjoying the ocean breezes and sea music.

On Friday and Saturday evenings, the esplanade hosts a Walking Street market, selling food, souvenirs and clothes.

North of Khao Chong Krajok, just over the bridge, the bay stretches peacefully to a toothy mountain that's less-visited than its in-town counterpart. There is a good, long sandy beach here running parallel with the road that only sees people on weekends, making it a fine place to idle and beachcomb. At the far northern end is a traditional fishing village and a pier where colourfully painted wooden trawlers tie up after a day or night at sea.

Wat Ao Noi BUDDHIST TEMPLE

(วัดอ่าวน้อย) FREE From Ao Prachuap, follow the coastal road 8km north as it skirts through the fishing village to reach this beautiful teak temple that straddles two bays (Ao Noi and Ao Khan Kradai). Limestone mountains pose photogenically in the background, while a dramatic nine-headed *naga* (mythical serpent) protects the temple's exterior. Inside are unique bas-relief murals depicting the *Jataka* (stories of Buddha's previous lives).

The temple grounds are forested with a variety of fruit trees (jackfruit, pomegranate, mango and rose apple) and a lotus pond filled with ravenous fish, eager to be fed by merit-makers. You'll catch an unpleasant odour nearby indicating that the temple is in the business of raising swiftlets for the profitable edible-bird's-nest industry; the punishment for stealing nests or eggs is severe (five years' imprisonment and 500,000B).

A craggy limestone mountain (Khao Khan Kradai) shelters the temple from the coast and contains a locally famous cave temple, known as Tham Phra Nawn (Sleeping Buddha Cave). The cave is accessible via a concrete trail that leads up and around the side of the hill, providing scenic views of Ao Khan Kradai and the foothills beyond. It is blissfully quiet and the forested hill is dotted with blooming cacti clinging to the craggy rocks. Inside the cave is a small cavern leading to a larger one that contains the eponymous reclining Buddha. If you have a torch (flashlight) you can proceed to a larger second chamber also containing Buddha images.

Ao Manao SWIMMING

(อ่าวมะนาว) On weekends, locals head to Ao Manao, an island-dotted bay 4km south of town ringed by a clean sandy beach. It is within Wing 5 of a Thai Air Force base and each and every week the beach is given a military-grade clean up.

There are the usual beach amenities: a restaurant as well as beach chairs, umbrellas and inner tubes for hire. En route to the beach you'll pass Thailand's Top Guns relaxing on a nearby golf course and driving range. You enter the base through a checkpoint on Th Suseuk from town; you may need to show your passport. The beach closes at 8pm.

Sleeping

There are an increasing number of oceanfront options, ranging from guesthouses to hotels, but with Prachuap becoming more popular, it's worth booking ahead. A number of homestays are scattered on and off Th Suseuk: look for the signs.

In Town

Thur Hostel HOSTEL $

(☎096 047 5622; Thurhostel@gmail.com; 58 Th Chai Thaleh; dm 350B, r 600-1000B;) A hostel right on the oceanfront that has small but well-maintained dorms with good, thick mattresses. The most expensive rooms have terraces with fine sea views.

Maggie's Homestay GUESTHOUSE $

(☎087 597 9720; 5 Soi Tampramuk; r 180-550B;) In the old-school backpacker tradition, owner Maggie oversees an eclectic collection of travellers who call her house home. Rooms in a converted traditional house mostly have shared bathrooms and range from the very basic to the comfortable, and there's a shady garden and shared kitchen facilities.

★**House 73** GUESTHOUSE $$

(☎086 046 3923; www.facebook.com/house73prachuab/info; 73 Th Suseuk; r 800-1300B;) Lovingly designed to within an inch of its life, this modernist boutique guesthouse is the most eye-catching building in town. There are only four (big) rooms here, all painted in pastel colours, with huge beds. There's a communal lounge and, best of all, a fantastic roof terrace with commanding views across the bay.

Sun Beach Guesthouse GUESTHOUSE $$

(☎032 604770; www.sunbeach-guesthouse.com; 160 Th Chai Thaleh; r 700-1000B;) With hotel amenities and guesthouse hospitality, Sun Beach is a superb midranger. Its neo-classical styling and bright-yellow paint liven things up, while the rooms are super-clean and come with large verandahs. Book ahead.

Prachuap Beach Hotel HOTEL $$

(☎032 601288; www.prachuapbeach.com; 123 Th Suseuk; r 700-1300B;) Crisp white linens and modern, comfortable rooms at this multistorey number. One side has fabulous sea views, while the other has decent, though not exciting, mountain views.

Out of Town

Natural Home GUESTHOUSE $

(☎032 602082; 149-151 Th Suanson; r 300-400B;) About 1km north of town, these bungalows are simple, but you are right across the

PRACHUAP KHIRI KHAN IN WORLD WAR II

Prachuap, and specifically Ao Manao, was one of seven points on the gulf coast where Japanese troops landed on 8 December 1941 during their invasion of Thailand. The Air Force base at Ao Manao was the site of fierce skirmishes, with the Japanese unable to capture it until the Thai government ordered its soldiers to stop fighting as an armistice had been arranged.

Several street names around town refer to that time, such as Phithak Chat (Defend Country), Salachip (Sacrifice Life) and Suseuk (Fight Battle), and an annual memorial service commemorates the soldiers and civilians who died in the battle.

road from Ao Prachuap's beach. The cheapest rooms are fan-only. Pleasant, English-speaking staff and a talkative parrot at reception.

Aow Noi Sea View HOTEL $$
(☎032 604440; www.aownoiseaview.com; Ao Noi; r 800-900B; ❄📶) North of town and close to the pier where fishing boats tie up, this secluded three-storey hotel has Ao Noi beach on its doorstep. Rooms with balconies are spacious, if a little old-fashioned.

Golden Beach Hotel HOTEL $$
(☎032 601626; www.goldenbeachprachuap.com; 113-115 Th Suanson; r 800B; ❄📶) A comfortable midrange option opposite Ao Prachuap's beach, and a decent deal these days for a sea view. The rooms are clean and sizeable.

Eating & Drinking

Restaurants in Prachuap are cheap and offer excellent seafood, while Western dishes are popping up more frequently. The **day market** (Th Maitri Ngam; ⏲daylight hours) is the place to get pineapples fresh from the orchards; ask the vendor to cut it for you. The **night market** (Th Kong Kiat; ⏲5-9pm) is small and has the usual stir-fry stalls.

Suan Krua VEGETARIAN $
(Soi Tampramuk; dishes from 35B; ⏲6.30am-3pm; 🌿) Super vegetarian, buffet-style eatery. Choose from an array of dishes, but they go fast and then the place shuts. Arrive here promptly and with an appetite.

Grandma's CAFE $
(☎081 743 9737; 238 Th Suseuk; dishes from 35B, coffee from 30B; ⏲7.30am-7pm; 📶) Cool cafe on the ground floor of a renovated 80-year-old traditional wooden house. Run by artists, it's a good spot for breakfast, or a coffee or smoothie break. There are also three tastefully decorated rooms for rent here (from 690B).

★**In Town** THAI $$
(118 Th Chai Thaleh; dishes from 80B; ⏲3-10pm) Now the go-to place for discerning locals, here you can eat outside while gazing at the bay. Great range of fresh seafood on display – barracuda, tuna, crab and shellfish – so you can point and pick, and they will tone down the spices if you ask.

Rim Lom SEAFOOD $$
(5 Th Suanson; dishes 90-190B; ⏲10am-10pm) Popular with the locals, the *pàt pǒng gà·rèe boo* (crab curry) comes with big chunks of sweet crab meat and the *yam tá-lair* (seafood salad) is spicy and zesty. It's 200m past the bridge on the left and right opposite Ao Prachuap beach.

Longmug-Paa Lord THAI $$
(Th Chai Thaleh; dishes from 100B; ⏲noon-10pm) Another open-air spot with great bay views that gets busy once the sun goes down. Choose from the wide selection of seafood on display.

Ciao Pizza ITALIAN $$
(Th Suseuk; pizzas from 180B; ⏲10am-2pm & 4-10pm) Ciao Pizza is Italian-owned; come here for pizzas, homemade pasta and gelato, as well as fresh bread baked daily and a takeaway selection of cheese, sausage and salami.

Top Deck BAR
(53 Th Chai Thaleh; beers from 60B, cocktails from 130B; ⏲1pm-midnight Thu-Tue; 📶) Prachuap is an early-to-bed town, but at the Top Deck

TRANSPORT TO/FROM PRACHUAP KHIRI KHAN

DESTINATION	BUS	MINIVAN	TRAIN
Ban Krut	70B; 1½hr; hourly	90B; 1hr; hourly; 6am-5pm	13B; 1 daily
Bang Saphan Yai	60B; 2hr; hourly	100B; 1½hr; hourly; 6am-5pm	16B; 8 daily
Bangkok Hualamphong			168-455B; 7-8hr; 8 daily; 12.14am-11.35pm
Bangkok Southern Bus Terminal	200B; 6-7hr; 3 daily; 9am, 12.30pm & 1am	220B; 5-6hr; hourly; 7am-5pm	
Bangkok Victory Monument		220B; 6hr; hourly; 6am-5pm	
Cha-am		120B; 2hr; hourly; 6am-5pm	14B; 2hr; 1 daily
Hua Hin		80B; 1½hr; hourly; 6am-5pm	19B; 1hr; 8 daily
Phetchaburi		150B; 3hr; hourly; 6am-5pm	32B; 3hr; 8 daily

WORTH A TRIP

DAN SINGKHON BORDER MARKET

A mere 12km southwest of Prachuap Khiri Khan is the Myanmar border and at the time of research there were persistent rumours that the frontier would be open for foreigners to cross in the very near future. If that is the case – and check before you try it – you'll need to have arranged a Myanmar visa beforehand.

In the meantime, you can still visit the town of Dan Singkhon on the Thai side of the border. Once a strategic military point, Dan Singkhon now hosts a lively **market** known for its many bargains.

Beginning at dawn on Saturday mornings, locals from Myanmar appear from a bend in the road just beyond the checkpoint, pushing handcarts piled high with the usual trinkets, market goods and plants. Short-term tourists might be befuddled as to what will fit in a suitcase, but locals and expats make frequent buying trips here for orchids, the market's speciality, and hardwood furniture. Even if you come to window-shop, the market has a festive vibe, with music blaring, colourful umbrellas lining the road and thatched 'sales booths' hidden under palms. You'll need to arrive well before noon to enjoy it, as the market closes at midday.

To get to Dan Singkhon from Prachuap Khiri Khan with your own vehicle, head south on Hwy 4. After several kilometres you'll see a sign for Dan Singkhon; from there head west about 15km to reach the border.

you can sip a libation until late while gazing out at the winking lights of the fishing boats in the bay. Also does Thai and Western comfort food (from 120B).

Information

Bangkok Bank (cnr Th Maitri Ngam & Th Sarachip; ⌚9.30am-3.30pm Mon-Fri)

Police Station (Th Kong Kiat) Just west of Th Sarachip.

Post Office (cnr Th Maitri Ngam & Th Suseuk; ⌚8.30am-4.30pm Mon-Fri, 9am-noon Sat)

Tourist Office (☎032 611491; Th Chai Thaleh; ⌚8.30am-4.30pm) At the northern end of town. The staff speak English and are very helpful.

Getting There & Away

Three air-conditioned buses run daily to Bangkok's southern terminal from Th Phitak Chat. Buses also leave from here for Ban Krut and Bang Saphan Yai.

Minivans leave from the corner of Th Thetsaban Bamrung and Th Phitak Chat.

Long-distance buses to southern destinations (such as Phuket and Krabi) stop at the new bus station, 2km northwest of town on the main highway; motorcycle taxis will take you for 40B to 50B.

The train station is on Th Maharat; there are frequent services to/from Bangkok.

Getting Around

Prachuap is small enough to get around on foot, but you can hop on a motorcycle taxi for 30B. A bike to Ao Noi and Ao Manao is 100B to 150B.

You can hire motorbikes for 250B per day and bicycles for 50B; the roads in the area are good and it's a great way to see the surrounding beaches.

Ban Krut & Bang Saphan Yai บ้านกรูด/บางสะพานใหญ่

POP 4198 / 15,134

What a nice surprise to find these lovely, low-key beaches (80km to 100km south of Prachuap Khiri Khan, respectively) so close to civilisation yet so bucolic. Dusk falls softly through the coconut trees and the crystalline blue sea laps at a long sandy coastline. No high-rises, no late-night bars and no speeding traffic to distract you from a serious regimen of reading, swimming, eating and biking.

Although both beaches are pleasantly subdued, they are also well known to Thais. Ban Krut, in particular, hosts bus tours as well as weekending families. During the week you'll have the beaches largely to yourself and a few long-tail boats.

Check out the websites Ban Krut Info (www.bankrutinfo.com) and Bang Saphan Guide (www.bangsaphanguide.com) for local information on the area.

Sights & Activities

Ban Krut is divided into two beaches by a temple-topped headland. To the north is **Hat Sai Kaew**, which is remote and private with only a few resorts in between a lot of jungle. To the south is **Hat Ban Krut**, with a string of bungalow-style resorts and restaurants sitting opposite the beach. Both are golden-sand beaches with clear, calm water but Hat Ban Krut is more social and developed (you'll find ATMs here) and easier to get around without private transport.

Bang Saphan Yai, 20km south of Ban Krut, fits that most famous beach cliché: it is Thailand 15 years ago before pool villas and package tourists pushed out all the beach bums. Once you settle into a simple beachfront hut, you probably won't need any shoes and the days will just melt away. Islands off the coast, including **Ko Thalu** and **Ko Sing**, offer good **snorkelling** and **diving** from the end of January to mid-May.

Sleeping & Eating

Ban Krut

You'll struggle to find true budget options here, but if you visit on a weekday you should secure a discount. In Hat Ban Krut, bicycles (100B per day) and motorcycles (300B per day) can be hired to run errands in town, and most accommodation options arrange snorkelling trips to nearby islands. If you stay in Hat Sai Kaew you'll need private transport.

NaNa Chart Baan Krut HOTEL **$$**
(032 695525; www.thailandhostel.com; 123 Th Ban Krut-Kohktahom; r 700-4800B;) Technically it is a hostel – although there are no dorms – but NaNa Chart easily qualifies as a resort with a variety of rooms and bungalows on a barely inhabited, superb stretch of beach. The cheapest are wooden huts with fans, while the ritzy beachfront ones have all the mod cons.

The resort caters to large groups so expect some company at peak times; in low season (May to September) it's much quieter. Hostel members receive discounted rates.

Proud Thai Beach Resort GUESTHOUSE **$$**
(089 682 4484; www.proudthairesort.com; Hat Ban Krut; r 800-1200B;) Eight well-maintained bungalows in a flower-filled garden, all with terraces. Prices rise at weekends and on public holidays, when you should book ahead.

Bayview Beach Resort HOTEL **$$$**
(032 695566; www.bayviewbeachresort.com; Hat Ban Krut; r 1600-5000B;) A great choice for families and popular with Bangkok Thais at the weekend, Bayview has handsome bungalows with large verandahs amid shady grounds. There's a beachside pool and a kid-friendly wading pool as well as a small playground. The resort also offers snorkelling and diving trips and rents kayaks and bikes.

Kasama's Pizza ITALIAN **$$**
(Hat Ban Krut; pizza from 190B; 7.30am-11pm Fri-Wed;) Has substantial, succulent baguettes (from 100B) for beach-snacking, and it's fine for breakfast or a New York–style pizza in the evening.

Bang Saphan Yai

The beach is 6km south of the town of Bang Saphan Yai. It's not as idyllic a strip of sand as Ban Krut, but there's both budget accommodation and high-end pool villas here. Walk north of the Why Not Bar for the cheaper places.

Roytawan GUESTHOUSE **$**
(087 670 8943; Hat Bang Saphan Yai; r from 300B;) Smack dab on the beach, this laid-back, bare-bones operation is run by a friendly local Muslim family. The bungalows are simple (fan-only) but adequate and the resident roosters kindly sleep until daybreak. There's wi-fi in the attached restaurant.

Suan Luang Resort GUESTHOUSE **$**
(032 691663; www.suanluangresort.com; Hat Bang Saphan Yai; bungalows 480-680B;) Family-run Suan Luang is the most professional of the guesthouses, with rustic wooden bungalows that are arranged around an interior garden, although it's located 700m from the beach. The air-con bungalows are a big step up from the fan rooms. The excellent restaurant serves Thai and French food, and motorbikes are available for rent (250B per day).

Coral Hotel HOTEL **$$$**
(032 817121; www.coral-hotel.com; Hat Bang Saphan Yai; r 2640-7705B;) Catering mostly to French tourists – the restaurant is decent – this upmarket hotel is right on the beach and has all the resort amenities, including organised diving and snorkelling tours and Thai cooking classes. The tastefully decorated rooms are very comfortable and the pool is big.

Getting There & Around

Public transport is either nonexistent or limited. When booking transport, don't confuse Bang Saphan Yai with Bang Saphan Noi, which is a fishing village 15km further south.

From Bangkok's southern terminal buses go to Bang Saphan Yai (275B, hourly, six hours).

Frequent minivans run from Prachuap Khiri Khan to Ban Krut (90B) and Bang Saphan Yai (100B). Most minivans to Ban Krut will stop on the highway, a 100B motorbike ride from the beach.

Many seasoned visitors prefer to take the train for closer proximity to the beaches, although trains in this region are increasingly prone to delays. Six trains run to Ban Krut daily from Bangkok's Hualamphong station (265B to 615B, five to seven hours): the 08.05am train gets in at 1.07pm and is the best option. The train station is also handy if you are continuing south to Chumphon to catch the ferry to Ko Tao.

A motorcycle taxi from town to Bang Saphan Yai is 70B. Talk to your hotel or guesthouse about arranging transport back to town for your onward travel.

Chumphon ชุมพร

POP 33,516

A transit town funnelling travellers to and from Ko Tao or westwards to Ranong or Phuket, Chumphon is also where the south of Thailand starts proper; Muslim headscarves are a common sight here.

While there's not a lot to do while you wait for your ferry, there's good seafood in town and the surrounding beaches are great places to step off the backpacker bandwagon for a few days. **Hat Thung Wua Laen** (15km north of town) is an excellent beach with plenty of traveller amenities and during the week you'll have it mostly to yourself.

For a transit hub, Chumphon is surprisingly unconsolidated: the main bus station and piers for boats to Ko Tao, Ko Samui and Ko Pha-Ngan are some distance from town. But travel agencies and all guesthouses can book tickets, provide timetables and point you to the right bus stop.

Festivals & Events

Chumphon Marine Festival CULTURAL

(Mar) Normally held in mid-March, Hat Thung Wua Laen hosts a variety of sea-related events – boat and fishing trips, diving and snorkelling – as well as exhibitions and beach displays.

Chumphon Traditional Boat Race CULTURAL

(Oct) To mark the end of Buddhist Lent in October (Ork Phansaa), traditional long-tail boats race each other on the Mae Nam Lang Suan (Lang Suan River), about 60km south of Chumphon. Other merit-making activities coincide with the festival.

Sleeping

As most people overnighting in Chumphon are backpackers, accommodation is priced accordingly. Th Tha Taphao is the local Th Khao San, with many guesthouses and travel agencies.

★ **Suda Guest House** GUESTHOUSE $

(080 144 2079; 8 Soi Sala Daeng 3; r 200-650B;) Suda, the friendly English-speaking owner, maintains her impeccable standards with six rooms, all with wooden floors and a few nice touches that you wouldn't expect for the price. It's very popular so phone ahead. Suda can also book tickets and rents motorbikes (200B to 300B).

Salsa Hostel HOSTEL $

(077 505005; www.salsachumphon.com; 25/42 Th Krom Luang Chumphon; dm 280-300B, d 650-750B;) Helpful hostel (the owner speaks good English) with cramped but bright, clean and modern dorms. The private rooms are big and comfortable, even if they are overpriced for this town.

Fame Guest House GUESTHOUSE $

(077 571077; www.chumphon-kohtao.com; 188/20-21 Th Sala Daeng; r 150-300B;) A *fa·ràng* (Westerner) depot, Fame does a little bit of everything, from providing basic rooms for people overnighting to booking tickets and renting motorbikes. The attached restaurant is a key backpacker hang-out, and offers a decent and wide range of Thai, Indian and Western food.

View Resort BUNGALOW $$

(077 560214; Hat Thung Wua Laen; r 700-1000B;) Sleepy bungalow operation outside town that's right on the beach. Bungalows aren't big and come with severely slanted roofs, but they're comfortable enough, and the attached restaurant is pretty good.

Chumphon Gardens Hotel HOTEL $$

(077 506888; www.chumphongarden.com; 66/1 Th Tha Taphao; r 590-750B;) Sports a 1970s-style design but has large, comfortable rooms and the bathrooms are a cut above the local competition.

Chumphon

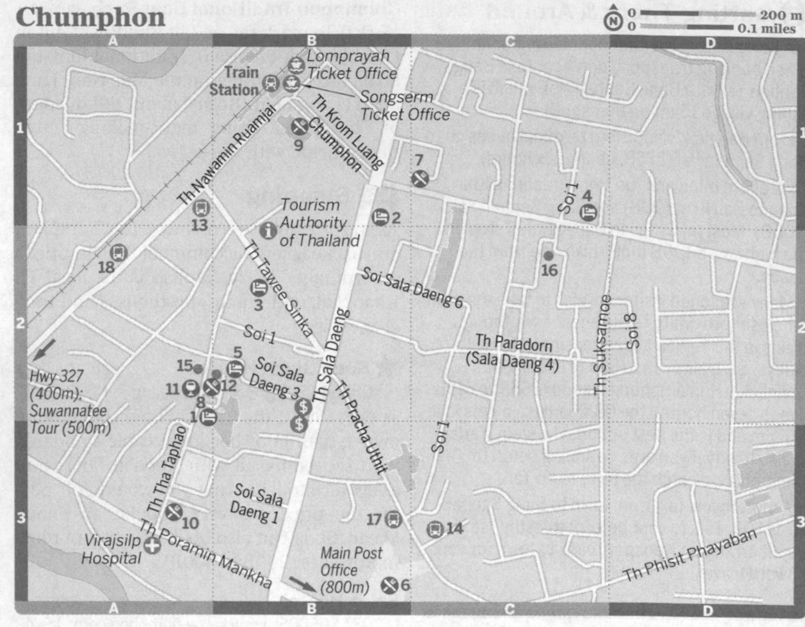

Chumphon

Sleeping
1 Chumphon Gardens Hotel A2
2 Fame Guest House B1
3 Morakot Hotel B2
4 Salsa Hostel C1
5 Suda Guest House B2

Eating
6 Day Market B3
7 Night Market C1
8 OK Restaurant A2
9 Papa Seafood B1
10 Prikhorm A3

Drinking & Nightlife
11 Farang Bar A2

Information
12 New Infinity Travel B2

Transport
13 Buses to Hat Yai A1
14 Choke Anan Tour C3
15 Minivans to Ranong A2
16 Minivans to Surat Thani, Bang Saphan Yai & Prachuap Khiri Khan C2
17 Sŏrng·tăa·ou to Hat Thung Wua Laen B3
18 Sŏrng·tăa·ou to Main Bus Terminal A2

Morakot Hotel HOTEL $$
(☎077 502999; www.morakothotel.com; 102-112 Th Tawee Sinka; r 490-890B; ❄📶) Spread across two buildings: the newer wing houses the better and more expensive rooms, but the older wing is acceptable for the price.

Chumphon Cabana Resort & Diving Centre HOTEL $$$
(☎077 560245; www.chumphoncabanaresort.com; Hat Thung Wua Laen; r 1850-2500B; ❄📶🏊) The most pleasant resort on the beach, despite the rather plain bungalows, Chumphon Cabana is ecofriendly, with the owner using traditional methods in an effort to be as green as possible. The grounds are devoted to raising the resort's own food with rice fields, hydroponic vegetable gardens and a chicken farm, while waste water is recycled through water-hyacinth ponds.

Even if you don't stay here, the home-grown food at **Rabieng Talay**, the resort's affiliated restaurant, is worth a try.

Eating & Drinking

Chumphon's **night market** (Th Krom Luang Chumphon; 4-11pm) is excellent, with a big variety of food options and good people-watching. There is also a **day market** (6am-4pm) on Th Pracha Uthit, while Th Sala Daeng and Th Pracha Uthit are both lined with hole-in-the-wall noodle joints.

OK Restaurant THAI $
(Th Tha Taphao; buffet 119B; 4-9pm) A new, open-air buffet-style restaurant where you can eat as much you like for the price. Unsurprisingly, it gets busy in the early evening.

Papa Seafood SEAFOOD $
(2-2/1 Th Krom Luang Chumphon; dishes from 70B; 8am-4am;) There's a huge display of seafood on offer at this big, open-air place that sometimes features live music; it's good without being exceptional. Foreigner-friendly, but many locals come here too. Next door is the affiliated club Papa 2000, where you can dance off dinner.

Pirates Terrace INTERNATIONAL, THAI $
(Hat Thung Wua Laen; dishes from 80B; 7.30am-10pm;) Opposite the beach, this is a popular spot for breakfast, a daytime coffee, or a drink in the evening. The menu mixes Thai classics with pizza and pasta. They can also book tickets and rent motorbikes for 200B a day.

★ **Prikhorm** SOUTHERN THAI $$
(32 Th Tha Taphao; dishes 150-450B; 11am-11pm) The place where the locals come for fiery and delicious southern Thai cuisine. Their *gaang sôm* is a superbly spicy and flavoursome fish curry, but all the dishes are delicious.

Farang Bar BAR
(077 501003; www.farangbarchumphon.com; 69/36 Th Tha Taphao; beers from 80B; 11am-midnight;) An agreeable hang-out for expat English teachers and passing travellers, the Farang Bar is an easy place to while away a few hours over a drink. The menu mixes Thai and Western dishes; the local ones are better. It closes in the depths of low season (July and August).

Information

There are banks along Th Sala Daeng with exchange facilities and ATMs.

Bangkok Bank (Th Sala Daeng; 9.30am-3.30pm Mon-Fri) Has an ATM.

Main Post Office (Th Poramin Mankha; 8.30am-4.30pm Mon-Fri, 9am-noon Sat) In the southeastern part of town.

New Infinity Travel (077 570176; 68/2 Th Tha Taphao; 8am-10pm;) A great travel agency with knowledgable and friendly staff. It's also the only secondhand bookshop in town.

Tourism Authority of Thailand (TAT; 077 501831; 111/11-12 Th Tawee Sinka; 8.30am-4.30pm) Hands out maps and brochures but you're likely to get better information from your guesthouse.

Virajsilp Hospital (077 503238; Th Poramin Mankha) Privately owned; handles emergencies.

Getting There & Away

Boats leave from different piers; bus transfer is sometimes included in the ticket price. Otherwise, you pay an extra 100B for transport to the pier.

BOAT

You have a number of boat options for getting to Ko Tao, though departure times are limited to mainly morning and night. Most ticket prices include pier transfer. If you buy a combination ticket, make sure you have a ticket for both the bus and the boat.

Car Ferry A comfortable ride with bunk or mattress options available on board.

Lomprayah Catamaran (077 558214; www.lomprayah.com; 5am-9pm) The best and most popular bus-boat combination; it leaves from Tha Tummakam, 25km from town. The ticket office is beside Chumphon train station.**Songserm Express Boat** (077 506205; www.songserm-expressboat.com; 9am-8pm) Faster, morning option leaving from Tha Talaysub, about 10km from town, but the company has a reputation for being poorly organised and not providing promised free transport into town if you are coming from the islands. The ticket office doesn't seem to open often; book tickets through guesthouses.

BUS

The main bus terminal is on the highway, an inconvenient 16km from Chumphon. To get there you can catch a *sŏrng·tăa·ou* (50B) from Th Nawamin Ruamjai. You'll have to haggle with the opportunistic taxi drivers for night transit to/from the station; no matter what they tell you, it shouldn't cost more than 200B.

There are several in-town bus stops to save you a trip out to the main bus station. **Choke Anan Tour** (077 511757; soi off Th Pracha Uthit), in the centre of town, has departures to Bangkok, Phuket and Ranong. **Suwannatee Tour** (077 504901), 700m southwest of the train station, serves Bangkok, Phetchaburi and Prachuap Khiri Khan. Buses to Hat Yai depart from near the petrol station on Th Nawamin Ruamjai.

TRANSPORT TO/FROM CHUMPHON

DESTINATION	BOAT	BUS	MINIVAN	TRAIN	AIR
Bang Saphan Yai			120B; 2hr; 1 daily; 2pm	20B; 2hr; 2 daily; 7am & 12.46pm	
Bangkok Don Mueang Airport					from 1720B; 1hr; 2 daily (Nok Air)
Bangkok Hualamphong				192-690B; 8hr; 11 daily	
Bangkok Southern Bus Terminal		300-591B; 8hr; 11 daily			
Hat Yai		400B; 7hr; 4 daily		269-652B, 6 hr; 7 daily	
Ko Pha-Ngan (Lomprayah)	1000B; 3¼hr; 2 daily; 7am & 1pm				
Ko Pha-Ngan (Songserm)	900B; 5½hr; 1 daily; 7am				
Ko Samui (Lomprayah)	1100B; 4½hr; 2 daily; 7am & 1pm				
Ko Samui (Songserm)	1000B; 6hr; 1 daily; 7am				
Ko Tao (car ferry)	400B; 6hr; 1 daily; 11pm Mon-Sat				
Ko Tao (Lomprayah)	600B; 1½hr; 2 daily; 7am & 1pm				
Ko Tao (Songserm)	500B; 3hr; 1 daily; 7am				
Phetchaburi		362B; 6hr; 5 daily		58-545B; 6-7hr; 11 daily	
Phuket		350B; 3½hr; 2 daily			
Prachuap Khiri Khan			180B; 4hr; 1 daily; 3pm	84B; 3-4hr; 10 daily	
Ranong		120B; 2½hr; 4 daily	120B; 2hr; frequent		
Surat Thani			170B; 3hr; hourly; 6am-5pm	100B; 2-3 hr; 12 daily	

All minivans for Surat Thani, Bang Saphan Yai and Prachuap Khiri Khan leave from the unnamed soi opposite Salsa Hostel.

TRAIN

There are frequent services to/from Bangkok (192B to 690B, 11 daily, eight hours).

Getting Around

Sŏrng·tăa·ou (40B per trip) and motorcycle taxis (20B to 30B per trip) can be taken around town. Yellow *sŏrng·tăa·ou* to Hat Thung Wua Laen cost 30B.

Motorcycles can be rented at travel agencies and guesthouses from 200B per day.

Ko Samui & the Lower Gulf

Includes ➡

Best Places to Eat

- Dining On The Rocks (p534)
- Chez François (p534)
- Pepenero (p532)
- Fisherman's Restaurant (p551)
- Baraccuda (p566)

Best Places to Stay

- Six Senses Samui (p528)
- Divine Comedie (p546)
- View Point Resort (p564)
- Place (p561)
- Sanctuary (p550)

Why Go?

The Lower Gulf features Thailand's ultimate island trifecta: Ko Samui, Ko Pha-Ngan and Ko Tao. This family of spectacular islands lures millions of tourists every year with their powder-soft sands and emerald waters. Ko Samui is the oldest sibling, who has made it big. Here, high-class resorts operate with Swiss efficiency as uniformed butlers cater to every whim. Ko Pha-Ngan is the slacker middle child with tangled dreadlocks and a penchant for hammock-lazing and all-night parties. Meanwhile Ko Tao is the outdoorsy, fun-loving kid with plenty of spirit and spunk – the island specialises in high-adrenalin activities, including world-class diving and snorkelling.

The mainland coast beyond the islands sees few foreign visitors, but is more authentic Thailand and in many ways more culturally enjoyable for that. From the pink dolphins and waterfalls of sleepy Ao Khanom to the Thai Muslim flavours of beach strolling Songkhla, this region will convince any naysayer that Thailand still holds a bevy of off-the-beaten-track wonders.

When to Go

- February to April celebrates endless sunshine after the monsoon rains have cleared.
- June to August, conveniently coinciding with the northern hemisphere's summer holidays, are among the most inviting months, with relatively short drizzle spells.
- October to December is when torrential monsoon rains rattle hot-tin roofs, and room rates drop significantly to lure optimistic beach goers.

Ko Samui & the Lower Gulf Highlights

1. Finding Nemo in the technicolour kingdom off **Ko Tao** (p555).
2. Paddling to the hidden bleach-blonde beaches of **Ang Thong Marine National Park** (p570).
3. Stringing up a cotton hammock and toeing the curling tide along a secluded beach on **Ko Pha-Ngan** (p538).
4. Enjoying five-star international cuisine and sipping fancy sunset cocktails on **Ko Samui** (p520).
5. Joining the masses of party pilgrims and trancing the night away at the **Full Moon Party** (p543) at Hat Rin on Ko Pha-Ngan.

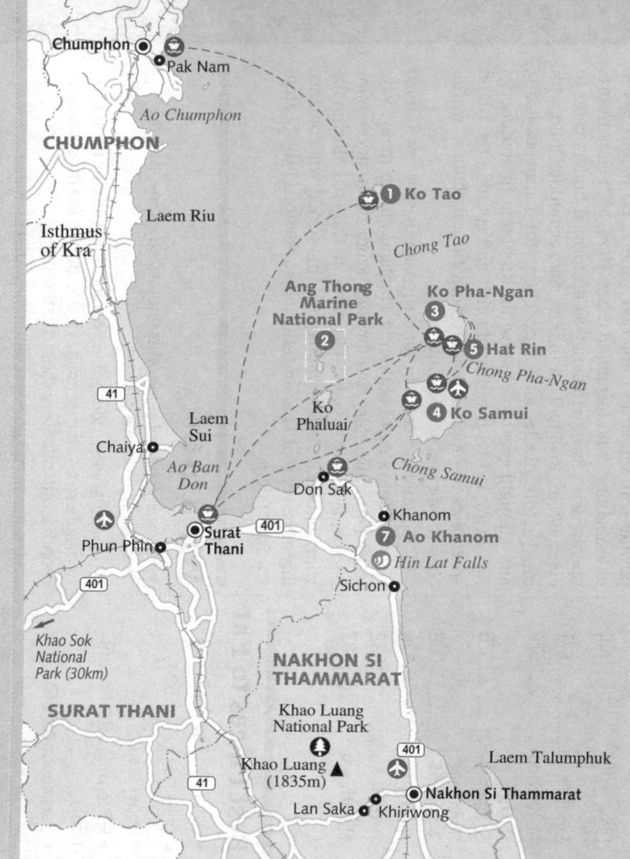

6 Savouring steaming street-stall seafood on the sands of **Songkhla** (p578).

7 Spotting elusive pink dolphins gliding along the shores of **Ao Khanom** (p574).

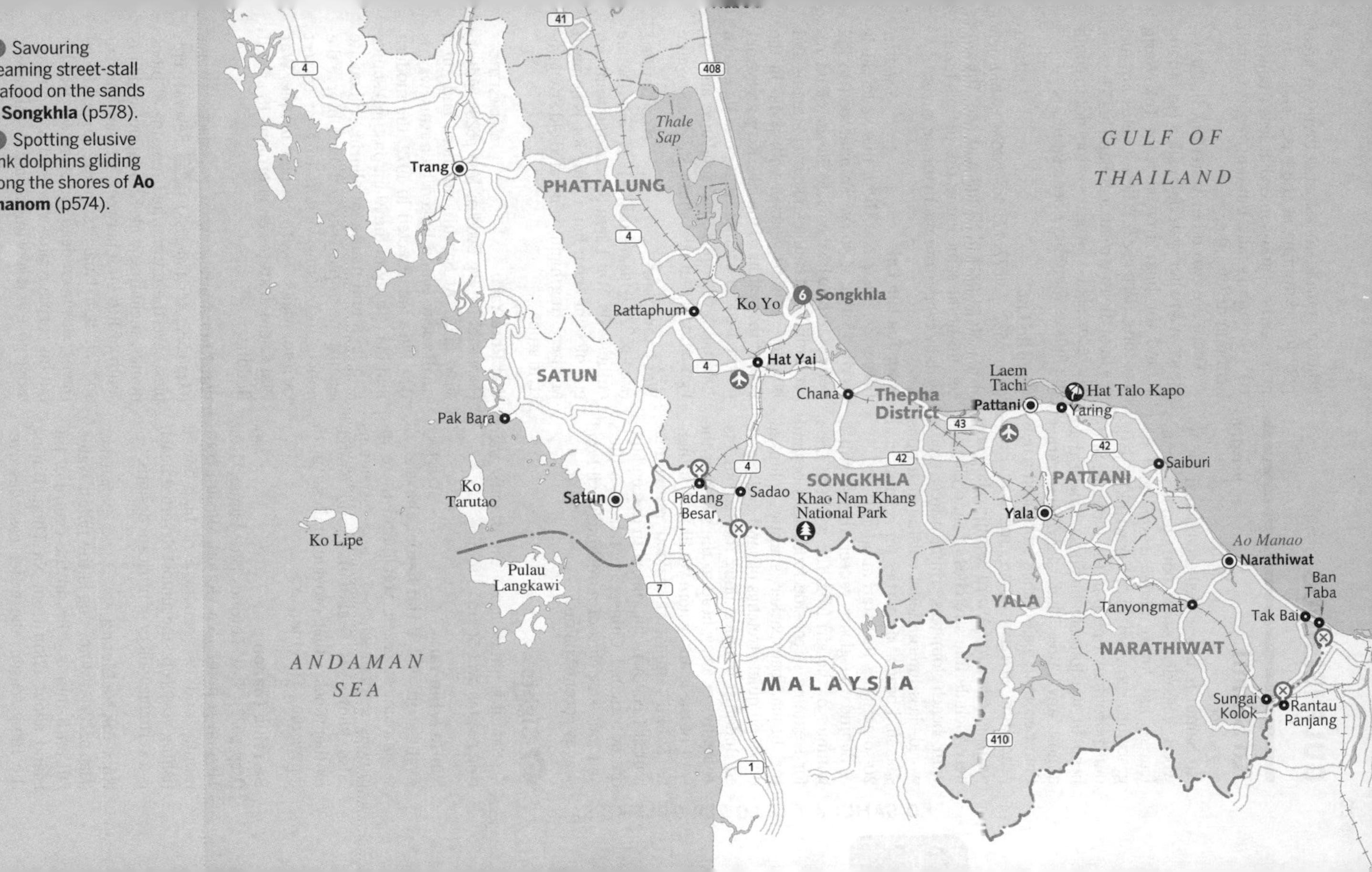

GULF ISLANDS

Ko Samui เกาะสมุย

POP 50,000

Ko Samui is like a well-established Hollywood celebrity: she's outrageously manicured, has lovely blond tresses and has gracefully removed all of her wrinkles without more than a peep in the tabloids. She's been in the tourism business longer than almost any other Thai island, but rather than becoming passé, she's embraced a new generation of resort goers, many of them upscale. Academy Award–winning holidays here include fine stretches of sand clogged with beach loungers, rubbish-free roads, world-class international cuisine, luxurious spas and beach bar parties for scantily clad 20-somethings that start at noon.

Behind the glossy veneer there's still a glimmer of the girl from the country. Look for steaming street-side food stalls beyond the beach, backpacker shanties plunked down on quiet stretches of sand and secreted Buddhist temples along the backstreets. To really get away, head to the south or the west of the island where you'll find authentic Samui family-run seafood restaurants, tourist-free towns buzzing with descendants of the original Chinese merchant settlers and long stretches of refreshingly wild and shaggy coconut palms.

Sights

Ko Samui is quite large – the island's main ring road is over 50km in total.

Hin-Ta & Hin-Yai LANDMARK

At the south end of **Hat Lamai**, the island's second-largest beach, you'll find these infamous genitalia-shaped stone formations (also known as Grandfather and Grandmother Rocks) that provide endless mirth for giggling Thai tourists.

Ban Hua Thanon AREA

(Map p522) Just beyond Hat Lamai, Hua Thanon is home to a vibrant Muslim community, and its anchorage of high-bowed fishing vessels by the almost deserted beach is a veritable gallery of intricate designs.

Nam Tok Na Muang WATERFALL

(Map p522) At 30m, this is the tallest waterfall on Samui and lies in the centre of the island about 12km from Na Thon. During the rainy season, the water cascades over ethereal purple rocks, and there's a great pool for swimming at the base. This is the most scenic – and somewhat less frequented – of Samui's falls, but don't expect much action in dry weather.

There are two other waterfalls in the vicinity: a smaller waterfall called **Na Muang 2**, and the high drop at **Nam Tok Wang Saotong** (Map p522). These chutes are just north of the ring road near Ban Hua Thanon. There are signs warning visitors not to climb the falls as there have been fatalities.

Wat Hin Lat TEMPLE

(Map p522; 077 423146; dawn-dusk) On the western part of Samui and near the waterfalls of the same name, this temple teaches daily *vipassana* meditation courses.

Nam Tok Hin Lat WATERFALL

(Map p522) Near Na Thon, this waterfall is worth visiting if you've an afternoon to kill before taking a boat back to the mainland. After a mildly strenuous hike over streams and boulders, reward yourself with a dip in the pool at the bottom of the falls. Keep an eye out for the Buddhist temple that posts signs with spiritual words of moral guidance and enlightenment, but take sturdy shoes and water.

Wat Laem Saw BUDDHIST TEMPLE

(Map p522; dawn-dusk) FREE For temple enthusiasts, Wat Laem Saw, at the southern end of Samui near Ban Phang Ka, is home to an interesting, highly venerated old Srivijaya-style stupa.

Wat Phra Yai BUDDHIST TEMPLE

(Temple of the Big Buddha; Map p528; dawn-dusk) FREE At Samui's northern end, on a small rocky island linked by a causeway, is Wat Phra Yai. Erected in 1972, the modern Buddha (sitting in the Mara posture) stands 15m high and makes an alluring silhouette against the tropical sky and sea. Observe the notices instructing visitors to wear correct garb for visits. Nearby, a new temple, **Wat Plai Laem**, features an enormous 18-armed Buddha.

Wat Khunaram BUDDHIST TEMPLE

(Map p522; dawn-dusk) FREE Several temples have the mummified remains of pious monks, including Wak Khunaram, which is south of Rte 4169 between Th Ban Thurian and Th Ban Hua. Its monk, Luang Phaw Daeng, has been dead for over two decades but his corpse is preserved sitting in a meditative pose and sporting a pair of sunglasses.

GULF ISLANDS IN...

One Week

After coming to terms with the fact that you only have a week to explore these idyllic islands, start on one of **Ko Pha-Ngan's** secluded western beaches or journey east to live out your ultimate castaway fantasies. For the second half of the week choose between partying in **Hat Rin**, pampering on **Ko Samui** or diving off little **Ko Tao**.

Two Weeks

Start on **Ko Tao** with a 3½-day Open Water certification course, or sign up for a few fun dives. Slide over to **Ko Pha-Ngan** and soak up the sociable vibe in party-prone Hat Rin. Then, grab a long-tail and make your way to one of the island's hidden coves for a few days of detoxing and quiet contemplation. **Ko Samui** is next on the agenda. Try **Bo Phut** for boutique sleeps or live it up like a rock star on Chaweng or Choeng Mon beach. And, if you have time, do a day trip to **Ang Thong National Marine Park**.

One Month

Follow the two-week itinerary at a more relaxed pace, infusing many extra beach-book-and-blanket days on all three islands. Be sure to plan your schedule around the Full Moon Party, which takes place at Hat Rin's Sunrise Beach on **Ko Pha-Ngan**.

Wat Samret BUDDHIST TEMPLE
(Map p522; ⌚dawn-dusk) FREE At Wat Samret, near Th Ban Hua, you can see a typical Mandalay sitting Buddha carved from solid marble – a common sight in India and northern Thailand, but not so common in the south.

Activities

Ko Samui is an excellent choice for families travelling with kids as there are many activities especially geared to the little ones.

Blue Stars KAYAKING, SNORKELLING
(Map p526; ☎077 300615; www.bluestars.info; Hat Chaweng; kayak & snorkelling tours adult/child 2500/1600B) There are many choices for snorkelling and kayak tours to Ang Thong Marine National Park, but Blue Stars has the best reputation and the coolest boat. Even if you don't go with this company, don't miss taking a trip to these islands.

Football Golf GOLF
(Map p522; ☎089 771 7498; www.samuifootballgolf.com; adult/child 730/350B; ⌚9am-6.30pm) At Hat Choeng Mon there's a curious hybrid called 'football golf' where you 'putt' your football into a rubbish-bin-sized hole. It's great for the kids and each game comes with a complimentary soft drink. It's a par 69.

Koh Samui Rum RUM TASTING
(Map p522; www.rum-distillery.com; Ban Bang Kao; tasting shots 50-75B; ⌚9am-6pm) The only rum distillery in Thailand produces Caribbean agricole style (distilled from fresh, fermented sugar cane juice) in a variety of all natural flavours, including a delectable coconut rum obtained from soaking coconut meat in the rum for several months. There's a video about the production process, a tasting area, an excellent French and Thai restaurant and a shop in beautiful palm-shaded surrounds.

Aquapark WATER PARK
(Map p526; www.aquaparkchaweng.com; Hat Chaweng; hourly/half-day/full-day 300/500/700B; ⌚10am-6pm) Let the kids loose on these gigantic green, climbable, slip-off-able and all-around-fun inflatables (including a UFO, an iceberg climbing wall and trampolines) anchored to a corded-off area of Ao Chaweng. All participants are required to wear life jackets. Meanwhile you can lounge on the beach and watch, or join them as many parents do.

Coco Splash Waterpark WATER PARK
(www.samuiwaterpark.com; Ban Lamai; admission over/under 1.3m 490/390B; ⌚10.30am-5.30pm) Kids under 10 will love this small park of fun painted concrete water slides. Towel hire is 60B (200B deposit) and there's mediocre food available. Note that if you're planning on watching the kids and not going in the water yourself, you get in for free.

Samui Dog & Cat Rescue Centre VOLUNTEERING
(Map p526; ☎077 413490; www.samuidog.org; Soi 3, Chaweng Beach Rd; ⌚9am-6pm) Donations of time and/or money are hugely appreciated at the aptly named Samui Dog & Cat Rescue

Ko Samui

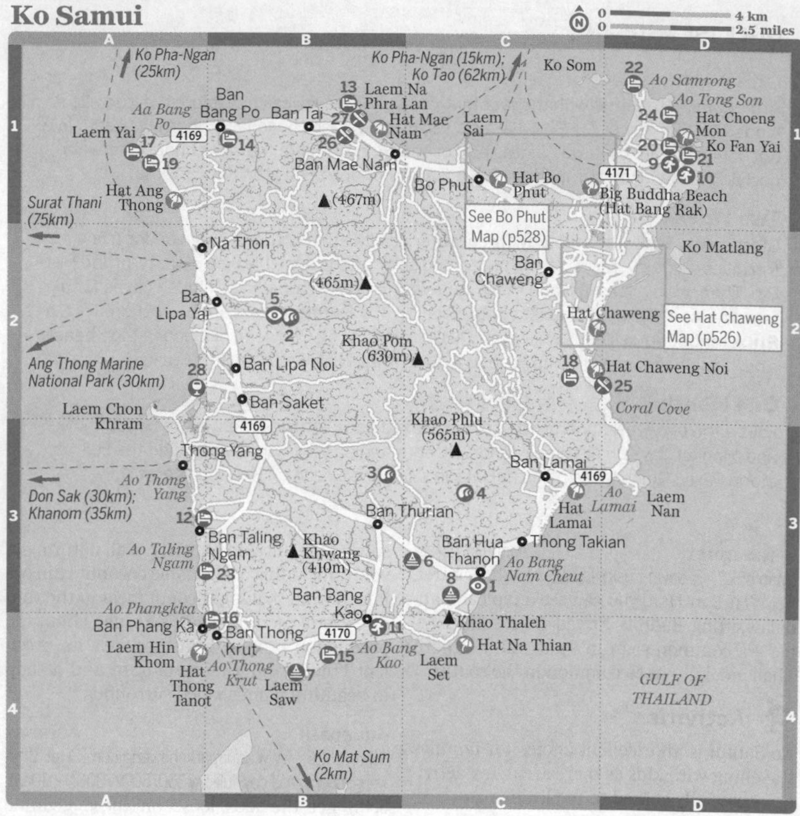

Centre. Volunteers are always needed to take care of the animals at their kennel/clinic in Ban Taling Ngam (but not at the smaller Hat Chaweng branch). Call the centre for volunteering details or swing by for additional info. Check the website for directions.

The organisation has played an integral role in keeping the island's dog population under control through an active spaying and neutering program. The centre also vaccinates dogs against rabies.

Diving

If you're serious about diving, head to Ko Tao and base yourself there. If you're short on time and don't want to leave Samui, there are plenty of operators who will take you to the same dive sites (at a greater fee, of course). Try to book with a company that has its own boat (or leases a boat) – it's slightly more expensive, but you'll be glad you did it. Companies without boats often shuttle divers on the passenger catamaran to Ko Tao, where you board a second boat to reach your dive site. These trips are arduous, meal-less and rather impersonal.

Certification courses tend to be twice as expensive on Ko Samui as they are on Ko Tao, due largely to use of extra petrol, since tiny Tao is significantly closer to the preferred diving locations. You'll spend between 14,000B and 22,000B on an Open Water certification, and figure on between 4500B and 6200B for a diving day trip including two dives, depending on the location of the site.

Ko Samui's hyperbaric chamber is at Big Buddha Beach (Hat Bang Rak).

100 Degrees East DIVING
(☎077 425936; www.100degreeseast.com; Hat Bang Rak; ⏲9am-6.30pm Dec-Oct) Highly recommended, with a dedicated team.

Ko Samui

Sights
1 Ban Hua Thanon C3
2 Nam Tok Hin Lat B2
3 Nam Tok Na Muang B3
4 Nam Tok Wang Saotong C3
5 Wat Hin Lat B2
6 Wat Khunaram C3
7 Wat Laem Saw B4
8 Wat Samret C3

Activities, Courses & Tours
9 Absolute Sanctuary D1
10 Football Golf D1
11 Koh Samui Rum B4

Sleeping
12 Am Samui A3
Belmond Napasai .... (see 13)
13 Coco Palm Resort B1
14 Code B1
15 Easy Time B4
16 Elements B4
17 Four Seasons Koh Samui A1
18 Jungle Club C2
19 Mövenpick Resort Laem Yai Beach Samui A1
20 Sala Samui D1
21 Samui Honey Cottages Resort D1
22 Six Senses Samui D1
23 Sunset Beach Resort & Spa B3
24 Tongsai Bay D1

Eating
Dining On The Rocks .... (see 22)
25 Dr Frogs D2
26 Farmer B1
Five Islands .... (see 12)
Hua Thanon Market .... (see 1)
27 John's Garden Restaurant B1

Drinking & Nightlife
28 Nikki Beach A2

Discovery Dive Centre DIVING
(Map p526; 077 300656; www.discoverydivers.com; Chaweng Beach Rd, Amari Palm Reef Resort; courses 5900-17,400B; 11am-11pm) This popular office offers dive courses from beginner to professional as well as dive trips and snorkelling.

Spas & Yoga

Competition between Samui's five-star accommodation is fierce, meaning spas are of the highest calibre. For top-notch pampering, try the spa at Anantara (p529) in Bo Phut, or the Hideaway Spa at the Six Senses Samui (p528). The Spa Resort (p527) in Lamai is the island's original health destination, and is still known for its effective 'clean me out' fasting regime.

Samahita Retreat YOGA, SPA
(077 920090; www.samahitaretreat.com; Laem Saw Beach; retreats around €840) Secreted away along the southern shores, Samahita Retreat has state-of-the-art facilities and a dedicated team of trainers for the growing band of therapeutic holidaymakers, wellness seekers and detoxers. Accommodation is in a comfy apartment block up the street while yoga studios, wellness centres and a health food restaurant sit calmly along the shore.

Tamarind Springs MASSAGE
(077 424221; www.tamarindsprings.com) Tucked away in a location far from the beach within a silent coconut-palm plantation, Tamarind's small collection of villas and massage studios is seamlessly incorporated into nature: some have granite boulders built into the walls and floors, while others offer private ponds or creative outdoor baths.

Absolute Sanctuary YOGA, SPA
(Map p522; 077 601190; www.absolutesanctuary.com; Choeng Mon) Detox, spa, yoga, pilates and lifestyle packages, in a Moroccan-inspired setting.

Courses

Samui Institute of Thai Culinary Arts COOKING COURSE
(SITCA; Map p526; 077 413172; http://sitca.com; Hat Chaweng; 1-day course 1850B) For Thai cooking skills, SITCA is the place to do it, with daily Thai-cooking classes and courses in the aristocratic Thai art of carving fruits and vegetables into intricate floral designs. Lunchtime classes begin at 11am, while dinner starts at 4pm (both are three-hour courses with three or more dishes).

Included is a tutorial about procuring ingredients in your home country. Of course you get to eat your projects, and can even invite a friend along for the meal. Complimentary DVDs with Thai cooking instruction are also available so you can practise at home.

Lamai Muay Thai Camp THAI BOXING
(087 082 6970; www.lamaimuaythaicamp.com; 82/2 Moo3, Lamai; 1-day/1-week training sessions 300/1500B; 7am-8pm) The island's best *moo·ay tai* (also spelt *muay Thai*) training (best for the seriously serious) is at this place,

which caters to beginners as well as those wanting to hone their skills. There's also a well-equipped gym for boxers and nonboxers who want to up their fitness levels.

Kiteboarding Asia KITEBOARDING
(☎083 643 1627; www.kiteboardingasia.com; 1-/3-day courses 4000/11,000B; ⏲9am-6pm) This pro place will get you kitesurfing on flat shallow water. The Na Thon location on the west side is for December to March winds (another in Hua Thanon in the south of the island is for April to October gusts).

Mind Your Language LANGUAGE COURSE
(☎077 960103; www.mindyourlanguagethailand.com) With lessons from 600B per hour, this accessible and professional language school in Lamai can gear you up with classes in Thai. There's another branch in Bo Phut.

Sleeping

The island's array of sleeping options is overwhelming. If you're looking to splurge, there is definitely no shortage of top-end resorts sporting exclusive bungalows, pampering spas, private infinity pools and top-notch dining. Bo Phut, on the island's northern coast, has an attractive collection of boutique lodging – the perfect choice for midrange travellers. Backpack-lugging visitors may have to look a little harder, but budget digs pop up periodically along all of the island's beaches.

Most visitors pre-book their resort, but outside peak season most midrange and budget places offer discounted walk-in rates equal or better to what you'll find online.

Private villa services have become popular in recent years; www.gosamuivillas.com is a good place to book the luxury variety.

Hat Chaweng

Busy, commercial Chaweng is packed wall-to-wall with every level of accommodation from cheap backpacker pads advertised with cardboard signs to futuristic villas with private swimming pools – and these might be just across the street from each other. There's little charm here, though: the northern half of the beach is the biggest party zone and nearby resorts are in ear-shot of the thumping bass pumping from Ark Bar at the centre of it all. If you're hoping for early nights, pick a resort near the southern half of the beach or bring earplugs. Bristling with selfie sticks and an assault course of low-hanging street signs that will clobber anyone over six foot, Chaweng Beach Road is crowded with souvenir shop owners, ads for wet T-shirt competitions, tattoo parlours and Heath Ledger *Joker* acrylic portraits, as jets roar overhead. Lamai is much quieter, less intense and altogether more pleasant.

Lucky Mother GUESTHOUSE $
(Map p526; ☎077 230931; 60 Moo 2; r & bungalows 800-1500B; ❄📶) The action-filled beachfront location, clean, bright rooms and popular bar out front that's prime for mingling with your toes in the sand all get the thumbs up. If you want a Chaweng beach location, it's a great deal (though some staff members could be friendlier).

P Chaweng HOTEL $
(Map p526; ☎077 230684; r from 600B, f 1000B; ❄@📶) At the end of a road off the main drag, this vine-covered cheapie has clean, pink-tiled rooms and wood-floored family rooms in two blocks, all decked out with air-con, hot water, TVs and fridges. It's a 10-minute walk to the bar zone and not particularly hip, but good luck finding a better room in the area for this price.

Queen Boutique Place HOTEL $
(Map p526; ☎077 413148; queensamui@yahoo.com; r 700-1500B; ❄@📶) With welcoming and well-mannered staff, the Queen serves up boutique sleeps at backpacker prices. Rooms are clean and well-equipped (with air-con, TVs and DVD players) and garner style points for colourful throw pillows, but the cheapest are boxy and windowless.

Pott Guesthouse GUESTHOUSE $
(Map p526; r with fan 300-400B, with air-con 500-600B; ❄📶) The bright cement rooms, all with attached hot-water bathrooms and balcony, in this apartment block are a steal. Reception is at an unnamed restaurant on the main drag right opposite across the alley.

Akwa GUESTHOUSE $
(Map p526; ☎084 660 0551; www.akwaguesthouse.com; r from 750B; ❄@📶) Akwa's funky rooms come with bright colours, cartoon paintings and soft toys, but things are a little past their prime. There's no shortage of character and friendly service, however, and the branch a five-minute walk to the north of the original is fresher and newer.

Samui Hostel HOSTEL $
(Map p526; ☎089 874 3737; dm 200-300B, d 850B; ❄@) It doesn't look like much from the front, but this very neat, tidy and friendly place has

clean fan and air-con dorm rooms and spruce air-con doubles. Service is a cut above the rest and there's a popular room at the front with wooden tables for lounging and chatting.

★Jungle Club BUNGALOW **$$**
(Map p522; ☎081 894 2327; www.jungleclubsamui.com; huts 800-1800B, houses 2700-4500B;) The drive up the slithering road is worthwhile once you take in the views from the top. With a relaxed back-to-nature vibe, this isolated mountain getaway is a huge hit among locals and tourists alike. Guests chill around the stunning horizon pool or catnap under the canopied roofs of an open-air *săh·lah* (often spelt as *sala*).

Call ahead for a pick up (from Chaweng only) – you don't want to spend your precious jungle vacation in a body cast.

Chaweng Garden Beach RESORT **$$**
(Map p526; ☎077 960394; www.chawenggarden.com; r 3600-33,000B;) A huge variety of room types hide amid the abundant foliage, from fine if rather bland standards with balcony to an indulgent 33,000B private beachfront pool villa. The best value is found in those such as the modern Asian-inspired 'Shinto' rooms and polished wood bungalows. The whole place is well-tended with greenery and serviced by an extra-smiley and helpful staff.

Tango Beach Resort RESORT **$$**
(Map p526; ☎077 300451; www.tangobeachsamui.com; r 1600-7400B;) The colourful lobby suggests a youngish vibe, but Tango is really more a standard string of bungalows arranged along a teak boardwalk meandering away from an excellent but busy stretch of beach. The dark tinted windows make the place look a little tacky from the outside (and the dated pool doesn't help) but the 39 rooms are fresh enough.

Ark Bar Beach Resort RESORT **$$**
(Map p526; ☎077 422047; www.ark-bar.com; r 1700-5200B;) You'll find two of every party animal at clean and well-tended 328-room Ark Bar – frat boys, chilled-out hippies, teenagers, 40-somethings and so on. Contemporary, brightly painted rooms all come with balcony, within staggering distance from the bar that pumps out music all day and well into the night.

★Library RESORT **$$$**
(Map p526; ☎077 422767; www.thelibrary.co.th; r from 9140B;) This library is too cool for school. The entire resort is a sparkling white mirage accented with black trimming and slatted curtains. Besides the futuristic iMac computer in each page (rooms are 'pages' here), our favourite feature is the large monochromatic wall art – it glows brightly in the evening and you can adjust the colour to your mood.

Life-size statues are engaged in the act of reading, and if you too feel inclined to pick up a book, the on-site library houses an impressive assortment of colourful art and design books. The large rectangular pool is not to be missed – it's tiled in piercing shades of red, making the term 'bloodbath' suddenly seem appealing. It has an on-site restaurant (p532).

Buri Rasa Village RESORT **$$$**
(Map p526; ☎077 230222; www.burirasa.com; r 4850-8900B;) Thai-style wooden doors lead to private villa patios and simple yet elegant rooms. This Zen-feeling place is beautifully landscaped with palms and frangipani, central, well-priced and on a good stretch of busy beach, but the real reason to stay here is the bend-over-backwards friendly and helpful service.

Chaweng Regent Beach Resort RESORT **$$$**
(Map p526; ☎077 422390, 077 422389; www.chawengregent.com; r 6000-15,000B;) This delightful oasis of tree, vegetation, shady foliage and tropical seclusion is a welcome respite from frantic Chaweng Beach Rd. Enticingly secluded, the resort is navigated via wooden boardwalks leading to the beach, with two pools, goldfish ponds and a wide range of rooms.

Baan Haad Ngam RESORT **$$$**
(Map p526; ☎077 231500; www.baanhaadngam.com; bungalows 8700-33,500B;) Very modern and stylish, with classy yet simple lime-green rooms, villas and pool villas tucked into a lush botanical garden cut with mini waterfalls and streams that lead to a small infinity pool that gazes over aqua sea. Its best asset, however, is its location, close to the action yet quiet and private.

Kirikayan Boutique Resort RESORT **$$$**
(Map p526; ☎077 332299; www.kirikayan.com; r from 4500B;) Simple whites, lacquered teak and blazing red accents set the colour scheme at this small, hip address along Hat Chaweng's southern sands. It's a smooth and restful composition: wander past thick palm trunks and sky-scraping foliage to find the relaxing pool deck at the back.

Hat Chaweng

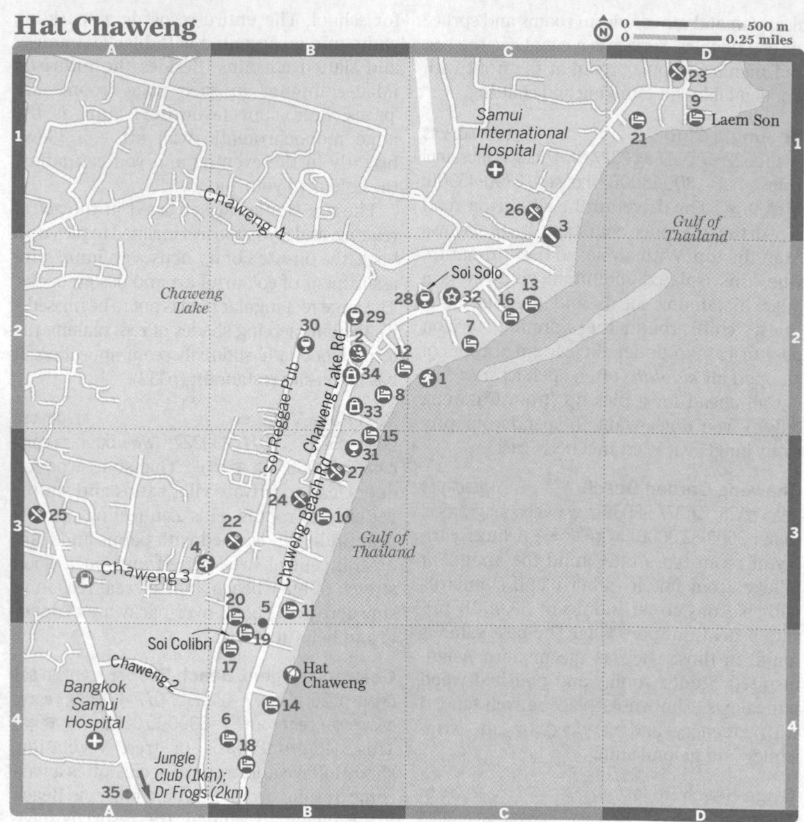

Centara Grand RESORT $$$

(Map p526; ☎077 230500; www.centralhotelsresorts.com; r 8900-21,500B; ❄@🛜🏊) Centara is a massive, manicured beachfront compound in the heart of Hat Chaweng, but the palm-filled property is so large you can safely escape the street-side bustle. Rooms are found in a hotel-like building, conspicuously Western in theme and decor. Babysitting and family-friendly services abound. Check online for big discounts out of high season.

Baan Chaweng Beach Resort RESORT $$$

(Map p526; ☎077 300564; www.baanchawengbeachresort.com; bungalows 4500-11,000B; ❄@🛜🏊) A bit of luxury without breaking the bank, Baan Chaweng draws in families and retired bargain-seekers who roast themselves on loungers along the lovely beach. The immaculate rooms are painted in various shades of peach and pear, with teak furnishings that feel both modern and traditional.

Hat Lamai

The central, powdery white area of Hat Lamai is packed with an amazing quantity of sunburned souls lounging on beach chairs, but head to the grainier northern or southern extremities and things get much quieter. Ban Lamai runs back from the main beach area. Unlike Hat Chaweng, the main party in Lamai takes place off the beach, so the sand here is generally free of a dance-beat soundtrack. However, the party scene that is here, mostly along the town's main drag and its smaller arteries, is of the seedier bar-girl-oriented variety.

Amarina Residence HOTEL $

(☎077 418073; www.amarinaresidence.com; r 1200-1800B; ❄🛜) A two-minute walk to the beach, this excellent-value small hotel has two storeys of big, tastefully furnished, tiled rooms encircling the lobby and an incongruous dipping pool.

Hat Chaweng

Activities, Courses & Tours
1 Aquapark ... C2
2 Blue Stars ... B2
3 Discovery Dive Centre ... C1
4 Samui Dog & Cat Rescue Centre ... A3
5 Samui Institute of Thai Culinary Arts ... B3

Sleeping
6 Akwa ... B4
7 Ark Bar Beach Resort ... C2
8 Baan Chaweng Beach Resort ... B2
9 Baan Haad Ngam ... D1
10 Buri Rasa Village ... B3
11 Centara Grand ... D3
12 Chaweng Garden Beach ... B2
13 Chaweng Regent Beach Resort ... C2
14 Kirikayan Boutique Resort ... B4
15 Library ... B3
16 Lucky Mother ... C2
17 P Chaweng ... B4
18 Pott Guesthouse ... B4
19 Queen Boutique Place ... B4
20 Samui Hostel ... B3
21 Tango Beach Resort ... D1

Eating
22 Laem Din Market ... B3
23 Larder ... D1
24 Ninja Crepes ... B3
Page ... (see 15)
25 Pepenero ... A3
26 Prego ... C1
27 Stacked ... B3

Drinking & Nightlife
Ark Bar ... (see 7)
28 Bar Solo ... C2
29 Green Mango ... B2
30 Reggae Pub ... B2
31 Tropical Murphy's Irish ... B3

Entertainment
32 Paris Follies Cabaret ... C2

Shopping
33 Bookazine ... B2
34 Central Festival ... B2

Transport
35 Bangkok Airways Office ... A4

New Hut BUNGALOW $
(☎077 230437; newhutlamai@yahoo.co.th; Lamai North; huts 300-800B;) A-frame huts right on the beach all share a big, clean block of bathrooms. There's a lively restaurant, friendly enough staff and one of the most simple and happy backpacker vibes.

Spa Resort BUNGALOW $$
(☎077 230855; www.spasamui.com; Lamai North; bungalows 720-1200B;) Programs at this friendly spa include colonics, massage, aqua detox, hypnotherapy and yoga, just to name a few. With rattan furniture, traditional wall art and balconies, rooms are comfortable and excellent value, but book up quickly. Nonguests are welcome to partake in the spa programs and dine at the excellent (and healthy) open-air restaurant by the beach.

★ **Rocky Resort** RESORT $$$
(☎077 418367; www.rockyresort.com; Hua Thanon; r 8000-20,000B;) With a supremely calm reception area and two swimming pools, Rocky effortlessly finds the right balance between an upmarket ambience and an unpretentious, sociable vibe. During quieter months prices are a steal, since ocean views abound, and each room (some with pool) has been furnished with beautiful Thai-inspired furniture that seamlessly incorporates a modern twist.

Banyan Tree Koh Samui RESORT $$$
(☎077 915333; www.banyantree.com/en/samui/overview; villas from 23,300B;) Occupying an entire bay, this sprawling over-the-top luxury delight encompasses dozens of pool villas hoisted above the foliage by spider-like stilts. Golf carts zip around the grounds carrying jet-setters between the myriad dining venues and the gargantuan spa (which sports a relaxing rainforest simulator). Service, however, could be improved.

Samui Jasmine Resort RESORT $$$
(☎077 232446; 131/8 Moo 3, Lamai; r & bungalows 4600-12,000B;) Smack dab in the middle of Hat Lamai, varnished-teak yet frilly Samui Jasmine is a great deal. Go for the lower-priced rooms – most have excellent views of the ocean and the crystal-coloured lap pool.

Choeng Mon

Choeng Mon is an area that holds several beaches that span the northeastern nub of the island. Samrong and Ton Son to the north are home to small communities and some of the most luxurious resorts in the world. Those with mortal budgets tend to stay on the beach at Choeng Mon proper whose perfect (although busy) half-moon of sand is considered by many to be the most beautiful beach on the island.

Bo Phut

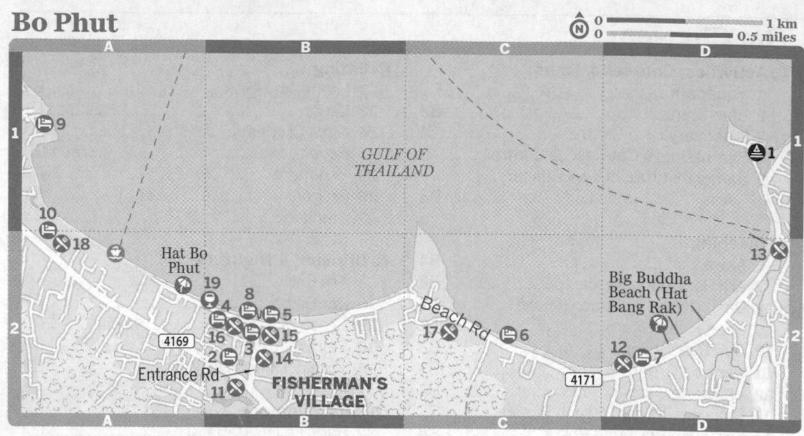

Samui Honey Cottages Resort RESORT $$
(Map p522; ☎077 427093; www.samuihoney.com; Choeng Mon; r incl breakfast 3500-6500B; ❄📶🏊) At the quieter southern part of the beach, this small resort (with an equally small pool) isn't anything that special but it's nicer than some of the other mediocre offerings in this price range on this beach. Expect attractive, classic Zen-style rooms.

★ **Six Senses Samui** RESORT $$$
(Map p522; ☎077 245678; www.sixsenses.com/hideaway-samui/index.php; Samrong; bungalows from 13,000B; ❄@📶🏊) This hidden bamboo paradise is worth the once-in-a-lifetime splurge. Set in 9 hectares along a rugged promontory, Six Senses strikes the perfect balance between opulence and rustic charm, and defines the expression 'barefoot elegance'. Most of the 66 villas have stunning concrete plunge pools and offer magnificent views of the silent bay below.

The regal, semi-outdoor bathrooms give the phrase 'royal flush' a whole new meaning. Golf buggies move guests between their cottages and the stunning amenities strewn around the property – including a world-class spa and two excellent restaurants.

Tongsai Bay RESORT $$$
(Map p522; ☎077 245480; www.tongsaibay.co.th; Tong Son; ste 11,800-38,000B; ❄📶🏊) For serious pampering, head to this secluded luxury gem. Impeccably maintained, the 10-hectare hilly grounds make the cluster of bungalows look more like a small village. All the split-level suites have day-bed rest areas, romantic decor, stunning views, large terraces and creatively placed bathtubs (you'll see).

Facilities include two pools, a tennis court, a spa, a dessert shop, several restaurants and a private beach, of course.

Sala Samui RESORT $$$
(Map p522; ☎077 245888; www.salasamui.com; Choeng Mon; r 6700B, villas 9700-23,200B; ❄@📶🏊) Is the hefty price tag worth it? Definitely. The dreamy, deluxe design scheme is exquisite and modern – clean whites and lacquered teaks are lavish throughout, while subtle turquoise accents draw on the colour of each villa's private plunge pool. Heavenly.

Big Buddha Beach (Hat Bang Rak)

Named after the huge golden Buddha that presides over the small nearby quasi-island of Ko Fan, this beach's western half is by far the best, with its relatively empty stretch of white sand. The closer you get to the busy pier areas, the coarser and browner the sand becomes and the murkier the water. Big Buddha Beach's proximity to the airport means some overhead roaring (but quick and cheap taxi rides for flight arrivals).

Secret Garden Beach Resort BUNGALOW $$
(Map p528; ☎077 245255; www.secretgarden.co.th; bungalows 1700-3700B; ❄📶🏊) This refurbished and renewed Dutch-owned establishment has an excellent beach restaurant and bar and fresh, well-equipped bungalows in the eponymous garden and by the pool. There's live music on Sundays when locals, expats and tourists come to chill out and imbibe, but it's fairly subdued the rest of the time.

Bo Phut

Sights

1 Wat Phra Yai....D1

Sleeping

2 Anantara....B2
3 Castaway Guesthouse....B2
4 Eden....B2
5 Hacienda....B2
6 Scent....C2
7 Secret Garden Beach Resort....D2
8 The Lodge....B2
9 W Retreat Koh Samui....A1
10 Zazen....A1

Eating

11 69....B2
12 Antica Locanda....D2
13 Catcantoo....D2
14 Chez François....B2
15 Karma Sutra....B2
16 Shack Bar & Grill....B2
17 The Hut....C2
18 Zazen Restaurant....A2

Drinking & Nightlife

Billabong Surf Club....(see 8)
19 Coco Tam's....B2
Woo Bar....(see 9)

★Scent RESORT $$$

(Map p528; ☎077 960123; www.thescenthotel.com; ste 8500-10,500B) Seek out the taste (and scent if you light your complimentary incense) of Indo-China at this tranquil gem that recreates the elegance of 1940s and '50s colonial Asia. The tall grey concrete structure is cut by elongated teak framed windows and surrounds a courtyard swimming pool and ornamental trees and plants.

Choose between European, Chinese or Thai-Chinese style rooms, each one spacious and decorated with tasteful opulence.

Bo Phut

Bo Phut's Fisherman's Village is a concentration of narrow Chinese shophouses, transformed into some of the island's trendiest (and often midrange) boutique hotels and eateries. The accompanying beach, particularly the eastern part, is slim and coarse but becomes whiter and lusher further west.

Hacienda GUESTHOUSE $$

(Map p528; ☎077 245943; www.samui-hacienda.com; r 1200-2800B, ste 2600-4450B;) Polished terracotta and rounded archways give the entrance a Spanish mission motif. Similar decor permeates the adorable rooms, which sport touches such as pebbled bathroom walls and translucent bamboo lamps. Hacienda Suites, the overflow property a few doors down, holds the cheaper 'eco' rooms which are minuscule and mostly window-less, but still clean and comfortable. The tiny rooftop pool has gorgeous ocean views.

The Lodge HOTEL $$

(Map p528; ☎077 425337; www.lodgesamui.com; r 2500-3000B;) The Lodge feels like a colonial hunting chalet with pale walls, hardwood floors and dark wooden beams jutting across the ceiling, except it all looks out over blue-green sea. Each of the eight rooms has scores of wall hangings and a private balcony overlooking the beach; the 'pent-huts' on the top floor are particularly spacious.

You're really in the heart of the Fisherman's Village, making this a lively spot but somehow still intimate. It's extremely popular so reservations are a must.

Castaway Guesthouse GUESTHOUSE $$

(Map p528; ☎098 464 6562; r with fan/air-con 650-1500B;) A block away from the beach, right in the Fisherman's Village, the newly renovated Castaway's 15 rooms are all clean, bright and cheery.

Eden BUNGALOW $$

(Map p528; ☎077 427645; www.edenbungalows.com; bungalows 1500-2300B;) The 10 bungalows and five rooms here are all tucked away in a garden with a small pool at its centre. Cheaper options are rather shabby but an upgrade gets you a more stylish suite with yellow walls and naturalistic wood furniture. It's about a two-minute walk to the beach.

★Anantara RESORT $$$

(Map p528; ☎077 428300; samui.anantara.com; r 6400-22,775B;) Anantara's stunning palanquin entrance satisfies fantasies of a far-flung oriental kingdom. Clay and copper statues of grimacing jungle creatures abound on the property's wild acreage, while guests savour wild teas in an open-air pagoda, swim in the lagoon-like infinity-edged swimming pool or indulge in relaxing treatments amid the lush tropical foliage of the beautiful spa.

Zazen RESORT $$$

(Map p528; ☎077 425085; www.samuizazen.com; r 6160-17,200B; ❄@☜≋) Welcome to one of the boutique-iest boutique resorts on Samui – every inch of this charming getaway has been thoughtfully and creatively designed. It's 'Asian minimalism meets modern rococo' with a scarlet accent wall, terracotta goddesses, a dash of feng shui and a generous smattering of good taste. Guests relax poolside or on loungers gently shaded by canvas parasols on the very best stretch of this beach. Even better, the service is as luxe as the setting.

Mae Nam & Bang Po

Mae Nam's slim length of white sand slopes down to an aqua sea. One of the island's prettiest stretches of beach, it's popular with families and older couples, giving it an unhurried yet still vibrant ambience perfect for reading under the shade of a coconut tree, sleeping or having beach massages. Bang Po, just around the tiny peninsula, is even quieter.

Shangri-la BUNGALOW $

(☎077 425189; Mae Nam; bungalows with fan/air-con from 500/1300B; ❄☜) A backpacker's Shangri La indeed – these are some of the cheapest huts around and they're on a sublime part of the beach. Grounds are sparsely landscaped but the basic concrete bungalows, all with attached bathrooms (only air-con rooms have hot water), are well kept and the staff is pleasant.

Coco Palm Resort BUNGALOW $$

(Map p522; ☎077 425095; www.cocopalmbeachresort.com; Mae Nam; bungalows 3000-9450B; ❄☜≋) The huge array of bungalows at this resort have been crafted with hard wood, bamboo and rattan touches. A rectangular pool is the centrepiece along the beach. The cheapest choices are the furthest from the beach, but even these are comfy; and if you want to make a real splash, aim for the beachfront pool villas.

Code HOTEL $$$

(Map p522; ☎077 602122; www.samuicode.com; Mae Nam; ste 3300-11,100B; ❄☜≋) All sleek modern lines and dust-free white contrasts against the turquoise sea and the hotel's large infinity pool, making for a stunning piece of architecture. The all-ocean-view suites are spacious and efficient and the service is just as grand.

Of course, as with any fine piece of machinery, everything you need is at your fingertips including a gym, spa and restaurant.

W Retreat Koh Samui RESORT $$$

(Map p528; ☎077 915999; www.starwoodhotels.com/whotels; Mae Nam; r from 19,500B; ❄@☜≋) A bejewelled 'W' welcomes guests on the curling road to the lobby, and upon arrival jaws immediately drop while staring out over the infinity pools and endless horizon. The trademark 'W glam' does its darnedest to fuse an urban vibe with tropical serenity throughout. Do note, though, that this hotel is on a hill and not on a beach.

Belmond Napasai RESORT $$$

(Map p522; ☎077 429200; www.napasai.com; Bang Po; r from 10,900B; ❄@☜≋) Gorgeously manicured grounds welcome weary travellers as they glide past grazing water buffalo and groundsmen donning cream-coloured pith helmets. A generous smattering of villas dot the expansive landscape – all sport traditional Thai-style decorations, from the intricately carved wooden ornamentation to streamers of luscious local silks.

Na Thon

Chytalay Palace Hotel HOTEL $$

(☎077 421079; 152 Nathon Moo 3; d with fan 400B, d with air-con, 550-950B, tr 800-1000B; ❄☜) This quiet hotel on the beachfront road a short walk south from the pier has spacious rooms with balcony overlooking the sea. The perfectly good, cheaper, lower-floor rooms have electricity cables partially blocking the view but are 400B less than the newer rooms upstairs. All rooms have attached shower rooms. Service is pleasant, if rather reserved.

West Coast

With more Thai tourists, Samui's west coast has skinny beaches of grainy sand but the sunsets can be breathtaking, while the blue seas and views out to the Five Islands and the shadowy greens of the mainland are beguiling. It's a welcome escape from the often-draining east-side bustle.

Am Samui BUNGALOW $$

(Map p522; ☎077 235165; Taling Ngam; bungalows 1600-6000B; ❄☜≋) Cast modesty aside, spread your curtains wide, and welcome sunshine and sea views in through your floor-to-ceiling windows. Getting out of the main tourist areas to this private beach with fantastic sunset views means your baht goes miles further in terms of room quality.

Sunset Beach Resort & Spa RESORT $$$
(Map p522; ☎077 428200; www.thesunsetbeachresort.com; Ban Taling Nam; r 6000-14,300B, villa 11,000-35,800B; ❄📶🏊) While the views over the Five Islands at sunset, quiet (though slightly pebbly) beach and extra-clean, simple yet luxurious rooms are a draw, it's the smiling, attentive service that makes this place stand out among resorts in this area. Free mountain bikes get you around the sleepy surrounding village, but you'll want a vehicle to get further afield.

Four Seasons Koh Samui HOTEL $$$
(Map p522; ☎077 243000; www.fourseasons.com/kohsamui; villas from 30,000B; ❄📶🏊) This hilly 17-hectare enclave of 60 villas, on a peninsula at the far western corner of Bang Po, feels more like a private village than a resort. Stunning views range out from the lobby, while each huge villa has a private plunge pool. A beautiful stretch of flaxen sand awaits, there's a Thai boxing ring and a gym with a view.

Mövenpick Resort Laem Yai Beach Samui RESORT $$$
(Map p522; ☎077 421722; www.moevenpick-hotels.com; r incl breakfast 8100-21,900B; ❄📶🏊) Splendid and serene, this boutique spot on the west coast is a top choice for out-of-the-action beachcombing, coupled with fine sunsets and a sparklingly high degree of service. Facilities, including three pools, are top notch, as are the villas. Cabarets and fire shows kick off in the evening, but if it's nightlife you want, look elsewhere.

South Coast

The southern end of Ko Samui is spotted with rocky headlands and smaller coves of pebble sand that are used more as parking lots for Thai fishing boats than for lounge chairs. It's a great area to take a leisurely cycle through coconut palm groves and small Thai villages that aren't ruled by tourism.

Easy Time BUNGALOW $$
(Map p522; ☎077 920111; www.easytimesamui.com; Phang Ka; villas 2300-4000B; ❄@📶🏊) Safely tucked away from the throngs of tourists, this little haven – nestled a few minutes' walk to the beach around a serene swimming pool – doesn't have well-oiled service so be prepared to be master of your own off-the-beaten-path getaway. Duplex villa units and a chic dining space create an elegant mood that is refreshingly unpretentious.

Elements RESORT $$$
(Map p522; ☎077 914678; www.elements-koh-samui.com; Phang Ka; r incl breakfast 7400-24,000B; ❄@📶🏊) Peaceful Elements occupies a lonely strand of sand with views of the Five Islands, and is the perfect place for a meditative retreat or quiet couples romantic getaway. Chic rooms are arranged in condo-like blocks while hidden villas dot the path down to the oceanside lounge area. Free kayaks and bikes plus excellent service add to the calm.

Eating

If you thought it was hard to pick a place to sleep, the island has even more options when it comes to dining. From roasted crickets to beluga caviar, Samui's got it and is not afraid to flaunt it.

Influenced by the mainland, Samui is peppered with *kôw gaang* (rice and curry) shops, usually just a wooden shack displaying large metal pots of southern Thai-style curries. Folks pull up on their motorcycles, lift up the lids to survey the vibrantly coloured contents, and pick one for lunch. *Kôw gaang* shops are easily found along the Ring Rd (Rte 4169) and sell out of the good stuff by 1pm. Any build-up of local motorcycles is usually a sign of a good meal in progress.

The upmarket choices are even more numerous and although Samui's swank dining scene is laden with Italian options, visitors will have no problem finding flavours from around the globe. Lured by high salaries and spectacular weather, world-class chefs regularly make an appearance on the island.

Hat Chaweng

Dozens of the restaurants on the 'strip' serve a mixed bag of local bites, international cuisine and greasy fast food, but there's nothing worth making a trip for. For the best ambience head to the beach, where many bungalow operators set up tables on the sand and have glittery fairy lights at night.

Laem Din Market MARKET $
(Map p526; dishes from 35B; ⏰4am-6pm, night market 6pm-2am) A busy day market, Laem Din is packed with stalls that sell fruits, vegetables and meats and stock local Thai kitchens. Pick up a kilo of sweet green oranges or wander the stalls trying to spot the ingredients in last night's curry. For dinner, come to the adjacent night market and sample the southern-style fried chicken and curries.

Ninja Crepes THAI **$**
(Map p526; dishes from 75B; ⊙11am-midnight) Rammed nightly, with flaming woks at the heart of things working double-time to keep the pace, this warehouse-sized restaurant serves up Thai seafood, curries, crepes, soups and desserts to throngs of eager patrons.

★ **Stacked** STEAK **$$**
(Map p526; www.stacked-samui.com; mains from 295B; ⊙noon-midnight;) All sharp lines, open grill, a team of busy staff plus a cracker of a menu, this burger restaurant is a visual and culinary feast. Burgers and steaks – bursting with flavour – are served up on slate slabs in generous portions. Go with a sizeable hunger as the inclination is to simply keep on ordering.

★ **Pepenero** ITALIAN **$$**
(Map p526; www.pepenerosamui.com; mains from 250B; ⊙5.30-10.30pm Mon & Wed-Sat, 6-10.30pm Sun) Pepenero has caused quite a stir on Ko Samui. What this excellent Italian restaurant lacks in views, is more than made up for by a terrific menu (including cutting boards with cheese and cold cuts) and the care and attention displayed to customers by the very sociable, hard-working hosts.

★ **Larder** EUROPEAN **$$$**
(Map p526; www.thelardersamui.com; mains 300-900B; ⊙noon-11pm;) This restaurant/bar/gastropub pulls out the stops in an invigorating menu of classic fare in a relaxing and tasteful setting, supported by a strong selection of wines and zesty cocktails. It's a winning formula, with dishes ranging from slow cooked lamb spare ribs to beer-battered snow fish and warm falafel with feta cucumber and chilli salad.

Page ASIAN FUSION **$$$**
(Map p526; www.thelibrary.co.th/the-page.html; dishes 300-1650B; ⊙7am-11.30pm;) If you can't afford to stay at the ultra-swanky Library (p525), have a meal at its beachside restaurant. It's not cheap, but lunch is a bit more casual and affordable.

Dr Frogs STEAK **$$$**
(Map p522; www.drfrogssamui.com; mains from 380B; ⊙noon-11pm) Perched atop a rocky overlook, Dr Frogs combines beautiful ocean vistas with international Italian grills, seafood, pasta, pizza and Thai favourites. Delectable steaks and crab cakes, and friendly owners, make it a winner. It's a romantic set-

SALT AND SPICE IN SOUTHERN THAI CUISINE

Don't say we didn't warn you: southern Thai cooking is undoubtedly the spiciest regional cooking style in a land of spicy regional cuisines. The food of Thailand's southern provinces also tends to be very salty, and seafood, not surprisingly, plays an important role, ranging from fresh fish that is grilled or added to soups, to pickled or fermented fish or served as sauces or condiments.

Two of the principal crops in the south are coconuts and cashews, both of which find their way into a variety of dishes. In addition to these, southern Thais love their greens, and nearly every meal is accompanied by a platter of fresh herbs and vegies, and a spicy 'dip' of shrimp paste, chillies, garlic and lime.

Dishes you are likely to come across in southern Thailand include the following:

Gaang đai Ƅlah An intensely spicy and salty curry that includes *đai Ƅlah* (salted fish stomach); much tastier than it sounds.

Gaang sôm Known as *gaang lĕu·ang* (yellow curry) in central Thailand, this sour/spicy soup gets its hue from the liberal use of turmeric, a root commonly used in southern Thai cooking.

Gài tôrt hàht yài The famous deep-fried chicken from the town of Hat Yai gets its rich flavour from a marinade containing dried spices.

Kà·nŏm jeen nám yah This dish of thin rice noodles served with a fiery curry-like sauce is always accompanied by a tray of fresh vegetables and herbs.

Kôo·a glîng Minced meat fried with a fiery curry paste is a southern staple.

Kôw yam A popular breakfast, this dish includes rice topped with sliced herbs, bean sprouts, dried prawns, toasted coconut and powdered red chilli, served with a sour/sweet fish-based sauce.

Pàt sà·đor This popular stir-fry of 'stink beans' with shrimp, garlic, chillies and shrimp paste is both pungent and spicy.

ting, and for harassed parents there's a kids playground in the front garden. Live guitar music from Tuesday to Thursday at 7.30pm.

Prego ITALIAN $$$
(Map p526; www.prego-samui.com; mains 280-860B; ⌚noon-11pm) Renovated and zestfully refreshed with a new bar/lounge zone, this cool restaurant serves up tantalising Italian cuisine, with a strong selection of vegetarian dishes, backed up by a tempting wine list.

Hat Lamai

As Samui's second-most populated beach, Hat Lamai has a surprisingly limited assortment of decent eateries when compared to Hat Chaweng next door. Most nights a few noodle and pancake stalls open up around the 'Lady Boxing' bars in the centre of town, and sell dishes from 50B that you can eat at outdoor plastic tables.

Hua Thanon Market MARKET $
(Map p522; dishes from 30B; ⌚6am-6pm) Slip into the rhythm of this village market slightly south of Lamai; it's a window into the food ways of southern Thailand. Vendors shoo away the flies from the freshly butchered meat and housewives load bundles of vegetables into their motorcycle baskets. Follow the market road to the row of food shops delivering edible Muslim culture: chicken *biryani,* fiery curries or toasted rice with coconut, bean sprouts, lemon grass and dried shrimp.

Lamai Day Market MARKET $
(dishes from 30B; ⌚6am-8pm) Lamai's market is a hive of activity, selling food necessities and takeaway food. Visit the covered area to pick up fruit or to see vendors shredding coconuts to make coconut milk. Or hunt down the ice-cream seller for homemade coconut ice cream. It's next door to a petrol station.

Pad Thai THAI $
(www.manathai.com/samui/phad-thai; mains from 70B; ⌚11am-11pm) On the corner of the huge Manathai hotel, this highly affordable, semi alfresco and smart restaurant is a fantastic choice for stir-fried and soup noodles, rounded off with a coconut ice cream.

Tandoori Nights INDIAN $
(mains from 150B; ⌚11am-11.30pm) The set meals at this welcoming Indian restaurant will only set you back 190B for a vegetable curry, soft drink and a papadum; otherwise select your spice level from the à la carte menu or take a deep breath and order up the eye-watering lamb vindaloo (290B).

★**La Fabrique** BAKERY $$
(set breakfasts from 120B; ⌚6.30am-10.30pm; 📶) Ceiling fans chop the air and service is snappy and helpful at this roomy French-styled boulangerie/patisserie away from the main drag, near Wat Lamai on Rte 4169. Choose from fresh bread, croissants, gratins, baguettes, meringues, yoghurts, pastries or unusually good set breakfasts that include fresh fruit and well-cooked eggs. Wash it down with a selection of coffees or teas. There's a smaller and noisier branch in Chaweng.

Baobab FRENCH $$
(☎084 838 3040; Hat Lamai; mains 150-380B; ⌚8.30am-6pm) Grab a free beach towel and crash out on a sun lounger after a full meal at breezy Baobab, or have a massage next door, but seize one of the beach tables (if you can). You'll need two hands to turn over the hefty menu, with its all-day breakfasts, French/Thai dishes, grills, pastas and popular specials, including red tuna steak (350B).

With the sound of the surf and lovely views, it's frequently a sell-out.

Radiance INTERNATIONAL $$
(meals 100-400B; ⌚7am-10pm; 📶✎) Even if you're not staying at the Spa Resort, or not even a vegetarian for that matter, healthy food rarely tastes this good. It's not all brown rice: you'll find everything from an amazing raw *thom kha* (coconut green curry soup) to chocolate smoothies that can jive with anyone's dietary restrictions. Plus the semi-outdoor beach-side setting is tranquil, relaxing and unpretentious.

The Dining Room FRENCH $$$
(www.rockyresort.com/en/dining/dining-room; dishes 300-950B; ⌚lunch & dinner) The signature beef Rossini at this beachfront restaurant at Rocky's Resort is like sending your taste buds on a Parisian vacation as the views pop you into seventh heaven.

Choeng Mon & Big Buddha Beach (Hat Bang Rak)

Choeng Mon's lively main drag that runs parallel to this main northern beach has lots of eating options, although price tags are high even without the beach view. There are fewer eating options around Big Buddha Beach, west of Choeng Mon, and the setting is less glamorous, but prices are more reasonable.

Antica Locanda ITALIAN $$
(Map p528; ☎077 245163; www.anticasamui.com; Hat Bang Rak; mains from 240B; ⊙1-11pm; 📶) This friendly trattoria has pressed white tablecloths and caskets of Italian wine. Try the *vongole alla marinara* (clams in white wine; 240B), but also consider the succulent specials of the day.

Catcantoo INTERNATIONAL $$
(Map p528; www.catcantoo.com; Hat Bang Rak; mains 90-350B; ⊙9am-2am) Enjoy good-value breakfasts in the morning, succulent ribs at noon, or shooting pool later in the day.

★Dining On The Rocks ASIAN FUSION $$$
(Map p522; ☎077 245678; reservations-samui@sixsenses.com; Choeng Mon; menus from 2200B; ⊙5-10pm) Samui's ultimate dining experience takes place on nine cantilevered verandahs of weathered teak and bamboo that yawn over the gulf. After sunset (and wine), guests feel like they're dining on a barge set adrift on a starlit sea. Each dish on the six-course set menu is the brainchild of the cooks who regularly experiment with taste, texture and temperature.

If you're celebrating a special occasion, you'll have to book well in advance if you want to sit at 'table 99' (the honeymooners' table) positioned on a private terrace, complete with surprise menu. Dining On The Rocks is at the isolated Six Senses Samui. The bar and lounge opens an hour earlier, with dining starting at 6pm.

Bo Phut

The Fisherman's Village is the nicest setting for a meal but you'll find heaps of cheaper options on the road leading inland towards the main road.

The Hut THAI $
(Map p528; mains 60-550B; ⊙1-10pm) Basic, reasonably priced Thai specialities share space with more expensive fresh seafood and Western treats here, but the dozen or so tables fill fast so get here early or late if you don't want to wait. If you're a fisherman this is the place to get your own catch cooked up.

Karma Sutra INTERNATIONAL $$
(Map p528; mains 180-700B; ⊙8am-2am; 📶) A haze of purples and pillows, beanbags and low tables, this charming chow spot straddles the heart of Bo Phut's Fisherman's Village and serves up good international and Thai eats, with alfresco seating by the wayside.

69 THAI FUSION $$
(Map p528; mains from 149B; ⊙1-10pm; 📶) The simply roaring roadside setting puts it on the wrong side of the tracks and the dated, eclectic decor is looking rather limp and tired; that said, almost unanimous rave reviews for its creative twists on Thai favourites make this a really popular choice.

★Chez François FRENCH $$$
(Map p528; www.facebook.com/chezporte; 33/2 Moo 1 Fisherman's Village; set meal 1700B; ⊙6-11pm Tue-Sat) With no à la carte menu, but a reputation for outstanding cuisine that has sent waves across the culinary map of Ko Samui, Chez François serves a three-course surprise meal. Book ahead using the Facebook page and if you're only on Ko Samui for a few days, book early to get a table. It's tiny (and cash only).

Chez François is hidden away behind a wooden door near a pharmacy.

Shack Bar & Grill STEAK $$$
(Map p528; www.theshackgrillsamui.com; mains 450-800B; ⊙5.30-11pm) The Shack imports the finest cuts of meat from Australia and slathers them in a rainbow of tasty sauces from red wine to blue cheese. Booth seating and jazz over the speakers give the joint a distinctly Western vibe, though you'll find all types of diners coming here to splurge.

Zazen Restaurant ASIAN FUSION $$$
(Map p528; dishes 540-900B, set menu from 1300B; ⊙lunch & dinner) This superb romantic dining experience at the Zazen Resort comes complete with ocean views, dim candle lighting and soft music. Thai dancers animate things on Thursday and Sunday nights from 8pm. Reservations recommended.

Mae Nam & Bang Po

Mae Nam has tonnes of eating options from beachside huts serving a mix of Thai, Western and seafood dishes to classier places tucked along the inland, lily-pad pond-dotted tangle of roads. It's a lovely place to wander and find your own surprises.

Fish Restaurant INTERNATIONAL $
(mains from 50B; ⊙noon-10pm) With elegant Thai tablecloths and a well-priced, tasty menu of Thai seafood and pan-Asian dishes and international appetisers, this popular concrete-floor eatery pulls in a regular stream of diners, although portions are a bit on the teeny side and the relaxing music edges into muzak territory.

Bang Po Seafood SEAFOOD $$
(Bang Po; dishes from 100B; ⏲dinner) A meal at Bang Po Seafood is a test for the taste buds. It's one of the only restaurants that serves traditional Ko Samui fare: recipes call for ingredients such as raw sea urchin roe, baby octopus, sea water, coconut and local turmeric.

John's Garden Restaurant THAI $$
(Map p522; ☎077 247694; www.johnsgardensamui.com; mains from 160B; ⏲1-10pm) This delightful garden restaurant is a picture, with tables slung out beneath bamboo and palms and carefully cropped hedges. The signature dish on the Thai and European menu is the excellent massaman chicken. Mosquito repellent is generally provided, but pack some in case. It's particularly romantic when lantern-lit at night, so reserve ahead.

Farmer INTERNATIONAL $$$
(Map p522; ☎077 447222; Mae Nam; mains 350-1000B; ⏲lunch & dinner) Magically set in front of a photogenic rice field, fantastic Farmer is a choice selection, especially when the candlelight flickers on a starry night. The mostly European-inspired food is lovely and well-presented, there's a free pick-up for nearby beaches and service is attentive. At the time of writing, new resort villas were being constructed around the rice field.

West & South Coasts

The quiet west coast features some of the best seafood on Samui. Na Thon has a giant **day market** on Th Thawi Ratchaphakdi – it's worth stopping by to grab some snacks before your ferry ride.

Ging Pagarang SEAFOOD $
(Thong Tanote; meals from 50B; ⏲11.30am-8pm) Locals know this is one of the island's best beachside places to sample authentic Samui-style seafood. It's simple and family-run, but the food and views are extraordinary. Try the sea algae salad with crab, fried dried octopus with coconut or the spectacular fried fish or prawns with lemon grass.

Five Islands SEAFOOD $$$
(Map p522; ☎077 415359; www.thefiveislandssamui.com; dishes 250-790B; ⏲noon-11pm) Five Islands offers a unique (yet pricey) eating experience. First, a long-tail boat (tours for two including meal 7500B to 9250B) will take you out into the turquoise sea to visit the haunting Five Sister Islands where you'll learn about the ancient art of harvesting bird nests to make bird's-nest soup, a Chinese delicacy. When you return, a deluxe meal is waiting for you on the beach.

Lunch tours departs around 10am, and the dinner programs leave around 3pm. Customers are also welcome to dine without going on the tour and vice versa but if you want the tour, book two days in advance.

Drinking & Nightlife

Samui's biggest party spot is, without a doubt, noisy Hat Chaweng. Lamai and Bo Phut come in second and third respectively, while the rest of the island is generally quiet, as the drinking is usually focused around self-contained resort bars.

Hat Chaweng & Hat Lamai

Making merry in Chaweng is a piece of cake. Most places are open until 2am and there are a few places that go strong all night long.

Every Saturday night around dinner hours it's lady boxing time at Lamai's thus named 'Lady Boxing' bars, when two bar girls duke it out in the ring after weeks of training. The rest of the week the girls writhe and dance at these central open-air bars, which is particularly depressing when there are no clients.

Beach Republic BAR
(www.beachrepublic.com; 176/34 Mu 4, Hat Lamai; ⏲7am-11pm) Recognised by its thatch-patched awnings, Beach Republic could be the poster child of a made-for-TV, beachside, booze swilling holiday. There's a wading pool, lounge chairs, an endless cocktail list and even a hotel if you never, ever want to leave the party. The Sunday brunches here are legendary.

Ark Bar BAR
(Map p526; www.ark-bar.com; Hat Chaweng; ☎7am-2am;) Drinks are dispensed from the multicoloured bar to an effusive crowd, guests recline on loungers on the beach, and the party is on day and night.

Bar Solo BAR
(Map p526; Hat Chaweng) Bar Solo's bubbly party mood, decent DJs and evening drink specials lure in front-loaders preparing for a late, late night at the dance clubs on Soi Solo and Soi Green Mango.

Tropical Murphy's Irish BAR
(Map p526; Hat Chaweng; ⏲8am-2am; 📶) Come night-time, the live music kicks on and this place turns into the most popular Irish bar on Ko Samui (yes, there are a few). On

the menu, there's steak-and-kidney pie, fish and chips, Ulster Fry (breakfast) and lamb chops and Irish stew (mains 60B to 300B).

Green Mango BAR

(Map p526; www.thegreenmangoclub.com; Hat Chaweng) This place is so popular it has an entire soi named after it. Samui's favourite power drinking house is very big, very loud and very *fa·ràng*. Green Mango has blazing lights, expensive drinks and masses of sweaty bodies swaying to dance music.

Reggae Pub BAR

(Map p526; Hat Chaweng; ⏲6pm-3am) This fortress of fun sports an open-air dance floor with music spun by foreign DJs. It's a towering two-storey affair with long bars, pool tables and a live-music stage. The whole place doubles as a shrine to Bob Marley; it's often empty early in the evening, getting going around midnight. The long road up to Reggae Pub is ladyboy central.

Northern & West Coast Beaches

Woo Bar BAR

(Map p528; Mae Nam; ⏲11am-1am; 📶) With serious wow factor, the W Retreat's signature lobby bar gives the word 'swish' a whole new meaning with cushion-clad pods of seating plunked in the middle of an expansive infinity pool that stretches out over the infinite horizon. This is, without a doubt, the best place on Samui for sunset cocktails. Mojitos are free-flow on Thursday nights (1300B).

Nikki Beach BAR

(Map p522; ☎077 914500; www.nikkibeach.com/kohsamui; Lipa Noi; 📶) The acclaimed luxury brand brings international *savoir faire* to the secluded west coast of Ko Samui. Think: haute cuisine, chic decor and jet-setters. Themed brunch and dinner specials keep the masses coming throughout the week, and sleek villa accommodation is also on offer.

Coco Tam's BAR

(Map p528; Bo Phut; shisha pipes 500B; ⏲5pm-1am) Plop yourself on a beanbag on the sand, order a cocktail served in a jar and take a toke on a shisha (water pipe). It's a bit pricey, but this boho, beach bum–chic spot oozes relaxation. There are fire dancers most nights.

Billabong Surf Club BAR

(Map p528; Bo Phut; ⏲9am-1am; 📶) Billabong's all about Aussie Rules football – it's playing on the TV and the walls are smothered with signed shirts and memorabilia from Down Undah. There are great views of Ko Pha-Ngan and hearty portions of ribs and chops to go with your draught beer.

☆ Entertainment

Paris Follies Cabaret CABARET

(Map p526; Hat Chaweng; ⏲8pm-midnight) This dazzling and fun cabaret offers one-hour *gà·teu·i* (ladyboys; also spelled *kàthoey*) cabaret every night at 8pm, 9pm, 10pm and 11pm and attracts a mixed clientele of both sexes. Admission is free, but you need to buy a drink (around 390B).

Shopping

Central Festival SHOPPING CENTRE

(Map p526; ⏲11am-11pm) This new monster-mall is stuffed with shops and restaurants.

Island Books BOOKS

(⏲9am-7pm) Tucked away on a lane off Rte 4169 and run by Liverpudlian Paul, Island Books in Lamai has the largest selection of used books on the island.

Bookazine BOOKS

(Map p526; ☎077 413616; Hat Chaweng; ⏲11am-10pm) Chaweng Chain outlet selling new books, magazines and Lonely Planet guides.

ℹ Information

DANGERS & ANNOYANCES

The rate of road accident fatalities on Ko Samui is quite high. This is mainly due to the large number of tourists who rent motorcycles only to find out that the winding roads, sudden tropical rains and frenzied traffic can be lethal. If you decide to rent a motorcycle, protect yourself by wearing a helmet, and ask for one that has a plastic visor. Be warned that if you don't have an international driving licence, you may have problems in the event of an accident and your insurer might not cover you.

Beach vendors are registered with the government and should all be wearing a numbered jacket. No peddler should cause an incessant disturbance – seek assistance if this occurs.

A car bomb exploded in the Central Festival shopping centre in 2015, wounding six people.

EMERGENCY

Tourist Police (☎077 421281, emergency 1155) Based at the south of Na Thon.

IMMIGRATION

Located about 2km south of Na Thon is Ko Samui's **Immigration Office** (☎077 421069; ⏲8.30am-noon & 1-4.30pm Mon-Fri). Officials here tend to issue the minimum rather than maximum visa extensions. During our visits here we've watched dozens of tourists wait through exhausting lines only to be curtly denied an extension for no particular reason. On a particularly bad day expect extensions to take the entire afternoon.

INTERNET ACCESS

Wi-fi is widespread at most accommodation choices, restaurants and bars. You may have to pay for wi-fi access at some high-end hotels, but it is provided free at most midrange and budget places.

MEDIA

Siam Map Company (www.siammap.com) Puts out quarterly booklets including a *Spa Guide*, *Dining Guide*, and an annual directory, which lists thousands of companies and hotels on the island. Its *Siam Map Company Samui Guide Map* is free and easily found throughout the island.

Samui Navigator (www.samuinavigator.com) This pamphlet is worth a look.

Samui Guide (www.samuiguide.com) This guide looks more like a magazine and features mostly restaurants and attractions.

MEDICAL SERVICES

Ko Samui has four private hospitals, all near Chaweng's Tesco Lotus supermarket on the east coast (where most of the tourists tend to gather). The government hospital (Samui Hospital) in Na Thon has seen significant improvements in the past couple of years but the service is still a bit grim because funding is based on the number of Samui's legal residents (which doesn't take into account the many illegal Myanmar workers).

Bandon International Hospital (☎077 245236, emergency 077 425748)

Bangkok Samui Hospital (Map p526; ☎077 429500, emergency 077 429555) Your best bet for just about any medical problem.

Hyperbaric Chamber (☎077 427427; Big Buddha Beach) The island's dive medicine specialists.

Samui International Hospital (Map p526; ☎077 230782; www.sih.co.th; Hat Chaweng) Emergency ambulance service is available 24 hours and credit cards are accepted. It's near the Amari Resort in Hat Chaweng.

MONEY

Changing money isn't a problem on the east and north coasts, and in Na Thon. Multiple banks and foreign-exchange booths offer daily services and there's an ATM every 200m. You should not have to pay credit card fees as you do on Ko Tao.

POST

In several parts of the island there are privately run post-office branches charging a small commission. You can almost always leave your stamped mail with your accommodation.

Main Post Office Near the TAT office; not always reliable.

TOURIST INFORMATION

Tourism Authority of Thailand (TAT; ☎077 420504; Na Thon; ⌚8.30am-4.30pm)

Getting There & Away

AIR

Ko Samui's **airport** (www.samuiairportonline.com) is in the northeast of the island near Big Buddha Beach. **Bangkok Airways** (www.bangkokair.com) operates flights roughly every 30 minutes between Samui and Bangkok's Suvarnabhumi International Airport (50 minutes). Bangkok Airways also flies direct from Samui to Phuket, Pattaya, Chiang Mai, Singapore, Kuala Lumpur, Hong Kong and other cities in Southeast Asia. **Firefly** (www.fireflyz.com.my) operates direct flights from Ko Samui to Kuala Lumpur's Subang airport and has three flights per week to Penang.

There is a **Bangkok Airways Office** (Map p526; ☎077 420519, 077 420512) in Hat Chaweng and another at the airport. The first (at 6am) and last (10pm) flights of the day are always the cheapest.

During the high season, make your flight reservations far in advance as seats often sell out. If the Samui flights are full, try flying into Surat Thani from Bangkok and taking the short ferry ride to Samui instead. Flights to Surat Thani are generally cheaper than a direct flight to the island, although they are much more of a hassle.

BOAT

To reach Samui, the main piers on the mainland are Ao Ban Don, Tha Thong, Don Sak and Chumphon – Tha Thong (in central Surat) and Don Sak being the most common. On Samui, the three oft-used ports are Na Thon, Mae Nam and Big Buddha Beach. Expect complimentary taxi transfers with high-speed ferry services.

To the Mainland

There are frequent boat departures between Samui and the mainland. Two options are the high-speed Lomprayah (p573; 450B), which departs from Na Thon, and the slower, stinkier Raja (☎022 768 2112; www.rajaferryport.com) car ferry (120B) to Don Sak, which departs from Thong Yang. Ferries take one to five hours, depending on the boat. A couple of these departures can connect with the train station in Phun Phin (for a nominal extra fee). The slow night boat to Samui (300B) leaves from central Surat Thani each night at 11pm, reaching Na Thon around 5am. It returns from Na Thon at 9pm, arriving at around 3am. Watch your bags on this boat.

To Ko Pha-Ngan & Ko Tao

There are almost a dozen daily departures between Ko Samui and Thong Sala on the west coast of Ko Pha-Ngan and many of these continue on to Ko Tao. These leave from the Na Thon, Mae Nam or Big Buddha Beach pier, take from 20 minutes to one hour and cost 200B to 300B to Ko Pha-Ngan, depending on the boat.

To go directly to Hat Rin, the *Haad Rin Queen* goes back and forth between Hat Rin and Big Buddha Beach four times a day, with double the number of sailings the day after the Full Moon Party and an extra trip laid on at 7.30am the same day. The voyage takes 50 minutes, costs 200B and the last boat leaves at 6.30pm.

Also for Hat Rin and the more remote east coast beaches of Ko Pha-Ngan, the small and rickety *Thong Nai Pan Express* runs once a day at noon from Mae Hat on Ko Samui to Hat Rin and then up the east coast, stopping at all the beaches as far as Thong Nai Pan Noi. Prices range from 200B to 400B, depending on the destination. The boat won't run in bad weather.

BUS & TRAIN

A bus–ferry combo is more convenient than a train–ferry package for getting to Ko Samui because you don't have to switch transportation in Phun Phin. However, the trains are much more comfortable and spacious – especially at night. If you prefer the train, you can get off at Chumphon and catch the Lomprayah catamaran service the rest of the way.

Several services offer these bus–boat combo tickets, the fastest and most comfortable being the Lomprayah which has two daily departures from Bangkok at 6am and 9pm and two from Samui to Bangkok at 8am and 12.30pm. The total voyage takes about 13½ hours and costs between 1400B and 1450B.

MOTORBIKE RENTAL SCAMS

Even if you escape unscathed from a motorbike riding experience, some shops will claim that you damaged your rental and will try to extort some serious cash. The best way to avoid this is to take copious photos of your vehicle (cars included) at the time of rental, making sure the person renting you the vehicle sees you do it (they will be less likely to make false claims against you if they know you have photos). If they still make a claim against you, keep your cool. Losing your temper won't help you win the argument and could significantly escalate the problem. The situation is just as bad on Ko Pha-Ngan, a bit less so on Ko Tao.

If things get really bad call the **tourist police** (p536), not the regular police.

Getting Around

You can rent motorcycles (and bicycles) from almost every resort on the island. The going rate is 150B to 200B per day, but for longer periods try to negotiate a better rate.

Drivers of *sŏrng·tăa·ou* (pick-up trucks) love to try to overcharge you, so it's always best to ask a third party for current rates, as they can change with the season. These vehicles run regularly during daylight hours. It's about 50B to travel between beaches, and no more than 100B to travel halfway across the island. Figure about 20B for a five-minute ride on a motorcycle taxi.

Taxi service is quite chaotic due to the plethora of cabs. In the past taxi fares were unwieldy; these days prices are more standardised across the islands (though fares are still ridiculously inflated compared to Bangkok). Taxis typically charge around 500B for an airport transfer. Some Hat Chaweng travel agencies can arrange minibus taxis for less.

Ko Pha-Ngan เกาะพงัน

POP 12,500

Hippie-at-heart Ko Pha-Ngan has become so synonymous with the massive Full Moon Party on Hat Rin that the rest of the island gets eclipsed, and forgotten. This is a massive shame, as there's so much else to enjoy and explore. For one week a month, the island sees some 30,000 people cramming one beach partying their minds out and then, off they all go on the next boat, and the beaches and accommodations are left half empty. It's at this time, however, that budget-conscious serenity seekers can retreat into a fog of the backpacker days of old and nab a fan-cooled beach shack from 400B (on the northern beaches at least). This may change overnight with the future opening of the island's airport, but for now this exceptionally gorgeous island is in a sleepy sweet spot where you can even find a solid bungalow on Hat Rin for around 1000B outside of full moon mania.

Ko Pha-Ngan has plenty to offer the more clean-cut, comfort-seeking traveller as well; its peace and quiet make it a great choice for families. Remote Hat Thong Nai Pan Noi in particular feels like a miniature version of Ko Samui with its elegant resorts fronted by rows of cushion-clad beach loungers, while the easier-to-access west coast has attracted a handful of new upscale resorts and a few older places have been revamped to attract a more ritzy market.

Ko Pha-Ngan

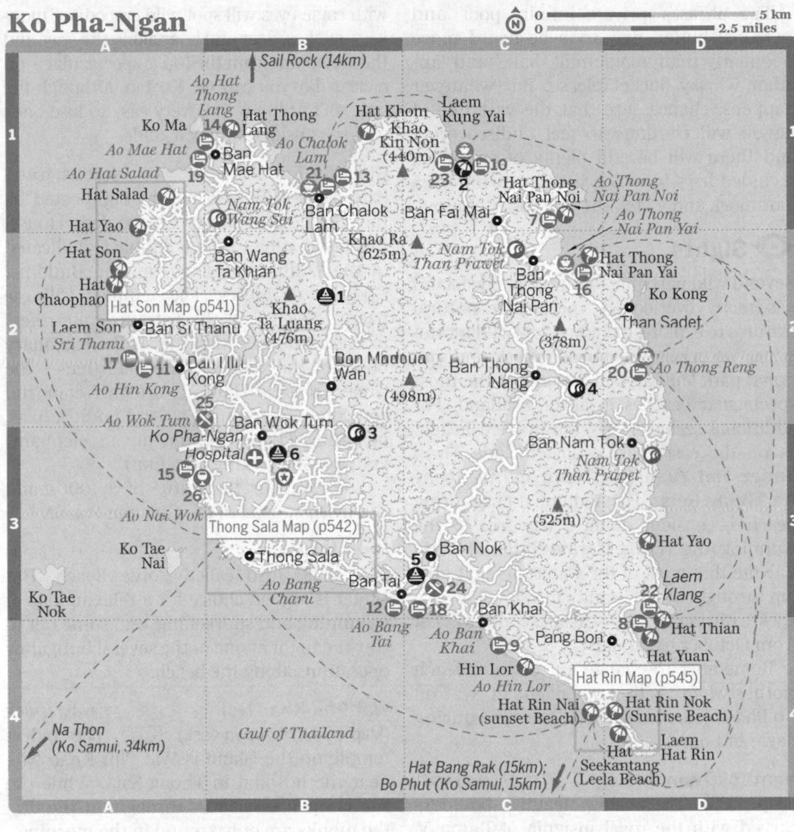

Ko Pha-Ngan

Sights

1 Guanyin Temple B2
2 Hat Khuat C1
Ko Pha-Ngan's tallest Yang Na Yai Tree ...... (see 5)
3 Nam Tok Phaeng B3
4 Nam Tok Than Sadet C2
5 Wat Pho C3
6 Wat Phu Khao Noi B3

Sleeping

7 Anantara Rasananda C1
8 Bamboo Hut D4
Barcelona ...... (see 8)
9 Bay Lounge & Resort C4
Boom's Cafe Bungalows ...... (see 9)
10 Bottle Beach II C1
11 Chills Resort A2
12 Divine Comedie B3
13 Fantasea B1
14 Island View Cabana B1
15 Kupu Kupu Phangan Beach Villa A3
16 Longtail Beach Resort C2
17 Loyfa Natural Resort A2
18 Mac Bay C3
19 Mae Hat Beach View Resort A1
20 Mai Pen Rai D2
21 Mandalai B1
Pariya Resort & Villas ...... (see 8)
22 Sanctuary D3
23 Smile Bungalows C1

Eating

Bamboo Hut ...... (see 8)
Cucina Italiana ...... (see 21)
24 Fabio's C3
Fisherman's Restaurant ...... (see 12)
25 JJ's Restaurant A2
Sanctuary ...... (see 22)

Drinking & Nightlife

26 Amsterdam A3
Flip Flop Pharmacy ...... (see 16)
Jam ...... (see 25)

The phrases 'private infinity pool' and 'personal butler' may soon be heard more frequently than 'magic milkshake' and 'another whisky bucket please'. But whatever happens, chances are that the vast inland jungle will continue to feel undiscovered, and there will be still plenty of stunning, secluded bays in which you can string up a hammock and watch the tide roll in. Enjoy!

Sights

Beyond wild partying, this large jungle island has many overlooked, spectacular natural features to explore, including tree-clad mountains, waterfalls, unspoiled forest and national park land as well as some of the most spectacular beaches in all of Thailand. For additional seclusion, try the isolated beaches on the east coast, which include **Than Sadet**, **Hat Yuan**, **Hat Thian** and the teeny **Ao Thong Reng**. For additional enchanting beaches, consider doing a day trip to the stunning **Ang Thong Marine National Park**.

Note that most of the waterfalls that glisten throughout the island's interior slow to a trickle during the dry season, so aim to visit from October to January.

Remember to change out of your beach clothes when visiting one of the 20 wát on Ko Pha-Ngan. Most temples are open during daylight hours.

Nam Tok Than Sadet WATERFALL

(Map p539) These falls feature boulders carved with the royal insignia of Rama V, Rama VII and Rama IX. King Rama V enjoyed this hidden spot so much that he returned over a dozen times between 1888 and 1909. The river waters of Khlong Than Sadet are now considered sacred and used in royal ceremonies. Also near the eastern coast, **Than Prawet** is a series of chutes that snake inland for approximately 2km.

Nam Tok Phaeng WATERFALL

(Map p539) Nam Tok Phaeng is protected by a national park; this waterfall is a pleasant reward after a short, but rough, hike. After the waterfall (dry out of season), it's a further exhilarating 15-minute climb up a root-choked path (along the Phaeng-Domsila Nature Trail) to the fantastic Domsila Viewpoint, with ranging views. The two- to three-hour trail then continues on through the jungle in a loop, past other waterfalls before bringing you back. Take water and good shoes.

It's possible to continue up to Khao Ra, the highest mountain on the island at 625m. Those with eagle-eyes will spot wild crocodiles, monkeys, snakes, deer and boar along the way, and the viewpoint from the top is spectacular – on a clear day you can see Ko Tao. Although the trek isn't arduous, it is very easy to lose one's way, so consider finding a guide.

Guanyin Temple BUDDHIST TEMPLE

(Map p539; 40B; ⏲7am-6pm) Signposted as the 'Goddess of Mercy Shrine Joss House', this fascinating Chinese temple is dedicated to the bodhisattva Guanyin, the Buddhist Goddess of Mercy. The temple's Chinese name (普岳山) on the entrance gate refers to the island in China that is the legendary home of the goddess. The main hall – the Great Treasure Hall – is a highly colourful confection, containing several bodhisattvas, including Puxian (seated on an elephant) and Wenshu (sitting on a lion).

Look out for the statue of a 1000-hand Guanyin, housed in the Guanyin Palace.

Hat Khuat BEACH

(Map p539) Also called Bottle Beach, Hat Khuat is a good choice for a relaxing day of swimming and snorkelling, and some opt to stay the night at one of the several bungalow operations along the beach.

Wat Phu Khao Noi BUDDHIST TEMPLE

(Map p539; ⏲dawn-dusk) FREE The oldest temple on the island is Wat Phu Khao Noi, near the hospital in Thong Sala. While the site is open to visitors throughout the day, the monks are only around in the morning.

Ko Pha-Ngan's Tallest Yang Na Yai Tree TREE

(Map p539) Near Wat Pho, Ko Pha-Ngan's tallest Yang Na Yai (dipterocarpus alatus; ยางนา) is an astonishing sight as you veer round the bend for the diminutive Wat Nok temple, a small shrine tucked away in the greenery. These colossal giants grow to over 50m in height and, for tree lovers, are real beauties. This imposing specimen is often garlanded with colourful ribbons.

Wat Pho BUDDHIST TEMPLE

(Map p539; ⏲herbal sauna 1-7pm) FREE With a dazzling gateway and extensive temple grounds, Wat Pho, near Ban Tai, has a **herbal sauna** (admission 50B) accented with natural lemon grass. When we last visited, a new temple hall was under construction.

Wat Khao Tham BUDDHIST TEMPLE

(Map p542; www.kowtahm.com; ⏲dawn-dusk) FREE With resident female monks, Wat

Khao Tham, near Ban Tai, sits among the trees high on a hill. A bulletin board details a meditation retreat at the temple; see the website for details. Don't miss the temple hall at the top of the steps with the colourful glass, housing a sleeping Buddha.

Activities

With Ko Tao, the high-energy diving behemoth, just a few kilometres away, Ko Pha-Ngan enjoys a much quieter, more laid-back diving scene focused on fun diving rather than certifications. A recent drop in Open Water certification prices has made local prices competitive with Ko Tao. Group sizes tend to be smaller on Ko Pha-Ngan since the island has fewer divers in general.

Like the other islands in the Samui Archipelago, Pha-Ngan has several small reefs dispersed around the island. The clear favourite snorkelling spot is **Ko Ma**, a small island in the northwest connected to Ko Pha-Ngan by a charming sandbar. There are also some rock reefs of interest on the eastern side of the island.

A major perk of diving from Ko Pha-Ngan is the proximity to **Sail Rock** (Hin Bai), the best dive site in the Gulf of Thailand and a veritable beacon for whale sharks. This large pinnacle lies about 14km north of the island. An abundance of corals and large tropical fish can be seen at depths of 10m to 30m, and there's a rocky vertical swim-through called 'The Chimney'.

Dive shops on Ko Tao sometimes visit Sail Rock; however, the focus tends to be more on shallow reefs (for newbie divers) and the deep-dive waters at Chumphon Pinnacle. The most popular trips departing from Ko Pha-Ngan are three-site day trips which stop at **Chumphon Pinnacle**, Sail Rock and one of the other premier sites in the area. These three-stop trips cost from around 3650B to 4000B and include a full lunch. Two-dive trips to Sail Rock will set you back around 2500B to 2800B.

Lotus Diving and Haad Yao Divers are the main operators on the island with a solid reputation.

Hiking and snorkelling day trips to **Ang Thong Marine National Park** generally depart from Ko Samui, but recently tour operators are starting to shuttle tourists from Ko Pha-Ngan as well. Ask at your accommodation for details about boat trips as companies often come and go due to unstable petrol prices.

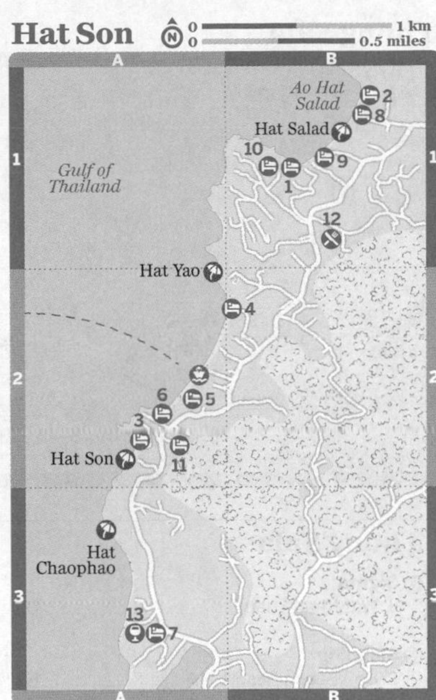

Hat Son

Sleeping

1 Cookies Salad B1
2 Green Papaya B1
3 Haad Son Resort & Restaurant A2
4 Haad Yao Bay View Resort B2
5 Haad Yao See Through Boutique Resort A2
6 High Life A2
7 Pha-Ngan Paragon A3
8 Salad Beach Resort B1
9 Salad Hut B1
10 Shiralea B1
11 Tantawan Bungalows A2

Eating

12 Peppercorn B1

Drinking & Nightlife

13 Belgian Beer Bar A3

Many of the larger accommodation options can hook you up with a variety of aquatic equipment such as jet skis and kayaks, and the friendly staff at Backpackers Information Centre (p554) can attend to any of your other water-sports needs.

Chaloklum Diving DIVING
(☎077374025; www.chaloklum-diving.com; ⊙6am-8pm) One of the more established dive shops on the island (based on the main drag in

Thong Sala

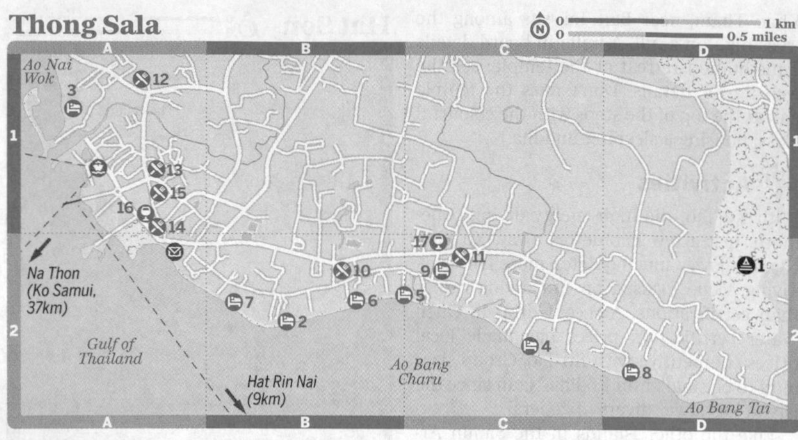

Thong Sala

Sights

1 Wat Khao Tham D2

Sleeping

2 B52 Beach Resort B2
3 Baan Manali Resort A1
4 Charu Bay Villas C2
5 Coco Garden B2
6 Hacienda Resort B2
7 Lime n Soda B2
8 Milky Bay Resort D2
9 V-View Beach Resort C2

Eating

10 Ando Loco B2
11 Food Factory C2
12 Mason's Arms A1
13 Night Market A1
14 Nira's A1
15 Vintage Burgers A1

Drinking & Nightlife

16 Harp A1
17 Outlaws Saloon C2

Ban Chalok Lam) has quality equipment and high standards.

Lotus Diving DIVING
(☎077 374142; www.lotusdiving.com) This dive centre gets the thumbs up from divers. Trips can be booked at its Ban Chalok Lam office, or at the Backpackers Information Centre.

Haad Yao Divers DIVING
(☎086 279 3085; www.haadyaodivers.com; Hat Yao) Established in 1997, this dive operator has garnered a strong reputation by maintaining European standards of safety and customer service.

Wake Up WAKEBOARDING
(☎087 283 6755; www.wakeupwakeboarding.com; ⊙Jan-Oct) Jamie passes along his infinite wakeboarding wisdom to eager wannabes at his water sports school in Chalok Lam. Fifteen minutes of 'air time' will set you back 1200B, which is excellent value considering you get one-on-one instruction. Kiteboarding, wakeskating and waterskiing sessions also available.

Jungle Gym GYM
(Map p545; Hat Rin) One of several Thai boxing places on Ko Pha-Ngan, this very conveniently located gym was one of the island's first and also offers yoga and well-maintained fitness equipment.

Tours

Eco Nature Tour TOUR
(☎084 850 6273) This popular outfit offers a selection of island day trips. We suggest the one-day 'safari' including snorkelling, a visit to a Chinese temple, a stunning viewpoint and Nam Tok Phaeng waterfall (1500B). Elephant trekking is also available, but it's worth reading up on the animal welfare issues involved before considering that option. Bookings can be made at its office in Thong Sala or at the Backpackers Information Centre.

Sleeping

Ko Pha-Ngan's legendary history of laid-back revelry has solidified its reputation as *the* stomping ground for the gritty backpacker lifestyle. Even so, many local mainstays have recently collapsed their bamboo huts and constructed newer, sleeker accommodation aimed at the ever-growing legion of 'flashpackers'.

On other parts of the island, new tracts of land are being cleared for Samui-esque five-star resorts. But backpackers fear not – it will still be a while before the castaway lifestyle goes the way of the dodo. For now, Ko Pha-Ngan can revel in having excellent choices to suit every budget. Pha-Ngan also caters to a subculture of seclusion seekers who crave a deserted slice of sand. The northern and eastern coasts offer just that – a place to escape.

Sleeping options start in Hat Rin, move along the southern coast, head up the west side, across the northern beaches and down the quiet eastern shore. The accommodation along the southern coast is the best bang for your baht on Ko Pha-Ngan, while the west coast is seeing a lot of development. The atmosphere here is a pleasant mix of quiet seclusion and a sociable vibe, although some of the beaches, particularly towards the south, aren't as picturesque as other parts of the island. Price tags are also higher than north or south of here.

Stretching from Chalok Lam to Thong Nai Pan, the dramatic northern coast is a wild jungle with several secluded beaches – it's the most scenic coast on the island.

The east coast is the ultimate hermit hang-out. For many of these refuges, you'll have to hire a boat from Thong Sala, Chalok Lam and Hat Rin, and 4WD taxis from Thong Sala are an option for those that have dirt roads. The *Thong Nai Pan Express* boat runs daily at noon from Hat Mae Nam on Ko Samui, stopping at Hat Rin and the east coast beaches as far as Thong Nai Pan Noi. The boat is a casual, rickety fishing-style vessel and won't run in rough weather.

Hat Rin

The thin peninsula of Hat Rin features three separate beaches. Beautiful blonde Hat Rin Nok (Sunrise Beach) is the epicentre of Full Moon tomfoolery, Hat Rin Nai (Sunset Beach) is the much less impressive stretch of sand on the far side of the tiny promontory, and Hat Seekantang (also known as Hat Leela), just south of Hat Rin Nai, is a smaller, lovely white and more private beach. The three beaches are linked by Ban Hat Rin (Hat Rin Town) – a small inland collection of restaurants and bars. It takes only a few minutes to walk from one beach to another.

Hat Rin sees Thailand's greatest accommodation crunch during the Full Moon festivities. At this time, bungalow operations expect you to stay for a minimum number of days (usually five). If you plan to arrive the day of the party (or even the day before), we strongly suggest booking a room in advance, or else you'll probably have to sleep on the beach (which you might end up doing anyway). A new breed of cattle car–style dorms stack and cram a seemingly impossible number of beds into dark small rooms and shared toilets are few. These start at around 200B outside of the Full Moon chaos then escalate to 650B and up for party times. Even though these grim options have added a significant number of beds to the town, everything still manages to fill up. Check hostel booking websites for dorm bed availability. Catering to the deluge, new operations constantly set up.

Full Mooners can also stay on Ko Samui or other beaches on Ko Pha-Ngan and take speedboat shuttles to access the festivities – prices will depend on how far away you're staying but the money you'll save on staying anywhere besides Hat Rin itself will probably make it worth it. With gory and often fatal accidents monthly, driving on Ko Pha-Ngan during the festivities is an absolutely terrible idea.

Expect room rates to increase by 20% to 300% during Full Moon.

Lighthouse Bungalows BUNGALOW **$**

(Map p545; ☎077 375075; www.lighthousebungalows.com; Hat Seekantang; bungalows 400-1000B; ❄📶) This outpost perched on the rocks has simple fan options and newer spacious air-con bungalows, all great value and with sweeping views of the sea; plus there's a cushion-clad restaurant/common area and high-season yoga classes. To get there, follow the wooden boardwalk southeast from Hat Leela or take the high road (motorbike). Beware the monthly techno parties (check), unless that's in your wishlist.

Seaview Sunrise BUNGALOW **$**

(Map p545; www.seaviewsunrise.com; Hat Rin Nok; r 500-1400B; ❄📶) Budget Full Moon revellers who want to sleep inches from the tide: apply here. Some of the options back in the jungle are sombre and musty, but the solid, beachfront models have bright, polished wooden interiors facing onto a line of coconut trees and the sea.

Paradise Bungalows BUNGALOW $
(Map p545; ☎077 375244; Hat Rin Nok; bungalows 1200-4500B; ❄📶🏊) The world-famous Full Moon Party was first hatched here way back, and the place has been milking it ever since, but the original plot has been divided up and what's left is a rather charmless series of hillside and poolside units and two-storey blocks, with more going up at the time of writing.

Same Same GUESTHOUSE $
(Map p545; ☎077 375200; www.same-same.com; Ban Hat Rin; dm 400B, r 650B; ❄📶) A sociable spot for Scandinavians during the Full Moon madness, Same Same offers simple but bright rooms and plenty of party fun.

Blue Marine BUNGALOW $$
(Map p545; ☎077 375079; www.bluemarinephangan.com; Hat Rin Nai; bungalows 1000-1200B; ❄📶) This cluster of identical concrete bungalows with blue tiled roofs surrounds a manicured green lawn; the best have dreamy views over the whitest and cleanest part of quiet Sunset Beach. Every unit is spacious, clean and has air-con, fridge, hot water and TV.

Cocohut Village RESORT $$
(Map p545; ☎077 375368; www.cocohut.com; Hat Seekantang; bungalows incl breakfast 2600-9500B; ❄@📶🏊) This super-social place on a stunning stretch of sand is very popular with Israelis, but prices are high. The most expensive options, including the cliff villas and beachfront bungalows, are some of the best bets in Hat Rin but budget choices are far less appealing. A fantastic buffet breakfast is included in the room rate.

Pha-Ngan Bayshore Resort RESORT $$
(Map p545; ☎077 375224; www.phanganbayshore.com; Hat Rin Nok; r 2300-6000B; ❄@📶🏊) This neat and well-maintained hotel-style operation soaks up an ever-increasing influx of Hat Rin flashpackers. Staff are on the ball and welcoming, while sweeping beach views and a giant swimming pool nudge it into one of the top addresses on Sunrise Beach, especially if you are able to nab a special promotion.

Delight GUESTHOUSE $$
(Map p545; ☎077 375527; www.delightresort.com; Ban Hat Rin; r 800-6400B; ❄📶🏊) In the centre of Hat Rin, friendly Delight offers some of the best lodging around. Spic-and-span rooms in a Thai-style building come with subtle designer details (such as peacock murals) and are sandwiched between an inviting swimming pool and a lazy lagoon peppered with lily pads.

Tommy Resort RESORT $$
(Map p545; ☎077 375215; www.tommyresort.com; Hat Rin Nok; r incl breakfast 1850-7500B; ❄📶🏊) Tommy is a trendy address in the heart of Hat Rin, striking a balance between chic boutique and carefree flashpacker hang-out. Wander down to a lovely strip of white sand, past flowering trees, an azure slab of a pool at the heart of things and helpful, obliging staff. Rooms come with air-con, fridge and safe.

Palita Lodge BUNGALOW $$
(Map p545; ☎077 375172, 077 375170; www.palitalodge.com; Hat Rin Nok; bungalows 1800-6400B; ❄📶🏊) Smack in the heart of the action, family-run Palita is notable for its welcoming service. Spacious concrete bungalows look a bit ramshackle from the outside but the wooden accents and modern design elements make the interiors very comfy. It's on a beachy wedge of sand and the restaurant serves good Thai food. Nonguests can use the pool for 200B.

Sea Breeze Bungalow BUNGALOW $$
(Map p545; ☎077 375162; Ban Hat Rin; bungalows 500-6000B; ❄📶🏊) Sea Breeze gets a good report card from our readers, and we agree; the labyrinth of secluded hillside cottages is a pleasant retreat for any type of traveller. Several bungalows, poised high on stilts, deliver stunning views of Hat Rin and the sea. There's a big range of options here from fan rooms up and a lovely forested setting.

Sarikantang RESORT $$$
(Map p545; ☎077 375055; www.sarikantang.com; Hat Seekantang; bungalows 2500-5600B; ❄📶🏊) Cream-coloured cabins, framed with teak posts and lintels, are sprinkled among swaying palms and crumbling winged statuettes on one of Hat Rin's best stretches of beach. Inside, the rooms are an Ikea chic that's not ageing well but still offers a comfy stay.

The Coast RESORT $$$
(Map p545; ☎077 951567; www.thecoastphangan.com; Hat Rin Nai; 3700-10,800B; ❄📶🏊) This dark-grey, sharp-angled and stylish resort leads to a slim but OK stretch of beach away from the party hub. Swanky room interiors are polished cement and beds topped with white duvets, while an infinity pool overlooks the sea and service pulls out the stops. Hip, cool and minimalist, but comfy.

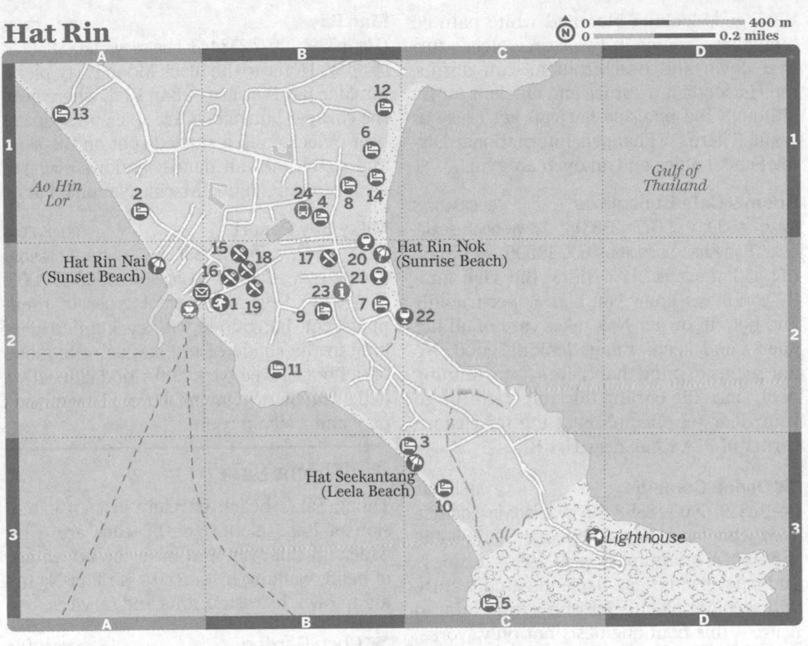

Hat Rin

Activities, Courses & Tours
1 Jungle Gym B2

Sleeping
2 Blue Marine A1
3 Cocohut Village C3
4 Delight B1
5 Lighthouse Bungalows C3
6 Palita Lodge B1
7 Paradise Bungalows B2
8 Pha-Ngan Bayshore Resort B1
9 Same Same B2
10 Sarikantang C3
11 Sea Breeze Bungalow B2
12 Seaview Sunrise B1
13 The Coast A1
14 Tommy Resort B1

Eating
15 Lazy House B2
16 Lucky Crab B2
17 Matt's Joint B2
18 Monna Lisa B2
19 Om Ganesh B2

Drinking & Nightlife
20 Cactus Bar B2
21 Drop-In Bar B2
22 Rock C2
Sunrise .... (see 8)
Tommy .... (see 14)

Information
23 Backpackers Information Centre B2

Transport
24 Sŏrng•tăa•ou to Thong Sala B1

Ban Khai to Ban Tai

The waters at Ban Tai tend to be shallow and opaque, especially during low season, but lodging options are well-priced compared to other parts of the island, and you're close to Thong Sala and not too far from Hat Rin. Like Ban Tai, Ban Khai's beaches aren't the most stunning, but the accommodation is cheap and there are beautiful views of Ang Thong Marine National Park in the distance.

These beaches are where many of the moon-but-not-full-moon parties happen so even if your resort seems quiet, there's probably some boozed-up action nearby.

Hacienda Resort BUNGALOW $

(Map p542; ☎077 238825; www.beachresorthacienda.com; dm 300B, r 500-1500B; ❄☜☒)

With good-looking blue and white painted bungalows, rooms in two-storey blocks further down and beachfront air-con dorms, the Hacienda is a spruce and efficient outfit, although the poolside bar can get noisy at night. There's a Phangan International Diving School office and an open air gym.

Boom's Cafe Bungalows BUNGALOW **$**
(Map p539; 077 238318; www.boomscafe.com; Ban Khai; bungalows 600-1000B) Staying at Boom's is like visiting the Thai family you never knew you had. Super-friendly and helpful owner Nok takes care of all her guests and keeps things looking good. No one seems to mind that there's no swimming pool, since the curling tide rolls right up to your doorstep. Boom's is at the far eastern corner of Ban Khai, near Hat Rin.

★**Divine Comedie** RESORT **$$**
(Map p539; 080 885 8789; www.ledivinecomedie.com; Ban Tai; r 1900-3600B, ste 3100-6900B) A stunning mix of 1920s Chinese and perhaps Mexican hacienda architecture with a colour palette that shifts from mint to ochre – this boutique oasis not only works, it's beguiling. Junior suites have rooftop terraces, the elongated pool runs to the slim beach and there's an on-site restaurant serving Myanmar specialities.

V-View Beach Resort BUNGALOW **$$**
(Map p542; 077 377436; r 600-2100B) An air of seclusion settles over this beach resort and although the sea can be a bit swampy, there are hammocks galore and a fine pool, decent bungalows and a helpful owner.

B52 Beach Resort BUNGALOW **$$**
(Map p542; www.b52-beach-resort-phangan.info; bungalows 1500-4200B) It doesn't cost a bomb at B52's campus of Thai-styled bungalows sporting plenty of thatch, polished concrete floors and rustic tropical tree trunks leading down to the sea.

Bay Lounge & Resort RESORT **$$**
(Map p539; 077 377892; www.bayloungeresort.com; Ban Khai; bungalows incl breakfast 3200-3700B) On a private white nugget of beach sandwiched by jungle-topped boulders, this is an intimate, chic choice. Bungalows mingle with the natural surroundings yet inside look quite urban with distressed concrete and modern art. It's midway between Hat Rin's Full Moon Party and the Half Moon Party in Ban Khai – the resort offers transport to each. Check-out time is late at 1pm.

Mac Bay BUNGALOW **$$**
(Map p539; 077 238443; bungalows 1200-8500B) Home to the Black Moon Party, pleasant Mac Bay is a slice of Ban Khai where even the cheaper bungalows are spic and span. At beer o'clock, grab a shaded spot on the sand and watch the sun dance shadows over the islands of Ang Thong Marine National Park.

Milky Bay Resort RESORT **$$$**
(Map p542; 077 238566; http://milkybaythailand.com; Ban Tai; bungalows 1800-13,200B) Several different types of minimalist chic bungalows with dark tinted glass hide in the shade of tall stands of bamboo on a floor of tree bark and wood chip. It's a delightful picture, with a covered swimming pool and a steam room.

Thong Sala

Thong Sala's beach is really just an extension of Ban Tai but the beaches are a bit wider up this way and have the advantage of being walking distance to Ko Pha-Ngan's main town, its restaurants and services.

★**Coco Garden** BUNGALOW **$**
(Map p542; 086 073 1147, 077 377721; www.cocogardens.com; Thong Sala; bungalows 550-1100B) The best budget hang-out along the southern coast, fantastic Coco Garden one-ups the nearby resorts with well-manicured grounds and 25 neat bungalows and an excellent beach bar.

Baan Manali Resort BUNGALOW **$$**
(Map p542; 077 377918; bungalows 2200-3150B) Quiet, clean and attractively laid out among the coconut trees, 14-bungalow Baan Manali is a convenient, relaxing and well-run choice with an infinity pool and excellent restaurant, close to the action at Thong Sala.

Lime n Soda RESORT **$$**
(Map p542; www.limesodathailand.com; bungalows 700-2300B) Clean and simple tiled bungalows hide in the shade of bamboo and coconut palms along a breakwater above the beach. Ignoring the 'Ko Pha-Ngan's first Eco-Friendly beachfront resort' waffle, it's all in all a solid, decent choice.

Charu Bay Villas VILLA **$$$**
(Map p542; 084 191 1266; www.backpackersthailand.com; villas 8640-11,520B) These fully equipped villas on the bay of Ao Bang Charu, just southeast of Thong Sala, are great value if you're a group. The Beachfront Villa is a three-bed with large Jacuzzi and

is big enough to sleep up to 10; the two-bed Seaview Villa sleeps up to four.

Ao Nai Wok to Ao Sri Thanu

Close to Thong Sala, the resorts peppered along this breezy west-coast strip mingle with small beaches between patches of mangroves. Despite the lack of sand, the prices are cheap and the sunsets are memorable.

Chills Resort RESORT **$$**
(Map p539; ☎089 875 2100; Ao Sri Thanu; r 1000-2300B;) Under new management and set along a stunning and secluded stretch of stony outcrops, Chills' cluster of delightfully simple-but-modern rooms all have peaceful ocean views letting in plenty of sunlight, sea breezes and gorgeous sunset views. Book through www.agoda.com.

Loyfa Natural Resort BUNGALOW **$$**
(Map p539; ☎077 349022; www.loyfanaturalresort.com; Ao Sri Thanu; r 750B, bungalows 1300-3100B, villas from 3825B;) Loyfa scores high marks for its friendly, French-speaking Thai staff, charming gardens and sturdy huts guarding sweeping ocean views. Modern bungalows tumble down the promontory onto an exclusively private sliver of ash-coloured sand. Cheapest rooms are in a hotel block.

Kupu Kupu Phangan Beach Villa RESORT **$$$**
(Map p539; ☎077 377384; www.kupuphangan.com; Ao Nai Wok; villas from 8500B;) This supreme Balinese-style resort is one of the island's most swoon-worthy, with lily ponds, tall palms, a swimming pool straight from a luxury magazine centrefold and rocky boulders that meet the sea. The gorgeous wooden villas have pools and elegant interiors.

Hat Chaophao

Like Hat Yao up the coast, this rounded beach on the west coast is lined with a variety of bungalow operations.

Pha-Ngan Paragon BUNGALOW **$$$**
(Map p541; ☎084 728 6064; bungalows 1750-12,000B;) A tiny hideaway with just seven rooms, the Paragon has decor that incorporates stylistic elements from ancient Khmer, India and Thailand, without forfeiting any modern amenities. The 'royal bedroom' deserves a special mention – apparently the canopied bed was imported from Kashmir.

Hat Yao & Hat Son

One of the busier beaches along the west coast, Hat Yao sports a swimmable beach, numerous resorts and a few extra services such as ATMs and convenience stores. With a delightful sense of seclusion, Hat Son is a quiet, smaller beach that feels like a big secret.

Tantawan Bungalows BUNGALOW **$**
(Map p541; ☎077 349108; www.tantawanbungalow.com; Hat Son; bungalows 900-3300B;) This relaxed and recently renovated 11-bungalow (fan and air-con) teak nest, tucked among jungle, has fantastic views and a fine pool but it's a bit of a steep climb with luggage.

High Life BUNGALOW **$**
(Map p541; ☎077 349114; www.haadyaohighlife.com; Hat Yao; air-con bungalows 1200-3500B;) We can't decide what's more conspicuous: the dramatic ocean views from the infinity-edged swimming pool, or the blatant double entendre in the resort's name. True to its moniker, the 25 bungalows, of various shapes and sizes, sit on a palmed outcropping of granite soaring high above the sea.

Shiralea BUNGALOW **$**
(Map p541; ☎080 719 9256; www.shiralea.com; Hat Yao; dm 250B, bungalows 600-1300B;) The fresh-faced poolside bungalows are simple but the new air-con dorms are great and the ambience, with an on-site bar with draught beer, is convivial. It's about 100m away from the beach and it fills up every few weeks with Contiki student tour groups.

Haad Son Resort & Restaurant RESORT **$$**
(Map p541; ☎077 349104; http://haadsonresort.net; Hat Son; bungalows 1000-8000B;) There's a mixed bag of rooms here from big, older wooden bungalows with terraces on the hillside to brand-new polished cement suites and rooms along the beachfront. The secluded beach setting is spectacular and is highlighted by one of the most beachy-chic restaurants on the island on a jungle- and boulder-clad peninsula overlooking the sea.

Haad Yao See Through Boutique Resort HOTEL **$$**
(Map p541; ☎077 349315; www.haadyao.net; Hat Yao; r 2350-2550B;) This towering polished cement double-storey complex with elongated Chinese-style wooden doors has a long but uninviting pool that's hard to access. The building looks bizarrely placed,

but room interiors are comfortable and the resort has a central beachfront location.

Haad Yao Bay View Resort RESORT $$$
(Map p541; 077 349193; www.haadyao-bayviewresort.com; Hat Yao; r & bungalows incl breakfast 1500-7000B;) This arrangement of bungalows and hotel-style accommodation looks like a tropical mirage on Hat Yao's northern headland. There's a huge array of options but our pick are the tiny but good-value rooms that hover right over the sea. For more luxe head up to the hillside sea-view bungalows. It's a busy, businesslike place.

Hat Salad

This slim, pretty beach on the northwest coast is fronted by shallow blue water – a clutch of photogenic long-tail boats tend to park at the southern end. It's slightly rustic, with local Thai fishermen coming out to throw their nets out at sunset, yet with plenty of amenities and comfortable accommodation.

Cookies Salad RESORT $$
(Map p541; 083 181 7125, 077 349125; www.cookies-phangan.com; bungalows 1800-3300B;) Sling out on a hammock at this resort with private Balinese-styled bungalows on a steep hill, orbiting a two-tiered lap pool tiled in various shades of blue. Shaggy thatching and dense tropical foliage give the realm a certain rustic quality, although you won't want for creature comforts. It's super friendly and books up fast.

Salad Hut BUNGALOW $$
(Map p541; 077 349246; www.saladhut.com; bungalows 2200-5000B;) Totally unpretentious despite sharing a beach with some distinctly upscale options, this small clutch of Thai-style bungalows sits but a stone's throw from the rolling tide, but the pool is rather small. Watch the sun gently set below the waves from your lacquered teak porch or the beach bar.

Salad Beach Resort BUNGALOW $$
(Map p541; 077 349149; www.phangan-saladbeachresort.com; bungalows 2000-3920B;) A full-service retreat along the sands of Hat Salad. Room decor employs an unusual palette of colours, but the grounds are tasteful and understated – especially around the pool.

Green Papaya BUNGALOW $$$
(Map p541; 077 374230; www.greenpapayaresort.com; bungalows 3600-10,200B;) In a tranquil and elegant setting, the polished wooden bungalows at Green Papaya are a clear stand-out along the lovely beach at Hat Salad; however, they come at quite a hefty price.

Ao Mae Hat

The relatively undeveloped northwest tip of the island has excellent ocean vistas, plenty of white sand and little Ko Ma is connected to Pha-Ngan by a stunning sandbar.

Island View Cabana BUNGALOW $
(Map p539; 077 374173; islandviewcabana@gmail.com; Ao Mae Hat; bungalows 400-1500B;) Well positioned for sunsets, the bungalows here are really big, though not that new, but this is a lovely spot at the end of the beach right at the isthmus to Ko Ma. Cheaper fan bungalows are at the rear.

Mae Hat Beach View Resort BUNGALOW $
(Map p539; 089 823 9756; bungalows 400-1500B;) At the listless southern end of the beach, this quiet but rather neglected spot sees little action. It's an option if you just want peace and quiet, with fan-cooled bamboo bungalows with solid tiled floors and a solitary air-con model.

Ban Chalok Lam (Chaloklum) & Hat Khom

In the north of the island, the cramped and quiet fishing village at Ban Chalok Lam is like no other place on Ko Pha-Ngan. The conglomeration of teak shanties and huts is being slowly infiltrated with the occasional European-style bakery and authentic Italian restaurant. For much of the time, locals still outnumber tourists and that's refreshing, but the new road is pumping up visitor numbers and there's not much of a beach.

Sŏrng·tăa·ou ply the route from here to Thong Sala for around 150B per person. There's a dirt road leading from Chalok Lam to Hat Khom, and water taxis are available to a number of beaches.

Fantasea BUNGALOW $
(Map p539; 089 443 0785; www.fantasea.asia; Chalok Lam; bungalows with fan/air-con 500/800B;) This friendly place is one of the better of a string of family-run bungalow operations along the quiet, eastern part of Chalok Lam. There's a thin beach out front with OK swimming and an elevated Thai-style restaurant area to chill out in.

Mandalai HOTEL $$$
(Map p539; ☎077 374316; www.mandalaihotel.com/web2014; Chalok Lam; r 1800-5600B; ❄@≋) With a couple of surreal-looking Louis XIV armchairs in reception, this lovely small boutique hotel quietly towers over the surrounding shantytown of fishermen's huts. Floor-to-ceiling windows command views of tangerine-coloured fishing boats in the bay, and there's a small but inviting pool in the main courtyard, mere steps from the sand.

Hat Khuat (Bottle Beach)

This isolated dune in the north of the island has a reputation as a low-key getaway, so it's pretty popular. During high season, places can fill up fast so it's best to arrive early. Grab a long-tail taxi boat from Chalok Lam for 100B to 150B (depending on the boat's occupancy).

Smile Bungalows BUNGALOW $
(Map p539; ☎085 429 4995; www.smilebungalows.com; Bottle Beach/Hat Khuat; bungalows 520-920B; ⊙closed Nov) At the far western corner of the beach, family-run Smile features an assortment of all-fan wooden huts climbing up a forested hill. The two-storey bungalows (920B) are our favourite.

Bottle Beach II BUNGALOW $
(Map p539; ☎077 445156; Bottle Beach/Hat Khuat; bungalows 600-1100B; ⊙closed Nov; 📶) At the far eastern corner of the beach, this string of basic bungalows is the ideal place to chill out – if you don't need many creature comforts.

Thong Nai Pan

The pair of rounded bays at Thong Nai Pan, in the northeast of the island, are some of the most remote yet busy beaches on the island; Ao Thong Nai Pan Yai (*yai* means 'big') is the southern half that has some excellent budget and midrange options, and Ao Thong Nai Pan Noi (*noi* means 'little') is Pha-Ngan's most upscale beach that curves just above. Both bays are equally beautiful and great for swimming and hiking. A taxi between the two is around 100B. The road from Thong Sala to Thong Nai Pan is now excellent, so visitor numbers are increasing.

Longtail Beach Resort BUNGALOW $
(Map p539; ☎077 445018; www.longtailbeachresort.com; Thong Nai Pan; bungalows with fan/air-con from 550/2590B; ❄📶) Tucked away at the southern end of the beach by the forest, Longtail offers backpackers charming abodes that wind up a lush garden path.

Anantara Rasananda RESORT $$$
(Map p539; ☎077 239555; http://phangan-rasananda.anantara.com; villas from 7500B; ❄@📶≋) Blink and you'll think you've been transported to Ko Samui. This five-star luxury resort is a sweeping sand-side property with a smattering of semi-detached villas – many bedecked with private plunge pools. A savvy mix of modern and traditional *săh·lah* styling prevails, and superb Anantara management assures service is polished.

Than Sadet

A new road runs all the way to Than Sadet, so the lovely bay here is totally accessible. Otherwise catch the *Thong Nai Pan Express* boat from Ko Samui.

Mai Pen Rai BUNGALOW $
(Map p539; ☎081 894 5076, 077 445090; www.thansadet.com; Than Sadet; bungalows 550-1200B; 📶) This quiet, beachy bay elicits nothing but sedate smiles. Trek up to Nam Tok Than Sadet falls, hike an hour to Thong Nai Pan or explore by sea with a rented kayak. Bungalows mingle with Plaa's next door on the hilly headland, and sport panels of straw weaving with gabled roofs. Family bungalows are available for 900B and there's a friendly on-site restaurant.

Hat Thian & Hat Yuan

Both Hat Thian and Hat Yuan, near the southeastern tip of the island, have a few bungalow operations, and are quite secluded. You can walk between the two in under 10 minutes via the rocky outcrop that seperates them. Hat Yuan is the more developed beach and has the whiter, wider stretches of sand, while Hat Thian is relatively empty and is back-to-nature pretty.

To get here hire a long-tail from Hat Rin (300B to 400B for the whole boat) or organise a boat pick-up from your resort. A dirt road to Hat Yuan has been cleared for 4WDs, but is only passable in the dry season; even then the voyage by sea is much easier.

Bamboo Hut BUNGALOW $
(Map p539; ☎087 888 8592; Hat Yuan; bungalows 400-1000B; 📶) Beautifully lodged up on the bouldery outcrops that overlook Hat Yuan and back into the jungle, groovy, hippie village, Bamboo Hut is a favourite for yoga retreats and meditative relaxation. Dark wood bungalows are small and have terraces.

Barcelona BUNGALOW $

(Map p539; ☎077 375113; Hat Yuan; bungalows 400-700B) Old, rickety wood bungalows with balconies – some with hammocks – climb up the hill on stilts behind a palm garden and have good vistas. Price depends on the view, but there's not a huge amount of variation, so grab a cheap one.

★ **Sanctuary** BUNGALOW $$

(Map p539; ☎081 271 3614; www.thesanctuarythailand.com; Hat Thian; dm 220B, bungalows 770-6000B) A friendly forested enclave of relaxed smiles, the Sanctuary is a haven of splendid lodgings, yoga classes and detox sessions. Accommodation, in various manifestations of twigs, is scattered along a tangle of hillside jungle paths while Hat Thian is wonderfully quiet and is great for swimming. Note that payment is cash only.

Pariya Resort & Villas RESORT $$$

(Map p539; ☎087 623 6678; www.pariyahaadyuan.com; Hat Yuan; villas 8000-17,000B; ❄📶🏊) The swankiest option on these beaches is found right in front of the softest sands of Hat Yuan in majestic burnt-yellow painted concrete, but it's not cheap. the octagonal, pagoda-topped bungalows are spacious yet sparsely furnished.

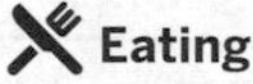

Eating

Most visitors quickly adopt the lazy lifestyle and wind up eating at their accommodation, which is a shame as Ko Pha-Ngan has some excellent restaurants scattered around the island; at the very least, it's another reason to get exploring.

Hat Rin

Hat Rin has the largest conglomeration of restaurants and bars on the island, yet most of them are pretty lousy so don't come here for the food. The infamous Chicken Corner is a popular intersection stocked with several faves and a decent new arrival or two.

Matt's Joint BARBECUE $$

(Map p545; mains from 189B; ⏲10.30am-midnight) With Marvel posters, tonnes of elbow room and choice positioning at the Chicken Corner intersection, this brash-looking US-styled newcomer is an obvious, if rather unsubtle, choice among very middling competition. The all-you-can-eat BBQ buffet (299B) at 6.30pm is a winner, and breakfasts and burgers pull in hungry punters throughout the day.

Lazy House INTERNATIONAL $$

(Map p545; Hat Rin Nai; dishes 90-270B; ⏲lunch & dinner) Back in the day, this joint was the owner's apartment – everyone liked his cooking so much that he decided to turn the place into a restaurant and hang-out spot. Today, Lazy House is easily one of Hat Rin's best places to veg out in front of a movie with a scrumptious shepherd's pie.

Lucky Crab SEAFOOD $$

(Map p545; Hat Rin Nai; dishes 100-450B; ⏲9am-11pm) Rows of freshly caught creatures are presented nightly atop miniature long-tail boats loaded with ice. Once you've picked your prey, grab a table inside amid dangling plants and charming stone furnishings.

Om Ganesh INDIAN $$

(Map p545; Hat Rin Nai; mains from 100B; ⏲9am-11pm) Seasoned old-timer Om Ganesh sees a regular flow of customers for its north Indian curries, *biryani* rice, roti and lassis, with a token spread of Chinese dishes for good measure. Set meals start at 300B.

Monna Lisa ITALIAN $$

(Map p545; Hat Rin Nai; pizza & pasta from 200B; ⏲1-11pm) Travellers rave about the pizza here, and the pasta gets a thumbs-up as well. It's run by a team of friendly Italians and has a basic, open-air atmosphere.

Southern Beaches

On Saturday evenings from 4pm to 10pm, a side street in the eastern part of Thong Sala becomes **Walking Street** – a bustling pedestrian zone mostly filled with locals hawking their wares to other islanders. There's plenty on offer, from clothing to food.

Night Market MARKET $

(Map p542; Thong Sala; dishes 25-180B; ⏲2-11pm) A heady mix of steam and snacking locals, Thong Sala's night market is a must for those looking for doses of culture while nibbling on low-priced snacks. Wander the stalls for a galaxy of Thai street food, from vegetable curry puffs to corn on the cob, spicy sausages, kebabs, spring rolls and coconut cake.

Nira's BAKERY $

(Map p542; snacks from 80B; ⏲7am-7pm) With outstanding service, a bright interconnected two-room interior, scrummy baked goodies, tip-top coffee (and rarities such as Marmite) and trendy furniture, Nira's is second to none in Thong Sala, and perhaps the entire island. This is *the* place for breakfast. Music is of the Grover Washington school.

Ando Loco MEXICAN $
(Map p542; www.andoloco.com; Ban Tai; mains from 50B; ⊙2-10.30pm Wed-Mon) This super-popular outdoor Mexican hang-out gets the universal thumbs up. Grab a jumbo margarita, down a drunken fajita, line up a quesadilla or two and sink a round of balls on the pool table.

★**Fisherman's Restaurant** SEAFOOD $$
(Map p539; ☎084 454 7240; Ban Tai; dishes 50-600B; ⊙1-10pm) Sit in a long-tail boat looking out over the sunset and a rocky pier. Lit up at night it's one of the island's nicest settings and the food, from the addictive yellow curry crab to the massive seafood platter to share, is as wonderful as the ambience. Reserve ahead, especially during party time.

★**Fabio's** ITALIAN $$
(Map p539; ☎083 389 5732; Ban Khai; dishes 150-400B; ⊙5-10pm Mon-Sat) An intimate, and delicious Italian place with golden walls, cream linens and bamboo furniture. There are only seven tables, so reserve in advance. House-made delicacies like seafood risotto, pizzas and iced limoncello are as artfully presented as they are fresh and delicious.

Vintage Burgers BURGERS $$
(Map p542; mains from 220B; ⊙5-10pm; 📶) This fantastic Portuguese-run gourmet burger spot in Thong Sala really hits the nail on the head with six types of superb patties, including a vegie, tuna and kids burger option, backed up by scrummy salt and oregano French fries and a sociable vibe.

Mason's Arms BRITISH $$
(Map p542; Thong Sala; mains 160-350B; ⊙10am-10.30pm, till midnight high season) Surreally emerging from the swaying palms, this Tudor-style black-and-white affair is seemingly plucked straight from Stratford-upon-Avon and deposited in the steamy jungle. It's one blood pudding away from being an official British colony, with a classic British menu – the fish 'n' chips (290B) is a winner every time and Marmite on toast (80B) awaits salt-deficient diners.

Food Factory INTERNATIONAL $$
(Map p542; mains from 180B; ⊙24hr; 📶) Serving up pizza and burgers around the clock on the busy road to Ban Tai and divided into restaurant and bar, this hard-working spot is all signed football shirts, sports TV check table cloths, '80s sounds, really terrific milkshakes and winning breakfasts (150B).

Other Beaches

★**Cucina Italiana** ITALIAN $$
(Jenny's; Map p539; Chalok Lam; pizzas 180-200B; ⊙5-10pm) If it weren't for the sand between your toes and the long-tail boats whizzing by, you might think you had been transported to the Italian countryside. The friendly Italian chef is passionate about his food, and creates everything from his pasta to his tiramisu daily, from scratch.

Sanctuary HEALTH FOOD $$
(Map p539; www.thesanctuarythailand.com; Hat Thian; mains from 130B; 📶) The Sanctuary's restaurant proves that wholesome food (vegetarian and seafood) can also be delicious. Enjoy a tasty parade of plates – from massaman curry to crunchy Vietnamese spring rolls. Don't forget to wash it all down with a blackberry, soya milk and honey immune booster. No credit cards.

Peppercorn STEAK $$
(Map p541; www.peppercornphangan.com; Hat Salad; mains 160-400B; ⊙4-10pm Mon-Sat; 🌿) Escargot and succulent steaks in a rickety jungle cottage? You bet. Peppercorn may be tucked in the brush away from the sea, but that shouldn't detract foodies from seeking out some of Pha Ngan's best international cuisine, with a fine selection of good vegetarian dishes to boot. No MSG or artificial ingredients.

Bamboo Hut WESTERN, THAI $$
(Map p539; Hat Yuan; dishes 100-300B; ⊙breakfast, lunch & dinner; 📶🌿) Lounge on a Thai-style cushion or sit at a teak table that catches sea breezes and looks over infinite blue. There are plenty of options from vegetarian specialities and fresh juices for those coming off a fast or cleanse, to classic, very well-prepared Thai dishes with all assortments of beef, chicken and prawns.

Two Brothers SEAFOOD $$
(Chalok Lam; barbecue sets from 250B; ⊙breakfast, lunch & dinner) One of the best of a string of Chalok Lam's seafood restaurants where fisher families serve you their bounty straight off the boats.

JJ's Restaurant THAI $$
(Map p539; ⊙9am-9pm) Drop off at JJ's come sunset to swoon before stirring visuals over the young mangroves at Ao Wok Tum while

devouring tasty treats from the kitchen and toasting it all with a chilled beer.

Drinking & Nightlife

Every month, on the night of the full moon, pilgrims pay lunar tribute to the party gods with trancelike dancing, wild screaming and glow-in-the-dark body paint. The throngs of bucket-sippers and fire twirlers gather on the infamous Sunrise Beach (Hat Rin Nok) and party until the sun replaces the moon in the sky.

A few other noteworthy spots can be found around the island for those seeking something a bit mellower.

Hat Rin

Hat Rin is the beating heart of the legendary Full Moon fun. When the moon isn't lighting up the night sky, partygoers flock to other spots on the island's south side. Most party venues flank Hat Rin's Sunrise Beach from south to north.

Rock BAR, CLUB
(Map p545) The superb views of the party from the elevated terrace on the far south side of the beach are matched by the best cocktails in town.

Drop-In Bar BAR, CLUB
(Map p545) This dance shack blasts the chart toppers that we all secretly love. This is one of the liveliest places but things go quiet on non–Full Moon nights.

Cactus Bar BAR, CLUB
(Map p545) Smack in the centre of Hat Rin Nok, Cactus pumps out a healthy mix of old-school tunes, hip-hop and R&B. It's popular and lively, although a DJ was shot dead here a few years back.

Sunrise BAR, CLUB
(Map p545) A spot on the sand where trance beats shake the graffiti-ed walls, with drum 'n bass coming into its own at Full Moon.

Tommy BAR, CLUB
(Map p545) One of Hat Rin's largest venues lures the masses with loungers, low tables, black lights and blaring Full Moon trance music.

Thong Sala

Harp PUB
(Map p542; 8am-midnight) With chatty staff and a prime location on the corner straight down from the pier, cavernous wood-floored Harp is the sports bar of choice for those crucial Premier League fixtures, draught beer and outstanding Sunday roasts (250B) plus other solid pub fare.

Other Beaches

Belgian Beer Bar BAR
(Map p541; www.seetanu.com; Surat Thani; 8am-10pm) Run by the affable Quentin, this enjoyable bar defies Surat Thani's appropriation by yogis and the chakra-balancing crowd with a heady range of Belgian beer, the most potent of which (Amber Bush) delivers a dizzying 12.5% punch. If the yogic flying doesn't give you wings, this might.

Jam BAR
(Map p539; Hin Kong; 8pm-2am Tue & Sat) It's DIY live music at this friendly nightspot on the west coast. Saturday nights are open mic, and the rest of the week you'll usually catch a few locals jamming on their guitars. By appointment, musicians can practise their songs from 6pm.

Outlaws Saloon BAR
(Map p542; 4pm-2am) With its buffalo skulls, US flags, sounds from Elvis and other American icons, this fun ranch-style saloon is quite a sight on a lively night. There's a meaty menu, excellent Sunday roast dinners and imported beers and ciders.

It's on the north side of the road between Thong Sala and Ban Tai.

Flip Flop Pharmacy BAR
(Map p539; Thong Nai Pan; noon-1am;) With flip flops on the wall, this open-air bar on the sands of Thong Nai Pan has a fine beach perspective (and a pool table).

Amsterdam BAR
(Map p539; Ao Plaay Laem) Near Ao Wok Tum on the west coast, Amsterdam attracts tourists and locals from all over the island, who are looking for a chill spot to watch the sunset.

Information

DANGERS & ANNOYANCES

Some of your fondest holiday memories can hatch on Ko Pha-Ngan; just be mindful of the following situations where things can go pear-shaped.

Drugs You're sunning on the beach when a local walks up and offers you some local herb at a ridiculously low price. 'No thanks,' you say, knowing that the penalties for drug use in

Thailand are fierce. But the vendor drops his price even more and practically offers you the weed for free. Too good to be true? Obviously. As soon as you take a toke, the seller rats you out to the police and you're whisked away to the local prison to pay a wallet-busting fine. This is a regular scenario on Ko Pha-Ngan so it's best to avoid the call of the ganja.

Another important thing to remember: your travel insurance does not cover drug-related injuries or treatment. Drug-related freak-outs *do* happen – we've heard firsthand accounts of partiers slipping into extended periods of delirium. Suan Saranrom (Garden of Joys) Psychiatric Hospital in Surat Thani has to take on extra staff during Full Moon and other party periods to handle the number of *fa·ràng* who freak out on magic mushrooms, acid or other abundantly available hallucinogens.

Women Travellers Female travellers should be particularly careful when partying on the island. We've received numerous reports about drug- and alcohol-related rape (and these situations are not limited to Full Moon Parties). Another disturbing problem is the unscrupulous behaviour of some of the local motorcycle taxi drivers. Several complaints have been filed about drivers groping female passengers; there are even reports of severe sexual assaults.

Motorcycles Ko Pha-Ngan has more motorcycle accidents than injuries incurred from Full Moon tomfoolery, although bad motorcycle driving coincides with the Full Moon revelries. Nowadays there's a decent system of paved roads (recently extended to Than Sadet), but some tracks remain rutted dirt-and-mud paths and the island is also hilly, with some steep inclines.The island now has a special ambulance that trawls the island helping injured bikers. If you don't have an international driving licence, you will also be driving illegally and your insurance may not cover you in the event of an accident, so costs could pile up fast.

Drowning Rip currents and alcohol don't mix well. Drownings are frequent; if swimming, it's advisable to be clear-headed rather than plunging into the sea on a Full Moon bender.

Fake Alcohol This is a common scam during the Full Moon mania at the bucket stalls on the beach and along the road. Buckets may be filled with low-grade moonshine rice whisky, or old bottles filled with homemade alcohol. Apart from obvious health risks, dodgy alcohol is also a prime mover in many of the accidents at the time of the Full Moon, from motorcycle accidents to drownings, fights and burns from jumping fire ropes.

Glass on the Beach Beware nasty cuts from broken glass in the sand at Full Moon Party time – don good footwear.

EMERGENCY

Main Police Station (Map p539; ☎077 377114, 191) Located about 2km north of Thong Sala. Come here to file a report. You might be charged between 110B and 200B to file the report, which is for insurance and refusing to pay may lead to complications. If you are arrested you have the right to an embassy phone call; you don't have to accept the 'interpreter' you are offered.

If you have committed a serious offence, do not sign anything written only in Thai, or write on the document that you do not understand the language and are signing under duress.

LAUNDRY

If you got fluorescent body paint on your clothes during your Full Moon romp, don't bother sending them to the cleaners – it will never come out. Trust us, we've tried. For your other washing needs, there are heaps of places that will gladly wash your clothes. Prices hover around 40B per kilo, and express cleanings shouldn't be more than 60B per kilo.

MEDICAL SERVICES

Medical services can be a little crooked in Ko Pha-Ngan – expect unstable prices and underqualified, mercenary doctors. Many clinics charge a 3000B entrance fee before treatment. Serious medical issues should be dealt with on nearby Ko Samui.

Ko Pha-Ngan Hospital (Map p539; ☎077 377034; Thong Sala; ⌚24hr) About 2.5km north of Thong Sala; has 24-hour emergency.

MONEY

Thong Sala, Ko Pha-Ngan's financial 'capital', has plenty of banks, currency converters and several Western Union offices. Hat Rin has numerous ATMs and a couple of banks at the pier. There are also ATMs in Hat Yao, Chalok Lum and Thong Nai Pan.

POST

Main Post Office (Map p542; ⌚8.30am-4.30pm Mon-Fri, 9am-noon Sat) In Thong Sala; there's a smaller office (Map p545) right near the pier in Hat Rin.

TOURIST INFORMATION

There are no government-run Tourist Authority of Thailand (TAT) offices on Ko Pha-Ngan; instead tourists get their information from local travel agencies and brochures. Most agencies are clumped around Hat Rin and Thong Sala. Agents take a small commission on each sale, but collusion keeps prices relatively stable and standardised. Choose an agent you trust if you are spending a lot of money – faulty bookings do happen on Ko Pha-Ngan, especially since the island does not have tourist police.

Several mini-magazines also offer comprehensive information about the island's accommodation, restaurants, activities and Full Moon Parties. Our favourite option is the pocket-sized quarterly Phangan Info (www.phangan.info), also available as a handy app.

Backpackers Information Centre (Map p545; ☎077 375535; www.backpackersthailand.com; Hat Rin; ⏰11am-8pm) A must for travellers looking to book high-quality tours (diving, live-aboards, jungle safaris etc) and transport. Not just for backpackers, it's an expat-run travel agency that offers peace of mind with every purchase – travellers are provided with the mobile phone number of the owners should any problems arise. Service is first rate and staff are forever helpful. It also runs the Crystal Dive shop next door.

WEBSITES

www.backpackersthailand.com Everything you need to know about Ko Pha-Ngan, from booking accommodation to finding out the Full Moon Party schedule. Doubles as a vast resource for the whole country as well.

www.phangan.info Handy and informative resource for Ko Pha-Ngan, with detailed maps and reviews.

Getting There & Away

As always, the cost and departure times are subject to change. Rough waves are known to cancel ferries between the months of October and December.

AIR

Ko Pha-Ngan's new airport was due to open in 2014, but when we stopped by in 2015 it was still not operational and no date was set for an official opening. At the time of writing, there were issues relating to the airport encroaching on land belonging to Than Sadet-Koh Phangan National Park, so everything was in the air, so to speak. If and when operational, it is expected that Kan Air flights will connect Ko Pha-Ngan with Bangkok, with flights taking 80 minutes. It's also expected that services will increase over the next few years to include more Bangkok flights and other destinations as well.

BOAT

To Bangkok, Hua Hin & Chumphon

The Lomprayah and Seatran Discovery services have bus–boat combination packages (from around 1300B) that depart from the Th Khao San area in Bangkok and pass through Hua Hin and Chumphon. The whole voyage takes about 17 hours.

It is also quite hassle-free (unless your train breaks down, which happens a lot) to take the train from Bangkok or Hua Hin to Chumphon and switch to a ferry service. In this case expect to pay 300B for a 2nd class seat on a train from Bangkok to Chumphon (about 8½ hours); the boat from Chumphon to Ko Pha-Ngan takes around 2½ hours and costs 800B to 1000B depending on the boat.

To Ko Samui

There are around a dozen daily departures between Thong Sala on Ko Pha-Ngan and Ko Samui. These boats leave throughout the day from 7am to 6pm, take from 20 minutes to an hour and cost 200B to 300B depending on the boat.

The **Haad Rin Queen** (☎077 484668) goes back and forth between Hat Rin and Big Buddha Beach on Ko Samui four times a day. The voyage takes 50 minutes and costs 200B.

The *Thong Nai Pan Express* is a wobbly old fishing boat (not for the faint-hearted) that runs once a day from Mae Hat on Ko Samui to Hat Rin on Ko Pha-Ngan and then up the east coast, stopping at all the beaches as far as Thong Nai Pan Noi. Prices range from 200B to 400B depending on the destination. The boat won't run in bad weather.

To Ko Tao

Ko Tao-bound **Lomprayah** ferries (500B to 600B) depart from Thong Sala on Ko Pha-Ngan at 8.30am, 1pm and 5.45pm and arrive at 9.45am, 2.15pm and 6.45pm. The **Seatran** service (430B, 90 minutes) departs from Thong Sala at 8.30am, 1.30pm and 5pm daily. Taxis depart Hat Rin for Thong Sala one hour before the boat departure. The cheaper-but-slower **Songserm** (350B) leaves Ko Pha-Ngan at 12.30pm and alights at 2.30pm, before continuing to Chumphon.

To Surat Thani & the Andaman Coast

There are approximately eight daily departures between Ko Pha-Ngan and Surat Thani on the **Songserm Express** (350B, 4½ hours) or **Lomprayah** (550B, 2¾ hours) services, both travelling via Ko Samui. These boats leave from Thong Sala throughout the day from 7am to 8pm. Every night, depending on the weather, a night boat runs from Surat (400B, seven hours), departing at 11pm. Boats in the opposite direction leave Ko Pha-Ngan at 10pm.

Combination boat–bus tickets are available at any travel agency. Simply tell them your desired destination and they will sell you the necessary links in the transport chain. Most travellers will pass through Surat Thani as they swap coasts.

Getting Around

You can rent motorcycles all over the island for 150B to 250B per day. Always wear a helmet – it's the law on Ko Pha-Ngan, and local policemen are starting to enforce it. But whatever the law, if you come off even at quite a low speed and hit your head, you can sustain serious injuries. Check that the motorcycle has enough space in the underseat compartment to store your helmet. If you plan on riding over dirt tracks it is imperative that you rent a bike comparable to a Honda MTX125 – gearless scooters cannot make the journey. Bicycle rentals are discouraged unless you're fit enough to take on the Tour de France.

Pick-up trucks and *sŏrng·tăa·ou* chug along the island's major roads and the rates double after sunset. Ask your accommodation about free or discount transfers when you leave the island. The trip from Thong Sala to Hat Rin is 100B; further beaches will set you back around 150B to 200B.

Long-tail boats depart from Thong Sala, Chalok Lam and Hat Rin, heading to far-flung destinations such as Hat Khuat (Bottle Beach). Expect to pay anywhere from 50B for a short trip, and up to 300B for a lengthier journey. You can charter a private boat ride from beach to beach for about 150B per 15 minutes of travel.

Ko Tao

เกาะเต่า

POP 2032

Once the baby of the Samui–Pha-Ngan–Tao trio, Ko Tao may still be the smallest in size but in many other ways it's grown up. The island is consistently gaining popularity and going more upscale, but for now this jungle-topped cutie has the busy vibe of Samui mixed with the laid-back nature of Pha-Ngan. But Tao also has its wild card, something the others don't: easy-to-get-to, diverse diving right off its shores. Cavort with sharks and rays in a playground of tangled neon coral, toast the day with sunset cocktails on a white beach then get up and do it all over again the next day. But even while the island may be synonymous with diving, there is much more to the place. Hikers and hermits can re-enact an episode from *Lost* in the dripping coastal jungles. And when you're Robinson Crusoe-ed out, hit the pumpin' bar scene that rages on until dawn.

Activities

Diving

If you've never been diving before, Ko Tao is *the* place in Thailand to lose your scuba virginity. The shallow bays scalloping the island are perfect for newbie divers to take their first stab at scuba; the waters are crystal clear, there are loads of neon reefs and the temperatures feel like bathwater. With many sheltered dive sites, waters around Ko Tao can be dived all year round, and it's only during the monsoon months that diving may stop for a day or two if the waters are too choppy, but this is actually quite rare. The best dive sites are found at offshore pinnacles within a 20km radius of the island, but seasoned scubaholics almost always prefer the top-notch sites along the Andaman coast. The local marine wildlife includes groupers, moray eels, batfish, bannerfish, barracudas, titan triggerfish, angelfish, clownfish (Nemos), stingrays, reef sharks and frequent visits by mighty whale sharks.

Onshore, over 40 dive centres are ready to saddle you up with gear and teach you the ropes in a 3½-day Open Water certification course. The intense competition among scuba schools means that certification prices are unbeatably low and the standards of service top-notch; dozens of dive shops vie for your baht, so be sure to shop around. The island issues more scuba certifications than anywhere else in the world.

ACE Marine Expeditions DIVING
(Map p562; ☎077 456547; www.divephotothai.com) The luxe choice. Go out on this James Bond–worthy speedboat and get to sites in a fraction of the time. The ingenious 'whaleshark watch' program keeps up-to-the-moment tabs on where sightings are taking place – they'll whisk you out to where the creatures are so your chances of seeing them are greatly increased.

Ban's Diving School DIVING
(Map p562; ☎077 456466; www.bansdivingresort.com; Sairee Beach) A well-oiled diving machine that's relentlessly expanding, Ban's is one of the world's most prolific diver certification schools yet it retains a five-star feel. Classroom sessions tend to be conducted in large groups, but there's a reasonable amount of individual attention in the water. A breadth of international instructors means that students can learn to dive in their native tongue.

Big Blue Diving DIVING
(Map p562; ☎077 456050; www.bigbluediving.com; Sairee Beach) If Goldilocks were picking a dive school, she'd probably pick Big Blue – this mid-size operation (not too big, not too small) gets props for fostering a sociable vibe while maintaining a high standard of service. Divers of every ilk can score dirt-cheap accommodation at their resort.

Buddha View DIVING
(☎077 456074; www.buddhaview-diving.com; Chalok Ban Kao) One of several big dive operations on Ko Tao, Buddha View offers the standard fare of certification and special programs for technical diving (venturing

Ko Tao

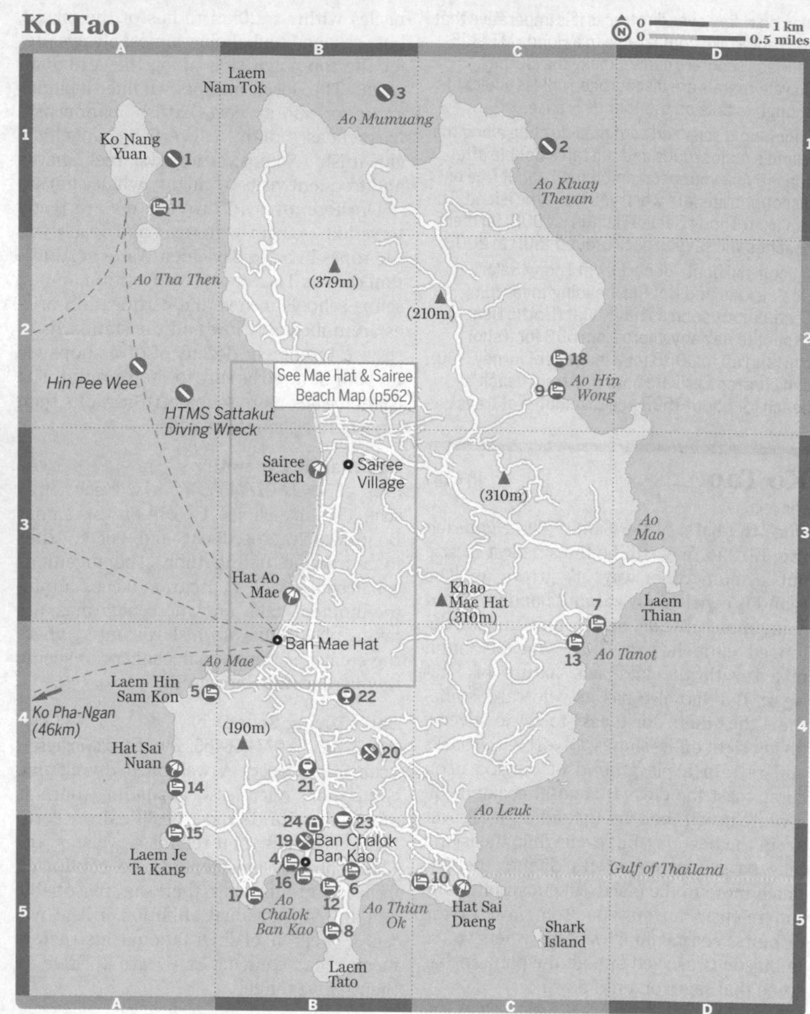

beyond the usual parameters of recreational underwater exploration). Discounted accommodation is available at its friendly resort.

Crystal Dive DIVING

(Map p562; ☎077 456106; www.crystaldive.com; Mae Hat) Crystal is the Meryl Streep of diving operators, winning all the awards for best performance year after year. It's one of the largest schools on the island (and around the world), although high-quality instructors and intimate classes keep the school feeling quite personal. Multilingual staff members, air-conditioned classes and two on-site swimming pools sweeten the deal. Highly recommended.

New Heaven DIVING

(☎077 457045; www.newheavendiveschool.com; Chalok Ban Kao) The owners of this small diving operation dedicate a lot of their time to preserving the natural beauty of Ko Tao's underwater sites by conducting regular reef checks and contributing to reef restoration efforts. A special CPAD research diver certification program is available in addition to the regular order of programs and fun dives.

Ko Tao

Activities, Courses & Tours
1 Japanese Gardens Dive Site A1
2 Light House Point C1
3 Mango Bay B1

Sleeping
4 Buddha View Dive Resort B5
5 Charm Churee Villa A4
6 Chintakiri Resort B5
7 Family Tanote C3
8 Freedom Beach B5
9 Hin Wong Bungalows C2
10 Jamahkiri Resort & Spa C5
JP Resort .... (see 16)
11 Ko Nangyuan Dive Resort A1
12 Ko Tao Resort B5
13 Poseidon C4
14 Sai Thong Resort A4
15 Tao Thong Villa A5
16 Tropicana B5
17 View Point Resort B5
18 View Rock C2

Eating
19 I (Heart) Salad B5
20 Long Pae B4
Viewpoint Restaurant .... (see 17)

Drinking & Nightlife
21 Castle B4
22 Earth House B4
23 Natural High Cafe B5

Shopping
24 Hammock Cafe Plaeyuan B5

Scuba Junction DIVING
(Scuba J; Map p562; ☎077 456164; www.scuba-junction.com; Sairee Beach) These instructors lure travellers that are looking for an intimate dive experience.The outfit guarantees a maximum of four people per group.

Snorkelling

Snorkelling is a popular alternative to diving, and organising your own snorkelling trip here is simple, since the bays on the east coast have bungalow operations offering equipment rental for between 100B and 200B per day.

Most snorkel enthusiasts opt for the do-it-yourself approach on Ko Tao, which involves swimming out into the offshore bays or hiring a long-tail boat to putter around further out. Guided tours are also available and can be booked at any local travel agency. Tours range from 500B to 800B (usually including gear, lunch and a guide/boat captain) and stop at various snorkelling hotspots around the island. **Laem Thian** is popular for its small sharks, **Shark Island** has loads of fish (and ironically no sharks), **Ao Hin Wong** is known for its crystalline waters, and **Light House Point** (Map p556), in the north, offers a dazzling array of colourful sea anemones. Dive schools will usually allow snorkellers on their vessels for a comparable price – but it's only worth snorkelling at the shallower sites such as Japanese Gardens. Note that dive boats visit the shallower sites in the afternoons.

Freediving

Over the last couple of years freediving (exploring the sea using breath-holding techniques rather than scuba gear) has grown rapidly in popularity. Several small schools have opened across the island. We recommend the capable staff at **Apnea Total** (Map p562; ☎081 956 5720, 081 956 5430; www.apneatotal.com; Sairee Beach) who have earned awards in the freediving world and have a knack for easing newbies into this sport. The student–teacher ratio of three to one also ensures plenty of attention to safety. Also worth a special mention is **Blue Immersion** (Map p562; ☎081 188 8488; www.blue-immersion.com; Sairee Beach) run by friendly Akim, a martial arts expert and a freediving pro – he was one of the first people in the world to freedive below 100m – where a one-day introduction to freediving costs 3000B. Freediving prices are standardised across the island as well – a 2½-day SSI beginner course will set you back 5500B.

Technical Diving & Cave Diving

Well-seasoned divers and hardcore Jacques Cousteaus should contact **Tech Thailand** (www.techthailand.com) or one of a handful of other tech diving schools if they want to take their underwater exploration to the next level and try a technical dive. According to PADI, tec diving, as it's often known, is 'diving other than conventional commercial or recreational diving that takes divers beyond recreational diving limits'. Technical diving exceeds depths of 40m and requires stage decompressions, and a variety of gas mixtures are often used in a single dive. You must be a certified tech diver to undertake tech dives; training courses are available at many schools on the island, offering various tech diving certifications.

TAKING THE PLUNGE: CHOOSING A DIVE SCHOOL ON KO TAO

It's no surprise that this underwater playground has become exceptionally popular with beginners. But before you dive in (so to speak) it's important to look around at the various dive schools available.

When you alight at the pier in Mae Hat, touts will try to coax you into staying at their dive resort with promises of a 'special price for you'. But there are dozens of dive centres on Ko Tao, so it's best to arrive armed with the names of a few reputable schools. If you're not rushed for time, consider relaxing on the island for a couple of days before making any decisions – you will undoubtedly bump into swarms of scubaphiles and instructors who will offer their advice and opinions.

Remember: the success of your diving experience will largely depend on how much you like your instructor. Other factors to consider are the size of your diving group, the condition of your equipment and the condition of the dive sites, to name a few.

For the most part, diving prices are somewhat standardised across the island, so there's no need to spend your time hunting around for the best deal. A **PADI** (www.padi.com) Open Water Diver (OWD) certification course costs 9800B; an **SSI** (www.ssithailand.com) OWD certificate is slightly less (9000B) because you do not have to pay for instruction materials. An Advanced Open Water Diver (AOWD) certification course will set you back 8500B, a rescue course is 9500B and the Divemaster program costs a cool 25,000B. Fun divers should expect to pay roughly 1000B per dive, or around 7000B for a 10-dive package. These rates include all dive gear, boat, instructors/guides and snacks. Discounts are usually given if you bring your own equipment. Be wary of dive centres that offer too many price cuts – safety is paramount, and a shop giving out unusually good deals is probably cutting too many corners.

Most dive schools will hook you up with cheap or even free accommodation. Almost all scuba centres offer gratis fan rooms for anyone doing beginner coursework. Expect large crowds and booked-out beds throughout December, January, June, July and August, and a monthly glut of wannabe divers after every Full Moon Party on Ko Pha-Ngan.

Several years ago, Tech Thailand's old boat, MV *Trident,* made a name for itself in the diving community after successfully locating dozens of previously undiscovered wrecks in the Gulf of Thailand. Its most famous discovery was the USS *Lagarto,* an American naval vessel that sank during WWII. The gulf has long been an important trading route and new wrecks are being discovered all the time, from old Chinese pottery wrecks to Japanese *marus* (merchant ships). In 2010 the *Trident* was purposefully sunk off the coast of Ko Tao to create an artificial reef. A miscalculation with the explosives has left the wreck a bit too deep for beginners. The HTMS *Sattakut* wreck and deeper pinnacle dive sites are also good for tech diving.

Cave diving has taken Ko Tao by storm, and the most intrepid scuba buffs are lining up to make the half-day trek over to Khao Sok National Park. Beneath the park's main lake lurks an astonishing submarine world filled with hidden grottos, limestone crags and skulking catfish. In certain areas divers can swim near submerged villages that were flooded in order to create a reservoir and dam. Most cave-diving trips depart from Ko Tao on the afternoon boat service and return to the island on the afternoon boat service of the following day. Overnight stays are arranged in or near the park.

Underwater Photography & Videography

If your wallet is already full of diving certification cards, consider renting an underwater camera or enrolling in a marine videography course. Many scuba schools hire professional videographers to film Open Water Diver certifications, and if this piques your interest, you could potentially earn some money after completing a video internship. Your dive operator can put you in touch with any of the half-dozen videography crews on the island. We recommend **ACE Marine Images** (Map p562; ☎077 457054; www.acemarineimages.com; Sairee Beach), one of Thailand's leading underwater videography studios. An introductory course including camera, diving and instruction is 4500B and can also be used towards an Advanced PADI certification. **Crystal Images** (☎092 476 4110; www.crystalimageskohtao.com) and **Oceans Below** (www.oceansbelow.net) offer videography courses and internships and each have their own special options.

Other Activities

★**Flying Trapeze Adventures** ACROBATICS
(FTA; Map p562; ☎080 696 9269; www.gtadventures.com; Sairee Beach; ⏰4-8pm, lessons 3.30-5.30pm) Find out if you're a great catch during a 90-minute small group beginner trapeze lesson (1200B). Afternoon courses are taught by super-friendly Gemma and her posse of limber sidekicks, who take you from circus neophyte to soaring savant in four jumps or less. There are occasional nightly shows, involving audience participation. Class times vary depending on sundown; reserve ahead.

Participants must be at least six years old.

The Gallery Spa MASSAGE
(Map p562; ☎077 456547; www.thegallerykohtao.com; 400B) The traditional Thai massage will make you feel brand-new. Book in advance.

Goodtime Adventures HIKING, ADVENTURE SPORTS
(Map p562; ☎087 275 3604; www.gtadventures.com; Sairee Beach; ⏰noon-late) Dive, hike through the island's jungle interior, swing from rock to rock during a climbing and abseiling session, or unleash your inner daredevil during an afternoon of cliff jumping (at your own risk). Alternatively, take a shot at all of them on the full-day Koh Tao Adventure (3500B). The Goodtime office, along the Sairee sands, doubles as a friendly cafe.

Dorms and doubles are also available.

Monsoon Gym & Fight Club MARTIAL ARTS
(Map p562; www.monsoongym.com) This Sairee Beach club combines Thai boxing programs

DIVE SITES AT A GLANCE

In general, divers don't have much of a choice as to which sites they explore. Each dive school chooses a smattering of sites for the day depending on weather and ocean conditions. Deeper dive sites such as Chumphon Pinnacle are usually visited in the morning. Afternoon boats tour the shallower sites such as Japanese Gardens. Recently, two large vessels have been sunk off the coast, providing scubaphiles with two new wreck dives. Divers hoping to spend some quality time searching for whale sharks at Sail Rock should join one of the dive trips departing daily from Ko Pha-Ngan.

Chumphon Pinnacle (36m maximum depth), 13km west of Ko Tao, has a colourful assortment of sea anemones along the four interconnected pinnacles. The site plays host to schools of giant trevally, tuna and large grey reef sharks. Whale sharks are known to pop up once in a while.

Green Rock (25m maximum depth) is an underwater jungle gym featuring caverns, caves and small swim-throughs. Rays, grouper and triggerfish are known to hang around. It's a great place for a night dive.

Japanese Gardens (Map p556; 12m maximum depth), between Ko Tao and Ko Nang Yuan, is a low-stress dive site perfect for beginners. There's plenty of colourful coral, and turtles, stingray and pufferfish often pass by.

Mango Bay (Map p556; 16m maximum depth) might be your first dive site if you are putting on a tank for the first time. Lazy reef fish swim around as newbies practise their skills on the sandy bottom.

Sail Rock (40m maximum depth), best accessed by Ko Pha-Ngan, features a massive rock chimney with a vertical swim-through, and large pelagics like barracuda and kingfish. This is one of the top spots in Southeast Asia to see whale sharks; in the past few years they have been seen year round, so there's no clear season.

Southwest Pinnacle (33m maximum depth) offers divers a collection of pinnacles that are home to giant groupers and barracudas, and whale sharks are sometimes spotted.

White Rock (29m maximum depth) is home to colourful corals, angelfish, clownfish and territorial triggerfish. Another popular spot for night divers.

HTMS Sattakut was sunk in 2011 southeast of Hin Pee Wee at a depth of 30m and has become one of the most popular wreck diving sites.

and air-con dorm accommodation (300B) for students signed up to get to grips with the fighting art. It's an excellent and exhilarating way to spend time in Ko Tao, if diving isn't your scene. The well-equipped concrete gym is right alongside the Muay Thai ring. Drop-in fight training costs 300B, monthly unlimited use is 7000B.

Shambhala YOGA
(Map p562; ☎084 440 6755; www.shambhalayogakohtao.com; Sairee Beach) Ko Tao's full-time yoga centre is housed in beautiful wooden *săh·lah* on the forested grounds of Blue Wind in Sairee Beach. The two-hour classes, led by Kester, the energetic yogi, cost 300B.

Ko Tao Bowling & Mini Golf BOWLING, GOLF
(☎077 456316; ⊙noon-midnight) On the main road between Mae Hat and Chalok Ban Kao, Ko Tao Bowling & Mini Golf has several homemade bowling lanes where the employees reset the pins after every frame (300B per hour). The 18-hole mini-golf course has a landmark theme – putt your ball through Stonehenge or across the Golden Gate Bridge.

Sleeping

If you are planning to dive while visiting Ko Tao, your scuba operator will probably offer you free or discounted accommodation to sweeten the deal. Some schools have on-site lodging, while others have deals with bungalows. It's important to note that you only receive your discount on the days you dive. So, for example, if you buy a 10-dive package, and decide to take a day off in the middle, your room rate will not be discounted on that evening. Also, a restful sleep is important before diving, so scope out these 'great room deals' before saying yes – some of them are one cockroach away from being condemned.

There are also many sleeping options that have absolutely nothing to do with the island's diving culture. Ko Tao's secluded eastern coves are dotted with stunning retreats that still offer a true getaway experience, but these can be difficult to reach due to the island's dismal network of roads. You can often call ahead of time and arrange to be picked up from the pier in Mae Hat.

Note that many budget rooms are only available on a first come, first served basis and often aren't even advertised on hotel websites. Many midrange resorts offer budget rooms so take a look at all our listings to see each resort's (usually very big) price range. These rooms book fast so it can be prudent to call ahead and find out what may be available before you arrive.

Sairee Beach

Giant Sairee is the longest and most developed strip on the island, with a string of dive operations, bungalows, travel agencies, minimarkets and internet cafes. The northern end is the prettiest and quietest while there's more of a party scene and noise from the bars to the south. For most people, this is the choice beach to stay since it has a great blend of scenery and action.

Blue Wind BUNGALOW $
(Map p562; ☎077 456116; bluewind_wa@yahoo.com; bungalows 350-1400B; ❄📶) Blue Wind is a great rustic but relaxing alternative to the high-intensity dive resorts strung along Sairee Beach. Sturdy bamboo huts are peppered along a dirt trail behind the beachside bakery. Large, tiled air-conditioned cabins and attractive rooms in blocks with balcony boast hot showers and TVs. Reception is shut in the evenings and wi-fi is limited to the beach area.

Spicytao Backpackers HOSTEL $
(Map p562; ☎082 278 7115; www.spicyhostels.com/Home.html; dm 200-250B; ❄📶) Like your own super-social country hang-out, Spicytao is hidden off the main drag in a rustic garden setting. Backpackers rave about the ambience and staff who are always organising activities. Book in advance!

Ban's Diving Resort RESORT $$
(Map p562; ☎077 456466; www.bansdivingresort.com; r 600-10,000B; ❄@📶🏊) This dive-centric party palace offers a wide range of quality accommodation from basic backpacker digs to sleek hillside villas, and it's growing all the time. Post-scuba chill sessions take place on Ban's prime slice of beach or at one of the two swimming pools tucked within the strip of jungle between the two-storey, pillared and terraced white hotel blocks.

Sairee Cottage BUNGALOW $$
(Map p562; ☎077 456374; www.saireecottagediving.com; bungalows 500-3000B; ❄📶🏊) Bungalows are connected by a sand path through a sun-splotched garden of palms and hibiscus. Even the smallest, most budget options here are of a higher standard than most and very good value. The beach out front is slim and under the shade of a giant ironwood tree.

Big Blue Resort BUNGALOW $$

(Map p562; ☎077 456050; www.bigbluediving.com; dm 400B, r 1000-7000B; ❄@) This scuba-centric resort has a summer camp vibe – diving classes dominate the daytime, while evenings are spent en masse, grabbing dinner or watching fire twirling. Both the basic fan bungalows and motel-style air-con rooms offer little when it comes to views, but you can grade up if you want ocean panoramas.

Palm Leaf Resort BUNGALOW $$

(Map p562; ☎077 456731; www.kohtaopalmleaf.com; bungalows 2000-3500B; ❄🛜🏊) Palm Leaf rooms are good though nothing spectacular, but the location, at the quieter northern section of silky Sairee Beach, can't be beat.

Seashell Resort BUNGALOW $$

(Map p562; ☎077 456271; www.seashell-kohtao.com; bungalows 1000-4000B; ❄🛜🏊) Another huge mix of lodging from simple wood fan bungalows to hotel-style rooms in a block, this is a busy resort with nicely tended grounds but prices are out of whack with what you can find elsewhere. It's a good backup, however, that welcomes divers and non-divers.

★ **Place** RESORT $$$

(Map p562; www.theplacekohtao.com; villas 8000-9000B; ❄🛜) About a 15-minute walk or five-minute taxi ride from its hilltop location to Sairee Beach, this romantic boutique choice has nine private luxury villas nestled in leaf-clad hills with sweeping ocean views. Honeymooners will rejoice: a private plunge pool is standard and private chef services satisfy those who choose to remain in their nuptial nest instead of venturing out for calories.

Ko Tao Cabana BUNGALOW $$$

(Map p562; ☎077 456505; www.kohtaocabana.com; bungalows 6100-16,700B; ❄@🛜🏊) This prime piece of quiet beachside property offers timber-framed villas and white adobe huts with woven roofs dotted along the beach and up the hill, as paths wind through the fern-laden, manicured jungle. The private villas are one of the more upscale options on the island, although service can be lacking and a bit of TLC wouldn't go amiss.

Mae Hat

All ferry arrivals pull into the pier at the busy village of Mae Hat and nearly all the resorts on this beach will have a view and be in earshot of the constant ebb and flow of boat arrivals and departures. As such this isn't the best beach for a tranquil getaway although it's a good hub if your main goal is diving. Accommodation is spread throughout, but the more charming options extend in both directions along the sandy beach, both north and south of the pier.

Sai Thong Resort BUNGALOW $

(Map p556; www.saithongresort.info; Hat Sai Nuan; bungalows 500-2500B; ❄🛜) As the rush of Mae Hat dwindles away along the island's southwest shore, Sai Thong emerges along quiet, sandy Hat Sai Nuan. Bungalows, in various, rustic incarnations of weaving and wood, have colourful porch hammocks and palm-filled vistas. It's secluded and serene: guests frequent the restaurant's relaxing sun deck. Wi-fi only in the restaurant.

The resort is accessed by a quick ride from the Mae Hat pier by long-tail boat, or a 25-minute walk.

Ko Tao Central Hostel HOSTEL $

(Map p562; ☎077 456925, 093 761 2398; www.kohtaohostel.com; dm 310B; ❄🛜) Identified by its London Underground–style logo, this clean, central and friendly Mae Hat hostel has good 12-bed dorms, if all you need is a handy dorm near to the pier. Check-out is at 11am. Reception is in Island Travel next door; no towel service, so bring your own.

Tao Thong Villa BUNGALOW $

(Map p556; ☎077 456078; Ao Sai Nuan; bungalows 400-1800B; ❄@🛜) Popular with long-termers seeking peace and quiet, these no-frills bungalows have killer views. Tao Thong actually straddles two tiny beaches on a craggy cape about halfway between Mae Hat and Chalok Ban Kao. To reach it, grab a boat taxi for a short ride from the Mae Hat pier.

Crystal Dive Resort BUNGALOW $$

(Map p562; ☎077 456106; www.crystaldive.com; bungalows 800-1500B; ❄🛜🏊) The bungalow and motel-style accommodation at Crystal is reserved for its divers, and prices drop significantly for those taking courses. Guests can take a dip in the refreshing pool when it isn't overflowing with newbie divers.

Ananda Villa HOTEL $$

(Map p562; ☎077 456478; www.anandavilla.com; r 500-1800B; ❄🛜) This friendly, two-storey hotel with verandahs and lined with decorative palms and plumeria has a colonial feel, not far from the jetty. The cheapest rooms are fan only and are in another older room block a bit further from the beach.

Mae Hat & Sairee Beach

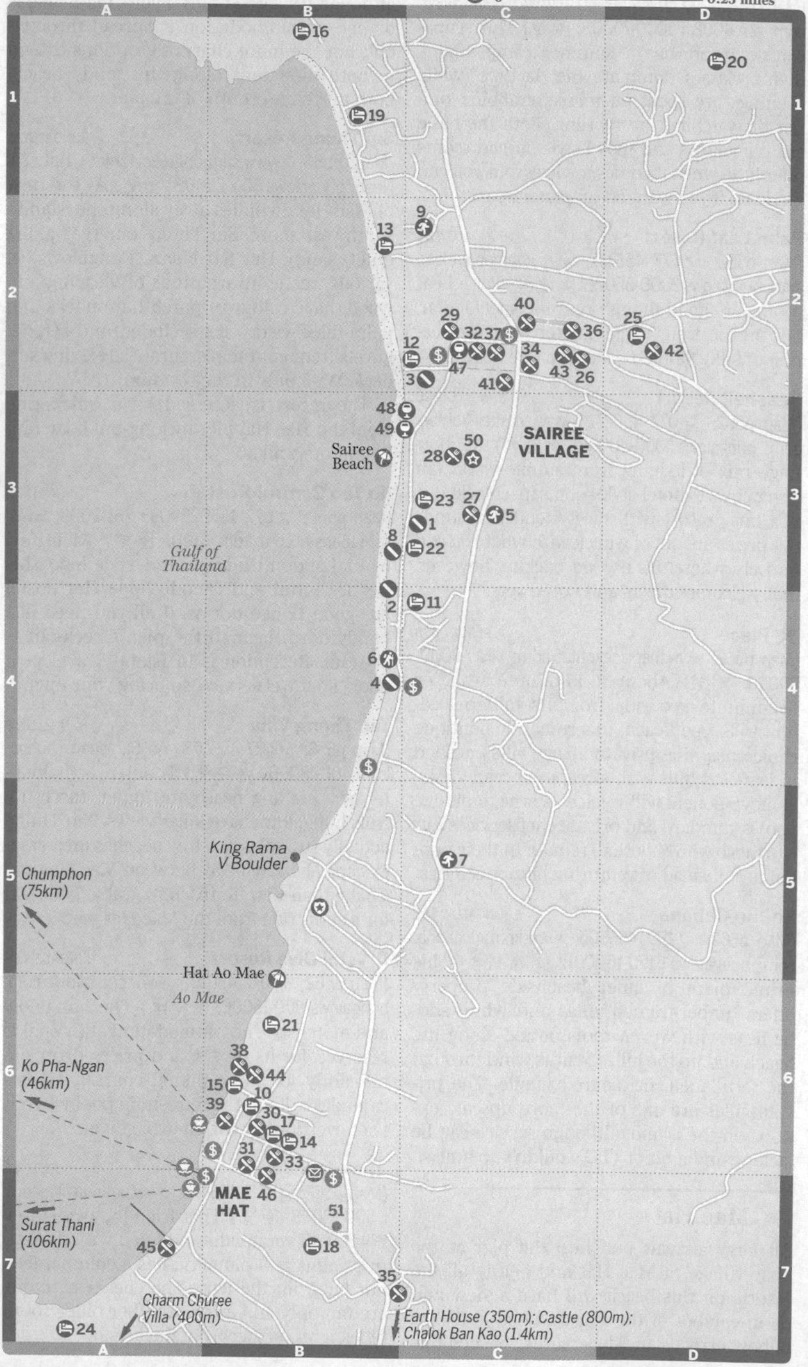
0 500 m
0 0.25 miles
A
B
C
D
1
2
3
4
5
6
7
SAIREE VILLAGE
Sairee Beach
Gulf of Thailand
King Rama V Boulder
Hat Ao Mae
Ao Mae
MAE HAT
Chumphon (75km)
Ko Pha-Ngan (46km)
Surat Thani (106km)
Charm Churee Villa (400m)
Earth House (350m); Castle (800m); Chalok Ban Kao (1.4km)
1
2
3
4
5
6
7
8
9
10
11
12
13
14
15
16
17
18
19
20
21
22
23
24
25
26
27
28
29
30
31
32
33
34
35
36
37
38
39
40
41
42
43
44
45
46
47
48
49
50
51

Mae Hat & Sairee Beach

Activities, Courses & Tours
ACE Marine Expeditions ....(see 43)
ACE Marine Images ....(see 43)
1 Apnea Total C3
2 Ban's Diving School B4
3 Big Blue Diving C2
4 Blue Immersion B4
Crystal Dive ....(see 15)
5 Flying Trapeze Adventures C3
6 Goodtime Adventures B4
7 Monsoon Gym & Fight Club C5
8 Scuba Junction B3
9 Shambhala C2
The Gallery Spa ....(see 43)

Sleeping
10 Ananda Villa B6
11 Ban's Diving Resort C4
12 Big Blue Resort C2
13 Blue Wind B2
14 Captain Nemo Guesthouse B6
15 Crystal Dive Resort B6
16 Ko Tao Cabana B1
17 Ko Tao Central Hostel B6
18 Nadapa Resort B7
19 Palm Leaf Resort B1
20 Place D1
21 Regal Resort B6
22 Sairee Cottage C3
23 Seashell Resort C3
24 Sensi Paradise Resort A7
25 Spicytao Backpackers D2

Eating
26 995 Roasted Duck C2
27 Bang Burgers C3
28 Barracuda Restaurant & Bar C3
29 Café Corner C2
30 Café del Sol B6
31 Cappuccino B6
32 Chopper's Bar & Grill C2
33 Dolce Vita B6
34 Farango's C2
35 Greasy Spoon B7
36 Los Pollos Hermanos C2
37 Oishi Kaiso C2
38 Pranee's Kitchen B6
39 Safety Stop Pub B6
40 Simple Life C2
41 Su Chili C2
42 Taste of Home D2
43 The Gallery C2
44 This is a Book Cafe B6
45 Whitening A7
46 Zest Coffee Lounge B7

Drinking & Nightlife
47 Diza C2
48 Fizz C3
49 Lotus Bar C3

Entertainment
50 Queen's Cabaret C3

Transport
51 Lederhosenbikes B7

Captain Nemo Guesthouse GUESTHOUSE $$
(Map p562; www.captainnemo-kohtao.com; d 1000-3000B;) With only five rooms, this popular, small choice a short walk from the pier is nearly always full, so book upfront. The owners are responsive, friendly and helpful and everything is kept clean.

Regal Resort RESORT $$
(Map p562; 077 456007; www.kohtaoregal.com; r 2000-4500B;) Just north of the pier, this resort gives you all the commotion along with your pretty stretch of white sand – the main pool (of three) is filled with divers most of the day. Rooms are large and some have beautiful sea views but things tend to break down. Decent value for the price though.

Nadapa Resort RESORT $$
(Map p562; 077 456495; www.nadaparesort.com; tw & d 1500B;) It's not really a resort and not the choice if what you want is a pool and a beach front, but reliable Nadapa is bright, clean and comfortable, with colour-coded rooms in a block with balcony and bungalows. Away from, but not far from, the action and close to the pier.

Charm Churee Villa RESORT $$$
(Map p556; 077 456393; www.charmchureevilla.com; bungalows 3600-39,100B;) Tucked under sky-scraping palms on a 48-hectare jungle plot away from the bustle of the pier, the luxuriant villas of Charm Churee are dedicated to the flamboyant spoils of the Far East. Staircases, chiselled into the rock face, dribble down a palmed slope revealing teak huts strewn across smoky boulders. The villas' unobstructed views of the swishing waters are beguiling.

Sensi Paradise Resort RESORT $$$
(Map p562; 077 456244; www.sensiparadise.com; bungalows 2100-7000B;) 'Natural chic' on the prettiest stretch of Mae Hat proper, right up against some boulder outcrops. You won't escape the noise of the pier, however. Rooms on the hillside are worn and not worth the price while newer models closer to the beach are quite lovely. Friendly

caretakers and several airy teak *săh·lah* add an extra element of charm.

Chalok Ban Kao

Ao Chalok Ban Ko, about 1.7km south of Mae Hat by road, has one of the largest concentrations of accommodation on Ko Tao. This is a slim stretch of sand in a scenic half-circle bay framed by boulders at either end. The milky blue water here is quite shallow and at low tide a sandbar is exposed that's fun to wade out to for prime sunbathing. This is the quietest of the main beaches but there's still a good selection of restaurants, diving and a more mellow but fun nightlife scene.

Tropicana GUESTHOUSE **$**
(Map p556; ☎077 456167; www.koh-tao-tropicana-resort.com; r 450-2500B) This friendly place has 56 basic, low-rise units peppered across a sandy, shady garden campus with fleeting glimpses of the ocean between fanned fronds and spiky palms.

JP Resort GUESTHOUSE **$**
(Map p556; ☎077 456099; r from 700-1300B; ❄@📶) A colourful but rather old menagerie of motel-style rooms stacked on a small scrap of jungle across the street from the sea.

★**View Point Resort** RESORT **$$**
(Map p556; ☎077 456444; www.kohtaoviewpoint.com; bungalows 2500-14,000B; ❄📶🏊) Lush grounds of ferns and palms meander across a boulder-studded hillside offering stunning views over the sea and the bay. All options, from the exquisite private suites that feel like Tarzan and Jane's love nest gone luxury to the huge, view-filled bungalows, use boulders, wood and concrete to create comfortable, naturalistic abodes. It's under new management and fantastic value.

Freedom Beach BUNGALOW **$$**
(Map p556; ☎077 456596; www.freedombeachresort.info; bungalows 700-3500B; ❄📶) On its own secluded beach shaded by tall bushes and connected to Ao Chalok Ban Kao by a boardwalk, Freedom feels like a classic backpacker haunt. Steep paths link the seaside bar to the accommodation (from wooden shacks to sturdier huts with air-con) that runs from the beach to high on the cliff. Reception is next door at Taahtoh Resort.

New Heaven Resort BUNGALOW **$$**
(☎077 456422; www.newheavenkohtao.com; r & bungalows 700-3800B; ❄📶) Just beyond the clutter of Chalok Ban Kao, New Heaven delivers colourful huts perched on a hill over impossibly clear waters. A steep path of chiselled stone tumbles down the shrubby rock face revealing views ripped straight from the pages of *National Geographic*.

Buddha View Dive Resort BUNGALOW **$$**
(Map p556; ☎077 456074; www.buddhaview-diving.com; r 800-1300B; ❄@📶🏊) Like other large diving operations on the island, Buddha View offers its divers discounted on-site digs in a super-social atmosphere. Wi-fi costs 100B.

Ko Tao Resort RESORT **$$$**
(Map p556; ☎077 456133; www.kotaoresort.com; r & bungalows 1900-6500B; ❄@📶🏊) Rooms at this resort are split between 'pool side' and 'paradise zone' – all are well stocked, water sports equipment is on offer, and there are several bars primed to serve an assortment of fruity cocktails.

Chintakiri Resort RESORT **$$$**
(Map p556; ☎077 456133; www.chintakiri.com; r & bungalows 3200-6200B; ❄@📶🏊) Perched high over the gulf waters overlooking Chalok Ban Kao, Chintakiri is one of Ko Tao's more luxurious properties, helping the island furtively creep upmarket. Rooms are spread around the inland jungle, and sport crisp white walls with lacquered finishing.

Hin Wong

A sandy beach has been swapped out for a boulder-strewn coast on the serene east side of the island, but the water is crystal clear. The road to Hin Wong is paved in parts, but sudden sand pits and steep hills can toss you off your motorbike. A taxi to Sairee Beach will cost you around 200B.

Hin Wong Bungalows BUNGALOW **$**
(Map p556; ☎077 456006; Hin Wong; bungalows 500-700B; 📶) Above boulders strewn to the sea, these 11 pleasant corrugated roof huts are scattered across a lot of untamed tropical terrain – it all feels a bit like *Gilligan's Island*. A rickety dock, jutting out just beyond the breezy restaurant, is the perfect place to dangle your legs and watch schools of black sardines slide through the cerulean water.

View Rock BUNGALOW **$**
(Map p556; ☎077 456549, 077 456548; viewrock@hotmail.com; Hin Wong; bungalows 500-2000B; ❄📶) When coming down the dirt road into Hin Wong, follow the signs as they lead you north of Hin Wong Bungalows. View Rock is

precisely that: views and rocks; the hodgepodge of wooden huts, which resembles a secluded fishing village, is built into the steep crags, offering stunning views of the bay.

Ao Tanot (Tanote Bay)

Boulder-strewn Ao Tanot is more populated than some of the other eastern coves, but it's still rather quiet and picturesque. Note that the road is paved quite a fair bit, but then dissolves into a deeply pitted dirt track, so go slow. Discounted taxis (around 100B) bounce back and forth between Tanote Bay and Mae Hat; ask at your resort for a timetable.

Poseidon BUNGALOW $
(Map p556; ☎077 456735; poseidonkohtao@hotmail.com; Ao Tanot; bungalows 800-1500B; wi-fi) Poseidon keeps the tradition of the budget bamboo bungalow alive with 150 or so basic-but-sleepable fan huts scattered near the sand. Wi-fi in restaurant.

Family Tanote BUNGALOW $$
(Map p556; ☎077 456757; Ao Tanot; bungalows 800-3500B; air-con, internet, wi-fi) This family-run scatter of hillside bungalows is a good choice for solitude seekers. Strap on a snorkel mask and swim around with the fish at your doorstep, or climb up to the restaurant for a tasty meal and beautiful views of the bay.

Ao Leuk & Ao Thian Ok

Jamahkiri Resort & Spa RESORT $$$
(Map p556; ☎077 456400; www.jamahkiri.com; bungalows incl breakfast 8400-30,000B; air-con, internet, wi-fi, pool) Wooden masks and stone fertility goddesses abound amid mosaics and multi-armed statues at this whitewashed estate. Hoots from monkeys confirm the jungle theme, as do the thatched roofs and tiki-torched soirees. There are lots of steps, but views are gorgeous, the spa is top-of-the-range and the dive centre is excellent.

Ko Nang Yuan

Photogenic Ko Nang Yuan, just off the northwest coast of Ko Tao, is easily accessible by the Lomprayah catamaran, and by water taxis that depart from Mae Hat and Sairee (100B each way). There's a 100B tax for all visitors to the island.

Ko Nangyuan Dive Resort BUNGALOW $$$
(Map p556; ☎077 456088; www.nangyuan.com; bungalows incl breakfast 1500-14,000B; air-con, wi-fi) The rugged collection of wood and aluminium bungalows winds its way across three coolie-hat-like conical islands connected by an idyllic beige sandbar. Yes, this is a private island paradise but note it gets busy with day trippers. Prices include round-trip to Ko Tao.

Eating

With super-sized Ko Samui lurking on the horizon, it's hard to believe that quaint little Ko Tao holds its own in the gastronomy category. Most resorts and dive operators offer on-site dining, and stand-alone establishments are multiplying at in Sairee Beach and Mae Hat. The diverse population of divers has spawned a broad range of international cuisine dining options, including Mexican, French, Italian, Indian and Japanese. On our quest to find the tastiest Thai fare on the island, we discovered, not surprisingly, that our favourite local meals were being dished out at small, unnamed roadside restaurants.

Sairee Beach

★ **995 Roasted Duck** CHINESE $
(Map p562; mains from 70B; ⏰9am-9pm) You may have to queue a while to get a seat at this shack and wonder what all the fuss is about. The fuss is excellent roast duck, from 70B for a steaming bowl of roasted waterfowl with noodles to 700B for a whole bird.

Bang Burgers BURGERS $
(Map p562; mains from 100B; ⏰10am-10pm) You may have to dig your heels in and wait in line at this terrific burger bar that does a roaring trade in Sairee. There's around a half dozen burgers on the menu, including a vegie choice for meat-free diners.

Su Chili THAI $
(Map p562; dishes 85-225B; ⏰10am-10.30pm) Inviting and bustling, Su Chili serves fresh and tasty Thai dishes, with friendly staff always asking how spicy you want your food. Try the delicious northern Thai specialities or Penang curries. There's a smattering of Western comfort food for homesick diners.

Oishi Kaiso JAPANESE $
(Map p562; mains from 90B; ⏰11.30am-10.30pm) This neat *gyoza* (dumpling) sized establishment is often full, doing a brisk trade in *nigiri*, *sashimi* and *maki*. A couple of Thai dishes are thrown in for good measure, but you can find them elsewhere. The *gyoza* are very tempting indeed.

Los Pollos Hermanos BARBECUE $
(Map p562; www.lospolloshermanos-kohtao.com; mains from 140B; ⏲8am-midnight) No, there's no Nandos on Ko Tao. But there's *Los Pollos Hermanos*, which does a mighty fine job of grilling up peri-peri chicken with sauces arriving in three different grades of spiciness. We hope they lose the wooden plates though. It's tucked away along an alley off the main drag.

Simple Life INTERNATIONAL $
(Map p562; mains from 80B; ⏲7.30am-10.30pm) The menu is kind of average but excellent deals are noteworthy here: the all-you-can-eat pizza buffet (199B) brings in crowds four nights a week (Sunday, Monday, Wednesday and Friday) and the all-you-can-eat breakfasts (170B) and free-flow coffees do a roaring trade each morning.

★**Barracuda Restaurant & Bar** ASIAN FUSION $$
(Map p562; ☎080 146 3267; mains 240-590B; ⏲6-10.30pm) Chef Ed Jones caters for the Thai princess when she's in town but you can sample his exquisite cuisine for mere pennies in comparison to her budget. Locally sourced ingredients are sourced for creative, fresh, fusion masterpieces. Try the seafood platter, sesame-seared tuna fillet or braised lamb shank – then wash it down with a lemon grass, ginger mojito.

There's another branch a five-minute walk away.

The Gallery THAI $$
(Map p562; ☎077 45654/; www.thegallerykohtao.com; mains 120-420B; ⏲noon-10pm) One of the most pleasant settings in town, next to owner Chris Clark's gallery of beautiful island photography, the food here is equally special. The signature dish is *mok maprao* (chicken, shrimp and fish curry served in a young coconut) but the white snapper fillet in creamy red curry sauce is also excellent.

Taste of Home INTERNATIONAL $$
(Map p562; mains 120-250B; ⏲11am-1pm & 6-11pm; 📶) German-run and serving a bit of everything (Swedish meatballs, Turkish kofta, Hungarian goulash and Wiener schnitzel to name a few), but everything is delicious and prepared with heart. It's a small, simple setting popular with expats.

Chopper's Bar & Grill INTERNATIONAL $$
(Map p562; www.choppers-kohtao.com; mains 160-300B; ⏲9am-midnight) Frequently rammed and a fixture on the Ko Tao pub crawl, Chopper's is a riotously popular two-storey hangout with live music, sports on the TVs, billiards, a cinema room and decent pub grub. Happy hour is 5pm to 8pm.

Café Corner CAFE $$
(Map p562; snacks & mains 30-180B; ⏲breakfast & lunch) Prime real estate, mod furnishings and tasty iced coffees have made Café Corner a Sairee staple over the last few years. Swing by at 5pm to stock up for tomorrow morning's breakfast; the scrumptious baked breads are buy-one-get-one-free before being tossed at sunset.

Farango's PIZZA $$
(Map p562; dishes 80-230B; ⏲lunch & dinner) Things are cookin' at his busy pizzeria doing a fine trade in Sairee Village with decent pizzas and other signature Italian fare. Payment is cash only.

Mae Hat

Zest Coffee Lounge CAFE $
(Map p562; dishes 70-200B; ⏲6am-6pm; 📶) All brick and wood with a scuffed red floor, Zest pulls out the stops to brew up some excellent coffee. Eggs Benedict gets the morning off on the right foot, while idlers and snackers can nibble on ciabatta sandwiches or sticky confections while nursing their creamy caffe latte. There's a second branch in Sairee, although we prefer this location.

Cappuccino CAFE $
(Map p562; Mae Hat; dishes from 30B; ⏲7am-6pm) With marble table tops, wall mirrors and good grooves, Cappuccino's decor falls somewhere between the New York deli on *Seinfeld* and a French brasserie – it's a great place to grab a coffee and croissant.

Safety Stop Pub INTERNATIONAL $
(Map p562; mains 60-250B; ⏲7am-11pm; 📶) A haven for homesick Brits, this pier-side restaurant and bar feels like a tropical beer garden. Stop by on Sundays to stuff your face with an endless supply of barbecued goodness; and the Thai dishes also aren't half bad.

Pranee's Kitchen THAI $
(Map p562; dishes 50-150B; ⏲7am-10pm; 📶) An old Mae Hat fave, Pranee's serves scrumptious curries and other Thai treats in an open-air pavilion sprinkled with lounging pillows, wooden tables and TVs. English-language movies are shown nightly at 6pm.

Greasy Spoon BREAKFAST $

(Map p562; English breakfast 140B; ⌚6.30am-3pm; 📶) Although completely devoid of character, Greasy Spoon stays true to its name by offering a variety of heart-clogging breakfast treats: black pudding, eggs, sausage, hash browns, chips (and vegie options) that'll bring a tear to any Brit's eye.

★Whitening INTERNATIONAL $$

(Map p562; dishes 150-400B; ⌚1pm-1am; 📶) This starched, white, beachy spot falls somewhere between being a restaurant and a chic seaside bar – foodies will appreciate the tasty twists on indigenous and international dishes. Dine amid dangling white Christmas lights while keeping your bare feet tucked into the sand. And the best part? It's comparatively easy on the wallet.

Café del Sol INTERNATIONAL $$

(Map p562; mains from 100B; ⌚8am-10.30pm; 📶) This corner cafe steps away from the pier is an excellent choice to down a French (120B), Full English (190B) or Divers (140B) breakfast and watch the morning Ko Tao world go by. Lunch and dinner dishes range from hearty pepper hamburgers to homemade pasta, though prices tend to be quite inflated.

This is a Book Cafe CAFE $$

(Map p562; ⌚7am-9pm; 📶) With lovely white walls, books on shelves, a small scattering of trendy furniture (and a dissonant 1970s fat-screen TV in the corner) and floral sofa, this charming and very quiet choice is perfect for a coffee, ice cream, baked goodies and doses of tranquillity.

Dolce Vita ITALIAN $$

(Map p562; pizzas 170-270B; ⌚noon-10pm) For the best Italian on Ko Tao, come and taste Dolce Vita's homemade pastas and fine pizzas.

Chalok Ban Kao

I ♥ Salad CAFE $$

(Map p556; mains from 120B; ⌚8am-9pm; 📶) This rustic choice offers a healthy array of salads using fresh ingredients, with a good supply of vegetarian and vegan dishes and sticky desserts to follow. There are also real fruit juices and healthy egg white–only breakfasts.

Viewpoint Restaurant INTERNATIONAL $$$

(Map p556; ☎077 456444; 250-1100B; ⌚7.30am-10pm) On a deck overlooking Ao Chalok Ban Kao, this is one of the most romantic settings on the island. The food is also the most upscale and holds its own against Samui's best – try the braised pork belly or the whole tuna from the oven. Apart from the Australian beef dishes, prices are reasonable.

Long Pae STEAK $$$

(Map p556; mains from 160B; ⌚10am-midnight) Ensconced off the radar from most of the island's tourist traffic, 'Uncle Pae' sits on a terrace in hilly jungle with distant views of the sea down below. The speciality here is steak, which goes well with a generous smattering of pan-Asian appetisers. If the weather's clear, try to tic in sunset, but if the winds blow, hold on to your napkins.

Drinking & Nightlife

After diving, Ko Tao's favourite pastime is drinking, and there's no shortage of places to get tanked. In fact, the island's three biggest dive centres each have bars – **Fishbowl Beach Bar**, **Crystal Bar** and **Buddha On The Beach** in Chalok Bak Kao – that attract swarms of travellers and expats alike. It's well worth stopping by even if you aren't a diver.

Flyers detailing upcoming parties are posted on various trees and walls along the island's west coast (check the two 7-Elevens in Sairee). Also keep an eye out for posters touting 'jungle parties' held on nondescript patches of scrubby jungle in the centre of the island. There's also a **Koh Tao Pub Crawl** (www.kohtaopubcrawl.com) that starts at Chopper's Bar & Grill (p566) on Hat Sairee every Monday, Wednesday and Friday at 6pm before departing at 7.30pm to four other watering holes, taking in cabaret, live music and fire shows. The 400B cover includes a bucket, two shots and a T-shirt, so it's not a bad deal. If you go again, it's 300B and then 200B.

Several places, such as Chopper's and Safety Stop Pub (p566), double as great hangout joints for a well-deserved post-dive beer.

Just remember: don't drink and dive.

Clumped at the southern end of Sairee Beach, **AC Party Pub**, **In Touch** and **Maya Bar** take turns reeling in the partiers throughout the week.

★Earth House BEER GARDEN

(Map p556; www.theearthhousekohtao.com; ⌚noon-midnight Mon-Sat) Run by Kelly from Worcester, this relaxing, secluded and rustic spot serves up a global selection of 40 beers, craft labels and ciders in a dreamy garden setting. With its own relaxing treehouse, there's also a restaurant for bites (9am to noon and 1pm to 6pm Monday to Saturday) and bungalows for going prone if you overdo it on the Green Goblin (cider).

Earth House is on the road to Ao Tanot, just before the turn-off for Ao Leuk.

★Fizz BAR

(Map p562; Sairee Beach) Sink into a bean bag, order up a designer cocktail and let the hypnotic surf roll in amid a symphony of ambient sounds. Fantastic.

Castle CLUB

(Map p556; www.thecastlekohtao.com; Mae Hat) Located along the main road between Mae Hat and Chalok Ban Kao, the three-floor Castle is the top hip-hop, garage, electro and funk party venue on the island, luring an array of local and international DJs to its triad of parties each month.

Lotus Bar BAR

(Map p562; Sairee Beach) Lotus is the de facto late-night hang-out spot along the northern end of Sairee. Muscular fire twirlers toss around flaming batons, and the drinks are so large there should be a lifeguard on duty.

Diza BAR

(Map p562; Sairee Beach) Diza is a packed hang-out at the crossroads of Sairee Village, flogging cheap beer and drowning and cranking the volume up as loud as it can go.

Natural High Cafe CAFE

(Map p556; ⏲10.30am-midnight) With a fine elevated open-air terrace and ranging views in all directions over the profuse island greenery, hammocks for lying around in, ambient chill-out sounds and coffee served up in enamel cups, this cafe is ideal for zoning out, but there's pool for fidgets. It's on a hill on the road to Hat Sai Daeng; look out or the signs.

☆ Entertainment

Queen's Cabaret CABARET

ap p562; ⏲10.15pm nightly) Every night different at this intimate bar where acts ge from your standard sparkling Abba leg kicks extravaganza to steamy top-croons. If you're male, note you may get ged' into the performance if you're sit- near the front. The show is free but it's ted that you will purchase a (pricey) – which is totally worth it.

rt Moovment LIVE MUSIC

m-late) A place for art, music, social- drinking and, most importantly, the Sunday Art Jam when the island's talented musicians perform and the vibe is like a big, fun (free!) party at someone's house (in fact the venue is part of owner's Denny and Lisa's house). The first chords are strummed at 7.30pm, but come by any time.

Shopping

Although most items are cheap when compared to prices back home, diving equipment is a big exception to the rule. On Ko Tao you'll be paying Western prices plus shipping plus commission on each item (even with 'discounts') so it's better to do your scuba shopping at home or on your computer. The main 7-Eleven at the intersection in Sairee Village is often rammed with punters waiting in line, especially at night; if you're after beer, soft drinks or anything else you might find at a smaller, local shop, it's quicker to hunt around. There are a few family-run shops up the road past the Gallery, for example. Ubiquitous pharmacists charge very high prices for imported sunscreen, shampoos, mosquito repellent and other items; check in smaller shops and branches of 7-Eleven to see if you can find better-priced equivalents.

Hammock Cafe Plaeyuan HOMEWARES

(Map p556; ⏲9am-6pm) This small cafe on the road to Chalok Ban Kao doubles as a hammock shop, selling a fantastic selection of vivid and brightly coloured Mlabri hand-woven hammocks, some with up to 3km worth of fabric. Prices start at around 1700B for a sitting hammock, and up to 5000B for the most elaborate.

Information

The ubiquitous *Koh Tao Info* booklet lists loads of businesses on the island and goes into some detail about the island's history, culture and social issues.

DANGERS & ANNOYANCES

There's nothing more annoying than enrolling in a diving course with your friends and then having to drop out because you scraped your knee in a motorcycle accident. The roads on Ko Tao are slowly being paved but some remain dangerous. While hiring a scooter is extremely convenient, this is not the place to learn how to drive. The island is rife with abrupt hills and sudden sand pits along gravel trails; if driving a scooter, stick to good roads and if you are unsure, turn back. Even if you escape unscathed, scamming bike shops may claim that you damaged your rental and will try to extort some serious cash from you (ensure you check the bike carefully prior to hire and identify scratches and dents).

Also be aware that mosquito-borne dengue fever is a real and serious threat. The virus can spread quickly due to tightly packed tourist areas and the small size of the island.

EMERGENCY

Police Station (Map p562; ☎ 077 456631) Between Mae Hat and Sairee Beach along the rutted portion of the beachside road.

INTERNET ACCESS

Wi-fi is widely available at resorts, bars and restaurants.

MEDICAL SERVICES

All divers are required to sign a medical waiver before exploring the sea. If you have any medical condition that might hinder your ability to dive (including mild asthma), you will be asked to get medical clearance from a doctor on Ko Tao. If you're unsure about whether or not you are fit to dive, consider seeing a doctor before your trip as there are no official hospitals on the island, and the number of qualified medical professionals is limited. Also, make sure your traveller's insurance covers scuba diving. On-island medical 'consultations' (and we use that term very lightly) cost 300B. There are several walk-in clinics and mini hospitals scattered around Mae Hat and Sairee, but all serious medical needs should be dealt with on Ko Samui. If you are diving, ask your outfitter to point you in the proper direction of medical advice. The nearest hyperbaric chamber is on Big Buddha Beach (Hat Bang Rak) on Ko Samui; in emergencies, a speedboat makes the journey.

MONEY

There are 24-hour ATMs at the island's 7-Elevens. There's also a cluster of ATMs orbiting the ferry docks at Mae Hat. There is a money exchange window at Mae Hat's pier and a second location near Chopper's in Sairee Beach. There are several banks near the post office in Mae Hat, at the far end of town along the island's main inland road. They are usually open 9am to 4pm on weekdays. Almost all dive schools accept credit cards, however there is usually a 3% or 4% handling fee.

POST

Post Office (Map p562; ☎ 077 456170; ⏰ 9am-5pm Mon-Fri, 9am-noon Sat) A 10- to 15-minute walk from the pier; at the corner of Ko Tao's main inner-island road and Mae Hat's 'down road'.

TOURIST INFORMATION

There's no government-run TAT office on Ko Tao. Transportation and accommodation bookings can be made at most dive shops or at any of the numerous travel agencies, all of which take a small commission on services rendered.

WEBSITES

www.kohtaocompleteguide.com Handy website and an excellent quarterly free hard copy guide in book form.

www.kohtaoonline.com An online version of the *Koh Tao Info* booklet.

ℹ Getting There & Away

As always, costs and departure times are subject to change. Rough waves are known to cancel ferries between the months of October and December. When the waters are choppy we recommend taking the Seatran rather than the Lomprayah catamaran if you are prone to seasickness. The catamarans ride the swell, whereas the Seatran cuts through the currents as it crosses the sea. Note that we highly advise purchasing your boat tickets *several* days in advance if you are accessing Ko Tao from Ko Pha-Ngan after the Full Moon Party.

AIR

Nok Air (www.nokair.com) jets passengers from Bangkok's Don Mueang airport to Chumphon once or twice daily in each direction while **Happy Air** (www.happyair.co.th) has several flights per day from Bangkok's Suvarnabhumi International Airport and a flight five days a week to Ranong. Flights to/from Bangkok are usually around 3300B. Upon arriving in Chumphon, travellers can make a seamless transfer to the catamaran service bound for Ko Tao.

BOAT

To Ko Pha-Ngan

The Lomprayah catamaran offers a thrice-daily service (500B to 600B), leaving Ko Tao at 6am, 9.30am and 3pm and arriving on Ko Pha-Ngan around 7am, 10.30am and 4pm. The Seatran Discovery Ferry (430B) offers a similar service, but its earliest boat departs at 6.30am. The Songserm express boat (350B) departs daily at 9.30am and arrives on Ko Pha-Ngan at 11.30am. Hotel pick-ups are included in the price.

To Ko Samui

The **Lomprayah** catamaran offers a twice-daily service (600B), leaving Ko Tao at 9.30am and 3pm and arriving at Mae Nam on Ko Samui via Ko Pha-Ngan, around 11.20am and 4.40pm. An earlier boat at 6am goes to Na Thon on Ko Samui, arriving at 7.45am. The **Seatran Discovery Ferry** (600B) offers a similar service, with departures at 6.30am, 9am and 3pm. The **Songserm** express boat (450B) departs daily at 9.30am and arrives on Samui (again via Ko Pha-Ngan) at 1.15pm. Hotel pick-ups are included in the price.

To Surat Thani & the Andaman Coast

The easiest option is to stop over on either Ko Pha-Ngan or Ko Samui to shorten the trip and lessen the number of connections. Otherwise, a combination bus–boat ticket from travel agents around the island shouldn't cost more than going it alone. But if you don't feel like being herded like a sheep onto a tourist bus, there are two routes you can take. The first, and more common, approach is to board a Surat-bound boat (you may have to transfer boats on Ko Pha-Ngan or Ko Samui), then transfer to a bus upon arrival.

The second option is to take a ferry to Chumphon on the mainland and then switch to a bus or train bound for the provinces further south.

BUS

Bus-boat package tickets to/from Bangkok are available from travel agencies all over Bangkok and the south; tickets cost around 1000B and the whole voyage takes around 12 hours. Buses switch to boats in Chumphon, and Bangkok-bound passengers can choose to disembark in Hua Hin (for the same price as the Ko Tao–Bangkok ticket).

TRAIN

Travellers can plan their own journey by taking a boat to Chumphon, then making their way to Chumphon's town centre to catch a train up to Bangkok (or any town along the upper southern gulf); likewise in the opposite direction. A 2nd-class ticket to Bangkok will cost around 300B and the trip takes around 8½ hours.

From Ko Tao, the high-speed Lomprayah catamaran departs for Chumphon at 10.15am and 2.45pm (600B, 1½ hours), and a Songserm express boat makes the same journey at 2.30pm (500B), arriving at 5pm. There may be fewer departures if the swells are high.

Getting Around

MOTORCYCLE

Renting a motorcycle is a dangerous endeavour if you're not sticking to the main, well-paved roads. Daily rental rates begin at 150B for a scooter. Larger bikes start at 350B. Discounts are available for weekly and monthly rentals. Try **Lederhosenbikes** (Map p562; ☎0817 528994; www.kohtaomotorbikes.com; Mae Hat; ⏲8.30am-6pm Mon-Sat). Reconsider renting all-terrrain-vehicles (ATVs) or jet skis – accidents are not uncommon.

SŎRNG·TĂA·OU

In Mae Hat *sŏrng·tăa·ou*, pick-up trucks and motorbikes crowd around the pier as passengers alight. If you're a solo traveller, you will pay 200B to get to Sairee Beach or Chalok Ban Kao. Groups of two or more will pay 100B each. Rides from Sairee to Chalok Ban Kao cost 150B per person, or 300B for solo tourists. These prices are rarely negotiable, and passengers will be expected to wait until their taxi is full unless they want to pay an additional 200B to 300B. Prices double for trips to the east coast, and drivers will raise the prices when rain makes the roads harder to negotiate. If you know where you intend to stay, we highly recommend calling ahead to arrange a pick-up. Many dive schools offer free pick-ups and transfers as well.

WATER TAXI

Boat taxis depart from Mae Hat, Chalok Ban Kao and the northern part of Sairee Beach (near Vibe Bar). Boat rides to Ko Nang Yuan will set you back at least 100B. Long-tail boats can be chartered for around 1500B per day, depending on the number of passengers carried.

Ang Thong Marine National Park

อุทยานแห่งชาติหมู่เกาะอ่างทอง

The 40-some jagged jungle islands of Ang Thong Marine National Park stretch across the cerulean sea like a shattered emerald necklace – each piece a virgin realm featuring sheer limestone cliffs, hidden lagoons and perfect peach-coloured sands. These dream-inducing islets inspired Alex Garland's cult classic novel, *The Beach*.

February, March and April are the best months to visit this ethereal preserve of greens and blues; crashing monsoon waves mean that the park is almost always closed during November and December.

Sights

Every tour stops at the park's head office on **Ko Wua Talap**, the largest island in the archipelago.

The naturally occurring stone arches on **Ko Samsao** and **Ko Tai Plao** are visible during seasonal tides and weather conditions. Because the sea is quite shallow around the island chain, reaching a maximum depth of 10m, extensive coral reefs have not developed, except in a few protected pockets on the southwest and northeast sides. There's a shallow coral reef near Ko Tai Plao and Ko Samsao that has decent but not excellent snorkelling. There are also several novice dives for exploring shallow caves and colourful coral gardens and spotting banded sea snakes and turtles. Soft powder beaches line **Ko Tai Plao**, **Ko Wuakantang** and **Ko Hintap**.

Viewpoint VIEWPOINT

The island's viewpoint might just be the most stunning vista in all of Thailand. From the top, visitors will have sweeping views of the jagged islands nearby as they burst through the placid turquoise water in easily anthropomorphised formations. The trek to the lookout is an arduous 450m trail that takes roughly an hour to complete. Hikers should wear sturdy shoes and walk slowly on the sharp outcrops of limestone. A second trail leads to **Tham Bua Bok**, a cavern with lotus-shaped stalagmites and stalactites.

Emerald Sea LAKE

The Emerald Sea (also called the Inner Sea) on **Ko Mae Ko** is a popular destination. This large lake in the middle of the island spans an impressive 250m by 350m and has an ethereal minty tint. You can look but you can't touch; the lagoon is strictly off limits to the unclean human body. A dramatic **viewpoint** can be found at the top of a series of staircases nearby.

Tours

The best way to experience Ang Thong is by taking one of the many guided tours departing Ko Samui and Ko Pha-Ngan. The tours usually include lunch, snorkelling equipment, hotel transfers and (with fingers crossed) a knowledgeable guide. If you're staying in luxury accommodation, there's a good chance that your resort has a private boat for providing group tours. Some midrange and budget places also have their own boats, and if not, they can easily set you up with a general tour operator. Dive centres on Ko Samui and Ko Pha-Ngan offer **scuba trips** to the park, although Ang Thong doesn't offer the world-class diving that can be found around Ko Tao and Ko Pha-Ngan.

Tour companies tend to come and go like the wind. Ask at your accommodation for a list of current operators.

Sleeping

Ang Thong does not have any resorts; however, on Ko Wua Talap the national park has set up five bungalows, each housing between two and eight guests. Campers are also allowed to pitch a tent in certain designated zones. Online bookings are possible, although customers must forward a bank deposit within two days of making the reservation. For advance reservations contact the **National Parks Services** (☎077 286025; www.dnp.go.th; bungalows 500-1400B).

Getting There & Around

The best way to reach the park is to take a private day tour from Ko Samui or Ko Pha-Ngan (28km and 32km away, respectively). The islands sit between Samui and the main pier at Don Sak; however, there are no ferries that stop off along the way.

The park officially has an admission fee (adult/child 400/200B), although it should be included in the price of every tour (ask your operator if you are unsure). Private boat charters are also another possibility, although high petrol prices will make the trip quite expensive.

SURAT THANI PROVINCE

Surat Thani อำเภอเมืองสุราษฎร์ธานี

POP 128,990

Known in Thai as 'City of Good People', Surat Thani was once the seat of the ancient Srivijaya empire. Today, this unglamorously typical Thai town is a busy transport hub moving cargo and people around the country. Travellers rarely linger here as they make their way to the popular islands of Ko Samui, Ko Pha-Ngan and Ko Tao, but it's a great stop if you enjoy real Thai working cities, good southern-style street food and nosing around colourful Chinese temples.

Sleeping

Staying in central Surat puts you in a bustling Thai city that can be refreshing, and indeed fascinating, after sojourns in the primped-for-tourists gulf islands. Prices are low and you get a lot for relatively few baht.

For more modern amenities, hop on a *sŏrng·tăa·ou* heading towards the Phang-Nga district. When you climb aboard, tell the driver 'Tesco Lotus', and you'll be taken about 2km to 3km out of town to a large, boxlike shopping centre. A handful of more upscale hotel options orbit the mall.

If you're on a very tight budget, consider zipping straight through town and taking the night ferry to reach your island destination.

My Place @ Surat Hotel HOTEL $

(☎077 272288; 247/5 Th Na Meuang; d 490-590B, f 620B; ❄📶) All smiles and nary a speck of dust at this excellent, central Chinese hotel,

Surat Thani

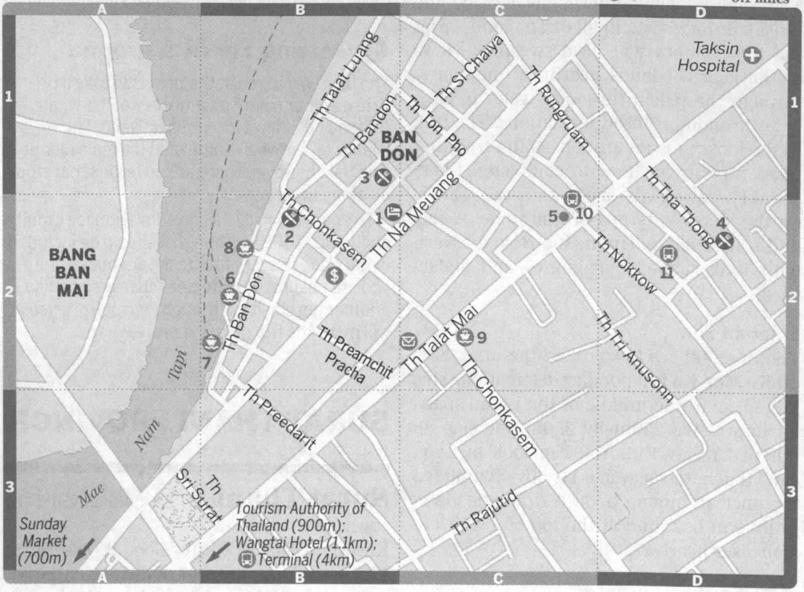

Surat Thani

Sleeping
1 My Place @ Surat Hotel B2

Eating
2 Milano B2
3 Night Market B1
4 Vegetarian Restaurant D2

Information
5 Pranthip Co C2

Transport
6 Ko Tao Night Ferry Pier B2
Lomprayah .... (see 8)
7 Night Boat to Ko Pha-Ngan B2
8 Seatran Discovery B2
9 Seatran Office C2
Songserm .... (see 8)
10 Talat Kaset 1 Bus Terminal C2
11 Talat Kaset 2 Bus Terminal D2

which offers spacious, very clean rooms, colourful throw cushions, modern art on the walls, power showers and value for money. It may be budget, but it will suit almost anyone. Breakfast is served in the cafe next door.

Wangtai Hotel HOTEL **$$**
(☎077 283020; 1 Th Talad Mai; r 790-2000B;) Across the river from the TAT office, the 230-room Wangtai is a smart, marbled choice in the centre of town, offering pleasant and comfortable, if rather generic, rooms with good views of the city.

Eating

Surat Thani is packed with delicious street food for lunch and dinner. Aside from the central night market, stalls near the departure docks open for the daily night boats to the islands, and there's an afternoon **Sunday market** (4-9pm) near the TAT office. During the day, many food stalls near the downtown bus terminal sell *kôw gài òp* (marinated baked chicken on rice).

Night Market MARKET **$**
(Sarn Chao Ma; Th Ton Pho; dishes from 35B; 6-11pm) A fantastic smorgasbord of food including masses of melt-in-your-mouth marinated meats on sticks, fresh fruit juices, noodle dishes and desserts. It's not that big so it's easy to browse the stalls before making a selection.

Milano PIZZA **$**
(Th Bandon; mains from 110B; noon-10pm) This Italian restaurant near the pier bakes up

a tasty selection of pizza, while pasta and a choice of other international dishes and comfort food round out a surprisingly good menu.

Vegetarian Restaurant VEGETARIAN $
(47/7 Th Tha Thong; mains from 30B; ⏲7am-3pm;) This simple but friendly vegie restaurant can serve you a bowl or rice and curried vegies, washed down with an enamelled cup of water for 30B. Look for the yellow banners with the Chinese character 斋 (meaning 'vegetarian').

Information

Th Na Meuang has a bank on virtually every corner in the heart of downtown.

Post Office (☎077 281966, 077 272013; ⏲8.30am-4.30pm Mon-Fri, 9am-noon Sat & Sun) West of Wat Thammabucha.

Taksin Hospital (☎077 273239; Th Talat Mai) The most professional of Surat's three hospitals. Just beyond the Talat Mai Market in the northeast part of downtown.

Tourism Authority of Thailand (TAT; ☎077 288818; 5 Th Talat Mai; ⏲8.30am-4.30pm) This friendly office southwest of town has useful brochures and maps, and staff speak good English.

Getting There & Away

In general, if you are departing Bangkok or Hua Hin for Ko Pha-Ngan or Ko Tao, consider taking the train or a bus–boat package that goes through Chumphon rather than Surat. You'll save time, and the journey will be more comfortable. Travellers heading to/from Ko Samui will most likely pass through town. If you require any travel services, try reliable **Pranthip Co** (Th Talat Mai; ⏲7.30am-5.30pm).

AIR

Although flights from Bangkok to Surat Thani are cheaper than the flights to Samui, it takes quite a bit of time to reach the gulf islands from the airport. Air Asia offers a convenient bus and boat shuttle with its flights that can alleviate some of the stress. There are daily shuttles to Bangkok on **Thai Airways** (☎077 272610; 3/27-28 Th Karunarat), **Air Asia** (www.airasia.com) and **Nok Air** (www.nokair.com).

BOAT

Various ferry companies offer services to the islands. Try **Lomprayah** (☎077 4277 656; www.lomprayah.com), **Seatran Discovery** (☎077 275063; www.seatrandiscovery.com) or **Songserm** (☎077 377704; www.songserm-expressboat.com).

Bus–Boat Combination Tickets

In the high season travellers can usually find bus–boat services to Ko Samui and Ko Pha-Ngan directly from the Phun Phin train station (which is 14km west of Surat). These services don't cost any more than those booked in Surat Thani and can save you some serious waiting time.

There are also several ferry and speedboat operators that connect Surat Thani to Ko Tao, Ko Pha-Ngan and Ko Samui. Most boats – such as the Raja and Seatran services – leave from Don Sak (about one hour from Surat; bus transfers are included in the ferry ticket) although the Songserm leaves from the heart of Surat town. Be warned that the Raja service can be a very frustrating experience, especially for travellers who are tight on time. The boat trip usually takes around 1½ hours to Ko Samui and 2½ hours to Ko Pha-Ngan, although often the captain will cut the engines to half propulsion, which means the journey can take up to five hours.

Night Ferry

From the centre of Surat there are nightly ferries to Ko Tao (600B, eight hours, departs at 11pm), Ko Pha-Ngan (400B, seven hours, departs at 11pm) and Ko Samui (300B, six hours, departs at 11pm). These are cargo ships, not luxury boats, so bring food and water and watch your bags.

BUS & MINIVAN

The most convenient way to travel around the south, frequent buses and minivans depart from two main locations in town known as Talat Kaset 1 and Talat Kaset 2. Talat Kaset 1, on the north side of Th Talat Mai (the city's main drag), offers speedy service to Nakhon (120B, 1½ hours). This is also the location of Pranthip Co, one of the more trustworthy agencies in town. Buses to Phun Phin also leave from Talat Kaset 1.

At Talat Kaset 2, on the south side of Th Talat Mai, you'll find frequent transportation.

The 'new' bus terminal (actually a few years old now, but still referred to as new by the locals) is 7km south of town on the way to Phun Phin. This hub services traffic to and from Bangkok (380B to 800B, 11 to 14 hours).

BUSES & MINIVANS FROM SURAT THANI

DESTINATION	FARE (B)	DURATION (HR)
Bangkok	421-856	10
Hat Yai	160-290	5
Khanom	100	1
Krabi	150	2½
Phuket	250	6
Trang	160	2

TRAIN

When arriving by train you'll actually pull into Phun Phin, a nondescript town 14km west of Surat. From Phun Phin, there are buses to Phuket, Phang-Nga and Krabi – some via Takua Pa, a junction for Khao Sok National Park. Transport from Surat moves with greater frequency, but it's worth checking the schedule in Phun Phin first – you might be lucky and save yourself a slow ride between towns.

If you plan on travelling during the day, go for the express train. Night travellers should opt for the air-con couchettes. Trains passing through Surat stop in Chumphon and Hua Hin on their way up to the capital, and in the other direction you'll call at Trang, Hat Yai and Sungai Kolok before hopping across the border. The train station at Phun Phin has a 24-hour left-luggage room that charges around 20B a day. The advance ticket office is open from 6am to 6pm daily (with a nebulous one-hour lunch break somewhere between 11am and 1.30pm). The trip to Bangkok takes over 8½ hours and costs 297B to 1379B depending on class.

Getting Around

Air-conditioned vans to/from Surat Thani airport cost around 100B per person and they'll drop you off at your hotel.

To travel around town, *sŏrng·tăa·ou* cost 10B to 30B (it's around 30B to reach Tesco Lotus from the city centre).

Fan-cooled Orange buses run from Phun Phin train station to Surat Thani every 10 minutes (15B, 25 minutes). For this ride, taxis charge a cool 200B for a maximum of four people, while share taxis charge 100B per person. Other taxi rates are posted just north of the train station (at the metal pedestrian bridge). If you have to overnight in Phun Phin, the Queen Hotel is very basic and unfriendly, but is cheap and can put a roof over your head for a similar price as a taxi to Surat Thani.

NAKHON SI THAMMARAT PROVINCE

Ao Khanom อ่าวขนอม

Lovely Ao Khanom, halfway between Surat Thani and Nakhon Si Thammarat, quietly sits along the blue gulf waters. Overlooked by tourists who flock to the jungle islands nearby, this pristine region, simply called Khanom, is a worthy choice for those seeking a serene beach setting unmarred by enterprising corporations.

The beach area is actually quite long and is comprised of two beaches: the main, long Hat Nadan and the smaller and more out of the way Hat Nai Plao.

Sights

This area is home to a variety of pristine geological features including **waterfalls** and **caves** but the highlight for many are the pink dolphins.

Caves CAVE

Two beautiful caves are along the main road (Hwy 4014) between Khanom and Don Sak. Khao Wang Thong has a string of lights guiding visitors through the network of caverns and narrow passages. A metal gate covers the entrance; stop at the house at the base of the hill to retrieve the key (and leave a small donation). Turn right off the main highway at Rd 4142 to find Khao Krot, with two large caverns (but bring a torch).

Samet Chun Waterfall WATERFALL

This is the largest waterfall in the area with tepid pools for cooling off, and great views of the coast. To reach the falls, head south from Ban Khanom and turn left at the blue Samet Chun sign. Follow the road for about 2km and, after crossing a small stream, take the next right and hike up into the mountain following the dirt road. After about a 15-minute walk, listen for the waterfall and look for a small trail on the right.

Hin Lat Falls WATERFALL

The scenic Hin Lat Falls is the smallest of the cascades in the area, but also the easiest to reach. There are pools for swimming and several huts providing shade. It's south of Hat Nai Plao.

Dat Fa Mountain MOUNTAIN

For a postcard-worthy vista of the undulating coastline, head to Dat Fa Mountain, about 5km west of the coast along Hwy 4014. The hillside is usually deserted, making it easy to stop along the way to snap photos.

Tours

Pink Dolphin Viewing Tours WILDLIFE WATCHING

(day tours 1700B) The most special feature of Khanom are the pink dolphins – a rare albino breed with a stunning pink hue. They are regularly seen from the old ferry pier and the electric plant pier around dawn and dusk but resorts are now offering full-day tours that include viewing the dolphins by boat and a car tour to the area's caves and waterfalls.

If you just want to see the dolphins you can hire a boat for a few hours (for up to six people) for 1000B. Enquire at your hotel.

Sleeping & Eating

Despite talk of further developing Khanom's beaches into a more laid-back alternative to the nearby islands, it remains a very low-key and quiet retreat. Many of the resorts see very few customers and constant disuse (not regularly flushing the toilets etc) means that some rooms are dank. In general, it's advisable to stay away from the large hotels and stick to beachside bungalow operations. Note that all options are spaced very far apart so unless you have your own wheels don't expect to just show up and wander around looking for a place to stay.

For some cheap eats, head to **Hat Kho Khao** at the end of Rd 4232 where you'll find a steamy jumble of barbecue stands offering some tasty favourites such as *mŏo nám đòk* (spicy pork salad) and *sôm·đam*. On Wednesday and Sunday there are markets further inland near the police station.

Suchada Villa BUNGALOW $
(075 528459; www.suchadavilla.com; Hat Naiplau; bungalows weekday/weekend incl breakfast 800/1000B;) Right off the main road and a five-minute walk to the beach, Suchada offers a cache of brightly coloured, quite cute bungalows. Friendly, English-speaking staff.

Khanom Hill Resort BUNGALOW $$
(075 529403, 081 956 3101; www.khanom.info; Hat Naiplau; bungalows 2900-3900B;) Travellers rave about this lovely spot on a very small hill, that leads to a half-circle of dreamy white beach. Choose from modern, concrete villas with thatched roofs, cheaper models with Thai-style architecture or big family-sized apartments; all are clean and comfy.

Talkoo Beach Resort BUNGALOW $$
(075 528397; yok_hana@yahoo.com; Hat Nadan; bungalows 1000-1500B;) An efficiently run place on Hat Nadan, Talkoo has a range of bungalows in a garden on the beach and cheaper ones across the main road in a more dry, sparse area. All are in good shape, spacious, comfortable and include charming touches like naturalistic bathrooms.

CC Beach Bar & Bungalows BUNGALOW $$
(www.ccbeachbarthai.wordpress.com; bungalows from 1500B;) A social spot that's sprung from a friendly, fun beach bar on a stunning stretch of Hat Nadan. The clean and modern concrete bungalows are priced higher for what you can find elsewhere, with a foreigner-specific, chummy ambience.

Racha Kiri RESORT $$$
(075 300245; www.rachakiri.com; bungalows 3550-7150B;) With spa and pool, Khanom's upscale retreat is a beautiful campus of rambling villas. The big price tag means no crowds, which can be nice, although the resort feels like a white elephant when the property isn't being used as a corporate retreat.

WORTH A TRIP

WÁT SUAN MOKKHAPHALARAM

Wát Suan Mokkhaphalaram (www.suanmokkh-idh.org; Wat Suanmokkh) Surrounded by lush forest, Wat Suan Mokkhaphalaram ('the Garden of Liberation'), charges 2000B for a 10-day program including food, lodging and instruction (although technically the 'teaching' is free). Retreats, run by the International Dharma Hermitage, begin on the first day of every month and registration takes place the afternoon before. Founded by Ajan Buddhadasa Bhikkhu, arguably Thailand's most famous monk, the temple's philosophical teachings are ecumenical in nature, comprising Zen, Taoist and Christian elements, as well as the traditional Theravada schemata.

For details on reaching the temple, located 7km outside of Chaiya, check out the website.

Information

The police station and hospital are just south of Ban Khanom at the junction leading to Hat Kho Khao. There's a 7-Eleven (with an ATM) in the heart of Khanom town.

Getting There & Away

Minivans from both Surat Thani and Nakhon leave every hour on the hour from 5am to 5pm daily and drop passengers off in Khanom town, which is several kilometres from the beach. From Khanom town you can hire motorcycle taxis out to the beaches for about 20B to 80B depending on the distance you're going. If you've booked in advance your hosts may offer to pick you up in Khanom town for free.

A taxi to/from Don Sak pier for the gulf islands is 1000B and a motorcyle taxi is 300B.

Once at your lodging you'll be stranded unless you hire your own transport or take a tour with your hotel.

Nakhon Si Thammarat

อำเภอเมืองนครศรีธรรมราช

POP 120,836

With one of the most significant temples in the kingdom, the historic city of Nakhon Si Thammarat (usually shortened to 'Nakhon') is a natural and rewarding stop between Hat Yai and Surat Thani.

Hundreds of years ago, an overland route between the western port of Trang and the eastern port of Nakhon Si Thammarat functioned as a major trade link between Thailand and the rest of the world. This ancient influx of cosmopolitan conceits is still evident today in the local cuisine, and housed in the city's temples and museums.

Sights

Most of Nakhon's commercial activity (hotels, banks and restaurants) takes place in the northern part of the downtown. South of the clock tower, visitors will find the city's awe-inspiring Wat Mahathat, while tantalising remains of the historic **red brick city walls** can be seen near the park and public square of **Sanam Na Muang** off the long, long main thoroughfare of Th Ratchadamnoen, itself teeming with cheap *sŏrng·tăa·ou* zipping north and south. Sanam Na Muang is a delightful sight in the late afternoon, when locals come out to play football and hacky sack and jog or walk in the cooler air. Note also the gold-coloured statues of the 12 animals of the Thai zodiac atop lampposts along Th Ratchadamnoen, each of which also represents one of the 12 city states that were tributary to the Nakhon Si Thammarat kingdom.

★ Wat Phra Mahathat Woramahawihaan TEMPLE

(Th Si Thamasok; 8.30am-4.30pm) The most important wát in southern Thailand, stunning Wat Phra Mahathat Woramahawihaan (simply known as Mahathat) boasts an imposing 77m white *chedi* (stupa) crowned by a gold spire piercing the sky. According to legend, Queen Hem Chala and Prince Thanakuman brought relics to Nakhon over 1000 years ago, and built a small pagoda to house the precious icons. The temple has since grown into a huge site, and today crowds gather daily to purchase the popular Jatukham amulets.

Within the courtyard beneath the towering *chedi* rise up scores of further grey *chedi*. Don't miss the hall enclosing a splendid stairway and the **museums** featuring antique statues from all eras and corners of Thailand including an 18th-century reclining Buddha. Frequently stuffed with visiting school kids who apply gold leaf to the temple statuary, the wát is a 10B *sŏrng·tăa·ou* ride from the Thai Hotel area.

Shadow Puppet Museum MUSEUM

(Th Si Thamasok Soi 3; 9am-4.30pm) There are two styles of local shadow puppets: *năng đà·lung* and *năng yài*. At just under 1m tall, the former feature movable appendages and parts; the latter are nearly life-sized, and lack moving parts. Both are intricately carved from cow hide. Suchart Subsin's puppet house has a small museum where staff can demonstrate the cutting process and performances for visitors (50B).

Look out for the shadow puppets from the 18th century upstairs and others from the WWII era which were smaller than the traditional size and include a bi-plane.

National Museum MUSEUM

(Th Ratchadamnoen; admission 150B; 9am-4pm Wed-Sun) When the Tampaling (also known as Tambralinga) kingdom traded with merchants from Indian, Arabic, Dvaravati and Champa states, the region around Nakhon became a melting pot of crafts and art. Today, many of these relics are on display in this absorbing national museum.

Sleeping & Eating

Nakhon is a great place to sample cuisine with a distinctive southern twist. In the evening, Muslim food stands sell delicious *kôw mòk gài* (chicken *biryani*), *má·đà·bà* (*murdabag;* Indian pancake stuffed with chicken or vegetables) and roti. A good hunting ground is along Th Neramit, which turns into Th Pak Nakhon – the street bustles with food stalls every night.

Thai Hotel HOTEL $

(075 341509; fax 075 344858; 1375 Th Ratchadamnoen; r with fan 350B, with air-con 430-550B;) The most central sleeping spot in town, and not far from the train station, the

DON'T MISS

KHAO LUANG NATIONAL PARK

Khao Luang National Park (อุทยานแห่งชาติเขาหลวง; ☎075 300494; www.dnp.go.th; adult/child 400/200B) Known for its beautiful mountain and forest walks, cool streams, waterfalls and orchards, Khao Luang National Park surrounds the 1835m peak of Khao Luang. A soaring mountain range covered in virgin forest and a habitat for a plethora of bird species, it's a good spot for any budding ornithologist. There are over 300 species of orchid in the park, some of which are found nowhere else on earth.

It's possible to rent **park bungalows** (per night 600-2000B), sleeping six to 12 people. There's a **restaurant** at park headquarters. **Camping** is permitted along the trail to the summit.

To reach the park, take a *sŏrng·tăa·ou* (around 35B) from Nakhon Si Thammarat to Lan Saka; drivers will usually take you the extra way to park headquarters. The entrance to the park and the offices of the Royal Forest Department are 33km from the centre of Nakhon on Rte 4015, an asphalt road that climbs almost 400m in 2.5km to the office and a further 450m to the car park. Plenty of up-to-date details are available on the park's website.

Thai Hotel is a semi-smart bargain. Walls may be a bit thin and the wi-fi twitchy, but rooms are clean and a good deal for the price. Each room has a TV and the higher floors have good views of the urban bustle, while staff are lovely.

Nakorn Garden Inn HOTEL $
(☎075 323777; 1/4 Th Pak Nakhon; r 445B; ❄📶) There's a lovely forested setting more like a shady jungle than the centre of town, but most of the bare brick rooms are gloomy, although they come with air-con, TV, hot water and fridge. It's a nice rustic change from a cement block, though, and prices are a steal, although staff speak zero English.

Twin Lotus Hotel HOTEL $$
(☎075 33777; www.twinlotushotel.net; 97/8 Th Phattanakan Khukhwang; r 1500-2500B; ❄📶🏊) It's looking a bit tired, but the 401-room Twin Lotus is still the place to go a little more upscale when in Nakhon. This 16-storey behemoth sits 2km southeast of the city centre.

★**Krua Talay** THAI $
(1204/29-30 Th Pak Nakhon; dishes 40-300B; ⏰4-10pm) Opposite the Nakorn Garden Inn, this fantastic restaurant serves awesome seafood dishes. Take a seat in the rear garden area and order up fried prawn cake, crispy cat fish with hot and spicy salad, or stir-fried vegetables in oyster sauce, and make a meal of it. There's no English sign, but look for the red, yellow and blue sign and potted plants outside.

Hao Coffee CAFE $
(☎075 346563; Bovorn Bazaar; dishes 30-60B; ⏰breakfast & lunch) This charming, shuttered and well-staffed cafe is always stuffed with talkative locals and decorated with an eclectic array of collectibles and knick-knacks from pith helmets to rifles and assorted ceramics. It's a great place for a scrambled eggs breakfast, a larger meal or a caffeine fix, either inside or at one of the tables out front.

Rock 99 INTERNATIONAL $
(1180/807 Bovorn Bazaar; mains from 65B; ⏰4pm-midnight) In Bovorn Bazaar, Rock 99 may be rather rough and ready, but has a good enough selection of international fare, from taco salads to pizzas (avoid the Thai fare though) and live music several nights a week. A glass of wine is 70B.

ℹ Information

Several banks and ATMs hug Th Ratchadamnoen in the northern end of downtown. There is an English-language bookstore on the 3rd floor of Robinson Ocean shopping mall.

Most hotels have free maps to give to guests, but not all are that useful.

Police Station (☎1155; Th Ratchadamnoen)

Post Office (Th Ratchadamnoen; ⏰8.30am-4.30pm Mon-Fri, 9am-noon Sat & Sun)

Tourism Authority of Thailand (TAR; ☎075 346515; ⏰8.30am-4.30pm) Housed in a fine 1926-vintage building in the northern end of the Sanam Na Muang (City Park), this office has some useful brochures, but spoken English is limited.

ℹ Getting There & Away

AIR

Several carriers such as Nok Air, Air Asia and Orient Thai Airlines (plus Thai Airways) fly from Bangkok to Nakhon everyday. There are about six daily one-hour flights. One-way fares are around 1500B.

BUS

Ordinary buses to Bangkok leave from the bus terminal (mostly in the afternoon or evening), but a couple of private buses leave from booking offices on Th Jamroenwithi, where you can also buy tickets. The journey takes 12 hours and costs 454B to 1142B depending on the class of bus.

When looking for minivan stops to leave Nakhon, keep an eye out for small desks along the side of the downtown roads (minivans and waiting passengers may or may not be present nearby). It's best to ask around as each destination has a different departure point. Krabi and Don Sak minivans are grouped together – just make sure you don't get on the wrong one. Stops are scattered around Th Jamroenwithi, Th Wakhit and Th Yommarat.

TRAIN

There are two daily train departures to/from Bangkok to Nakhon (133B to 652B; stopping through Hua Hin, Chumphon and Surat Thani along the way). All are 12-hour night trains. These trains continue on to Hat Yai and Sungai Kolok.

Getting Around

Sŏrng·tăa·ou run north–south along Th Ratchadamnoen and Th Si Thammasok for 10B (a bit more at night). Motorcycle-taxi rides start at 30B and cost up to 50B for longer distances.

SONGKHLA PROVINCE

Songkhla Province's two main commercial centres, Hat Yai and Songkhla, are less affected by the political turmoil plaguing the cities further south, although some state travel advisories warn against travel here. You won't be tripping over foreign backpackers, but you'll see a fair number of tourists drawn to wandering through local markets, savouring Muslim-Thai fusion cuisine, relaxing on breezy beaches and tapping into Hat Yai's fun and eclectic urban vibe.

Songkhla & Around สงขลา

POP 90,780

'The great city on two seas' is photogenic in parts; however, slow-paced Songkhla doesn't see much in the way of foreign tourist traffic. Although the town hasn't experienced any of the Muslim separatist violence plaguing the provinces further south, it's still catching the same bad press.

The population is a mix of Thais, Chinese and Malays, and the local architecture and cuisine reflect this fusion at every turn.

Sights

The **aquarium** (สงขลาอะควาเรี่ยม; www.songkhlaaquarium.com; admission adult/child 300/200B; ⌚9.30am-3.45pm Tue-Fri, 9.30am-4.45pm Sat & Sun) is a good outing if you have kids in tow.

★National Museum MUSEUM

(พิพิธภัณฑสถานแหงชาติสงขลา; Th Wichianchom; admission 150B; ⌚9am-4pm Wed-Sun, closed public holidays) This 1878 building was originally built in a Chinese architectural style as the residence of a luminary. The museum is easily the most picturesque national museum in Thailand and contains exhibits from all Thai art-style periods, particularly the Srivijaya. Walk barefoot on the wood floors to view elaborate wood carvings, historical photos and pottery salvaged from a shipwreck.

Hat Samila BEACH

(หาดสมิหลา) Stroll this beautiful strip of white sand with the giggling local couples and enjoy the kite flying (a local obsession). A bronze **Mermaid sculpture**, in tribute to Mae Thorani (the Hindu-Buddhist earth goddess), sits atop some rocks at the northern end of the beach. Locals treat the figure like a shrine, tying the waist with coloured cloth and rubbing the breasts for good luck.

Don't expect to sunbathe here – the local dress code is too modest – but it's a wholesome spot to meet locals and enjoy a distinctly Thai beach scene, and it's a gorgeous spot for a wander at sundown.

Ko Yo ISLAND

(เกาะยอ) A popular day trip from Songkhla is this island in the middle of Thale Sap. It is actually connected to the mainland by bridges and is famous for its cotton-weaving industry. There's a roadside market selling cloth and ready-made clothes at excellent prices.

If you visit Ko Yo, don't miss **Wat Phrahorn Laemphor**, with its giant reclining Buddha, and check out the **Thaksin Folklore Museum** (☎074 591618; admission 100B; ⌚8.30am-4.30pm), which actively aims to promote and preserve the culture of the region.

The pavilions here are reproductions of southern Thai–style houses and contain folk art and traditional household implements.

Tours

Singora Tram Tour TRAM TOUR
(9am-3pm) FREE These free 40-minute tours (six daily) in an open-air tram leave from next to the National Museum. You'll be lucky if you get any English narration but you will get a drive through the old part of town past the Songkhla mosque, a Thai temple, Chinese shrine and then out to Hat Samila.

Sleeping & Eating

Songkhla's hotels tend to be lower priced than other areas in the gulf, which makes going up a budget level a relatively cheap splurge.

For quality seafood, head to the street in front of the BP Samila Beach Hotel – the best spot is the restaurant directly in the roundabout. If market munching is your game, you'll find a place to sample street food most days of the week. On Sundays try the bustling market that encircles the Pavilion Hotel. Monday, Tuesday and Wednesday feature a night market (which closes around 9pm) near the local fish plant and bus station, and the Friday morning market sits diagonally opposite the City Hall.

Sook Soom Boon 2 HOTEL $
(074 323809; 14 Th Saiburi; d 550B;) The owner speaks good English and rooms are excellent value at this centrally located choice.

BP Samila Beach Hotel HOTEL $$
(074 440222; 8 Th Ratchadamnoen; r 1600-2500B;) This landmark hotel is a great deal – you'd pay nearly double for the same amenities on the islands. The beachfront establishment offers large rooms with fridges, satellite TVs and a choice of sea or mountain views (both are pretty darn good), although it's rather set in its ways and checking on wi-fi reception in your room first is prudent.

★ **Blue Smile Cafe** CAFE $
(254 Th Nakhonnai; mains from 100B; 10am-10pm Tue-Fri & Sun, 10am-midnight Sat) A fine place for a snack, some alcohol or cool beats; we're not sure what we like best at this Canadian-owned place: the roof garden, *The Blues Brothers* poster, the B52s and Bob Dylan pics, the live jazz (from 7.15pm Friday and Saturday) or the homemade waffles. There's even a double room if you need to crash out.

Ong Heap Huad CAFE $
(Th Nakhonnai; 8am-6pm) This astonishing family-run curiosity shop-slash-cafe has a mesmerising museum-like collection of ancient Chinese and Thai shop signs, antiques, statuette, lamps, stuffed animal heads and more. It's an enchanting place for a glass of tea. Look for the shop with the urns and bric-a-brac outside and the Chinese shop sign saying 黄協發, opposite No 239.

Information

Banks can be found all over town.

Indonesian Consulate (074 311544; www.kemlu.go.id/songkhla; 19 Th Sadao)

Malaysian Consulate (074 311062; 4 Th Sukhum, Songkhla; 8.15am-noon & 1-4pm Mon-Thu, 8.15am-noon & 2-4pm Fri)

Police Station (074 321868; Th Laeng Phra Ram) North of the town centre.

Post Office (Th Wichianchom) Opposite the market; international calls can be made upstairs.

Getting There & Around

BUS

The bus and minibus station is a few hundred metres south of the Viva Hotel. Three 2nd-class buses go daily to Bangkok (693B to 1070B), stopping in Nakhon Si Thammarat and Surat Thani, among other places. For Hat Yai, buses (21B) and minivans (30B to 40B) take around 40 minutes, and leave from Th Ramwithi. *Sŏrng·tăa·ou* also leave from here for Ko Yo.

TRAIN

From Songkhla you'll have to go to Hat Yai to reach most long-distance destinations in the south (trains no longer pass through town).

Hat Yai หาดใหญ่

POP 191,696

Welcome to the urban hub of southern Thailand, where Western-style shopping malls mingle with wafts of Cantonese street eats and curry from the eclectic range of busy street food stalls as Old Chinese men sit and watch the world go by on rickety chairs outside junk shops. It's a mix of busy city and laid-back tropics and Hat Yai has long been a favourite stop for Malaysian men on their weekend hooker tour. You'll notice that the town's tourism scene is still predominantly Malaysian mixed with a few Western expats. Come evenings, Hat Yai's cosy pubs and bouncing clubs come into their own.

The town is often said to be safe from the violent hullabaloo of the far south; however' it hasn't been ignored. The Lee Gardens Plaza Hotel was bombed in 2012, killing four people in a subsequent fire and injuring 400. Three bombs exploded in Hat Yai in 2014, injuring eight. In earlier years pubs, malls, department stores and hotels have been targeted in other bombings.

It's up to you if you want to stop here, but changing transport shouldn't be too risky. Those who get out and explore will be rewarded with some of the best food in the region and the dynamic flavour of the big smoke of southern Thailand.

Sleeping

Hat Yai has dozens of business-style hotels in the town centre, within walking distance of the train station.

Cathay Guest House HOSTEL $

(074 243815; 93/1 Th Niphat Uthit 2; s 200B, d & tw 240B, tr 290B;) There are very helpful staff and plentiful information about onward travel at this central cheapie; although rooms are simple (with squat loos), prices are rock bottom. Wi-fi is 30B for one hour.

Hat Yai Backpackers HOSTEL $

(www.hatyaibackpackershostel.com; 226 Th Niphat Uthit 1; dm 240B, d 350B;) With four-bed female dorms, eight-bed mixed dorms and double rooms (all fan), this new central choice is a decent bet, and there's helpful staff at hand for Hat Yai pointers.

Red Planet HOTEL $

(074 261011; www.redplanethotels.com; 152-156 Th Niphat Uthit 2; r from 900B;) In a great, central location, this hotel offers cleanliness, affordability and good service, with uncluttered, functional rooms. The atmosphere and theme is generically charmless and prices depend a lot on how far in advance you book. The 200B upgrade for the room with the kettle is not worth it.

Centara HOTEL $$$

(074 352222; www.centarahotelsresorts.com; 3 Th Sanehanusorn; r 4000-4700B, apt 5300-7000B, ste 8500B;) The centrally located, 244-room Centara is a particularly smart choice with pool, excellent rooms, terrific service and some fine views from the upper floors. Evening live jazz in the foyer bar brings some style.

Eating

The city is the unofficial capital of southern Thailand's cuisine, offering Muslim roti and curries, Chinese noodles, duck rice and dim sum, and fresh Thai-style seafood from both the gulf and Andaman coasts. You'll find hawker stalls everywhere but a particularly good hunting ground is along Th Supasarnrangsan. Meals here cost between 25B to 80B.

Night Market MARKET $

(Th Montri 1) The night market boasts heaps of local eats including several stalls selling the famous Hat Yai–style deep-fried chicken and *kà·nŏm jeen* (fresh rice noodles served with curry), as well as a couple of stalls peddling grilled seafood.

Daothiam CAFE $

(79/3 Thammanoonvithi Rd; mains from 60B; 7am-7pm;) Serving Hat Yai patrons since 1959, this traditional Chinese cafe has framed bank notes on its walls, friendly staff, a reliable menu of Thai/Chinese dishes and fine breakfasts. Curiously, its name means 'Satellite'. It's opposite the Odean Shopping Mall.

Gedi Chadian CHINESE $

(134-136 Th Niphat Uthit 3; mains from 50B) This big, open, spacious and very busy restaurant serves steaming bowls of scrumptious *won-ton* noodles, chicken rice, *chā shāo* pork and other filling Chinese staples.

Drinking

Hive Bar BAR

(127 Th Niphat Uthit 2; 3pm-midnight) A cut above the rest, Hive bar is a decent downtown hang-out in Hat Yai with a traveller, expat and local fan base, serving up a solid menu of pub food. Pool enthusiasts won't be disappointed.

Information

Immigration Office (Th Phetkasem) Near the railway bridge, it handles visa extensions.

Tourism Authority of Thailand (TAT; www.tourismthailand.org/hatyai; 1/1 Soi 2, Th Niphat Uthit 3; 8.30am-4.30pm) The very helpful staff here speak excellent English and have loads of info on the entire region.

Tourist Police (Th Niphat Uthit 3; 24hr) Near the TAT office.

Getting There & Away

AIR

Air Asia (www.airasia.com) and **Nok Air** (www.nokair.com) have daily flights to and from Bangkok.

Thai Airways International (THAI; www.thaiairways.com; 182 Th Niphat Uthit 1) Runs several flights daily between Hat Yai and Bangkok.

BUS

Most interprovincial buses and southbound minivans leave from the bus terminal 2km southeast of the town centre, while most northbound minivans now leave from a minivan terminal 5km west of town at Talat Kaset, a 60B túk-túk ride from the centre of town. Buses link Hat Yai to almost any location in southern Thailand.

Prasert Tour (Th Niphat Uthit 1) runs quicker minibuses to Surat Thani (4½ hours, 8am to 5pm), and **Cathay Tour** (93/1 Th Niphat Uthit 2) can also arrange minivans to many places in the south.

BUSES FROM HAT YAI

DESTINATION	FARE (B)	DURATION (HR)
Bangkok	688-1126	15
Krabi	182-535	5
Nakhon Si Thammarat	140	4
Pak Bara	130	2
Phuket	360	7
Songkhla	40	1½
Sungai Kolok	200	4
Surat Thani	235	5
Trang	100	2

TRAIN

There are four overnight trains to/from Bangkok each day (259B to 945B), and the trip takes at least 16 hours; trains go via Surat Thani (105B). There are also seven trains daily that run along the east coast to Sungai Kolok (92B) and two daily trains running west to Butterworth (332B) and Padang Besar (57B), both in Malaysia.

There is an advance booking office and left-luggage office at the train station; both are open 7am to 5pm daily.

Getting Around

An **Airport Taxi Service** (182 Th Niphat Uthit 1; 100B per person; ⏲6.30am-6.45pm) makes the run to the airport six times daily (6.45am, 10am, 12.15pm, 1.45pm, 3pm and 6.15pm). A private taxi for this run costs 320B.

Sŏrng·tăa·ou run along Th Phetkasem (10B per person). Túk-túk and motorcycle taxis around town cost 20B to 40B per person.

DEEP SOUTH

Yala ยะลา

POP 61,250

Landlocked Yala wiggles its way south to the Malaysian border, making it Thailand's southernmost province. Its eponymous capital appears very different from other Thai metropolises. The city's big boulevards and well-organised street grid are set around a huge circular park and feel distinctly Western. Around three-quarters of the population are Muslim and it is a university town; the educational centre of the Deep South.

Sights

Yala's biggest attraction is **Wat Kuha Pi Muk** (also called Wat Na Tham or Cave-front Temple), one of the most important pilgrimage points in southern Thailand. Located 8km west of town on the road connecting Yala to Hat Yai (Rte 409), the Srivijaya-period cave temple features a reclining Buddha that dates back to AD 757. A statue of a giant guards the temple's entrance and, inside, small natural openings in the cave's roof let in the sun's rays to illuminate a variety of ancient Buddhist cave drawings.

Further south, Betong is home to the largest **mail box** in Thailand, first built in 1924. Betong also functions as a legal, but inconvenient, border crossing to Malaysia; contact Yala's **immigration office** (☎073 231292; ⏲8.30am-4.30pm).

Sleeping & Eating

Many of Yala's cheapest lodgings double as unofficial brothels. There are excellent restaurants that are scattered around the park's perimeter.

Yala Rama HOTEL $
(☎073 212815; 21 Th Sri Bumrung; r 600B; ❄📶) Like most hotels in the region, this central and reputable place would be more expensive if it weren't in the tourist-free Deep South. Clean, comfortable rooms and an OK attached restaurant.

TRAVEL IN THE DEEP SOUTH: SHOULD YOU GO?

Despite the conflict, almost everyone in the Deep South – whether ethnic Malay Muslim or a Thai soldier – is happy to see a *fa·ràng*. So few foreigners make it here that you're guaranteed a lot of attention from the locals.

Nor have tourists, or any Westerners, ever been targeted by the insurgents; this is a very insular war.

Yet, by nature insurgencies are unpredictable, and bombs kill indiscriminately. Explosive devices planted on parked motorbikes outside shops, or in markets, are a common tactic of the separatists and are frequently used in the city centres of Yala, Pattani, Narathiwat and Sungai Kolok.

It's best not to linger on the streets for too long; you could be in the wrong place at the wrong time. Nor is travel in the countryside in the early morning or after dark advisable. This isn't an area to be driving a motorbike in if you can't be identified as a foreigner.

But perhaps the biggest drawback to travel in the region is that the insurgency has stifled tourism to such an extent that there is very little infrastructure for visitors. Travel between the major centres apart, you'll need private transport to get around. There are few hotels and restaurants, and almost no nightlife, while those beautiful beaches have absolutely no facilities.

If you do want to travel here, research the current situation carefully and take advice from your embassy.

Getting There & Around

Yala's bus station is south of the city centre. There are three daily buses to and from Bangkok's southern bus terminal (711B to 1422B, 14 hours). The 4pm bus from Bangkok carries onto Betong.

Four trains a day run between Bangkok and Yala (22 hours). Two trains travel daily between Yala and Sungai Kolok (three to four hours). The train station is just north of the city centre.

Buses to Hat Yai (160B, 2½ hours) stop several times a day on Th Sirirot, outside the Prudential TS Life office.

Minivans to Betong and Sungai Kolok (100B, two hours) depart hourly from opposite the train station.

Pattani ปัตตานี

POP 44,234

Once the heart of a large Muslim principality that included the neighbouring provinces of Yala and Narathiwat, Pattani Province has never adjusted to Thai rule. Although today's political situation has stunted the area's development, Pattani Town has a 500-year history of trading with the world's most notorious imperial powerhouses. The Portuguese established a trading post here in 1516, the Japanese passed through in 1605, the Dutch in 1609 and the British flexed their colonial muscle in 1612.

Yet despite the city's fascinating past, there's little of interest in Pattani. There are some decent beaches nearby, but the ongoing insurgency has made most of these sandy destinations unsafe for the independent traveller.

Sights

The Mae Nam Pattani (Pattani River) divides the older town to the east and the newer town to the west. Along Th Ruedi you can see what is left of old Pattani **architecture** – the Sino-Portuguese style that was once so prevalent in this part of southern Thailand. On Th Arnoaru there are several ancient but still quite intact, Chinese-style homes.

Pattani could be one of the better beach destinations in the region. The coastline between Pattani Town and Narathiwat Province is stunning: untouched and deserted apart from fishing villages. But exploring much of this area independently is not a safe option at this time.

Locals frequent **Laem Tachi**, a sandy cape that juts out over the northern end of Ao Pattani. It can be reached by boat taxi from Pattani pier. **Thepha district**, 35km northwest of Pattani, is the most developed beach destination in the area, although it is technically in Songkhla Province. There you'll find a few resorts and beachfront restaurants that cater mostly to middle-class Thais. To reach Thepha, hop on any Songkhla-bound bus from Pattani (or vice versa); mention the name of your resort and you'll be deposited at the side of the road for the brief walk to the beach.

Matsayit Klang MOSQUE
(Th Naklua Yarang) Thailand's second-largest mosque is the Matsayit Klang, a traditional structure with a green hue that is probably still the south's most important mosque. It was built in the 1960s. Non-Muslims can enter outside of prayer times.

Sleeping & Eating

Palace Hotel HOTEL $
(☎073 349171; 10-12 Pipit Soi Talattewiwat 2; r 200-350B; ❄) There's nothing palatial about this place. But it is the only budget option in town for foreigners and close to the night market. Go for the air-con rooms with hot water.

CS Pattani Hotel HOTEL $$
(☎073 335093; www.cspattanihotel.com; 299 Moo 4, Th Nong Jik; r from 1400B; ❄@🛜≈) The safest and best hotel, with soldiers outside and a metal detector in the lobby, this is where Thai politicians stay on their rare visits to the Deep South. The paucity of tourists mean you get great rooms and facilities for a bargain price. It's 2km north of the centre of town.

Night Market SOUTHERN THAI $
(Soi Talattewiwat; ⏲4-9pm) Pattani shuts down far earlier than most Thai towns, but the night market offers solid seafood, as well as southern Thai-style curries and the usual noodle and fried-rice options.

Information

There are several banks along the southeastern end of Th Pipit, near the Th Naklua Yarang intersection.

Pattani Hospital (☎073 323411, 073 323414; Th Nong Jik)

Police Station (☎073 349018; Th Pattani Phirom)

Getting There & Around

Minivans and buses depart from Pattani's bus station on the western fringes of town. There are frequent daytime departures to Hat Yai (100B, 1½ hours), Narathiwat (100B, 1½ hours) and Sungai Kolok (140B, 2½ hours).

There are two daily buses to and from Bangkok's southern bus terminal (920B to 1220B, 15 hours).

Motorbike taxis charge 30B for hops around town, but they become very scarce after dark.

Narathiwat นราธิวาส

POP 41,342

Sitting on the banks of the Bang Nara River, Narathiwat is probably the most Muslim city in Thailand, with many mosques scattered around town. There are still a few old Sino-Portuguese buildings lining the riverfront (although blink and you'll miss them), and there are some excellent beaches just outside town. But few tourists pass through, due to the security situation.

Sights

Matsayit Klang MOSQUE
Towards the southern end of Th Pichitbumrung stands Matsayit Klang, a wooden mosque built in the Sumatran style and known locally as the 'central mosque'. It was reputedly built by a prince of the former kingdom of Pattani over a hundred years ago. Non-Muslims can enter outside of prayer times.

Ao Manao BEACH
Five kilometres south of town, Ao Manao is a superb strip of palm tree-fringed sand. You'll likely have it all to yourself, unless it's a public or Muslim holiday.

Hat Narathat BEACH
Just north of town is Hat Narathat, a 5km-long sandy beach fronted by towering pines, which serves as a public park for locals. The beach is only 2km from the town centre – you can easily walk there or take a săhm·lór.

Wat Khao Kong BUDDHIST TEMPLE
(⏲9am-5pm) FREE The tallest seated-Buddha image in southern Thailand is at Wat Khao

MOBILE PHONES

At the time of writing, Thailand was unveiling a nationwide mobile (cell) phone registration program. It's a scheme that started in the Deep South, where mobile phones are frequently used by insurgents to set off bombs. If you buy a Thai SIM card, your number should be registered automatically. But if you reach the Deep South and your phone stops working, then you'll need to visit any local phone shop to reactivate it. Hand over your passport and your details will be noted and, an hour later, your phone will work again.

THAILAND'S FORGOTTEN WAR

It may seem fantastic as you laze on the beach, or meditate at a peaceful hilltop temple, but the Deep South is home to one of Southeast Asia's longest-running and bloodiest conflicts.

Just 300km or so south of the party islands of Ko Samui and Ko Pha-Ngan, a guerrilla war between ethnic Malay Muslims and the overwhelmingly Buddhist Thai state has claimed almost 6000 lives since 2004.

The Deep South, which borders Malaysia, is a different world from the rest of the country. Foreign visitors are nonexistent and the pristine beaches deserted. Military convoys rumble through the villages and towns, checkpoints dominate the roads and residents are subject to compulsory DNA tests designed to make identifying suspected insurgents easier.

Around 80% of the 1.8 million people who live in Thailand's three southernmost provinces of Pattani, Narathiwat and Yala are ethnic Malay Muslims. They speak a Malay dialect and many want their own independent state, as the region once was hundreds of years ago.

For the estimated 12,500 to 15,000 separatist fighters here, the Deep South is 'Patani': the name given to the Qatar-sized sultanate during its glory days in the 14th and 15th centuries. The insurgents view the Thai government as a colonial power and Thai Buddhists as interlopers in their land.

Ranged against the separatists are around 150,000 soldiers, police and militias. Targeted in ambushes along the coconut tree–lined roads of the region, or by increasingly sophisticated IEDs (improvised explosive devices), barely a week goes by without a member of the Thai security forces being killed or wounded.

At the same time, the insurgency has set neighbours against each other. Gruesome tit-for-tat killings occur, with both Buddhist and Muslim civilians being gunned down as they ride home on their motorbikes or beheaded in the rubber plantations that are the mainstay of the local economy. Bombs are planted outside shops and in the markets of the towns, claiming random victims. The few remaining Buddhist monks in the region have to be escorted by the army when they collect alms every morning for fear they will be assassinated, while mosques are riddled with bullet holes.

Yet despite the appalling violence, the insurgency remains little known both at home and overseas. With almost 25 million visitors a year, Thailand is fiercely proud and protective of its reputation as the 'Land of Smiles'. The media downplay the security situation, while Thai politicians act as if they are in denial about the sheer scale of the conflict.

The insurgents, too, have resisted attacking targets outside the Deep South, a tactic that would do huge damage to the Thai psyche and would garner them far more attention

Kong, 6km southwest on the way to the train station in Tanyongmat. Located in a park, the image is 17m long and 24m high, and made of reinforced concrete covered with tiny gold-coloured mosaic tiles that glint magically in the sun.

Sleeping & Eating

Most of the town's accommodation is located on and around Th Puphapugdee along the Bang Nara river.

Ocean Blue Mansion HOTEL $
(073 511109; 297 Th Puphapugdee; r 400-500B;) The decent-sized rooms are a little beaten up, but some have fine river views and this is still the best budget choice.

Tanyong Hotel HOTEL $$
(073 511477; www.tanyonghotel.com; 16/1 Th Sophaphisai; r 690-890B;) Respectable, welcoming hotel with big, comfortable rooms and an OK attached restaurant. Some English spoken.

Ang Mo CHINESE $
(cnr Th Puphapugdee & Th Chamroonnara; dishes 50-150B; 10am-10pm) This popular Chinese restaurant is both cheap and tasty, and has even fed members of the Thai royal family.

Mangkorntong THAI $
(433 Th Puphapugdee; dishes 55-200B; 11am-9pm) Perched over the river, there are two terraces to dine on here. There's a wide selection of seafood dishes plus a number of vegie options, and it serves alcohol.

around the world. Nor do they appear to be connected to the more extreme Islamic militants of Indonesia and the Philippines.

Instead, they stay in the shadows, rarely issuing statements or talking to the press. Operating in independent cells, they belong to a number of different organisations all likely linked to each other. But there seems to be no common leader of the groups. That renders the sporadic peace talks that take place between the separatists and the Thai government meaningless, as no one is really sure if the representatives of the insurgents have any true control over them.

While the insurgency kicked into life in earnest in 2004, after 32 suspected Muslim rebels were cornered in an ancient mosque in Pattani Town and brutally killed by the Thai army, its roots go back hundreds of years. From the 16th century on, the sultanate of Patani was unwillingly under Thai rule for brief periods. But it wasn't until the Anglo-Siamese Treaty of 1909 that the Deep South was absorbed into Thailand proper. Britain recognised Thai sovereignty over the region, in return for Bangkok abandoning its claims to other parts of what were then the British-ruled Malay States.

Since then, Thailand, the most populous Buddhist country in the world, has set about attempting to remake the Deep South in its own image. Muslim schools have been shut down and all children made to study in Thai, even though most of them speak it only as a second language. They are also forced to learn about Buddhism, a part of the Thai national curriculum, despite following Islam. Officials from other parts of the country are imported to run the region.

By turns heavy-handed and paternalistic, the Thai government's policies began to fuel a separatist movement. Having their children subject to the Thai school system remains a huge source of resentment for many Muslims. Regarded as symbols of the hated Thai state by the insurgents, over 300 schools have been burned down in recent years, while more than 150 Buddhist teachers have been assassinated.

But with the insurgency entirely confined to just three provinces, and a small part of neighbouring Songkhla Province, few Thais are even aware of why the fighting is taking place. Nor are they willing to contemplate giving into the separatists' demands. Imbued with the nationalism taught in their schools, the idea that the Deep South should want to secede from Thailand is unthinkable, both to ordinary Thais and the authorities.

Yet, some form of autonomy for the region is likely the only way to end the violence. Until that happens, Thailand's forgotten war will carry on and the grim list of casualties will continue to grow.

Information

The **Tourism Authority of Thailand** (TAT; ☎ Narathiwat 073 522411, nationwide call centre 1672) is inconveniently located a few kilometres south of town, just across the bridge on the road to Tak Bai.

Getting There & Around

Air Asia (☎ nationwide call centre 02 515 9999; www.airasia.com) flies daily to and from Bangkok (from 1783B, 1½ hours).

Minivans and buses leave from Narathiwat's **bus terminal** (☎ 073 511552), 2km south of town on Th Rangae Munka. There are two daily buses to and from Bangkok's southern bus terminal (860B to 1338B, 15 to 17 hours).

There are frequent minivans heading to Hat Yai (170B, three hours), Pattani (100B, two hours), Sungai Kolok (70B, one hour) and Yala (100B, 1½ hours).

Narathiwat is small enough to navigate by foot. Motorcycle taxis charge 30B to get around.

Sungai Kolok สุไหงโกลก

POP 41,590

It's not the most prepossessing place to enter or exit the 'Land of Smiles', but Sungai Kolok is the main gateway between Thailand and Malaysia. As such, it's a scuzzy border town best known for smuggling and prostitution. Less of a target than the other major towns in the region, the unstable situation in the Deep South has nevertheless severely diminished its 'sin city' reputation in recent years, with the Malaysian men who once came here for wild weekends now

GETTING TO MALAYSIA: SUNGAI KOLOK TO RANTAU PANJANG

Getting to the Border The Thai border (open 5am to 9pm) is about 1.5km from the centre of Sungai Kolok or the train station. Motorbike taxis charge 30B.

At the Border This is a hassle-free border crossing. After completing formalities, walk across the Harmony Bridge to the Malaysian border post.

Moving On Shared taxis and buses to Kota Bharu, the capital of Malaysia's Kelantan State, can be caught 200m beyond the Malaysian border post. Shared taxis cost RM$10 per person (90B) or RM$50 (450B) to charter the whole car yourself. The ride takes around 40 minutes. Buses make the hour-long journey for RM$5.10 (45B).

It's possible to continue south by the so-called 'jungle train', but the closest station is at Pasir Mas, located along taxi/bus routes to Kota Bharu.

Tak Bai, also in Narathiwat Province, and Betong, further south in Yala, are also legal crossing points for foreigners, but Sungai Kolok is by far the most convenient place to cross the border.

favouring safer Hat Yai. Fewer travellers, too, leave Thailand here now; more come in the opposite direction and immediately hop on a train heading north.

Sleeping & Eating

Most hotels here are uniform in quality and price. Many of the real cheapies won't accept foreigners.

Stand-out restaurants are in short supply, although there is some tasty Malaysian and Chinese food around.

Merlin Hotel HOTEL **$$**
(073 611003; 68 Th Charoenkhet; r 600B;) Fixtures and furniture from a different age, but clean and handy for the train station.

Genting Hotel HOTEL **$$**
(073 613231; 250 Th Asia 18; r 700B;) More respectable than most hotels in town and, if you're the nervous type, the security is efficient. But the midrange rooms are rather scuffed for the price. It's a few hundred metres west of the train station on the other side of the road.

Kakyah Restaurant MALAYSIAN **$**
(43/11 Th Charoenkhet; dishes from 30B; 10am-10pm) Decent Malaysian food is on offer at this reliable, alcohol-free, Muslim-run place.

Information

There is an **immigration office** (073 614114; Th Charoenkhet; 8am-5pm Mon-Fri) opposite the Merlin Hotel with helpful, English-speaking staff. A tourist police office sits at the border. There are ATMs and foreign-exchange booths close to the train station.

Getting There & Away

The long-distance **bus station** (Th Asia 18) is 3km east of the train station. There are four buses daily to and from Bangkok's southern bus terminal (707B to 1414B, 17 to 20 hours). Minvans to Hat Yai (200B, four hours) leave from here too.

Minivans heading north to Narathiwat (70B, one hour), Pattani (130B, 2½ hours) and Yala (120B, two hours) depart from opposite the train station.

Two daily trains (11.30am and 2.20pm, 24 hours) connect Sungai Kolok with Bangkok. Trains in the Deep South are often delayed and subject to army and police searches.

Getting Around

Motorcycle taxis zoom around town for a flat rate of 30B.

Phuket & the Andaman Coast

Includes ➡

Best Places to Eat

➡ Suay (p621)
➡ Aziamendi (p608)
➡ Krua Thara (p654)
➡ Pad Thai Shop (p634)
➡ Trang Night Market (p681)

Best Places to Stay

➡ Point Yamu by Como (p647)
➡ Iniala Beach House (p608)
➡ Pak-Up Hostel (p649)
➡ Six Senses Hideaway (p612)
➡ Castaway Resort (p700)

Why Go?

The Andaman is Thailand's turquoise coast; one of those places you see on a postcard that makes you want to quit your job and live in flip-flops...forever. For once, the beauty exceeds the hype. Pure-white beaches, some of the world's softest sand, cathedral-esque limestone cliffs and hundreds of jungle-covered isles extend down the Andaman Sea from the border of Myanmar to Malaysia. Phuket is the glitzy show-stealer, but head north and you'll uncover world-class dive sites, little-visited isles and Ranong's Thai-Myanmar flavour. To the south, you can lazily island-hop past karst towers down to the Malaysian border.

The catch? The Andaman Coast is no secret and its beaches are becoming increasingly crowded with backpackers, package tourists, high-end jet-setters and everyone in between. Flashy resorts are pushing out the bamboo shacks, and authenticity largely now hides in the backwaters. But your postcard dream is still here – if you're willing to look.

When to Go

➡ May to October is the rainy season. At this time, swells pick up, some islands become inaccessible, many resorts close and others slash their prices. In Phuket, Trang and other southern towns, the Vegetarian Festival is held in late September or October and involves parades of pierced-faced worshippers, endless firecrackers and fantastic meat-free food.

➡ December to January is the peak season for tourism and conditions are ideal for diving and snorkelling. Prices soar, transport links increase, and accommodation and transport must be booked well in advance.

Phuket & the Andaman Coast Highlights

1 Buzzing glassy waters between white-sand beaches in the **Trang Islands** (p684).

2 Exploring a heady mix of luxury lodgings and street-food treats on **Phuket** (p613).

3 Traipsing through the real-life Jurassic Park of **Khao Sok National Park** (p600).

4 Snorkelling over colourful corals off **Ko Lipe** (p697).

5 Scaling limestone cliffs above blissful jade waters in **Railay** (p655).

6 Blending into the laid-back beach scene on **Ko Lanta** (p670).

7 Floating in a cerulean sea, then

dancing into the night on **Ko Phi-Phi** (p660).

8 Looking for elusive whale sharks in the **Surin** (p598) and **Similan Islands** (p606).

9 Kayaking into the spectacular *hôrng* (island caves) of jaw-dropping **Ao Phang-Nga** (p609).

10 Falling into the mellow beach-bar vibe of **Ko Phayam** (p594).

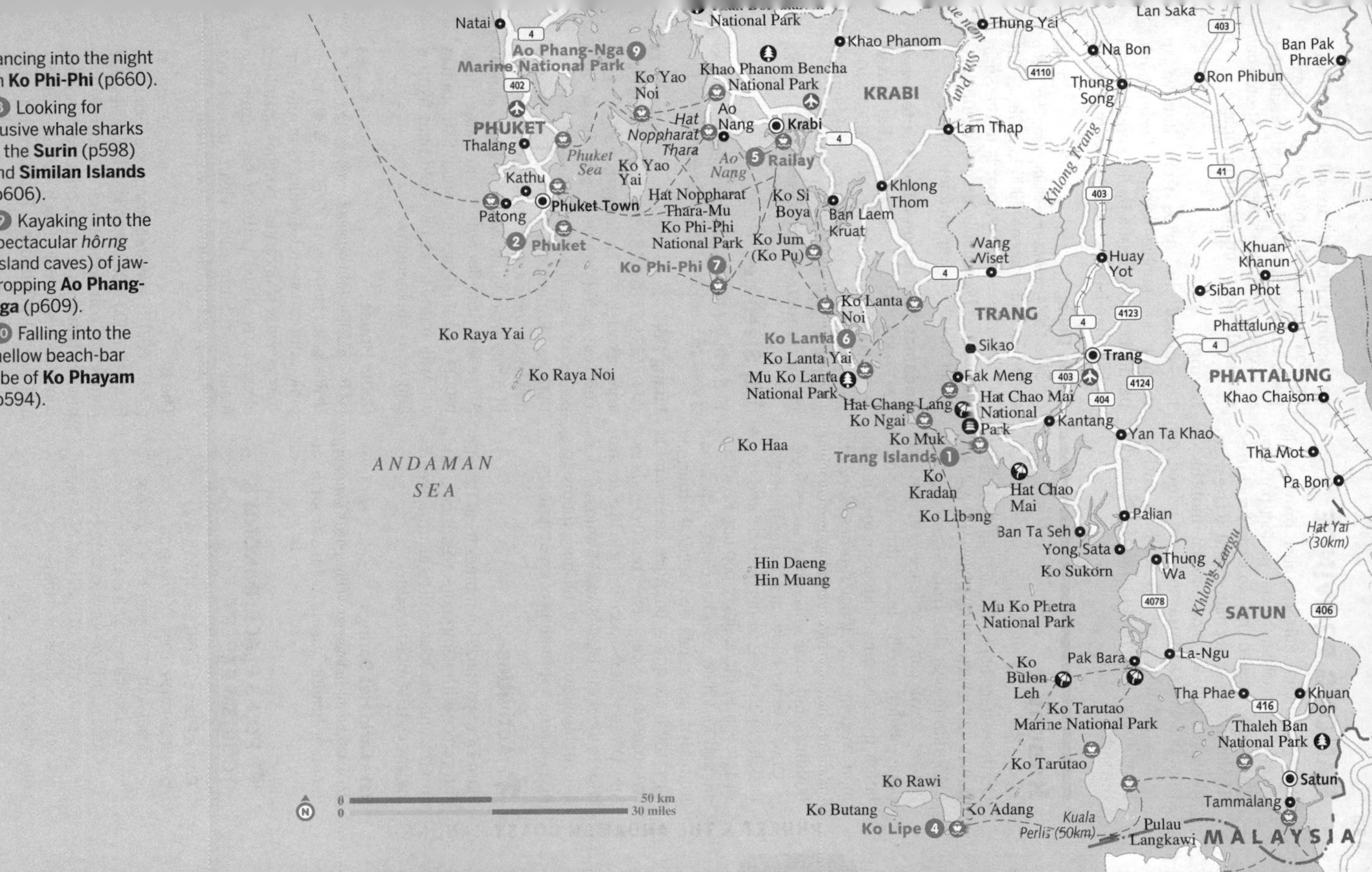

RANONG PROVINCE

The Andaman's northernmost province is a different package to the perfect-paradise Andaman flogged on tourist brochures. Thailand's least populated and wettest region gets up to eight annual months of rain; beaches along the coast are scarce. As a result, Ranong's forests are lush and its beautiful islands remain *relatively* under the radar.

Ranong ระนอง

POP 53,000

On the eastern bank of Mae Nam Pak Chan's turbid, tea-brown estuary, Ranong lies just a 45-minute boat ride from Myanmar. This border town par excellence (shabby, frenetic, slightly seedy) has a thriving population from Myanmar (keep an eye out for men wearing traditional sarongs, *longyi*), bubbling hot springs, crumbling historical buildings and some sensational street food.

Once a gritty backwater, today Ranong is basking in border-crossing business and transit tourism to increasingly popular Ko Phayam and Ko Chang, and has clearly benefitted from Myanmar's stabilised political situation. Now there are quirky boutique hotels and a style-conscious local scene (relatively speaking). Dive operators specialising in live-aboard trips to the Surin Islands and Myanmar's Mergui Archipelago are establishing themselves here, adding a sprinkling of expat flavour.

Activities

Siam Hot Spa (p622) combines local flavour and prices with sumptuous treatments and an atmospheric location (right on a steaming river). It's fantastic value.

Rakswarin Hot Springs HOT SPRING
(Th Phetkasem; admission 40B; ⏲6.30am-9pm) Ranong's healing waters bubble from a sacred spring hot enough to boil eggs (65°C), on the southeastern side of town. The riverside pools are blessed with chequered mosaic tiles, showers, towels and sunbeds. Just stretch out and let the heat work its natural magic.

> **PON'S PLACE: RANONG'S TOURISM EXPERT**
>
> **Pon's Place** (☎081 597 4549; www.ponplace-ranong.com; Th Ruangrat; ⏲7.30am-7pm; wi-fi) Ranong's go-to spot for everything from wi-fi and European breakfasts (40B to 70B) to flight bookings, visa runs (1300B), airport pick-ups and bus schedules. Pon himself is a high-energy, friendly guy.

Diving

Live-aboard dive trips from Ranong to world-class bubble-blowing destinations, particularly the Burma Banks and the Surin and Similan Islands, are deservedly popular.

A-One-Diving DIVING
(☎077 832984; www.a-one-diving.com; 256 Th Ruangrat; 3-day live-aboard 17,900-18,900B; ⏲Oct-Apr) Specialises in live-aboards to the Surin Islands and Myanmar's Mergui Archipelago, plus PADI diving certification courses.

Andaman International Dive Center DIVING
(☎089 814 1092; www.aidcdive.com; Bus Terminal, Th Phetkasem; 4-day live-aboard 19,000B; ⏲Oct-Apr) Live-aboards to the Surins and Similans and the Mergui Archipelago in Myanmar, focusing on extensive excursions (six to 14 days).

Sleeping

Red *sŏrng·tăa·ou* (passenger pick-up truck) 3 goes to places on Th Phetkasem (Hwy 4).

Luang Poj GUESTHOUSE $
(☎077 833377, 087 266 6333; www.facebook.com/luangpojhostel; 225 Th Ruangrat; r 500B; air-con, wi-fi) This self-styled 'boutique guesthouse' is a gorgeous remodel of a 1920s-era building that was Ranong's first hotel. Though windowless, rooms are spotless, comfy and cosy, in signature colours (we like the hot orange). All share tile-floored warm-water bathrooms and mod-meets-vintage flair: Indian art, wall murals, one-of-a-kind light fixtures and retro photography.

Dahla House GUESTHOUSE $
(☎077 812959; http://dahla.siam2web.com; 323/5 Th Ruangrat; r fan/air-con 400/500B; air-con, wi-fi) Baby-pink, mint-green and sky-blue concrete bungalows with fridges and porches sprinkled along a tree-lined path set back from the main road. Simple and clean (though not spotless), with a friendly down-to-earth feel.

The B BOUTIQUE HOTEL $$
(☎077 823111; www.thebranong.com; 295/1-2 Th Ruangrat; r 1100-1600B; air-con, wi-fi, pool) This good-value chunk of polished-concrete modernism is proof of Ranong's new era. Impeccably stylish, comfy rooms have floating beds, rain showers and tasteful, bright decor. Extra points for the

Ranong

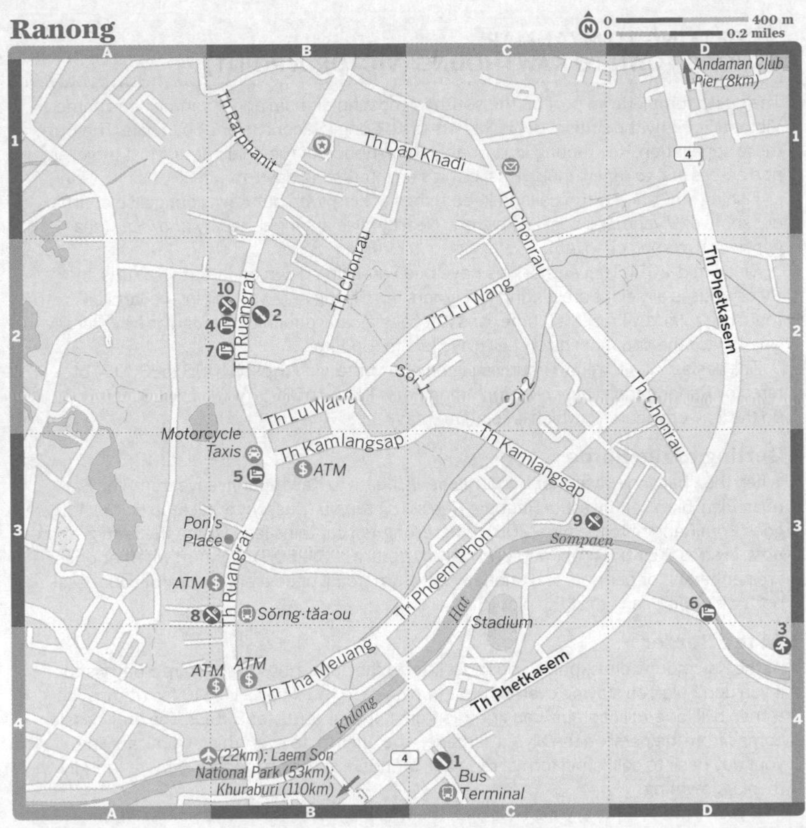

snooker bar, the open-air **bar-restaurant** (mains 100-250B; 7am-1am;), and, particularly, the rooftop infinity pool overlooking Ranong and the surrounding green hills.

Thansila HOTEL $$
(081 797 4674, 077 823405; www.facebook.com/thansilahotspringresort; 129/2 Th Phetkasem; r fan/air-con 1000/1600B;) A homely spot with artsy flair, 800m west of the hot springs on the southeast edge of town. The best digs are exposed-stone, lodge-style rooms overlooking the river, with grotto-like hot-water bathrooms and wooden mirrors. It's owned by a Thai architect who renovated over two years.

Ranong

Activities, Courses & Tours
1 Andaman International Dive Center C4
2 A-One-Diving B2
3 Rakswarin Hot Springs D4

Sleeping
4 Dahla House B2
5 Luang Poj B3
6 Thansila D3
7 The B B2

Eating
8 Day Market B3
9 Night Market C3
10 Ranong Hideaway B2
The B Restaurant .... (see 7)

Eating & Drinking

Ranong has a lively, young, very local drinking scene involving lots of karaoke.

★ **Day Market** MARKET $
(Th Ruangrat; dishes 40-50B; 5am-midnight) Ranong's bubbly day market offers delicious, inexpensive Thai and Burmese meals. It's a wonderfully local scene.

GETTING TO MYANMAR: RANONG TOWN TO KAWTHOUNG (VICTORIA POINT)

The dusty, tumbledown port on the southernmost tip of mainland Myanmar was named Victoria Point by the British, but is known as Ko Song (Second Island) by Thais. The Burmese appellation, Kawthoung, is probably a corruption of the Thai name. Most travellers pop across just to renew their visas, but it's an interesting day trip.

Fishing and trade with Thailand keep things ticking over, but Kawthoung also churns out some of Myanmar's best kickboxers. Nearby isles are inhabited by *chow lair* (sea gypsies; also spelt *chao leh*).

Since mid-2014, Thai authorities have been cracking down on in-out visa runs. In theory, this is aimed at preventing foreigners from living and working in Thailand on tourist visas and, at research time, was not causing any difficulty for regular travellers. Do monitor the situation; ask other travellers for updates.

The easiest way to renew your visa is on one of the 'visa trips' (1100B to 1300B) offered by Ranong travel agencies, including Pon's Place (p590). You'll save 200B if you do the legwork yourself, which is relatively easy.

Getting to the Border

When the Thailand–Myanmar border is open, boats to Kawthoung leave from Tha Saphan Plaa, 5km southwest of Ranong. Red *sŏrng·tăa·ou* (passenger pick-up truck) 4 goes from Ranong to the pier (20B), where long-tail captains lead you to the immigration post, then to their boat (per person one-way/return 125/250B). Confirm whether prices are per person or per ride, and one-way or return. You'll need a photocopy of your passport, which you can get at the pier (5B).

At the Border

At the Kawthoung checkpoint, you must inform the authorities that you're a day visitor if you don't plan on staying overnight – in which case you'll pay a US$10 fee (it must be a crisp bill; long-tail captains can get this from harbour touts for 500B). The only hassle comes from 'helpers' on the Myanmar side, who offer to do everything from carrying your day pack to collecting forms, then ask for tips, but they're generally more friendly than aggravating.

If you're just renewing your Thai visa, the whole process takes two hours. When returning to Thailand, bear in mind that Myanmar's time is 30 minutes behind Thailand's. This has previously caused problems for returning travellers who got through **Myanmar Immigration** (⏲7am-5pm) before its closing time only to find the Thai Immigration post (p593) closed. It's worth checking Thai immigration closing hours when leaving the country; if you don't get stamped in you'll have to return to Myanmar the next day.

A quicker, easier and much more polished alternative (albeit sterilised and less interesting) is via the **Andaman Club Pier** (☎077 871081; www.andamanclub.com; off Rte 4004; ⏲8.30am-4pm), 8km northwest of town, off Rte 4004. At the terminal, you'll get your passport stamped immediately, and a Myanmar-bound speedboat (950B return, 15 minutes each way) leaves hourly from 8.30am to 3.30pm, docking at a flash casino. The whole trip takes one hour. For an additional 550B you can add a two-hour tour along Myanmar's coast from the casino.

Moving On

It's possible to stay overnight in one of Kawthoung's dingy, overpriced hotels, but you'd probably rather not. If you have a valid Myanmar visa, which you'll have to apply for in advance at the Myanmar Embassy in Bangkok (or a third country), you'll be permitted to stay for up to 28 days and exit anywhere you like.

Night Market MARKET $

(Th Kamlangsap, off Hwy 4; dishes 30-50B; ⏲2-7pm) The night market, which is located just northwest off the highway, sizzles up some brilliant Thai dishes offered at killer prices.

BUSES FROM RANONG

DESTINATION	FARE (B)	DURATION (HR)	FREQUENCY
Bangkok	445-692	9-10	hourly 7am-1pm, 3pm, 5pm, 7pm & 8pm (VIP)
Chumphon	120	2	hourly 7am-5pm
Hat Yai	420	7	6am, 10am & 8pm
Khao Lak	180	3½	hourly 6.30am-5.45pm
Krabi	197	6	7.30am, 10.15am & 2pm
Phang-Nga	190	5	7.30am, 10.15am & 2pm
Phuket	250	5-6	hourly 6.30am-5.45pm
Surat Thani	190	4-5	6am & 2pm

Ranong Hideaway THAI, INTERNATIONAL **$$**
(077 832730; www.ranonghideaway.com; 323/7 Th Ruangrat; mains 90-300B; 10am-11pm;) A long-time favourite of expats and border businessmen, this attractive (if weathered) international eatery unfurls beneath a stilted bamboo roof, offering decent pastas, meaty mains, Thai curries and international breakfasts along with a pizza oven, a pool table and a well-stocked bar.

Information

Most guesthouses and restaurants have wi-fi. ATMs are clustered around the intersection of Th Ruangrat and Th Tha Meuang.

Ranong Immigration Office (Th Chalermprakiat; 8.30am-5pm) Main immigration office, 4km southwest of town; handles visa extensions.

Ranong Immigration Post (Tha Saphan Plaa; 8am-5pm) If you're just popping in and out of Myanmar's Kawthoung, visiting this small immigration post, 5km southwest of town, is sufficient.

Getting There & Away

AIR

Ranong Airport is 22km south of town. **Nok Air** (02 900 9955; www.nokair.com) flies twice daily to Bangkok (Don Muang).

BUS

The **bus terminal** (Th Phetkasem) is 1km southeast of the centre. *Sŏrng·tăa·ou* 2 (blue) passes the terminal. From here, minivans head to Surat Thani (190B, 3½ hours, 6am and 2pm) and Chumphon (150B, two hours, hourly 7am to 5pm).

Getting Around

Motorcycle taxis (50B) take you almost anywhere in town, including **Tha Saphan Plaa**, 5km southwest of the centre, for boats to Myanmar, and **Tha Ko Phayam**, 6km southwest of the centre, for Ko Chang and Ko Phayam. *Sŏrng·tăa·ou* 4 (red) stops near the piers (20B).

Pon's Place (p590) helps with motorcycle and car rentals and offers shuttle vans from its office/the airport to the piers (70/200B).

Ko Chang เกาะช้าง

This little-visited rustic isle is a long way (in every respect) from its much more popular Trat Province namesake. The speciality here is no-frills living, and, yes, electricity and wi-fi are frills here, but their absence from most places gives as much as it denies. An all-pervading quiet saturates 'Little Ko Chang'. The buzz of modern life is replaced by the slosh of the sea, the murmur of cicadas or the far-off rumbling of a long-tail. In the fringe and low-season months, it's beyond mellow.

Wide west-coast **Ao Yai** (Long Beach) has gorgeous marbled white-black sand in the south, which obscures the otherwise clear sea. White-sand snobs will be happiest on Ao Yai's north end. A short trail leads south over the bluff to **Ao Tadaeng**, a boulder-strewn beach and the island's best sunset spot.

Stroll the beaches, explore the tiny village capital (halfway between east and west coasts) or wind around the island's dirt trails. If you're lucky, you'll spot sea eagles, Andaman kites and hornbills floating above the mangroves and the jungled east coast. Trails lead south from the village and Ao Yai to west-coast **Ao Kai To** and the park ranger station, where you'll find the island's best stretch of intact jungle; elsewhere it's been tamed into cashew orchards and rubber plantations.

Activities

Aladdin Dive Safari DIVING
(087 274 7601; www.aladdindivesafari.com; Cashew Resort, Ao Yai; 2/3 dives 4900/6500B,

3-day live-aboard 15,800-19,800B; ⌚10am-6pm Nov-Apr) A relatively flash live-aboard operation that runs day trips to the Surin and Similan Islands, Open Water Diver (OWD) courses (18,700B to 19,800B) and live-aboards to Myanmar's Mergui Archipelago, the Surins, the Similans, Ko Phi-Phi, Hin Daeng and Hin Muang.

Om Tao YOGA
(☎085 470 9312; www.omtao.net; Ao Yai; class 300B) German-run studio with daily yoga (8.30am) November to April. Classes are by request at other times; tai chi and qi-gong also offered.

Sleeping & Eating

Basic bamboo huts reign supreme on Ko Chang. They're mostly only open from November to mid-April. Electricity is limited; a few places have solar and wind power.

Ao Yai is where you'll find most lodgings. A few more places are tucked away on Ao Tadaeng, immediately south, and linked to Ao Yai via a short walking track. More isolated options lie on the beaches to the north and far south of the island.

★**Crocodile Rock** GUESTHOUSE $
(☎080 533 4138; tonn1970@yahoo.com; Ao Yai; bungalows 400-700B) Outstanding bamboo bungalows perched on Ao Yai's serene southern headland with superb bay views. The classy kitchen turns out homemade yoghurt, breads, cookies, good espresso, and a variety of vegie and seafood dishes. It's popular, so book ahead.

Little Italy BUNGALOW $
(☎084 851 2760; daniel060863@yahoo.it; Ao Yai; r 400-650B) Just three immaculate bungalows attached to an Italian restaurant amid the trees towards the southern end of Ao Yai. Two are stilted split-level concrete-and-wood jobs encircled by wraparound verandas. The third concrete bungalow is back on earth, with a tiled bathroom. At research time, the friendly Italian owner was planning upgrades, so prices may rise. Book well ahead.

Sunset Bungalows BUNGALOW $
(☎084 339 5224; Ao Yai; bungalows 300-500B; ⌚Oct–mid-Apr) Sweet wooden bungalows with bamboo decks and attached Thai-style bathrooms sit back in the trees along Ao Yai's finest (northern) patch of beach. Staff are as friendly as they come.

Sawasdee BUNGALOW $
(☎086 906 0900; www.sawadeekohchang.com; Ao Yai; bungalows 350-950B; ⌚Nov–mid-Apr) A-frame wooden bungalows have vented walls to keep things cool, sunken bathrooms painted bright colours and hammocks on terraces, at the southern end of Ao Yai.

Eden BUNGALOW $
(☎080 628 7590; Ao Yai; r 200-300B) These rickety, barebones-basic bungalows (forget bathrooms doors) and no-frills shared-shower rooms at the north end of Ao Yai are kept clean by a friendly family who'll whip you up a sensational massaman curry. It's popular with returnees, electricity runs 6pm to 11pm and there's a social beachside bar-restaurant.

Information

There are no banks or cars, but wi-fi has arrived at a few shops and resorts, including Koh Chang Resort (southern Ao Yai).

Getting There & Around

From Ranong, *sŏrng·tăa·ou* (20B) or motorcycle taxis (50B) go from Th Ruangrat to Tha Ko Phayam (p593) near Saphan Plaa.

Two daily long-tail taxi boats (150B, two hours) leave for Ko Chang at 9.30am and 1pm. In high season, they stop at the west-coast beaches, returning at approximately 8.30am and 1.30pm. During the monsoon, only morning long-tails make the crossing (weather permitting), docking at the main pier on the northeast coast.

During the November-to-April high season, several daily speedboats (350B, 30 minutes, 8am to 4.30pm) run between Ranong's Tha Ko Phayam and Ko Chang's northeast-coast pier.

High-season Ko Phayam–Ranong speedboats often drop off and pick up passengers in Ko Chang (350B) on request, though they're unreliable; get your resort to make (and confirm!) the booking. You can charter long-tails to Ko Phayam (2000B) through Koh Chang Resort.

Motorcycle taxis meet boats, charging 100B between the northeast-coast pier and Ao Yai.

Ko Phayam เกาะพยาม

Technically part of Laem Son National Park (p596), increasingly popular Ko Phayam is fringed with beautiful soft-white beaches and, for now, is continuing to go mainstream while still holding onto its soul. If you're coming from Phuket or Ko Phi-Phi, it'll feel refreshingly wild and dozy. The spectacular northwest and southwest coasts are dotted with rustic bungalows, small-scale resorts, breezy sand-side restaurants and barefoot beach bars. Fauna includes wild pigs, monkeys, snakes and tremendous bird life (sea eagles, herons, hornbills).

The island's one 'village' (on the east coast, beside the main pier) caters mostly to tourists. But hit it during a festival (say the February Cashew Festival) and you'll see that islanders still have a firm grip on their homeland.

Narrow motorcycle pathways, concrete roadways and dirt trails run across the island's wooded interior; some are rutted to the point of hazardous – drive slowly.

Sights & Activities

Ko Phayam's main drawback is that the snorkelling isn't great; high sea temperatures have killed off all the coral. But the Surin Islands are close, and you can hop on live-aboard dive expeditions or speedboat transfers.

Wat Phayam BUDDHIST TEMPLE
(วัดเกาะพยาม; dawn-dusk) FREE Shrouded in jungle just north of the main pier, on Ko Phayam's east coast, you'll find a majestic golden Buddha flanked by a three-headed *naga* (mythical serpent).

Phayam Divers DIVING
(086 995 2598; www.phayamlodge.com; Ao Yai; 2 dives 6400B, 3-day live-aboard 16,000-17,000B; Nov-Apr) At the north end of Ao Yai. Offers one-day snorkelling (4000B) and dive trips to the Surins, plus multi-day live-aboards to the Surins, Ko Tachai and Ko Bon.

Aladdin Dive Safari DIVING
(087 274 7601; www.aladdindivesafari.com; Ao Yai; 2/3 dives 4900/6500B, 3-day live-aboard 15,800-19,800B; 8am-8pm Nov-Apr) A relatively flash live-aboard operation, 500m inland from central Ao Yai. It runs day trips to the Surin and Similan Islands, Open Water Diver courses (18,700B to 19,800B) and live-aboards to Myanmar's Mergui Archipelago, the Surins, the Similans, Ko Phi-Phi, Hin Daeng and Hin Muang.

Sleeping & Eating

Room capacity has sky-rocketed in recent years. Many resorts now stay open year-round, with attached eateries serving middling Thai fare. The best, cheapest Thai eats are in town near the pier. Plenty of resorts have 24-hour power, though some still have limited electricity.

The most popular beaches to use as a base are Ao Yai, to the southwest, and Ao Khao Kwai to the northwest. Other quieter, less known options are the east-coast beaches of Ao Hin Khow and Ao Mea Mai, north and south of the pier respectively

Ao Yai อ่าวใหญ่

Aow Yai Bungalows BUNGALOW $
(083 389 8688; www.aowyai.com; bungalows 400-800B;) This French-Thai operation, southeast end of Ao Yai, is the thatched bamboo bungalow pioneer that kicked it all off two decades ago. Choose between decent, rustic small wooden-and-bamboo bungalows amid towering palms and pines, and larger beachfront wood models or concrete bungalows. Electricity 10am to 3am.

Frog Beach House HOTEL $
(083 542 7559; www.frogbeachhouse.com; bungalows 500-1400B;) Well-kept, traditional Thai-style hardwood chalets with wooden floors, outdoor bathrooms, glass sinks and mosquito nets line up behind a nice slab of sand beside a small stream at the north end of Ao Yai.

Cede BOUTIQUE HOTEL $$
(081 622 6464; cedekohphayam@gmail.com; r 2000-2400B;) A 2015 baby, Italian-run Cede brings a dash of low-key sophistication to northwest end of Ao Yai. Interiors are gleaming, boutique-y and inviting; two front rooms soak in sea panoramas. Star of the show is the sprawling wide-open beachfront bar-restaurant deck. There's 24-hour electricity, along with evenings-only air-con, a coffee shop and motorbike rental (200B).

Ban Nam Cha INTERNATIONAL $
(dishes 100-180B; 9am-6.30pm, hours vary;) Twinkling lights, prayer flags and driftwood signs adorn this artsy, easygoing food shack. Tuck into fantastic homemade panini (garlic mushroom, cashew-nut pesto), sandwiches, cakes and a range of Burmese, European and vegetarian treats, and peruse a paperback from the lending library. It's 500m inland from central Ao Yai.

Ao Khao Kwai อ่าวเขาควาย

Heaven Beach BUNGALOW $$
(082 806 0413; www.ppland-heavenbeach.com; r 1500-2000B;) A sweet four-year-old resort on an idyllic slice of central beachfront real estate. Tiled bungalows in shades of pastel are cutesy, characterful and super-spacious without losing comfort, and feature flower motifs, open-air bathrooms, hot showers,

all-day electricity and wide decks with rattan lounges.

Mr Gao BUNGALOW $$

(☎077 870222; www.mr-gao-phayam.com; bungalow 1200-1600B; ⊙Nov-Apr;) These sturdy, varnished wood-and-brick or bamboo bungalows in the centre of Ao Khao Kwai are popular with activity-oriented couples and families and have character, mosquito nets, tiled bathrooms and front decks. The owner arranges kayak rental, snorkelling and multiday trips to the Surin Islands. A makeover (including 24-hour electricity) was underway at research time in 2015.

Baan Klong Kleng BUNGALOW $$

(☎089 772 5090; www.baanklongkleng.com; r 1200-1700B; ⊙mid-Oct–Apr;) Simple, clean wooden bungalows cascade through trees to a luscious chunk of beach. They're comfy, if not overly exciting, with stylish ceramic-bowl sinks and semi-open bathrooms. The fabulous open-walled beachside **restaurant** (mains 140-180B; ⊙8am-10pm mid-Oct-Apr;) has a fun vibe, dishing up fragrant Thai curries (veg versions available), delicious breakfasts and fusion specials like green-curry pasta. It's in the centre of Ao Khao Kwai.

Ao Hin Khow & Ao Mea Mai อ่าวหินขาว/อ่าวแม่หม้าย

★PP Land BUNGALOW $

(☎081 678 4310; www.ppland-heavenbeach.com; Ao Hin Khow; bungalows 700-1400B;) A stunning Thai-Belgian–owned ecolodge, just north of the pier on the little-visited east coast. Beautifully designed concrete bungalows are powered by wind and sun, with 24-hour electricity and hammocks on terraces overlooking the sea. The knowledgeable owners bake cakes, run an organic garden, treat sewage and make their own all-natural laundry detergent. Excellent value.

Sabai Sabai BUNGALOW $

(☎087 895 4653; www.sabai-bungalows.com; Ao Mea Mai; bungalows 250-1400B;) Five minutes' walk south of the east-coast pier, this fab, social travellers' hideaway has heaps of clean, (mostly) fan-cooled, budget-friendly options. Cheap and cheerful bamboo huts share bathrooms. Simple doubles come with sea views, sunken bathrooms and plenty of style. Best is the two-floor, loft-style room with balcony. There's a chilled-out bar, plus hammocks, movie nights and electricity 8am to 1am.

Information

Many resorts now have wi-fi. There are no ATMs; get cash out in Ranong before heading over to Ko Phayam.

Getting There & Away

A daily 10am ferry runs from Ranong's Tha Ko Phayam (p593), 6km southwest of town, to Ko Phayam itself (200B, two hours), returning at 3pm. During the November-to-April high season, speedboats (350B, 35 minutes) make the run at least hourly from 7.45am to 4.30pm, returning to the mainland at 8am, 9am, 9.30am, 11.30am, noon, 3.30pm, 4pm and 4.30pm. High-season speedboats go from Ko Phayam to Ko Chang (350B, 20 minutes) en route to Ranong at 8.30am, 9am, noon, 12.30pm, 3pm and 3.30pm, though they aren't 100% reliable.

Getting Around

Ko Phayam has no cars. Motorcycle taxis from the pier to Ao Khao Kwai/Ao Yai cost 50/80B. Walking distances are long; it's about 45 minutes from the pier to Ao Khao Kwai, the nearest bay. You can rent motorbikes (200B) in the village (best) and from larger resorts; you'll need one to explore properly.

Laem Son National Park อุทยานแห่งชาติแหลมสน

This serene 315-sq-km **national park** (☎077 861431; www.dnp.go.th; adult/child 200/100B; ⊙8am-4.30pm) covers 60km of Andaman coastline (Thailand's longest protected shore) and over 20 islands, including much-loved Ko Phayam (p594). It's 85% open sea. Much of the coast is fringed by mangroves and laced with tidal channels, home to fish, deer, macaques, civets, giant squirrels and over 100 bird species, including white-bellied sea eagles.

The most accessible beach is gorgeous, casuarina-backed 3km **Hat Bang Ben**, home to the park headquarters and accommodation. To the south, peninsulas jut out into the ocean concealing isolated coves accessible only by long-tail. All these beaches are allegedly safe for swimming year-round. From Hat Bang Ben, spot Ko Kam Yai, Ko Kam Noi, Mu Ko Yipun, Ko Khang Khao and, to the north, Ko Phayam. If there's a prettier sunset picnic spot in the northern Andaman, we missed it.

Hat Praphat, 56km south of Hat Bang Ben, is a turtle nesting ground.

Activities

Nature trails wind off from the park headquarters, where you can arrange one-day boat trips (2500B, maximum 10 people) to nearby islands. Turn left (south) towards the pier just before park headquarters to access the beach without paying park fees.

Sleeping & Eating

Most accommodation is at Hat Bang Ben.

Wasana Resort BUNGALOW **$**
(077 861434; www.wasanaresort.org; Hat Bang Ben; bungalow fan 450B, air-con 650-750B;) A family-run ring of cosy concrete bungalows with bamboo beds wraps around the colourful on-site **restaurant** (mains 80-200B; 7.30am-9pm). The welcoming Dutch-Thai owners make a gloriously authentic gado-gado, organise Laem Son day trips, lend bicycles and are full of fantastic ideas for exploring the park (ask about the stunning 10km trek around the headland). If you've booked, they'll collect you from the highway.

There are larger four-person bungalows for families.

Laem Son National Park Accommodation BUNGALOW, CAMPGROUND **$$**
(077 861431, in Bangkok 02 562 0760; www.dnp.go.th; Hat Bang Ben; d/q 1000/1800B, camp site per person 30B, with tent hire 270B;) Simple air-conditioned concrete bungalows under a shady beachside casuarina canopy, or camping in the grounds or on the sand.

Getting There & Away

The Laem Son National Park turn-off is 44km south of Ranong on the west side of Hwy 4, between the Km 657 and Km 658 markers. Buses heading south from Ranong will drop you here (ask for Hat Bang Ben; 65B, one hour). You'll have to flag down a vehicle going towards the park or grab a taxi (200B) at the roadside agency. It's 10km from Hwy 4 to the park entrance.

PHANG-NGA PROVINCE

Phang-Nga's jungle mountains are carved up by muddy rivers leading to aqua bays sprinkled with limestone karsts and, below, some of Thailand's finest underwater treasures.

More than a decade after the 2004 Boxing Day tsunami, Phang-Nga's touristy areas feel pretty much back to normal. There's a tangible sense of progress, especially around Khao Lak, which has surpassed all prior expectations of development. Many fishing communities, however, have had their way of life changed forever, either by the loss of key family members, the destruction of fishing equipment or being forced to relocate inland.

Phang-Nga remains very seasonal. From mid-October to mid-April, visitors descend en masse for its clear waters, white beaches and colourful reefs. Many establishments close during the May-to-October monsoon, when the region feels slightly haunted.

Khuraburi คุระบุรี

Blink and you'll miss it. But, if you keep your eyes wide open, you'll enjoy this soulful, roadside gateway to the Surin Islands and some of southern Thailand's best community-based tourism opportunities. For local inhabitants, Khuraburi is a market town relied on by hundreds of squid fishermen.

For tourist information, contact **Tom & Am Tour** (086 272 0588; 298/1 Mu 1, Hwy 4; 24hr), opposite the bus station road.

Tours

Andaman Discoveries TOUR
(087 917 7165; www.andamandiscoveries.com; 120/1 Mu 1, Khuraburi; 3-day trip per person 6000B; 8.30am-5.30pm Mon-Fri) Highly recommended community-based one- and multi-day tours, featuring cycling, cultural and handicraft activities, snorkelling trips, village homestays on Ko Phra Thong and ecotours to Khao Sok National Park. They also manage community projects that take volunteers.

Sleeping & Eating

★**Boon Piya Resort** GUESTHOUSE **$**
(081 752 5457; 175/1 Th Phetkasem; bungalows 650B;) In a garden compound just off the main road at Khuraburi's north end, these spacious, modern concrete bungalows with tiled floors, hot-water bathrooms and little balconies are a wonderful surprise. The helpful owner books transport to/from the Surin Islands and Ko Phra Thong.

Morning Market MARKET **$**
(Hwy 4; dishes 20-40B; 6-10am) Don't miss the morning market at the north end of town. Stalls fry chicken, grill coconut waffles, and bubble kettles with Thai doughnuts to be dipped in thick, sugary green curry. Tea (10B) arrives caramel coloured and floating on a layer of condensed milk. You'll be among very few *fa·ràng* (Westerners) here.

Getting There & Around

Most buses running between Ranong (105B, two hours) and Phuket (150B, four hours) stop in Khuraburi. Take a Phuket-bound bus to Takua Pa (70B, 1½ hours), 55km south, to transfer to further destinations including Khao Sok National Park.

The pier for the Surin Islands and Ko Phra Thong is 9km northwest of town. Whoever books your boat to the islands will arrange free pier transfer.

Surin Islands Marine National Park

อุทยานแห่งชาติหมู่เกาะสุรินทร์

The five gorgeous isles of the **Surin Islands Marine National Park** (☎076 472145; www.dnp.go.th; adult/child 500/300B; ⏱mid-Oct–mid-May) sit 60km offshore, 5km from the Thailand–Myanmar marine border. Healthy rainforest, pockets of white-sand beach in sheltered bays and rocky headlands that jut into the ocean characterise these granite-outcrop islands. Perfectly clear water makes for easy marine-life spotting, with underwater visibility of up to 30m outside monsoon. These shielded waters attract *chow lair* (sea gypsies; also spelt *chao leh*), an ethnic group of Malay origin who live on Ko Surin Tai during the May-to-November monsoon. Here they're known as Moken, from the local word *oken* ('salt water').

The spectacular flaxen sand, the purpling depths, the sparkling bays in never-ending shades of jade and turquoise, and the sheer granite peninsulas that tumble down in a permanent geological avalanche, forming arrow-like points and natural breakwaters, are what you'll remember.

Ko Surin Tai (south) and Ko Surin Neua (north) are the two largest islands. Park headquarters, an **information office** (⏱7.30am-8.30pm mid-Oct–mid-May) and all visitor facilities are at Ao Chong Khad on southwest Ko Surin Neua.

Khuraburi is the park's jumping-off point. The pier is 9km northwest of town, alongside the helpful mainland **national park office** (☎076 472145; www.dnp.go.th; Tha Khuraburi; ⏱8.30am-4.30pm mid-Oct–mid-May).

Sights & Activities

Ban Moken VILLAGE

(Ao Bon, Ko Surin Tai) Ban Moken on east Ko Surin Tai welcomes visitors. Post-tsunami, the Moken (from the Sea Gypsy ethnic group) have re-settled in this sheltered bay, where a major ancestral worship ceremony, **Loi Reua** takes place each April. The colourfully carved *labong* poles dotted around embody Moken ancestors. This population experienced no casualties during the 2004 Boxing Day tsunami that wiped out the village, because they understood nature's signs and evacuated to the hilltop.

The Surin Islands Marine National Park runs two-hour trips from Ko Surin Neua to Ban Moken (per person 150B, minimum five people). You'll stroll through the stilted village, where you can ask permission/guidance for hiking the 800m **Chok Madah trail** over the jungled hills to an empty beach. Handicrafts for sale help support the local economy and clothing donations are accepted. Please refrain from bringing along alcohol and sweets; alcoholism is a growing problem among Moken.

Diving & Snorkelling

The park's dive sites include **Ko Surin Tai**, **Ko Torinla** (south) and **HQ Channel** between the two main islands. **Richelieu Rock**, a seamount 14km southeast, is also technically in the park and happens to be one of the Andaman's best dive sites (if not *the* best). Manta rays pay visits and whale sharks are sometimes spotted here during March and April.

There's no dive facility inside the park, so dive trips (four-day live-aboards from 20,000B) must be booked through centres in Khao Lak (p602), Phuket (p613) and Ranong (p590). Transfers are usually included. There's a 200B park diving fee per day, plus the national park fee (adult/child 500/300B), which is valid for five days.

Though recent bleaching of hard corals means snorkelling isn't quite as fantastic as it once was, you'll still see plenty of colourful fish and soft corals. The most vibrant soft corals we saw were at **Ao Mai Yai**, off southwest Ko Surin Neua. There's good snorkelling at **Ao Sabparod** and **Ao Pak Kaad**, where you might spot turtles, off east and south Ko Surin Tai. More fish swim off tiny **Ko Pajumba**, but the coral isn't great. **Ao Suthep**, off north Ko Surin Tai, has hundreds of colourful fish.

The nearest decompression chamber is in Phuket. In the case of an accident, dive operators will contact the chamber's Khao Lak–based SSS Ambulance (p606), which meets boats and rushes injured divers south to Phuket.

Half-day snorkelling trips (per person 150B, snorkel hire 160B) leave the island headquarters at 9am and 2pm. You'll be mostly in the company of Thais, who generally splash around fully clothed in life jackets. For more serene snorkelling, charter a long-tail from the national park (per day 3000B) or, better yet, directly from the Moken in Ban Moken (p598).

Tour operators in Khuraburi (p597) and Khao Lak (p602) organise snorkelling day trips to the park (adult/child 3500/2100B).

Greenview SNORKELLING

(☎076 472070; greenviewtour99@gmail.com; Tha Khuraburi; adult/child one-day tour 3500/2100B; ⏲7.30am-9pm) Impressive in safety, service and value, Greenview runs excellent Surin Islands snorkelling day trips with knowledgeable guides. Rates include transfers, snacks, equipment and a delicious lunch. Also organises multi-night stays in the Surins.

Wildlife & Hiking

Around park headquarters, you can explore the forest fringes and spot crab-eating macaques and some of the 57 resident bird species, including the beautiful Nicobar pigeon, endemic to the Andaman islands, and the elusive beach thick-knee. Along the coast you're likely to see Brahminy kites and reef herons. Twelve species of bat live here, most noticeably the tree-dwelling fruit bat (flying fox).

Nature Trail WALKING

(Ko Surin Neua) FREE Behind Ao Chong Khad's campground, a rough-and-ready nature trail winds 2km along the coast and through forest to the campsite at Ao Mai Ngam. At low tide, it's easy to stroll along the coast between the two campsites.

Sleeping & Eating

Park accommodation is decent, though it can feel seriously crowded when full (around 300 people). The clientele is mostly Thai, giving the place a lively holiday-camp vibe.

Surin Islands Marine National Park Accommodation BUNGALOW, CAMPGROUND $$

(☎076 472145; www.dnp.go.th; Ko Surin Neua; d/q 2000/3000B, camping site per person 80B, with tent hire 300B; ⏲mid-Oct–mid-May; ❄) Bungalows, at Ao Chong Khad, have wooden floors, private bathrooms, front terraces and fans from 9.30pm to 7am or air-con from 6pm to 9.30pm. Electricity runs 6pm to 7am. You can camp on Ao Chong Khad and Ao Mai Ngam. The former has the more spectacular beach; the latter fills up last, is more secluded and, with its narrow shallow white-sand bay, feels wilder.

Book ahead online or through the mainland national park office.

Ao Chong Khad Restaurant THAI $$

(Ko Surin Neua; mains 80-180B, set menu 120-280B; ⏲7.30-9am, noon-2pm & 6.30-8pm) The park restaurant on Ko Surin Neua serves authentically good Thai food. This is where day trips stop for lunch.

Ao Mai Ngam Restaurant THAI $$

(Ko Surin Neua; mains 80-180B, set menu 120-280B; ⏲7.30-9am, noon-2pm & 6.30-8pm) The national park's restaurant at Ao Mai Ngam does decent Thai food.

Getting There & Away

Tour operator speedboats (return 1700B, 1¼ hours one-way) leave around 9am, return between 1pm and 4pm and honour open tickets. Return whenever you please, but confirm your ticket with Ko Surin Neua's park office the night before.

Ko Phra Thong & Ko Ra

เกาะพระทอง/เกาะระ

According to legend, many centuries ago, pirates buried a golden Buddha beneath the sands at Ko Phra Thong (Golden Buddha Island). The statue was never found, but the island's modern-day treasures are its endless sandy beaches, mangroves, vast bird life and rare orchids.

This long, slender, wooded island is as quiet as a night on the open ocean. Fishing (squid, prawns, jellyfish) remains its key industry; the local delicacy is pungent *gà·Ъì* (fermented prawn paste). On the southern west coast lies 10km of virgin golden-sand beach kissed by blue sea.

Immediately north is even quieter Ko Ra, encircled by golden beaches and mangroves. This small isle is a mountainous jungled slab with impressive wildlife (including over 100 bird species, leopard cats, flying lemurs, wild pigs, monitor lizards, scaly anteaters and slow lorises) and a welcoming population of fisherfolk.

Sleeping & Eating

Mr Chuoi's BUNGALOW $

(☎084 855 9886, 087 898 4636; www.mrchuoibarandhut.com; Ko Phra Thong; bungalows 500-1200B) Simple, wood-and-bamboo bungalows, on the island's northwest coast, with evening electricity. You'll also find a fun bar and excellent restaurant, enlivened by Mr Chuoi himself. Call ahead and he'll arrange transport to Ko Phra Thong.

Horizon BUNGALOW $$
(081 894 7195; www.horizonecoresort.com; Ko Phra Thong; d 1300-1900B) This northwest beach ecolodge has seven roomy, shaggy-haired, wood-and-bamboo bungalows made from natural local products from renewable sources (wherever possible); they only use fansa and sleep two or four. Horizon organises hiking tours to neighbouring Ko Ra (1600B, minimum three people) and has the island's only dive school, **Blue Guru** (080 144 0551; www.blue-guru.org; 2 dives 4500-6500B), ideally positioned for underwater explorations of the nearby Surin Islands.

★ **Golden Buddha Beach Resort** BUNGALOW $$$
(081 895 2242, 081 892 2208; www.goldenbuddharesort.com; Ko Phra Thong; bungalows 2700-14,000B;) The area's poshest resort attracts yogis, couples and families keen for a secluded getaway. Accommodation is in uniquely designed, naturalistic-chic, privately owned wooden houses, short- or long-term; there are big family-sized house options too. Rooms have open-air bathrooms, wood-carved interiors and glimpses of the fabulous 10km beach through surrounding forest and gardens. Everyone congregates at the mosaic-floored club house **restaurant-bar** (mains 220-300B; 7.30am-9.30pm;).

Getting There & Away

You could theoretically charter a long-tail from the Khuraburi pier to Ko Phra Thong (one-way around 1500B); but boatmen are hard to find. It's worth enquiring in Khuraburi about the 'daily local ferry' to the island, though timings and reliability vary. It's easiest to contact your resort in advance to arrange transport.

Khao Sok National Park อุทยานแห่งชาติเขาสก

If your leg muscles have atrophied after too much beach-bumming, venture inland to the wondrous 738-sq-km **Khao Sok National Park** (077 395154; www.khaosok.com; adult/child 300/150B; 8am-5pm), halfway between the Andaman and Gulf coasts. Many believe this lowland jungle (Thailand's rainiest spot) is over 160 million years old, one of the world's oldest rainforests. Dramatic limestone formations and waterfalls cascade through juicy thickets drenched with rain and morning dew. A network of dirt trails snakes through, allowing visitors to spy on an exciting array of indigenous creatures.

Khao Sok's vast terrain makes it one of the last viable habitats for large mammals. During rainy months you may spot bears, boars, gaurs, tapirs, gibbons, deer, marbled cats, wild elephants and perhaps even a tiger. And you'll find more than 300 bird species, 38 bat varieties and one of the world's largest (and smelliest) flowers, the increasingly rare *Rafflesia kerrii*, which, in Thailand, lives only in Khao Sok. These giant flowers can reach 80cm in diameter.

The best time to visit is during the December-to-April dry season. During the June-to-October monsoon, trails get slippery, flash flooding is common and leeches come out in force, though European summer holidays keep the park busy. Animals leave their hidden reservoirs throughout the wet months, so you're more likely to stumble across big fauna.

Sights & Activities

Kayaking (700B), rafting (1100B; high season) and tubing (400B; rainy season) are popular activities. Elephant rides are available, but it's worth reading up on the animal welfare issues involved (p327) if you're considering these.

The road leading 1.8km northeast from Rte 401 to park headquarters is lined with simple, sweet guesthouses offering park tours and guide services. We recommend a two-day, one-night canoeing and hiking trip (per person 2500B) to Chiaw Lan, where you sleep on the lake in floating huts. Book through the park headquarters (p602) or any tour agency.

Chiaw Lan Lake LAKE
(เขื่อนเชี่ยวหลาน; day/overnight trip 1500/2500B) This stunning 165-sq-km lake sits 65km (an hour's drive) east of park headquarters. It was created in 1982 by an enormous shale-clay dam called Ratchaprapha (Kheuan Ratchaprapha or Chiaw Lan). Limestone outcrops protruding from the lake reach up to 960m, over three times higher than Phang-Nga's formations. Most lake visits involve a day or overnight tour (including transfers, boats and guides). Charter boats (per day 2000B) from local fishermen at the

dam's entrance to explore the coves, canals, caves and cul-de-sacs along the lakeshore.

Two caves can be accessed by foot from the southwestern shore. **Tham Nam Thalu** FREE, contains striking limestone formations and subterranean streams. Visiting during the rainy season isn't recommended; there have been fatalities. **Tham Si Ru** FREE features four converging passageways used as a hideout by communist insurgents between 1975 and 1982.

Hiking

Khao Sok hiking is excellent. Most guesthouses and agencies arrange hiking tours (full day 1500B to 2000B); just ensure you find a certified guide (they wear official badges).

The park headquarters (p602) hands out hiking maps. You can hike independently from the headquarters to waterfalls at **Wing Hin** (2.8km) and **Bang Hua Rad** (3km). Hikes to the waterfalls at **Than Sawan** (6km) and **Than Kloy** (7km) require guides. At research time, the 4km trail to the 11-tiered waterfall at **Sip-Et Chan** was off-limits.

Sleeping & Eating

Jungle Huts BUNGALOW $

(077 395160; www.khaosokjunglehuts.com; 242 Mu 6; r fan 300-700B, air-con 1000B;) This popular budget hang-out, 1km northeast off Rte 401, contains an ever-growing collection of decent, individually styled bungalows, all with bathrooms and porches. Choose from plain stilted bamboo huts, bigger wooden editions, pink-washed concrete bungalows, or air-con rooms along vertiginous walkways.

Art's Riverview Jungle Lodge GUESTHOUSE $$

(098 826 6967, 090 167 6818; www.facebook.com/Arts-Riverview-Lodge-Travel-1562090180732965; 54/3 Mu 6; bungalows fan 650-1000B, air-con 1200-1500B;) In a monkey-filled jungle bordering a rushing river with a limestone cliff-framed swimming hole, Art's enjoys Khao Sok's prettiest setting. Stilted brick, shingled and all-wood bungalows are spacious and comfy, many with river views, though they could use a refresh. There's a variety of rooms, including family-sized options, and a host of family-friendly activities. It's signposted 1.5km northeast off Rte 401.

Tree Tops River Huts BUNGALOW $$

(077 395129, 087 862 9656; www.treetopsriverhuts.com; d fan/air-con 1000/1300B;) Clean and sturdy, if ageing, fan-cooled bungalows with porches sit high on stilts in the trees at this busy riverside spot overlooking park headquarters. Stone-walled air-con rooms are perfectly comfy, though less exciting. All have hot showers.

> **KHAO SOK TOURS**
>
> Tours in and around Khao Sok can be up to 50% cheaper when booked through guesthouses or travel agents around the park itself. Tours booked from further-afield destinations (Phuket or Khao Lak) include higher-priced transport and tour agent commissions.

★ **Elephant Hills** RESORT $$$

(076 381703; www.elephanthills.com; 170 Mu 7, Tambon Klong Sok; d all-inclusive from 13,585B;) Whether you're a five-strong family, honeymooning backpacker couple or a soloist, this resort makes everyone smile. Above Mae Nam Sok, at the foot of stunning limestone mountains draped in misty jungle, Khao Sok's only top-end tented camp offers rootsy Serengeti-style luxury. Airy tents have wood furnishings, full bathrooms, skylights and hammocks on porches.

All-inclusive prices cover meals, guided hikes and canoe trips downriver to its elephant camp, where 12 lovely ladies (rescues from other camps where they were forced to carry tourists around) are treated kindly. You can't ride them, but you get to feed, bathe, and spend quality time with them. It's a special experience. Consider adding a night at their floating **Rainforest Camp** (076 381703; www.elephanthills.com; Chiaw Lan Lake; d all-inclusive from 19,355B). Reservations only.

Jasmine Garden RESORT $$$

(082 282 3209; www.khaosokjasmine.com; 35/6 Mu 6; d/q 2200/3000B;) A 2015 arrival, family-run Jasmine hosts some of Khao Sok's classiest non-luxury lodgings, plus cooking classes (800B). Orange-toned concrete bungalows open onto roomy terraces overlooking a warm-blue pool with sensational cliff vistas. Delicate interiors involve wood-carved beds, Buddha paintings, tiled floors and plenty of teak. It's 1km northeast off Rte 401.

Pawn's Restaurant THAI $

(park access road; mains 100-150B; 9am-9pm;) A friendly all-female team heads up this humble eatery: your go-to spot for deliciously spiced curries, from searing red pumpkin-and-veg to beautifully creamy tofu or chicken massaman, and huge hearty breakfasts. It's 500m southwest of park headquarters.

Information

There are many ATMS. Most guesthouses have wi-fi.

Khao Sok National Park Headquarters (077 395154; www.khaosok.com; 8am-5pm) About 1.8km northeast off Rte 401, exiting near the Km 109 marker; helpful maps and information.

Getting There & Around

From Surat catch a bus going towards Takua Pa; from the Andaman coast, take a Surat Thani–bound bus. Buses stop on Rte 401, 1.8km southwest of the visitors centre. If touts don't meet you, you'll have to walk to your chosen guesthouse (50m to 2km).

Daily minivan departures include the following:

DESTINATION	FARE (B)	DURATION (HR)
Bangkok	850	11
Khao Lak	150	1¼
Ko Lanta	750	5
Ko Tao	1100	8
Krabi	350	3
Surat Thani	250	1

Khao Lak & Around เขาหลัก

When people refer to Khao Lak, they're usually talking about a series of white-sand beaches hugging Phang-Nga's west coastline, backed by forested hills, about 70km north of Phuket. With easy day trips to the Similan and Surin Islands, Khao Sok and Khao Lak/Lam Ru National Parks, or even Phuket, the area is a central, kick-back base for exploring the northern Andaman.

Southernmost **Hat Khao Lak** gives way to **Hat Nang Thong**, making up a beach for those who shun the glitz and cheesiness of Phuket's bigger resort towns, but still crave comfort, shops and plenty of facilities. Khao Lak proper (Khao Lak Town), a jumble of restaurants, tourist markets and low-rise hotels along grey Hwy 4, is bland but convenient; you'll probably spend your days further afield.

About 2.5km north, **Hat Bang Niang** is a quieter version of sandy bliss with skinnier beaches. **Hat Pakarang** and **Hat Bang Sak**, 12km to 13km north of Hat Khao Lak, are a sleepy, unbroken sandy stretch surrounded by thick mangroves, rolling pasture and plantations of rubber trees forming a wide buffer between the coast and highway. You'll feel like you've really escaped it all here.

Sights

Khao Lak/Lam Ru National Park NATIONAL PARK
(อุทยานแหงชาติเขาหลัก-ลำรู่; 076 485243; www.dnp.go.th; adult/child 200/100B; 8am-4.30pm) Immediately south of Hat Khao Lak, this vast 125-sq-km park is a collage of sea cliffs, 1000m-high hills, beaches, estuaries, waterfalls, forested valleys and mangroves. Wildlife includes hornbills, drongos, tapirs, serows, monkeys, Bengal monitor lizards and Asiatic black bears. The park office and visitors centre, 3km south of Khao Lak proper off Hwy 4, has little printed information, but there's a scenic open-air **restaurant** (mains 100-200B; 8.30am-8.30pm) perched on a shady slope overlooking the sea. From here, there's an easy 3km (one-hour) round-trip nature trail south along the cape to often-deserted **Hat Lek**.

Boat 813 MEMORIAL
(Bang Niang) This police boat was hurled into an open field 1km inland from Hat Bang Niang (2.5km north of central Khao Lak) by the powerful 2004 Boxing Day tsunami. A decade later, it remains the region's most prominent reminder of the disaster. There's a regal monument-worthy entryway and an information booth with a tsunami timeline in Thai and English.

International Tsunami Museum MUSEUM
(พิพิธภัณฑ์สึนามิระหวางประเทศ; Hwy 4, Bang Niang; adult/child 100/50B; 9am-7pm) On Hwy 4, 2.5km north of Khao Lak proper and just north of Boat 813, is the International Tsunami Museum, with English-language displays, photos and videos that spare no detail about the effects of the disaster in one of Thailand's worst hit regions.

Activities

Diving and snorkelling day excursions to the Similan and Surin Islands are immensely popular but, if you can, go for a live-aboard. The islands are around 70km from the mainland (1½ hours by speedboat), so live-aboards allow you a more relaxing trip sans masses of day trippers. Dive shops offer live-aboard trips from around 19,000/35,000B for three-/six-day packages and day trips for 5000B to 6000B.

On these three- to seven-day trips, you'll slink below the ocean's surface up to four

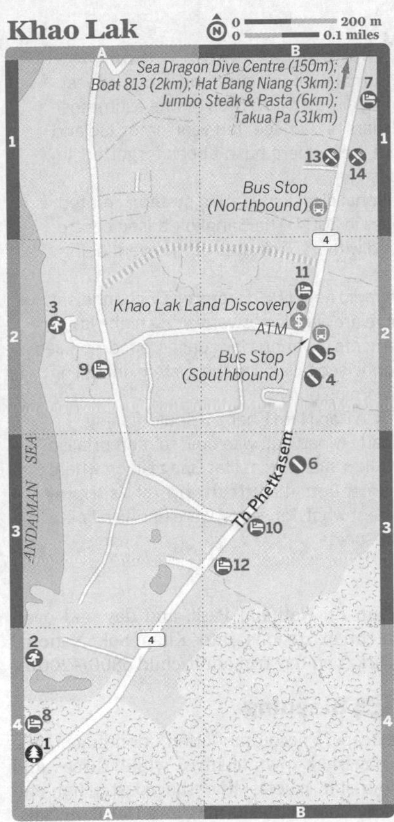

Khao Lak

Sights

1 Khao Lak/Lam Ru National Park........A4

Activities, Courses & Tours

2 Hat Khao Lak........A4
3 Hat Nang Thong........A2
4 IQ Dive........B2
5 Sea Bees........B2
6 Wicked Diving........B3

Sleeping

7 Fasai House........B1
8 Khao Lak/Lam Ru National Park Accommodation........A4
9 Nangthong Bay Resort........A2
10 PhuKhaoLak........B3
11 To Zleep........B2
12 Walker's Inn........B3

Eating

13 Go Pong........B1
14 Jai........B1
Khao Lak/Lam Ru National Park Restaurant........(see 8)
PhuKhaoLak........(see 10)

times daily in what's commonly considered one of the world's top 10 diving realms. While both the Similan and Surin Islands have experienced vast coral bleaching recently, Richelieu Rock (p598) in the Surin Islands is still the crème de la crème of the region's dive sites, frequented by whale sharks from March to April. Ko Bon (p606) and Ko Tachai (p606) are rewarding Similan sites due to the traffic of giant manta rays.

Most dive shops welcome snorkellers on selected day dives and live-aboards, with around 30% discount. Otherwise, tour agencies offer cheaper snorkelling trips to the Similans (1900B). Open Water certification costs between 10,500B and 18,000B, depending on where you dive. Beginners can join one-day Similans Discover Scuba trips for around 6500B. Rates exclude the 700B national park diving fee.

The Similans' dive season runs from mid-October to mid-May, when the national park is open. April and May trips are weather dependent.

★ Wicked Diving DIVING

(☎076 485868; www.wickeddiving.com; Th Phetkasem, Khao Lak; 2 dives 5700B, snorkelling day/overnight trip 2900/8100B; ⊙Oct-May) An exceptionally well-run, environmentally conscious outfit that offers diving and snorkelling day and overnight trips, a range of live-aboards (three-day Similans trip from 20,700B) and conservation trips, and a range of dive courses (PADI Open Water certification costs 17,000B).

★ Fantastic SNORKELLING

(☎076 485998; www.fantasticsimilan.com; adult/child 2300/1700B; ⊙mid-Oct–mid-May) Fantastic is an over-the-top frolic of a Similans snorkelling tour featuring players from the local cross-dressing cabaret as guides. It's a trip duplicated nowhere else on earth; they get you to the prime snorkel sites too. Prices include hotel pick-ups from Phuket or Khao Lak. Bookings essential online or by phone.

Sea Dragon Dive Centre DIVING

(☎076 485420; www.seadragondivecenter.com; Th Phetkasem, Khao Lak; 2 dives 5100B, snorkelling day trip 2700B; ⊙Oct-May) One of Khao Lak's older dive centres, super-efficient Sea Dragon maintains high standards, running

TSUNAMI EARLY WARNING SYSTEM

On 26 December 2004, an earthquake off the Sumatran coast sent enormous waves crashing into Thailand's Andaman coast, claiming almost 5400 lives (some estimates have it much higher) and causing millions of dollars of damage. Ten years later, life and business on this stretch have bounced back, but the incident hasn't been forgotten. In fact, it's inspired action to prevent a repeat disaster.

In 2005, Thailand officially inaugurated a national disaster warning system, created in response to the country's lack of preparedness in 2004. The Bangkok-based centre anticipates that a tsunami warning can be issued within 15 minutes of the event being detected by existing international systems.

The public will be warned via the nationwide radio network, dozens of TV channels and SMS messages. For non-Thai speakers, there are warning towers along high-risk beachfront areas that will broadcast announcements in various languages, accompanied by flashing lights. Recent reports (2014) have criticised failings in the system, including insufficient alert towers and two out-of-action warning buoys.

The wave-shaped **Tsunami Memorial Park** in Ban Nam Khem, a squid-fishing village 26km north of Hat Khao Lak that was nearly wiped out, was built to memorialise those who lost their lives. **Boat 813** (p602) lies 1km inland from Hat Bang Niang where it was deposited by the wave, just around the corner from the **International Tsunami Museum** (p602). The moving memorials augment what, for years, were unofficial pilgrimage sites for those who came to pay their respects.

diving and snorkelling day trips, wreck dives (2600B), Open Water Diver certification (10,500B to 17,500B) and an array of Similan and Surin Islands live-aboards (three-day trip from 12,600B).

Sea Bees DIVING

(☎076 485434; www.seabees.com; Th Phetkasem, Khao Lak; 2 dives 5600B; ⊙mid-Oct–May) This well-organised German-run dive operation offers two-dive Similan day trips, one-day tasters (9600B), Open Water courses (18,050B) and advanced diver courses, plus Similans live-aboards (three-day trip from 18,900B). Snorkellers can join day trips (2800B).

IQ Dive DIVING

(☎076 485614; www.iq-dive.com; Th Phetkasem, Khao Lak; 2/3 dives 5000/6000B) A quality dive school focused on diving and snorkelling (2700B) day trips. Also offers Open Water certification (15,000B to 17,000B), one-day Discover Scuba (6500B), and low-season dives off Phuket and Ko Phi-Phi.

Tours

Khao Lak Land Discovery ADVENTURE TOUR

(☎076 485411; www.khaolaklanddicovery.com; 21/5 Mu 7, Th Phetkasem, Khao Lak; ⊙9am-8pm) This multilingual agency, one of Khao Lak's most reliable, runs adventure-activity day trips (adult/child 2500/1800B) to Khao Lak/Lam Ru National Park, and day and overnight excursions into Khao Sok National Park (two-day trip adult/child 5800/4200B).

Sleeping

Cheaper accommodation dominates the congested town centre, while three- and four-star resorts line the coast. High-end hotels dot Hat Pakarang and Hat Bang Sak.

Fasai House GUESTHOUSE $

(☎076 485867, www.fasaihouse.com; 5/54 Mu 7, Khao Lak; r 650-900B; ❄@≋) Arguably Khao Lak's top budget choice, Fasai wins us over with its delightful staff and immaculate, motel-style air-con rooms set in a warm yellow-washed block framing a little pool. It's signposted west off Hwy 4 towards the northern end of Khao Lak.

To Zleep GUESTHOUSE $

(☎076 485899; www.tozleep.com; Th Phetkasem, Khao Lak; r 700-1200B; ❄📶) If you can forgive the name, this chequered roadside block is a tasteful, hostel-feel guesthouse full of colourful wall murals and small, spotlessly smart rooms. Some have bunks, others doubles. All come coolly kitted out with minimalist Ikea-style furnishings, concrete floors and colour-on-white themes. Biggest and brightest are corner mountain-view doubles.

Walker's Inn GUESTHOUSE $
(084 840 2689; www.walkersinn.com; 26/61 Mu 7, Th Phetkasem, Khao Lak; dm/r 200/600B;) A long-running backpacker fave and classic old-school guesthouse that features bright, spacious air-con rooms, decent single-sex dorms, and a popular downstairs pub dishing up full English breakfasts. It also does laundry and hire motorbikes (per day 200B).

Khao Lak/Lam Ru National Park Accommodation BUNGALOW $
(076 485243, in Bangkok 02 562 0760; www.dnp.go.th; Hat Khao Lak; bungalows fan/air-con 800/2000B;) Just beyond the southern end of Khao Lak Town, the national park headquarters has a handful of no-frills two-, four- and 10-person bungalows. Nothing fancy, but the shady hillside setting and low-key vibe will suit anyone after an eco-experience.

Nangthong Bay Resort RESORT $$
(076 485088; www.nangthong.com; 13/5 Mu 7, Hat Nang Thong; r 1800-3000B;) The massive turquoise pool dominates lush grounds that ramble to the beach and service is good. Free-standing bungalows follow a minimalist black-and-white chic design, with open-air showers. Cheaper rooms are set back from the beach, but are still fantastic value. It's popular with holidaying Thai families for the lovely big pool and four-person rooms, and an absolute steal in low season.

PhuKhaoLak BUNGALOW $$
(089 874 1018, 076 485141; www.phukhaolak.com; Mu 7, Th Phetkasem, Khao Lak; r fan/air-con 800/1800B; Oct-May;) Air-con rooms are stylish stand-alone casitas with high ceilings, dark-wood furnishings, ceramic-tiled floors, huge bathrooms, and beanbags loaded on verandahs. Fan rooms, fronted by porches, are basic but spotless. All curve around an aqua-tiled pool and a palm grove sprawling back against jungled hills. The open-walled Thai restaurant (p606) is good.

★ **Sarojin** HOTEL $$$
(076 427900; www.sarojin.com; Hat Pakarang; r 13,100-24,100B;) A gloriously peaceful and romantic retreat with stellar service and an elegant, intimate setting amid lotus ponds, 12km north of Khao Lak proper. The very private spa (p622), which takes in views of coconut groves and mangroves, is one of the Andaman's best. Glossy-chic rooms are impeccably styled in warm woods, with huge swish bathrooms sporting free-standing circular tubs. No kids allowed.

Both the beachside **Thai seafood kitchen** and the gorgeous candle-lit **Mediterranean restaurant** tucked into the trees are exceptional, and there are weekly guests-only cocktail parties. **Cooking classes** happen on the banks of Mae Nam Takua Pa, where you can watch water buffalo amble by. The resort contributes to local community projects, including animal welfare and landscape replanting.

Casa de La Flora DESIGN HOTEL $$$
(076 428999; www.casadelaflora.com; 67/213 Mu 5, Hat Bang Niang; r incl breakfast 12,420-24,050B;) Folded into trim seaside grounds dotted with contemporary art, this sleekly modern belle is composed of smart cube-like glass-and-concrete villas and suites adorned with warm-wood-panelled walls, double-sided mirrors, chunky concrete bathtubs and private plunge pools. Thoughtful touches include iPod docks, in-room espresso machines, hairdryers and, of course, pillow menus. Pod-style lounge beds fringe the sea-view infinity pool.

The service strikes that perfect friendly-but-efficient balance.

Eating & Drinking

This is no culinary capital, but tourists congregate at a few local haunts to rehash the day's diving. Early-morning divers will struggle to find breakfast before 8.30am.

Go Pong THAI $
(Th Phetkasem, Khao Lak; dishes 40-120B; 10am-11pm) Get a real taste of local flavours at this terrific streetside diner where they stir-fry noodles and sensational spicy rice dishes and simmer aromatic noodle soups that attract a loyal lunch following. Dishes are packed full of flavour.

Jai THAI $
(5/1 Mu 7 Th Phetkasem, Khao Lak; mains 80-250B; 8am-9pm;) Under a soaring peaked roof at the northern end of central Khao Lak, this semi-open-air, family-run eatery has a gigantic menu of fresh grilled seafood, spiced stir fries and all the curries, rices and noodles. Satisfying, friendly and convenient.

Takieng THAI $$
(26/43 Mu 5, Bang Niang; mains 120-350B; noon-10pm;) Of two open-air Thai restaurants beneath stilted tin roofs on Hwy 4, 2.5km north of Khao Lak Town,

Takieng is the most popular and attractive. It steams fresh fish in sweet green curry, does a scintillating chicken or pork *lâhp*, bubbles up beautifully spiced curries, and fries squid in a delicious chilli paste. Service is impeccable.

Jumbo Steak & Pasta ITALIAN **$$**
(☎098 059 8293; Th Phetkasem, Ban Khukkhuk; mains 70-280B; ⊙noon-10.30pm Thu-Tue) A hole-in-the-wall joint on the west side of Hwy 4, 6km north of Khao Lak proper, launched by a former Le Meridien line chef who does beautiful pasta dishes in all kinds of flavours: penne arrabiata, hot-and-spicy seafood spaghetti, creamy spinach tagliatelle, a host of pizzas and terrific steaks. Dishes are great value in terms of quality, though portions aren't huge.

PhuKhaoLak INTERNATIONAL, THAI **$$**
(☎076 485141; www.phukhaolak.com; Mu 7, Th Phetkasem, Khao Lak; mains 100-350B; ⊙7am-10pm Oct-May;) With cloth-covered tables spilling to the lawn edge at the south end of Khao Lak's highway strip, it's hard to miss. And you shouldn't, because there's a never-ending, well-prepared Thai-European menu of fried/grilled/steamed fish, sirloin steaks, pastas and sandwiches, and a dedicated veg section featuring such delights as spicy tofu with peanut sauce.

Information

SSS Ambulance (☎076 209 347, emergency 081 081 9000) For diving-related emergencies, the SSS Ambulance rushes injured persons to Phuket International Hospital (p617), and can also be used for car or motorcycle accidents.

Getting There & Around

Any bus following Hwy 4 between Takua Pa (55B, 45 minutes) and Phuket (100B, two hours) will stop at Hat Khao Lak if you ask.

Khao Lak Land Discovery (p604) runs shared minibuses to Phuket International Airport (600B, 1¼ hours). Alternatively, you can take **Cheaper Than Hotel** (☎085 786 1378, 086 276 6479; cheaperkhaolak1@gmail.com) taxis to Phuket airport (1000B) and points south. Otherwise, taxis cost 1500B from Khao Lak to the airport. Or tell a Phuket-bound bus driver to drop you at the 'airport'; you'll be let off at an intersection from which motorcycle taxis usually take you to the airport (10 minutes, 100B).

Numerous travel agencies and guesthouses rent motorbikes (per day 250B), including Khao Lak Land Discovery.

Similan Islands Marine National Park

อุทยานแห่งชาติหมู่เกาะสิมิลัน

Known to divers the world over, the beautiful 70-sq-km **Similan Islands Marine National Park** (☎076 453272; www.dnp.go.th; adult/child 500/300B ; ⊙mid-Oct–mid-May) lies 70km offshore from Phang-Nga Province. Its smooth granite islands are as impressive above the bright-aqua water as below, topped with rainforest, edged with blindingly white beaches and fringed by coral reefs. Unfortunately, coral bleaching has killed off many hard corals, but soft corals are still intact, the fauna is there and it remains a lovely (popular) place to dive.

In 1998, the nine-island park was expanded to include **Ko Bon** and **Ko Tachai**. Two of the 11 islands, Ko Miang (Island 4) and **Ko Similan** (Island 8), have accommodation. The park visitors centre and most facilities are on Ko Miang. 'Similan' comes from the Malay *sembilan*, meaning 'nine'; while each island is named, they're more commonly known by numbers.

Hat Khao Lak, home to most dive schools, is the park's jumping-off point. The pier and mainland **national park headquarters** (☎076 453272; www.dnp.go.th; 93 Mu 5, Thap Lamu; ⊙8am-5pm mid-Oct–mid-May) are at Thap Lamu, 12km south (Hwy 4, then Rte 4147). There's a **visitors centre** (Ko Miang; ⊙7.30am-8pm mid-Oct–mid-May) on Ko Miang's north-coast beach.

Sadly, the onslaught of mass tourism means that many Similan beaches and dive/snorkel sites get completely packed with day trippers. It's clear that nobody is monitoring these numbers, to the park's detriment. There are huge queues to climb viewpoints and some snorkelling outfits even feed the fish, a big ecological no-no. That would never happen if this were a national park! Oh, wait...

Sights & Activities

Diving & Snorkelling

The Similans offer diving for all levels, at depths from 2m to 30m. There are rock reefs at **Ko Hin Pousar** (Island 7) and dive-throughs at **Hin Pousar** (Elephant Head Rock), with marine life ranging from tiny plume worms and soft corals to schooling fish, manta rays and rare whale sharks. **Ko Bon** and **Ko Tachai**, largely unscathed

Similan Islands Marine National Park

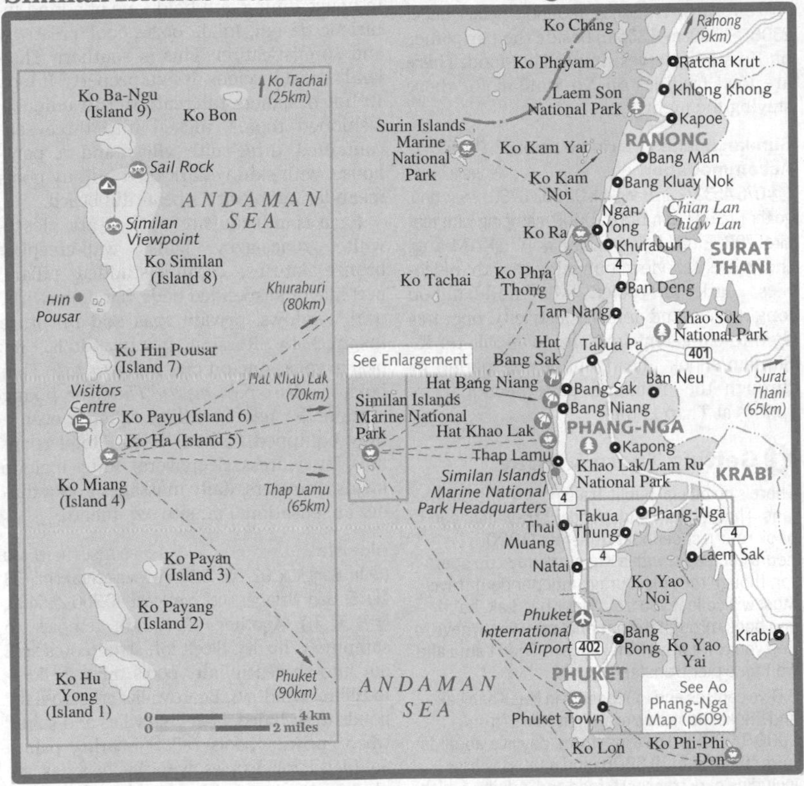

by coral bleaching, are some of the better diving and snorkelling areas. There are dive sites at each of the six islands north of **Ko Miang**. The park's southern section (Islands 1, 2 and 3) is an off-limits turtle nesting ground.

No facilities for divers exist in the national park, so you'll be taking a dive tour. Dive schools in Hat Khao Lak (p602) book day trips (two dives 5000B to 6000B) and live-aboards (three-/six-day trip from around 19,000/35,000B), as do Phuket dive centres (two-dive day trip from 5600B, three-day live-aboard from 19,000B).

Agencies situated in Khao Lak offer snorkelling-only day/overnight trips from 1900/4700B. Day-trip operators usually visit three or four snorkelling sites.

Wildlife & Hiking

The forest around Ko Miang's visitors centre has some walking trails and great wildlife. The fabulous Nicobar pigeon, with its wild mane of grey-green feathers, is common here. Endemic to the islands of the Andaman Sea, it's one of the park's 39 bird species. Hairy-legged land crabs and fruit bats (flying foxes) are relatively easy to spot in the forest, as are flying squirrels.

A small beach track, with information panels, leads 400m east from the visitors centre to a tiny snorkelling bay. Detouring from the track, the **Viewpoint Trail**, about 500m or 30 minutes of steep scrambling, has panoramic vistas from the top. A 500m (20-minute) walk west from the visitors centre leads through forest to smooth west-facing granite platform **Sunset Point**.

On Ko Similan, there's a 2.5km forest hike to a **viewpoint**, and a shorter, steep scramble off the north-coast beach to **Sail Rock** (Balance Rock), during daylight it's clogged with visitors.

Sleeping & Eating

A **restaurant** (dishes 120-150B, lunch buffet 230B; ⌚7.30am-8.30pm) beside the park office on Ko Miang serves simple Thai food. There are food facilities on Ko Similan for those staying the night.

Similan Islands Marine National Park Accommodation BUNGALOW $$
(☎076 453272, in Bangkok 02 562 0760; www.dnp.go.th; r fan/air-con 1100/2000B, camping with tent hire 570B; ⌚mid-Oct–mid-May; ❄) On Ko Miang, there are sea-view bungalows with balconies, dark fan-cooled wood-and-bamboo longhouses, and tents. Electricity operates 6pm to 6am. Tents are also available on Ko Similan. Book ahead online, by phone or through the mainland park headquarters (p606) at Thap Lamu.

Getting There & Away

There's no official public transport to the Similans. Theoretically, independent travellers can book return speedboat transfers (1900B, 1½ hours each way) with a Khao Lak day-trip operator, though they discourage independent travel. Most will collect you from Hat Khao Lak, but if you book through the national park you'll have to find your own way to the office in Thap Lamu and wait for a pier transfer.

Dive centres and tour agents in Hat Khao Lak and Phuket book day/overnight tours (from 2900/5000B), dive trips (three-day live-aboards from 16,000B to 19,000B) and multi-day trips including park transport, food and lodging, which cost little more than what you'd pay getting to the islands independently, which is not encouraged.

Natai นาใต้

Officially in Phang-Nga Province, Natai is like a misleadingly laid-back outpost of high-life Phuket – but, in reality, even more fabulous. Just 26km north of Phuket International Airport, this budding luxury bolthole lies within easier reach of Phuket than parts of Phuket itself. There's little else out here yet, apart from a delicious broad blonde beach that disappears into turquoise waters. And, of course, some of southern Thailand's finest dining and lodgings.

Sleeping & Eating

★Iniala Beach House DESIGN HOTEL $$$
(☎076 451456; www.iniala.com; 40/14 Mu 6, Ban Natai; d all-inclusive $1290-2820; ❄📶🏊👪) From expertly concocted passion-fruit welcome drinks to highly personal service, in-house dining and bold, one-of-a-kind futuristic design, Iniala oozes cool, creativity and sophistication. This is southern Thailand's most luscious design property. It took 10 hot designers to create the 10 uniquely fashioned rooms, tucked into three self-contained three-suite villas and a penthouse, with skinny dark-tiled infinity pools meandering to Natai's beautiful beach.

Each is an exquisite work of art: glossy-white space-agey pads, wall-creeping bronze lotuses, ceramic-studded pillars, pod-like or suspended beds, bamboo twirls, oval windows, private spas and furniture inspired by Russian nesting dolls. Try beach yoga, one-on-one *moo·ay tai* (Thai boxing; also spelt *muay Thai*) or biking around the nearby village. There's even a fully equipped 24-hour Kids' Hotel (nannies, fancy dress, sleepovers). Rates include meals, transfers, daily massages and a dinner at sensational on-site Aziamendi.

Aleenta BOUTIQUE HOTEL $$$
(☎in Bangkok 02 514 8112; www.aleenta.com; 33 Mu 5, Ban Natai; r incl breakfast 10,300-21,540B; ❄📶🏊👪) Another of Natai's temples to sumptuous luxury. Sleek loft-style rooms spill out into shared infinity pools through floor-to-ceiling windows. Boardwalks crisscross lily ponds to secluded, uber-chic villas and suites, where private pools reflect soaring palms. Split-level quadruples with kitchenettes are ideal for families. Swish cabanas dot the black-tiled seafront infinity pool and there's an elegant spa, plus brand-new villas on the way.

★Aziamendi FUSION $$$
(☎083 006 5277; www.aziamendi.com; Iniala Beach House, 40/14 Mu 6, Ban Natai; 10-course tasting menu from 5300B; ⌚6.30-9pm Tue-Sat Dec-Apr) Topping many fine-dining dream lists, the south's hottest new restaurant comes courtesy of three-Michelin-star Basque chef Eneko Atxa (of Azurmendi, Spain, fame) and an internationally acclaimed culinary team. Dining at avant-garde Aziamendi takes the shape of ambitious, inventive 10-course tasting menus that fuse Basque techniques with Thai flavours, unearthing such wonderful complex creations as truffled eggs, deconstructed picnics and sea bass with tsuyu tartare.

It all unfolds alongside a prize-winning wine list, in a stunning space loaded with gold Andaman-inspired ceilings, fluffy black carpets and elaborate Southeast Asian art.

Getting There & Away

Taxis to/from Phuket airport cost 700B.

Ao Phang-Nga อ่าวพังงา

Between turquoise bays peppered with craggy limestone towers, brilliant-white beaches and tumbledown fishing villages, Ao Phang-Nga is one of the Andaman's most spectacular landscapes. Little wonder then that it was here, among looming cliffs and swifts' nests, that James Bond's nemesis, Scaramanga *(The Man with the Golden Gun)*, chose to build his lair. Modern-day wanted assassins with world-domination goals would doubtless skip the place, as it's swarming with tourists, motorboats and sea kayaks year-round. Much of the bay, and some of the coastline, makes up Ao Phang-Nga National Park (p610).

Phang-Nga พังงา

POP 12,000

Phang-Nga is a scruffy, unremarkable town set against sublime limestone cliffs. There isn't much to see or do unless you're here during the annual **Vegetarian Festival** (late September or October). Hotels and amenities are mostly on Th Phetkasem.

Tours

Although it's nice to create your own Ao Phang-Nga itinerary by chartering a boat (p610), it's easier (and cheaper) to join a tour with one of Phang Nga's agencies, most of which are at the bus station. Quality varies, but all offer near-identical itineraries and prices.

Sayan Tours BOAT TOUR
(☎090 708 3211, 076 430348; www.sayantour.com; bus station, off Th Phetkasem; half/full day 800/1100B) A long-standing Ao Phang-Nga tour company offering day trips to Ko Panyi, Ko Phing Kan and Tham Lod (covered in stalactites), and overnight stays on Ko Panyi (1350B).

Mr Kean Tour BOAT TOUR
(☎076 430619, 089 871 6092; bus station, off Th Phetkasem; half/full day 800/1100B) Mr Kean has been running tours of Ao Phang-Nga for over 20 years. Half- and full-day tours include Tham Lod, Ko Phing Kan and Ko Panyi. You can add kayaking and trekking, or spend the night on Ko Panyi (1450B to 1750B).

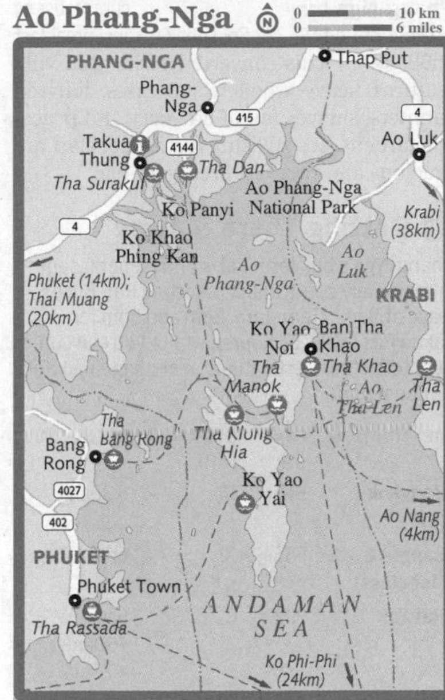

Sleeping & Eating

Several food stalls along Th Phetkasem sell delicious *kà·nŏm jeen* (thin wheat noodles) with chicken curry, *nám yah* (spicy ground-fish curry) or *nám prík* (spicy sauce). There's a small night market on Th Phetkasem just north of the bus station, beside 7-Eleven.

Thaweesuk Hotel GUESTHOUSE $
(☎076 412100; www.thaweesukhotel.com; 76 Th Phetkasem; r incl breakfast with fan 450B, air-con 700-800B; ❄📶) A welcoming, family-run guesthouse tucked behind a colourful mosaic-floor lobby, on north Th Phetkasem. Ground-floor cold-water fan/air-con rooms are simple and clean. Hot-water air-con pads on the 1st floor are significantly more stylish, with varnished-wood floors and lots of tiles.

Baan Phang Nga GUESTHOUSE $$
(☎076 413276; baanphangngabandb@gmail.com; 100/2 Th Phetkasem; r 650-850B; ❄📶) This is a homey, retro-style place with spacious, bright, spotless rooms in an old relic towards the north end of Th Phetkasem. Ceilings are high, varnished-concrete floors are colourful and hot-water bathrooms have rain showers. Good coffee, European breakfasts and Thai fare are served in the delightful downstairs **bakery** (dishes 65-160B; ⏱8am-9pm; 📶).

Phang-Nga Inn GUESTHOUSE $$
(☎084 851 4444; 2/2 Soi Lohakit; r incl breakfast 850B; ❄📶) This converted residential villa features heavy wooden staircases, louvred cabinets, shelves full of crockery and peaceful gardens. It's stylishly furnished, staff are gracious and there's a breezy lounge.

ℹ Getting There & Away

Phang-Nga's bus terminal is off Th Phetkasem, immediately south of Soi Bamrung Rat. Buses leave at 9am, 11am, 1pm, 3pm and 5pm for Takua Pa (150B, 1½ hours), where you can connect to further destinations, including Khao Sok National Park.

DESTINATION	FARE (B)	DURATION (HR)	FREQUENCY
Bangkok (VIP)	916	12	5.30pm
Bangkok (1st class)	585	12	6pm & 7pm
Hat Yai	292	6	hourly 7.30am-4.20pm
Krabi	80	1½	hourly 7.30am-6pm
Phuket	90	1½	hourly 9am-4pm
Ranong	170	5	10.30am & 1.30pm
Surat Thani	150	4	9.30am, 11.30am, 1.30pm & 3.30pm
Trang	185	3½	hourly 7.30am-4.20pm

Ao Phang-Nga National Park อุทยานแห่งชาติอ่าวพังงา

Established in 1981, 400-sq-km **Ao Phang-Nga National Park** (☎076 481188; www.dnp.go.th; adult/child 300/100B; ⏰8am-4pm) is famous for its classic karst scenery. Huge vertical cliffs frame 42 islands, some with caves accessible only at low tide and leading into hidden *hôrng* (semi-submerged island caves). The bay is composed of large and small tidal channels (Khlong Ko Phanyi, Khlong Phang-Nga, Khlong Bang Toi and Khlong Bo Saen), which run north to south through vast mangroves functioning as aquatic highways for fisherfolk and island inhabitants. These are Thailand's largest remaining primary mangrove forests.

Ao Phang-Nga's marine limestone environment conceals reptiles like Bengal monitor lizards, two-banded monitors (reminiscent of crocodiles when swimming), flying lizards, banded sea snakes, shore pit vipers and Malayan pit vipers. Mammals include serows, crab-eating macaques, white-handed gibbons and dusky langurs.

In high season (November to April) the bay becomes a clogged package-tourist superhighway. But if you explore in the early morning (ideally from the Ko Yao Islands) or stay out later, you might just find a slice of beach, sea and limestone karst of your own. The best way to explore is by kayak.

👁 Sights & Activities

You can charter boats to explore Ao Phang-Nga's half-submerged caves and oddly shaped islands from Tha Dan, 9km south of central Phang-Nga.

Two- to three-hour tours (per person 1000B) head to well-trodden Ko Phing Kan, Ko Panyi and elsewhere in the park. Tha Surakul, 13km southwest of Phang-Nga in Takua Thung, has private boats for hire at similar prices to tours. From the national park headquarters, you can hire boats (1400B, maximum four passengers) for three-hour islands tours. From Phuket, John Gray's Seacanoe (p620) is the top choice for Ao Phang-Nga kayakers.

Ko Khao Phing Kan ISLAND
(เกาะเขาพิงกัน, James Bond Island) Ao Phang-Nga's top tourist drawcard is known to Thais as Ko Phing Kan ('Leaning on Itself Island'). Once used as a location setting for *The Man with the Golden Gun*, today the island is packed with photo-snapping visitors and vendors hawking coral and shells that should have stayed in the sea.

Ko Panyi ISLAND
(เกาะปันหยี) A stilted Muslim village clings to this small karst island, where most tours dock for lunch. It's busy, but several Phang-Nga town tours (p609) enable you to stay overnight and soak up the scenery without crowds.

🛏 Sleeping & Eating

Ao Phang-Nga National Park Accommodation BUNGALOW $
(☎076 481188, in Bangkok 02 562 0760; www.dnp.go.th; Rte 4144; bungalows 700-1000B) Simple aircon bungalows sleep two to three, in quiet

shady grounds 8.5km south of central Phang-Nga. There's a basic waterside Thai restaurant.

Getting There & Around

From central Phang-Nga, drive 7km south on Hwy 4, turn left onto Rte 4144 (the road to Tha Dan) and travel 2.6km to the park headquarters. Otherwise take a *sŏrng·tăa·ou* to Tha Dan (30B).

Ko Yao เกาะยาว

With mountainous backbones, unspoilt shorelines, hugely varied birdlife and a population of friendly Muslim fisherfolk, Ko Yao Yai and Ko Yao Noi are laid-back vantage points for soaking up Ao Phang-Nga's beautiful karst scenery. The islands are part of Ao Phang-Nga National Park (p610), but most easily accessed from Phuket (30km away).

Despite being the relative pipsqueak of the Ko Yao Islands, Ko Yao Noi is the main population centre, with fishing, coconut farming and tourism sustaining its small, year-round population. Bays on the east coast, where most resorts are, recede to mud flats at low tides. That said, **Hat Pasai**, on the southeast coast, and **Hat Paradise**, on the northeast coast, are both gorgeous, and **Hat Tha Khao**, on the east coast, has its own dishevelled charm. **Hat Khlong Jark** is a beautiful sweep of sand with good sleeping options.

Ko Yao Yai is more remote and less developed; it's twice the size of Yao Noi with a fraction of the infrastructure. The most accessible beaches are slightly developed **Hat Lo Pared**, on the southwest coast, and powder-white **Hat Chonglard** on the northeast coast.

Please respect local beliefs and dress modestly away from the beaches.

Sights & Activities

Cycling

Amazing Bike Tours (p630) runs popular small-group day trips to Ko Yao Noi from Phuket. If you're keen to explore the numerous dirt trails on Ko Yao Noi or Ko Yao Yai independently, most guesthouses rent mountain bikes (per day 200B), though they're more readily available on Ko Yao Noi.

Diving & Snorkelling

Half-day three-island snorkelling tours (1800B) of Ao Phang-Nga are easily arranged through guesthouses or at the piers.

Elixir Divers DIVING
(087 897 0076; www.elixirdivers.com; Glow Elixir, 99 Mu 3, Ko Yao Yai; 2 dives 3500-5500B, 4-day live-aboard 17,900-22,900B; Oct-Apr) Ko Yao Yai's only dive school is an on-the-ball operator covering a range of PADI courses, two-dive day trips locally and to Ko Phi-Phi, and live-aboards to Hin Daeng, Hin Muang and the Similans, plus snorkelling excursions to Ao Phang-Nga, Krabi and Ko Phi-Phi. If you're staying on Ko Yao Noi, they'll help with transfers.

Yoga

Island Yoga YOGA
(089 290 0233; www.thailandyogaretreats.com; 4/10 Mu 4, Hat Tha Khao, Ko Yao Noi; class 600B; classes 7.30am & 4.30pm) A popular yoga school hosting daily drop-in classes, and multi-day yoga and tai chi retreats. Enquire ahead for schedules.

Kayaking

Kayaks (per day 500B) are widely available on Ko Yao Noi, including at Sabai Corner (p612).

Rock Climbing

Mountain Shop Adventures ROCK CLIMBING
(083 969 2023; www.themountainshop.org; Tha Khao; half-day 3200B) There are over 150 climbs on Ko Yao Noi; Mountain Shop owner Mark has routed most of them himself. Trips range from beginner to advanced and many involve boat travel to remote limestone cliffs.

Sleeping & Eating

Ko Yao Noi

Suntisook BUNGALOW $$
(089 781 6456, 075 582750; www.facebook.com/suntisookresort; 11/1 Mu 4, Hat Tha Khao; r 2200B;) Suntisook's comfy, stylish varnished-wood bungalows are sprinkled across gorgeous butterfly-filled gardens just metres from a quiet beach. All have spacious hammock-laden verandahs, clear-glass sinks, mugs, drinking water, fridges and pot plants. It's efficiently run by a helpful English-speaking Thai family, who offer a good authentic **restaurant** (mains 70-140B; 7.30am-9pm;) and kayak hire. Rates include motorbike use.

Hill House BUNGALOW $$
(089 593 9523; www.hillhouse-kohyaonoi.com; Hat Tha Khao; r 1000-1200B;) A friendly, simple hillside spot where dark-wood, hot-water, fan-cooled bungalows are swathed in mosquito nets and have beautiful views

through trees to Ao Phang-Nga's limestone karsts from hammock-loaded terraces.

Sabai Corner Bungalows GUESTHOUSE $$
(076 597497; www.sabaicornerbungalows.com; Hat Khlong Jark; bungalows 1800B) Pocketed into a rocky headland, these super-clean no-fuss bungalows with whizzing fans, mosquito nets and hammocks on terraces are blessed with gorgeous sea views. The good, chilled-out waterside **restaurant** (mains 85-260B; 8am-10pm) is a bubbly place to hang out, and it rents kayaks.

★ **Six Senses Hideaway** RESORT $$$
(076 418500; www.sixsenses.com; 56 Mu 5, btwn Hat Khlong Jark & Hat Tha Khao; villa incl breakfast 27,485-61,500B;) This elegant five-star property, with 56 hillside pool villas and an exquisite spa (p622) built into an existing rubber plantation, exceeds every expectation. Views of Ao Phang-Nga are as jaw-dropping at pink tinged-sunset as at fresh-blue morning; its clifftop infinity pool is a dream; its lounge bar and white-sand beach are well worthy of the frequenting fashionistas; and its commitment to sustainability is unparalleled among global high-end hotels.

Ko Yao Island Resort RESORT $$$
(076 597474; www.koyao.com; 24/2 Mu 5, Hat Khlong Jark; villa 6500-21,600B;) Open-concept thatched bungalows offer serene views across a palm-shaded garden and beach-facing infinity pool to a white strip of sand. We love the graceful, airy, near safari-esque feel of the villas, with their fan-cooled patios and indoor-outdoor bathrooms. There's a snazzy bar-restaurant area and service is stellar.

Chaba Café INTERNATIONAL $
(www.facebook.com/Chaba-Café-and-Gallery-481886365211171; Hat Khlong Jark; mains 90-120B; 9am-5pm Mon-Sat;) Rustic-cute Chaba is a haven of pastel-painted prettiness, with driftwood walls, mellow music and a small gallery. Organic-oriented offerings include honey-sweetened juices, coconut-milk-and-avocado shakes, chrysanthemum tea and home-baked paninis, cookies and cakes, plus soups, pastas and Thai dishes. It's just beyond northern Hat Khlong Jark.

★ **Rice Paddy** INTERNATIONAL, THAI $$
(082 331 6581, 076 454255; Hat Pasai; mains 180-280B; noon-10.30pm Tue-Sun Oct-Apr, 6-10.30pm Tue-Sun May-Sep;) On the roadside corner at the southwest end of Hat Pasai, this sweet, all-wood, German-owned Thai-international kitchen is very special. Chunky wooden menus reveal flash-fried *sôm đam*, fantastic falafel and hummus, spicy whole-fish coconut curry and fresh salads. There are excellent vegie dishes with meat substitutes like shiitake 'lamb'. The massaman curry is divine. So are the mojitos.

Ko Yao Yai

Thiwson Beach Resort BUNGALOW $$$
(081 956 7582; www.thiwsonbeach.com; 58/2 Mu 4, Hat Chonglard; bungalows with fan & breakfast 1800B, air-con & breakfast 2300-3600B;) Easily the sweetest of the island's humbler bungalow properties. Here are proper wooden thatch- or tin-topped huts with polished floors, outdoor bathrooms and wide patios overlooking the island's prettiest, northeast-coast beach, fronted by an aqua pool. Beachfront bungalows are biggest, but fan rooms are excellent low-season value.

Glow Elixir RESORT $$$
(087 808 3838; www.glowbyzinc.com; 99 Mu 3, Prunai; bungalows incl breakfast 4000-14,900B;) Beside its own silky beach in the southwest corner of the island, the oldest of Yao Yai's four-star resorts offers tasteful beachfront and hillside peaked-roof villas steeped in classic Thai style: dark-wood floors, outdoor showers and fish-patterned ceramic-bowl sinks. Some have private pools. You'll also enjoy a high-season dive centre (p611), massage pagodas and spectacular sunsets over Phuket.

Information

There are a few ATMs in Ta Khao, Ko Yao Noi's largest settlement, and there's an east-coast ATM opposite the Six Senses Hideaway entrance.

On Ko Yao Yai, three ATMs were operating at research time. It's still wise to carry plenty of cash in low season; resupplying can be an issue.

Getting There & Away

TO/FROM AO NANG

From November to April, there's an 11am speedboat from the pier at Hat Noppharat Thara to Ko Yao Noi and Ko Yao Yai (both 650B, 45 minutes). It continues to Phuket's Tha Bang Rong, returning at 3pm.

TO/FROM PHUKET

From Phuket's Tha Bang Rong, there are daily speedboats (200B, 30 minutes) to Ko Yao Noi at 7.50am, 8.40am, 9.50am,11.30am, 1pm, 1.30pm, 2.30pm, 3pm and 5.40pm, plus long-tails (120B, one hour) at 9.15am, 12.30pm and 5pm. They stop en route at Tha Klong Hia on Ko Yao Yai (200B, 25 minutes). Boats return to Phuket between 6.30am and 4.40pm.

Returning to Phuket from Ko Yao, taxis run from Tha Bang Rong to Phuket's resort areas for 600B to 800B, and *sŏrng·tăa·ou* (50B) leave for Phuket Town at 7am, 8.30am, 11am and 2.30pm daily.

TO/FROM KO PHI-PHI

Three weekly speedboats run to/from Ko Phi-Phi (1500B), October to April.

TO/FROM KRABI

From 9am to 5.30pm daily, there are frequent long-tails (150B) between Ko Yao Noi's Tha Khao and Krabi's Tha Len (33km northwest of Krabi Town). *Sŏrng·tăa·ou* (100B) run between Tha Len and Krabi's Th Maharat via Krabi's bus terminal.

TO/FROM PHANG-NGA

From Tha Dan in Phang-Nga there's a 1pm ferry to Ko Yao Noi (200B, 1½ hours), returning at 7.30am.

Getting Around

Frequent shuttle boats run from Ko Yao Noi's Tha Manok to Ko Yao Yai's Tha Klong Hia (per person 50B). On the islands, túk-túk (pronounced *đúk đúk*) rides cost about 150B, and most guesthouses rent motorbikes (per day 250B to 300B). It's 100B for *sŏrng·tăa·ou* transport to the resorts.

PHUKET PROVINCE

The island of Phuket has long been misunderstood. Firstly, the 'h' is silent. And secondly, Phuket doesn't feel like an island at all. It's so huge (49km long, the biggest in Thailand) that you rarely feel surrounded by water, which is probably why Ko ('island') was dropped from its name. Branded the 'pearl of the Andaman', this is Thailand's original flavour of tailor-made fun in the sun.

Phuket's sin city of Patong is the biggest town and busiest beach. It's the ultimate gong show where beachaholics sizzle off their hangovers and go-go girls play ping pong… without paddles. But there's space for all kinds here. Phuket Town has morphed into an artsy, culturally rich capital, while Rawai on the island's southern tip remains blissfully laid-back, despite development. The twin west-coast beaches of Kata and Karon reel in holidaymakers who like their trips easy. An upmarket twist awaits along Hat Surin and Ao Bang Thao, while, further north, things quieten down as you thread through Sirinat National Park and Khao Phra Thaew reserve.

Ultimately, the island's affinity for luxury far outshines its other stereotypes. Jet-setters swing through in droves, getting pummelled during swanky spa sessions and sipping sundowners at fashion-forward nightspots or on rented yachts. And you don't have to be an heiress to tap into Phuket's style-packed to-do list. With deep-sea diving, high-end dining, luxury shopping, fabulous white beaches and some of Thailand's swankiest hotels at your fingertips, you might forget to leave.

Activities

Diving & Snorkelling

Phuket enjoys an enviable central location relative to the Andaman's top diving destinations. The much-talked-about Similan Islands lie 100km northwest, while dozens of dive sites orbit Ko Phi-Phi and Ko Lanta, 40km and 72km southeast. Trips from Phuket to these awesome destinations cost slightly more than from places closer to the sites, as you'll be forking out extra baht for boat petrol. Most Phuket operators take divers to the nine decent sites orbiting the island, like **Ko Raya Noi** and **Ko Raya Yai** (Ko Racha Noi and Ko Racha Yai), but these spots rank lower on the wow-o-meter. The reef off the southern tip of Raya Noi is the best spot, with soft corals and pelagic fish species aplenty, though it's usually reserved for experienced divers. Manta and marble rays are frequently glimpsed here and, if you're lucky, you might spot a whale shark.

One-day two-dive trips to nearby sites typically cost 3000B to 4000B. Nondivers (and snorkellers) can tag along for a significant discount. Open Water certification costs 12,000B to 18,000B for three days' instruction. Some schools charge 500B extra for equipment.

From Phuket, you can join a huge range of live-aboard diving expeditions to the Similan Islands (p606) and Myanmar's Mergui Archipelago.

Snorkelling isn't wonderful off Phuket proper, though mask, snorkel and fins (per day 200B) are available in most resort areas. As with diving, you'll find better snorkelling (with greater visibility and variety of marine life) along the shores of small outlying islands, such as Ko Raya Yai and Ko Raya Noi.

As elsewhere in the Andaman Sea, the best diving months are November to April when weather is good and seas smooth and clear, though most dive shops power on

Phuket Province

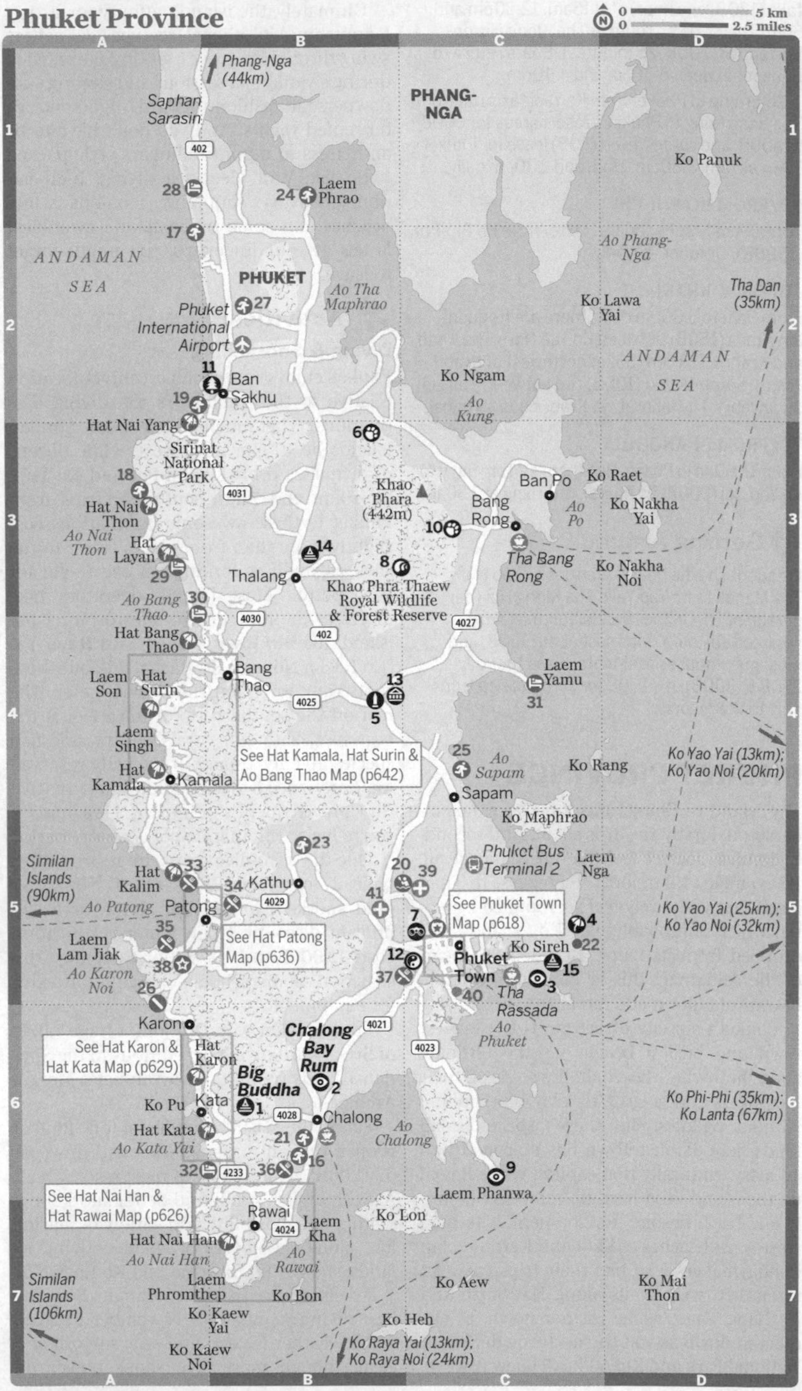

0 5 km
0 2.5 miles

Phang-Nga (44km)
Saphan Sarasin
PHANG-NGA
402
Ko Panuk
28
24 Laem Phrao
17
ANDAMAN SEA
Ao Phang-Nga
PHUKET
Ao Tha Maphrao
Tha Dan (35km)
Phuket International Airport
27
Ko Lawa Yai
ANDAMAN SEA
11
Ban Sakhu
Ko Ngam
19
Ao Kung
Hat Nai Yang
6
Sirinat National Park
18
Khao Phara (442m)
Ban Po
Ko Raet
4031
Hat Nai Thon
Bang Rong
Ao Po
Ko Nakha Yai
10
Ao Nai Thon
Hat Layan
14
8
Tha Bang Rong
Ko Nakha Noi
29
Thalang
Khao Phra Thaew Royal Wildlife & Forest Reserve
Ao Bang Thao
30
4030
402
4027
Hat Bang Thao
Bang Thao
Laem Son
Hat Surin
13
Laem Yamu
4025
5
31
Laem Singh
25
Ao Sapam
Ko Rang
Ko Yao Yai (13km); Ko Yao Noi (20km)
Hat Kamala
Kamala
Sapam
Ko Maphrao
23
Similan Islands (90km)
Hat Kalim
33
34
Kathu
20
39
Phuket Bus Terminal 2
Laem Nga
Ao Patong
Patong
4029
41
7
4
Ko Yao Yai (25km); Ko Yao Noi (32km)
35
Laem Lam Jiak
12
Ko Sireh
22
Phuket Town
15
38
37
3
40
Ao Karon Noi
26
Tha Rassada
Karon
4021
Ao Phuket
Chalong Bay Rum
4023
Hat Karon
Big Buddha
2
Ko Phi-Phi (35km); Ko Lanta (67km)
Ko Pu
Kata
1
4028
Chalong
Hat Kata
21
Ao Chalong
Ao Kata Yai
16
32
4233
36
9
Laem Phanwa
Rawai
Laem Kha
Ko Lon
4024
Hat Nai Han
Ao Nai Han
Ao Rawai
Similan Islands (106km)
Laem Phromthep
Ko Bon
Ko Aew
Ko Mai Thon
Ko Kaew Yai
Ko Heh
Ko Kaew Noi
Ko Raya Yai (13km); Ko Raya Noi (24km)

See Hat Kamala, Hat Surin & Ao Bang Thao Map (p642)
See Phuket Town Map (p618)
See Hat Patong Map (p636)
See Hat Karon & Hat Kata Map (p629)
See Hat Nai Han & Hat Rawai Map (p626)

Phuket Province

Top Sights

1 Big Buddha B6
2 Chalong Bay Rum B6

Sights

3 Chow Lair Village C5
4 Hat Teum Suk C5
5 Heroines Monument B4
6 Khao Phra Thaew Royal Wildlife & Forest Reserve B3
7 Khao Rang C5
Nam Tok Bang Pae .... (see 10)
8 Nam Tok Ton Sai B3
9 Phuket Aquarium C6
10 Phuket Gibbon Rehabilitation Project C3
11 Sirinat National Park B2
12 Sui Boon Tong Shrine C5
13 Thalang National Museum B4
14 Wat Phra Thong B3
15 Wat Sireh C5

Activities, Courses & Tours

Asia Marine .... (see 24)
Banyan Tree Spa .... (see 30)
16 Bob's Kite School B6
Bua Luang Spa .... (see 28)
Cool Spa .... (see 9)
Coqoon Spa .... (see 19)
17 Hat Mai Khao A2
18 Hat Nai Thon A3
19 Hat Nai Yang A2
20 John Gray's Seacanoe B5
Kite Zone .... (see 19)
Kiteboarding Asia .... (see 19)
21 Phuket Riding Club B6
22 Phuket Thai Cookery School C5
23 Phuket Wake Park B5
24 Phuket Yacht Haven Marina B1
25 Royal Phuket Marina C4
Sea Bees .... (see 35)
26 Sea Fun Divers A5
27 Soi Dog B2

Sleeping

28 Anantara Phuket A1
29 Anantara Phuket Layan A3
30 Banyan Tree A3
Dewa .... (see 19)
Discovery Beach Resort .... (see 19)
Indigo Pearl .... (see 19)
Panwa Beach Resort .... (see 9)
31 Point Yamu by Como C4
Pullman .... (see 18)
Sirinat National Park Accommodation .... (see 11)
Sri Panwa .... (see 9)
32 The Shore at Katathani B6

Eating

Breeze Restaurant .... (see 31)
Elements .... (see 18)
33 Home Kitchen A5
34 Kaab Gluay B5
35 La Gritta A5
Mr Kobi .... (see 19)
36 Som Tum Lanna B6
Terrace Grill .... (see 19)
37 Weekend Market B5

Drinking & Nightlife

Baba Nest .... (see 9)

Entertainment

38 Phuket Simon Cabaret A5

Information

39 Bangkok Hospital Phuket C5
40 Phuket Immigration Office C5
41 Phuket International Hospital B5

(weather permitting) through the low season, with good discounts.

Highly recommended dive schools have branches across Phuket, including in Patong (p635), Kata (p629) and Karon (p633).

Sea Kayaking

Several Phuket-based companies offer canoe tours of scenic Ao Phang-Nga. Kayaks can enter semi-submerged caves inaccessible to long-tail boats. A day paddle (per person around 4000B) includes meals, equipment and boat transfer. Some outfits run all-inclusive, three-day (from 13,500B) or six-day (from 23,500B) kayaking and camping trips, covering Ao Phang-Nga and Khao Sok National Park. John Gray's Seacanoe (p620) is the island's star operator.

Surfing

Phuket is an undercover surf destination. With the monsoon's midyear swell, glassy seas fold into barrels. The best waves arrive between June and September, when annual competitions are held on Hat Kata Yai (p628), Phuket's most popular surf spot, and Hat Kalim, just north of Patong. Phuket Surf (p629) is based at the south end of Kata Yai near the best break, which tops out at 2m. Hat Nai Han (p627) gets bigger waves (up to 3m), in front of the yacht club. Both Kata and Nai Han have vicious undertows that can claim lives.

Hat Kalim is sheltered and has a consistent break that gets up to 3m. This is a hollow wave, and is considered the best break on the island. The northernmost stretch of

Hat Kamala (p639) has a nice 3m beach break. Laem Singh (p639), 1km north, gets very big and fast, plus it's sheltered from wind by a massive headland. Hat Surin (p640) gets some of Phuket's most challenging waves.

Hat Nai Yang (p644) has a consistent (if soft) wave that breaks more than 200m offshore. Hat Nai Thon gets better shape. Swells get up to 3m high a few times per year.

In the low season, you can rent surfboards (per hour 250B to 300B) on most of these beaches.

Kitesurfing

One of the world's fastest-growing sports is also one of Phuket's latest addictions. The best kitesurfing spots are Hat Nai Yang (p644) from April to October and Rawai (p627) from mid-October to March. All listed kitesurfing outfitters are affiliated with the International Kiteboarding Organization (www.ikointl.com).

Adventure Sports

There's no shortage of adrenaline-fuelled activities on Phuket (bungee jumps, zip lines). Equipment quality and safety levels vary, and there have been serious, even fatal, accidents. Ask for recommendations and, if you have any doubts, don't proceed.

Yachting

Phuket is one of Southeast Asia's main yachting destinations. You'll find all manner of craft anchored along its shores, from 80-year-old wooden sloops to the latest in high-tech motor cruisers.

Marina-style facilities with year-round anchorage are available at several locations. Marinas can advise in advance on the latest port-clearance procedures. Expect to pay from 14,500B per day for a high-season, bareboat charter.

Royal Phuket Marina BOATING
(Map p614; ☎076 360811; www.royalphuketmarina.com; off Hwy 402) The US$25 million east-coast Royal Phuket Marina is 13km north of Phuket Town. It's luxurious, with high-end condos and upscale restaurants overlooking 350 berths, and does repairs.

Phuket Yacht Haven Marina BOATING
(Map p614; ☎076 206704; www.pyhmarina.com; 141/2 Mu 2, Laem Phrao) This recently revamped marina, on Phuket's northeastern tip, boasts 320 high-tech berths with deep-water access. Popular with superyachts.

Asia Marine BOATING
(Map p614; ☎076 206653; www.asia-marine.net; Phuket Yacht Haven Marina, 141/2 Mu 2, Laem Phrao) One of Phuket's first yacht charters and with a diverse Andaman fleet, Asia Marine has a boat for everyone, from sleek fibreglass catamarans to wooden junks. High-season bareboat charters start at 14,3000B.

Courses

Popular Thai cooking classes are held in Kata (p630), Phuket Town (p620), Ko Sireh (p625) and Patong (p635).

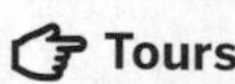

Tours

We recommend opting for a bike tour (p630) instead of supporting the questionable animal welfare and environmental standards of Phuket's elephant ride and 4WD tour operators. For more on the elephant debate see p327 and p759.

Information

DANGERS & ANNOYANCES

Assaults We've had reports of late-night motorbike muggings and stabbings on the road leading from Patong to Karon and from Kata to the Rawai–Hat Nai Han area. Random sexual assaults on women can also happen. Think twice before sunbathing topless (a big no-no in Thailand anyway) or alone, especially on isolated beaches. It can also be dangerous to run alone at night or early in the morning.

Jet skis Keep an eye out for jet skis when you're swimming. Although the Phuket governor declared jet skis illegal in 1997 and they've been re-banned as part of the recent island clean-up, enforcement of the rule is another issue. Long-tails can be hazardous; do not expect the boatman to see you!

Motorcycles Renting a motorbike can also be hazardous. Thousands of people are injured or killed every year on Phuket's highways. If you must, make sure you at least know the basics and wear a helmet. Rental rarely includes insurance.

Undertows During the May-to-October monsoon, large waves and fierce undertows sometimes make swimming dangerous. Dozens of drownings occur every year on Phuket's beaches, especially Laem Singh, Kamala, Karon and Patong. Heed the red flags signalling serious rips.

MEDIA

The weekly English-language *Phuket Gazette* (www.phuketgazette.net) publishes information on island-wide activities, dining and entertainment, plus the latest scandals. *Phuket Wan*

PHUKET TAXIS

Since taking over in 2014, the Thai military has cracked down on Phuket's infamous 'taxi mafia', an organisation of overpriced chartered cars which, until recently, had a monopoly on the island's transport industry. Numerous drivers suspected of extortion and intimidation have been arrested, and taxi salas, where drivers gathered, have been torn down. Some drivers deny involvement, saying they are simply earning a living.

Price boards around the island outline *maximum* journey rates; you're free to negotiate down. Meters have been introduced but, at research time, metered taxis remained tricky to find.

To avoid being overcharged, jot down the phone number of a metered taxi and use the same driver throughout your stay. The best way to do this is to take a metered taxi from the airport (the easiest place to find them) when you arrive. Metered taxis are 50m to the right as you exit airport arrivals. Set rates are 50B for the first 2km, 12B per kilometre for the next 15km and 10B per kilometre thereafter, plus a 100B 'airport tax'. That's no more than 700B to anywhere on the island from the airport.

Driver-booking apps Uber and GrabTaxi have landed on Phuket, opening up more transport options, though not necessarily at lower prices.

(www.phuketwan.com) is frequently juicier and more newsworthy. *Phuket News* (www.thephuketnews.com) is another excellent source on up to date island life.

MEDICAL SERVICES

Local hospitals are equipped with modern facilities, emergency rooms and outpatient-care clinics. Both hospitals listed below have hyperbaric chambers.

Bangkok Hospital Phuket (Map p614; ☎076 254425; www.phukethospital.com; Th Hongyok Uthit) Reputedly the favourite among locals, 3km north of Phuket Town.

Phuket International Hospital (Map p614; ☎076 361818, 076 249400; www.phuketinternationalhospital.com; 44 Th Chalermprakiat) International doctors rate this hospital as the island's best.

USEFUL WEBSITES

Jamie's Phuket (www.jamie-monk.blogspot.com) A fun, intelligent insider's blog written by a long-time Phuket expat, with excellent photos and travel tips.

Phuket Dot Com (www.phuket.com) A compendium of island-wide information and recommendations, including accommodation.

Getting There & Away

AIR

Phuket International Airport (Map p614; ☎076 327230; www.phuketairportthai.com) is 30km northwest of Phuket Town. It takes 45 minutes to an hour to reach the southern beaches from here. A number of carriers serve domestic destinations:

Air Asia (Map p636; ☎02 515 9999; www.airasia.com; 39 Th Thawiwong, Hat Patong; ⊙11am-9.30pm)

Bangkok Airways (Map p618; ☎076 225033; www.bangkokair.com; 158/2-3 Th Yaowarat, Phuket Town; ⊙8am-5.30pm Mon-Sat)

THAI (Map p618; ☎076 360444; www.thaiairways.com; 78/1 Th Ranong, Phuket Town; ⊙8am-4.30pm)

BUS

Interstate buses depart from **Phuket Bus Terminal 2** (Map p614; Th Thepkrasattri), 4km north of Phuket Town.

FERRY & SPEEDBOAT

Phuket's **Tha Rassada** (Map p614), 3km southeast of Phuket Town, is the main pier for boats to Ko Phi-Phi, Krabi, Ao Nang, Ko Lanta, the Trang Islands, Ko Lipe and even as far as Pulau Langkawi in Malaysia (which has ferry connections to Penang). Additional services to Krabi and Ao Nang via Ko Yao leave from **Tha Bang Rong** (Map p614), 26km north of Tha Rassada.

MINIVAN

Phuket travel agencies sell tickets (including ferry fare) for air-con minivans to destinations across southern Thailand, including Krabi, Ranong, Trang, Surat Thani, Ko Samui and Ko Pha-Ngan. Prices are usually slightly higher than for buses.

Getting Around

Local Phuket transport is terrible. The systems in place make tourists either stay on their chosen beach, rent a car or motorbike or take overpriced taxis or túk-túk. *Sŏrng·tăa·ou* run from Phuket Town to the beaches, but often you'll have to go via Phuket Town to get from one beach to another (say Hat Surin to Hat Patong), which takes hours.

That said, thanks to the recent crackdown on Phuket's 'taxi mafia' (p617), the stranglehold local drivers have enjoyed may be coming to an end, particularly when it comes to transport to and from the airport.

Phuket Town เมืองภูเก็ต

POP 77,600

Long before flip-flops and selfie sticks, Phuket was an island of rubber trees, tin mines and cash-hungry merchants. Attracting entrepreneurs from the Arabian Peninsula, China, India and Portugal, Phuket Town was a colourful blend of cultural influences, cobbled together by tentative compromise and cooperation. Today the city is testament to the island's historical soul. Wander down streets clogged with Sino-Portuguese architecture housing arty coffee shops, eccentric galleries, bright textiles stores, fantastic cheap restaurants and inexpensive boutique-chic guesthouses, and peek down alleyways to serene incense-cloaked Chinese Taoist shrines.

But it's not just some lost-in-time cultural archive. Bubbling up throughout the emerging Old Town is an infusion of current art, music and food attracting a very style-conscious, mostly Thai crowd. Investors have finally caught on that culture, not just beaches and girly bars, is a commodity. Century-old shophouses and homes, once left to rot, have been restored, resulting in flash-forward gentrification. It *can* feel like every other building is now a trendy polished-concrete cafe or a quirky guesthouse, but the city is still a wonderfully refreshing cultural break from Phuket's beaches.

Despite inflated real estate prices, Phuket Town has the island's best lodging bargains, and regular *sŏrng·tăa·ou* run to most beaches. Stay a few days to soak it all up, if you can.

Phuket Town

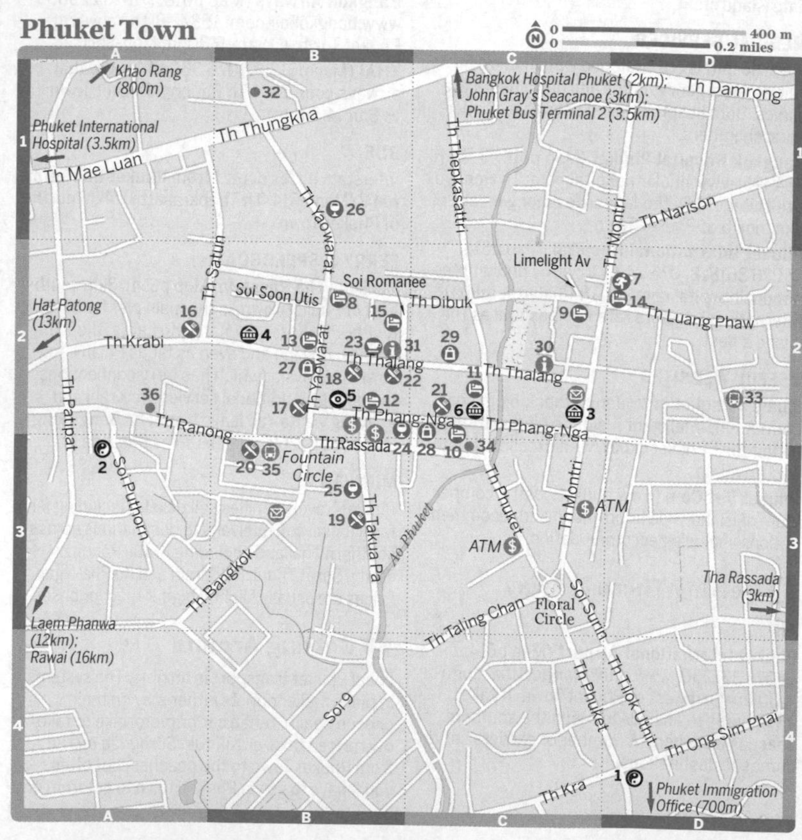

Sights

Phuket Thaihua Museum MUSEUM

(พิพิธภัณฑ์ภูเก็ตไทยหัว; Map p618; ☎076 211224; 28 Th Krabi; admission 200B; ⏰9am-5pm) Formerly a Chinese language school, this flashy museum is filled with photos and English-language exhibits on Phuket's history, from the Chinese migration (many influential Phuketian families are of Chinese origin) and the tin-mining era to local cuisine, fashion and literature. There's an overview of the building's history, which is a stunning combination of Chinese and European architectural styles, including art deco, Palladianism and a Chinese gable roof and stucco.

Shrine of the Serene Light CHINESE SHRINE

(ศาลเจ้าแสงธรรม, Saan Jao Sang Tham; Map p618; Th Phang-Nga; ⏰8.30am-noon & 1.30-5.30pm) FREE A handful of Chinese temples pump colour into Phuket Town, but this restored shrine, tucked away up a 50m alley, is particularly atmospheric, with its Taoist etchings on the walls and the vaulted ceiling stained from incense plumes. The altar is always fresh with flowers and burning candles. The shrine is said to have been built by a local family in the 1890s.

Khao Rang VIEWPOINT

(เขารัง, Phuket Hill; Map p614; P) For a bird's-eye view of the city, climb (or drive) up Khao Rang, 3km northwest of the town centre. A new viewing platform has opened up the commanding panoramas across Phuket Town and all the way to Chalong Bay, Laem Phanwa and Big Buddha. It's at its best during the week, when the summit is relatively peaceful. There are a few restaurants up here. It's about an hour's walk, but don't try it at night. A taxi up costs 700B.

Sino-Portuguese Architecture

Stroll along Ths Thalang, Dibuk, Yaowarat, Ranong, Phang-Nga, Rassada and Krabi for a glimpse of Phuket Town's Sino-Portuguese architectural treasures. The most magnificent examples are the **Standard Chartered Bank** (Map p618; Th Phang-Nga), Thailand's oldest foreign bank; the THAI office (p617); and the **old post office building**, which now houses the **Phuket Philatelic Museum** (Map p618; Th Montri; ⏰10am-5pm Mon-Sat) FREE. Some of the most colourfully revamped buildings line Soi Romanee, off Th Thalang, once home to brothels, gamblers and opium dens.

Phuket Town

Sights

1	Bang Niew Shrine	D4
2	Jui Tui Shrine	A3
3	Phuket Philatelic Museum	C2
4	Phuket Thaihua Museum	B2
5	Shrine of the Serene Light	B2
6	Standard Chartered Bank	C2

Activities, Courses & Tours

	Blue Elephant Cooking School	(see 16)
7	Raintree Spa	D2
	Suay Cooking School	(see 19)

Sleeping

8	Ai Phuket Hostel	B2
9	Baan Suwantawe	C2
10	Best Stay Hostel	C2
11	Casa Blanca	C2
12	Memory at On On Hotel	B2
13	RomManee Classic	B2
14	Sino House	D2
15	The RomManee	B2

Eating

16	Blue Elephant	A2
17	Gallery Cafe	B2
18	Kopitiam by Wilai	B2
19	Suay	B3
20	Thanon Ranong Day Market	B3
21	The Cook	C2
22	Walking St	B2

Drinking & Nightlife

23	Bo(ok)hemian	B2
24	Comics	B2
25	Ka Jok See	B3
26	Timber Hut	B1

Shopping

27	Ban Boran Textiles	B2
28	Drawing Room	C2
29	Ranida	C2

Information

30	Tourism Authority of Thailand	C2
31	Tourist Information Centre	B2

Transport

32	Bangkok Airways	B1
33	Phuket Bus Terminal 1	D2
34	Pure Car Rent	C3
35	Sŏrng·tăa·ou to Beaches	B3
36	THAI	A2

PHUKET FOR CHILDREN

While the seedier side of Thailand's sex industry is on show in Patong (we'd be reluctant to bring our kids here, though many people do), the rest of Phuket is fairly G-rated.

Visits to **Phuket Aquarium** (p625), **Soi Dog** (p645) and the **Phuket Gibbon Rehabilitation Project** (p646) are terrific animal-themed activities for kids. Adrenaline-addled older kids can tackle kitesurfing in **Rawai** (p625) and **Hat Nai Yang** (p644).

Phuket's main family-flogged feature is **Phuket Fantasea** (p640) which, while popular, does not set an ecologically sound (let alone responsible) example to kids big or small. Elephant rides are particularly plentiful on Phuket, but carry complex yet significant animal welfare concerns (p759). For those with children who insist, ask around about more responsible outfits.

Phuket Wake Park (Map p614; ☎089 873 0187; www.phuketwakepark.com; 86/3 Mu 6, Th Vichitsongkram, Kathu; adult/child 2hr 650/350B, day pass 1150/550B; ⏰7.30am-11pm; 👪) Buzz Kathu's marvellous hill-backed lake on a wakeboard. This outfit, mostly aimed at teenagers and older kids, offers rides in two-hour blocks, by the day or as lessons (per hour 1000B). Gear rental is available (from 350B), as are hotel transfers.

Surf House (Map p629; ☎081 979 7737; www.surfhousephuket.com; 4 Mu 2, Th Pak Bang, Hat Kata; ⏰9.30am-11.30pm; 👪) Across the street from Hat Kata Yai, this bar-entertainment spot serves both beer and artificial waves. Kids will love the sloped surf slide on which riders show off wakeboarding skills for as long as they can stay upright. The bar pours icy Chang and serves pub grub.

The best-restored residential properties lie along Ths Thalang, Dibuk and Krabi. The fabulous 1903 **Phra Phitak Chyn Pracha Mansion** has been refurbished into the upscale Blue Elephant restaurant (p622) and culinary school.

Activities

★John Gray's Seacanoe KAYAKING
(Map p614; ☎076 254505; www.johngray-seacanoe.com; 86 Soi 2/3, Th Yaowarat; adult/child from 3950/1975B) 🍃 The original, the most reputable and by far the most ecologically sensitive kayaking company on Phuket. The Hong by Starlight trip dodges the crowds, involves sunset paddling and will introduce you to Ao Phang-Nga's famed after-dark bioluminescence. Like any good brand in Thailand, John Gray's 'Seacanoe' name and itineraries have been frequently copied. He's 3.5km north of Phuket Town.

Courses

★Suay Cooking School COOKING COURSE
(Map p618; ☎081 797 4135; www.suayrestaurant.com; 50/2 Th Takua Pa; per person 1800B) Learn from one of Phuket's top chefs at the most laid-back, soulful and fun cooking school around. Noy Tammasak will lead you through the local market and teach you how to make three dishes, before cracking open a bottle of wine to enjoy with your culinary creations. Highly recommended; minimum three people.

Blue Elephant Cooking School COOKING COURSE
(Map p618; ☎076 354355; www.blueelephant.com; 96 Th Krabi; half-day class 3270B) Master the intricate art of royal Thai cooking in a stunningly restored Sino-Portuguese mansion. Options range from half-day group lessons to private eight-dish vegetarian classes (7000B). Morning sessions visit the market. Book ahead.

Sleeping

Phuket Town is a treasure trove of affordable lodging. Head to the beaches for midrange and top-end options.

Ai Phuket Hostel HOSTEL $
(Map p618; ☎076 212881; www.aiphukethostel.com; 88 Th Yaowarat; dm 259B, d 650-850B; ❄@📶) Doubles are tight but characterful with wood floors, black-and-white photos, muralled ceilings and, for some, private bathrooms. Dorms are bright, colourful and clean, sleeping six (girls only) to eight. All share polished-concrete hot-water bathrooms and a cramped downstairs hangout lounge.

Best Stay Hostel HOSTEL $
(Map p618; ☎099 301 9499; www.beststayhostel.com; 88 Th Phang-Nga; dm/r 250/600B; ❄📶) Another fresh Phuket Town hostel, featuring

shiny-white eight- to 10-person dorms with gleaming green floors and chunky-framed bunks with individual lamps and white duvets, plus boxy doubles. It's friendly and has a cute tile-floored cafe downstairs.

★The RomManee BOUTIQUE HOTEL $$
(Map p618; ☎089 728 9871; www.therommanee.com; Th Romanee; r 1200B; ❄📶) On Phuket Town's prettiest street, this 'boutique guesthouse' definitely packs in plenty of style with its turquoise-toned exterior, varnished-concrete floors and wood-block reception bar. The four spacious rooms have an arty modern feel with wood floors, flat screens, colour feature walls, neon-washed chairs and tasteful lighting. Stairs are steep and there's no lift. There's another comfy, less-friendly **branch** (Map p618; ☎076 355488; 4-6 Th Krabi; r 1000-1200B; ❄📶) a block away.

Casa Blanca BOUTIQUE HOTEL $$
(Map p618; ☎076 219019; www.casablancaphuket.com; 26 Th Phuket; r 2300-2800B; ❄📶🏊) All whites and pastels, this elegantly revamped Sino-Portuguese beauty gets extra boutique spark from Spanish-themed touches like patterned tiles and a plant-lined patio. Modern art adorns smart rooms, in soft greens and pale blues. Deluxes have balconies with city panoramas; superiors overlook the little pool. A teensy cafe doles out fresh-from-the-oven pastries in the bubbly bright lobby.

Memory at On On Hotel HOTEL $$
(Map p618; ☎076 216161; www.thememoryhotel.com; 19 Th Phang-Nga; dm 300B, r incl breakfast 1700-3400B; ❄📶) This longtime bare-bones classic played a dingy backpacker dive in *The Beach* (2000). But a smart revamp put the antiquated shine on Phuket's first hotel, transforming it into a contemporary budget-to-midrange guesthouse. Four- to six-bed dorms are fantastic, thanks to wooden flooring, ceramic sinks, old-school office desks, draped bunks and excellent shared facilities.

Stylish private rooms have concrete floors, rain showers, flat screens and vibrant shutters (though some seem stuffy).

Baan Suwantawe HOTEL, APARTMENT $$
(Map p618; ☎076 212879; www.baansuwantawe.com; 1/10 Th Dibuk; r 1800-3200B; P❄@📶🏊) With Zen art, hardwood floors, good-sized bathrooms, colourful bedspreads and comfy lounge areas, these spacious studio-style rooms are a steal. Higher-priced rooms have terraces overlooking the pool and lily pond, and the whole place basks in a lemongrassy scent that seems to be synonmous of many upmarket Asian hotels.

Sino House HOTEL $$
(Map p618; ☎076 232494; www.sinohousephuket.com; 1 Th Montri; r incl breakfast 1600-2500B; P❄@📶) Shanghai style meet 1960s chic at this impressive Phuket Town offering. Massive airy rooms are more like small apartments, with modern furnishings, handmade ceramic basins, tea/coffee sets, unique wall murals and quarter-moon showers in the bathrooms. The on-site Raintree Spa (p622) is excellent. Long term discounts available.

Eating

There's great food in Phuket Town; meals here cost a lot less than at the beach.

Kopitiam by Wilai THAI $
(Map p618; ☎083 606 9776; www.facebook.com/kopitiambywilai; 18 Th Thalang; mains 80-120B; ⏰11am-10pm Mon-Sat; 📶) Kopitiam serves Phuket soul food. It does Phuketian *pàt tai* (thin rice noodles with egg, tofu and/or shrimp) with a kick, and a fantastic *mee sua*: noodles sautéed with egg, greens, prawns, chunks of sea bass, and squid. Wash it all down with fresh chrysanthemum or passionfruit juice.

The Cook THAI, FUSION $
(Map p618; ☎076 258375; 101 Th Phang-Nga; mains 65-240B; ⏰8am-9.30pm Tue-Sun) The Thai owner-chef used to cook Italian at a mega-resort, so when he opened this ludicrously inexpensive Old Town restaurant he successfully fused the two cultures. Try one of the sensational green chicken curry or *đôm yam* (spicy Thai soup) pizzas, or a classic pasta plate, and you'll see what the fuss is about.

★Suay INTERNATIONAL, THAI $$
(Map p618; ☎081 797 4135; www.suayrestaurant.com; 50/2 Th Takua Pa; mains 15-400B; ⏰5pm-midnight) Fabulous fusion at this converted house, just south of old town proper, means mouth-melting glass noodle salad, bright pomelo salad with salmon carpaccio and roasted chilli dressing, lamb-chop massaman curry, turmeric-infused sea bass wrapped in banana leaf, smoked eggplant with chilli-coconut dressing and crab meat, and an innovative *sôm·đam* (spicy green papaya salad) featuring flavour-popping mangosteen.

Tables are sprinkled across the romantically lit house, garden and wraparound porch. Don't miss the flamed mango with sticky rice and black sesame ice cream.

DON'T MISS

FIVE SPARKLING SPAS OF THE NORTHERN ANDAMAN

There's a massage shop on every Andaman corner, especially on Phuket. Most are low-key family affairs where traditional one-hour 300B Thai massages are a real steal. Service quality varies and staff turnover is high. Go with your gut instinct or ask locally for recommendations.

If you fancy a more Europen-style spa experience, book into one of Phuket's resort spas. Though often affiliated with a glitzy hotel, most of these high-class affairs with sumptuous Zen designs and extensive treatment menus accept nonguests. Of course there are gorgeous spas to be found across the northern Andaman.

Siam Hot Spa (077 813551; www.siamhotsparanong.com; 73/3 Th Phetkasem, Ranong Town; treatment 300-750B; 11am-8pm) This is a highly recommended, classier mineral bath experience than the public hot springs opposite in Ranong Town. Soak in a private hot tub, then add a salt scrub or a classic Thai massage.

Cool Spa (Map p614; 076 371000; www.coolspaphuket.com; Sri Panwa, 88 Mu 8, Th Sakdidej, Laem Phanwa, Phuket; massages 2400-4000B; 10am-8.30pm) An elegant wonderland of fruit-infused wraps, facials and scrubs, and hilltop ocean-view pools. Oh, and then there's the dreamy setting, on the southernmost tip of Phuket's Laem Phanwa.

Six Senses Spa (076 418500; www.sixsenses.com; 56 Mu 5, btwn Hat Khlong Jark & Hat Tha Khao, Ko Yao Noi; massage 3900-6500B; 8am-9pm) No luxury brand presents back-to-nature elegance like the Six Senses stilted 'spa village'. Therapists are trained in massage traditions and organic-fuelled treatments from China, India and Thailand. The 'Signature Yao Noi Ritual' is a blissful 3½-hour scrub, massage and facial blend.

Pathways Spa (076 427900; www.sarojin.com; Sarojin, Hat Bang Sak, Khao Lak; massage 2100-2600B; 10am-9pm) One of the finest massage settings of your life awaits. Sala-style treatment rooms wander to the edge of mangroves and coconut groves, open to the ocean breeze. Relax and let the talented therapists take you through signature Sarojin flower scrubs and herbal wraps, and royal oriental massages.

Raintree Spa (Map p618; 081 892 1001; www.theraintreespa.com; Sino House, 1 Th Montri, Phuket Town; massages 600-1000B; 10am-9.30pm) Tucked into tranquil tropical grounds, Raintree is a step up in price, quality and atmosphere from Phuket Town's storefront spas. Skilled therapists don't just go through the motions here. Get silky-smooth with an aloe-cucumber body wrap or indulge in a two-hour 'fruit salad' scrub (pineapple, papaya, mango).

The wine list is short but proper, and affable chef/owner Noy Tammasak offers good cooking classes (p620).

Gallery Cafe CAFE $$
(Map p618; www.gallerycafe-phuket.com; 19 Th Yaowarat; mains 160-270B; 8am-8pm;) Settle in on comfy cushions at this popular brunch cafe, surrounded by varnished-wood booths and yellow walls hung with art. The menu is full of hearty international and Thai goodies: all-day egg breakfasts, pizzas, pastas, salads, sandwiches, smoothies, homemade veggie burgers. We're still dreaming about the brilliant breakfast bagels and zingy passionfruit, lemongrass and ginger juices.

Blue Elephant THAI $$$
(Map p618; 076 354355; www.blueelephant.com; 96 Th Krabi; mains 670-1000B, set menus 1350-2400B; 11.30am-2.30pm & 6.30-10.30pm;) Royal Thai cuisine in royal Thai surrounds. Set in the beautifully restored, mustard-yellow Phra Phitak Chyn Pracha Mansion overlooking manicured lawns, Blue Elephant is elegant in every way, from the brass cutlery and ornately carved doors to the chequered tiled floors, stellar service and superbly prepped and presented dishes.

Choose a tasting menu, a three-main set or go à la carte: it's all exquisite. The Blue Elephant Cooking School (p620) is also here.

Drinking & Nightlife

Phuket Town is where you can party like a local. Bars buzz until late, patronised almost exclusively by Thais and local expats.

Timber Hut CLUB
(Map p618; 076 211839; 118/1 Th Yaowarat; 6pm-2am) Thai and expat locals have been

packing out this two-floor pub-club nightly for 25 years, swilling whiskey and swaying to live bands that swing from hard rock to pure pop to hip-hop. No cover charge.

Comics BAR

(Map p618; www.facebook.com/Comics-Cafe-Bar-358086567609208; 44 Th Phang-Nga; ⏲6pm-midnight) A youthful all-Thai clientele crams into this bubbly, blue-lit, comic-covered space for mellow live music enjoyed with Thai and international beers, ciders, wines and cocktails.

Bo(ok)hemian CAFE

(Map p618; ☎098 090 0657; www.bookhemian.com; 61 Th Thalang; ⏲9am-7pm Mon-Fri, to 8.30pm Sat & Sun; 📶) Every town should have a coffee house this cool, with a split-level design that feels simultaneously warm and cutting-edge. Used books (for sale) line the front room, bicycles hang from the wall, and it does gourmet coffee and tea, and damn good chocolate cake.

Ka Jok See CLUB

(Map p618; ☎076 217903; kajoksee@hotmail.com; 26 Th Takua Pa; buffet per person 2500B; ⏲8pm-1am Nov-Apr, reduced hours May-Oct) Dripping with Old Phuket charm and the owner's fabulous trinket collection, this intimate century-old house has two identities: half glamorous eatery, half crazy party venue. There's good Thai food, but once the tables are cleared it becomes a bohemian madhouse party with top-notch music and – if you're lucky – some sensationally extravagant cabaret. Book a month or two ahead. There's no sign.

Shopping

There are some gorgeous bohemian-chic boutiques scattered throughout Old Town selling jewellery, women's fashions, fabrics and souvenirs, plus an ever-growing number of whimsical art galleries.

★Ranida ANTIQUES, FASHION

(Map p618; 119 Th Thalang; ⏲10.30am-7.30pm Mon-Sat) An elegant antique gallery and boutique featuring antiquated Buddha statues and sculpture, organic textiles, and ambitious, exquisite high-fashion clothing inspired by vintage Thai garments and fabrics.

Drawing Room ARTS

(Map p618; isara380@hotmail.com; 56 Th Phang-Nga; ⏲10am-9pm) With a street-art vibe reminiscent of pre-boom Brooklyn or East London, this wide-open cooperative is by far the stand-out gallery in a town full of them. Canvases might be vibrant abstract squiggles or comical pen-and-ink cartoons. Metallic furniture and bicycles line concrete floors. House music thumps at low levels.

Ban Boran Textiles TEXTILES

(Map p618; ☎076 211563; 51 Th Yaowarat; ⏲11am-6.30pm) Shelves at this hole-in-the-wall are stocked high with quality silk scarves, Burmese lacquerware, sarongs, linen shirts, cute colourful bags and cotton textiles from Chiang Mai.

Information

There are numerous ATMs on Ths Phuket, Ranong, Montri and Phang-Nga.

FLIGHTS TO/FROM PHUKET

DESTINATION	AIRLINE	FREQUENCY	FARE (B)
Bangkok (Don Muang)	Air Asia	14 daily	1400
Bangkok (Don Muang)	Nok Air	8 daily	1600
Bangkok (Suvarnabhumi)	Bangkok Airways	7-9 daily	1790
Bangkok (Suvarnabhumi)	THAI	9-10 daily	1800
Chiang Mai	Air Asia	3 daily	1900
Dubai	Emirates	1-2 daily	15,000
Hat Yai	Bangkok Airways	daily	1400
Hong Kong	Air Asia	daily	3700-6000
Ko Samui	Bangkok Airways	4-5 daily	3200
Kuala Lumpur	Air Asia	5 daily	2000-3000
Seoul	Korean Air	daily	13,000
Shanghai	China Eastern	2 daily	9800
Singapore	Air Asia	daily	1500-2500

BUSES FROM PHUKET BUS TERMINAL 2

DESTINATION	BUS TYPE	FARE (B)	DURATION (HR)	FREQUENCY
Bangkok	VIP	1011	13	5pm, 5.20pm, 6.20pm, 6.30pm & 7pm
	air-con	650	13-14	hourly 3.30pm-7pm
Chiang Mai	VIP	1826	22	3pm
Hat Yai	VIP	560	7	9.45pm
	air-con	360	7	hourly 7.30am-12.30pm, 7.30pm & 9.30pm
Ko Samui	air-con	450	8 (bus/boat)	9am
Ko Pha-Ngan	air-con	550	9½ (bus/boat)	9am
Krabi	air-con	155	3½	hourly 6.20am-7pm
Phang-Nga	air-con	85	2½	8.15am, 10.15am, 12.15pm & 8.15pm
Ranong	air-con	250	6	hourly 5.30am-6.10pm
Satun	air-con	364	7	8.15am, 10.15am, 12.15pm & 8.15pm
Surat Thani	air-con	195	5	8am, 10am, noon & 2pm
Trang	air-con	252	5	hourly 7.30am-12.30pm, 7.30pm & 9.30pm

Phuket Immigration Office (Map p614; ☎076 221905; www.phuketimmigration.go.th; 482 Th Phuket; ⏰8.30am-4.30pm Mon-Fri) Handles visa extensions.

Police (Map p614; ☎076 212046, 191; Th Chumphon)

Post Office (Map p618; Th Montri; ⏰8.30am-4.30pm Mon-Fri, 9am-noon Sat & Sun)

Tourism Authority of Thailand (TAT; Map p618; ☎076 211036; www.tourismthailand.org/Phuket; 191 Th Thalang; ⏰8.30am-4.30pm) Has maps, brochures, transport advice and info on boat trips to nearby islands.

Tourist Information Centre (Map p618; Th Thalang; ⏰9am-4.30pm) Maps, brochures, historical displays.

ℹ Getting There & Around

TO/FROM THE AIRPORT

Despite what airport touts say, an hourly bright-orange government airport bus (www.airportbusphuket.com) runs between the airport and Phuket Town (100B, one hour) via the Heroines Monument from 6.30am to 8.30pm. Taxis from the airport to Phuket Town cost 550B.

BUS

Phuket Bus Terminal 1 is mostly used by minivans. From here, a 'local bus' (actually a minivan) to Patong (50B) operates from 7am to 5pm.

Interstate buses depart from **Phuket Bus Terminal 2** (p617), 4km north of Phuket Town. Taxis or túk-túk do the run from Phuket Town for 300B.

CAR & MOTORCYCLE

Th Rassada has cheap car-rental agencies near **Pure Car Rent** (Map p618; ☎076 211002; www.purecarrent.com; 75 Th Rassada; ⏰8am-7pm), a good central choice. Cars cost around 1200B per day (including insurance), though rates drop in low season and for rentals of over three days.

Rates are usually better at local places than at the better-known internationals (which have desks at the airport), though you might find deals with familiar companies if you book ahead.

You can rent motorcycles on Th Rassada, including at Pure Car Rent, or from countless places at the beaches, for 250B to 300B per day. Bigger bikes (over 125cc) can be rented at shops in Patong, Kata, Rawai and Karon.

MINIVAN

From **Phuket Bus Terminal 1** (Map p618; Th Phang-Nga), 500m east of Phuket Town centre, minivans run to destinations across southern Thailand. Departures include the following:

DESTINATION	FARE (B)	DURATION (HR)
Hat Yai	360	7
Ko Lanta	280	5
Krabi	140	3
Surat Thani	200	4

SŎRNG·TĂA·OU & TÚK-TÚK

Large bus-sized *sŏrng·tăa·ou* run regularly from Th Ranong near the day market to Phuket's beaches (per person 25B to 40B, 30 minutes to 1½ hours), from 7am to 6pm; otherwise you'll have to charter a túk-túk to the beaches, which costs 400B (Rawai, Kata and Ao Bang Thao), 500B (Patong, Karon and Surin) or 600B (Kamala). Beware of tales about the tourist office being 5km away, or that the only way to reach beaches is by taxi.

For a ride around town, túk-túk drivers charge 100B to 200B and motorcycle taxis 30B.

Ko Sireh เกาะสิเหร่

This tiny island, 4km east of Phuket Town and connected to Phuket by a bridge, is known for its hilltop reclining Buddha at **Wat Sireh** (Map p614; Th Sireh; dawn-dusk) FREE and its **chow lair village** (Map p614).

Thailand's largest settlement of *chow lair* (sea gypsies) is little more than a poverty-stricken cluster of stilted tin shacks. The Urak Lawoi, the most sedentary of the three *chow lair* groups, live only between here and the Tarutao-Langkawi archipelago, and speak a mixture of Malay and Mon-Khmer.

A single road loops the island, passing a few villas, prawn farms, rubber plantations, a bit of untouched forest and east-coast **Hat Teum Suk** (Map p614).

Courses

Phuket Thai Cookery School COOKING COURSE
(Map p614; 076 252355; www.phuketthaicookery.com; 1-day course 2900B; 8am-3pm) Get intimate with aromatic Thai spices at this terrific cooking school on a quiet seafront plot on Ko Sireh's east coast, 7km east of Phuket Town. Courses take in a market tour and a cookbook and last up to six hours. Hotel pick-up is provided.

Laem Phanwa แหลมพันวา

An elongated jungle-covered cape jutting into the sea just south of Phuket Town, Laem Phanwa is an all-natural throwback. Some say this is the last vestige of Phuket as it once was. The biggest bloom of development is near the harbour at the cape's tip, 12km south of Phuket Town. On either side of the harbour, the beaches and coves remain rustic, protected by rocky headlands and mangroves and reached by a dreamy, sinuous coastal road. If you're seeking peace and quiet on Phuket, head here by taking Rte 4021 south, then heading southeast down Rte 4023 just south of Phuket Town.

Sights

Phuket Aquarium AQUARIUM
(สถานแสดงพันธุ์สัตว์น้ำภูเก็ต; Map p614; 076 391126; www.phuketaquarium.org; 51 Th Sakdidej; adult/child 180/100B; 8.30am-4.30pm; P) Get a glimpse of Thailand's wondrous underwater world at Phuket's popular aquarium, by the harbour on the tip of Laem Phanwa. There's a varied collection of tropical fish, sharks and other marine life, with helpful English-language displays. Check out the blacktip reef shark, the tiger-striped catfish resembling a marine-like zebra and the electric eel with up to 600V.

Sleeping & Eating

The seafood restaurants (mains 100B to 300B) along the harbour waterfront are a great place to relax and watch painted fishing boats bobbing by.

★**Sri Panwa** RESORT $$$
(Map p614; 076 371000; www.sripanwa.com; 88 Mu 8, Th Sakdidej; d incl breakfast 18,090-38,000B; P) From the mosaic-filled lobby and classy orange-grey colour scheme to the sensational pool-lined Cool Spa (p622), Sri Panwa is as decadent as the cape gets, poised idyllically on its jungle-cloaked southernmost tip. Multi-room villas feature hot tubs, outdoor showers, private pools and personal sound systems. More affordable rooms are still wonderfully comfy.

There is a games room, several pools, tennis courts and two-bedroom villas designed for families. The rooftop **Baba Nest** (5-9pm) lounge-bar, flooded with unimaginably beautiful ocean-and-island views, is magical. On-site food offerings range from all-day international staples to Mexican tapas and Japanese specialities.

Panwa Beach Resort RESORT $$$
(Map p614; 076 393300; www.thepanwabeachresort.com; 5/3 Mu 8, Ao Yon; r incl breakfast 4500-5500B; P) With its own stretch of beachfront and views of Chalong, Rawai and Big Buddha, this slightly dated resort on the cape's west coast offers seclusion, sizeable rooms and four-star service at good-value rates.

Rawai ราไวย์

Now this is a place to live, which is exactly why Phuket's rapidly developing south coast is teeming with retirees, artists, Thai and

Hat Nai Han & Hat Rawai

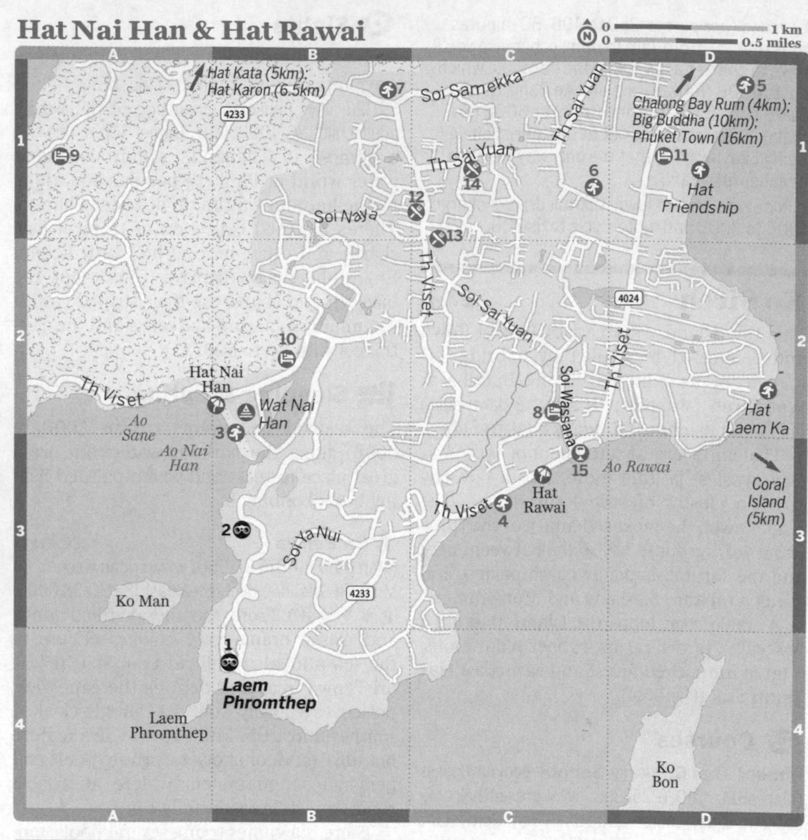

Hat Nai Han & Hat Rawai

Top Sights
1 Laem Phromthep B4

Sights
2 Secret Viewpoint B3

Activities, Courses & Tours
Boat Charters .... (see 4)
3 Hat Nai Han B2
4 Hat Rawai C3
5 Kite Zone D1
6 Rawai Supa Muay Thai C1
7 Sinbi Muay Thai B1

Sleeping
8 Good 9 at Home C2
9 Sabai Corner A1
10 Sunsuri B2
11 Vijitt D1

Eating
12 Da Vinci C1
13 German Bakery C1
14 Rum Jungle C1
Sabai Corner .... (see 9)

Drinking & Nightlife
15 Nikita's C3

expat entrepreneurs, and a service sector that, for the most part, moved here from somewhere else.

The region is defined not just by its beaches but also by its lush coastal hills that rise steeply and tumble into the Andaman Sea, forming **Laem Phromthep** (Map p626; Rte 4233) Phuket's beautiful southernmost point; for a more secluded sunset spot, seek out the **secret viewpoint** (Map p626; Rte 4233) 1.5km north. These hills are home to pocket neighbourhoods and cul-de-sacs knitted together by just a few roads – although more are being carved into the hills each year and you can almost envision real-estate money chasing away all the seafood grills and tiki bars. Let's hope that's several decades off. Or at least one. Even with the growth you can still feel nature, especially when you hit the beach.

Activities

Rawai is the centre of Phuket's growing *moo·ay tai* mania, home to half a dozen schools where students (of both sexes) live and train traditional-style in camps with professional *moo·ay tai* fighters.

Hat Rawai is an excellent place to arrange **boat charters** (Map p626) to neighbouring islands. Destinations include quiet Ko Bon (long tail/speedboat 1200/2100B) and Coral island (1800/3500B, maximum eight people) for snorkelling.

Hat Nai Han BEACH

(Map p626) Ask a Phuket local or expat which their favourite beach is and they should say Hat Nai Han, though they'll probably send you off somewhere else and keep this one to themselves. One of Rawai's great swimming spots (be careful of rips in low season), this is a beautifully curved white crescent on the west side of the cape, with minimal development and backed by casuarinas and a seafront wát.

Hat Rawai BEACH

(Map p626) Not really good for lounging, Hat Rawai is a rocky long-tail and speedboat harbour with a string of seafood grills on the east side of the cape. This is where most of the luxury condo development seems to be proliferating.

Rawai Supa Muay Thai THAI BOXING

(Map p626; ☎076 226495; www.supamuaythai phuket.com; 43/42 Mu 7, Th Viset; per session/week 300/3000B; ⏰7am-7pm Mon-Sat, 9am-6pm Sun) Strap up those wrists and get fired up at this Thai boxing gym opened by a former *moo·ay tai* champion (he doesn't teach here). People come from around the world to learn how to fight alongside seasoned Thai professionals. It's a mix of Thais and foreigners who live in on-site dorms, but tourists can join drop-in classes and yoga (400B).

Sinbi Muay Thai THAI BOXING

(Map p626; ☎083 391 5535; www.sinbi-muay thai.com; 100/15 Mu 7, Th Sai Yuan; per session/week 400/4800B; ⏰7.30am-7pm Mon-Sat) A well-respected boxing training camp for both men and women.

Kite Zone KITESURFING

(Map p626; ☎083 395 2005; www.kitesurfthailand.com; Hat Friendship; 1hr lesson 1100B, 3-day course 10,000-15,000B) Rawai is a fine place to tackle kitesurfing and this cool young school has a tremendous perch on Hat Friendship. Courses range from one-hour tasters to three-day, 10-hour courses. From April to October, classes happen at Hat Nai Yang (p644) on the northwest side of the island. Also rents kit (per hour/day 1200/3500B) and runs stand-up paddle trips (from 700B).

Bob's Kite School KITESURFING

(Map p614; ☎092 459 4191; www.kiteschool phuket.com; Rte 4024; 1hr lesson 1500B, 3hr course 3500B; ⏰Nov-Apr) Phuket's very first, German-run kite school is still going strong with keen, friendly staff. From May to mid-October they operate on the northwest of the island at Hat Nai Yang (p644). Equipment hire costs 1000B per hour.

Phuket Riding Club HORSE RIDING

(Map p614; ☎076 288213; www.phuketridingclub.com; 95 Th Viset; 1/2hr 1000B/2000B; ⏰7.30am-6.30pm) The perfect opportunity to live out that horse-riding through the tropics dream. Phuket Riding Club offers fun one- to two-hour rides in the jungle around Rawai. Book a day ahead.

Sleeping

Good 9 at Home GUESTHOUSE $

(Map p626; ☎088 457 6969; www.facebook.com/good9athome; 62 Mu 6, Soi Wassana; r incl breakfast 900B; ❄📶) Beside a cute patio, these seven small but wonderfully fresh, gleaming contemporary-style rooms spiced up with colour feature walls, tiled bathrooms and the odd bit of artwork make for good-value digs, 300m up the street from Hat Rawai. The lime-green-and-grey house is kept clean, cosy and friendly, with a thoughtful little coffee corner thrown into the mix.

Vijitt RESORT $$$

(Map p626; ☎076 363600; www.vijittresort.com; 16 Mu 2, Th Viset; villa incl breakfast 6800-27,500B; P❄📶🏊) Arguably the area's most elegant property, peaceful Vijitt is sprinkled with frangipani trees and deluxe villas that boast limestone floors, large bathtubs, outdoor showers and gorgeous sea views from private terraces (some with their own pools). The stunning, multilevel, black-bottom infinity pool overlooks Hat Friendship.

Sunsuri RESORT $$$
(Map p626; ☎076 336400; www.sunsuri-phuket.com; 11/5 Mu 1, Hat Nai Han; r 4600-5000B; P ❄ @ 📶 🏊) Sprawling over a ridge behind Hat Nai Han, this luxe 132-room compound is made up of vaguely modernist cubes swathed in earthy tones that make it feel a bit like Jurassic Park. Almost all of the smart, straight-lined rooms enjoy ocean views, along with free-standing baths, plush linens and hardwood-on-limestone decor. Three huge swimming pools round off the package.

Eating

Hat Rawai is lined with a dozen locally owned seafood grills sizzling fresh catch along the roadside (mains 90B to 300B), with seating on plastic chairs or blankets on the floor.

Som Tum Lanna THAI $
(Map p614; ☎081 597 0569; 3/7 Th Sai Yuan; mains 80-150B; ⏲9am-5pm Tue-Sun) When it comes to *sôm·đam*, order it mild – it'll still bring some serious heat. And while the fish at this Isan soul food shack is good, its equal exists elsewhere. The chicken on the other hand is outstanding.

German Bakery EUROPEAN $
(Map p626; Th Viset; mains 80-140B; ⏲7.30am-4.30pm) This fun, friendly restaurant run by a German-Thai couple does the best pastries in the area. It makes fine brown bread, serves excellent breakfasts (try the pineapple pancakes) and has amazing bratwurst and sauerkraut. Surfers come here to fuel up before an early session.

Da Vinci ITALIAN $$
(Map p626; ☎076 289574; www.davinciphuket.com; 28/46 Mu 1, Th Viset; mains 320-900B; ⏲5.30-10.30pm; 👪) Alfresco wining and dining on crisp white-linen tables at this modern, authentic Italian kitchen is perfect on a balmy night. Staff are lovely and warm, the pizza is wood-fired, breads are fresh and pastas arrive full of flavour. The world-roaming wine list is excellent and there's complimentary after-dinner limoncello up for grabs. Popular with families for the kids' play area.

★**Rum Jungle** INTERNATIONAL $$$
(Map p626; ☎076 388153; www.facebook.com/Rum-Jungle-Cafe-Rawai-Phuket-173738946050909; 69/8 Mu 1, Th Sai Yuan; mains 240-620B; ⏲11.30am-2pm & 6-10.30pm; 🌿) One of Rawai's finest, this semi-open thatched-roof restaurant with an exceptional world-beat soundtrack is family-run and spearheaded by a terrific Aussie chef. The New Zealand lamb shank is divine, as are the steamed clams, and the pasta sauces are all made from scratch. Tempting veggie choices include eggplant parmigiana and pasta Gorgonzola.

Drinking & Nightlife

Nikita's BAR
(Map p626; ☎076 288703; www.nikitas-phuket.com; Hat Rawai; mains 150-350B; ⏲10am-midnight; 📶) This beautifully chilled-out open-air hang-out gazes over the sea just west of Rawai's pier, with coffee, green tea and a good selection of shakes and cocktails. A mango margarita, perhaps? If you're hungry, it also does decent watering-hole food such as omelettes, pastas, burgers and wood-fired pizzas.

Getting There & Away

Rawai is 18km southwest of Phuket Town. *Sŏrng·tăa·ou* (40B) run to Rawai from Phuket Town's Th Ranong between 7am and 5.30pm. Some continue to Hat Nai Han (40B), but not all, so ask first. Taxis from Rawai to Nai Han cost 200B.

Taxis go from Rawai and Hat Nai Han to Phuket airport (750B), Patong (700B) and Phuket Town (500B).

Hat Kata หาดกะตะ

Classier than Karon and without Patong's seedy hustle, Kata attracts travellers of all ages and walks of life for its shopping, surfing and lively beach. While you won't bag a secluded strip of sand, you'll still find lots to do.

Enjoy surfing in the shoulder and wet seasons, terrific day spas, fantastic (if pricey) food, and a top-notch yoga studio. The gold-sand beach is carved in two by a rocky headland. **Hat Kata Yai** lies on the north side; more secluded **Hat Kata Noi** unfurls to the south. The road between them is home to Phuket's original millionaire's row.

The main commercial street, Th Kata, runs parallel to the beach. There are cheaper restaurants, bars and guesthouses on Th Thai Na, which branches inland just south of where Th Kata heads up over the hill into Karon.

Sights & Activities

The small island of **Ko Pu** is just offshore, but be careful of rip tides, heed the red flags and don't go past the breakers in the rainy

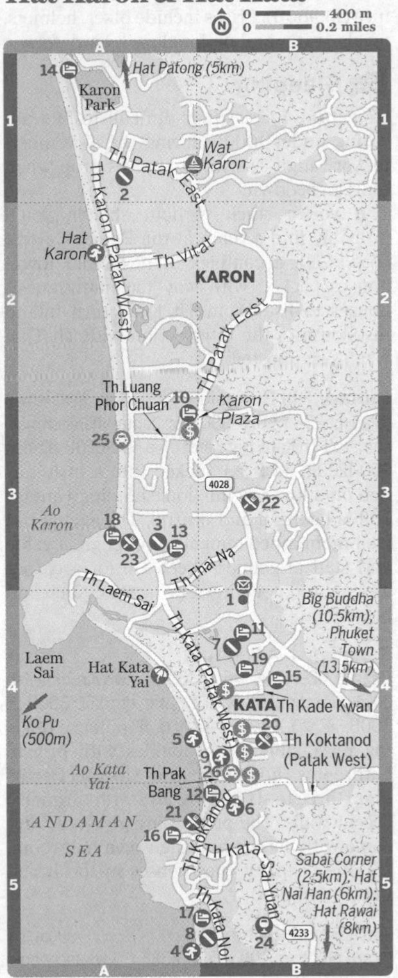

Hat Karon & Hat Kata

Activities, Courses & Tours

- **1** Amazing Bike Tours B4
- Baray Spa .... (see 19)
- Boathouse Cooking Class .... (see 12)
- **2** Dive Asia A1
- **3** Dive Asia A3
- **4** Hat Kata Noi A5
- **5** Hat Kata Yai A4
- Infinite Luxury Spa .... (see 16)
- **6** Kata Hot Yoga B5
- Phuket Surf .... (see 21)
- Re Ká Ta Beach Club .... (see 12)
- **7** Rumblefish Adventure B4
- **8** Sea Fun Divers B5
- Sunrise Divers .... (see 10)
- **9** Surf House B4

Sleeping

- **10** Bazoom Haus A3
- **11** Beach Centre B4
- **12** Boathouse B5
- **13** Fantasy Hill Bungalow A3
- **14** In On The Beach A1
- **15** Kata Beach Homestay B4
- **16** Kata Rocks A5
- **17** Katathani Resort & Spa B5
- **18** Marina Phuket A3
- Pineapple Guesthouse .... (see 10)
- Rumblefish Adventure .... (see 7)
- **19** Sawasdee Village B4

Eating

- Boathouse Wine & Grill .... (see 12)
- **20** Capannina B4
- **21** Kata Mama A5
- Mama Noi's .... (see 10)
- **22** Pad Thai Shop B3
- **23** Red Chopsticks A3

Drinking & Nightlife

- **24** After Beach Bar B5
- Ska Bar .... (see 21)

Transport

- **25** Sŏrng•tăa•ou & Taxi Stop A3
- **26** Sŏrng•tăa•ou & Taxi Stop B4

season unless you're a strong, experienced ocean swimmer.

Both Kata's beaches offer decent surfing from April to November. Hiring stand-up paddle kit or kayaks costs 300/900B per hour/day.

There's a branch of highly rated **Sea Fun Divers** (Map p629; ☎076 330124; www.seafundivers.com; Katathani, 14 Th Kata Noi; ⏰9am-6pm) on Kata Noi.

Phuket Surf SURFING
(Map p629; ☎087 889 7308; www.phuketsurfing.com; Hat Kata Yai; lesson 1500B, board rental per hr/day 150/500B; ⏰8am-7pm Apr-late Oct) Offers private 1½-hour surf lessons plus board rentals. Check the website for info on local surf breaks.

Rumblefish Adventure DIVING
(Map p629; ☎095 441 8665; www.rumblefishadventure.com; 98/79 Beach Centre, Th Kata; 2/3 dives 2900/3700B; ⏰10am-7pm) A terrific boutique dive shop offering all the standard courses, day trips and live-aboards from its Beach Centre location in Kata. The PADI

Open Water course costs 11,900B. There's a hostel attached.

Dive Asia DIVING

(Map p629; ☎076 330 598; www.diveasia.com; 24 Th Karon; 2/3 dives 3400/3900B; ⊙10am-9pm) Runs an extensive range of PADI certification courses (Open Water 11,600B to 16,020B) plus day-trip dives to Ko Phi-Phi and live-aboards to the Similan and Surin Islands (from 21,000B). There's another branch (p633) in Karon.

Kata Hot Yoga YOGA

(Map p629; ☎076 605950; www.katahotyoga.com; 217 Th Koktanod, Hat Kata; per class 550B; ⊙classes 9am, 5.15pm & 7.15pm Mon-Fri, 9am & 5.15pm Sat & Sun) Craving more heat? At Kata Hot Yoga, Bikram's famous asana series is taught over 90 minutes in a sweltering room by the expert owner and an international roster of visiting instructors. All levels welcome; no bookings needed. Multi-class packages offer good deals.

Re Ká Ta Beach Club BEACH CLUB

(Map p629; ☎076 330421; www.rekataphuket.com; 184 Th Koktanod, Hat Kata; day pass 1500B) Of Phuket's (controversially) popular beach clubs, gleaming-white Re Ká Ta is one of the chicest. It's part of the Boathouse family. Entry bags you a day of glamour, lounging on faux-leather beds or sipping passionfruit mojitos in the beachfront infinity pool surrounded by colour-changing lamps – and goes towards drinks and food (mains 300B to 1000B). Wednesdays mean free admission and manicures for girls.

Courses

Boathouse Cooking Class COOKING COURSE

(Map p629; ☎076 330015; www.boathousephuket.com; 182 Th Koktanod; 1-/2-day class 2570/4095B; ⊙class 10am Wed, Sat & Sun) Kata's top fine-dining restaurant offers fantastic Thai cooking classes with its renowned chef.

Tours

Amazing Bike Tours CYCLING

(Map p629; ☎087 263 2031; www.amazingbiketoursthailand.asia; 191 Th Patak East; day trip adult/child 2900/2500B) This highly popular Kata-based adventure outfitter leads small groups on half-day bicycle tours through Khao Phra Thaew Royal Wildlife & Forest Reserve. It also runs terrific day trips around Ko Yao Noi and more challenging three-day adventures rides around Khao Sok National Park (14,900B) and Krabi Province (15,900B). Prices include bikes, helmets, meals, water and national park entry fees.

Sleeping

It's getting increasingly difficult to find anything under 1000B during the November-to-April high season, but prices drop when tourism is down.

If you're stuck without shelter, you'll probably find a room at the **Beach Centre** (Map p629), a complex of new-build townhouses packed with way too many guesthouses to list. From Th Kata, turn inland just south of the intersection with Th Thai Na; it's signposted.

Fantasy Hill Bungalow BUNGALOW $

(Map p629; ☎076 330106; fantasyhill@hotmail.com; 8/1 Th Kata, Hat Kata; r fan 500-650B, air-con 900-1200B; P❄🛜) Tucked into a lush garden on a low-rise hill, longstanding Fantasy Hill is peaceful and central. The ageing but well-maintained bungalows offer great value and staff are super sweet. Go for a corner air-con room with views across Kata and beyond.

Rumblefish Adventure HOSTEL $

(Map p629; ☎076 330315; www.rumblefishadventure.com; 98/79 Th Kata; dm 250-300B, d 800B; ❄🛜) A water-sports flop house offering reasonably clean doubles with private bathrooms, hot water and air-con. Dorms sleep three to six and are airy with turquoise accent walls. The priciest are girls-only and come with air-con and their own bathroom. It's one of many guesthouses in the Beach Centre complex.

Kata Beach Homestay HOSTEL $

(Map p629; ☎093 574 8586; www.facebook.com/Kata-Beach-Homestay-490941801079830; 9 Th Kade Kwan; dm 250B, d 650-950B; 🛜) This modern-feel hostel-guesthouse offers cheap sleeps in a spotless, chequered-floor, eight-bed dorm with two bathrooms. Tile-floored super-clean doubles, in shared- or private-bathroom editions, have fridges, colourful cushions and purple walls, and there's a large communal lounge. Enter through the ground-floor herb shop/travel agency.

Sabai Corner BUNGALOW $$

(Map p626; ☎089 875 5525; www.facebook.com/Sabai-Corner-150517525037992; Hat Kata, off Rte 4233; r 2000B; P🛜) No room on this island offers the fabulous 270-degree ocean view available from these three isolated hillside

DON'T MISS

CHALONG BAY RUM: THE SPIRIT OF PHUKET

When Marine Lucchini and Thibault Spithakis, each born into a prestigious French wine family, met and fell in love, they bonded over booze – fine rum, in particular. Which is why they became master distillers and launched their own distillery, **Chalong Bay Rum** (Map p614; ☎093 575 1119; www.chalongbayrum.com; 14/2 Mu 2, Soi Palai 2; tour 300B; ⊙tours hourly 2-6pm; P).

They knew they wanted to make natural rum in the French style, the kind they make in Martinique, which meant distilling sugarcane juice, rather than molasses (as is used for most rum). Thailand is the world's fourth-largest sugarcane producer with over 200 varieties currently in cultivation and, in 2012, nobody was distilling anything at all on Phuket, so they imported 40-year-old copper Armagnac stills and incorporated one of the world's great islands into their brand.

For now, their rum is white, though there's dark rum on the horizon. It has great flavour, took a gold medal at the 2015 San Francisco World Spirits Competition, and makes a mean mojito – which you'll be sipping as you tour the facility, learning way more about rum than you could ever imagine.

Book ahead, because you'll need directions. About 3km north of Chalong Circle, turn east at the signs to the zoo; it's signposted shortly after.

chalets. Each is a spacious independent concrete studio with pebbled bathroom, canopied four-poster bed, wall-mounted TV, fridge, sofa and safe, as well as a large outdoor terrace with lounge chairs. There's a fourth, wooden bungalow on the way.

From Kata, head 2.5km south on Rte 4233 (towards Rawai/Hat Nai Han). Though it isn't signposted, turn right (downhill) immediately beyond Karon Viewpoint and after 1.5km you're here.

★Sawasdee Village BOUTIQUE HOTEL **$$$**
(Map p629; ☎076 330979; www.phuketsawasdee.com; 38 Th Kade Kwan, Hat Kata; r 4400-7400B, villa 9800-16,500B; ❄@🛜🏊) This opulent boutique resort mixes classic Thai style with Moroccan-esque flourishes and is immersed in a lush tropical landscape laced with canals, waterfalls, Buddhist art installations and a stunning **spa** (massage 1300-2600B; ⊙10am-10pm). Ornate, peaked-roof bungalows have wooden floors, beamed ceilings and lots of character.

Villas are exquisite two-floor homes with free-standing baths, super-comfy beds, elaborate domed ceilings and direct access to one of two romantic pools.

Kata Rocks DESIGN HOTEL **$$$**
(Map p629; ☎076 370777; www.katarocks.com; 186/22 Th Koktanod, Hat Kata; d 24,900-33,300B; P❄🛜🏊) Kata's newest luxury offering is a coolly contemporary all-white beauty, poised on cliffs between the two beaches. Villas are insanely modern, minimalist-chic apartments with iPad-controlled sound systems, full kitchens, Nespresso machines, private pools and electric blinds. Semi-submerged sunbeds dot the pale-turquoise sea-view infinity pool. The innovative **Infinite Luxury Spa** (massages 4200B; ⊙10am-10pm) blends traditional therapies with bang-up-to-date technology like anti-jetlag pods.

Katathani Resort & Spa RESORT **$$$**
(Map p629; ☎076 330124; www.katathani.com; 14 Th Kata Noi, Hat Kata Noi; r incl breakfast 6400-12,300B, ste 8600-18,000B; P❄🛜🏊👪) Taking over a huge portion of (relatively) quiet Hat Kata Noi, this glitzy resort offers all the usual trimmings in stylish surrounds. It features six pools and heaps of space and activities, though rooms could be smarter. **The Shore** (Map p614; ☎076 330124; www.theshore.katathani.com; Hat Kata Noi; villa incl breakfast 19,000-24,200B; ❄🛜🏊) complex is an ultra-luxurious and peaceful, private world of pastel-painted villas fronted by a luscious infinity pool practically on the beach.

Excellent low-season deals are often available. There are several child-friendly pools, a kids' club, kids' menus, a host of activities and babysitting service.

Boathouse BOUTIQUE HOTEL **$$$**
(Map p629; ☎076 330015; www.boathousephuket.com; 182 Th Koktanod; r incl breakfast 7650-9775B, ste 14,300-17,600B; P❄🛜🏊) For Thai politicos, pop stars, artists and celebrity authors, the intimate, elegant boutique Boathouse is still the only place to stay on Phuket. Dark-wood rooms are grand, spacious and gorgeous, some sporting large

BIG BUDDHA

Big Buddha (พระใหญ่; Map p614; www.mingmongkolphuket.com; off Rte 4021; ⏲6am-7pm; 🅿) High atop the Nakkerd Hills, northwest of Chalong circle, and visible from half of the island, the 45m-high Big Buddha sits grandly on Phuket's finest viewpoint. Though it's a tad touristy, tinkling bells and flapping flags give this space an energetic pulse. Pay your respects at the tented golden shrine, then step up to Big Buddha's glorious plateau, where you can peer into Kata's perfect bay, glimpse the shimmering Karon strand and, to the southeast, survey the pebble-sized channel islands of Chalong Bay.

Construction began on Big Buddha in 2007. He's dressed in Burmese alabaster, which isn't cheap. All in all, the price tag is around 100 million baht (not that anybody minds). Phuketians refer to the Big Buddha as Phuket's most important project in the last 100 years, which means a lot considering that construction on Phuket hasn't stopped for the last 20 years.

From Rte 4021, follow signs 1km north of Chalong circle to wind 6km west up a steep country road, passing terraces of banana groves and tangles of jungle.

breezy verandahs. The on-site Boathouse Wine & Grill is one of the island's top restaurants and the attached Re Ká Ta Beach Club (p630) oozes glamour.

Eating

There's some surprisingly classy cuisine in Kata, though you'll be paying for it. For cheaper eats, head to Th Thai Na or the cluster of casual seafood restaurants at the southern end of Hat Kata Yai.

Kata Mama THAI $
(Map p629; Hat Kata Yai; mains 50-400B; ⏲8am-9pm) Our pick of several cheapie seafood huts hidden at the southern end of Hat Kata Yai, Kata Mama keeps busy thanks to its charming management, reliably tasty Thai standards and the low-key beachside setting.

★**Sabai Corner** INTERNATIONAL, THAI $$
(Map p626; ☎089 875 5525; www.facebook.com/Sabai-Corner-150517525037992; Hat Kata, off Rte 4233; mains 100-400B; ⏲10am-10pm; 📶) There's no better Phuket view than the one you'll glimpse from this wide deck: all the way to Karon in one direction and an endless horizon of blue ocean wrapping around the island in the other. It's rare that a location like this gets the restaurant it deserves, but this popular Thai-Swiss-American–owned indoor-outdoor eatery is a stellar nature-fringed find frequented by local expats.

Here are a soaring thatched roof, a pool table, an island bar and a flatscreen for sports. The menu isn't innovative – wandering from fried rice, grilled fish and searing Thai curries to salads, pastas and pizza – but it satisfies. From Kata, head 2.5km south towards Rawai/Hat Nai Han on Rte 4233, turn downhill right behind Karon Viewpoint and drive 1.5km.

Capannina ITALIAN $$
(Map p629; ☎076 284318; www.capannina-phuket.com; 30/9 Mu 2, Th Kata, Hat Kata; mains 160-800B; ⏲11am-11pm Nov-Apr, 5.30-11pm May-Oct) Everything at this modern semi-open-air eatery – from pastas to sauces – is made fresh. Service can be inconsistent, but the four-cheese ravioli is memorable, the risotto comes highly recommended, and there are excellent pizzas, calzones and bruschettas, plus weekly specials on the board. It gets crowded during the high season, so you may want to book ahead.

★**Boathouse Wine & Grill** INTERNATIONAL $$$
(Map p629; ☎076 330015; www.boathousephuket.com; 182 Th Koktanod, Hat Kata; mains 470-1750B, tasting menu 1800-2200B; ⏲11am-10.30pm) The perfect place to wow a special date, this is the pick of the bunch for many a local foodie. The atmosphere can feel a little old-school stuffy, but it's all very glam – plus the Thai and Mediterranean food (think: tiger prawn risotto and lobster soufflé) is fabulous, the wine list famously expansive and the sea views sublime. Special sharing platters are prepared at your table.

Drinking & Nightlife

Kata's nightlife is pretty mellow.

★**Ska Bar** BAR
(Map p629; www.skabar-phuket.com; 186/12 Th Koktanod; ⏲noon-late) Tucked into rocks on the southernmost curl of Hat Kata Yai and seemingly intertwined with the trunk of a

grand old banyan tree, Ska is our choice for seaside sundowners. The Thai bartenders add to the laid-back Rasta vibe, and buoys, paper lanterns and flags dangle from the canopy. Hang around if there's a fire show.

After Beach Bar BAR
(Map p629; ☎081 894 3750; Rte 4233; ⊙9am-10.30pm) It's impossible to overstate how glorious the 180-degree views are from this stilted, thatched reggae bar clinging to a cliff above Kata: rippling sea, rocky peninsulas and palm-dappled hills. Now wack on the Bob Marley and you've got the perfect sunset-watching spot. When the fireball finally drops, lights from fishing boats blanket the horizon. It also does some flavour-bursting *pàt tai*.

Information

There are plenty of ATMs and wi-fi along Kata's main drag.

Post Office (Map p629; Rte 4028; ⊙8.30am-4.30pm Mon-Fri, 9-11am Sat)

Getting There & Around

Sŏrng·tăa·ou run from Th Ranong in Phuket Town to Kata (per person 35B) from 7.30am to 6pm, stopping on Th Pak Bang (opposite Kata Beach Resort).

Taxis from Kata go to Phuket airport (1200B), Phuket Town (600B), Patong (500B) and Karon (300B). There's a minibus service from the airport to Kata (per person 200B, minimum 10 people).

Motorbike rentals (per day 300B) are widely available.

Hat Karon หาดกะรน

Hat Karon is like Hat Patong and Hat Kata's baby: chilled-out, reaching for glamour and a tad sleazy. Despite the megaresorts, there's still more sand space per capita here than at Patong or Kata. The further north you go the more beautiful the broad golden beach gets, culminating at the northernmost edge (accessible from a rutted road past the roundabout) where the water is like turquoise glass.

Within the inland network of streets and plazas you'll find a harmless mess of good local food, more Russian signage than seems reasonable, low-key girly bars, T-shirt vendors and pretty Karon Park, with its artificial lake and mountain backdrop. The northern end of town, near the roundabout, feels tatty, while southern Karon filters into more sophisticated Kata.

Activities

During the April-to-October low season, you can take surf lessons (one hour 1200B) and rent surfboards/bodyboards (per hour 250/100B) at the south end of Hat Karon.

Kata-based Dive Asia has an **office** (Map p629; ☎076 396 199; Th Patak East) in north Karon.

Sunrise Divers DIVING
(Map p629; ☎084 626 4646, 076 398040; www.sunrise-divers.com; 269/24 Th Patak East, Hat Karon; 2/3 dives 3200/3800B, live-aboards from 12,900B; ⊙9am-5pm) Managed by a long-time Phuket blogger, Phuket's biggest live-aboard agent organises a range of budget to luxury multi-day dives to the Similan and Surin Islands, Myanmar's Mergui Archipelago and Ko Phi-Phi. Also arranges day-trip dives, including to Ko Phi-Phi and the Similans.

Sleeping

Pineapple Guesthouse GUESTHOUSE $
(Map p629; ☎076 396223; www.pineapplephuket.com; 291/4 Karon Plaza; dm 280B, r fan/air-con 500/1100B; ❄📶) Pocketed away 400m inland from Hat Karon, Pineapple is an excellent budget choice under warm Thai-English management. It's full of brilliantly kept, bright hot-water rooms adorned with colourful feature walls, fridges and, in some cases, small balconies, and there's a simple, clean 10-bed dorm.

★ **Bazoom Haus** GUESTHOUSE $$
(Map p629; ☎076 396414; www.bazoomhostel.com; 269/5 Mu 3, Karon Plaza; dm 400B, r 2300-3500B; ❄📶) The bold modern exterior suggests something special. Fabulous doubles have wood floors and furnishings, concrete walls, recessed lighting, mosaic showers and, for some, private terraces. There are DJ decks and colourful art in the polished-concrete, in-house Korean restaurant (the helpful young owners are Korean), plus a dive shop. Dorms sleep six. Up to 60% off in low season.

Marina Phuket RESORT $$$
(Map p629; ☎076 330625; www.marinaphuket.com; 47 Th Karon; r incl breakfast & dinner 8100-11,800B; P❄📶🏊) Stilted boardwalks lead through lush, hushed gardens to comfy, secluded sea-

and jungle-facing rooms and villas decked out in classic Thai style. All enjoy breezy terraces, warm-wood decor, teak furniture and silk throws. Villas have hot tubs. Garden rooms were getting an upgrade at research time. The modern-Asian Red Chopsticks restaurant is excellent. Up to 50% discount in low season.

In On The Beach HOTEL **$$$**
(Map p629; ☎076 398220; www.karon-inonthebeach.com; 695-697 Mu 1, Th Patak West, Hat Karon; r incl breakfast 3500B; P ❄ 📶 🏊) Though nothing fancy, this is a sweet, tasteful inn on Karon Park. The slightly dated, cream-walled rooms line a deep-blue pool and come with marble floors, air-con, ceiling fans and sea views. The wonderful location is the thing. With substantial low-season discounts, it's an ideal surf lair.

Eating

There are cheap Thai and seafood places at the north end of Hat Karon and on the main road near south Hat Karon.

★Pad Thai Shop THAI **$**
(Map p629; Th Patak East, Hat Karon; dishes 50B; ⌚9am-6pm) This glorified roadside food shack does rich, savoury chicken stew and absurdly good *kôw pàt Ъoo* (crab fried rice), *pàt see·éw* (fried noodles) and noodle soup. It also serves up some of the best *pàt tai* we've ever tasted: spicy and sweet, packed with tofu, egg and peanuts, and plated with a side of spring onions, beansprouts and lime. Don't miss the house-made chilli sauces.

Mama Noi's THAI, ITALIAN **$**
(Map p629; Karon Plaza; mains 90-185B; ⌚9am-10pm; 📶) This simple tile-floored cafe with faded Italy photos, a good local vibe and dangling pot-plants has been feeding the expat masses for a generation. They do fantastic versions of all the Thai dishes plus a huge list of popular pastas – anyone for red-curry spaghetti? Cheap, tasty and friendly.

Red Chopsticks THAI **$$**
(Map p629; ☎076 330625; 47 Th Karon; mains 80-250B; ⌚noon-midnight; 📶) This great contemporary-Thai eatery, just beyond south Hat Karon, is a welcome breath of sophistication. Dine in a smart, fashionable food lounge full of cosy striped chairs, thick wood pillars and dangling low-light lamps, where busy waiters deliver clay-pot seafood grills, light bubbling curries and herb-infused stir-fries from the open-plan kitchen. The cocktail list is suitably long.

Getting There & Around

Sŏrng·tăa·ou run frequently from Th Ranong in Phuket Town to Hat Karon (per person 30B) from 7.30am to 6pm. Taxis from Karon go to Phuket airport (1000B), Phuket Town (550B), Patong (400B) and Kata (200B). A minibus runs from the airport to Karon (per person 200B, minimum 10 people). Motorbike rental costs 250B per day.

THE BIG PHUKET BEACH CLEAN-UP

As of Thailand's 2014 military takeover, the governing Thai junta has been tackling Phuket's notoriously widespread corruption. Most noticeably, this has involved a firm crackdown on illegal construction and consumer activity on the island's overcrowded beaches, and on its 'taxi mafia' (p617).

Initially, all rental sunbeds, deckchairs and umbrellas were banned, with thousands removed under the watch of armed soldiers. Vendors, masseuses and restaurants on the sand were ordered off the beach. Illegally encroaching buildings were bulldozed, including well established beach clubs and restaurants, and others dramatically reduced in size.

How does all this affect travellers? At the time of writing, beach mats and umbrellas are still available to rent, in limited numbers and in '10%' allocated areas; sunbeds remain banned. Tourists may pitch their own umbrellas and chairs within the '10%' zone. Of course, people aren't necessarily following these new regulations. Jet skis, which were suspended to begin with, are still very much operating on Patong and Kamala. Some businesses have defied close-down orders and popped back up elsewhere.

For now, you'll be enjoying Phuket's beautiful beaches in refreshingly tidier, less-hassle versions, albeit with more limited amenities. This is a trial run that may be extended to other parts of Thailand, and the situation is complex and open to change.

Hat Patong หาดป่าตอง

Sun-scorched Russians in bad knock-off T-shirts, an overwhelming disregard for managed development and a knack for turning the midlife crisis into a full-scale industry make Patong rampant with unintentional comedy. But for all the concrete, silicon and moral bending, there's something honest about this place.

Patong is a free-for-all. Anything, from a Starbucks venti latte to, ahem, companions for the evening, is available for the right price. And while that's true of dozens of other destinations, Patong doesn't try to hide it.

Of course, that doesn't mean you're going to like it. But when you arrive you'll take one look at the wide white-sand beach and its magnificent crescent bay, and you'll at least understand how the whole thing started.

Diving and spa options abound, along with upscale dining, streetside fish grills, extravagant cabaret, Thai boxing, dusty antique shops, one of Thailand's coolest shopping malls and, obviously, dusk-'til-dawn parties.

Activities

★ Sea Fun Divers DIVING
(Map p614; ☎076 340480; www.seafundivers.com; 29 Soi Karon Nui; 2/3 dives 4100/4500B, Open Water certification 18,400B; ⏲9am-6pm) An outstanding, very professional diving operation, with high standards, impeccable service and keen, knowledgeable instructors. It's based at Le Meridien resort at the southern end of Patong; there's a second location (p629) in Kata Noi.

Sea Bees DIVING
(Map p614; ☎076 292969; www.sea-bees.com; Amari Coral Beach Resort; 2 dives 3750B; ⏲9am-6pm) An excellent German-managed diving school offering fun dives to Ko Phi-Phi and King Cruiser Wreck, Open Water certification (15,000B) and Similan Islands liveaboards (from 18,900B). Branches across Phuket and Khao Lak.

Courses

Pum Thai Cooking School COOKING COURSE
(Map p636; ☎076 346269; www.pumthaifoodchain.com; 204/32 Th Rat Uthit; class 500-7500B) This restaurant and cookery school (with branches in Thailand, France and the UK) holds several daily one-dish (30 minutes) to six-hour classes. Popular, four-hour 'Little Wok' classes include a market tour and a take-home cookbook.

Sleeping

It's getting tricky to find anything in Patong under 1000B between November and April. Outside this time rates drop by 40% to 60%.

★ Lupta Hostel HOSTEL $
(Map p636; ☎076 602462, 092 934 6453; www.luptahostel.com; 138 Th Tawiwong; dm 490-590B, d 1200B; @ wifi) Just 100m from Th Bangla, this wonderful, warm, modern newcomer feels more European posh-tel than Patong crashpad. Small, comfy four- to eight-person dorms in light woods and whites share smartish bathrooms. Each bed gets its own locker, plug socket and tiny shelf. Enjoy light breakfast in the social lobby loaded with cushions, high stools and rattan lamps. There's a girls-only dorm.

Patong Backpacker Hostel HOSTEL $
(Map p636; ☎076 341196; 140 Th Thawiwong; dm 250-450B; ❄ wifi) This busy budget spot has a great location across the road from the beach and a welcoming communal lounge. Colour-walled dorms sleep three to 10. The top floor is brightest, but dorms on the lower floors each have their own attached bathrooms.

Baipho GUESTHOUSE $$
(Map p636; ☎076 292074; www.baipho.com; 205/12-15 Th Rat Uthit ; r incl breakfast 2000-4500B; ❄ wifi) Tucked into a quiet soi, this artsy, characterful boutique guesthouse overflows with Buddha imagery, paintings of dancers, floral motifs and Zen-like trimmings that mingle with modern art and urban touches. The dimly lit but stylish nest-like rooms are all unique, so ask the friendly management if you can see a few.

Merrison Inn HOTEL $$
(Map p636; ☎076 340383; www.merrisoninn.com; 5/35 Th Hat Patong; r incl breakfast 1500-2000B; ❄ wifi) Polished-concrete floors, colourful-tiled bathrooms, wall-mounted flat-screen TVs, queen-sized beds, friendly staff and more than a little Asian kitsch make this place an excellent deal.

Red Planet HOTEL $$
(Map p636; ☎076 341936; www.redplanethotels.com; 56 Th Rat Uthit; r 1200-2500B; P ❄ wifi) Part of a budding Southeast Asian brand, this red-and-white block offers no-frills, tidy, three-star living. And it works. Rooms

Hat Patong

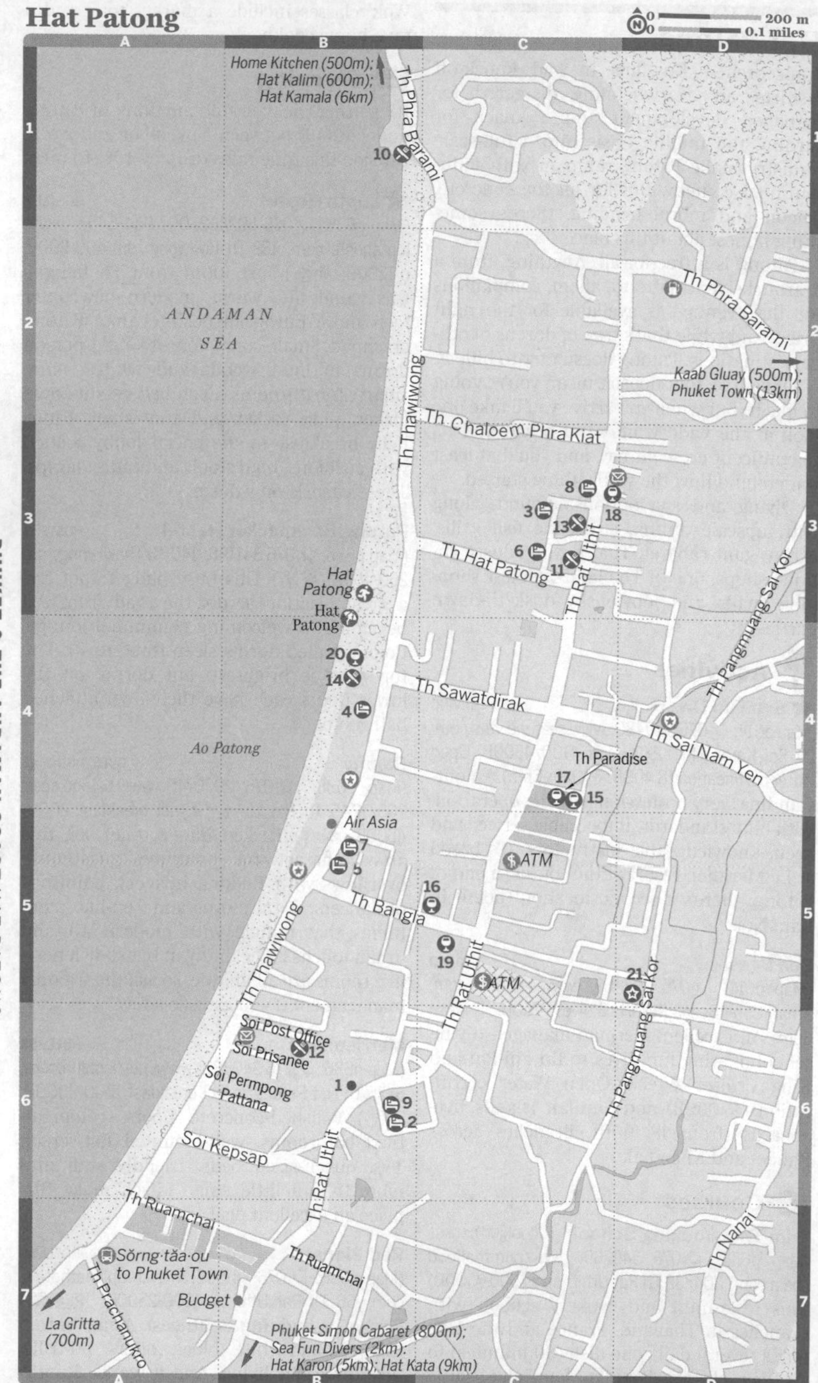

0 200 m
0 0.1 miles
Home Kitchen (500m); Hat Kalim (600m); Hat Kamala (6km)
Th Phra Barami
ANDAMAN SEA
Th Phra Barami
Kaab Gluay (500m); Phuket Town (13km)
Th Thawiwong
Th Chaloem Phra Kiat
Th Hat Patong
Th Rat Uthit
Hat Patong
Hat Patong
Th Sawatdirak
Th Pangmuang Sai Kor
Th Sai Nam Yen
Ao Patong
Th Paradise
Air Asia
ATM
Th Bangla
ATM
Th Thawiwong
Th Rat Uthit
Th Pangmuang Sai Kor
Soi Post Office
Soi Prisanee
Soi Permpong Pattana
Soi Kepsap
Th Rat Uthit
Th Ruamchai
Th Ruamchai
Th Nanai
Sŏrng·tăa·ou to Phuket Town
Th Prachanukro
Budget
La Gritta (700m)
Phuket Simon Cabaret (800m); Sea Fun Divers (2km); Hat Karon (5km); Hat Kata (9km)

Hat Patong

are a tight fight, but smart, cushy and well-equipped with wood floors, hairdryers and plush linens.

Sino House GUESTHOUSE $$
(Map p636; ☎076 293272; 205/10-11 Th Rat Uthit; r 1400-1800B;) A sweet guesthouse with Chinese art hanging on the flagstone hallway walls, an elaborately tiled lobby, and clean and large, if basic, rooms with wood furnishings, burgundy drapes, safety boxes and floor-to-ceiling headboards.

★ **BYD Lofts** APARTMENT $$$
(Map p636; ☎076 343024; www.bydlofts.com; 5/28 Th Hat Patong; apt 6500-17,400B;) Three-block BYD feels like it's been torn straight out of an upmarket interior design magazine. If style and comfort win over beachfront location (it's only a minute's walk), look no further. Urban-chic apartments coated in white (floors, walls, blinds), sharp lines and colourful art feel angelic compared to the seedy world outside. Some rooms have private pools. For everyone else there's a turquoise rooftop pool.

Impiana Phuket Cabana HOTEL $$$
(Map p636; ☎076 340138; www.impiana.com; 41 Th Thawiwong; r 5300-10,600B, ste 12,750-29,700B;) Cabana-style and bang on the best (north) part of the beach, Impiana's rooms are laden with sophisticated creature comforts and still close to all the action. There's good Asian-Mediterranean fusion food at poolside **Sala Bua** (mains 300-1900B; 11am-11pm), while indulgent treatments at the on-site **Swasana Spa** (massage 1100-1900B; 10am-9pm) see you nestled in a cool glass cube with ocean views.

Eating

Patong has loads of restaurants, for all budgets. The trick is to steer around the abundant watered-down Thai and poorly executed Western kitchens. The swishest restaurants are huddled together above the cliffs on the north edge of town.

Bargain seafood and noodle stalls pop up across town at night. Try the sois around Th Bangla, and **Patong Food Park** (Map p636; Th Rat Uthit; dishes 50-200B; 4.30pm-midnight) once the sun drops.

Kaab Gluay THAI $
(Map p614; ☎076 346832; 58/3 Th Phra Barami; dishes 60-165B; 11am-2am;) It's hardly Patong's most peaceful spot, but this easy-going roadside eatery is a hit for its authentic, affordable Thai food, with switched-on staff and well-spelt (!) menus to match. Unpretentious dining happens under a huge tin roof. Expect red-curry prawns, chicken satay, sweet-and-sour fish, deep-fried honeyed chicken, classic noodles and stir-fries, and 30-plus takes on spicy Thai salads.

Chicken Rice Briley THAI $
(Map p636; ☎081 597 8380; Patong Food Park, Th Rat Uthit; meals 50-60B; 6am-9pm) One of few diners in Patong Food Park to offer sustenance while the sun shines. Steamed chicken breast is served on a bed of rice with a bowl of chicken broth with crumbled bits of meat; dip it in the fantastic chilli sauce. It does a popular stewed pork on rice, plus

mango with sticky rice. There's a reason it's perennially packed.

Ella INTERNATIONAL **$$**
(Map p636; ☎076 344253; www.facebook.com/EllaBistro; 100/19-20 Soi Post Office; mains 200-400B; ⊙9am-11pm; 📶) A moulded-concrete, industrial-feel bistro-cafe that's a lovely surprise. Inventive all-day breakfasts feature spicy Rajasthani scrambled eggs, massaman chicken tacos, omelettes stuffed with chicken and veg, and baguette French toast with caramelised banana. It has similarly styled **rooms** (r 3200-5400B; ❄📶) upstairs.

The Beach THAI, SEAFOOD **$$**
(Map p636; ☎076 345944; 49 Th Thawiwong; mains 180-350B; ⊙8am-11.30pm) If you fancy decent Thai food and a string of predictable, reliable seafood choices by the beach, wander over to this long-running shack. It's slightly overpriced, but the setting is fantastic.

★Home Kitchen INTERNATIONAL **$$$**
(Map p614; ☎093 764 6753; www.facebook.com/HOME.kitchen.bar.bed; 314 Th Phra Barami, Hat Kalim; mains 300-800B; ⊙5am-1am; 📶) White leather, faded tables, floaty fabrics, burning lanterns and neon lighting crash together with Mediterranean flair. This crazily beautiful, quirky-chic dining room/cocktail bar shaped like a ship's hull is a stunning work of art. And the creative Thai-Mediterranean food is fab too. Try avocado and crabmeat salad, squid-ink pasta with salmon, massaman Wagyu beef, deep-fried *pá·aang*-curry sea bass and perfectly crispy Parmesan coated chips.

Baan Rim Pa THAI **$$$**
(Map p636; ☎076 340789; www.baanrimpa.com; 223 Th Phra Barami; mains 290-750B; ⊙noon-10pm) Refined Thai fare is served with a side order of spectacular views at this institution. Standards are high, with prices to match, but romance is in the air, with candlelight and piano music aplenty. Book ahead, button up and tuck in.

La Gritta ITALIAN **$$$**
(Map p614; ☎076 292697; www.lagritta.com; Amari Coral Beach Resort; mains 400-800B; ⊙10am-midnight; 📶) A spectacularly positioned, modern Italian restaurant serving up huge portions of deliciously creamy pastas and gourmet pizzas. With comfy booths, gorgeous beach views and a deck just centimetres above the boulder-strewn shore at the south end of Hat Patong, there are few better settings for a sunset Chalong Bay Rum mojito (p631).

🍷 Drinking & Nightlife

Some visitors may find that Patong's bar scene puts them off their *pàt tai*, but, if you're in the mood for plenty of winking neon and short skirts, it's certainly a once-in-a-lifetime experience.

Th Bangla is beer and bar-girl central, featuring spectacular go-go extravaganzas with the usual mix of gyrating Thai girls and often red-faced Western men. The techno is loud, the clothes are all but nonexistent and the decor is typically slapstick with plenty of phallic imagery. The atmosphere is more carnival than carnage and you'll find plenty of peers fighting through the throng to the bar.

ℹ TIGER KINGDOM

At some point during your stay, you'll inevitably be handed a brochure flaunting Phuket's controversial Tiger Kingdom. Launched in 2013, Tiger Kingdom Phuket (like its original in Chiang Mai) offers hundreds of daily visitors the chance to stroke, feed and pose over-enthusiastically with its 'domesticated' tigers, both tiny cubs and full-grown adults.

As with Thailand's other tiger-centric attractions, worries of animal welfare and human safety abound, and there are constant concerns about animals being maltreated, confined to small cages and sedated to keep them docile. Like the infamous Tiger Temple (p184) in Kanchanaburi, Tiger Kingdom denies all allegations that its tigers are mistreated.

In 2014, an Australian tourist was seriously mauled while visiting Tiger Kingdom. The tiger in question was 'retired'.

Given the significant animal welfare issues involved, Lonely Planet does not recommend visiting Tiger Kingdom. For more on the thorny issues surrounding Thailand's animal attractions, see p492.

★ Seduction CLUB
(Map p636; www.facebook.com/seductiondisco; 70/3 Th Bangla; ⏲10pm-5am) International DJs, professional-grade sound system and forever the best dance party on Phuket, without question.

Illuzion CLUB
(Map p636; www.illuzionphuket.com; 31 Th Bangla; ⏲10pm-6am) Patong's hottest new mega-club is a sparkly multi-level mishmash of dance and gymnastics shows, international DJs, regular ladies' nights, all-night electronic beats, and more bars than you could ever count.

Sole Mio BAR
(Map p636; ☎081 5378116; Th Thawiwong; ⏲10am-midnight;) A whimsically decorated Caribbean-feel bar, crafted from reused corrugated tin, strings of shells and reclaimed pastel-washed wood. It's right by the beach, pulses with pop songs and is fuelled by middling cocktails and Chang draught. There are worse ways to spend an afternoon.

Nicky's Handlebar BAR
(Map p636; ☎076 343211; www.nickyhandlebars.com; 41 Th Rat Uthit ; ⏲7.30am-1am;) This fun biker bar welcomes all, wheels or no wheels. Once a bit of a dive, Nicky's has never looked better. Ashtrays crafted from bike parts rest on the metal bar and weighty menus are made from hubcaps and heavy disk brakes. You can get your own wheels here by asking about Harley tours and hire (from 4800B).

☆ Entertainment

Cabaret shows and Thai boxing are Patong's specialities.

Phuket Simon Cabaret CABARET
(Map p614; ☎076 342114; www.phuket-simoncabaret.com; 8 Th Sirirach; adult 700-800B, child 500-600B; ⏲shows 6pm, 7.45pm & 9.30pm) About 500m south of town, Simon puts on fun colourful trans cabarets. The 600-seat theatre is grand, the costumes are glittery, feathery extravaganzas and the ladyboys are convincing. It's noticeably geared towards an Asian audience and the house is usually full – book ahead.

Bangla Boxing Stadium SPECTATOR SPORT
(Map p636; ☎076 273416; www.banglaboxingstadiumpatong.com; Th Pangmuang Sai Kor; admission 1700-2500B; ⏲9pm Wed, Fri & Sun) Old name, same game: a packed line-up of competitive *moo·ay tai* bouts featuring Thai and foreign fighters.

ℹ Information

There are ATMs, currency-exchange facilities and wi-fi across town.

Post Office (Map p636; Th Rat Uthit; ⏲8.30am-4.30pm Mon-Fri, 9am-noon Sat & Sun)

Tourist Police (Map p636; ☎1669, 076 342719; cnr Th Thawiwong & Th Bangla)

ℹ Getting There & Around

Túk-túks circle Patong for around 200B per ride. Numerous places rent motorbikes (250B); Nicky's Handlebar (p639) rents Harleys (from 4800B). The mandatory helmet law is strictly enforced in Patong, where roadblocks/checkpoints can spring up suddenly. **Budget** (Map p636; ☎089 873 0234; www.budget.co.th; Patong Merlin Hotel, 44 Th Thawiwong; ⏲8am-6pm) hires cars at the south end of town.

Sŏrng·tăa·ou from Th Ranong in Phuket Town go to the south end of Hat Patong (30B) from 7am to 6pm. From here you can walk or hop on motorbike taxis (30B per ride) or túk-túk. After-hours túk-túk charters from Phuket Town cost 500B. A 'local bus' runs between Phuket Town's Bus Terminal 1 (p624) and Patong (50B) from 7am to 5pm.

Taxis to/from the airport cost 800B. There's a shared minibus from the airport to Patong (per person 180B, minimum 10 people).

Hat Kamala หาดกมลา

A chilled-out hybrid of Hat Karon and Hat Surin, Kamala lures in a mix of longer-term, low-key visitors, families and young couples. The bay is magnificent and serene. Palms and pines mingle on the leafy, rocky northern end, where the water is a rich emerald green and the snorkelling around the rock reef is halfway decent. The entire beach is backed by a paved path and lush rolling hills, which one can only hope are left alone…forever. Flashy new resorts are carved into the southern bluffs and jet skis make an appearance, but Kamala is quietish and laid-back, by Phuket standards.

Activities

During the May-to-October monsoon, you can hire surfboards (per hour 300B) and take surf classes (1500B) on south Hat Kamala.

Laem Singh BEACH
(Map p642) Local beach addicts will tell you that cliff-framed Laem Singh, 1km north of Kamala, conceals one of the island's most beautiful beaches. Park on the headland and clamber down a steep jungle-frilled path, or

PHUKET FANTASEA

It's impossible to ignore the brochures, billboards and touts flogging **Phuket Fantasea** (Map p642), the US$60 million 'cultural theme park' located just east of Hat Kamala and relentlessly promoted as one of the island's top 'family-friendly' attractions. We recommend reading up on the numerous animal welfare issues associated with this Vegas-style spectacle, at which animals are forced to 'perform' here daily, before choosing to support it.

you could charter a long-tail (1000B) from Hat Kamala. It gets crowded.

Sleeping

Papa Crab BOUTIQUE HOTEL **$$**
(Map p642; ☎076 385315; www.phuketpapacrab.com; 93/5 Mu 3; r 1900B;) This elegant boutique guesthouse combines homey lodgings, peaceful location and discreet, friendly service. A wooden bridge trails over the lobby's lily pond to tastefully styled terracotta-floor rooms with darkwood beds, Lemongrass toiletries and soothing lime-green-and-white colour schemes, topped up by fresh frangipani flowers.

Cape Sienna HOTEL **$$$**
(Map p642; ☎076 337300; www.capesienna.com; 18/40 Mu 6, Th Nakalay; r 4950-16,900B;) This flashy, romantic hotel sprawls up the southern headland offering magnificent azure bay views from the lobby, the pool, the sunken in-pool cabanas and every room. Rooms are bright, smart and modern, with all amenities and splashes of orange and turquoise. Deluxes have balcony hot tubs. Up above is Kamala's breeziest cocktail bar, **Vanilla Sky** (5pm-midnight), and there's polished Mediterranean-Thai cuisine at on-site **Plum** (mains 400-1000B; 6-11pm, closed Mon May-Oct;).

Layalina Hotel BOUTIQUE HOTEL **$$$**
(Map p642; ☎076 385944; www.layalinahotel.com; 75-75/1 Mu 3, Hat Kamala; r incl breakfast 6050-8500B;) Bag one of the split-level suites with private rooftop terraces at this beachfront boutique spot for sunset views. The decor is simple, Thai and chic, full of fluffy white duvets and honey-toned wooden furniture. The pool is ridiculously tiny, but that aqua ocean *is* only steps away. Good low-season discounts.

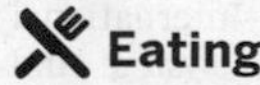

Eating

Meena Restaurant THAI **$**
(Map p642; mains 80-150B; 9am-5pm) This family-run beachside shack with rainbow-striped and leopard-print sarongs for tablecloths is a real find. The owners couldn't be more welcoming. The tasty authentic Thai food is exceptional and so are the fresh fruit shakes. The rustic setting is exactly what you (most likely) came to Kamala for. It's at the north end of the beach.

Mam's Restaurant THAI, INTERNATIONAL **$$**
(Map p642; ☎089 032 2009; 32/32 Soi 8; mains 90-280B; noon-10pm) There's no beach view, but local expats swear by this quiet, simple place with just a handful of tables sprinkled across the patio of a family home. Mam's plates up all the usual Thai suspects in meat, shrimp or vegie versions packed full of flavour, along with burgers, pastas, kebabs, sandwiches and, yes, even fish 'n' chips. It's about 400m east (inland) from the main highway.

Getting There & Away

Sŏrng·tăa·ou run between Phuket Town's Th Ranong and Kamala (35B) from 7am to 5pm. *Sŏrng·tăa·ou* also go from Kamala to Hat Surin (20B). Taxis to/from the airport cost 700B.

Hat Surin หาดสุรินทร์

With a wide, blonde beach, water that blends from pale turquoise in the shallows to a deep blue on the horizon, and lush, boulder-strewn headlands, Surin could easily attract visitors on looks alone. Ah, but there are stunning galleries, fabulous boutiques, five-star spa resorts, wonderful beachfront dining and a fun party vibe too.

Phuket's beach clean-up operation (p634) has hit Surin particularly hard. At research time, all establishments on the sand had been cleared away (leaving behind a scruffy mess), and there were mixed messages about the fate of remaining businesses. *In theory*, this means you'll now enjoy Hat Surin's full untarnished beauty.

Sleeping

Hat Surin hosts some of Phuket's classiest resorts, but little for those on a budget.

Benyada Lodge HOTEL $$
(Map p642; ☎076 271261; www.benyadalodge-phuket.com; 106/52 Mu 3, Hat Surin; r incl breakfast 2800-5500B; ❄📶🏊) Stellar service and stylish, modern rooms – with black louvred closets, tiled bathrooms, lounging corners and vibrant silk pillows on tight white sheets – make Benyada one of Surin's better deals. Admire the sunset from the rooftop bar. It's just a couple of minutes' walk from the beach.

Surin Bay Inn HOTEL $$
(Map p642; ☎076 271601; 106/11 Mu 3; r incl breakfast 1800-3000B; ❄📶) A welcoming no-frills midranger 300m back from the beachfront. Tiled floors, white sheets and colourful cushions smarten up spacious, simple kettle-equipped rooms. Larger rooms at the front, with terraces and sea glimpses, are best.

★Twin Palms RESORT $$$
(Map p642; ☎076 316500; www.twinpalms-phuket.com; 106/46 Mu 3; r incl breakfast 8100-18,400B, ste 14,100-29,100B; ❄@📶🏊) Classic yet completely contemporary, Twin Palms is what Surin is all about. Delicate white frangipani trees fringe a maze of artsy minimalist pools. Even the simplest rooms are modern and extra spacious, with oversized bathrooms, free-standing baths, sublimely comfortable beds and a supreme sense of calm. Staff are professional, the **Sun Spa** (treatment 1500-2400B; ⏰11am-9pm) is fantastic, and the beach lies just minutes away.

There's a popular Sunday brunch (1970B).

★Surin Phuket RESORT $$$
(Map p642; ☎076 316400; www.thesurinphuket.com; 118 Mu 3, Hat Pansea; r incl breakfast 10,500-41,200B; P❄📶🏊) Almost any establishment on a secluded beach this quiet and stunning would be a top pick. But bungalows at the Surin, hidden beneath hillside foliage, offer homey, earthy, luxurious interiors that make the site that much better, and the six-sided sea-view pool is gorgeously abstract. It's quite a walk up hills and over wooden walkways to many of the 'cottages'.

Amanpuri Resort RESORT $$$
(Map p642; ☎076 324333; www.amanresorts.com; Hat Pansea; villa US$990-3450; P❄📶🏊) Understated, luxurious and unbelievably peaceful, celebrity magnet Amanpuri is one of Phuket's most exclusive hotels. Graceful traditional-design bungalows are all about the location, with sea-facing cabanas, warm-wood decor and enormous bathrooms. There's a huge array of activities on offer (yoga, kayaking, surfing), plus a jet-black pool, first-rate service and a well-stocked library.

Eating & Drinking

Surin has some excellent upmarket restaurants. For cheap seafood, head to the numerous delicious seafront dining rooms. The most affordable eats are at the food stalls in the beachside parking lot and the couple of roadside shacks heading inland on Rte 4025.

Twin Brothers THAI $$
(Map p642; Hat Surin; mains 120-350B; ⏰11am-10pm) By day, one brother mans the wok, stirring up decent seafood-focused Thai food at (almost) local prices. At night, the other fires up a fresh seafood grill. It's more down to earth than Surin's other options.

Taste FUSION $$
(Map p642; ☎076 270090; www.tastesurinbeach.com; dishes 200-420B; ⏰noon-11pm Tue-Sun; 📶) Minimalist modern lines, top-notch service, a sophisticated but chilled-out vibe and delicious Thai-Mediterranean fusion food make this urban-meets-surf eatery an outstanding choice. Dine indoors or alfresco on meal-sized salads (try the goats' cheese with smoked almonds), weekly specials or a variety of creative starters and mains. Ceramic fish swim above the bathroom door.

Sugo ITALIAN $$
(Map p642; ☎076 386599; www.sugo-phuket.com; 117 Mu 3, Th Srisoonthorn; mains 250-570B; ⏰5-10.30pm Tue-Sun) A Sicilian chef leads this popular new 'rustic Italian' spot, 700m east of Hat Surin on Rte 4025. It's smart and full of style, with specials chalked up on the walls. Slip into a bright-red booth or sneak into the back courtyard to feast on carefully crafted wood-fired pizza, pasta, bruschetta, meaty mains or antipasti platters.

★Catch INTERNATIONAL $$$
(Map p642; ☎076 316567; www.catchbeachclub.com; mains 400-600B; ⏰noon-2am; 📶) Throw on your breeziest island-chic outfit to dine overlooking the sea at Surin's glitziest beach club. It's classy at every turn, from ambience to cocktails and international cuisine (pastas, salads, burgers, pizzas). Club admission (low/high season 1000/2000B) buys you a beach mat and pillow for the day, and goes towards food

Hat Kamala, Hat Surin & Ao Bang Thao

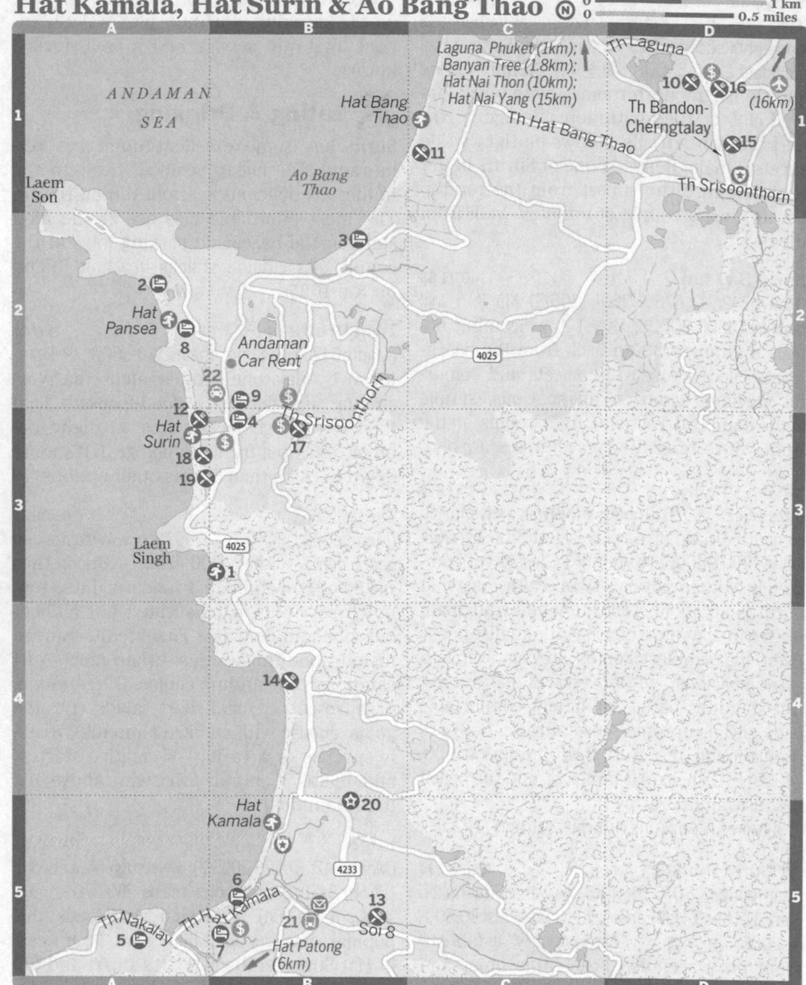

and drinks. Or just grab a table and order off the menu.

Getting There & Away

Sŏrng·tăa·ou go from Phuket Town's Th Ranong to Hat Surin (30B) from 7am to 5pm, continuing to Hat Kamala; túk-túk charters cost 500B. Taxis to/from the airport cost 700B.

Andaman Car Rent (Map p642; 076 621600; www.andamancarrent.com; 112/12 Mu 3, Hat Surin; 9am-7pm) This agency, 300m north of Twin Palms, rents vehicles (per day 800B).

Ao Bang Thao อ่าวบางเทา

Even more beautiful than Hat Patong, stunning 8km-long white-sand Hat Bang Thao is the glue that binds this area's disparate elements. The southern half of the region is dotted with three-star bungalow resorts, plus the swanky Bliss Beach Club. Further inland you'll find an old fishing village laced with canals, a number of upstart villa subdivisions and some stellar restaurants. If you see a herd of water buffalo grazing beside a gigantic construction site...well, that's how fast Bang Thao has developed.

Hat Kamala, Hat Surin & Ao Bang Thao

Activities, Courses & Tours
1 Laem Singh ... B3
Sun Spa ... (see 9)

Sleeping
2 Amanpuri Resort ... A2
3 Andaman Bangtao Bay Resort ... B2
4 Benyada Lodge ... B3
5 Cape Sienna ... A5
6 Layalina Hotel ... B5
7 Papa Crab ... B5
Surin Bay Inn ... (see 4)
8 Surin Phuket ... A2
9 Twin Palms ... B2

Eating
Andaman Restaurant ... (see 3)
10 Bampot ... D1
11 Bliss Beach Club ... C1
12 Catch ... A3
13 Mam's Restaurant ... B5
14 Meena Restaurant ... B4
15 Pesto ... D1
Plum ... (see 5)
16 Siam Supper Club ... D1
17 Sugo ... B3
18 Taste ... A3
Tatonka ... (see 16)
19 Twin Brothers ... A3

Drinking & Nightlife
Vanilla Sky ... (see 5)

Entertainment
20 Phuket Fantasea ... B5

Transport
21 Sŏrng·tăa·ou to Hat Surin & Phuket Town ... B5
22 Taxi Stop ... B2

Smack in the centre of it all is the somewhat bizarre Laguna Phuket complex, a network of five four- and five-star resorts tied together by an artificial lake (patrolled by tourist shuttle boats) and a paved nature trail. At the northern end, nature reasserts itsself, and a lonely stretch of powder-white sand and tropical blue sea extends past the bustle into the peaceful bliss you originally had in mind.

Sleeping

Laguna Phuket has seven luxury resorts, an 18-hole golf course and over 30 restaurants. Guests can use the dining and recreation facilities at all of them. Frequent shuttle buses make the rounds of the hotels, as do pontoon boats (via the linked lagoons).

★ **Anantara Phuket Layan** RESORT **$$$**
(Map p614; ☎076 317200; www.anantara.com; 168 Mu 6, Soi 4, Hat Layan; P ❄ ☎ ≋ ♿) On its own secluded, wild-feel bay just north of Hat Bang Thao, this is an exquisite top-end addition. Chic, contemporary-Thai rooms come decked out with dark woods, marble floors, ceramic-bowl sinks and Apple gadgets. Villas have dark-tiled pools and 24-hour butlers. A laid-back lounge-bar overlooks the bubbling beachside pool. Dine at two excellent on-site restaurants (Thai, international/Italian) or in a private beach cabana.

An arts and crafts kids' club keeps the little ones happy.

Banyan Tree RESORT **$$$**
(Map p614; ☎076 372400; www.banyantree.com; 33 Mu 4, Th Srisoonthorn, Laguna Phuket; d incl breakfast 18,600-28,250B; P ❄ @ ☎ ≋) One of Phuket's finest hotels, and the first to introduce bungalows with their own personal pools, the sprawling Banyan Tree is a lushly shaded oasis of sedate, understated luxury. Accommodation is situated in sophisticated villas, with free-standing, open-air baths and private pools, and there's also an adults-only pool. Don't miss the on-site **spa** (treatment 2900-7000B; ⊙8am-9pm).

Andaman Bangtao Bay Resort HOTEL **$$$**
(Map p642; ☎076 270246; www.andamanbangtaobayresort.com; 82/9 Mu 3, Hat Bang Thao; r incl breakfast 2000-8450B; P ❄ ☎ ≋) Most bungalows have sea views and there's a summer-camp vibe at this pleasant little resort at the southern end of Hat Bang Thao. The design is very Thai, with woodcarvings on the walls and coconuts hanging from the roofs, but we'd expect a little more luxury at these prices. Tuck into BBQ seafood and Thai curries at the simple sand-side **restaurant** (mains 195-295B; ⊙8am-10pm; ☎).

Eating & Drinking

Some of Phuket's finest restaurants are just outside Laguna's main gate.

Pesto THAI, INTERNATIONAL $$
(Map p642; 082 423 0184; Th Bandon-Cherngtalay; mains 69-479B; 11.30am-11pm Sun-Fri, 5-11pm Sat;) Mix a Paris-trained Thai chef with a tiny roadside shack and you've got a fantastic find for delicious, wallet-friendly Thai and international food. Light pesto pasta, lobster lasagne and roast-pumpkin salad whizz you across the Mediterranean. Otherwise, stay local with *đôm yam gûng* (spicy-sour prawn soup), deep-fried turmeric fish of the day, and all your favourite curries.

★ **Bampot** INTERNATIONAL $$$
(Map p642; 093 586 9828; www.bampot.co; 19/1 Mu 1, Th Laguna; mains 500-600B; 6pm-midnight Tue-Fri, noon-3pm & 6pm-midnight Sat & Sun) The latest fabulous arrival on Bang Thao's food scene is suitably classy with a modern, urban edge. Cool-blue booths, dangling pans, black-topped tables and white brick walls hung with art set the scene for ambitious European-inspired meals (lobster mac and cheese, sea bass ceviche with pomelo) straight from the open-plan kitchen. Creatively concocted cocktails and international wines round things off.

Bliss Beach Club INTERNATIONAL $$$
(Map p642; 076 510150; www.blissbeachclub.com; 202/88 Mu 2; mains 400-720B; 11am-late;) Even if you don't commit to the Sunday party or a day indulging in these plush turquoise-and-orange-on-white surrounds (per person 300B), swing by Bliss for a tasty lunch or dinner. The Thai-international menu of 13in wood-fired pizzas, roast pumpkin and quinoa salad, chicken satay, burgers and quesadillas is served on a breezy beachside deck with gorgeous sea views.

Siam Supper Club INTERNATIONAL $$$
(Map p642; 076 270936; www.siamsupperclub.com; 36-40 Th Laguna; mains 290-1250B; 6pm-1am;) One of the swishest spots on Phuket, where the glamorous come to sip cocktails, listen to jazz and eat an excellent meal. The menu is predominantly international with gourmet pizzas, grilled goats' cheese and hearty mains such as barbecued Tasmanian salmon, plenty of pastas and truffle-honey roast chicken.

Tatonka INTERNATIONAL $$$
(Map p642; 076 324349; 382/19 Mu 1, Th Laguna; dishes 180-790B; 6-10pm Mon-Sat;) Tatonka bills itself as the home of 'globetrotter cuisine', which owner-chef Harold Schwarz has developed by combining local products with cooking techniques learned in Europe, Colorado and Hawaii. The eclectic, tapas-style selection includes inventive vegetarian and seafood dishes and such delights as Peking duck pizza, green-curry pasta and eggplant 'cookies' with goats' cheese. Book ahead in high season.

Getting There & Away

Sŏrng·tăa·ou run between Phuket Town's Th Ranong and Ao Bang Thao (25B) from 7am to 5pm. Túk-túk charters are 400B. Taxis to/from the airport cost 700B.

Sirinat National Park

อุทยานแห่งชาติสิรินาถ

Comprising the exceptional beaches of Nai Thon, Nai Yang and Mai Khao, along with the former Nai Yang National Park and Mai Khao wildlife reserve, **Sirinat National Park** (Map p614; 076 327152, 076 328226; www.dnp.go.th; adult/child 200/100B; 8.30am-4pm) encompasses 22 sq km of coastline and 68 sq km of sea, stretching from the north end of Ao Bang Thao to Phuket's northernmost tip. This is one of the sweetest slices of the island.

The whole area is 15 minutes or under from Phuket International Airport.

Activities

During the April-to-October monsoon, Hat Nai Yang is great for kitesurfing. Three fine schools include **Kiteboarding Asia** (Map p614; 081 591 4594; www.kiteboardingasia.com; Hat Nai Yang; 1hr lesson 1300B, 3-day course 11,000B; Apr-Oct), **Kite Zone** (Map p614; 083 395 2005; www.kitesurfthailand.com; Hat Nai Yang; 1hr lesson 1100B, 3-day course 10,000-15,000B; May–late-Oct) and Rawai-based Bob's Kite School (p627).

Hat Nai Thon BEACH
(Map p614) If you're after a lovely arc of fine golden sand, away from Phuket's busy buzz, come to west-coast Hat Nai Thon, 7km south of the airport. Swimming is good (except at the height of the monsoon), and there's coral near the headlands at either end of the bay. Many beach restaurants here have been demolished by the island clean-up.

Hat Nai Yang BEACH
(Map p614) Hat Nai Yang's bay, 3km south of the airport, is sheltered by a reef that slopes 20m below the surface – which means good

snorkelling in high season and fantastic surfing/kitesurfing during the monsoon. Behind is a seemingly endless strip of seafood restaurants, hotels and mellow bars.

Hat Mai Khao BEACH
(Map p614) Phuket's longest beach is a beautiful, secluded 10km stretch of sand extending from just south of the airport to the island's northernmost point. Except on weekends and holidays, you'll mostly have it to yourself. Sea turtles lay eggs here between November and February. Take care with the strong year-round undertow.

Soi Dog VOLUNTEERING
(Map p614; ☎081 788 4222; www.soidog.org; 167/9 Mu 4, Soi Mai Khao 10, admission by donation; ⏰9am-noon & 1-3.30pm Mon-Fri, tours 9.30am, 11am & 1.30pm) This nonprofit foundation, 2km inland from Hat Mai Khao, protects 50 cats and 450 dogs (many rescued from the illegal dog-meat trade), focusing on sterilisation, castration, re-homing and animal welfare awareness. Visits are by in-depth tour. The 'old dogs' enclosure can be upsetting, but they're in a happy home. Visitors can play with the animals, or become a dog-walking or long-term volunteer.

Sleeping & Eating

Hat Nai Thon หาดในทอน

Pullman RESORT $$$
(Map p614; ☎076 303299; www.pullmanphuketarcadia.com; 22/2 Mu 4; r 6500-32,350B; P ❄ @ 📶 🏊) Set high on cliffs above northern Hat Nai Thon, this 227-room resort is a belle. The lobby alone will send you into relax mode, with its arched bridge, soothing grey-and-lavender colour scheme, treasure-chest desks and exposed rough-cut limestone walls. A dreamy network of reflection pools extends out above the sea. Service is divine. Cool two- and three-storey chalets are spacious and modern, with terraces.

Enjoy upmarket Thai cuisine and Friday seafood BBQs at the on-site **Elements** (mains 320-1100B; ⏰6.30-11pm) restaurant.

Hat Nai Yang หาดในยาง

Sirinat National Park Accommodation CAMPGROUND, BUNGALOW $
(Map p614; ☎076 327152, in Bangkok 02 562 0760; www.dnp.go.th; camping per person 30B, bungalow 700-1000B) At the park headquarters at the north end of Hat Nai Yang you'll find campsites (bring your own tent) and large, concrete, air-con bungalows just back from the beach on a gorgeous, shady, white-sand bluff. Book ahead online or by phone.

Discovery Beach Resort GUESTHOUSE $
(Map p614; ☎082 497 7500; discovery-phuket@hotmail.com; 90/34 Mu 5; r fan/air-con 800/1500B; ❄ 📶) With wooden Thai accents featured on the facade, lacquered timber handrails and furnishings, and fridges in the rooms, this spotless budget place is a perfectly decent choice. It's nothing fancy, but the location – right on the beach – makes it great value.

★**Dewa** BOUTIQUE HOTEL $$$
(Map p614; ☎076 372300; www.dewaphuketresort.com; 65 Mu 1; r from 7000B; P ❄ 📶 🏊) An independently owned boutique property that offers one- and two-bedroom apartments and luscious pool villas, just steps from the national park. Full-kitchen apartments are more spacious, but villas are secluded pods with reclaimed wood accents, vintage wrought-iron motifs and huge outdoor bathrooms with soaker tubs that spill into gorgeous gardens dominated by sizeable plunge pools.

The **Terrace Grill** (mains 250-440B; ⏰6.30am-10.30pm; 📶) is sensational and borders the sultry common pool/bar area. Service could not be better.

Indigo Pearl RESORT $$$
(Map p614; ☎076 327006; www.indigo-pearl.com; 116 Mu 1; r 8250-16,500B; P ❄ 📶 🏊) One of Phuket's most unique megaresorts takes its design cues from the island's tin-mining history. Hardware (vices, scales and other mining tools) feature in the delicate decor – even the toilet-paper rolls are big bolts – and common lounge areas are infused with indigo light. Perks include a sports bar, a pool oasis, cooking classes (3000B) and the fantastic **Coqoon Spa** (treatment 2200-7000B; ⏰9am-8pm).

Mr Kobi THAI $$
(Map p614; mains 150-200B; ⏰10am-10pm) The sign says, 'Broken English spoken here perfect', but the ever-popular Mr Kobi speaks English very well. Tuck into inexpensive Thai faves in refreshingly scruffy surrounds. One wall is dedicated to telling the story of the 2004 tsunami.

Hat Mai Khao หาดไม้ขาว

Anantara Phuket HOTEL $$$

(Map p614; 076 336100; www.phuket.anantara.com; 888 Mu 3; villa from 13,125B;) This romantic all-villa property opens onto a serene lotus-filled lagoon crisscrossed by timber boardwalks beneath swaying palms. Luxurious, classic Thai pool villas are impeccably elegant, some with private lagoon salas. It also offers a handsome **spa** (treatment 3500-5900B; 10am-10pm) and every activity under the sun (yoga, pilates, cycling, tennis, *moo·ay tai*).

Getting There & Away

Taxis to/from the airport cost 200B. A túk-túk charter from Phuket Town costs 550B.

Khao Phra Thaew Royal Wildlife & Forest Reserve

อุทยานสัตว์ป่าเขาพระแทว

This **reserve** (Map p614; off Rte 4027 & Hwy 402; adult/child 200/100B) protects 23 sq km of virgin island rainforest on north Phuket. Because of its royal status, it's better protected than the average Thai national park. The highest point is Khao Phara (442m).

Tigers, Malayan sun bears, rhinos and elephants once roamed here, but nowadays residents are limited to humans, wild boar, monkeys, slow loris, langurs, gibbons, deer, civets, flying foxes, cobras, pythons, squirrels and other smaller creatures.

A German botanist discovered the rare 3m to 5m white-backed palm (*langkow* palm) in Khao Phra Thaew about 50 years ago. This fan-shaped plant is found only here and in Khao Sok National Park.

To get to Khao Phra Thaew from Phuket Town, take Th Thepkasattri 13km north to Thalang District. At the Heroines Monument, drive 9km northeast on Rte 4027, turn left (west) towards Nam Tok Bang Pae and after 1km you're at the Phuket Gibbon Rehabilitation Project (p646). The reserve is also accessible off Hwy 402, 6km northwest of the Heroines Monument.

Sights & Activities

There are pleasant hill hikes and some photogenic waterfalls, including **Nam Tok Ton Sai** (Map p614; 076311998; off Hwy 402; adult/child 200/100B) and **Nam Tok Bang Pae** (Map p614; off Rte 4027; adult/child 200/100B) (300m along a jungle-fringed path from the Gibbon Project). The falls are most impressive during the June-to-November monsoon. Park rangers may guide hikers in the park on request; payment is negotiable.

Phuket Gibbon Rehabilitation Project WILDLIFE SANCTUARY

(โครงการคืนชะนีสู่ป่า; Map p614; 076 260492; www.gibbonproject.org; off Rte 4027; admission by donation; 9am-4.30pm, to 3pm Thu;) Financed by donations (1800B cares for a gibbon for a year), this tiny sanctuary adopts gibbons that have been kept in captivity in the hope that they can be reintroduced to the wild. The centre has volunteer opportunities that include providing educational information to visitors, cleaning cages, feeding and tracking released gibbons. Swing by around 9am to hear the gibbons' morning song. Note that you can't get too close to them, which may disappoint kids, but the volunteer work done here is outstanding.

Gibbon poaching is a big problem on Phuket, fuelled in no small part by tourism: captive gibbons are paraded around tourist bars. Phuket's last wild white-handed gibbon was poached in the early 1980s. You can help by choosing not to have your photo taken with Phuket's captive gibbons.

Thalang District อำเภอถลาง

Unfolding around the **Heroines Monument** (Map p614; Hwy 402), 13km north of Phuket Town, untouristed Thalang has some worthwhile cultural attractions.

Sights & Activities

Thalang National Museum MUSEUM

(พิพิธภัณฑสถานแหงชาติ ถลาง; Map p614; 076 379895; Th Srisoonthorn (Rte 4027); admission 100B; 9am-4pm Wed-Sun;) This excellent museum chronicles Phuket's history, from prehistoric Andaman inhabitants to the tin-mining era, with Thai and English displays. It traces southern Thailand's varied ethnicities and dialects, and recounts the legend of the 'two heroines' (immortalised on the nearby Heroines Monument), who supposedly drove off an 18th-century Burmese invasion by convincing the island's women to dress like men. The prize entrance-hall artefact is a 2.3m-tall 9th-century stone statue of Vishnu, found in Takua Pa in the early 20th century.

It's 200m northeast of the Heroines Monument, on Rte 4027.

Wat Phra Thong BUDDHIST TEMPLE

(วัดพระทอง; Map p614; off Hwy 402; dawn-dusk; P) FREE About 7km north of the Heroines Monument, Phuket's 'Temple of the Golden Buddha' is half buried, so only the head and shoulders are visible. According to legend, those who have tried to excavate the image have become very ill or encountered serious accidents. The temple is particularly revered by Thai-Chinese, who believe the image hails from China. During Chinese New Year, pilgrims descend from Phang-Nga, Takua Pa and Krabi. Also here are a **crematorium** and a **historical museum**.

Sleeping & Eating

★Point Yamu by Como RESORT $$$

(Map p614; 076 360100; www.comohotels.com/pointyamu; 225 Mu 7, Pa Klok, Laem Yamu; d incl breakfast 7060-47,480B; P) Breeze into the soaring lobby, where chunky white-mosaic pillars frame ponds reflecting encircling palms, and fall in love. This five-star stunner blends Thai influences (monk-robe orange, lobster traps as lamps) into a coolly contemporary, Italian-designed creation. A huge array of rooms, some with private pools, comes in royal-blue or turquoise, intensifying the endless sea and Ao Phang-Nga panoramas from the entire property.

Laze in the soft-blue pool, the aqua-tiled spa and the private beach club, or join complimentary yoga, pilates, tai chi and bike tours. Two- and three-bedroom villas accommodate families, and there's a babysitting service. Two fantastic restaurants provide southern Italian and refined southern Thai fare. It's 20km northeast of Phuket Town, but you'll never want to leave.

★Breeze Restaurant INTERNATIONAL $$$

(Map p614; 081 271 2320; www.breezecapeyamu.com; Laem Yamu; mains 275-750B; noon-10pm Wed-Sat, to 4pm Sun ;) Classy yet understated, one of Phuket's finest restaurants sits in glorious hilltop, sea-surrounded seclusion, 20km northeast of Phuket Town. Blue beanbags overlook pool and sea from the pillared open-walled dining hall. Mini upside-down graffitied cars patrol the log ceiling. Weekly-changing menus triumph with divine, inventive European-style dishes infused with local produce. Pair with classic cocktails given a Thai twist. Book for Sunday brunch (1930B).

KRABI PROVINCE

When travellers talk dreamily about the amazing Andaman, they usually mean Krabi, with its trademark karst formations curving along the coast like a giant limestone fortress of adventure. Rock climbers will find their nirvana in Railay, while castaway wannabes should head to Ko Lanta, Ko Phi-Phi or any of the other 150-plus islands swimming off this 120km-long bleach-blonde shoreline.

Krabi Town กระบี่

POP 30,500

Bustling Krabi Town is majestically situated among impossibly angular limestone karsts jutting from the mangroves, but mid-city you're more likely to be awe-struck by the sheer volume of guesthouses, travel agencies and building work packed into this quirky, compact town. It's a key transport hub, around which a busy traveller scene continues to evolve. Western restaurants and free wi-fi are ubiquitous, as are gift shops selling the usual trinkets.

And yet, if you hang around a while, you'll see that there's also a very real provincial scene going on between the cracks.

Sights & Activities

★Wat Tham Seua BUDDHIST TEMPLE

(วัดถ้ำเสือ, Tiger Cave Temple) This sprawling hill and cave temple complex 9km northwest of Krabi Town is an easy, worthwhile day trip. At the park entrance you'll come to a gruellingly steep 1260-step staircase leading to a 600m karst peak. After a 30- to 40-minute climb, the fit and fearless are rewarded with golden Buddha statues, a gilded stupa and spectacular views out to sea beyond Ao Nang. Start early and bring water; there are drinking taps at the top.

The best of the rest of the grounds can be found by following a loop trail through a little forest valley behind the ridge where the *bòht* (central sanctuary) is located. Here you'll find several limestone caves that are hiding Buddha images, statues and altars.

Krabi Town

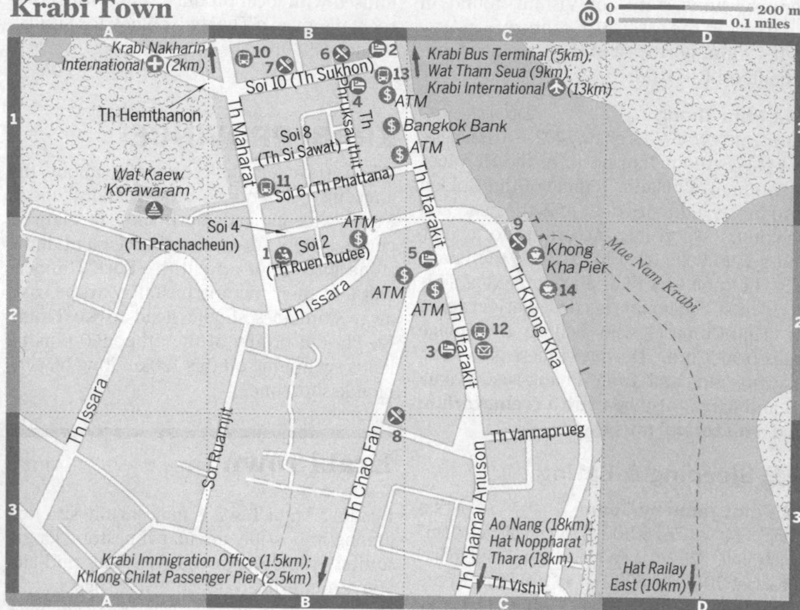

Krabi Town

Activities, Courses & Tours
1 Sea Kayak Krabi B2

Sleeping
2 Apo B1
3 Chan Cha Lay C2
4 Hometel B1
5 Pak-Up Hostel C2

Eating
6 Day Market B1
7 May & Mark's B1
8 Mr Krab-i B3
9 Night Market C2

Drinking & Nightlife
Playground .... (see 5)

Transport
10 Sŏrng·tăa·ou to Ao Luk B1
11 Sŏrng·tăa·ou to Ao Nang & Hat Noppharat Thara B1
12 Sŏrng·tăa·ou to Ao Nang & Hat Noppharat Thara C2
13 Sŏrng·tăa·ou to Krabi Bus Terminal B1
14 Tha Khong Kha C2

This is a sacred area of worship: please dress appropriately by covering shoulders to knees and avoiding tight outfits.

Motorcycle taxis or túk-túk from Krabi cost 100B. A *sŏrng·tăa·ou* from Krabi's Th Utarakit is 50B.

Sea Kayak Krabi KAYAKING
(☎089 724 8579, 075 630270; www.seakayak-krabi.com; 40 Th Ruen Rudee) A wide variety of sea-kayaking tours, including to Ao Tha Len (half/full day 1050/1500B), which has looming sea cliffs; Ko Hong (full day 2200B), famed for its emerald lagoon; and Ban Bho Tho (full day 1700B), which has karsts and sea caves with 2000- to 3000-year-old cave paintings. Rates include guides, transfers, lunch and water.

Tours

Many companies offer day trips to Khlong Thom, 45km southeast of Krabi on Hwy 4, taking in hot springs and freshwater pools, for 1200B to 2000B (including transport, guides, lunch and beverages). Bring decent shoes. Various other 'jungle tours' and mangrove and island trips are available.

Sleeping

Exceptional cheap sleeps abound in Krabi. Head to Ao Nang if you crave luxury.

★Pak-Up Hostel HOSTEL $
(075 611955; www.pakuphostel.com; 87 Th Utarakit; dm 280-390B, d 400-500B;) This snazzy hostel features contemporary, polished-cement four- to 10-bed air-con dorms with big wooden bunks built into the wall, each with its own locker. Massive, modern shared bathrooms have cold-water stalls and hot-water rain showers. The two doubles share bathrooms and women-only dorms are available. There are two on-site bars and a young, fun-loving, club-like vibe; you'll never want to leave.

Chan Cha Lay GUESTHOUSE $
(075 620952; www.lovechanchalay.com; 55 Th Utarakit; r fan 350-600B, air-con 450-800B;) The en-suite, air-con rooms at ever-busy Chan Cha Lay, done up in Mediterranean blues and whites with white-pebble and polished-concrete open-air bathrooms, are among Krabi's most comfortable and characterful. Shared-bathroom, fan-only rooms are plainer but spotless, with firm beds. Service ranges from rude to delightful.

Hometel GUESTHOUSE $
(075 622301; hometel_2012@hotmail.com; 7 Soi 10, Th Maharat ; r 750B;) A modern, friendly boutique sleep with 10 rooms on three floors crafted entirely from polished concrete. Abstract art brings colour, some rooms have two terraces and all have rain showers and high ceilings. The lack of windows might not suit everyone. There's a tour/transport desk plus a sunny cafe serving international breakfasts.

Apo HOTEL $$
(075 631189; www.apohotel.com; 189 Th Utarakit; r 1500-2000B;) The best-value of several fresh, modern guesthouses in this otherwise unremarkable block, Apo has gleaming, minimalist-smart rooms decorated with a single colourful swirl and wall-mounted TVs, spread across two buildings. Some have river views from little balconies.

Eating & Drinking

★Night Market MARKET, THAI $
(Th Khong Kha; meals 30-60B; 4-10pm) Beside Tha Khong Kha, this market is the most popular, pleasant spot in town for an evening meal. Try authentic *sôm·đam*, wok-fried noodles, *đôm yam gûng* (prawn and lemon grass soup), grilled snapper, all things satay, plus creamy Thai desserts and freshly pressed juices. English menus are a bonus.

Day Market MARKET, THAI $
(Th Sukhon; meals 20-60B; noon-8pm) Among bouquets of flowers and weighty tropical-fruit stands are simmering curry pots and banquet trays of steaming noodles with fried squid, sautéed beef, fried fish and boiled corn. Eat daringly.

May & Mark's INTERNATIONAL, THAI $
(34 Th Sukhon; mains 85-150B; 7am-10.30pm;) A classic travellers' spot with a bold varnished concrete coffee bar, May and Mark's is always busy. We love it for the delicious espresso and excellent breakfast omelettes, pancakes and home-baked bread. It also does popular Thai meals, plus international salads, sandwiches and mains.

Mr Krab-i INTERNATIONAL $$
(www.facebook.com/MrKRAB-i-Thailand-518357558204883; 27-29 Th Chao Fah; mains 150-280B; 11am-1am Mon-Sat, 5pm-1am Sun;) A sociable, open-brick lounge bar and chilled-out eatery that hits all the right traveller notes: oven-baked pizzas, pastas, salads, and burgers, plus cool cocktails, friendly management and a pool table. Good vegie options.

Playground BAR
(www.facebook.com/krabiplaygroundbar; 87 Th Utarakit; 5.30pm-2am;) The rollicking downstairs courtyard bar at Pak-Up Hostel is where Krabi fun happens. From beer pong and open-mic nights to live music and giant Jenga, there's always something going on.

Information

There are numerous banks and ATMs. Most guesthouses and restaurants offer free wi-fi.

Krabi Immigration Office (075 611097; 382 Mu 7, Saithai; 8.30am-4.30pm Mon-Fri) Handles visa extensions; 4km southwest of Krabi.

Krabi Nakharin International Hospital (075 626555; www.krabinakharin.co.th; 1 Th Pisanpob) Located 2km northwest of town.

Post Office (Th Utarakit; 8.30am-4.30pm Mon-Fri, 9am-noon Sat & Sun)

Getting There & Away

AIR

The airport is 14km northeast of Krabi on Hwy 4. Most domestic carriers fly between Bangkok and Krabi. Bangkok Air (www.bangkokair.com) flies daily to Ko Samui and Air Asia (www.airasia.com) to Chiang Mai.

BUS

Krabi Bus Terminal (☎075 663503; cnr Th Utarakit & Hwy 4) is 5km north of central Krabi at Talat Kao, near the Th Utarakit and Hwy 4 junction.

BOAT

Ferries to Ko Phi-Phi and Ko Lanta leave from the Khlong Chilat Passenger Pier (Tha Khlong Chilat), 4km southwest of Krabi. Travel agencies selling boat tickets include free transfers.

Hat Railay East Long-tail boats (150B, 45 minutes) leave from Krabi's Tha Khong Kha between 7.45am and 6pm. Boatmen wait until eight people arrive before leaving; otherwise, you can charter the whole boat (1200B). Boats to Hat Railay West leave from Ao Nang.

Ko Jum From November to late April, Ko Lanta boats stop at Ko Jum (400B, one hour), where long-tails shuttle you to shore.

Ko Lanta From November to late April, one daily boat (400B, two hours) leaves at 11.30am. During the rainy season, you can only get to Ko Lanta by frequent air-con minivans (250B to 300B, 2½ hours), which also run in high season.

Ko Phi-Phi Year-round boats (250B to 300B, 1½ to two hours) leave at 9am, 10.30am, 1.30pm and 3pm, returning at 9am, 10.30am, 1.30pm and 3.30pm. Ferries may be cancelled in low season.

Phuket & Ko Yao Islands The quickest route is with direct boats from the pier at Hat Noppharat Thara (p654), 19km southwest of Krabi. *Sŏrng·tăa·ou* (50B) run between Krabi's Tha Khong Kha and the pier at Hat Noppharat Thara; taxis cost 600B. Boats also run several times daily to Ko Yao Noi from Tha Len, 33km northwest of Krabi Town.

MINIVAN

Travel agencies run air-con minivans and VIP buses to popular southern tourist centres, but you'll end up crammed cheek-to-jowl with other backpackers. Most offer combined minivan-boat tickets to Ko Samui (500B, five hours) and Ko Pha-Ngan (650B, seven hours). More (usually cheaper) minivans depart from the bus terminal. Departures from Krabi include the following:

DESTINATION	FARE (B)	DURATION (HR)
Hat Yai	230	4
Ko Lanta	250-300	2½
Phuket	140-450	2-3
Satun	200	4
Surat Thani	180	2½
Trang	150	2

SŎRNG·TĂA·OU

Sŏrng·tăa·ou run from the bus station to Krabi (20B) and on to Hat Noppharat Thara (50B), Ao Nang (50B) and the Shell Cemetery at Ao Nam Mao (50B) between 6am and 7pm. In high season there are less frequent services until 10pm for a small surcharge. For Ao Luk (80B, one hour) there are frequent *sŏrng·tăa·ou* from Th Maharat, just north of Th Sukhon; the last service leaves around 3pm.

Getting Around

You can explore central Krabi on foot. *Sŏrng·tăa·ou* between the bus terminal and Krabi (20B) stop on Th Utarakit, outside the River View Hotel.

TO/FROM THE AIRPORT

Taxis between the airport and Krabi Town cost 350B; motorcycle taxis cost 200B. Agencies and Pak-Up Hostel (p649) can arrange seats on the airport bus (130B).

CAR & MOTORCYCLE

Most travel agencies and guesthouses, including Pak-Up Hostel (p649), rent motorbikes (per day 200B). Several international car-rental companies have offices at the airport (vehicle hire per day 1000B to 1200B).

BUSES FROM KRABI

DESTINATION	FARE (B)	DURATION (HR)	FREQUENCY
Bangkok (VIP)	955	12	5pm
Bangkok (air-con)	640-650	12	8am, 8.20am, 4pm, 5.30pm & 6pm
Hat Yai	230	4½	hourly 9am-3.20pm
Phuket	150	3	every 30min 7.30am-5.30pm
Ranong	210	5	8.30am & noon
Satun	234	5	11am, 1pm & 3pm
Surat Thani	150	2½	hourly 4.30am-4.30pm
Trang	120	2	hourly 9am-3.20pm

Ao Nang อ่าวนาง

POP 12,200

First, the hard truths. Thanks to its unchecked and unsightly development huddled in the shadows of stunning karst scenery, Ao Nang is ugly pretty, but it's an easy, if blandly touristy, destiantion to visit. There's a slightly seedy undercurrent too, with booze crawls and naughty bar-girl sois.

So, yes, it's a little trashy, but if you forgive all that and focus on the beaches, framed by limestone headlands tied together by narrow strips of golden sand, there's an awful lot to like. In the dry season the sea glows a turquoise hue; during the monsoon, currents stir up the mocha shallows. If you're hankering for a swim in clearer waters, you can easily book a trip to the little local islands that dot the horizon, which generally enjoy less-murky water, at any time of the year.

Ao Nang is compact and straightforward to navigate. The surge of attractive, midrange development means accommodation standards are high (and substantial discounts possible). It's nowhere near as cheap or authentic as Krabi Town, but it's cleaner, sunnier and, obviously, beach-ier. With plenty to do (dive trips, mangrove tours, snorkelling, kitesurfing) and only 40 minutes away from Krabi airport and a smooth 15-minute long-tail boat ride from dramatic Railay, it's easy to see why visitors flock here year-round.

Sights

Shell Cemetery NATURE RESERVE

(สุสานหอย, Gastropod Fossil, Su-San Hoi; adult/child 200/100B; 8am-6pm) About 8km east of Ao Nang at the eastern end of Ao Nam Mao is the Shell Cemetery: giant slabs formed from millions of tiny 75-million-year-old fossil shells. There's a dusty **visitors centre** (8am-4.30pm), with mildly interesting geological displays, plus stalls selling snacks. *Sŏrng·tăa·ou* from Krabi/Ao Nang cost 60/40B.

Activities

Loads of activities are possible at Ao Nang. Kids under 12 typically get a 50% discount.

Diving & Snorkelling

Ao Nang has numerous dive schools offering trips to 15 local islands, including Ko Si, Ko Ha, Ko Poda, Yava Bon and Yava Son. Two local dives cost 2700B to 3400B. Ko Mae Urai is one of the more unique local dives, with two submarine tunnels lined with soft and hard corals. As of 2013, the area has three new wreck dives created by the deliberate sinking of three decommissioned Thai navy ships, though these are only suitable for advanced-level divers and trips are very limited.

Other trips run further afield to King Cruiser Wreck (p662) for 3600B to 4700B, to Ko Phi-Phi (p662) for 3600B to 4500B, and Hin Daeng, Hin Muang and Ko Haa (p671) south of Ko Lanta for 5700B to 6600B. An Open Water course costs 14,900B. Most dive companies also arrange snorkelling trips (from 1800B).

Aqua Vision DIVING

(086 944 4068; www.diving-krabi.com; 76/12 Mu 2, Ao Nang; 2/3 dives 2700/3600B; 9am-7pm) A reliable, well-informed dive school offering local dives, two-dive trips to Ko Phi-Phi (3600B to 4400B), a realm of diving courses courses (OWD 14,900B) and 'safaris' to Hin Daeng, Hin Muang and Ko Haa (5700B to 6600B), plus local snorkelling trips (1800B).

The Dive DIVING

(082 282 2537; www.thediveaonang.com; 249/2 Mu 2; 2/3 dives 2700/3600B; 11am-8pm) This relatively new, keen Ao Nang diving team with an excellent reputation runs trips to Ko Phi-Phi (3500B), which snorkellers can join (2500B), and Ko Haa (6200B). Open Water certification costs 14,900B.

Kon-Tiki DIVING

(075 637826; www.kontiki-krabi.com; 161/1 Mu 2; 2/3 dives 3400/4000B; 9am-9pm) A well regarded, large-scale operation, Kon-Tiki does fun dives to Ko Phi-Phi (3900B) and Ko Haa (6300B), local after-dark dives (3800B), snorkelling 'safaris' (2700B) and Open Water courses (14,900B).

Cycling

Krabi Eco Cycle CYCLING

(081 607 4162, 075 637250; www.krabiecocycle.com; 309/5 Mu 5; half-/full-day tour 800/2000B) The recommended full-day 20km pedal leads you through rubber and oil plantations, small villages, hot springs and, finally, to the 'Emerald Pool'. Lunch is included on all tours except the half-day bike-only tour. It also rents bikes (per day 250B).

Kayaking

Several companies offer kayaking tours to surrounding mangroves and islands. Popular destinations include the hidden lagoon at Ko Hong (1800B to 2500B) to view collection points for sea swallow nests (spurred by the ecologically dubious demand for bird's-nest soup). There are also trips to the lofty sea cliffs at Ao Tha Len (half/full day 700/1100B) and to the sea caves and 2000- to 3000-year-old paintings at Ban Bho Tho (half/full day 1000/1500B). Rates vary (some companies use speedboats), but always include lunch, water, kayaks and guides.

Last Café (p653), at the southeastern end of Hat Ao Nang, rents kayaks (250B).

Kitesurfing

Kiteboarding Asia (p654) offers lessons and courses from nearby Hat Noppharat Thara.

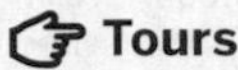

Tours

All agencies can book you on popular four- or five-island tours for 900B to 1200B, depending on whether you choose long-tail or speedboat. Ao Nang Long-Tail Boat Service and Ao Nang Long-Tail Boat Service Club (p653) offer private charters to Hong Island (2500B) and Bamboo Island (3800B), the standard five-island tour (2200B) and half-day trips to Ko Kai (Chicken Island) and Ko Poda (1700B); maximum six people.

Tour agencies offer half-day tours to Khlong Thom (adult/child 800/1200B), including visits to freshwater pools and hot springs.

You can arrange speedboat day tours to Ko Phi-Phi (adult/child 1800/1200B) with Green Planet (p654), departing at 9am and visiting Ao Maya, Ao Pileh and Bamboo Island.

Sleeping

Prices drop by 50% during low season.

★ Glur HOSTEL $

(075 695297, 089 001 3343; www.krabiglurhostel.com; 22/2 Mu 2, Soi Ao Nang; dm/d 600/1500B;) A sneaky, fabulous Krabi-area hostel that's much better value than many nearby 'hotels'. Designed, built, owned and operated by a talented Thai architect and his wife, this gleaming white lodge complex incorporates shipping containers, glass, and moulded and polished concrete to create sumptuous dorms, with curtained-off turquoise beds, bright-orange pillows, and airy doubles. The pale-blue pool is fringed by tropical gardens.

It's a walkable 1.5km northeast of Ao Nang proper.

Slumber Party Hostel HOSTEL $

(075 637089; www.slumberpartyhostel.com; Th Ao Nang; dm 400-500B;) You're here for the social scene not the z's. Catering to a lively young crowd, Slumber Party's pod-like, purple-washed, 12-bed air-con dorms with private bathrooms are straightforward but comfy and contemporary. Booze cruises, beer pong, pub crawls, island trips, cultural tours – it does it all. Reception is the downstairs bar.

It's 2km northeast of central Ao Nang, where there's another **branch** (075 656850; Th Ao Nang;) just back from the beach.

Mini House BOUTIQUE HOTEL $$

(075 810678; www.minihouseaonang.com; 675 Mu 2; r incl breakfast 1850-2100B;) Local-life murals, warm-wood furnishings, an airy reception lounge and a trickling river feature bring a boutique-y edge to this fresh grey-washed block. Slickly minimalist modern rooms are delicately kitted out with chunky wooden beds, feature walls, tiled bathrooms and balconies; some suites are loft-style abodes reached by smart ladders. It's 900m up the main road leading northeast out of Ao Nang.

Anawin BUNGALOW $$

(081 677 9632, 075 637664; www.anawinbungalows.com; 263/1 Mu 2; bungalow 1400B;) This zingy-yellow collection of clean, compact concrete cabins with TVs and fronted by little verandahs is tucked into a quiet flowery corner 400m northeast of Ao Nang beach.

Ban Sainai RESORT $$$

(075 819333; www.bansainairesort.com; 11/1 Mu 2, Soi Ao Nang; bungalow incl breakfast 4950-7200B;) A relatively new property 1.5km northeast of the main strip, Ban Sainai sports cushy, thatched faux-adobe bungalows in burnt orange, sprinkled amid the palms and crushed up so close to the cliffs you can almost kiss them. Expect high-end tiled floors, coloured-concrete bathrooms, timber wash basins and pebbled showers. Low-season deals (2625B) are wonderful.

Phra Nang Inn HOTEL $$$

(075 637130; www.vacationvillage.co.th; Th Ao Nang; r incl breakfast 2800-5500B;) A thatched explosion of rustic coconut wood,

shell curtains, bright orange and purple paint and elaborate Thai tiles with Mexico-inspired flair. There are two pools, and a similarly styled branch across the road from the original. Some rooms could use a refresh, but it's a sweet perch with plenty of life and a beachfront bar.

Red Ginger Chic HOTEL $$$
(075 637999; www.redgingerkrabi.com; 168 Mu 3; r 3200-8000B;) On a hotel-filled boulevard at the far western end of Ao Nang, Red Ginger is fashionable and colourful with detailed tiles, red paper lanterns, draped fabrics and a frosted glass bar in the lobby. Spacious rooms feature elegant wallpaper, modern furnishings and big balconies overlooking an expansive pool.

Eating

Ao Nang is full of mediocre roadside restaurants serving overpriced Italian, Scandinavian, Indian, Thai and fast food. For budget meals, stalls pop up in the evening on the road to Krabi (near McDonald's). You'll find *roti* (pancakes), *gài tôrt* (fried chicken), hamburgers and the like, and around lunchtime street stalls set up just north of Krabi Resort. The best meal in the area (and beyond) is at Krua Thara (p654), in nearby Hat Noppharat Thara.

Soi Sunset SEAFOOD $$
(Soi Sunset; dishes 200-450B; noon-10pm) At the northwest end of the beach is this packed pedestrian-only alley where several samey seafood restaurants with gorgeous sea views show off the day's catch. One of the best (and most popular) is **Krua Ao Nang Cuisine** (075 695260; mains 200-450B; 7.30am-10pm), at the far end.

Wang Sai Seafood SEAFOOD, THAI $$
(075 638128; Hat Noppharat Thara; mains 80-300B; 10.30am-10pm) Come to this huge open-walled dining hall (just beyond the northwestern end of Ao Nang) for the breezy seaside setting. Fresh seafood and no-fuss Thai fare keep the masses happy: red-curry snapper, cashew-nut fried prawns, lemon-steamed squid and garlic-infused fish cooked every which way. Cutesy cafe attached.

Drinking & Nightlife

Last Café BAR
(Hat Ao Nang; 11am-late) For a welcome blast of natural Ao Nang, hit this barefoot beach bar with cold beer, cool breezes and plastic tables in the far southern corner of Hat Ao Nang. 'Open until sunrise'.

Information

All information offices on the strip are private tour agencies. Cafes and hotels have wi-fi. Several banks on the main drag have ATMs and foreign-exchange windows (open approximately 10am to 8pm).

Getting There & Around

TO/FROM THE AIRPORT

White airport buses (150B) run hourly from 9am to 5pm, stopping outside McDonald's on the Krabi road. Private taxis (600B) and minivans (150B) go to/from the airport.

BOAT

Boats to Railay's Hat Railay West (15 minutes) are run by **Ao Nang Long-Tail Boat Service** (northwestern end of Hat Ao Nang; 8am-4pm, to 2pm May-Oct) and **Ao Nang Long-Tail Boat Service Club** (southeastern end of Hat Ao Nang; 8am-midnight, to 8pm May-Oct). Fixed rates are 100B per person from 8am to 6pm or 150B per person from 6pm to midnight. Boats leave with eight passengers; you can charter the whole boat for the eight-person price.

Boats leave for Ko Phi-Phi, Ko Lanta, Phuket and the Ko Yao Islands from the pier at Hat Noppharat Thara (p654).

CAR

Dozens of agencies along the main strip rent out motorcycles (200B). Budget Car Hire (www.budget.co.th) has desks at bigger resorts and the airport (vehicle rental per day 1200B to 1500B).

MINIVAN

Minivans (often combined boat-minivan tickets) go to destinations across southern Thailand.

DESTINATION	FARE (B)	DURATION (HR)
Khao Sok	350	3
Ko Lanta	350	3
Ko Lipe	1000	6
Ko Samui	500	4
Ko Tao	800	7
Ko Pha-Ngan	600	5
Phuket	300-350	3

SŎRNG·TĂA·OU

Sŏrng·tăa·ou run to/from Krabi (50B, 20 minutes). The route goes from Krabi's bus terminal via Th Maharat to Krabi's Tha Khong Kha and on to Hat Noppharat Thara, Ao Nang and the Shell Cemetery. From Ao Nang to Hat Noppharat Thara or the Shell Cemetery it's 30B.

Hat Noppharat Thara หาดนพรัตน์ธารา

North of Ao Nang, the golden beach turns more au naturel as it curves 4km around a less developed headland, until the sea eventually spills into a busy natural lagoon at **Hat Noppharat Thara-Mu Ko Phi-Phi National Park** (อุทยานแห่งชาติหาดนพรัตน์ธารา-หมู่เกาะพีพี; ☎075 661145; www.dnp.go.th; adult/child Ko Phi-Phi 400/200B, other islands 200/100B) headquarters. The **visitors centre** (⏱8.40am-4pm) has displays on coral reefs and mangrove ecology in Thai and English.

Several resorts here deceptively advertise a 'central Ao Nang' location though you may well prefer it if you end up a little out of town here anyway.

Activities

Kiteboarding Asia KITESURFING
(☎084 628 5786; www.kiteboardingasia.com; 1-day course 4000B; ⏱May-Sep & Nov–mid-Mar) Thailand's kitesurfing craze has hit Krabi. Here you can test the waters with one-hour private lessons (2000B) or jump straight in with one-/three-day courses (4000/11,000B).

Sleeping & Eating

Several restaurants serving typical Thai snacks (fried chicken, papaya salad) cluster near the national park headquarters. There are seafood restaurants along the seafront road.

Hat Noppharat Thara-Mu Ko Phi-Phi National Park Accommodation BUNGALOW, CAMPGROUND $$
(☎075 661145; www.dnp.go.th; bungalow 1000B, camping per person 30B, incl tent hire 250B) Rustic but well maintained concrete, air-con, 24-hour-electricity bungalows, located just over the road from the beach. Camping is just behind the park headquarters, near the harbour. Prices stay the same year-round. Book ahead online or at the visitors centre.

Sabai Resort HOTEL $$
(☎075 637791; www.sabairesort.com; 79/2 Mu 3; bungalow fan 1300-1600B, air-con 1600-2200B; ❄@📶🏊👪) This is the most professionally run of the area's bungalow properties. Tiled-roof, mint-green bungalows come in fan-cooled or air-coniditioned editions, with pebbled concrete patios thatt are overlooking a palm-shaded pool and flower-filled gardens. There are four-person family-sized rooms.

★**Krua Thara** SEAFOOD $$
(☎075 637361; 82 Mu 5; mains 100-400B; ⏱11am-10pm) This cavernous, tin-roof delight is one of the best restaurants in the South Andaman and one of the finest seafood kitchens in southern Thailand (which places it high in the running for best worldwide). There's no style or pretension, just the freshest fish, crab, clams, oysters, lobster, squid and prawns done dozens of ways, some of them very special.

The crab stir-fried in yellow curry and topped with curry scramble is spectacular. The fried rice is fluffy and light. The snapper fried in red curry is one of the best fish dishes we've ever eaten in Thailand (and we've had hundreds). If seafood isn't your thing, there are lip-smacking versions of all your other Thai faves too. Service is super-efficient and the place is packed.

Getting There & Away

Sŏrng·tăa·ou between Krabi (50B) and Ao Nang (30B) stop in Hat Noppharat Thara. In April 2015, an *Ao Nang Princess* ferry sank en route from Krabi to Phuket; one passenger died. At research time, these ferries were still operating despite the incident.

Ko Phi-Phi The *Ao Nang Princess* runs between Hat Noppharat Thara's pier, beside the national park headquarters, and Ko Phi-Phi (450B, two hours) daily from around November to April, and on Wednesday, Friday and Sunday from May to October. Boats leave at 9.30am, returning from Ko Phi-Phi at 3.30pm, via Railay.

Ko Lanta In high-season only, a 10.30am *Ao Nang Princess* boat runs to Ko Lanta (550B, 2¾ hours).

Phuket From November to April, the fastest option to Phuket is the **Green Planet** (☎075 637488; www.krabigreenplanet.com) speedboat from Hat Noppharat Thara to Tha Bang Rong (1200B, 1¼ hours), via Ko Yao Noi and Ko Yao Yai (both 650B, 45 minutes). The boat leaves Hat Noppharat Thara's pier at 11am, returning from Phuket at 3pm; transport to your Phuket accommodation is included. There's also a 3pm *Ao Nang Princess* boat to Phuket (700B, three hours; reduced services May to October).

Railay ไร่เล

Krabi's fairy-tale limestone crags come to a dramatic climax at Railay (also spelt Rai Leh), the ultimate jungle gym for rock-climbing fanatics. Accessible only by boat, this slice of paradise fills in the sandy gaps between each craggy flourish. It's just around the bend from Ao Nang, so the tourist hustle sometimes spills over, but the atmosphere here remains one of laid-back, Thai-Rasta bliss.

Sights

Tham Phra Nang CAVE

(ถ้ำพระนาง, Princess Cave; Hat Tham Phra Nang) At the eastern end of the beach, Tham Phra Nang is an important shrine for local fishermen (Muslim and Buddhist), who make offerings of carved wooden phalluses in the hope that the inhabiting spirit of a drowned Indian princess will provide a good catch. According to legend, a royal barge carrying the princess foundered here in a storm during the 3rd century BC. Her spirit took over the cave, granting favours to all who paid their respects.

Sa Phra Nang LAGOON

(Holy Princess Pool) Halfway along the trail linking Hat Railay East to Hat Tham Phra Nang, a sharp 'path' leads up the jungle-cloaked cliff wall to this hidden lagoon. The first section is a steep 10-minute uphill climb (with ropes for assistance). Fork right for the lagoon, reached by sheer downhill climbing. If you fork left, you'll quickly reach a dramatic cliffside **viewpoint**; this is a strenuous but generally manageable, brief hike.

Tham Phra Nang Nai CAVE

(Inner Princess Cave, Diamond Cave; adult/child 200B/free; ⏲9am-4.30pm) A wooden boardwalk leads through this series of illuminated caverns full of beautiful limestone formations (and squeaking bats) but, with shifting rain patterns, the water is gone and with it the luminescent effects that won it the diamond moniker. It's pricey for what you see. Follow signs north off Walking St (five minutes' walk).

Activities

Overnight trips to deserted islands can be arranged with local boat owners, but you'll need your own camping gear and food.

Rock Climbing

With over 700 bolted routes, ranging from beginner to challenging advanced climbs, all with unparalleled cliff-top vistas, it's no surprise that Railay is among the world's top climbing spots. You could spend months climbing and exploring – many people do. Deep-water soloing, where free-climbers scramble up ledges over deep water, is incredibly popular. If you fall you'll probably just get wet, so even daring beginners can try.

Most climbers start at **Muay Thai Wall** and **One, Two, Three Wall**, at the southern end of Hat Railay East, which have at least 40 routes graded from 4b to 8b on the French system. The **Thaiwand Wall** sits at the southern end of Hat Railay West, offering a sheer limestone cliff with some of the most challenging climbing routes, graded from 6a to 7c+.

Other top climbs include **Hidden World**, with its classic intermediate routes, **Wee's Present Wall**, an overlooked 7c+ winner, **Diamond Cave**, a busy beginner-to-intermediate favourite, and **Ao Nang Tower**, a three-pitch climbing wall reached only by boat. There's excellent climbing information online at www.railay.com.

Climbing courses cost 800B to 1000B for a half-day and 1500B to 2000B for a full day. Private instruction runs 3000B for a half-day and 4500B to 5000B for a full-day. Three-day courses (6000B) involve lead climbing, where you clip into bolts on the rock face as you ascend. Experienced climbers can rent gear sets for two people from the climbing schools for around 1000B per day (quality can vary); the standard set consists of a 60m rope, two climbing harnesses and climbing shoes. If you're planning to climb independently, you're best off bringing your own gear, including plenty of slings and quickdraws, chalk (sweaty palms are inevitable in the tropics) and a small selection of nuts and cams as backup for thinly protected routes. If you forget anything, some climbing schools sell a limited range of imported climbing gear.

Several locally published books detail climbs in the area. *Rock Climbing in Thailand and Laos* (2014; Elke Schmitz) is one of the more complete and up-to-date guides.

★**Basecamp Tonsai** ROCK CLIMBING

(☎081 149 9745; www.tonsaibasecamp.com; Hat Ton Sai; half/full day 800/1500B, 3-day course 6000B; ⏲8am-5pm & 7-9pm) Arguably Railay's most professional outfit and big on deep-water soloing (700B).

Highland Rock Climbing ROCK CLIMBING

(☎084 443 9539; www.highlandrockclimbingthailand.weebly.com; Railay Highlands; half/full day

Railay

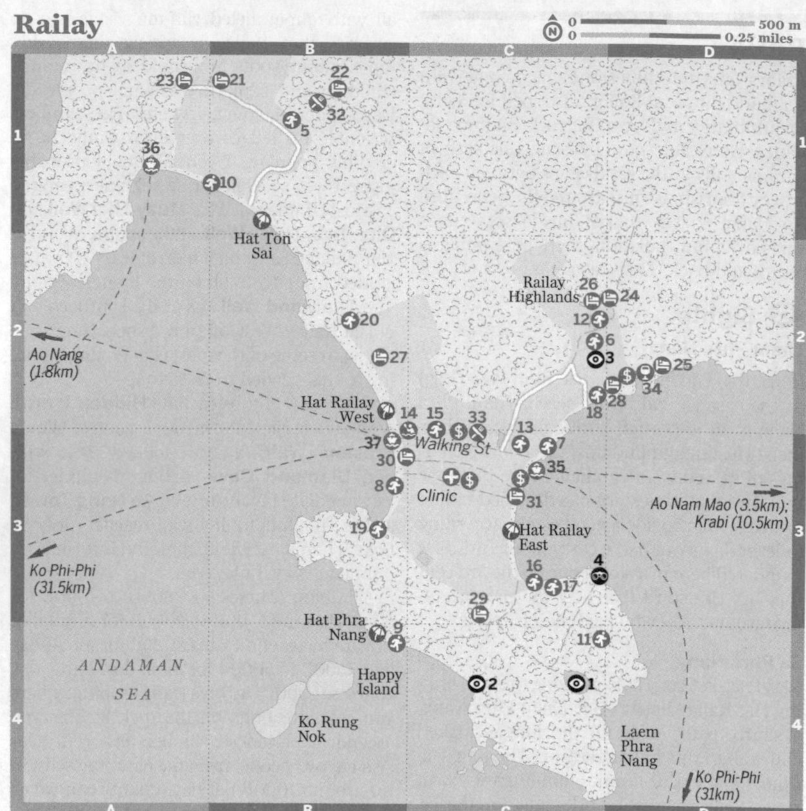

1000/1800B, 3-day course 6000B; ⌚8am-10pm) If you're sleeping on the mountain, Mr Chao is the man to climb with.

Hot Rock ROCK CLIMBING
(☎085 641 9842; www.railayadventure.com; Hat Railay East; half/full day 1000/2000B, 3-day course 6000B; ⌚9am-8pm) Owned by one of the granddaddies of Railay climbing, Hot Rock has a good reputation.

King Climbers ROCK CLIMBING
(☎081 797 8923; www.railay.com; Walking St; half/full day 1000/1800B, 3-day course 6000B; ⌚8.30am-9pm Mon-Fri, to 6pm Sat & Sun) One of the biggest, oldest, most reputable and commercial schools.

Real Rocks ROCK CLIMBING
(Hat Railay East; half/full day 1000/1800B, 3-day course 6000B; ⌚8am-10pm) A newer, Thai-American–run operation that's efficiently managed and gets good reports.

Diving & Snorkelling

Dive operations in Railay run trips out to local dive sites, including Ko Poda. Two dives cost 2500B; an Open Water dive course is 13,500B. There are also dive trips to Ko Phi-Phi (4000B) and King Cruiser Wreck (p662) for 4500B. Most dive operators in Ao Nang, where there's more choice, will pick up from Railay.

Full-day, multi-island snorkelling trips to Ko Poda, Ko Hong, Ko Kai and beyond can be arranged through resorts and agencies for 450B to 1400B, or you can charter a long-tail (half/full-day 1800/2800B) from Hat Railay West. One-day snorkelling tours to Ko Phi-Phi cost 1400B to 2000B. If you're just snorkelling off Railay, most resorts rent mask sets and fins for around 150B each.

Kayaking

Rent kayaks on Hat Railay West or Hat Ton Sai (per hour/day 200/800B).

Railay

Sights
1 Sa Phra Nang ... C4
2 Tham Phra Nang ... C4
3 Tham Phra Nang Nai ... C2
4 Viewpoint ... C3

Activities, Courses & Tours
5 Basecamp Tonsai ... B1
6 Diamond Cave ... C2
7 Hat Railay East ... C3
8 Hat Railay West ... B3
9 Hat Tham Phra Nang ... B4
10 Hat Ton Sai ... B1
11 Hidden World ... C4
12 Highland Rock Climbing ... C2
13 Hot Rock ... C3
Kayak Rental ... (see 36)
14 Kayak Rental ... C3
15 King Climbers ... C3
16 Muay Thai Wall ... C3
17 One, Two, Three Wall ... C3
18 Real Rocks ... C2
19 Thaiwand Wall ... B3
20 Wee's Present Wall ... B2

Sleeping
21 Chill Out ... B1
22 Forest Resort ... B1
23 Paasook ... A1
24 Railay Cabana ... D2
25 Railay Garden View ... D2
26 Railay Phutawan Resort ... C2
27 Railei Beach Club ... B2
28 Rapala Rockwood Resort ... D2
29 Rayavadee ... C3
30 Sand Sea Resort ... B3
31 Sunrise Tropical Resort ... C3

Eating
32 Mama's Chicken ... B1
33 Mangrove Restaurant ... C3
Sunset Restaurant ... (see 30)
The Grotto ... (see 29)
The Terrace ... (see 29)

Drinking & Nightlife
Chill Out ... (see 21)
Highland Rock Climbing ... (see 12)
34 Last Bar ... D2

Transport
35 Ferry Jetty ... C3
Long-Tail Boats to Ao Nam Mao ... (see 35)
36 Long-Tail Boats to Ao Nang ... A1
37 Long-Tail Boats to Ao Nang ... B3
Long-Tail Boats to Krabi ... (see 35)

Sleeping & Eating

Hat Railay East หาดไร่เลย์ทิศตะวันออก

Rapala Rockwood Resort BUNGALOW $
(075 622586; bungalow 800-900B;) These ramshackle wooden bungalows have been spruced up with gleaming paint and hammocks on verandahs. Within lie colourful linens, cold-water bathrooms, mosquito nets and fans. There's a teensy paddling pool beside a couple of sun loungers. The hilltop location means breezes, sea panoramas and some steep steps. Walk-ins only.

Railay Garden View BUNGALOW $$
(085 888 5143; www.railaygardenview.com; bungalow incl breakfast 1450-1950B;) A collection of tin-roof, woven-bamboo and shiny-wood bungalows, stilted between tropical gardens high above the mangroves at the northeastern end of the beach. Some look weather-beaten from outside, but all are spacious and decently clean, graced with Thai fabrics, creative concrete bathrooms and floor cushions. Bring mosquito repellent and a torch for after-dark walks.

Sunrise Tropical Resort RESORT $$$
(075 819418; www.sunrisetropical.com; bungalow incl breakfast 3200-6950B;) Swish 'chalets' and 'villas' here rival some of the finest on Hat Railay West but are priced for Hat Railay East – so we reckon this is one of the best deals in Railay. Expect soothing smart decor, hardwood floors, four-poster beds or wooden mattress-platforms, lush bathrooms with aqua-tiled floors and private balconies or patios.

Mangrove Restaurant THAI $
(Walking St; dishes 80-150B; 9am-10pm;) This humble, heaving, local-style place, set beneath a stilted thatched roof between east and west beaches, turns out all the spicy Thai favourites cheaply, from glass-noodle salad and cashew-nut stir-fry to curries, *sôm đam* and the wonderful creation that is egg-grilled sticky rice. Praise goes to the kitchen's matriarch.

Hat Railay West หาดไร่เลย์ทิศตะวันตก

You can't go wrong with any of the beachfront resort restaurants.

WHERE TO STAY IN RAILAY

There are four beaches around Railay, or you can sleep up on the headland. It's a five-minute walk between Hat Railay East, Hat Railay West, Hat Tham Phra Nang and the highlands.

Hat Railay East (Hat Sunrise) Railay's most developed beach, this shallow, muddy, mangrove-lined bay recedes to mud flats during low tide, gets steamy hot if the breezes aren't blowing and isn't appealing for swimming. That said, it's lined with affordable hotels, guesthouses and restaurants and is only a five-minute walk to better beaches. Rates drop by 50% for low season.

Hat Railay West A near flawless white wonder and the best place to swim, join an afternoon pick-up football game or watch a fiery sunset. It's all tasteful midrange and top-end resorts here, but rates can drop by up to 50% in low season. Long-tail boats to/from Ao Nang pick up and drop off here.

Hat Tham Phra Nang Quite possibly one of the world's most beautiful beaches, on the southwest side of the headland and with a crescent of pale, golden sand, framed by cave-carved karst cliffs and Ko Kai (Chicken Island) and Ko Poda peeking out of the cerulean sea. There's only one place to stay here – the peninsula's most exclusive resort, Rayavadee. Anyone can drop a beach towel.

Hat Ton Sai The grittier climbers' and budgeteers' retreat. The beach itself isn't spectacular, but with so many good climbs all around, most people don't mind. Bars and bungalows are nestled further back in the jungle and it's a lively, fun scene.

At research time, a private development had walled off and ripped up a vast section of the jungle fringing the beach, unearthing mountains of rubbish; Ton Sai lovers have retaliated with witty wall graffiti. It's a pretty ugly mess.

To get to the other beaches you'll need to take a long-tail (50B) or hike – it takes about 20 minutes to scramble over the rocks from Hat Railay West at low tide or 30 minutes through the jungle with lots of up and downs.

Railay Highlands About 500m inland from Hat Railay West or East, this is Railay's most recently developed area. Sea breezes cool the jungle canopy and lodgings are good value. From Hat Railay West, follow Walking St and veer left (north) onto the path to Tham Phra Nang Nai (Diamond Cave). From Hat Railay East head right (north) on the cement road accessible via Diamond Cave Resort.

Sand Sea Resort RESORT **$$$**
(075 819463; www.krabisandsea.com; Hat Railay West; bungalow incl breakfast 3990-6800B;) The lowest-priced resort on this sublime beach offers everything from ageing 'superior' bungalows to newly remodelled cottages and smart, sparkly, contemporary rooms with every amenity. The grounds aren't as swanky as the neighbours', but rooms are comfy and there are two peaceful foliage-enclosed pools, one with karst views.

At the recommended beachfront **Sunset Restaurant** (mains 180-400B; 11am-9pm;), red-shirted waiters take seafood-grill and Thai-curry orders on iPads.

★**Railei Beach Club** VILLA **$$$**
(086 685 9359; www.raileibeachclub.com; house 3000-20,000B;) At the northern end of the beach, hidden in forested grounds that stretch back to luscious limestone cliffs, is this collection of individually designed Thai-style homes for six to eight people, rented out on behalf of absent owners. They come with patios, kitchens and amenities, and there are also a few smaller but impeccably stylish dark-wood doubles. Only a few homes have air-con.

It's a superb, unique deal and a romantic location; book well ahead. In-house chefs prepare fresh Thai meals on request.

Hat Tham Phra Nang
หาดถ้ำพระนาง

★**Rayavadee** HOTEL **$$$**
(075 620740; www.rayavadee.com; pavilion incl breakfast 16,900-50,300B, villa 106,500-162,600B;) Arguably one of Thailand's finest chunks of beachfront property, this exclusive resort sprawls across grounds filled with banyan trees, flowers and meandering

ponds. The two-storey, mushroom-domed pavilions are packed with antique furniture, locally sourced spa products and every mod con (including butler service). Some have private pools.

There are yoga classes, tours in luxury speedboats and a first-rate spa, plus a range of kids-only activities, and family-sized villas. Nonguests are welcome for pricey but divine cuisine courtesy of the four on-site eateries. **The Grotto** (mains 460-820B; ⏲noon-10pm) plates up Mediterranean treats half-inside an illuminated cave fronting Hat Tham Phra Nang, where you might alternatively dine on upscale Thai fare at **the Terrace** (mains 400-1100B; ⏲6-11pm; ✎).

Railay Highlands

Railay Cabana BUNGALOW $

(☎075 621733, 084 534 1928; Railay Highlands; bungalow 500B) Superbly located in a bowl of karst cliffs, this is your tropical hippie mountain hideaway. Creaky yet clean thatched-bamboo bungalows with 24-hour electricity are surrounded by mango, mangosteen, banana and guava groves. It's just north of Tham Phra Nang Nai, inland from Hat Railay East.

Railay Phutawan Resort HOTEL $$

(☎084 060 0550, 075 819479; www.railayphutawan.com; Railay Highlands; r fan 800B, air-con 2500-3500B; ❄@🛜🏊) The spacious cottages highlighted with creamy yellow walls and big rain-shower bathrooms offer all the trimmings of a high-end resort, though the surly service doesn't. Tiled rooms in an apartment-style block are a step down in luxury, but comfortable. Musty but decent-value fan bungalows are for walk-ins only. Watch rock-climbers in action from the sea-and-cliff-view infinity pool.

Hat Ton Sai หาดต้นไทร

For the best cheap eats, follow the path leading inland beyond bungalows.

Chill Out BUNGALOW $

(☎087 699 4527, 084 186 8138; www.chilloutbarkrabi.com; Hat Ton Sai; dm/d 400/600B; 🛜) While no more luxurious than Ton Sai's other offerings, Chill Out's bungalows bring a sociable, laid-back atmosphere and a pinch more style. Vibrantly painted international flags are plastered across the doors of basic tin-topped, wood-floored huts, which have terraces, cold-water bathrooms and mosquito nets. The bar gets busy. Electricity and wi-fi in evenings only.

Paasook BUNGALOW $

(☎081 893 9220; juaaup@gmail.com; bungalow 600-900B) Cheaper, concrete-floored bungalows are clean and just about do-able, but the wooden cottages are huge, with floor-to-ceiling windows and tiled bathrooms. The gardens are lush and management is friendly.

Forest Resort BUNGALOW $$

(☎084 440 4335; www.basecamptonsai.com; r 600-900B, bungalow 600-1200B) The bamboo bungalows are slightly less scruffy than the sparse three-person, concrete-floor cells. The best bet are the wood-and-brick bungalows with tiled floors, red-brick bathrooms, private porches and tin roofs. All are fan cooled when the electricity is running (6pm to 1am). If there's no one around, ask at Basecamp Tonsai (p655), which manages the place.

Mama's Chicken THAI $

(70-100B; ⏲7am-10pm; ✎) Relocated to the jungle path leading inland to Hat Railay East and West, Mama's remains one of Ton Sai's favourite food stops for its international breakfasts, fruit smoothies and extensive range of cheap Thai dishes, including a rare massaman tofu and other vegetarian-friendly adaptations.

Drinking & Nightlife

There's a bunch of beachside places where you can unwind.

★Last Bar BAR

(Hat Railay East; ⏲11am-late) A reliably packed-out multi-level tiki bar that rambles to the edge of the mangroves, with bunting, balloons and cushioned seats on one deck, candlelit dining tables on another, live music at the back and waterside fire shows.

Highland Rock Climbing CAFE

(☎084 443 9539; Railay Highlands; ⏲8am-8pm) Part climbing school, part cafe, this driftwood-clad place sources beans from sustainable farms in Chiang Rai and serves some of the peninsula's best coffee.

Chill Out BAR

(Hat Ton Sai; ⏲11am-late, hours vary; 🛜) Kick back over some cold beers, live music, DJ beats and frenzied fire shows at Ton Sai's top jungle reggae bar.

Information

There's lots of local information on www.railay.com. There are ATMs on Hat Railay East and on the paths leading to Hat Railay West. Bigger resorts change cash. Wi-fi is widely available.

Clinic (☎084 378 3057; Railay Bay Resort, Hat Railay West; ⏲8am-10pm) For minor injuries.

Getting There & Around

Long-tails run to Railay from Krabi's Tha Khong Kha and from the seafront at Ao Nang and Ao Nam Mao. Boats between Krabi and Hat Railay East leave between 7.45am and 6pm when they have eight people (150B, 45 minutes). Chartering the boat costs 1200B.

Boats to Hat Railay West or Hat Ton Sai from the southeastern end of Ao Nang (15 minutes) cost 100B from 8am to 6pm or 150B from 6pm to midnight. Boats don't leave until eight people show up. Private charters cost 800B. Services stop as early as 5pm May to October.

During exceptionally high seas, boats from Ao Nang and Krabi stop running; you may still be able to get from Hat Railay East to Ao Nam Mao (100B, 15 minutes), where you can pick up a *sŏrng·tăa·ou* to Krabi or Ao Nang.

A year-round ferry runs to Ko Phi-Phi (400B, 1¼ hours) from Hat Railay East at 9.45am; long-tails motor over to meet it. Boats to Ko Lanta (500B, two hours, 10.45am daily) operate only during the October-to-April high season. For Phuket (700B, 2¼ hours), there's a year-round ferry at 3.15pm. Some ferries pick up off Hat Railay West.

Ko Phi-Phi Don เกาะพีพีดอน

Oh, how beauty can be a burden. About 38km southwest of Krabi, the insanely pretty islands of Ko Phi-Phi Don and Ko Phi-Phi Leh are Thailand's Shangri-La: a hedonistic paradise where tourists cavort in azure seas, party all night long on packed-out sands and snap pictures of long-tails puttering between craggy cliffs. With its flashy, curvy, bleach-blonde beaches and bodacious jungles, it's no wonder Phi-Phi has become the darling of the Andaman coast.

Unfortunately, nothing can withstand this pace forever. Phi-Phi's stunning looks have become its own demise and, unless limits are set, these beloved islands will continue speeding towards ecological disaster.

Ko Phi-Phi Don is practically two islands joined together by a narrow isthmus, flanked on either side by Ao Ton Sai and Ao Lo Dalam. Boats dock at Ao Ton Sai and a narrow path, crammed full of tour operators, restaurants and souvenir shops, stretches east along the beach to **Hat Hin Khom** (Map p661). This central sandbar is a cramped, chaotic mess of relentless construction and overpriced accommodation. **Hat Yao** (Long Beach; Map p661), facing south, is more attractive.

On the island's more isolated eastern coast it's a slightly different story: here you'll still find sensational snow-white coves and a beachy scene unpolluted by pounding bass. The beautifully languid, long eastern bays of **Hat Laem Thong** (Map p661) and **Ao Lo Bakao** (Map p661) are reserved for top-end resorts, while the smaller bays of **Hat Phak Nam** (Map p661) and **Hat Rantee** (Map p661) host low-key bungalows.

Choose carefully, tread lightly, manage your expectations, and Phi-Phi may well seduce you as it has thousands of other travellers. You might, equally, find you can't wait to leave.

Sights

★Phi-Phi Viewpoint VIEWPOINT
(จุดชมวิวเกาะพีพีดอน; Map p661; admission 30B) The strenuous Phi-Phi viewpoint climb is a steep, rewarding 20- to 30-minute hike up hundreds of steps and narrow twisting paths. Follow the signs on the road heading northeast from Ton Sai Village; most people will need to stop for a break (don't forget your water bottle). The views from the top are exquisite: Phi-Phi's lush mountain butterfly brilliance in full bloom.

From here, head over the hill through the jungle to the peaceful eastern beaches.

Activities

Watersports Experience WATER SPORTS
(www.watersportsexperience.com; per person without/with sports 1500/2500B; ⏲tour 10am) Zip around in a speedboat and stand-up paddle (SUP), wakeboard, water ski, cliff-jump and snorkel the waters around Phi-Phi Don and Phi-Phi Leh. Anyone who doesn't fancy getting sporty is welcome at a discount. Book at any Ton Sai Village agency.

Diving

Crystalline water and abundant marine life make the perfect recipe for top-notch scuba (p662).

Phi-Phi has fixed island-wide dive prices. Open Water certification costs 13,800B, while standard two-dive trips cost 2500B to

Ko Phi-Phi Don

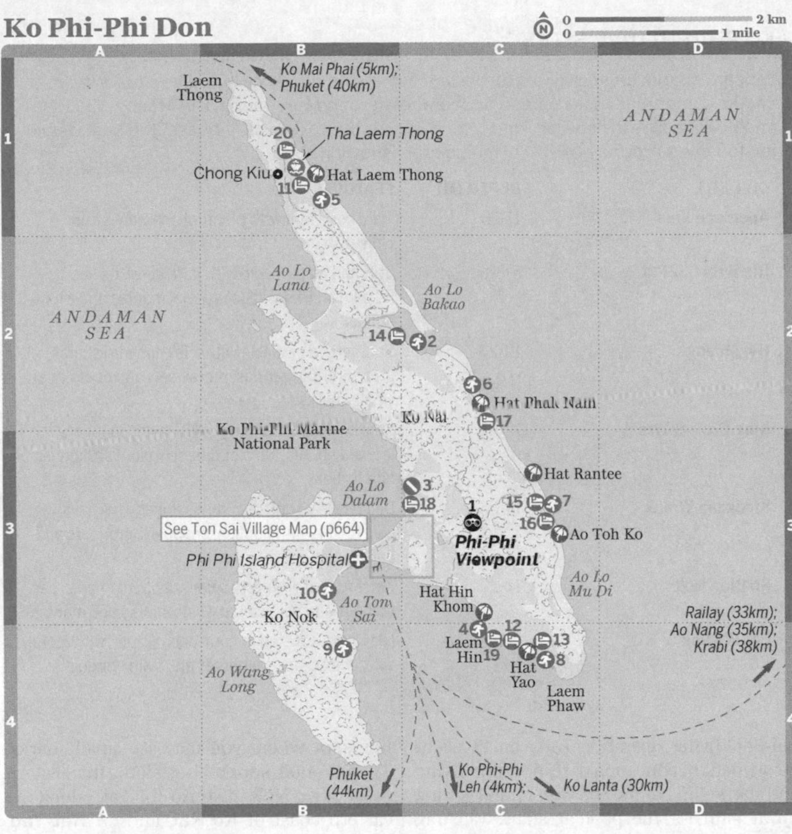

Ko Phi-Phi Don

Top Sights
1 Phi-Phi Viewpoint........C3

Activities, Courses & Tours
2 Ao Lo Bakao........C2
3 Blue View Divers........C3
4 Hat Hin Khom........C4
5 Hat Laem Thong........B1
6 Hat Phak Nam........C2
7 Hat Rantee........C3
8 Hat Yao........C4
9 Hin Taak Climbing Area........B4
10 Ton Sai Tower Climbing Area........B3

Sleeping
11 P.P. Erawan Palms Resort........B1
12 Paradise Pearl Bungalow........C4
13 Paradise Resort Phi Phi........C4
14 Phi Phi Island Village........B2
15 PP Rantee........C3
16 Rantee Cliff Beach Resort........C3
17 Relax Beach Resort........C2
18 Sunflower Boathouse........C3
19 Viking Natures Resort........C4
20 Zeavola........B1

Eating
Paradise Pearl Bungalow........(see 12)
Relax Beach Resort........(see 17)

Drinking & Nightlife
Sunflower Bar........(see 18)

3500B and Discover Scuba costs 3400B. Hin Daeng and Hin Muang, 60km south, are expensive ventures from Ko Phi-Phi (5500B); it's slightly cheaper to link up with a dive crew in Ko Lanta.

★ **Adventure Club** DIVING
(Map p664; 081 895 1334; www.diving-in-thailand.net; Ton Sai Village; 2 dives 2500B, Open Water certification 13,800B; 8am-10pm) Our favourite

KO PHI-PHI DIVE SITES

Leopard sharks and hawksbill turtles are common on Ko Phi-Phi's dive sites. Whale sharks sometimes make cameo appearances around Hin Daeng, Hin Muang, Hin Bida and Ko Bida Nok in February and March. November to February boasts the best visibility. Top dives around Ko Phi-Phi include the following:

DIVE SITE	DEPTH (M)	FEATURES
Anemone Reef	17-26	Hard coral reef with plentiful anemones and clownfish
Hin Bida Phi-Phi	5-30	Submerged pinnacle with hard coral, turtles, leopard sharks and occasional mantas and whale sharks
Hin Muang	19-24	Submerged pinnacle with a few leopard sharks, groupers, barracudas, moray eels and occasional whale sharks
King Cruiser Wreck	12-30	Sunken passenger ferry (1997) with snappers, leopard sharks, barracudas, scorpionfish, lionfish and turtles
Kledkaeo Wreck	14-26	Deliberately sunk decommissioned Thai navy ship (2014) with lionfish, snappers, groupers and barracudas
Ko Bida Nok	18-22	Karst massif with gorgonians, leopard sharks, barracudas and occasional whale sharks and mantas
Phi-Phi Leh	5-18	Island rim covered in coral and oysters, with moray eels, octopuses, seahorses and swim-throughs

Phi-Phi diving operation runs an excellent assortment of educational, responsible diving and snorkelling tours. You won't mind getting up at 6am for the popular shark-watching snorkel trips (800B) on which you're guaranteed to cavort with at least one reef shark.

Blue View Divers DIVING
(Map p661; ☎075 819 395; www.blueviewdivers.com; Phi Phi Viewpoint Resort, Ao Lo Dalam; 2 dives 2500B; ⏲10am-8pm) A professional, well-organised outfit that focuses on community involvement, beach clean-ups and environmental conservation, with two-dive trips, night dives (1900B), Open Water courses (13,800B) and Discover Scuba (3400B).

Sea Frog Diving DIVING
(Map p664; ☎087 920 0680, 075 601073; www.ppseafrog.com; Ton Sai Village; 2 dives 2500B; ⏲7am-10pm) A long-running dive shop with a solid reputation. Offers Open Water certification (13,800B) and Discover Scuba (3400B), plus the standard two-dive trips.

Snorkelling

Ko Mai Phai (Bamboo Island), 6km north of Phi-Phi Don, is a popular shallow snorkelling spot where you may see small sharks. There's good snorkelling along the eastern coast of **Ko Nok** (near Ao Ton Sai), along the eastern coast of **Ko Nai**, and off **Hat Yao**. Most resorts rent out snorkel, mask and fins sets (per day 200B).

Snorkelling trips cost 700B to 2500B, depending on whether you travel by long-tail or motorboat. You can tag along with dive trips, and many dive operators also offer specialised snorkelling tours. Those with the Adventure Club (p661) come highly recommended.

Rock Climbing

Yes, there are good limestone cliffs to climb on Phi-Phi, and the views are spectacular. The main climbing areas are **Ton Sai Tower** (Map p661), at the western edge of Ao Ton Sai, and **Hin Taak** (Map p661), a short long-tail boat ride around the bay.

Ibex Climbing & Tours ROCK CLIMBING
(Map p664; ☎075 601370, 084 309 0445; www.ibexclimbingandtours.com; Ton Sai Village; half/full day 1100/1950B) One of Phi-Phi's newest and best rock-climbing operators. Rates include instruction and gear.

Courses

Pum Restaurant & Cooking School COOKING COURSE
(Map p664; ☎081 521 8904; www.pumthaifoodchain.com; 125/40 Mu 7, Ton Sai Village; per person 500-4000B; ⊙classes 11am, 4pm & 6pm) Thai-food fans can take highly recommended cooking courses ranging from half-hour, one-dish sessions to five-hour 'healthy lifestyle' extravaganzas. You'll learn the secrets behind some of the excellent dishes served in their Ton Sai Village restaurant and go home with a cookbook.

Tours

Ever since Leo (DiCaprio) smoked a spliff in the film rendition of Alex Garland's *The Beach*, Phi-Phi Leh has been something of a pilgrimage site. Aside from long-tail boat trips to Phi-Phi Leh and Ko Mai Phai, tour agencies organise sunset tours around Phi-Phi Leh that include Monkey Bay and the beach at Wang Long.

PP Original Sunset Tour BOAT TOUR
(Map p664; Ton Sai Village; per person 900B; ⊙tour 1pm) A sensational sunset cruise that sees you bobbing around Phi-Phi Leh aboard a double-decker boat to mellow beats, snorkelling and kayaking between Ao Pi Leh's sheer-sided cliffs and dining on fried rice off Maya Beach, led by an enthusiastic, organised team. Bliss.

Maya Bay Sleepaboard BOAT TOUR
(www.mayabaytours.com; per person 3000B) You can no longer camp on Phi-Phi Leh's Maya Beach, but you can spend the night just offshore. Prices include food, sleeping bags and national park entry fees; tours depart at 3pm, returning at 10am the following morning. The same team runs the popular **Plankton Sunset Cruise** (www.mayabaytours.com; per person 1200B; ⊙3-8pm) to Phi-Phi Leh. Book at any Ton Sai travel agent.

Captain Bob's Booze Cruise BOAT TOUR
(Map p664; ☎084 848 6970; www.phiphiboozecruise.com; women/men 2500/3000B; ⊙tour 1pm) Phi-Phi's latest buzz-worthy excursion: you're cruising the waters around Phi-Phi Don and Phi-Phi Leh, on a sail boat, adult beverage in hand.

Sleeping

Finding accommodation on this popular island has never been easy. Expect serious room shortages and extortionate rates, especially at peak holiday times. Masses of touts meet incoming boats and, while often annoying, can make your life easier.

Break-ins are a problem: lock the door while you sleep and close all windows when you go out.

Ton Sai Village & Ao Lo Dalam บ้านต้นไทร/อ่าวโละดาลัม

The flat, packed-out, hourglass-shaped land between Ao Ton Sai and Ao Lo Dalam is crammed with lodging options. Central Ton Sai is called the 'Tourist Village'.

Framed by stunning karst cliffs, the beach at Ao Lo Dalam is arguably Phi-Phi's prettiest. But it's clogged with people and long-tail boats, and polluted by beach bars and day visitors.

There's an insane amount of (loud) construction going on in this area. More and more identical, basic-job dorm rooms are popping up, particularly behind popular clubs on Ao Lo Dalam.

Blanco HOSTEL $
(Map p664; ☎093 638 3781; Ao Lo Dalam; dm 470-625B; ❄📶) This bare-bones (bring your own top sheet!) but modern party hostel offers four- to eight-bed dorms in concrete-floor bamboo chalets. Digs are cramped, there's usually sand on the floor and mattresses are gym-mat hard, but this is where the hard core revellers stay, thanks to the fun-loving vibe and super-sociable beach bar with cushioned lounges and a pool table.

Prepare to keep vampire hours.

Ibiza House HOSTEL, HOTEL $
(Map p664; ☎075 601274, 080 537 1868; ibizahouseppth@gmail.com; Ao Lo Dalam; dm 450-700B, r incl breakfast 2000-5500B; ❄📶🏊) Ibiza House stacks up points for its popular, well-kept (slightly sandy) 10-bed air-con dorms with hot showers, safes and wi-fi, and lively party atmosphere, and also has a collection of shiny white doubles and 'villas'. All guests can use the pool – which hosts regular Sunday parties.

Rock Backpacker HOSTEL $
(Map p664; ☎081 607 3897; Ton Sai Village; dm 300B, r fan/air-con 800/1600B; ❄📶) A proper hostel on the village hill, with clean dorms lined with bunk beds, tiny private rooms, an inviting restaurant-bar and a rugged, graffiti-scrawled exterior. It's still one of Ton Sai's cheaper pads and there's a buzzing backpacker scene – just don't expect a friendly welcome. Walk-ins only.

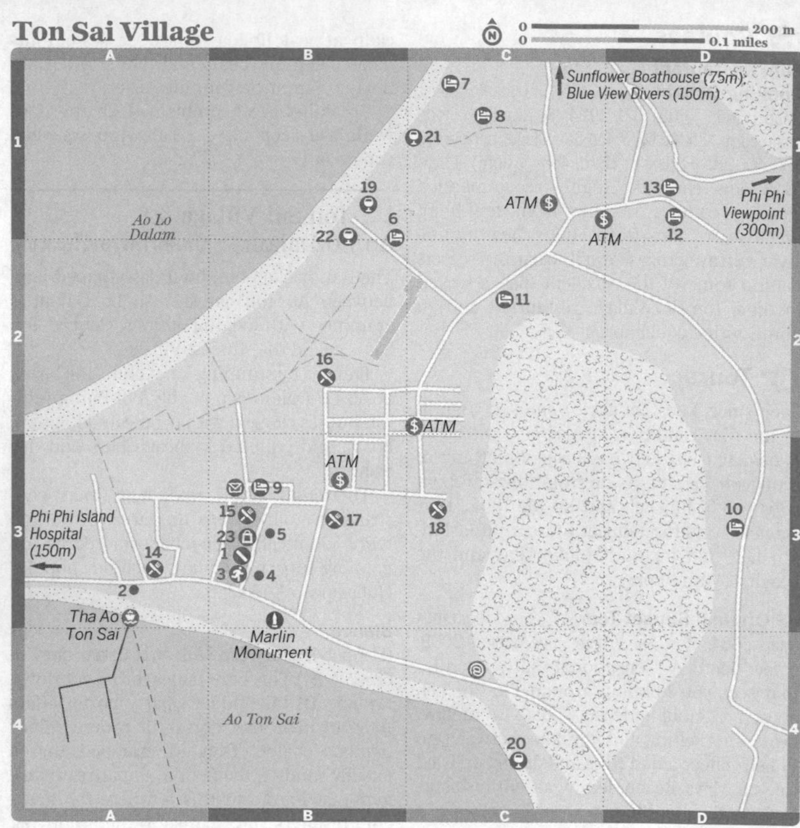

Ton Sai Village

Activities, Courses & Tours

1 Adventure Club B3
2 Captain Bob's Booze Cruise A3
3 Ibex Climbing & Tours B3
4 PP Original Sunset Tour B3
5 Pum Restaurant & Cooking School B3
Sea Frog Diving .... (see 15)

Sleeping

6 Anita Resort B1
7 Blanco C1
8 Ibiza House C1
9 JJ Residence B3
10 Oasis Guesthouse D3
11 Rock Backpacker C2
12 Tropical Garden Bungalows D1
13 Up Hill Cottage D1

Eating

14 Le Grand Dleu A3
15 Local Food Market B3
16 Only Noodles B2
17 Papaya 2 .... B3
18 Papaya Restaurant C3
Unni's .... (see 15)

Drinking & Nightlife

19 4Play B1
20 Carlito's C4
21 Ibiza C1
22 Slinky B1

Shopping

23 D's Bookshop B3

Oasis Guesthouse GUESTHOUSE **$**
(Map p664; ☎075 601207; 115 Mu 7, Ton Sai Village; r 700-800B; ❄📶) Up the side road east of central Ton Sai you'll find this cute, simple guesthouse with wooden shutters, surrounded by trees. Freshly painted rooms have

gleaming bathrooms. Staff can be surly. No reservations: it's first-come, first-served.

JJ Residence HOTEL $$
(Map p664; 075 601098; www.jjresidence.com; 95 Mu 7, Ton Sai Village; r 2500B;) Spacious tiled rooms with smart wood panelling, beamed ceilings, duvets, mini fridges, built-in desks and wardrobes and private terraces make this one of Ton Sai's better choices. Rooms on the 1st floor spill out onto the pool with its feature waterfall. A new, similar-style block directly opposite should be ready by the time you read this.

Up Hill Cottage BUNGALOW $$
(Map p664; 075 601124; www.phiphiuphillcottage.com; 140 Mu 7, Ton Sai Village; r fan 1200B, air-con 2000-2500B;) These newly renovated, cream-painted wood-panelled bungalows come in cute pastels offset by colourful bed runners and snazzily tiled bathrooms. Most enjoy island views from private balconies. Cheaper fan rooms are simple but still clean. It's *slightly* beyond the madness, at the eastern end of the main street heading north from Ton Sai Village. Beware the hundreds of stairs.

Tropical Garden Bungalows BUNGALOW $$
(Map p664; 089 729 1436; www.thailandphiphitravel.com; Ton Sai Village; r fan 1100-1300B, air-con 1400-2300B;) If you don't mind walking 10 minutes to eat, drink or sunbathe, you'll love Tropical Garden, near the viewpoint path. Rooms are offered in a million shapes, sizes and budgets: frontier-style log cabins, modern concrete air-con rooms, and even the smallest options have a bit of character. There's a flower-fringed pool with a swim-up bar.

Anita Resort RESORT $$
(Map p664; 075 601282; www.phiphianitaresort.com; Ao Lo Dalam ; r 2700-4500B;) Just back from Ao Lo Dalam, this three-star resort has shiny-floored bungalows tastefully done up with pink-tiled bathrooms, wood-carved-elephant lamps, those rare floor-to-ceiling headboards and sliding glass doors that open onto private decks overlooking the pool. Opposite, newer 'deluxe' rooms with flat-screen TVs are more contemporary.

Sunflower Boathouse GUESTHOUSE $$
(Map p661; 080 038 3374; www.facebook.com/pages/Sunflower-Boathouse-Phi-Phi/101127755691; Ao Lo Dalam; r fan/air-con 1200/1500B;) Lovingly built, varnished dark-wood rooms with a bit of space and character sporting colourful bed-throws are spread across a thatch-roofed, ship-like structure, cosied up to the wonderfully chilled-out Sunflower Bar (p667) at the northern end of Ao Lo Dalam. Simple and welcoming.

Hat Hin Khom หาดหินคม

A 15-minute beach or jungle walk east of Ao Ton Sai, this area has a few small white-sand beaches in rocky coves.

Viking Natures Resort BUNGALOW $$
(Map p661; 083 649 9492, 075 819399; www.vikingnaturesresort.com; Hat Hin Khom; bungalow 1200-6000B;) OK, it's wacky in every way (and definitely not the place to stay if you're afraid of jungle critters), but if it's character you're after, Viking's wood, thatch and bamboo bungalows (decorated with driftwood, shell curtains, stone-cut sinks and hammock-decked lounging spaces that enjoy fabulous views of Phi-Phi Leh) are just the ticket.

We say splurge on the large wooden lodge rooms that open onto inviting verandas.

Hat Yao หาดยาว

This lively stretch of pure-white south-coast beach is perfect for swimming, but don't expect it to yourself. You can walk here in 30 minutes from Ton Sai via Hat Hin Khom or take long-tails (100B to 150B) from Ton Sai pier.

Paradise Pearl Bungalow RESORT $$
(Map p661; 075 601248; www.phiphiparadisepearl.com; Hat Yao; r incl breakfast 3000-6000B;) A sprawling complex of dark-wood Thai chalets, decked out with art and updated electronics, tucked into the rocky headland on the northern curl of Hat Yao. Delightfully old-fashioned beach-facing wooden 'houses' have four-poster beds, lace curtains and tea/coffee stands. The loungey **restaurant** (mains 120-400B; 7.30am-10pm;), typically packed with young couples, rambles to the edge of the sand.

★**Paradise Resort Phi Phi** HOTEL $$$
(Map p661; 081 968 3982; www.paradiseresort.co.th; Hat Yao; bungalow 2900-6500B;) Freshly built, impeccably kept seafront villas at this sparkly white resort are plush with floor-to-ceiling windows, massive semi-open-air bathrooms, indoor-outdoor showers, colour feature walls, kettles, fridges, hairdryers and wooden sun loungers on the front deck. Older villas at the back are per-

fectly comfy, bright and clean, and they also have smart wood-panelled 'Thai-modern' rooms. Superb low-season deals. Online bookings only.

Hat Rantee หาดรันตี

Still low-key, this small, remote, grey-gold eastern bay has modest family bungalows and good snorkelling. Arrive by long-tail from Ton Sai's pier (600B; return per person 200B, minimum four people; resorts provide free pick up if you've booked) or via the strenuous 45-minute hike over the viewpoint.

Rantee Cliff Beach Resort BUNGALOWS $$
(Map p661; 087 474 7770; www.phiphirantee-cliff.com; bungalow incl breakfast 2500-5000B;) Fronted by swaying orange and purple hammocks, Rantee's newest offering surprises with character-packed, pointy-roofed chunky bamboo bungalows overlooking a gorgeous patch of sand. All have bright-blue throws, in-room sinks, soaring thatched ceilings, sunken bathrooms, gauzy mosquito netting, tea/coffee kits and fridges. It's tucked into the headland at the southern end of Hat Rantee.

PP Rantee BUNGALOW $$
(Map p661; 092 124 0599; bungalow fan 1500B, air-con 2500-4500;) Basic, acceptable woven bamboo bungalows and newer, clean, tiled concrete bungalows with air-con and wide porches overlooking a trim garden path that leads to the sand. It also has an excellent restaurant and a wooden tree-swing out front.

Hat Phak Nam หาดผักน้ำ

This gorgeous white-sand beach shares its bay with a small fishing hamlet. Charter a long-tail from Ao Ton Sai (1000B; 200B by shared taxi boat to return) or make the sweaty one-hour hike over the viewpoint.

★ **Relax Beach Resort** BUNGALOW $$
(Map p661; 089 475 6536; www.phiphirelaxresort.com; bungalow 2100-5200B;) These 47 lacquered Thai-style bungalows, with wood floors, thatched roofs, two-tiered terraces with lounging cushions and mosaic bathrooms (in the best rooms), are rimmed by lush jungle. There's a good seafood-focused Thai/international **restaurant** (Map p661; Hat Phak Nam; dishes 100-350B; 7.30am-9pm;) and breezy bar, and it's run by charming staff who treat guests like family.

Ao Lo Bakao อ่าวโละบาเกา

Ao Lo Bakao's fine stretch of northeastern palm-backed sand, ringed by dramatic hills, is one of Phi-Phi's loveliest, with offshore views over aqua bliss to Bamboo and Mosquito Islands. A long-tail charter from Ao Ton Sai costs 1000B.

Phi Phi Island Village BUNGALOW $$$
(Map p661; 075 628900; www.phiphiislandvillage.com; r incl breakfast 8400-22,000B;) The 156 wood-and-concrete bungalows take up most of the beachfront, with palms swaying between them. Amenities vary from the family-friendly and casual to romantic dining experiences, pampering spa treatments and dozens of activities. If you have the means, it's good living with a hint of old-school luxury. The resort arranges long-tail transfers to/from Ton Sai.

SLEEPING (OR TRYING TO) ON KO PHI-PHI

Noise pollution on Phi-Phi is terrible and focused on central Ao Ton Sai and Ao Lo Dalam. Don't expect an early night on Hat Hin Khom either. At research time, bars in Dalam and Ton Sai had a 2am curfew (which is more or less observed) though that doesn't stop inebriated revellers from making plenty of other noise (door slamming, dry heaving) or builders bashing away at all hours.

For a shot at peaceful Phi-Phi accommodation, try one of the following:

- Phi-Phi's east coast
- the back road connecting southeast Ao Ton Sai with Ao Lo Dalam
- the hill near the road up to Phi-Phi Viewpoint (p660)
- Hat Yao (p660)

Of course, the best option is probably to grab a bucket and join the fun.

Hat Laem Thong หาดแหลมทอง

Despite the upmarket offerings, this north-eastern white-sand beach is busy and has a small, rubbish-strewn *chow lair* (sea gypsy) settlement at its northern end. Long-tail charters from Ao Ton Sai cost 1200B; hotels arrange transfers.

★Zeavola HOTEL **$$$**
(Map p661; 075 627000; www.zeavola.com; bungalow incl breakfast 10,600-21,800B;) Hibiscus-lined pathways lead to shady teak bungalows with sleek, distinctly Asian indoor-outdoor floorplans. Each comes with floor-to-ceiling windows on three sides, beautiful 1940s fixtures and antique furniture, huge ceramic sinks, indoor/outdoor showers, tea and coffee pods on a private terrace and impeccable service. The finest villas enjoy their own infinity pools and there's a fabulous couples-oriented spa.

P.P. Erawan Palms Resort HOTEL **$$$**
(Map p661; 075 627500; www.pperawanpalms.com; r incl breakfast 4200-9000B;) Step onto the grounds and let the stress fall away as you follow a meandering path through gardens to bright, spacious, modern yet traditional-feel 'cottages' and smaller rooms decorated with Thai art and handicrafts. There's an inviting pool bar plus excellent service.

Eating

Most resorts and bungalows have restaurants. Ao Ton Sai is home to some reasonably priced restaurants, but don't expect haute cuisine.

Local Food Market MARKET, THAI **$**
(Map p664; Ton Sai Village; meals 60-80B; 7am-10pm) Phi-Phi's cheapest, most authentic eats are at the market (which was being renovated at research time), on the narrowest sliver of the isthmus. A handful of enthusiastic local stalls serve up scrumptious *pàt tai*, fried rice, *sôm·đam* and smoked catfish.

Only Noodles THAI **$**
(Map p664; Ton Sai Village; dishes 60-120B; 11am-10pm) The name tells no lies. You're at this popular tucked-away spot for straightforward, flavour-packed *pàt tai*, served up with your choice of noodles in meat, seafood or veg format at just two simple streetside tables.

Papaya Restaurant THAI **$**
(Map p664; 087 280 1719; Ton Sai Village; dishes 100-350B; 10am-10.30pm) Cheap, tasty and spicy. Here's some real-deal Thai food served in heaping portions. It has your basil and chilli, all the curries, *sôm·đam* and *đôm yam,* too. There's a second branch, **Papaya 2** (dishes 100-350B; 10am-10pm), a block away.

★Unni's INTERNATIONAL **$$**
(Map p664; 081 979 2865; Ton Sai Village; mains 200-350B; 8am-midnight;) Swing by this local expat fave for homemade breakfast bagels topped with everything from smoked salmon to meatballs or specials like avocado-and-feta toast. Other excellent global treats include massive Greek salads, pastas, burritos, nachos, burgers, tapas, cocktails and more. It's a chic cafe-lounge–style place with contemporary mood music.

Le Grand Bleu THAI, FRENCH **$$**
(Map p664; 081 979 9739; 137 Mu 7, Ton Sai Village; mains 160-360B; 6.30-11pm) Thai-French fusion in a charming wooden house with a trickling fountain, wall art and a colourful concrete bar, just off the main pier. Here you can get duck oven-roasted with honey, shrimp as ravioli, king prawns cooked in pesto and creamy mushroom tagliatelle, plus a selection of southern Thai specialities, accompanied by international wines.

Drinking & Nightlife

A rowdy party scene saturates Phi-Phi. Buckets of cheap whiskey and Red Bull and sickly-sweet cocktails make this the domain for gap-year craziness and really bad hangovers. If you're crashing within earshot of the party, you might as well enjoy it.

★Sunflower Bar BAR
(Map p661; Ao Lo Dalam; 11am-2am;) Poetically ramshackle, this driftwood gem is still Phi-Phi's most chilled-out bar. Destroyed in the 2004 tsunami, it was rebuilt with reclaimed wood. The long-tail booths are named for the four loved ones the owner lost in the deluge.

Slinky CLUB
(Map p664; Ao Lo Dalam; 9pm-2am) Forever the beach dancefloor of the moment. One of several Dalam nightspots with standard over-the-top fire shows, buckets of candy-juice cocktails and throngs of Thais, expats and tourists mingling, flirting and flailing to throbbing bass on the sand.

BOATS TO/FROM KO PHI-PHI DON

DESTINATION	FARE (B)	DURATION (HR)	TO KO PHI-PHI	FROM KO PHI-PHI
Ao Nang	350	1¾	9.30am	3.30pm
Ko Lanta	250-700	1½	8am, 12.30pm, 1pm & 4pm	11.30am & 3pm
Krabi	250-300	1½-2	9am, 10.30am, 1.30pm & 3	9am, 10.30am, 1.30pm & 3.30pm
Phuket	250-300	1¼-2	9am, 11am & 3pm	9am, 2pm, 2.30pm & 3.30pm
Railay	350-400	1¼	9.45am	3.30pm

Ibiza CLUB
(Map p664; Ao Lo Dalam; ⏲9pm-2am) Another of Dalam's beach dens of inebriation and iniquity (but, you know, in a good way). Relax on beachside cushions and marvel at expert fire twirlers and drunken daredevils as they jump through fiery hoops and limbo beneath a fiery cane, while everyone else dances and fist-pumps to bone-rattling bass.

4Play CLUB
(Map p664; Ao Lo Dalam; ⏲9pm-2am) If Dalam's frenzied clubs start to feel the same after a few (buckets), that's because they're pretty much identical: 4Play has the usual mix of electrifying fire throwing, tight-rope walking and throbbing bass.

Carlito's BAR
(Map p664; www.carlitosbar.net; Ao Ton Sai; ⏲11am-1am) For a (slightly) toned-down take on Dalam's fire-twirling madness, pull up a plastic chair on the sand at this fairy-light-lit beachside bar, which puts on fun fire shows and attracts beer- and cocktail-seeking *fa·ràng* (Westerners). It can get a bit rowdy on party nights.

Shopping

D's Bookshop BOOKS
(Map p664; Ton Sai Village; ⏲10am-10pm) Swaps and sells new and used fiction and travel guides (English, German, French, Italian).

ℹ Information

ATMs are spread thickly throughout the Tourist Village but aren't available on the eastern beaches. Wi-fi is everywhere.

Phi Phi Island Hospital (Map p661; ☎075 622 151; Ao Ton Sai) Emergency care, at the west end of Ao Ton Sai. For anything truly serious, you're on the first boat to Krabi or Phuket.

Post Office (Map p664; Ton Sai Village; ⏲9am-5pm Mon-Fri & 9am-1pm Sat)

ℹ Getting There & Away

Ko Phi-Phi can be reached from Ao Nang, Krabi, Phuket, Railay and Ko Lanta. Most boats moor at Ao Ton Sai, though a few from Phuket use isolated, northern Tha Laem Thong (Map p661). Phuket, Krabi and Ao Nang ferries operate year-round, while Ko Lanta boats only run from October to April.

There are also combined boat-minivan tickets to destinations across Thailand, including Bangkok (550B to 600B, 11 hours, 5pm and 5.30pm), Ko Samui (400B to 500B, 6½ hours, 11am and 4pm) and Ko Pha-Ngan (500B to 600B, seven hours, 11am and 4pm).

ℹ Getting Around

There are no roads on Ko Phi-Phi Don. Transport is mostly by foot, though long-tails can be chartered at Ao Ton Sai for short hops around both islands.

Long-tails leave Ao Ton Sai pier for Hat Yao (100B to 150B), Hat Rantee (600B), Hat Phak Nam and Ao Lo Bakao (1000B), Laem Thong (1200B) and Viking Cave (on Ko Phi-Phi Leh; 600B). Chartering a long-tail for three/six hours costs 1500/3000B; a half-day speedboat charter costs 5000B.

Ko Phi-Phi Leh เกาะพีพีเล

Rugged Phi-Phi Leh is the smaller of the two Phi-Phi Islands, protected on all sides by soaring, jagged cliffs. Coral reefs crawling with marine life lie beneath the crystal-clear waters and are hugely popular with day-tripping snorkellers (so there's some coral damage and a huge amount of rubbish).

There are no places to stay on Phi-Phi Leh. Most people visit on a day trip or sunset cruise with one of the ludicrously popular tours (p663) out of Phi-Phi Don. Tours last half a day, including various snorkelling stops around the island and detours to Viking Cave and Ao Maya. Long-tail trips cost 700B to 800B; by motorboat you'll pay 2500B. The national park day-use fee (adult/child 400/200B) is payable upon landing.

You can no longer camp on Phi-Phi Leh, but you can still swing by Maya Beach at dusk and sleep on a boat bobbing offshore with Maya Bay Sleepaboard (p663).

Sights & Activities

Viking Cave CAVE

(Tham Phaya Naak) On the northeastern tip of the island, Viking Cave is a major collection point for outrageously valuable swifts' nests, the key components of Chinese speciality bird's-nest soup. Nimble collectors scamper up fragile bamboo scaffolding to the roof of the cave to gather the nests. Before ascending, they pray and make offerings of tobacco, incense and liquor. The cave gets its misleading moniker from the 400-year-old boat graffiti created by crews of passing Chinese fishing junks.

At research time, visitors were not allowed inside the cave, but most tour boats slow down for a good glimpse.

Ao Pileh LAKE

Of the two gorgeous emerald lagoons that await in Phi-Phi Leh's interior, Pileh lies on the eastern coast. It's predictably busy, but the thrill of kayaking between these towering limestone walls never gets old.

Ao Maya BAY

(Maya Bay; adult/child 400/200B) Dramatically flanked by green-clad cliffs, majestic Ao Maya sits on Phi-Phi Leh's western shoreline. In 1999, its beautiful sands were controversially used as a set for *The Beach*, based on Alex Garland's cult novel. Natural sand dunes were flattened and extra palm trees planted to increase the paradisaical backdrop and, although the production's team restored things, many claim the damage to the ecosystem has been permanent.

The level of boat traffic here nowadays somewhat detracts from the serenity, but the setting is still spectacular.

Ko Jum & Ko Si Boya เกาะจำ/เกาะศรีบอยา

Just north of Ko Lanta, Ko Jum and its low-lying neighbour Ko Si Boya have surprisingly little development; what's there is tucked away in the trees. There's little more to do than wander the long, broad beaches and soak up the islands' refreshingly rustic beauty.

Ko Jum was once the exclusive domain of Lanta's *chow lair* people, but ethnic Chinese began arriving after Chairman Mao came to power in the 1950s. At the time there were no Thai people living here at all, but eventually the three cultures merged into one, a mix best sampled early in the morning amid the ramshackle poetry of Ban Ko Jum, the fishing village on the southeast side of the island.

Although technically one island, local people consider only the flatter southern part of Ko Jum to be Ko Jum. The northern hilly bit is Ko Pu.

Activities

Koh Jum Divers DIVING

(☎082 273 7603; www.kohjum-divers.com; Koh Jum Beach Villas, Ko Jum; 2 dives 4600-5500B, Open Water certification 15,800B; ⏲10am-7pm) Ko Jum's only, west-coast dive operation hits all the Lanta and Phi-Phi sites. Snorkellers can tag along for about half price.

Sleeping & Eating

Accommodation is strung out along Ko Jum's west coast. Most resorts have on-site restaurants; some close for the May-to-October low season.

Bodaeng BUNGALOW $

(☎081 494 8760; Hat Yao, Ko Jum; bungalow 250-300B) A good old-fashioned hippie vortex with dirt-cheap bamboo bungalows and a couple of slightly newer wood huts, sprinkled in the trees. Expect squat toilets in the corrugated-tin bathrooms and very limited electricity. Nonetheless, it's a hit with returning travellers, who bring along a sociable high-season scene, and the owner is a charmer.

Siboya Bungalows BUNGALOW $

(☎081 979 3344; www.siboyabungalows.com; Ko Si Boya; bungalow 350B, house 500-1200B; @ 🛜 👪) OK, Ko Si Boya's beach isn't spectacular. But the mangrove setting is wild and full of life, the bungalows and private homes are large, stylish and affordable, and the excellent restaurant is wired with high-speed internet. No wonder ever-smiling, secretive 50-somethings flock here like it's a retiree's version of Alex Garland's *The Beach*. There are family-friendly homes that sleep four people.

★ **Woodland Lodge** BUNGALOW $$
(☎081 893 5330; www.woodland-koh-jum.com; Hat Yao, Ko Jum; standard/family bungalow 1100/1500B; 📶) Tasteful, clean, fan-cooled bamboo huts with proper thatched roofs, polished wood floors and verandahs, spaciously laid out across shady grounds, make this our favourite spot on Ko Jum. Concrete-and-wood family bungalows sleep three. The friendly British-Thai owners organise boat trips and run the excellent on-site **Fighting Fish Restaurant** (mains 100-200B; ⏰8am-4pm & 6-10pm; 📶).

Koh Jum Beach Villas VILLA $$$
(☎086 184 0505; www.kohjumbeachvillas.com; Hat Yao, Ko Jum; villa incl breakfast 12,800-26,900B; 📶) Spacious, elegant privately owned wooden homes with four-poster beds, cosy decks and sea views sprawl back among frangipani- and bougainvillea-filled gardens from a luscious golden beach. Some have romantic private infinity pools. The team keeps things as environmentally and socially responsible as possible. Staff are delightful, the **restaurant** (mains 190-350B; ⏰8am-10pm; 📶) and bar scrumptious.

There's no air-con, but villas are built to catch ocean breezes. Some have up to five bedrooms, making them ideal for families.

Koh Jum Lodge RESORT $$$
(☎089 921 1621; www.kohjumlodge.com; Hat Yao, Ko Jum; bungalow incl breakfast 4500-7000B; ⏰Nov-Apr; 📶) An ecolodge with style: lots of hardwoods and bamboo, gauzy mosquito netting, coconut palms, Thai carvings, silk throws, manicured grounds, massage pavilions and a hammock-strewn curve of white sand out front. It strikes that hard-to-get balance of authenticity and comfort.

Hong Yong Restaurant THAI $
(Ban Ting Rai, Ko Jum; mains 80-100B; ⏰8am-10pm) Local food talk sends you inland to this pastel-pink makeshift village restaurant, where bubbly Rosa sizzles up huge portions of delicious Thai curries, stir fries and international breakfasts. Try the fragrant massaman curry or the seasonal seafood specials. Also known as Rosa's.

Getting There & Away

From November to May, the boat from Krabi to Ko Lanta will drop you at Ko Jum, for the full fare (400B, one hour, 11.30am); boats return from Lanta at 8.30am. In high season, daily boats run from Ko Jum to Ko Phi-Phi (600B, 1½ hours) at 8.30am, collecting guests from the Hat Yao resorts; boats return from Phi-Phi at 2.30pm.

There are year-round long-tails to Ko Jum from Ban Laem Kruat, 38km southeast of Krabi at the end of Rte 4036, off Hwy 4. Boats (100B, 30 minutes) leave at 9am, 10am, 11.30am, 1pm, 2.30pm, 4pm, 5.30pm and 6.15pm, and return at 6.30am, 7.15am, 7.35am, 7.55am, 8.10am, 1.30pm, 2.30pm and 4pm.

If you're arriving on Ko Jum via Laem Kruat, note that boats run to three different piers; Ban Ko Jum and Mu Tu piers are most convenient. Guesthouses will arrange transfers from the piers if you call in advance. Otherwise, you're relying on the kindness of strangers.

Daily boats to Ko Si Boya (50B, 15 minutes) run from Laem Kruat every hour between 8am and 5.30pm, returning hourly from 6.15am to 5pm. Call Siboya Resort (p669) to arrange transfer from the pier.

Sŏrng·tăa·ou meet boats at Laem Kruat and go to Krabi (100B), via Krabi airport and Nua Khlong (where you can connect for Ko Lanta).

Getting Around

Several places in Ban Ko Jum and some Ko Jum guesthouses rent bicycles (100B) and motorbikes (250B).

Ko Lanta เกาะลันตา

POP 26,800

Once the domain of backpackers and sea gypsies, Lanta has morphed from a luscious southern Thai backwater into a mid-range-to-luxury getaway for mostly-European tourists, who come for the divine miles-long beaches unpolluted by jet skis (though the northern coast is alarmingly eroded) and nearby dive spots of Hin Daeng, Hin Muang and Ko Haa.

Within eyeshot of Phi-Phi, charming Lanta remains far more calm, real and culturally rich, and effortlessly caters to all tastes and budgets. It's also relatively flat compared to its karst-formation neighbours, and laced with good roads that run 22km from north to south, so is easily explored by motorbike. A quick loop reveals a colourful crucible of cultures – fried-chicken stalls sit below slender minarets, stilted *chow lair* villages cling to the island's east side, and small Thai wát hide within green-brown tangles of curling mangroves.

Ko Lanta is technically called Ko Lanta Yai. Boats pull into dusty two-street Ban Sala Dan, on the northern tip of the island.

Sights

★ Ban Si Raya — VILLAGE

(บ้านศรีรายา, Lanta Old Town; Map p674) Halfway down Lanta's eastern coast, Ban Si Raya was the island's original port and commercial centre, providing a safe harbour for Arabic and Chinese trading vessels sailing between Phuket, Penang and Singapore. It was Lanta's administrative capital from 1901 to 1998. Some of the gracious, well-kept wooden century-old stilt houses and shopfronts have been transformed into beautifully dated guesthouses. Pier restaurants offer fresh catch overlooking the sea, and there are some cute bohemian shops dotted around.

Tham Khao Maikaeo — CAVE

(ถ้ำเขาไม้แก้ว; Map p674; ☎089 288 8954; tour 300B) Monsoon rains pounding away at limestone crevices for millions of years have created this complex of caverns and tunnels. There are cathedral-size chambers, dripping with stalactites and stalagmites, tiny passages you have to squeeze through on hands and knees, and even a subterranean pool. A local family runs hourly treks to the caves (with headlamps). The full trip takes two hours; sensible shoes essential. It's signposted off the main road from Hat Khlong Tob to the east coast. Phone ahead for timings.

Tham Seua — CAVE

(ถ้ำเสือ, Tiger Cave; Map p674; tour 200B; ⏲Oct-Apr) Reached via a signposted track heading east off the national park headquarters road, 2km south of Hat Khlong Nin, Tham Seua has interesting tunnels to explore via guided one-to-two-hour tours (with individual headlamps).

Activities

Diving & Snorkelling

Some of Thailand's top diving spots are within arm's reach of Lanta. The best diving can be found at the undersea pinnacles of Hin Muang (p662) and **Hin Daeng**, 45 minutes away by speedboat. These lone mid-sea coral outcrops act as important feeding stations for large pelagic fish such as sharks, tuna, barracudas and occasionally whale sharks and manta rays. Hin Daeng is commonly considered to be Thailand's second-best dive site after Richelieu Rock (p598), near the Myanmar border.

The sites around **Ko Haa** have consistently good visibility, with depths of 18m to 34m, plenty of marine life (including turtles) and a three-chamber cave known as 'the Cathedral'. Lanta dive outfitters run trips up to King Cruiser Wreck (p662), Anemone Reef (p662) and Ko Phi-Phi (p662).

Lanta's dive season is November to April, though some operators run weather-dependent dives during low season. Trips to Hin Daeng and Hin Muang cost 3400B to 4500B; Ko Haa dives are 3100B to 4000B. PADI Open Water courses cost 13,900B to 17,900B. Rates usually exclude national park fees.

From mid-October to April, agencies across Lanta offer four-island snorkelling and kayaking tours (1200B to 1800B) to Ko Rok Nok (p678), the Trang Islands and other nearby isles.

Scubafish — DIVING

(Map p674; ☎075 665095; www.scubafish.com; Ao Kantiang; 2 dives 3500B; ⏲8am-8pm) A long-running southern-based operator with a stellar reputation, Scubafish offers personable, personal programs, including the Liquid Lense underwater photography courses. The three-day dive packages (9975B) are popular. One-day Discover Scuba is 3200B; Open Water certification costs 15,900B to 17,900B; for Hin Daeng/Hin Muang you'll pay 4500B for two dives.

Blue Planet Divers DIVING
(Map p673; ☎075 668165; www.divinglanta.com; 3 Mu 1, Ban Sala Dan; 2 dives 3100B; ⏰8.30am-9pm) The first Lanta school to specialise in free-diving instruction (from 2700B). Also does Open Water certification (13,700B), Discover Scuba (4300B) and snorkelling tours (1500B).

Lanta Diver DIVING
(Map p673; ☎075 668058; www.lantadiver.com; 197/3 Mu 1, Ban Sala Dan; 2 dives 2900B, Open Water certification 13,900B; ⏰10am-6pm) A very professional Scandinavian-run operator, based near the pier and with smaller resort concessions. Two-dive day trips to Hin Daeng and Hin Muang run 3900B to 4700B; two-dive Discover Scuba is 4500B.

Go Dive DIVING
(Map p673; ☎075 668320; www.godive-lanta.com; 6 Mu 1, Ban Sala Dan; 2 dives 3300B; ⏰Oct-Apr) One of Lanta's newer outfitters. Fun dives (two for 4200B at Hin Daeng/Hin Muang), two-dive Discover Scuba (3900B) and Open Water certification (PADI/SSI 13,900/12,900B).

Yoga

Relax Bay (p673) offers high-season drop-in classes (400B), as does Sri Lanta (p675) for 500B.

Oasis Yoga YOGA
(Map p673; ☎085 115 4067; www.oasisyoga-lanta.com; Hat Khlong Dao; class 400B) A dedicated studio halfway down Hat Khlong Dao, with up to four daily high-season drop-in Hatha, Ashtanga or flow yoga, plus detox retreats and teacher training. Reduced schedule May to October; check its website.

Volunteering

Lanta Animal Welfare VOLUNTEERING
(Map p673; ☎084 304 4331; www.lantaanimalwelfare.com; 629 Mu 2, Ban Phra Ae; tour by donation; ⏰9am-5pm) This long-standing animal rescue centre cares for 30 dogs and 60 cats through feeding, sterilising and re-homing, and vaccination and local awareness campaigns. Visitors can join hourly 40-minute facilities tours (low season noon and 3pm only) and play with kittens. The centre also welcomes casual dog-walking visitors and volunteers for longer placements.

Courses

Time for Lime COOKING COURSE
(Map p673; ☎075 684590; www.timeforlime.net; Hat Khlong Dao; class 1800B; ⏰class 4pm) On south Hat Khlong Dao, this popular school-restaurant offers excellent cooking courses with a slightly more exciting recipe selection than most Thai cookery schools, in a professional moulded-concrete kitchen. Five-hour courses can be adapted for vegetarians and there are multiple-class discounts. Profits finance Lanta Animal Welfare. Book ahead.

Sleeping

Ban Sala Dan ท่าศาลาด่าน

Lanta House GUESTHOUSE $
(Map p673; ☎095 547 3873, 075 656277; lantahouse@gmail.com; r fan/air-con 350/450B; ❄📶) A fine budget choice run by an exceptionally friendly family, Lanta House has windowless but sparkling-clean, fan-cooled rooms with dark walls, bamboo beds and lots of style for this price. An extra 100B gets you air-con, a window and a balcony. All share bathrooms.

Hat Khlong Dao หาดคลองดาว

★**Costa Lanta** HOTEL $$$
(Map p673; ☎075 668186; www.costalanta.com; r incl breakfast 6800-9900B; ❄📶🏊) These Zen-like standalone abodes are nestled in a coconut-palm garden laced with tidal canals at the north end of Hat Khlong Dao. Everything from the floors to the walls to the washbasins is polished concrete, and the barn doors of each minimalist-chic cabana open on two sides to maximise space and breezes.

The restaurant is stunning, as is the service and the black sand-edge spill-over pool. Discounts are available if booked online; low-season rates are excellent.

Hat Phra Ae หาดพระแอ

Andaman Sunflower BUNGALOW $
(Map p673; ☎089 969 2610, 075 684668; bungalow 750-1350B; ⏰Oct-Mar; 📶) Hidden amid bougainvillea- and palm-filled gardens, this is a terrific set of wood and bamboo bungalows with built-in platform beds, high palm-leaf ceilings, polished-wood floors, glass-bowl bathroom sinks and hammock-laden verandas. Set back from the beach, these are some of the best upper-budget bungalows around Hat Phra Ae.

Ko Lanta North

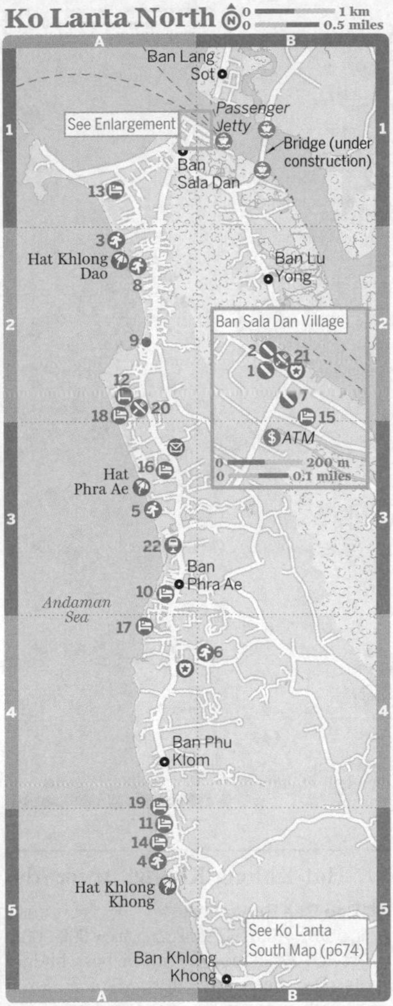

Ko Lanta North

Activities, Courses & Tours

1 Blue Planet Divers ... B2
2 Go Dive ... B2
3 Hat Khlong Dao ... A2
4 Hat Khlong Khong ... A5
5 Hat Phra Ae ... A3
6 Lanta Animal Welfare ... B4
7 Lanta Diver ... B2
8 Oasis Yoga ... A2
9 Time for Lime ... A2

Sleeping

10 Andaman Sunflower ... A3
11 Bee Bee Bungalows ... A5
12 Chill Out House ... A2
13 Costa Lanta ... A1
Hutyee Boat ... (see 10)
14 Isara Lanta ... A5
15 Lanta House ... B3
16 Layana Resort ... A3
17 Relax Bay ... A4
18 Somewhere Else ... A2
19 Where Else! ... A4

Eating

20 Cook Kai ... A2
21 Lanta Seafood ... B2
Manao ... (see 17)
Red Snapper ... (see 10)

Drinking & Nightlife

Feeling Bar ... (see 19)
22 Irish Embassy ... A3

Chill Out House HOSTEL $
(Map p673; ☎082 183 2258; www.facebook.com/ChillOutHouse; dm 150B, d 220-275B;) This buzzing backpacker 'treehouse community' has simple four-bed dorms, shared bathrooms, chalkboard doors and rickety en-suite doubles. It's basic, but you can't beat the laid-back vibe (or the price): swings at the bar, a communal iPod dock, and a wonderful (yes) chill-out lounge heavy on hammocks.

Hutyee Boat BUNGALOW $
(Map p673; ☎083 633 9723; bungalow 500-700B) A hidden, hippie paradise of big, solid bungalows on stilts with tiled bathrooms, mini fridges and swinging hammocks in a forest of palms and bamboo. It's just back from the beach (behind Nautilus Resort) and run by a friendly Muslim family.

Relax Bay HOTEL $$
(Map p673; ☎075 684194; www.relaxbay.com; Ao Phra Ae; bungalow incl breakfast with fan 1600-2450B, air-con 2450-5100B, luxury tent 2750-3250B;) This gorgeous French-run place sprawls over a tree-covered headland by a small beach. Yellow- and red-toned, wood-and-bamboo bungalows sit on stilts with large decks overlooking the bay. There's a lovely tropical-feel pool, plus the good, stylish semi-open-air **Manao restaurant** (mains 140-400B; 7am-9.30pm;) and bar and high-season yoga (400B). It's sightly overpriced, but an absolute steal in low season.

Ko Lanta South

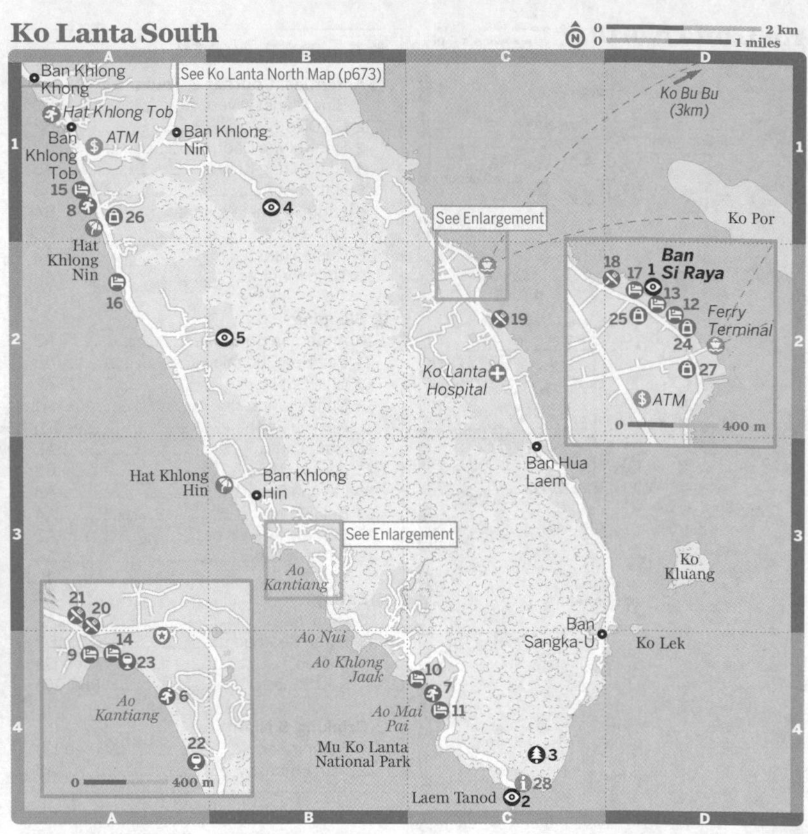

Somewhere Else BUNGALOW $$
(Map p673; ☎081 536 0858; bungalow 800-1700B; 📶) Choose between basic thatched bamboo huts with terracotta-tiled bathrooms and bigger octagonal polished-concrete bungalows, all of which dot a shady lawn right on a very popular, social and lounge-worthy stretch of beach.

Layana Resort RESORT $$$
(Map p673; ☎075 607100; www.layanaresort.com; r incl breakfast 16,900-28,100B; ❄📶🏊) The beachfront location, fabulous palm-lined pool and impeccable service make anyone lucky to stay at the slickly contemporary adults-only Layana. Comfy, spacious hardwood rooms with soothing neutral decor, complimentary fruit bowls and a pillow menu mean it's all the more attractive. Rack rates are steep but internet deals can make it a bargain; expect 50% discounts in low season.

Hat Khlong Khong หาดคลองโขง

★Bee Bee Bungalows BUNGALOW $
(Map p673; ☎081 537 9932; bungalow 600-900B; ⊙Oct-Apr; 📶) One of Lanta's best budget spots, Bee Bee's is comprised of a dozen creative bamboo cabins managed by superfriendly staff. Each bungalow is unique; a few are stilted in the trees. The on-site restaurant has a library of tattered paperbacks to keep you occupied while you wait for your delicious Thai staples.

Where Else! BUNGALOW $
(Map p673; ☎075 667173, 081 536 4870; where else_lanta@yahoo.com; bungalow 800-2000B) One of Lanta's little slices of bohemia, thatched bungalows with semi-outdoor cold-water bathrooms are pretty shaky; if you're trying to avoid late-night parties and tropical critters look elsewhere. Still, the place buzzes with backpackers

Ko Lanta South

Top Sights
1 Ban Si Raya....D2

Sights
2 Laem Tanod....C4
3 Mu Ko Lanta National Park....C4
4 Tham Khao Maikaeo....B1
5 Tham Seua....B2

Activities, Courses & Tours
6 Ao Kantiang....A4
7 Ao Mai Pai....C4
8 Hat Khlong Nin....A1
Scubafish....(see 9)

Sleeping
9 Baan Laanta Resort & Spa....A4
10 Baan Phu Lae....C4
11 La Laanta....C4
12 Mango House....D2
Mu Ko Lanta National Park Accommodation....(see 28)
13 Old Times....D2
14 Phra Nang Lanta....A4
15 Round House....A1
16 Sri Lanta....A2
17 Sriraya....D2

Eating
18 Beautiful Restaurant....D2
19 Caoutchouc....C2
20 Drunken Sailors....A3
La Laanta....(see 11)
21 Phad Thai Rock'n'Roll....A3

Drinking & Nightlife
22 Same Same But Different....A4
23 Why Not Bar....A4

Shopping
24 Hammock House....D2
25 Malee Malee....D2
26 Monkey Biziness....A1
27 Sunday Market....D2

Information
28 Mu Ko Lanta National Park Headquarters....C4
Mu Ko Lanta National Park Visitors Centre....(see 28)

and there's a fun barefoot-beach vibe that culminates in the popular Feeling Bar (p679). Pricier bungalows are multilevel abodes sleeping up to four.

Low season rates drop by 50% to 70%.

Isara Lanta BUNGALOW **$$**
(Map p673; ☎088 823 2184; www.isaralanta.com; bungalow fan 500-1300B, air-con 1200-2500B;) A popular little set of neat, pastel-painted, tin-roofed concrete bungalows with woven bamboo flourishes lining a simple flowery path that spreads back behind a rustic blue-and-white-washed restaurant-bar.

Hat Khlong Nin หาดคลองนิน

Round House GUESTHOUSE **$$**
(Map p674; ☎086 950 9424; www.lantaroundhouse.com; r 1600B, bungalow without/with bathroom 600/1500B, house 3000B;) A cute multi-option find on the north end of the beach. Stilted bamboo and wood fan bungalows are simply styled with (mostly) shared hot-water bathrooms, and are just behind the breezy beachfront restaurant. Also available is a cool two-person adobe round house, concrete rooms fronted by porches and an air-con beach house perfect for families. Good low-season and solo-traveller discounts.

Sri Lanta BOUTIQUE HOTEL **$$$**
(Map p674; ☎075 662688; www.srilanta.com; r 3400-6900B; Sep-May;) At the southern end of the beach, this decadent ecospot consists of minimalist wooden villas in wild gardens stretching from the beach to a landscaped hillside. There's a chic flower-fringed beachside area with an infinity pool, restaurant and private massage pavilions. The resort strives for low environmental impact by using biodegradable products and minimising energy use and waste.

It also hosts yoga classes (500B) and some retreats.

Ao Kantiang อ่าวกันเตียง

★ **Baan Laanta Resort & Spa** HOTEL **$$**
(Map p674; ☎075 665091; www.baanlaanta.com; bungalow incl breakfast 2500-4500B;) Landscaped grounds wind around stylish wooden bungalows with terraces and a sultry dark infinity pool refreshed by elephant fountains and surrounded by frangipani trees, all overlooking an idyllic white sandy beach. The bungalows' centrepiece is a futon-style bed on a raised wooden platform under a delicate veil of mosquito netting, beside which lie lounge sofas on varnished terracotta tiles. The Scubafish (p671) dive school is on-site.

WHERE TO STAY ON KO LANTA

Ko Lanta has masses of long good-looking golden beaches, most on the western coast. You'll experience the island in different incarnations depending on where you bed down. Some resorts close for the May-to-October low season; others drop rates by 50%. Resorts usually have their own restaurants and tour-booking facilities.

The building boom means that there are now dozens of good-value roadside spots available, though views are lacking. Reservations are essential in high season.

Ban Sala Dan Decent budget accommodation has sprung up in characterful Ban Sala Dan. It's handy for local-flavoured seafood restaurants and boat arrivals/departures, but not on the beach.

Hat Khlong Dao Once an outstanding 2km white-sand stretch perfect for swimming, this beach has become so eroded that at high tide there's no sand at all. That's a big issue throughout northern Lanta.

Hat Phra Ae (Long Beach) A large travellers' village (*fa·ràng*-oriented restaurants, beach bars, tour offices) has grown up along sandy Hat Phra Ae, 3km south of Ban Sala Dan. The beach has suffered erosion recently, but there's a nice stretch on its northern flank.

Hat Khlong Khong This is thatched-roof, Rasta-bar bliss with beach volleyball, moon parties and the occasional well-advertised mushroom shake, 9km south of Ban Sala Dan. It's all pretty low-key. The thinning yet ample stretch of beach goes on forever in either direction lapped by turquoise shallows.

Hat Khlong Nin The main road heading south forks 13km south of Ban Sala Dan (after Hat Khlong Tob). The left road leads to the east coast; the right road hugs the coastline for 14km to Ko Lanta's southernmost tip. On the right fork the first beach is lovely white-sand Hat Khlong Nin, which has lots of small, flashpacker-type guesthouses at its north end. Shop around.

Ao Kantiang This superb southwestern sweep of sand backed by mountains is also its own self-contained village with mini-marts, motorbike rental and restaurants. It's upmarket-ish and far from everything. Don't expect to move much.

Ao Mai Pai A lush nearly forgotten cove at the southwestern curve just before the cape, Ao Mai Pai is one of Lanta's finest beaches. Backed by elegant palm groves, with a rock reef jutting north, a jungle-swathed headland to the south and jade waters between.

Laem Tanod The wild, jungled, mountainous southern tip of the island has sheer drops and massive views.

Ban Si Raya There are a handful of guesthouses in Lanta's oft-ignored, wonderfully dated and incredibly rich east-coast Old Town, which has its own bohemian groove.

Phra Nang Lanta HOTEL **$$$**
(Map p674; 075 665025; www.vacationvillage.co.th/phrananglanta; r 5900-9500B;) These 15 gorgeous, Mexican-style, adobe-looking concrete studios are straight off the pages of an interiors magazine. Think: clean lines, hardwoods and whites accented with vibrant colours, lounge cushions and ceramic sinks. Outside, flowers and foliage climb over bamboo lattice sunshades, and the pool and restaurant-bar look over the beautiful beach. Excellent low-season deals.

Ao Mai Pai อ่าวไม้ไผ่

Baan Phu Lae BUNGALOW **$$**
(Map p674; 075 665100, 085 474 0265; www.baanphulaeresort.com; Ao Mai Pai; bungalow fan 1800B, air-con 2000-2400B;) Set on secluded rocks at the northern end of the final beach before Lanta's southern cape, this collection of cute, canary-yellow concrete fan and air-con bungalows have thatched roofs, colourful art, bamboo beds and private porches. Just behind stand stilted, wooden, air-con bungalows. They also arrange div-

ing and snorkelling trips, cooking classes, massages and transport.

★La Laanta BOUTIQUE HOTEL $$$
(Map p674; ☎087 883 9977, 087 883 9966; www.lalaanta.com; bungalow incl breakfast 2800-6200B;) Operated by a young English-speaking Thai-Vietnamese couple, this is the grooviest spot on Lanta. Thatched bungalows have polished-concrete floors, platform beds, floral-design murals and decks overlooking a sandy volleyball pitch, which blends into a rocky beach. The laid-back **restaurant** (mains 120-350B; 8am-9pm;) does a tasty Thai menu with lots of vegie-friendly choices. It's the last turn before the national park, far from everything else.

They provide extra beds for children and there's a kids' swimming pool. Steep low-season discounts.

Laem Tanod แหลมโตนด

Mu Ko Lanta National Park Accommodation BUNGALOW, CAMPGROUND $
(Map p674; ☎075 660711, in Bangkok 02 561 4292; www.dnp.go.th; bungalow 1500-3000B, camp site per person 40B, with tent hire 300B) Engulfed by craggy outcrops and the sound of crashing waves, the secluded national park headquarters grounds are a gloriously serene place to stay, in simple four- to eight-person bungalows or tents. There are toilets, running water and a shop, but bring your own food. You can also get permission for camping on Ko Rok here.

The road to the marine national park headquarters fords the *klorng* (canal; also spelt *khlong*), which can get deep during the monsoon.

Ban Si Raya บ้านศรีรายา

Sriraya GUESTHOUSE $
(Map p674; ☎075 697045; punpun_3377@hotmail.com; r with shared bathroom 500B) Sleep in a simple but beautifully restored, thick-beamed Chinese shophouse with plenty of style and a friendly welcome. Walls are brushed in earth tones and sheets are bright. Go for the street-front balcony room overlooking the Old Town's characterful centre.

Old Times GUESTHOUSE $$
(Map p674; ☎075 697255, 098 567 2855; www.theoldtimeslanta.com; Ban Si Raya; r fan 900B, air-con 1200-2000B;) A fabulous new Old Town addition, tucked into two stylishly revamped 100-year-old teak houses facing each other across the street. Impeccably styled rooms grace various sizes and budgets, under music-inspired names like 'Yellow Submarine'. The best – bright and decked with black-and-white photos – jut out over the sea on the jetty, where there's a cushioned communal chill-out area. Fun, fresh and friendly.

★Mango House GUESTHOUSE $$$
(Map p674; ☎095 014 0658; www.mangohouses.com; ste 2500-3000B, 2-person villa 4000B;) These century-old Chinese teak pole houses and former opium dens are stilted over the harbour. The original time-worn wood floors are intact, ceilings soar and the three, house-sized suites are kitted out with kitchenettes, satellite TVs, DVD players and ceiling fans. There are also newly built Old Town–style seafront villas sleeping two to six people. Rates drop by 50% in low season.

Eating

The best-value places for a feed are the seafood restaurants along the northern edge of Ban Sala Dan, which offer fresh seafood sold by weight (including cooking costs) on verandahs over the water.

Phad Thai Rock'n'Roll THAI $
(Map p674; www.facebook.com/phadthairock77; Ao Kantiang; mains 90-150B; 11am-9pm) It's not every day you get your spiced-to-taste *pàt tai* whipped up streetside by a guitarist. Choose from just six options ('jazz' fried rice, 'blues' fried noodles; veg, meat or seafood), swiftly and artfully prepared in simple contemporary surrounds. With about as many tables as dishes, it's deservedly popular, so you may have to wait.

Cook Kai THAI $
(Map p673; www.cook-kai.com; Hat Phra Ae; mains 75-350B; 8am-10pm;) A huge family-run eatery where shells dangle from a thatched roofed. Cook Kai is best for its wide selection of straightforward local staples, which takes in everything from spicy Thai salads, noodle soups and fried rice to sizzling seafood hotpans and deep-fried or steamed fish.

★Drunken Sailors INTERNATIONAL, THAI $$
(Map p674; ☎075 665076; www.facebook.com/DrunkenSailors; Ao Kantiang; mains 90-150B; 9am-3pm & 6-10pm;) This relaxed octagonal pod is smothered in beanbags, hammocks and low-lying tables spilling out onto a terrace. The global, want-to-eat-it-all

WORTH A TRIP

MU KO LANTA NATIONAL PARK

Mu Ko Lanta National Park (อุทยานแห่งชาติหมู่เกาะลันตา; Map p674; ☎075 660711, in Bangkok 02 561 4292; www.dnp.go.th; adult/child/motorbike 200/100/20B; ⊙8am-6pm) Established in 1990, this marine national park protects 16 islands in the Ko Lanta group, including the southern tip of Ko Lanta Yai. The park is increasingly threatened by the runaway development on west-coast Ko Lanta Yai, though other islands in the group have fared slightly better.

Ko Rok Nai is still very beautiful, with a crescent-shaped bay backed by cliffs, fine coral reefs and a sparkling white-sand beach. Camping is permitted on adjacent **Ko Rok Nok** with permission from the park headquarters. On the eastern side of Ko Lanta Yai, **Ko Talabeng** (Map p671) has some dramatic limestone caves that you can visit on sea-kayaking tours (1300B). National park fees apply if you visit any of the islands. Ko Rok Nai, Ko Rok Nok and **Ko Haa** (p671) are off limits to visitors from 16 May to 31 October.

The **national park headquarters** (Map p674; ☎075 660711, in Bangkok 02 561 4292; ⊙8am-4pm) and **visitors centre** (Map p674; ⊙8am-6pm) are at Laem Tanod, on the southern tip of Ko Lanta Yai, reached by a steep paved road. There are some basic hiking trails, two twin beaches and a gorgeously scenic lighthouse, plus camping facilities and bungalows amid wild, natural surroundings.

menu roams from pastas, baguettes and burgers to top-notch Thai, starring perfectly spiced ginger stir fries and red curries cooked to personal taste. Coffees, cakes and juices are another forte.

Lanta Seafood SEAFOOD $$
(Map p673; Ban Sala Dan; mains 80-250B; ⊙11am-9pm) The best of Ban Sala Dan's seafood-by-weight options, with all your other Thai favourites too. Try the *Ƀlah tôrt kà-mîn:* deep-fried white snapper rubbed with fresh, hand-ground turmeric and garlic.

Beautiful Restaurant SEAFOOD $$
(Map p674; ☎086 282 1777; Ban Si Raya; mains 100-350B; ⊙10am-9pm; 📶) Tables are scattered on four piers that extend into the sea at the northwest end of the Old Town. Fish is fresh and exquisitely prepared.

Caoutchouc INTERNATIONAL, THAI $$
(Map p674; ☎075 697060; www.facebook.com/Caoutchouc-125216317555399; Ban Si Raya; dishes 150-300B; ⊙10am-9pm) For Thai-international flavours blended into delectable creative concoctions, hunt down this rustic-chic, French-run restaurant with a short but special changing menu served on a panoramic stilted deck, 800m south of the Old Town pier. You might just uncover a deliciously fresh feta-and-rice or shrimp curry salad, served alongside mango or pineapple lassi.

Red Snapper INTERNATIONAL $$$
(Map p673; ☎087 885 6965; www.redsnapper-lanta.com; Hat Phra Ae; tapas 60-295B, mains 315-625B; ⊙5-11pm Thu-Tue; ✍) When local expats fancy a splurge, they head to this Dutch-run roadside tapas restaurant, serving everything from Indian lentil-and-pumpkin curry and house marinated olives to a popular beef tenderloin steak and a huge variety of cheese platters, in a romantic garden setting. Decent vegetarian choices too. When we stopped by, there were plans to relocate nearby in mid-2016.

Drinking & Nightlife

If you're after heaving clubs, pick another island. If you fancy a more low-key bar scene with music wafting well into the night, Lanta has options on most beaches, and particularly around Hat Phra Ae. Things move around depending on the day, so check out posters island-wide for upcoming events. Low season is beyond mellow.

Why Not Bar BAR
(Map p674; www.facebook.com/WhyNotBarKohLanta; Ao Kantiang; ⊙11am-midnight) A buzzing, driftwood-clad hang-out that keeps things simple with a killer mix of fire twirlers, sturdy cocktails, bubbly bar-staff and fantastic nightly live music jams, best enjoyed at low-slung wooden tables on a raised deck.

Feeling Bar BAR

(Map p673; Hat Khlong Khong; ⏰11am-late) Joined to the rickety but much-loved Where Else! (p674) bungalows, Feeling keeps that original Lanta hippie-backpacker vibe alive with its 'Friday Feeling' beach parties.

Same Same But Different BAR

(Map p674; ☎081 787 8670; www.facebook.com/samesamebutdifferentlanta; Ao Kantiang; ⏰10am-10pm) In an island-chic seaside setting, you can sample middling Thai cuisine (mains 120B to 300B) and sip cocktails beneath massive trees, thatched pagodas or in a bamboo chair sunk into the sand. The location is the thing.

Irish Embassy PUB

(Map p673; www.irishembassylanta.com; Ban Phra Ae; ⏰4pm-midnight) Few may come to Lanta looking for a pub, but this warm, friendly expat favourite has all the quiz nights, sports screens, pool competitions and darts fun you could ask for if you do.

Shopping

★**Malee Malee** FASHION

(Map p674; ☎075 697235; 55/3 Mu 2, Ban Si Raya; ⏰9am-9pm) A bohemian wonderland of quirky homemade goods, from silk-screened and hand-painted T-shirts and silk scarves to journals, toys, baby clothes, paintings, jewellery and handbags. Prices are low, it's super fun to browse and a sweet cafe (coffees around 80B) sits on the doorstep.

Hammock House HOMEWARES

(Map p674; www.jumbohammock.com; Ban Si Raya; ⏰10am-5pm) For unique, quality, colour-bursting hammocks, crafted by rural villagers and threatened Mlabri tribespeople in northern Thailand, don't miss Hammock House. It sometimes closes for low season (May to October).

Monkey Biziness FASHION

(Map p674; Hat Khlong Nin; ⏰10am-7pm Sep-May; 📶) Floaty, soft-toned Thai-made women's clothing and accessories, plus home decor pieces and a relaxed cafe (drinks 60B).

Sunday Market MARKET

(Map p674; Ban Si Raya; ⏰8-11am) There's a small Sunday market in Ban Si Raya.

Information

Ban Sala Dan has plenty of ATMs, restaurants, mini-marts, travel agencies, dive shops and motorcycle rentals. There are 7-Elevens spread along the island's west coast, most with ATMs. Lanta Pocket Guide (www.lantapocketguide.com) is helpful.

Ko Lanta Hospital (Map p674; ☎075 697017; Ban Si Raya) About 1km south of the Ban Si Raya Old Town.

Police Station (Map p673; ☎075 668192; Ban Sala Dan)

Getting There & Away

Transport to Ko Lanta is by boat or air-con minivan. If arriving independently, you'll need to use the frequent **vehicle ferries** (motorcycle/pedestrian/car 20/20/200B; ⏰6am-10pm) between Ban Hua Hin and Ban Khlong Mak (Ko Lanta Noi) and on to Ko Lanta Yai.

BOAT

Ban Sala Dan has two piers. The passenger jetty is 300m from the main strip of shops; vehicle ferries leave from a **jetty** (Map p673) 2km east.

From mid-October to mid-April, the high-speed **Tigerline** (☎075 668428; www.tigerlinetravel.com) ferry runs between Phuket (1500B, two hours) and Ban Sala Dan (Ko Lanta) and on to Ko Lipe (1700B, five hours), via Ko Ngai (750B, one hour), Ko Kradan (850B, 1½ hours) and Ko Muk (850B, two hours). The service heads south at 10am, returning from Lipe at 10am the following day and stopping on Ko Lanta around 3pm before continuing north.

Ko Phi-Phi Ferries between Ko Lanta and Ko Phi-Phi run only during the October-to-April high season. Boats leave Ko Lanta at 8am and 1pm (250B, 1½ hours), returning from Ko Phi-Phi at 11.30am and 3pm. There are also high-season speedboats between Lanta and Phi-Phi (700B to 800B, one hour).

Krabi From November to late April, boats leave Ko Lanta for Krabi's Khlong Chilat (p650) pier at 8.30am and 1.30pm (400B, two hours) and return from Krabi at 11.30am. During high season, they stop at Ko Jum (400B, one hour).

Phuket From Ko Phi-Phi you can transfer to ferries to Phuket; you can book tickets all the way through to Phuket from Lanta. Ko Lanta to Ko Phi-Phi is 250B to 350B. From Ko Lanta to Phuket it's 700B.

Trang Islands From November to early April, speedboats buzz from Ko Lanta to the Trang Islands, including the **Satun Pak Bara Speedboat Club** (☎099 404 0409; www.tarutaolipeisland.com) and **Bundhaya Speedboat** (☎075 668043; www.bundhayaspeedboat.com). Stops include Ko Ngai (650B, 30 minutes), Ko Muk (900B, one hour), Ko Kradan (1150B, 1¼ hours), Ko Bulon Leh (1600B, two hours) and Ko Lipe (1900B, three hours).

MINIVAN

Minivans, your easiest option from the mainland, run year-round, but they're particularly packed in this region and traffic jams for vehicle ferries can cause delays. Most minivans offer pick ups from resorts. Frequency is reduced in low season.

Minivans to Krabi airport (300B, 2½ hours) and Krabi Town (300B, three hours) run hourly between 7am and 4pm in both directions. You can connect in Krabi for further destinations, including Khao Lak and Bangkok. Departures from Lanta include the following:

DESTINATION	FARE (B)	DURATION (HR)	FREQUENCY
Ko Pha-Ngan	1000-1200	8½	8am & 10.30am
Ko Samui	900-1100	6½	8am & 10.30am
Phuket	400	6	9am, 10am & 1.30pm
Trang	380	3	8am, 9.20am, 10.40am, noon & 1.30pm

Getting Around

Most resorts send vehicles to meet the ferries – a free ride to your resort. In the opposite direction expect to pay 100B to 400B. Alternatively, take a motorcycle taxi from outside 7-Eleven in Ban Sala Dan; fares run from 50B to 400B, depending on distance.

Motorbikes (per day 250B) can be rented everywhere (without insurance). Agencies in Ban Sala Dan rent out small 4WDs (per day 1300B).

TRANG PROVINCE

South of Krabi, Trang Province has an impressive limestone-covered Andaman coast with several sublime islands. For the adventurous, there's plenty of big nature to explore in the lush interior, including dozens of scenic waterfalls and limestone caves. And it's nowhere near as popular as Krabi, which means you're more likely to see working rubber plantations here than rows of T-shirt vendors. Transport links continue improving every year, and during the high season you can easily island-hop all the way to Malaysia.

Trang ตรัง

POP 60,590

Most visitors to Trang are in transit to nearby islands, but if you're an aficionado of culture, Thai food or markets, stay a day or more. Here is an easy-to-manage, old-school Thai town where you can get lost in wet markets, hawker markets and late-night Chinese coffee shops. At nearly any time of year, there'll be some minor festival that oozes local colour.

Most tourist facilities lie along Th Praram VI, between the **clock tower** and the train station.

Sights

Trang is more a business centre than a tourist town. The lively, colourful wet and dry markets on **Th Ratchadamnoen** and **Th Sathani** are worth exploring.

Wat Tantayaphirom BUDDHIST TEMPLE

(วัดตันตยาภิรม; Th Tha Klang) FREE Wat Tantayaphirom has a huge white-and-gold *chedi* (stupa) enshrining a footprint of the Buddha that's mildly interesting.

Meunram Shrine CHINESE TEMPLE

(ศาลเจ้าพ่อหมื่นราม; btwn Th Visetkul & Th Ratsada) FREE Hazy with incense smoke, the Chinese Meunram Shrine conceals a surprisingly elaborate interior behind a blander facade and sometimes sponsors southern Thai shadow theatre.

Activities

Tour agencies around the train station and Th Praram VI offer boat trips to Hat Chao Mai National Park and the Trang Islands (750B, plus park fees), snorkelling trips to Ko Rok (per person 1300B) and private car trips to local caves and waterfalls (1500B, maximum three people).

Festivals & Events

Vegetarian Festival CULTURAL

(late Sep-Oct) Trang's Chinese population celebrates this wonderful festival to coincide with Phuket's Vegetarian Festival (p138).

Sleeping & Eating

Trang is famous for its *mŏo yâhng* (crispy barbecued pork), spongy cakes, early-morning dim sum breakfasts and *ráhn go·Ъii* (coffee shops) that serve real filtered coffee. You can find *mŏo yâhng* in the mornings at some

Trang Province

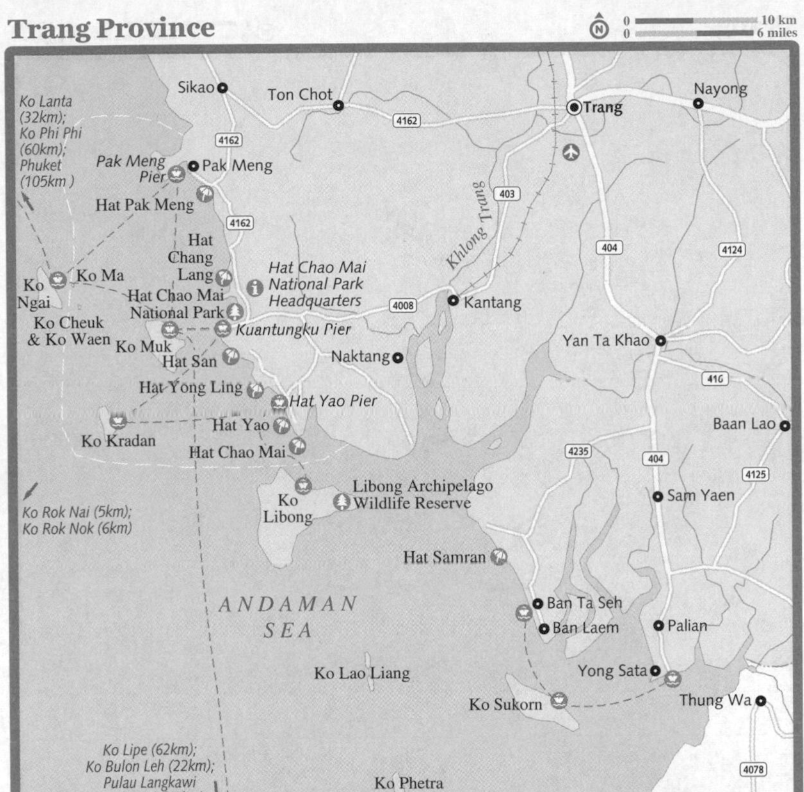

coffee shops or by weight at the wet market on Th Ratchadamnoen. To really get into the local scene, stay out late at the coffee shops along Th Ratsada.

Yamawa Guesthouse GUESTHOUSE **$**
(☎099 402 0349, 075 216617; www.yamawaguesthouse.blog.com; 94 Th Visetkul; r fan/air-con 350/450B; ❄📶) With simple, spotless fan or air-con rooms equipped with fridges, and sweet local owners who hand out detailed Trang maps, this popular budget spot is often full.

Sri Trang Hotel HOTEL **$$**
(☎075 218122; www.sritranghotel.com; 22-26 Th Sathani; r 600-800B; ❄📶) This renovated old building (which has been open for business since 1952) hosts a range of fan-cooled and air-con rooms, playing up its dated design with retro travel trunks, high ceilings, a winding wooden staircase and colourful paint jobs. Downstairs is the cosy contemporary-style **1952 Café** (dishes 65-250B; ⌚8am-8pm; 📶), perfect for coffee and mushroom omelettes while studying the Trang map wall mural.

Rua Rasada Hotel HOTEL **$$$**
(☎075 214230; www.ruarasadahotel.com; 188 Th Phattalung; r incl breakfast 2900-7100B; ❄📶🏊) Trang's slickest choice is handily located opposite the bus station, a 10-minute 3.5km (40B) túk-túk ride northeast from the train station. Modern, corporate-smart rooms come in dusky blue, dark mauve and grey, with huge windows, rectangular sinks and comfy beds.

★ **Night Market** MARKET **$**
(btwn Th Praram VI & Th Ratchadamnoen; dishes around 30B; ⌚4-9pm) The finest night market on the Andaman coast will have you salivating over bubbling curries, fried chicken and fish, deep-fried tofu, *pàt tai* and an array of Thai desserts. Go with an empty stomach

Trang

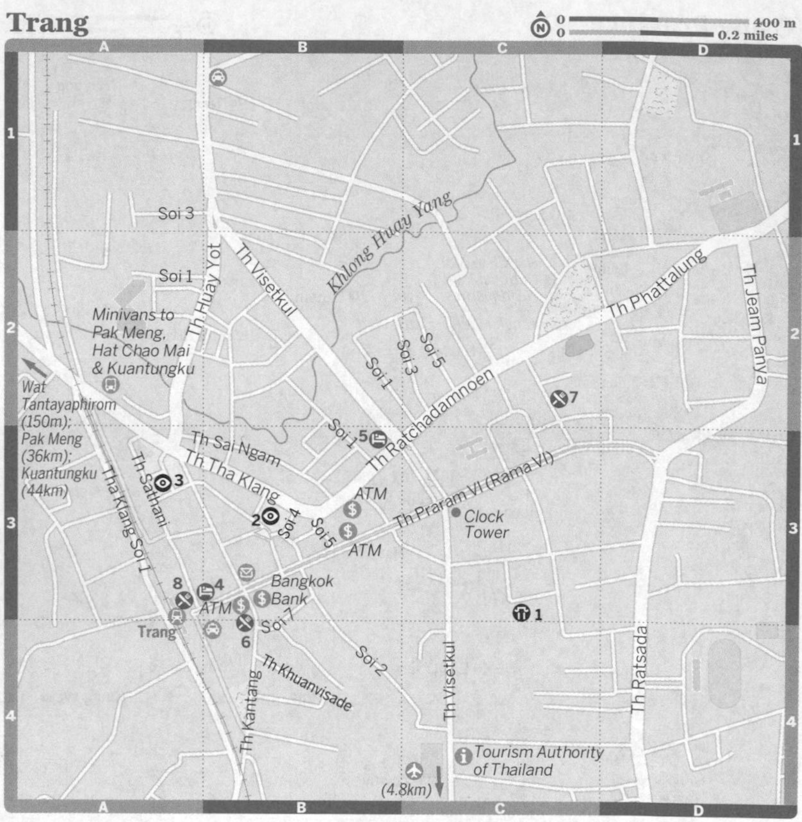

Trang

Sights

1 Meunram Shrine.......C3
2 Wet & Dry Market.......B3
3 Wet & Dry Market.......A3

Sleeping

4 Sri Trang Hotel.......B3
5 Yamawa Guesthouse.......B3

Eating

1952 Café.......(see 4)
6 Asia Ocha.......B4
7 Night Market.......C2
8 Night Market.......A3

and a sense of adventure. There's a second, equally glorious weekend **night market** (Train Station; dishes around 30B; 6-10pm Thu-Sun) opposite the train station.

Asia Ocha THAI $

(Th Kantang; dishes 35-50B; 6.30am-5pm) In business for 60 years, this antiquated spot serves filtered coffee (20B) to an all-Thai clientele who sit at vintage marble tables. Come here for delicious roast duck, crispy pork and noodle soups.

Information

ATMs and foreign-exchange booths line Th Praram VI. Hotels have wi-fi.

Post Office (cnr Th Praram VI & Th Kantang; 8.30am-4.30pm Mon-Fri, 9am-noon Sat)

Tourism Authority of Thailand (TAT; 075 211580, 075 215867; www.tourismthailand.org; 199/2 Th Visetkul; 8.30am-4.30pm)

Getting There & Away

AIR

Nok Air (02 900 9955; www.nokair.com) and **Air Asia** (02 900 9999; www.airasia.com) fly

BUSES TO/FROM TRANG

DESTINATION	FARE (B)	DURATION (HR)	FREQUENCY
Hat Yai	100	3	every 30min 5.30am-5.30pm
Krabi	120	2	hourly 5.30am-6.30pm
Phang-Nga	185	4	hourly 5.30am-6.30pm
Phuket	252	5	hourly 5.30am-6.30pm

daily from Bangkok (Don Muang) to Trang. The airport is 5km south of Trang.

Minivans to town (90B) meet flights. In the reverse direction, taxis, motorbike taxis or túk-túk cost 100B to 120B. Agencies at airport arrivals sell combined taxi-boat tickets to Trang's islands, including Ko Ngai (1000B).

BUS

Buses leave from Trang's **New Bus Terminal** (Th Phattalung), 3.5km northeast of the train station. There are 1st-class air-con buses to Bangkok (646B, 12 hours) at 8.30am, 9.30am, 4.30pm and 5pm, and more comfortable VIP 24-seat buses at 5pm and 5.30pm (1050B). From Bangkok, VIP/air-con buses leave between 6.30pm and 7.30pm. There are plenty of services to other destinations.

MINIVAN

Minivans depart from Trang's New Bus Terminal. Agencies sell minivan tickets including in-town pick-up.

Local transport is by air-con minivan rather than *sŏrng·tăa·ou*. From the bus station, minivans leave regularly from 7.30am to 4pm for Pak Meng (80B, one hour), Hat Chao Mai (100B, one hour) and Kuantungku (100B, one hour), stopping in town just east of where Th Tha Klang crosses the railway tracks.

Other departures include the following:

Hat Yai (120B, two hours, hourly 6am to 6pm)

Ko Lanta (250B, 2½ hours, five daily 9.50am to 4.30pm)

Krabi (100B, two hours, hourly 7am to 5pm)

Satun (120B, two hours, every 40 minutes 6am to 6pm)

Surat Thani (160B, three hours, hourly 7am to 5pm)

TRAIN

Only two trains run between Bangkok and Trang: the express 83 and the rapid 167, which leave from Bangkok's Hualamphong station at 5.05pm and 6.30pm and arrive in Trang the next morning at 8.05am and 10.30am respectively.

From Trang, trains leave at 1.30pm and 5.25pm, arriving in Bangkok at 5.35am and 8.35am the following morning. Fares are around 1480/761B for a 1st-/2nd-class air-con sleeper and 285B for 3rd class.

Getting Around

Túk-túk and motorbike taxis congregate near the train station, charging 40B for local trips. Travel agencies rent motorbikes (per day 250B). Most agencies arrange car rental (per day 1200B). You can rent cars at the airport.

An orange 'local bus' runs from the train station to the New Bus Terminal (12B).

Trang Beaches

Trang's beaches are mostly just jumping-off points to the Trang Islands, but, if you have time, stop and enjoy the scenery: limestone karsts rising from steamy palm-studded valleys and swirling seas.

Sights & Activities

Thirty-nine kilometres west of Trang in Amphoe Sikao (Sikao District) you'll hit Hat Pak Meng; immediately south is **Hat Chang Lang**.

Pak Meng's tour agencies organise one-day boat tours to Ko Muk, Ko Cheuk, Ko Ma and Ko Kradan, and snorkelling day tours, all including lunch (per person 750B, plus Hat Chao Mai National Park fees). Mask and snorkel sets and fins can be rented by the pier (50B each).

Hat Chao Mai National Park NATIONAL PARK

(อุทยานแห่งชาติหาดเจ้าไหม; ☎075 203308; www.dnp.go.th; adult/child 200/100B; ⏰9am-4pm) This 231-sq-km park covers the shoreline from Hat Pak Meng to Laem Chao Mai, and encompasses the islands of Ko Muk, Ko Kadran and Ko Cheuk (plus a host of small islets). While touring the coast and islands, you may spot endangered dugongs and rare black-necked storks, as well as more common species like barking deer, sea otters, macaques, langurs, wild pigs, pangolins, little herons, Pacific reef egrets, white-bellied sea eagles and monitor lizards.

Park headquarters are at the southern end of Hat Chang Lang, where the beachfront road turns inland.

Hat Pak Meng BEACH

There's a wild-looking stretch of coastline at Hat Pak Meng, 39km west of Trang. Though the beach is scruffy, the spectacular jutting limestone karsts here rival the best of Railay and Phi-Phi. Pak Meng's pier, the jumping-off point for Ko Ngai, is at the north end of the beach. Several seafood restaurants, popular with Thai day trippers and weekenders, stand where Rte 4162 meets the coast.

Sleeping & Eating

Hat Chao Mai National Park Accommodation CAMPGROUND, BUNGALOW $

(075 203308; www.dnp.go.th; Hat Chang Lang; bungalow 800B, camp site per person 30B, with tent hire 225B) Simple fan-cooled cabins sleep two to six people or you can camp under the casuarinas. There's also a restaurant.

Anantara Si Kao HOTEL $$$

(075 205888; www.sikao.anantara.com; Hat Chang Lang; r incl breakfast 6500-11,200B, ste 13,300-18,250B; P) Deluxe oceanfront rooms with rich wood floors, floating desks and delicious views of Pak Meng's signature karsts bring Anantara's trendy glamour to northern Hat Chang Lang. Impressive timber columns and Balinese furnishings line the lobby, there's a host of activities on offer, and the sea-views from Italian restaurant **Acqua** (mains 300-700B; 6.30-10.30pm) are jaw-dropping.

Shuttle over to the guests-only beach club on seductive Ko Kradan.

Getting There & Away

Air-con minivans run regularly from Trang's New Bus Terminal to Hat Pak Meng (80B, one hour) and Hat Chao Mai (100B, one hour) between 7.30am and 4pm, via Trang's Th Tha Klang. Taxis from Trang cost 1000B.

Boats leave Ko Ngai for Pak Meng at 9.30am daily, returning to Ko Ngai at noon (350B, one hour). Long-tail charters cost 1500B.

The Hat Chao Mai National Park headquarters is 1km off the main road, down a clearly signposted track.

Trang Islands

The mythical Trang Islands feel like lost fragments of the Andaman's iconic limestone that have tumbled into the sea. Most have tangles of verdant jungle and pure white-sand beaches home to roving sea gypsies.

Ko Ngai เกาะไหง (ไห)

Encircled by coral and clear waters, densely forested Ko Ngai (Ko Hai) is the most developed of the Trang Islands. The long blonde wind-swept beach on the eastern coast spills into turquoise water with a sandy bottom (perfect for children) that ends at a reef drop-off with good snorkelling. It's a stunning place. With no indigenous population, a bunch of snazzy resorts have the whole island to themselves.

Although technically part of Krabi Province, Ko Ngai's mainland link is with Pak Meng, 16km northeast. Pricier resorts have wi-fi.

Activities

Ko Ngai has a couple of dive centres (dives from 1300B). Resorts rent snorkel sets and fins (50B each) and sea kayaks (per hour 150B), or you can join half-day snorkelling tours of nearby islands (from 600B).

Sleeping & Eating

Most places are decidedly upper-midrange, with restaurants and 24-hour electricity. The pier is at Koh Ngai Resort, but long-tails usually drop you at your resort. Most resorts arrange transfers.

Ko Ngai Seafood Bungalows BUNGALOW $$

(081 367 8497, 095 014 1853; kob_1829@hotmail.com; bungalow 1000-1500B; year-round) Boosted by its friendly family-style set-up in the middle of main beach, this collection of simple, well-kept, fan-cooled bungalows with sea-view porches is essentially a few rooms tacked onto a popular seafood-focused **restaurant** (081 367 8497; mains 80-280B; 7am-9pm Sep-Apr). Its coconut-milk crab curry with chunks of de-shelled fresh crab is a dream come true.

★**Coco Cottage** BUNGALOW $$$

(089 724 9225; www.coco-cottage.com; bungalow 3400-5000B; Oct-May; @) Cottages at the north end of main beach are coconut thatched-roof extravaganzas with coconut-wood walls and coconut-shell lanterns. Wake up to twinkling Andaman vistas through floor-to-ceiling windows in sea-view bungalows. It's impeccably styled, with decks and interiors catching plenty of breezes. Other perks include bamboo

BOATS TO/FROM KO NGAI

DESTINATION	BOAT COMPANY	FARE (B)	DURATION
Ko Lanta	Tigerline	750	1hr
	Speedboat	650	30min
Ko Lipe	Tigerline	1300	4hr
	Speedboat	1600	2½hr
Ko Kradan	Tigerline	450	30min
	Satun Pakbara Speedboat Club	400	25min
Ko Muk	Tigerline	350	1hr
	Speedboat	350	30min
Ko Phi-Phi	Tigerline	1200	2½hr
	Satun Pakbara Speedboat Club	1350	2hr
Phuket	Tigerline	1800	3½hr
	Satun Pakbara Speedboat Club	2350	3hr

loungers, massage pavilions and a fantastic Thai/fusion beachfront **restaurant-bar** (mains 160-280B; ⏲7-10am, 11am-4pm & 6-9.30pm).

Thanya Resort BUNGALOW **$$$**
(☎086 950 7355, 075 206967; www.kohngaithanyaresort.com; south end of main beach; r incl breakfast 3500-5200B; ⏲Oct-Apr; ❄@📶🏊) Ko Ngai's Bali-chic choice has dark but stylish, spacious teak bungalows that have indoor hot showers and outdoor country-style bucket showers (don't knock it until you've tried it). Laze in the gorgeous beachside pool and gaze across the frangipani-filled lawn rolling out towards the sand from your terrace. There's an on-site **dive centre** (☎085 056 3455; 1 dive 1300-1500B) plus a breezy Thai **restaurant** (mains 170-310B; ⏲7am-10pm Oct-Apr; 📶).

Thapwarin Resort RESORT **$$$**
(☎081 894 3585; www.thapwarin.com; north end of main beach; garden/sea view bungalow incl breakfast 2700/4700B; ⏲mid-Jun–mid-May; ❄📶) Thapwarin's airy, attractive bamboo cottages sprawl back into trees. With private decks, tumbling mosquito netting, paper lanterns and semi-outdoor showers, they're comfy and cosy, if a tad overpriced. Catch evening fire shows at the beach-facing **bar-restaurant** (mains 200-500B; ⏲7am-10pm mid-Jun–mid-May; 📶), which tackles everything from grilled snapper to pizza and pasta.

ℹ Getting There & Away

Ko Ngai Villa runs daily boats from Ko Ngai to Pak Meng (350B, one hour) at 9.30am, returning to Ko Ngai at noon. You can also charter long-tails to/from Pak Meng (1500B), Ko Muk (1500B), Ko Kradan (1800B) and Ko Lanta (2000B); enquire at Ko Ngai Seafood (p684) or Ko Ngai Villa.

From mid-October to mid-April, **Tigerline** (☎075 590490, 081 358 8989; www.tigerlinetravel.com) ferries stops just off Ko Ngai en route between Phuket and Ko Lipe. From November to early April, **Satun Pakbara Speedboat Club** (☎099 414 4994, 099 404 0409; www.tarutaolipeisland.com) and **Bundhaya Speedboat** (☎083 653 0323, 075 668043; www.bundhayaspeedboat.com) offer faster/comfier island-hopping transport.

Ko Muk เกาะมุก

Motoring toward jungle-clad Ko Muk is unforgettable, whether you land on sugary white eastern sand bar **Hat Sivalai**, on humble, local-flavoured **Hat Lodung** or on southwest **Hat Farang** (Hat Sai Yao, Charlie's Beach), where jade water kisses a perfect beach.

Unfortunately, the lodging options aren't amazing, and there's a steady stream of Speedo-clad package tourists tramping the beach and day-tripping over to Tham Morakot (p686) from Ko Lanta. Still, the west-coast sunsets are glorious, it's an easy hop from here to every island in the province, and you'll be mixing in with a blend of travellers more likely to relish the calm than party all night.

Sights & Activities

Between Ko Muk and Ko Ngai are two small karst islets, **Ko Cheuk** and **Ko Waen**, both with small sandy beaches and good snorkelling (though there's some coral damage).

Koh Mook Garden Resort rents out bikes (per day 100B) with self-guided maps, several resorts rent kayaks (per hour 100B to 300B) and motorbikes (per day 250B), and you can spend hours walking through rubber plantations and the island's devout Muslim sea shanty villages (remember to cover up).

Tham Morakot CAVE

(ถ้ำมรกต, Emerald Cave) This beautiful limestone tunnel leads 80m into a *hôrng* on Ko Muk's west coast. No wonder long-gone pirates buried treasure here. You have to swim or paddle through the tunnel, part of the way in pitch blackness, to a small white-sand beach surrounded by lofty limestone walls. A piercing shaft of light illuminates it around midday. National park fees (adult/child 200/100B) apply.

The cave features prominently on most tour itineraries, so it can get ridiculously crowded in high season. It's best to charter a long-tail boat (800B to 1000B) or rent a kayak and zip over at daybreak or late afternoon when you'll have it to yourself, but note that you can't get inside at high tide.

Sleeping & Eating

Most places on Hat Sivalai and Hat Lodung are a short walk from the main pier, on Ko Muk's eastern side. Hat Lodung is west of the pier beyond a stilt village and mangroves; Hat Sivalai wraps around the peninsula to the east. Though beautiful, these shores get lapped by murky backwash from the mainland mangrove villages.

The sea is cleaner on Hat Farang, where budget-friendly resorts lie inland from the beach. Most boats will pick up and drop off here; otherwise it's a 10-minute motorbike taxi to/from the pier (50B).

Koh Mook Garden Resort GUESTHOUSE $

(☎081 748 3849; kohmookgardenresort@hotmail.com; Hat Lodung; r 400-800B; 📶) In shady grounds, the tile-floored, concrete, semi-sea-view rooms and new bungalows here are clean and airy, while older bamboo bungalows are small and basic. You'll be looked after by an enthusiastic local family who take guests snorkelling, lend bikes, rent kayaks (per hour 200B), organise transport and give out detailed maps of the island's secret spots.

Pawapi Resort BUNGALOW $$

(☎089 662 3169; www.pawapi.com; Hat Sivalai; bungalow 2800-5000B; ❄📶) These upscale bamboo bungalows with balconies are perched on stilts 1.5m off the ground so that breezes ventilate the room, but it's the insane 180-degree view of islands, white sand and sparkling sea that steals the show. At research time, new rooms were under construction, so expect a hike in rates.

Sivalai HOTEL $$$

(☎089 723 3355; www.komooksivalai.com; Hat Sivalai; bungalow incl breakfast 5000-7000B; ❄📶🏊) Straddling an arrow-shaped white-sand peninsula framed by views of karst islands and the mainland, Sivalai wins the award for Ko Muk's most fabulous location. Elegant, exotic thatched-roof cottages splashed with colour are almost encircled by glass doors and many have wraparound verandas. The pool lacks style, but the beach is exquisite and there's a handy spa (massages from 700B).

Kayak rental is 300B per hour.

Hilltop Restaurant THAI $

(mains 50-300B; ⏲9am-10pm) About 800m inland from Hat Farang, this welcoming, family-run operation serves up all your Thai favourites with an extra kick (on request) at wooden picnic-style benches in an open-air jungle-cloaked setting.

Getting There & Away

Boats to Ko Muk (100B to 300B, 30 minutes) leave daily from the pier at Kuantungku at noon, 1pm and 5pm November to April, returning to

THE 50B SURCHARGE

Tigerline (p687) ferries and speedboats often stop in the sea off the Trang and Satun islands. There's a 50B surcharge for long-tail transfers on/off islands, which you'll be asked for once you're aboard the long-tail; boatmen usually refuse to continue until you pay up. Yes, it's frustrating, but it'll hardly ruin your trip, so it's worth keeping change handy.

the mainland at 8am, 9am and 2pm. Services peter out in November and April, but the cheapest, 1pm 'local' ferry runs year-round. Minibus-boat combo tickets take you to/from Trang (250B to 450B, 1½ hours) and Trang airport (500B, 1½ hours). You can also charter long-tails to/from Kuantungku (600B to 800B, 30 minutes).

From November to early April, Ko Muk is a stop on the speedboats connecting Ko Lanta (900B, one hour), Ko Ngai (350B to 400B, 30 minutes) and Ko Lipe (1400B, two hours). The Phuket–Ko Lipe **Tigerline** (☎075 590490, 081 358 8989; www.tigerlinetravel.com) stops off Hat Farang mid-October to mid-April.

Long-tail charters from Ko Muk to Ko Kradan (600B, 30 minutes), Ko Ngai (1000B, one hour) and Pak Meng (1500B, 45 minutes to one hour) are easily arranged on the pier or on Hat Farang at Rubber Tree Bungalow or Ko Yao Viewpoint.

Ko Kradan เกาะกระดาน

Beautiful Ko Kradan is dotted with slender, silky, white-sand beaches, bathtub-warm shallows and dreamy views across the twinkling turquoise sea to Ko Muk, Ko Libong and limestone karsts from its main, east-coast beach. The water is clean, clear and inviting, and there's a small but lush tangle of remnant jungle inland.

Activities

Hat Sunset BEACH

A short signposted track at the south end of the main beach leads past Paradise Lost guesthouse and over the ridge to Sunset Beach, a mostly wet and rocky patch of sand facing open seas – and a fun place to get a little beachside privacy over a flaming pink sunset.

Hat South SNORKELLING

Although some of Kradan's coral structure has been decimated, there's good snorkelling off the island's South Beach, which you can reach in a 10-minute walk along a jungly path from Paradise Lost, signposted at the south end of the main beach.

Sleeping & Eating

Kradan's lodgings and restaurants are overpriced; blame the idyllic location.

Paradise Lost GUESTHOUSE $$

(☎089 587 2409; www.kokradan.wordpress.com; dm 300B, bungalow with/without bathroom 1200/700B) One of Kradan's first lodgings, this inland, Thai-American founded property has easy access to more secluded beaches. Despite a little wear, it's still your best lower-range choice, with 24-hour electricity, a friendly vibe, and an airy new five-bed, fan-cooled dorm. Small bamboo huts have wood floors, mosquito nets and shared bathrooms; bigger wooden bungalows come with private facilities.

The open-plan **kitchen** (mains 120-300B; ⏰8am-9pm) dishes up Kradan's tastiest homemade food in giant portions.

Seven Seas Resort HOTEL $$$

(☎082 490 2552, 082 490 2442; www.sevenseasresorts.com; r incl breakfast 7000-7980B, villa 11,300-15,100B; ❄️📶🏊) This boutique resort's super-sleek rooms have terrazzo floors, indoor-outdoor bathrooms blending into tropical gardens, enormous low-slung beds and, for some, private cabanas. Hugging the jet-black infinity pool, the breezy **restaurant** (mains 330-520B; ⏰7am-10pm; 📶) serves pricey Thai-international dishes. Beach

BOATS TO/FROM KO KRADAN

DESTINATION	BOAT COMPANY	FARE (B)	DURATION
Hat Yao	Tigerline	550	1hr
Ko Lanta	Tigerline	850	1½hr
	Satun Pakbara Speedboat Club	1150	1¼hr
Ko Lipe	Tigerline	1450	3½hr
	Satun Pakbara Speedboat Club	1400	2hr
Ko Muk	Satun Pakbara Speedboat Club	300	15min
Ko Ngai	Tigerline	450	30min
	Satun Pakbara Speedboat Club	400	45min

bums will love this sandy stretch, halfway up Kradan's main beach.

Reef Resort HOTEL $$$

(086 948 8559; www.reefresortkradan.com; r incl breakfast 3500-4000B;) Bright, minimalist, modern-design rooms frame a palm-lined pool at this fresh Italian-run arrival, steps from aqua waters at the northern, wooded end of Kradan's main beach. The thatched-roof beach bar is perfect sundowner land; the Thai-Italian **restaurant** (mains 170-300B; 8-10am, noon-3pm & 6-9pm;) is decent.

Getting There & Away

For boat tickets (and wi-fi), visit Kradan Beach Resort. From November to April, daily boats to Kuantungku leave at 9am and noon; tickets include connecting minibuses to Trang (450B) or Trang airport (550B). From Trang, minibus-boat services depart for Ko Kradan at 11am and 4pm. You can charter long-tails to/from Kuantungku (1500B, 45 minutes to one hour), Ko Muk (800B, 30 minutes) and Ko Ngai (1800B, one hour).

The Phuket–Ko Lipe **Tigerline** (075 590490, 081 358 8989; www.tigerlinetravel.com) stops off Ko Kradan from mid-October to mid-May. November to early April, **Satun Pakbara Speedboat Club** (099 404 0409, 099 414 4994; www.tarutaolipeisland.com) offers faster links (p687).

Ko Libong เกาะลิบง

Trang's largest island is just 30 minutes by long-tail from mainland Hat Yao. Less visited than neighbouring islands, it's a gorgeous, lush mountainous pearl, wrapped in rubber trees, thick with mangroves and known for its captivating flora and fauna (especially the resident dugongs and migrating birds) more than its thin gold-brown beaches. The island is home to a small Muslim fishing community and has a few west-coast resorts. With its scruffy sweetness and untouristy backwater charm, Libong has a way of drawing you in, if you let it.

Sights

Libong Archipelago Wildlife Reserve NATURE RESERVE

This large mangrove area on Ko Libong's east coast at Laem Ju Hoi is protected by the Botanical Department. The sea channels are one of the last habitats of the endangered dugong: over 100 graze on the sea grass that flourishes in the bay. Most of Ko Libong's resorts offer dugong-spotting boat tours, led by trained naturalists, for 1000B to 1500B.

Sleeping & Eating

Libong Sunset Resort BUNGALOW $

(089 766 3341, 087 276 5484; www.libongsunsetresort.com; r 500B, bungalow fan/air-con 1000/2000B; Oct–mid-Apr;) Tucked up against a headland on its own rocky, sandy beach, the simple spotless air-con and fan-cooled bungalows at this sweet family-owned resort make good-value (though potentially isolated) crash pads. All have private sea-view porches. The biggest air-con options come with sofas and TVs, while basic shared-bathroom doubles do a straightforward budget job.

Libong Beach Resort BUNGALOW $$

(084 849 0899, 081 747 4600; bungalow fan 800-1000B, air-con 1000-2000B;) This cute spot has everything from bland slap-up shacks behind a murky stream to comfy varnished wood-and-thatch beachfront chalets with semi-outdoor bathrooms. It also offers wildlife-spotting trips, transport info and motorbike rental (per day 300B). We love the restaurant; try the *pàt see·éw* (fried noodles) or the *đôm yam kà·mîn* (turmeric fish soup).

Libong Relax Beach Resort BUNGALOW $$

(091 825 4886, 094 582 5113; www.libongrelax.com; r incl breakfast fan 1200-2300B, air-con 2500-3000B;) Top choice at this friendly, laid-back resort are rustic-stylish wood-and-bamboo bungalows with terracotta sinks, shiny floors and shuttered doors that open up to the sea. Fan-cooled cottages come simply but smartly designed, and there's a selection of bird- and dugong-spotting and snorkelling trips, plus kayak rental (per hour 200B). The low-key, thatch-roofed beachside **restaurant** (mains 80-350B; 7.30am-3pm & 5-9pm;) does a good line in Thai staples.

Getting There & Around

During daylight hours, long-tail boats to Ban Ma Phrao on Ko Libong's east coast leave hourly from Hat Yao (per person 50B, 30 minutes). On Ko Libong, motorcycle taxis run across to the west-coast resorts (per person 100B). Chartered long-tails from Hat Yao to the resorts cost 900B. You can charter boats to Ko Kradan (1800B), Ko Muk (1500B) and Ko Ngai (2300B).

Ko Sukorn เกาะสุกร

Little-visited Ko Sukorn is a cultural paradise of tawny beaches, light-green sea, jungle-shrouded black-rock headlands, and stilted shack neighbourhoods home to 2600 Muslim inhabitants whose rice fields, watermelon plots and rubber plantations unfurl along narrow concrete roads. Spin past fields occupied only by water buffalo, through pastel villages where people are genuinely happy to see you and sleep soundly through deep, silent nights. Sukorn's stillness is breathtaking, its authenticity a tonic to the jaded, road-weary soul.

With few hills, expansive panoramas, plenty of shade and lots of opportunities to meet islanders, Sukorn is best explored by rented bike (200B). The main beach, dotted with a few low-key resorts, extends along the island's southwestern coast. Please cover up away from the beach.

Sleeping & Eating

★ Yataa Island Resort RESORT $$
(☎081 444 9989, 089 647 5550; www.yataaresort.com; bungalow incl breakfast 1350-3000B;) Rebranded under new management, these pastel-painted, green-roofed concrete air-con bungalows frame a cool blue pool and have tasteful varnished-wood verandahs. Older concrete-and-wood, air-con bungalows amid bougainvillea-filled gardens are comfy too. Staff offer Sukorn maps, guided island tours (per person 500B) and bicycle/motorbike rental (150/200B). Enjoy fiery pink sunsets over outlying islands from the gorgeous long beach out front. The **restaurant** (mains 100-150B; 7.30am-9pm;) is excellent.

Sukorn Cabana BUNGALOW $$
(☎089 724 2326; www.sukorncabana.com; bungalow incl breakfast 900-1500B;) Sloping landscaped grounds dotted with papaya, frangipani and bougainvillea hold large, clean, well-managed bungalows sporting thatched roofs, fridges, polished-wood interiors and plush verandahs. On the hill up above are spacious modern-style rooms overlooking the pretty beach and Ko Phetra through floor-to-ceiling windows.

Getting There & Around

The easiest way to get to Sukorn is by private transfers from Trang, arranged through your resort (per person 1900B). The cheapest way is to take a *sŏrng·tăa·ou* from Trang to Yan Ta Khao (80B, 40 minutes), then transfer to Ban Ta Seh (50B, 45 minutes), from where long-tails to Ban Saimai (50B), Sukorn's main village, leave when full. Trang guesthouses and travel agents arrange *sŏrng·tăa·ou*-and-boat transfers (250B to 350B) to Ban Saimai via Ban Ta Seh, departing Trang at 11am daily.

Otherwise, book a taxi from Trang to Ban Ta Seh (1200B). The resorts are a 3km walk or 100B moto-taxi ride from Ban Saimai. You can charter long-tails directly to the beach resorts (1000B).

SATUN PROVINCE

The Andaman's southernmost region, Satun was until recently mostly overlooked, but that's all changed thanks to the dynamic white sands of Ko Lipe – a one-time backpacker secret turned mainstream beach getaway. Beyond Ko Lipe, the rest of the province passes by in the blink of an eye, as visitors rush north to Ko Lanta or south to Pulau Langkawi (Malaysia). Which means, of course, that they miss the untrammelled beaches and sea caves of Ko Tarutao, the rugged trails and ribbon waterfalls of Ko Adang, the rustic beauty of Ko Bulon Leh and the scruffy urban buzz of Satun itself.

Largely Muslim in make-up, Satun has seen little of the political turmoil (p584) that plagues neighbouring Yala, Pattani and Narathiwat. Around 60% of inhabitants speak Yawi or Malay as a first language, and the few humble wát in the region are vastly outnumbered by mosques.

Satun สตูล

POP 23,610

Lying in a steamy jungle valley surrounded by limestone cliffs and a murky river, isolated Satun is a surprisingly bustling little city: the focal point of a province home to over 300,000 people. Most visitors whizz through en route to Malaysia; Malaysia-based yachties, dropping in for cheap repairs in Satun's acclaimed boat yard, are the only travellers who hang around. But if you explore before you leave, you'll uncover intriguing religious architecture, deliciously authentic food, lots of friendly smiles and plenty of gritty charm.

Sights & Activities

Satun National Museum MUSEUM
(พิพิธภัณฑสถานแห่งชาติสตูล, Kuden Mansion; Soi 5, Th Satun Thanee; admission 50B; 9am-

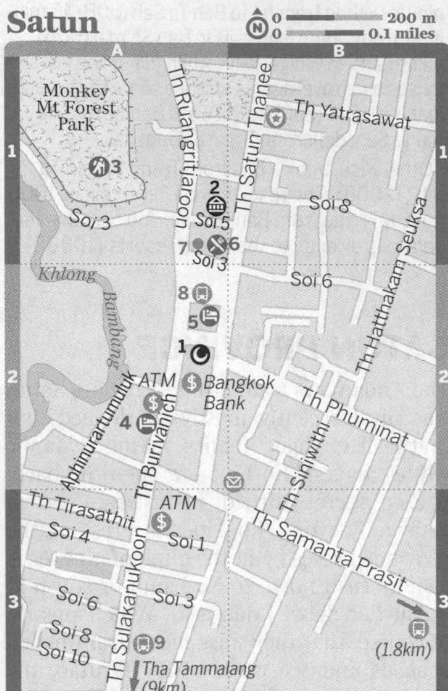

Satun

Sights
1 Masjid Mambang A2
2 Satun National Museum A1

Activities, Courses & Tours
3 Monkey Mountain A1

Sleeping
4 On's Guesthouse A2
5 Satun Tanee Hotel A2

Eating
@On's the Kitchen .... (see 4)
6 Night Market A1

Information
7 Immigration Office A1

Transport
8 Buses to Trang and Hat Yai A2
9 Sŏrng•tăa•ou to Tha Tammalang A3

4pm Wed-Sun) Housed in a restored bright white, mint-green-windowed 1902 Sino-Portuguese mansion, Satun's excellent museum was originally constructed as a home for King Rama V during a royal visit, but the governor snagged the pad when the king failed to show up. The building exhibits feature dioramas with soundtracks covering every aspect of Muslim life in southern Thailand.

Monkey Mountain WALKING
Soak up Satun's refreshing shabby beauty by hiking this jungled mound of limestone teeming with macaques. You can also walk over a bridge here to a stilted fishing village 1km west of town.

Sleeping

On's Guesthouse GUESTHOUSE $
(☎074 724133; onmarch13@hotmail.com; 36 Th Burivanich; dm/r 250/650B; ❄📶) Satun's dynamic tourism matriarch, On, has transformed an old downtown shophouse into a sparkling, affordable guesthouse of spacious air-con rooms featuring wood furnishings, cute end tables and desks, plus other homey touches. Now she's added a massive, spotless six-bed dorm decked out in pastel wallpaper, with lockers.

Satun Tanee Hotel GUESTHOUSE $
(☎074 711010, 074 712309; www.satuntaneehotel.com; 90 Th Satun Thanee; r fan 300B, air-con 350-570B) Behind this jazzed-up, lime-green-and-orange exterior lie newly revamped, fresh-painted rooms modernised by tight white sheets and wood-panelled floors, plus dingier, cheaper, unrenovated air-con and fan rooms. It's a bit institutional, but the updated rooms are good value and you get a warm welcome.

Eating

Quick, cheap Chinese and Muslim restaurants are on Th Burivanich and Th Samanta Prasit. Chinese food stalls specialise in *kôw mŏo daang* (red pork with rice); Muslim restaurants offer roti with southern-style chicken curry.

★**Night Market** MARKET $
(off Th Satun Thanee; dishes around 35B; ⏲5-9pm) Satun's popular, bubbly night market springs to life with flavour-packed *pàt tai*, fried fish, chicken satay and spicy, southern-style curries. There's a larger Saturday night market on Th Burivanich.

@On's the Kitchen THAI, INTERNATIONAL $$
(☎074 724133; 36 Th Burivanich; mains 60-250B; ⏲8am-10pm; 📶) Frequented by visiting yachties, young expat English teachers and a few locals, the lively ground-floor cafe at On's Guesthouse dishes out tasty baguettes, pastas, pizzas, salads and Thai mains, along

with popular steak dinners and European breakfasts.

Information

Most hotels have wi-fi. ATMs line Th Burivanich.

Immigration Office (☎074 711080; Soi 3, Th Burivanich; ⊙8.30am-4.30pm Mon-Fri) Handles visa issues and extensions. It's easier for tourists to exit and re-enter Thailand via the border checkpoint at Tha Tammalang (p691).

Post Office (cnr Th Satun Thanee & Th Samanta Prasit; ⊙8.30am-4.30pm Mon-Fri, 9am-noon Sat)

Getting There & Away

BUS

Buses leave from Satun Bus Terminal, 2km south of town. Buses to Hat Yai (70B, two hours, hourly 5am to 5pm) and local (non air-con) buses to Trang (100B, two hours, hourly 5am to 4.30pm) pick up passengers on Th Satun Thanee.

Departures include the following:

Bangkok – VIP (1150B, 14 hours, 4.30pm)

Bangkok – air-con (731B to 742B, 14 hours, 6am and 4pm)

Krabi (234B, five hours, 8.15am, 10.15am, 12.15pm and 8pm)

Phuket (364B, eight hours, 8.15am, 10.15am, 12.15pm and 8pm)

MINIVAN

Minivans run from Satun Bus Terminal to Hat Yai (100B, two hours, 6am to 5pm), Krabi (200B, five hours, 7am and 2pm) and Trang (120B, two hours, hourly 5am to 5pm). Direct minivans run between Tha Tammalang and Hat Yai (86B, two hours, 6.30am to 7pm).

Getting Around

Orange *sŏrng·tăa·ou* to Tha Tammalang (30B, 15 minutes; for boats to Malaysia) leave from the 7-Eleven on Th Sulakanukoon every 30 to 40 minutes. Motorcycle taxis from here cost 80B. *Sŏrng·tăa·ou* to the bus station cost 40B per person.

GETTING TO MALAYSIA

Since mid-2014, Thai authorities have been clamping down on in-out visa runs. This is particularly aimed at foreigners living/working in Thailand on tourist visas and, at research time, was not causing any problems for regular travellers. Do monitor the situation carefully and research latest updates.

Keep in mind that Malaysia is one hour ahead of Thai time.

Ko Lipe to Pulau Langkawi

From mid-October to mid-April, **Tigerline** (p701), **Bundhaya Speedboat** (p701) and **Satun Pakbara Speedboat Club** (☎099 414 4994, 099 404 0409; www.tarutaolipeisland.com) run daily from Ko Lipe to Pulau Langkawi in Malaysia (1000B to 1400B, 1½ hours). Departures are at 10am, 10.30am, 11am and 4pm. Head to the **immigration office** (Map p698; ⊙8am-6pm) at Bundhaya Resort (east end of Hat Pattaya) 1½ hours ahead to get stamped out. In reverse, boats leave Pulau Langkawi for Ko Lipe at 9am, 9.30am, 2pm and 2.30pm Malaysian time.

Satun to Kuala Perlis or Pulau Langkawi

Daily boats to Malaysia's Pulau Langkawi leave from Tha Tammalang (10km south of Satun) at 9.30am, 1.30pm and 4pm (300B, 1½ hours). In the reverse direction, boats (M$30) return from Pulau Langkawi at 9am, 1pm and 5pm Malaysian time. Get stamped out in advance at Satun's immigration office or, much easier, exit Thailand via the Tammalang border checkpost. If you're just doing a visa run, the whole process is doable in a day.

Public long-tails no longer run from Tha Tammalang to Kuala Perlis in Malaysia. It's possible to take a 9am minivan from Satun to Kuala Perlis (400B) via the Wang Prajan/Wang Kelian border crossing; On's Guesthouse sells tickets.

At the Border

Citizens of the US, EU, Australia, Canada and several other countries may enter Malaysia for up to 90 days without prior visa arrangements. If you have questions about your eligibility, check with the nearest Malaysian embassy or consulate and apply for a visa in advance.

Pak Bara ปากบารา

Pak Bara, 60km northwest of Satun, is the main jumping-off point for the dazzling southern islands in the Mu Ko Phetra and Ko Tarutao Marine National Parks. Facilities are slowly improving as Pak Bara becomes increasingly packed with tourists. The peaceful fishing town has forgettable sleeping options, and, aside from great seafood, there's no pressing reason to stick around.

The main road from La-Ngu (Rte 4052) terminates at the pier, which is basically a massive passenger waiting terminal for Lipe- and Tarutao-bound speedboats, with travel agencies, cheap restaurants, ATMs and stalls flogging beach gear. The Ko Tarutao Marine National Park **visitors centre** (Map p694; ☎074 783485; ⊙8am-5pm) is by the pier; here you can book Ko Tarutao and Ko Adang accommodation, buy speedboat tickets and obtain camping permission. Local travel agents arrange one-day tours (2000B) to the parks' islands.

Getting There & Away

BUS

From Satun, take an ordinary Trang bus and get off at La-Ngu (50B, 30 minutes), continuing by *sŏrng·tăa·ou* to Pak Bara (20B, 15 minutes).

MINIVANS

Air-con minivans run every 45 minutes between 7.30am and 6.30pm from Hat Yai to Pak Bara pier (130B, two hours). Minivan services may be reduced mid-May to mid-October. Departures from Pak Bara include the following:

Hat Yai (150B, two hours, 11.30am and 3.30pm)

Hat Yai Airport (250B, two hours, 11.30am and 3.30pm)

Ko Lanta (450B, three hours, 11.30am)

Krabi (450B, four hours, 11.30am)

Phuket (650B, six hours, 11.30am)

Trang (200B, two hours, 11.30am)

BOAT

From mid-October to mid-May speedboats run from Pak Bara to Ao Pante Malacca on Ko Tarutao (450B, 30 minutes), and on to Ko Lipe (650B, 1½ hours) at 10.30am and 11.30am. There are further speedboats to Ko Lipe at 9.30am, 12.30pm, 2pm and 3pm. Boats return from Ko Lipe at 9am, 9.30am, 12.15pm, 1pm, 1.30pm and 4pm.

For Ko Bulon Leh (400B, 30 minutes), boats depart at 12.30pm and buzz on to Ko Lipe. If you miss the Bulon boat, you can charter long-tails from local fishermen (2000B, 1½ hours). D uring low season, services to Ko Lipe are weather dependent, but generally leave daily from Pak Bara at 11.30am, returning at 9.30am.

Ko Bulon Leh เกาะบุโหลนเล

Gracious Ko Bulon Leh, 23km west of Pak Bara, is surrounded by the Andaman's signature clear waters and has its share of faultless alabaster beaches with swaying casuarinas. This gorgeous island is in that perfect phase of being developed enough to offer comfortable facilities, yet it's not so popular that you have to book beach-time days in advance (though bungalow numbers are on the rise).

The exceptional, main white-sand beach extends along the east coast from Bulone Resort (p693), on the northeast cape, to Pansand Resort. In places it narrows, especially where buffered by gnarled mangroves and strewn with thick sun-bleached logs, making it easy to find a secret shady spot with dreamy views.

Sights & Activities

Bulon's lush interior is interlaced with tracks and trails that are fun to explore, though the dense, jungled rock that makes up the western half remains inaccessible on foot. The island's wild beauty is accessible on the northern coast at blue, coral-gravel-laden **Ao Panka Yai**, which has decent snorkelling. This bay is linked by a small paved path to **Ao Panka Noi**, a fishing village with beautiful karst views, long-tails docking on a gravel beach and a clutch of good, simple restaurants, on the eastern half of the northern coast. Follow a signposted trail nearby west through remnant jungle and rubber plantations – with eyes open wide lest you miss one of Bulon's enormous monitor lizards – to wind your way south to **Ao Muang** (Mango Bay), where there's an authentic *chow lair* squid-fishing camp.

There's good coral off **Laem Son** on the northeastern edge of the island and down the eastern coast. You can rent masks, snorkels and fin sets (200B) and kayaks (per hour 200B) at Bulone Resort and Pansand Resort. Snorkelling is best at low tide.

Resorts can arrange guided snorkelling trips (1700B, four hours, maximum six people) to other islands in the Ko Bulon group.

Tours usually take in the glassy emerald waters of **Ko Gai** (Map p694) and **Ko Ma** (Map p694), whose gnarled rocks have been ravaged by wind and time. But the most stunning sight is **White Rock** (Map p694): bird-blessed spires shooting out of the open sea. Beneath the surface is a mussel-crusted rock reef teeming with colourful fish.

Sleeping & Eating

Most places close from mid-April to November. For food, it's worth wandering over to Ao Panka Noi. There are a few local restaurants and shops in the Muslim village between Ao Panka Noi and Ao Panka Yai.

Chaolae Homestay BUNGALOW $

(Map p694; 086 967 0716, 086 290 2519; Ao Panka Yai; bungalow 500-600B; Dec-Apr) These classy, good-value, bamboo-and-wood bungalows have varnished wood interiors, thatched roofs and polished-cement bathrooms (with squat toilets). It's a blissfully quiet, shady spot, run by a welcoming *chow lair* family, and steps away from decent snorkelling at Ao Panka Yai.

Bulon Hill Resort BUNGALOW $$

(Map p694; 086 960 3890, 086 296 5809; www.bulonhill.com; bungalow 1300-1800B; Oct–mid-Apr) A collection of spacious, Thai-German–owned, concrete-and-wood bungalows and smaller bamboo ones, all with fans, stilted on the flower-strewn hill just inland from the northeast end of Bulon's main beach (it's signposted behind Bulone Resort). Electricity runs from 6pm to 6am. The recommended restaurant was being renovated at research time.

Bulone Resort HOTEL $$

(Map p694; 081 897 9084; www.bulone-resort.com; Main Beach; bungalow incl breakfast with fan 3500B, air-con 3000-4000B; Nov-Apr;) Perched on Bulon's northeast cape with access to two exquisite white-sand stretches, Bulone Resort steals the island's top location. Cute whitewashed-wood bungalows (some fan, some air-con) come with queen-sized beds, iron frames and ocean breezes. Huge new alpine-chalet-style air-con rooms tower behind on stilts, with glorious views. Enjoy 24-hour electricity, a Thai-international **restaurant** (Map p694; mains 180-250B; 7.30-10am & 6-10pm;) and a coffee corner.

Su's Corner THAI, BREAKFAST $

(Map p694; 081 189 7183; Ao Panka Noi; dishes 80-100B; 7am-8pm) Anyone who can transform vegie fried rice into something magical deserves high praise. This simple open-air cafe, with only a few tables scattered under palms just inland from Ao Panka Noi, is deservedly popular for its baguettes, shakes, cakes and Thai staples done with flair.

Information

Bulone Resort and Pansand Resort have wi-fi (nonguests per minute 3B). Bulone Resort also offers battery-charging services (free for restaurant clients).

Getting There & Away

From November to April, speedboats to Ko Bulon Leh (400B, 30 minutes) leave from Pak Bara at 12.30pm daily. Long-tail ship-to-shore transfers cost 50B; ask to be dropped off on the beach closest to your resort. In the reverse direction, the boat moors in the bay in front of Pansand Resort at 9am. You can charter long-tails to/from Pak Bara (2000B, 1½ hours).

From November to April, daily speedboats (600B, one hour) run from Ko Bulon Leh to Ko Lipe at 1pm, stopping in front of Pansand Resort. Boats originate in Ko Lanta (1600B, two hours) and make stops at Ko Ngai (1050B, 1½ hours), Ko Muk (900B, one hour) and Ko Kradan (900B, one hour), returning from Lipe at 9am.

Ko Tarutao Marine National Park

อุทยานแห่งชาติหมู่เกาะตะรุเตา

One of Thailand's most exquisite, unspoilt regions, **Ko Tarutao Marine National Park** (074 783485; www.dnp.go.th; adult/child 200/100B; mid-Oct–mid-May) encompasses 51 islands blanketed by well-preserved rainforest teeming with fauna, surrounded by healthy coral reefs and radiant white beaches. Born in 1974, it's the country's second marine national park. Within, you might spot dusky langurs, crab-eating macaques, mouse deer, wild pigs, sea otters, fishing cats, tree pythons, water monitors, Brahminy kites, sea eagles, hornbills, reef egrets and kingfishers.

The park's main accommodation consists of small, ecofriendly, government-run cabins. Pressure from big developers to build resorts on the islands has so far (mostly) been ignored, though concessions were made for the filming of American reality-TV series

Ko Tarutao Marine National Park & Around

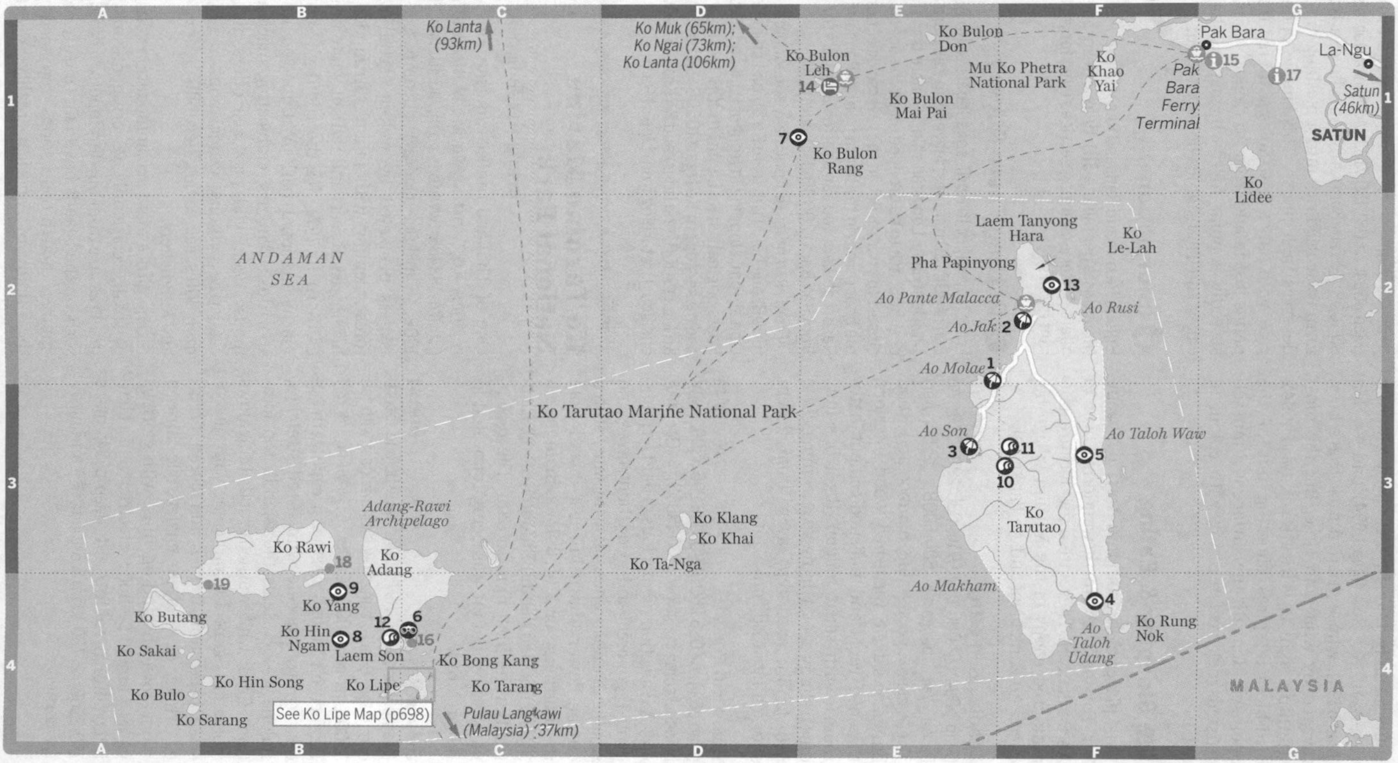

0 10 km
0 5 miles

Ko Lanta (93km)
Ko Muk (65km); Ko Ngai (73km); Ko Lanta (106km)
Ko Bulon Don
Ko Bulon Leh
14
Mu Ko Phetra National Park
Ko Bulon Mai Pai
Ko Khao Yai
Pak Bara
15
Pak Bara Ferry Terminal
17
La-Ngu
Satun (46km)
SATUN
7
Ko Bulon Rang
Ko Lidee
ANDAMAN SEA
Laem Tanyong Hara
Ko Le-Lah
Pha Papinyong
13
Ao Pante Malacca
Ao Rusi
Ao Jak
2
Ao Molae
1
Ko Tarutao Marine National Park
Ao Son
3
11
10
Ao Taloh Waw
5
Ko Tarutao
Adang-Rawi Archipelago
Ko Klang
Ko Khai
Ko Rawi
18
Ko Adang
Ko Ta-Nga
19
9
Ko Yang
Ao Makham
4
Ko Butang
12
6
Ko Hin Ngam
8
16
Laem Son
Ao Taloh Udang
Ko Rung Nok
Ko Sakai
Ko Bong Kang
Ko Hin Song
Ko Lipe
Ko Tarang
Ko Bulo
MALAYSIA
Ko Sarang

See Ko Lipe Map (p698)

Pulau Langkawi (Malaysia) (37km)

Ko Tarutao Marine National Park & Around

Sights
1 Ao Molae E2
2 Ao Pante Malacca F2
3 Ao Son E3
4 Ao Taloh Udang F4
5 Ao Taloh Waw F3
6 Chado Cliff C4
7 Ko Gai D1
8 Ko Hin Ngam B4
Ko Ma (see 7)
9 Ko Yang B4
10 Nam Tok Lo Po F3
11 Nam Tok Lu Du F3
12 Pirate's Falls B4
13 Tham Jara-Khe F2
Toe-Boo Cliff (see 2)

Activities, Courses & Tours
White Rock (see 7)

Sleeping
Ao Molae National Park Accommodation (see 1)
Ao Pante Malacca National Park Accommodation (see 2)
Ao Son National Park Accommodation (see 3)
Bulon Hill Resort (see 14)
14 Bulone Resort E1
Chaolae Homestay (see 14)
Ko Tarutao Marine National Park Accommodation (see 16)

Eating
Ao Pante Malacca Canteen (see 2)
Ao Son Canteen (see 3)
Bulone Resort (see 14)
Su's Corner (see 14)

Information
Ao Molae Ranger Station (see 1)
Ao Son Ranger Station (see 3)
Ao Taloh Udang Ranger Station (see 4)
Ao Taloh Waw Ranger Station (see 5)
Ko Tarutao Marine National Park Headquarters (see 2)
15 Ko Tarutao Marine National Park Visitors Centre G1
Ko Tarutao Visitors Centre (see 2)
16 Laem Son Ranger Station C4
17 Mu Ko Phetra National Park Headquarters G1
18 Ranger Station B3
19 Ranger Station B4

Survivor (2002). And there is the minor issue of a private resort on Ko Adang, which is supposedly off-limits to developers. It was originally scheduled to open in 2010, but local environmentalists have managed to keep it shut, so far.

Rubbish on the islands is a problem. Removal of beach and visitor refuse only happens sporadically, though successful Trash Hero (p699) clean-ups are improving things. Do your part and tread lightly.

Ko Tarutao is the biggest and second-most visited island in the group (after Ko Lipe). It's home to the park headquarters (p696) and most government-run accommodation. There are no foreign-exchange facilities on Ko Tarutao; you can change cash at travel agencies in Pak Bara and there are ATMs in Pak Bara and La-Ngu.

Most travellers choose to stay on Ko Lipe (p697) which, despite being inside the park, has rapidly morphed into a popular, increasingly paved resort island overflowing with tourist facilities and hotels. Curiously, the island has managed to evade the park's protection because it is home to communities of *chow lair*, making it exempt from zero development laws.

Long-tail tours to outlying islands can be arranged through travel agencies in Satun or Pak Bara, through the national park headquarters on Ko Tarutao, or through Ko Lipe's resorts and long-tail boat operators.

Ko Tarutao เกาะตะรุเตา

Most of Ko Tarutao's whopping 152 sq km is covered in old-growth jungle, rising sharply to the park's 713m peak. Just 22km southwest of Pak Bara, this is one of Thailand's wildest islands. Mangrove swamps and impressive limestone cliffs circle much of Tarutao. The western coast is dotted with caves and peaceful white-sand beaches.

Tarutao's sordid history partly explains its preservation. Between 1938 and 1948, more than 3000 Thai criminals, including 70 political rebels, were incarcerated here. Among them were interesting inmates such as So Setabutra, who compiled the first Thai–English dictionary while imprisoned on Tarutao, and Sittiporn Gridagon, son of Rama VII. During WWII, food and medical supplies from the mainland were severely depleted and hundreds of prisoners died from malaria, starvation and maltreatment. Prisoners and guards allied and mutinied, taking to piracy in the nearby Strait of Malacca until they were suppressed by British troops in 1946.

The park entrance fee (adult/child 200/100B) is payable on arrival at **park headquarters** (Map p694; Ao Pante Malacca; ⏲8am-5pm) on Tarutao's northwest side. The **visitors centre** (Map p694; ⏲8am-5pm) here hands out maps and has detailed displays on local history, geography, fauna and flora, plus a fascinating dusty library.

Sights & Activities

With a navigable river and long paved roads, Tarutao is perfect for independent exploration. Hire kayaks (per hour/day 200/500B) or mountain bikes (50/250B) from park headquarters.

Ao Pante Malacca BEACH
(อาวพันเตมะละกา; Map p694) Ao Pante Malacca, on the northwest Ko Tarutao, is the island's main arrival and departure point, with a lovely creamy beach shaded by pandanus and casuarinas. It is also home to the park headquarters and most park accommodation.

Toe-Boo Cliff VIEWPOINT
(จุดชมวิวผาโต๊ะบู; Map p694) Behind park headquarters at Ao Pante Malacca, on the northwest side of the island, a steep 500m (20-minute) trail winds through the jungle below a limestone karst dripping with precipitation, then climbs a series of stone-cut steps to this dramatic rocky outcrop with fabulous views across Ko Tarutao towards Ko Adang and other surrounding isles.

Tham Jara-Khe CAVE
(ถ้ำจระเข, Crocodile Cave; Map p694) The large stream flowing inland from Ao Pante Malacca, on northwest Ko Tarutao, leads to Tham Jara-Khe, once home to deadly saltwater crocodiles. The cave is navigable for 1km at low tide and can be visited on long-tail tours (500B) from Ao Pante Malacca's jetty.

Ao Molae BEACH
(อาวเมาะและ; Map p694) Quiet, wonderfully secluded and unbelievably beautiful, Ao Molae has an exquisite white-sand beach backed by a ranger station, bungalows and a campsite, all a (very) hilly 4km walk/cycle south of Ao Pante Malacca.

Ao Son BEACH
(อาวสน; Map p694) On the western coast, a 30-minute boat ride (1500B) or 8km walk/cycle south of Ao Pante Malacca, is this isolated bay. A signposted track 300m inland from the beach leads to **Nam Tok Lu Du** (Lu Du Waterfall; Map p694) (3km, 1½ hours each way). You can also hike inland to **Nam Tok Lo Po** (Lo Po Waterfall; Map p694) (5km, 2½ hours each way) via a trail that starts 500m south down Ao Son's beach.

Ao Taloh Waw BAY
(อาวตะโละวาว; Map p694) The prison camp for civilian prisoners was on Ko Tarutao's isolated eastern coast, 12km southeast of Ao Pante Malacca. A historical trail leads through Ao Taloh Waw's old **prison site**, though the original buildings are long gone. Long-tails from Ao Pante Malacca charge 2500B return.

Ao Taloh Udang BAY
(อาวตะโละอุดัง; Map p694) The overgrown ruins of Tarutao's **political prisoners' camp** can be seen at Ao Taloh Udang, 24km southeast of the park headquarters. Return long-tail charters from the jetty at Ao Pante Malacca cost 3500B (about three hours).

Sleeping & Eating

There's government-run accommodation at Ao Pante Malacca, Ao Molae and Ao Son. Water is rationed, rubbish is (sporadically) transported back to the mainland and electricity runs from 6.30pm to 6am.

Camping (site per person 30B, with tent hire 225B) is permitted under casuarinas at Ao Molae and Ao Son, where there are toilets and showers, and on the wild beaches of Ao Makham, Ao Taloh Waw and Ao Taloh Udang, where you'll need to be self-sufficient. Monkeys often wander into tents, destroying or eating everything they find inside, so shut it all tight.

Accommodation can be booked online or, more easily, at the park's visitors centre (p692) in Pak Bara.

Ao Pante Malacca National Park Accommodation BUNGALOW $
(Map p694; Ao Pante Malacca; r 500-1000B; ⏲Nov–mid-May) The biggest spread of government-run sleeping options, conveniently near the facilities and park offices. Newer, fan-cooled bungalows with balconies sleep two. Simpler longhouse rooms with shared bathroom fit up to four people. The semi-open-air **canteen** (mains 80-180B; ⏲7.45am-2.30pm & 5.30-8.30pm) does good, straightforward Thai cooking. There's beer at the small convenience shop.

Ao Molae National Park Accommodation BUNGALOW $

(Map p694; www.dnp.go.th; Ao Molae; r 600B; ⏲Nov–mid-May) Simple and reasonably clean (not spotless) one- and two-room duplexes with classic mint-green national-park bedding stand right on the edge of the beach amid palms and casuarinas. Thai meals are available at the small **canteen** (mains 70-140B; ⏲7am-2pm & 5-9pm).

Ao Son National Park Accommodation BUNGALOW $

(Map p694; www.dnp.go.th; Ao Son; r 300-500B; ⏲Nov–mid-May) Basic, clean-enough, concrete rooms with shared showers and toilets, just back from isolated Ao Son's beautiful beach. Also here is a **canteen** (mains 60-140B; ⏲7am-8pm) offering simple Thai fare, drinks and snacks.

Getting There & Around

From 21 October to mid-May, the 10.30am and 11.30am speedboats from Pak Bara to Ko Lipe stop at Ko Tarutao (450B, 30 minutes). Only the 9am boat from Lipe to Pak Bara drops passengers at Tarutao. The island officially closes from mid-May to mid-October. During high season, you can visit on speedboat day tours from Pak Bara (around 2000B; includes park fees, lunch, drinks and snorkelling).

If you're staying at Ao Molae, take a shared van from Ao Pante Malacca at 11am or 1pm daily (per person 50B; demand-dependent).

Ko Lipe เกาะหลีเป๊ะ

Ko Lipe is this decade's poster child for untamed development in Thailand's islands. Blessed with two wide white-sand beaches separated by jungled hills and within spitting distance of protected coral reefs, seven or eight years ago the island was only spoken about in secretive 'rising star' whispers. Then the whispers became small talk, which quickly turned into a roar – you know, the kind generally associated with bulldozers. The biggest losers have been the 700-strong community of *chow lair* (sea gypsy) villagers, whose ancestors were gifted Lipe as a home by King Rama V in 1909, but eventually sold to a Thai developer with suspected mafia ties in the 1970s.

The big fear continues to be whether or not Lipe will become another Phi-Phi: a victim of its own beauty. Those fears were stoked back in 2009 when a bass-heavy nightclub arrived on Hat Pattaya. Although the club was shut down, development hasn't stopped. Walking St arrived in 2010 and, in between the glorious beaches, there's an ever-expanding concrete maze of cafes, travel agencies, shops and salons. Even 7-Eleven has landed.

But there's still plenty to love, and love deeply, about Lipe: gorgeous salt-white sand crescents, perfectly chilled-out reggae bars, some sensational dive sites, a jungle-clad interior, a contagiously friendly vibe and a good few inhabitants keen to minimise their environmental impact. You'll just have to look a little harder to find it all.

There are ATMS on Walking St. Most hotels offer free (often slow) wi-fi.

Activities

There are few experiences as relaxing as put-putting between the jungled gems of Ko Rawi, Ko Adang and surrounding islets. The best way to see the archipelago is to hire a *chow lair* captain from the **Taxi Boat** (Map p698) stand on Hat Sunrise. You can rent kayaks (per hour 250B) across the island, including at Sabye Divers (p699) and Daya's (p701).

Beaches

Be careful while swimming, especially in low season. A swimmer was killed in 2013 when a long-tail ran him down. Don't expect boats to see you!

Do not try to swim the narrow strait between Lipe and Adang at any time of year; currents are swift and can be deadly.

Hat Pattaya BEACH

(Map p698) Busy Hat Pattaya on Lipe's southern coast has some terrific beach bars, seafood and a party vibe during the high season, though long-tails often crowd out swimmers.

Hat Sunrise BEACH

(Map p698) Windswept Hat Sunrise, a sublime long stretch of powder-fine sand, runs along the island's east coast. From its northernmost point you'll have spectacular Ko Adang views.

Hat Sunset BEACH

(Map p698) With its golden sand, gentle jungled hills and serene bay that spills into the Adang Strait on the western side of the island, Hat Sunset has an altogether different feel to Lipe's other beaches and, blissfully, retains the island's wild soul.

Ko Lipe

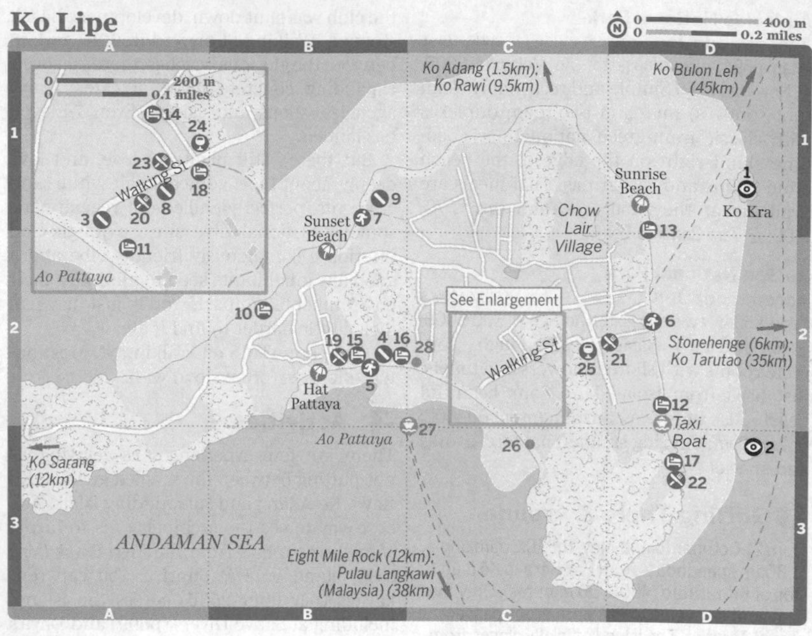

Ko Lipe

Sights
1 Ko Kra ... D1
2 Ko Usen ... D3

Activities, Courses & Tours
Castaway Divers ... (see 12)
Davy Jones' Locker ... (see 15)
Forra Dive ... (see 13)
3 Forra Dive ... A1
4 Forra Dive ... B2
5 Hat Pattaya ... B2
6 Hat Sunrise ... D2
7 Hat Sunset ... B1
8 Ko Lipe Diving ... A1
9 Sabye Divers ... B1

Sleeping
10 Bila Beach ... B2
11 Blue Tribes ... A2
12 Castaway Resort ... D2
13 Forra Dive ... D1
Forra Dive 2 ... (see 4)
14 Gecko Lipe ... A1
15 Koh Lipe Backpackers Hostel ... B2
16 Mali Resort ... B2
17 Serendipity ... D3
18 The Box ... A1

Eating
19 Daya's ... B2
20 Elephant Coffee House ... A1
21 Nee Papaya ... D2
22 On The Rocks ... D3
23 Papaya Mom ... A1
The Box ... (see 18)

Drinking & Nightlife
24 Maya Bar ... A1
25 Pooh's Bar ... C2

Information
26 Immigration Office ... C3

Transport
27 Ferry Jetty ... C2
28 Satun Pak Bara Speedboat Club ... C2

Diving

While it would be a stretch to call the diving here world-class most of the year, it's outstanding when the visibility clarifies, somewhat counter-intuitively, in the early part of the wet season (15 April to 15 June). There are some fun drift dives and two rock-star dive sites.

Eight Mile Rock is a deep pinnacle that attracts devil rays and (very) rare whale sharks. It's the only site in the area to see pelagics. **Stonehenge** is popular because of its beautiful soft corals, resident seahorses, rare leopard sharks and the reef-top boulders behind its inspired name. **Ko Sarang** is another stunner with gorgeous soft corals, a ripping current and solar flares of fish that make it many people's favourite Lipe dive spot.

Forra Dive DIVING
(Map p698; ☎084 407 5691; www.forradiving.com; Hat Sunrise; 1/2 dives 1500/2800B; ⊙Nov-mid-May) French-owned Forra is one of Lipe's longest running outfitters. It offers snorkelling trips (from 650B), Discover Scuba (2500B), Open Water Diver courses (13,500B) and Lipe's only live-aboard operation (three-day trip 10,000B). These 'marine safaris' visit Hin Daeng and Hin Muang, one of Thailand's top dive sites, en route north to Ko Phi-Phi. Branches on **Walking St** and **Hat Pattaya**.

Castaway Divers DIVING
(Map p698; ☎087 478 1516; www.kohlipedivers.com; Castaway Resort, Hat Sunrise; 1/2 dives 1600/3000B; ⊙10am-8pm) Offers a range of specialised courses (night diving, underwater photography) along with the usual, and more intimate dives off long-tail boats. Maximum four people per group.

Ko Lipe Diving DIVING
(Map p698; ☎088 397 7749, 087 622 6204; www.kolipediving.com; Walking St; 1/2 dives 1700/2800B; ⊙8am-10pm) Well-organised, professional dive operator with consistently glowing reviews for its selection of specialist courses and fun dives focused on diving education. Two-dive Discover Scuba costs 3000B; SSI/PADI OWD certification is 14,000/14,500B.

Sabye Divers DIVING
(Map p698; ☎089 464 5884; www.sabyesports.com; Hat Sunset; 2/3 dives 2700/3500B; ⊙8.30am-8pm) Longstanding Sabye Divers is a small Greenfins-certified shop owned by a long-time expat. They're experienced and do a selection of PADI certification courses (from 10,500B) plus fun dives and Discover Scuba (2400B).

Snorkelling

There's good coral located along the southern coast and around **Ko Kra** (Map p698) and **Ko Usen** (Map p698), the islets that are opposite Hat Sunrise (be careful with oncoming long-tailed boats). Most resorts rent out mask and snorkel sets and fins (200B), and arrange various four-point snorkelling trips to Ko Adang, Ko Rawi and other coral-fringed islands (a group trip per person 550B; private 1700B, a maximum of five people).

Volunteering

Trash Hero VOLUNTEERING
(www.trashhero.org) The pioneering, increasingly successful brainchild of a Thai-Swiss duo, Trash Hero organises regular Monday volunteer clean-ups to preserve Lipe's beloved white-sand beaches and others in Ko Tarutao Marine National Park. The program launched in December 2013 with the straightforward aim of protecting the islands' beaches using only materials and people-power to hand. Local businesses quickly pledged support, supplying long-tailed boats, food, drinks and rubbish bags.

Over 1000 volunteers (locals and tourists) have since removed 21,000kg of rubbish from local beaches. Trash Hero now runs weekly clean-ups at 11 official points across Thailand and Indonesia.

Yoga

Swing by Castaway Resort (p700) for high-season yoga (450B; 7am and 4.30pm).

Sleeping

More and more Ko Lipe resorts are staying open year-round. A few humble bamboo bungalows still stand strong, but charmless package-tour type resorts are colonising, particularly on Hat Pattaya. Book well ahead during high season and holidays, when prices skyrocket.

Koh Lipe Backpackers Hostel HOSTEL $
(Map p698; ☎085 361 7923; www.kohlipebackpackers.com; Hat Pattaya; dm 400-500B, r 2500-3000B; ❄📶) The first of its kind on Lipe, this classic 21st-century backpacker pad houses spotless, spacious, air-conditioned eight-bed dorms in a contemporary-style concrete block on west Hat Pattaya. Showers are shared, but you get private lockers, wi-fi, an on-site **Davy Jones' Locker dive school** (dives from 2500B) and a fun young vibe. Upstairs are comfy air-con doubles brushed in pastels.

The Box BOUTIQUE HOTEL $$
(Map p698; ☎086 957 2480; www.theboxlipresort.com; Walking St; r incl breakfast with fan 1200-1900B, air-con 1600-2900B; ❄📶) Bang in the middle of Walking St is this alluring boutique hotel crafted from shipping containers,

dressed up in natural wood panelling and connected by wooden paths through gardens. Interiors are stylishly minimalist with bamboo beds, colour feature walls and square wash basins. Linger over tasty tapas in the superb Spanish-Mediterranean restaurant (p701) out front.

Forra Dive BUNGALOW **$$**
(Map p698; 084 407 5691; www.forradiving.com; Hat Sunrise; bungalow 1000-1400B;) Forra captures the look of Lipe's pirate spirit with a range of those beloved bamboo bungalows and lofts, the best of which sport indoor-outdoor bathrooms and hammock-strung terraces. Divers get same-day 25% off lodging and there's a second location with similar-style bungalows on Hat Pattaya. Sometimes it's divers-only.

Bila Beach BUNGALOW **$$**
(Map p698; 087 570 3684; www.bilabeachresort.com; Hat Sunset; bungalow 1500B) A killer bamboo reggae bar and beachfront restaurant lurk below stylish shaggy-haired cliffside bungalows set above a tiny, secluded white-sand cove, which is strewn with boulders and adjacent to Hat Sunset. It's the perfect setting for your hippie honeymoon and a short sweaty walk over the hill from Hat Pattaya.

Gecko Lipe BUNGALOW **$$**
(Map p698; 087 810 7257; www.geckolipe.com; 61 Mu 7, Walking St; r small 800-1200B, large 1630-2530B;) Here is a wonderful hilltop collection of fan-cooled bamboo bungalows in two sizes nestled among trees. The smaller white-washed variety offers blonde floors and colourful-walled, cold-water bathrooms. The larger, thatch-topped golden-bamboo edition has stylish hot-water bathrooms and thicker mattresses. Good low-season discounts.

Blue Tribes BUNGALOW **$$**
(Map p698; 083 654 0316, 080 546 9464; www.bluetribeslipe.com; Hat Pattaya; bungalow 1400-2800B; Aug-May;) Tucked into flower-filled gardens, Blue Tribes is one of Hat Pattaya's more attractive small resorts. The best choices are two-storey thatched wooden bungalows with downstairs living rooms and top-floor bedrooms fronted by sliding doors opening to sea views. Some rooms have minor wear and tear but all are comfy and most have breezy porches.

★ **Castaway Resort** HOTEL **$$$**
(Map p698; 081 170 7605, 083 138 7472; www.castaway-resorts.com; Hat Sunrise; bungalow 3400-5400B;) Roomy dark-wood bungalows with hammock-laden terraces, cushions everywhere, overhead fans and fabulous, modern-meets-natural bathrooms embody Lipe at its barefoot-beach-chic best. This welcoming resort is also one of Lipe's most environmentally friendly, run on solar water heaters and lights (there's no AC). There's a super-chilled beachside cafe, plus high-season yoga classes (450B) and a good dive school (p699).

Mali Resort RESORT **$$$**
(Map p698; 091 979 4600; www.maliresortkohlipe.com; Hat Pattaya; bungalow incl breakfast 3700-9945B;) Chic, laid-back and Bali-inspired, the gorgeous new bungalows at this American-owned resort offer dark-wood floors, thatched beamed ceilings, built-in day beds, carved-wood elephant lamps, colourful wall art and giant outdoor bathrooms with dual shower heads. All rooms offer access to the stunning, sophisticated beach bar and an ideal slab of Pattaya beachfront. Best deals online.

There are also older, more affordable garden cottages done up in plush linens.

Serendipity BUNGALOW **$$$**
(Map p698; 088 395 5158; www.serendipityresort-kohlipe.com; Hat Sunrise; r 7800-19,000B;) An exquisitely designed orange-themed spot, delightfully isolated by draping itself up above the boulder-strewn southern point of Hat Sunrise and accessed via a wooden boardwalk. Spacious dark-wood thatched bungalows feature private patios, seating areas inside and out, brass-bowl sinks, tea and coffee sets and air-con. The two penthouse suites include private pools with swoon-worthy views. The Thai/international **bar-restaurant** (mains 165-375B; noon-9.30pm;) clings to the cliffside.

Eating

Find cheap eats at the roti stands and small Thai cafes along Walking St. Please take advantage of the waste-reducing water refill points at many resorts and eateries.

★ **Nee Papaya** THAI **$**
(Map p698; mains 80-150B; 9am-9.30pm) Delightful Nee offers an affordable fish grill nightly, all the standard curries (including a dynamite beef *pá·naang*), noodles and stir

fries (beef, chicken, seafood or vegie), along with a tremendous array of fiery Isan dishes. She'll tone down the chilli quotient on request, but her food is best when spiced for the local palate, which is why she attracts droves of in-the-know Thai tourists.

Papaya Mom THAI $
(Map p698; Walking St; mains 90-200B; ⏲9am-10pm; ✎) A cute Isan food stall notable for its authentic eats and especially succulent meat dishes popular with local Thais (grilled spicy pork neck, *lâhp*). Vegetarians can raid the luscious fruit stand and thoughtful veg menu featuring a delicious bean-curd-and-bean-sprouts stir-fry.

The Box SPANISH, MEDITERRANEAN $$
(Map p698; ☎086 957 2480; www.theboxliperesort.com; Walking St; tapas 170-235B, mains 300-380B; ⏲7am-10.30pm; 📶) If you fancy a break from flaming-hot curries and seafood grills (it happens), rustle up a *tinto de verano* (red wine with lemonade) and a parade of authentically good Spanish tapas specials at this casually elegant, modern, wood-clad space. Top of the list are Spanish potato omelette, garlic prawns, Iberian ham, brie-and-caramelised-onion toast and some highly recommended (not-so-Spanish) burgers.

Daya's SEAFOOD, THAI $$
(Map p698; Hat Pattaya; mains 150-300B; ⏲7am-10pm) One of few places still locally run, Daya's is arguably the best of the fresh seafood barbecues put on nightly by Hat Pattaya's resorts.

Elephant Coffee House INTERNATIONAL $$
(Map p698; www.facebook.com/ElephantKohLipe; Walking St; dishes 180-440B; ⏲8am-1am) The bar is a long-tail, secondhand books are for sale and black-and-white local-life photos are plastered across varnished-concrete walls. Pop into this contemporary cafe for fabulous all-day breakfasts of thick French toast, excellent coffee and homemade muesli loaded with tropical fruit. Otherwise choose from fresh salads, sandwiches, burgers and the like. Also hosts live music.

Drinking & Nightlife

Good espresso-based coffee has become Lipe's thing. Coffee shops are sprinkled all over the island, particularly on Walking St.

Thankfully, driftwood-clad Rasta bars can still be found on all beaches. At least some things never change.

Maya Bar BAR
(Map p698; Walking St; ⏲6pm-late) A forever-packed, open-air cocktail bar that feels sultrily modern-rustic thanks to faded log stools, chunky-wood tables, flickering candles and a bamboo 'wall'. DJs spin dance/electronic beats after dark.

Pooh's Bar BAR
(Map p698; ☎074 750345, 089 463 5099; www.poohlipe.com; Walking St; ⏲10am-10.30pm; 📶) This expansive complex (which includes bungalows, a dive shop and several restaurants) was built by a Lipe pioneer and remains a popular local expat hang-out. Nightly films and sports are projected onto the big screen and there's often live music.

Getting There & Away

From 21 October to mid-May, speedboats run from Pak Bara to Ko Lipe via Ko Tarutao or Ko Bulon Leh at 9.30am, 10.30am, 11.30am, 2pm and 3pm (650B, 1½ hours). Boats return to Pak Bara at 9am, 9.30am, 12.15pm, 1pm, 1.30pm and 4pm. Low-season transport is weather dependent, but there's usually a direct daily boat from Pak Bara to Lipe at 11.30am, returning at 9.30am.

From November to late April, the high-speed **Tigerline** (☎081 358 0808, 089 737 0552; www.tigerlinetravel.com) ferry departs Ko Lipe at 10am for Phuket (2400B, eight hours), via Ko Phi-Phi (1950B, seven hours), Ko Lanta (1700B, five hours), Ko Muk (1600B, 3½ hours), Ko Kradan (1800B, 3½ hours) and Ko Ngai (1600B, 4½ hours).

From mid-November to late March, **Bundhaya Speedboat** (☎081 678 2826, 074 7503889; www.bundhayaspeedboat.com) and **Satun Pak Bara Speedboat Club** (Map p698; ☎099 404 0409, 099 414 4994; www.tarutaolipeisland.com) leave Ko Lipe at 9am for Ko Lanta (1900B, three hours), via Ko Bulon Leh (600B, one hour), Ko Kradan (1400B, two hours), Ko Muk (1400B, two hours) and Ko Ngai (1600B, 2½ hours). Speedboats return from Lanta at 10.30am.

Boats also run from Ko Lipe to Pulau Langkawi (p691) in Malaysia, mid-October to mid-April.

No matter which boat you end up using, you'll have to take a 50B long-tail shuttle to/from the **floating ferry jetty** (Map p698) off Hat Pattaya, and pay a 20B 'entrance fee'. It's part of a local agreement to share the flow. Speedboats *may* drop you directly on Hat Pattaya.

Ko Adang & Ko Rawi เกาะอาดัง/เกาะราวี

Ko Adang, the 30-sq-km island immediately north of Ko Lipe, has brooding, densely forested hills, white-sand beaches and healthy coral reefs. Lots of snorkelling tours make a stop here. Inland are a few short jungle trails and tumbling waterfalls, including **Pirate's Falls** (Map p694; Ko Adang), which is rumoured to have been a freshwater source for pirates (more of a cascading river than a waterfall). There are great views from **Chado Cliff** (Map p694; Ko Adang), a half-hour hike above the main beach; apparently pirates plotted attacks on commercial ships from this viewpoint.

Ko Rawi, a rocky, 29-sq-km jungled ellipse 1km west of Ko Adang, has first-rate beaches and large coral reefs offshore. Excellent snorkelling spots include north **Ko Yang** (Map p694), 1km south of Ko Rawi's southeastern end, and tiny **Ko Hin Ngam** (Map p694), 3km further south, which has underwater fields of giant clams, vibrant anemones and striped pebble beaches. Legend has it that these stones are cursed: anyone who removes one will experience bad luck until the stone is returned.

Sleeping & Eating

Camping (site per person 30B) at Ao Lik on Ko Rawi is allowed, with park permission.

Ko Tarutao Marine National Park Accommodation BUNGALOW $
(Map p694; www.dnp.go.th; Ko Adang; d 600B, 6-person 1800B, camp site per person 30B, with tent hire 225B; ⏲Nov–mid-May) Ko Adang's park accommodation is near Laem Son ranger station in the island's southeast. There are attractive, fan-cooled doubles and six-person family bungalows, all with attached cold-water bathrooms, plus camping facilities. Book ahead, online or at the Pak Bara park visitors centre (p692). A small restaurant provides good Thai meals.

Getting There & Away

Long-tails from Ko Lipe take you to Ko Adang for around 200B or Ko Rawi for 500B, though you may have to bargain. Even a short stop on the islands will cost you the park entrance fee.

Understand Thailand

Thailand Today

These are troubled times for Thailand. With the military in charge again and no real prospect of elections before 2017, the country remains divided politically between the rural poor at one end and the traditional elite and urban middle classes at the other. A slowing economy and a poor human rights record have also helped tarnish Thailand's image as an oasis of relative stability in Southeast Asia. Tourism, however, hasn't taken much of a hit, with visitors – especially from China – still arriving in droves.

Best in Non-fiction Books

Very Thai (Philip Cornwel-Smith) Photos and essays on Thailand's quirks.

A Kingdom in Crisis: Thailand's Struggle for Democracy in the Twenty-First Century (Andrew MacGregor Marshall) Banned in Thailand, so read it before you go.

Bangkok Days (Lawrence Osborne) A witty and insightful account of living in Bangkok.

Best in Thai Literature

Pisat, Evil Spirits (Seni Saowaphong) Deals with conflicts between the old and new generations.

Lai Chiwit (Many Lives) (Kukrit Pramoj) A collection of short stories.

Monsoon Country (Pira Sudham) Brilliantly captures the northeast's struggles against nature and nurture.

The Judgment (Chart Korbjitti) A drama about a young village man wrongly accused of a crime.

Jasmine Nights (SP Somtow) An upbeat coming-of-age novel that fuses traditional ideas with modern Thai pop culture.

Married to the Demon King (Sri Daoruang) Adaptation of the *Ramayana* into modern Bangkok.

Another Day, Another Coup

On 22 May 2014, the Thai military under General Prayuth Chan-o-cha overthrew the elected Puea Thai government led by Yingluck Shinawatra. It was the 13th coup in Thailand since 1932 and brought to an end months of political crisis that saw parts of central Bangkok occupied by anti-government protesters. Prayuth said the coup was necessary to restore stability and to end the risk of violence between the supporters of Yingluck and her exiled brother and former prime minister Thaksin Shinawatra, and their opponents who regard Thaksin as the Lord Voldemort of Thailand. But while the coup was hailed by the urban middle classes and traditional elite, who accuse the Shinawatras of massive corruption, they are far outnumbered by the legions of rural poor who regard Thaksin as the only politician to have ever done anything for them.

Prayuth, who speaks to the country weekly on his Friday evening TV show *Returning Happiness to the People*, is now the civilian head of the Orwellian-sounding National Council for Peace and Order (NCPO), the name the junta have given to their government. Since taking power, the NCPO has muzzled the media, detained and imprisoned political opponents, and repealed the 2007 constitution and ordered a new one – Thailand's 20th since 1932 – to be drafted.

Despite assurances that the NCPO would only run the country temporarily, at the time of research there has been no announcement of when elections are likely to be held. What is certain is that they will not be staged until the new constitution is finalised. The first draft version was rejected by the committee set up to approve it, in part because of provisions that appeared designed to dilute Thailand's already shaky version of democracy. They included allowing an unelected prime minister to be installed and for more than half of all senators in parliament to be appointed rather than elected.

Few observers believe that an election is likely before 2017, and even fewer are confident that the the new constitution will end Thailand's political divisions. The NCPO appears to be trying to return the country to the paternalistic model that once dominated Thai politics, where the military and elite run the show on behalf of the monarchy, while everyone else stays silent. But Thaksin's major achievement was to politicise the poor, and there is little likelihood of them putting up with any system that attempts to turn the clock back to the old days.

The NCPO is also under increasing pressure for its failure to address Thailand's slumping economy. With foreign investment down since the coup, and much needed infrastructure upgrades delayed, there is real concern about the country's economic future. Thailand's international image has also been hurt by increasing criticism of its human rights record, with human trafficking scandals and the alleged poor treatment of migrant workers highlighted by both the EU and the US.

Speak No Evil

One of the first actions of the junta was to assert its control over the media. With martial law in place, domestic newspapers and TV stations were told not to publish or broadcast any stories critical of the coup. Some 15 TV and radio stations were taken off the air altogether, 100 websites were blocked (including Facebook temporarily) and internet providers were ordered to block any content that violated the junta's orders. Even now, some websites, including the Thailand section of the Human Rights Watch website, remain inaccessible inside Thailand. Following threats from the NCPO – in March 2015 Prayuth told journalists that he would 'execute' those who did not toe the official line – the domestic media now self-censors their stories to ensure they don't get into trouble.

Accompanying the assault on press freedom has been a general crackdown on dissent. More than 1000 people – opposition politicians, academics, journalists, bloggers and students – have been detained for various periods since the coup. Some have been tried by military courts, others have had their passports taken away. In March 2015, this prompted the UN's High Commissioner for Human Rights to claim the military are using martial law to silence opposition and to call for 'freedom of expression to ensure genuine debate'.

There has also been a notable rise in the number of people being prosecuted under Thailand's *lèse-majesté* laws. They are some of the strictest in the world and critics have accused the army of using them to silence political opponents. Recent cases have seen two university students imprisoned for appearing in a play said to have defamed the monarchy, while in

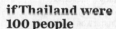

POPULATION: **68.65 MILLION**

GDP: **US$373.8 BILLION**

GDP PER CAPITA: **US$5560**

UNEMPLOYMENT: **0.9%**

EDUCATION SPENDING: **6.4% OF GDP**

if Thailand were 100 people

75 would be Thai
14 would be Chinese
11 would be Other

belief systems

(% of population)

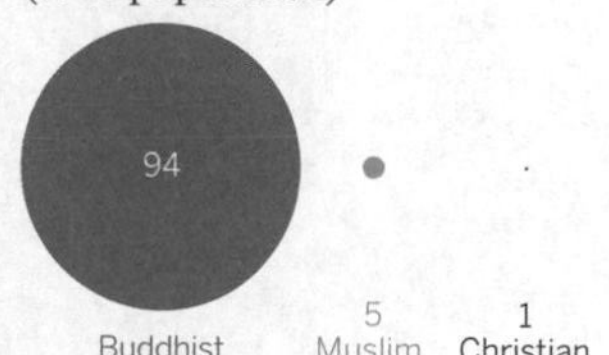

population per sq km

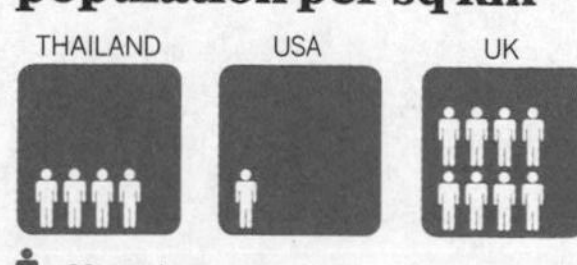

Best on Film

Paradoxocracy (Pen-ek Ratanaruang; 2013) Documentary tracing the country's political history from the 1932 revolution on.

Tom-Yum-Goong (Prachya Pinkaew; 2005) Tony Jaa, the Jackie Chan of Thailand, stars in this martial arts movie, the most successful Thai film ever released in the US.

36 (Nawapol Thamrongrattanarit; 2012) A love affair told through 36 static camera set-ups.

Tropical Malady (Apichatpong Weerasethakul; 2004) This rural romance and drama won the Jury Prize at the Cannes Film Festival.

Best News Analysis Sites

The Diplomat (thediplomat.com) Current affairs magazine covering Asia Pacific.

New Mandala (asiapacific.anu.edu.au/newmandala) Commentary on news, society and culture in Southeast Asia.

Asia Times Online (atimes.com) Solid Southeast Asia reporting.

August 2015 one man received a 30-year prison sentence for insulting the monarchy on his Facebook page.

Hello Neighbour

By the end of 2015 it was expected that the ASEAN Economic Community (AEC) will have united the association's 10 Southeast Asian countries in a liberalised marketplace where goods, services, capital and labour are shared across borders with little or no country-specific impediments. In theory, the AEC will make it easier to buy and sell goods, hire non-nationals and invest within ASEAN. Each member country is required to meet certain standards in order to comply with AEC agreements. Thailand has already opened a new bridge across the Mekong to facilitate trade with Laos and it is expected that more land crossings between Thailand and Myanmar will open in the near future. But there are still barriers ranging from restrictive labour codes (Thai law excludes non-nationals from 39 occupations) to undeveloped infrastructure (in countries like Laos, Cambodia and Myanmar) and language barriers. While Thailand is expected to benefit economically from the AEC, some observers are concerned that the kingdom lags behind its neighbours (Malaysia especially) in English and Chinese language skills, making it less competitive in the common pool. Many analysts cite the EU as a model for the AEC, but it is unclear how effective a single market will be in a region with much greater economic disparity between countries than in Europe. There are also questions over the undefined role of China, whose influence looms over the entire region.

History & Politics

Thai history began as a story of migrants heading into a frontier land claimed by distant empires for trade, forced labour and patronage. Eventually the nascent country developed powerful entities that united feuding localities and began fusing a national identity. The kings resisted colonisation from Western powers on its border only to cede absolute grip on the country when challenged from forces within. Since the 1932 transition to a constitutional monarchy the military has predominantly ruled the country, with a few democratic hiccups in between.

History

Ancient History

Little evidence remains of the cultures that existed in Thailand before the middle of the 1st millennium AD. *Homo erectus* fossils in Thailand's northern province of Lampang date back at least 500,000 years, and the country's most important archaeological site is Ban Chiang, outside Udon Thani, which provides evidence of one of the world's oldest agrarian societies. It is believed that the Mekong River Valley and Khorat Plateau were inhabited as far back as 10,000 years ago by farmers and bronze-workers. Cave paintings in Pha Taem National Park near Ubon Ratchathani date back some 3000 years.

Relief carvings at Angkor Wat depict Tai mercenaries serving in Khmer armies. The Khmer called them 'Syam'. The name was transliterated to 'Siam' by the English trader James Lancaster in 1592.

Early Empires

Starting around the 10th century, the 'Tai' people, considered to be the ancestors of the contemporary Thais, began migrating from southern China into present-day Southeast Asia. These immigrants spoke Tai-Kadai, said to be the most significant ethno-linguistic group in Southeast Asia. Some settled in the river valleys of modern-day Thailand while others chose parts of modern-day Laos and the Shan state of Myanmar.

They settled in villages as farmers, hunters and traders and organised themselves into administrative units known as *meu·ang*, under the rule of a lord, that became the building blocks of the Tai state. Over time, the Tai expanded from the northern mountain valleys into the central plains and northeastern plateau, where there existed several important trading

TIMELINE

4000–2500 BC

Prehistoric people develop pottery, rice cultivation and bronze metallurgy in northeastern Thailand.

6th–11th centuries

Dvaravati establish city-states in central Thailand, develop trade routes and Mon culture and practise Theravada Buddhism.

9–13th centuries

Angkor extends control across parts of Thailand, building Hindu-Buddhist sanctuaries.

centres ruled by various indigenous and 'foreign' empires, including the Mon-Dvaravati, Khmer (Cambodia) and Srivijaya (Malay).

Ancient Sites

- *Ayuthaya Historical Park*
- *Sukhothai Historical Park*
- *Chiang Saen Historical Park*
- *Lopburi Khmer ruins*
- *Nakhon Si Thammarat National Museum*
- *Phimai Historical Park*

Dvaravati

The Mon dominated parts of Burma (present-day Myanmar), western Thailand and into the central plains. In the 6th to 9th centuries, the Dvaravati culture emerged as a distinct Buddhist culture associated with the Mon people. Little is known about this period but it is believed that Nakhon Pathom might have been the centre, and that overland trade routes extended to Burma, Cambodia, Chiang Mai and Laos as evidenced by findings of distinctive Dvaravati Buddha images, temples and stone inscriptions in the Mon language.

The Dvaravati was one of many Indian-influenced cultures that established themselves in Southeast Asia, but scholars single out the Dvaravati because of its artistic legacy and the trade routes that might have provided an early framework for what would become the core of the modern-day Thai state.

Khmer

The Khmers were Southeast Asia's equivalent of the Roman Empire. This kingdom became famous for its extravagant sculpture and architecture and had a profound effect on the art and religion of the region. Established in the 9th century, the Khmer kingdom built its capital in Angkor (modern-day Cambodia) and expanded westward across present-day central and northeastern Thailand. Administrative centres anchored by Angkor-style temples were built in Lopburi (then known as Lavo), Sukhothai and Phimai (near Nakhon Ratchasima) and linked by road to the capital.

The Khmer's large-scale construction projects were a symbol of imperial power in its frontier lands and examples of the day's most advanced technologies. Khmer elements – Hinduism, Brahmanism, Theravada Buddhism and Mahayana Buddhism – mark this period in Thailand.

Top History Reads

- *Thailand: A Short History (2003) – David K Wyatt*
- *A History of Thailand (2009) – Chris Baker & Pasuk Phongpaichit*
- *Chronicle of Thailand: Headlines Since 1946 (2010) – William Warren*

Srivijaya

While mainland Thailand was influenced by forces from the north and west, thc Malay peninsula was economically and culturally fused to cultures further south. Between the 8th and 13th centuries, the Malay peninsula was under the sway of the confederation of the Srivijaya, which controlled maritime trade between the South China Sea and Indian Ocean. The Srivijaya capital is believed to have been in Palembang on Sumatra.

Of the series of Srivijaya city-states along the Malay peninsula, Tambralinga established its capital near present-day Nakhon Si Thammarat

10th century	1240–1438	1283	1292
Arrival of Tai peoples in Thailand.	Approximate dates of Sukhothai kingdom.	Early Thai script invented by King Ramkhamhaeng of Sukhothai.	Chiang Mai becomes the capital of Lanna, the historic northern kingdom.

RAMKHAMHAENG'S STONE INSCRIPTION

In an inscription of 1292, King Ramkhamhaeng gives a picture of his kingdom as idyllic and free of constraints, and of himself as a benevolent patriarch:

In the time of King Ramkhamhaeng this land of Sukhothai is thriving. There are fish in the water and rice in the fields...whoever wants to trade in elephants, does so; whoever wants to trade in horses, does so;...if any commoner in the land has a grievance... it is easy; he goes and strikes the bell which the king has hung there; King Ramkhamhaeng...hears the call; he goes and questions the man, examines the case, and decides it justly for him.

Translation by AB Griswold and Prasert Na Nagara, *Journal of the Siam Society* (July 1971)

and adopted Buddhism in the 13th century, while the states further south adopted Islam, creating a religious boundary which persists to this day. Remains of Srivijaya culture can be seen around Chaiya and Nakhon Si Thammarat. Many art forms of the Srivijaya kingdom – such as *năng đà·lung* (shadow play) and *lá·kon* (classical dance-drama) – persist today.

Emerging Tai Kingdoms

In the 13th century, the regional empires started to decline and prosperous Tai city-states emerged with localised power and military might. The competing city-states were ultimately united into various kingdoms that began to establish a Thai identity. Scholars recognise Lanna, Sukhothai and Ayuthaya as the unifying kingdoms of the period.

Lanna

The Lanna kingdom, based in northern Thailand, dates its formation to the upper Mekong River town of Chiang Saen in the middle of the 13th century by King Mengrai. He migrated south to Chiang Mai (meaning 'New City') in 1292, and four years later made it his capital. The king was a skilled diplomat and forged important alliances with potential rivals, such as King Ngam Muang of Phayao and King Ramkhamhaeng of Sukhothai; a bronze statue commemorating this confederation stands in Chiang Mai today. King Mengrai is also credited for successfully repulsing the Mongol invasions in the early 14th century.

The Lanna kingdom is recognised for its royal patronage of the Sinhalese tradition of Theravada Buddhism that is now widely practised in Thailand and of the distinctive northern Thai culture of the region. The

Phibul Songkhram officially changed the name of the country in 1939 from 'Siam' to 'Prathet Thai' (or 'Thailand' in English); it was considered an overt nationalistic gesture intended to unite all the Tai-speaking people.

1351–1767
Reign of Ayuthaya and rise of the Siamese.

1511
Portuguese found foreign mission in Ayuthaya, followed by other European nations.

1688
King Narai dies, followed by the Palace Revolution and the expulsion of the French.

1700
Ayuthaya's population is estimated to be one million, making it probably the largest city in the world at the time.

Lanna kingdom didn't experience an extensive expansion period as it was plagued by dynastic intrigues and wars with rival powers.

Sukhothai

During the 13th century, several principalities in the central plains united and wrested control from the dying Khmer empire, making their new capital at Sukhothai (meaning 'Rising of Happiness'). Thais consider Sukhothai the first true Thai kingdom and the period is recognised as an artistic and cultural awakening.

The most revered of the Sukhothai kings was Ramkhamhaeng, who is credited for developing the modern Thai writing system, which is based on Indian, Mon and Khmer scripts. He also established Theravada Buddhism as the official religion.

In its prime, the Sukhothai kingdom extended as far as Nakhon Si Thammarat in the south, to the upper Mekong River Valley in Laos and to Bago (Pegu) in southern Burma. For a short period (1448–86) the Sukhothai capital was moved to Phitsanulok, but by that time another star was rising in Thailand, the kingdom of Ayuthaya.

Ayuthaya

In the mid-14th century, the Ayuthaya kingdom began to dominate the Chao Phraya River basin during the twilight of the Khmer period. It survived for 416 years, defining itself as Siam's most important kingdom with an expansive sphere of influence (including much of the former Khmer empire) and a fundamental role in organising the modern Thai state and social structure.

With a strategic island location formed by encircling rivers, Ayuthaya grew wealthy through international trade during the 17th century's age of commerce and fortified itself with superior Portuguese-supplied firearms and mercenaries. The river system connected to the Gulf of Thailand and to the hinterlands as well.

This is the period when Western traders 'discovered' Southeast Asia, and Ayuthaya hosted many foreign settlements. Accounts by foreign visitors mention Ayuthaya's cosmopolitan markets and court. In 1690 Londoner Engelbert Campfer proclaimed, 'Among the Asian nations, the kingdom of Siam is the greatest'.

Ayuthaya adopted Khmer court customs, honorific language and ideas of kingship. The monarch styled himself as a Khmer *devaraja* (divine king) rather than Sukhothai's *dhammaraja* (righteous king); and Ayuthaya continued to pay tribute to the Chinese emperor, who rewarded this ritualistic submission with generous gifts and commercial privileges.

The kingdom functioned according to a strict and complex hierarchy, much of which was defined by King Trailok (r 1448–88). Elaborate lists

1767
Ayuthaya is sacked by the Burmese.

1768
King Taksin establishes a new capital in Thonburi.

1782
Founding of the Chakri dynasty and Bangkok as the new capital.

1826
Thailand allies with Britain during the first Anglo-Burmese War.

FRIENDS OF THE KING

In the 1680s many foreign emissaries were invited to Ayuthaya by King Narai, who was keen to acquire and consume foreign material, culture and ideas. His court placed orders for spyglasses, hourglasses, paper, walnut trees, cheese, wine and marble fountains. He joined the French Jesuits to observe the eclipse at his palace in Lopburi and received a gift of a globe from France's King Louis XIV.

Also at this time, Narai recruited the services of the Greek adventurer Constantine Phaulkon, who was later accused of conspiring to overthrow the ailing king. Instead, the accusers led a coup and executed Constantine.

of official posts with specific titles and ranks were established. Individual social status was measured in numerical units of how much land one possessed. Fines and punishments were proportional to the person's rank. Ayuthaya society consisted of royalty, nobility and commoners. Commoners were further divided into freemen and slaves. Freemen were assigned to a royal or noble overseer. For six months of each year they owed labour to the ruling elite, doing personal errands, public works or military service. Despite the clear social hierarchy, social mobility was possible, depending on personal skills, connections (including marriage) and royal favour. These societal divisions are reflected in the feudal elements that persist in Thai society today.

The glories of Ayuthaya were interrupted by the expansionist Burmese. In 1569 the city had fallen to the great Burmese king, Bayinnaung, but regained independence under the leadership of King Naresuan. Then, in 1765, Burma's ambitious and newly established Kongbaung dynasty pushed eastward to eliminate Ayuthaya as a political and commercial rival. Burmese troops laid siege to the capital for a year before destroying it in 1767. The city was devastated, its buildings and people wiped out. The surrounding areas were deserted. So chilling was this historic sacking and razing of Ayuthaya that the perception of the Burmese as ruthless aggressors still persists in the minds of many Thais to this day.

King Naresuan is portrayed as a national hero and has become a cult figure, especially worshipped by the Thai army. His story inspired a high-budget, blockbuster film trilogy, *King Naresuan*, funded in part by the Thai government.

The Bangkok Era

With Ayuthaya in ruins, the line of succession of the kings was broken and chaos ensued. A former general, Taksin, claimed his right to rule, defeated potential rivals and established his new capital in Thonburi, a settlement downriver from Ayuthaya with better access to trade. King Taksin, the son of a Chinese father and Thai mother, strongly promoted trade with China. After 15 years, the king was deposed in 1782 by the military.

1851–68
Reign of King Mongkut (Rama IV) and a period of Western influence.

1855
Bowring Treaty concluded between Siam and Britain, stimulating the Thai economy and granting extraterritorial rights to British subjects in Siam.

1868–1910
Reign of King Chulalongkorn (Rama V) and increased European imperialism in neighbouring countries.

1874
Slavery is abolished.

Landmarks of the Bangkok Era

Wat Arun

Wat Phra Kaew & Grand Palace

Dusit Palace Park

One of the coup organisers, Chao Phraya Chakri, assumed the throne as King Yot Fa (Rama I) and established the Chakri dynasty, which still rules today. The new monarch moved the capital across Chao Phraya River to modern-day Bangkok. The first century of Bangkok rule focused on rebuilding the cultural, political and military might of Ayuthaya. The new rulers extended their influence in every direction. Destroying the capital cities of both Laos and Cambodia, Siam contained Burmese aggression and made a vassal of Chiang Mai. Defeated populations were resettled and played an important role in increasing Siam's production of rice, much of which was exported to China.

Unlike the Ayuthaya rulers who identified with the Hindu god Vishnu, the Chakri kings positioned themselves as defenders of Buddhism. They undertook compilations and Thai translations of essential Buddhist texts and constructed many royal temples.

In the meantime, a new social order and market economy was taking shape in the mid-19th century. Siam turned to the West for modern scientific and technological ideas and reforms in education, infrastructure and legal systems. One of the great modernisers, King Mongkut (Rama IV; r 1851–68) never expected to be king. Before his ascension he had spent 27 years in a monastery, founding the Thammayut sect based on the strict disciplines of the Mon monks.

During Mongkut's reign, Siam concluded treaties with Western powers that integrated the kingdom into the world market system, ceded royal monopolies and granted extraterritorial rights to British subjects.

In 1868 King Mongkut (Rama IV) abolished a husband's right to sell his wife or her children without her permission. The older provision, it was said, treated the woman 'as if she were a water buffalo'.

Mongkut's son, King Chulalongkorn (Rama V) was to take much greater steps in replacing the old political order with the model of the nation-state. He abolished slavery and the corvée system (state labour), which had lingered on ineffectively since the Ayuthaya period. Chulalongkorn's reign oversaw the creation of a salaried bureaucracy, a police force and a standing army. His reforms brought uniformity to the legal code, law courts and revenue offices. Siam's agricultural output was improved by advances in irrigation techniques and increasing peasant populations. Schools were established along European lines.

Chulalongkorn relied greatly on foreign advisers, mostly British. Within the royal court, much of the centuries-old protocol was abandoned and replaced by Western forms. The architecture and visual art of state, like the new throne halls, were designed by Italian artists.

Like his father, Chulalongkorn was regarded as a skilful diplomat and is credited for successfully playing European powers off one another to avoid colonisation. In exchange for independence, Thailand ceded territory to French Indochina (Laos in 1893, Cambodia in 1907) and British Burma (three Malayan states in 1909). In 1902, the former Patani king-

1890

Siam's first railway connects Bangkok with Nakhon Ratchasima.

1893

French blockade Chao Phraya River over disputed Indochina territory and intensify threat of colonisation.

1902

Siam annexes Yala, Pattani and Narathiwat from the former sultanate of Patani.

1909

Anglo-Siamese Treaty outlines Siam's boundaries.

THE THAI MONARCHY

After the 1932 revolution, King Prajadhipok (Rama VII) abdicated the throne in 1935, but was replaced shortly thereafter by his nephew Ananda Mahidol. He was crowned Rama VIII, though he was only 10 years old and had spent much of his childhood studying abroad. After returning to Thailand, he was shot dead under mysterious circumstances in his bedroom in 1946.

His brother Bhumibol Adulyadej (pronounced *phuumíphon adunyádèt*) assumed the throne the same year and has gone on to become the longest-reigning king in Thai history, as well as the world's longest-reigning living monarch. Although he has no official direct role in politics, he has intervened behind the scenes in times of political crisis. The king enjoys great respect, even worship, among his subjects and has served as a role model for the modern Thai man: educated, family oriented, philanthropic and even stylish.

Now 87, the king rarely appears in public. Hospitalised in Bangkok between 2009 and 2013, he spends much of his time at his seaside palace in Hua Hin. Queen Sirikit is also struggling with old age, having suffered a stroke.

The King's heir, Crown Prince Vajiralongkorn, has assumed many of the royal duties, along with the king's eldest daughter Princess Sirindhorn. After the king, she is now perhaps the most popular member of the royal family with the Thai public.

dom was ceded to the British, who were then in control of Malaysia, but control reverted back to Thailand five years later.

Defying old traditions, Chulalongkorn followed in his father's footsteps in allowing himself to be seen in public, photographed in peasant garb and consented to his image being reproduced on coins, stamps and postcards. He was also well travelled and visited Europe, Singapore, Java, Malaya, Burma and India. He collected art and inspiration from these travels and built fanciful palaces as architectural scrapbooks.

Siam was becoming a geographically defined country in a modern sense. By 1902, the country no longer called itself Siam but Prathet Thai (the country of the Thai) or Ratcha-anachak Thai (the kingdom of the Thai). By 1913, all those living within its borders were defined as 'Thai'.

Democracy vs Military

In 1932 a group of young military officers and bureaucrats calling themselves Khana Ratsadon (People's Party) mounted a successful, bloodless coup which marked the end of absolute monarchy and introduced a constitutional monarchy. The leaders of the group were inspired by the democratic ideology they had encountered during their studies in Europe.

In the years after the coup, rival factions (royalists, military, civilians) struggled for the upper hand in the new power regime. Even the People's

1913
King Vajiravudh requires all citizens to adopt surnames.

1916
The first Thai university, Chulalongkorn University, is established.

1917
Siam sends troops to join the Allies in WWI.

1932
Bloodless coup ends absolute monarchy.

LIBERAL COUNTERWEIGHT

Pridi Phanomyong (1900–83) was a French-educated lawyer and a civilian leader in the 1932 revolution and People's Party. His work on democratic reforms in Thailand was based on constitutional measures and attempts to restrict by law military involvement in Thai politics. He supported nationalisation of land and labour, state-led industrialisation and labour protection. In 1934, he founded Thammasat University. He also served as the figurehead of Seri Thai (the resistance movement against WWII Japanese occupation of Thailand) and was Thai prime minister (1946).

Though acknowledged as a senior statesman, Pridi Phanomyong was a controversial figure and a major foe of Phibul and the military regimes. He was accused of being a communist by his critics and forced out of the country under suspicion of regicide. Since the thawing of the Cold War, his legacy has been re-examined and recognised for its democratic efforts and the counterbalancing effects it had on military interests. He was named one of Unesco's great personalities of the 20th-century world in 2000.

Party was not unified in its vision of a democratic Thailand, and before general elections were held the military wing of the party seized control of the government. The leader of the civilian wing of the People's Party, Pridi Phanomyong, a French-educated lawyer, was forced into exile in 1933 after introducing a socialist-leaning economic plan that angered the military generals. Thailand's first popular election was held in 1937 for half of the seats in the People's Assembly, the newly instated legislative body. General Phibul Songkhram, one of the military leaders, became prime minister, a position he held from 1938 to 1944 and again from 1948 to 1957.

Phibul's regime coincided with WWII and was characterised by strong nationalistic tendencies of 'nation' and 'Thai-ness'. He collaborated with the Japanese and allowed them to use Thailand as a staging ground for their invasion of other Southeast Asian nations. The Phibul government was hoping the allegiance would restore historical territory lost during France's expansion of Indochina. Thailand intended to declare war on the US and Britain during WWII. But Seni Pramoj, the Thai ambassador in Washington and a member of Seri Thai (the Thai Liberation Movement), refused to deliver the formal declaration of war, thus saving Thailand from bearing the consequences of defeated-nation status. Phibul was forced to resign in 1944 and was tried for war crimes.

For a brief period after the war, democracy flourished: full elections for the People's Assembly were held and the 1946 constitution sought to reduce the role of the military and provide more democratic rights. It lasted until the death of King Ananda, the pretext the military used to return to power with Phibul at the helm.

1935

King Prajadhipok (Rama VII) becomes the only Thai king to abdicate. The government chooses Prince Mahidol to replace him.

1939

The country's English name is officially changed from Siam to Thailand.

1941

Japanese forces enter Thailand during WWII.

1945

WWII ends; Thailand cedes seized territory from Laos, Cambodia and Malaysia.

Military Dictatorships

In 1957 Phibul's successor, General Sarit Thanarat, subjected the country to a true military dictatorship: abolishing the constitution, dissolving the parliament and banning all political parties. In the 1950s, the US partnered with Sarit and subsequent military dictators Thanom Kittikachorn and Praphat Charusathien (who controlled the country from 1964 to 1973), to allow the US military to develop bases in Thailand during the war in Vietnam in exchange for economic incentives.

By 1973, an opposition group of left-wing activists, mainly intellectuals and students, organised political rallies demanding a constitution from the military government. On 14 October that year the military brutally suppressed a large demonstration in Bangkok, killing 77 people and wounding more than 800. The event is commemorated by a monument on Th Ratchadamnoen Klang in Bangkok, near the Democracy Monument. King Bhumibol stepped in and refused to support further bloodshed, forcing Thanom and Praphat to leave Thailand.

In the following years, the left-oriented student movement grew more radical, creating fears among working-class and middle-class Thais of home-grown communism. In 1976 Thanom returned to Thailand (ostensibly to become a monk) and was received warmly by the royal family. In response, protesters organised demonstrations at Thammasat University against the perceived perpetrator of the 14 October massacre. Right-wing, anti-communist civilian groups clashed with the students, resulting in bloody violence. In the aftermath, many students and intellectuals were forced underground, and joined armed communist insurgents – known as the People's Liberation Army of Thailand (PLAT) – based in the jungles of northern and southern Thailand.

Military control of the country continued through the 1980s. The government of the 'political soldier', General Prem Tinsulanonda, enjoyed a period of political and economic stability. Prem dismantled the communist insurgency through military action and amnesty programs. But the country's new economic success presented a challenging rival: prominent business leaders who criticised the military's role in government and their now-dated Cold War mentality. Communists, they maintained, should be business partners, not enemies.

Thailand has had 19 constitutions, all rewritten following various miltary coups. Constitution number 20 was being drafted in late 2015. Each new version seeks to allocate power within the branches of government with a bias for the ruling interest (military, royalist or civilian) and against their political foes.

It's Just Business

In 1988, Prem was replaced in fair elections by Chatichai Choonhavan, leader of the Chat Thai Party, who created a government dominated by well-connected provincial business people. His government shifted power away from the bureaucrats and set about transforming Thailand into an 'Asian Tiger' economy. But the business of politics was often bought and sold like a commodity and Chatichai was overthrown by the military

1946
King Bhumibol Adulyadej (Rama IX) ascends the throne; Thailand joins the UN.

1957
Sarit Thanarat leads a coup that introduces military rule that lasts until 1973.

1959
The first tourist authority is created.

1965
Thailand hosts US military bases during the Vietnam War.

on grounds of extreme corruption. This coup demarcated an emerging trend in Thai politics: the Bangkok business community and educated classes siding with the military against provincial business-politicians and their money politics.

In 1992, General Suchinda Kraprayoon inserted himself as prime minister. This was met with popular resistance and the ensuing civilian-military clash was dubbed 'Black May'. Led by former Bangkok mayor Chamlong Srimuang, around 200,000 protesters (called the 'mobile phone mob', representing their rising urban affluence) launched a mass demonstration in Bangkok that resulted in three nights of violence with armed soldiers. On the night of 20 May, King Bhumibol called an end to the violence.

After Black May, a new wave of democracy activists advocated for constitutional reforms. For most of the 1990s, the parliament was dominated by the Democrat Party, which represented the urban middle class and business interests. Its major base of support came from the southern Thai population centres, formerly port towns now dominated by tourism and exports (rubber, tin and fishing). On the other side of the spectrum were the former pro-military politicians based in the central plains and the people of the agrarian northeast in new provincial towns who focused on state-budget distributions. These political lines still exist today.

In 1997, the boom years ended and the Asian economic crisis unfolded. The country's economy was plagued by foreign-debt burdens, a real-estate bubble and a devalued currency. Within months of the crisis, the Thai currency plunged from 25B to 56B per US$1. The International Monetary Fund (IMF) stepped in to impose financial and legal reforms and economic liberalisation programs in exchange for more than US$17 billion to stabilise the Thai currency.

In the aftermath of the crisis, the Democrats returned to power uncontested, but were viewed as ineffective as the economy worsened.

Thaksinocracy & the 2006 Coup

Thaksin Shinawatra was the first prime minister in Thai history to complete a four-year term of office. His sister Yingluck managed three years in power before being deposed.

In 2000, the economic slump began to ease. Thaksin Shinawatra, a telecommunications billionaire and former police officer, and his Thai Rak Thai (TRT or 'Thai Loving Thai') party, won a majority in the elections of 2001. Self-styled as a CEO-politician, Thaksin swiftly delivered on his campaign promises for rural development, including agrarian debt relief, village capital funds and cheap health care.

Thanks to the 1997 constitutional reforms designed to strengthen the prime minister's position, Thaksin's was one of Thailand's most stable elected governments. The surging economy and his bold, if strong-arm, leadership won an outright majority in 2005, introducing one-party rule. His popularity among the working class and rural voters was immense.

1968

Thailand is a founding member of the Association of Southeast Asian Nations (ASEAN).

1973

Thai students, workers and farmers demonstrate for the reinstallation of a democratic government.

1976

Violent suppression of the student movement by the military.

1979

After three years of military rule, elections and parliament are restored.

In 2006 Thaksin was accused of abusing his powers and of conflicts of interest, most notably in his family's sale of their Shin Corporation to the Singaporean government for 73 billion baht (US$1.88 billion), a tax-free gain thanks to legislation he helped craft. Demonstrations in Bangkok called for his ousting and on 19 September 2006, the military staged a bloodless coup that forced Thaksin into exile. General elections were held shortly thereafter, with Thaksin's political allies forming a government led by Samak Sundaravej.

This was an unsatisfactory outcome to the military and the anti-Thaksin group known as People's Alliance for Democracy (PAD), comprised of mainly urban elites nicknamed 'Yellow Shirts' because they wore yellow (the king's birthday colour). It was popularly believed that Thaksin was consolidating power during his tenure so that he could interrupt royal succession.

In September 2008, Samak Sundaravej was unseated by the Constitutional Court on a technicality: while in office, he hosted a TV cooking show deemed to be a conflict of interest. Concerned that another election would result in a Thaksin win, the Yellow Shirts seized control of Thailand's main airports, Suvarnabhumi and Don Mueang, for a week in November 2008 until the military manoeuvred a silent coup and another favourable court ruling that further weakened Thaksin's political proxies. Through last-minute coalition building, Democrat Abhisit Vejjajiva was elected in a parliamentary vote, becoming Thailand's 27th prime minister.

Thaksin supporters organised their own counter-movement as the United Front for Democracy Against Dictatorship (UDD), better known as the 'Red Shirts'. Supporters hail mostly from the north and northeast, and include anti-coup, pro-democracy activists; anti-royalists; and die-hard Thaksin fans. There is a degree of class struggle, with many working-class Red Shirts expressing bombastic animosity towards the aristocrats.

The Red Shirts' most provocative demonstration came in 2010, when Thailand's Supreme Court ordered the seizure of US$46 billion of Thaksin's assets after finding him guilty of abusing his powers as prime minister. The Red Shirts occupied Bangkok's central shopping district for two months and demanded the dissolution of the government and reinstatement of elections. In May 2010 the military used force to evict the protesters, resulting in bloody clashes where 91 people were killed and shopping centres were set ablaze (US$1.5 billion of crackdown-related arson damage was estimated).

In 2011, general elections were held and Thaksin's politically allied Puea Thai party won a parliamentary majority, with Thaksin's sister Yingluck Shinawatra elected as prime minister.

The Thai national anthem is played on TV and radio stations at 8am and 6pm. The video that accompanies the TV broadcast shows a multi-ethnic, multi-religious Thailand living in harmony under the national flag.

1980

Prem Tinsulanonda's government works to undermine the communist insurgency movement and eventually ends it with a political solution.

1988

Chatichai Choonhavan becomes first elected PM since 1976.

1991–2

General Suchinda attempts to seize power; King Bhumibol intervenes to halt civil turmoil surrounding 'Black May' protests.

1997

Asian economic crisis; passage of historic 'people's constitution'.

The Yingluck Years

Yingluck Shinawatra became both the first female prime minister of Thailand and the country's youngest-ever premier after her Puea Thai party won a landslide victory in the 2011 election. But throughout her time in power, Yingluck faced accusations that she was just a proxy for her older brother Thaksin, forced into exile following the 2006 coup. Accounts of his influence over the Yingluck government circulated in Bangkok, with Thaksin said to be joining cabinet meetings by Skype from his homes in London, Dubai and Hong Kong.

Certainly, Puea Thai under Yingluck continued the same focus on economic policies designed to help the rural poor of the north and northeast of Thailand, the Shinawatra power base, that had characterised the Thaksin-dominated governments of the previous decade. That, and the belief that the Yingluck government was a Thaksin administration in all but name, ensured that Yingluck faced bitter opposition to her rule from the very start.

It was one of those controversial policies that helped spark the protests that resulted in Yingluck becoming the second Shinawatra to be ousted in a coup. The so-called rice-pledging scheme was designed to boost the incomes of small farmers: the government would buy their rice at above market rates, stockpile it – forcing global prices up – and then sell it at a handsome profit. But the scheme went disastrously wrong, when India lifted its ban on rice exports and flooded the world market with grains. Thailand, the world's biggest rice exporter until 2012, could only watch as prices sank. The damage to the economy was huge, while millions of baht were alleged to have disappeared into the hands of the politicians and officials overseeing the policy. In May 2014, Yingluck was indicted on charges relating to the scheme.

Equally contentious was Yingluck's misguided attempt to introduce an amnesty bill that would have pardoned various politicians, including Thaksin, for charges dating back to 2004. This was widely seen as the prelude to the return of Thaksin to Thailand. Street demonstrations against the government began in October 2013, led by former deputy prime minister Suthep Thaugsuban and his coalition of anti-government groups known as the People's Democratic Reform Committee. Calling for Yingluck and the government to step down and for an end to corruption, the protesters started occupying government buildings, Lumphini Park and several key intersections in central Bangkok.

The Democrat Party (Phak Prachathipat), founded in 1946, is now the longest-surviving political party in Thailand.

In January 2014, Yingluck declared a state of emergency in Bangkok. The following month, a snap general election was boycotted by the opposition Democrat Party. With sporadic violence between Yingluck's supporters and opponents breaking out, Yingluck and nine of her ministers were forced to step down by the Constitutional Court on 7 May. Fifteen

2001

Telecommunications tycoon Thaksin Shinawatra is elected prime minister.

2004

Indian Ocean tsunami kills over 5000 people in Thailand and damages tourism and fishing industries; Muslim insurgency reignites in the Deep South.

2006

King Bhumibol celebrates 60th year on the throne; Thaksin government overthrown in a coup and prime minister forced into exile.

2008

Cambodia successfully petitions Unesco to list Phra Wihan as a World Heritage Site, reigniting border tensions; Yellow Shirt, pro-royalist activists seize Bangkok's international airports, causing a weeklong shutdown.

PROTESTERS FOR HIRE

Anyone who saw the central Bangkok street demonstrations by anti-government protesters in 2013 and 2014 might have thought they were witnessing genuine people power in action. But many of the demonstrators were paid to be there: bussed in from southern Thailand (the stronghold of the Democrat Party) and given wages to sit and block key intersections for months in an effort to force the Puea Thai government from power.

days later, the military launched a coup and took over Thailand for the 13th time since 1932.

Troubles in the Border Regions

Since 2001, Thailand has been fighting a low-level war with ethnic Malay Muslim separatist insurgents in the southernmost provinces of Pattani, Narathiwat and Yala, collectively known as the Deep South. These provinces once comprised the historic sultanate of Patani until it was conquered by the Chakri kings. During WWII, a policy of nation-building set out to transform the multi-ethnic, multi-religious society into a unified and homogeneous Thai Buddhist nation. This policy was resisted in the Deep South and gave birth to an ongoing separatist movement. In the 1980s and '90s, the assimilation policy was abandoned and Prem, prime minister at the time, brokered peace through support for Muslim cultural rights and religious freedoms, amnesty to the armed insurgents and economic development for the historically impoverished region.

The Thaksin regime took another approach to the region. Greater central control from Bangkok was exerted, and was viewed as a thinly disguised policy to break up the traditional stronghold of the Democrat Party. The Muslim population of the Deep South did not respond favourably. In 2002, the government dissolved the long-standing inspectorate and the joint civilian-police-military border-security office – a unit often lauded for maintaining peace and stability and providing a communication link between the Thai government and the southern Muslims. In its place the Thai provincial police assumed control of security, though they lacked perceived moral authority and the support of the local population. In 2004, the government responded harshly to demonstrations that resulted in the Krue Se Mosque and Tak Bai incidents, which together cost the lives of at least 180 Muslims, many of them unarmed civilians. In 2005, martial law was declared in the area.

In 2015, the different insurgent groups united under the umbrella-group title of Mara Patani and began negotiating directly with the government, with talks being held in Malaysia. But after more than a

2009

Red Shirt protesters force the cancellation of the Fourth East Asia Summit in Pattaya. A state of emergency is declared in Bangkok.

2010

Red Shirt, pro-Thaksin activists occupy central Bangkok for two months; military crackdown results in 91 deaths.

2011

Yingluck Shinawatra becomes Thailand's first female prime minister; devastating floods inundate industrial region.

2012

Multiple car bombings across the Deep South in March leave 16 people dead and over 300 injured.

decade of violence, there is still no end in sight to the conflict. Successive governments have not made ending the insurgency a priority, and many Thais are only dimly aware of why their army continues to fight in the Deep South.

Politics & Government

Much of the political drama that has unfolded since the 2006 coup involves a long-standing debate about how to structure Thailand's legislative body and, ultimately, who gets greater control. The National Assembly (or parliament of Thailand) currently has 630 members divided into two chambers (the House of Representatives and Senate), with a mix of seats being popularly elected and elected by party vote. The ratio of seats being popularly elected changes with each replacement constitution. The 1997 version, dubbed the 'People's Constitution', called for both chambers to be fully elected by popular vote. This power to the people paved the way for Thaksin and his Thai Rak Thai party to gain nearly complete control. The military and the elites have since questioned the benefits of full democracy in Thailand.

Voting in Thailand is compulsory for all eligible citizens, apart from monks and other religious figures who are barred from participating in elections.

When Thai voters go to the polls they cast a ballot for the constituency member of parliament (MP) and for their preferred party, the results of which are used to determine individual winners and proportional representation outcomes for the positions assigned by party vote. The prime minister is the head of the government and is elected via legislative vote by the majority party.

Voting in Thailand is compulsory for all eligible citizens (over the age of 18), but members of the clergy are not allowed to vote. Voter turnout for national elections was 75% in 2011, down from 78% in 2007. Charges of vote-buying typically accompany every election. Anecdotally, local party leaders make their rounds through the villages handing out money for the promise of a vote. In some cases, villagers will accept money from competing parties and report that they have no loyalty at the ballot box.

The ballots include a 'no' vote if the voter wishes to choose 'none of the above', intended as an option for compulsory voters who dislike all of their options. It is also common to 'spoil' the ballot, or disqualify it, by writing on it or defacing it. During the 2005 general election a large number of ineligible ballots contained anti-Thaksin messages. In the 2011 election, Yellow Shirts mounted a 'vote no' campaign as a political demonstration against the current political system that they charged was corrupt. The Democrat Party went a step further in the February 2014 election, refusing to participate at all.

2013
Peace talks start, then stall, with southern militants.

2014
The military stage their 13th coup since 1932, overthrowing Yingluck Shinawatra's Puea Thai government.

2015
The military's proposed new constitution is rejected by lawmakers, delaying elections until 2017.

2016
ASEAN common market goes into effect, tying Thailand closer to its neighbours.

People & Culture

Thailand's cohesive national identity provides a unifying patina for ethnic and regional differences that evolved through historical migrations and geographic kinships with ethnically diverse neighbours.

Ethnic Makeup

Some 75% of the citizens of Thailand are ethnic Thais, providing a superficial view of sameness. But subtle regional differences exist. In the central plains (Chao Phraya delta), Siamese Thais united the country through its historic kingdoms and promulgated its culture and language. Today the central Thai dialect is the national standard and Bangkok exports a unified culture through popular media and standardised education.

Above Akha girl

The northeast (Isan) has always stood apart from the rest of the country, sharing closer ethnic and cultural ties with Laos and the Thai Lao people. In the northeastern provinces that border Cambodia, there is a distinct Khmer influence as many families migrated across the border during historical tumult. A minority tribe, known as Suay, lives near Surin and Khorat (Nakhon Ratchasima) and are traditional elephant mahouts.

Thailand Demographics

Population: 67.9 million

Fertility rate: 1.6

Percentage of people over 65: 9.9%

Urbanisation rate: 3%

Life expectancy: 74.4 years

Thai Pak Tai people define the characteristics of the south. The dialect is a little faster than standard Thai and there is more mixing of Muslim folk beliefs into the regional culture thanks to the geographic proximity to Malaysia and the historic Muslim population.

If you were to redraw Thailand's borders according to ethnicity, northern Thailand would be united with parts of southern China and northern Myanmar. The traditional homeland of the Tai people was believed to be the Yúnnán region of China. There are also many sub-groups, including the Shan (an ethnic cousin to the Thais who settled in the highlands of Burma) and the Tai Lü (who settled in Nan and Chiang Rai Provinces as well as the Vietnam highlands).

After the Thai Chinese – the most numerous ethnic minority in Thailand, with a population of just under 9.5 million – the second-largest group is the Malays (4.6%), most of whom reside in the provinces of the Deep South. The remaining minority groups include smaller percentages of non-Thai-speaking people such as the Vietnamese, Khmer, Mon, Semang (Sakai), Moken (*chow lair,* also spelt *chao leh;* people of the sea, or 'sea gypsies'), Htin, Mabri, Khamu and a variety of hill tribes. A small number of Europeans and other non-Asians reside in Bangkok and the provinces.

Thai Chinese

People of Chinese ancestry – second- or third-generation Hakka, Teochew, Hainanese or Cantonese – make up 14% of the population, the world's largest overseas Chinese population. Bangkok and the nearby coastal areas have a large population of immigrants from China who came for economic opportunities in the early to mid-20th century. Historically wealthy Chinese introduced their daughters to the royal court as consorts, developing royal connections and adding a Chinese bloodline that extends to the current king.

The mercantile centres of most Thai towns are run by Thai-Chinese families and many places in the country celebrate Chinese festivals such as the annual Vegetarian Festival.

ECONOMIC MIGRANTS

Thailand unofficially hosts up to 3 million migrant workers, mainly from Myanmar (an estimated 2 million) and to a lesser extent Laos and Cambodia. The majority are low-skilled workers from economically depressed or politically unstable areas, with little to no formal education. Often in the country illegally, they frequently have no labour protections; labour rights groups estimate that most work for half the minimum wage, if they are paid at all, and medical insurance may be nonexistent. Fisheries, garment factories and construction sites depend heavily on migrant labour. Although the Thai government maintains a national verification process that has registered about half of the estimated guest workers, the rules require them to return home for up to four years before being allowed to return for a renewed work permit. Such punitive measures and expensive brokerage fees deter many migrants from becoming legitimate workers.

Mien women

Chinese Buddhist temples, often highly colourful and displaying an allegiance again to southern Chinese folklore and belief, are widespread, especially in the south. Temples to Mazu (Tianhou; Tienhau) – the Queen of Heaven and goddess of fisherfolk and those who make their living from the sea – are common and typical of the southern seaboard provinces of China from where many Thai Chinese can trace their ancestors. You will also encounter temples to Guandi, colloquially known as the God of War and frequently red-faced, as well as a host of other Taoist deities, some deeply obscure. Guanyin – the Buddhist Chinese Goddess of Mercy – is also widely venerated by the Thai Chinese as are other bodhisattvas who enjoy similar adoration throughout China. Chinese guildhalls and ancestral halls are also plentiful.

Thai Muslims

At around 4% of the population, Muslims make up Thailand's largest religious minority, living side by side with the Buddhist majority. To this day, many of Thailand's Muslims reside in the south, but an ever greater number is scattered through the nation. Most of Thailand's southern Muslims are ethnically Malay and speak Malay or Yawi (a dialect of Malay written in the Arabic script) in addition to Thai. In northern Thailand there is also a substantial number of Chinese Muslims who emigrated from Yúnnán in the late 19th century.

Hill Tribes

Ethnic minorities in the mountainous regions of northern Thailand are often called 'hill tribes', or in Thai vernacular, *chow kŏw* (mountain people). Each hill tribe has its own language, customs, mode of dress and spiritual beliefs.

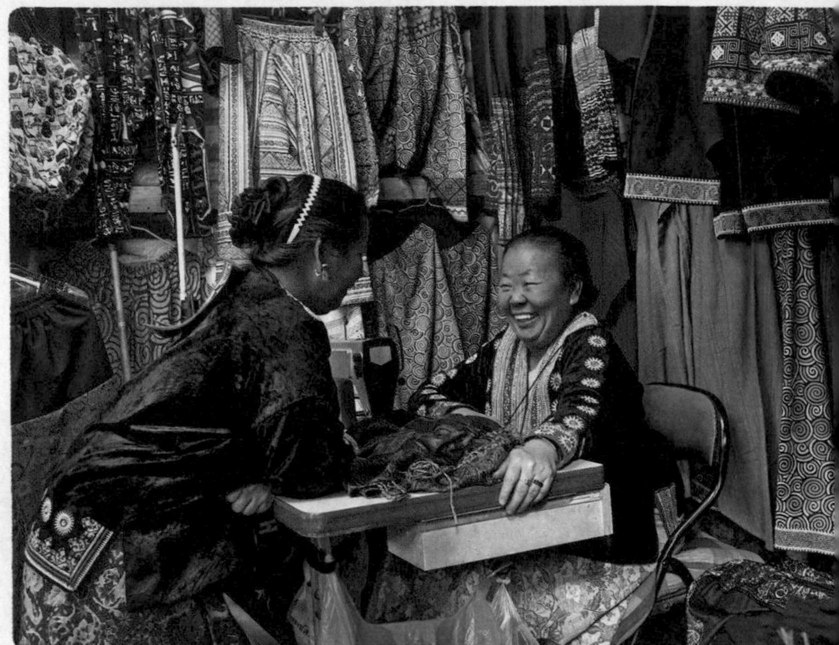

Hmong women

Most are of semi-nomadic origin, having come from Tibet, Myanmar, China and Laos during the past 200 years or so. They are 'fourth-world' people in that they belong neither to the main aligned powers nor to the developing nations. Language and culture constitute the borders of their world. Some groups are caught between the 6th and 21st centuries, while others have assimilated into modern life. The Tribal Research Institute in Chiang Mai recognises 10 different hill tribes but there may be up to 20. Hill tribes are increasingly integrating into the Thai mainstream and many of the old ways and traditional customs are disappearing.

Akha (I-kaw)

Population: 70,000
Origin: Tibet
Present locations: Thailand, Laos, Myanmar, Yunnan
Belief system: Animism with an emphasis on ancestor worship; some groups are Christian
Cultural characteristics: The Akha are among the poorest of Thailand's ethnic minorities and reside mainly in Chiang Mai and Chiang Rai Provinces, along mountain ridges or steep slopes 1000m to 1400m in altitude. They're regarded as skilled farmers but are often displaced from arable land by government intervention. The well-known Akha Swing Ceremony takes place from mid-August to mid-September, between rice planting and harvest time. Akha houses are constructed of wood and bamboo, usually atop short wooden stilts and roofed with thick grass. At the entrance of every traditional Akha village stands a simple wooden ceremonial 'spirit gate' to which Akha shamans affix various charms made from bamboo strips to prevent malevolent spirits from entering.

Standing next to each village gateway are crude wooden figures of a man and a woman, each bearing exaggerated sexual organs, in the belief that human sexuality is abhorrent to the spirit world.

Akha are focused on family ties and will recite their personal genealogies upon first meetings to determine a shared ancestor.

Their traditional clothing consists of a headdress of beads, feathers and dangling silver ornaments.

With many different dialects, the tonal Akha language belongs to the Lolo branch of the Tibeto-Burman family. The language has no written form.

Hmong (Mong or Maew)

Population: 151,000
Origin: South China
Present locations: South China, Thailand, Laos, Vietnam
Belief system: Animism
Cultural characteristics: Divided into two subgroups (White Hmong and Blue Hmong), the Hmong are Thailand's second-largest hill-tribe group and are especially numerous in Chiang Mai Province with smaller enclaves in the other northern Thai provinces. They usually live on mountain peaks or plateaus above 1000m. Kinship is patrilineal and polygamy is permitted.

Hmong tribespeople wear simple black jackets and indigo or black baggy trousers with striped borders (White Hmong) or indigo skirts (Blue Hmong) and silver jewellery. Sashes may be worn around the waist, and embroidered aprons draped front and back. Most women wear their hair in a bun.

A MODERN PERSPECTIVE ON THE HILL TRIBES

Hill tribes tend to have among the lowest standards of living in Thailand. Although it could be tempting to correlate this with traditional lifestyles, their situation is compounded, in most cases, by not having Thai citizenship. Without the latter, they are technically illegal residents in the country of their birth. Without legal status they don't have the right to own land, educate their children, earn a minimum wage or access health care. In the last decades some hill-tribe groups have been issued Thai identification cards, which enable them to access national programs (in theory, though, extra 'fees' might prevent families from being able to afford public schooling and health care). Other hill-tribe families have received residency certificates that restrict travel outside of an assigned district, in turn limiting access to job opportunities associated with a mobile modern society.

Furthermore, the Thai government has pursued a 30-year policy of hill-tribe relocation, often moving villages from fertile agricultural land to infertile land, in turn removing the tribes from a viable subsistence system in which tribal customs were intact to a market system in which they can't adequately compete and in which tribal ways have been fractured.

In the past decade, the expansion of tourism into the mountainous regions of the north presents a complicating factor to the independence of hill-tribe villages. City speculators will buy land from hill-tribe farmers for fairly nominal sums only to be resold, usually to resorts, for much higher costs if the documentation of ownership can be procured. (In many cases the hill-tribe farmer doesn't own the land rights and has very little bargaining power when approached by outsiders.) The displaced farmer and his family might then migrate to the city, losing their connection to their rural and tribal lifestyle, and with few resources to succeed in the lowland society.

Karen (Yang or Kariang)

Population: 500,000
Origin: Myanmar
Present locations: Thailand, Myanmar
Belief system: Animism, Buddhism, Christianity, depending on the group
Cultural characteristics: Numbering about 47% of the total tribal population, the Karen are the largest hill-tribe group in Thailand. They tend to live in lowland valleys and practise crop rotation rather than swidden (slash-and-burn) agriculture. Their numbers and proximity to mainstream society have made them the most integrated and financially successful of the hill-tribe groups. Karen homes are built on low stilts or posts, with the roofs swooping quite low. There are four distinct Karen groups: the Skaw (White) Karen, Pwo Karen, Pa-O (Black) Karen and Kayah (Red) Karen.

Thickly woven V-neck tunics of various colours are typically worn (though unmarried women wear white). Kinship is matrilineal and marriage is monogamous.

Karen languages are tonal and belong to the Sino-Tibetan family.

The Lahu people are known for their strict adherence to gender equality.

Lahu (Musoe)

Population: 103,000
Origin: Tibet
Present locations: Southwest China, Thailand, Myanmar
Belief system: Theistic animism; polytheistic; some groups are Christian
Cultural characteristics: The Thai term for this tribe, *moo·seu,* is derived from a Burmese word meaning 'hunter', a reference to their skill in the forest. The Lahu, originating in the Tibetan plateau, tend to live at about 1000m in remote areas of Chiang Mai, Chiang Rai and Tak Provinces. They typically live in mixed ethnic villages and are an ethnically diverse group with five main subsets: Red Lahu (the most numerous Lahu group in Thailand), Black Lahu, White Lahu, Yellow Lahu and Lahu Sheleh. Houses are built of wood, bamboo and grass, and usually stand on short wooden posts. Lahu food is probably the spiciest of all the hill-tribe cuisines.

Traditional dress consists of black-and-red jackets with narrow skirts worn by women; bright green or blue-green baggy trousers worn by men.

The tonal Lahu language belongs to the Lolo branch of the Tibeto-Burman family.

Lisu (Lisaw)

Population: 55,000
Origin: Tibet
Present locations: Thailand, Yunnan (China)
Belief system: Animism with ancestor worship and spirit possession
Cultural characteristics: Lisu villages are usually in the mountains at an elevation of about 1000m and occur in eight Thai provinces: Chiang Mai, Chiang Rai, Mae Hong Son, Phayao, Tak, Kamphaeng Phet, Sukhothai and Lampang. Patrilineal clans have pan-tribal jurisdiction, which makes the Lisu unique among hill-tribe groups (most of which have power centred with either a shaman or a village headman). Homes are built on the ground and consist mostly of bamboo and thatched grass.

The women wear long multicoloured tunics over trousers and sometimes black turbans with tassels. Men wear baggy green or blue pants pegged in at the ankles.

Closely related to Akha and Lasu, the tonal Lisu language belongs to the Lolo branch of the Tibeto-Burman family.

Lisu people

Mien (Yao)
Population: 35,500
Origin: Central China
Present locations: Thailand, south China, Laos, Myanmar, Vietnam
Belief system: Animism with ancestor worship, Taoism, Buddhism and Christianity
Cultural characteristics: The Mien are highly skilled at crafts such as embroidery and silversmithing. They settle near mountain springs at between 1000m and 1200m with a concentration in Nan, Phayao and Chiang Rai Provinces and a few communities elsewhere. Migration into Thailand increased during the American War era when the Mien collaborated with the CIA against Pathet Lao; 50,000 Mien refugees were resettled in the US. The Mien are influenced by Chinese traditions and use Chinese characters to write their language, although a unified script was also developed in the 1980s. Kinship is patrilineal and marriage is polygamous. Houses are built at ground level, out of wood or bamboo thatch.

Women wear trousers and black jackets with intricately embroidered patches and red furlike collars, along with large dark-blue or black turbans. Men wear black tunics and black pants.

Mien is a tonal language and belongs to the Hmong-Mien language family.

The Thai Character

Much of Thailand's cultural value system is hinged upon respect for the family, religion and monarchy. Within that system each person knows his or her place and Thai children are strictly instructed in the importance of group conformity and suppressing confrontational views. In most social situations, establishing harmony often takes a leading role and Thais take personal pride in making others feel at ease.

Sà·nùk

In general, Thais place high value on *sà·nùk*, which means 'fun'. It is often regarded as a necessary underpinning of anything worth doing. Even work and studying should have an element of *sà·nùk,* otherwise they automatically become drudgery. This doesn't mean Thais don't want to work, but they labour best as a group, so as to avoid loneliness and ensure an element of playfulness. Nothing condemns an activity more than *mâi sà·nùk* (not fun). Thais often mix their job tasks with a healthy dose of socialising, from the back-breaking work of rice farming to the tedium of long-distance bus driving.

Thais are fastidious in their personal appearance, often bathing twice a day, and are confused that seemingly wealthy foreigners are so unkempt.

Saving Face

In a similar vein to Chinese people, Thais believe strongly in the concept of saving face, ie avoiding confrontation and endeavouring not to embarrass themselves or other people (except when it's *sà·nùk* to do so). The ideal face-saver doesn't bring up negative topics in conversation, doesn't express firm convictions or opinions and doesn't claim to have an expertise. Agreement and harmony are considered to be the most important social graces.

While Westerners might think of heated discussion as social sport, Thais regard any instance where voices are raised as rude and potentially volatile. Losing your temper causes a loss of face for everyone and Thais who have been crossed may react in extreme ways. Minor embarrassments, such as tripping or falling, might elicit giggles from a crowd of Thais. In this case they aren't taking delight in your mishap, but helping you save face by laughing it off.

Status & Obligation

All relationships in traditional Thai society – and those in the modern Thai milieu as well – are governed by social rank defined by age, wealth, status and personal or political position. The elder position is called *pôo yài* (literally, the 'big person') and is used to describe parents, bosses, village heads, public officials etc. The junior position is called *pôo nóy* (little person) and describes anyone who is subservient to the *pôo yài.* Although this tendency towards social ranking is to some degree shared by many societies around the world, the Thai twist lies in the set of mutual obligations linking the elder to the junior.

Pôo nóy are supposed to show obedience and respect (together these concepts are covered by the single Thai term *greng jai*) towards the elder. Those with junior status are not supposed to question or criticise those with elder status. In the workplace, this means younger staff members are not encouraged to speak during meetings and are expected to do their bosses' bidding.

In return *pôo yài* are obligated to care for or 'sponsor' the *pôo nóy*. It is a paternalistic relationship in which *pôo nóy* can ask for favours involving money or job access. *Pôo yài* reaffirm their rank by granting requests when possible; to refuse would risk a loss of face and status.

The Thai equivalent of giving someone the middle finger is to show them the bottom of the foot.

The protocol defined by the social hierarchy governs almost every aspect of Thai behaviour. Elected or appointed officials occupy one of the highest rungs on the social ladder and often regard themselves as caretakers of the people, a stark contrast to the democratic ideal of being the voice of the people. The complicated personal hierarchy in Thailand often prevents collaboration, especially between those with competing status. This is why Bangkok has several modern-art museums with somewhat anaemic collections rather than one consolidated powerhouse.

Songkran (p30), Bangkok

Most foreign visitors will interact with a simplified version of this elder-junior relationship in the form of *pêe* (elder sibling) and *nórng* (younger sibling). All Thais refer to each other using familial names. Even people unrelated by blood quickly establish who's *pêe* and who's *nórng*. This is why one of the first questions Thais ask new acquaintances is 'How old are you?'

Lifestyle

Individual lifestyles vary according to family background, income and geography. In many ways Bangkok is its own phenomenon where upper- and middle-class Thais wake up to an affluent and modern lifestyle: smartphones, fast food, K-pop music and fashion addictions. The amount of disposable income in Bangkok is unparalleled elsewhere in the country, though affluence throughout the nation is on the rise.

There continues to be a migration from the countryside or small towns to the urban job centres. It was once standard for Thais to send a portion of their pay home to support their parents or dependent children left behind to be raised in the village. This still happens today in some socio-economic strata, but increasingly affluent parents don't need financial help from their adult children. In fact, an important social shift has occurred: parents continue to support their adult children with big-ticket purchases of cars and real estate that entry-level salaries can't afford. As a result, the older generation often criticises today's youth as having an inflated sense of entitlement.

In the provincial capitals, life is more traditional, relatively speaking. The civil servants – teachers and government employees – make up the backbone of the Thai middle class and live in nuclear families in terrace housing estates outside the city centre. Some might live in the older in-town neighbourhoods filled with front-yard gardens growing papayas,

Lifestyle Statistics

Average marriage age for a Thai man/woman: 27/24 years

Minimum daily wage: 300B

Entry-level professional salary: 9000B to 12,000B per month

Monk visiting giant buddha at Wat Si Chum (p256), Sukhothai Historical Park

mangoes and other fruit trees. The business class lives in the city centre, usually in apartments above shops, making for an easy commute but a fairly urban life.

One of the best places to view the Thai 'lifestyle' is at the markets. Day markets sell kitchen staples as well as local produce and regional desserts. Night markets are good for dinner and people-watching as few Thais bother to cook for themselves.

From a demographic perspective, Thailand, like most of Asia, is greying. The 25- to 54-year-old segment of Thai society represents 47% of the total population, a bulge that – as it moves into old age – will grey the country further. Women are pursuing careers instead of husbands; unmarried women now comprise 30% of the population (plus they start to outnumber men in their 30s). With a current growth rate of only around 0.35%, Thailand's population growth rate is low. Successful government-sponsored family-planning efforts and professional opportunities have reduced the fertility rate so successfully – from six children in the 1960s to 1.5 children today – that analysts are now warning of future labour shortages and overextended pension systems.

The official year in Thailand is reckoned from 543 BC, the beginning of the Buddhist Era, so that AD 2013 is BE 2556, AD 2014 is BE 2557 etc.

Religion

Colourful examples of daily worship can be found on nearly every corner. Walk the streets early in the morning and witness the solemn procession of Buddhist monks, with shaved heads and orange-coloured robes, engaged in *bin·dá·bàht*, the daily house-to-house alms food gathering.

Although the country is predominantly Buddhist, other religions often practise alongside one another. Beyond the substantial Muslim minority population of Thailand, there is also a community of around 70,000 Sikhs. More primordial animist beliefs, which long predate Buddhism and Hinduism, survive most noticeably in 'spirit houses' but also in festivals such as animal sacrifice in the Pu Sae Ya Sae festival in Chiang Mai. Loi Krathong also has its origins in animist belief, honouring the spirit of the water.

Buddhism

Approximately 95% of Thai people are Theravada Buddhists, a branch of Buddhism that came from Sri Lanka during the Sukhothai period.

The ultimate end of Theravada Buddhism is *nibbana* ('nirvana' in Sanskrit), which literally means the 'blowing out' or extinction of all grasping and thus of all suffering *(dukkha)*. Effectively, *nibbana* is also an end to the cycle of rebirths (both moment-to-moment and life-to-life) that is existence. In reality, most Thai Buddhists aim for rebirth in a 'better' existence rather than the supramundane goal of *nibbana*. The concept of rebirth is almost universally accepted in Thailand, even by non-Buddhists.

The idea of reincarnation also provides Thais with a sense of humility and interconnectedness. They might observe a creepy-crawly in the bushes and feel that perhaps they too were once like that creature or that a deceased relative now occupies a non-human body. Reflecting Thailand's social stratification, reincarnation is basically a reward or punishment. This is essentially the Buddhist theory of karma, expressed in the Thai proverb *tam dee, dâi dee; tam chôoa, dâi chôoa* (good actions bring good results; bad actions bring bad results). A good person can improve their lot in life today and in future lives by making merit *(tam bun)*.

The Buddhist hierarchy in Thailand is made up of the Tiratana (Triple Gems) – the Buddha, the *dhamma* (the teachings) and the *sangha* (the Buddhist community). Historically, the Thai king has occupied a revered position in Thai Buddhism, often viewed as semi-divine. Thai royal ceremonies remain almost exclusively the domain of Brahman priests, bestowed with the duty of preserving the three pillars of Thai nationhood, namely sovereignty, religion and the monarchy.

Thai Buddhism has no particular Sabbath day but there are holy days *(wan prá)*, which occur every seventh or eighth day depending on phases of the moon. There are also religious holidays, typically marking important events in the Buddha's life.

Merit-Making

Pilgrimages to famous temples are an important feature of domestic tourism. During these visits, merit-making is an individual ritual rather than a congregational affair. Worshippers buy offerings such as lotus buds, incense and candles and present these symbolic gifts to the temple's primary Buddha image. Other merit-making activities include offering food to the temple *sangha*, meditating (individually or in groups), listening to monks chanting *suttas* (Buddhist discourse), and attending a *têht* or *dhamma* talk by the abbot or another respected teacher. Though Thailand is increasingly secular, merit-making remains an important cultural activity often linked to wish fulfilment (finding love or academic success) rather than religious devotion.

Monks & Nuns

Socially, every Thai male is expected to become a monk (*bhikkhu* in Pali; *prá* or *prá pík·sù* in Thai) for a short period in his life, optimally between the time he finishes school and the time he starts a career or marries. A family earns great merit when one of its sons 'takes robe and bowl'. Traditionally, the length of time spent in the wát is three months, during the *pan·săh* (Buddhist lent), which begins in July and coincides with the rainy season. However, nowadays men may spend as little as a week to

Good Reads

Being Dharma: The Essence of the Buddha's Teachings (2001; Ajahn Chah)

Thai Folk Wisdom: Contemporary Takes on Traditional Proverbs (2010; Tulaya Pornpiriyakulchai and Jane Vejjajiva)

Sacred Tattoos of Thailand (2011; Joe Cummings)

HOUSES OF THE HOLY

Many homes or inhabited dwellings in Thailand have an associated 'spirit house', built to provide a residence for the plot of land's *prá poom* (guardian spirits). Based on animistic beliefs that predate Buddhism, guardian spirits are believed to reside in rivers, trees and other natural features and need to be honoured (and placated). The guardian spirit of a particular plot of land is the supernatural equivalent of a mother-in-law, an honoured but sometimes troublesome family member. To keep the spirits happily distracted, Thais erect elaborate dollhouse-like structures where the spirits can 'live' comfortably separated from humans. To further cultivate good relations and good fortune, daily offerings of rice, fruit, flowers and water are made to the spirit house. If the human house is enlarged the spirit house must also be enlarged, so that the spirits do not feel slighted. Spirit houses must be consecrated by a Brahman priest.

accrue merit as monks. Most temporary ordinations occur under the age of 20 years old, when a man may enter the *sangha* as a 10-vow novice *(nairn)*.

Monks are required to shave their heads, eyebrows and any facial hair during their residence in the monastery as a sign of renouncing worldly concerns. They are also required to live an ascetic life free of luxury and eat one meal per day (sometimes two, depending on the temple traditions). Monks who live in the city usually emphasise study of the Buddhist scriptures, while those who opt for the forest temples tend to emphasise meditation. Fully ordained monks perform funeral and marriage rites, conduct sermons and instruct monastic teachings.

The monastery sometimes still serves its traditional role as a social welfare institution. Male children can enter the monastery and receive a free education, a tradition that has been largely replaced by public schooling.

In Thai Buddhism, women who seek a monastic life are given a minor role in the temple that is not equal to full monkhood. A Buddhist nun is known as *mâa chee* (mother priest) and lives as an *atthasila* (eight-precept) nun, a position traditionally occupied by women who had no other place in society. Thai nuns shave their heads, wear white robes and take care of temple chores. Generally speaking, *mâa chee* aren't considered as prestigious as monks and don't have a function in the merit-making rituals of lay people. An increasing number of foreigners come to Thailand to be ordained as Buddhist monks and nuns. If you want to find out more, visit the Buddha Net website (www.buddhanet.net).

Islam

There are some 3000 mosques in Thailand – over 200 in Bangkok alone. Of these mosques, 99% are associated with the Sunni branch of Islam (in which Islamic leadership is vested in the consensus of the Ummah, or Muslim community), and 1% with the Shi'ite branch (in which religious and political authority is given to descendants of the Prophet Mohammed).

Islam was introduced to Thailand's southern region between AD 1200 and 1500 through the influence of Indian and Arab traders and scholars.

Food & Drink

There's an entire universe of amazing dishes once you get beyond 'pad Thai' and green curry, and for many visitors, food is one of the main reasons for choosing Thailand as a destination. Even more remarkable, however, is the locals' own love for Thai food: Thais get just as excited as tourists when presented with a bowl of perfectly prepared noodles, or when seated at a renowned hawker stall. This unabashed enthusiasm for eating, as well as an abundance of fascinating ingredients and influences, has generated one of the most fun and diverse food scenes anywhere in the world.

Staples & Specialities

Rice & Noodles

In Thailand to eat is to eat rice, and for most of the country, a meal is not acceptable without this staple. Thailand maintains the world's fifth-largest area of land dedicated to growing rice, an industry that employs more than half the country's arable land and a significant portion of its population. Rice is so central to Thai food culture that the most common term for 'eat' is *gin kôw* (literally 'consume rice') and one of the most common greetings is *Gin kôw rĕu yang*? (Have you consumed rice yet?).

There are many varieties of rice in Thailand and the country has been among the world's leading rice exporters since the 1960s. The highest grade is *kôw hŏrm má·lí* (jasmine rice), a fragrant long grain so coveted by neighbouring countries that there is allegedly a steady underground business in smuggling out fresh supplies. The grain is customarily served alongside main dishes such as curries, stir-fries or soups, which are lumped together as *gàp kôw* (with rice). When you order plain rice in a restaurant you use the term *kôw bplòw* ('plain rice') or *kôw sŏo·ay* ('beautiful rice'). Residents of Thailand's north and northeast eat *kôw nĕe·o* ('sticky rice'), a glutinous short-grained rice that is cooked by steaming, not boiling. In Chinese-style eateries, *kôw đôm* ('boiled rice'), a watery porridge sometimes employing brown or purple rice, is a common carb.

Thailand is the world's second-largest exporter of rice, and in 2014 exported approximately 10.8 million tonnes of the grain.

Curries & Soups

In Thai, *gaang* (it sounds somewhat similar to the English 'gang') is often translated as 'curry', but it actually describes any dish with a lot of liquid and can thus refer to soups (such as *gaang jèut*) as well as the classic chilli-paste-based curries for which Thai cuisine is famous. The preparation of the latter begins with a *krêu·ang gaang,* created by mashing, pounding and grinding an array of fresh ingredients with a stone mortar and pestle to form an aromatic, extremely pungent-tasting and rather thick paste. Typical ingredients in a *krêu·ang gaang* include dried chilli, galangal, lemongrass, Kaffir lime zest, shallots, garlic, shrimp paste and salt.

Another food celebrity that falls into the soupy category is *đôm yam,* the famous Thai spicy-and-sour soup. Fuelling the fire beneath *đôm yam's* often velvety surface are fresh *prík kêe nŏo* (tiny chillies) or, alternatively, half a teaspoonful of *nám prík pŏw* (a roasted chilli paste). Lemongrass, Kaffir lime leaf and lime juice give *đôm yam* its characteristic tang.

THAI NOODLES 101

In Thailand, noodles are ubiquitous, cheap and tasty. But they're also extremely varied and somewhat complicated to order. So with this in mind, we've provided a crash course in Thai noodles.

The Noodles

You'll find four main kinds of noodle in Thailand. When ordering, it's generally necessary to specify which noodle you want.

Bà·mèe Made from wheat flour and egg, this noodle is yellowish in colour and sold only in fresh bundles.

Kà·nŏm jeen This fine, round noodle is produced by pushing a rice-based dough through a sieve into boiling water.

Sên gŏo·ay đĕe·o The most common type of noodle in Thailand is made from rice flour mixed with water to form a paste, which is then steamed to form wide, flat sheets. The sheets are folded and sliced into various widths ranging from *sên lék* (thin) to *sên yài* (wide).

Wún·sên An almost-clear noodle made from mung-bean starch and water, it features occasionally in noodle soups.

The Dishes

Bà·mèe These eponymous Chinese-style wheat-and-egg noodles are typically served with slices of barbecued pork, a handful of greens and, if you like, wontons.

Gŏo·ay jáp Rice noodles and pork offal served in a fragrant, peppery broth; a dish popular among the Thai-Chinese.

Gŏo·ay đĕe·o kaang A Thai-Islamic dish of rice noodles served with a curry broth, often including garnishes such as tofu, hard-boiled egg and peanuts.

Gŏo·ay đĕe·o lôok chín This dish combines rice noodles in a generally clear broth with pork- or fish-based (or less commonly, beef or chicken) balls; one of the most common types of noodles across the country.

Gŏo·ay đĕe·o reu·a Known as boat noodles because they were previously served from the canals of central Thailand, these intense pork- or beef-based bowls are among the most full flavoured of Thai noodle dishes.

Kà·nŏm jeen This dish, named after its noodle, combines thin rice threads and typically mild, curry-like broth, served topped with a self-selection of fresh and pickled vegetables and herbs. *Kà·nŏm jeen* varies immensely from region to region, and also tends to be one of the cheapest noodle dishes in the country.

Kôw soy Associated with northern Thailand, this dish combines wheat-and-egg noodles and a fragrant, rich, curry-based broth.

Yen đah foh Combining a slightly crimson broth with a variety of meatballs, cubes of blood and crispy greens, this dish is probably the most intimidating and popular noodle dish in Bangkok.

The Seasoning

Thai noodle dishes are often served slightly underseasoned. In these cases it's seen as the eater's job to season the dish, typically using some or all of four common condiments: *prík nám sôm* (sliced mild chillies in vinegar), *nám Ƀlah* (fish sauce), *prík Ƀòn* (dried red chilli, flaked or ground to a near powder) and *nám·đahn* (plain white sugar). In typically Thai fashion, these condiments offer three ways to make the soup hotter – hot and sour, hot and salty, and just plain hot – and one to make it sweet. Many shops also include a shaker of white pepper, and more obscure noodle dishes may be served with condiments such as ground peanuts, ground chilli fried in oil, or Chinese vinegar.

Stir-Fries & Deep-Fries

The simplest dishes in the Thai culinary repertoire are the various *pàt* (stir-fries), introduced to Thailand by the Chinese, who are famed for being able to stir-fry a whole banquet in a single wok.

The list of *pàt* dishes seems endless. Many cling to their Chinese roots, such as the ubiquitous *pàt pàk bûng fai daang* (morning glory flash-fried with garlic and chilli), while some are Thai-Chinese hybrids, such as *pàt pèt* (literally 'spicy stir-fry'), in which the main ingredients, typically meat or fish, are quickly stir-fried with red curry paste.

Tôrt (deep-frying in oil) is mainly reserved for snacks such as *glôo·ay tôrt* (deep-fried bananas) or *Ƀò·Ƀée·a* (egg rolls). An exception is *Ƀlah tôrt* (deep-fried fish), which is a common way to prepare fish.

Thai Food by David Thompson is widely considered the most authoritative English-language book on Thai cooking. Thompson's follow-up, *Thai Street Food*, focuses on more casual street cuisine.

Hot & Tangy Salads

Standing right alongside curries in terms of Thai-ness is the ubiquitous *yam*, a hot and tangy 'salad' typically based around seafood, meat or vegetables.

Lime juice provides the tang, while the abundant use of chilli generates the heat. Most *yam* are served at room temperature, or just slightly warmed by any cooked ingredients. The dish functions equally well as part of a meal or on its own as *gàp glâam*, snack food to accompany a night of boozing.

Nám Prík

Although they're more home than restaurant food, *nám prík*, spicy chilli-based 'dips', are, for the locals at least, among the most emblematic of all Thai dishes. Typically eaten with rice and steamed or fresh vegetables and herbs, they're also among the most regional of Thai dishes – you could probably pinpoint the province you're in by simply looking at the *nám prík* on offer.

Fruits

Being a tropical country, Thailand excels in the fruit department. *Má·môo·ang* (mangoes) alone come in a dozen varieties that are eaten at different stages of ripeness. Other common fruit include *sàp·Ƀà·rót* (pineapple), *má·lá·gor* (papaya) and *đaang moh* (watermelon), all of which are sold from ubiquitous vendor carts and accompanied by a dipping mix of salt, sugar and ground chilli. A highlight of visiting Thailand is sampling the huge variety of indigenous fruits of which you've probably never heard. Many are available year-round nowadays, but April and May is peak season for several of the most beloved varieties, including durian, mangoes and mangosteen.

Bangkok's Top 50 Street Food Stalls by Chawadee Nualkhair also functions well as a general introduction and guide to Thai-style informal dining.

Custard apple Known in Thai as *nóy nàh*, the knobbly green skin of this fruit conceals hard black seeds and sweet, gloopy flesh with a granular texture.

Durian Known in Thai as *tú·ree·an*, the king of fruit is also Thailand's most infamous, due to its intense flavour and odour, which can suggest everything from custard to onions.

Guava A native of South America, *fa·ràng* is a green, apple-like ball containing a pink or white flesh that's sweet and crispy.

Jackfruit The gigantic green pod of *kà·nŭn* – it's considered the world's largest fruit – conceals dozens of waxy yellow sections that taste like a blend of pineapple and bananas (it reminds us of Juicy Fruit chewing gum).

Langsat Strip away the yellowish peel of this fruit, known in Thai as *long·gong*, to find a segmented, perfumed pearlescent flesh with a lychee-like flavour.

Longan *Lam yai* takes the form of a tiny hard ball; it's like a mini lychee with sweet, perfumed flesh. Peel it, eat the flesh and spit out the hard seed.

Maintained by a Thai woman living in the US, She Simmers (www.shesimmers.com) is a good resource for those wanting to make Thai food outside of Thailand.

Lychee The pink skin of *lín·jèe* conceals an addictive translucent flesh similar in flavour to a grape. It's generally only available between April and June.

Mangosteen The hard purple shell of *mang·kút*, the queen of Thai fruit, conceals delightfully fragrant white segments, some containing a hard seed.

Pomelo Like a grapefruit on steroids, *sôm oh* takes the form of a thick pithy green skin hiding sweet, tangy segments. Cut into the skin, peel off the pith and then break open the segments and munch on the flesh inside.

Rambutan People have different theories about what *ngó* look like, not all repeatable in polite company. Regardless, the hairy shell contains sweet translucent flesh that you scrape off the seed with your teeth.

Rose apple Known in Thai as *chom·pôo*, rose apple is an elongated pink or red fruit with a smooth, shiny skin and pale, watery flesh. It's a good thirst quencher on a hot day.

Salak Also known as snake fruit because of its scaly skin. The exterior of *sàlà* looks like a mutant strawberry and the soft flesh tastes like unripe bananas.

Starfruit The star-shaped cross-section of *má·feu·ang* is the giveaway. The yellow flesh is sweet and tangy and believed by many to lower blood pressure.

Sweets

English-language Thai menus often have a section called 'Desserts', but Thai-style sweets are generally consumed as breakfast or a sweet snack, not directly following a meal. Sweets also take two slightly different forms in Thailand. *Kŏrng wăhn,* which translates as 'sweet things', are small, rich sweets that often boast a slightly salty flavour. Prime ingredients for *kŏrng wăhn* include grated coconut, coconut milk, rice flour (from white rice or sticky rice), cooked sticky rice, tapioca, mung-bean starch, boiled taro and various fruits. Egg yolks are a popular ingredient for many *kŏrng wăhn,* including the ubiquitous *fŏy torng* (literally 'golden threads'), probably influenced by Portuguese desserts and pastries introduced during the early Ayuthaya era.

Lonely Planet's *From the Source: Thailand* features authentic recipes straight from the Thai kitchens where they were perfected.

Thai sweets roughly similar to the European concept of pastries are called *kà·nŏm*. Probably the most popular type of *kà·nŏm* in Thailand are the bite-sized items wrapped in banana leaves, especially *kôw đôm gà·tí* and *kôw đôm mát.* Both consist of sticky rice grains steamed with *gà·tí* (coconut milk) inside a banana-leaf wrapper to form a solid, almost taffy-like, mass.

Regional Variations

One little-known (at least outside of Thailand) characteristic of Thai food is its regional diversity. Despite having evolved in a relatively small area, Thai cuisine is anything but a single entity and takes a slightly different form every time it crosses a provincial border. For more on the regional specialities of Thailand, see p44.

Drinks

Coffee, Tea & Fruit Drinks

Thais are big coffee drinkers, and good-quality arabica and robusta are cultivated in the hilly areas of northern and southern Thailand. The traditional filtering system is nothing more than a narrow cloth bag attached to a steel handle. This type of coffee is served in a glass, mixed with sugar and sweetened with condensed milk – if you don't want either, be sure to specify *gah·faa dam* (black coffee) followed with *mâi sài nám·đahn* (without sugar).

Thai Hawker Food by Kenny Yee and Catherine Gordon is an illustrated guide to recognising and ordering street food in Thailand.

Black tea, both local and imported, is available at the same places that serve real coffee. *Chah tai,* Thai-style tea, derives its characteristic orange-red colour from ground tamarind seed added after curing.

Fruit drinks appear all over Thailand and are an excellent way to rehydrate after water becomes unpalatable. Most *nám pŏn·lá·mái* (fruit juices) are served with a touch of sugar and salt and a whole lot of ice. Many foreigners object to the salt, but it serves a metabolic role in helping the body to cope with tropical temperatures.

Beer & Spirits

There are several brands of beer in Thailand, ranging from domestic brands (Singha, Chang, Leo) to foreign-licensed labels (Heineken, Asahi, San Miguel). They are all largely indistinguishable in taste and quality.

Domestic rice whisky and rum are favourites of the working class, struggling students and family gatherings as they're more affordable than beer. Once spending money becomes a priority, Thais often upgrade to imported whiskies. These are usually drunk with lots of ice, soda water and a splash of cola. On a night out, buying a whole bottle is the norm in most of Thailand. If you don't finish it, it will simply be kept at the bar until your next visit.

Pok Pok by Andy Ricker with JJ Goode features recipes of the rustic, regional Thai dishes served at Ricker's eponymous Portland, Oregon, New York City and Los Angeles restaurants.

Vegetarians & Vegans

Vegetarianism isn't a widespread trend in Thailand, but many of the tourist-oriented restaurants cater to vegetarians, and there are also a handful of *ráhn ah·hăhn mang·sà·wí·rát* (vegetarian restaurants) in Bangkok where the food is served buffet-style and is very inexpensive. Dishes are almost always 100% vegan (ie no meat, poultry, fish or fish sauce, dairy or egg products).

During the Vegetarian Festival, celebrated by Chinese Buddhists in September/October, many restaurants and street stalls in Bangkok go meatless for one month.

The phrase 'I'm vegetarian' in Thai is *pŏm gin jair* (for men) or *dì·chăn gin jair* (for women). Loosely translated it means 'I eat only vegetarian food', which includes no eggs and no dairy products – in other words, total vegan.

The downloadable Vegetarian Thai Food Guide (www.eatingthaifood.com/vegetarian-thai-food-guide) is a handy resource for vegetarians visiting Thailand.

Habits & Customs

Like most of Thai culture, eating conventions appear relaxed and informal but are orchestrated by many implied rules.

Whether at home or in a restaurant, Thai meals are always served 'family style' – that is, from common serving platters, with the plates appearing in whatever order the kitchen can prepare them. When serving yourself from a common platter, put no more than one spoonful onto your plate at a time. Heaping your plate with all 'your' portions at once will look greedy to Thais unfamiliar with Western conventions. Another important factor in a Thai meal is achieving a balance of flavours and textures. Traditionally the party orders a curry, a steamed or fried fish, a stir-fried vegetable dish and a soup, taking great care to balance cool and hot, sour and sweet, salty and plain.

Originally Thai food was eaten with the fingers, and it still is in certain regions of the kingdom. In the early 1900s Thais began setting their tables with fork and spoon to affect a 'royal' setting, and it wasn't long before fork-and-spoon dining became the norm in Bangkok and later spread throughout the kingdom. To use these tools the Thai way, use a serving spoon, or alternatively your own, to take a single mouthful of food from a central dish and ladle it over a portion of your rice. The fork is then used to push the now-food-soaked portion of rice back onto the spoon before entering the mouth.

If you're not offered chopsticks, don't ask for them. Chopsticks are reserved for eating Chinese-style food from bowls, or for eating in all-Chinese restaurants. In either case, you will be supplied with chopsticks without having to ask. Unlike their counterparts in many Western countries, restaurateurs in Thailand won't assume you don't know how to use them.

Appon's Thai Food (www.khiewchanta.com) features nearly 1000 authentic and well-organised Thai recipes – many with helpful audio recordings of their Thai names – written by a Thai.

Food Spotter's Guide

Spanning four distinct regions, influences from China to the Middle East, a multitude of ingredients and a reputation for spice, Thai food can be more than a bit overwhelming. So to point you in the direction of the good stuff, we've put together a shortlist of the country's must-eat dishes.

1. Đôm yam
The 'sour Thai soup' moniker featured on many English-language menus is a feeble description of this mouth-puckeringly tart and intensely spicy herbal broth.

2. Pàt tai
Thin rice noodles fried with egg, tofu and shrimp, and seasoned with fish sauce, tamarind and dried chilli, have emerged as the poster boy for Thai food – and justifiably so.

3. Gaang kĕe·o wăhn
Known outside of Thailand as green curry, this intersection of a piquant, herbal spice paste and rich coconut milk is single-handedly emblematic of Thai cuisine's unique flavours and ingredients.

4. Yam
This family of Thai 'salads' combines meat or seafood with a tart and spicy dressing and fresh herbs.

5. Lâhp
Minced meat seasoned with roasted rice powder, lime, fish sauce and fresh herbs is a one-dish crash course in the strong, rustic flavours of Thailand's northeast.

6. Bà·mèe
Although Chinese in origin, these wheat-and-egg noodles, typically served with roast pork and/or crab, have become a Thai hawker-stall staple.

7. Kôw mòk
The Thai version of *biryani* couples golden rice and tender chicken with a sweet and sour dip and a savoury broth.

8. Sôm·đam
'Papaya salad' hardly does justice to this tear-inducingly spicy dish of strips of crunchy unripe papaya pounded in a mortar and pestle with tomato, long beans, chilli, lime and fish sauce.

9. Kôw soy
Even outside of its home in Thailand's north, there's a cult following for this soup that combines flat egg-and-wheat noodles in a rich, spice-laden, coconut-milk-based broth.

10. Pàt pàk bûng fai daang
'Morning glory', a crunchy green vegetable, flash-fried with heaps of chilli and garlic, is, despite the spice, Thai comfort food.

1

6

8

AUSTIN BUSH ©

AUSTIN BUSH ©

AUSTIN BUSH ©

AUSTIN BUSH ©

AUSTIN BUSH ©

AUSTIN BUSH ©

AUSTIN BUSH ©

Arts & Architecture

Thailand possesses an intensely visual culture where an appreciation of beauty and aesthetics infuses everything from extravagant temple buildings and humble old-fashioned houses to the high arts conceived for the royal court. Temple architecture and Buddhist sculpture define the bulk of Thailand's ancient arts but the modern era has seen creativity expressed in multiple forms from social commentary in contemporary paintings to sky-piercing towers in Bangkok. Musical traditions range from classical orchestras to teenage dance anthems and all melodic and harmonic points in between.

Above Wat Phra Kaew (p61), Bangkok

Architecture

The most striking aspect of Thailand's architectural heritage is its frequently magnificent Buddhist temples (wát). As with many Chinese Buddhist temple pagodas, one of the most distinctive features of Buddhist temple architecture is the *chedi* (stupa), a mountain-shaped monument that pays tribute to the enduring stability of Buddhism. Many contain relics of important kings or the historical Buddha or the remains of notable monks or nuns. Thai temples freely mix different foreign influences, from the corn-shaped stupa inherited from the Khmer empire to the bell-shaped stupa of Sri Lanka.

Thai temples are replete with Hindu-Buddhist iconography. *Naga,* a mythical serpentlike creature who guarded Buddha during meditation, is often depicted in entrance railings and outlining roof gables. On the tip of the temple hall roof is the *chôr fâh:* a golden bird-shaped silhouette suggesting flight.

A venerated Buddhist symbol, the lotus bud is another sacred motif that often decorates the tops of temple gates, verandah columns and the spires of Sukhothai-era *chedi*. Images of the Buddha often depict him meditating in a lotus pedestal. It carries with it a reminder of the tenets of Buddhism. The lotus can bloom even from the mud of a rancid pond, illustrating the capacity for religious perfection in a defiled environment.

Thais began mixing traditional architecture with European forms in the late 19th and early 20th centuries. The port cities, including Bangkok and Phuket, acquired fine examples of Sino-Portuguese architecture –

THAILAND'S ARTISTIC & ARCHITECTURAL PERIODS

PERIOD	TEMPLE & CHEDI STYLES	BUDDHA STYLES	EXAMPLES
Dvaravati Period (7th–11th centuries)	Rectangular-based *chedi* (stupas) with stepped tiers	Indian influenced; thick torso, large hair curls, arched eyebrows (like flying birds), protruding eyes, thick lips and flat nose	Phra Pathom Chedi, Nakhon Pathom; Lopburi Museum, Lopburi; Wat Chama Thewi, Lamphun
Srivijaya Period (7th–13th centuries)	Mahayana Buddhist–style temples; Javanese-style *chedi* with elaborate arches	Indian influenced; heavily ornamented, human-like features and slightly twisted at the waist	Wat Phra Mahathat Woramahawihaan and National Museum, Nakhon Si Thammarat
Khmer Period (9th–11th centuries)	Hindu-Buddhist temples; corn-cob shaped *prang* (Khmer-styled *chedi*)	Buddha meditating under a canopy of the seven-headed *naga* and atop a lotus pedestal	Phimai Historical Park, Nakhon Ratchasima; Phanom Rung Historical Park, Surin
Chiang Saen–Lanna Period (11th–13th centuries)	Teak temples; square-based *chedi* topped by gilded umbrella; also octagonal-based *chedi*	Burmese influences with plump figure, round, smiling face and foot-pads facing upwards in meditation pose	Wat Phra Singh, Chiang Mai; Chiang Saen National Museum, Chiang Saen
Sukhothai Period (13th–15th centuries)	Khmer-inspired temples; slim-spired *chedi* topped by a lotus bud	Graceful poses, often depicted 'walking', no anatomical human detail	Sukhothai Historical Park, Sukhothai
Ayuthaya Period (14th–18th centuries)	Classical Thai temple with three-tiered roof and gable flourishes; bell-shaped *chedi* with tapering spire	Ayuthaya-era king, wearing a gem-studded crown and royal regalia	Ayuthaya Historical Park, Ayuthaya
Bangkok-Ratanakosin Period (19th century)	Colourful and gilded temple with Western-Thai styles; mosaic-covered *chedi*	Reviving Ayuthaya style	Wat Phra Kaew, Wat Pho and Wat Arun, Bangkok

Robot Building, Bangkok

buildings of stuccoed brick decorated with an ornate facade – a style that followed the sea traders during the colonial era. It is locally known as 'old Bangkok' or 'Ratanakosin'.

Bangkok Today

Bangkok's skyscrapers are a textbook portfolio of postmodern dos and don'ts. In the 1960s and '70s Thai architecture was inspired by the earlier European Bauhaus movement, promoting stark functionalism – the average building resembled a giant egg carton turned on its side. When Thai architects began experimenting with form over function during the mid-1980s building boom, the result was high-tech designs such as ML Sumet Jumsai's famous machine-age 'Robot Building' (1986) on Th Sathon Tai in Bangkok. Rangsan Torsuwan, a graduate of the Massachusetts Institute of Technology (MIT), introduced the neoclassic (or neo-Thai) style. Rangsan Torsuwan designed the Sathorn Unique Tower; construction commenced in 1990 before grinding to a halt in 1997 and the tower remains derelict today, after being four-fifths completed.

Bangkok today has evolved a more sophisticated architectural aesthetic. Shopping malls, skyscrapers and hotels all incorporate current architectural trends: rounded glass towers, patterned facades, hyper geometry and stark minimalism. Adapting modern architecture to the extremes of a tropical climate has restored some of the functionalism that was lost during the country's rush towards modernisation in decades past. Reclaiming and restoring old buildings is another architectural trend for vintage-oriented youth who view traditional architecture as novel and nostalgic rather than outdated and outmoded.

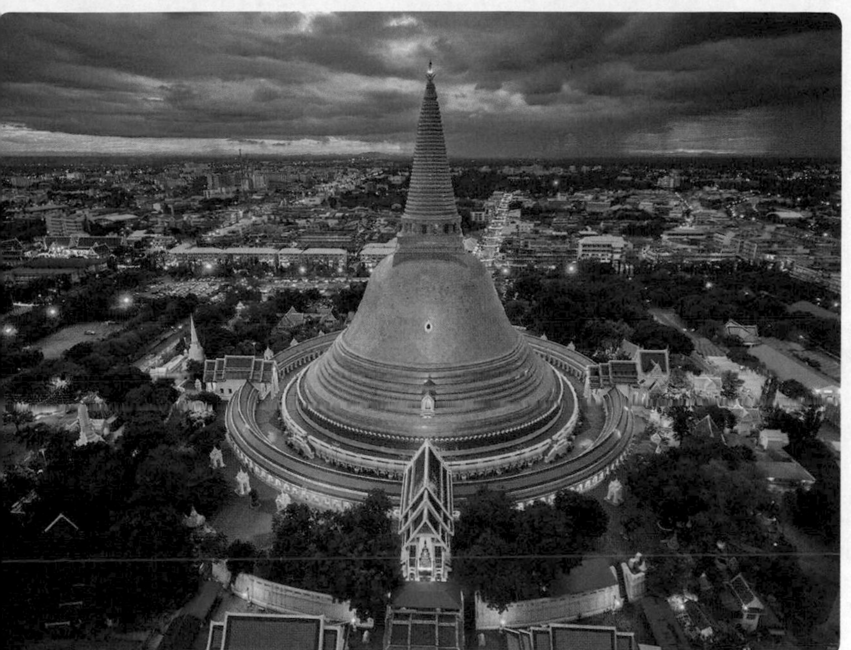

Phra Pathom Chedi (p152), Nakhon Pathom

Arts

Much of Thailand's best ancient art is on display inside the country's myriad hallmark temples, while Bangkok's many national and commercial museums curate more contemporary collections.

Traditional Painting & Sculpture

Thailand's artistic repository resides in its temples, where Buddha sculptures and murals communicate a continuous visual language of the religion. These Buddha images trace Thailand's historical and artistic evolution from a conquered backwater to a sovereign nation.

The country first defined its own artistic style during the Sukhothai era, famous for its graceful and serene Buddha figures. Temple murals are the main form of ancient Thai art. Always instructional in purpose, murals often depict the *jataka* (stories of the Buddha's past lives) and the Thai version of the Hindu epic *Ramayana*. Lacking the durability of other art forms, pre-20th-century religious painting is limited to very few surviving examples. The earliest examples are found at Ayuthaya's Wat Ratburana, but Bangkok is home to some of the best surviving examples.

The development of Thai religious art and architecture is broken into different periods defined by the patronage of the ruling capital. The best examples of a period's characteristics are seen in the variations of the *chedi* shape and in the features of the Buddha sculptures, including facial features, the top flourish on the head, the dress and the position of the feet in meditation.

Bangkok Art Museums & Galleries

- *National Museum*
- *Bangkok Art & Culture Centre*
- *100 Tonson Gallery*
- *H Gallery*
- *Kathmandu Photo Gallery*
- *Museum of Contemporary Art*
- *Silom Galleria*

Contemporary Art

Adapting traditional themes to the secular canvas began around the turn of the 20th century as Western influence surged in the region. In general,

Top Art Books

The Thai House (2002; Ruethai Chaichongrak)

The Arts of Thailand (1998; Steve Van Beek)

Flavours: Thai Contemporary Art (2005; Steven Pettifor)

Bangkok Design (2006; Brian Mertens)

Buddhist Temples of Thailand (2010; Joe Cummings)

Thai painting favours abstraction over realism and continues to preserve the one-dimensional perspective of traditional mural paintings. There are two major trends in Thai art: the updating of religious themes and tongue-in-cheek social commentary, with some artists overlapping the two.

Italian Corrado Feroci is often credited as the father of modern Thai art. He was invited to Thailand by Rama VI in 1923 and built Bangkok's Democracy Monument and other monuments in Bangkok.

In the 1970s Thai artists tackled the modernisation of Buddhist themes through abstract expressionism. Leading works include the colourful surrealism of Pichai Nirand and the mystical pen-and-ink drawings of Thawan Duchanee. Internationally known Montien Boonma uses the ingredients of Buddhist merit-making, such as gold leaf, bells and candle wax, to create installation pieces.

Politically motivated artwork defined a parallel movement in Thai contemporary art. In Thailand's rapidly industrialising society, many artists watched as rice fields became factories, the forests became asphalt and the spoils went to the politically connected. Manit Sriwanichpoom is best known for his Pink Man on Tour series, in which he depicted artist Sompong Thawee in a pink suit with a pink shopping cart amid Thailand's most iconic attractions. Graduate of the College of Fine Art in Bangkok, outspoken artist and poet Vasan Sitthiket is more blatantly controversial and uses mixed-media installations to condemn exploitation and corruption. His often powerful works have been banned in Thailand and criticised as anti-Thai.

In the 1990s there was a push to move art out of museums and into public spaces. Navin Rawanchaikul started his 'in-the-streets' collaborations in his hometown of Chiang Mai and then moved to Bangkok where he filled the city's taxi cabs with art installations, a show that literally went on the road. His other works have a way with words, such as the mixed-media piece *We Are the Children of Rice (Wine)* (2002) and his rage against the commercialisation of museums in his epic painting entitled *Super (M)art Bangkok Survivors* (2004). Up-and-coming artists use a variety of media and take on more introspective topics, like Maitree Siriboon who uses collage and photography to explore personal identity, sexuality and transformation. Born in 1979, Thai-Japanese artist Yuree Kensaku creates allegorical, sometimes surreal cartoon-like paintings with vivid pop culture references. Of her art, she says 'In terms of content, I am often interested in issues of change, relationships with others and my surroundings'.

Historically most closely associated with Buddhist statuary, Thai sculpture today is often considered to be the strongest of the contemporary arts. Influenced by Henry Moore, who taught him, Khien Yimsiri created

HANDMADE ART

Thailand has a long tradition of fascinating handicrafts, often regionally and even village specific. Thai ceramics include the greenish celadon products, red-earth clay pots of Dan Kwian, and central Thailand's *ben·jà·rong* or 'five-colour' style, employing elaborate, multi-coloured enamels on white porcelain. Once exclusively manufactured for the royal court, *ben·jà·rong* is based on Chinese patterns, while celadon is of Thai origin.

Northern Thailand has long produced regionally distinctive lacquerware thanks to the influence of Burmese artisans.

Each region in Thailand has its own silk-weaving style. In ancient times woven textiles might have functioned much like business cards do today – demarcating tribal identity and sometimes even marriage status. Today, village weaving traditions continue but have become less geographically specific.

Top Democracy Monument, Bangkok
Bottom Traditional Thai pottery

ANIRUT RASSAMEESRITRAKOOL / ALAMY STOCK PHOTO ©

Mŏr lam music performance

elegant human and mythical forms from bronze. Manop Suwanpinta moulds the human anatomy into fantastic shapes that often intersect with technology, such as hinged faces that open to reveal inanimate content. Kamin Lertchaiprasert explores the subject of spirituality and daily life in his sculptures. His *Ngern Nang* (Sitting Money) installation included a series of figures made from discarded paper bills from the national bank embellished with poetic instructions on life and love.

Music

Throughout Thailand you'll encounter a rich diversity of musical genres and styles, from the serene court music that accompanies classical dance-drama to the bass-heavy house music shaking dance clubs across the nation.

Classical Music

The classical orchestra is called the *Ъèe âht* and was originally developed to accompany classical dance-drama and shadow theatre, but these days can be heard in straightforward performances at temple fairs and tourist attractions. The ensemble can include from five to more than 20 players. Prior to a performance the players offer incense and flowers to the *đà·pohn* (or *thon*), a double-headed hand drum that sets the tempo for the entire ensemble.

The standard Thai scale divides the eight-note octave into seven full-tone intervals, with no semitones. Thai scales were first transcribed by the Thai-German composer Peter Feit (also known by his Thai name, Phra Chen Duriyang), who composed Thailand's national anthem in 1932.

Lôok Tûng & Mŏr Lam

The best-selling modern musical genre in Thailand is *lôok tûng* (literally 'children of the fields'), which dates to the 1940s. Analogous to country and western music in the USA, it appeals to working-class Thais. Traditional subject matter are tales of lost love, tragic early death, and the dire circumstances of struggling farmers. The plaintive singing style ranges from sentimental to anguish and singers are often backed by Las Vegas-style showgirl dancers.

Mŏr lam is Thailand's blues; it's a folk tradition firmly rooted in northeast Thailand and Laos and is based on the songs played on the *kaan* (a wind instrument devised of a double row of bamboo-like reeds fitted into a hardwood soundbox). The oldest style is most likely to be heard at a village gathering and has a simple but insistent bass beat and is often sung in Isan dialect. With songs frequently dwelling on unrequited love and the hardships of life, *mŏr lam* has jumped the generational fence with an electrified pop interpretation and a seriously silly side.

As economic migrants moved from across the country to Bangkok, the two genres merged with each other as well as with other forms, leading to hybridisation and cross-pollination. Contemporary singers might sing about city woes, factory work or being too fat backed up by a dance club beat.

Thailand's most famous *lôok tûng* singer was Pumpuang Duangjan, a vocalist who received a royally sponsored cremation and a major shrine at Suphanburi's Wat Thapkradan when she died just aged 30 in 1992. Gravelly voiced Siriporn Ampaipong helped carry the tradition afterwards and is still much loved. The new *lôok tûng* princesses are Yingli Sijumpon, a sweetheart from Buriram, and Baitoi R Siam, who has crossed over into sexy pop. Pai Pongsaton and Tai Orathai are other stalwarts while Auu Jeerawat has an acoustic take on the genre.

Music Sources

E Thai Music (www.ethaicd.com) is an online Thai music store

Popular Thai radio stations include Fat FM 104.5 (alt-rock), Seed FM 97.5 (T-pop) and Luk Thung FM95.0 (lôok tûng and mŏr lam)

Thai Rock & Pop

The 1970s ushered in the politically conscious folk rock of the USA and Europe, which the Thais dubbed *pleng pêu·a chee·wít* ('songs for life'). Chiefly identified with the Thai band Caravan, this style defined a major contemporary shift in Thai music, with political and environmental topics replacing the usual love themes. During the authoritarian dictatorships of the '70s many of Caravan's songs were officially banned. Another long-standing example of this style, Carabao, mixed in rock and heavy metal and spawned a whole generation of imitators.

Thailand's thriving teen-pop industry – sometimes referred to as T-pop – first surfaced in the 1970s and 1980s, centred on artists chosen for their good looks, which often means they are half-Thai, half-*fa·ràng* and sport English names. Thailand's king of pop is Thongchai 'Bird' Mcintyre (also known as Pi Bird). His first album hit the shelves in 1986 and he has followed up with an album almost every year since. With

TRADITIONAL INSTRUMENTS

Ɓée High-pitched woodwind, often heard at Thai-boxing matches

rá·nâht èhk Bamboo-keyed percussion that resembles a xylophone

kórng wong yài Tuned gongs arranged in a semicircle

đà·pohn (tohn) A double-headed hand-drum

pĭn Four-stringed instrument plucked like a guitar

sor Slender bowed instrument with a coconut-shell soundbox

klòo·i Wooden flute

George Michael's staying power coupled with a nice-guy persona, he is highly popular with Thais in their 30s and 40s.

The 1990s gave birth to an alternative pop scene – known as 'indie' – pioneered by the independent record label Bakery Music. During indie's heyday, Modern Dog, composed of four Chulalongkorn University graduates, orchestrated the generation's musical coming of age. Another indie fixture was Loso (from 'low society' as opposed to 'hi-so' or socialites), which updated Carabao's affinity for Thai folk melodies and rhythms. The noughties saw these bands move towards classic rock status, while Bakery Music was bought by a conglomerate.

The alt scene lives in a variety of forms – lounge pop, garage rock and electronica. Tattoo Colour hailing from Khon Kaen managed to score several hits from a small indie label. The female trio Yellow Fang has a following for its once-a-year single releases. The revived disco sound of Groove Riders has brought down the tempo but upped the funky factor. Electro-rock band Futon announced their arrival with a catchy version of Iggy Pop's 'I Wanna Be Your Dog' in 2003. Endorphine was a feel-good noughties band led by sweet-faced Da with almost a decade's worth of hits; Da later went solo. Bangkok rockers Ebola have notched up two decades' worth of song writing, while hip hop band Thaitanium have been rapping since the millennium.

The current crop of pop stars imitate Korean pop stars' (Japan pop, or J-pop, is out) signature dance moves. Apple Girl Band (as in Apple products) uses Apple apps to make music. Other contemporary stars include girl duo Four-Mod, who have enjoyed a string of hit singles, poster trio FFK (Faye Fang Kaew) and twin sisters Neko Jump.

Thailand Playlist

- *That Song (Modern Dog)*
- *The Sound of Siam: Leftfield Luk Thung, Jazz & Molam in Thailand 1964–1975 (Soundway Records compilation)*
- *Made in Thailand (Carabao)*
- *Best (Pumpuang Duangjan)*
- *Romantic Comedy (Apartment Khunpa)*
- *I Wanna Be Your Dog (Futon)*

Dance & Theatre

Thailand's high arts have endured decline since the palace transitioned from a cloistered community, although some endangered art forms have been salvaged and revived for a growing tourist community. Folk traditions enjoy broader appeal, though the era of village stage shows is sadly long gone.

Thailand's most famous dance-drama is *kŏhn*, which depicts the *Ramakian*, the Thai version of India's *Ramayana*. The central story revolves around Prince Rama's search for his beloved Princess Sita, who has been abducted by the evil 10-headed demon Ravana and taken to the island of Lanka. Dancers are clothed in elaborate costumes with some characters masked.

Every region has its own traditional dance style performed at temple fairs and provincial parades. Occasionally temples also provide shrine dancers, who are commissioned by merit-makers to perform. School-aged children often take traditional Thai dance lessons.

Most often seen at Buddhist festivals, *lí·gair* is a gaudy, raucous theatrical art form thought to have descended from drama rituals brought to southern Thailand by Arab and Malay traders. A colourful mix of folk and classical music, outrageous costumes, melodrama, slapstick comedy, sexual innuendo and up-to-date commentary, it's partly improvised.

Puppet theatre also enjoyed royal and common patronage. *Lá·kon lék* (little theatre) used marionettes of varying sizes for court performances similar to *kŏhn*. Two to three puppet masters are required to manipulate the metre-high puppets by means of wires attached to long poles. Stories are drawn from Thai folk tales, particularly *Phra Aphaimani*, and occasionally from the *Ramakian*.

Shadow-puppet theatre – in which two-dimensional figures are manipulated between a cloth screen and a light source at night-time performances – has been a Southeast Asian tradition for perhaps five centuries, originally brought to the Malay Peninsula by Middle Eastern

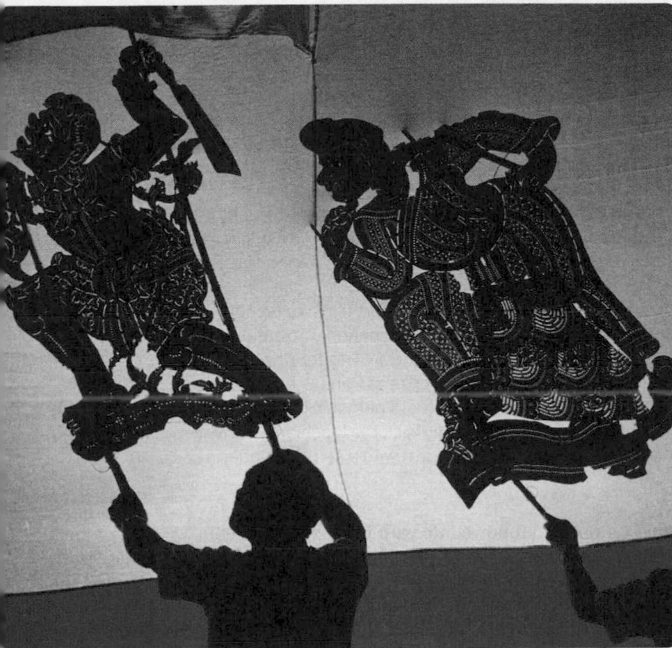

Shadow-puppet theatre show

traders. In Thailand it is mostly found in the south. As in Malaysia and Indonesia, shadow puppets in Thailand are carved from dried buffalo or cow hides *(năng)*. The capital of shadow puppetry today is in Nakhon Si Thammarat, which has regular performances at its festivals. While sadly a dying art, puppets are popular souvenirs for tourists. If visiting Nakhon Si Thammarat, stop by the fantastic Shadow Puppet Museum (p576) for excellent examples of shadow puppets, including one from the 18th century.

Cinema

When it comes to Thai cinema, there are usually two concurrent streams: movies that are financially successful and films that are considered cinematically meritorious. Only rarely do they successfully overlap.

Popular Thai cinema ballooned in the 1960s and '70s, especially when the government levied a tax on Hollywood imports which kick-started a home-grown industry. The majority of films were cheap action flicks that were typically dubbed *nám nôw* ('stinking water'), but the fantastic (even nonsensical) plots and rich colours left a lasting impression on modern-day Thai filmmakers.

Thai cinema graduated into international film circles in the late 1990s and early 2000s, thanks in part to the output of Pratt Institute–educated arthouse director and screenwriter Pen-Ek Ratanaruang and his gritty and engrossing oeuvre. Apichatpong Weerasethakul is Thailand's leading *cinéma-vérité* director and has garnered three Cannes accolades, including the Palme d'Or (the festival's highest prize) for his *Uncle Boonmee Who Can Recall His Past Lives* (2010).

International film festivals today play host to a new crop of experimental directors from Thailand. Nawapol Thamrongrattanrit gained acclaim for his modern-girl-in-the-city screenplay *Bangkok Traffic Love*

Classic Thai Movies

6ixtynin9 (1997)

Yam Yasothon (2005)

Ruang Rak Noi Nid Mahasan (Last Life in the Universe; 2003)

Fah Talai Jone (Tears of the Black Tiger; 2000)

Mekhong Sipha Kham Deuan Sip-et (Mekong Full Moon Party; 2002)

Uncle Boonmee Who Can Recall His Past Lives (2010)

KICK THE MACHINE: THE FILMS OF APICHATPONG WEERASETHAKUL

Winner of the 2010 Cannes Palme D'or for his *Uncle Boonmee Who Can Recall His Past Lives*, Bangkok-born independent film director Apichatpong Weerasethakul has made a point of ruffling feathers at home in defence of his art. Joint founder of the Free Thai Cinema Movement, formed to oppose the 2007 draft law devising ratings for films that encouraged censors to demand cuts to his film *Syndromes and a Century*, the *enfant terrible* of Thai movie-making has said he does not wish his latest feature-length film *Cemetery of Splendour* (2015) to be screened in Thailand, fearing calls for censorship. The film's theme – a group of soldiers receiving treatment in a clinic after suffering from a form of sleeping sickness – has been widely read as a metaphor for Thailand's dysfunctional political culture.

Of Thai Chinese stock and a prolific creator of short films, full-length films and installations, 45-year-old Weerasethakul first came to international attention with his 2002 erotic romance *Blissfully Yours*, which won the Un Certain Regard prize at Cannes in 2002 and *Tropical Malady*, which scooped the Jury prize at Cannes two years later, despite an opinion-dividing reception. Weerasethakul favours personal themes and social issues in his films – all produced by his film company Kick the Machine – conveyed in an often hypnotic, dreamlike and sometimes surreal form with a spiritual underlay.

Story (2009) and followed up with his directorial debut *36* (2012), which uses 36 static camera shots to explore lost love and lost memories. *Mary is Happy, Mary is Happy* (2013) is a film festival hit that adapted the Twitter feed of a Thai teen into a movie. His most recent work includes *Heart Attack* (2015) and the documentary *The Master* (2014).

Film fest fare has been bolstered by independent film clubs and self-promotion through social media. This is how low-budget filmmakers bypass the big studios, the ever-vigilant cinema censors and the skittish, controversy-averse movie theatres. In 2007 the film board introduced a rating system with seven classifications (including banned). Being censored may seem like the kiss of death, but it often guarantees indie success and cult status. Two political documentaries of 2013 challenged the board's sensitivities. Pen-ek's historical *Paradoxocracy* had to mute objectionable dialogue while Nontawat Numbenchapol's *Boundary* was initially banned, though the ban was lifted after an appeal. The Thai horror *Arbat* was banned in 2015 because it depicted improper 'misconduct' by Thai monks, which was considered a slur against Buddhism.

The big studios like ghost stories, horror flicks, historic epics, sappy love stories and camp comedies. Elaborate historical movies and epics serve a dual purpose: they can be lucrative and they promote national identity. Criticised as a propaganda tool, the *Legend of King Naresuan* epic, which comprises four instalments, focuses on the Ayuthaya-era king who repelled an attempted Burmese invasion. Each chapter (five have been released so far) has been a box-office winner.

Top Fiction

- *The Lioness in Bloom: Modern Thai Fiction about Women* (1996; translated by Susan Fulop Kepner)
- *Four Reigns* (1991; Kukrit Pramoj)
- *Bangkok 8* (2003; John Burdett)
- *Fieldwork: A Novel* (2007; Mischa Berlinski)
- *Bangkok Bound* (2012; Ellen Boccuzzi)

Literature

The written word has a long history in Thailand, dating back to the 11th or 12th century when the first Thai script was fashioned from an older Mon alphabet. The 30,000-line *Phra Aphaimani*, composed by poet Sunthorn Phu in the late 18th century, is Thailand's most famous classical literary work. Like many of its epic predecessors around the world, it tells the story of an exiled prince who must complete an odyssey of love and war before returning to his kingdom in victory.

Of all classical Thai literature, however, *Ramakian* is the most pervasive and influential in Thai culture. The Indian source, *Ramayana*, came to Thailand with the Khmers 900 years ago, first appearing as stone reliefs on

Wat Phra Kaew (p61), Bangkok

Prasat Hin Phimai and other Angkor temples in the northeast. Eventually the Thais developed their own version of the epic, which was first written down during the reign of Rama I (r 1782–1809). This version contained 60,000 stanzas and was a quarter longer than the Sanskrit original.

Although the main themes remained the same, the Thais embroidered the *Ramayana* with more biographical detail on arch-villain Ravana (called Thotsakan, or '10-necked' in the *Ramakian*) and his wife Montho. Hanuman, the monkey god, differs substantially in the Thai version in his flirtatious nature (in the Hindu version he follows a strict vow of chastity). One of the classic *Ramakian* reliefs at Bangkok's Wat Pho depicts Hanuman clasping a maiden's bared breast as if it were an apple.

Thai literature is usually written in Thai; however, some modern works you may find translated include:

- *Pisat, Evil Spirits* by Seni Saowaphong. Deals with conflicts between the old and new generations.
- *Lai Chiwit* (*Many Lives*; translation 1996) by Kukrit Pramoj. A collection of short stories.
- *Monsoon Country* (1988) by Pira Sudham. Brilliantly captures the northeast's struggles against nature and nurture.
- *The Judgement* (1982) by Chart Korbjitti. A drama about a young village man wrongly accused of a crime.
- *Jasmine Nights* (1994) by SP Somtow. Upbeat coming-of-age novel that fuses traditional ideas with modern Thai pop culture.
- *Married to the Demon King* (2005) by Sri Doruang. Adapts the *Ramayana* into modern Bangkok.

Environment & Wildlife

Thailand spans a distance of 1650km from its northern tip to its southern tail, a distance that encompasses 16 latitudinal degrees and a variety of ecological zones, making it one of the most environmentally diverse countries in Southeast Asia.

The Land

Thailand's odd shape is often likened to the head of an elephant, with the shaft of the trunk being the Malay peninsula and the head being the northern mountains. Starting at the crown of the country, northern Thailand is dominated by the Dawna-Tenasserim mountain range, a southeast-trending extension of the Himalayan mountains. Dropping into the central region, the topography mellows into rice-producing plains fed by rivers that are as revered as the national monarchy. Thailand's most exalted river is Chao Phraya, which is formed by the northern tributaries of Ping, Wang, Yom and Nan – a lineage as notable as any aristocrat's. The country's early kingdoms emerged around Chao Phraya basin, still the seat of the monarchy today. The river delta is in cultivation for most of the year.

Tracing the contours of Thailand's northern and northeastern border is another imposing watercourse: Mekong. From its source in the Tibetan Plateau and then flowing through China's Yúnnán province as the Lancang River (Láncāng Jiāng), the Mekong courses through Myanmar, Laos, Thailand, then Cambodia and Vietnam before reaching the South China Sea. Mekong both physically separates and culturally fuses Thailand with its neighbours. As the artery of Southeast Asia, it is a workhorse river that has been dammed for hydroelectric power, and swells and contracts based on the seasonal rains. In the dry season, farmers plant vegetables in the muddy floodplain, harvesting their crops before the river reclaims its territory.

The landscape of Thailand's northeastern border is occupied by the arid Khorat Plateau rising some 300m above the central plain. This is a hardscrabble land where the rains are meagre, the soil is anaemic and the red dust stains as stubbornly as the betel nut chewed by the ageing grandmothers.

WHERE THE WILD ELEPHANTS ROAM

Many of the national parks host wild elephant herds that congregate in the evenings at salt ponds and watering holes. Here are a few parks known for their elephant herds:

Kuiburi National Park (p507), near Prachuap Khiri Khan.

Khao Yai National Park (p410), northeast of Bangkok in Nakhon Ratchasima Province.

Kaeng Krachan National Park (p490), south of Bangkok in Phetchaburi.

The kingdom's eastern rivers dump their waters into the Gulf of Thailand, a shallow basin off the neighbouring South China Sea. The warm, gentle gulf is an ideal cultivation ground for coral reefs. Sliding further south is the Malay peninsula, a long trunk-like landmass. On the western side extends the Andaman Sea, a splendid tropical setting of stunning blue waters and dramatic limestone islands. Onshore, the peninsula is dominated by some final remaining stands of rainforest and ever-expanding rubber and palm-oil plantations.

Flora & Fauna

In the northern half of Thailand, most indigenous species are classified zoologically as Indo-Chinese, referring to fauna originating from mainland Asia, while those of the south are generally Sundaic, typical of peninsular Malaysia, Sumatra, Borneo and Java. There is also an interesting overlap that provides habitat for plants and animals from both zones starting in Uthai Thani and extending south to the gulf region around Prachuap Khiri Khan.

Thailand is particularly rich in bird life, with over a thousand recorded resident and migrating species, approximately 10% of the world's bird species. The cool mountains of northern Thailand are populated by montane species and migrants with clear Himalayan affinities such as flycatchers and thrushes. The arid forests of Khao Yai National Park in northeastern Thailand are favourites for hornbills. Marshland birds prefer the wetlands of the central region, while Sundaic species such as Gurney's pitta flock to the wetter climate of southern Thailand.

Flowing through six nations, the Mekong River rivals the Amazon River in terms of biodiversity, and shelters endangered and newly discovered species, such as the Khorat big-mouthed frog, which catches prey with its fangs.

In addition to abundant bird life, visitors to the country's national parks are most likely to spot monkeys. Thailand is home to five species of macaque (including the crab-eating macaque and the pig-tailed macaque), four species of the smaller leaf-monkey and three species of gibbon. Although they face the same habitat loss as other native species, monkeys sometimes survive in varying states of domestication with humans. The long-armed gibbons were once raised alongside children in rural villages, and macaques can be found living in small wooded patches or unused temples in population centres.

Other species that are found in the kingdom's parks and sanctuaries include gaur (Indian bison), banteng (wild cattle), serow (an Asiatic goat-antelope), sambar deer, muntjac (barking deer), mouse deer and tapir – to name a few.

Thailand has six venomous snakes: the common cobra, king cobra, banded krait, green viper, Malayan viper and Russell's pit viper. Although the relatively rare king cobra can reach up to 6m in length, the nation's largest snake is the reticulated python, which can reach a whopping 10m.

The country's many lizard species include two common varieties – *đúk·gaa,* a reclusive and somewhat homely gecko heard in the early evening coughing its name; and *jîng·jòk,* a spirited house lizard that is usually spotted on ceilings and walls chasing after bugs. The black jungle monitor, which resembles a miniature dinosaur, inhabits some of the southern forests.

The oceans are home to hundreds of species of coral, and the reefs created by these tiny creatures provide the perfect living conditions for fish, crustaceans and tiny invertebrates. You can find some of the world's smallest fishes (the 1cm-long dwarf pygmy goby) and the largest cartilaginous fish (the 12m-long whale shark), plus reef denizens such as clownfish, parrotfish, wrasse, angelfish, triggerfish and lionfish. Deeper waters are home to grouper, barracuda, sharks, manta rays, marlin and tuna. You might also encounter turtles, whales and dolphins.

Thailand's most famous animals are also its most endangered. The Asian elephant, a smaller cousin to the African elephant, once roamed the forests of Indochina in great herds. But the wild elephant faces extinction due to habitat loss and poaching. The population of wild elephants in Thailand is estimated at about one thousand.

Queen Sirikit Botanic Garden (p355), outside of Chiang Mai, includes a beautiful collection of orchids and lotus.

Reclusive wild tigers stalk the hinterlands between Thailand and Myanmar, but in ever-decreasing numbers. It is notoriously difficult to obtain an accurate count, but experts estimate that around 200 to 300 wild tigers remain in Thailand. Although tiger hunting and trapping is illegal, poachers continue to kill the cats for the overseas wildlife trade.

Weighing up to 1000kg, the rare dugong (also referred to as 'sea cows') – a herbivorous marine mammal once thought extinct in Thailand – survives in a few small pockets around Trang, but is increasingly threatened by habitat loss and the lethal propellers of tourist boats.

The remaining jungles of Thailand can be divided into two forest types: monsoon (with a distinct dry season of three months or more) and rainforest (where rain falls more than nine months per year). The most heavily forested provinces are Chiang Mai and Kanchanaburi.

Monsoon forests in the northern parts of the country are comprised of deciduous trees, which are green and lush during the rainy season but dusty and leafless during the dry season. Teak is one of the most highly valued monsoon forest trees, but it now exists only in limited quantities.

In southern Thailand, where rainfall is plentiful and distributed evenly throughout the year, forests are classified as rainforests with a few areas of monsoon forest. One remarkable plant found in some southern forests is *Rafflesia kerrii,* a squat plant with a huge flower that reaches 80cm across; you can see it at Khao Sok National Park near Surat Thani.

Thailand is home to nearly 75 coastal mangrove species, small salt-tolerant trees that provide an incubator for many coastal fish and animal species. Reforestation programs of mangrove areas have gained popularity thanks to their protective role during the 2004 Asian tsunami.

Orchids are Thailand's most exquisite native flora. There are over 1100 native species and they live in a variety of habitats: some are ground dwellers, while others anchor high up in trees, and still others cling to rocky outcrops.

Environmental Issues

Deforestation

Thailand has put enormous pressure on its ecosystems through cultivation of land into cities and farms. According to the World Bank, natural forest cover constituted about 32% of land area in 2013, compared to 70% some 50 years ago. The rapid depletion of the country's forests coincided with the shift towards industrialisation, urbanisation and commercial logging. Although these statistics are alarming, forest loss has slowed since the turn of the millennium to about 0.4% per year and total forest cover is up from 27.4% in 1990.

Environmental Statistics

Thailand encompasses 514,000 sq km, slightly larger than Spain.

Bangkok sits at N14° latitude, level with Madras, Manila, Guatemala City and Khartoum.

In response to environmental degradation, the Thai government created a large number of protected areas, starting in the 1970s, and establishing a goal of 40% forest cover by the middle of this century. In 1989 all logging was banned in Thailand following disastrous mudslides in Surat Thani Province that buried villages and killed more than a hundred people. It is now illegal to sell timber felled in the country, but this law is frequently flouted by local populations living near forest complexes and by those with well-connected interests.

A corollary problem to deforestation is habitat loss. Wildlife experts agree that the greatest danger faced by Thai fauna and flora is neither hunting nor the illegal wildlife trade, but habitat loss. Species that are notably extinct in Thailand include the kouprey (a type of wild cattle), Schomburgk's deer and the Javan rhino, but innumerable smaller species have also disappeared with little fanfare.

Coastal & Marine Degradation

With the majority of manufacturing industry located along the eastern seaboard and the upper Gulf of Thailand, the country's coastal region has experienced higher population and economic growth than the national average, increasing pressure on the environment.

Soil erosion is a major coastal problem. According to the World Bank, Thailand is losing 2 sq km from its coastline every year, partly due to coastal development (construction of jetties, breakwaters, oceanfront hotels and roads), land subsiding (due to groundwater depletion) and rising sea levels. Accurate data is lacking on coastal water quality, but analysts admit that wastewater treatment facilities are outpaced by the area's population and that industrial wastewater is often insufficiently treated.

Fed on up to 540,000 metric tonnes of wild caught trash fish, a staggering 250,000 to 300,000 metric tonnes of shrimp are harvested from fish farms each year in Thailand, according to the World Wide Fund for Nature.

Coastal degradation puts serious pressure on Thailand's diverse coral reef system and marine environment. It is estimated that about 50% of Thailand's coral reefs are classified as highly threatened, indicating a disproportionate number of dead coral to living coral, according to a World Bank 2006 environmental report. The 2010 global bleaching phenomenon, in which El Niño weather conditions contributed to warmer sea temperatures, exacerbated the health problems of Thailand's reefs. Eighteen areas in seven marine parks that had experienced widespread bleaching were closed to tourism by the Thai government. Many of the reefs, especially in shallow water, will never recover.

An important part of the Thai economy, the overall health of the ocean is further impacted by large-scale fishing and global warming. Fisheries continue to experience declining catches as fish stocks plummet, and an industry once dominated by small family fisherfolk has shifted to big commercial enterprises that can go into deeper waters, focus more resources on a profitable catch and are less troubled by fines imposed on vessels that flout laws designed to protect fish stocks. In 2013 a pipeline unloading an oil tanker off the coast of Rayong spilled 50,000L of crude into the sea, coating the western side of Ko Samet. While the outward condition of beaches quickly recovered with the use of dispersants, experts say there may be considerable long-term effects of the spill on both human health and the marine ecosystem.

With much of the city around 1.5m above sea level, low-lying Bangkok has been sinking at a rate of 2cm per year, and some scientists estimate that the city may face submersion within 15 years due to rising sea levels.

Energy Consumption

Thailand's increasingly affluent society is expected to consume 75% more energy in the forthcoming decades, according to the Oxford Business Group. As Southeast Asia's second-largest energy consumer (Indonesia ranks first in the region), Thailand is looking to increase and diversify its energy supply and production, by expanding oil and gas resources or developing alternative fuel sources, including nuclear. Currently, three quarters of Thailand's energy derives from natural gas. Most of the existing oil and gas fields are in the Gulf of Thailand in an area known as the Pattani Trough; the government is also working with Cambodia on the development of reserves in the upper Gulf of Thailand near the Thailand-Cambodia border.

Thailand also produces biofuels, including ethanols from molasses and cassava, and biodiesel from palm oil. Power generation, agriculture and industrial activity account for the largest proportion of the country's greenhouse gas emissions. While the energy sector searches for additional fuel supplies to feed the economy, the country's greenhouse gas

ILLEGAL WILDLIFE TRADE

Thailand is a signatory to the UN Convention on International Trade in Endangered Species (Cites), but the country remains an important transport link and marketplace for the global wildlife trade, the third-largest black-market activity after drugs and arms dealing. Endangered animals and animal parts are poached from local forests or smuggled from neighbouring countries through Thailand en route to the lucrative markets of China or the US. Despite police efforts, Bangkok's Chatuchak Market contains a clandestine exotic species section.

Though the country's efforts to stop the trade are more impressive than those of its neighbours, corruption and weak laws hinder law enforcement. Another complicating factor is that Thai law allows the trade of wild species bred in captivity, designed ostensibly to take the pressure off wild populations. This is especially problematic with elephants; criminal gangs steal baby elephants from wild herds or smuggle them across the Burmese borders and then forge registration papers so that the elephant appears to have been born to a captive mother and can be 'legally' sold to elephant camps.

management division is pushing for a voluntary carbon market in an attempt to meet international standards set for 2020.

Thailand is aiming to boost its production of renewable energy by a quarter by 2021. The Energy Generating Authority of Thailand (EGAT) is set to buy 90% of the US$3.5 billion Thai-built Xayaburi Dam's electrical output in northern Laos, one of 11 dams along the lower Mekong, when it becomes operational. Damming of the Mekong for hydroelectric power may generate 'clean' electricity, but at great environmental cost, including contributing to the extinction of the endangered Mekong giant catfish and the disappearance of the Irrawaddy dolphin from Mekong waters.

Flooding

Seasonal flooding is a common natural occurrence in some parts of Thailand due to the nature of the monsoon rains. But high-level floods are an almost annual occurrence. The record-busting 2011 floods were unlike anything the country has ever experienced before. Prior to the start of the rainy season, a two-week period of heavy rainfall presaged trouble ahead, causing flooding in southern Thailand, and temporarily stranding tourists on resort islands. By mid-year, tropical storms brought an inundation of rain that triggered a domino flood effect spanning nearly three months and drowning almost every region of the country. Of Thailand's 77 provinces, 65 were declared flood disaster zones; there were 815 deaths and an estimated US$45.7 billion worth of damages, one of the world's costliest natural disasters.

The 2011 flood trumped the previous year's record-setting event in which late-arriving rains transformed reservoirs in Nakhon Ratchasima Province from parched pits into overflowing disaster zones. There were 177 deaths in the 2010 floods, and a massive disaster relief response that lasted for several months after waters subsided. Another record flood occurred in 2006 with 46 affected provinces, mainly in the north, and again in 2008 along the Mekong.

These extreme weather patterns are blamed on a variety of causes. Many environmental experts attribute human alteration of natural flood barriers and watercourses and deforestation as contributory factors. Increased incidents of flooding along the Mekong is often linked to upstream infrastructure projects, such as dams and removal of rapids for easier navigation, and increasing human populations along the river that infringe on forested floodplains and wetlands. Another emerging and possibly crucial component is the role of climate change in the increase of seasonal rains.

Survival Guide

Responsible Travel

Cultural Etiquette

The monarchy and religion (which are interconnected) are treated with extreme deference in Thailand. Thais avoid criticising or disparaging the royal family for fear of offending someone or, worse, being charged with a violation of the country's very strict *lèse majesté* laws, which carry a jail sentence.

Buddha images are sacred objects. Thais consider it bad form to pull a silly pose in front of one for a photo, or to clamber upon them (in the case of temple ruins). Instead they would show respect by performing a *wâi* (a prayer-like gesture) to the figure no matter how humble it is. As part of their ascetic vows, monks are not supposed to touch or be touched by women. If a woman wants to hand something to a monk, the object is placed within reach of the monk or on the monk's 'receiving cloth'.

From a spiritual viewpoint, Thais regard the head as the highest and most sacred part of the body and the feet as the dirtiest and lowest. Many of the taboos associated with the feet have a practical derivation as well. Traditionally Thais ate, slept and entertained on the floor of their homes with little in the way of furniture. To keep their homes and eating surfaces clean, the feet (and shoes) contracted a variety of rules.

Shoes aren't worn inside private homes and temple buildings, as a sign of respect and for sanitary reasons. Thais can kick off their shoes in one fluid step and many lace-up shoes are modified by the wearer to become slip-ons. Thais also step over – not on – the threshold, which is where the spirit of the house is believed to reside. On some buses and 3rd-class trains, you'll see Thais prop their feet up on the adjacent bench, and while this isn't the height of propriety, do notice that they always remove their shoes before doing so. Thais also take off their shoes if they need to climb onto a chair or seat.

Thais don't touch each others' heads or ruffle hair as a sign of affection. Occasionally you'll see young people touching each others' heads, which is a teasing gesture, maybe even a slight insult, between friends.

Social Conventions & Gestures

The traditional Thai greeting is made with a prayer-like, palms-together gesture known as *wâi*. The depth of the bow and the placement of the fingers in relation to the face is dependent on the status of the person receiving the *wâi*. Adults don't *wâi* children and in most cases service people (when they are doing their jobs) aren't *wâi-ed*, though this is a matter of personal discretion.

In the more traditional parts of the country, it is not proper for members of the opposite sexes to touch one another, either as lovers or as friends. Hand-holding is not acceptable behaviour outside the major cities such as Bangkok. But same-sex touching is quite common and is typically a sign of friendship, not sexual attraction. Older Thai men might grab a younger man's thigh in the same way that buddies slap each other on the back. Thai women are especially affectionate with female friends, often sitting close to one another or linking arms.

Thais hold modesty in personal dress in high regard, though this is changing among the younger generation. The importance of modesty extends to the beach as well. Except for urbanites, most provincial Thais swim fully clothed. For this reason, sunbathing nude or topless is not acceptable and in some cases is even illegal. Remember that swimsuits are not proper attire off the beach; wear a cover-up in between the sand and your hotel.

Tourism

Most forms of tourism, despite the prevailing prejudices, have a positive economic effect on the local economy in Thailand, providing jobs for young workers and business opportunities for entrepreneurs. But in an effort to be more than just a consumer, many travellers look for opportunities to spend where their money might be needed, either on charitable causes or activities that preserve traditional ways of life. Thailand has done a surprisingly good job at adapting to this emerging trend by promoting village craft programs and homestays. Unfortunately, much of this is aimed at the domestic market rather than international visitors. But more and more, foreign tourists can engage in these small-scale tourism models that offer an insight into traditional ways.

Diving

The popularity of Thailand's diving industry places immense pressure on fragile coral sites. To help preserve the ecology, adhere to these simple rules.

- Avoid touching living marine organisms, standing on coral or dragging equipment (such as fins) across the reef. Coral polyps can be damaged by even the gentlest contact.
- When treading water in shallow reef areas, be careful not to kick up clouds of sand, which can easily smother the delicate reef organisms.
- Take great care in underwater caves where your air bubbles can be caught within the roof and leave previously submerged organisms high and dry.
- Join a coral clean-up campaign that's sponsored by dive shops.
- Don't feed the fish or allow your dive operator to dispose of excess food in the water. The fish become dependent on this food source and don't tend to the algae on the coral, causing harm to the reef.

Elephant Encounters

Throughout Thai history, elephants have been revered for their strength, endurance and intelligence, working alongside their mahouts harvesting teak, transporting goods

ESSENTIAL ETIQUETTE

Do

Stand respectfully for the national anthem It is played on TV and radio stations as well as public and government places at 8am and 6pm.

Rise for the royal anthem It is played in movie theatres before every screening.

Smile a lot It makes everything easier.

Bring a gift if you're invited to a Thai home Fruit, drinks or snacks are acceptable; flowers are usually for merit-making purposes, not home decor.

Take off your shoes When you enter a home, temple building or wherever there are sandals piled up at the door.

Lower your head slightly When passing between two people having a conversation or when passing near a monk; it is a sign of respect.

Dress modestly for temple visits Cover to the elbows and ankles and always remove your shoes when entering any building containing a Buddha image.

Give and receive politely Extend the right hand out while the left hand gently grips the right elbow when handing an object to another person or receiving something – truly polite behaviour.

Respect all Buddha images and pictures of the monarchy Signs of disrespect can have serious consequences.

Sit in the 'mermaid' position inside temples Tuck your feet beside and behind you so that your feet aren't pointing at the Buddha image.

Don't

Get a tattoo of the Buddha It is considered sacrilegious.

Criticise the monarchy The monarchy is revered and protected by defamation laws.

Prop your feet on tables or chairs Feet are considered dirty and people have to sit on chairs.

Step on a dropped bill to prevent it from blowing away Thai money bears a picture of the king. Feet + monarchy = grave offence.

Step over someone or their personal belongings Aaah, attack of the feet.

Tie your shoes to the outside of your backpack They might accidentally brush against someone; gross.

Touch a Thai person on the head It is considered rude, not chummy.

Women cannot touch monks or their belongings Step out of the way when passing one on the footpath and do not sit next to them on public transport.

through mountainous terrain or fighting ancient wars.

But many of the elephants' traditional roles have either been outsourced to machines or outlawed (logging was officially banned in 1989, although it still goes on along the Thai/Myanmar border), leaving the 'domesticated' animals and their mahouts without work. Some mahouts turned to begging on the streets in Bangkok and other tourist centres, but most elephants find work in Thailand's tourism industry. Their jobs vary from circus-like shows to elephant camps giving rides to tourists, to 'mahout-training' schools, while sanctuaries and rescue centres provide modest retirement homes to animals that are no longer financially profitable to their owners.

It costs about 30,000B (US$1000) a month to provide a comfortable living for an elephant, an amount equivalent to the salary of Thailand's upper middle class. Welfare standards within the tourism industry are not standardised or subject to government regulations, so it's up to the conscientious consumer to encourage the industry to ensure safe conditions for elephants.

With more evidence available than ever to support claims by animal welfare experts that elephant rides and shows are harmful to these gentle giants, who are often abused to force them to perform for humans, a small but growing number of sanctuaries offer more sustainable interactions, such as walking with and bathing retired and rescued elephants. If you're still bent on riding one, however, ask the right questions to ensure you choose a well-run operation.

For more information about ethical elephant interactions, see p327.

- **Does the camp employ a veterinarian?** Good camps keep their elephants under regular medical supervision.
- **What is its policy on procuring new elephants?** Some camps buy illegally caught elephants with forged registration so they appear to have been born in captivity.
- **How many hours per day do the elephants work?** A brisk walk for about four hours per day (with breaks for eating and drinking in between) is considered adequate exercise.
- **How many adults do the elephants carry?** An Asian elephant can carry a maximum of 150kg on its back, plus a mahout on its neck. Tally up the combined weight of you and your partner and request a separate elephant if you tip the scales.
- **Are the elephants kept in a shady spot near fresh water and a food source? What do they eat?** A balanced diet includes a mixture of fruit, grasses, bamboo and pineapple shoots.
- **Do the elephants have noticeable wounds?** This is often a sign of mistreatment.
- **What kind of a seat is used for elephant riding?** Wooden seats, custom-made to fit the elephant's back, cause less irritation and stress on the animal.
- **What is the camp's birth/death rate?** Happy elephants have babies.

Hill-Tribe Hikes

Though marginalised within mainstream society, Thailand's hill-tribe minorities remain a strong tourism draw, with large and small businesses organising 'trekking' tours (these can range from proper hikes to leisurely walks) to villages for cultural displays and interactions. Economically it is unclear whether hill-tribe trekking helps alleviate the poverty of the hill-tribe groups, which in turn helps to maintain their separate ethnic identity. Most agree that a small percentage of the profits from trekking filters down to individual families within hill-tribe villages, giving them a small source of income that might prevent urban migration.

In general, the trekking business has become more socially conscious than in past decades. Most companies now tend to limit the number of visits to a particular area to lessen the impact of outsiders on the daily lives of ordinary villagers. But the industry still has a long way to go. It should be noted that trekking companies are Thai owned and employ Thai guides, another bureaucratic impediment regarding citizenship for ethnic minorities. Without an identification card, guides from hill tribes do not qualify for a Tourist Authority of Thailand (TAT) tour guide licence and so are less than desirable job candidates.

Trekkers should also realise that the minority tribes maintain their own distinct cultural identity and many continue their animistic traditions, which define social taboos and conventions. If you're planning on visiting hill-tribe villages on an organised trek, talk to your guide about acceptable behaviour.

Here is a general prescription to get you started.

- Always ask for permission before taking any photos of tribes people, especially at private moments inside their dwellings. Many traditional belief systems regard photography with suspicion.
- Show respect for religious symbols and rituals. Don't touch totems at village entrances or sacred items hanging from trees. Don't participate in ceremonies unless invited.
- Avoid cultivating the practice of begging, especially among children. Talk to your guide about donating to a local school instead.
- Avoid public nudity and be careful not to undress near an open window where village children might be able to peep in.

- Don't flirt with members of the opposite sex unless you plan on marrying them.
- Don't drink or do drugs with the villagers; altered states sometimes lead to culture clashes.
- Smile at villagers even if they stare at you. Ask your guide how to say 'hello' in the tribal language.
- Avoid public displays of affection, which in some traditional systems are viewed as offensive to the spirit world.
- Don't interact with the villagers' livestock, even the free-roaming pigs; these creatures are valuable possessions, not entertainment. Also avoid interacting with jungle animals, which in some belief systems are viewed as visiting spirits.
- Don't litter.
- Adhere to the same feet taboos that apply to Thai culture. Don't step on the threshold of a house, prop your feet up against the fire or wear your shoes inside.

Homestays

A visit to a homestay is one of the best ways to experience Thailand's rural culture, not to mention a way to ensure that your baht are going directly to locals. More popular with domestic tourists, homestays differ from guesthouses in that visitors are welcomed into a family's home, typically in a small village that isn't on the tourist trail. Accommodation is basic: usually a mat or foldable mattress on the floor, or occasionally a family will have a private room. Rates include lodging, meals with the family and cultural activities that highlight the region's traditional way of life, from rice farming to silk weaving. English fluency varies, so homestays are also an excellent way to exercise your spoken Thai.

TOP HOMESTAYS

Ban Kham Pia Homestays (☎087 861 0601; www.bunloedhuts.jimdo.com; s 170-270B, d 200-300B, meals 50-90B), Bueng Kan

Prasat Muang Tam Homestay (☎089 070 8889; per person with 3 meals 500B), Buriram

Mae Kampong Homestay Program (☎089 559 4797; r 580B), Chiang Mai

Sichang Healing House (☎081 572 7840; off Th Makham Thaew), Ko Si Chang

Dan Sai Homestay (☎086 862 4812, 042 892339; dm/tw or d 170/550B, with air-con 650B), Loei

Muang Pon Homestay Program (☎084 485 5937; per night incl breakfast & dinner 350B), Mae Hong Son

Ban Prasat Homestay (☎081 725 0791; per person incl 2 meals 400B), Nakhon Ratchasima (Khorat)

Ban Na Ton Chan Homestay Program (☎089 885 1639; http://homestaynatonchan.blogspot.com; per person incl breakfast & lunch 500B), Sukhothai

Elephant Study Centre (☎044 145050; admission 100B; ⌚8.30am-4pm), Surin

Volunteering

There are a myriad of volunteer organisations in Thailand to address both the needs of the locals and visitors' desires to help. A regularly updated resource for grassroots-level volunteer opportunities in Thailand is **Volunteer Work Thailand** (www.volunteer-workthailand.org). Be aware though that so-called 'voluntourism' has become a big business and that not every organisation fulfils its promise of meaningful experiences. Lonely Planet does not endorse any organisations we do not work with directly, so it is essential that you do your own thorough research before agreeing to volunteer with any organisation.

Environmental & Animal Welfare Work

A number of NGOs undertake local conservation efforts and run rescue and sanctuary centres for wild animals that have been adopted as pets or veterinarian clinics that tend to the domesticated population of dogs and cats. At centres and sanctuaries that rely on volunteer labour, your hard work is often rewarded with meaningful interactions with the animals.

- **Elephant Nature Park** (☎053 818754; www.elephantnaturepark.org; 1 Th Ratchamankha; 1-/2-day tour 2500/5800B) This popular and well-run elephant sanctuary offers seven-day volunteer programs at its Chaing Mai base, and at its sister organisation, the Surin Project.
- **Elephants World** (☎086 335 5332; www.elephantsworld.org) Has regular one- (2500B per person) and two-day (4500B) work-for-the-elephants programs, and also accepts volunteers for month-long stays.
- **Highland Farm Gibbon Sanctuary** (☎081 727 1364; www.gibbonathighlandfarm.org; Mae Sot) Gives a permanent home to orphaned,

abandoned and mistreated gibbons. Volunteers are asked for a one-month commitment and to help with daily farm chores.

➡ **Koh Chang Animal Project** (☎089 042 2347; www.kohchanganimalproject.org; Ban Khlong Son; ⏲9am-5.30pm Mon-Sat) Travelling vets and vet nurses often drop by to volunteer here, while non-vets are needed to help with numerous odd jobs. Call to make an appointment.

➡ **Lanta Animal Welfare** (☎084 304 4331; www.lantaanimalwelfare.com; 629 Mu 2, Ban Phra Ae; tour by donation; ⏲9am-5pm) This centre on Ko Lanta welcomes both casual dog-walking visitors and volunteers for longer placements.

➡ **Phuket Gibbon Rehabilitation Project** (โครงการคืนชะนีสู่ป่า; ☎076 260492; www.gibbonproject.org; off Rte 4027; admission by donation; ⏲9am-4.30pm, to 3pm Thu; Ⓟ) This Phuket centre has volunteer opportunities that include providing educational information to visitors, cleaning cages, feeding and tracking released gibbons.

➡ **Samui Dog & Cat Rescue Centre** (☎077 413490; www.samuidog.org; Soi 3, Chaweng Beach Rd; ⏲9am-6pm) Donations of time and/or money are hugely appreciated at this centre. Volunteers are always needed to take care of the animals at its kennel/clinic in Ban Taling Ngam (but not at the smaller Hat Chaweng branch). Call the centre for volunteering details or swing by for additional info. Check the website for directions.

➡ **Soi Dog** (☎081 788 4222; www.soidog.org; 167/9 Mu 4, Soi Mai Khao 10; admission by donation; ⏲9am-noon & 1-3.30pm Mon-Fri, tours 9.30am, 11am & 1.30pm) This Phuket centre welcomes visitors to play with the animals, or become a dog-walking or long-term volunteer.

➡ **Trash Hero** (www.trashhero.org) A volunteer outfit that runs weekly clean-ups at 11 official points across Thailand.

➡ **Wild Animal Rescue Foundation** (WARF; ☎02 712 9715; www.warthai.org) Operates the Phuket Gibbon Rehabilitation Project, as well as several other programs across the country.

➡ **Wildlife Friends of Thailand Rescue Centre** (☎032 458135; www.wfft.org; Phetchaburi) Puts volunteers to work caring for sun bears, macaques and gibbons at its animal rescue centre in Phetchaburi.

Humanitarian & Educational Work

Northern Thailand, especially Chiang Mai and Chiang Rai, has a number of volunteer opportunities working with disadvantaged hill-tribe groups. Chiang Mai, Mae Sot and Sangkhlaburi have distressed communities of Burmese refugees and migrants. There are also many volunteer teaching positions in northeastern Thailand, the country's agricultural heartland.

When looking for a volunteer placement, it is essential to investigate what your chosen organisation does and, more importantly, how it goes about it. If the focus is not primarily on your skills and how these can be applied to help local people, that should ring alarm bells. Any organisation that promises to let you do any kind of work, wherever you like, for as long as you like, is unlikely to be putting the needs of local people first.

For any organisation working with children, child protection is a serious concern, and organisations that do not conduct background checks on volunteers should be regarded with extreme caution. Experts recommend a three-month commitment for volunteering with children. Visit www.thinkchildsafe.org for more information.

➡ **Baan Unrak** (บ้านอุ่นรัก; www.baanunrak.org) A home and school that cares for over 140 orphaned or abandoned children. Regardless of their religion, the children follow a neohumanist philosophy of vegetarianism (volunteers must also during their stay), meditation and universal love.

➡ **Cultural Canvas Thailand** (www.culturalcanvas.com; Chiang Mai) Places volunteers in migrant learning centres, art programs and other social-justice projects in northern Thailand.

➡ **Khok Pia Village Volunteering** (www.isanexplorer.com/khok-pia-village-volunteering.html) A one-village program run by a dedicated local that accepts teaching assistants with homestay accommodation.

➡ **Khon Kaen Education & Travel Programs** (☎083 359 9115; www.kketp.com) A volunteer teaching program in Khon Kaen.

➡ **LemonGrass** (☎081 977 5300; www.lemongrass-volunteering.com) A well-run Surin-based outfit that places native English speakers in local primary schools, where they work alongside the regular teachers.

➡ **Open Mind Projects** (☎088 564 0734; www.openmindprojects.org) Offers volunteer positions in IT, health care, education and community-based ecotourism across Thailand.

➡ **Starfish Ventures** (www.starfishvolunteers.com) Places volunteers in building, health care and teaching programs across Thailand.

➡ **Travel to Teach** (☎092 818 5929; www.travel-to-teach.org) Organisation that links volunteer teachers with positions across Thailand.

➡ **Volunthai** (www.volunthai.com) A family-run operation that places volunteers in teaching positions at rural schools with homestay accommodation.

Directory A-Z

Accommodation

Thailand offers a wide variety of accommodation, from cheap and basic to pricey and luxurious. In places where spoken English might be limited, it is handy to know the following: *hôrng pát lom* (room with fan) and *hôrng aa* (room with air-con).

> **BOOK YOUR STAY ONLINE**
>
> For more accommodation reviews by Lonely Planet authors, check out http://lonelyplanet.com/hotels/. You'll find independent reviews, as well as recommendations on the best places to stay. Best of all, you can book online.

Hostels, Guesthouses & Homestays

In the larger tourist destinations, those counting every baht can get a dorm bed with a shared bathroom for as little as 200B. Increasingly popular is the 'flashpacker' hostel, which has dressed up the utilitarian options of the past with stylish decor and more creature comforts. Expect an upper-budget or lower-midrange price tag.

Many budget-oriented hostels also offer private rooms. Rates vary according to facilities and location. In small towns, 200B to 300B is about the cheapest rate around and these rooms will usually have shared bathroom and a rickety fan. Private facilities, air-con and sometimes a TV can be had for 600B to 800B. But prices are much higher in the beach resorts, where a basic fan room starts at 700B to 800B. Many budget places make their bread and butter from their on-site restaurants, which serve the classic backpacker fare (banana pancakes and fruit shakes). Although these restaurants are convenient and a good way to meet other travellers, don't measure Thai food based on these dishes. Likewise with the typical guesthouse breakfast of white bread and instant coffee; if you want good food, you're better off going to the morning market.

A homestay is a slightly less commercial budget option, generally found only in rural areas. As the name suggests, you'll be staying in a family home, with food and often activities included in the fee. See also p761.

In Thailand it's worth noting that 'guesthouse' has come to refer to any sort of budget accommodation rather than a room in a family home, although we use it to describe the latter.

> **SLEEPING PRICE RANGES**
>
> A two-tiered pricing system has been used to determine the accommodation price ranges (budget, midrange, top end) in Thailand. Note that rates we list are high-season walk-in rates.
>
> **Big Cities & Beach Resorts**
>
> **$** less than 1000B
>
> **$$** 1000–3000B
>
> **$$$** more than 3000B
>
> **Small Towns**
>
> **$** less than 600B
>
> **$$** 600–1500B
>
> **$$$** more than 1500B

ADDITIONAL RESOURCES

Agoda (www.agoda.com/city/bangkok-th.html) Asia-based hotel booking site with a lowest price guarantee.

Airbnb (www.airbnb.com/s/Bangkok--Thailand) A large and growing number of listings across Thailand, ranging from condos and apartments to small hotels masquerading as condos and apartments.

Travelfish (www.travelfish.org/country/thailand) Independent reviews with lots of reader feedback.

Hotels

In provincial capitals and small towns, the only options are often ageing Thai-Chinese hotels, once the standard in all of Thailand. Most cater to Thai guests and English is usually limited. These hotels are multistorey buildings generally offering rooms ranging from bare, fan-cooled cheapies to ones with private bathrooms, air-con and TV. Although some Thai-Chinese hotels have got tonnes of accidental retro charm, we've found that, unless the establishment has been recently refurbished, they are generally too old and worn to represent good value compared to guesthouses.

Increasingly, midrange has come to mean a room with air-con, fridge, hot water, TV and free wi-fi. It's not uncommon for a room to boast all of these but lack a view, or even windows. Breakfast can range from 'buffets' based around toast and oily fried eggs (often referred to as 'ABF', meaning 'American breakfast') to healthier meals involving yoghurt or tropical fruit. Midrange and chain hotels, especially in major tourist destinations, can be booked in advance and some offer discounts through their websites or online agents. They also accept most credit cards, but only a few deluxe places accept American Express.

International chain hotels can be found in Bangkok, Chiang Mai, Phuket and other high-end beach resorts. The more thoughtful places have amenities such as in-room computers and free wi-fi; otherwise, it's not uncommon to have to pay a premium for the latter. Pools are almost standard, not to mention fitness and business centres, restaurants and bars. Breakfast is often buffet-style. Most top-end hotels and some midrange hotels add a 7% government tax (VAT) and an additional 10% service charge. The additional charges are often referred to as 'plus plus'.

National Parks Accommodation

Most national parks have bungalows or campsites. Bungalows typically sleep as many as 10 people and rates range from 600B to 3000B, depending on the park and the size of the bungalow. These are popular with extended Thai families who bring enough provisions to survive the Apocalypse.

Camping is available at many parks for around 100B per night. Some parks rent tents and other sleeping gear, but the condition of the equipment can be poor.

Reservations for all park accommodation must be

Climate

Bangkok

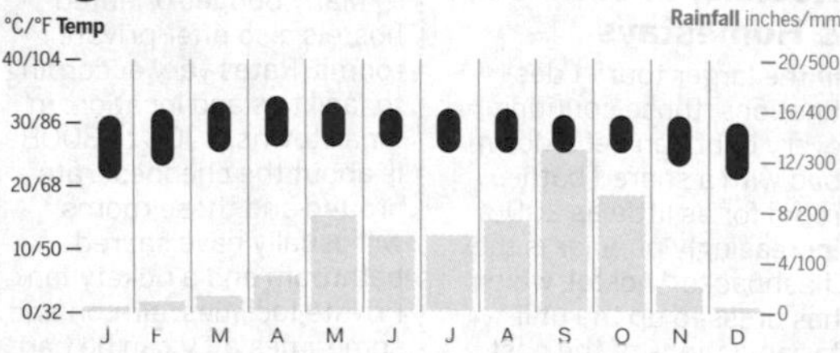

Chiang Mai

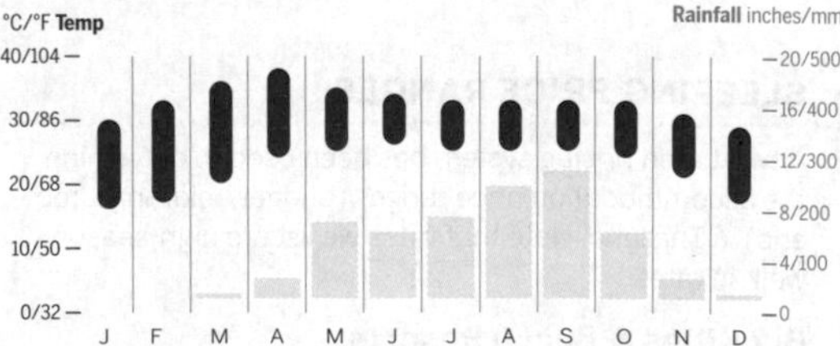

Phuket

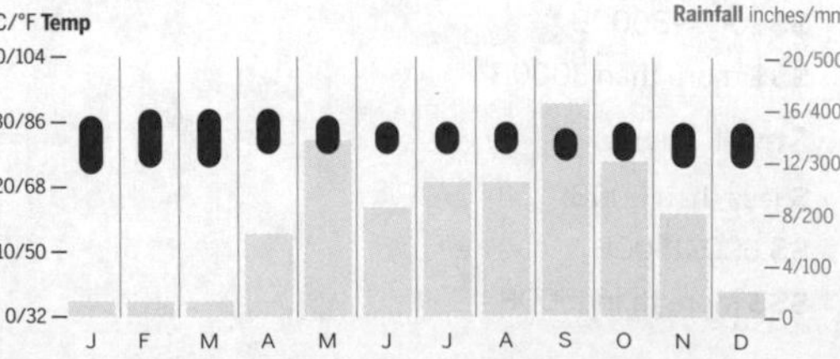

made in advance through the **Royal Forest Department** (02 561 0777; www.dnp.go.th/parkreserve/nationalpark.asp?lg=2) in Bangkok. Note that reservations for campsites and bungalows are handled on different pages within the website.

Children

There aren't a whole lot of attractions in Thailand meant to appeal specifically to the little ones, but there's no lack of locals willing to provide attention. This means kids are welcome almost anywhere and you'll rarely experience the sort of eye-rolling annoyance often seen in the West. For more on travelling Thailand with children, see p51.

Customs Regulations

The **customs department** (www.customs.go.th) maintains a helpful website with specific information about customs regulations for travellers. Thailand allows the following items to enter duty free:

- reasonable amount of personal effects (clothing and toiletries)
- professional instruments
- 200 cigarettes
- 1L of wine or spirits

Thailand prohibits the import of the following items:

- firearms and ammunition (unless registered in advance with the police department)
- illegal drugs
- pornographic media

When leaving Thailand, you must obtain an export licence for any antique reproductions or newly cast Buddha images (except personal amulets). Submitting two front-view photos of the object(s), a photocopy of your passport, the purchase receipt and the object(s) in question, to the **Office of the National Museum** (02 224 1370, 02 224 7493; National Museum, 4 Th Na Phra That; 9am-4pm Tue-Fri; Chang Pier, Maharaj Pier, Phra Chan Tai Pier). Allow four days for the application and inspection process to be completed.

Electricity

Thailand uses 220V AC electricity. Power outlets most commonly feature two-prong round or flat sockets.

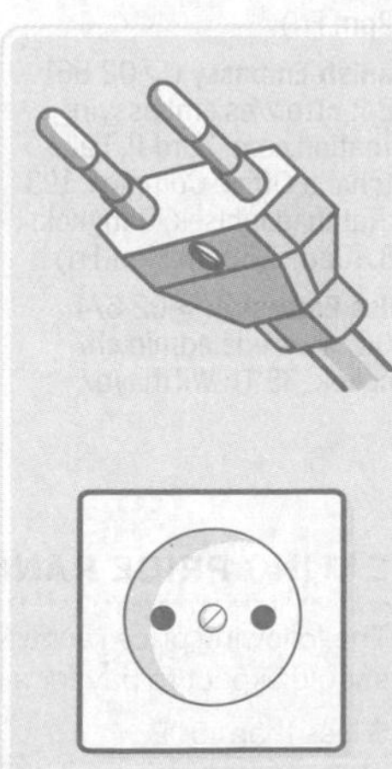

Embassies & Consulates

Foreign embassies are located in Bangkok; some nations also have consulates in Chiang Mai, Pattaya, Phuket or Songkhla.

Australian Embassy (02 344 6300; www.thailand.embassy.gov.au; 37 Th Sathon Tai/South, Bangkok; 8.30am-4.30pm Mon-Fri; M Lumphini exit 2)

Cambodian Embassy (02 957 5851; 518/4 Th Pracha Uthit/Soi Ramkhamhaeng 39, Bangkok; 9am-noon Mon-Fri; M Phra Ram 9 exit 3 & taxi) Consulate in Sa Kaew.

Canadian Embassy Bangkok (02 646 4300; www.thailand.gc.ca; 15th fl, Abdulrahim Pl, 990 Th Phra Ram IV, Bangkok; 7.30am-12.15pm & 1-4.15pm Mon-Thu, to 1pm Fri; M Si Lom exit 2, S Sala Daeng exit 4); Chiang Mai (053 850147; 151 Superhighway, Tambon Tahsala, Chiang Mai; 9am-noon Mon-Fri)

Chinese Embassy Bangkok (02 245 0888; www.chinaembassy.or.th/eng; 57 Th Ratchadaphisek, Bangkok; 9am-noon & 3-4pm Mon-Fri); Chiang Mai (053 276125; www.chiangmai.chineseconsulate.org/eng; 111 Th Chang Lor, Tambon Haiya, Chiang Mai; 9-11.30am Mon-Fri) Also has consulates in Khon Kaen and Songkhla.

Danish Embassy (02 343 1100; http://thailand.um.dk; 10 Soi 1, Th Sathon Tai, Bangkok; 10am-noon & 1-3pm Mon-Thu) Consulate in Phuket.

French Embassy Bangkok (02 657 5100; www.ambafrance-th.org; 35 Soi 36, Th Charoen Krung, Bangkok; 8.30am-noon Mon-Fri; Oriental Pier); Chiang Mai (053 281466; 138 Th Charoen Prathet, Chiang Mai; 10am-noon Mon-Fri) Consulates also in Chiang Rai, Ko Samui, Pattaya and Phuket.

German Embassy (02 287 9000; www.bangkok.diplo.de; 9 Th Sathon Tai/South, Bangkok;

⌚8.30-11.30am Mon-Fri; MLumphini exit 2)

Indian Embassy Bangkok (☎02 258 0300; www.indianembassy.in.th; 46 Soi 23, Th Sukhumvit, Bangkok; ⌚9am-noon & 3-4.30pm Mon-Fri); Bangkok Visa Centre (☎02 664 1200; www.indiavisathai.com; IVS Global Services, 22nd fl, 253 Soi 21/Asoke, Th Sukhumvit, Bangkok; ⌚8.30am-2pm & 4.30-5.30pm Mon-Fri); Chiang Mai (☎053 243066; 33/1 Th Thung Hotel, Wat Gate, Chiang Mai; ⌚9am-noon Mon-Fri)

Indonesian Embassy (☎02 252 3135; www.kemlu.go.id/bangkok; 600-602 Th Phetchaburi, Bangkok; ⌚9am-noon & 2-4pm Mon-Fri) Consulate in Songkhla.

Irish Embassy (☎02 632 6720; www.irelandinthailand.com; 12th fl, 208 Th Witthayu/Wireless Rd, Bangkok; ⌚8.30am-12.30pm Mon-Fri; SPhloen Chit exit 1)

Israeli Embassy (☎02 204 9200; http://embassies.gov.il/bangkok-en; 25th fl, Ocean Tower 2, 75 Soi 19, Th Sukhumvit, Bangkok; ⌚9am-noon)

Japanese Embassy Bangkok (☎02 207 8500; www.th.emb-japan.go.jp; 177 Th Witthayu/Wireless Rd; ⌚8.30am-noon & 1.30-4pm Mon-Fri); Chiang Mai (☎053 203367; Airport Business Park, 90 Th Mahidol, Chiang Mai)

Laotian Embassy (☎02 539 6667; www.laoembassybkk.gov.la/index.php/en; 502/1-3 Soi Sahakarnpramoon, Th Pracha Uthit/Soi Ramkhamhaeng 39, Bangkok; ⌚8am-noon & 1-4pm Mon-Fri; MPhra Ram 9 exit 3 & taxi)

Malaysian Embassy (☎02 629 6800; www.kln.gov.my/web/tha_bangkok/home; 33-35 Th Sathon Tai/South, Bangkok; ⌚8am-4pm Mon-Fri; MLumphini exit 2) Consulate in Songkhla.

Myanmar Embassy (☎02 233 7250; www.myanmarembassybkk.com; 132 Th Sathon Neua/North , Bangkok; ⌚9am-noon & 1-3pm Mon-Fri; SSurasak exit 3)

Nepalese Embassy (☎02 391 7240; http://nepalembassybangkok.com; 189 Soi 71, Th Sukhumvit, Bangkok; ⌚9am-noon Mon-Fri)

Netherlands Embassy (☎02 309 5200; http://thailand.nlembassy.org; 15 Soi Ton Son, Bangkok; ⌚8.30-11.30am Mon-Thu; SChit Lom exit 4)

New Zealand Embassy (☎02 254 2530; www.nzembassy.com/thailand; 14th fl, M Thai Tower, All Seasons Pl, 87 Th Witthayu/Wireless Rd, Bangkok; ⌚8am-noon & 1-2.30pm Mon-Fri; SPhloen Chit exit 5)

Philippine Embassy (☎02 259 0139; www.bangkokpe.dfa.gov.ph; 760 Th Sukhumvit, Bangkok; ⌚9am-noon & 1-6pm Mon-Fri)

Russian Embassy (☎02 234 2012; www.thailand.mid.ru; 78 Th Sap, Th Surawong, Bangkok; ⌚9am-11.45am Mon, Tue, Thu & Fri) Consulates in Pattaya and Phuket.

Singaporean Embassy (☎02 286 2111; www.mfa.gov.sg/bangkok; 129 Th Sathon Tai (South), Bangkok; ⌚9am-noon & 1-5pm Mon-Fri)

South African Embassy (☎02 659 2900; www.dirco.gov.za/bangkok; 12th A fl, M Thai Tower, All Seasons Place, 87 Th Witthayu/Wireless Rd, Bangkok; ⌚8am-4.30pm Mon-Thu, to 2pm Fri)

Spanish Embassy (☎02 661 8284; http://es.embassyinformation.com; 23rd fl, Lake Ratchada Office Complex, 193 Th Ratchadaphisek, Bangkok; ⌚8.30am-3.30pm Mon-Fri)

Swiss Embassy (☎02 674 6900; www.eda.admin.ch/bangkok; 35 Th Witthayu/Wireless Rd, Bangkok; ⌚9-11.30am Mon-Fri)

UK Embassy Bangkok (☎02 305 8333; www.gov.uk/government/world/organisations/british-embassy-bangkok; 14 Th Witthayu/Wireless Rd, Bangkok; ⌚8am-4.30pm Mon-Thu, to 1pm Fri; SPhloen Chit exit 5); Chiang Mai (☎053 263015; 198 Th Bamrungrat, Chiang Mai; ⌚8am-4.30pm Mon-Thu, to 1pm Fri) Consulate also in Pattaya.

US Embassy Bangkok (☎02 205 4000; http://bangkok.usembassy.gov; 120-122 Th Witthayu/Wireless Rd, Bangkok; ⌚7am-4pm Mon-Fri; SPhloen Chit exit 5); Chiang Mai (☎053 107700; http://chiangmai.usconsulate.gov; 387 Th Wichayanon, Chiang Mai; ⌚7.30am-4pm Mon-Fri)

Vietnamese Embassy (☎02 251 3552; www.vietnamembassy-thailand.org; 83/1 Th Witthayu/Wireless Rd, Bangkok; ⌚9-11.30am & 2-4.30pm Mon-Fri)

Food

For in-depth information on Thailand's glorious cuisine, see p733.

LGBT Travellers

Thai culture is relatively tolerant of both male and female homosexuality. There are fairly prominent LGBT scenes in Bangkok, Pattaya and Phuket. With regard to dress or mannerism, the LGBT community are generally accepted without comment. However, public displays of affection – wheth-

EATING PRICE RANGES

The following price ranges indicate how much you should expect to pay for a main dish in Thailand.

$ less than 150B

$$ 150–350B

$$$ more than 350B

er heterosexual or homosexual – are frowned upon.

It's worth noting that, perhaps because Thailand is still a relatively conservative place, lesbians generally adhere to rather strict gender roles. Overtly 'butch' lesbians, called *tom* (from 'tomboy'), typically have short hair, bind their breasts and wear men's clothing. Femme lesbians refer to themselves as *dêe* (from 'lady'). Visiting lesbians who don't fit into one of these categories may find themselves met with confusion.

Insurance

A travel-insurance policy to cover theft, loss and medical problems is a good idea. Policies offer differing medical-expense options. There is a wide variety of policies available, so check the small print. Be sure that the policy covers ambulances or an emergency flight home. Some policies specifically exclude 'dangerous activities', which can include scuba diving, motorcycling and even trekking. A locally acquired motorcycle licence is not valid under some policies. You may prefer a policy that pays doctors or hospitals directly rather than you having to pay on the spot and claim later. If you have to claim later, make sure you keep all documentation.

Worldwide travel insurance is available at www.lonelyplanet.com/travel-insurance. You can buy, extend and claim online any time – even if you're already on the road.

Internet Access

As more people travel with mobile devices, internet cafes have begin to disappear, but wi-fi is almost standard in guesthouses and cafes. Signal strength deteriorates in the upper floors of a multistorey building; you can always request a room near a router.

Legal Matters

In general Thai police don't hassle foreigners, especially tourists. They usually go out of their way to avoid having to speak English with a foreigner, especially regarding minor traffic issues.

One major exception is drugs, which most Thai police view as either a social scourge against which it's their duty to enforce the letter of the law, or an opportunity to make untaxed income via bribes.

If you are arrested for any offence, the police will allow you the opportunity to make a phone call, either to your embassy or consulate in Thailand if you have one, or to a friend or relative if not. There's a whole set of legal codes governing the length of time and the manner in which you can be detained before being charged or put on trial, but a lot of discretion is left to the police. In the case of foreigners the police are more likely to bend these codes in your favour. However, as with police worldwide, if you don't show respect you will make matters worse.

Thai law does not presume an indicted detainee to be either 'guilty' or 'innocent' but rather a 'suspect', whose guilt or innocence will be decided in court. Trials are usually speedy.

The **tourist police** (☎1155) can be very helpful in cases of arrest. Although they typically have no jurisdiction over the kinds of cases handled by regular cops, they may be able to help with translations or with contacting your embassy. You can call the hotline number 24 hours a day to lodge complaints or to request assistance with regards to personal safety.

Money

The basic unit of Thai currency is the baht. There are 100 satang in one baht. Coins include 25-satang and 50-satang pieces and 1B, 2B, 5B and 10B coins. The 2B coin is similar in size to the 1B coin but is gold in colour. The two satang coins are typically only issued at supermarkets where prices aren't rounded up to the nearest baht.

Paper currency notes are issued in 20B (green), 50B (blue), 100B (red), 500B (purple) and 1000B (beige) denominations.

ATMs & Credit/Debit Cards

Debit and ATM cards issued by a bank in your own country can be used at ATMs around Thailand to withdraw cash (in Thai baht only) directly from your account back home. ATMs are widespread throughout the country and can be relied on for the bulk of your spending cash.

The downside is that Thai ATMs charge a 150B foreign-transaction fee on top of whatever currency conversion and out-of-network fees your home bank charges. That means ATMs are now a lot more expensive to use than in the past. Before leaving home, shop around for a bank account that has free international ATM usage and reimburses fees incurred at other institutions' ATMs.

Aeon is the only bank we know of in Thailand that doesn't charge the 150B usage fee on foreign accounts, but its distribution of national ATMs is somewhat limited, largely relegated to Big C stores.

Credit cards as well as debit cards can be used for purchases at some shops, hotels and restaurants. The most commonly accepted cards are Visa and MasterCard. American Express is typically only accepted at high-end hotels and restaurants.

Contact your bank and your credit card provider before you leave home and notify them of your upcoming trip so that your accounts aren't suspended due to suspicious overseas activity.

To report a lost or stolen credit/debit card, call the following hotlines in Bangkok:

American Express (☎02 273 5500)

MasterCard (☎001 636 722 7111)

Visa (☎001 800 11535 0660)

Foreign Currency Regulations

There is no limit on the amount of foreign currency that can be brought into Thailand, but people arriving or departing with amounts over US$20,000 need to declare this to the customs officer. The law also requires foreigners to demonstrate adequate funds for their visit. Usually this is only required when applying in advance for a tourist or other type of visa.

Moneychangers

Banks or private moneychangers offer the best foreign-exchange rates. When buying baht, US dollars is the most accepted currency, followed by British pounds and euros. Most banks charge a commission and duty for each travellers cheque cashed. Current exchange rates are posted at exchange counters.

Taxes & Refunds

Thailand has a 7% value-added tax (VAT) on many goods and services. Mid-range and top-end hotels and restaurants might also add a 10% service tax. When the two are combined this becomes the 17% king hit known as 'plus plus', or '++'.

You can get a refund on VAT paid on shopping, though not on food or hotels, as you leave the country. For how-to info, go to www.rd.go.th/vrt/engindex.html.

Tipping

Tipping is not generally expected in Thailand, though it is appreciated. The exception is loose change from a large restaurant bill – if a meal costs 488B and you pay with a 500B note, some Thais will leave the 12B change. It's not so much a tip as a way of saying 'I'm not so money grubbing as to grab every last baht'. At many hotel restaurants or other upmarket eateries, a 10% service charge will be added to your bill.

Opening Hours

The following are standard hours for different types of businesses in Thailand. All government offices and banks are closed on public holidays.

Banks 9.30am to 3.30pm Monday to Friday. Banks in shopping centres and tourist areas are often open longer hours (generally until 8pm) and on weekends. ATMs are accessible 24 hours.

Bars & clubs Open until midnight or 1am, although those in designated entertainment zones can stay open until 2am. Bars and clubs close during elections and certain religious public holidays.

Government offices 8.30am to 4.30pm Monday to Friday; some close for lunch (noon to 1pm), while others are open Saturday (9am to 3pm).

Restaurants Local places often serve food from morning until night (10am to 8pm or 9pm), while more formal restaurants serve only during lunch (from around 11am to 2pm) and dinner (6pm to 10pm).

Stores Large shops usually open from 10am to 7pm; shopping centres open until 10pm. In some small towns, local stores close on Sunday.

Photography

Memory cards for digital cameras are widely available in the electronic sections of most shopping malls.

Be considerate when taking photographs of locals. Learn how to ask politely in Thai and wait for an embarrassed nod. In some of the regularly visited hill-tribe areas, be prepared for the photographed subject to ask for money in exchange for a picture. Other hill tribes will not allow you to point a camera at them.

PRACTICALITIES

Newspapers & Magazines

Thailand's predominate English-language newspapers are the Bangkok Post (www.bangkokpost.com) and the business-heavy Nation (www.nationmultimedia.com). The *International New York Times* and weeklies such as the *Economist* and *Time* are sold at news stands.

Smoking

Smoking in restaurants and bars has been banned since 2008.

Weights & Measures

Thailand follows the international metric system. Gold and silver are weighed in *bàat* (15g).

Post

Thailand has a very efficient postal service and local postage is inexpensive. Typical provincial post offices open from 8.30am to 4.30pm weekdays and 9am to noon on Saturdays. Larger main post offices in provincial capitals may also be open for a half-day on Sundays.

Most provincial post offices will sell do-it-yourself packing boxes. Don't send cash or other valuables through the mail.

Thailand's poste restante service is generally very reliable, though these days few tourists use it. When you receive mail, you must show your passport and fill out some paperwork.

Public Holidays

Government offices and banks close their doors on the following public holidays. For the precise dates of lunar holidays, see the Events & Festivals page of the Tourism Authority of Thailand's website (www.tourismthailand.org/see-do/event-festival).

1 January New Year's Day

February (date varies) Makha Bucha day, Buddhist holy day

6 April Chakri Day, commemorating the founder of the Chakri dynasty, Rama I

13–15 April Songkran Festival, traditional Thai New Year and water festival

1 May Labour Day

5 May Coronation Day, commemorating the 1950 coronation of HM the King and HM the Queen

May/June (date varies) Visakha Bucha, Buddhist holy day

July/August (date varies) Khao Phansa, beginning of the Buddhist Lent

12 August Queen's Birthday

23 October Chulalongkorn Day

October/November (date varies) Ork Phansaa, the end of Buddhist Lent

5 December King's Birthday/Father's Day

10 December Constitution Day

31 December New Year's Eve

GOVERNMENT TRAVEL ADVICE

As Thailand has recently been the site of both violent political protest and military coups, it's wise to check the situation before planning your trip. The following government websites offer travel advisories and information on current hot spots.

Australian Department of Foreign Affairs (www.smarttraveller.gov.au)

British Foreign Office (www.gov.uk/foreign-travel-advice)

US State Department (www.travel.state.gov/content/travel/en.html)

Safe Travel

Although Thailand is not a dangerous country to visit, it is smart to exercise caution, especially when it comes to dealing with strangers (both Thai and foreigners) and travelling alone. In reality you are more likely to be ripped off or have a personal possession surreptitiously stolen than you are to be physically harmed. Motorcycle accidents are another common injury.

Assault

Assault of travellers is relatively rare in Thailand, but it does happen. Causing a Thai to 'lose face' (feel public embarrassment or humiliation) can sometimes elicit an inexplicably strong and violent reaction. Often alcohol is the number-one contributor to bad choices and worse outcomes.

Women, especially solo travellers, need to be smart and somewhat sober when interacting with the opposite sex, be they Thai or *fa·ràng* (foreigners). Opportunists pounce when too many whisky buckets are involved. Also be aware that an innocent flirtation might convey firmer intentions to a recipient who does not share your culture's sexual norms.

Border Issues & Hot Spots

Thailand now enjoys much better relations with its neighbours, and most land borders are fully functional passages for goods and people. However, the ongoing violence in the Deep South has made the crossing at Sungai Kolok into Malaysia dangerous and the entire Muslim-majority provinces (Yala, Pattani and Narathiwat) should be avoided by casual visitors.

Cross-border relations between Thailand and Myanmar have normalised with unprecedented open land access. The long-contested area at Khao Phra Wihan (known as 'Preah Vihear' in Cambodia), along the Thai–Cambodian border, is still a source of military clashes and should be avoided until a lasting peace is found.

Check with your government's foreign ministry for current travel warnings (p769).

Drug Possession

Belying Thailand's anything-goes atmosphere are severely strict punishments for possession and trafficking that are not relaxed for foreigners. It is illegal to buy, sell or possess opium, heroin, amphetamines, hallucinogenic mushrooms and marijuana in Thailand. Possession of drugs can result in a year or more of prison time. Drug smuggling – defined as attempting to cross a border with drugs in your possession – carries considerably higher penalties, including execution.

Scams

Thais can be so friendly and laid-back that some visitors are lulled into a false sense of security, making them vulnerable to scams of all kinds. Bangkok is especially good at long-involved frauds (p143) that dupe travellers into thinking they've made a friend and are getting a bargain, when in fact they are getting ripped off.

Follow Tourism Authority of Thailand's (TAT) number-one suggestion to tourists: *Disregard all offers of free shopping or sightseeing help from strangers*. These invariably take a commission from your purchases.

Theft & Fraud

Exercise diligence when it comes to your personal belongings. Ensure your room is securely locked and carry your most important effects (passport, money, credit cards) on your person. Take care when leaving valuables in hotel safes.

Follow the same practice when you're travelling. A locked bag will not prevent theft on a long-haul bus.

When using a credit card, don't let vendors take your card out of your sight to run it through the machine. Unscrupulous merchants have been known to rub off four or more receipts with one purchase. Sometimes they wait several weeks – even months – between submitting each charge receipt to the bank, so that you can't remember whether you'd been billed by the same vendor more than once.

To avoid losing all of your travel money in an instant, use a credit card that is not directly linked to your bank account so that the operator doesn't have access to immediate funds.

Contact the **tourist police** (☎1155) if you have any problems with consumer fraud.

Touts & Commissions

Touting is a long-time tradition in Asia, and while Thailand doesn't have as many touts as, say, India, it has its share. In Bangkok, túk-túk drivers and other new 'friends' often take new arrivals on city tours. These almost always end up in high-pressure sales situations at silk, jewellery or handicraft shops.

Touts also steer customers to certain guesthouses that pay a commission. Travel agencies are notorious for talking newly arrived tourists into staying at inconveniently located, overpriced hotels.

Some travel agencies masquerade as TAT, the government-funded tourist information office. They might put up agents wearing fake TAT badges, or have signs that read TAT in big letters to entice travellers into their offices where they can sell them bus and train tickets for a commission. Be aware that the official TAT offices do not make hotel or transport bookings. If such a place offers to do this for you then they are a travel agent, not a tourist information office.

BARGAINING

If there isn't a sign stating the price for an item then the price is negotiable. Bargaining is common in street markets and some small shops. Prices in department stores, minimarts, 7-Elevens and so forth are fixed.

Thais respect a good haggler. Always let the vendor make the first offer, then ask 'Can you lower the price?'. This usually results in a discount. Now it's your turn to make a counter-offer. Always start low, but don't bargain at all unless you're serious about buying. If you're buying several of an item, you have much more leverage to request and receive a lower price.

It helps immeasurably to keep the negotiations relaxed and friendly, and always remember to smile. Don't lose your temper or raise your voice as drama is not a good leverage tool.

Shopping

Many bargains await you in Thailand, but don't go shopping in the company of touts, tour guides or friendly strangers as they will inevitably take a commission on anything you buy, thus driving prices up beyond an acceptable value and creating a nuisance for future visitors.

Antiques

Real Thai antiques are increasingly rare. Today, most dealers sell antique reproductions or items from Myanmar. Bangkok and Chiang Mai are the two centres for the antique and reproduction trade.

Real antiques cannot be taken out of Thailand without a permit. No Buddha image, new or old, may be exported without the permission of the **Office of the National Museum** (☎02 224 1370, 02 224 7493; National Museum, 4 Th Na Phra That; ⏱9am-4pm Tue-Fri; ⛴Chang Pier, Maharaj Pier, Phra Chan Tai Pier).

Ceramics

Many kinds of hand-thrown pottery, old and new, are available throughout the kingdom. Bangkok is full of modern ceramic designs, while Chiang Mai sticks to traditional styles. Ko Kret and Dan Kwian are two traditional pottery villages.

Clothing

Clothes tend to be inexpensive in Thailand, but ready-made items are not usually cut to fit Westerners' body types. Increasingly, larger-sized clothes are available in metropolitan malls or tourist centres. Markets sell cheap everyday items and are handy for picking up something when everything else is dirty. For chic clothes, Bangkok leads the country with design-minded fashions. Finding shoes that fit larger feet is also a problem. The custom of returns is not widely accepted in Thailand, so be sure everything fits before you leave the store.

Fake Goods

In Bangkok, Chiang Mai and other tourist centres there's a thriving black-market street trade in fake designer goods. No one pretends they're the real thing, at least not the vendors. Technically it is illegal for these items to be produced and sold and Thailand has often been pressured by intellectual-property enforcement agencies to close down the trade. Rarely does a crackdown by the police last, however, and often the vendors develop more surreptitious means of distribution.

Furniture

Rattan and hardwood furniture items are often good purchases and can be made to order. Chiang Mai is the country's primary furniture producer with many retail outlets in Bangkok. Due to the ban on teak harvesting and the subsequent exhaustion of recycled teak, 70% of export furniture produced in Thailand is made from parawood, a processed wood from rubber trees that can no longer be used for latex production.

USEFUL NUMBERS

Thailand country code ☎66

Bangkok city code ☎02

Mobile numbers ☎06, ☎08, ☎ 09

Operator-assisted international calls ☎100

Free local directory assistance ☎1133

Gems & Jewellery

Thailand is a leading exporter of gems and ornaments, rivalled only by India and Sri Lanka. Although rough-stone sources in Thailand have decreased dramatically, stones are now imported from Myanmar, Sri Lanka and other countries to be cut, polished and traded.

Lacquerware

Chiang Mai is known for gold-on-black lacquerware. Lacquerware furniture and decorative items were traditionally made from bamboo and teak, but these days mango wood might be used as the base. If the item is top quality, only the frame is bamboo and horse or donkey hairs will be wound round it. With lower-quality lacquerware, the whole object is made from bamboo.

Textiles

The northeast is famous for *mát·mèe* cloth, a thick cotton or silk fabric woven from tie-dyed threads, similar to Indonesia's *ikat* fabrics. Surin Province is renowned for its *mát·mèe* silk, often showcasing colours and geometric patterns inherited from Khmer traditions.

In the north, silks reflect the influence of the Lanna weaving traditions, brought to Chiang Mai and the surrounding mountains by the various Tai tribes.

Fairly nice batik is available in the south in patterns that are more similar to the batik found in Malaysia than in Indonesia.

Telephone

The telephone country code for Thailand is 66 and is used when calling the country from abroad. All Thai telephone numbers are preceded by a '0' if you're dialling domestically (the '0' is omitted when calling from overseas). After the initial '0', the next three numbers represent the provincial area code, which is now integral to the telephone number. If the initial '0' is followed by a '6', an '8' or a '9' then you're dialling a mobile phone.

Domestic Calls

Inside Thailand you must dial the area code no matter where you are. In effect, that means all numbers are nine digits. In Bangkok they begin with 02, then a seven-digit number. Calling the provinces will usually involve a three-digit code beginning with 0, then a six-digit number. The only time you drop the initial 0 is when you're calling from outside Thailand.

International Calls

If you want to call an international number from a telephone in Thailand, you must first dial an international access code plus the country code followed by the subscriber number.

In Thailand there are various international access codes charging different rates per minute. The standard direct-dial prefix is ☎001; it is operated by CAT and is considered to have the best sound quality. It connects to the largest number of countries, but is also the most expensive. The next best is ☎007, a prefix operated by TOT with reliable quality and slightly cheaper rates. Economy rates are available through different carriers – do an internet search to determine promotion codes.

The following are some common international country codes: ☎61 Australia, ☎44 UK and ☎1 US.

Dial ☎100 for operator-assisted international calls or reverse-charge (collect) calls.

Mobile Phones

The easiest phone option in Thailand is to acquire a mobile (cell) phone equipped with a local SIM card. Buying a prepaid SIM is as difficult as finding a 7-Eleven. The market is super competitive and deals vary so check websites first, but expect to get a SIM for as little as 49B. More expensive SIMs might come with preloaded talk time; if not, recharge cards are sold at the same stores and start from as little as 10B. Domestic per-minute rates start at less than 50 satang.

Thailand is on the GSM network and mobile phone providers include AIS (1 2 Call), DTAC and True Move. Thailand finally has a 4G network. Coverage and quality of the different carriers varies from year to year based on network upgrades and capacity. Carriers usually sell talk-data packages based on usage amounts.

The main networks:

- **AIS (1 2 Call)** (www.ais.co.th/12call/th)
- **DTAC** (www.dtac.co.th)
- **TrueMove** (www.truemove.com)

Time

Thailand's time zone is seven hours ahead of GMT/UTC (London). Times are often expressed according to the 24-hour clock, eg 11pm is written '23.00' in most cases.

The official year in Thailand is reckoned from the Western calendar year 543 BC, the beginning of the Buddhist Era (BE), so that AD 2016 is 2559 BE, AD 2017 is 2560 BE etc.

Toilets

Increasingly, the Asian-style squat toilet is less of the norm in Thailand. There are still specimens in rural places, provincial bus stations, older homes and modest restaurants, but the Western-style toilet is becoming more prevalent and appears wherever foreign tourists can be found.

If you encounter a squat, here's what you should know. You should straddle the two foot pads and face the door. To flush use the plastic bowl to scoop water out of the adjacent basin and pour into the toilet bowl. Some places supply a small pack of toilet paper at the entrance (5B), otherwise bring your own stash or wipe the old-fashioned way with water.

Even in places where sit-down toilets are installed, the septic system may not be designed to take toilet paper. In such cases there will be a waste basket where you're supposed to place used toilet paper and feminine hygiene products. Some toilets also come with a small spray hose – Thailand's version of the bidet.

Tourist Information

The government-operated tourist information and promotion service, **Tourism Authority of Thailand** (TAT; ☎1672; www.travelthailand.tourismthailand.org), was founded in 1960 and produces excellent pamphlets on sightseeing. TAT's head office is in Bangkok and there are 35 regional offices throughout the country; check the website for contact information.

Travellers with Disabilities

Thailand presents one large, ongoing obstacle course for the mobility impaired. With its high kerbs, uneven footpaths and nonstop traffic, Thai cities can be particularly difficult. In Bangkok many streets must be crossed on pedestrian bridges flanked with steep stairways, while buses and boats don't stop long enough even for the fully abled. Rarely are there any ramps or other access points for wheelchairs.

A number of more expensive top-end hotels make consistent design efforts to provide disabled access to their properties. Other deluxe hotels with high employee-to-guest ratios are usually good about accommodating the mobility impaired by providing staff help where building design fails. For the rest, you're pretty much left to your own resources.

Some organisations and publications that offer tips on international travel include the following:

Accessible Journeys (www.disabilitytravel.com)

Asia Pacific Development Centre on Disability (www.apcdfoundation.org)

Lonely Planet Accessible Travel (http://lptravel.to/accessible travel)

Mobility International USA (www.miusa.org)

Society for Accessible Travel & Hospitality (www.sath.org)

Wheelchair Holidays @ Thailand (www.wheelchairtours.com)

Visas

The **Ministry of Foreign Affairs** (☎02 203 5000; www.mfa.go.th) oversees immigration and visa issues. Check the website or the nearest Thai embassy or consulate for application procedures and costs. In the past five years there have been new rules nearly every year regarding visas and extensions. The best online monitor is **Thaivisa** (www.thaivisa.com).

Tourist Visas & Exemptions

Citizens of 62 countries (including most European countries, Australia, New Zealand and the USA) can enter Thailand at no charge. Depending on nationality, these citizens are issued a 14- to 90-day visa exemption if they arrive by air (most nationalities receive 30 days), or 15 to 30 days by land.

Without proof of an onward ticket and sufficient funds for your projected stay, you can be denied entry, but in practice this is a formality that is rarely checked.

If you plan to stay in Thailand longer than 30 days, you should apply for the 60-day tourist visa from a Thai consulate or embassy before your trip. Contact the nearest Thai embassy or consulate to obtain application procedures and determine fees for tourist visas.

Non-Immigrant Visas

The non-immigrant visa is good for 90 days and is intended for foreigners entering the country for business, study, retirement and extended family visits. There are multiple-entry visas available in this visa class. If you plan to apply for a Thai work permit, you'll need to possess a non-immigrant visa first.

Visa Extensions & Renewals

If you decide you want to stay longer than the allotted time, you can extend your visa by applying at any immigration office in Thailand. The usual fee for a visa extension is 1900B. Those issued with a standard stay of 15 or 30 days can extend their stay for 30 days if the extension is handled before the visa expires. The 60-day tourist visa can be extended by up to 30 days at the discretion of Thai immigration authorities.

Another visa-renewal option is to cross a land border. A new 15- or 30-day visa exemption will be issued upon your return, although the authorities are starting to crack down on frequent and repeated 'visa runs'.

If you overstay your visa, the usual penalty is a fine of 500B per day, with a 20,000B limit. Fines can be paid at the airport, or in advance at an immigration office. If you've overstayed only one day, you don't have to pay. Children under 14 travelling with a parent do not have to pay the penalty.

Foreign residents in Thailand should arrange visa extensions at the immigration office closest to their in-country address.

THAILAND'S IMMIGRATION OFFICES

The following are two immigration offices where visa extensions and other formalities can be addressed. Remember to dress in your Sunday best when doing official business in Thailand and do all visa business yourself (don't hire a third party). For all types of visa extensions, bring along two passport-sized photos and one copy each of the photo and visa pages of your passport.

Bangkok Immigration Office (☎02 141 9889; www.bangkok.immigration.go.th/intro1.html; Bldg B, Government Centre, Soi 7, Th Chaeng Watthana; ⌚8.30am-noon & 1-4.30pm Mon-Fri; Ⓜ Chatuchak Park exit 2 & taxi, Ⓢ Mo Chit exit 3 & taxi)

Chiang Mai Immigration Office (☎053 201755; http://chiangmaiimm.com; off Rte 1141 (Th Mahidol); ⌚8.30am-4.30pm Mon-Fri)

Volunteering

For information about volunteering in Thailand, see p761.

Women Travellers

Women face relatively few problems in Thailand. With the great amount of respect afforded to women, an equal measure should be returned.

Thai women, especially the younger generation, are showing more skin these days. That means almost everyone is now dressing like a bar girl and you can wear spaghetti strap tops and navel-bearing shirts without offending Thais' modesty streak. But to be on the safe side, cover up if you're going deep into rural communities. And certainly cover up if visiting temples.

Attacks and rapes are not common in Thailand, but incidents do occur, especially when an attacker observes a vulnerable target: a drunk or solo woman. If you return home from a bar alone, be sure to have your wits about you. Avoid accepting rides from strangers late at night or travelling around in isolated areas by yourself – common-sense stuff that might escape your notice in a new environment filled with hospitable people.

Be aware that frivolous flirting could unintentionally cause a Thai man to feel a loss of face, especially when the involved parties have different intentions. Always bear in mind that what may seem commonplace in your culture may be received very differently abroad.

Transport

GETTING THERE & AWAY

Flights and tours can be booked online at www.lonelyplanet.com/bookings.

Entering the Country

Entry procedures for Thailand, by air or by land, are straightforward: you'll have to show your passport and and boarding pass, and you'll need to present completed arrival and departure cards.

You do not have to fill in a customs form on arrival unless you have imported goods to declare. In that case you can get the proper form from Thai customs officials at your point of entry.

Air

Airports

Bangkok is Thailand's primary international and domestic gateway. Thailand's provincial airports support an extensive domestic and growing international network. Those offering international destinations include the following:

Suvarnabhumi International Airport (☎02 132 1888; www.suvarnabhumiairport.com) The country's main air terminal, although most domestic flights operate out of Don Mueang International Airport. It's located in Samut Prakan, 30km east of Bangkok and 110km from Pattaya. The airport's name is pronounced *su·wan·na·poom*, and it inherited the airport code (BKK) previously held by the old airport at Don Mueang. The airport website has real-time details of arrivals and departures.

Don Mueang International Airport (☎02 535 1253; www.donmueangairportthai.com) Located 25km north of central Bangkok, Don Mueang was retired from service in 2006 only to reopen later as the city's de facto budget and domestic hub.

Phuket International Airport (☎076 327230; www.phuketairportthai.com) Several domestic and international destinations.

Chiang Mai International Airport (☎053 270222; www.chiangmaiairportthai.com) International destinations include Hong Kong, Kuala Lumpur, Luang Prabang, Macau, Mandalay, Seoul, Singapore, Taipei and Yangon, as well as Beijing, Shanghai and several other cities in China.

Chiang Rai International Airport (Mae Fah Luang International Airport;☎053 798000; www.chiangraiairportonline.com) International destinations include Kunming, Macau and Singapore.

Hat Yai International Airport (☎074 227131; www.hatyaiairportthai.com) International destinations are limited to Kuala Lumpur and Singapore.

Mae Sot Airport (☎055 563620; Th Asia) Flights to/from Yangon.

CLIMATE CHANGE & TRAVEL

Every form of transport that relies on carbon-based fuel generates CO_2, the main cause of human-induced climate change. Modern travel is dependent on aeroplanes, which might use less fuel per kilometre per person than most cars but travel much greater distances. The altitude at which aircraft emit gases (including CO_2) and particles also contributes to their climate change impact. Many websites offer 'carbon calculators' that allow people to estimate the carbon emissions generated by their journey and, for those who wish to do so, to offset the impact of the greenhouse gases emitted with contributions to portfolios of climate-friendly initiatives throughout the world. Lonely Planet offsets the carbon footprint of all staff and author travel.

Land

Thailand shares land borders with Laos, Malaysia, Cambodia and Myanmar (Burma). Land travel between all of these countries can be done at sanctioned border crossings. With improved highways and new bridges, it is also easier to travel from Thailand to China via Laos.

Border Crossings

CAMBODIA

Cambodian tourist visas are available at the border for US$30. Bring a passport photo and ignore the runner boys who want to issue a health certificate or other paperwork for additional fees.

Aranya Prathet to Poipet The most direct land route between Bangkok and Siem Reap (for Angkor Wat), now connected by direct government bus.

Hat Lek to Krong Koh Kong The coastal crossing for travellers heading to/from Ko Chang/Sihanoukville.

Ban Pakard to Psar Pruhm A back-door route from Ko Chang (via Chanthaburi) to Battambang and Angkor Wat.

Remote crossings include O Smach to Chong Chom (periodically closed due to fighting at Khao Phra Wihan) and Choam to Chong Sa-Ngam, but they aren't as convenient as you'll have to hire private transport on the Cambodian side of the border.

CHINA

The interior of southern China is now linked with Laos and northern Thailand, making it possible to travel somewhat directly between the two countries. You'll need to arrange your Chinese visa prior to departure, ideally in Bangkok or Chiang Mai.

Chiang Khong to Mengla The China–Thailand highway (AH3) was a former opium smuggling trail that has been modernised into a major transnational trade route. The 1800km of paved road between Kunming, in China's Yunnan Province, and northern Laos to Bangkok has been facilitated by the construction of the fourth Thai-Lao Friendship Bridge (at Chiang Khong-Huay Xai) across the Mekong River in 2014.

Chiang Saen to Jinghong It was previously possible to take a passenger boat along the Mekong River from northern Thailand to China's Yunnan Province, but at the time of writing the service had been suspended.

LAOS

It is fairly hassle free to cross into Laos from northern and northeastern Thailand. Lao tourist visas (US$30 to US$42) can be obtained on arrival and applications require a passport photo. Try to have crisp, clean bills. There are increasing numbers of direct buses that link major towns on both sides of the border, making the border towns just a formality stop.

Nong Khai to Vientiane The first Thai-Lao Friendship Bridge to span the Mekong River is one of the main gateways between the two countries. Nong Khai is easily reached by train or bus from Bangkok.

Chiang Khong to Huay Xai The fourth Thai-Lao Friendship Bridge has increased the popularity of this crossing that links northern Thailand with Luang Prabang via boat. Direct buses from Chiang Mai and Chiang Rai to Laos use this crossing.

Mukdahan to Savannakhet The second Thai-Lao Friendship Bridge provides a trilateral link between Thailand, Laos and Vietnam.

Nakhon Phanom to Tha Khaek The third Thai-Lao Friendship Bridge connects northeastern Thailand to southern Laos.

Chong Mek to Vangtao The border is best accessed via Ubon Ratchathani (Thailand) and is a good option for transiting to Pakse (Laos). Direct buses from Ubon are now available.

In northeastern Thailand, remote crossings include Bueng Kan to Paksan (Lao visas must be arranged in advance) and Tha Li to Kaen Thao (requires chartered transport). In northern Thailand, a remote crossing links Ban Huay Kon, in Nan, and Muang Ngeun.

MALAYSIA

Malaysia, especially the west coast, is easy to reach by bus, train and even boat.

Hat Yai to Butterworth The western spur of the train line originating in Bangkok terminates at Butterworth, the mainland transfer point to Penang.

Hat Yai to Padang Besar Buses and trains originate out of the southern transit town of Hat Yai en route to a variety of Malaysian destinations. Border formalities are handled at Padang Besar.

Sungai Kolok to Rantau Panjang While this border crossing is a possibility, the continued violence in Thailand's Deep South means that we do not recommend it.

Ko Lipe to Langkawi Boats provide a convenient high-season link between these two Andaman islands. Most travellers opt for this route instead of that linking the mainland port of Satun (Thailand) to the Malaysian island of Langkawi and the mainland town of Kuala Perlis.

There are a few other minor crossings along this border, but a private vehicle is a necessity.

MYANMAR

As part of the AEC (ASEAN Economic Community) integration goals, Myanmar has lifted travel restrictions at four of its borders with Thailand, meaning that foreign visitors can now enter the country with a prearranged Myanmar visa and exit via a different border (previously all visitors had to enter and exit via the same controlled point). The Phu Nam Ron to Htee Khee crossing is new and requires a major infrastructure investment. The Thai government intends to develop this route as a link between Bangkok and Myanmar's Dawei port in the Andaman Sea.

Mae Sai to Tachileik This is a popular border-run crossing. It also hosts a popular border market that can be visited on a day trip from Thailand without a prearranged visa. For further travel, a prearranged visa is required.

Ranong to Kawthoung This is a popular visa-renewal point in the southern part of Thailand and can be used to enter/exit southern Myanmar.

Mae Sot to Myawaddy One of the most accessible land borders for points within Myanmar.

Bus, Car & Motorcycle

Road connections exist to all of Thailand's neighbours, and these routes can be travelled by bus, shared taxi and private car. In some cases you'll take a bus to the border point, pass through immigration and then pick up another bus or shared taxi on the other side. In other cases, especially when crossing the Malaysian border, the bus will stop for immigration formalities and then continue to its destination across the border.

Taking a private vehicle across an international border requires some paperwork; it's generally not allowed to take a hired vehicle abroad.

Train

Thailand's and Malaysia's state railways meet at Butterworth (93km south of the Thai–Malaysian border), which is a transfer point to Penang (by boat), or to Kuala Lumpur and Singapore (by Malaysian train).

There are several border crossings for which you can take a train to the border and then switch to car transport on the other side. The Thai–Cambodian border crossing of Aranya Prathet to Poipet and the Thai–Lao crossing of Nong Khai to Vientiane are two examples.

Another rail line travels to the Malaysian east-coast border town of Sungai Kolok, but because of ongoing violence in Thailand's Deep South we don't recommend this route for travellers.

GETTING AROUND

Air

Hopping around the country by air continues to be affordable. Most routes originate from Bangkok (both Don Mueang and Suvarnabhumi International Airports), but Chiang Mai, Hat Yai, Ko Samui, Phuket and Udon Thani all have a few routes to other Thai towns.

Airlines

Air Asia (☎02 515 9999; www.airasia.com) Don Mueang to Buriram, Chiang Mai, Chiang Rai, Hat Yai, Khong Kaen, Krabi, Loei, Nakhon Phanom, Nakhon Si Thammarat, Nan, Narathiwat, Phitsanulok, Phuket, Roi Et, Sakhon Nakhon, Surat Thani, Trang, Ubon Ratchathani and Udon Thani; Chiang Mai to Hat Yai, Krabi, Phuket and Surat Thani; and Phuket to Udon Thani.

Bangkok Airways (☎1771; www.bangkokairways.com) Suvarnabhumi to Chiang Mai, Chiang Rai, Krabi, Lampang, Pattaya, Phuket, Ko Samui, Sukhothai, Trat and Udon Thani; and Chiang Mai to Ko Samui, Phuket and Udon Thani.

Happy Air (☎02 216 5151; www.happyair.co.th) Suvarnabhumi to Chumphon and Ranong.

Kan Air (☎02 551 6111; www.kanairlines.com) Don Mueang to Chiang Mai, Chiang Rai, Hua Hin, Khon Kaen, Nakhon Ratchasima, Nan, Phitsanulok, Mae Sot, Pattaya, Ubon Ratchathani and Udon Thani; and Chiang Mai to Chiang Rai, Pai and Mae Hong Son.

Nok Air (☎1318; www.nokair.com) Don Mueang to Buriram, Chiang Mai, Chiang Rai, Chumphon, Hat Yai, Khon Kaen, Krabi, Lampang, Loei, Mae Sot, Nakhon Phanom, Nakhon Si Thammarat, Nan, Phitsanulok, Phrae, Phuket, Ranong, Roi Et, Sakhon Nakhon, Surat Thani, Trang, Ubon Ratchathani and Udon Thani; and Chiang Mai to Udon Thani.

Orient Thai (☎02 229 4100; www.flyorientthai.com/en/home) Don Mueang to Phuket.

Solar Air (☎02 535 2456; www.solarair.co.th) Don Mueang to Chumphon.

Thai Lion Air (☎02 529 9999; www.lionairthai.com) Don Mueang to Chiang Mai, Chiang Rai, Hat Yai, Krabi, Nakhon Si Thammarat, Phuket, Surat Thani, Ubon Ratchathani and Udon Thani; and Hat Yai to Udon Thani.

Thai Smile (☎02 118 8888; www.thaismileair.com) Don Mueang to Chiang Mai, Phuket and Khon Kaen; Suvarnabhumi to Chiang Mai, Chiang Rai, Hat Yai, Phuket, Khon Kaen, Narathiwat, Surat Thani, Ubon Ratchathani and Udon Thani; and Chiang Mai to Phuket.

Boat

The true Thai water transport is the *reu·a hăhng yow* (long-tail boat), so-called because the propeller is mounted at the end of a long driveshaft extending from the engine. The long-tail boats are a staple of transport on rivers and canals in Bangkok and neighbouring provinces, and between islands.

Between the mainland and small, less-touristed islands, the standard craft is a wooden boat, 8m to 10m long, with an inboard engine, a wheelhouse and a simple roof to shelter passengers and cargo. To more popular destinations, faster hovercraft (jetfoils) and speedboats are the norm.

Bus & Minivan

The bus network in Thailand is prolific and reliable. The Thai government subsidises the Transport Company (*bò·rí·sàt kŏn sòng*), usually abbreviated to Baw Khaw Saw (BKS). Every city and town in Thailand linked by bus has a BKS station, even if it's just a patch of dirt by the side of the road.

By far the most reliable bus companies in Thailand are the ones that operate out of the BKS stations. In some cases the companies are entirely state owned; in others they are private concessions.

We do not recommend using bus companies that operate directly out of tourist centres, such as Bangkok's Th Khao San, because of repeated instances of theft and commission-seeking stops. Be sure to be aware of bus scams and other common problems.

For some destinations, minivans are increasingly superseding buses. Minivans are run by private companies and because their vehicles are smaller, they can depart from the market (instead of the out-of-town bus stations) and in some cases will deliver guests directly to their hotel. Just don't sit in the front – that way you can avoid having to watch the driver's daredevil techniques!

Bus Classes

The cheapest and slowest buses are the *rót tam·má·dah* (ordinary fan buses) that stop in every little town and for every waving hand along the highway. Only a few of these ordinary buses still exist, mostly in rural locations or for local destinations.

Rót aa (air-con buses) come in a variety of classes, depending on the destination's distance. Short distances are usually covered by the basic 2nd-class bus, which does not have an on-board toilet. For longer routes, buses increase in comfort and amenities, ranging from 1st class to 'VIP' and 'Super VIP'. The latter two have fewer seats so that each seat reclines further; sometimes these are called *rót norn* (sleeper buses).

Bring a jacket for long-distance bus trips as air-con keeps the cabin at arctic temperatures. The service on these buses is usually quite good and on certain routes sometimes includes a beverage and video, courtesy of an 'air hostess'.

On overnight journeys the buses usually stop somewhere en route for a midnight meal.

Reservations

You can book air-con BKS buses at any BKS terminal, or even by phone with a payment at 7-Eleven. Ordinary (fan) buses cannot be booked in advance. Privately run buses can be booked through most hotels or any travel agency, but it's best to book directly through a bus office to be sure that you get what you pay for.

Car & Motorcycle

Driving Licence

In theory, short-term visitors who wish to drive vehicles (including motorcycles) in Thailand need an International Driving Permit. In reality this is rarely enforced.

Fuel & Spare Parts

Modern petrol (gasoline) stations are plentiful. In more rural areas *ben·sin/nám·man rót yon* (petrol containing benzene) is usually available at small roadside or village stands. All fuel in Thailand is unleaded, and diesel is used by trucks and some passenger cars. Thailand also uses several alternative fuels, including gasohol (a blend of petrol and ethanol that comes in either 91% or 95% octane levels) and compressed natural gas, used by taxis with bi-fuel capabilities.

Hire & Purchase

Cars, 4WDs and vans can be hired in most major cities and airports from local companies as well as all the international chains. Local companies tend to have cheaper rates, but the quality of their fleets varies. Check the tyre tread and general upkeep of the vehicle before committing.

BICYCLE TRAVEL IN THAILAND

For exploring the more rural, less-trafficked corners of Thailand – Ayuthaya Historical Park, Pai, Sukhothai Historical Park – bicycles are a great way to get around. They can usually be hired from guesthouses for as little as 50B per day, though they aren't always high-quality. A security deposit isn't usually required.

Elsewhere, lack of infrastructure and dangerous roads mean that cycling isn't generally recommended as a means of transport for the casual tourist. Exceptions are the guided bicycle tours of Bangkok and some other large cities that stick to rural routes.

Yet despite the risks, bicycle touring is an increasingly popular way to see Thailand, and most roads are sealed and have roomy shoulders. Because duties are high on imported bikes, you'll do better to bring your own bike to Thailand rather than purchasing locally. No special permits are needed for bringing a bicycle into the country. It's advisable to bring a well-stocked repair kit. A good resource for cycling in the country is **Bicycle Thailand** (www.bicyclethailand.com).

Motorcycles can be hired in major towns and tourist centres from guesthouses and small mum-and-dad businesses. Hiring a motorcycle in Thailand is relatively easy and a great way to independently tour the countryside. For daily hires most businesses will ask that you leave your passport as a deposit. Before hiring a motorcycle, check the vehicle's condition and ask for a helmet (which is required by law).

Insurance

Thailand requires a minimum of liability insurance for all registered vehicles on the road. The better hire companies include comprehensive coverage for their vehicles. Always verify that a vehicle is insured for liability before signing a rental contract; you should also ask to see the dated insurance documents. If you have an accident while driving an uninsured vehicle, you're in for some major hassles.

Road Rules & Hazards

Thais drive on the left-hand side of the road (most of the time!). Other than that, just about anything goes, in spite of road signs and speed limits.

The main rule to be aware of is that right of way goes to the bigger vehicle – this is not what it says in the Thai traffic laws, but it's the reality. Maximum speed limits are 50km/h on urban roads and 80km/h to 100km/h on most highways – but on any given stretch of highway you'll see various vehicles travelling as slowly as 30km/h and as fast as 150km/h.

Indicators are often used to warn passing drivers about oncoming traffic. A flashing left indicator means it's OK to pass, while a right indicator means that someone's approaching from the other direction. Horns are used to tell other vehicles that the driver plans to pass. When drivers flash their lights, they're telling you not to pass.

In Bangkok traffic is chaotic, roads are poorly signposted and motorcycles and random contraflows mean you can suddenly find yourself facing a wall of cars coming the other way.

Outside of the capital, the principal hazard when driving in Thailand, besides the general disregard for traffic laws, is having to contend with so many different types of vehicles on the same road – trucks, bicycles, túk-túk (pronounced *đúk đúk*) and motorcycles. This danger is often compounded by the lack of working lights. In village areas the vehicular traffic is lighter but you have to contend with stray chickens, dogs and water buffaloes.

ROAD SAFETY

Thailand's roads are dangerous: in 2014 the University of Michigan's Transportation Research Institute declared the country's roads the second deadliest in the world, with 44 road deaths per 100,000 people – more than double the world average. Several high-profile bus accidents involving foreign tourists have prompted some Western nations to issue travel advisories for highway safety due to disregard for speed limits, reckless driving and long-distance bus drivers' use of stimulants.

Fatal bus crashes make headlines, but nearly 75% of vehicle accidents in Thailand involve motorcycles. Less than half of the motorcyclists in the country wear helmets and many tourists are injured when riding motorcycles because they don't know how to handle the vehicles and are unfamiliar with local driving conventions. British consular offices cited Thailand as a primary destination for UK citizens experiencing road-traffic accidents, often involving motorcyclists.

If you are a novice motorcyclist, familiarise yourself with the vehicle in an uncongested area of town and stick to the smaller 100cc automatic bikes. Drive slowly, especially when roads are slick or when there is loose gravel. Remember to distribute weight as evenly as possible across the frame of the bike to improve handling. And don't expect that other vehicles will look out for you: motorcycles are low on the traffic totem pole.

Hitching

Hitching is never entirely safe in any country and we don't recommend it. Travellers who decide to hitch should understand that they are taking a small but potentially serious risk. Other than at some national parks where there isn't public transport, hitching is rarely seen these days in Thailand, so most passing motorists might not realise the intentions of the foreigner standing on the side of the road with a thumb out. Indeed, Thais don't 'thumb it'; instead, when they want a ride they wave their hand with the palm facing the ground. This is the same gesture used to flag a taxi or bus, which is why some drivers might stop and point to a bus stop if one is nearby.

Local Transport

City Bus & Sŏrng·tăa·ou

Bangkok has the largest city-bus system in the country, while Udon Thani and a few other provincial capitals have some city-bus services. The etiquette for riding public buses is to wait at a bus stop and hail the vehicle by waving your hand palm-side downward. You typically pay the fare once you've taken a seat or, in some cases, when you disembark.

Elsewhere, public transport is provided by *sŏrng·tăa·ou* ('two rows'; a small pick-up truck outfitted with two facing benches for passengers). They sometimes operate on fixed routes, just like buses, but they may also run a share-taxi service where they pick up passengers going in the same general direction. In tourist centres, *sŏrng·tăa·ou* can be chartered just like a regular taxi, but you'll need to negotiate the fare beforehand. You can usually hail a *sŏrng·tăa·ou* anywhere along its route and pay the fare when you disembark.

Depending on the region, *sŏrng·tăa·ou* might also run a fixed route from the centre of town to outlying areas, or even points within the provinces.

Mass Transit

Bangkok is the only city in Thailand to have an above-ground (BTS) and underground light-rail (MRT) public transport system.

Motorcycle Taxi

Many cities in Thailand have *mor·đeu·sai ráp jâhng*, motorcycle taxis that can be hired for short distances. If you're empty-handed or travelling with a small bag, they can't be beaten for transport in a pinch.

In most cities, you'll find motorcycle taxis clustered near street intersections. Usually they wear numbered jerseys. Fares tend to run from 10B to 50B, depending on distance. You'll need to establish the price beforehand.

> **SĂHM·LÓR & TÚK-TÚK**
>
> Săhm·lór are three-wheeled pedicabs that are typically found in small towns where traffic is light and old-fashioned ways persist.
>
> The modern era's version of the human-powered săhm·lór is the motorised túk-túk. They're small utility vehicles, powered by screaming engines (usually LPG-powered) with a lot of flash and sparkle.
>
> With either form of transport the fare must be established by bargaining before departure. In tourist centres, túk-túk drivers often grossly overcharge foreigners, so have a sense of how much the fare should be before soliciting a ride. Hotel staff are helpful in providing reasonable fare suggestions.
>
> Readers interested in pedicab lore and design may want to have a look at Lonely Planet's hardcover pictorial book, *Chasing Rickshaws*, by Lonely Planet founder Tony Wheeler.

Taxi

Bangkok has the most formal system of metered taxis, although other cities have growing 'taxi meter' networks. In some cases, fares are set in advance or require negotiation.

In bigger cities, traditional taxi alternatives and app-based taxi hailing initiatives are also available – sort of.

Uber (www.uber.com/cities/bangkok), undoubtedly the most well-known ride service in the world, was introduced to Thailand in 2014. It quickly gained popularity among those looking to avoid the usual Bangkok taxi headaches: communication issues, perpetual lack of change and reckless drivers. Yet in late 2014 Thailand's Department of Land Transport deemed the app-based outfit illegal, declaring that its vehicles weren't properly registered, its fares unregulated and its drivers unlicensed. At the time of writing, the situation seemed to have reached a stalemate, with Uber still operating in Bangkok, albeit less conspicuously.

The good news is that other outfits such as **GrabTaxi** (www.grabtaxi.com/bangkok-thailand) and **Easy Taxi** (www.easytaxi.com/th), both of which operate via already-registered taxis, haven't been affected by the ruling. And in 2015, a domestic alternative, **All Thai Taxi** (www.allthaitaxi.com), had even been introduced.

Tours

Many operators around the world can arrange guided tours of Thailand. Most of them simply serve as brokers for tour companies based in Thailand. The better tour companies build their own Thailand itineraries from scratch and choose their local suppliers based on which best serve these itineraries.

Asian Trails (☎02 626 2000; www.asiantrails.travel) Tour operator that runs programs for overseas brokers. Trips include a mix of on- and off-the-beaten-path destinations.

Eastern & Oriental Express (www.belmond.com/eastern-and-oriental-express) Luxury train travel in Thailand.

i-to-i (www.i-to-i.com) Volunteer tourism and gap-year programs.

Intrepid Travel (www.intrepidtravel.com) Specialises in small-group travel geared towards young people.

Isan Explorer (☎087 643 9018; www.isanexplorer.com) Custom tours to the northeast.

Mekong Cruises (www.cruisemekong.com) Float down the mighty river aboard an elegant vessel.

Spice Roads (☎02 381 7490; www.spiceroads.com) Variety of regional cycling programs.

Tour de Thailand (☎081 173 4469; www.tourdethailand.com) Charity bike ride organiser covering touring routes throughout the country.

Tours with Kasma Loha-Unchit (www.thaifoodandtravel.com) Thai cookbook author offers personalised 'cultural immersion' tours of Thailand.

Train

Thailand's train system connects the four corners of the country and is a convenient and scenic, if slow, alternative to buses for the long journey north to Chiang Mai or south to Surat Thani. The train is also ideal for short trips to Ayuthaya and Lopburi from Bangkok, where traffic is a consideration.

The 4500km rail network is operated by the **State Railway of Thailand** (☎1690; www.railway.co.th) and covers four main lines: northern, southern, northeastern and eastern. All long-distance trains originate from Bangkok's Hualamphong station.

Classes

The SRT operates passenger trains in three classes – 1st, 2nd and 3rd – but each class varies considerably depending on whether you're on an ordinary, rapid or express train.

First Class Private, two-bunk cabins define the 1st-class carriages, which are available only on rapid, express and special-express trains.

Second Class The seating arrangements in a 2nd-class, nonsleeper carriage are similar to those on a bus, with pairs of padded seats, usually recliners, all facing towards the front of the train. On 2nd-class sleeper cars, pairs of seats face one another and convert into two fold-down berths. The lower berth has more headroom than the upper berth and this is reflected in a higher fare. Children are always assigned a lower berth. Second-class carriages are found only on rapid and express trains. There are air-con and fan 2nd-class carriages.

Third Class A typical 3rd-class carriage consists of two rows of bench seats divided into facing pairs. Each bench seat is designed to seat two or three passengers, but on a crowded rural line nobody seems to care. Express trains do not carry 3rd-class carriages at all. Commuter trains in the Bangkok area are all 3rd class.

Costs

Fares are determined on a base price with surcharges added for distance, class and train type (special express, express, rapid, ordinary). Extra charges are added if the carriage has air-con and for sleeping berths (either upper or lower).

Reservations

Advance bookings can be made from one to 60 days before your intended date of departure. You can make bookings in person from any train station. Train tickets can also be purchased at travel agencies, which usually add a service charge to the ticket price. If you are planning long-distance train travel from outside the country, you should email SRT (passenger-ser@railway.co.th) at least two weeks before your journey. You will receive an email confirming the booking. Pick up and pay for tickets an hour before leaving at the scheduled departure train station.

It is advisable to make advanced bookings for long-distance sleeper trains between Bangkok and Chiang Mai, or from Bangkok to Surat Thani, as seats fill up quickly.

For short-distance trips you should purchase your ticket at least a day in advance for seats (rather than sleepers).

Partial refunds on tickets are available depending on the number of days prior to your departure that you arrange a cancellation. These arrangements can be handled at the train station booking office.

Station Services

You'll find that all train stations in Thailand have baggage-storage services (or 'cloak rooms'). Most stations have a ticket window that will open between 15 and 30 minutes before train arrivals. There are also newsagents, small snack vendors and some full-service restaurants.

Most train stations have printed timetables in English, though this isn't always the case for smaller stations.

Health

Health risks and the quality of medical facilities vary depending on where and how you travel in Thailand. The majority of cities and popular tourist areas have adequate, and even excellent, medical care. However, travel to remote rural areas can expose you to some health risks and less adequate medical care.

Travellers tend to worry about contracting exotic infectious diseases when visiting the tropics, but these are far less common than problems with pre-existing medical conditions, such as heart disease, and accidental injury (especially as a result of traffic accidents).

Other common illnesses are respiratory infections, diarrhoea and dengue fever. Fortunately most common illnesses can be prevented or are easily treated.

Our advice is a general guide and does not replace the advice of a doctor trained in travel medicine.

BEFORE YOU GO

Pack medications in clearly labelled original containers and obtain a signed and dated letter from your physician describing your medical conditions, medications and syringes or needles. If you have a heart condition, bring a copy of your electrocardiogram (ECG) taken just prior to travelling.

If you take any regular medication bring double your needs in case of loss or theft. In Thailand you can buy many medications over the counter without a doctor's prescription, but it can be difficult to find the exact medication you are taking.

Contact your home country's Department of Foreign Affairs or the equivalent and register your trip; this is a helpful precaution in the event of a natural disaster.

Insurance

Even if you're fit and healthy, don't travel without health insurance – accidents *do* happen. You may require extra cover for adventure activities such as rock climbing or diving, as well as scooter/motorcycle riding. If your health insurance doesn't cover you for medical expenses abroad, ensure you get specific travel insurance. Most hospitals require an upfront guarantee of payment (from yourself or your insurer) prior to admission. Enquire before your trip about payment of medical charges and retain all documentation (medical reports, invoices etc) for claim purposes.

Recommended Vaccinations

You should arrange your vaccines six to eight weeks prior to departure through a specialised travel-medicine clinic.

The Centers for Disease Control and Prevention (www.cdc.gov) has a traveller's health section that contains recommendations for vaccinations. The only

FURTHER READING

- International Travel & Health (www.who.int/ith) is published by the World Health Organization (WHO).
- Centers for Disease Control & Prevention (www.cdc.gov) has country-specific advice.
- *Traveller's Health: How to Stay Healthy Abroad* by Dr Richard Dawood is considered the 'health bible' for international holidays.
- *Travelling Well* by Dr Deborah Mills is a health guidebook and website (www.travellingwell.com.au).
- *Healthy Living in Thailand,* published by the Thai Red Cross, is recommended for long-term travellers.

vaccine required by international regulations is yellow fever. Proof of vaccination will only be required if you have visited a country in the yellow-fever zone within the six days prior to entering Thailand. If you are travelling to Thailand *from* Africa or South America you should check to see if you require proof of vaccination.

Medical Checklist

Recommended items for a personal medical kit include the following, most of which are available in Thailand.

- antifungal cream, eg Clotrimazole
- antibacterial cream, eg Muciprocin
- antibiotic for skin infections, eg Amoxicillin/Clavulanate or Cephalexin
- antibiotics for diarrhoea include Norfloxacin, Ciprofloxacin or Azithromycin for bacterial diarrhoea; for giardiasis or amoebic dysentery take Tinidazole
- antihistamine – there are many options, eg Cetrizine for daytime and Promethazine for night-time
- antiseptic, eg Betadine
- antispasmodic for stomach cramps, eg Buscopan
- contraceptives
- decongestant
- DEET-based insect repellent
- oral rehydration solution for diarrhoea (eg Gastrolyte), diarrhoea 'stopper' (eg Loperamide) and antinausea medication
- first-aid items such as scissors, Elastoplasts, bandages, gauze, thermometer (but not one with mercury), sterile needles and syringes (with a doctor's letter), safety pins and tweezers
- hand gel (alcohol based) or alcohol-based hand wipes
- ibuprofen or another anti-inflammatory
- indigestion medication, eg Quick-Eze or Mylanta
- laxative, eg Coloxyl
- migraine medicine – for migraine sufferers
- paracetamol
- permethrin to impregnate clothing and mosquito nets if at high risk
- steroid cream for allergic/itchy rashes, eg 1% to 2% hydrocortisone
- sunscreen, sunglasses and hat
- throat lozenges
- thrush (vaginal yeast infection) treatment, eg Clotrimazole pessaries or Diflucan tablet
- Ural or equivalent if prone to urine infections

IN TRANSIT

Deep-Vein Thrombosis

Deep-vein thrombosis (DVT) occurs when blood clots form in the legs during long trips such as flights, chiefly because of prolonged immobility. The longer the journey, the greater the risk. Though most blood clots are reabsorbed uneventfully, some may break off and travel through the blood vessels to the lungs, where they can cause life-threatening complications.

The chief symptom of DVT is swelling or pain of the foot, ankle or calf, usually but not always on one side. When a blood clot travels to the lungs, it may cause chest pain and difficulty in breathing. Travellers with any of these symptoms should immediately seek medical attention.

To prevent the development of DVT on long flights you should walk about the cabin, perform isometric compressions of the leg muscles (ie contract the leg muscles while sitting) and drink plenty of fluids (nonalcoholic). Those at higher risk should speak with a doctor.

Jet Lag & Motion Sickness

Jet lag is common when crossing more than five time zones. It results in insomnia, fatigue, malaise or nausea. To avoid jet lag, drink plenty of fluids (nonalcoholic) and eat light meals. Upon arrival, seek exposure to natural sunlight and readjust your schedule. Some people find melatonin helpful.

Sedating antihistamines such as dimenhydrinate (Dramamine) or Prochlorperazine (Phenergan) are usually the first choice for treating motion sickness. Their main side effect is drowsiness. A herbal alternative is ginger. Scopolamine patches are considered the most effective prevention.

IN THAILAND

Availability & Cost of Health Care

Bangkok is considered a centre of medical excellence in Southeast Asia. Private hospitals are more expensive than other medical facilities, but offer a superior standard of care and English-speaking staff. The cost of health care is relatively cheap in Thailand compared to most Western countries.

Infectious Diseases

Cutaneous Larva Migrans

This disease, caused by dog or cat hookworm, is particularly common on the beaches of Thailand. The

RARE BUT BE AWARE

Avian Influenza Most of those infected have had close contact with sick or dead birds.

Filariasis A mosquito-borne disease that is common in the local population; practice mosquito-avoidance measures (p784).

Hepatitis E Transmitted through contaminated food and water and has similar symptoms to hepatitis A. Can be a severe problem in pregnant women. Follow safe eating and drinking guidelines.

Japanese B Encephalitis Viral disease transmitted by mosquitoes, typically occurring in rural areas. Vaccination is recommended for travellers spending more than one month outside cities, or for long-term expats.

Meliodosis Contracted by skin contact with soil. Affects up to 30% of the local population in northeastern Thailand. The symptoms are very similar to those experienced by tuberculosis (TB) sufferers. There is no vaccine, but it can be treated with medications.

Strongyloides A parasite transmitted by skin contact with soil; common in the local population. It is characterised by an unusual skin rash – a linear rash on the trunk that comes and goes. An overwhelming infection can follow. It can be treated with medications.

Tuberculosis Medical and aid workers and long-term travellers who have significant contact with the local population should take precautions. Vaccination is recommended for children spending more than three months in Thailand. The main symptoms are fever, cough, weight loss, night sweats and tiredness. Treatment is available with long-term multidrug regimens.

Typhus Murine typhus is spread by the bite of a flea; scrub typhus is spread via a mite. Symptoms include fever, muscle pains and a rash. Follow general insect-avoidance measures; Doxycycline will also prevent it.

rash starts as a small lump, and then slowly spreads like a winding line. It is intensely itchy, especially at night. It is easily treated with medications and should not be cut out or frozen.

Dengue Fever

This mosquito-borne disease is increasingly problematic in Thailand, especially in the cities. As there is no vaccine it can only be prevented by avoiding mosquito bites. The mosquito that carries dengue is a daytime biter, so use insect-avoidance measures at all times. Symptoms include high fever, severe headache (especially behind the eyes), nausea and body aches (dengue was previously known as 'breakbone fever'). Some people develop a rash (which can be very itchy) and experience diarrhoea. Chiang Mai and the southern islands are particularly high-risk areas. There is no specific treatment, just rest and paracetamol – do not take aspirin or ibuprofen as they increase the risk of haemorrhaging. See a doctor to be diagnosed and monitored.

Dengue can progress to the more severe and life-threatening dengue haemorrhagic fever, but this is very uncommon in tourists. The risk of this increases substantially if you have previously been infected with dengue and are then infected with a different serotype.

Hepatitis A

The risk in Bangkok is decreasing, but there is still significant risk in most of the country. This food- and waterborne virus infects the liver, causing jaundice (yellow skin and eyes), nausea and lethargy. There is no specific treatment for hepatitis A. In rare instances it can be fatal for those over the age of 40. All travellers to Thailand should be vaccinated against hepatitis A.

Hepatitis B

The only sexually transmitted disease (STD) that can be prevented by vaccination, hepatitis B is spread by body fluids, including sexual contact. In some parts of Thailand up to 20% of the population are carriers of hepatitis B, and usually are unaware of this. The long-term consequences can include liver cancer, cirrhosis and death.

HIV

HIV is now one of the most common causes of death in people under the age of 50 in Thailand. Always practise safe sex, and avoid getting tattoos or using unclean syringes.

Influenza

Present year-round in the tropics, influenza (flu) symptoms include high fever, muscle aches, runny nose, cough and sore throat. Flu is the most common vaccine-preventable disease contracted by travellers and everyone should consider vaccination. There is no specific treatment, just rest and paracetamol. Complications such as bronchitis or middle-ear infection may require antibiotic treatment.

Leptospirosis

Leptospirosis is contracted from exposure to infected surface water – most commonly after river rafting or canyoning. Early symptoms are very similar to flu and include headache and fever. It can vary from a very mild ailment to a fatal disease. Diagnosis is made through blood tests and it is easily treated with Doxycycline.

Malaria

There is an enormous amount of misinformation concerning malaria. Malaria is caused by a parasite transmitted by the bite of an infected mosquito. The most important symptom of malaria is fever, but general symptoms such as headache, diarrhoea, cough or chills may also occur – the same symptoms as many other infections. A diagnosis can only be made by taking a blood sample.

Most parts of Thailand visited by tourists, particularly city and resort areas, have minimal to no risk of malaria, and the risk of side effects from taking antimalarial tablets is likely to outweigh the risk of getting the disease itself. If you are travelling to high-risk rural areas (unlikely for most visitors), seek medical advice on the right medication and dosage for you.

Measles

This highly contagious viral infection is spread through coughing and sneezing. Most people born before 1966 are immune as they had the disease in childhood. Measles starts with a high fever and rash and can be complicated by pneumonia and brain disease. There is no specific treatment. Ensure you are fully vaccinated.

Rabies

This disease, fatal if left untreated, is spread by the bite or lick of an infected animal – most commonly a dog or monkey. You should seek medical advice immediately after any animal bite and commence post-exposure treatment. Having a pretravel vaccination means the postbite treatment is greatly simplified.

If an animal bites you, gently wash the wound with soap and water, and apply iodine-based antiseptic. If you are not prevaccinated you will need to receive rabies immunoglobulin as soon as possible, followed by five shots of vaccine over 28 days. If prevaccinated you need just two shots of vaccine given three days apart.

MOSQUITO AVOIDANCE TIPS

Travellers are advised to prevent mosquito bites by taking these steps:

- use a DEET-containing insect repellent on exposed skin
- sleep under a mosquito net, ideally impregnated with permethrin
- choose accommodation with screens and fans
- impregnate clothing with permethrin in high-risk areas
- wear long sleeves and trousers in light colours
- use mosquito coils
- spray your room with insect repellent before going out

STDs

Sexually transmitted diseases most common in Thailand include herpes, warts, syphilis, gonorrhoea and chlamydia. People carrying these diseases often have no signs of infection. Condoms will prevent gonorrhoea and chlamydia, but not warts or herpes. If after a sexual encounter you develop any rash, lumps, discharge or pain when passing urine, seek immediate medical attention. If you have been sexually active during your travels, have an STD check on your return home.

Typhoid

This serious bacterial infection is spread through food and water. It gives a high and slowly progressive fever, severe headache and may be accompanied by a dry cough and stomach pain. It is diagnosed by blood tests and treated with antibiotics. Vaccination is recommended for all travellers spending more than a week in Thailand, or travelling outside of the major cities. Be aware that vaccination is not 100% effective, so you must still be careful with what you eat and drink.

Traveller's Diarrhoea

Traveller's diarrhoea is by far the most common problem affecting travellers. In over 80% of cases, traveller's diarrhoea is caused by a bacteria (there are numerous potential culprits) and responds promptly to treatment with antibiotics.

Here we define traveller's diarrhoea as the passage of more than three watery bowel movements within 24 hours, plus at least one other symptom such as vomiting, fever, cramps, nausea or feeling generally unwell.

Treatment consists of staying well hydrated; rehydration solutions such as Gastrolyte are the best for this. Antibiotics such as Norfloxacin, Ciprofloxacin or Azithromycin will kill the bacteria quickly. Seek medical attention if you do not respond to an appropriate antibiotic.

Loperamide is just a 'stopper' that only treats the symptoms. It can be helpful, for example, if you have to go on a long bus ride. Don't take Loperamide if you have a fever, or blood in your stools.

Giardia lamblia is a parasite that is relatively common. Symptoms include nausea, bloating, excess gas, fatigue and intermittent diarrhoea. 'Eggy' burps are often attributed solely to giardiasis. The treatment of choice is Tinidazole, with Metronidazole being a second-line option.

Amoebic dysentery is very rare in travellers, but may be misdiagnosed by poor-quality labs. Symptoms are similar to bacterial diarrhoea. You should always seek reliable medical care if you have blood in your diarrhoea. Treatment involves two drugs: Tinidazole or Metronidazole to kill the parasite in your gut and then a second drug to kill the cysts. If left untreated complications, such as liver abscesses, can occur.

Environmental Hazards

Food

Eating in restaurants is the biggest risk factor for contracting traveller's diarrhoea. Ways to avoid it include eating only freshly cooked food and avoiding food that has been sitting around in buffets. Peel all fruit and cook vegetables. Eat in busy restaurants with a high turnover of customers.

Heat

For most people it takes at least two weeks to adapt to the hot climate. Prevent swelling of the feet and ankles as well as muscle cramps caused by excessive sweating by avoiding dehydration and excessive activity in the heat of the day.

Heat stroke requires immediate medical treatment. Symptoms come on suddenly and include weakness, nausea, a hot dry body with a body temperature of more than 41°C, dizziness, confusion, loss of coordination, fits and eventually collapse and loss of consciousness.

Insect Bites & Stings

Bedbugs live in the cracks of furniture and walls and then migrate to the bed at night to feed on humans. You can treat the itch by using an antihistamine.

Ticks are contracted when walking in rural areas. They are commonly found behind the ears, on the belly and in armpits. If you've been bitten by a tick and a rash develops at the site of the bite or elsewhere, along with fever or muscle aches, see a doctor. Doxycycline prevents tick-borne diseases.

Leeches are found in humid rainforests. They do not transmit disease, but their bites are often itchy for weeks afterwards and can easily become infected. Apply an iodine-based antiseptic to the bite to help prevent infection.

Bee and wasp stings mainly cause problems for people who are allergic to them. Anyone with a serious allergy should carry an injection of adrenaline (eg an EpiPen) for emergencies. For others, pain is the main problem – apply ice to the sting and take painkillers.

Parasites

Numerous parasites are common in local populations in Thailand, but most of these are rare in travellers. To avoid parasitic infections, wear shoes and avoid eating raw food, especially fish, pork and vegetables.

Skin Problems

Prickly heat is a common skin rash in the tropics, caused by sweat being trapped under the skin. Treat by taking cool showers and using powders.

Two fungal rashes commonly affect travellers. The first occurs in the groin, armpits and between the toes. It starts as a red patch that slowly spreads and is usually itchy. Treatment involves keeping the skin dry, avoiding chafing and using an antifungal cream such as Clotrimazole or Lamisil. The fungus *Tinea versicolor* causes small and light-coloured patches, most commonly on the back, chest and shoulders. Consult a doctor.

Cuts and scratches become easily infected in humid climates. Immediately wash all wounds in clean water and apply antiseptic. If you develop signs of infection, see a doctor. Coral cuts can easily become infected.

Snakes

Though snake bites are rare for travellers, there are more than 85 species of venomous snakes in Thailand. Wear boots and long pants if walking in an area that may have snakes.

The Thai Red Cross produces antivenom for many of the poisonous snakes in Thailand.

Sunburn

Even on a cloudy day, sunburn can occur rapidly. Use a strong sunscreen (at least factor 30+), making sure to reapply after a swim, and always wear a wide-brimmed

JELLYFISH STINGS

Box jellyfish stings are extremely painful and can even be fatal. There are two main types of box jellyfish – multitentacled and single-tentacled.

Multitentacled box jellyfish are present in Thai waters – these are the most dangerous and a severe envenomation can kill an adult within two minutes. They are generally found along sandy beaches near river mouths and mangroves during the warmer months.

There are many types of single-tentacled box jellyfish, some of which can cause severe symptoms known as the Irukandji syndrome. The initial sting can seem minor; however, severe symptoms such as back pain, nausea, vomiting, sweating, difficulty breathing and a feeling of impending doom can develop between five and 40 minutes later.

There are many other jellyfish in Thailand that cause irritating stings but no serious effects. The only way to prevent these stings is to wear protective clothing.

First Aid for Severe Stings

For severe, life-threatening envenomations, experts say the first priority is keeping the person alive. Send someone to call for medical help and start immediate CPR if they are unconscious. If the victim is conscious, douse the stung area liberally with vinegar for 30 seconds.

Vinegar can also reduce irritation from minor stings. It is best to seek medical care quickly in case any other symptoms develop over the next 40 minutes.

Australia and Thailand are now working in close collaboration to identify the species of jellyfish in Thai waters, as well as their ecology – hopefully enabling better prediction and detection of the jellyfish.

hat and sunglasses outdoors. If you become sunburnt stay out of the sun until you have recovered, apply cool compresses and take painkillers for the discomfort. One-percent hydrocortisone cream applied twice daily is also helpful.

Travelling With Children

Thailand is relatively safe for children. Consult a doctor who specialises in travel medicine prior to travel to ensure your child is appropriately prepared. A medical kit designed specifically for children includes liquid medicines for children who can not swallow tables. Azithromycin is an ideal paediatric formula used to treat bacterial diarrhoea, as well as ear, chest and throat infections.

Good resources include Lonely Planet's *Travel with Children* and, for those spending longer away, Jane Wilson-Howarth's *Your Child's Health Abroad*.

Women's Health

Pregnant women should receive specialised advice before travelling. The ideal time to travel is in the second trimester, when pregnancy-related risks are low. Avoid rural areas with poor transport and medical facilities. Ensure travel insurance covers all pregnancy-related possibilities, including premature labour.

Malaria is a high-risk disease in pregnancy. Pregnant women should *not* travel to areas with chloroquine-resistant malaria. None of the more effective antimalarial drugs are completely safe in pregnancy.

Traveller's diarrhoea can lead to dehydration and result in inadequate blood flow to the placenta. Azithromycin is considered one of the safest anti-diarrhoea drugs in pregnancy.

In Thailand's urban areas, supplies of sanitary products are readily available. Bring adequate supplies of your personal birth-control option. Heat, humidity and antibiotics can all contribute to thrush, which can be treated with antifungal creams and Clotrimazole. A practical alternative is one tablet of fluconazole (Diflucan). Urinary-tract infections can be precipitated by dehydration or long bus journeys without toilet stops; bring suitable antibiotics for treatment.

Language

Thailand's official language is effectively the dialect spoken and written in central Thailand, which has successfully become the lingua franca of all Thai and non-Thai ethnic groups in the kingdom.

In Thai the meaning of a single syllable may be altered by means of different tones. In standard Thai there are five: low tone, mid tone, falling tone, high tone and rising tone. The range of all five tones is relative to each speaker's vocal range, so there is no fixed 'pitch' intrinsic to the language.

➡ **low tone** – 'Flat' like the mid tone, but pronounced at the relative bottom of one's vocal range. It is low, level and has no inflection, eg bàht (baht – the Thai currency).

➡ **mid tone** – Pronounced 'flat', at the relative middle of the speaker's vocal range, eg dee (good). No tone mark is used.

➡ **falling tone** – Starting high and falling sharply, this tone is similar to the change in pitch in English when you are emphasising a word, or calling someone's name from afar, eg mâi (no/not).

➡ **high tone** – Usually the most difficult for non-Thai speakers. It's pronounced near the relative top of the vocal range, as level as possible, eg máh (horse).

➡ **rising tone** – Starting low and gradually rising, sounds like the inflection used by English speakers to imply a question – 'Yes?', eg săhm (three).

WANT MORE?

For in-depth language information and handy phrases, check out Lonely Planet's *Thai Phrasebook*. You'll find it at **shop.lonelyplanet.com**, or you can buy Lonely Planet's iPhone phrasebooks at the Apple App Store.

The Thai government has instituted the Royal Thai General Transcription System (RTGS) as a standard method of writing Thai using the Roman alphabet. It's used in official documents, road signs and on maps. However, local variations crop up on signs, menus etc. Generally, names in this book follow the most common practice.

In our coloured pronunciation guides, the hyphens indicate syllable breaks within words, and some syllables are further divided with a dot to help you pronounce compound vowels, eg mêu·a-rai (when).

The vowel a is pronounced as in 'about', aa as the 'a' in 'bad', ah as the 'a' in 'father', ai as in 'aisle', air as in 'flair' (without the 'r'), eu as the 'er' in 'her' (without the 'r'), ew as in 'new' (with rounded lips), oh as the 'o' in 'toe', or as in 'torn' (without the 'r') and ow as in 'now'.

Most consonants correspond to their English counterparts. The exceptions are b (a hard 'p' sound, almost like a 'b', eg in 'hip-bag'); đ (a hard 't' sound, like a sharp 'd', eg in 'mid-tone'); ng (as in 'singing'; in Thai it can occur at the start of a word) and r (as in 'run' but flapped; in everyday speech it's often pronounced like 'l').

BASICS

The social structure of Thai society demands different registers of speech depending on who you're talking to. To make things simple we've chosen the correct form of speech appropriate to the context of each phrase.

When being polite, the speaker ends his or her sentence with kráp (for men) or kâ (for women). It is the gender of the speaker that is being expressed here; it is also the common way to answer 'yes' to a question or show agreement.

The masculine and feminine forms of phrases in this chapter are indicated where relevant with 'm/f'.

Hello.	สวัสดี	sà-wàt-dee
Goodbye.	ลาก่อน	lah gòrn
Yes./No.	ใช่/ไม่	châi/mâi
Please.	ขอ	kŏr
Thank you.	ขอบคุณ	kòrp kun
You're welcome.	ยินดี	yin dee
Excuse me.	ขออภัย	kŏr à-pai
Sorry.	ขอโทษ	kŏr tôht

How are you?
สบายดีไหม — sà-bai dee măi

Fine. And you?
สบายดีครับ/ค่า แล้วคุณล่ะ — sà-bai dee kráp/ kâ láa·ou kun lâ (m/f)

What's your name?
คุณชื่ออะไร — kun chêu à-rai

My name is ...
ผม/ดิฉันชื่อ... — pŏm/dì-chăn chêu ... (m/f)

Do you speak English?
คุณพูดภาษา อังกฤษได้ไหม — kun pôot pah-săh ang-grìt dâi măi

I don't understand.
ผม/ดิฉันไม่ เข้าใจ — pŏm/dì-chăn mâi kôw jai (m/f)

ACCOMMODATION

Where's a ...?	... อยู่ที่ไหน	... yòo têe năi
campsite	ค่ายพักแรม	kâi pák raam
guesthouse	บ้านพัก	bâhn pák
hotel	โรงแรม	rohng raam
youth hostel	บ้าน เยาวชน	bâhn yow-wá-chon

Do you have a ... room?	มีห้อง ... ไหม	mee hôrng ... măi
single	เดี่ยว	dèe·o
double	เตียงคู่	đee·ang kôo
twin	สองเตียง	sŏrng đee·ang

air-con	แอร์	aa
bathroom	ห้องน้ำ	hôrng nám
laundry	ห้องซักผ้า	hôrng sák pâh
mosquito net	มุ้ง	múng
window	หน้าต่าง	nâh đàhng

Question Words

What?	อะไร	à-rai
When?	เมื่อไร	mêu·a-rai
Where?	ที่ไหน	têe năi
Who?	ใคร	krai
Why?	ทำไม	tam-mai

DIRECTIONS

Where's ...?
... อยู่ที่ไหน — ... yòo têe năi

What's the address?
ที่อยู่คืออะไร — têe yòo keu à-rai

Could you please write it down?
เขียนลงให้ได้ไหม — kĕe·an long hâi dâi măi

Can you show me (on the map)?
ให้ดู (ในแผนที่) ได้ไหม — hâi doo (nai păan têe) dâi măi

Turn left/right.
เลี้ยวซ้าย/ขวา — lée·o sái/kwăh

It's ...	อยู่...	yòo ...
behind	ที่หลัง	têe lăng
in front of	ตรงหน้า	đrong nâh
next to	ข้างๆ	kâhng kâhng
straight ahead	ตรงไป	đrong bai

EATING & DRINKING

I'd like (the menu), please.
ขอ (รายการ อาหาร) หน่อย — kŏr (rai gahn ah-hăhn) nòy

What would you recommend?
คุณแนะนำอะไรบ้าง — kun náa-nam à-rai bâhng

That was delicious!
อร่อยมาก — à-ròy mâhk

Cheers!
ไชโย — chai-yoh

Please bring the bill.
ขอบิลหน่อย — kŏr bin nòy

I don't eat ...	ผม/ดิฉัน ไม่กิน ...	pŏm/dì-chăn mâi gin ... (m/f)
eggs	ไข่	kài
fish	ปลา	Ƀlah
red meat	เนื้อแดง	néu·a daang
nuts	ถั่ว	tòo·a

Key Words

bar	บาร์	bah
bottle	ขวด	kòo·at
bowl	ชาม	chahm
breakfast	อาหารเช้า	ah-hăhn chów
cafe	ร้านกาแฟ	ráhn gah-faa
chopsticks	ไม้ตะเกียบ	mái đà-gèe·ap
cold	เย็น	yen
cup	ถ้วย	tôo·ay
dessert	ของหวาน	kŏrng wăhn
dinner	อาหารเย็น	ah-hăhn yen
drink list	รายการ เครื่องดื่ม	rai gahn krêu·ang dèum
fork	ส้อม	sôrm
glass	แก้ว	gâa·ou
hot	ร้อน	rórn
knife	มีด	mêet
lunch	อาหาร กลางวัน	ah-hăhn glahng wan
market	ตลาด	đà-làht
menu	รานการ อาหาร	rai gahn ah-hăhn
plate	จาน	jahn
restaurant	ร้านอาหาร	ráhn ah-hăhn
spicy	เผ็ด	pèt
spoon	ช้อน	chórn
vegetarian (person)	คนกินเจ	kon gin jair

Signs

ทางเข้า	Entrance
ทางออก	Exit
เปิด	Open
ปิด	Closed
ที่ติดต่อสอบถาม	Information
ห้าม	Prohibited
ห้องสุขา	Toilets
ชาย	Men
หญิง	Women

with	มี	mee
without	ไม่มี	mâi mee

Meat & Fish

beef	เนื้อ	néu·a
chicken	ไก่	gài
crab	ปู	ɓoo
duck	เป็ด	ɓèt
fish	ปลา	ɓlah
meat	เนื้อ	néu·a
pork	หมู	mŏo
seafood	อาหารทะเล	ah-hăhn tá-lair
squid	ปลาหมึก	ɓlah mèuk

Fruit & Vegetables

banana	กล้วย	glôo·ay
beans	ถั่ว	tòo·a
coconut	มะพร้าว	má-prów
eggplant	มะเขือ	má-kĕu·a
fruit	ผลไม้	pŏn-lá-mái
guava	ฝรั่ง	fa-ràng
lime	มะนาว	má-now
mango	มะม่วง	má-môo·ang
mangosteen	มังคุด	mang-kút
mushrooms	เห็ด	hèt
nuts	ถั่ว	tòo·a
papaya	มะละกอ	má-lá-gor
potatoes	มันฝรั่ง	man fa-ràng
rambutan	เงาะ	ngó
tamarind	มะขาม	má-kăhm
tomatoes	มะเขือเทศ	má-kĕu·a têt
vegetables	ผัก	pàk
watermelon	แตงโม	đaang moh

Other

chilli	พริก	prík
egg	ไข่	kài
fish sauce	น้ำปลา	nám ɓlah
ice	น้ำแข็ง	nám kăang

noodles	เส้น	sên
oil	น้ำมัน	nám man
pepper	พริกไทย	prík tai
rice	ข้าว	kôw
salad	ผักสด	pàk sòt
salt	เกลือ	gleu·a
soup	น้ำซุป	nám súp
soy sauce	น้ำซีอิ๊ว	nám see-éw
sugar	น้ำตาล	nám đahn
tofu	เต้าหู้	đôw hôo

Drinks

beer	เบียร์	bee·a
coffee	กาแฟ	gah-faa
milk	นมจืด	nom jèut
orange juice	น้ำส้ม	nám sôm
soy milk	น้ำเต้าหู้	nám đôw hôo
sugarcane juice	น้ำอ้อย	nám ôy
tea	ชา	chah
water	น้ำดื่ม	nám dèum

EMERGENCIES

Help!	ช่วยด้วย	chôo·ay dôo·ay
Go away!	ไปให้พ้น	ɓai hâi pón

Call a doctor!
เรียกหมอหน่อย rêe·ak mŏr nòy

Call the police!
เรียกตำรวจหน่อย rêe·ak đam·ròo·at nòy

I'm ill.
ผม/ดิฉันป่วย pŏm/dì-chăn ɓòo·ay (m/f)

I'm lost.
ผม/ดิฉัน หลงทาง pŏm/dì-chăn lŏng tahng (m/f)

Where are the toilets?
ห้องน้ำอยู่ที่ไหน hôrng nám yòo têe năi

SHOPPING & SERVICES

I'd like to buy ...
อยากจะซื้อ ... yàhk jà séu ...

I'm just looking.
ดูเฉย ๆ doo chĕu·i chĕu·i

Can I look at it?
ขอดูได้ไหม kŏr doo dâi măi

How much is it?
เท่าไร tôw-rai

That's too expensive.
แพงไป paang ɓai

Can you lower the price?
ลดราคาได้ไหม lót rah-kah dâi măi

There's a mistake in the bill.
บิลใบนี้ผิด นะครับ/ค่ะ bin bai née pìt ná kráp/kâ (m/f)

TIME & DATES

What time is it?
กี่โมงแล้ว gèe mohng láa·ou

morning	เช้า	chów
afternoon	บ่าย	bài
evening	เย็น	yen
yesterday	เมื่อวาน	mêu·a wahn
today	วันนี้	wan née
tomorrow	พรุ่งนี้	prûng née

Monday	วันจันทร์	wan jan
Tuesday	วันอังคาร	wan ang-kahn
Wednesday	วันพุธ	wan pút
Thursday	วันพฤหัสฯ	wan pá-réu-hàt
Friday	วันศุกร	wan sùk
Saturday	วันเสาร์	wan sŏw
Sunday	วันอาทิตย์	wan ah-tít

TRANSPORT

Public Transport

bicycle rickshaw	สามล้อ	săhm lór
boat	เรือ	reu·a
bus	รถเมล์	rót mair
car	รถเก๋ง	rót gĕng
motorcycle taxi	มอร์เตอร์ไซค์ รับจ้าง	mor-đeu-sai ráp jâhng
plane	เครื่องบิน	krêu·ang bin
train	รถไฟ	rót fai
túk-túk	ตุ๊ก ๆ	đúk đúk

Numbers

1	หนึ่ง	nèung
2	สอง	sŏrng
3	สาม	săhm
4	สี่	sèe
5	ห้า	hâh
6	หก	hòk
7	เจ็ด	jèt
8	แปด	bàat
9	เก้า	gôw
10	สิบ	sìp
11	สิบเอ็ด	sìp-èt
20	ยี่สิบ	yêe-sìp
21	ยี่สิบเอ็ด	yêe-sìp-èt
30	สามสิบ	săhm-sìp
40	สี่สิบ	sèe-sìp
50	ห้าสิบ	hâh-sìp
60	หกสิบ	hòk-sìp
70	เจ็ดสิบ	jèt-sìp
80	แปดสิบ	bàat-sìp
90	เก้าสิบ	gôw-sìp
100	หนึ่งร้อย	nèung róy
1000	หนึ่งพัน	nèung pan
10,000	หนึ่งหมื่น	nèung mèun
100,000	หนึ่งแสน	nèung săan
1,000,000	หนึ่งล้าน	nèung láhn

When's the ... bus?	รถเมล์คัน ... มาเมื่อไร	rót mair kan ... mah mêu·a rai
first	แรก	râak
last	สุดท้าย	sùt tái
next	ต่อไป	đòr bai

A ... ticket, please.	ขอตั๋ว ...	kŏr đŏo·a ...
one-way	เที่ยวเดียว	têe·o dee·o
return	ไปกลับ	bai glàp

I'd like a/an ... seat.	ต้องการ ที่นั่ง ...	đôrng gahn têe nâng ...
aisle	ติดทางเดิน	đìt tahng deun
window	ติดหน้าต่าง	đìt nâh đàhng

platform	ชานชาลา	chan-chah-lah
ticket window	ช่องขายตั๋ว	chôrng kăi đŏo·a
timetable	ตารางเวลา	đah-rahng wair-lah

What time does it get to (Chiang Mai)?
ถึง (เชียงใหม่) กี่โมง — tĕung (chee·ang mài) gèe mohng

Does it stop at (Saraburi)?
รถจอดที่ (สระบุรี) ไหม — rót jòrt têe (sà-rà-bù-ree) măi

Please tell me when we get to (Chiang Mai).
เมื่อถึง (เชียงใหม่) กรุณาบอกด้วย — mêu·a tĕung (chee·ang mài) gà-rú-nah bòrk dôo·ay

I'd like to get off at (Saraburi).
ขอลงที่(สระบุรี) — kŏr long têe (sà-rà-bù-ree)

Driving & Cycling

I'd like to hire a ...	อยากจะ เช่า ...	yàhk jà chôw ...
car	รถเก๋ง	rót gĕng
motorbike	รถ มอร์เตอร์ไซค์	rót mor-đeu-sai

I'd like ...	ต้องการ ...	đôrng gahn ...
my bicycle repaired	ซ่อมรถ จักรยาน	sôrm rót jàk-gà-yahn
to hire a bicycle	เช่ารถ จักรยาน	chôw rót jàk-gà-yahn

Is this the road to (Ban Bung Wai)?
ทางนี้ไป (บ้านบุ่งหวาย) ไหม — tahng née bai (bâhn bùng wăi) măi

Where's a petrol station?
ปั๊มน้ำมันอยู่ที่ไหน — bâm nám man yòo têe năi

Can I park here?
จอดที่นี้ได้ไหม — jòrt têe née dâi măi

How long can I park here?
จอดที่นี้ได้นานเท่าไร — jòrt têe née dâi nahn tôw-rai

I need a mechanic.
ต้องการช่างรถ — đôrng gahn châhng rót

I have a flat tyre.
ยางแบน — yahng baan

I've run out of petrol.
หมดน้ำมัน — mòt nám man

Do I need a helmet?
ต้องใช้หมวกกันน็อกไหม — đôrng chái mòo·ak gan nórk măi

GLOSSARY

This glossary includes Thai, Pali (P) and Sanskrit (S) words and terms frequently used in this guidebook. For definitions of food and drink terms, see p780.

ajahn – *(aajaan)* respectful title for 'teacher'; from the Sanskrit term *acarya*
amphoe – *(amphur)* district, the next subdivision down from province
AUA – American University Alumni

bâhn – *(ban)* house or village
baht – *(bàat)* the Thai unit of currency
bàht – a unit of weight equal to 15g; rounded bowl used by monks for receiving alms food
BKS – Baw Khaw Saw (Thai acronym for the Transport Company)
bodhisattva (S) – in Theravada Buddhism, the term used to refer to the previous lives of the Buddha prior to his enlightenment
bòht – central sanctuary in a Thai temple used for the monastic order's official business, such as ordinations; from the Pali term *uposatha (ubohsòt);* see also *wí·hăhn*
bòr nám rórn – hot springs
Brahman – pertaining to Brahmanism, an ancient religious tradition in India and the predecessor of Hinduism; not to be confused with 'Brahmin', the priestly class in India's caste system
BTS – Bangkok Transit System (Skytrain); Thai: *rót fai fáh*
ɓah·đé – batik

CAT – CAT Telecom Public Company Limited
chedi – see *stupa*
chow – folk; people
chow lair – *(chow nám)* sea gypsies
CPT – Communist Party of Thailand

doy – mountain in the Northern Thai dialect; spelt 'Doi' in proper names
đròrk – *(trok)* alley, smaller than a soi

fa·ràng –a Westerner (person of European origin); also guava

gà·teu·i – *(kàthoey)* Thailand's 'third gender', usually cross-dressing or transsexual males; also called ladyboys
gopura (S) – entrance pavilion in traditional Hindu temple architecture, often seen in Angkor-period temple complexes

hàht – beach; spelt 'Hat' in proper names
hŏr đrai – a Tripitaka (Buddhist scripture) hall
hôrng – *(hong)* room; in southern Thailand this refers to semi-submerged island caves

Isan – *(ee·săhn)* general term used for northeastern Thailand

jataka (P) – *(chah·dòk)* stories of the Buddha's previous lives
jeen – Chinese
jeen hor – literally 'galloping Chinese', referring to horse-riding Yunnanese traders

kàthoey – see *gà·teu·i*
klorng – canal; spelt 'Khlong' in proper nouns
kŏhn – masked dance–drama based on stories from the Ramakian
kŏw – hill or mountain; spelt 'Khao' in proper names
KMT – Kuomintang
KNU – Karen National Union
ku – small *stupa* that is partially hollow and open
kùti – monk's dwelling

lăam – cape; spelt 'Laem' in proper names
làk meu·ang – city pillar
lék – little, small (in size); see also *noi*
longyi – Burmese sarong
lôok tûng – Thai country music
lôw kŏw – white whisky, often homemade rice brew

mâa chee – Thai Buddhist nun
mâa nám – river; spelt Mae Nam in proper names
mahathat – *(má·hăh tâht)* common name for temples containing Buddha relics; from the Sanskrit–Pali term *mahadhatu*
masjid – *(mát·sà·yít)* mosque
mát·mèe – technique of tie-dyeing silk or cotton threads and then weaving them into complex patterns, similar to Indonesian *ikat*; the term also refers to the patterns themselves
meu·ang – city or principality
mon·dòp – small square, spired building in a wát; from Sanskrit *mandapa*
moo·ay tai – *(muay thai)* Thai boxing
mŏr lam – an Isan musical tradition akin to *lôok tûng*

naga (P/S) – *(nâhk)* a mythical serpent-like being with magical powers
ná·kon – city; from the Sanskrit-Pali *nagara;* spelt 'Nakhon' in proper nouns
nám – water
nám đòk – waterfall; spelt 'Nam Tok' in proper nouns
neun – hill; spelt 'Noen' in proper names
nibbana (P/S) – nirvana; in Buddhist teachings, the state of enlightenment; escape from the realm of rebirth; Thai: *níp·pahn*
noi – *(nóy)* little, small (amount); see also *lék*
nôrk – outside, outer; spelt 'Nok' in proper names

ow – bay or gulf; spelt 'Ao' in proper nouns

pâh mát·mèe – *mát·mèe* fabric
pěe – ghost, spirit

pík·sù – a Buddhist monk; from the Sanskrit *bhikshu*, Pali *bhikkhu*

PLAT – People's Liberation Army of Thailand

prá – an honorific term used for monks, nobility and Buddha images; spelt 'Phra' in proper names

prá krêu·ang – amulets of monks, Buddhas or deities worn around the neck for spiritual protection; also called *prá pim*

prá poom – earth spirits or guardians

prang – *(ɓrahng)* Khmer-style tower on temples

prasat – *(ɓrah·sàht)* small ornate building, used for religious purposes, with a cruciform ground plan and needlelike spire, located on temple grounds; any of a number of different kinds of halls or residences with religious or royal significance

rót aa – blue-and-white air-con bus

rót norn – sleeper bus

săh·lah – open-sided, covered meeting hall or resting place; from Portuguese term *sala*, literally 'room'

săhm·lór – three-wheeled pedicab

samsara (P) – in Buddhist teachings, the realm of rebirth and delusion

sangha – (P) the Buddhist community

satang – *(sà·đahng)* a Thai unit of currency; 100 satang equals 1 baht

serow – Asian mountain goat

sêua môr hôrm – blue cotton farmer's shirt

soi – lane or small street

Songkran – Thai New Year, held in mid-April

sŏrng·tăa·ou – (literally 'two rows') common name for small pick-up trucks with two benches in the back, used as buses/taxis; also spelt '*săwngthăew*'

SRT – State Railway of Thailand

stupa – conical-shaped Buddhist monument used to inter sacred Buddhist objects

tâh – pier, boat landing; spelt 'Tha' in proper nouns

tâht – four-sided, curvilinear Buddha reliquary, common in Northeastern Thailand; spelt 'That' in proper nouns

tâm – cave; spelt 'Tham' in proper nouns

tam bun – to make merit

tambon – see *đam·bon*

TAT – Tourism Authority of Thailand

Thammayut – one of the two sects of Theravada Buddhism in Thailand; founded by King Rama IV while he was still a monk

thanŏn – *(tà·nŏn)* street; spelt 'Thanon' in proper noun and shortened to 'Th'

T-pop – popular teen-music

tràwk – see *đròrk*

trimurti (S) – collocation of the three principal Hindu deities, Brahma, Shiva and Vishnu

Tripitaka (S) – Theravada Buddhist scriptures; (Pali: *Tipitaka*)

túk-túk – *(đúk-đúk)* motorised săhm·lór

vipassana (P) – *(wí·ɓàt·sà·nah)* Buddhist insight meditation

wâi – palms-together Thai greeting

wan prá – Buddhist holy days, falling on the days of the main phases of the moon (full, new and half) each month

wang – palace

wát – temple-monastery; from the Pali term *avasa* meaning 'monk's dwelling'; spelt 'Wat' in proper nouns

wí·hăhn – *(wihan, viharn)* any large hall in a Thai temple, usually open to laity; from Sanskrit term *vihara*, meaning 'dwelling'

Yawi – traditional language of Malay parts of Java, Sumatra and the Malay Peninsula, widely spoken in the most southern provinces of Thailand; the written form uses the classic Arabic script plus five additional letters

yài – big

Behind the Scenes

SEND US YOUR FEEDBACK

We love to hear from travellers – your comments keep us on our toes and help make our books better. Our well-travelled team reads every word on what you loved or loathed about this book. Although we cannot reply individually to postal submissions, we always guarantee that your feedback goes straight to the appropriate authors, in time for the next edition. Each person who sends us information is thanked in the next edition – the most useful submissions are rewarded with a selection of digital PDF chapters.

Visit **lonelyplanet.com/contact** to submit your updates and suggestions or to ask for help. Our award-winning website also features inspirational travel stories, news and discussions.

Note: We may edit, reproduce and incorporate your comments in Lonely Planet products such as guidebooks, websites and digital products, so let us know if you don't want your comments reproduced or your name acknowledged. For a copy of our privacy policy visit lonelyplanet.com/privacy.

OUR READERS

Many thanks to the travellers who used the last edition and wrote to us with helpful hints, useful advice and interesting anecdotes:

A Alma Asuai, Andrea Zanchi, Anne Légaré **B** Bill Weir **C** Charlotte Toolan, Clare Blenkinsop **D** Daniëlle Wolbers, David Cross, Déan Smits, Des Moriarty **E** Elisa Fernandez, Eric Bitencourt **F** Francesco Agnelli, Francesco Franceschi **G** Geoffrey Taylor, Grant Jarvis **H** Hans van Ek **I** Isabella Capel-Timms **J** Jarosław Śmietana, Jeroen Reitsma, Jessica Meier, Jildau van den Berg, Jocelyn Bulgin, John Zachariassen, Jourdan Shapiro, Julian Rudd, Juliane Dicke, July Marín **K** Karen Fogh, Karlie Drutz, Keith Freeman, Kerry O'Connor **L** Leah Kroes, Louis Aarts, Lucia Urgell **M** Maria Clavero , Marielle Boivin, Matthew Huxtable, Michael Roos, Michelle Tan, Mike Kear **N** Nicholas Jarvis **P** Peter Lilley **R** Rob Falloon, Roscoe Ward **S** Samantha Jeffery, Sarah North, Sharon Dayan, Shira Rotem , Simon Partridge, Stéphanie Visser, Stig Buch **U** Ursula Rose **V** Veronika Stalz **W** Wendy Chrisman, Willemijn Schneyder **Z** Zdenek Klusacek

AUTHOR THANKS

Mark Beales

Firstly, thanks to Sarah Reid for offering me the chance to return to this guide. In Bang Saen, Michiel and Mynd had some great tips and on Ko Kut, Seren was a star. On Ko Chang, thanks to Ian, Lisa and Olivier, who all helped immensely while Eric and Issac had some great ideas. The staff at TAT were as helpful as ever, especially K.Suladda and K.Kesorn. Lastly, thanks to Ann and Daniel.

Tim Bewer

A hearty *kòrb kun kráp* to the many people who helped me out during this update. In particular Prapaporn Sompakdee provided great help. And, of course, a special thanks to Suttawan for many things.

Joe Bindloss

Thanks as always to Linda and Tyler, for helping me get the authoritative answer on which elephant centres, restaurants, monasteries and waterfalls are truly family-friendly, and for holding the fort at home while I finished up research. In Chiang Mai, thanks to the Tourist Authority of Thailand, the staff of Awana House, the many patient red car drivers who put up with stop/start trips around the hills, and the locals and travellers who helped me find new and surprising things to see and do.

Austin Bush

My thanks to the previous authors of this guide, Joe Cummings and China Williams – believe it or not, some of your words live on! Destination Editor, Sarah Reid; this edition's Local Knowledgers 'Bi', Pongtawat 'Ian' Chalermkittichai and Joe Cummings; part-time research assistants Kathy MacLeod and Maher Sattar; and the rest of the kind folks on the ground in Bangkok and northern Thailand.

David Eimer

Thanks to Sarah Reid and all the LP crew. As ever, much gratitude to everyone who passed on tips, whether knowingly or unwittingly.

Bruce Evans

I was especially fortunate to have two good friends help me on this trip: Gamontip Prayoontong (Dukata) and one of my old associates from my Buddhist monk days, Thanom Kongphet, who took me on a road trip through Nong Khai, Udon Thani and Bueng Kan (his home town). Thanks also to Khun Sutchaniphat and Khun Banphot for the trip to Phu Thok. At Lonely Planet, thanks to Destination Editor, Sarah Reid for taking a chance on me, and to Anthony Ham for providing valuable authoring tips. In Thailand, author Tim Bewer provided information about his home region.

Damian Harper

Many thanks to all who eased the way and came up with ideas, help and suggestions; most notably, gratitude to Neal Bambridge, Charoon Juntra, Brigitte Gomm, Matt Rubin, Jessica Meier, Eveline Fortuin, Amanda, Suwatchai Praesomboon, Stanley Chang and Mark Tewari. Loved the company of the charming family on the train from Hat Yai to Surat Thani, you are fine people and I wish you every good fortune. Cheers also to my brother and Thailand enthusiast, John. Thanks to Daisy, Tim and Emma, as always.

Isabella Noble

Thanks to everyone who helped out on the road, whether knowingly or not, particularly Jamie Monk and Lee Cobaj for the stellar Phuket intel. Cheers to Paul on Ko Phayam, elephant expert John Roberts, the Gibbon Rehab Project crew and Ann for Thai language tips. Thanks to my hardworking co-authors, especially fellow island experts Mark Beales and Damian Harper. Extra special thanks to Andrew, Raquel and Papi for pitching in, and to my favourite research assistant Jack Noble.

ACKNOWLEDGMENTS

Climate map data adapted from Peel MC, Finlayson BL & McMahon TA (2007) 'Updated World Map of the Köppen-Geiger Climate Classification', *Hydrology and Earth System Sciences*, 11, 1633–44.

Illustrations pp62-3 and pp64-5 by Michael Weldon.

Cover photograph: Buddhist monks light floating lanterns, lifeispixels/Getty ©.

THIS BOOK

This 16th edition of Lonely Planet's *Thailand* guidebook was researched and written by Mark Beales, Tim Bewer, Joe Bindloss, Austin Bush, David Eimer, Bruce Evans, Damian Harper and Isabellea Noble. This guidebook was produced by the following:

Destination Editor Sarah Reid

Product Editors Elin Berglund, Alison Ridgway

Regional Senior Cartographer Diana Von Holdt

Book Designer Cam Ashley

Assisting Editors Andrew Bain, Judith Bamber, Nigel Chin, Gabrielle Innes, Anne Mulvaney, Monique Perrin, Christopher Pitts, Vicky Smith, Gabrielle Stefanos

Assisting Cartographers David Kemp, Valentina Kremenchutskaya

Cover Researcher Naomi Parker

Thanks to Daniel Corbett, Bruce Evans, Andi Jones, Karyn Noble, Ellie Simpson, Tasmin Waby, Lauren Wellicome, Tony Wheeler

Index

Map Pages **000**
Photo Pages **000**

D

E

L

M

Map Pages **000**
Photo Pages **000**

Map Legend

Sights

- Beach
- Bird Sanctuary
- Buddhist
- Castle/Palace
- Christian
- Confucian
- Hindu
- Islamic
- Jain
- Jewish
- Monument
- Museum/Gallery/Historic Building
- Ruin
- Shinto
- Sikh
- Taoist
- Winery/Vineyard
- Zoo/Wildlife Sanctuary
- Other Sight

Activities, Courses & Tours

- Bodysurfing
- Diving
- Canoeing/Kayaking
- Course/Tour
- Sento Hot Baths/Onsen
- Skiing
- Snorkelling
- Surfing
- Swimming/Pool
- Walking
- Windsurfing
- Other Activity

Sleeping

- Sleeping
- Camping

Eating

- Eating

Drinking & Nightlife

- Drinking & Nightlife
- Cafe

Entertainment

- Entertainment

Shopping

- Shopping

Information

- Bank
- Embassy/Consulate
- Hospital/Medical
- Internet
- Police
- Post Office
- Telephone
- Toilet
- Tourist Information
- Other Information

Geographic

- Beach
- Gate
- Hut/Shelter
- Lighthouse
- Lookout
- Mountain/Volcano
- Oasis
- Park
- Pass
- Picnic Area
- Waterfall

Population

- Capital (National)
- Capital (State/Province)
- City/Large Town
- Town/Village

Transport

- Airport
- Border crossing
- Bus
- Cable car/Funicular
- Cycling
- Ferry
- Metro/MRT/MTR station
- Monorail
- Parking
- Petrol station
- Skytrain/Subway station
- Taxi
- Train station/Railway
- Tram
- Underground station
- Other Transport

Note: Not all symbols displayed above appear on the maps in this book

Routes

- Tollway
- Freeway
- Primary
- Secondary
- Tertiary
- Lane
- Unsealed road
- Road under construction
- Plaza/Mall
- Steps
- Tunnel
- Pedestrian overpass
- Walking Tour
- Walking Tour detour
- Path/Walking Trail

Boundaries

- International
- State/Province
- Disputed
- Regional/Suburb
- Marine Park
- Cliff
- Wall

Hydrography

- River, Creek
- Intermittent River
- Canal
- Water
- Dry/Salt/Intermittent Lake
- Reef

Areas

- Airport/Runway
- Beach/Desert
- Cemetery (Christian)
- Cemetery (Other)
- Glacier
- Mudflat
- Park/Forest
- Sight (Building)
- Sportsground
- Swamp/Mangrove